D0931586

FROM THE GULAG TO THE KILLING FIELDS

From the Gulag
to
the Killing Fields

PERSONAL ACCOUNTS OF
POLITICAL VIOLENCE AND REPRESSION
IN COMMUNIST STATES

Edited by Paul Hollander

ISI Books
2006

This book was supported in part by a gift given by Matthew and Brooke Haas
in the memory of John F. Lulves Jr.

Editor's acknowledgments, introduction, and headnotes © 2006 Paul Hollander
Foreword © 2006 Anne Applebaum

All rights reserved. No part of this publication may be reproduced or transmitted in any
form or by any means, electronic or mechanical, including photocopy, or any information
storage and retrieval system now known or to be invented, without permission in writing
from the publisher, except by a reviewer who wishes to quote brief passages in connection
with a review written for inclusion in a magazine, newspaper, or broadcast.

From the Gulag to the killing fields : personal accounts of political violence and
repression in communist states / edited by Paul Hollander. — 1st ed. — Wilmington,
DE : ISI Books, 2006.

    p. ; cm.

    ISBN-13: 978-1-932236-78-1
    ISBN-10: 1-932236-78-3
    Includes bibliographical references.

    1. Political violence—Former communist countries. 2. Political persecution—
Former communist countries. 3. Civil rights and socialism—Former communist
countries. 4. Political crimes and offenses—Former communist countries. I.
Hollander, Paul.

JC328.65.F6 F76 2006   2005937234
323/.044/09171/7—dc22   0601

Book design by Kara Beer

Published in the United States by:

    ISI Books
    Intercollegiate Studies Institute
    Post Office Box 4431
    Wilmington, DE 19807-0431
    www.isibooks.org

Manufactured in the United States of America

Contents

Acknowledgments   xi

Anne Applebaum
     Foreword   xiii

Editor's Introduction
     The Distinctive Features of Repression in Communist States   xv

❖

THE SOVIET UNION

Janusz Bardach
     Man Is Wolf to Man: Surviving the Gulag   3

F. Beck and W. Godin
     Russian Purge and the Extraction of Confession   21

Vladimir Bukovsky
     To Build a Castle   39

Eugenia Ginzburg
     Journey into the Whirlwind   53

Jerzy Gliksman
     Tell the West   66

Gustav Herling
     A World Apart   80

Anna Larina
     This I Cannot Forget   104

Anatoly Marchenko
     My Testimony   120

Aleksandr Solzhenitsyn
    One Day in the Life of Ivan Denisovich   137

❀

EASTERN EUROPE

ALBANIA

Nika Stajka
    The Last Days of Freedom   151

BULGARIA

Georgi Markov
    The Truth That Killed   169
Tzvetan Todorov
    Voices from the Gulag   183

CZECHOSLOVAKIA

Arthur London
    The Confession   193
Eugene Loebl
    My Mind on Trial   214

EAST GERMANY

Mike Dennis
    The Stasi   234

HUNGARY

Paul Ignotus
    Political Prisoner   255
Gyorgy Paloczi-Horvath
    The Undefeated   268

POLAND

Jan Mur
    A Prisoner of Martial Law   277

Contents

ROMANIA

Lena Constante
  The Silent Escape: Three Thousand Days
    in Romanian Prisons   286

YUGOSLAVIA

Venko Markowski
  Goli Otok: Island of Death   303

❁

CHINA

James Cameron
  Mandarin Red   319
Bao Ruo-Wang
  Prisoner of Mao   324
Harry Wu
  Bitter Winds: A Memoir of My Years in China's Gulag   345
Pu Ning
  Red in Tooth and Claw: Twenty-Six Years in
    Communist Chinese Prisons   364
Tenzin Choedrak
  Jiuzhen Prison—A Tibetan Account   382
Wei Jingsheng
  Q1—A Twentieth-Century Bastille   393
Gao Yuan
  Born Red   402
Palden Gyatso
  Autobiography of a Tibetan Monk   414

❁

CAMBODIA

Haing Ngor
  A Cambodian Odyssey   439

JoAn D. Criddle and Teeda Butt Mam
  To Destroy You Is No Loss   448
Pin Yathay
  Stay Alive, My Son   465
Dith Pran (compiler)
  Children of Cambodia's Killing Fields   478

✿

Vietnam

Jade Ngoc Quang Hu'ynh
  South Wind Changing   503
James M. Freeman (editor)
  Hearts of Sorrow   513
Doan Van Toai and David Chanoff
  The Vietnamese Gulag   533
Tran Tri Vu
  Lost Years: My 1,632 Days in Vietnamese
     Reeducation Camps   549

✿

Cuba

Reinaldo Arenas
  Before Night Falls   569
Charles J. Brown and Armando M. Lago (editors)
  The Politics of Psychiatry in Revolutionary Cuba   584
Armando Valladares
  Against All Hope   603
Jorge Valls
  Twenty Years and Forty Days: Life in a Cuban Prison   628

✿

Contents

NICARAGUA

Roger Miranda and William Ratliff
   The Civil War in Nicaragua   655

   Fleeing Their Homeland: A Report on the
      Testimony of Nicaraguan Refugees   666

❀

NORTH KOREA

Kang Chol-Hwan
   The Aquariums of Pyongyang   683

❀

ETHIOPIA

Myles F. Harris
   Breakfast in Hell   701
D. W. Giorgis
   Red Tears   715

Notes   737

Acknowledgments

In 1993, John O'Sullivan, then editor of *National Review,* encouraged me to write an article about the Western perceptions of and moral responses to the Holocaust, on the one hand, and the mass murders committed by various Communist systems, on the other. The result was an article titled "Soviet Terror, American Amnesia" (originally titled: "Moral Responses to the Great Mass Murders of Our Century"), which was published by *National Review* on May 2, 1994. Subsequently, the idea occurred to me (and was again encouraged by John O'Sullivan) that it would be worthwhile—given the limited public awareness and information about these matters—to put together an anthology, or sourcebook, that would be based on excerpts from memoirs and would thus constitute a sampling of personal experiences of repression in different Communist states. The Historical Research Foundation kindly provided a grant for the initial research expenses associated with the project.

By the late 1990s the volume was more or less completed and I therefore searched for a publisher. None of those approached was interested, although one took the trouble to send the materials to reviewers, who evaluated the project very positively; nevertheless, the publisher decided not to proceed. After these disappointments the project languished for a while. At last, on the advice of Professor George Panichas, editor of *Modern Age*, I contacted ISI Books, which was interested and offered a contract.

A remaining problem was the cost of permissions from publishers to reprint the many excerpts I wanted to include. Earhart Foundation (a generous supporter of my work for almost a quarter century) agreed to underwrite these expenses. In the end, these costs exceeded the amount I originally anticipated and requested; fortunately, ISI was willing to cover the difference. Without the support of Earhart Foundation and ISI the volume could not have come into existence.

Several individuals helped in various ways. My old friend Peter Kenez (University of California, Santa Cruz) read the introduction and made useful comments; Ying Hong Cheng (University of Delaware) advised me on Chinese sources; I received advice on Cuban sources from Frank Calzone (Center for a Free Cuba, Washington, D.C.) and Mark Falcoff (American Enterprise Institute). Mark Kramer (Davis Center for Russian and Eurasian Studies, Harvard University) helped to uncover biographical information about some Soviet authors. Two Hungarian historians, Gyorgy Litvan and Krisztian Ungvari (both associated with the Research Institute of the 1956 Hungarian Revolution), provided biographical information about Hungarian authors included in the volume. Phil Guillon (at the time a graduate student in sociology at the University of Massachusetts, Amherst) helped in the initial stages of collecting and sampling source materials; Rebecca Jost (Smith College) has been my research assistant for the last two years, and she helped with a wide range of tasks associated with the volume, including the collection of biographical information about various authors, which was often difficult to find.

This volume appears at a time when there is a worldwide resurgence of political violence in the service of ideals and causes, political and religious, which has come to preoccupy the public and policymakers in much of the Western world. This violence has been legitimated in ways that bear some resemblance to the justifications and rationalizations of the political violence and repression practiced by Communist systems, different as the latter were in their scope and manifestations. It is my hope that these chronicles and narratives—aside from documenting neglected chapters of twentieth-century history—will offer some help in better understanding the type of political violence and repression that originate in the determination to force people into more virtuous and meritorious ways of life. I am well aware that there is a long way between better understanding and remedial action.

Paul Hollander
Northampton, Massachusetts
December 2005

Foreword

Anne Applebaum

Since the archives of the Soviet concentration camp system first became accessible in the early 1990s, a wave of historians and journalists has rushed to make use of them, and rightly so. In a few short years, the once-secret archives have achieved what eight decades' worth of polemics could not, quietly laying to rest a host of myths about the camps and establishing them as a central part of the Soviet economy and political system. Archives have put an end to any remaining questions about the size of the camp system, which was vast, and have established that the victims numbered in the millions, not the thousands. Most of all, archives have made it impossible for anyone to take seriously the propaganda of the Communist regimes of China, North Korea, and Cuba about their remaining concentration camps. For archives not only document Soviet terror, they do so with enormous precision. Inspection reports, carefully filed in Moscow, outline the horrors of life in the Soviet Gulag in great detail: the epidemics, the starvation rations, the impossible work norms. The means by which the regime concealed the camps' existence are also meticulously described, including the secret codes, the official lies, and the cryptic telegraphic addresses.

What archives could not do, and will never be able to do, is replace the extraordinary body of camp literature that was produced in the Soviet Union, in Eastern Europe, and in Asian, African, and Latin American Communist countries over the past century and is still being written today. Archives can describe what the authorities believed was happening, should be happening, inside the camps. But a decade's worth of scholarship has also shown that archives cannot describe the myriad ways in which the prisoners themselves altered the rules of the often bizarre, surreal world that they had been forced to inhabit. Since historians first began to work in the Soviet archives, it has become more clear than ever that memoirs, while they may not be a reliable source of names, dates, and numbers, are the only source of other kinds of information about life in the camps. Prisoners' relationships with one another and with their guards, conflicts between national groups and criminal gangs, even the existence of love and passion—these are topics that are only properly covered by memoirists.

In this superb collection, Paul Hollander has gathered together some of the most famous memoirists—Eugenia Ginzburg, Aleksandr Solzhenitsyn, Vladimir Bukovsky, Gustave Herling—with lesser-known writers from Eastern Europe, China, Cambodia, Vietnam, Cuba, Nicaragua, North Korea, and Ethiopia. This is the first time anyone has published these authors together, and that Hollander chose to do so is also an important sign of the times. For only now, in the wake of the collapse of the USSR, is it truly possible to understand the cross-cultural, multinational history of communism as a single phenomenon. While we have not perhaps reached the end of the story that began with the Bolsehvik revolution, it already has a clear beginning and a clear middle: it is now possible to trace the direct lines of influence, ideological and financial, from Lenin to Stalin to Mao to Ho Chi Minh to Pol Pot, from Castro to the MPLA in Angola.

It is also possible to trace the links between their remarkably similar systems of repression. The use of concentration camps spread directly from Russia to China and North Korea. The Cuban secret police were specifically set up along Soviet lines. Artificial famines have characterized Communist regimes in Ukraine, China, Cambodia, Ethiopia, and now North Korea. Without exception, the Leninist belief in the one-party state was and is characteristic of every Communist regime, from Russia to China to Cuba to Mozambique. Without exception, the Bolshevik use of violence was repeated in every Communist revolution. Words and phrases invented by Lenin and his chief of secret police, Feliks Dzerzhinsky, were deployed with uncanny predictability all over the world. As late as 1976, Mengistu launched a "Red Terror" in Ethiopia. Memoirs help make it possible to find patterns of Communist repression, as indeed Hollander has done in the comprehensive, wide-ranging introduction to this book, and to show what each of these systems had in common.

In the end, though, camp memoirs are more remarkable for their differences than for their similarities. For above all, memoirs are the only source that can shed light on one of the most fascinating and morally controversial aspects of the camp system—namely, what methods prisoners used to survive. Prisoners stayed alive by cheating one another, by lying about their work norms, by becoming informers, by helping their guards control other prisoners; prisoners also survived thanks to friendship, love, intellectual passions, or religious faith. Camps have brought out the very worst in human nature, and the very best. Every person who entered them discovered qualities in themselves, both good and evil, that they hadn't previously known they had. Ultimately, that self-discovery is the true subject of most camp memoirs, and the true subject of this book.

Editorís Introduction: The Distinctive Features of Repression in Communist States
Paul Hollander

I: Objectives and Criteria for Source Selection

The political violence and repression produced by Communist systems in the twentieth century was one of the most consequential and destructive phenomena of history.[1] Yet relatively little is known about them, especially in comparison with the Holocaust, the other major chapter in political violence of our times (and all history). The collapse of Soviet communism has made no significant difference to this state of affairs.[2]

Arthur Waldron wrote:

> The twentieth century was remarkable not only for the number
> and scale of the atrocities it witnessed but also for the slowness
> with which these frightful events were recognized for what they
> were, let alone condemned. Of these crimes, which began with
> the mass murders by Lenin and Stalin ... and continued through
> the Nazi Holocaust and the democides in China and Cambo-
> dia, only the Nazi horror is regularly acknowledged and truly
> well known.[3]

While there is a vast literature on the Holocaust (as well as photographic documentation, surviving physical evidence, memorials, and museums), and while it has justifiably stimulated a huge and continued outpouring of research, moral outrage, and soul searching, the mass murders and other atrocities committed in the Soviet Union under (and after) Stalin have inspired little corresponding concern and interest.[4] It is not because there is insufficient information about these matters.[5] (A further indication of this limited interest has been the extremely modest review attention given to Alexander Yakovlev's impassioned indictment of Soviet repression, *A Century of Violence in Soviet Russia,* published in 2002.)

Even less is known about repression in the other Communist states (with the possible exception of Cambodia under Pol Pot), and no definitive Western social scientific or historical studies are available on these topics. It is hard to escape the conclusion that, as one writer recently noted, "communism . . . is the deadliest fantasy in human history, and even Americans, for all our struggles against it, have not yet looked it full in the face."[6] For different reasons, in the former Soviet Union too there has been a reluctance to confront the past.[7] Given these circumstances, this volume is a new attempt to draw attention to and document these matters.

There are various ways to approach the subject. Statistics could be presented about those killed, imprisoned, deported, and otherwise brutalized in the different Communist states. Official policies and statements regarding the struggle against "the enemies" of these states could be described at length. Archival materials, when available, can be mined for data and information.

Instead, I have chosen here to illuminate repression in Communist states through the recollected personal experiences of the surviving victims.[8] There are several reasons for taking this approach. In the first place, these personal accounts are readily available (and have been for a long time); secondly, many of them are not merely of documentary value but also of considerable literary merit. Thirdly, the personal experiences and the qualitative specifics of victimization provide a superior way to grasp the human costs and consequences of these historical events and processes. Such experiences, when clearly articulated and eloquently recalled, tend to be more informative and memorable than quantitative data and scholarly analysis—though of course the latter too are vital for a full understanding of the phenomenon.[9]

The experiences related in the selections to follow include arrest, interrogation, trials, transportation to the place of detention, varieties of physical mistreatment, life in the prisons and camps, various types of labor, circumstances of death, and impressions of the social, psychological, and demographic characteristics of the victim groups and those in charge of them.

These memoirs (even in excerpted form) help the reader to form a vivid picture of the dimensions and human consequences of the political repression engaged in by Communist states. These accounts are also timeless repositories of the processes of suffering, coping with injustice, and adjusting to hopelessness, as well as reflections of human bonding and solidarity, of the relationship between the powerless and the powerful, and the insoluble problem of facing death, especially when it is violent and unnatural.

The amount and types of repression here considered preclude comprehensive treatment in this volume. The use of excerpts is a compromise and cannot be a substitute for reading the entire works from which they are drawn; on the other hand, few readers, even if in search of painful enlightenment on the subject, can be expected to locate, sample, and read the vast literature that is available. Limiting the collection to one volume, even if substantial, is thus a necessary practical compromise; many volumes of such materials could be assembled in search of comprehensiveness and to do justice to the subject matter.

More specifically, this anthology seeks to accomplish the following:

(1) to make available for the general public as well as for specialists a substantial comparative historical sampling of the experiences and facts of political victimization in Communist states. No such collection or sourcebook exists at the present time;

(2) to bring together in one volume personal (autobiographical) and historical as well as social scientific information (as provided in this introduction) about these events and policies and the institutions created to carry them out;

(3) to narrow the gap between information and analysis that is available about the political violence perpetrated by Nazi and Communist regimes and thereby make it possible to compare, and better understand, the two major political outrages of our century;[10]

(4) to stimulate research about the political violence that occurred within different Communist systems, extinct and surviving—an especially compelling task since it is difficult to identify a single American scholar specializing in Communist political violence, either as a comparative endeavor or as one focused on a particular Communist system. Robert Conquest is the only exception: see his pioneering studies of political violence in the Soviet Union, such as *The Great Terror, The Soviet Deportation of Nationalities, Kolyma: Arctic Death Camps,* and *The Harvest of Sorrow.* Anne Applebaum has joined him of late in this endeavor.

(5) to honor the memory of the tens of millions who, in different parts of the world, suffered and perished in the past century as a result of both the intended and the unintended consequences of the pursuit of power and political utopia by Communist political systems. As Martin Malia puts it, "at a time ... when historical writing is turning increasingly to retrospective affirmative action, to fulfilling our 'duty of remembrance' to all the oppressed of the past," there should be room for compassion for these victims of inhumanity as well.[11]

But of all the reasons for this undertaking, the desire to fill a gap—both moral and informational—may be the most compelling. The Western awareness of repression in Communist states remains very limited, even in this post-Communist era when new sources of information have become abundant. Much information was also available before the collapse of Soviet communism (as the dates of publication borne by many selections in this volume indicate), but it attracted little attention and led to little sustained reflection regarding the moral, historical, and political significance of these matters.[12]

Treating Communist mass murders as comparable to the Holocaust need not cast doubt on the uniqueness of the latter. Nonetheless, when close to one hundred million people die in order to achieve certain political ends, a new threshold in political violence is crossed that stimulates comparison with the other mass murders of our times.[13]

There are good reasons why relatively little has been learned in the West about Communist political repression. These systems not only withheld information about their policies and institutions of repression but sometimes went to great length to misinform and deceive international public opinion about them. The Soviet Union, China, Cuba, Nicaragua, and Vietnam (and possibly other Communist states as well) created atypical, model penal institutions for the benefit of visiting delegations from abroad, facilities in which inmates (mostly nonpolitical criminals) were treated humanely and their rehabilitation was the ostensible goal.[14]

One such project was described and praised at length in a volume produced by Soviet writers (thirty-four of them, including Maxim Gorky, Vera Inber, V. Kataev, Alexei Tolstoy, and M. Zoshchenko). It was the building of the Belomor canal—carried out by forced laborers without the benefit of any machinery. Gorky in particular "toured concentration camps and admired their educational value." He visited the Belomor project in the company of Yagoda (head of the political police) and congratulated him for its splendid educational accomplishments.[15] Amabel Williams-Ellis, author of the introduction to the American edition of the book on the Belomor Canal, called it a "tale of the accomplishment of a ticklish engineering job . . . by tens of thousands of enemies of the State . . . guarded . . . by only thirty-seven GPU officers. . . . [O]ne of the most exciting stories that has ever appeared in print."[16]

In support of this official denial and concealment, the once famous Alexei Stakhanov, originally a "simple" coal miner (after whom a mass movement to increase production was named in the Soviet Union), sent an indignant letter to the British socialist publication *Tribune* to rebut allegations about the Soviet penal system and especially its characteristic feature, forced labor. He was specifically indignant about David J. Dallin and Boris I. Nicolaevsky's *Forced Labor in the Soviet Union* (1948), the first study of this subject. Stakhanov (or whoever composed the letter to which his name was appended) wrote in the inimitable style of self-righteousness and injured innocence peculiar to the Soviet propaganda of the times: "You can hardly imagine what indignation and disgust such vile and utterly false tales about our country arouse in a man like myself, who has devoted and is devoting all his efforts to serve his country." The authors he denigrated had "published a disgusting book piled high with all sorts of monstrous fabrications about the Soviet Union."[17]

Witholding or suppressing information about Communist human rights violations was not limited to Communist states. Victor Serge (a former Russian Communist and émigré) found it difficult in the 1940s to publish his memoirs in the United States because they were critical of the Soviet system. And in the 1970s, reported Shirley Hazzard at the time, "the embargo imposed upon Solzhenitsyn's writings in his native land has been . . . reproduced on the international territory of the United Nations, ... which banned the sale of his *Gulag Archipelago* from bookshops on United Nations premises."[18]

The defectors' and refugees' accounts of Soviet repression and the camp system were often publicly questioned by Western supporters of Communist states—and sometimes not only by such sympathizers. The best-known (although now forgotten) case was that of Victor Kravchenko, a Soviet government official who defected to the United States after World War II and wrote two books about his experiences in the Soviet Union. The latter included information acquired in the course of his career as manager of various industrial enterprises located near labor camps, some of which enterprises used convict labor. Kravchenko was subjected to especially vicious attacks in France by local Communists and Soviet officials. He was also regarded with undisguised contempt in the United States by numerous liberal journalists and intellectuals.[19]

In the 1970s Noam Chomsky scornfully dismissed "the tales of Communist atrocities" that had been related by Cambodian refugees.[20] In a similar spirit, J. Arch Getty deplored the use of defectors' accounts in historical research.[21] More recently, Nicholas Kristof, a correspondent for the *New York Times*, cautioned against taking at face value the uncorroborated reports of former inmates of North Korean camps who had managed to escape from that country during the famines of the mid-1990s.[22]

By contrast, few (if any) questions were raised about the reliability or authenticity of the reports of the survivors of Nazi concentration camps,[23] nor has it been suggested that the personal accounts of the victims of racial discrimination (in this or other countries) are to be approached with reservations given their subjective nature.

The enormous literature describing Communist repression made it difficult to decide which authors to choose and which parts of their volumes to excerpt here. The following considerations were paramount:

(1) representativeness; I intended to provide readings by eyewitnesses from as many Communist states as possible, preferably every one of them, in order to document that while the instances of repression here examined are best known in the Soviet setting—thanks largely to Aleksandr Solzhenitsyn—they were not confined to it but rather existed in every Communist state, though not always simultaneously.

(2) I sought writings that would shed light on different aspects of political violence and coercion, e.g., procedures of arrest, extraction of confessions, and conditions of life in prisons and labor camps, as well as excerpts informative about both victims and victimizers;

(3) I also sought selections that would illuminate the nature of repression in different periods and among less-known victim groups and settings (e.g., Albania, North Korea, Romania, Yugoslavia).

(4) The identity and literary reputation of the authors was also taken into account; other things being equal I was inclined to select writings by major,

recognized figures familiar to at least some Western readers. The quality of the writings played an important part in my decision regardless of the author's renown.

Reading these accounts may prove difficult for some readers, as they graphically illustrate and remind us of the unfathomable and distressing capacity of human beings to inflict pain and suffering on one another, often cheerfully and enthusiastically, some times vindictively, more often matter-of-factly and indifferently.

Contemplating the matters detailed in this voume also provides an opportunity to reconsider the concept of evil, which is especially appropriate since, as Lance Morrow has written,

> In enlightened political conversation, the word "evil" had been disreputable for a long time—and still is, to a large extent, despite 9/11. The word "evil," in many minds, still smacks of an atavistic, superstitious simplism, of a fundamentalist mindset. . . .
>
> The secular, educated, cosmopolitan instinct . . . tends to shun the word "evil" and, as an optimist and creature of the Enlightenment, approaches the world's horrors as individual problems that can be solved. . . .[24]

It is always one's hope that information leads to better understanding, and that the latter may influence political attitudes and behavior. To search for meaning even—or especially—in the most horrendous and bewildering events and atrocities appears to be a deeply rooted human impulse: we are instinctively reluctant to believe that such events hold no meaning or provide no lessons.

II: The Question of Moral Equivalence

Unlike Nazi Germany, Communist states did not attempt to eradicate, in a premeditated, systematic, and mechanized fashion, any particular ethnic group or class of people. This policy was nonetheless compatible with the systematic mistreatment of particular ethnic groups suspected of disloyalty. Major examples include the Soviet treatment of Baltic and Caucasian ethnic groups and the so-called Volga Germans and the Chinese treatment of Tibetans.[25] There is a second important difference: Communist regimes, unlike the Nazis, did not seek to murder children.

Communist systems did not invest any single, identifiable group with an omnipotent evil that required its total eradication, nor did they fixate obsessively on any one group, as did the Nazis. The victims of Communist systems came from a wide variety of groups; no particular ethnic, religious, social, or political affiliation and no particular background conferred immunity—this was the major and highly distinctive characteristic of the Communists' policies of victimization. Anybody could be designated as "the enemy" and treated accordingly, including former supporters, functionaries, and leaders.[25] It does not follow, however, that victimization was random, but rather that the criteria for being assigned to the "enemy" category varied over time and among different systems.

There was another morally significant difference between the Nazi and Communist approach to liquidating undesirable groups. In theory, if not often in practice, in the Communist states it was sometimes possible to escape an undesirable social-political designation by demonstrating loyalty to the system; under the Nazis, racial-ethnic categories conferred an immutable condition and inescapable death sentence to the members of such groups.[26]

Richard Pipes summed up the differences as follows:

> The Russians murdered even more people than the Germans, and they murdered their own, but they did it without the mechanical precision, the rational calculation of the Germans who "harvested" human hair and gold fillings. Nor were they proud of their murders. I have never seen a photograph of a Soviet atrocity. . . . [T]he Germans took countless photographs of theirs.[27]

The Nazi mass murders were further distinguished from all other cases of actual or attempted genocide and massive political violence by taking place in what used to be considered the civilized heart of Europe; they were initiated, planned, and carried out by members of a nation that used to be seen as torchbearer of the highest Western cultural traditions and ideals, the descendants of Goethe, Heine, Schiller, Thomas Mann, Kant, Bach, Beethoven, Brahms, and other giants of German and European culture.

The settings of Communist political violence were for the most part countries with large illiterate populations and autocratic traditions, nations either completely isolated from Western cultural influences (as China was for centuries) or harboring a highly ambivalent attitude toward them (as Russia had).

The similarities between the two types of mass murder are also noteworthy, the most significant being their association with the pursuit of some kind of utopia. As Alan Ryan observes, "What is common to all Communist states . . . is the perversion of utopia." Eric Weitz writes, "The movements and regimes discussed . . . promised to create utopia in the here and now. . . . In their overarching drive to found utopia [they] . . . sought to create the 'new man' and the 'new woman.'" In Michael Ignatieff's view, "The danger of genocide lies in its promise to create a world without enemies. . . . [G]enocide [is] a crime in service of a utopia, a world without discord, enmity, suspicion, free of the enemy without or the enemy within. . . . [T]his utopia is the core of the genocidal intention. . . ."[28]

Nazi and Communist mass murders also have in common a cleansing, purifying intention and aspect. As Lance Morrow puts it, "The Nazis justified their extermination as necessities of racial purification. . . . Pol Pot's Khmer Rouge justified its slaughters on the ground of cultural/ideological purification. . . . [E]vil so often justifies itself as a necessary purification. . . ."

He could have added the Soviet "purges," which sought to cleanse society of the many alleged enemies of the system.

The quest for purification and utopia are also linked: ". . . much evil emanates from the discrepancy between the daydream of a golden age and the disappointments of the present. It is one of the great lessons of evil that it flourishes in the subjective self-righteousness and grievance of a highly developed victim culture," writes Morrow. "Evil portrays itself, almost without exception, as injured innocence, fighting back." Aggressors typically define themselves as the injured party.[29]

The Nazis derived their sense of victimhood from the Versaille Treaty, the Soviet Union from being abused and encircled by capitalist countries, China from the experiences of colonial exploitation, Castro's Cuba from American domination, etc., etc. In a similar spirit, George Steiner writes that

> messianic socialism. Even where it proclaims itself to be atheist, the socialism of Marx, of Trotsky, of Ernst Bloch, is directly rooted in messianic eschatology. Nothing is more religious, nothing is closer to the ecstatic rage for justice in the prophets, than the socialist vision of the destruction of the bourgeois Gomorrah and the creation of a new, clean city for man.

As for the Chinese variant, "Mao . . . had a vision, a utopian dream of the total transformation of China . . . 'Even as his policies caused the death of millions, Mao never entirely lost his belief in the . . .possibility of redemption.'" Explicitly comparing Mao to Hitler, Ian Buruma further argues that "the carnage arose from a similar kind of quasi-artistic impulse, an aesthetic vision based on pseudoscience. . . . Anything standing between the vision and the artist had to be eliminated."[30] The Nazi utopia rested on the propagation and supremacy of the racially pure and the elimination or subordination of the racially inferior.

More generally speaking—and again, for both the Nazi and the Communist systems—Charles Simic writes,

> Never before have so many classes of human beings been regarded as having no intrinsic value and therefore having no right to exist. These ambitious programs for depopulating the planet of some national, ethnic, racial or religious group would have been impossible without the accompanying idea that bloodshed

was permissible for the sake of some version of future happiness.[31]

This was also the case in Cambodia under Pol Pot, whose methods of coercion, violence, and establishing guilt generously borrowed not only from the Moscow Trials and Chinese campaigns of "reeducation" but even from the Spanish Inquisition and the eighteenth-century French Revolutionary terror. There are further striking similarities between the Cambodian and Nazi concerns with secrecy.[32]

Most recently, the fusion of mass murder (albeit on a smaller scale) with religious-utopian impulses has been demonstrated by those Islamic suicide bombers and pilots who have eagerly destroyed themselves and others in pursuit of individual salvation and what they consider to be social-political redemption and justice.

There is a shared and profound irrationality in all these policies and actions designed to eliminate their perceived enemies in the expectation that such slaughters will pave the way to superior social-political arrangements (or in the case of Islamic fanatics, to individual salvation and otherworldy rewards).

The determination to provide the necessary resources for these endeavors even under conditions of great scarcity testifies to the unwavering irrationality of these commitments. A well-known example is the Nazis' diverting (in 1943–44) railroad cars from military use to transport Jews to the gas chambers when such rolling stock was badly needed in the faltering war effort. But it is not well known that "in 1943 and 1944, in the middle of the war, Stalin diverted thousands of trucks and hundreds of thousands of soldiers serving in the special NKVD troops from the front . . . in order to deport various peoples living in the Caucasus." Earlier in the war, "when the Red Army was retreating on all fronts [in 1941] and losing tens of thousands every day . . . Beria diverted more than 14,000 men from the NKVD for this operation [the deportation of German speaking minorities]. . . ."[33]

It is another important similarity between Nazi and Communist mass murders that in both cases victimization was often based not on actions or behavior but on belonging to certain categories or groups that automatically conferred an "enemy" designation. In the Nazi case these categories were primarily racial, in the Communist they were mostly related to social status, class, or kinship.

Both systems treated ordinary criminals far better than those assigned to the political-enemy categories. The persecution of homosexuals was another policy shared by Nazi, Soviet, Cuban, and Chinese penal systems. Lesser but not insignificant similarities include the numbering of prisoners (instead of using names), but the Nazi practice of tattooing numbers into the skin was far more brutal than merely affixing the numbers clothing, as was the practice in Communist camps.

There is also a similarity in the theoretical and putatively scientific legitimizations of Nazi and Communist political violence: both served a vision of history, one defined by racial theories in the case of the Nazis, and "scientific socialism" in the case of Communist states.

Chronologically, the Soviet camps preceded the Nazis' and in some ways might have provided a model for the latter. Rudolf Hess, the commander of Auschwitz, wrote:

> The Reich security Head Office issued to the commandants [of camps] a full collection of reports concerning the Russian concentration camps. These described in great detail the conditions in, and organization of, the Russian camps. . . . Great emphasis was placed on the fact that the Russians, by their massive employment of forced labor, had destroyed whole peoples.[34]

Elena Bonner believed that "there was an amazing resemblance between the two punitive bureaucracies—the SS and the NKVD—both in how they were above the law and how their officials were selected."[35]

There are also points of similarity in the mistreatment associated with the interrogation of political prisoners. A former inmate of Soviet prisons and labor camps wrote, "I have met people who went through both Hitler's interrogation and ours. They stated that there must have been an exchange of experience, for the methods were very similar."[36] However, those interrogated by the Nazis were not forced to sign fabricated confessions, as were many in the Communist states. It also appears that, for the most part, Nazi camp guards were more brutal and sadistic than their Communist counterparts.

III: The Attention Gap and Selectivity in Moral Concerns

It is not entirely clear why some historical outrages and atrocities become the focus of public concern and indignation—as well as scholarly attention and research—while others remain largely overlooked, barely known, or forgotten. The mass murders (including the use of chemical weapons against civilians) committed in Iraq under Saddam Hussein, for example, inspired relatively little indignation and concern in Western countries. Paul Berman writes:

> In the twentieth century, crimes on the highest scale took place in the open, yet somehow, through the alchemies of political ideology, the crimes were rendered invisible. . . . This has been Iraq's experience precisely. Saddam launched his slaughters twenty-five years ago, and in Western countries everyone knew, yet most people managed not to see and no one ever succeeded in organizing a truly mass protest.
>
> A truly large and powerful protest movement took to the streets

all over the Western world only in February 2003—and this was not to denounce the terrible dictatorship but to prevent an invasion from overthrowing the terrible dictatorship.[37]

Another notable example, this one from the more distant past, is the case of the Chinese civilians massacred by the Japanese military in Nanking in 1937.[38] The reasons for overlooking this exceptionally repugnant episode of modern history may also shed some light on the limited attention Communist atrocities have received in the Western world.

The "rape of Nanking" was probably ignored in part because of the cultural remoteness of the setting (it took place China rather than in Europe) and the apparent lack of ideological motivation on the part of the perpetrators. The massacres were seen as a by-product of war (making them seem more "normal"), and no particular segment of the population was singled out on racial, ethnic, or political grounds. At the same time, this was not just an instance of victorious troops getting out of hand: "it was not a temporary lapse of military discipline since it lasted for seven weeks," points out one historian, and it was conducted in public with no attempt to hide it.[39]

The Japanese biological and germ warfare experiments (including vivisection of mostly Chinese prisoners of war) likewise attracted little attention, although an estimated 200,000 Chinese prisoners were killed in field experiments. In the course of these studies prisoners were locked "inside a pressure chamber to see how much the body can withstand before the eyes pop from their sockets. . . ." On other occasions, writes Nicholas Kristof,

> Victims were taken to a proving ground . . . where they were tied to stakes and bombarded with test weapons to see how effective the new technologies were. Planes sprayed the zone with a plague culture or dropped bombs with plague-infested fleas to see how many people would die.[40]

Another mass murder committed by the Japanese and described as "one of World War II's least publicized atrocities" took place in the Indonesian province of what is now called West Kalimantan. It "could legitimately be described as 'genocidal' in that whole sectors of society seemed to be picked out for execution," wrote Barbara Crosette. "[U]p to 20,000 people may have been put to death by firing squad or the sword. . . . Among them . . . scholars, doctors, former government officials, business leaders—anyone who might one day have opposed Japanese rule."[41]

Until very recently there has been little soul-searching in Japan concerning these massacres (or, for that matter, the others carried out by Japanese forces during World War II); they have been altogether denied or their magnitude disputed.

A contrasting example of a mass killing of civilians in war that did generate lasting moral indignation was the U.S.'s dropping of two atomic bombs on Japan in 1945. These bombings have not only become the focus of worldwide public attention but also the source of enduring soul-searching in the Western world (especially in the United States), although the number of their combined victims (140,000 in Hiroshima and 78,000 in Nagasaki)[42] was eclipsed by those of Nanking, where the casualties are estimated at between 260,000 and 350,000. (Comparable numbers of civilians were also killed in the conventional aerial bombardment of German cities during World War II, and this without provoking moral concern in the West.) The victims of the American atomic bombs arguably met their deaths faster, and under less painful conditions, than did the Chinese civilians of Nanking. Moreover, defensible military considerations also played a part in the decision to use atomic bombs; the invasion of Japan by U.S. military forces could have cost more lives, Japanese as well as American, than did the bombing.

Another largely forgotten catastrophic chain of events claimed hundreds of thousands of victims in Ethiopia in the 1980s (an Ethiopian author has called it "the Ethiopian holocaust"). It combined governmental coercion and economic mismanagement inspired partly by Marxist doctrine and partly by a desire to bring the population under more thorough political control. The forcible resettlement, collectivization, and disruption of agricultural production resulted in famine, as had similar policies pursued in the former Soviet Union in the early 1930s.[43]

The treatment of civilians in Afghanistan by the Soviet armed forces and the Afghan political police (the KHAD) offers another example of large-scale atrocities (these from the 1970s and '80s) that have resulted in little but inattention and moral indifference among the Western public. As one of the reports on these events summed it up:

> Just about every conceivable human rights violation is occurring in Afghanistan and on an enormous scale. The crimes of indiscriminate warfare are combined with the worst excesses of unbridled state-sanctioned violence against civilians. The ruthless savagery in the countryside is matched by the subjection of a terrorized urban population to arbitrary arrest, torture, imprisonment and execution.[44]

These acts of violence against the civilian population were sparked by anti-Soviet guerilla activities, but Soviet troops made few distinctions between armed guerillas and unarmed civilians they suspected of supporting them; they killed civilians as retribution for guerilla attacks.[45] Soviet soldiers taken prisoner by the guerillas recounted the atrocities they witnessed or participated in:

"If one of ours was killed or wounded, we would kill women, children and old people as revenge. We killed everything, even the animals. . . ."

Once they [Soviet soldiers] entered a village where only old men and women with children were left. . . . The lieutenant ordered his platoon to herd all these women, children and old men together into one room and throw in hand grenades. . . .[46]

It is important to stress that "the [r]epression was not simply a response to resistance . . . it preceded, and indeed helped to inspire, the revolt." As in other Communist states, criteria unrelated to actual behavior but supposedly suggestive of hostile predisposition were sufficient:

Reasons for suspicion can be quite diverse: past friendship with an American Peace Corps volunteer, possession of an opposition leaflet, having relatives suspected of opposition, or being named by a paid spy or a prisoner under torture. In June 1983 a group of handicapped teenage boys who had been cared for by a French priest were arrested and interrogated under torture about their alleged work for French intelligence.[47]

Muslim clerics and liberal, westernized intellectuals alike were hunted down with particular fervor.[48] Torture was widely used:

The methods of torture are . . . beatings, death threats, pulling out of hair and fingernails, near-drownings, sleep deprivation, strangling, and most common . . . electric shocks. The electric shock equipment has been upgraded since the Soviet invasion. . . . Several sources tell of a new equipment introduced in 1984, such as the [electric] chair that was used to torture an eighteen year old who had distributed anti-Soviet leaflets. . . .[49]

According to another source, "the most commonly reported methods of torture are sleep deprivation, prolonged beatings and electric shocks . . . sometimes intensified by dousing the prisoner with water."[50] Among the more unusual forms of pressure brought to bear on the detainees was showing them the badly tortured corpses of other prisoners and torturing others in front of them.[51] Burying prisoners alive was also widely reported.[52] Notwithstanding these unusually brutal tactics, the Western condemnation of the Soviet Union was muted.

The atrocities committed by Soviet troops in Eastern Europe and especially East Germany during and in the aftermath of World War II were likewise overlooked, and to this date few people in the West are aware of them.

The mistreatment of civilians in these countries took three major forms: 1) the widespread raping of women; 2) large-scale authorized looting; 3) the killing of civilians who attempted to interfere with the above activities.

These Soviet policies were reflected in the remarks of Stalin recorded by Milovan Djilas. Even in Yugoslavia, which was an ally of the Soviet Union and had been occupied by Germany, such atrocities occurred. The Yugoslav Communist leaders visiting Moscow raised the issue with Stalin, tactfully pointing to the *political damage* done by such behavior, rather than to its morally problematic nature. Stalin was not impressed: "And such an army [the Soviet one] was insulted . . . by Djilas. . . . Can't he understand it if a soldier who has crossed thousands of kilometers through blood and fire and death has fun with a woman or takes some trifle?"[53]

Djilas also wrote:

> Soon after my return from Moscow, I heard . . . of a far more significant example of Stalin's "understanding" attitude toward the sins of Red Army personnel. Namely, while crossing East Prussia, Soviet soldiers, especially tank units, pounded and regularly killed all German civilian refugees—women and children. Stalin was informed of this and asked what should be done. He replied: "We lecture our soldiers too much; let them have some initiative."[54]

Stalin displayed a similar attitude when the problem of rape and plunder in East Germany was brought to his attention by East German Communist leaders: "Stalin replied with an old Russian proverb: 'In every family there is a black sheep.' He said nothing more. When one of us tried to put the matter more seriously . . . he was interrupted by Stalin: 'I will not allow anyone to drag the reputation of the Red Army in the mud.' That was the end of the conversation."[55] Thus, for Stalin mass rapes were but "fun," vast sprees of looting simply "taking some trifles," and the mass killing of civilians nothing but a display of "initiative."[56]

It is not surprising that the most serious acts of violence were inflicted on the people of East Germany, given the German attack on the Soviet Union in World War II and the brutal treatment of the Soviet population by German troops. The behavior of the Soviet troops reflected a confluence of spontaneous personal feeling and official policy. Soviet propaganda encouraged the troops to act brutally, as for example the "road signs [which] urged Soviet soldiers to hurt the Germans: 'Soldier you are in Germany, take revenge on the Hitlerites.'" Moreover, writes Norman Naimark, "throughout the Soviet press, the idea was widespread that the Germans—women on the homefront included—would have to 'pay' for their evil deeds."[57] Official connivance was reflected in the persistence of these incidents "at least until the beginning of

1947."[58] The scope of these atrocities was huge, with estimates of rape victims ranging from hundreds of thousands to two million.[59] As Naimark puts it:

> It was not atypical for Soviet troops to rape every female over the age of twelve or thirteen in a village, killing many in the process; to pillage homes for food, alcohol and loot; and leave the village in flames. The reports of women subjected to gang rapes . . . are far too numerous to be considered isolated incidents. Lev Kopelev, then a captain in the Soviet Army, tried to stop a group of rampaging soldiers and was accused of having engaged in "bourgeois humanism."[60]

Soviet policy toward its own troops was no less brutal: in World War II surrender was treated as treason and punished accordingly; military tribunals sentenced to death the astonishing number of 157,000 soldiers; "most of the condemned," writes Alexander Yakovlev, "had escaped from prisoner of war camps or broken out of encirclement."[61]

Soviet atrocities against civilians were also widespread in Hungary during and after World War II. According to one estimate, approximately 10 percent of all women in Hungary were raped by Soviet soldiers.[62]

The repression that followed the Communist victory in South Vietnam is another example of large-scale political violence in recent times that received little attention in the Western world and especially the United States. More than one million Vietnamese sought escape (the so-called boat people) *after the war ended.* In other words, it was not the hardships of war but Communist rule they fled; hundreds of thousands of those who remained were imprisoned in various types of "reeducation" camps, and probably hundreds of thousands were executed.[63]

Another more recent and persisting case of public indifference toward what one writer has called "arguably the greatest humanitarian catastrophe of our lifetime"[64] has been the civil war and associated instances of repression in the Sudan, which have reportedly claimed at least two million lives and created more than twice that many refugees. The victims have been the southerners (who are different in religion and ethnicity) and the victimizers a radical Islamic regime in the north.

Finally, the widespread "hacking off hands and feet of ordinary people" by a rebel group in Sierra Leone in 1999 was another unique atrocity that generated little attention or moral indignation in Western countries.[65]

These examples make clear that the public (and scholarly) responses to the great historical outrages of our times are not necessarily proportional either to the number of victims or the quality of the suffering inflicted. The adverse reaction to the American use of atomic weapons against Japan (a reaction that has actually intensified over time) was probably conditioned by an aversion toward the military use of advanced technology, and possibly also by the circumstance that annihilation was inflicted by a Western nation upon a non-Western one. A diffuse, collective sense of guilt and a distaste toward modern technology among large portions of American (and Western) intellectuals, opinion-makers, and the educated public help to explain these sentiments. Similar attitudes contributed to the vehement criticism of U.S. bombing in Vietnam by huge planes flying at high altitudes, as if such ways of inflicting damage were inherently more repugnant than the use of small arms, land mines, or poisoned bamboo sticks, methods favored by the Vietcong.

The primary example of this asymmetry in public reaction pertains to Western attitudes toward Nazism and the various Communist states and the atrocities perpetrated by each. By contrast, Tzvetan Todorov argues: "Communism . . . lasted longer . . . spread more widely, to almost every continent . . . and it killed an even greater number of people. It is also more important to condemn it from our present perspective: it has a greater power to confuse and seduce. . . . But there is an obvious imbalance in the way the two regimes are . . . described. The Nazi regime is universally abhorred . . . whereas Communism (in France in its Trotskyist variant) still enjoys wide respect. Antifascism is obligatory, whereas anti-Communism remains suspect. . . . In contemporary France and Germany Holocaust denial is an offense punishable by law, whereas denying Communist crimes—indeed praising the ideology that commanded them—remains perfectly legitimate." Anne Applebaum recalls Western tourists eagerly decking themselves out in the paraphernalia of the defunct Soviet system that is sold on the streets of Prague and Moscow, all of whom "would be sickened by the thought of wearing a swastika" but think nothing of "wearing the hammer and sickle on a T-shirt." She also notes that nobody in Hollywood has chosen to make a movie about Soviet concentration camps, while many have been made about those of the Nazis and Japanese. And while pro-Nazi sympathies inflicted serious damage on the reputation of some Western intellectuals, Jean Paul Sartre (and many others like him) did not experience comparable damage to their reputations on account of their support for Communist systems, including that of Stalin. As Applebaum concludes, "to many people the crimes of Stalin [and one may add, those of Mao, Pol Pot, Castro, Ho Chi Minh etc.] do not inspire the same visceral reaction as do the crimes of Hitler." A large part of the reason for these discrepant attitudes was that "to condemn the Soviet Union too thoroughly would be to condemn a part of what some of the Western left once held dear as well."[66] Or as Tony Judt put it: "To many Western European intellectuals communism was a failed variant of a common progressive heritage."[67]

Alain Besançon has asked with good reason: ". . . how is it that today the two systems are treated so unequally in historical memory, to the point when one of them, Soviet communism, though a still-recent presence on the world scene, has already been all but forgotten?"[68]

None of this discussion implies that there was anything questionable or irrational about the profound and durable moral abhorrence the Holocaust inspired. Rather, I am simply suggesting that the Communist atrocities are as deserving of moral attention and condemnation as are the Nazi ones. As Alain de Benoist writes:

> The victims of communism do not cancel out the victims of Nazism anymore than the victims of Nazism cancel out the victims of communism. . . . [T]he crimes of one regime cannot be used to justify or diminish the importance of the crimes perpetrated by the other. . . .[69]

Another notable example of the asymmetrical reactions we are discussing is found in a theoretical examination of what one author called "sanctioned massacres . . . directed at groups that have not themselves threatened or engaged in hostile action against the perpetrators of the violence." In this text, juxtaposed to an ample discussion of the Nazi mass murders and American atrocities in Vietnam is but one brief, perfunctory reference to Soviet mass murders ("the liquidation of the kulaks and the great purges in the Soviet Union"), alongside others committed in this century in Indonesia, Biafra, Burundi, etc. There is not a single reference to any source dealing with Soviet or other Communist mass murders.[70] Professor Kelman's apparent unfamiliarity with Communist mass violence leads him to believe that "sanctioned massacres" in those systems are "entirely outside of the realm of moral discourse," since they don't have a defensive justification. In fact Communist governments vastly extended the notion of self-defense and obliterated the line between actual and potential threats to their rule: people were persecuted and killed not for their actual but for their *potentially* threatening behavior. Kelman's unfamiliarity with Communist mass murders severely restricts the scope of his generalizations.

A further illustration of these attitudes appears in a symposium on the work of Stanley Milgram, the social psychologist famous for his experiments illustrating obedience to authority. Not one of the fourteen contributors entertains the idea that his experiments might have some applicability or relevance to the highly organized political violence of Communist systems.[71]

Similarly revealing is a 1987 program on public television (titled "The Faces of the Enemy" and produced by Sam Keen, a California psychologist) that purported to explore the connections between political propaganda and the dehumanization of various groups. While the program examined the attitudes, atrocities, and propaganda associated with Nazis, right-wingers, and the U.S. military in Vietnam, there was no reference whatsoever to the mass murders of Stalin, Mao, or Pol Pot, or the Communist propaganda associated with these atrocities.[72]

This inattention or selectivity is all the more remarkable since the number of victims of Communist systems significantly exceeds those of Nazism.[73] These systems were in power for a much longer time than were the Nazis and controlled much larger populations.

The discrepancy in reaction to the Nazi and Communist horrors is even more striking if one considers the responses to the combined mass murders (and other forms of victimization) committed in Communist states other than the Soviet Union, such as China, Cuba, Ethiopia, North Korea, Vietnam, and others. The mass murders in Vietnam, in fact, provoked perhaps the least public indignation or moral outrage, with the exception of Cambodia. The latter, not quite incidentally, came to attract attention and moral indignation only after the system was overthrown (and thereby delegitimated) by another Communist state, Vietnam. The Vietnamese government eagerly publicized the Cambodian horrors: coming as it did from a Communist source, the information appeared more credible to many Western intellectuals and opinion makers than it was when provided by the refugees, as the views of Chomsky (cited earlier) illustrate.[74] Prior to the war with Vietnam, pro–Pol Pot apologies like this one, from Malcolm Caldwell, were more typical:

> The new Government [of Pol Pot] fighting for its survival against all this counter-revolutionary activity had to deal swiftly and sternly with every instance of sabotage and subversion. Undoubtedly this was a bloody process that may well have entailed some excesses and mistakes. But without revolutionary violence against the enemy, the revolution itself would have been crushed in its infancy.[75]

This has been the classic apology for every instance of Communist political violence ever since the Russian Revolution of 1917.

Chomsky was the most famous and voluble Western sympathizer with the government of Pol Pot. He self-assuredly disputed the higher and far more accurate estimates of the number of Pol Pot's victims and scornfully dismissed the refugees' accounts. Nonetheless, his intellectual and moral reputations have suffered little. As Martin Malia has written: "The status of 'ex-Communist' [in Chomsky's case, 'ex-apologist'] carries with it no stigma, even when unaccompanied by any expression of regret. Past contact with Nazism, however, no matter how marginal or remote, confers an indelible stain."[76]

Malia proposes several explanations for what he calls "the dual perception" of Nazism and communism. In the first place there was the World War II alliance of the Western powers and the Soviet Union against Nazism, which muted potential criticism of the Soviet system. Secondly, the defeat (in World War II) cut Nazism down in the prime of its iniquity, thereby eternally fixing its memory in full horror. By contrast communism, at the peak of *its* iniquity, was rewarded with an epic victory (in World War II)—thereby gaining a half-century to . . . half-repent of Stalin and even . . . to attempt giving the system a "human face." These contrasting endgames thus bared all Nazism's secrets fifty years ago while we are only beginning to explore Soviet archives, and those of East Asia and Cuba remain sealed.[77]

An obvious source of the different moral judgments of Nazism and communism is the reluctance—or refusal, as the case may be—to recognize that there were significant structural and attitudinal similarities between the Nazi and the Soviet (and, by extension, other Communist) systems. For the same reason (often unacknowledged), in the 1960s the concept of totalitarianism came under criticism from many Western scholars and intellectuals because it provided a conceptual bridge, and suggested a moral equivalence, between Nazi and Communist systems.

This is the place to recall Edward Shils's little known inventory of the similarities between the beliefs and attitudes of the authoritarian supporters of the Nazi and Soviet systems. On the extreme Right (as specified by the study of the authoritarian personality), we find:

(1) Extreme hostility towards "outgroups". . . .
(2) Extreme submissiveness towards "ingroups."
(3) Establishment of sharp boundaries between the group one is a member of and other groups.
(4) The tendency to categorize persons with respect to certain qualities. . . .
(5) . . . a vision of the world as a realm of conflict.
(6) Disdain for purely theoretical . . . activities.
(7) A repugnance for the expression of sentiments. . . .
(8) Belief that oneself and one's group can survive only by the manipulation of others.
(9) The ideal of a conflictless, wholly harmonious society. . . .

As for what Shils called the Bolshevik outlook, we see:

(1) The demand for complete and unqualified loyalty to the party.
(2) The insistence on the necessary conflict of interest between the working class of which the party is the leader and all other . . . classes. . . .

(3) The continuous application of the criteria of party interests in judging every person and situation. . . .

(4) A stress on the class characteristics of individuals. . . .

(5) The belief that all history is the history of class conflicts.

(6) The denial of the existence of pure truth. . . .

(7) The belief that the expression of sentiment is an expression of weakness. . . .

(8) The belief in the ubiquitousness of the influence of "Wall Street" . . . "Big Banks" . . . "200 families," etc., and their masked control. . . .

(9) The ideal of the classless society . . . without conflict. . . .[78]

In all probability, the most important and emotive reason for the divergence in moral judgments examined here is that Communist systems were associated with the idealistic and universalistic ideology of Marxism, whereas no ideology of comparable respectability was utilized by the Nazi regime. But as Tzvetan Todorov argued, "Much has been made of the seemingly unbridgeable ideological abyss separating the two systems, yet as soon as one begins to look not at abstract ideological pronouncements but at the ideologies that can be deduced from actions, the gap narrows." Todorov also wrote,

Communism seeks the happiness of humanity but only once the 'bad guys' have been separated out of it, and that is what Nazism envisaged too. How is it possible to believe in the universal validity of the doctrine when it asserts that it is based on struggle, violence, permanent revolution, hatred, dictatorship and war? It justifies itself on the grounds that the proletariat is the majority and bourgeoisie the minority—but that already takes us a long way away from universal ideals. . . .

We must . . . stress that the renunciation of universalism is no less characteristic of Communism, which professes universal ideals, than it is of Nazism, which . . . openly declares its own particularism. . . . In practice Communism was as 'particularist' as Nazism since it explicitly asserted that its stated ideal did not extend to the whole of humanity. . . . The only real difference is that in one case the division of humanity is 'horizontal,' based on national frontiers, and in the other it is 'vertical,' between different layers of a society: national and racial war for Nazism, and class war for Communism.[79]

Benoist further explicates this point:

> Stalin's crimes were the result of the perversion of communism, which was "an ideal of human liberation," while Hitler's crimes followed directly from his ideology.... [C]ommunism betrayed its promises, Nazi practices followed directly from its doctrine. ... [T]he practices of Soviet communism constituted ... "a misguided application of a sound ideology." ...[80]

This was a belief apparently shared by Eric Hobsbawm, who was unembarrassed to admit that even if he had known in 1934 that "millions of people were dying in the Soviet experiment" he would not have renounced it, because "the chance of a new world being born in great suffering would still have been worth backing," even if it had required the sacrifice of fifteen or twenty million.[81] Hobsbawm (like Chomsky) continues to enjoy an excellent moral and intellectual reputation in Western academic circles. His quotation above illustrates and corroborates Malia's observation about those fearful of "shut[ting] the door on utopia," those who "in this unjust world cannot abandon hope for an absolute end to inequality...."[82]

Hobsbawm and kindred spirits have focused on the morality of intentions, on what François Furet calls "the founding promise" that protected the reputation of the movements and systems built upon it.[83] But Milovan Djilas (more closely acquainted with these matters than Hobsbawm and most Western intellectuals) pointed out that

> communism brims over with humanistic injunctions touching on brotherhood, solidarity, equality and so on. But ... the humanitarian elements as a rule have no significance beyond legitimizing stern methods.... Communism's humanistic elements nourish the illusion that they themselves will become a reality once the final goal ... is reached.[84]

Joseph Brodsky (a Soviet exile and Noble prize–winning poet) believes that the Western refusal to fully acknowledge "Soviet reality" (i.e., the enormity of repression) is a matter of "mental self preservation.... [A] mental fence was constructed especially by the Western left. It was mostly among the intellectuals."[85]

The difference in the West's moral judgments of Nazism and communism is also linked to the distinction made between "extermination practiced to achieve a political objective, no matter how perverse [the Communist case] and extermination as an end itself [the Nazi policy]."[86] This distinction, however, may become blurred when one considers that the extermination of the Jews, while an end in itself, was for the Nazis a precondition for creating a better, purified world. In short, it was also an idealistic goal, however perverted and irrational. Benoist has also pointed out that no regime has ever seen the massacres it engaged in as an "end in itself." ... Both the utopia of a classless society and of pure race required the elimination of those presumed to be obstacles to the realization of a "grandiose" project, impediments to the realization of a radically better society. In both cases, the ideology (racial or class struggle) led to a bad principle: the exclusion of whole categories ("inferior" races or "harmful" classes) composed of people whose only crime was to belong to one of these categories.[87]

Ian Buruma also raises a relevant, thought-provoking question:

[I]s it categorically different to murder people because of their class than because of their race? There is a distinction to be sure: Hitler wanted to kill every Jewish man, woman or child. Mao still believed that at least some reactionaries could be redeemed through "reeducation." And yet when one thinks that Mao's victims included the children and even grandchildren of class enemies, persecuted simply because of their background, the difference may not disappear entirely but surely becomes less categorical.[88]

Some East European dissidents have in fact argued that "mass murder in the name of a noble ideal is more *perverse* than in the name of a base one. The Nazis, after all, never claimed to be virtuous. The Communists, by contrast, trumpeting their humanism, hoodwinked millions around the world for decades."[89]

At last, as I have argued elsewhere,[90] the repellent "moral distinction" the Nazi mass murders have achieved is closely linked to their highly premeditated, efficient, and technologically advanced character.[91] A much higher *proportion* of inmates survived the Gulag and similar establishments in various Communist states than did their counterparts in the Nazi camps. The Gulag and similar institutions in Communist states were not designed for extermination, although they accomplished this through the high mortality rates that resulted from their living and working conditions. To be sure, substantial numbers in Communist states were also executed (by shooting) or eliminated by famines, which were either the result of deliberate government policy (as in the Ukraine) or of the unanticipated consequences of policies such as the collectivization of agriculture, population transfers, and the assignment of agricultural workers to tasks such as the collection of scrap metal: famines caused by these policies occurred in the Soviet Union, Ethiopia, and China, respectively.

The large number of victims deliberately killed has been confirmed by the post-Soviet discoveries of numerous mass burial sites, among them the Kuropaty graves. As Robert Conquest notes, "the revisionist estimates for the whole USSR could be tucked into a single corner of this one gravesite. . . ."[92]

The secretiveness of Communist systems made the gathering of information on these matters difficult and at times impossible—a circumstance that partially explains why Communist atrocities generated disproportionately less moral indignation. Nonetheless, none of these systems was completely successful in concealing *all* such information. Much was revealed in individual accounts smuggled out, or by those who managed to escape. Considerable information of this type accumulated over the decades, despite the efforts of Communist governments. Following their collapse much more has become available.

The least known among the remaining Communist states is North Korea, rated by Freedom House "as 'the worst of the worst' in terms of political rights and civil liberties." As Christopher Hitchens (who managed to visit) puts it, North Korea "might easily be described as the world's protoype Stalinist state . . . where individual life is *absolutely pointless,* and where everything that is not absolutely compulsory is absolutely forbidden."[93] Because of the famine of the mid-1990s, which produced thousands of refugees, new information about the specifics of North Korean repression has begun finally to emerge.[94] It is emblematic of longstanding Western attitudes that a reporter from the *New York Times* expressed the type of misgivings about these refugee reports that Chomsky voiced two decades ago about the accounts of Cambodian refugees, and still earlier skeptics expressed about Soviet refugee accounts. Nicholas D. Kristof wrote:

> Mrs. Li and other defectors portray the North Korean camps as unremittingly savage but it is difficult to know how accurate this portrait is. North Korea is sealed off from the rest of the world and virtually all of those who claim any contact with the prison system are defectors. . . . Thus it is impossible to know if the defectors are describing what they really endured or what South Korean intelligence officials told them to recount.[95]

Mr. Kristof evidently forgot or never learned that refugee reports of Communist repression proved to be accurate in virtually all cases over a long period of time. *The Aquariums of Pyongyang* (excerpted in this volume) certainly substantiates the claims of the North Korean defectors and suggests that the North Korean Gulag has been among the most inhumane.

It is possible that the limited Western attention paid to Communist atrocities and their victims may in part be explained by the fact that a large proportion of them did not die as a result of execution. On the other hand, as Tony Judt has pointed out, "These mass murders were not the accidental by-product of misguided policies but the outcome of willful, sometimes genocidal calculation and intent. . . . Mass murder . . . was not an unintended consequence but part of the project from the start."[96]

It remains debatable what precise moral distinctions should be attached to the fact that in the Nazi extermination camps people died as a result of highly purposeful, mechanized ways of killing, whereas in the Soviet (and other Communist) systems most deaths resulted—over a far longer period of time—from the impossibility of surviving long sentences in the labor camps. It may well be argued that the deliberate, programmatic extermination of entire groups is more repugnant than a death toll attained in a less purposeful manner, for example, from harsh living conditions and forced labor. It is not easy to decide which was worse: years of starvation, ill health, and hard labor in the camps or prisons culminating in death, or a quick end in the gas chambers or in front of the firing squads.

It is hard to know—as far as the Communist camps were concerned—what carried more weight in the minds of those who designed them: the desire to provide a large pool of cheap labor for important construction projects or the intention to gradually eliminate perceived enemies. An early victim of Soviet repression believed that physical elimination was the goal:

> I gathered from the candid statements of the Chekhists that the GPU has now no need to make a regular practice of mass shootings, because more humane measures—slow murder from starvation, work beyond the prisoner's strength, and "medical help"—are perfectly adequate substitutes.

As to rehabilitation:

> The leaders of the Communist Party declare that the Northern Camps for Special Purposes are something in the nature of a reformatory. The punishments administered in these establishments, they would have the world to believe, are intended to make the prisoners mend their ways an become useful citizens.
>
> . . .
>
> In reality, the camp punishments, like the camp medical arrangements, are based upon no other calculation than that of sending the largest possible number of prisoners . . . to "the other side."[97]

V. T. Shalamov, a major chronicler and inmate of the Gulag (quoted by Roy Medvedev), wrote:

> [I]t took twenty to thirty days to turn a healthy man into a wreck. Working in the camp mine sixteen hours a day, without any

days off, with systematic starvation, ragged clothes, sleeping in
a torn tent at sixty below zero, did the job. Beating by the foremen, by the ringleaders of the thieves, by the guards, speeded
up the process.

While, according to Roy Medvedev, the mining camps were the most lethal, after 1937 "the corrective labor camps were turned into hard-labor camps,
calculated not so much to correct as to destroy the prisoners. . . . [T]he regime
of most Kolyma and northern camps was deliberately calculated to destroy
people."[98] Avraham Shifrin pointed out that some of the camps were "death
camps," in the sense that "prisoners, forced to work under dangerously un-
healthy conditions . . . face virtually certain death." They included uranium
mines, uranium enrichment plants, and military nuclear plants, among others.[99]

All in all, the moral differences and similarities between Nazi and Soviet
death camps may be summed up in the words of Irving Louis Horowitz:

> [O]f the two systemic horrors of the century, the Communist
> regimes hold a measurable edge over fascist regimes in their
> life-taking propensities. . .
>   . . . those for whom the technology of death remains central
> may . . . prefer to think of the Nazis as worse offenders, whereas
> those for whom an elaborate prison system forever enshrined as
> the Gulag by Solzhenitsyn will see Communists as worse of-
> fenders.[100]

IV: Characteristics of Repression in Communist States

HISTORICAL BACKGROUND AND IDEOLOGICAL ROOTS

Communist systems existed in areas of diverse historical and cultural traditions inhabited by different ethnic groups. As time went by these systems
became more differentiated in their policies, including the degree of repression they engaged in. Nonetheless, it is possible to make certain generalizations about them (see note 1) and the type of political repression they per-
petuated.

These systems ranged in size and population from Albania to China, in
longevity from the Soviet Union (seventy-four years) to Sandinista Nicaragua
(ten years), in economic development and level of urbanization from Czechoslovakia and East Germany to Ethiopia and Angola. Most of these systems
could also be described—at least in their origins—as "revolutionary."[101] Of
such systems it has been observed:

> What is strikingly similar about the twenty-two cases of con-
> temporary revolutions ... is not their structural origins, but the
> common values and shared behavior of their leaders. . . .
> [S]uccessful revolutionaries, once in control ... proved to have
> had remarkably similar ideas about how to remake their societ-
> ies. . . .The shared intellectual culture of contemporary revolu-
> tions centered on a commitment to "socialism."[102]

Communist political violence ebbed and flowed, surged and diminished over time. There are identifiable high points (as for example the 1930s in the Soviet Union and the 1960s in China) and long periods of routine, less life-threatening policies of repression. But the common ideological foundations of Communist systems shaped their policies of repression, which centered on the crucial—theoretical as well as practical—distinction between supporters and opponents. As Igal Halfin wrote:

> Far from dispensing with the division of human souls into good
> and evil, Communism endowed this tradition with the status of
> a thoroughly scientific observation. The Communist concep-
> tual architectonics was full of black-and-white oppositions: pro-
> letariat versus bourgeoisie, revolution versus counterrevolution,
> progress versus reaction. . . .[103]

Another widely shared philosophical premise was that "the leaders of the Communist Party, unfettered by a 'bourgeois' legal code or a capricious judicial system, were fully entitled to punish enemies of the state. They were empowered to do so because of their privileged relationship to historical laws."[104]

The common heritage of the Marxist-Leninist worldview also enabled the rulers and planners of repression to think in abstract, impersonal categories and overlook the specific, empirical consequences of their policies for particular groups and individuals. Simon Leys observed (in the Chinese context):

> [T]he Communists always believed that mankind mattered more
> than man. In the eyes of the party leaders individual lives were
> merely a raw material in abundant supply—cheap, disposable and
> easily replaceable. Therefore ... they came to consider that the
> exercise of terror was synonymous with the exercise of power.[105]

The political police forces (or "state security" organs) Communist states developed to perform these tasks were larger, more powerful, and more highly differentiated than regular police forces charged with ordinary crime control and prevention. They had similar organizational structures because the first Communist state, the Soviet Union, was the model for such forces and provided assistance in establishing them. Police and military officers attended Soviet training schools; Soviet advisers assisted their East European counterparts in the preparation of the post–World War II show trials. The East German state security arm (the Stasi) came to play a prominent role in Third World Communist systems. As a former high-ranking Vietnamese Communist functionary wrote, "the state of our security forces owes a lot to the East German Stasi and the Soviet KGB. These two organizations trained our cadres in various specialized subjects and exchanged experience about methods of detection and investigation. . . . [T]he Cong [the Vietnamese political police] became just as overmanned as the armed forces."[106]

All Communist penal systems made a sharp distinction between political and nonpolitical crimes and criminals. In every one of them the latter were treated better and were often given, informally, power over the political prisoners. The authorities considered political criminals a much greater threat than ordinary criminals, who were not accused of calling into question the nature of the system or of trying to undermine it. Sometimes those classified as political criminals were also accused of common, nonpolitical crimes, including, in the Soviet case, "hooliganism." The purpose of such accusations was either to obscure the political origins of the persecution of particular individuals (especially if they were known in the West) or to complete their moral discreditation.

In at least four Communist states—the Soviet Union, Cuba, China, and Romania—those accused of political crimes were sometimes simultaneously classified as suffering from some mental illness and thus were detained in special psychiatric institutions. The most widely practiced and best known was the Soviet detention of outspoken dissidents in psychiatric hospitals,[107] but in China, too, according to recent reports, there is "a secretive system of psychiatric hospitals around the country that are affiliated with local public security bureaus [the Chinese political police]. . . ." In one instance, a Chinese dissident was held for seven years in such a hospital for unfurling a protest banner in Tiananmen Square in 1992.[108] Spurious attributions of mental illness in Communist systems are probably made for two reasons. One is to make the system appear more humane and less punitive; the other, more sinister and totalitarian in its implications, is the belief that questioning and criticizing the system *itself* amounted to a kind of mental disease.

It is among the remarkable paradoxes of history that Communist systems claimed the lives of vast numbers of their citizens in spite of the ideologically derived expectation that they would be far less repressive than both their historical predecessors and contemporary non-Communist societies. This expectation rested on the belief that Communist governments would enjoy unparalleled popular support and social legitimacy, that they would be veritable embodiments of consensus and harmony and therefore would have little need to resort to force in dealing with their citizens. As Engels wrote (and as Lenin quoted approvingly):

> Society, thus far based upon class antagonism, had need of the state... for the purpose of forcibly keeping the exploited classes in the condition of oppression. . . . [But] when at last it [the state] becomes the real representative of the whole of society, it renders itself unnecessary. As soon as there is no longer any social class to be held in subjection . . . nothing more remains to be repressed, and a special force, the state is no longer necessary. The first act by virtue of which the state really constitutes itself the representative of the whole of society—the taking possession of the means of production in the name of society— this is at the same time, its last independent act as a state. State interference in social relations becomes, in one domain after another, superfluous and then withers away of itself. . . .[109]

This presumption of unfolding social harmony was at the heart of the optimistic assessments of the future of the state as an agency of coercion; the same presumption also served as the theoretical basis for establishing a one-party system that would be adequate to represent all interests in a society that had banished major divisions and conflicts. In more recent times, even in Communist Ethiopia, which rapidly embraced overt terror, "the Revolution began with a famous slogan and song: 'Without blood, without blood. . . .'"[110]

Admittedly, the use of force was not expected to disappear at once but gradually—hence the expression, "the withering away of the state." This anticipation was predicated on the elimination of social contradictions, "antagonisms" associated with the conflict-ridden, exploitative class societies of the past; in the new socialist system there was going to be little conflict requiring massive state regulation and little discontent to be repressed (and this applied not only to political conflicts but also to antisocial or criminal behavior, which was expected to disappear since its root causes, exploitation and inequality, were to be eliminated).

The remaining opponents of the new society were expected to be a mere handful—a notion rooted in Marx's mistaken idea that a fundamental polarization of capitalist societies was destined to take place, leading to a huge increase in the size of the exploited masses and a decline in the number of the exploiters. After the revolution the few former exploiters that remained were to be annihilated as a class (though in practice, many of them were annihilated as individuals as well) and deprived of the means to cause trouble for the new government. In other words, the new system was supposed to rest on such overwhelming popular support that it would require little coercion to maintain itself. Lenin wrote:

> What class must the proletariat suppress? Naturally only [!] the exploiting class, i.e. the bourgeoisie. The toilers need a state only to suppress the resistance of the exploiters.... [Whereas] the exploiting classes need political rule in order to maintain exploitation ...[t]he exploited classes need political rule in order completely to abolish all exploitation, i.e. in the interests of the vast majority of the people, and against the insignificant minority consisting of the modern slaveowners—the landlords and capitalists.

Lenin (before the October Revolution) was also exceedingly and unrealistically optimistic about the prospects for the elimination of bureaucracy (the mainstay of coercion and organized political violence in this century): "since the majority of the people *itself* suppresses its oppressors a 'special force' for suppression is *no longer necessary.*" He also wrote that

> the suppression of the minority of exploiters by the majority of wage slaves of *yesterday* is comparatively so easy, simple and natural a task that it will entail far less bloodshed than the suppression of the risings of slaves, serfs or wage slaves and it will cost mankind far less.... The exploiters are naturally unable to suppress the people without a highly complex machine for performing this task: but the *people* can suppress the exploiters even with a very simple "machine," almost without a machine, without a special apparatus....[111]

These were extraordinarily groundless beliefs and anticipations, and Lenin himself rapidly abandoned them after his seizure of power. Thus, for example, in 1922 he demanded the arrest and execution of a "very large number" of residents of the small town of Shuya because they had opposed the confiscation of consecrated articles from local churches. Lenin wrote: "Now it is the time to teach these people such a lesson that for decades to come they will not dare to even think of such opposition."[112]

Indeed, it quickly became apparent that none of the predictions cited above were correct: conditions in the Soviet Union (and in the other Communist states to emerge later) were far from conducive to the shrinking of bureaucracy and the restrained use of coercion by the party-state. On the contrary, Communist states created coercive agencies of unprecedented size and complexity, agencies that came to be charged not merely with tracking down and punishing those suspected of political unreliability (manifest, potential, or imaginary), but also with overseeing vast construction projects utilizing the labor of those arrested.

The major reason for these developments was that the popular support that had been anticipated quickly evaporated—or, arguably, never existed; the programs and policies of the Soviet Communist Party (and those of most other Communist states) did not elicit the wholehearted support of the majority. In fact, these policies—the collectivization of agriculture, for example—stimulated increasing opposition. At every step of the way people had to be pushed, prodded, and coerced along the path of rapid, state-controlled industrialization and political regimentation.

Secondly, Communist governments placed a high premium on total conformity, which could not be achieved by persuasion but only by intimidation. The political culture of the party was therefore one of intolerance and dogmatism; means were unflinchingly subordinated to ends that could not be questioned.

By the early 1930s the resistance to collectivization and the purges (in the USSR) called for a new justification of intensified repression already institutionalized, on a smaller scale, under Lenin. The new theory of political conflict promulgated by Stalin claimed that it was the very successes of socialism which called forth the vicious resistance of the enemy (sometimes called the cornered enemy). This resistance called for stern measures. Even if it was only the resistance of a minority, it remained, or could become, especially dangerous, and it sought to undermine the new system. Stalin said:

> We must smash and throw out the rotten theory that with each forward movement we make, the class struggle will die down more and more, that in proportion to our successes the class enemy will become more and more domesticated.
>
> This is not only a rotten theory but a dangerous theory, for it lulls our people to sleep, leads them into a trap and makes it possible for the class enemy to rally for the struggle against Soviet power.
>
> On the contrary, the more we move forward, the more success we have, then the more wrathful become the remnants of the beaten exploiter classes. . . . [T]he more mischief they do the Soviet state, the more they grasp the most desperate means of struggle as the last resort of the doomed.[113]

This became the official theoretical justification of the waves of terror unleashed during the 1930s.

The isolation of the Soviet Union contributed to its besieged mentality: it was plausible to claim, as Soviet leaders repeatedly did, that internal enemies were conspiring with those abroad. "Conspiracies" were integral parts of the widely publicized show trials and essential for justifying the mass terror. Conspiracy themes were also incorporated into routine accusations against the anonymous victims of the terror. "Who recruited you?" was a standard question in countless interrogations. The "organs of the state security" (Cheka, NKVD, GPU, MVD, KGB, etc.) were in effect counter-conspiracies seeking to uncover and smash those of the enemy. In all this, there was an element of psychological projection: "totalitarian regimes see other regimes [and one may add, groups and individuals as well] as being as ruthless, duplicitous as themselves, and they act accordingly...."[114]

It is important to note that although the repression inflicted by Communist states had not been anticipated in the theoretical blueprints, these policies nonetheless had idealistic roots: they were by-products of the urgent desire to reshape societies (and human beings) and to remove all obstacles from, and opposition to, this endeavor. As Solzhenitsyn wrote:

> To do evil a human being must first of all believe that what he is doing is good.... The imagination and the spiritual strength of Shakespeare's evildoers stopped short at a dozen corpses. Because they had no *ideology*.
>
> Ideology—that is what gives evildoing its long-sought justification and gives the evildoer the necessary steadfastness and determination. That is the social theory which helps to make his acts seem good instead of bad in his own and other's eyes....
>
> That is how the agents of the Inquisition fortified their wills: by invoking Christianity; the conquerors of foreign lands by extolling the grandeur of their Motherland; the colonizers by civilization, the Nazis, by race; and the Jacobins (early and late) by equality, brotherhood and the happiness of future generations.[115]

More recently, Alexander Yakovlev, former member of the highest Soviet political elite (in charge of ideology and propaganda under Gorbachev), has come to the conclusion that the roots of Soviet political violence could be discerned in the Marxist-Leninist ideological legacy and inspiration: "Fundamentally, the responsibility for the genocide ... that took place in Russia and the entire Soviet Union rests on the ideology of Bolshevism."[116] He does not believe that the mass killings could be ascribed to a siege mentality, the backwardness of Russia, or Stalin's personality. He writes:

> Marxists who sincerely believed that the revolution was the locomotive of history and violence was its midwife could no longer doubt the truth of Marxism once they had taken up arms....
>
> ... [B]elief in the inevitability of the coming Communist world served to justify the numerous and senseless victims of the class struggle....
>
> The idea that one should not fear creating victims in the course of serving the cause of progress, that the revolutionary

spirit of the proletarian masses must be preserved at any cost is very characteristic of Marx. . . .

Moral criteria are simply not appropriate under the conditions of a revolutionary coup d'état; they are "revoked" by the brutality and directness of class warfare. . . . This special "class"morality . . . leads to indulgence of any actions. . . . Its justification comes from the special vision of the historical path of development, its final goals for the full renaissance of humanity.

Yakovlev repeatedly stressed the idealistic underpinnings of Communist political violence:

Dostoevsky's Grand Inquisitor speaks of love for humanity. But complete contempt for an actual individual flows from this love.
. . .

. . . [A]ll of this was committed under the guise of concern about humankind, but with complete disregard for the specific individual. Terror is the way of remaking human material in the name of the future. . . .

Marx finally shed the discussion about humanity and love. . . . He no longer spoke of moral justice. . . . All this grew into the conviction that everything that corresponded to the interests of the revolution and communism was moral. That is the morality with which hostages were executed . . . concentration camps were built, and entire peoples forcibly relocated. . . .

Can everything be justified in the name of progress? And is it really progress? What gives one group of people the right to sentence to death civil society, or popular custom centuries in the making?[117]

Yakovlev's reflections reaffirm the distinctive feature of Communist political violence: its idealistic origin and intent—that is to say, in its origins, at any rate, it was violence with a higher purpose. By contrast, much historic violence, including recent outbreaks of ethnic hostility, have little or no idealistic justification. The Nazis, the Turks, the Hutus, the Serbs, and others (engaged respectively in slaughtering Jews, Armenians, Tutsis, and Albanians) had no interest in "remaking human material in the name of the future"—they just wished to get rid of those belonging to groups considered different, threatening, competing, or inferior, although sometimes even these types of violence were colored by the conviction that a better world would be created after the inferior or poisonous group was removed. But most intergroup (ethnic) violence is based on a visceral, taken-for-granted group hostility aggravated by competition for some important and scarce resource, usually land. In Rwanda, Bosnia, Kosovo, the Sudan, Cyprus, Sri Lanka, and Israel (and Palestine), groups have sought greater control over their lives while other groups have sought to prevent them from achieving this goal. Schemes for improving human nature, or a desire for major social transformation and utopian social arrangements, play a negligible part in these conflicts and massacres.

Communist political violence flowed from a utopian vision of the future, from the great goals pursued, and from the intolerance the service of these ideals inspired, as well as from an intense attachment to power. The means had to be subordinated to historically unparalleled ends that required extraordinary measures. In a nutshell, this is the part played by ideology or belief in the repression Communist states employed.

The future orientation of the revolutionaries and their successors helped to resolve or reduce the tension between ends and means: the Bolsheviks did not "consider the chance of attaining certain goals to be lessened by the . . . protracted and large-scale use of means which [were] . . . at extreme variance to them. . . ."[118] The accomplishments unfolding in the future were going to outweigh and cleanse the questionable means employed in their pursuit—this was the unshakeable conviction of generations of Communist leaders and revolutionaries in the Soviet Union and other Communist states. The committed revolutionary steeled himself in the face of the pain and suffering his policies caused. Lenin said that "there are no . . . serious battles without field hospitals near the battlefields. It is altogether unforgivable to permit oneself to be frightened or unnerved by field hospital scenes. If you are afraid of the wolves, don't go into the forest."[119] This was an attitude Edward Ochab, a Polish functionary, shared:

> I became . . . a professional revolutionary. I read Lenin's *What Is To Be Done* . . . where Lenin maintains that the socialist revolution needs "professional revolutionary" cadres . . . who would be prepared to spend months crawling along sewers and would be in charge . . . of organizing the masses. That was when I said to myself: that's me.[120]

Self-discipline, mastery of personal feelings, and committment to the cause made it possible to transcend reservations or revulsion about the means used. Again, as Leites put it:

> The Bolshevik must eschew free-floating empathy. . . . Bolshevism shares the feeling expressed by a character in Dostoevsky's *A Raw Youth*: "It doesn't matter if one has to pass through filth to get there as long as the goal is magnificent. It will all be washed off, it will all be smoothed away afterward."[121]

Leites also wrote that "Bolshevik doctrine rejects the virtue of empathy with and pity for all human beings. . . . The awareness of distress of others would reduce one's capacity to perform those acts which would ultimately abolish it."[122] This might be called the surgeon's view of pain; he must remain indifferent to the bodily sensations of the patient in order to heal him. Thus, in the political struggle, "instead of feeling guilty about the sufferings which one imposes on others . . . one attempts to feel self-righteous about directly and actively imposing suffering on others—for the sake of the future abolition of suffering."[123]

Hence the political violence of Communist systems was instrumental rather than expressive or passionate, not the kind that would satisfy some personal instinct or impulse, although occasionally and illicitly it might have done so.[124]

The use of violent means was also made easier by perceiving them as both defensive and revolutionary. Trotsky wrote:

> The man who repudiates terrorism in principle—i.e., repudiates measures of suppression and intimidation toward determined and armed counter-revolution, must reject all idea of political supremacy of the working class and its revolutionary dictatorship. The man who repudiates the dictatorship of the proletariat repudiates the Socialist revolution. . . .

Earlier, Trotsky pointed out that the dictatorship of the proletariat is a necessity because no agreement is possible with the bourgeoisie: "only force can be the deciding factor."[125]

Leites grasped with great clarity the mentality required by impersonal, deliberate, ideologically motivated mass murder, the willingness to "dirty ones' hands." Still, there remained, in all probability, a lingering awareness of the dissonance between ends and means.[126] This awareness helps to explain the secretiveness surrounding much of the political violence in most Communist systems, and probably the Nazi secretiveness as well.

The uninhibited use of political violence and coercion also followed from the paternalism of professional revolutionaries (subsequently transformed into functionaries) who believed that they were acting on behalf of, and in the interest of, the masses, while in fact they were sharply separated from them. The deep class cleavages in Russia (and in other similarly or even more backward Communist countries) bolstered this elitism.

Even Stalin's extraordinary power-hunger and vindictiveness toward his real or imagined enemies is in part explained by his conviction that he was a chosen instrument of history, the executor of great and lofty goals bequeathed by both Marxist-Leninist theory and Russian history. Similar beliefs doubtless also motivated Mao, Castro, Kim Il Sung, Ho Chi Minh, and other Communist leaders. These convictions did not inspire restraint or attention to proper procedure.

Despite the controversies that have surrounded it since the late 1960s, it is the theory of totalitarianism which best explains the principal characteristics of Communist political violence and coercion. The latter were inseparable from the unconstrained exercise of power, from the urge to dissolve distinctions between the public and private realm (by completely subordinating the latter to the former), and from the attempted politicization of every aspect of life. Because political meaning was attached to virtually everything citizens did, political crime and deviance became defined very broadly, leading to the mistreatment of vast numbers of people, most of whom had not the slightest interest in politics and were not inclined to question let alone endanger the power of the party-state.

Communist leaders were (at least in the beginning) inspired by ideas promising secular redemption; they possessed enormous concentrated power unchecked by any institutional arrangement, countervailing social force, or tradition.[127] At the same time, in all probability the personalities of the supreme leaders also played a part in the forms political violence took. Stalin, Mao,[128] Castro, Mengistu (of Ethiopia),[129] and Mathias Rakosi (of Hungary) were exceptionally ruthless, deceitful, and vindictive individuals who attached little value to individual human lives. They each had the proven capacity to turn on or betray their closest collaborators, friends (if any they could be said to have), or comrades in arms if they were suspected of the slightest disagreement or diminished loyalty.

SCOPE AND SCALE

Possibly the most distinctive characteristic of Communist political repression was its vast scope. Tens of millions of people were affected; thousands of penal establishments were created.[130] The large numbers of the imprisoned resulted from the systems' preventative or prophylactic intent, from the notion of "objective crime," and from the assumption that "prisoners were guilty of something because they had been accused, and subhuman because they had been arrested."[131]

The authorities typically sought to identify certain attributes of various groups that were supposed to be conducive to political misbehavior as defined by the rulers.[132] Repressive measures were aimed not merely at those who were actually opposed to the system and did something to show this opposition, but more often at all those "guilty" of the *potential* for opposition, that is, of "objective crimes."[133] In Cambodia "the hunt for internal enemies" rested on the belief that "[i]nsidious 'bourgeois' ideas, preferences and attitudes were ... buried in everybody's consciousness." A former associate of Pol Pot recalled: "[Pol Pot] saw enemies as rotten flesh, as swollen flesh. Enemies surrounding. Enemies in front, enemies behind, enemies to the north ... to the south ... to the west ... to the east ... enemies coming from all nine directions, closing in, leaving no space for breath."[134]

The official belief that huge numbers were susceptible to some questionable political disposition prompted, in the Soviet Union during the "Great Terror," the organs of repression to establish quotas to be met, that is to say, certain numbers of people to be arrested.[135]

The Marxist-Leninist background of the leaders and designers of the Communist system of repression greatly contributed to its vast sweep: these were individuals used to thinking in large, impersonal social and political categories; individual behavior and guilt was irrelevant once the person was classified as belonging to a class or group of people designated as actually or potentially hostile to the system.

A witness to the implementation of these policies, Jerzy Gliksman, wrote:

> The arm of the Soviet punitive apparatus endeavors to reach not only all real offenders but also the probable and doubtful ones, and even—as a measure of social prophylaxis—the potential ones. . . .
>
> In order to avoid risks attendant on exonerating dubious cases they adopted . . . the system of elimination of all potential deviators. . . .The definition of a "socially dangerous act" is very broad. . . . The articles of the code devoted to "counter-revolutionary" crimes are formulated in an especially comprehensive way so as to include . . . even actions tending toward "weakening" of the power of the government (Article 58).[136]

These systems sought merely not to restrain or annihilate their actual enemies but to destroy even the potential for resistance and dissent. The founder of the Soviet political police, Felix Dzerzhinsky, expressed this idea succinctly and explicitly: "We are terrorizing the enemies of the Soviet government so as to suppress crime in embryo."[137] Political attitudes were inferred from socioeconomic and sometimes ethnic characteristics, as well as from kinship ties and social connections, rather than from behavior or utterances of opinion.

In the Soviet Union, "arrestworthy categories" included former members of the party, old Bolsheviks, former political convicts (under the Tsar), army officers, transport workers, technicians, various industrial or agricultural specialists, and people with ties to foreigners.[138] Potential enemies, or those deemed "socially dangerous," were also described as "anyone whose social group contained the prefix 'ex-' . . . ex-kulaks, ex-criminals, ex-tsarist civil servants, ex-members of the Menshevik Part, ex-Socialist Revolutionaries, and so on."[139] In the same period, "anyone who had any contacts outside the country . . . who owned a radio transmitter, collected stamps or spoke Esperanto stood a very good chance of being accused of espionage."[140] Grounds for prosecution were also based on categories such as "anti-Soviet element, active member of the Church, member of a religious sect, rebel—anyone who in the past was in any way involved in anti-Soviet uprisings, anyone with contacts abroad."[141] At the construction sites of the Danube–Black Sea Canal in Romania there were "prisoners from every walk of life: members of the professional classes rubbed shoulders with dispossessed farmers, Orthodox priests with Zionist leaders, Yugoslavs from the Banat with Saxons from Transylvania...."[142]

Collective responsibility was vastly expanded. *Pravda,* the official newspaper of the Soviet Communist Party, wrote in 1934:

> Individual members of his family are also responsible for the acts of traitors. In the case of escape or flight across the border of a person in military service, all mature members of his family, if they are implicated in aiding the criminal, or knew of his intentions and did not report them to the authorities, the punishment is imprisonment from five to ten years with confiscation of all their property.
>
> The other members of the family of the traitor and all his dependents at the time he committed treason are subject to disfranchisement and exile to some remote regions in Siberia for five years.... One cannot be a neutral observer where the interests of the country or the workers and peasants are concerned. This is a terrible crime: this is complicity in the crime.[143]

Half a century later in Communist Vietnam similar principles prevailed: the "main basis for deporting people to the camps was the set of administrative categories.... Anyone who fell into the wrong categories—in effect, anyone the Communists feared or suspected, however groundlessly—was ipso facto classified as deportable."[144] More peculiarly, the Vietnamese authorities suspected those who wore glasses: "determining who was an enemy ... was often so arbitrary that simply by wearing glasses one could be persecuted as an intellectual or a 'bourgeois elitist.'"[145] The persecution (on similar grounds) of those who wore glasses in Cambodia under Pol Pot was more widespread and better known.[146]

In Communist China, "Mao's enemy list expanded from 'landlords, bureaucratic-capitalists and imperialist agents' in the 1920s to '(former) landlords, rich peasants, reactionaries, bad characters, rightists,' in the 1950s, and again to '(former) landlords, rich peasants, reactionaries, bad characters, rightists, traitors, enemy agents and capitalist-roaders' during the Cultural Revolution."[147]

The 1957 decision establishing Chinese labor reeducation camps (as distinct from the already existing labor reform camps) specified in equally broad terms the characteristics of the inmates, as for example "those who do not engage in proper employment ... [and] behave like hooligans ...," "counterrevolutionaries and antisocialist reactionaries ... people who interfere with public order. . . who. . . do not obey work assignment . . . who . . .make trouble and interfere with public order. . . ."[148] In Cambodia,

> the Khmer Rouge began to murder all those who fit into certain social and political categories.
> . . . Those who were regarded as corrupted by their education, class or employment—civil servants, doctors, lawyers, soldiers and teachers were identified and eliminated. . . . The killing of soldiers' wives and children is also alleged to have occurred frequently. A Khmer Rouge slogan advanced the maxim that "Their line must be annihilated down to the last survivor."[149]

Moreover, "for the Khmer Rouge, as for the Chinese Communists, some social groups were criminal by nature, and this criminality was seen as transmittable from husband to wife, as well as an inherited trait." It was estimated by a student of the Cambodian genocide that 82 percent of the officers in the former army, 51 percent of all "intellectuals" (a term rather broadly used by the Khmer Rouge), and 41 percent of all residents of Phnom Penh perished.[150]

In North Korea, "immediate family members as well as distant relatives are also punished as political criminals because they are considered guilty by association."[151] Somewhat unusually, in North Korea the handicapped too have suffered discrimination and social exclusion, have not been allowed to live in the capital and have been exiled to various remote locations.[152] In Pol Pot's Cambodia, "people with handicaps were simply treated as shirkers and executed."[153]

These broad definitions of political enemies and the policies based upon such definitions were rooted in the mentality of Communist leaders and the political culture they created. This outlook can be traced to the conspiratorial tradition of the founders of the Soviet Union, which exaggerated the power and malevolence of political adversaries; those who used to conspire against the Tsarist government could not help continuing to conspire against those whom they designated as *their enemies* after they seized power. But unlike the Nazis, who were obsessed with the conspiracy of a particular group (the Jews), Communist leaders were prepared to feel mortally threatened by a wide and changing constellation of enemies whose only common feature was a projected potential for nonconformity or resistance. These attitudes were not confined to the Soviet leaders and functionaries.

Communist policies of repression further rested upon an exceptionally intense attachment to power and apprehension about the possibility of losing it. In the Soviet case, the civil war (in the early 1920s) and subsequent isolation from the rest of the world made these attitudes more plausible: in contrast to the early expectations of Lenin and Trotsky, the October Revolution failed to spark uprisings in the West, and consequently the hoped-for Western influ-ences on—and help for—the Russian revolution didn't materialize.[154]

Trotsky (following his break with Stalin) associated the repressiveness of the Soviet system with its progressive bureaucratization. The latter, at least in part, was a response to material scarcities. He wrote:

> When there is enough goods in a store, the purchasers can come whenever they want to. When there is little goods, the purchas-ers are compelled to stand in line. When the lines are very long, it is necessary to appoint a policeman to keep order. Such is the starting point of the power of the Soviet bureaucracy.

More generally Trotsky regarded the rise of bureaucracy as a reflection of "sharp antagonisms" that had to be regulated and repressed. He also observed, "Bureaucracy and social harmony are inversely proportional to each other."[155]

Other Communist states, too, had similar historical experiences of isola-tion and civil war, notably China and Cambodia. The Cuban regime, emerging from a guerilla war, also had reason to feel threatened by the United States and has led a partially isolated existence. The isolation of North Korea and North Vietnam was largely self-imposed. (During the 1980s and 1990s, Vietnam, like China, opened up economically.)

The Communist regimes in Eastern Europe were well protected by the Soviet armed forces from any external or internal threat until the late 1980s.[156] The conspiratorial view of the world they entertained was part of a political culture that had been transplanted from the Soviet Union. Because of their manifest dependence on Soviet forces, East European Communist leaders were especially aware of their shaky legitimacy.

Arguably, the insecure and therefore all the more intense attachment to power of the Communist rulers was rooted in the fundamental illegitimacy of their systems—these rulers knew or sensed that their power was not the result of popular mandate (except perhaps initially in Cuba and China), and they never considered submitting their rule to electoral endorsement or legitimiza-tion.

The famines that several Communist states experienced (notably the Soviet Union, China, and Ethiopia) added millions to their victims. These events were largely results of government policy, not "acts of God." In parts of the Soviet Union food supplies were deliberately withheld from the peasants, or else they were not allowed to move to areas better supplied.[157] According to Alexander Orlov, a former high ranking NKVD official, "this terrible disaster was caused not by uncontrollable elements of nature, but by the stupidity and willfulness of a dictator unable to foresee the consequences of his actions and indifferent to human suffering."[158]

In Ethiopia, the forcible resettlement of peasants associated with collectivization directly contributed to the onset of famine, insofar as, as in the Soviet Union, these collective farms were highly unproductive and inefficient. These measures were not *intended* to kill but nonetheless caused the death of millions. Neither the Ethopian regime, nor the Soviet, nor the Chinese, was concerned with the human costs of these policies.[159]

In China, the huge famine of the late 1950s resulted from the bizarre policy of pressuring peasants to collect and melt scrap metal at the expense of performing agricultural work; this was intended to be a part of "the Great Leap Forward." Instances of cannibalism were unique by-products of that famine (this recurred later during the Cultural Revolution).[160]

The scope and scale of repression in Communist states were also related to these states' widespread reliance on denunciation, or on the use of informers to ferret out disloyalty. Communist systems encouraged their citizens to inform on one another and to place loyalty to the party-state above loyalty to family or friends. In China, denunciation boxes on the street (complete with forms) were available to make denunciation convenient.[161] In Cuba, denunciation was made easier

> by providing a special form which can be filled out by CDR [Committee for the Defense of the Revolution] activists. . . . On one side, the form records the opinion that a person may have expressed on a political subject. On the other side, it records such data as the person's age and profession; where the opinion was expressed; whether the person is considered a revolutionary, disaffected, or this is unknown; whether the listeners approved, disapproved, were indifferent and so forth.[162]

The Committees for the Defense of the Revolution (CDR) in Cuba were "an all-purpose institution for repression" that shouldered the task of informing on fellow citizens and was concerned with every aspect of their lives: work, housing, immigration, applications to university and trade school, and all other matters in which the observation of citizens' political reliability played an important part.[163] Similar tasks were performed in China by the neighborhood, street, and district committees.[164] In Cambodia, "all that was required for an arrest was a total of three denunciations as a 'CIA Agent.' . . ."[165]

In the Soviet Union, twelve-year-old Pavel Morozov, who informed on his own family, was made into a role model and national hero. In East Germany (a country of seventeen million), the Stasi created an exceptionally large network of full- and part-time informers (95,000 full-time and 160,000 part-time, according to one source). The Gestapo, supervising a nation of over sixty million, had half as many full-time agents.[166]

Communist states made wide use of informers for several reasons. One was to maximize information about dissent or political deviance; political systems on the lookout for conspiracies needed conspiratorial methods to counter them. Secondly, the knowledge that informers might lurk everywhere had a powerful, intimidating impact on the population; it was part of the system of social control. The widespread presence of informers discouraged people from sharing criticism of or expressing their dissatisfaction with the authorities, which in turn increased the stability of these systems. Thirdly, all those providing this type of information (even on a part-time basis) became implicated in the system; this was a form of political participation totalitarian systems appreciated.

The collection of such information by ordinary citizens was a form of civic duty that also helped to establish their own political credentials and prove their loyalty, especially during periods of terror, when anybody could be accused of disloyalty.

Given the belief in the ubiquitousness of the enemy and the readiness to define every accident as sabotage, it was official policy not to ignore or dismiss denunciations, however outlandish or implausible. This, too, swelled the numbers who became accused of and punished for political crimes they did not commit. Reliance on denunciation was particularly helpful when the political police had quotas of arrest to fulfill, as in the Soviet Union during the 1930s.

CONTROL OVER POPULATION MOVEMENTS

Tight control of population movements both within the country and especially across international borders was a key characteristic of Communist states. These controls took various forms. The internal passport was one major device; it had to be carried by every adult and shown to the police on request. It contained information about one's residence. To change one's residence required registering with the police. Certain areas were off limits: border areas, capitals, those with military installations. In China under Mao, food rations were tied to residence and were not available if people moved without official permission.

Regular passports for travel abroad were not generally available and were issued only under exceptional circumstances; following a trip abroad, these passports usually had to be surrendered. Ordinary citizens could not aspire to take trips to non-Communist countries, although such policies changed over time in some of the countries here discussed. More typically, delegations or groups made such trips, and the members of these groups were carefully screened and supervised by police agents or informants. In Eastern Europe in the 1970s and '80s, it became easier to visit neighboring countries that also belonged to the "Socialist Commonwealth." Since the 1980s, travel from China to Western countries has also become much easier.

Control over population movements was accomplished not only by administrative measures regulating and minimizing legal travel; unauthorized border crossings were prevented by what came to be known in Europe as the Iron Curtain, the complex of obstacles (including mine fields), fortifications, and observation posts that was created along much of the boundary of the Soviet empire, including the East European countries under Soviet control.[167] Best known of these installations was the Berlin Wall. These countries also maintained large, special border-police forces.

The forcible removal and resettlement of populations was another method by which Communist states asserted and consolidated their rule: ethnic groups or those judged unreliable on the basis of class and political criteria were often resettled or exiled en masse, in both Eastern Europe and the Soviet Union, to more inaccessible areas that they were not allowed to leave.[168] Exile often followed release from jail or labor camp. In Cambodia, entire cities were emptied and their inhabitants moved to the countryside in an effort to remold urban populations by immersing them in rural life and agricultural labor. In China during the Cultural Revolution, millions of urban residents, white-collar workers, students, and party officials judged to be in need of political character reform were sent to villages to learn from the peasants and to become better socialist citizens by performing manual labor. In Ethiopia, resettlement was associated with the collectivization of agriculture, but it also served to extend the authorities' political control. Cuba, while at times permitting large numbers of its citizens to depart legally and occasionally exiling prominent dissidents, also has maintained tight controls, which has led to the recurring attempts of refugees to reach the United States on the most rudimentary flotation devices. Most remarkably, in 1969 one Cuban escaped by hiding in the landing gear of a plane that flew to Spain.[169]

Communist policies to prevent, minimize, and carefully regulate movements across international boundaries were prompted by several motives. The most important, in all probability, was the fear of symbolic ideological repudiation: to have citizens leave what were supposed to be the historically most advanced and just societies was intolerable and inadmissible for those in power. Just as people were not allowed to choose among competing political parties in elections, they were not allowed "to vote with their feet" either. Those who managed to escape or were exiled were subjected to extensive vilification. Defectors from the Soviet Union were sometimes kidnapped from abroad or assassinated.[170]

The second reason for investing vast human and material resources in order to prevent escape was that not only would escape discredit the system at home, but abroad as well, since the escapees often made public the sources of their unhappiness with the system and the conditions they had left behind. The dramatic and dangerous circumstances under which some of the escapes took place reflected the despair these regimes generated.[171] The numbers involved were substantial, running into the millions.[172]

Thirdly, these regimes sought to prevent the loss of productive and highly skilled strata of the population.[173] Such a drain was most pronounced in the case of East Germany and was ended with the building of the Berlin Wall in 1961 and other fortifications erected along the border with West Germany.

At last, these regimes, which drastically curtailed or eliminated personal and group freedoms, could not afford to allow the freedom of movement to survive. The freedom to leave one's country represents a fundamental freedom of choice, and its availability or unavailability has great bearing on the citizen's attitude toward the political system under which he lives. Adjustment and acceptance of the status quo are more readily forthcoming when all alternatives, including departure, have been foreclosed.

All Communist states considered illegal border crossing, or its attempt, a serious crime. In the Soviet Union it was classified as treason. "Flight abroad or refusal to return from abroad to the USSR" was listed, alongside treason and espionage, as an "especially dangerous crime against the state."[174]

Border controls (and the associated restrictions on internal travel and legal emigration) were an integral part of the system of political control and are arguably a key characteristic of all totalitarian regimes, Communist and otherwise. "Closed societies" must not only literally close themselves off from subversive influences from abroad, but must also deny their people the most subversive alternative of removing themselves from the society altogether.

THE ENEMY: DEHUMANIZATION AND DEMONIZATION

In the twentieth century politically motivated mass murders came to require elaborate explanation and justification; contemporary sensibilities, perhaps even moral progress of a sort, demand that a good case be made for large-scale extermination: "in order to perform genocide the perpetrator has always had to first organize a campaign that redefined the victim group as worthless, outside the web of human obligations, a threat to other people, immoral sinners and/or subhuman."[175] Such dehumanization in our time has been readily embraced by a variety of different political ideologies, movements, and systems.

In Communist states the preoccupation with the enemy had a second source. Given the commitment to create a "new man," the superior socialist human being, the eradication of his opposite—the enemy—was a step all the more logical and urgent. There was a compelling reciprocal relationship between creating the new man and destroying the old.

An obsessive preoccupation with the enemy—especially an internal or domestic one—characterizes all totalitarian systems. Tzvetan Todorov observed: "Totalitarian doctrines always divide humanity into two groups of unequal worth.... [U]nder them all men do not have the same rights.... A class enemy in one case, a race enemy in the other ... against whom a war of extermination is justified."[176]

lvii

Communist systems were not content with punishing and exterminating their perceived enemies; campaigns of repression were preceded and accompanied by lengthy campaigns of dehumanization and demonization performed by the propaganda apparatus. These campaigns were embedded in official ideology. Eduard Shevardnadze wrote: "Tanks and machine guns may only be employed as arguments within the appropriate ideological frame. . . . [T]he executioner has always been preceded by the inquisitor, the axe and block foreshadowed by the dogmas of faith."[177]

These campaigns took two major forms. One required that some individuals of political importance be singled out and subjected to intensive public denunciation, usually in conjunction with their arrest, trial, and sentencing, as in the case of the defendants in the Moscow Trials of the 1930s. Secondly, more general propaganda campaigns were directed at "the enemy" identified not as specific individuals but as certain social-political groups—e.g., "kulaks," Trotskyites, Titoists, or "capitalist-roaders." These campaigns were coupled with demands on the population to be vigilant, that is to say, to be ready to denounce, unmask, and expose the enemy.

In China, during the early years of the regime as well as during the Cultural Revolution, denunciation and mistreatment of the enemy were often compressed: landowners were simultaneously denounced, tried, and executed in proceedings that took place before mass audiences. During the Cultural Revolution, similar techniques were used with an even stronger emphasis on various forms of public humiliation, followed by punishment.

Central to these efforts was the mythic image of the enemy, the incarnation of unmitigated political evil. Virtually any individual or group could be placed into this category, depending on the historical-political circumstances and their interpretation by the leaders in power.

Both political propaganda and the arts, regimented under the auspices of "socialist realism," were used to acquaint the population with the character and types of the enemy and to dehumanize him.[178] Implicit in these portrayals was the justification and demand for merciless punishment. In an early Soviet novel of Ilia Ehrenburg, the so-called positive hero "signed these things [death sentences] many times and with confidence. It was simple: he weeded the gigantic garden, pulling out various weeds."[179] In Communist Hungary, a critic of an aspiring socialist-realist novel complained that "the characters whose role was to personify the Tito regime, although contemptible, are not sufficiently hateful. . . ." Another critic, the cultural commissar of the period, Joseph Revai (also known as the Hungarian Zhdanov), criticized the novelist Tibor Dery because he "does not unmask the enemy, he discovers some positive human traits even in the unequivocally negative characters."[180]

During the 1930s Moscow Trials, the prosecutors provided authoritative specifications and elaborations of the traits of the enemy. These statements became the model for corresponding prosecutorial disquisitions in Eastern Europe after World War II and inspired the propaganda apparatuses in these countries in their politically correct portrayals of the enemy.

The speeches of the most notorious Soviet prosecutor exude and exemplify the dehumanizing and demonizing intent of this strategy. Thus spoke Andrei Vyshinski in 1938 at the trial of what was called "The Anti-Soviet Trotskyite Center":

> With every day and every hour that passed, as the Court investigation ... proceeded, it brought to light ever more of the horrors of the chain of shameful, unparalleled, monstrous crimes committed by the accused ... heinous deeds before which the base deeds of the most inveterate, vile, unbridled and despicable criminals fade. . . . [W]hat trial ... can compare with the present trial in the monstrosity, brazenness and cynicism of the crimes committed by these gentlemen? . . .
>
> It is a gang of bandits, robbers, forgers, diversionists, spies and murderers in the literal sense of the word! . . . These people have lost all shame. . . .
>
> . . . [They] conspired to commit the blackest treason ... sold their native land for thirty pieces of silver. . . . these Trotskyite Judases. . . . Nobody has mastered the art of cynical double-dealing to such a degree as they have. . . . [T]hese [are] the most unprincipled and degraded people. . . .[181]

Not accidentally, the prosecutor's presentation closely paralleled the corresponding characterizaton of the accused found in the iconic *History of the Communist (Bolshevik) Party of the Soviet Union,* which refered to the defendants as "the monsters of the Bucharinite-Trotskyite Gang" and also described them as "crawling, sneaking snakes ... a more dangeous enemy, more to be hated than any before."[182] The imagery was further developed by Vyshinski, who commented on the "reptile cold-bloodedness" and the "brutal claws and ferocious fangs" of the defendants.[183]

Bukharian, who fell victim to the purveyors of these images, was a product of the same political culture. He declared "after the execution of his old party comrades Zinoviev and Kamanev ... 'I am so happy that they have been shot like dogs.'"[184] Needless to say, this remark preceded his own arrest and trial.

A Hungarian journalist covering the trial of Laszlo Rajk and his "accomplices" (the Hungarian equivalent of the Moscow Trials) wrote in the official newspaper of the Hungarian Communist Party:

> Is there any word which can capture the nature of the monsters who wanted to enslave us anew? Is there such a hatred that could make them feel even a ... fraction of the ... torture, suffering,

misery and death they prepared once more for the people. . . . Never before has the fist of the people struck upon more detestable vermin. . . . [I]t is painful to breathe the same air with them—but it will not last much longer.[185]

Another Hungarian writer urged his fellow writers to "portray the monster [Rajk] so that future generations can also feel revulsion." His own contribution to the enlightenment of these generations included the following:

> Slowly it becomes clear that we are not facing here a human being, neither an animal—whose instinct is straightforward—but a third type of creature, the enemy of the working-class, the agent of the bourgeosie . . . a product of the imperialist-capitalist system . . . the vilest creature that ever existed.[186]

Pol Pot, for his part, compared his enemies to "microbes" that had infiltrated the body of the party and had to be eradicated.[187]

These characterizations of the "enemy" conform precisely to Aldous Huxley's definition of dehumanizing propaganda: "All propaganda directed against an opposing group has but one aim: to substitute diabolical abstractions for concrete persons. The propagandist's purpose is to make one set of people to forget that certain other sets of people are human."[188]

Political expediency and hate-mongering were not the sole reasons for these vilifications. The political culture and ideological traditions of Communist states supported an apocalyptic, irrational image of the enemy that was genuinely threatening, not unlike the Nazi conviction that the Jews were an incipient, mortal threat. Although Marxism-Leninism rejects the role of accident in history and human suffering, despite its historical-economic determinism it dwells on and stresses the culpability and malevolence of particular groups (classes) and individuals. Whenever Communist systems and their rulers felt threatened—and they often did—their aggressiveness intensified:

> [I]t is not rational cost-benefit analysis, but emotional impulse . . . that precipitates aggression. . . . The sense of moral virtue, with which all these regimes are imbued, especially in their early decades in power, gives psychological comfort to, and reinforces the emotional impulses of the regime leaders.[189]

Even conflicts between Communist states, such as Cambodia and Vietnam,

> were considered by the participants not as reasonable disagreements of interest between states led by political comrades, but Manichean life-and-death struggles against "international re-

actionaries" and "agents of imperialism." . . . Marxist-Leninist
regimes seem to share a view of conflict in history not as the
outcome of "impersonal historical foces" as Marx would have
it, but rather as the outcome of deliberate conspiracy. . . .[190]

Also of interest here (especially in light of the similarity with Nazi notions
of the enemy) is that "references to cleanliness and purification dominated
Khmer Rouge rhetoric . . . [and] the belief in internal conspiracies . . . drove the
Cambodian holocaust."[191] The same applies to the Soviet waves of arrest and
mass murder in the 1930s and to aspects of the Chinese Cultural Revolution.

In most Communist regimes, and especially Cambodia, China, and the
Soviet Union under Stalin, the failure of economic policies intensified irrational, conspiratorial scapegoating and punitiveness. In these societies the enemy
was always said to be responsible for such difficulties; the enemy's role was
almost invariably hidden and disguised and had therefore to be unmasked and
ferreted out—and it was all the more to be hated for representing a hidden
menace.

In Pol Pot's Cambodia, hatred of the mythical enemy was incorporated
into the Khmer Rouge anthem:

> Bright red Blood which covers towns and plains
> Of Kampuchea, our Motherland,
> Sublime Blood of workers and peasants,
> Sublime Blood of revolutionary men and women fighters!
> The Blood changing into unrelenting hatred.[192]

The confluence of ideology and paranoia—and the associated preoccupation with control, domination, and demonized images of the enemy—are among
the distinctive attributes of political violence in Communist states.

PUBLICITY AND SECRECY

Communist states sought to balance publicity and secrecy in their policies of
repression. Publicized repression was useful for intimidation and to impress
on citizens the power of the party-state; secretiveness, on the other hand, made
the exercise of unchecked power smoother and lent a certain unpredictability
to repression that also helped to terrorize the populace. Furthermore, secretiveness was part of a conspiratorial political culture in which all major political decisions were made in private. Information was knowledge; depriving
people of information was an exercise of power; it was dangerous to allow the
enemy to know of one's plans.

The secretiveness surrounding the treatment of political prisoners was part
of a broader political pattern that included the vast expansion of official secrets in Communist countries. There was a prohibition against taking photo-

graphs not only of military installations but of industrial ones as well: bridges, railroad stations, radio towers, etc. Recruits in the Soviet army were not supposed to tell their families where they were garrisoned or what food they ate, let alone any aspect of their training. (Presumably, similar policies prevailed in other Communist armies.) Information or data about industrial or agricultural production were official secrets, too. Secretiveness was linked to the concept and attitude of "vigilance" that party members and all good citizens were to display in guarding the secrets. Mikhail Heller, a Soviet émigré historian, wrote:

> Everything in the Soviet Union is secret, from the plans of arms factories to the personal lives of Party leaders, from the size of the army or the number of people in prison to last year's *Pravda* and books by Solzhenitsyn. A permit is needed to enter all institutions and a special pass is needed for access to library books in the "closed fund." . . . Party members are brought together at closed Party meetings and the Central Committee informs the rank and file members . . . of the Party's activity in sealed letters. . . .[193]

The amount and kind of publicity given to the punishment of the enemy varied among different Communist states. In the Soviet Union the punishment of prominent political criminals was given much publicity, as in the show trials of the 1930s, but ordinary trials (or quasi-judicial procedures leading to sentencing) in the vast majority of cases were held in secret: no relatives, no press, no defense attorneys, and no publicity was permitted. Millions of anonymous victims were dispatched secretively in these proceedings to camps or the prison cellars or secluded forest clearings used for mass shootings (as in the famous case of the Polish officers killed in the Katyn Forest in April 1940). Large numbers of mass graves in such locations have been found since the collapse of the Soviet Union.[194] There were no public executions in the Soviet Union, except during the civil war.

Nocturnal arrests were typical in the USSR and in the East European Communist states. These were designed not solely for secrecy but also to demoralize those arrested: to be awakened in the middle of the night to face a house search and arrest left victims helpless and bewildered. Those arrested were usually transported in unmarked cars, while more numerous prisoners were put in trucks that gave no hint of their function; sometimes they were disguised as delivery vans with the labels "bread" or "meat." One prisoner reported being transported in a van that bore on its side the advertisement "drink Soviet champagne," with a picture of the bottle. In Afghanistan during the Soviet occupation, the corpses of political prisoners were sometimes put in "trucks . . . painted with flowers or pictures of children so the villagers would not know what was in them. . . ."[195]

By contrast, in China during the Cultural Revolution and during the first years of solidifying Communist rule public executions and humiliations were common,[196] especially when the countryside was cleansed of "class enemies," mostly landlords. These executions by shooting were preceded by public trials that included few judicial niceties. In later years, victims were drawn from a wider cross-section of the population. During the Cultural Revolution those with higher education were singled out.

In Ethiopia during its own "Red Terror" in 1978, "bullet ridden bodies were left in the streets [of Addis Ababa, the capital] or publicly exhibited to . . . intimidate rival factions."[197] In Cuba in the early days of the Castro regime, public trials were held "in a carnival-like atmosphere."[198]

Much of the Communist political violence was didactic and therefore in tension with the requirements of secrecy. Punishment for political misbehavior had to be publicized in order to deter and to demonstrate the power of the authorities (especially in exacting false confessions) and to teach the public particular political-ideological lessons. For example, it was alleged that the old Bolsheviks (in the Soviet Union) camouflaged themselves as party loyalists, while in fact they were agents of hostile powers from the beginning of their polical careers; Trotskyism supposedly led to conspiring against the system and to alliances with the USSR's foreign enemies; the nationalistic deviation of Tito culminated in cooperation with the CIA or the Vatican; Rajk and Slansky (the major Hungarian and Czech victims of the show trials respectively) were Tito's lackeys; and so on.

The public trial and sentencing of the designated enemies of the state and party provided an important opportunity for clarifying for the masses which crimes or types of political deviance deserved severe retribution; these occasions also helped to inform the population about the personal and social characteristics of the "enemy."

The pursuit of secrecy, as well as other considerations discussed below, often led to locating places of detention and especially forced labor in remote, inaccessible areas. Many of these locations were generally unknown until de-Stalinization in the USSR and corresponding changes in other Communist states. Relatives rarely got permission to visit. It was easier to find such remote areas in the former Soviet Union and China than in more densely populated Eastern Europe or Cuba; the latter sited one of its major penal colonies on an island called Isle of Youth.[199] In the Soviet Union, camps were primarily located in Siberia, in or near the Arctic Circle, and the Soviet Far East.[200] Chinese camps too were located in remote and inhospitable areas such as "the semi-desert zones of northern Manchuria, Inner Mongolia, Tibet, Xinjiang, and above all Qinghai, which was a genuine penal province, the Chinese equivalent of the Russian Kolyma, with a climate that was scorching in the summer and freezing in the winter."[201]

Security was another consideration dictating these locations; it was difficult if not altogether impossible to escape from these camps, to survive and reach human settlements. The location of these camps was also determined by the economic purposes they served, such as opening up distant areas where free labor was scarce and difficult to attract. In these areas inmates cut timber and built roads, canals, hydroelectric plants, and assorted industrial plants; they also mined coal, uranium, and precious metals.

The relationship between secretiveness and the desire to intimidate remained somewhat problematic. Unless people knew how their fellow citizens were treated and mistreated they could not be properly intimidated. In most Communist states the specifics were kept secret but the general outlines of the systems of repression were easy to grasp: individuals were arrested in large numbers and for unknown reasons and disappeared to unknown destinations. At any rate, this was the case in the Soviet Union. In China, political violence to this day is less concealed; nonpolitical criminals are often executed in public, and such executions are sometimes televised.

CONFESSION, SHOW TRIALS, AND INSTITUTIONALIZED BRUTALITY

A prominent characteristic of Communist "judicial" proceedings was the centrality of confession as the main and often single proof of the alleged crimes. This was true for the widely publicized show trials as well as in the cases of the anonymous millions dispatched to the camps, who were convicted on the basis of standardized, thematic, signed confessions.

The widely publicized confessions of well-known political figures were integral to the didactic purpose of the trials: the confession was supposed to reveal and prove the evil personified by the perpetrators while simultaneously demonstrating the power of the state that extracted them. The confession also illustrated some larger political theme or conveyed a particular message. Bertold Brecht, the German Communist writer, well understood this principle, having observed in connection with the Moscow trials, "It is necessary to bring to light behind the deeds of the accused a political concept that can credibly be attributed to them and that has led them into the swamps of common criminality. . . ."[202]

The confessions of well-known figures were also designed to discredit the accused not only politically but also morally. In addition, confessions were relied upon because as a rule they were the only "proof" of the alleged crimes and were easy to obtain under heavy physical pressure and deprivation. Confession could also be used to implicate others and to uncover and ferret out alleged and imaginary conspiracies.

In the Soviet Union as of 1937, torture was officially acknowledged as a legitimate means to important ends. According to an official document, the Central Committee of the party deemed methods of physical pressure in NKVD practice permissible from 1937 on.... [A]ll bourgeois intelligence services use methods of physical influence against representatives of the socialist proletariat.... The question arises as to why the socialist intelligence service should be more humanitarian against the mad agents of the bourgeoisie, against the deadly enemies of the working class and the collective farm workers.[203]

In addition to sleep deprivation and beatings, another simple method favored in the Soviet Union to extract confession was to make the prisoner stand. Walter Krivitsky, a high-ranking defector from the military intelligence service (GRU), wrote: "I knew personally one prisoner who was kept standing during his examinations, with brief interruptions, for a total of fifty-five hours under glaring and blinding lights. This was perhaps the commonest form of the third degree."[204] Another method reportedly ordered by Yagoda (head of the political police at the time) to soften up Zinoviev and Kamenev was to overheat their cells in the summer.[205]

In Hungary, operatives of the AVH (political police) were given lectures by a physician on "investigatory practices" that sanctioned and explained beating without causing death.[206]

Confession was an integral part of "thought reform" in China both in formal criminal proceedings and on the occasions when group pressure was informally applied to prisoners during so-called "struggling" sessions.[207] For example, during the "Four Clean Ups" campaign in 1964, "inmates [were] directed to confess whether they were clean or unclean in regard to the following four questions ...: satisfaction with their sentences, thoughts of escaping, participation in any secret oppositional cliques within the camp, and behavior after their release."[208] In Mao's China the confession was seen by the authorities both as a tool of reeducation or character reform and as a weapon in the struggle against privacy. In Cambodia, too, political guilt was established entirely by confession, and the procedures used bore close resemblance to the Soviet model.[209] In Albania, interrogators used tapes "with voices of members of his [the detainee's] family pretending they had all been arrested and tortured. Listening to the screams many prisoners broke down completely ... and told the Communists anything they wanted to hear."[210]

Since few confessions were made voluntarily of hideous crimes not committed, physical and psychological pressure—torture—played an important part in their extraction. A partial exception to this generalization was the qualified willingness of some high-ranking defendants—motivated by a residual loyalty to the cause and the party—to cooperate in the Soviet and other show trials. Such ideologically induced cooperation is the central theme of Arthur Koestler's novel *Darkness at Noon*. In the 1949 Hungarian show trial of Laszlo Rajk, similar arguments were used to persuade Rajk to confess his treacherous activities.[211]

Aside from sleep and food deprivation and beatings, methods ranged from verbal denunciation to solitary confinement in small spaces to threats of violence against members of the family of the accused and sometimes to more elaborate physical torture. Roy Medvedev wrote:

> NKVD personnel were specially trained to be capable of carrying out any order, even the most criminal. The special brigades of torturers . . . usually included students from the NKVD schools. . . . They were taken to torture chambers as medical students are to dissection laboratories. . . .

Medvedev believed that many of the guards were "sadists," while others were motivated by "the fear of becoming prisoners themselves" unless they performed their duties zealously and brutally. There was "a terrible selection [process], sifting out some officials, leaving the worst."[212]

Torture designed to extract confession is to be distinguished from the generally brutal treatment of prisoners. Such mistreatment included overwork, harsh living conditions, inadequate food, deprivations of medical care and proper clothing, punitive solitary confinement (in unheated and often cramped cells, as a rule), and occasional beatings.

In Romania, prisoners were subjected to "ferocious discipline" and

> punished for the slightest deviation from prison rules. . . . Transgressors were flogged . . . or placed into solitary confinement in a cell without windows. . . . A feature of incarceration was the permanent sensation of hunger.
>
> . . . Physical torture during interrogations by the Securitate [the Romanian political police] was common. An internal report of the Ministry of Interior noted that at the notorious Danube Black Sea Canal construction camps "many prisoners were beaten . . . with iron bars, shovels, spades and whips. . . . Prisoners were put naked or skimpily dressed in isolation cells in winter . . . punished by making them stand in frozen water. . . . Prisoners were tied by the hands and exposed naked in the summer to be bitten by mosquitos.[213]

The Cuban mistreatment of political prisoners is among the least known in the West, even the United States, even though it was especially cruel. The guards apparently engaged in brutalities with relish and many seemed sadistic. As Carlos Alberto Montaner wrote, "Cuba needs a patient Solzhenitsyn to recount the history of the Caribbean Archipelago."[214] It was a fairly common practice for the guards to "prod and jab" prisoners with bayonets, to beat them with "rubber hose covered iron bars" and "woven electrical cables," to keep them in their cells naked over long periods of time (months), to pour urine and excrement on them (from the ceilings of cages made of chain-link), to poke them from above with what was called "the Ho-Chi Minh pole" in order to prevent them from sleeping, and to prohibit them from wearing shirts while working in mosquito-infested swamps.[215] These activities were unrelated to efforts to make the prisoners confess. Another more unusual feature of Cuban repression was the vindictive mistreatment of political prisoners who refused to undergo political reeducation or "rehabilitation."[216]

Torture and gratuitous cruelty in Cambodia was, according to one author,

> more widespread than in any other Communist regime. . . . [T]o save bullets, and also to satisfy the sadistic instincts of executioners, shooting was not the most common means of execution. . . . [O]nly 29% of the victims died that way. . . . 53% . . . died from blows to the head, inflicted with iron bars, pick-ax handles or agricultural implements; 6% were hanged or asphyxiated with plastic bags; and 5% had their throats slit.[217]

Electric shock (as a means of torture) was favored in Cambodia (notwithstanding the antitechnological bent of its rulers), while "forcing prisoners to eat excrement" appears to have been a Cambodian specialty, as it is not encountered elsewhere in the relevant literature.[218]

In Cambodia, such types of mistreatment, among others, could be inflicted for an unusually wide variety of behavioral reasons (in addition to the predetermined political criteria that had nothing to do with behavior but with classification): "People suffered beatings and executions, mock and real, because they stole vegetables, roots or crabs from fields; hoarded rice; visited family members; or had sex outside marriage."[219]

In China under Mao,

> "watching television" meant being forced to hold one's head over a bucket of excrement; . . . "looking in the mirror" is placing a tube of toothpaste between one's forehead and the wall without letting it drop for hours on end and "doing the airplane"—a form of torture devised during the Cultural Revolution—involves arms suspended at forty-five degree angles to the shoulder blades. The use of electric cattle prods or truncheons to discipline prisoners is commonplace and well documented by Asia Watch, [and] Amnesty International. . . . Among guards or warders contests are sometimes held to find out who can fit a pair of handcuffs on a prisoner the tightest.[220]

In China, more than in any other Communist state, public humiliation of "the enemy" was widespread, especially during the "Cultural Revolution." These "enemies" were paraded on the street with signs hanging from their necks specifying their crimes; they had to wear "dunce caps" and stand for hours with bowed heads in front of abusive crowds, listening to their denunciations. Public confessions were extracted.[221] Such public shaming was a Chinese specialty.

As for North Korea, in addition to the wide range of brutalities detailed in *Aquariums of Pyongyang* (including occasional public executions), one scientist, recently defected, "told the BBC that he used experimental chemical weapons on political prisoners, taking notes as they died in agony. Such experiments were apparently used to determine how much gas would be necessary to annihilate the city of Seoul."[222]

Repression and the Economy

The integration of coercive economic institutions and policies was a central characteristic of Communist systems. As Anne Applebaum puts it: "a society allegedly inspired by Marx and Marxism had taken the commodification of labor to new heights."[223] The majority of those arrested and sentenced were sent to forced or "corrective" labor camps located near various construction projects. Many of the most acclaimed construction projects in these countries were built with such convict labor, as for example the Belomor or White Sea–Baltic canal in the USSR; the road to Lhassa (Tibet) from China proper; the Danube–Black Sea Canal in Romania; the first nuclear research institute in Hungary; etc.[224] Prisoners in Czechoslovakia worked in uranium mines. In China, inmates worked in "mining, farming, manufacturing, quarrying, forestry, [and] railway construction," among other projects.[225] The Chinese use of such labor was more efficient and wide-ranging than was the Soviet, and unlike other Communist states China exported many products of forced labor to Western countries. The products of forced labor in China included

> coal, matches, trucks, toothpaste, cosmetics, livestock, vegetables, sugar cane, bricks, flashlights, batteries, shoes, gypsum, tea, knitted goods, nylon socks, wine grapes, prawns, industrial chemicals, bed sheets, glass, lead, cement, paper, opium poppies, auto parts, plastics, crop sprayers, liquor, mercury, tractors, pottery and porcelain, rubber, fans, leather and furs, asbestos, gunnysacks, milk products, firefighting equipment, motorcycles, gloves, embroidery, diesel engines and even the "launch plate" for one of China's early intercontinental missiles.[226]

There were many reasons for the widespread use of convict labor. One was the low level of technology: human beings were more readily available than machinery; there was an abundant supply of them, especially in the USSR and China. Communist governments made especially good use of prisoners on labor-intensive projects in remote areas involving considerable physical hardship.

The best-known embodiment of these policies, thanks to Solzhenitsyn, was the Soviet Gulag, an abbreviation of the administrative authority controlling the labor camps. The magnitude of this system is revealed in the book of Shifrin (referred to earlier) based on information supplied by former inmates, which includes maps showing the location of these establishments, four of which are reproduced following this introduction. Harry Wu, another former inmate, listed 990 such camps in China, and this is estimated to represent only between one-sixth and one-fourth of the total number.[227]

Using forced labor for large economic projects was cheap, since no attempts were made to make working conditions humane or to prolong the lives of workers. It was, moreover, a labor force that could be easily and quickly mobilized and replenished and sent to remote projects for which it was difficult to recruit free workers. Located for the most part in inaccessible areas, these camps also removed those defined as politically unreliable from the proximity of population centers. Often the inmates who had served their sentences remained confined to the area where the camp was located. The camps were also favored because the high mortality rates diminished the number of alleged enemies. To what degree this was a calculated policy or merely a welcome by-product of the system of labor camps remains to be determined.

ì REHABILITATIONî AND ìTHOUGHT REFORMî

In the early days of the various Communist states it was an article of the official faith that work was therapeutic and the best device for rehabilitation and redemption. All Communist political systems, and in particular the first among them, the Soviet, initially proposed ambitious schemes aimed at the rehabilitation of all criminals, including sometimes even political wrongdoers. Felix Dzerzhinsky (the first head of the Soviet political police) called the forced labor camps "schools of labor." It was supposed to be possible even for hardened criminals (especially those not guilty of political offenses) to gain readmittance to the community of good citizens if they proved themselves through hard work. Posted at the entrance of numerous Soviet labor camps was the slogan "Honest labor: the road home,"[228] reminiscent of the better-known signs at the gates of Nazi concentration camps which promised that "work will set you free." At a prison entrance in Cuba a large poster declared: "When these bars are no longer necessary, the Revolution will have triumphed—Fidel Castro." Vietnamese labor camps were adorned with the ironic assurance of Ho Chi Minh: "Nothing is more precious than independence and liberty."[229]

Maxim Gorky, the famous Soviet writer, visited the first labor camps in the Solovki islands (located near the Arctic circle) in order to chronicle their great reformative achievements. His observations included: "For the first time I saw horse and cow stables kept in a state of such cleanliness that the sharp stench emanating from such places cannot be detected at all.... The rough lyricism of these islands... awakens a longing to work more rapidly and fervently towards creating a new reality...." As another observer pointed out, "Under Gorky's pen life in the concentration camp could be the cause of envy on the part of inhabitants of the ordinary Soviet reality on the other side of the barbed wire." Gorky wrote in the visitors' book (which had been specially made for his visit):

> I am not in a state of mind to express my impressions in just a few words. I would not want... to permit myself banal praise of the remarkable energy of people who, while remaining vigilant and tireless sentinels of the Revolution, are able at the same time to be remarkably bold creators of culture.[230]

Presumably these people were the guards.

The Soviet writers who were sent in 1933 on a "fact-finding mission" to the construction site of the Belomor canal also found guards devoted to the well-being and political-ideological transformation of their prisoners, as well as inmates seeking to refashion themselves "on the anvil of unremitting work." They concluded that from "the unruly human material ... the Bolshevik genius is able to construct the most homogeneous harmonious, just and happy society on earth."[231] This was also the message of Nicholas Pogodin's play *The Aristocrats*, which dealt with the successful efforts of the NKVD personnel to rehabilitate both ordinary and political prisoners during the construction of the same canal. The play portrayed Commandant Gromov, who "resemble[d] a kindly, good-hearted pedagogue. His understanding for the prisoners placed in his charge is boundless. He treats them like a clever and attentive father.... [H]is main task is to find the proper way of reaching the soul of every individual."[232]

Imprisonment thus combined punishment, work, and political education. In the Soviet case, efforts at rehabilitation became increasingly a formality, while in China under Mao "thought reform" was pursued avidly. Similar attempts were also made in Vietnam.[233]

As time went by, the distinction between political and nonpolitical offenders hardened (especially in the USSR), and the rehabilitation of the former was taken off the agenda. Even the policies of rehabilitation of ordinary criminals were gradually abandoned and replaced by a harsh, punitive orientation. These changes originated in the shifting theoretical premises regarding individual responsibility. Initially, the Soviet authorities maintained the conventional Marxist position that crime and other forms of antisocial behavior were responses to exploitation, inequality, and the brutalized social relations that prevailed in capitalist societies permeated by the profit motive.[234]

By the early 1930s the major socioeconomic transformations were completed in the Soviet Union—most importantly, the private ownership of the means of production had been abolished—which in theory should have put an end to the conditions supposedly breeding antisocial attitudes and behavior. Since this failed to happen, Soviet ideologues invented the concept of "survivals": bad behavior was now blamed not on capitalist institutions or social relations (they had, after all, been abolished) but on their lingering after-effects. How long these "survivals" were going to pollute the minds and behavior of Soviet citizens was not made clear. A Soviet official said in 1966: "It would be a mistake to think that the very fact of living in the land of the Soviets, in the conditions of socialist reality, presupposes a Communist worldview in a young person."[235] Marx's proposition about existence determining consciousness no longer applied in Soviet society. Soviet penologists and political authorities reached the conclusion that individuals misbehaving in an established socialist system were to be held responsible and could no longer be regarded as products of society responding to inexorable social forces. Punishment conceived of as a matter of social justice and as a deterrent was fully restored.

There was no explicit discussion of how these principles applied to political as distinct from nonpolitical criminals; Soviet official discourse had almost from the beginning suggested that the behavior of political criminals was not socially determined; they were fully responsible for their abominable crimes and deserved stern punishment. In a thoroughly un-Marxist fashion, the Soviet and other Communist systems maintained what amounted to the position that there was evil in human nature as far as political criminals or class enemies were concerned, and this evil had little to do with the social environment. It had to be eradicated without mercy.

While attempts to rehabilitate or reeducate political wrongdoers faded over time, especially in the Soviet Union and Eastern Europe, work—that is, "corrective labor"—remained officially defined as the instrument of therapeutic rehabilitation for both political and nonpolitical offenders. In reality there was little or no political education in Soviet prisons and labor camps,[236] and few attempts were made to mobilize group pressure among prisoners in the service of political-ideological reeducation, such as the practice of "struggling" in China. The struggle session was defined by one who had experienced it as

> a peculiarly Chinese invention combining intimidation, humiliation and sheer exhaustion ... an intellectual gang-beating of one man by many ... in which the victim has no defense. ... [T]he technique ... was a thing of utter simplicity: a fierce and pitiless crescendo of screams demanding that the victim confess. ...[237]

In Communist China, Vietnam, and Cuba, political reeducation, or thought reform, was taken far more seriously and applied to both political and nonpolitical prisoners. Inmates in Chinese labor camps reportedly spent two to three hours daily "in some sort of political study session."[238] A precondition of rehabilitation was a freely expressed sense of guilt or penitence for the transgressions of which the inmate had been accused, hence the centrality of confession in the reeducation process.

A plausible explanation of the difference between Chinese, Vietnamese, and Cuban approaches as opposed to the Soviet and East European is that the former were newer, more revolutionary, and in some ways more idealistic systems (initially, at any rate), more seriously committed to the idea of creating new human beings; they were also less inspired by orthodox Marxism. Political will or voluntarism was their guiding principle. China's oppressive collectivism also had stronger cultural roots in the pre-Communist Chinese tradition of subjecting the individual to the group. As in all traditional societies, the lines between the private and the public realm were less sharply drawn.

The Cuban regime also avidly pursued a program of "political rehabilitation" comparable to the Chinese in its intensity:

> At first the objective . . . was to reduce the number of men in prison who continued to repudiate the government. Therefore the authorities promised better treatment, frequent family visits, correspondence . . . prompt return to freedom and reintegration into the new society. . . . [Y]ou had to turn in reports and make a self-criticism, write an apology for your previous counterrevolutionary activity and confess everything. . . . [T]he ultimate aim . . . was the internal annihilation of the prisoner, the destruction of all his principles. . . . The men who agreed to join [the Program] had to sign a little form renouncing all their beliefs and adopting Marxism as their new philosophy.[239]

The policies of reeducation (or thought reform) can also be explained with reference to the concept of totalitarianism: Communist China under Mao, Cuba under Castro, and Vietnam until the late 1980s were indisputably totalitarian, certainly more so than were the Soviet Union and its East European allies after the death of Stalin. This meant a greater determination to maximize the power of the state and obliterate sanctuaries of personal freedom in the private realm. These third-world political systems were more serious about creating a "new socialist man" suited to living in the totalitarian-collectivistic society being created. While the Soviet system, especially under Stalin, also claimed to be engaged in the creation of the new socialist man, it had made fewer tangible efforts to implement this goal. In the long Brezhnev era the system became even more conservative and reluctant to experiment.

It remains an open question what is more inhumane: to attempt to radically transform human beings by the kind of relentless pressure and invasion of privacy entailed in thought reform, or to discard them (literally or figuratively) in the manner of the Soviet-type penal systems.

THE PERPETRATORS

One may distinguish at least three types of motivation and mindset among those involved in the planning, administration, and execution of political violence and coercion in Communist systems.[240] At the highest level there were ideologically driven, puritanical, and ruthless individuals exemplified in the Soviet case by Felix Dzerzhinsky (his Nazi counterpart might be Heinrich Himmler).[241] Such individuals tended to be more prominent in the earlier periods of Communist systems. They seemed immune to doubt, inner conflict, and reservations about the use of harsh, even murderous methods seen as essential for the achievement of their great goals and for staying in power. As Lance Morrow has written: "There is always a professor of violence—realist, zealot, ideologue . . . who lays it down that evil is the price of change. . . . Intellectuals, alas, have an immense tolerance for—even an attraction to—evil if they see it as part of a means to a socially and intellectually satisfying end. . . . [T]he professors of violence, the theoreticians . . . preside over armies of brutal morons. . . ."[242] George Lukacs, the Hungarian Marxist philosopher, himself not involved in the dirty business of keeping the system in power, expressed this mindset with great precision: "The highest duty for Communist ethics is to accept the necessity of acting immorally. This is the greatest sacrifice that the revolution demands of us. The conviction of the true Communist is that evil transforms itself unto bliss through the dialectics of historical evolution."[243] The same attitude is captured by Montefiore:

> The Bolsheviks were atheists but they were hardly secular politicians. . . . [T]hey stooped to kill from the smugness of the highest moral eminence. . . . They would die and kill for their faith in the inevitable progress toward human betterment, making sacrifices of their own families with the fervour only seen in religious slaughters and martyrdoms of the Middle Ages—and the Middle East.[244]

Lenin was the supreme embodiment of this type of human being. The Russian historian Dmitri Volkogonov wrote of him: "It is difficult to fathom how a man who loved Beethoven and Spinoza, who read Kant . . . could reconcile himself to a system permeated with police rule. How could Lenin, who claimed to be the leader of a new world, personally write orders to hang, to shoot, to take hostages, to imprison in concentration camps. . . ?"[245]

The human capacity to compartmentalize and selectively highlight or dismiss empirical facts is also reflected in the advice of a Hungarian Communist regarding the Soviet show trials: "Do not look at the details . . . but consider them in their total political context."[246] Molotov's view of the Purges was similar: "of course there were excesses but all that was permissible, to my mind, for the sake of the main objective—keeping state power. . . ."[247] Pol Pot, the geno-cidal Cambodian leader, shared this outlook and conveyed it to an interviewer shortly before his death: "I do not reject responsibility—our movement made mistakes, like every movement in the world. But . . . [w]e had no other choice . . . we had to defend ourselves . . . my conscience is clear. Everything I have done . . . is first for the nation and the people of Cambodia."[248]

The second type of individual, exemplified by Adolf Eichman, is the pro-verbial cog in the bureaucratic machinery; he is the embodiment of ordinari-ness and symbolizes the "banality of evil"—a concept popularized by Hannah Arendt in the Nazi context but equally applicable to the Communist setting. He follows orders rather then being driven by strong convictions. Such indi-viduals were to be found in many authoritarian systems. A former veteran of the Japanese army in World War II who participated in the atrocities in China observed that "the torturers themselves . . . were regular people who simply did their job." In a similar spirit, Kang Kek Ieu, head of the Khmer Rouge Secret Police and commandant of a prison where 14,000 people were tortured and killed, averred that he merely "wanted to be a good Communist" and "sought to make clear that he had not tortured or killed for the fun of it. . . . [H]e portrayed himself as a harried bureaucrat, constantly concerned about the quality of his product."[249]

Communist systems made it particularly easy to shift responsibility for carrying out morally problematic tasks to higher authority, given the myth of the infallibility of the party and its leaders and the attendant requirement for obedience just as rigid and unthinking as that demanded by the Nazi and Japa-nese authorities. This attitude was not limited to those at the lower reaches of the hierarchy: Georgi Piatakov, a leading Bolshevik revolutionary, reportedly said, "If the Party demands it . . . I will see black where I saw white . . . because for me there is no life outside the Party." George Kennan's characterization of Andrei Gromyko captures the same mindset: "The Party became . . . his mother, his father, his teacher, his conscience and his master. . . . And if it turned out that what the Party required to be done . . . involved apparent injustice or cruelty—well, one might regret that it was found necessary. . . . But it was not one's own responsibility."[250]

The third type of individual drawn to the mechanics of repression repre-sents the least attractive: the amoral or unmistakably malevolent individual, motivated at his highest by the lust for power, at his lowest by the enjoyment of inflicting pain and of being in total control of those at his mercy. This group of individuals includes the anonymous guards, interrogators, and torture special-ists whose profiles often emerge from the recollections of their former victims. It is this group which has attracted the least social scientific attention, although the general idea that in every society there are people who possess or develop a personality and mentality congenial to the practices of political repression has been expressed by several authors. For example, Antonio Candido, a Brazilian writer, has observed that to carry out these tasks "society needs thousands of individuals with appropriately deformed souls. . . . [S]ociety draws from these people the brutality, the need, the frustration, the depravity, the defect—and gives them the repressive function." Dennis Deletant has come to the conclusion that "brutality was the characteristic feature of the men chosen by the NKVD/MGB [the Soviet political police] to head Romania's security police." Joseph Skvorecky, the Czech writer, has perceived among the hardcore supporters of both Nazi and Communist systems "people scarred by private hatreds, grounded in deeply negative personal experience . . . [people] with physical or psychological malformations . . . haunted by a feeling of insecurity . . . exploit [ing] ideas and movements to achieve a feeling of self-worth." Another Czech author, Peter Hruby, has written: "Every nation has a small percentage of potential criminals in its population. In totalitarian dictatorships these people . . . get their best chance and can really enjoy themselves, at the same time feeling proud that they are serving a great cause." Victor Serge has observed that during the early years of the Soviet state, the apparatus of repression had already attracted two types of individuals, a small number of "incorruptible men like . . .Dzerzhinsky, a sincere idealist, ruthless but chivalrous. . . . But the Party had few men of this stamp . . . ," and gradually selection came to be based on more unappealing traits:

> The only temperaments that devoted themselves willingly and tenaciously to this task of "internal defense" were those characterized by suspicion, embitterment, harshness and sadism. Longstanding social inferiority-complexes and memories of humiliations and suffering . . . rendered them intractable . . . perverted men tending to see conspiracy everywhere.

This was also the conclusion of Walter Krivitsky: "As the . . . Secret Police gained more power . . . fearless revolutionists were slowly replaced by hardened, dissolute and demoralized executioners."[251] Orlov thought that there were three major types among "Stalin's inquisitors": "sadists . . . unscrupulous careerists . . . and men with a dual mind . . . who have put their conscience on the altar of the party and carried out with broken heart the criminal orders of Stalin."[252]

While unattractive personality types and traits have been quite readily detected and discussed among both the Nazi elite and lower-ranking Nazi specialists in coercion, only the former victims or citizens of Communist states have made similar observations about the characteristics of those performing corresponding functions in Communist systems. Western social scientists, while readily ascribing certain pathologies to leading Nazis, have resisted recognizing similar traits among Communist leaders, functionaries, or heads of police forces. This attitude has something to do with the divergent perceptions of the evils Nazism and communism respectively represented; the perception that Nazism was the greater evil has allowed, or predisposed, scholars to focus more readily on their individual pathologies.

Another explanation of this difference in the attribution of personal pathology lies in the fact that while many of the Nazi executioners and torturers were brought to trial and were sometimes objects of study during their incarceration, hardly any member of the Communist apparatuses of repression has been brought to trial and thus subjected to public or social scientific scrutiny. Even when such individuals were removed from power and liquidated, as happened to virtually every head of the Soviet political police, their treatment was secretive, and neither the general public nor social scientists were given a chance to learn about their personalities or the possible social-psychological causes leading to their career patterns and behavior.

Aside from ideological conviction, the propensity to obey the authorities, lust for power, and sadism, one more motive should be noted that often combined with or complemented the others, namely, material incentives. Members of the Communist repressive apparatus, and in particular those at its highest echelons, could count on numerous benefits: better pay, better housing, career opportunities, a wide assortment of privileges and rewards. Access to such privileges depended on the kind of service performed and the position occupied in the hierarchy. There was, for example, a great difference between the lifestyle of an important camp commander and the enlisted men guarding the prisoners;[253] being a guard in a remote camp was no path to privilege, but being an officer in the NKVD, KGB, or the East German Stasi surely was ("the Stasi men were always an elite, a group that benefited from opportunities for training and education . . ."). The memoirs of Oleg Kalugin (a former high-ranking KGB officer) testify to the privileges of the KGB elite. In Communist Czechoslovakia, state security operatives were given bonuses and promotions for increasing their "output" of arrests and confessions. Hungarian state security officials "could fill their pockets with various allowances, bonuses and benefits."[254]

V: Conclusions

No Communist system was free of repression, but the severity of repression fluctuated over time (North Korea may be an exception, since its repressive policies seem to have changed little over the years). The routine reliance on political violence and coercion was at once a defining characteristic of Communist systems and a telling indicator of the failure of their policies and their lack of (or limited) legitimacy. Communist systems' habitual reliance on repressive policies may also be seen as the institutionalization of their leaders' intolerance.

The decline and fall of Communist states coincided with declining repression, growing corruption, and the underlying weakening of the political will of their ruling elites.[255] Those still in power—in China, Cuba, North Korea, and Vietnam—did not and would not hesitate to use force to crush and stifle dissent or opposition and have remained highly repressive. Nonrepressive, noncoercive, tolerant Communist systems "with a human face" have never existed. Hungary in the late Kadar years approached the possibility of such a system, but it eventually fell apart.

In the final analysis, the repressive character of Communist states can be explained by a combination of universal and historically specific factors. The first includes the longstanding and entrenched human potential and disposition to dehumanize, demonize, and mistreat others (those defined as outsiders, strangers, and enemies) without compunction and for a wide variety of reasons; most commonly such hatreds and scapegoating are associated with conditions of scarcity and competition for scarce resources (not only material). Social, ethnic, and physical distances between groups aggravate such dispositions.

Preconditions for the type of massive violence and coercion described in this volume must also include the availability of certain minimal technological and administrative means for carrying out large-scale repression, lethal or nonlethal. Victims must be transported (on trains, trucks, or boats) to particular locations (for incarceration or execution); firearms are required for the rapid and efficient killing of large numbers (absent gas chambers); barbed wire is an essential ingredient for the creation of concentration camps and for rapidly confining large numbers of people.

The second set of factors consists of more specific historical, and ideological elements. Most Communist states had no democratic, liberal, or individualistic political culture or traditions; reflexive submission to authority was more readily forthcoming in these societies. Most of these countries were also economically underdeveloped, inegalitarian, and scarcity-ridden.

Arguably, ideology—that is to say, certain structured and militant beliefs—was most important in channeling frustrations and resentments into politically defined and legitimated violence and aggression; such beliefs led to the mistreatment of designated groups in the service of bringing about a radical break with past deprivations and injustices—although these beliefs were held only by small elite groups.

Communist systems were relentlessly ends-oriented. Their ends provided the assurance and legitimation needed to coerce, or outright eliminate, all those who stood in the way of the great experiment in human liberation, the creation of a better world. In each of these societies small but determined minorities (mostly politicized intellectuals or quasi-intellectuals) found new meaning for themselves in the attempt to radically transform societies and human beings; politics became, at least initially, a quasireligious quest that stimulated ruthlessness and intolerance. As Hilton Kramer, among others, has pointed out: "Socialism had indeed supplanted religion as the source of 'political idealism,' and from that fateful shift there have flowed many of the horrors of the modern age."[256] To be sure, this idealism or utopianism did not endure, but the practices and institutions created in its pursuit remained in place decades after revolutionary fervor had gradually given way to the love of power and privilege among the ruling elites.

The decline and fall of Communist systems shows that the love of power and privilege bereft of ideological and moral certainties is insufficient for keeping such systems going when they are incapable of realizing either their original idealistic aspirations or meeting the less than utopian needs of their people. As Forrest Colburn has written:

> Politically intoxicated ... revolutionaries have shoved their poor societies into an unsustainable recasting of state and economy that has left the majority of people disoriented, politically cynical, and materially more impoverished. .... The brutal confrontation of dreams with intractable political and ... economic realities ... explains the dispiriting outcomes of contemporary revolutions.[257]

In the final analysis the inhumanities discussed in this introduction and detailed in the writings that follow were, for the most part, unintended byproducts of the desire to radically and rapidly change the human condition through the inherently limited and crude means at the disposal of human beings.

Note on the Organization of this Volume

The readings included in this volume are organized according to the setting of the writing. For example, a Polish author who was imprisoned in the Soviet Union would be included in the Soviet Union section, not Poland.

The statements that introduce each reading and its author vary in length because of the uneven amount of information available. Some authors have written numerous books; others wrote little aside from the memoir here excerpted. Some have become prominent figures; others were or remain reclusive individuals. Many are still alive; others have died.

Biographical information on the authors was obtained from many sources, including the Internet, prefaces to their books, individuals familiar with their lives and work, and sometimes the authors themselves. In spite of these efforts it was not possible in every instance to provide all essential biographical information, such as dates of birth (or death).

Map 1: Kazakh S.S.R. Penal Facilities, ca. 1980

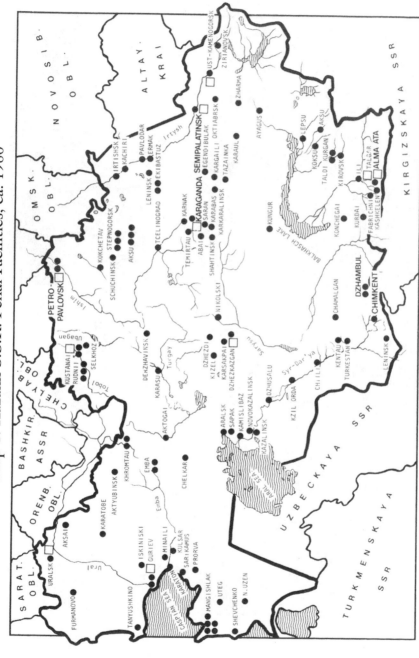

Maps from Avraham Shifrin, The First Guidebook to Prisons and Concentration Camps of the Soviet Union, © 1980 by Stephanus Edition Verlags AG. Drawings by Jorge Martinez.

Map 2: Psychiatric Prisons of the USSR, ca. 1980

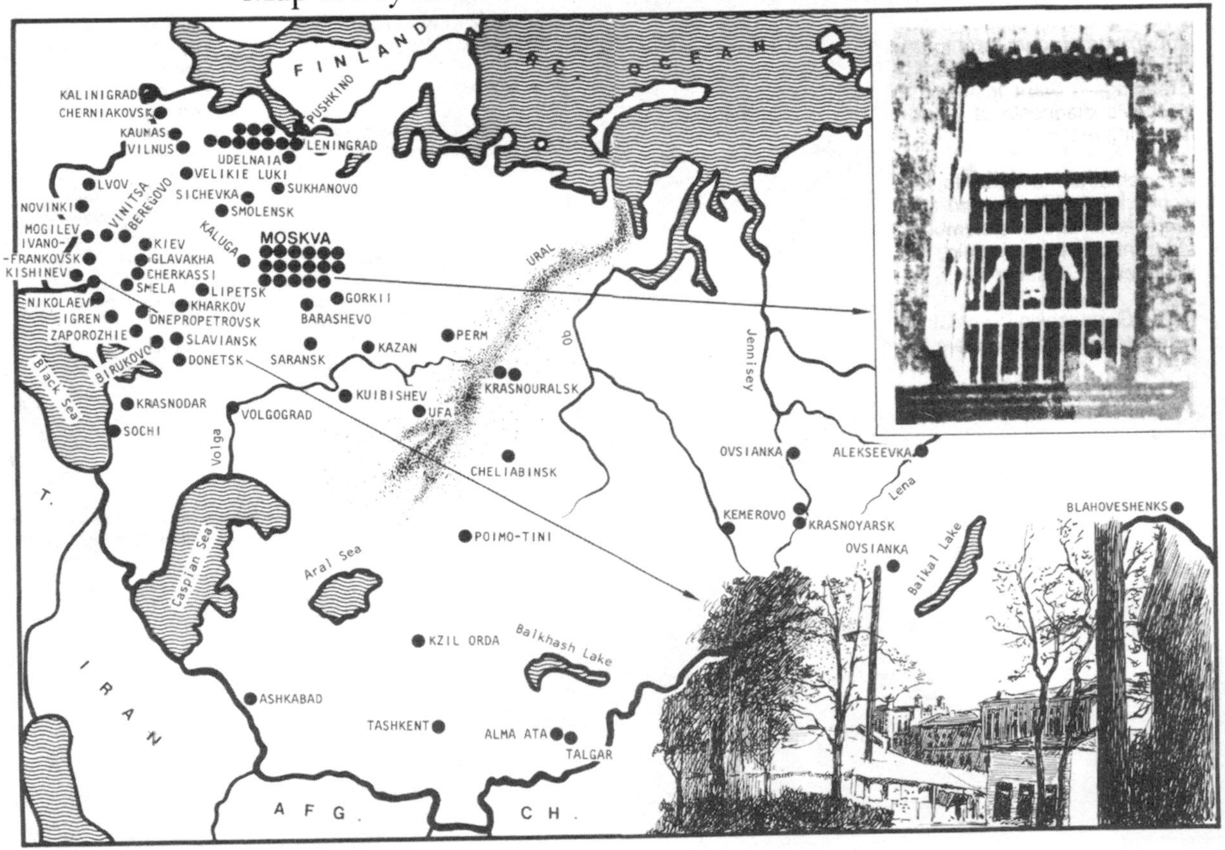

Inset photo: *Imprisoned dissident in "Belye Stolby" psychiatric prison in Moscow (1975).*

Map 3: Death Camps of the USSR, ca. 1980

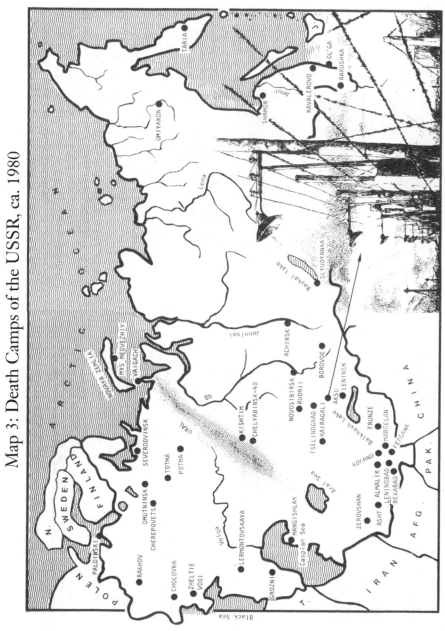

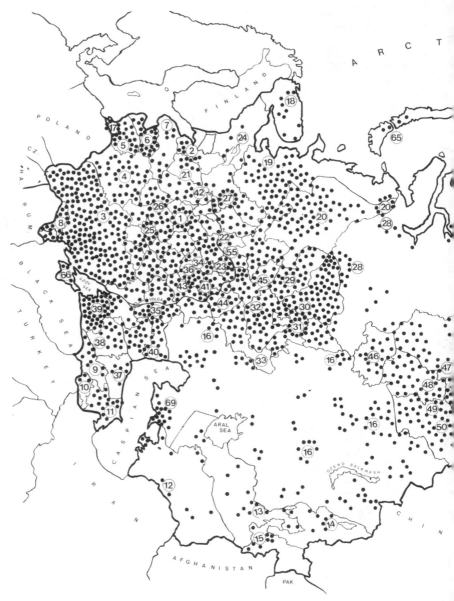

1. Moscow Region (RSFSR)
2. Leningrad Region (RSFSR)
3. Ukrainian S.S.R.
4. Belorussian S.S.R.
5. Lithuanian S.S.R.
6. Latvian S.S.R.
7. Estonian S.S.R.
8. Moldavian S.S.R.
9. Georgian S.S.R.
10. Armenian S.S.R.

11. Azerbaidzhan S.S.R.
12. Turkmen S.S.R.
13. Uzbek S.S.R.
14. Kirghiz S.S.R.
15. Tadzhik S.S.R.
16. Kazakh S.S.R.
17. Kaliningrad Region (RSFSR)
18. Murmansk Region (RSFSR)
19. Arkhangel'sk Region (RSFSR)
20. Komi A.S.S.R.

21. Novgorod Region (RSFSR)
22. Gor'kii Region (RSFSR)
23. Tatar A.S.S.R.
24. Petrozavodsk Region
25. Orel, Kursk, Tula, Kaluga, Lipetsk Regions (RSFSR)
26. Pskov, Vladimir, Bryansk, Kalinin, Smolensk Regions (RSFSR)
27. Vologda, Kostroma, Kirov, Izhevsk Regions (RSFSR)
28. Tyumen' Region (RSFSR)
29. Perm' Region (RSFSR)
30. Sverdlovsk Region (RSFSR)

31. Chelyab
32. Bashkir
33. Orenbu
34. Mordov
35. Volgogr
36. Penza R
37. Kalmyk A.S.S.R
38. Stavrop
39. Krasnoe and Ros
40. Astrakh

Map 4: Concentration Camps, Prisons, and Psychiatric Prisons (USSR), ca. 1980

SR)	41. Ul'yanovsk Region (RSFSR)
	42. Yaroslavl' Region (RSFSR)
)	43. Saratov Region (RSFSR)
	44. Kuibyshev Region (RSFSR)
)	45. Udmurt A.S.S.R.
	46. Omsk Region (RSFSR)
	47. Tomsk Region (RSFSR)
	48. Novosibirsk Region (RSFSR)
	49. Altai Territory
	50. Gorno-Altai Autonomous Region (RSFSR)

51. Krasnoyarsk Territory
52. Tuva A.S.S.R.
53. Irkutsk Region
54. Buryat A.S.S.R.
55. Chuvash A.S.S.R.
56. Chita Region
57. Amur Region
58. Yakutsk A.S.S.R.
59. Magadan Region
60. Kamchatka Region

61. Khabarovsk Territory
62. Primorsk Territory
63. Sakhalin Region (RSFSR)
64. Wrangel Island
65. Novaya Zemlya Island
66. Crimean Region
67. Taishet „Ozerlag"
68. BAM
69. Mangyshlak Peninsula
70. Mongolia

THE SOVIET UNION

Man Is Wolf to Man: Surviving the Gulag

Janusz Bardach

JANUSZ BARDACH (1919–2002), born in Poland, was drafted into the Soviet army in 1940 after the Soviet occupation of eastern Poland in 1939. Following an accident in which a tank he drove overturned, he was sentenced to ten years of hard labor, serving half of the sentence. He spent several years in various Soviet penal establishments, including Kolyma, in the Far East, the site of what Robert Conquest called "Arctic death camps." His survival was in part the result of his pretending to be a former medical student, which allowed him to work as a feldsher, *or doctor's assistant. He thoroughly sampled the worst aspects of the Gulag.*

After World War II Bardach received medical training in Moscow, and he later practiced in Poland. He came to the U.S. in 1972 and worked in Iowa as a plastic surgeon.

· · · · ·

Our *etap*[1] was on foot and lasted for two days. We followed a dirt road through a forest and arrived at a small camp affiliated with Burepolom. The compound, smaller than a school yard, contained two barracks, one log cabin, and an iron hand pump in the middle. Both barracks were windowless and made of rotting boards. The roofs were coated with tar and topped by several rusty smoke pipes. One barracks was half the size of the other and was situated against the barbed-wire fence. A *predurok*[2] led a group of us to this barracks and told us to find a place on the bed boards.

Three continuous tiers of rough, warped boards lined the long sides of the barracks, which appeared to sleep several hundred prisoners. As in the cattle car, there were no mattresses, pillows, or blankets. The floor was nothing but damp, packed dirt, which, along with the moldy wooden walls and bed boards, suffused the barracks with a musty smell. The stale air was made thicker by the heavy odors of sweat, urine, and excrement. A breeze came through gaps in the wooden walls, but it wasn't enough to circulate and freshen the air.

Dozens of prisoners lay on the bed boards in their clothes, some stretched out like logs, others curled up like worms. Their fetid bodies and pale, translucent skin and sunken eyes made me think of Anatoly. I wondered how ill they

From Janusz Bardach, Man Is Wolf to Man: Surviving the Gulag *(Berkeley, CA: University of California Press, 1998),* © *1998 by The Regents of the University of California. Reprinted by permission.*

were and how long they'd gone unfed and uncared for. Most of all, I wondered how quickly they had deteriorated to this state. It appeared as though nothing was being done to help them. One of them begged repeatedly for water, and I filled a dirty tin cup and gave it to him. Out of his rags, the man extended a skeletal hand with long nails caked with dirt. He turned his head to look at me and tried to say something but started to hiccough. He drank the water and asked for more, and I brought him another cup. Other prisoners moaned or mumbled over and over. I bent over a young man and tried to understand what he was saying, but his disjointed words made no sense. His skin was yellow, his face covered with sweat; he was shivering, and his teeth chattered. His putrid breath seemed to emanate from his bowels. I thought it was the smell of death.

My heart grew heavy as I looked around at the dying prisoners, my new living quarters, and the tiny compound in which my every move would be monitored by armed guards. I had believed there would be a base level of humanity in the camps—a regard for human life to keep prisoners from dying unnecessarily—but no one cared.

The door banged open, and a crowd of coughing, sniffling, spitting prisoners crept into the barracks. Like their ill counterparts, these moving figures appeared ravaged and log-like, barely able to raise their eyes or lift their legs as they shuffled across the room and hoisted themselves onto the boards. The arrogance and crudeness of the *urkas*[3] had vanished; only their tattoos set them apart. The prisoners' hands were bent, as though around an ax or saw handle. They looked menacing but were dead tired, falling asleep the moment they lay down.

What sounded like a church bell rang in the courtyard to announce *poverka*.[4] Everyone who could rolled promptly off the boards and shuffled outside, grumbling and cursing. The brigades lined up in blocks, five people deep. Guards with German shepherds patrolled the periphery. A man named Kovalov was in charge of the brigade to which I had been assigned. He was a bulky man with large, tough hands, Slavic cheekbones, and a gruff manner. He had no tattoos, so I knew he wasn't an *urka*, but he wasn't a political prisoner, either. From his crude manners and language, I gathered he'd probably worked in a factory or in construction. He picked out the newcomers to his unit and put our names on the list.

Despite the cool autumn weather, many prisoners—including me—wore only light clothing: tattered civilian shirts, army or prison tunics, ill-fitting army or prison pants. Those without jackets pulled their arms in close to their bodies and squeezed their hands between their thighs to keep warm. A few of the new arrivals and *predurkis* were dressed well, wearing winter jackets, warm hats, gloves, and boots. There was a great assortment of footwear—boots, galoshes, wooden clogs, and *laptys*.[5]

Darkness had fallen, but there was no sign of the camp commander. Floodlights shone down from the towers, illuminating a sea of pale, lifeless faces.

Nearly an hour later the camp commander, accompanied by several guards and *predurkis,* stomped onto the porch. Stout and red-faced, he held an NKVD cap in his hand and tried to steady himself on a guard's shoulder. His long military coat of gray-green wool flapped open, and his green scarf hung unevenly outside the collar of his coat. One of the guards shouted, "Attention! The camp commander will receive the reports."

One by one the brigadiers stepped up to the porch and, in military fashion, loudly reported the count of the brigade. Each report included the same formula, reminding me of roll call in the Red Army. Kovalov remained at attention, looking straight at the commander. He read from his clipboard in a raspy voice, loudly articulating every word. "Citizen Commander. Brigadier Kovalov reports the state of the seventh brigade. There were thirty-seven prisoners at work. Three members of the brigade were sick and remained in the barracks. One of them died. Two prisoners died at work. One was severely injured. Another committed the crime of self-injury. There are four new prisoners in the brigade. The total count at this time is forty-one. Two people are still sick in the barracks. The injured prisoner was sent to the hospital. The self-injured prisoner was arrested and is in the isolator. Tomorrow's work force will be thirty-seven." I couldn't imagine the kind of labor that would result in so many deaths and injuries.

As the reports droned on, the commander's head bobbed from side to side. "That's enough," he interrupted. "Go on," he said to several brigadiers after they had barely spoken. At the end of the reports, the drunk, impatient commander and his entourage stepped off the porch and staggered along the line of prisoners. The commander looked into the faces of the men, stepping deeply into the formation as though he were looking for someone special. No one met the commander's gaze.

"You," he shouted, poking a prisoner in the chest. "Speak."

A thin, graying man responded with his name, code, and sentence.

"Speak up. What's your code?"

"KRTD. Fifteen and five." He nervously tugged at the bottom of his dirty jacket.

"Trotskyite," the commander slurred, slapping a baton into his gloved hand. The man seemed to step back in formation, but the commander nodded at two guards, and they pulled the prisoner out into the middle of the courtyard.

"You," he shouted. A prisoner who appeared to be about my age and fresh from freedom stepped boldly up to the commander and recited his code.

The commander walked on. When he came to my row, he chose a young man in the back. "You. Code and term."

The man whimpered the letters more than he spoke them. "KRTD. Ten."

The commander gestured with his baton for the man to step into the middle of the courtyard.

During the two-hour ordeal, the commander chose about ten more prisoners, all with the code KRD or KRTD. KRD signified counterrevolutionary activity; KRTD stood for counterrevolutionary Trotskyite activity. Several guards, restraining dogs on silver choke-chains, led them through the gate and outside the zone. They appeared to be heading toward the commander's and guards' quarters.

No one said a word until we were back in the barracks, where tense but hushed conversations erupted. I crawled onto the bed board and lay on my side with my arm under my head as a pillow. Two prisoners lay down next to me, whispering anxiously to each other.

"I feel like I'm losing my mind. I tremble so hard when I see this animal."

"What are we going to do? I'd rather be shot than go through this everyday."

"I can't stop thinking of killing myself. Only you and Sergei gave me the strength to go on. Now I have only you."

"He was so devoted, a real Bolshevik. What's happening to us, Viktor? What's happened to the ideals we fought for? I'll go crazy unless we make *etap* soon."

At 4:00 a.m. the ringing rail sounded for us to get up. Despite my fatigue and the cold, I kept the exercise routine I had followed at home and in the Red Army, washing my face and hands at the hand pump. I wanted to retain as much pride in myself as I could, separate myself from the many prisoners I had seen give up day by day. They'd stop caring first about their hygiene or appearance, then about their fellow prisoners, and finally about their own lives. If I had control over nothing else, I had control over this ritual, which I believed would keep me from degradation and certain death.

Each morning four searchlights lit up the courtyard, shining on the procession of prisoners shuffling between the barracks and outhouse. The evening before I had visited the latrine and, seeing the overflowing holes and the thousands of maggots, decided to wait until we left the camp to relieve myself. The ten or so holes were hardly enough to accommodate the nearly one thousand prisoners in the camp. Prisoners stricken with diarrhea relieved themselves while waiting in line.

I went to the kettles and lined up for my morning ration, which consisted of a ladle full of coarse oatmeal and *paika*[6] weighing five hundred grams. Accusations and cursing burst out behind me: "You steal my bread, you steal my life! I'll kill you! I'll dig your eyes out!"

I heard the beatings and the cries of the accused, but no one paid attention. Another group surrounded a man lying on the ground and kicked him repeatedly—in the head, face, back, stomach. One man aimed for his genitals. The prisoner lay motionless while they shouted, "To a thief, a thief's death. To a dog, a dog's death! You'll die for this, motherfucker!"

A man with feral eyes held his bread in his brigadier's face. "Is this my five hundred grams? Is this my whole portion for the day's work? I want to weigh it. I want to know who's stealing from me. I saw how you gave bigger portions to your friends."

The brigadier pushed him away. "The prick is always thicker in someone else's hand." He turned back toward the loaves of bread.

The prisoner tried to grab the knife, but the brigadier cuffed him hard. The man stopped arguing and walked away, cursing the brigadier, the commander, all of life.

The brigades left the courtyard in numerical order. Outside the camp we stopped by a wooden building to pick up tools, then walked down a newly cleared path into the forest, each of us carrying shovels, handsaws, iron wedges, and sledgehammers. I slipped on the clay and sank into the mud, even though I was wearing my military boots. The stragglers greatly irritated the guards and their barking dogs. *"Davay! Davay! Podtyanis!"*[7] The guards stood on the sides of the path on firmer ground, kicking and hitting with their rifle butts those who slipped and fell. The snapping dogs and shouting guards made us scramble forward. On a hill, an older man slipped and slid backward, taking down three other men. Guards kicked them hard and threatened to shoot them if they didn't hurry up.

I was able to keep pace fairly easily despite my convalescing limbs. After walking for about an hour, we reached a newly paved road. The partially dug ditches were filled with rainwater. My brigade moved on. Where the pavement stopped, wooden planks began. Footprints and wheelbarrow marks meandered in all directions. Pyramids of sand and gravel were piled next to the road. We continued deeper into the forest, the brigades behind ours dropping off at their work sites. The wooden planks stopped where the road was still being cleared of rocks and branches, and logs of equal length were piled high. Several brigades extracted the stumps and roots of the newly felled trees. I was amazed to see that the roots of trees could extend so far out and be so enormous, some of them as thick as tree trunks themselves.

Our work site was at the end of the road, deep in the woods, and we had the longest way to walk. My brigade was assigned to cut down trees and clear out brush; small yellow flags indicated where the trees were to be cut down. The brigades behind ours stripped the trees of their branches and sawed the branches and trunks into pieces. Kovalov told two prisoners to build a fire and gave the rest of us our assignments. I was paired with another young prisoner who looked pale and exhausted. He appeared to be nearsighted, squinting when Kovalov showed us which trees we had to cut down to fulfill the norm for the day. Upon closer inspection, my partner, whom Kovalov called Pike, appeared gangly and childlike, and I was disappointed to have such a weak work mate.

"Get the saw," Pike flatly commanded. I grabbed a saw, and we took up positions around the first tree. The rusted teeth pierced the bark, releasing a bitter scent. I pushed and pulled with all my strength, thinking that the faster we worked, the sooner we'd be done.

"Slow down, idiot!" Pike yelled. His hostility startled me. "Do you want to kill both of us before noon? We work for twelve hours, and we don't eat until we return to camp. Now, follow my rhythm."

Pike knew a lot about cutting down trees. He knew not to cut too deeply into one side but to cut evenly from three sides and to cut so that the tree would fall into an open space. As we got closer to the center of the trunk, the saw became stuck. We pulled it out, and Pike hacked out a wedge with the ax to clear a deeper path.

The most dangerous moment in tree felling came when the trunk lost its connection with the stump. When this happened, the base of the tree often jumped sideways, and you never knew which way it would go. This was riskier than the actual falling of the tree. The thundering and cracking sounded like an approaching storm, and the tree would crash down and strike the forest floor like a bolt of lightning—fast and final.

At noon we had a half-hour *perekur,* or smoke break. Prisoners clustered in groups and smoked *makhorka,* the cheapest, crudest tobacco rolled in newspaper. Others dried ash leaves or weeds in the fire and rolled and smoked them. I never smoked and wasn't about to start. The noon tea was nothing but *kipyatok,*[8] boiled water with leaves of various trees added for taste. The dirty brown concoction tasted bitter, but everyone said it had vitamin C, which would prevent scurvy, and I gulped it down.

After a full day of labor I was exhausted, and we still had to make the long march back to the barracks. The route seemed longer and more difficult than in the morning. The light rain that had started in the afternoon was still sprinkling, and the mud and clay were deeper. Each step of my leaden boots sent a searing pain through my twisted back. At the barracks everyone hurried to lie down and rest until the evening meal. Then we had another head count. The commander, drunk as the night before, slapped and hit prisoners at random and selected another dozen or so men to leave with him and his entourage. The fear and anxiety among the prisoners as we walked to the head count filled me with terror. Everyone kept to himself, and I realized something horrible was going on in the camp.

In the darkness of the barracks, a political prisoner lying next to me explained that the commander sought to purge the camp of political prisoners—Trotskyites, Bukharinites, and Zinovievites, all of whom were given the code KRD or KRTD. These acronyms stood for counterrevolutionary activity or counterrevolutionary Troskyite activity. The camp commander felt it was his obligation to finish Stalin's extermination of these traitors, and he made it into a game, trying to distinguish the political prisoners by their faces and leading them off to their deaths outside the camp. No one ever returned, and it was rumored that he didn't simply shoot them.

· · · · ·

I soon learned that this was one of the worst camps in the Soviet Union. The hard labor and sadistic commander earned it the nickname *dokhodilovka.*[9]

Starvation was routine. We weren't given enough food to sustain us through-out one day of hard work, let alone weeks and months. Starving prisoners hunted for mice and rats with sticks and stones. They cooked them on the wood-burning stove and peeled off the fur before engulfing them. It made me sick to watch, despite the emptiness in my own stomach. At times I felt I could eat anything, and I learned from experienced prisoners how to ease this in-tense hunger. They pulled out certain weeds and chewed on their roots, wash-ing them with their saliva and spitting out the dirt until the grit was gone. I found a few small roots and chewed on them. Most were tasteless, but some were so bitter I couldn't swallow them. I found a few wormy mushrooms. They weren't poisonous, and the impulse to eat them was great, but I couldn't stom-ach them. Some prisoners ate them anyway, saying the worms provided pro-tein. Gradually I learned that anything I could chew—even a leaf or fresh twig—gave the illusion of eating.

The evening meal was generally watery soup with pieces of rotten pota-toes, beets, and cabbage. Everyone watched everyone else, hoping to grab some-thing left by a neighbor. I couldn't help but drink the watery soup in big gulps, but the thick harsh oats I chewed carefully, pushing them with my tongue between my clenched teeth before swallowing. I frequently recalled an image from my childhood: the large garbage bins filled with discarded food from the restaurant below our flat in Wlodzimierz-Wolynski. The garbage was removed daily by pig farmers, but at dawn I sometimes spotted vagrants digging through the refuse and eating it. The first time I saw them I couldn't believe that a human being could fall so low as to eat garbage. I asked my mother how this could be, and she told me about the many hungry and homeless people in the world. But, she added, the Communists in the Soviet Union were building a new society where no one would starve or be homeless.

The rich garbage pile from the restaurant now seemed like a feast. The camp kitchen lay outside the zone, so the garbage wasn't available for foraging, but I knew that if I could reach it, I would dig right in.

. . . . .

Although I became more efficient with the saw, ax, and wedge, the pain in my back became excruciating. The muscles cramped frequently and unexpect-edly, and pain shot through my legs with every movement. The pads on my palms and fingers blistered and broke; finally thick, tough calluses formed, and I developed the same frozen, claw-like grip I'd seen on the prisoners the first day in the camp. I was frightened that I was approaching the state of exhaus-tion reached by many other prisoners, who were no longer able to walk. As Pike and I grew weaker, we fulfilled less and less of our norm and received less and less to eat. One afternoon Kovalov took me aside and said, "Let me have your boots. Then I'll put you back on full rations. I'll also give you an extra *paika,* or even two."

My boots were my only treasure. But the sucking in my intestines nearly drove me to eat boiled shoe leather or the bark from a tree, and in the evening I gave Kovalov my boots. In return he gave me extra rations and camp shoes made out of worn leather, with tire tread for the soles.

The weather turned colder and wetter, but no additional clothing or footwear was issued. I still wore the green tunic and pants the NKVD guards had given me, plus the shoes from Kovalov. Coughing, hacking, and sneezing filled the barracks. The only medical care in the camp was provided by the camp's *feldsher*.[10] This man, also a prisoner, was crude and frequently drunk, with a pockmarked face and bloodshot eyes. It was rumored that he drank the disinfectant alcohol called "Blue Night." When ingested in large doses it supposedly caused blindness or even death, but the *feldsher* seemed to suffer no ill effects. He was the only one who could excuse someone from work; under extraordinary circumstances he could send someone to the hospital at the central camp. There was a limit on how many prisoners he could keep from work or send to the hospital each day, so he essentially had the power to decide life or death.

Many prisoners mutilated themselves in order to escape from the camp and be sent to the hospital. This usually happened at the work site; the ax came in handy not only for cutting wood. One man smashed the bones in his hand with a heavy stone. Another chopped off his toes and half of his foot. A prisoner in my brigade asked another prisoner to cut off all four fingers on his right hand. Such injuries were considered criminal acts of sabotage, and those who committed them were sentenced to additional time.

For the first two weeks I was in camp I slept next to Stepan Kulikov, a history student from Leningrad. He was infected with tuberculosis, and although he was spitting blood, he wasn't released from work. His eye sockets and cheeks grew more hollow each day. He was aware of what was happening and talked to me with great sadness and despair. Every morning he said as in prayer that maybe he would be called to *etap*. Stepan went to see the *feldsher* twice but was never sent to the hospital, and one day he didn't appear in the evening. I was told that while walking to work, he had stepped out of the column and walked slowly into a nearby field. The guards barked out several warnings, then fired several shots.

. . . . .

During my fifth week I was paired with Vasia, a man about ten years older than me. We worked together for three weeks, and I got to know him quite well. He was tall and muscular and had a pleasant smile on his broad Slavic face. His humped nose and protruding ears made me feel sympathetic toward him.

In 1938 he had been arrested with a group of other students and several professors, all of whom were accused of organizing a Trotskyite cell aimed at overthrowing the government and assassinating members of the Politburo and even Stalin himself. He told me part of his story during breaks, but most of our conversation was carried on at night, when we lay whispering next to each other on the bed board.

Vasia had spent two months in Lefortovo prison in Moscow, where he was beaten daily and denied sleep for weeks. For two months he wouldn't sign a confession, because the entire case had been fabricated. Then his interrogators told him that his parents and younger sister would be arrested as accomplices. Although this was a common practice, Vasia couldn't believe that his father, a leading aviation engineer and devoted member of the Communist Party, would be arrested and falsely accused as he himself had been, and so he didn't relent. But two months later he was shown confessions signed by his fiancée, two close friends, and one of his professors. He signed the confession and was given a KRTD sentence with fifteen years in the camps and five in exile. Forbidden correspondence and contact with the outside world, he didn't know what had happened to those arrested with him.

When we met, he was in good physical condition and had an optimistic outlook on life. He believed he would be out before his sentence was up, repeating again and again that the day Stalin died, all political prisoners would be rehabilitated and freed. I did not share this view. Even though I was beginning to think that many of Stalin's opinions were extreme, I still thought the NKVD and lower-level Party leaders were responsible for the mass arrests, sentences, and executions. And I thought that if only this information could reach Stalin or his close associates—Molotov, Kalinin, or any other Politburo member—the false accusations, arrests, interrogations, and executions would be stopped and many prisoners, including me, would be released.

At noon break one cool autumn day, Vasia and I went to the edge of the clearing with a cup of hot tea to talk in privacy. The ash and maple trees had shed their red and gold leaves, which blew across the dry, hardened ground. My body had conformed to the demands of tree-felling; my chest and arms bulged, my coarse hands had stiffened, my back was permanently bent. My neck and lower back ached persistently, but I no longer experienced excruciating pain.

In the distance a whistle shrieked. Then other whistles blew repeatedly. The guards ordered us to gather immediately near the kettle for a head count. Kovalov bounded into the nearby brush to retrieve anyone wandering out there. Everyone was present in our brigade, but two prisoners from another brigade had escaped. One of our guards took two dogs and joined the search team as they ran past our brigade and into the woods. The other guard aimed his cocked rifle at the lineup and ordered everyone to sit down. We weren't allowed to return to work until further orders were issued from the commander. The guard boasted, "It won't take long before they drag these sons of bitches back, if our dogs don't tear 'em apart first."

The manhunt made me think how desperate my own escape attempt had been. It was painful to wait for the prisoners' capture—the only outcome possible. We were so deep in the forest and so far from any city that they'd never get away. I could almost feel their bursting hearts as they stumbled over bushes and fallen trees. As we sat around the kettle drinking *kipyatok*, no one talked very much. Everyone was silently cheering on the escapees, hoping by some miracle they would succeed, but three hours later whistles blew in the distance, announcing the return of the search party. "I told you," the guard smiled triumphantly. "They got 'em."

Several guards dragged in the two limp bodies. The escapees' faces were unrecognizable, bloody pulps with hanging bits of flesh and hair. The German shepherds had shredded their shirts and pants and limbs. Blood was everywhere on their bodies. The guards threw them on the ground and kicked them repeatedly. One of them still moaned and cried loudly. The other made no sound. Each nerve in my body throbbed, as though I were being beaten all over again.

All brigades were summoned to witness the consequences of trying to escape. The commander got up on a stump and waved his pistol recklessly. "Guards, assemble your brigades. I want an exact count of all the prisoners. Defiance, insubordination, or attempted escapes are punished by the worst possible means—"

A prisoner holding an ax stepped up on a stump and called out, "You cocksucking murderer! Motherfucking fascist! You've killed so many of us! I'm not going to wait for you!" He swung the ax over his head and rushed toward the commander, scattering prisoners as he went. Several guards fired on him. The commander raised his pistol and shot him in the face. No one moved toward him; the commander walked slowly up to the prisoner, murmuring something, and fired several more times at the man's head. Not a word or breath could be heard. The commander ordered everyone to form a column and return to camp.

That night *poverka* was more terrifying than ever. The commander fired shots randomly into the air. Everyone could feel his murderous craving. Nearby, a prisoner sobbed quietly; the rest of us were quiet, hanging our heads, closing our eyes, trying to travel far away. The commander shot three prisoners in the formation and chose another group to be led outside the gate. Vasia and I linked arms as we walked back to the barracks.

Talk about *etap* with Vasia was never-ending. Every day we both became more exhausted, and the hunger that consumed us grew greater. Days extended into weeks, and still neither of us was called. Every night at *poverka* I worried about him; his political sentence put him in mortal danger, making me feel more desperate for his departure than for mine. But I sensed the limits of my own reserve approaching and was becoming extremely anxious for myself. Then, one morning, my name was called for *etap*. . . .

· · · · ·

The isolator was a windowless, gray concrete building with a flat tar roof. I passed it twice every day, going to and returning from the mines. The solitary building was outside the zone and encircled by a double row of barbed wire.

Every time I passed the building I felt disturbed and slightly frightened. I always feared that one day I, too, would be locked inside. The feeling was like a premonition; that in some unknowable way, my fate was connected to the isolator, and I superstitiously believed that by looking away from it when I walked by, I could escape the force it had over my life. The guard fiddled with the padlock and pushed open the iron door. We stepped into a small vestibule. A single encaged light bulb burned through a film of dust, cobwebs, and dead insects. An unfinished bench sat against the left wall, and above it was a board with ten nails. Prison garb dangled from four of them, beneath which were four pairs of boots. On the opposite side were a table and chair.

"Take off your clothes," the guard ordered. "Keep only your underwear and undershirt."

A hallway led out from the vestibule. Through the murky light from another encaged light bulb, I could see five doors on each side of the corridor. "Second on the left," the guard ordered. He never looked me in the eyes but gripped my arm tightly as he pushed open the door. The dim light from the hallway illuminated rippling water on the floor. I stepped inside. With a loud slam, the door closed. Everything became dark. The guard slid the bolt across the door and clicked the padlock.

The ice-cold water numbed my feet and sent spasms into my calves, I grabbed onto the bucket next to the door to catch my breath, then sloshed over to a wooden bench against the opposite wall. Light seeped through a slat in the door. The wall was slimy. The odor of mildew filled my nose. I lay down with my face away from the wall, brought my knees up to my chest, and huddled into a ball. Tucking each hand under the opposite armpit, I squeezed my arms close to my sides and tried to fall asleep.

The water was a permanent feature of the isolator; I could tell by the thickness of the slime on the walls and floor. It kept me confined not only to the cell but also to the bench, the effect obviously intended. At least this isolator had a roof—I'd heard of other isolation cells that had no roofs, leaving the prisoner at the mercy of the elements and insects. The most torturous cells were designed so that the prisoner had only enough room to stand. After three to five days in this cell, the prisoner's knees were badly strained, if not permanently injured.

Condensation dripped from the ceiling into the pool of water at a slow but steady rate. I counted the drops that landed on my hip. My underwear and undershirt were already damp, and I was shivering. My neck and shoulders got stiff and cramped. The soggy raw wood was decaying, especially on the edges of the bench, exposing soft but pointed splinters. I figured out the direction of the grain and moved with it to avoid getting stuck. The bench was so narrow I

13

could not lie on my back, and when I lay on my side, my legs hung over the edge; I had to keep them bent all the time. It was difficult to decide which side to lie on—on one side my face was pressed up against the slimy wall; on the other, my back became damp. Pulling the bench away from the wall was out of the question—the legs were embedded in the cement floor. Sitting was difficult because there was no place to put my feet, and I didn't want to lean against the wall, so I hugged my knees to my chest, wedging my heels against the edge of the bench. The water on the floor was an ingenious touch. I pictured the NKVD architect who designed the cell discussing its features with his superiors; how to deprive the prisoner of rest, agonize him, maybe drive him insane—even kill him—all without leaving a mark on his body. I lay with my back to the wall, preferring a cold, wet back to a face full of mold and mildew.

My legs began to ache. I slowly sat up and lay down on the other side, protecting my face with my hands. I ran my finger along a thick, moist, jelly-like ridge on the wall that burst when I pressed too hard. The water's slow, hypnotic drip was the only sound in the cell. I shouted, wanting to fill the thick, stifling silence. "One! Two! Three! Four!" It didn't sound like my voice. I counted to twenty, then counted backward from one hundred. Suddenly I was screaming, "Ruchka! You fucking dog's prick! You bastard! I hope you die with an ax in your skull and your balls ripped out! You should be here. You were the instigator. You son of a whore!" My voice echoed off the cement walls, stirring me into a frenzy. I swore at Ruchka some more, then at Gromov, then at the whole fucking world. The guard didn't respond. He probably wasn't even in the building. Hearing my sharp, amplified voice comforted me, made me feel less isolated, less afraid. Calmer, I went back to thinking about Ruchka. I should have struck back the first few times he tripped and pushed me. But he was bigger and stronger, and if I started a fight no one would interfere. This was one of the codes of camp life: prisoners fought one on one to settle their own disputes. If I'd gotten entangled with Ruchka, he'd have beaten me badly for sure. But I was beginning to see that even if I'd been beaten, I'd have established myself among the *urkas* and gained the respect of the other prisoners— and I wouldn't have wound up in the isolator. I wasn't afraid of fighting back, but I wasn't born a street fighter. I could put up with being harassed verbally and physically, but I had a bottom line, and Ruchka crossed it when he insulted my mother. I needed to recognize that bottom line and defend it, fighting fiercely without becoming enraged and striking with an intent to kill. My violent outbursts would lead me nowhere except to the isolator, and that would turn me into a *dokhodyaga*[11] faster than working in the gold mine.

Did I really intend to kill Ruchka? Certainly I wanted to hurt him badly, but I didn't really want to kill him. Many guards and prisoners looked for the opportunity to hurt, torture, and kill, but I didn't have a killer instinct. Rage could result in killing, but it was different from the desire to kill.

14

In the Red Army I once antagonized the master sergeant—a fat, stupid, ugly lout—by correcting him when he lectured about international affairs. I had no idea he was quoting from *The Agitator's Booklet,* the party's official instruction manual on how to present ideological issues to the population. His presentations were spotty and inaccurate; he knew nothing about international politics; he couldn't even locate Portugal on the map. He got back at me by making me do extra physical exercises after the rest of the battalion was sent home. I crawled through the mud, water, and snow, jumped over obstacles, and sprinted to the next course while he swore and shouted at me, saying he'd make me beg for forgiveness for my arrogant behavior.

One afternoon my classmates and I were cleaning out shotguns and bayonets. The sergeant casually inspected mine and glared at me. "Take it apart and clean it again." When he dismissed everyone else, he jeered in my face, "I'm going to run you down. I'll make you hang or shoot yourself just like the other soldiers who crossed me." I cleaned and reassembled the shotgun again, rage building inside. Without looking at it, he picked it up and slammed it down on the desk. "Do it again."

I grabbed the bayonet, forced him against the wall, and held the blade against his neck. I hissed two inches from his face, "One more word, and you'll never see your family again." I plunged the bayonet into a wooden desk.

He turned pale. "Quiet down," he mumbled nervously. "I'm just doing my job. I know you're a smart guy. Okay? It's over between us." I pulled the bayonet out of the desk and left.

That night I lay awake, certain to be arrested, but the military intelligence officers never came.

The damp cold air penetrated my body. It wasn't a cold that would leave me frostbitten, but it made it difficult to sleep, and I had to urinate frequently, which meant getting my feet wet again and again to get to the bucket. The darkness, cold, hunger, and silence put me in a state of semi-hibernation. My thoughts slowed and scattered. I didn't even think of bringing the bucket next to the bench so I wouldn't have to get my feet wet. I tried to settle and fall asleep but searched in vain for a comfortable position. The confinement of the bench was causing pain and agony. I counted thousands of water droplets, hoping to put myself in a trance and fall asleep. I used to be so irritated by a dripping faucet, especially when trying to fall asleep, but in the isolator it was comforting, entrancing, like the ticking of a grandfather clock.

The rattling and clicking of a lock pierced the heavy silence. A door opened. *"Podyom! Podyom!"*[12] Pound, pound, pound. The footsteps, pounding, and shouting were repeated at other doors and, finally, at mine. "Get your ration," a voice said. I waded over to the door and found a diminished clump of bread and can of camp tea. I consumed the *paika* before I thought of leaving even a crumb for later hours. It was less than half of my normal bread ration, and there would be no soup or oatmeal served later in the day.

Another bang on the door was followed by the unlatching of the lock and the command, "Get your bucket." I waded over to the barrel, picked it up, and followed the guard to the end of the hallway, with the contents sloshing dangerously close to the rim. The guard ordered me to dump the contents in a hole through the cement floor. As I tipped the bucket, I overshot the target.

"Clean it up," the guard ordered angrily. I looked at him for a moment. "With your shirt. Wipe up the mess." I obeyed. Back in the cell I rinsed out the T-shirt in the water on the floor, wrung it out, and put it back on.

The next morning I woke up thirsty. With no drinking water in the cell, my mouth became parched. At first I could keep my lips moist, but then my saliva began to dry up. My lips became chapped, my tongue stuck to the roof of my mouth, my throat became sticky. I could hardly swallow. I wanted to dip my fingers in the water or lick the moisture from the walls, but the thought of the billions of bacteria incubating there made my stomach lurch. I remembered reading about octogenarians in India and in the mountains of Georgia who drank their own urine to purify themselves. I'd never tasted my own, but if I became desperate it seemed preferable to the water on the floor.

The cell was as dark and quiet as a coffin. I didn't know if it was day or night. My cheek pressed against the damp wooden bench, my body contracted, I lay as though on a slow-moving river, on the surface of time, which I could no longer comprehend. I became weightless, suspended; my thoughts like clouds, whirling, changing shape, climbing on top of each other. I wanted to slow them down, to stop them, but could hardly focus on one thing. I was not only hungry, thirsty, and cold but also physically and mentally exhausted from the incessant shivering. Sensations and feelings waned. I became sluggish, dull, and drowsy. I dozed, came to, dozed again. There were no days, no hours, only minutes and seconds, millions of them, as heavy as the water droplets falling steadily to the floor.

Sleep, which had been so inconsequential before my arrest, was now a desperately needed harbor. I didn't care anymore that my bed was an unfinished board or that bedbugs fell on me from the ceiling, bloated with blood. Lice didn't bother me when I was asleep. Sleep was the only comfort I had known since my arrest. It took me away from the noise of the barracks, the filthy, dying prisoners around me, the stench thick in the air. Sleep was the only time I felt safe, not threatened by the guards or violent *urkas*. I developed a ritual: upon awakening, I would close my eyes again and count slowly to sixty, giving myself one more minute of comfort. The sound of the ringing rail early in the morning was the most bitter sound of all. If only I could fall asleep for these five days and wake up in another place, another time. But the hunger and cold kept me awake. My stomach growled. The knowledge that I was locked in the cell germinated fear, manageable at first but more difficult to conquer as time passed.

. . . . .

Muffled thumps sounded on the door across the hall. "Fascists! Fascists!" That was all I understood. The rest came out frenzied and in a language I couldn't understand. The thumping continued. No one responded. My heart raced. I wondered if I, too, would scream, pound my fists against the door, splash around the cell, howl into the murky silence. Escape was impossible, and no matter how much my neighbor and I might shout, no one would hear. What if I were to faint? choke? have a heart attack? go crazy? hang myself? Nothing. No one would care. I was a wild animal trapped in a cage. I wanted to thrash against the walls of the cell until I lost consciousness and died. Was my neighbor pounding the door with his fists or his head?

Agony screamed at me from all corners of the cell; searing pain exploded in my neck and temples. My muscles didn't obey as usual; some of them were quivering. My teeth chattered uncontrollably, and my tongue was dry and swollen. Out of saliva, unable to swallow, I feared I would choke. So much urine in the bucket—I didn't drink it. I still needed to urinate but could only spill a few painful drops. Diarrhea had taken away all my strength. I squeezed my belly hard to stop the pain, but it just went to a different place. Inhaling made it worse. I couldn't stop thinking about food—not ham, duck, or fried chicken but bread, oats, kasha.

I wanted to see or talk to someone, to know I hadn't been forgotten, wouldn't be left to die. The minutes felt like hours; the hours, like weeks and months. Is this unbearable, or is it something I can survive? I wondered. What is unbearable? How am I to decide where my limit is? How much can I bear? How much suffering must I take before I reach the point of self-destruction? No one can tell me where the edge is. Only I know how much physical and mental torture I can take. One day the cold, hunger, work, vicious guards, and *urkas* are bearable; the next day they could break me down. What is it like to break down?

I thought of the many pale, gaunt, death-like figures I had encountered in the prisons. Some confessed to crimes they had not committed, implicated their parents and children, and signed the most outrageous accusations after the first broken tooth or cigarette burn. Others survived months of interrogation, sleepless nights, pulled-out fingernails, and mutilated genitals but found the camps unbearable. Some people committed suicide within several days of their arrest. In Novosibirsk, two newly arrested Romanians, still wearing their fur coats, were both hanging by their scarves in the corner of the barracks at the end of the first day.

My arrest and trial on the front line had spared me from interrogation, and I wondered how I would react to it. I knew I could survive deprivation and vicious beatings, but what about torture?

The oppressive work regimen was a form of torture in itself. Sometimes I thought hacking the cement-hard soil with a wrought-iron crowbar was unbearable. I felt the limits of my endurance approaching when I couldn't fulfill the norm, when Gromov assigned me the most difficult jobs, when hunger made me weak and defenseless, when the wind blew in my face and through my clothes. I still wanted to live, but I thought about injuring myself as so many other prisoners had done, hoping to win several days in the hospital, to be assigned to a lighter job, to be transferred to another camp. But self-mutilation scared me. I didn't know if I'd be capable of cutting off a finger or toe. I once saw a man dragging a partially severed foot as he walked to the guards. He had tried to cut it off but couldn't finish the job. Blood gushed out and sank into the earth. I could probably cut off one finger, but that wouldn't be enough to get out of work. The thought of cutting into myself revolted me. I'd never do it. And inevitably the act would lead to another prison term, which scared me more than anything else.

The one thing I would never do, no matter how bad it got, was give myself an infection by forcing pus, saliva, or kerosene into my flesh. Prisoners used to inject a piece of straw or grass containing the substance under their skin or cut themselves and smear the substance in the wound. I'd witnessed many *mastirkas*,[13] and they always resulted in a blazing infection or septicemia. Sometimes limbs had to be amputated. Sometimes the infection spread throughout the body and the prisoner died—hardly the intended result.

It was becoming more and more difficult to make the norm. Would I reach the day, as so many others had, when I'd look for extra food in the garbage piles? It was the most common form of degradation. Rummaging through the garbage, eating rancid scraps of meat, chewing on fish skeletons—such behavior was so common that no one noticed. *Dokhodyagas* searched for food with half-human expressions and ate everything chewable. I was surprised by how quickly some prisoners fell into this state. Many men who seemed bigger and stronger than I did rapidly deteriorated and began sifting frantically through fetid garbage. They ate decomposed material, stuffing it in their mouths and grabbing it out of each others' hands. Why some and not others? Why some and not all? The hard work, weather, rations, and living conditions were the same for everyone. The majority survived, but many gave up. At first I thought the *dokhodyagas* lacked inner strength, mental resistance, or faith in themselves, or in God, but I was beginning to understand that they had simply lost hope and didn't want to be hungry anymore. The instinct for survival kept them from committing suicide. But I would rather kill myself than become a vermin-eater.

There were moments when I lost hope, when I felt as if I were hanging from a cliff and my hands were slipping. In the barracks in Buchta Nakhodka, I once caught an *urka* with his hand in my pocket trying to steal a wallet given to me by one of the political prisoners in Burepolom before he died. In it was a faded photo of his wife and daughter, and it had become very precious to me. As soon as I caught the *urka* trying to steal it, he began accusing me of stealing it from him. His buddies jumped me and took the wallet, but no one came to my aid. I was new. For the next few days they stole my bread, beat me, spat on me. More than the physical pain, it was the cruelty and hatred that drove me to despair.

After this incident I wanted to die, to kill myself, but I was too weak and injured to move. My plan was to go to the fence near a watchtower and start to climb. It would be over in a second. But these dark thoughts and feelings were foreign to me, and they passed after a brief time. Until the camps, I'd never thought of suicide. I believed in myself, in my luck, in my fate. Even now, after all I'd been through, hope circled back, though I didn't know how or why.

· · · · ·

On the fourth day in the isolator, a curious thing happened—I began to miss the mine. I missed pushing the wheelbarrow. I missed the pickax, the shovel, the crowded barracks, the camp—everything I had hated. Even with the work, filth, violence, and senseless death, I wanted to go back to the camp, to tree-felling or mining. There, at least I was among people—some good, many bad, but a few who actually cared about me. The daily fight to survive—to make the norm, keep the full ration, prevent frostbite, remain strong in spite of the gnawing hunger, get along with the brigadier and his friends, avoid clashing with the *urkas* and being singled out by the guards—often made me think only of myself. There was no room left for human feelings such as friendship, compassion, generosity. This was why there were so many fights; why the weak were trodden upon—everyone was looking for someone on whom to take out his anger. In Burepolom I felt myself becoming a different person, isolated from others, less apt to give help to someone who needed it. I began losing what had been instilled in me since childhood—warmth, sensitivity, readiness to help. My humanity was slipping.

In Buchta Nakhodka, Dr. Semyonov and Dr. Popugajeva taught me how to defy this seemingly inevitable degradation. I was able to catch myself on the way down and reverse the process. If I hadn't been helped along the way, I probably would have become cold and devoid of any civil or human impulse. Perhaps it was my fate to meet people who not only saved my life but also showed me how to remain sensitive to those around them. Meeting them gave me something to strive for besides survival and gave me hope to keep on going. Kolyma had taught me that degradation was not merely a by-product of the conditions we lived in; it was part of the plan. The intent wasn't simply to extract as much labor as possible but also to force the prisoners to devolve into animals.

In the dark cell, hungry and shivering, I thought of all I had been through: the Red Army, the tank accident, the trial, Efim Polzun, Burepolom, the cattle car, Buchta Nakhodka, Kolyma, the isolator. Home. What lay ahead? Where was my fate taking me? I felt at peace. I would fight for my life. I would stay out of the isolator. It had brought me closer to the edge than I'd ever been before.

Late in the evening of the fifth day the guard released me. The night was bright, the full moon glowing in the deep blue sky. I was stunned by the cold air filling my lungs; it was only the middle of September. Such an early winter, I thought. I blew on my hands and wiggled my cold toes. At the gate, I checked through the guardhouse and entered the zone.

Alone in the isolator, I'd felt somewhat heroic. But going back to the tent, I felt scared. I was afraid Gromov and Ruchka would take advantage of my weakened condition. I wanted to make peace, but how could I make peace with people who despised me, who wanted to hurt me?

Gromov was sitting on a bed board next to the stove with some of his *urka* friends. He patted me on the shoulder as I walked by. "I see you're doing well. You're probably tired, though. Tomorrow, instead of running the wheelbarrow, you'll load the conveyor belt. That'll give you time to recuperate. Then we'll talk."

Russian Purge and the Extraction of Confession

F. Beck and W. Godin

F. BECK (Fritz Houtermans, 1903–66) and W. GODIN (Konstantin Shtepa, dates not available) are the authors of a classic examination of the Soviet purges and the unique role played by the confession in those proceedings.

Houtermans was born in Germany but grew up in Vienna. He earned a doctorate in physics at Göttingen University and a second doctorate in Berlin in 1932. He was a member of the German Communist Party from 1920 to 1921 and again after 1926. In 1933 he left Nazi Germany because he was concerned with his safety, given his leftist beliefs and affiliations; he went to England, where he found a position in a research laboratory. In 1934 he moved to the Soviet Union (he had visited in 1930 on the occasion of a scientific conference), where he was invited to work at the Ukrainian Physico-Technical Institute in Kharkov, a leading research institution. After he was fired in 1937, he applied for and received an exit visa, but he was arrested in Moscow just before his departure. He was interrogated continuously for eleven days and threatened that his wife would be arrested and his children sent to an orphanage unless he confessed to imaginary crimes of espionage, which he finally did. In 1939, after the Nazi-Soviet pact, he was extradited to Germany (along with other refugees from Nazism). In 1940 he was released but kept under observation by the Gestapo, and in 1941 he obtained a research position in a private laboratory. In 1952 he became a professor at the University of Bern, Switzerland, where he died. (Information about him comes from Josif B. Khriplovich, "The Eventful Life of Fritz Houtermans," Physics Today, *July 1922.)*

Konstantin Shtepa had been a professor of history at Kiev University; the two authors met and became friends while sharing a prison cell.

The book excerpted below is a matter-of-fact, almost clinical survey of the methods used in the extraction of confession by Soviet authorities

From *F. Beck and W. Godin,* Russian Purge and the Extraction of Confession, *trans. Eric Mosbacher and David Porter,* © 1951 by Viking Press, Inc., © renewed 1979. Used by permission of Viking Penguin, a division of Penguin Group (USA) Inc.

in the 1930s. The authors' methodical investigation is based on information they gathered during their imprisonment from other prisoners, including former prosecutors with whom they shared cells. Among their findings was that each of those arrested was required "to build up the whole case against himself," and "everyone was required to denounce at least one other person who had 'recruited' him."

Illuminating case studies of their cellmates, including the informers among them, lend authenticity and interest to the narrative.

· · · · ·

Interrogation

When a man was arrested he was completely isolated from the outside world; everything connected with the NKVD was shrouded in darkness and mystery. Those who regained their freedom did not speak about their prison experiences, even to their closest friends, for the NKVD had warned them not to. But by the beginning of the Yezhov period rumors had begun to seep through to the population that the confessions quoted at the *prorabotka* meetings and heard at the show trials were extorted by maltreatment, beatings, and threats. Whole blocks of houses around the NKVD buildings and prisons were cleared of foreigners and others from whom there were special reasons for concealing what was going on. Night after night prisoners' screams could be heard coming from the interrogation cells.

All political arrests were made under a regulation warrant signed by a State attorney. They were usually made at night at the homes of the accused. Cases were not infrequent, however, of people being arrested at work or in the street, or being summoned to make depositions in the NKVD building and then never returning. The indictment was usually based on Article 58 of the penal code of the Russian Republic or on the corresponding article of the code of some other Soviet republic. Article 58, the only political article in the statute book, consists of about fourteen paragraphs, of which we need only mention here paragraph one (high treason); three (armed revolt); six (espionage); seven (sabotage); eight (terror); ten (counterrevolutionary propaganda); eleven (association with a counterrevolutionary organization).

The arrest was followed, after a period of anything from a few days to a year, by the first interrogation. According to regulations this should have taken place at the latest within ten days. Each prisoner was carefully isolated from fellow prisoners who knew him. Consultation with defense counsel was unheard of, and in the overwhelming majority of cases no defense of any kind was permitted. When counsel for the defense was permitted, his role was purely formal. The judiciary played no noticeable part in either the arrest or the fate of the accused. Lists of those to be arrested, or warrants for their arrest, were laid for signature before a State attorney, who would be acquainted neither with the reason for the arrest nor with the nature of the charge. We know this from the accounts of several State attorneys, who were themselves later arrested and shared our cell.

It was said that in the past arrested foreigners had in some cases been granted interviews with representatives of their embassies in the presence of an NKVD official, if they desired such interviews or the embassies asked for them; we have no knowledge of any such case. The majority of foreign nationals arrested during the Yezhov period, however, were either Germans or Poles, for the most part political émigrés and the like, whose politics prevented their appealing to their embassies.

The charge was strictly secret and, if the case ever came to trial, was only presented to the prisoner for cursory examination in the interrogation cell a few days before trial began. If interrogation led to a quick confession, it would last for only a few days. Otherwise it would last for weeks or months—often, with interruptions, for as much as a year. A rule to which there were practically no exceptions was that no interrogation could be concluded except with a confession from the accused. The extraction of a confession was thus the essential purpose of questioning.

In a relatively small percentage of cases the arrest was based on some actual occurrence, such as factory or railway accident, the destruction of goods in store or in transit, or even only an incautious remark or expression of opinion. A typical case based on an event was that of a young peasant who, after a drunken party at a collective farm, picked up an ax and threw it at another peasant of whom he was jealous. As luck would have it, the ax missed its mark and hit a portrait of Stalin, whereupon the man was arrested, accused of terrorism, and condemned to eight years' forced labor. In such cases interrogation was directed toward extracting a confession that attributed the occurrence to deliberate political intention.

The great majority of cases, however, had no such basis in fact. In every case, of course, the NKVD had at its disposal innumerable reports of unwise expressions of opinion, among which there were bound to be some that could be represented as coming within a sufficiently broad interpretation of the terms "espionage" or "counterrevolutionary agitation." If, however, the accused wished to make such things the subject of his confession, the examining magistrate would reply that he knew all about them already and attached not the slightest importance to them; everybody said that sort of thing, and such confessions were "not accepted."

In by far the largest number of cases the reason for arrest was some so-called "objective characteristic." An "objective characteristic" could be a man's social extraction, the past or present nature of his work, his being related to or friendly with someone, often simply his membership or activity in some official Soviet organization, his nationality, or some connection with a foreign country. A man's objective characteristic was immediately recognizable by his cellmates on his first appearance in a cell, but was never admitted by the examining magistrates as the real reason for the arrest.

The method of interrogation, proudly referred to by officials of the NKVD as the Yezhov method, consisted of making it the arrested man's primary task to build up the whole case against himself, more or less with his own inventive powers. Every arrested man had not only to invent his own "legend" but at the same time to do his utmost to make it plausible in every detail, relating it to actual events or giving them the desired twist.

The grotesque result of this was that the accused strained every nerve to convince their examining magistrates that their invented legends were true and represented the most serious political crimes possible, so that the stories should not be rejected as too improbable or insignificant. If they were rejected, it meant only a continuation of the interrogation until the legend was altered or replaced by a new one involving a sufficiently serious political crime. What was demanded of the individual depended less on his confession than on his personality, social position, education, party membership, and so forth. Most peasants and unskilled workers, for example, escaped with a simple confession that for purposes of counterrevolutionary agitation they had alleged that there was a shortage of certain foods or of petrol, or that shoes manufactured in Soviet factories were of inferior quality, or something of the kind. This was sufficient for a sentence of from three to seven years' forced labor under Article 58, paragraph 10 (counterrevolutionary agitation).

These legends were occasionally distinguished by a high degree of creative imagination. A Kiev workman, for instance, described in detail how he had tried to blow up a kilometer-long bridge over the Dnieper with several kilograms of arsenic, but, because of rainy weather, had had to abandon the attempt. A worker in an educational supplies factory in which blackboards and globes were manufactured maintained that he belonged to an organization whose object was the construction of artificial volcanoes to blow the entire Soviet Union sky-high. There were also some most remarkable cases of espionage. A Greek doctor, writing to relatives in Salonika, had revealed to the Greek government the names and characteristics of certain small fish which were being bred with a view to the extermination of malarial mosquitoes in Russia. Another accused had copied and communicated to the Polish consul the weather forecast regularly posted up in a public park. Professor Byelin, of Kiev University, explained in the course of self-criticism at a public meeting that he had inadvertently mentioned in a textbook the depth of the Dnieper at various places, whereupon he was arrested as a spy and confessed that the motive for this action had been espionage—i.e., to help the German army in case of war. Another professor, a Jewish refugee from Germany, had, while traveling abroad, given German agents details about the navigability of the River Ob by armored cruisers; a third had indirectly forwarded to the Japanese consul reports about the political attitudes of Jewish children.

But, with the best will in the world, the imagination of the accused was in many cases not up to devising a suitable legend. Sometimes the examining magistrate helped, and cellmates were nearly always consulted, whereupon the whole cell would get together to produce an adequate confession. There were real artists and specialists in this line, who were often moved from cell to cell by the magistrate for the purpose of helping with confessions. Some were men who had completely lost all self-respect and were prepared to give advice for a small reward in the form of food or cigarettes. We also met others who responded to prisoners' requests out of sheer pity, and helped to compose and phrase their legends so as to incriminate as few others as possible. "As much fiction and as few facts as possible" was the advice such a friend gave to one of us, and to this day we have never ceased to be grateful to him.

Everyone was required to denounce at least one other person who had "recruited" him—i.e., had persuaded him to engage in counterrevolutionary activity and had directed him. Everyone was also required to denounce as many other people as possible whom he had himself recruited and induced to commit political crimes, or who had worked with him in the same counterrevolutionary organization. Again and again during the hour- and often day-long interrogations the prisoner was asked, "Who recruited you?" and "Whom did you recruit?"

Answering these questions necessarily incriminated others, and to the conscientious they presented a terrible moral problem. The best way out was to name people who were dead or had left the Soviet Union forever. An Armenian priest we came across had an excellent memory and was able to confess to having recruited every single Armenian he had buried during the past three years. Frequently the cell into which the prisoner was put had a list available of dead people whose names could be drawn on. The occupants of cells changed rapidly, and the lists of names were passed from mouth to mouth; knowledge of them saved many. The denunciation of people who were known to have been arrested and sentenced was regarded as a disagreeable necessity, but was not discreditable. The examining magistrate often helped by showing the accused the written statements of other prisoners, which he then had only to confirm. Sometimes confrontations between prisoners were arranged at which an arrested acquaintance told you to your face, in the presence of the examining magistrate, either that you had persuaded him or that he had persuaded you to commit some serious political crime in the course of a conversation that had in fact been completely innocent. According to the otherwise fairly strict code of honor of the cells, this kind of statement was not regarded as particularly discreditable.

There were some who had no inhibitions whatever about incriminating others. They denounced hundreds of people, in some cases regarding it as a form of sport, or hoping thereby to reduce the whole interrogation system to a farce. One divisional commander, for instance, declared that he had recruited every officer in his division down to and including the company commanders.

But even without such exaggerations the number of those who were thus added to the lists of counterrevolutionaries inevitably grew like an avalanche. The NKVD lists ended by including practically the entire adult population of the Soviet Union; this point must have been reached about the middle of 1938. By this time the system had reduced itself to absurdity as a basis for further arrests. But the collection of "evidence" incriminating nearly every inhabitant of the country, and in particular everyone in an important position, was not just an arithmetical consequence of the methods employed; it was also a deliberate NKVD policy, providing a pretext for the arrest of any Soviet citizen at any time.

The NKVD had a dossier for every important official, stamping him as a counterrevolutionary, spy, and traitor. We know of cases, even after the appointment of Beriya as People's Commissar for Internal Affairs and the concomitant changes in the leading personnel of the NKVD, in which statements were explicitly demanded from and made by prisoners, charging leading scientists and men of learning with being foreign spies at the very time when they were being awarded the Stalin Prize and other high honors. They were not arrested. One of them may be mentioned here, as he has since died. At the time of his death he was president of the Ukrainian Academy of Sciences; he was the celebrated physiologist Professor Bogomolets, whose researches into the prolongation of life have been frequently reported in the non-Soviet press. At least ten statements were obtained from arrested scientists, denouncing him as a fascist and a spy.

To secure the confessions and incriminating statements required, a detailed technique was developed by the NKVD. It was applied according to the individual peculiarities of the accused, depending on his political importance and what he was accused of. Methods were based on central instructions and not left to the inventive powers of individual officers; apart from unimportant local variations, they were simultaneously employed throughout the Soviet Union, from Kiev to Vladivostok and from Leningrad to Tiflis. When alterations were introduced from time to time, they were felt simultaneously everywhere. Shortly after Beria's appointment, for instance, while beatings were not completely given up, their incidence was reduced to comparatively few cases.

The first stage was the so-called "persuasion" stage. The examining magistrate tried to persuade the prisoner to make a voluntary admission of guilt, generally by promising him complete freedom from punishment, or at least a very light sentence. The magistrate's efforts at persuasion were acutely conducted and were based on an exact knowledge of human nature and of the mentality of the Soviet individual; and they were specially adapted to the character of the accused. In many cases this phase was sufficient to make the accused give in. Certain types of intellectuals submitted very easily to persuasion, above all because this phase generally lasted for a very long time. Besides persuasion, intimidation and threats played a considerable role; they were generally employed after the persuasion phase was over. The prisoner was threatened with serious consequences because of his obstinacy and resistance; and the prospect of severe penalties, even of being shot, was held out.

Indirect methods were often applied. During an interrogation in which the magistrate was trying to extract a confession by "peaceful" means, for instance, unearthly female screams and shrieks for help would ring out from the next room. If the official saw that they severely upset the prisoner, he would go to the door and order the "disturbance" to be stopped. Shortly afterward, however, it would begin again, and so it would continue for several hours. The screams which issued from the interrogation rooms and were audible every night in nearly all the cells of the remand prisons throughout the years 1937 and 1938 served the same purpose. It was difficult to believe that a man could get used to them and end by being able to sleep peacefully through them.

In rare cases the whole paraphernalia of condemning a person to death by shooting would be staged. One case we remember was seventeen-year-old Serko-Byelinsky, son of a Russian émigré, who had been influenced by the intensive propaganda carried out in expatriate circles about the possibilities of finding work and obtaining higher education in the Soviet Union; he had illegally crossed the frontier from Poland and had been arrested as a spy. A "court" was set up for his benefit, complete with prosecuting counsel and the usual trimmings. It was, however, presided over by his examining magistrate, and he was condemned to death. He was then put for several months in one of the "death cells," in which those sentenced to death awaited either execution or reprieve. Finally a "sentence" was read out to him, letting him off with twenty-five years' forced labor. He was then returned to the remand cells and was interrogated again. In the process, he was called on to write letters to friends in Poland, saying that things were going well with him, that he had found work in a sugar factory and hoped shortly to be allowed to study at a university as a worker-student.

The most frequent threats were of reprisals against members of the prisoner's family. His wife or parents would be threatened with arrest, and he would be told that his children were to be put into homes for waifs and strays under false names, so that they could never be found again. A woman of Swiss nationality, who was able to return to Switzerland after 1945, supplied us with proof that such threats were actually carried out and that after release it was impossible to trace children who had been put into such homes.

Indeed it should be stated that during the Yezhov period cases in which prisoners' families were not subjected to reprisals were exceptions. If a prisoner's family occupied a better-than-average flat, they would invariably be evicted

27

immediately after the arrest and as a rule would lose their right to live in the city altogether. There were even different grades of deportation, very precisely regulated. The mildest form was to refuse a prisoner's family the right to live in the fifteen largest cities of the Soviet Union; a more severe form was to refuse the right to live in the forty biggest cities. The milder form was comparatively rare, at any rate in the case of intellectuals, particularly if the wife had some professional occupation. As a rule "free deportation" was to a specific area chosen by the NKVD—usually to Central Asia or Siberia, in particular to Karaganda in the Central Asian Republic of Kazakhstan. Some towns—Alma Ata in Central Asia, for instance, were said at times to be so crowded with deported women that the female part of the population greatly exceeded the male. The arrest of a senior party or government official was almost invariably followed by the arrest of his wife; the children were frequently put into special children's homes.

It cannot be maintained that the NKVD systematically set about getting prisoners' children into its power, except in a few cases of children of highly placed officials. Relatives and kindhearted neighbors were able in most cases to look after the children, and the NKVD officials who carried out the arrests were often helpful in finding accommodations.

The effect of deportation was made severe by the difference between the standards of living in large and small towns and between highly and less skilled work, but what was harder to bear was the abrupt change in the attitude of friends and acquaintances. Any kind of contact with relatives of enemies of the people was studiously avoided. Many acquaintances would cease to know them, and only a few individuals dared to visit them after dark to offer them help and sympathy.

Relatives of prisoners were generally dismissed from their jobs. At school the children were ostracized. Sometimes the examining magistrate, or some other NKVD official, would actually intervene on behalf of an ostracized wife and help her to find work and somewhere to live. But so far as we know this only occurred after the prisoner had confessed. In many cases the promise to help was used as the principal means of extracting the confession. The NKVD code, or sometimes the humanity of individual officials, generally ensured that such a promise was fulfilled. After arrests had become really widespread and prisoners' children were beginning to form sizable groups, the ostracizing of children and young people at schools and universities was officially forbidden.

An important part of the process of inducing confession was the moving of prisoners from cell to cell. A man who stubbornly refused to confess would be put into an especially crowded cell, or into a cell in which conditions were particularly unpleasant, and sometimes he would be kept there for many months without being interrogated at all. Prisoners were often moved for the sole purpose of demonstrating to them the various degrees of pressure at the disposal of the authorities and the effects that these had on prisoners. A man would, for instance, be put in a cell containing prisoners who were at the stage of interrogation during which severe beatings took place; all his cellmates would bear the marks of recent maltreatment; and shortly afterward he would be transferred to a cell all the inmates of which had already composed their legends and made the required confessions. Among his companions would be some who had been granted permission to receive food parcels and clothing, or had actually been allowed to see members of their families or to receive news about them, or had been told about what the NKVD had done in finding their relatives work and accommodations. Tremendous optimism was often to be found in these cells about the punishments to be expected as a result of confessing, and about conditions in the camps; you would be told, for instance, that in some remote area to which you would be banished you would be able to work at your own job, that your family would be able to join you later, or even that there was going to be an amnesty soon—at latest in the autumn of 1937, on the twentieth anniversary of the October Revolution.

One of the commonest and most important devices was the systematic prevention of sleep by protracted interrogation, which would often be kept up for days and nights, with three or more interrogators relieving one another and incessantly asking the accused questions about who had recruited him and whom he had recruited. Ordinary interrogations were mostly held at night. Years of experience had enabled the NKVD to develop a technique of protracted interrogation that practically no one was able to resist. There were various degrees of severity. The prisoner might be allowed to sit, or he might be made to stand, sometimes in awkward and uncomfortable positions. Continued lack of sleep has a severe toxic effect. The need for sleep ultimately displaces every other sensation, even hunger and thirst, and overcomes all resistance and all power of mental concentration. Among the Chinese and in the Middle Ages prevention of sleep was regarded as the worst form of torture; Campanella, who withstood all other tortures, succumbed to lack of sleep. Hallucinations frequently occur if a man is kept awake; he sees flies buzzing about, he is surrounded by beetles or mice, smoke seems to rise before his eyes; and, as he is usually forced to stand during the concluding days of interrogation, his feet swell into shapeless lumps. It was scarcely credible that some prisoners endured as long as they did. We know of a case in which interrogation went on without any break whatever for eleven days, during the last four of which the prisoner was forced to stand; and of another in which it went on for forty-eight days, with occasional breaks of two hours, during which the prisoner was not allowed to lie down but could sleep in a sitting position. Toward the end, of course, he collapsed, unconscious, almost every twenty minutes, and had to be brought around with cold water or slapping.

All the methods so far mentioned are referred to in NKVD terminology as "cultural"—i.e., as respectable methods of interrogation as opposed to other, more violent methods.

The NKVD did not always take the time and trouble to apply "cultural" methods. Interrogation frequently began with beating, particularly in the cases of simple people, or those whose occupation or character suggested great powers of resistance, such as soldiers or officials of the NKVD itself. Beating was by far the most frequent of the violent methods employed. Mild cases were beaten by hand, but in most cases any convenient objects were used—broken-off chair legs, for instance. It was no accident that more suitable implements, such as whips or rubber truncheons, were not provided. Also, the fact that only the examining magistrates or their assistants did the beating—never the prison staff—indicated a desire to maintain the fiction that beating was not a regulation method, but was used only at the whim of the individual magistrate.

A high official of the NKVD who had himself been arrested told us that, though the practice of beating had been systematically introduced and applied throughout the Soviet Union, there were no written instructions about it, and no mention was made of violence at the NKVD training schools; it was merely implied in verbal instructions that in all circumstances confessions must be obtained, and that beating and other forms of violence would be tolerated. It is also noteworthy that, though prisoners often suffered permanent injury—for example, to the kidneys—special care was generally taken to see that the interrogation left no permanent visible marks.

Methods of torture other than beating were used with relative infrequency; they included feeding the prisoner on highly salted foods and then letting him thirst, the use of bright spotlights, and many others. These methods were used in special cases in provincial prisons. The harshest methods, according to our information, seem to have been employed in the Lefortovo military prison near Moscow, where special cases from the whole Soviet Union were assembled.

The question of why the NKVD took such trouble to extort confessions is obviously more important than the particular methods employed. The NKVD was evidently concerned to eliminate certain suspicious categories of people among whom real and potential opponents of the regime were likely to be found. Such situations have been not infrequent in history. After the French Revolution the Jacobins enacted the famous "law against suspects," which enabled them to use the guillotine against all elements that appeared to be dangerous to the regime. The Nazis aimed at the extermination of certain categories of people, such as Jews, gypsies, and educated Poles, and devised machinery for the purpose. . . .

. . . . .

There are plenty of examples in history of confessions having been required as indispensable proof of guilt—for instance, the Inquisition and the seventeenth-century witches' trials, with their tortures and improbable self-accusations. Precise instructions for the extortion of confessions and for the interrogation of witches have been handed down to us in the *Malleus maleficorum*; it is doubtful whether the interrogators themselves believed in the "legends" they extorted.

The number of NKVD examining magistrates who were perfectly aware of the falseness of the legends and were occasionally cynical enough to admit as much was not inconsiderable. Most of them, though they did not believe the details, professed to believe that the legends contained grains of truth; and this sufficed to justify their actions in their own eyes. But practically all the officials who conducted these interrogations disappeared, partly during the Yezhov period itself, partly in the months that followed. They were succeeded by younger men, for the most part simple people who never doubted the guilt of the accused, except in a few cases, which were denounced as resulting from "excess of zeal."

The best historical analogy to the Soviet purge of 1936–39 is probably the famous case of the Knights Templars in fourteenth-century France. The French government set out to deprive the Order of Templars of all claim to its great wealth, so that the revenue could be confiscated for the Crown. Appropriate measures of interrogation insured that all the accused confessed to having committed the most appalling crimes, in the service of Satan. . . .

. . . . .

The *Seksot*

The most revolting phenomenon of Soviet life, which gave it a special stamp of its own, was that of the *seksot*, the worker or informer for the secret police— formerly the GPU, later the NKVD, and then the MVD.

Secret political agents are not a Bolshevik invention. Political espionage, false evidence, and faked accusations, even faked self-accusations and false extorted confessions, to say nothing of coercion, were not invented by the Bolsheviks. Bolshevism merely carried these things to fantastic extremes. That is what it did with the *seksots*.

It is said that if three Soviet citizens meet, one is a *seksot*. I do not know whether this is true. Perhaps two of them may be *seksots*; perhaps all three; or this may be an exaggeration. The fact remains that every Soviet citizen at every step, wherever he may be, feels himself under constant observation by the *seksots*. Subjectively, at any rate, he is never free from this secret observation, at work or in the street or talking to friends or among his family. Moreover, every Soviet citizen knows that his comfort, however limited that may be, his social position, his liberty, and his life depend on these *seksots*. People have grown used to them; they are regarded as an inevitable, almost natural evil, like disease germs, or accidents, to which everyone is subject. They constitute the most painful and evil phenomenon in Soviet life, bringing calamity and ruin to everyone alike, to the *seksots* as well as to their victims.

31

Who are the people who volunteer for such work? From what social strata and types of human beings are they recruited? Their services, incidentally, are not as a rule paid for; they are rendered as a "social duty." Here we must at once distinguish between two different kinds of *seksot*, the voluntary and the involuntary. The voluntary *seksots* consist of various types, prominent among whom are vicious, malevolent, morally weak, and degenerate people, who are ready to injure their neighbors out of spite, envy, jealousy, selfishness, or any sort of moral perversion. Among them also are some would-be idealists and busybodies who are convinced that their activities are somehow useful and indispensable—*ad maiorem Dei gloriam*—to the greater glory of world revolution and Soviet power.

But other *seksots* have their work more or less forced on them by the direct or indirect influence of the machine whose cogs they become. These too are often weak and characterless people, or such as have special reason to be afraid of the secret police. For the most part they are recruited from the enormous number of people who hope, by working for the police, to win favor with that organization, and believe they will thereby avert the terrible lot of "class enemies." But this is a miscalculation. Not infrequently they are people of special characteristics, such as women and girls of exceptional beauty and spirit, who are subjected to pressure by the police and induced to go into the work, often in the hope of rescuing friends or close relations. The police generally abide strictly by such bargains, at any rate until a new turn of events renders these people's services superfluous, whereupon the *seksots* are arrested.

Before my release I expected to be tried by a court-martial. I was transferred to another cell, where I met a new companion, who, like me, was awaiting early trial. He was a man of indeterminate middle age, perhaps in the middle forties. My first impression was that he was a typical intellectual, such as were frequently to be met with in Soviet prisons at that time. They were known ironically as "Trotskyists."

He proved to be sociable and talkative. He had been in solitary confinement for many months and was delighted at having someone to talk to. After the usual introductory questions such as "Who are you? How long have you been in prison? What are you charged with, or what article are you charged under?" we started really to get to know each other and soon we felt we were friends. The man was a former engineer and he told me his story, which was tragic but instructive.

Kovalenko came from a wealthy and intelligent family. After many vacillations and changes of heart, he had at last come to believe firmly and wholeheartedly in communism. As he himself had had connections with the Whites, and several of his relatives had been White officers, he could not join the party. On the advice of a responsible and respected Communist he decided to serve the party in another capacity, that of a *seksot*. The well-known Communist assured him that this service was at least as worthwhile as being a party member. Indeed, in some respects the position was even more important and responsible.

Kovalenko overcame his moral scruples by the reflection that his new work was justified in the service of the cause, the cause of world communism. There was actually something alluring, exciting, adventurous, about taking the plunge into collectivist morality and devoting oneself to an ideal. Also it was agreed with his superiors that the *seksot*'s normal work of petty espionage was not to be expected of him. His duties were to be more serious than eavesdropping or observing the facial expressions of his closest friends. Moreover, "Communism could not be built with kid gloves," and *à la guerre, comme à la guerre.* The die was cast, and progress down the slippery slope began.

At first Kovalenko was able to remain true to his conscience. He told no lies in his reports, he bore no false witness against his neighbor, and he avoided denouncing close friends and acquaintances—that is to say, people who trusted him and would have suffered by such an abuse of confidence. He merely observed objectively and impartially and recorded his observations with the detachment and accuracy of a photographic plate. His conscience felt no guiltier than if he had been a photographic plate, and if people suffered as the result of what he recorded it was their fault, not his, and they had only themselves to blame. He was only doing his duty, and doing one's duty is always pleasurable. When he had occasionally to overcome his own scruples or likes and dislikes he felt a positive hero.

He was exposed to not a few temptations. Sometimes he would want to protect a friend and whitewash him or keep quiet about something he had said or done, and sometimes the reverse would happen, and he would be tempted to harm someone he disliked by exaggerating some dangerous statement or item of behavior. There was, therefore, a certain element of subjectivity about the "photographic plate," but this he always tried to combat. During the first phase he was more or less able to reconcile himself to the more unpleasant aspects of his work. But this grew more and more difficult, and he was plunged into more and more agonizing struggles with his conscience; and it was not always his conscience that won.

His superiors soon ceased to be satisfied with the reporting of objective facts. The kind of thing that his colleagues and friends and acquaintances said in conversation, their discontent with Soviet rule in general and Soviet measures in particular, were well known to the NKVD already. The Bolsheviks have no illusions in this respect; they are too realistic to rely on popular sympathy; Machiavelli and Guicciardini warned them against taking any such risk. What the NKVD required of its secret agents, the *seksots*, was reports about actions. But Kovalenko was no good at supplying these. His reports were concerned exclusively with people's ideas and feelings, not with actions. His circle of friends was too frightened to be inclined to counterrevolutionary activity.

Kovalenko did not yet realize that such activity was nearly always invented by the NKVD, that the attempted assassinations, outrages, risings, diversionary activities, and so forth were faked by the security police to justify preventive measures.

In the whole of my long prison career, apart from a few cases of frontier-jumping by minor Polish or Rumanian agents, I did not come across anything whatever that pointed to the real existence of any kind of counterrevolutionary activity. Factory accidents occurred often enough and were obviously results of error or negligence, and often enough explicit warnings against the negligence which caused the accident had been issued by the man subsequently held to be responsible for it. But all the innumerable assassination plots, diversionary activities, and uprisings had remained at the "attempted" stage. At the last moment something always went wrong. The weather was too wet, or something else intervened.

An unequal battle began between the NKVD, which demanded reports of "actions," and the *seksot*, who had nothing to report but words. The tragedy was the NKVD's complete lack of interest in the truth. It wanted reports about actions, without caring in the least whether such reports corresponded with the facts. But the unlucky *seksot* insisted on sticking to the facts. His relations with his superiors consequently became increasingly strained. They treated him more and more rudely and started threatening him. They let him know that he was distrusted and was actually suspected of being a counterrevolutionary himself. He was aware in his own mind that his role had changed fundamentally; he had set out to be a sincere supporter of communism but had turned out to be nothing but a common police spy. He would have liked to give up the job and accept the consequences but he lacked the strength. He thought of taking his own life, but was too weak. The easiest way out was to drown his conscience in drink. That was the beginning of his downfall. From then on he gradually lost the last vestiges of conscience and feeling for truth.

On the advice of an ingenious NKVD superior, he set to work on "analytical deductions" from the facts. This meant that in his reports he started "interpreting" the things that people said and reading hidden meanings into them. A remark that the shops were empty and that there was nothing to buy would be interpreted as "dissatisfaction with and criticism of the party's economic policy." If someone said anything to a foreigner about Soviet housing conditions the remark was expanded into espionage, and a man who passed on a joke about Stalin became "the instigator of a terrorist state of mind." Unsuspecting groups of friends and colleagues were transformed into "political groups," "groupings," "organizations," and so on. It was merely a matter of altering a few words and phrases here and there, a matter of giving things a different twist. But this process gradually wiped out the distinction between truth and falsehood, fact and fiction. The facts were completely buried in the imagination.

Such "lawyer's methods," however, helped but little. For one thing, the NKVD kept making bigger and bigger demands and ceased to be satisfied with reports about possibilities and states of mind. It wanted facts about "real" organizations and "real" espionage. For another thing, the people of the Soviet Union were becoming more suspicious and cautious. The effect of perpetual intimidation, and of feeling that *seksots* were perpetually peering over their shoulders, made them more and more reserved and taciturn, even in private conversation.

The *seksot* was thus caught between the Scylla of the more and more demanding and suspicious NKVD and the Charybdis of the utterly intimidated and incredibly cautious Soviet citizen. What was he to do?

The outcome was that the borderline between fact and fiction grew hazier and hazier, and the real was increasingly displaced by the potential. From this point it was but a step to outright invention and lies. Kovalenko now proceeded from "lawyer's methods" to the unrestricted use of his imagination. He gave up worrying about truth, or even its shadow. He merely concerned himself with remaining within the bounds of plausibility. Was it possible for so-and-so, in view of his education, social position, general conduct, past, to have acted or spoken or behaved in such-and-such a manner in such-and-such circumstances? If the answer was yes, that was enough. Whether the man had in fact so acted or spoken was immaterial and interested neither the *seksot* nor the NKVD. There were no facts any longer; imagination reigned supreme.

All these inventions, which flowed in from every quarter, were collected by the NKVD, which erected on them a fantastic edifice of anti-Soviet organizations, planned risings, diversionary activities, espionage, and sabotage; and all these fantasies were later confirmed by the familiar interrogation methods. Thus did imagination materialize and put on flesh and blood.

Kovalenko's flights of fancy only partly satisfied the NKVD. There still remained limits beyond which he was not prepared to go. These were the limits of inherent plausibility. He insisted on remaining a realist, if only in the artistic sense. Why? He did not know. He had long been convinced that the end justified the means, but he could not believe that the means he was now brought up against could be justified by anything, and that was the source of his tragedy.

Kovalenko was unwilling to report to the NKVD revolts and conspiracies which lacked the slightest verisimilitude, and strained relations with his superior officers continued. So it went on until his arrest, and then he had to do what he had held out against doing for years. He had to confess to the "reality" of all the things he had put down in his reports as merely "potential." From the NKVD point of view Kovalenko had outlived his usefulness. Such is the pitiless law of life.

It was strange that, in spite of the NKVD's inexhaustible appetite for counterrevolutionary "facts," the technique of the *agent provocateur* as it was exploited at the time of the Czarist Okhrana played only an insignificant part. The *seksots* would frequently, indeed as a matter of course, lead conversation round to disparaging and derogatory remarks about the Soviet regime, to make the people they were watching feel safe and encourage them to unburden their souls in the true Russian manner. But, in spite of my many years of imprisonment, I did not come across a single example of real *agent-provocateur* technique, i.e., the organization by government agents of counterrevolutionary activity, assassination plots, and so forth. Rumor had it that such things were done as having illegal leaflets printed for some of the show trials, and there seemed to be signs that that sort of thing became more frequent after the end of the Yezhov period, when the interrogation procedure had relapsed into more normal channels. It sounds paradoxical, but it seems to be a fact that the activities of the *agent provocateur* presuppose the existence of at least the outer framework of a state governed by the rule of law. During the Yezhov period the NKVD had no need whatever laboriously to organize "facts." It was satisfied with the *seksots'* legends and prisoners' subsequent confessions. There was no need for facts when paper facts were sufficient. The exceptions mentioned seem only to confirm this theory.

To return to Kovalenko. Did he feel remorse for what he had done? Did he renounce the cause which had led him down the slippery slope? Yes and no. His attitude was roughly this: The road was difficult and frequently dirty, but the existence of the system depended on the use of such means; they were a grim necessity. He acknowledged that the supreme necessity was liberty. Therefore, he had nothing to repent, nothing to be sorry for. Would he return to his work after his release? No, he didn't want to, he was too tired. But if the Soviet government demanded it of him, he would be willing.

The loyal or "convinced" Soviet citizen, as he calls himself, may be dissatisfied with Soviet rule and hurt by it, but losing faith in it would mean losing faith in himself. In his faith lies his salvation. Every Communist must sacrifice his conscience, his natural moral feelings, to the Soviet ideal. What would become of a believer in Moloch who lost his faith in his idol after sacrificing his only beloved son to it?

Another *seksot* whom I met during my pilgrimage through the cells belonged to the category of has-beens. He had been a deputy minister in one of the many anti-Soviet governments in the Ukraine at the time of the civil war. He had therefore had to redeem himself by working as a *seksot*. But this had not saved him from periodic arrests. He had already been in prison five or six times.

Before his last arrest in 1937, Matviyevsky had been given a very delicate task. He had to report on visits he paid to a number of highly placed Communists in their homes, the anti-Soviet conversations he had had with them, and the instructions he had received from them for the preparation of anti-Soviet risings, and so forth. Needless to say, there was no shred of truth in these reports, but after his arrest he had had to confirm them all.

This leads us into the subject of the notorious Soviet show trials. The chief characteristic of these is not the exaggerated publicity given to them, or their propagandist purpose, but the fact that the charges against the prisoners have not the remotest connection with the real reason for putting them out of circulation. The sole purpose is to justify the elimination of political opponents in the eyes of public opinion and paint them in the blackest possible light for the people and for posterity. The real facts are entirely immaterial.

How simple it all was! Ten people such as Matviyevsky would be ordered to declare that some high party official, with those of his colleagues who had been selected for martyrdom with him, had joined them in a counterrevolutionary plot to prepare for the armed overthrow of Soviet power or a terrorist attack on Stalin, Voroshilov, or some other official. In one case the victims chosen, for some inscrutable reason, were Demtshenko, secretary of the Kharkov party committee, and other important officials. They were said to have joined in a plot with, among others, Matviyevsky, a former associate of Petlyura.

On the basis of such secret reports Demtshenko and his colleagues were arrested one night and taken in the "black raven" to the NKVD inner prison. To his extreme astonishment, this fighter in the October Revolution, companion of Lenin and of Stalin, one of the leading Bolsheviks, learned that he was no Bolshevik but a mere member of the "counterrevolutionary rabble," a "rebel" and a "terrorist." Then the interrogation began. After eight to ten months of the process—if necessary, nineteen or twenty—he finally came to trial; and at the trial he confessed, before his people, his party, and the whole world, to some crime of the most monstrous, incredible, and hair-raising kind, only to be sentenced to the supreme penalty. It made no difference whether he made his confession under the influence of the chair leg, as we in the cells all believed, or was sacrificing himself to an "acknowledged political necessity" for the sake of the cause and the power of the Soviet. The result was the same.

The completeness of the prisoners' confessions in Soviet political trials is not easy to understand. The explanation is to be found partly in the psychology of Soviet man. One thing is indisputable: the prisoners' docility in court is not to be explained solely by the impact on them of the interrogation process. It is true that the interrogation methods, particularly when applied for months or years, are capable of breaking the strongest will. But the decisive factor is something else. It is that the majority of convinced Communists must at all costs preserve their faith in the Soviet Union. To renounce it would be beyond their powers. For great moral strength is required in certain circumstances to renounce one's long-standing, deep-rooted convictions, even when these turn out to be untenable. Most prisoners, sometimes old revolutionaries who had defied the Czar, did not have the strength. The explanation of this remarkable phenomenon, which has led to so many puzzled conjectures, is not secret drugs or even the mysterious tendency of the Russian soul to self-accusation. These people cannot regard themselves as victims of and martyrs to a political enemy. They are the victims and martyrs of their own regime, which they fought for and set up themselves. In the past they may well have been opposed to Stalin and the party leadership in their own hearts, even if they have not admitted it, but they have made too many compromises with the regime, often perhaps against their better judgment, and shared too much of the guilt for mistakes and acts which they must have come to regard as criminal, to be able to revolt openly against it.

I was spared having to appear in a show trial. The proposed mass trial on a charge of bourgeois nationalism of a number of the highest party officials in the Ukraine, including Postychev and Kossior, as well as many scholars, scientists, and technicians, did not take place. The period of show trials was over. They had lost their effect. No one in the Soviet Union had any faith left in the plausibility of either the accusations or the confessions. People had started talking about "witch trials," and even the most faithful and consistent supporters of the Soviet abroad found the public confessions exasperating.

Not long afterward I was released and was able to return to my family. I was sent to the Crimea to convalesce and was reappointed to my former post. I was received with acclamation by the same students who had so pitilessly criticized me before and after my arrest, and I went back to my lecturing.

To Build a Castle

Vladimir Bukovsky

VLADIMIR BUKOVSKY *(1942–) was a well-known Soviet dissident during the Brezhnev era. Before his arrests he studied at Moscow State University. He was in and out of various penal institutions (including a psychiatric one), was arrested and rearrested several times, exiled from Moscow, and at last released in 1976 in exchange for the release of a Chilean Communist, Luis Corvalan. After his release he studied neuroscience at Cambridge University in the U.K. and at Stanford University, where he obtained an M.A. in biology.*

Bukovksy's recollections illuminate the characteristics of post-Stalin repression, which was less life-threatening and arbitrary than the terror of the previous decades, as the authorities made during the 1960s and '70s half-hearted attempts to introduce a new "Soviet socialist legality." Arrest and imprisonment in this period had something to do with actual behavior and, as such, was more selective. Genuine dissidents were arrested—people who expressed critical views of the system, rather than individuals deemed, on the basis of abstract criteria, to be potentially hostile towards the system, as was the case under Stalin.

The detention of dissidents in psychiatric institutions was an innovation of this period. They were "diagnosed" with various mental illnesses on account of engaging in political dissent.

The conditions of imprisonment, while still harsh, were more humane than in earlier decades; torture was no longer routine. Judicial procedures were not totally arbitrary; prisoners were entitled to complain if regulations were violated, and occasionally the authorities responded positively. In short, the system was no longer totalitarian but authoritarian.

Upon his arrival in the West, Bukovsky became an advocate of human rights in the Soviet Union, and he remains outspoken on human rights violations in post-Communist Russia. He has been a critic of the Putin government and persona non grata in Russia since 1996. He lives in England.

· · · · ·

From Vladimir Bukovsky, To Build a Castle *(Washington, DC: Ethics and Public Policy Center, 1977).*

I can't say that prison hunger was particularly agonizing—it wasn't a biting hunger but, rather, a prolonged process of chronic undernourishment. You very quickly stopped feeling it badly and were left with a kind of gnawing pain, like a quietly throbbing toothache. You even lost awareness that it was hunger, and only after several months did you notice it hurt to sit on a wooden bench, and at night, no matter which way you turned, something hard seemed to be pressing into you or against you—you would get up several times in the night and shake the mattress, toss and turn from side to side, and still it hurt. Only then did you realize that your bones were sticking out. But by then you didn't care anymore. Nevertheless, you didn't get out of your bunk too quickly in the mornings, otherwise your head would spin.

The most unpleasant thing of all was the sensation of having lost your personality. It was as if your soul, with all its intricacies, convolutions, hidden nooks and crannies, had been pressed by a giant flatiron, so that it was now as smooth and flat as a starched dickey. Jail makes you anonymous. As a result, every man strives to stand out from the crowd, to stress his individuality, to appear better and superior to the rest. There used to be constant fights in the criminals' cells, constant struggles for leadership, culminating even in murder. Among the political prisoners, of course, there was none of that, but after four or five months of sitting in the same cell with the same people, you got to know them so well that you came to detest them, and they you. At any moment of the day you knew what they were going to do next, what they were thinking, what question they were about to ask you. And it usually ended up with nobody saying anything to anybody, because they already knew all there was to know. You wondered at the paucity of man's resources, if after six months we have nothing left to say to each other.

It was particularly irritating when one of your cellmates had an unconscious tic—of sniffing his nose, say, or tapping his foot. After a couple of months you couldn't bear it any longer and were ready to kill him. Yet if you were separated and put in different cells, or if you did a spell in the box, and met again after some time apart, you were like bosom pals—you smothered one another with questions, stories, bits of news, reminiscences, and celebrated for a whole week. There are cases, of course, of total psychological incompatibility, when men can't bear to live two days in the same cell with one another yet are destined to spend years. In general it is possible to divide mankind into two categories—those you could share a cell with and those you couldn't. But then *your* opinion is never asked. You are obliged to be extraordinarily tolerant of your cellmates and to suppress your own habits and peculiarities: you have to adapt yourself to everybody and get along with everybody, otherwise life becomes unbearable.

Now multiply all these burdens by years and years, square them, add all the years you've served in other camps and investigation prisons, and you will understand why it is essential to fill every spare minute of your time with constant activity—best of all with studying some complex subject that demands enormous concentration. From the unremitting electric light, your eyelids start to itch and grow inflamed. You read the same phrase dozens and dozens of times and still you can't grasp it. With a superhuman effort you master a page, but no sooner have you turned it than you've forgotten it again. Go back. Read it twenty, thirty times. Don't allow yourself a cigarette until you've finished the chapter, don't allow yourself to think of anything else, don't dream, don't get distracted, don't even allow yourself to go to the toilet—nothing in the world is more important than to finish what you have set yourself for that day. And if, by the next day, you've forgotten it all, go back and read it again. And if you've finished a whole book, you can allow yourself the luxury of a day off—but only one, because after the first day your memory starts to slacken again, your attention wanders, and you slowly start to go under, like a drowning man—down, down, until there's a roaring in your ears and you see spots before your eyes, and it's touch and go whether you will ever come up again.

This is particularly noticeable when you are alone in the punishment cell, in the box. There, you get no paper, no pencil, and no books. They don't take you out for exercise or to the bathhouse; you get fed only every other day; the only window is blocked; and the one electric light bulb is set in a niche right at the top of the wall, where it meets the ceiling, so that its feeble light barely illuminates the ceiling. A ledge jutting out from the wall is your table, another your chair—ten minutes is as long as you can sit on it. At night they issue you a bare wooden duckboard for a bed; blankets or warm clothes are forbidden. In the corner there is usually a latrine bucket, or else simply a hole in the floor that stinks to high heaven all day. In short, it's a concrete box. Smoking is forbidden. The place is indescribably filthy. Dried gobs of bloody saliva adorn the walls from the TB sufferers who have been incarcerated here before you. And right here is where you start to go under, to slip down to the very bottom, into the ooze and the slime. The words they have for it in jail express it exactly—you "go down" to the box, and you "come up" again.

You spend your first two or three days down there groping around the entire cell—maybe somebody has managed to smuggle some tobacco in and has left a bit behind, or has tucked away a fag end somewhere. You poke into every little hollow and crack. Day and night still mean something to you. You spend most of the day walking up and down, and at night you try to sleep. But the cold and hunger and boredom wear you down. You can doze off for only ten to fifteen minutes at a time before leaping up again and running in place for three-quarters of an hour to get yourself warm. Then you doze off for fifteen minutes again, huddled either on your duckboard (at night) or on the concrete floor (by day), with one knee drawn up under you and your back to the wall, until it's time to jump up again and start running.

Gradually you lose all sense of reality. Your body stiffens, your movements become mechanical, and the more time passes the more you turn into some sort of inanimate object. Three times a day they bring you a drink of hot water, and that water affords you indescribable pleasure, melting your insides, as it were, and bringing you temporarily to life. For about twenty minutes or so, an exquisite ache permeates your entire being. Twice a day, before you use the latrine, they give you a scrap of old newspaper and you read it greedily, devouring every word, several times over. In your mind's eye you run over every book you have ever read, every person you have ever met, every song you have ever heard. You begin doing additions and multiplications in your head. You remember snatches of tunes and conversations. Time comes to a halt. You fall into a stupor, starting up and running about the cell for a while, then lapsing into a daze again, but it doesn't help the time to pass. Gradually the patches on the walls start to weave themselves into faces, as if the entire cell were adorned with the portraits of prisoners who have been here before you—it is a picture gallery of all your predecessors.

You can spend hours making them out, questioning them, arguing with them, quarreling, and making up again. But after a while they don't help to pass the time either. You know everything there is to know about them, as if you've been cellmates for half a lifetime. Some of them irritate you, while others are still bearable. There are some that need to be cut short right at the beginning, otherwise you can't get rid of them. They will bore you to tears with miserable, stupid stories about their miserable, stupid lives. They will spin yarns and invent things about themselves if they detect that you're not listening to them. They are disgustingly fidgety and servile. Others stay silent and glower at you—with them you have to keep a sharp eye open: the moment you drop off they'll swipe your rations. There are also friendly, sociable lads, usually the younger ones—with them it's possible to swap a joke. They are easygoing, never downhearted, and will do anything just to keep you company. They are usually in for hooliganism, gang rape, or a gang robbery. The corner place, over the latrine bucket, belongs to a veteran crook who knows all the ropes. Before you know where you are, he is scheming, setting groups at one another, and all of them at you. He whispers in the corners with them, exchanges meaningful glances. Underlining his own importance and authority and addressing no one in particular, he tells tall stories about the old days, reminiscing about transit prisons, labor camps, murdered prisoners. He is clearly out to start a fight, to set it up the way he wants it. He knows who should get what and who not. There is no way of avoiding a serious confrontation with him, and the sooner you get it over with the better, before he forms his little gang and consolidates his authority. But then all this too recedes, disappears, and leaves you alone with eternity, alone in the abyss.

It is hard to understand where you yourself end and infinity begins. Your body is no longer you, your thoughts are no longer yours, they come and go of their own accord, independently of your wishes. But do you have any wishes? I am absolutely convinced that death is not a cosmic void, not a blissful zero.

No, that would be too comforting, too simple. Death must be an agonizing repetition, an unbearable sameness. And that is why you fall prey to a monotonous, obsessive state somewhere between a waking dream and meditating in your sleep. This agonizing sense of emptiness festers in your consciousness like an open wound, and it is a long, long time before the scar tissue forms in your soul. Nothing at all remains in your memory from this period—it is a total blank. . . .

. . . . .

We in Vladimir Prison had been culled from the camps as the most recalcitrant and obstinate cases—hunger strikers, sit-down strikers, troublemakers. Almost none of us was there by accident, and the few who were took their places willy-nilly in our line of defense.

The cons around us were on the same special regime and had been convicted under the same articles of the Criminal Code as we had been.[1] But the majority of them were here by chance—they were mainly crooks who had reneged on gambling debts or had in some other way sinned against their cellmates according to the underworld code. Then, to escape retribution, they had put up political posters or tattooed themselves with anti-Soviet slogans— thus getting their sentences increased but enabling them to get transferred as "political recidivists" to this special regime. Of course, psychologically they had remained crooks. And the wonder is that in their case, special regime was an exact replica of the regime in Stalin's camps. The same officers, the same guards treated them completely differently from the way they treated us: they were beaten and humiliated, they fought over crusts of bread, betrayed one another to the guards—and there was no question of solidarity!

Until 1975 political prisoners in Vladimir Prison were not obliged to work— the prison authorities regarded it as inexpedient: they knew the majority simply wouldn't do it, and even those that did never met the quotas. It was too much of a loss for the prison to maintain the workshops, hire skilled foremen from outside, and work out additional targets for us without getting any real income from it. In the spring of 1975, however, Moscow decreed otherwise. It was decided to force us to work.

Forced labor is always degrading. But in prison conditions, where sixty percent of your earnings are deducted to pay for the armed guards, where further deductions are made to cover the cost of your food, clothing, and maintenance, where work is said to be one of the means of your re-education, where it robs you of eight hours a day six days out of every seven, and where the productivity quotas are artificially raised to a point where you can't possibly meet them—working under such conditions is intolerable to a man with any self-respect.

Naturally we refused. And the long siege started. The whole lot of us were treated as vicious malingerers and repeatedly subjected to every imaginable form of punishment. I, for instance, spent eighteen months (out of a total of less than two years) on strict regime, while others saw more of the punishment cells, some spending as many as sixty and even seventy-five full days in them. Our letters home were cut off, and we were deprived of visits and food parcels. It was a war without quarter, a war of attrition. We all understood that we dare not lose. Therefore, besides the normal defense tactics—hunger strikes, the smuggling out of information about the violations taking place in the prison— we resorted to a weapon that took the authorities completely by surprise: we overwhelmed official channels with a veritable avalanche of complaints.

You need to know the Soviet system of bureaucracy to understand how effective this was. Under Soviet law, every prisoner has the right to petition any state or public institution and any public official with a complaint. Every complaint has to be forwarded by the prison administration within three days of its receipt. In the interim, the administration has to write an explanation to accompany the complaint, add relevant details from the prisoner's dossier, and put everything into the same envelope for further dispatch. The public official or institution that receives the complaint records it in a daily register of incoming documents and must answer within a month. If the official or institution is not competent to deal with the matter complained of, he has to pass it on to someone who is. Repeated complaints set the whole machinery in motion each time they are made. The order in which complaints are scrutinized is regulated by a battery of laws and ordinances. In practice, it is never very effective to write just one complaint. Your complaint is invariably sent to the "competent official," in other words the person you are complaining of, and he quite naturally finds the complaint unfounded. It is even more likely, however, that no one reads it at all, and it is simply sent back down the chain, from office to office. This is why most people have no faith in the system of complaints.

However, complaints can be decidedly effective, even in prison, provided certain rules are observed. All you have to do is to know the law and the system under which complaints are examined; have a detailed knowledge of all the regulations pertaining to the prison regime; and compose your complaint so that it is brief and to the point, preferably on not more than a single page— otherwise no one will read it. The complaint should merely state the fact that a law or regulation has been infringed, the date when the infringement occurred, the names of the people responsible, and the nature of the law or regulation in question. It should be written in large clear letters, with generous margins. If you want your complaint to be examined by a high official, complain about his immediate subordinate. In other words, if you want an answer from the Ministry of the Interior, complain not about the prison governor but about the head of the local Ministry office. And to get to that point you need to progress patiently up the bureaucratic ladder, complaining one rung higher each time about the reply received from the person immediately below. You should never complain about two different matters in the same letter. You should always send complaints by registered mail, with confirmation of delivery. And, most importantly of all, you should write enormous numbers of complaints and send them to the officials least equipped to deal with them.

At the height of our war, each of us wrote from ten to thirty complaints a day. Composing thirty complaints in one day is not easy, so we usually divided up the subjects among ourselves and each man wrote on his own subject before handing it around for copying by all the others. If there are five men in a cell and each man takes six subjects, each of them has the chance to write thirty complaints while composing only six himself. Copying out thirty lines of text in large letters takes about one and a half to two hours.

It is best to address your complaints not to run-of-the-mill bureaucrats, but to the most unpredictable individuals and organizations: for instance to all the deputies of the Supreme Soviet, or of the Soviets at republican, regional, or city levels; to newspapers and magazines; to astronauts, writers, artists, actors, ballerinas; to all the secretaries of the Central Committee; all generals, admirals; productivity champions; shepherds, deer breeders, milkmaids; sportsmen, and so on and so forth. In the Soviet Union, all well-known individuals are state functionaries.

The next thing that happens is that the prison office, inundated with complaints, is unable to dispatch them within the three-day deadline. For overrunning the deadline they are bound to be reprimanded and to lose any bonuses they might have won. When our war was at its hottest the prison governor summoned every last employee to help out at the office with this work—librarians, bookkeepers, censors, political instructors, security officers. And it went even further. All the students at the next-door Ministry of the Interior training college were pressed into helping out as well.

All answers to and dispatches of complaints have to be registered in a special book, and strict attention has to be paid to observing the correct deadlines. Since complaints follow a complex route and have to be registered every step of the way, they spawn dossiers and records of their own. In the end they all land in one of two places: the local prosecutor's office or the local department of the Interior Ministry. These offices can't keep up with the flood either and also break their deadlines, for which they too are reprimanded and lose their bonuses. The bureaucratic machine is thus obliged to work at full stretch, and you transfer the paper avalanche from one office to another, sowing panic in the ranks of the enemy. Bureaucrats are bureaucrats, always at loggerheads with one another, and often enough your complaints become weapons in internecine wars between bureaucrat and bureaucrat, department and department. This goes on for months and months, until, at last, the most powerful factor of all in Soviet life enters the fray—statistics.

It is reported to some senior functionary—along with details of other figures, tables, reports, and memoranda on the progress of communism—that, say, Vladimir Prison or maybe Vladimir Region has been the recipient over a given period of seventy-five thousand complaints. No one has read these complaints, but it's an unheard-of figure. It immediately spoils the entire statistical record and the various indicators of socialist competition among collectives, departments, and even regions. Everybody suffers. The entire region drops from its leading place in the tables and becomes one of the worst, losing its red markers, pennants, and prize cups. The workers start seething with discontent, there is panic in the regional party headquarters, and a senior commission of inquiry is dispatched to the prison.

This commission won't help the prisoner personally; at the most it will resolve a few minor points raised in the complaints. But it is bound to find a mass of shortcomings and defects in the work of the prison administration. That's why it has been sent here, its members paid traveling allowances, expenses, and bonuses. Admin is taken to pieces. Individuals are fired, demoted, bawled out. The commission reports back to its superiors and with a sigh of relief goes home. Meanwhile, to the extent that you have petitioned sundry milkmaids, deputies, ballerinas, and deer breeders, they too are obliged to respond, investigate, and comply with protocol, informing you of the commission's decisions and the measures taken.

You go on writing and writing, spoiling the statistics for the next period under review and drumming up a new commission, and so on for years. Add to this the commissions and reprimands provoked by the leaking of information abroad, the directives, circulars, and counterorders, the petitions of relatives, the campaigns and petitions abroad, and you will have some idea of what our prison administration endured in warring with us to make us go out to work. What prison governor, what prosecutor, what regional Party secretary would relish such a life? If it had depended only on them, the blockade would soon have been lifted. But the orders had come from Moscow.

My God, what didn't they do with our complaints! They confiscated them by the sackful, they refused to give us paper or sell us envelopes and stamps, they forbade us to send them by registered mail with recorded delivery (so as to make it easier to steal them), they issued a special order making it an offense to petition anyone other than the Public Prosecutor and the Ministry of the Interior, they threw us into the punishment cells. And the answers—you should have seen the answers we got! It was fantastic. The bemused bureaucrats, having no time to read our complaints properly, answered completely at sixes and sevens, mixing up the complainants and confusing their complaints. They so twisted and garbled our poor laws that they could have been jailed for it themselves. A colonel in the local branch of the Interior Ministry, for example, overwhelmed by this paper hurricane, wrote to me that the Congress of the Communist Party was not a social organization and therefore could not be the recipient of complaints. Naturally I followed this up with a whole gamut of complaints against the colonel, and he sank in the ensuing whirlpool. Meanwhile the Vladimir judges, driven berserk by the mountains of suits and demands for criminal investigation pressed by us, replied that officers of the Interior Ministry do not come under the jurisdiction of Soviet judges. Sometimes two different offices gave diametrically opposed answers to the same complaint, and then we would set them at one another's throats. Finally they washed their hands of the whole business and instead of answers started to send us receipts, which read approximately like this: "During the past month 187 complaints have been received from you and refused," followed by the signature. The entire bureaucratic system of the Soviet Union found itself drawn into this war. There was virtually no government department or institution, no region or republic, from which we weren't getting answers. Eventually we had even drawn the criminal cons into our game, and the complaints disease began to spread throughout the prison—in which there were twelve hundred men altogether.

I think that if the business had continued a little longer and involved everyone in the prison, the Soviet bureaucratic machine would have simply ground to a halt: all Soviet institutions would have had to stop work and busy themselves with writing replies to us. But they surrendered. In 1977 the siege was lifted after two years of struggle. The governor of our prison was removed and pensioned off, some transfers were made within admin, and everything died down. Moscow had retreated from its orders. Our poor Colonel Zavyalkin! He suffered for nothing, the victim of an administrative injustice. As a matter of fact, he wasn't a bad man, merely a bureaucrat who carried out orders. He had barely understood what was going on. Faced with the innumerable commissions and contradictory instructions that had rained down on his head, he had evolved a most original line of defense: he pretended to be a simpleton, a mere simpleton who did as he was told and wanted all to be for the best, though somehow or other things always seemed to go wrong. He was hauled over the coals, but he took it all with the air of an innocent down on his luck....

· · · · ·

Late one night, after one of our readings, I was on my way home when a car suddenly drew up beside me. A group of young men bundled me inside and drove off with me. We had often been picked up before this and detained for several hours and questioned, so I wasn't surprised at first. After quite a long time, a half hour or more, we drove into a courtyard where there was a sort of office in a basement. It was curious that nobody was in the basement at all, apart from the people who had brought me here. I was led into a big windowless room with no furniture.

We had barely got inside when the man on my right suddenly punched me in the face. Almost simultaneously another tried to punch me in the solar plexus and knock me down, but I was already on my guard and turned away. I swiftly leaped into the corner, pressed my back to the wall, and attempted to guard my face and my solar plexus with my arms.

They beat me for hours. One of them grabbed my hair and pulled my head downward, trying to smash his knee into my face at the same time. Another took this opportunity to punch me in the back as hard as he could, aiming for my kidneys. All I thought of was how to keep myself from going down onto the floor, for then they would have crippled me with their boots. I hardly knew where I was, my head was spinning, and I had difficulty breathing. They stopped for a moment, and one of them leaned over me and stroked my cheek, smiling voluptuously. Then they started beating me again.

It was four in the morning when they pushed me out into the street. "Don't ever go to the square again, the next time we'll kill you," was all they said.

The last days of the readings were upon us. Bystanders had somehow been sifted out and disappeared, and the groups were dwindling, but this led to an even greater intimacy among the remaining few. It grew harder and harder to organize the readings, and even more complicated than before to get the readers away safely and unnoticed, one at a time. Many of them no longer lived at home, but had gone into hiding with friends. Still, every performance left us with an inexpressible sense of freedom and joy. There was something mystical in this reading of poetry to the nocturnal city, the isolated windows in which lights still burned, and the late-night trolleybuses. Even now, many years later, I feel a special, intimate attachment to the friends who held out to the bitter end in Mayakovsky Square.

On the morning of October 6, 1961, three days before the Twenty-Second Congress was due to open, we were all arrested. I suddenly woke up in bed with the feeling that someone was staring at me. It was true. Captain Nikiforov of the KGB—the one who had interviewed me in the spring—was sitting at the foot of my bed. How he had entered the apartment I do not know. A car was waiting by the front door to take us to the Lubyanka, the chief investigation prison and headquarters of the KGB.

Offices, corridors, staircases, and people everywhere, bustling back and forth with papers, folders, briefcases. In one office I was cross-examined, in another threatened, and in another I found not KGB officers at all but kindly father figures and dear friends. I was tempted with jokes and treated to tea. Then there was more shouting and fists banging on desks: "Quit being so obstinate, we know everything!" No beatings. No torture. That, I supposed, was still to come. I was led from one office to another, and everywhere there were crowds of people. . . .

. . . . .

Coercion in the camp was unbridled. We were forced to go to work almost without surcease and were lucky to get one rest day a month. Almost every Saturday they would read out an order proclaiming Sunday a working day because of the non-fulfillment of the week's production target. Safety equipment existed only on paper, and apart from the deliberate hornswogglers there were many who lost a hand because of this. Three men had been crippled by my lathe during the preceding months and nobody wanted to work on it.

I was put on that particular lathe as a punishment to break me down. Thanks to my reputation as someone who could "read and write," I had fairly soon started writing everybody's complaints for them. Quite unexpectedly I won a very important case for us all, namely, the right to receive visits.

Under the law we were supposed to get two extended (up to three days) visits a year, but admin regarded this not as a right, but as a reward. In practice, the only people allowed visits were those who had "started on the road to reform," and the rest were told they had behaved so badly they didn't deserve visits. Having gathered together a couple of dozen such instances, I began writing all over the place—at first, of course, without success. But I managed to persuade two hundred prisoners to write the same sort of complaint, and suddenly it worked: a colonel came from head office and gave instructions for visits to be allowed—but only to those who had complained. Now I had an enormous queue to contend with, and since there wasn't time to write on behalf of all of them, I simply composed a specimen text and circulated it.

On one occasion, a young fellow was beaten up by some guards in the guardhouse in the presence of a drunken officer. Fortunately there were several witnesses to this incident, and the young fellow himself, without them noticing, had contrived to smear some blood on the order committing him to the box. This affair took a couple of months to be resolved, but in the end the officer was punished with an official reprimand. Another prisoner was punished for not cutting his hair—he was letting it grow in anticipation of a visit from his wife. They deliberately humiliated him in front of everybody by shearing off a strip of hair right down the middle of his head. I advised him not to have the rest cut, but to leave it like that for at least a month. Sure enough, about three weeks later some official came from the regional camp administration in answer to his complaint, and seeing for himself that the complaint was justified, ordered the culprit to be punished. There was no shortage of these amazing cases passing through my hands until, at last, admin caught on to who was behind them all.

The lathe I was forced to work on as a punishment for all these complaints stood in a cold, unheated workshop. In winter you were even afraid to go near it—it seemed to exude cold, and if you touched it with your hands your fingers would instantly be glued to it by the frost and you couldn't get them off again without tearing your skin away. The exposed and unguarded blades rotated with furious speed right next to your fingers, and if you got a piece of wood that was splintered or had a knot in it, your right hand would immediately slip toward them. On top of this, the work quota had been set artificially high.

Admin's calculation was simple: if I refused to work on the lathe, they would grind me down with spells in the box for insubordination; if I did work, they'd do the same for failure to meet the norm. After trying it for about a month and seeing that I would never make it, I announced a hunger strike. Admin decided to ignore the strike and I starved for twenty-six days in all. Every day they demanded I go to work, pretending not to know whether I was still on hunger strike or not. On the seventeenth day I was put in the box for refusal to work.

The cold was arctic at that time—it was November. The box was hardly heated and one wall was covered with ice. There were eleven of us in there; we tried to keep warm by huddling together in a bunch. Only at night was it possible to warm up a bit, when they issued us duckboards and our jackets. There was barely room for us all to fit on the boards, lying on our sides, and we had to all turn over at once when the word was given. We were also lucky to have some tobacco. Criminals have this side of things well organized. If you've got a friend in the box, come what may your duty is to get some smokes to him, and something to eat too if you can.

You had to hand it to them, they were desperate characters. The solitary was situated in the free-fire zone, enveloped in barbed wire and tripwires, yet every evening, before lights-out, someone would sneak out of the compound, break the barbed wire unnoticed, creep up to the box window and push some tobacco through the bars. If he was caught, he himself would be flung in the box and somebody else would take his place. Later, after I had been let out, I too took part in these raids, and I must say that it was a desperately dangerous business. The guard in the watchtower might think you were trying to escape and fire on you. And to do it all without attracting attention was terribly difficult: the free-fire zone was lit up with searchlights, there were tripwires all over the place, as fine as a spider's web, and the barbed wire hooked in your clothing.

Sometimes, it's true, we managed to bribe a guard or a food server, and then it was easier. But without tobacco it would have been very bad, especially for me after such a long hunger strike. As luck would have it I had a strong constitution and I didn't lose consciousness once, or need to have the doctor called.

On the twenty-sixth day my spell in the box ended (they had given me eight days), and I went to the door, but my head spun, probably from the fresh air, everything went dark, and I crawled along the base of the wall and into the corridor, where I lay on the floor. . . .

. . . . .

At this point I announced a hunger strike. In fact, I was quite satisfied with the present situation: a forged accusation, no charges read, and no defense lawyer provided. All right, you can carry me starving into the courtroom if you like, on a stretcher. It will be as good as a play! I'll prepare a hundred identical applications for the advocate Kaminskaya to be summoned and every five minutes will hand one to the judge without a word.

Now the trouble began. The authorities always turn savage when you get them into a corner. But that is precisely the moment to break their backs.

I was put in an isolation cell and they confiscated my books, paper, pencils, and smokes. No newspapers, no exercise, not even a bath. Not even an aspirin for a headache. The deputy prison governor, Lieutenant Colonel Stepanov, came to see me and announced in his comical provincial accent that no medical treatment was available to hunger strikers.

"You are in the position of a suicide," he said. "Suicides are not allowed to have medical treatment. Stop your hunger strike."

That same day they started force-feeding me—through the nostrils! About a dozen guards led me from my cell to the medical unit. There they straitjacketed me, tied me down to a bed, and sat on my legs so that I wouldn't jerk. The others held my shoulders and my head. My nose is bent a bit to one side—I used to be a boxer as a boy and damaged it. The feeding tube was thick—thicker than my nostril—and wouldn't go in for love or money. Blood came gushing out of my nose and tears down my cheeks. I must say a nose is incredibly sensitive—I can think of only one other organ that equals it. But they kept pushing until the cartilages cracked and something burst—enough to make you howl like a wolf. But fat chance there was of howling when the tube was in your throat and you could breathe neither in nor out. I wheezed like a drowning man—my lungs were ready to burst. The doctor watching me also seemed ready to burst into tears, but she kept on shoving the tube farther and farther down. Then she poured some sort of slops through a funnel into the tube—you'd choke if it came back up. They held me down for another half hour so that the liquid was absorbed by the stomach and couldn't be vomited back, and then began to pull the tube out bit by bit. As they say in our country, like a razor across your balls.

There had just been time for everything to heal during the night and the blood to stop flowing when the brutes came back again. And did it all over again. Every day they found it harder and harder. Everything swelled up until it was agony to touch. And always the terrible smell of raw meat. And so on every day.

Around the tenth day, the guards could stand it no longer. As it happened it was a Sunday and no bosses were around. They surrounded the doctor: "Hey listen, let him drink it straight from the bowl, let him sip it. It'll be quicker for you too, you silly old fool."

She almost threw a fit. "If I do that he'll never end his blasted hunger strike. Do you think I want to go to jail because of you guys? From tomorrow on I'll feed him twice a day."

The only consolation I had was that I knew my mother was due to bring a parcel any day now. Without my signature they couldn't accept the parcel, and Mother would be bound to guess what was going on. And then the fellows would think of something to do.

For twelve days they tore at my nostrils, and I too was growing quite savage. I could think of nothing in the world except my nasopharynx. I would pace up and down my cell all day, gurgling through my nose. I had lived my whole life and never suspected that there was a link between my nose and the Moscow College of Advocates.

On the evening of the twelfth day the authorities surrendered. I received a visit from Deputy General Prosecutor Ilyukhin. "I just happened to drop in—by chance, you know—and suddenly I hear you're on hunger strike! What 'permits,' who told you such rubbish? There are no such things, I guarantee you."

"And what about Kaminskaya?" I said with a pronounced French accent. The sounds wouldn't go through my nose, only bubbles.

"Well, what about Kaminskaya, what about her?" said the Prosecutor fussily. "A good lawyer. I know her personally, we've met in court. We have nothing against her. But that's a bit tricky now, you know. As a matter of interest, why are you making such an issue of Kaminskaya? The world's large enough, we have plenty of excellent lawyers."

"I wasn't making an issue of it. Anyway, take your choice: Kaminskaya, Kallistratova, Shveisky. Any lawyer who's had his permit taken away will do for me."

"Oh, there you go again with those permits!"

It was a long wrangle before we settled on Shveisky.

"What the hell." The Prosecutor shrugged. "Let it be Shveisky. At least he's a Party member."

Shveisky had defended Amalrik before me, and the Ministry of Justice had already taken a decision to have him struck off the register. . . .

Journey into the Whirlwind

Eugenia Ginzburg

EUGENIA GINZBURG (1906–77) was a dedicated Communist and the wife of Pavel Aksyonov, a high-ranking provincial party functionary in the Soviet Union. Her case exemplifies the fate of countless loyal and idealistic supporters of the system, including the original, old revolutionaries, whom the authorities persecuted on account of wholly imaginary and contrived conspiracies. Ginzburg was specifically accused of conspiring with "the bourgeois-nationalist elements of the Tartar intelligentsia" (an ethnic group in the area where she lived). She was also charged with unspecified "terrorism" and sentenced to ten years in solitary confinement in court proceedings that lasted less than ten minutes.

This excerpt illustrates a peculiarity of Soviet repression during this period, namely its step-by-step nature (also revealed in the Larina reading). Prominent public figures to be liquidated were first expelled from the party, then suspended from their jobs, subjected to denunciation in the press, and finally arrested and tried in highly choreographed, prearranged, pseudo-judicial proceedings where they confessed to fantastic charges. Thus, there was a period of suspense (vividly captured in this selection) preceding the arrest that was often combined with a thorough search of the suspect's home.

On occasion, as in the case of Ginzburg, the suspects were invited to the offices of the political police and assured that it was to be a short, informal visit for the purpose of information gathering. It is not clear why such deceptions were used in some cases but not others. Ginzburg's memoir also describes the so-called "conveyor belt" technique (nonstop interrogation by different officials), an integral part of Communist political police procedures.

Ginzburg, like many other surviving victims of Stalin-era repression, was released (after serving eighteen years) and "rehabilitated" under Khrushchev. Such symbolic rehabilitation was also extended to those who did not survive, and their dependents were given a small pension. This was a gesture doubtless designed to distance the successors of, and erstwhile collaborators with, Stalin from his policies and personality.

From Eugenia Ginzburg, Journey into the Whirlwind *(New York: Harcourt, Brace, and World, 1967). Reprinted by permission of Harcourt, Inc.*

That Day

After my expulsion from the party, eight days went by before my arrest. All those days I sat at home, shut in my room and not answering the telephone. I was waiting; so were all my family. What for? We told each other that we were waiting for the leave my husband had been promised at this unusual time. When it came we would go again to Moscow and try to get people to help me. We would ask Razumov, who was a member of the Central Committee, to help us.

In our hearts we knew perfectly well that none of this would happen, that we were waiting for something quite different. My mother and my husband took turns watching over me. My mother sometimes fried some potatoes. "Do have some, darling. Remember how you liked them done this way when you were little?" Every time my husband had been out and came home he rang in a special way and shouted through the door:

"It's only me, open up!"

It was as if he were saying:

"It's still only me, not them."

We started a purge of our books. Our old nurse carried out pail after pailful of ashes. We burned Radek's *Portraits and Pamphlets,* the *History of Western Europe* by Friedland and Slutsky, Bukharin's *Political Economy.*

The "Index" grew longer and longer, and the scale of our *auto da fé* grander and grander. We even had to burn Stalin's *On the Opposition.* This too had become illegal under the new dispensation.

A few days before my arrest, Biktagirov, second secretary of the party municipal committee, was summarily removed from a meeting at which he was presiding. His secretary came in:

"Comrade Biktagirov, you are wanted."

"In the middle of a meeting? What nonsense. Tell them I'm busy."

But the secretary came back:

"They insist."

So he went, and was invited to put on his coat and go "for a short drive."

My husband was even more puzzled and shaken by this event than by my own expulsion from the party. A secretary of the municipal committee! And he too had "turned out to be an enemy of the people" . . . .

"Really, the Cheka[1] is getting a bit above itself. They'll have to let a good many of these people out again."

He was trying to convince himself that it was all no more than a checkup, or a misunderstanding of some sort, temporary and almost ludicrous. Surely on our next free day we would find Biktagirov sitting once more at table at Livadia, telling with a smile how he had almost been mistaken for an enemy of the people.

But the nights were very unpleasant. The windows of our bedroom faced the street and cars drove past all the time. And how we listened in fear and trembling when it seemed as though one of them might be pulling up in front of our house. At night, even my husband's optimism would give way to terror—the great terror that gripped our whole country by the throat.

"Paul! A car!"

"Well, what of it, darling? It's a big town, there are plenty of cars."

"It's stopped. I'm sure it has."

My husband, barefooted, would leap across to the window. He was pale but spoke with exaggerated calm:

"There, you see, it's only a truck."

"Don't they use trucks sometimes?"

We would fall asleep only after six, and when we woke there was the latest news about who had been "exposed."

"Have you heard? Petrov has turned out to be an enemy of the people! How cunning he must have been to get away with it for so long."

This meant that Petrov had been arrested overnight.

Sheaves of newspapers would arrive, and by now there was no telling which was the *Literary Gazette* and which, say, *Soviet Art*. They all ranted and raved in the same way about enemies, conspiracies, shootings. . . .

The nights were terrifying. But what we were waiting for actually happened in the daytime.

We were in the dining room, my husband, Alyosha, and I. My stepdaughter Mayka was out skating. Vasya was in the nursery. I was ironing some laundry. I often felt like doing manual work; it distracted me from my thoughts. Alyosha was having breakfast, and my husband was reading a story by Valeria Gerasimova aloud to him. Suddenly the telephone rang. It sounded as shrill as on that day in December 1934.

For a few moments, none of us picked it up. We hated telephone calls in those days. Then my husband said in that unnaturally calm voice he so often used now:

"It must be Lukovnikov. I asked him to call."

He took the receiver, listened, went as white as a sheet, and said even more quietly:

"It's for you, Genia. Vevers, of the NKVD."

Vevers, the head of the NKVD department for special political affairs, could not have been more amiable and charming. His voice burbled on like a brook in spring.

"Good morning, dear comrade. Tell me, how are you fixed for time today?"

"I'm always free now. Why?"

"Oh, dear, always free, how depressing. Never mind, these things will pass. So anyway, you'd have time to come and see me for a moment. The thing is, we'd like some information about that fellow Elvov . . . some additional information. My word, he did land you in a mess, didn't he! Oh, well, we'll soon sort it all out."

"When shall I come?"

"Whenever it suits you best. Now, if you like, or if it's more convenient, after lunch."

"How long is it likely to take?"

"Oh, say forty minutes, perhaps an hour."

My husband, who was standing beside me and could hear, was making signs and whispering to me to go at once, so that Vevers shouldn't think I was afraid—there was nothing to be afraid of.

I told Vevers I'd go at once.

"Perhaps I'll just stop at Mother's on the way," I said to my husband.

"No, don't. Go at once. The sooner it's all cleared up, the better."

He helped me to get quickly into my things. I sent Alyosha off to the skating rink. He went without saying good-by. I never saw him again.

For some strange reason, little Vasya, who was used to my going and coming and always took it perfectly calmly, ran out into the hall after me and kept asking insistently:

"Where are you going, Mother, where? Tell me. I don't want you to go!"

But I could not so much as look at the children or kiss them—if I had, I would have died then and there. I turned away and called out to the nurse:

"Fima, do take him. I haven't time for him now."

Perhaps it was just as well not to see my mother either. What must be must be, and there's no point in trying to postpone it. The door banged shut. I still remember the sound. That was all. . . . I was never again to open that door behind which I had lived with my dear children.

On the stairs we met Mayka, back from the skating rink. She was a child who understood everything intuitively. She said nothing, and didn't seem to wonder where we could be going at that unusual hour. Her enormous blue eyes wide open, she pressed herself against the wall, and so deep an understanding of pain and horror showed in her twelve-year-old face that I dreamed of it for years afterward.

Our old nurse Fima caught up with us at the front door. She had run down to tell me something. But she looked at me and said nothing. She only made the sign of the cross after us as we moved away.

"Let's walk, shall we."

"Yes, let's, while we still can."

"Don't be silly. That's not the way they arrest people. They want some information, that's all."

We walked for a long time in silence. It was a lovely, bright, February day. Snow had fallen that morning and was still very clean.

"It's our last walk together, Paul darling. I'm a state criminal now."

"Don't talk nonsense, Genia. I told you before, if they arrested people like you they'd have to lock up the whole Party."

"I sometimes have the crazy idea that that's what they mean to do."

I waited for my husband's usual reaction, thinking he would scold me for my blasphemous words. But instead, he himself gave way to "heresy" and said he was sure of the innocence of many of those who had been arrested as enemies, and he talked indignantly about very highly placed people indeed.

I was glad we were once again of one mind. I imagined then that everything was quite clear to me, though in fact many bitter discoveries still lay before me.

But here we were at the well-known address in Black Lake Street.

"Well, Genia, we'll expect you home for lunch."

How pathetic he looked, all of a sudden, how his lips trembled! I thought of his assured, masterful tone in the old days, the tone of an old Communist, an experienced Party worker.

"Good-by, Paul dear. We've had a good life together."

I didn't even say "Look after the children." I knew he would not be able to take care of them. He was again trying to comfort me with commonplaces—I could no longer catch what he was saying. I walked quickly toward the reception room, and suddenly heard his broken cry:

"Genia!"

He had the haunted look of a baited animal, of a harried and exhausted human being—it was a look I was to see again and again, *there.* . . .

· · · · ·

The Investigators Have Conclusive Evidence

I have often thought about the tragedy of those by whose agency the purge of 1937 was carried out. What a life they had! They were all sadists, of course. And only a handful found the courage to commit suicide.

Step by step, as they followed their routine directives, they traveled all the way from the human condition to that of beasts. Their faces, as time went by, defied description. I, at any rate, cannot find words to convey the expression on the faces of these un-men.

But all this happened only gradually. That night, Interrogator Livanov, who had summoned me, looked like any other civil servant with perhaps a little more than the usual liking for red tape. Everything about him confirmed this impression—the placid, well-fed face, the neat writing with which he filled the left-hand side (reserved for questions) of the record sheet in front of him, and his local, Kazan accent. Certain turns of speech, provincial and old-fashioned, reminded me of our nurse Fima and aroused a host of memories of home.

In that first moment I had a flash of hope that the madness might be over, that I had left it behind me, down there, with the grinding of padlocks and the pain-filled eyes of the golden-haired girl from the banks of the river Sungari.

Here, it seemed, was the world of ordinary, normal people. Outside the window was the old familiar town with its clanging streetcars. The window had neither bars nor a wooden screen, but handsome net curtains. And the plate with the remains of Livanov's supper had not been left on the floor but stood on a small table in a corner of the room.

He might be a perfectly decent man, this quiet official who was slowly writing down my answers to his straightforward, insignificant questions: Where had I worked between this year and that, where and when had I met this or that person. . . ? But now the first page had been filled and he gave it to me to sign.

What was this? He had asked me how long I had known Elvov, and I had answered, "Since 1932." But here it said, "How long have you known the Trotskyist Elvov?" and my reply was put down as "I have known the Trotskyist Elvov since 1932."

"This isn't what I said."

He looked at me in amazement, as though it really were only a question of getting the definition right.

"But he *is* a Trotskyist!"

"I don't know that."

"But we do. It's been established. The investigators have conclusive evidence."

"But I can't confirm something I don't know. You can ask me when I met *Professor* Elvov, but whether he is a Trotskyist, and whether I knew him as a Trotskyist—that's a different question."

"It's for me to ask the questions, if you please. You've no right to dictate to me the form in which I should put them. All you have to do is answer them."

"Then put the answers down exactly as I give them, and not in your own words. In fact, why don't we have a stenographer to put them down?"

These words, the height of naïveté, were greeted by peals of laughter—not, of course, from Livanov but from the embodiment of lunacy which had just entered the room in the person of State Security Lieutenant Tsarevsky.

"Well, well, what do I see! You're behind bars now, are you? And how long is it since you gave us a lecture at the club, on Dobrolyubov?[2] Eh? Remember?"

"Yes, I do. It was very silly, I agree. What could you possibly want with Dobrolyubov?"

My sarcasm was wasted on the lanky, tousled youth with the face of a maniac.

"So you want a stenographer! No more and no less! What a joke! Think you're back in your editorial office?"

With quick, jerky steps he went up to the desk, ran his eyes over the record, and looked up at me. His eyes, like Vevers's, were those of a sadist who took pleasure in his work, but there was also in them a lurking anxiety, a latent fear.

"So you're behind bars," he sneered again, in a tone of hatred as intense as though I had set fire to his house or murdered his child.

"You realize, of course," he went on more quietly, "that the regional committee has agreed to your arrest. Everything has come out. Elvov gave you away. That husband of yours, Aksyonov—he's been arrested too, and he's come clean. He's a Trotskyist too, of course."

I mentally compared this statement with Vevers's about Aksyonov disowning me. Yes, Lyama was right. They really were brazen liars.

"Is Elvov here, in this prison?"

"Yes! In the very cell next to yours. And he's confirmed all the evidence against you."

"Then confront me with him. I want to know what he said about me. Let him repeat it to my face."

"Like to see your friend, eh?" He added such a scurrilous obscenity that I could hardly believe my ears.

"How dare you! I demand to see the head of your department. This is a Soviet institution where people can't be treated like dirt."

"Enemies are not people. We're allowed to do what we like with them. People indeed!"

Again he roared with laughter. Then he screamed at me at the top of his voice, banged the table with his fist, exactly like Vevers, and told me I'd be shot if I didn't sign the record.

I noticed with amazement that Livanov, so quiet and polite, looked on unmoved. Obviously, he had seen it all before.

"Why do you allow this man to interfere with a case you're in charge of?" I asked.

His smile was almost gentle.

"Tsarevsky's right, you know. You can make things better for yourself if you honestly repent and make a clean breast of it. Stubbornness won't help you. The investigators have conclusive evidence."

"Of what?"

"Of your counterrevolutionary activity as a member of the secret organization headed by Elvov. You'd much better sign the record. If you do you'll be treated decently. We'll allow you to have parcels, and we'll let you see your children and your husband."

While Livanov spoke Tsarevsky kept quiet in readiness for his next attack. I thought he had just happened to come into Livanov's office. But after the two of them had been at me for three or four hours, I realized that it was part of a deliberate technique.

The blue light of a February dawn was casting its chill on the room by the time Tsarevsky rang for the warder. The same words ended the interrogation as those of Vevers the day before, but Tsarevsky's voice rose to a falsetto:

"Off to the cell with you! And there you'll sit until you sign."

Going down the stairs, I caught myself hurrying back to my cell. It seemed, after all, that I was better off there, in the human presence of a companion in misfortune—and the grinding of locks was better than the demented screams of un-men. . . .

· · · · ·

The "Conveyor Belt"

They started on me again. I was put on the "conveyor belt"—uninterrupted questioning by a changing team of examiners. Seven days without sleep or food, without even returning to my cell. Relaxed and fresh, they passed before me as in a dream—Livanov, Tsarevsky, Krokhichev, Vevers, Yelshin and his assistant, Lieutenant Bikchentayev, a chubby, curly-haired, pink-cheeked young man who looked like a fattened turkey cock.

The object of the conveyor belt is to wear out the nerves, weaken the body, break resistance, and force the prisoner to sign whatever is required. The first day or two I still noticed the individual characteristics of the interrogators—Livanov, calm and bureaucratic as before, urging me to sign some monstrous piece of nonsense, as though it were no more than a perfectly normal, routine detail; Tsarevsky and Vevers always shouting and threatening—Vevers sniffing cocaine and giggling as well as shouting.

"Ha-ha-ha! What's become of our university beauty now! You look at least forty. Aksyonov wouldn't recognize his sweetheart. And if you go on being stubborn we'll turn you into a real grandma. You haven't been in the rubber cell yet, have you? You haven't? Oh well, the best is still to come."

Major Yelshin was invariably courteous and "humane." He liked to talk about my children. He had heard I was a good mother, yet it didn't look as if I cared what happened to them. He asked me why I was so "becomingly pale" and was "amazed" to hear that I had been questioned without food or sleep for four or five days on end:

"Is it really worth torturing yourself like that rather than signing a purely formal, unimportant record? Come on now, get it over and go to sleep. Right here, on this sofa. I'll see you're not disturbed."

The "unimportant record" stated that, on Elvov's instructions, I had organized a Tartar writers' branch of the terrorist group of which I was a member; there followed a list of Tartar writers I had "recruited," starting with Kavi Nadzhimi.[3]

"Anxious to spare Nadzhimi? He didn't spare you," said the Major enigmatically.

"That's between him and his conscience."

"What are you, an Evangelist or something?"

"Just honest."

Again the Major couldn't miss the chance to display his learning, and gave me a lecture on the Marxist-Leninist view of ethics. "Honest" meant useful to the proletariat and its state.

"It can't be useful to the proletarian state to wipe out the first generation of Tartar writers, who are all Communists at that."

"We know for a fact that these people are traitors."

"Then why do you need my evidence?"

"Just for the record."

"I can't put on record what I don't know."

"Don't you trust us?"

"How can I do that when you arrest me without cause, keep me in jail, and use illegal methods of interrogation?"

"What are we doing that's illegal?"

"You've kept me without sleep, drink, or food for several days to force me to give false evidence."

"Have your dinner, I'm not stopping you. They'll bring it this minute. Just sign here. You're only torturing yourself."

Lieutenant Bikchentayev, who now always accompanied the Major, evidently as a trainee, stood by "in readiness," repeating the final words of Yelshin's sentences like an infant learning to talk.

"It's all your own fault," said the Major.

"Your own fault," echoed the Lieutenant.

One day the Major prepared a questionnaire on my contacts with Tartar intellectuals.

"You're an educated woman, you speak French and German, why should you have wanted to learn Tartar?"

"So that I could do translations."

"But it's an uncivilized language. . . ."

"Is it? Is that what you think too, Lieutenant?"

The turkey cock smiled sheepishly and said nothing.

After this preamble I was invited to sign a statement to the effect that, on the orders of Trotskyist headquarters, I had tried to organize an opportunist alliance with bourgeois-nationalist elements of the Tartar intelligentsia.

I ventured on irony: "That's right! All my life it's been my dream to unite the Moslem world for the greater glory of Islam!"

The Major laughed, but he didn't give me anything to eat or drink, or let me go away to sleep.

It seemed to me then that my suffering was beyond measure. But in a few months' time I was to realize that my spell on the conveyor belt had been child's play compared with what was meted out to others, from June 1937 on. I was deprived of sleep and food but allowed to sit down and, occasionally, given a sip of water from the jug on the interrogator's desk. I was not beaten.

It is true that once Vevers nearly killed me, but that was under the influence of cocaine, when he was not responsible for his actions, and it gave him a great fright.

It happened, I think, on the fifth or sixth night. By then I was half delirious.

As a means of "psychological pressure," the prisoner was customarily made to sit a long way off from the interrogator, sometimes at the opposite end of the room. On this occasion Vevers sat me down against the far wall and shouted his questions at me right across the vast office. He asked me in what year I had first met Professor Korbut, who had joined the Trotskyist opposition in 1927.

"I don't remember the exact year but it was a long time ago, before he voted for the opposition."

"Wha-at!" Excited by cocaine and my stubbornness, Vevers was beside himself with rage. "Opposition d'you call it, that gang of spies and murderers? Why, you. . . ."

A large marble paperweight flew straight at me. Only when I saw the hole in the wall half an inch from where my temple had been did I realize what a narrow escape I had had.

Vevers was so frightened that he actually brought me a glass of water. His hands were shaking. Killing prisoners under interrogation was not yet allowed. His feelings had run away with him.

On the seventh day I was taken to the floor below, to a colonel whose name I cannot remember. Here, for the first time, I was made to stand throughout the interrogation. As I kept falling asleep on my feet, the guards placed on either side of me had continuously to shake me awake, saying: "You're not allowed to sleep."

A similar scene from a film called *Palace and Fortress* floated through my mind. The hero, Karakozov, was interrogated in exactly this way; he, too, was deprived of sleep. Then my head began to swim. As through a thick fog, I saw the Colonel's disgusted expression, and the revolver on his desk, evidently put there to frighten me. What particularly annoyed me, I remember, were the circles on the wallpaper, the same as in Vevers's office. They kept dancing before my eyes.

I have no idea what answers I gave the Colonel. I think I was silent most of the time, only repeating occasionally: "I won't sign." He alternated threats and persuasion, promising that I would see my husband, my children. Finally I blacked out.

I must have been unconscious for so long that they had to stop the "belt." When I awoke I was on my bunk and saw Lyama's dear, tear-stained face bending over me. She was feeding me drops of orange juice, which Ira had just received in a parcel.

Soon I heard anxious inquiries from Garey and Abdullin next door.

"Thank heaven she's come around. Splendid. Kiss her for us."

Supper was brought, and I ate two portions of the disgusting slop that passed for fish stew. By way of dessert, Ira triumphantly produced two small squares of chocolate from her parcel.

I had only just enough time to think how kind people were when I was called out for another spell on the conveyor belt. . . .

. . . . .

In the Lefortovo prison, all the doors open noiselessly. Soft carpets drown the sound of footsteps, and the warders are exquisitely polite. The "kennels" have stools on which one can sit, and their tiled walls are so dazzlingly white that they remind one of an operating theater.

The solitary cell in which I was put that morning of the first of August was as clean as a private room in a hospital, and the wardress resembled the matron of a holiday home. Here I was to await my trial. I remembered Garey's rule of thumb: "The cleaner and more polite, the nearer to death."

Nevertheless, the atmosphere of the place made me want to smarten up my own appearance. I got out of my bundle my blue "afternoon" dress, spent a long time straightening its folds, used my fingers as curlers, and put tooth powder on my nose. All this I did more or less mechanically. There was nothing strange about it: Charlotte Corday made herself look pretty before she was guillotined, and so did Madame Camille Desmoulins, not to mention Mary Queen of Scots. But all these thoughts about my appearance were quite self-contained and had no effect on the great black toad which sprawled close to my heart, and which nothing would drive away.

My hour had come. The military tribunal of the Supreme Court—three officers and a secretary—faced me across a table. On either side of me were two warders. Such were the "fully public"[4] conditions in which my "trial" was conducted.

I looked intently at my judges' faces, and was struck by the fact that they closely resembled one another and also for some reason reminded me of the official at Black Lake who had taken my watch. They all looked alike, although one of them was dark and another's hair was graying. Yes, I saw what it was they had in common—the empty look of a mummy, or a fish in aspic. Nor was this surprising. How could one carry out such duties day after day without cutting oneself off from one's fellow men—if only by that glazed expression?

Suddenly I found that it was easy to breathe. A summer breeze of extraordinary freshness was blowing through the wide-open window. The room was a handsome one, with a high ceiling. So there were, after all, such places in the world!

Outside the windows there were some large, dark-green trees: their leaves were rustling and I was moved by the cool, mysterious sound. I could not remember having heard it before. It was strangely touching—why had I never noticed it?

And the clock on the wall—large and round, its shiny hands like a gray mustache—how long was it since I had seen anything like it?

I checked the time at the beginning and end of the trial. Seven minutes. That, neither more nor less, was the time it took to enact this tragicomedy.

The voice of the president of the court—Dmitriev, People's Commissar for Justice of the Russian Republic—resembled the expression of his eyes. If a frozen codfish could talk, that is undoubtedly what it would sound like. There was not a trace here of the animation, the zest which my interrogators had put into their performances: the judges were merely functionaries earning their pay. No doubt they had a quota, and were anxious to over-fulfill it if they could.

"You have read the indictment?" said the president in tones of unutterable boredom. "You plead guilty? No? But the evidence shows . . ."

He leafed through the bulky file and muttered through his teeth: "For instance the witness Kozlov . . ."

"Kozlova. It's a woman—and, I may add, a despicable one."

"Kozlova, yes. Or again, the witness Dyachenko . . ."

"Dyakonov."

"Yes. Well, they both state . . ."

But what they stated the judge was too pressed for time to read. Breaking off, he asked me:

"Any questions you wish to ask the court?"

"Yes, I do. I am accused under section 8 of Article 58, which means that I am charged with terrorism. Will you please tell me the name of the political leader against whose life I am supposed to have plotted?"

The judges were silent for a while, taken aback by this preposterous question. They looked reproachfully at the inquisitive woman who was holding up their work. Then the one with grizzled hair muttered:

"You know, don't you, that Comrade Kirov was murdered in Leningrad?"

"Yes, but I didn't kill him, it was someone called Nikolayev. Anyway, I've never been in Leningrad. Isn't that what you call an alibi?"

"Are you a lawyer by any chance?" said the gray-haired man crossly.

"No, I'm a teacher."

"You won't get anywhere by quibbling. You may never have been in Leningrad, but it was your accomplices who killed him, and that makes you morally and criminally responsible."

"The court will withdraw for consultation," grunted the president. Whereupon they all stood up, lazily stretching their limbs. . . .

I looked at the clock again. They couldn't even have had time for a smoke! In less than two minutes the worshipful assembly was back in session. The president had in his hand a large sheet of paper of excellent quality, covered with typescript in close spacing. The text, which must have taken at least twenty minutes to copy, was my sentence: the official document setting forth my crimes and the penalty for them. It began with the solemn words: "In the name of the Union of Soviet Socialist Republics," followed by something long and unintelligible. Oh, yes, it was the same preamble as in the indictment, with its "restoration of capitalism," "underground terrorist organization," and all the rest. Only wherever that document had said "accused," this one said "convicted." . . .

The president went on in a whining nasal voice. How slowly he read! He turned over the page. Here it comes . . . any moment now he would utter the words "supreme penalty. . . ."

Again I heard the trees rustling. For a moment I felt as if all this were part of a film. How could they possibly be going to kill me for no reason at all—me, Mother's Genia, Alyosha's and Vasya's mother. By what right . . .

I thought I must have screamed, but no—I stood and listened in silence, and all these other strange things were taking place inside me.

A sort of darkness came over my mind; the judge's voice sounded like a muddy torrent by which I might be swamped at any moment. In my delirium I noticed a thoughtful move by the two warders who were joining hands behind my back—evidently so that I should not hit the floor when I fainted. Why were they so sure I would faint? Oh, well, they must know from experience, doubtless many women fainted when they heard their death sentence read out.

The darkness closed in again—for the last time, surely. And then, all of a sudden—

What was it? What had he said? Like a blinding zigzag of lightning cutting across my mind. He had said . . . Had I heard right? . . .

"Ten years' imprisonment in solitary confinement with loss of civil rights for five years. . . ."

The world around me was suddenly warm and bright. Ten years! That meant I was to live!

". . . and confiscation of all personal property."

To live! Without property, but what was that to me? Let them confiscate it—they were brigands anyway, confiscating was their business. They wouldn't get much good out of mine, a few books and clothes—why, we didn't even have a radio. My husband was a loyal Communist of the old stamp, not the kind who had to have a Buick or a Mercedes. . . . Ten years! . . . Do you, with your codfish faces, really think you can go on robbing and murdering for another ten years, that there aren't people in the party who will stop you sooner or later? I knew there were—and in order to see that day, I must live! In prison, if needs be, but I must at all costs live!

If the "judges" ever looked at their victims' faces, they could not have failed to read all these silent exclamations in mine. But they did not look at me. Having read the sentence, they rose and hurried away. In single file they trooped out of the room. This time, no doubt, they would have time for a smoke, and then back to the grindstone. A hard day's work . . .

I looked around at the guards, whose hands were still clasped behind my back. Every nerve in my body was quivering with the joy of being alive. What nice faces the guards had! Peasant boys from Ryazan or Kursk, most likely. They couldn't help being warders—no doubt they were conscripts. And they had joined hands to save me from falling. But they needn't have—I wasn't going to fall.

I shook back the hair curled so carefully before facing the court, so as not to disgrace the memory of Charlotte Corday. Then I gave the guards a friendly smile. They looked at me in astonishment.

Tell the West

Jerzy Gliksman

JERZY GLIKSMAN (1902–58) was born in Warsaw. He earned a law degree at Warsaw University and also studied at the Sorbonne in Paris. In Poland, he was a member of a Jewish-Socialist organization. He had the highly unusual experience of both being taken on a conducted tour of a Soviet model prison as a tourist and later being imprisoned under conditions more typical of the Soviet penal system.

In 1935 he spent a month in the Soviet Union as a sympathetic political tourist on a trip organized by the official Intourist travel bureau. Before his visit to Bolshevo, the model prison established for the delectation of foreign visitors, Gliksman saw in Moscow a play titled The Aristocrats *by the playwright Pogodin. It dealt with the uplifting moral transformation of prisoners working on the Belomor Canal built to connect the White and Baltic seas. The convicts in the play were reborn and rehabilitated by their kind and therapeutically inclined guards and supervisors. The play was a typical product of socialist-realist literature, which was designed to portray social conditions not as they actually existed but as they were supposed to be according to the official blueprints. The play stimulated Gliksman's desire to see "the real thing," and so he asked the Intourist guide to set up a visit to a "corrective labor" camp. His wish was readily granted.*

Gliksman's experiences at Bolshevo confirmed the message of the play: the inmates worked in specialties freely chosen by themselves; the setting was pleasant; the food was tasty and nourishing; there were hardly any

From Jerzy Gliksman, Tell the West *(New York: Gresham Press, 1948).*

guards; and the inmates interviewed were totally satisfied with their treatment and on the way to complete rehabilitation and reintegration into society. It was socialist realism in action.

Four years later in 1939, after the Soviet occupation of Eastern Poland, Gliksman learned first-hand the realities of the Soviet penal system, which were diametrically opposed in every detail to the make-believe presented at Bolshevo.

After World War II Gliksman came to the United States. In the early 1950s he was a fellow at the Russian Research Center at Harvard University; later he worked at the Rand Corporation in California on the subject of forced labor in the Soviet Union.

Gliksman was the half-brother of Victor Alter, a Jewish labor leader in Poland who was executed by the authorities in the Soviet Union during World War II.

· · · · ·

If the inmates of Soviet jails were asked to select the worst feature of their imprisonment, they would undoubtedly name the lack of air to breathe as the most terrible. We found the poisoned air in our cell worse than the hunger, the filth, and the lice; worse even than the occasional beatings.

The *kartser* and some of the night interrogations were, perhaps, more cruel than the lack of fresh air, but not all prisoners were subjected to these special questionings, and not all were put into solitary confinement. Yet almost all who chanced to be interned in Soviet prisons had to suffer the unbearably stuffy air in the exceedingly overcrowded rooms.

When I first came into the cell, the windows were kept open day and night and the air was, therefore, endurable.

To prevent us from observing the goings-on in the courtyard, however, we had to close the windows several times during the day. The panes were covered with thick, white, opaque paint.

The forbidden sights in the courtyard were the prisoners of other cells. The admission of new prisoners as well as the transfer of old ones took place in the yard, as did the prisoners' exercises.

Sometimes, however, we did manage to break the rule forbidding us to peep into the yard. Since the windows were high, we formed, whenever the need arose—and if the guard happened not to be looking—a "human pyramid." The one on top observed the courtyard through a hole scratched in the paint with a small piece of glass.

Thus Druker, the graduate from the Warsaw Jewish Teachers' Seminary, once saw his younger brother being led through the courtyard. They had been arrested together, separated immediately, and for several months had not known of each other's whereabouts.

In the same way, Dr. Polonis, former head physician of the Oshmiana hospital, saw his wife and two small daughters being brought into prison. The family had intended to flee to Lithuania, and the doctor had hoped that his wife and children, at least, would be saved. It turned out, however, that they were locked up in the women's section of the prison.

A friend of mine, Bronek Bloch, a Warsaw student, thus saw his cousin Edek, the son of the Warsaw Jewish Bund leader Nathan Szafran. Edek and Bronek had both been captured at the border while attempting to reach their families in Vilna. Bronek was worried about his cousin, who was at the time only fifteen years old. After his arrest, Edek was placed in a special prison cell for juvenile prisoners.

On this occasion I, too, looked into the yard. It was heartbreaking to watch the fifty or sixty "juveniles." Most of them were young boys, the oldest perhaps sixteen, several not more than thirteen or fourteen.

Several days later one of the "look-outs" told me that a group of about a hundred women was walking in the yard. Among them I recognized Perel, the wife of Herman Kruk, a well-known cultural leader and the director of the largest workers' library in Warsaw, who was later murdered by the Gestapo. Perel and I had both been arrested at the same time while trying to cross the border and reach Vilna.

Our peeping into the yard was considered a great crime and whenever one of the prisoners was caught red-handed, he was severely punished by the guards.

With the beginning of spring we were struck a heavy blow. Our prison officials decided that we were not sufficiently isolated from the outside world; that the paint-covered windowpanes did not bar us adequately from viewing the activities in the courtyard; and that prison regulations were thereby being violated. For these reasons one of the most wretched decrees in our prison life was issued.

One morning several guards brought a carpenter into our cell. This man proceeded to cover both our windows with wooden planks while the guards took care that he neither looked at us nor talked. From our room the carpenter went to repeat his work in other cells, and all day long we could hear his hammering as well as the vainly protesting voices of the prisoners. As far as we were concerned, the shutting of the windows was nothing short of a disaster. We now felt ourselves to be in a subterranean dungeon. No longer were we able to see the sky, no longer could we benefit from the meager rays of the sun. Now there was no daylight at all in our cell, and the electric bulb had to be lit day and night.

These, however, were not the most important considerations. Much more vital was that the only source of fresh air for almost a hundred human beings in our cell was now gone.

In the daytime as well as at night we were now unable to breathe freely. Here I understood what was meant by "heavy air." Never before had I experienced anything of the kind.

The stuffiness and stench of the air in the cell were most noticeable when one entered it from the outside after returning from the latrine, from an interrogation, or from the "exercises." The first few instants after entering, a prisoner would be unable to breathe at all. Then, after a while, one's lungs adapted themselves to the foul air, but even then one's breathing remained panting and unnaturally shallow. One had the impression that all inmates were asthmatic, or that all had just finished running. Some of the prisoners, particularly the sick, breathed with their mouths wide open, like fish out of water.

The weather outside was still chilly, but the heat inside the cell was such that we all sweated profusely. Most of the prisoners undressed to their underwear and some, who cared little, remained almost entirely naked and barefooted. Our underwear was always soaking wet—not just damp, but literally drenched through.

The only advantage of our sweating was that our lice were unable to bear it. Lice apparently cannot endure perspiration, and we got rid of many of them.

The guard officers now made it a habit to appear at the regular *poverkas* with perfumed handkerchiefs, which they held to their noses, trying to filter the foul air in which we had to live. The inspections were now quickly over, and the officers would escape from the cell as if pursued by the plague.

There still remained narrow cracks between the planks covering our windows. These were too narrow to enable us to see through, but they were nevertheless the only tiny source of fresh air in the cell. The space immediately under the windows was consequently slightly more airy than the rest of the room. All places on the floor under the window were now occupied by the criminals and their "invited guests" from among the other prisoners, whom the criminals happened to like for one reason or another. Several times I, too, was honored by permission to sit under the windows. I paid for that privilege by telling them stories which they liked.

The shutting of the windows also brought about a basic change in our sleeping habits. Almost the entire upper floors of the berths, where the heat was most acute—worse than at the top shelf of a Turkish bath—were vacated. Some people remained on the lowest tier of the sleeping shelves, but most prisoners took to the floor.

We were now even more cramped on the floor than we had been on the berths. When we tried to go to sleep the first evening after the shutting of the windows, only part of the sleepers found it possible to stretch out; some had to lie with their legs bent, while others found no room at all.

After several hours of wrangling and fighting which the guards pretended neither to see nor hear, we finally, late at night, evolved a system which, with difficulty, provided everybody with room in which to lie down. We stretched out in two tightly packed rows, every two prisoners head-to-foot, the feet of one row near the heads of the other, and vice versa.

This system made use of every available inch. It is hardly possible to imagine, however, what it meant to have a pair of unwashed and perspiring feet near one's nose all night. Our hot bodies constantly bumped against one another, and unconsciously—some of us purposely—we shoved and kicked one another. . . .

. . . . .

We were, then, deep in the Russian interior.

Some of my Polish companions in the prison car frequently remarked that, after all, there had been a time when they would have given a great deal for an opportunity to visit the Soviet state, that mysterious land of gigantic social experiments. The Soviet Union had always attracted foreigners by being different, by the new principles she promised to introduce into the life of mankind. No other country on earth was the subject of so much human curiosity, so many legends, and so many illusions.

I was the only one among my companions who had previously been to Soviet Russia. That had been in November, 1935, when I had spent a month on a tour organized by the Soviet Intourist travel bureau.

That trip had been quite an event. Friends and acquaintances envied me. After my return I had to answer innumerable questions concerning Soviet life; I told of my experiences in several lectures delivered to trade-union locals and professional groups. And I had indeed had a great deal to tell.

During my excursion I had visited both Moscow and old, beautiful Leningrad. The Intourist had made all the arrangements for a predetermined and not too excessive fee. We traveled in comfortable sleeping cars belonging to an international express train; we lived in elegant hotels, each tourist accommodated in single rooms with private baths. In these hotels there were handsome and expensively furnished dining rooms which differed little from the ones I had visited in the capitals of Western Europe. The food was tasty and plentiful; we lacked neither fine Crimean fruits nor famous Russian fish nor excellent caviar from Astrakhan. There was music with every meal and Western dances in the evening. And we could buy whatever our hearts desired in a special store for foreigners. True, we had to pay in American dollars, but the prices were not especially high. I had bought a silver fox as a gift for my wife.

The participants in the excursion were also given an opportunity of witnessing the anniversary celebrations of the Russian Revolution, on Red Square adjoining the Kremlin and the Lenin Mausoleum. I marveled at the parade of the best Soviet regiments with their thousands of guns and tanks, at the planes overhead, at the tremendous throngs of Moscow workers marching with their banners and huge portraits of Stalin past the reviewing stand, where were assembled the most prominent leaders of Soviet Russia, with Stalin at their head.

Every day we were taken from our hotel to visit various points of interest. The program for these visits was prepared for us by a special government agency,

VOKS, whose duty it was to promote "cultural ties" with foreigners. VOKS representatives always accompanied us to all places we visited. A young girl, a pretty brunette, was assigned to me as my guide. She was a student at the University of Moscow.

I was shown large factories employing tens of thousands of workers where there were impressive workers' clubs, youth homes, and up-to-date nurseries for the convenience of mothers employed there. I visited a modern, well-equipped public school, institutions for the blind and for deaf-mutes, hospitals, clinics providing free medical care, art galleries, museums. I found especially interesting the Anti-Religious Museum, housed in a former Russian Orthodox Church, and the Museum of the Revolution.

In the latter I saw among other exhibits the portraits of the seven founders of the Russian Social Democratic Party called into being at a congress in Minsk, in 1898. Among these was the picture of Kazimierz Petrusevitch. Until the war Petrusevitch lived in Vilna, Poland, where he was a professor at the University and a noted jurist. After the Soviets occupied Vilna in 1940 they put Petrusevitch in the Lukishki Prison. His picture in the Museum of the Revolution had not saved him from arrest.

But then, at the time of my first trip to Russia, while sauntering in the Museum of the Revolution, I had not foreseen such developments. I had admired and enjoyed the exhibits.

I had spent almost every evening in Moscow at the theater.

The famous Moscow theaters! It was not an easy matter for an ordinary citizen to secure a seat, but the VOKS took good care of us. I most enjoyed Stanislavsky's Moscow Art Theater. The theater of Vakhtangov gave interesting and original performances, and so did that of Tairov. I admired the scope of the scenic experiments undertaken by these world-famous theaters and I was thrilled by the unsurpassed acting of the casts.

One day I was told of a sensational event in the Moscow theatrical world— a new play in one of the theaters based upon life in the Soviet camps. I could hardly believe my ears. The Soviet *lagers* were one of the most closely guarded secrets. It was considered dangerous even to mention their existence; and now— a play? But it was true. The play was called *The Aristocrats;* it was by Nicolas Pogodin, a famous Soviet playwright. I was extremely curious about this play, and I was successful in obtaining reservations for its performance....

The auditorium itself was arranged in an original manner. Instead of being in the usual place, the stage was built in the center of the edifice, the audience sitting in a circle around it. The director's aim was to draw the audience closer to the action of the play, to bridge the gap between actor and spectator. There was no curtain, and the stage settings were exceedingly simple, almost as in the Elizabethan theater.

The play by Pogodin contains four long acts and a large number of scenes. The performance lasted almost four hours, but it seemed only a minute before it was over. It was a real pleasure to watch the perfect acting and the new, bold approach to the art of directing and production. And the topic—life in a labor camp—was thrilling in itself.

The action of the play takes place in one of the camps of the so-called *Byelomor-Stroy*, the building enterprise which constructed the famous Stalin Canal connecting the White Sea (*Byeloye Morye*) with the Baltic Sea. This canal was considered one of the main accomplishments of Soviet construction. It shortened the water route between the two seas by more than two thousand miles.

The characters in the play are prisoners sentenced to various terms at hard labor. Most of them are underworld hoodlums of the worst kind, the "aristocrats" of iniquity. The author brings to the stage a collection of professional criminals—thieves, counterfeiters, harlots, highwaymen, and murderers. Among this conglomeration there is a sprinkling of counterrevolutionaries—saboteurs and obstructionists. This mob is brought into the camp and entrusted to the care of the CHEKA-men (CHEKA, OGPU, NKVD, and now MVD, are successive names for the same organizations). The convicts are to build the canal and, at the same time, to be re-educated to become good and honest citizens. . . .

· · · · ·

There are many touching scenes in the play. One sees, for instance, the old mother of one of the chief saboteurs, engineer Sadovsky, arrive in the camp after having received permission to live with her son. Gromov receives the mother of the camp inmate almost tenderly, and the old woman cannot cease praising Gromov and marveling at the *lager*. Everything is so clean, so comfortable, the food is so excellent (her son looks well, he even gained weight!), the treatment of the prisoners is so humane, they work just as if they were free.

Another time Kostya distinguishes himself at some important work. The Commandant sends for an accordion to the capital itself and Kostya plays sad Russian tunes for his companions.

Camp life, indeed, is one unbroken idyll.

However, before the happy ending takes place, complications are naturally in order. There is in the camp a group of rascals so far gone that they can no longer be brought back to the path of honesty. These characters have to be treated more harshly, and they have to be isolated from the remainder of the inmates. One of them, "The Lemon," manages to induce Kostya to leave everything and escape with him.

On their way, however, Kostya's conscience bothers him greatly. Finally he comes to the conclusion that he cannot leave the camp where he was treated so well and where he had become an honest man once again. But "The Lemon" refuses to let Kostya return, and the latter has to fight his companion before he can go back to the camp and repent.

The Soviet authorities know how to reward those who deserve it. The canal is finally constructed and the longed-for moment of reward arrives. Four prisoners—Sonya, Kostya "The Captain," Sadovsky, and another engineer, a former saboteur with the name of Botkin—are freed before their time is up and receive, in addition, important Soviet decorations for faithful work.

Towards the end of the play an impressive meeting of all camp inmates takes place. As Gromov publicly takes leave of the four freed prisoners, his former charges, they are all overcome by emotion. They weep as Gromov says:

"Why will the *Byelomor* Canal be famous? Because here people like you were brought back to socialist construction with unheard-of bravery, with Bolshevist strictness, and Stalinist sweep. People held in contempt, despised, lost, even our open enemies, became here faithful citizens of their fatherland."

How beautiful it all sounded from the stage!

. . . . .

After I left the theater and freed myself from the suggestive influence of art, I could clearly perceive what feeling it was that had gnawed at my mind throughout the entire performance, spoiling my enjoyment of the play. What we were shown was too beautiful—and it rang false in my ears.

I continued to ponder the problem of the camps. My curiosity as to the actual state of affairs gave me no rest. On the day following the performance I approached a VOKS representative and told him that I wished to visit a *lager*.

I had little hope of having my request granted. I felt certain that a more or less plausible excuse to refuse it would easily be found. I was convinced that such scenes could be shown on the stage but never in real life.

However, I was due for a surprise. The VOKS representative smiled.

"You are very welcome," he told me very politely indeed. "You may visit a corrective camp. We often have such requests from foreigners. On the day after tomorrow, in the morning, we are organizing an excursion to Bolshevo, not far from Moscow, to a camp for young men named after Felix Dzerzhinski. I shall reserve a seat for you in the bus."

. . . . .

I awaited the trip to the prison camp at Bolshevo with great impatience. Neither the Intourist nor the VOKS customarily included such a visit in their excursion schedules. I was assured that I had been granted a special privilege.

And, indeed, I traveled to the camp with a distinguished group of people which included correspondents of great foreign newspapers, several writers, artists, labor leaders, etc. My companions were Britishers, Americans, Frenchmen, Belgians—all were guests for the November 7th anniversary celebrations in Moscow. My immediate neighbor in the luxurious Intourist bus taking us to the camp was a noted Mexican painter.

Most of the conversation during the ride concerned the good will shown by the Soviet authorities in consenting to show to foreigners even the detention places of their criminals. What other government in the world would as easily agree to such a visit?

Several among the foreign guests understood some Russian, and these had seen *The Aristocrats.* The performance was, of course, greatly praised. A bold, elderly, well-dressed man with a small pince-nez spoke in French.

"Unfortunately I have not seen Pogodin's play," he said, "but I did study several professional books on Soviet law, and I am really charmed. We, the Western European jurists, talk a great deal about reforming the old, rusty penal codes; but they, in Russia, actually did something about it. We punish our criminals, we lock them up in prisons. But do these people improve as a result? What advantage does our society at large derive from their treatment? The Russian system of labor camps is an ideal solution. It gets important construction work done for the country, and it changes the character of the criminals through labor. The Russians may indeed be proud of accomplishments such as the Bye! . . . Bye! . . . —well, I always forget the name of the canal."

"You have in mind the *Byelomor* Canal," the VOKS representative who was in charge of our excursion cut in. Then he added with a smile, "So that you might recall this name with greater ease, I have something for you here." He then distributed to every person two packages of excellent Russian cigarettes which it was very difficult to obtain in the stores. On each box was an inscription reading *Byelomor Canal Cigarettes.*

· · · · ·

After a short ride, we arrived at Bolshevo. The day was sunny and beautiful. I recall that our bus entered a lovely park containing numerous trees and flower beds.

"I am sorry you see it in autumn," our guide remarked. "In summer it is even more beautiful here. Greenery and flowers are then all over the camp."

Several buildings were erected in the park. These were mostly wooden structures, but there were also some brick houses. All impressed us favorably.

We started our inspection in one of the buildings containing the inmates' dormitories. We saw nice white beds and bedding, fine washing rooms. Everything was spotlessly clean. All the bedrooms were empty, their occupants at work.

Then we visited the various workshops where the young people were occupied during the day. Everyone worked at a special occupation chosen by him of his own free will: some in metalworking shops, others at carpentry, still others at tailoring. The young men worked, and at the same time gained experience in their chosen trade under the surveillance of qualified instructors.

We were conducted to a large hall where wooden skis and snow sleds were being manufactured for the approaching winter sports season. The young men were working eagerly, with interest. Our entrance did not impress them in the least—apparently they were used to such visits. Cardboard placards with the names of those who had distinguished themselves in filling their work quotas—those who produced 120% of their quota, 150%, or even 200% of the work allotted to them—hung near the door. I asked about the working hours. Six hours a day was the maximum—the boys also had to study. The very young did not work at all, their time being wholly taken up by school.

We next visited the school, where we found large, light classrooms and likable young teachers. Then we were shown the clubhouse where the inmates spent their free time. Here we saw a reading room, a gymnasium, and an auditorium used by the dramatic group, the choir, and the mandolin ensemble to hold their performances. There was also a movie-house in the camp, and nearby were the tidy rooms of the educational KOMSOMOL (Communist Youth Movement) cells. Strict order prevailed wherever we went.

Finally we were taken to a large dining hall. At dinner we partook of the same food as prepared for the inmates; it was tasty and nourishing.

While we sat at the tables sipping our coffee, our guide, the VOKS representative, gave a short lecture in French. Later he himself translated it into English. He told us that most of the camp inhabitants had once been *bezprizornye* children, that is, mostly orphans, tens and perhaps hundreds of thousands of whom had wandered across Russia in bands—an aftermath of revolution and civil war. The youths in these bands were utterly demoralized. They drank, plundered, stole, committed arson and often murder, and presented a major problem for the Soviet government. However, instead of sending these unfortunate juvenile delinquents into prisons or houses of correction, Felix Dzerzhinski called into being camps similar to the one we were visiting. Now the problem of the *bezprizornye* was solved. Through proper education, Soviet justice had managed to save the children from the abyss of crime. And the most important principles of the new education were self-government and voluntary action.

The principle of self-government expressed itself in the fact that the entire administration of the camp was in the hands of the inmates themselves. The most modern teachings of the science of education were applied here. Every year the young men in the camp elected administrators and officials from their midst. Only the chief warden of the camp was an adult appointed by the authorities. He was an officer of the NKVD, but an educator by profession. He collaborated harmoniously with the elected youthful officials in running the camp, and only very infrequently did he have to impose his will on them. There was, indeed, no ground for conflict or even for a lack of smooth cooperation. And if a camp inmate did something improper—as some must, occasionally—he was tried and sentenced by a court also elected by the inmates from among themselves. The system gave excellent results and the number of misdemeanors was continually diminishing.

The second principle of the educational system employed was the stress put on voluntary action. It sounded incredible, but the camp was not guarded and the gate stood open. The camp inmates even enjoyed the privilege of going to Moscow every once in a while, to take care of their affairs. A group composed of the most capable inmates studied at the Moscow University and attended lectures there almost every day. And yet nobody escaped from the camp! In all the years that the camp was in operation only a few had done so, and almost all of these had later returned, greatly ashamed of themselves.

The influence of the educational methods was tremendous. By means of mild psychological measures the very characters of the youthful delinquents were changed. In their inner souls the inmates broke with their past, found new interests, a new aim in life. They became worthy, socially useful citizens permeated by a new moral sense and new ethical values—the morals and ethics of socialism. They were changed into new, reborn beings.

After our guide had finished his really touching speech, I saw tears in the eyes of an elderly English lady. They were tears of appreciation and joy. "Wonderful! Wonderful!" she kept repeating.

"How beautiful the world could be!" a French movie director who happened to be sitting at my side whispered into my ear.

Our guide had something more to offer. "I should like to convince you of the truth of my statements," he told us. "I should like to call a group of the young people into the room and leave them here with you, all by themselves. Before, in the working rooms, I asked you not to talk to them in order not to interfere with their work. Now, however, those of you who speak Russian may chat with the inmates."

Our guide left, and a dozen or so young people entered the room. Since I spoke Russian, most of our group gathered around me.

The inmates repeated almost everything we had been told by our guide. They were happy in the camp, they said. Everything was just ideal, nothing could be better. The youths offered to tell us of their pasts. They did not seem ashamed of the worst deeds. On the contrary, one had the impression that they wished to gain our undivided attention.

One of the boys told us that he used to steal travelers' baggage on the railway stations, together with a band of other *bezprizornye*. He had started when he was thirteen, and had "worked" at it for almost two years. He was finally caught—and now, after one and a half years in the camp, he understood his mistake. He would never steal again, he said. He would become an engineer. He was working in a machine shop and studying at the same time.

Another had belonged to a band that used to break into government and cooperative food stores and plunder the supplies. Now, after two years of camp education, he was the administrator of the camp food storeroom. He was never even a crumb short—we could ask the others about him. The other young men agreed that he was indeed an exceedingly honest keeper of supplies.

A third—a tall, sallow youth who avoided our eyes—admitted that he had wanted to kill a girl who had been his mistress but was about to leave him. He had been sixteen years old then, and he had wounded her with a knife. Now he had been in camp upwards of a year. He had gained everybody's confidence and had even been elected to the camp court.

Then the boys showed us a large picture of a group of laughing, well-dressed, and handsome children of different races handing a bunch of flowers to Stalin. The inscription read: "We thank Stalin for our happy childhood." This poster is very popular in Soviet Russia. It can be seen in many Soviet offices, particularly in children's homes and in schools.

Our visit to Bolshevo took up almost the entire day. During the return trip the participants exchanged lively comments about the wonderful institution. Our guide's face glowed with joy.

"If you are not tired," he told us, "we could visit still another institution today, one that should complete in your minds the picture of our educational homes. I propose that we visit the home for former prostitutes."

We were, of course, enthusiastic about the proposal, and instead of driving to the hotel our bus turned into one of the side streets.

"We shall arrive just at the right time," our guide told us, "for the working hours in this home are in the evening, when old habits tend to draw the women into the street. This is according to a well-thought-out method."

And, indeed, in the roomy, clean halls of the corrective home for former prostitutes we found several dozen women busily working at sewing machines.

The directress of the home, an elderly, stoutish, intelligent-looking woman, received us with the utmost friendliness. And, what good fortune! she spoke English, French, and German. Politely she explained to us the working of the home.

"In the Soviet Union prostitution is considered a crime," she told us, "but we do give the arrested prostitutes an opportunity to regain a decent station in life, to cultivate new habits. In our institution—and in similar ones throughout the Soviet Union—the women are taught a useful trade. That is the most important matter at hand. But simultaneously a course of lectures is given, a series of talks designed to awake intellectual interests in the fallen women, to raise them morally by teaching them an appreciation of music and poetry, and thus draw them into the normal life of the country. Such is the drawing power of our home that many prostitutes come to us of their own free will."

"This is the way the Soviet Union fights this plague and shame of mankind, prostitution," the VOKS representative proudly emphasized. "Not by means of harsh police methods like in your capitalist countries, but through proper education!"

The foreign guests with whom I visited the place, and particularly the women among them, were mightily impressed.

But we were all concerned about one matter. Were we not guilty of a lack of delicacy? Perhaps the fallen women thought it humiliating to be visited and stared at? True, they did not seem to mind at all and quietly continued their sewing. . . . One of the girl attendants reassured us.

"It does not matter," she said; "they are used to these visits. Foreign tourists are brought on a visit here almost every evening."

. . . . .

Back in my hotel room, I tried to bring some order into the multitude of new impressions. Pogodin's *Aristocrats*, the camp at Bolshevo, the home for former prostitutes—all this was really wonderful. These were not only examples of humane treatment of prisoners, but also audacious experiments in tune with the latest accomplishments of educational and criminological thought.

I had read and known a great deal about Soviet malpractices. But I was beginning to doubt.

Was it really possible that all I had seen was only artful propaganda, make-believe, mere fiction?

Perhaps the Great Russian Revolution had achieved something new and progressive in the treatment of prisoners, if only criminal prisoners. Perhaps we had not fully realized Russia's accomplishments in this field.

I found an answer to these questions five years later when I was myself a Soviet prisoner. But then, in 1935 in Moscow, I never dreamt that I should be in a position to study at close quarters and in great detail Soviet justice and especially Soviet prisons and camps, and see how prisoners, guilty and not guilty, criminals and "counterrevolutionaries," adults and adolescents, honest and "fallen" women alike, were really treated. . . .

. . . . .

Remolding of the fallen individual through productive work and suitable educational approach—it was a noble-sounding idea indeed.

There can be no doubt that the countries of the Western World have not found the proper answer to the problem of crime and punishment, that prisons fail to better the convict or to deter him from committing new crimes.

How beautiful, how humanitarian, therefore, did the notion sound that crime was the result of an intrinsically bad social order and that, for this reason, felons were not to be punished and made to suffer; that, on the contrary, their sick souls, rather, were to be cured, their bad inclinations uprooted, and they themselves later returned to society as useful citizens. The corrective labor camps were to be the means of accomplishing this end. Work was to be not a punishment but an educational method. There were even plans for abolishing all prisons, for erasing the very word from the dictionary.

Unfortunately, like many other plans of revolutionary Russia, this concept was also in practice a far cry from the ideal. In its application it turned out as such a caricature of the original idea that the conscience of the world should feel pangs of shame.

The Soviet *lagers* are in fact institutions practicing slave labor. They are closely tied to various industrial or other enterprises which, in turn, are part of the over-all Soviet economy. They are expected to fulfill their part in the general economic plan, and are a tremendous source of cheap labor for this plan. Openly and cynically, without any trace of concern for appearances, the camp inmate is therefore treated simply as a forced supplier of needed work.

With primitive machinery and working methods, mostly in severe climates, making use of undernourished, inexperienced slave labor, the quotas assigned for the camps are wholly unattainable. Work becomes the most wretched punishment, a veritable curse.

So hard are living conditions there that all human effort is expended in the struggle for survival, in the fight to pull through and, at least, keep alive. The work forced upon the inmates is far above their endurance, and instead of morally raising the individual, it makes of every prisoner a dazed, unhappy, working beast.

As the camp commanders and officers are responsible for the fulfillment of their assignments, they goad their slaves, swindle, fix their reports and their books, bribe their superiors, and accept bribes from their underlings.

The influence of the *lagers* on criminality in the country is disastrous. I do not here refer to political prisoners, millions of whom are kept in the camps, but to the real criminals, the ordinary convicts, for even insofar as they are concerned the labor camp is not a corrective institution but, on the contrary, a place where demoralizing influences reach their climax.

Education in the camps is limited to cheap, unconvincing propaganda—empty phrases, every single one obviously false. The support accorded professional criminals, the shameful condoning of their evil ways, the system of bribery and pull—all these practices deeply influence every phase of life in the camps. It is very infrequently that an individual is found capable of withstanding the venomous influence of this camp morality.

The treatment he receives from the camp authorities hurts and kills all vestiges of a man's inner moral values. In practice, the living, feeling, and thinking human being does not exist. The camp authorities are interested solely in extracting the maximum of labor from the prisoner whose value is measured by the number of cubic feet of earth dug or the amount of timber felled. And since the supply of camp inmates is almost inexhaustibly large, and the expended and weakened can easily be replaced by fresh human material, hardly anybody concerns himself with the prisoners' lives and health. The human being, the individual, is only an insignificant unit, a dead cipher in the involved account of this kind of planned economy.

A World Apart

Gustav Herling

*GUSTAV HERLING (1919–2000) was a student at Warsaw University
studying Polish literature and aesthetics when Nazi Germany attacked
Poland in 1939. He headed east to escape the invading German troops
and was arrested by Soviet forces, who were in the process of occupying
the eastern parts of Poland in accordance with the 1939 Nazi-Soviet
nonaggression pact, which divided Poland between Germany and the
Soviet Union.*

*Herling was at first accused of being a high-ranking officer in the
Polish army (on account of the boots he was wearing), as well as being
a relative of Goering (due to a misspelling of his name). The charge
was reduced to attempting to cross illegally the Soviet-Lithuanian
border. He was sentenced to five years imprisonment and sent to a camp
in the north near Archangelsk. He benefitted from the amnesty granted
in 1942 to Polish prisoners in the Soviet Union, after which he enlisted
in the Polish forces assembled in the USSR to join the fight against
Nazi Germany. Following his participation in the war he lived in
England and later in Italy, where he died.*

His A World Apart, *first published in 1951 (seven years before
Solzhenitsyn's* One Day in the Life of Ivan Denisovich), *has been
compared to the latter in quality, although it is far less known and "its
impact was blunted by Soviet sympathizers in the West who denied or
minimized the existence of the chain of Soviet prisons and labor camps.
. . ." (Obituary,* New York Times, *July 6, 2000, A25).*

*The excerpts reprinted here portray not only the harsh living and
working conditions in the camps but their social hierarchy as well,
which resulted from the official policy favoring common criminals over
political prisoners. These writings also illuminate the use of food rations
to reward, punish, or motivate prisoners—a widespread practice in the
Soviet and other Communist penal systems. Herling is also the author
of a novel titled* The Island, *published in 1992.*

· · · · ·

From Gustav Herling, A World Apart, *trans. Joseph Marek, © 1951, 1986 by Gustav Herling.
Used by permission of Viking Penguin, a division of Penguin Group (USA) Inc.*

The summer of 1940 was nearly over when I was in Vitebsk. In the afternoons the sun still shone for a while on the paving-stones of the prison courtyard, and later set behind the red wall of the neighboring block. Inside the cell familiar sounds reached us from the courtyard: the heavy tread of prisoners making their way to the bathhouse, mingled with Russian words of command and the jingling of keys. The warder in the corridor sang quietly to himself; every now and then he put down his newspaper and, without undue hurry, came up to the little round window in the cell door. As if at a given signal two hundred pairs of eyes abandoned their indifferent scrutiny of the ceiling and transferred their gaze to the small pane of the judas. An enormous eye peered into the cell, looked round at all of us, and disappeared again; the small tin shield which covered the glass on the other side fell back into place. . . . Three kicks on the door meant: "Get ready for supper."

Half-naked, we would get up from the cement floor—the supper signal had put an end to our afternoon nap. While waiting with clay bowls in our hands for the liquid mess which was to be our supper, we took the opportunity to relieve ourselves of the liquid mess which had been our lunch. Six or eight streams of urine crossed in the air like the jets of a fountain, and met in a miniature whirlpool at the bottom of a high pail before us, raising the level of foam along its sides. Before buttoning up our trousers, some of us would look curiously at our shaved flesh: it was like seeing a tree, bent by the wind, standing solitary on the barren slopes of a field.

If I were asked what else we did in Soviet prisons, I should find it difficult to add anything to the above account. We were woken in the morning by a knock on the door, and soon our breakfast—a pail of cabbage-water—was brought into the cell, together with a basket containing our daily ration of bread. We munched the bread until lunch and our conversational capacity reached its peak. The Catholics would then gather round an ascetic priest, the Jews round an army rabbi with fish-like eyes and folds of skin, which had once been his belly, hanging loosely from his body; simple people told each other their dreams and talked nostalgically about the past, while the intellectuals searched the cell for cigarette-ends which could be made into one common cigarette. Two kicks on the door put an end to the chatter, and the groups of prisoners, headed by their spiritual leaders, trooped out into the corridor and crowded round the pail of soup. But one day a dark Jew from Grodno joined us in the cell, and weeping bitterly announced that Paris had fallen. From that moment the patriotic whisperings and the political discussions on the palliasses came to an end.

Toward evening the air became cooler, woolly clouds sailed across the sky, and the first stars gleamed faintly. The rust-colored wall opposite our window would burst briefly into a reddish flame, which was then suddenly extinguished by the sunset. Night came, and with it cool air for the lungs, rest for the eyes, and moisture for parched lips.

Just before evening roll call the electric light came on in the cell, and its sudden brilliance accentuated the darkness of the sky outside. But only a moment later the night was pierced by the criss-crossing beams of searchlights, patrolling the darkness from the corner towers of the prison. Before the fall of Paris, a tall woman, her head and shoulders wrapped in a shawl, would pass at just about this hour through the small section of the street visible from our cell window. She would stop by the lamp-post opposite the prison wall to light a cigarette, and several times it happened that she lifted the burning match into the air like a torch and held it for a moment in that incomprehensible pose. We decided that this was a sign of Hope. After Paris fell, we did not see her for two months. It was not until an evening late in August that the sound of her hurried footsteps, echoing in the silence of the small street, woke us from our dreams; as before, she stood under the street-light and after she had lit her cigarette, she put out the match with a zig-zagging movement of the hand, like the motion of connecting-rods on railway-engine wheels. We all agreed that this could only mean a transfer, perhaps that very night. But they were in no hurry and we all remained in Vitebsk for another two months.

· · · · ·

The investigations and hearings of my case had been completed some months ago, in the prison at Grodno. I did not behave heroically during those hearings, and I still admire those of my prison friends who had the courage to engage their interrogators in subtle verbal duels and dialectic colloquies. My answers were short and direct, and it was not until I was outside in the corridor, being led back to my cell, that glorious-sounding phrases from the catechism of Polish political martyrdom suggested themselves to my fevered imagination.

All that I desired during those hearings was sleep. Physically I cannot endure two things, an empty stomach and a full bladder. Both were torturing me when, woken in the middle of the night, I took my place on a hard stool before the officer in charge of my examination, with an incredibly strong light shining straight in my eyes.

The first accusation in my indictment was based on two points of evidence. First, the high leather boots which I wore supposedly proved that I was a major of the Polish Army. (These boots had been given to me by my younger sister when I decided to try and make my way abroad after Poland had been defeated and partitioned between Germany and Russia in September 1939. I was then twenty, and the war had interrupted my university studies.) Secondly, my name, when transcribed into Russian, became Gerling[1] and this supposedly made me the relative of a well-known Field-Marshal of the German Air Force. The accusation therefore read: "Polish officer in the pay of the enemy." But fortunately it did not take me long to convince the interrogator that these accusations were quite without foundation, and we were able to dispense with them entirely. There remained the one undisputed fact—when arrested, I had been trying to cross the frontier between the Soviet Union and Lithuania. Then: "May I ask why you were trying to do that?"

"I wanted to fight the Germans."

"Yes. And are you aware that the Soviet Union has signed a pact of friendship with Germany?"

"Yes, but I am also aware that the Soviet Union has not declared war on France and England."

"That has not the slightest significance."

"Then how, finally, does the indictment stand?"

"Attempting to cross the Soviet-Lithuanian frontier in order to fight against the Soviet Union."

"Could you not substitute the words 'against Germany' for 'against the Soviet Union'?" A blow in the face brought me back to my senses. "It comes to the same thing, anyway," the judge consoled me as I signed the confession of guilt which had been placed in front of me.

It was not until the end of October, when I had already spent five months inside the Vitebsk prison, that, together with fifty of the two hundred prisoners in my cell, I was called out to hear my sentence. I walked to the office calmly, without a trace of excitement. After a sentence of five years' imprisonment had been read out to me, I was taken to a different cell, in the side-wing of the Vitebsk prison, to wait for my transport. There for the first time I came into contact with Russian prisoners. When I came in, several boys, aged between fourteen and sixteen, were lying on wooden bunks, and by the window, through which I could see a scrap of dark, lead-colored sky, sat a small man with red eyes and a hooked nose, munching in silence a piece of stale brown bread. It had been raining for several days. The autumn sky hung over Vitebsk like a swollen fish-bladder; streams of dirty water poured down through the gutter and trickled over the netting which covered the lower half of the bars on our window.

Juvenile delinquents, like the boys in the cell, are the plague of the Soviet prisons, though they are almost never found in labor camps. Unnaturally excited, always ferreting in other men's bunks and inside their own trousers, they give themselves up passionately to the only two occupations of their lives, theft and self-abuse. Almost all of them either have no parents or else know nothing of their whereabouts. Throughout the vast expanse of the Russian police state they manage to lead with astounding ease the typical life of "bzeprizornye" ("the homeless"), jumping goods-trains, constantly on the move from town to town, from settlement to settlement. They make a living by stealing and selling goods from government stores, and frequently they steal back what they have just sold, blackmailing unsuspecting purchasers with the threat of laying information against them. They sleep in railway stations, in municipal parks, in tram terminuses; often all their belongings can be wrapped in a small bundle tied with a leather strap. Only later I discovered that the bezprizornye constitute a most dangerous semi-legal mafia, organized on the pattern of masonic lodges, and surpassed only by the more powerful organization of "urkas," or criminal prisoners. If in Russia anything like a black market exists, it is only thanks to the efforts of these urchins, always weaving in and out of crowds, besieging the "spectorgs" (special shops supplying exclusively the *élite* of the Soviet bureaucracy), creeping at dusk towards stores of corn and coal. The Soviet authorities wink at all this activity; they regard the bezprizornye as the only true proletariat free of the original sin of counterrevolution, as a plastic mass of raw material which can be molded into any shape they choose. These young boys have come to look on prison as something like a holiday-camp, and they take advantage of a prison sentence to rest after the exertions of their life outside. Occasionally, a vospitatel [education officer], with an angelic face, flaxen hair, and blue eyes, would come into our cell, and, in a voice which sounded like the gentle whisper of the confessional, call the handful of bezprizornye out for a "lesson": "Come, children, let us go and learn a little." When the "children" came back from their instruction, our ears burned at the obscenities which they mixed freely with the stock phrases of Soviet political propaganda. Accusations of "Trotskyism," "nationalism," and "counterrevolution" were constantly flung out at us from their corner, then assurances that "Comrade Stalin did well to lock you up," or that "the power of the Soviets will soon conquer the whole world"—all this repeated again and again with the cruel, sadistic persistence typical of homeless youth. Later in the labor camp I met an eighteen-year-old boy who had been appointed chief of the local "Kulturno-Vospitatelnaya Tchast" [cultural and educational section] only because once, as a bezprizorny, he had gone through such a course of instruction in prison. . . .

· · · · ·

At half-past five in the morning the barrack doors opened with a clatter, and the silence, disturbed only by the last sighs of sleep, was broken by a loud shout of "Padyom—let's go." A moment later the "razvodchyk," a prisoner responsible for the march-out of the brigades to work, walked briskly along the rows of bunks, tugging the sleepers by their legs. The prisoners moved heavily on their bunks, threw aside the coats covering their heads, and slowly, as if their bodies were held down by invisible bonds, sat up, only to fall back on to the bunks with moans of pain a moment later. Then the "dnevalny," the barrack orderly, walked slowly up and down, repeating "To work, children, to work" in a monotonous whisper; he had to see that all the occupants of the barrack were up and on their feet before the kitchens opened. He performed his work gently and politely, not like the razvodchyk, but more as befits a man who, himself free from work, is forced to send others to it, and whose low status of a slaves' servant does not allow him to speak with the harshness used by free men and their camp servants when they address the prisoners.

Those few minutes after reveille, while the inhabitants of each barrack lay on their bunks without moving, were devoted to our peculiar form of prayer. It began invariably with swearing and curses, and ended almost as invariably with the sacramental formula: "Oh, what a bloody life...!" That expression, which I heard repeated every day on all sides, was a hideous complaint which contained everything that a prisoner knew and could say about his living death. In other lands and other conditions, in normal prisons, the place of this short cry of despair is taken by a real prayer or by the remission of one day of the total sentence, for it is only too understandable that a man robbed of everything but hope should begin his day by turning his thoughts to hope. Soviet prisoners have been deprived even of hope, for not one of them can ever know with any certainty when his sentence will come to an end. He can remember literally hundreds of cases where sentences have been prolonged by another ten years with one stroke of a pen at the Special Council of the NKVD in Moscow. Only someone who has been in prison can appreciate the whole implication of cruelty in the fact that during my year and a half in the camp only a few times did I hear prisoners counting aloud the number of years, months, days, and hours which still remained of their sentences. This silence seemed to be a tacit agreement not to tempt providence. The less we talked about our sentences, the less hope we cherished of ever regaining freedom, the more likely it seemed that "just this once" everything would be well. Hope contains the terrible danger of disappointment. In our silence, rather like the taboo which forbids the men of certain primitive tribes to pronounce the names of vengeful deities, humility was combined with a quiet resignation and anticipation of the worst. Disappointment was a fatal blow to a prisoner who lacked this armor against fate. I remember an old railwayman from Kiev, called Ponomarenko, who had spent ten years in various Soviet camps, and who alone among us all talked of his approaching release with a confidence that dispelled fear, excluding all uncertainty. In July 1941, two weeks after the outbreak of the Russo-German war, he was summoned to the NKVD office beyond the zone on the last day of his sentence to hear that it had been prolonged "indefinitely." When we came back from work that evening, he was already dead. Dimka told us later that he had come back from the Second Section looking pale,[2] and had seemed suddenly aged by the ten years which he had spent in the camp. He lay down on his bunk without a word, and to all questions would answer only: "My life is finished, it's all over"; and he, an old bolshevik, alternately prayed soundlessly or beat his grey head against the planks of the bunk. He died between four and five in the afternoon, when Dimka as usual went out for hvoya and hot water. I can only guess what was happening in his heart, but one thing is certain—that besides despair, pain, and helpless anger, he felt also regret for his thoughtless faith in hope. In his last moments, looking back on his wasted life, he must have reproached himself bitterly for provoking fate by his light-hearted confidence. In the barrack I heard more condemnation than sympathy for him. He had suffered, yes: but had he not brought it upon himself? Was it not playing with fire to talk freely about his release? Did he not invoke freedom, instead of putting his faith humbly in the sentences of destiny? He was no inexperienced novice, for he himself, in 1936, had seen men who were due for release at four o'clock in the afternoon cut the veins of their wrists when, at twelve o'clock, an order had come from Moscow abolishing the system of remission of two days for every day of stakhanovite work. He had told us this himself, laughing and pleased because his own good sense had always told him to work only so much that a day should be counted as a day. And now he had been cheated of 3,650 days of unfailing, honest work. It was considered that he had been deservedly punished for breaking the prisoners' code.

Everything went on as before: Ponomarenko's bunk was taken by another prisoner, the place of his faith in justice by the old taboo, and the place of his daily sentence-litany by the only words which we used to express hopelessness without provoking hope.

By a quarter to six only those prisoners who had obtained a medical dispensation from work on the previous day were still lying on their bunks, while the rest were beginning to dress. Prisoners bent over their bare legs, attempting to construct from rags, pieces of string, or lengths of wire, torn felt boots and scraps of car tires, a warm and enduring foot-covering which would last for an eleven-hour day of work. Only the specially picked brigades, mine among them, engaged in work directly concerned with the camp's production plan, were issued with new clothing and allowed to exchange it when it was worn out. But about three-quarters of all prisoners walked out to work in rags which exposed parts of their legs, arms, and chests. It was not surprising, then, that many of them did not undress at night for fear that their clothing, put together with difficulty, would simply disintegrate. For them the morning reveille was like a signal in the waiting room of a railway station. They shook the sleep out of themselves, dragged themselves off the bunks, moistened their eyes and mouths in the corner of the barrack, and walked out to the kitchen. They left the zone for work with a surreptitious hope that this time the frostbite on the exposed parts of their bodies would be bad enough to merit at least a few days' dispensation from work.

The zone was still quite dark. Only just before the morning roll call the sky became pink on the edge of the horizon, melting after a while in the steel-blue glare of the snow. It was difficult to distinguish faces even at the distance of an extended hand. We all walked in the direction of the kitchen, bumping into each other and clanging our mess-cans. By the well and round the small hut where the hot drinking water was boiled could be heard the jangling of buckets, the crunching of frozen snow, and the quiet whispers of the imprisoned priests, who, like Dimka, usually did the work of barrack orderlies, calmly conducting their morning exchange of courtesies. The somber ceiling of the sky closed upon us from above, and the still invisible barbed wire separated us from the outer world which was beginning to go about its business by the light of electric lamps.

On the raised platform in front of the kitchen formed three queues, epitomizing the social divisions of the camp proletariat. Before the serving-hatch with the inscription "third cauldron" stood the best-dressed and fittest prisoners—stakhanovites, whose daily production capacity reached or surpassed 125 per cent of the prescribed norm: their morning meal consisted of a large spoonful of thick boiled barley and a scrap of salted "treska" (a large northern fish similar in flavor to the cod) or herring. The second cauldron was for prisoners with a daily production capacity of 100 per cent of the norm—a spoonful of barley without the piece of fish. At the front of this queue stood old men and women from those brigades where it was impossible to reckon the work in terms of percentages, who were therefore automatically issued with the second cauldron. But the most terrible sight was the first cauldron queue, a long row of beggars in torn rags, shoes tied with string, and worn caps with earflaps, waiting for their spoonful of the thinnest barley. Their faces were shriveled with pain and dried like parchment, their eyes suppurating and distended by hunger, their hands convulsively gripping the billy-cans as if their stiff fingers had frozen to the tin handles. Dazed with exhaustion and swooning on their thin legs, they pushed their way through to the hatch, whined plaintively, begging for an extra dribble, and peered greedily into the cans of second- and third-cauldron prisoners as they left the hatches. In this queue arguments were most frequent, here the humble whining changed most frequently into the shrill falsetto of anger, envy, and hatred. The queue for the first cauldron was always the longest in the camp. Apart from the most numerous class of prisoners, those who with the best will in the world could not attain 100 per cent of the norm because their physical condition was too poor, there were many who purposely spared themselves at work, convinced that it was better to work little and eat little than to work hard and eat almost as little. All the barrack orderlies, and a few prisoners from the staff and administration of the camp, also belonged to the first cauldron.

Prisoners who left the zone without an escort, by special passes, had their breakfast before six. Besides water-carriers and servants employed in the houses of free administrative staff, this group also included the technical experts and engineers who had to be at their places before the arrival of the brigades. The meal of their special "iteerovski" (I.T.R.—engineering and technical work) cauldron surpassed in quantity and to some extent in quality the rations even of stakhanovites on general work. At half-past six all the serving-hatches were closed, though they opened again, after the brigades had left for work, to feed prisoners with medical dispensations from work, the inhabitants of the mortuary, and those working inside the zone itself on the second cauldron.

Very few prisoners had enough strength of will to carry their meals from the kitchen all the way back to the barracks. For the most part they ate standing up at the bottom of the platform, swallowing in two or three hasty gulps all that the cook's ladle had poured into the dirty can. Small groups of prisoners began to join the black crowd gathering by the guard-house immediately after breakfast. The zone was already light, and from the dispersing darkness could be made out first the frost-rimmed wires, then the enormous sheet of snow, extending to the hardly visible line of the forest on the horizon. In the village and in the barracks the lights were going out and the chimneys were sending dirty yellow clouds of smoke into the air. The moon was fading gently, frozen in the icy sky like a slice of lemon in a jelly, and the last stars still twinkled. The morning "razvod"—the brigades' march out to work—was starting.

At a given signal the prisoners drew themselves up into brigades, standing in twos. In normal brigades the old were at the front and the young at the back, but in brigades whose output did not come up to the prescribed norm the order was reversed. This practice must be explained more fully. There were very few prisoners who believed that it was better to work less and eat less, and in the overwhelming majority of cases the cauldron system was successful in obtaining the maximum physical effort from the prisoners for an insignificant increase in their rations. A hungry man does not stop to think, but is ready to do anything for an extra spoonful of soup. The fascination of the norm was not the exclusive privilege of the free men who imposed it, but also the dominating instinct of the slaves who worked to it. In those brigades where the work was done by teams of men working together, the most conscientious and fervent foremen were the prisoners themselves, for there the norms were reckoned collectively by dividing the total output by the number of workers. Any feeling of mutual friendliness was completely abolished in favor of a demented race for percentages. An unqualified prisoner who found himself assigned to a coordinated team of experienced workers could not expect to have any consideration shown to him; after a short struggle he was forced to give up and transfer to a team in which he in his turn frequently had to watch over weaker comrades. There was in all this something inhuman, mercilessly breaking the only natural bond between prisoners—their solidarity in face of their persecutors. The formation of brigades in the morning brought this system to monstrous cruelty. In brigades which failed to come up to the norm the pace of the march was set by the youngest prisoners to save time, while the older and feebler ones were dragged behind. This natural selection resulted in rapid rejuvenation of the brigades in question, for the old ones who could not keep up gradually disappeared for good.

The first to leave the zone were the brigades of foresters, who had to walk between five and seven kilometers to their work; leaving the camp at half-past six, they would arrive at their sector of the forest at half-past seven, and finish work at five. The razvodchyk, who acted as the master of ceremonies at the morning roll call, standing with a board and a pencil exactly on the borderline between the zone and free territory, called each brigade in turn to the gates and reported its presence to the officer of the guard. Beyond the gate waited with mounted bayonets a detachment of the "Vohra" (the labor camp garrisons) in long greatcoats and fur caps. The chief officer of the guard formally handed the brigade over to its permanent escorting soldier, who stepped out of his rank, called out his name and the number of his brigade, checked the number of prisoners and repeated it aloud to the officer, acknowledging the receipt of so many men for such and such work. From that moment he was responsible for them with his own life, so that a moment before marching off he repeated to the prisoners the sacred, invariable formula: "Brigade such and such, I am warning you: one single step to the right or the left, and you get a bullet through the head." Then he gave the signal to move off, and lowering his rifle as if for attack, with his finger on the trigger, sent the brigadier to the front and himself brought up the rear. After the forest brigades went those for the saw mill, the brigades of joiners going to the town, then the digging, the food-center, the road-building, the water-works, and the electricity-plant brigades. From the gates of the camp black crocodiles of men—stooping, shivering with cold, and dragging their legs—dispersed in all directions and disappeared on the horizon after a few minutes like scattered lines of letters, gathered with one pull of the hand from a white sheet of paper.

The journey to work was exhausting, but contained some variety compared with the work itself. Even prisoners whose brigades worked at a distance of less than a mile from the zone found great pleasure in passing familiar places, trees, frozen streams, dilapidated sheds, and wolf-traps, perhaps asserting their own existence by observation of the unchanging laws of nature. In some brigades, too, the degree of friendliness between the prisoners and their guard was so close that, as soon as they were out of sight of the guard-house, the "strelok" put his rifle on his shoulder and began to chat pleasantly with the last few pairs. This insignificant expression of human feelings gave us not so much the pleasure of raising ourselves from humiliation and contempt, but rather excitement at an infringement of prison rules. Occasionally the guard treated his brigade with politeness, and even showed signs of a rudimentary guilty conscience towards them. Therefore the days when the guard of a particular brigade was changed were among the most memorable for the prisoners, and were eagerly discussed in the barracks. Some time had always to pass before a fresh understanding could develop between the slaves and their new overseer. It was quite a different case if the escorting guard looked upon the prisoners as his natural enemies and treated them accordingly; that brigade did not miss the slightest opportunity of annoying him and making his work difficult.

The first hours of the day were always the most difficult to bear. Our bodies, stiffened rather than rested by sleep on hard bunks, had to struggle against great pain in order to recapture the rhythm of work. Besides, there was really nothing to wait for in the morning. Only the stakhanovites received a midday meal—a spoonful of boiled soya-beans and a hundred grams of bread; this "extra" was brought by one of the water-carriers, under the supervision of a cook, in a large bucket fixed to sledge runners. Other workers spent the mid-day break sitting round the fire in a position where they could not see the stakhanovites' "extra," smoking one common cigarette which was passed from hand to hand.

It was rarely that a prisoner had saved a slice of bread from the previous evening's meal. Bread rations were issued daily according to the cauldrons: third—700 grams, second—500 grams, and first—400 grams.[3] Bread—apart from the spoonful of boiled barley in the mornings and the portion of weak soup in the evenings—was the camp's basic food. To restrain oneself from gulping all of it down immediately after receiving it required a superhuman effort of will. Only those prisoners who walked out again to the kitchen after their evening meal, and bought additional portions of soup from the cooks with the rapidly vanishing items of their pre-camp clothing, could bring them-selves to put a little bread by for the morning.

Two hours before their return to the zone the prisoners came to life again. The prospect of rest and of momentary satisfaction of tormenting hunger had such an effect on us that not only the return, but even the anticipation of it was the day's most important event. As in every idealized picture, there was more illusion than reality in the expectation. The agony of prison life did not end for us when we returned to the barracks, but on the contrary became the agony of waiting for death. Yet it contained a mysterious attraction in the intimacy of suffering. Lying alone on one's bunk, one was at last free—free from work, from the company of one's fellow-prisoners, free, finally, from time, which dragged so slowly for us. Only in prison is it easy to understand that life with-out any expectation of the future becomes meaningless and flooded with de-spair. We feared solitude while waiting for it. It was our only substitute for freedom, and in moments of complete relaxation it gave us the relief and the almost physical pain of tears.

The first, instinctive reaction of hopelessness is always the faith that in loneliness suffering will become hardened and sublimated as in a purgatory fire. Though many long for solitude as their last refuge, few are capable of bearing it. The idea of loneliness, as that of suicide, is most frequently the only protest which we can make when everything else has failed us, and before death has begun to hold more attraction than terror for us. It is never more than an idea, for despair enlightened by consciousness would be greater than the despair of torpidity. A prisoner walking back to the zone was like a drown-ing man who has survived a shipwreck and is swimming with a last effort of will towards a desert island. As long as he is struggling with the waves and catching gusts of air into lungs which are already bursting with pain, but al-ways nearer and nearer to the land, his life is still worth living, for he still has hope. But there is no torture worse than the sudden realization that this hope itself was only the delusion of unsteady senses. To find oneself on a desert island, without the slightest prospect of rescue and salvation, after the efforts to survive in the sea—that may indeed be called suffering. We lived through that every day; every day shortly before the return to the zone, the prisoners laughed and talked like free men; and every day they would lie down on their bunks after work like men choking with despair.

In the forest brigades, which in the north were the basis of the labor camps' production plan, the work was divided among several teams of four or five prisoners. The functions of each prisoner were constantly varied so that each would in turn perform the heavier and the lighter tasks: thus, one felled the pines with a thin curved saw, one cleared them of bark and boughs, one burnt the cleared branches and bark on the fire (this was a form of rest which was taken in turn), and the remaining two sawed the felled trunks into logs of a prescribed length, stacking them in piles a yard or two in height. Under this system of division of labor the most important person at the wood-cutting was the foreman, a prisoner who walked about without an escort or a free supervisor, who measured the cut wood, and stamped the counted logs with the camp seal. His reckonings became the basis on which the brigadier calculated the output of each team in his brigade. I can no longer remember what the prescribed norm was in the forest, but I do know that the Finns, who are deservedly reputed to be the world's best woodcutters, considered it to be excessively high even for free and well-fed workers. It was impossible for a forest brigade to surpass its norm except with the help of what was known as "toufta," a whole system of ingenious cheating. The authority of a brigadier among his workers was measured by his talents in this direction, which were also a source of income to him in the form of bribes from weaker prisoners. Various methods were used; the logs were stacked so that the piles would look full from outside and yet be loose inside, with spaces between logs—this could be successful only when the foreman was himself a prisoner, and for a bribe of bread would ignore the hollowness of the piles. If the foreman happened to be an incorruptible free official (though even these could occasionally be bribed, usually with a civilian suit), we would saw off thinly the stamped end of the log and insert this "new" log into an uncounted pile, while the shavings were quickly burnt in the fire. In any case it is a fact that without the toufta and its accompanying bribery, on all sectors of the camp's industry, no brigade could ever have reached even a hundred per cent output.

Forest work was considered to be one of the heaviest forms of labor in the camp. The distance from work to the camp was usually about three miles: the prisoners worked all day under the open sky, up to their waist in snow, drenched to the skin, hungry, and exhausted. I never came across a prisoner who had worked in the forest for more than two years. As a rule they left after a year, with incurable disease of the heart, and were transferred to brigades engaged at lighter work; from these they soon "retired"—to the mortuary. Whenever a fresh transport of prisoners arrived in Yercevo, the youngest and strongest were always picked to be "put through the forest." This selection of slaves was some-times similar even in the details of its decor to the illustrations of books about negro slavery, when the chief of the Yercevo camp section, Samsonov, honored the medical examination with his presence, and with a smile of satisfaction felt the biceps, shoulders, and backs of the new arrivals. . . .

. . . . .

The whole system of forced labor in Soviet Russia—in all its stages, the inter-rogations and hearings, the preliminary imprisonment, and the camp itself—is intended primarily not to punish the criminal, but rather to exploit him eco-nomically and transform him psychologically. Torture is applied at the hear-ings not on principle, but as an auxiliary instrument. The real object of a hear-ing is not the extortion from the accused of the prisoner's signature to a ficti-tious indictment, but the complete disintegration of his individual personality.

A man woken up in the middle of the night, unable to satisfy his most elementary physical needs during the hearing, sitting for hours at a time on a small hard stool, blinded by the light of a powerful bulb directed straight at his eyes, surprised by sudden, cunning questions, and by an overwhelming cre-scendo of fictitious accusations, sadistically taunted with the sight of cigarettes and hot coffee on the other side of the table, and all this going on for months, sometimes even years—under these circumstances he is ready to sign any-thing. That, however, is not the essential point. A prisoner is considered to have been sufficiently prepared for the final achievement of the signature only when his personality has been thoroughly dismantled into its component parts. Gaps appear in the logical association of ideas; thoughts and emotions become loosened in their original positions and rattle against each other like the parts of a broken-down machine; the driving-belts connecting the past with the present slip off their wheels and fall sloppily to the bottom of the mind; all the weights and levers of mind and will-power become jammed and refuse to func-tion; the indicators of the pressure gauges jump as if possessed from zero to maximum and back again. The machine still runs on larger revolutions, but it does not work as it did—all that had a moment before appeared absurd now becomes probable even though still not true, emotions lose their color, will-power its capacity. The prisoner is now willing to admit that he had betrayed the interests of the proletariat by writing to his relatives abroad, that his slack-ness at work was sabotage of socialist industry. This is the crucial moment for the examining judge. One final blow at the rusty mechanism of resistance, and the machine will stop altogether. A man sleeping under an anesthetic remains for a split-second suspended in a vacuum, when he feels, thinks, and under-stands nothing. When the patient's heart stops beating for that fraction of a second, then is the time for immediate action. A trifling oversight, a slight delay, and the patient will regain consciousness on the operating table and then either rebel and shout out, or break down and retire into perpetual apathy. For the judge it is now or never. His eyes glance at the single piece of factual evidence, prepared for just this moment, his hands pick up the document like a scalpel. Only a few hours ago it could have been dismissed as insignificant, but as it is the only proof which has any foundation in fact, it grows now in the scorched imagination of the accused to gigantic proportions. The scalpel has found the right spot and the incision deepens. In feverish haste the surgeon cuts out the heart, his probing instruments transplant it to the body's right side, strip flakes of infected tissue from the brain, graft small patches of skin, change the direction of the blood flow, repair the torn network of the nervous system. The human mechanism, arrested at its lowest ebb and taken to pieces, is reconstructed and altered: those gaps between disjointed ideas are filled by new connections: thoughts and feelings settle in new bearings: the driving belts start to turn in the opposite direction, transmitting not the past to the present, but the present to the past: the efforts of mind and will are directed to different purposes: the arrows of the gauges will always point to maximum. The prisoner wakes from his trance, turns an exhausted but smiling face towards his benefactor, and with a deep sigh admits that now everything is clear to him, that he had erred all his life, but that now all will be well. The operation has been successful, the patient is reborn. Only once more, after his return to the cell, as he stands over the bucket and relieves his long-suffering bladder, when he feels drops of sweat on his forehead and the relaxation of tension in his whole body, he hesitates, and wonders whether he has dreamt or really lived through this re-incarnation. For the last time in his life he falls asleep with a sensation of tormenting uncertainty—the next morning he wakes feeling empty as a nut without a kernel and weak after the inhuman strain to which his whole organism has been subjected during the past few months, but dazzled by the thought that everything is already behind him. When a prisoner walks between the bunks without saying a word to anyone, it is easy for the others to guess that he is a convalescent with rapidly healing scars and a newly assembled personality, taking his first uncertain steps in a new world.

In the period between the hearings and the sentence (which will be passed in his absence and probably send him on a quick journey to the camp), the prisoner becomes acclimatized in the cell to his new situation. Instinct warns him against talking to prisoners who have not yet undergone the Great Change, for the stitches on his scars are still too fresh to withstand the sharp pulls of ruthless tearing hands. He is afraid above all of the moment when the whole of his new reality will topple from one blow like a house of cards, when the old brain, ruining the patient work of months, shows enough determination to understand that the new heart beats differently and elsewhere than before, and some atavistic voice, echoing from the rubble of the past, sends him rushing at the cell door with clenched fists and a desperate cry: "I lied, I lied! I withdraw everything! I'm innocent, take me to the judge! I want to see the judge, I'm innocent!" If he is fortunate enough to be spared that crisis, the prisoner can lie for days on his bunk, calm and indifferent to everything, simply waiting for a transfer to his camp. In this somnambulistic state he notices the feeble light of his last hope seeping into his own prison through a narrow breach in its cold wall: he begins to long for the camp, timidly at first, then with growing impatience. An unknown voice—a precious relic of his old personality, an assurance that he had been and still could be different—deceives him with the illusion of a free life in the camp, among men of whom some must surely still remember the past. He now needs only two things: work and pity. It is not pity for himself that he requires, since he regards what he has just gone through as basically his own victory. He feels dimly that if he is to save the slight thread that still binds him to the buried past in which he was a different person, he must at all costs generate in himself a feeling of pity for his companions in misery, and of compassion for the suffering of others, which could prove to him that, despite his inner transformation, he has remained a human being. "Can one live without pity?" he asks himself at night, turning from side to side and mopping his forehead anxiously as he tries to remember whether once, in that obliterated past, his only reaction to human suffering had been the same painful indifference that he has felt since his rebirth. Can one live without pity?

In the camp he learns that it is only too easy. At first he shares his bread with hunger-demented prisoners, leads the night-blind on the way home from work, shouts for help when his neighbor at work in the forest has chopped off two fingers, and surreptitiously carries cans of soup and herring-heads to the mortuary. After several weeks he realizes that his motives in all this are neither pure nor really disinterested, that he is following the egoistic injunctions of his brain and saving first of all himself. The camp, where prisoners live at the lowest level of humanity and follow their own brutal code of behavior toward others, helps him to reach this conclusion. How could he have supposed, back in the prison, that a man can be so degraded as to arouse not compassion but only loathing and repugnance in his fellow-prisoners? How can he help the night-blind, when every day he sees them being jolted with rifle-butts because they are delaying the brigade's return to work, and then impatiently pushed off the paths by prisoners hurrying to the kitchen for their soup; how visit the mortuary and brave the constant darkness and the stench of excrement; how share his bread with a hungry madman who on the very next day will greet him in the barrack with a demanding, persistent stare? After two or three months of this struggle, the prisoner who has undergone the Great Change and is now making a desperate attempt to recover some of the past conceptions which were submerged at the hearing finally gives in. He listens without contradiction to the daily grumbling in his barrack: "Those bastards in the mortuary stuff themselves with our bread, and don't even work for it"; "Those night-blind lower our norms after dark and then sprawl all over the paths so that you can't even move"; "Those madmen ought to be locked up in the punishment cells, they'll be stealing our bread soon." He remembers and believes the words of his examining judge, who told him that the iron broom of Soviet justice sweeps only rubbish into its camps, and that men worthy of the name are able to prove that their imprisonment is due to a judicial error. The last thread has snapped, the prisoner's education is complete. There remains only the exploitation of his cheap labor, and if he survives eight or ten years of the work, he will be fit to take the place of the examining judge behind a table, confronting the future prisoner who will be sitting where he had once sat.

There are, however, some who wake suddenly during this final trial, and stand at the crossroads of their lives to look back and realize clearly that they have been cheated, not convinced or converted, only destroyed as human beings, their feelings cauterized with a hot poker. They are still capable of one emotional effort. It is too late to jump at the door with raised fists and the cry "I want the judge, I am innocent!" but there is still time to blow the dying embers of his human feelings into a flame which will take the place of defeated compassion—the flame of voluntary and almost artificial martyrdom.

· · · · ·

The last stage of a prisoner's life in the camp was the mortuary, a large barrack situated between the kitchen and the maternity hut, where prisoners no longer capable of working were directed before their names were finally crossed off the list of the living.

A prisoner was transferred to the mortuary on the basis of a medical examination, which could be repeated, when he stopped being a "working man" and became a "dokhadyaga"—a word which can best be translated as "one who is dying by inches." Women prisoners who were unfit for work were either left in their barracks or sent from Yercevo to some unknown destination, as there was no separate mortuary for them. In theory, the mortuary provided an opportunity for the exhausted organism to recover its strength, but rest and idleness alone, without better nourishment, were not sufficient to revive even the youngest and healthiest prisoners. The mortuary brought release from the torture of daily work, but no relief from the agonies of daily hunger. On the contrary, hunger becomes really dangerous, and leads men to the verge of madness, particularly during long periods of idleness, when one has time to become fully conscious of it, when thoughts of it invade and fill every moment of the endless rest on the bunks. The crowd of beggars which gathered round the kitchen every evening, waiting for the dregs of soup from the cauldrons to be given out, came for the most part from the mortuary.

The originally intended function of the mortuary was probably to make sick and exhausted prisoners fit enough to go back to work, to serve as a kind of miniature health resort; in practice, however, its nature was summed up in the nickname given to it by the prisoners—a mortuary, a charnel-house. The mortuary food ration, although, as a shame-faced compensation for years of labor, was usually fixed at the level of the second cauldron, was insufficient to stop the disintegration of body tissues; the occasional coveted spoonful of raw vegetables could not cure the usual diseases of the north—scurvy and pellagra. Only a man with a very strong constitution, exhausted by work but still free from disease, could hope to regain strength in the mortuary, to live and work for a short time until he broke down again. Regular medical inspections divided the inhabitants of the mortuary into the "weaklings" and the "incurables." The weaklings were prisoners like myself who, it was considered, still had a prospect of returning to work after a period of rest; we were given a small additional ration, the so-called "weaklings' extra," and formed into a special brigade used for occasional light work inside the zone. The second category involved a diagnosis of "incurability in camp conditions," or in practice a sentence of slow death in the mortuary; the incurables were not forced to work, but neither did they receive any additional food. They could only wait patiently for the end.

There were so few cases of recovery and return to work even among the weaklings that this division into categories was no more than a polite fiction, yet the inhabitants of the mortuary, though fully realizing that despite artificial differentiations they were all doomed, always begged to be included in the first division. They were not so much eager for the additional food, as terrified by the death sentence contained in the word incurable.

The hard price of complete peace and idleness was the irrevocable loss of all remaining hope. No one, thinking of the barrack to which sooner or later all the paths of the camp led, would have dared to compare its aimless idleness with the restfulness of the hospital. It stood a little apart from the zone, snowbound, solitary, abandoned by hope, and avoided by the living, with frosted windows gleaming opaquely like the eyes of a blind man, and a white rag of smoke hanging over its roof like the flag of surrender. One might have said that it was not even in the camp, but beyond the wires, already on the side of eternal freedom. . . . And yet a prisoner in the mortuary did not even have the sympathy of others to accompany him on the last stage of his life's journey. "That rubbish, that shit, they eat our bread and do nothing for it. Better for us and for them if they were put out of their misery"—that was the usual comment whenever the mortuary was mentioned in the barracks.

My feelings as I walked to the mortuary for the first time from the hospital must have differed from those of my Russian fellow-prisoners in the same situation. Five days in hospital had not cured the swelling of my whole body or healed the sores on my legs; my nerves were relaxed after the tension of the hunger strike, my whole organism open to a fresh attack of scurvy; but the taste of victory was still fresh enough to revive my hopes of survival. The mortuary seemed to be the best solution for me, as without a temperature I had no formal right to occupy a bed in the hospital, and with the prospect of a speedy release from the camp before me I preferred to spend my remaining days there in idleness, even in the constant presence of death, than to cling to the appearance of life by going out to work. I felt as if I was entering a leper colony, protected against the disease by impenetrable armor. And now, as once before, I felt ashamed because my fate was pushing me off the paths trodden before me by thousands of swollen and scrofulous legs like mine.

I walked past the infirmary, past the new outbuilding of the technical barrack, past the maternity hut. I stopped at every few steps, laying down the bundle with all my possessions, to look back at the zone. Below me, lit up by the frosty December sun and surrounded by a high wall of drifted snow, stood my old barrack, to which I knew that I should never return. Two pregnant women walked slowly to the infirmary, clasping their dumpy stomachs with red, frostbitten hands. Beyond the wire, as far as the eye could see, stretched the white desert plain, bounded on the horizon by the thick line of the forest. As I stopped before the door of the mortuary to get my breath back, I saw the porters' brigade leaving the barrack and walking towards the bathhouse. So much time had passed since I had marched out to work with them, so many new, unknown faces had taken the place of those whose names now dimly rattled in my memory like stones in an empty box. When they were passing the mortuary one of the porters recognized me, waved his hand in greeting and gaily called out: "Hullo, friend! Dying already?"

In the mortuary I was greeted by curious glances from both the rows of two-tiered bunks. I laid my bundle on the table and started to look for Dimka. I found him in a far corner, on a lower bunk as usual (he believed that lying above other prisoners gave one a valuable sense of superiority, but his pin leg made it difficult for him to climb into the upper bunks), sleeping peacefully with his old wooden spoon in his hand. He had grown thinner since he had been classified as an incurable, but his graying beard was beautifully trimmed and pointed, and gave to his angular face an expression of mental resignation and inward peace. He woke when I touched his arm lightly. For a moment he seemed not to recognize me, painfully screwing up his eyes, hazy with sleep and so pale as to seem almost colorless, but then he raised himself on the bunk and welcomed me with a friendly smile. I am ashamed to say that I had not tried to see him from the moment when, having gathered up his things in our barrack, he shook my hand before leaving for the mortuary. Now he said almost through tears: "My son, my son, I've heard about everything. You're a brave boy!" and added, looking at my bundle: "Did they give you back the bread for those eight days?" He was indignant when I told him that after my hunger strike the pile of untouched bread from my cell had been sent back to the bread store, on Samsonov's express orders. Dimka did not once ask me why I had moved into the mortuary; he had already guessed it all with that sixth sense which allows veteran prisoners to read everything in the faces of their companions.

Near Dimka's bunk I found M., the Polish engineer, who had visited us in hospital twice, but had avoided mentioning the hunger strike. Thanks to his tact the whole business was passing into oblivion, giving every one of us six Poles an equal share of hope. His silence, his forbearance to ask questions and require explanations, was a sincere, convincing gesture of solidarity. M. was also a new arrival at the mortuary, for until then, despite his inclusion in the weaklings' category, he had been allowed to go on living in one of the general barracks. He was lying on an upper bunk, and I recognized him from a distance by his long legs, wrapped in rags and hanging out beyond its edge. When I shook his leg he awoke from his dreams, or possibly his prayers, and made room for me on the bunk. There I stayed, sleeping and living on three narrow planks, since my neighbor on my right, the school teacher from Novosybirsk who had once worked in the bathhouse, refused to give up another inch of space for me.

About midday Sadovski came back to the mortuary from the zone. They had already told me that he went out every day, morning and evening, to beg for soup by the kitchen. He always returned with an empty can, though not necessarily with an empty stomach, for he had reached that stage of hunger when he could not even wait until he had carried the soup back to the barrack, but gulped it down where he stood, rapidly and burning his lips. In his rare moments of sanity Sadovski's stories and his conversation were lively and interesting as before, but there were whole days when he seemed to notice nothing, and sat immovable on a bench at the table or by the fire, staring at one point with a fanatic stubbornness, crouching back as if ready to jump at the throat of anyone who interfered with him; from this demented reverie he was roused only at meal times by the tinkling of mess-cans outside. A silent but nonetheless passionate rivalry had developed between him and Dimka, for both had the reputation of being the most successful beggars at the kitchen and they must frequently have got in each other's way. Dimka treated Sadovski with unconcealed dislike, occasionally, without reason, justifying it by political arguments. But Sadovski, the old Bolshevik, had long ago given up the brilliant displays of dialectic reasoning which had sometimes led him to logical self-annihilation, and if he talked at all it was only to recall the past. After my arrival at the mortuary relations between them improved considerably, so much so that in the evenings the three of us, together with M., would often sit down at the table to play draughts or talk. But I never saw them talking to each other when alone, and they never went out to the kitchen with the other inhabitants of the mortuary.

The interior of the mortuary differed in its appearance from all other barracks. About a hundred and fifty of us lived in there. The first, and to some extent accurate, impression was that of a hostel for tramps and beggars. In the daytime some of the prisoners went out into the zone to look for food or to do the light work assigned to them, while the rest lay on their bunks talking in whispers, darning clothes, playing cards or writing letters. The most striking thing about the mortuary was the silence. No one commanded or enjoined it, but it was observed as strictly as if it had been enforced with regulations. We talked only in whispers, and then politely, with that typical guilty courtesy and consideration for others which is at once noticed in hospitals for the incurably sick. But for the fact that most of its inmates were no longer capable of controlling their natural functions, the mortuary could also have passed for the cleanest and tidiest barrack in the whole camp. We did not have our own orderly, but every day a different prisoner scrubbed the floor, washed down the tables and benches, wiped the windowpanes with a wet rag, lit the fire, and brought in the water. Pictures cut out of newspapers and family photographs in tin frames, decorated with a faded field flower, were pinned to the walls over some bunks. The room was bright, in good repair, with spaces between the bunks at every tenth sleeping-place. Frequently, after breakfast, arguments broke out between prisoners who each wanted to do the day's cleaning, for time hung on our hands dreadfully, and seemed to be seeping slowly away from us with our lives. Only towards evening, when the prisoners from the weaklings' brigade returned with news and gossip from the zone, and the electric lights went on, the mortuary came to life for a time with quite unsuspected reserves of energy. The very sight of prisoners playing draughts round the table or gathering in groups in the spaces between bunks was encouraging and comforting. Heat filled the barrack, opening the sores on our legs, opening too our hearts and our mouths. The bulbs shone above us, handfuls of light thrown at the frosted white tiles of windowpanes. Voices were raised above a whisper, laughter was heard, and even the tentative harmonies of mouth organs circled in the air, fluttering like moths in the bright circles of light. After nightfall the mortuary was silent again, but its accumulated suffering burst out with screams and babblings more piercing and more desperate than in any other barrack. The atmosphere was a stifling compound of exhaled breath, feverish sleep, and fetid excrements.

But the peaceful illusion of normality was a mask which hid a brutal reality, seen and recognized only after a longer stay in the mortuary. Even the beggars and tramps of a prison camp had evolved a code of existence, a set of rules of behavior which were themselves a caricature of the laws governing the lives of ordinary prisoners. For instance, in other barracks universal envy and greed were checked by the fact that everyone ate only as much he had earned by his work; mutual hatred was forgotten in common work and the consciousness of a common fate; even despair was sometimes drowned by fatigue. But in the mortuary, where time dragged unbearably slowly, all these emotions were given full rein, and in the emptiness of an aimless life without hope the barrack became charged with an atmosphere of malice and hatred which grew in intensity like a flooding river behind the dam of artificial courtesy, almost, but never quite, sweeping it completely away. Sitting on those bunks in rotting clothes, with unshaven faces and dangling, swollen legs, the prisoners watched each other with suspicion, followed each other's every movement, wanted to know everything about each other. Those who were dying could not avoid the unspoken question "When?" reflected in the eyes of their companions; those who were returning to life bragged cruelly of their health. Expiring human emotions revealed themselves here in their primordial form, distorted and deformed but horribly vivid. One evening when I came into the barrack I found the Novosybirsk schoolteacher mercilessly tormenting two incurables, both in the last stages of pellagra. Once, for a pinch of tobacco, he used to tell us about the naked women he saw in the bathhouse; now he was leaning back against a vertical beam, with his hands in his pockets and a cigarette-end in the corner of his mouth, and shouting at the incurables in his squeaky voice, encouraged by laughter from the neighboring bunks: "That's what women are—legs, thighs, breasts! It's no good even dreaming about it, brothers, you're no good for that sort of thing any more." Without even noticing it myself I was also beginning to accept and obey the cruel unwritten code of mortuary behavior. I shall never forget the day when I was fortunate enough to be taken on to help in the kitchen for a few hours. I was forbidden to take food out from the kitchen and into the zone with me; but in the evening, when I had scrubbed all the cauldrons clean, and had eaten my fill in there, I suddenly saw, behind the frozen window-pane, Dimka's face, then Sadovski's, and two hands holding out empty mess-cans through the serving hatch under the window-pane. One of the cooks walked up to the window and suddenly slammed the hatch-cover down over the opening; the begging hands jerked with a spasm of pain, but rapidly withdrew outside without dropping their cans. I looked at the wretches on the other side of the glass with disgust, with loathing, although not long before I myself had started to come out in the evenings to beg for dregs of soup at the kitchen. It is a mistake to suppose that only a beggar who has broken away from it can understand the misery and suffering of his former companions. On the contrary, nothing repels a man so much and rouses him to rebellion as the picture of his own human condition carried to the lowest extreme of degradation, suddenly brought before his eyes.

Nevertheless the mortuary gave prisoners who had known each other previously in the zone better opportunities for closer friendship. For over a year my relations with Dimka had been those of father and son, but it was only during our long conversations in the mortuary that I found out something about his old life. When the Revolution broke out, he was a very young priest in Verkhoyansk; they left him alone during the first few years, but then he himself rebelled, threw off his cassock, and became a notary's clerk. About 1930 he married and went to the south of Russia, where he found work as a manual laborer. He worked hard, having in his own fashion become reconciled to communism, and forgot the past almost completely. He was the only man that I met in the whole camp who had wiped out thirty years from his memory so thoroughly that he seemed to grope with difficulty among the indistinct and vague recollections of his youth. The renunciation of his priestly calling in 1925 was the "second birth" to which he owed his youthfulness, but at the same time he had the mature wisdom of an old man which was rooted in a dim and already nonexistent past. He was a strange combination of two personalities, and he himself often did not know which was the genuine one. From his youth he retained an understanding, sympathetic, instinctively religious attitude to human suffering, but whenever he became conscious of this, his fear expressed itself by a cynical scoffing at every kind of faith. The most important thing for him—and this was the echo of a young man, deformed by a premature struggle with life—was to eat and sleep as much as possible, to "take good care of yourself," as he would say. But like most atheists, he did not even suspect that his great gesture of religious rebellion was fundamentally more Christian than a thousand miraculous conversions. One evening I asked him when he had definitely stopped believing in God, and he told me that it was in 1937, when he had chopped off his foot with an axe in Yercevo forest, in order to go to the hospital and save his faith in his own will, faith in himself, faith in man. In this respect he was the very antithesis of Sadovski, who until his last conscious moment in the mortuary retained his deep contempt for the human personality and his faith in an abstract philosophical system devised by the human brain. Dimka was arrested in 1936 for the crime of "priesthood" which he himself had forgotten, and belonged to the almost extinct "old guard" of the Kargopol pioneers. His wife and his two children were arrested with him and transported to Central Asia. For five years he had heard nothing of them, and, what is stranger, did not want to know anything of them.

A completely different type was M., who had the appearance and the bearing of an aristocrat even in his prison rags. Very tall and slim, with a well-bred, narrow face, and deep-set eyes which expressed sadness and pride at the same time, he moved about the barrack slowly and meditatively and did not speak to anyone there. The prisoners disliked yet respected him. He was able to remain aloof from them without offending or hurting anyone, though he did not avoid the discussion of any question which had some lasting importance. Anyone who did not know him better might have laughed at his comic aspect: incredibly long legs and arms seemed to trail behind him like those of a broken puppet, and from his eyes and nose thin streams issued and ran down his haggard face towards his mouth. Heart disease was not his only affliction; more painful were the frequent migraines connected with disturbances of the brain, when he sat over the table, supporting his head with his hands, his eyes convulsively closed, as if he was trying desperately to fall asleep. Sometimes it happened that he would suddenly stop by the bunks, lean back against a beam, close his eyes, and put his hand to his forehead; then I knew that he was preparing to resist another attack. He also suffered from bad circulation, and it was pathetic to see him trying vainly to warm his limbs by the fire, crouching over it like his own shadow. But I never heard a word of complaint from his lips, and he did not allow hunger to dominate and distort his actions. He was hungry—we knew that well enough—but he ate what was given to him with dignity and calmness. His only passion, of which he could not cure himself until the end, was tobacco. Sometimes, having first looked all around, he would pick up a cigarette-end and hide it quickly in his pocket; I knew, too, that every other day he cut off half his starvation ration of bread to sell in the zone for a little tobacco. In one sense it was smoking that finished him, for he owed his prolonged detention in the camp, after the amnesty, to a denunciation by the camp official whom he had frequently visited for a cigarette and a chat. His political opinions were conservative, but he was interested deeply in only three things: God, Poland, and his wife. He had been arrested by the Russians on September 20th, 1939, three days after their entry into Poland, in one of the eastern regions where he had been working as a high official of the Ministry of Agriculture. He was sentenced first to death, then to ten years' hard labor. While he was in prison in Baranoviche he learnt that his wife had been sent into the depths of Russia, and when, in the camp, he was at last allowed to write her a monthly letter, all his attempts to contact her proved unsuccessful. His frightful headaches were, I am sure, largely caused by the effort of concentration with which, in moments of solitude and loneliness, he recalled to his memory one image to the exclusion of all others—that of his wife. At night—I slept next to him on the bunk—he found full consolation in prayer. I have never in my life heard a man pray more beautifully than M. Sitting up on the bunk, his face hidden in his hand, he pronounced the words of prayer in a whisper so moving, so pregnant with tears and pain, that he might have been prostrated at the foot of the Cross in a trance of adoration for Him whose martyred body had never broken out with a word of complaint.... "Who are you praying for so hard?" I once asked him when I could not sleep. "For all mankind," he answered calmly. "Even for those who are keeping us here?" He thought for a while, and then replied: "No, those are not men."

So in the evening we would sit down at one table, Dimka, Sadovski, M., and myself. Dimka enjoyed a game of draughts, and I played with him even though the monotony of the moves wearied me. Sadovski and M. cautiously discussed the latest developments at the front and watched our game. Sadovski, himself a Pole by origin (he had been born in Poland, and taken to Russia by his parents before the 1917 Revolution), hated M. for his inherent "lordliness" and his religious fervor. Dimka also mistrusted M., and yet we formed the closest and most friendly group in the whole mortuary. Sometimes, when the light came on in the barrack and we left the bunks for the table, the empty place in our corner looked like a painful gap in a row of teeth.

Just before Christmas all of us six Poles were given to read and acknowledge by signature a short verdict: "Detained in the camp by order of the Special Council of the NKVD in Moscow." This decision violently cut short our hopeful expectations of the future. I began to look at the mortuary in a different light, for it seemed that I would have to make my home there for a long time, if not for the rest of my days.

Christmas was celebrated in the camp unofficially and surreptitiously. All religious holidays and festivals have been scrupulously abolished and erased from the Soviet calendar, and replaced with historical anniversaries connected with the October Revolution and with the lives of Communist heroes; at liberty in Russia Sunday was an ordinary working-day, followed by the official "day off" on Monday. Among younger prisoners, brought up in the Bolshevik mentality, there were some who did not even know the Christian traditions underlying the divisions of the week and the annual festivals. But older prisoners preserved the old calendar in their hearts and memories, carrying out its injunctions humbly and in secret. During my first Christmas in Yercevo, in 1940, I was struck by the festive appearance of the barrack on Christmas Eve, and the large number of prisoners whose eyes were reddened by weeping. "All the best to you," they would say, shaking my hand, "for the next year—at liberty." That was all. But anyone who knows a Russian prison camp will understand how much this meant. In Russia the name of liberty is not taken in vain.

In 1941 we, i.e. the six Poles left in Yercevo, decided to celebrate Christmas together because the feeling of utter despair with which we greeted it was a common bond between us. The other four came to the mortuary in the evening, and before we broke the piece of bread which had been saved for this occasion, Miss Z. gave to each of us a handkerchief which she had embroidered with a Polish eagle, a fir branch, the date, and a monogram. It was impossible to guess how she had got hold of the thread and the thin linen to make them, and difficult to believe that despite her heavy work at the saw-mill she had devoted at least five evenings to sewing them. Timidly and happily we handled these gifts (I have kept mine to this day), and thanks to them we were able for a moment to forget that our whole Christmas dinner was to consist of a piece of bread and a mugful of hot water. The sight of that small group of people, sitting round an empty table and crying with longing for their distant country, must have commanded the unwilling respect of the mortuary's other inhabitants, who watched us from their bunks with gravity, while Dimka and Sadovski quickly went out into the zone. Late in the evening our conversation became more animated, and to this day I can remember the story of B., who, as a former officer of reserve of the Polish army, was arrested in his barrack in Yercevo on the day after the outbreak of the Russo-German war and detained in the central prison. B. started talking unwillingly (most prisoners are superstitiously afraid of recalling their prison hearings and the whole period between their arrest and the passing of sentence), but as he continued he talked faster and eagerly, as if this revelation of events usually shrouded in mystery among prisoners was giving him relief. When he had finished the mortuary was already plunged in sleep.

This I Cannot Forget

Anna Larina

ANNA LARINA (1914–96) *was the wife of Nikolai Bukharin, a major defendant and victim in the show trials of the 1930s who was executed in 1938. She was a young, largely apolitical woman who had the misfortune of being married to one of the original revolutionaries and a member of the ruling elite whom Stalin decided to discredit and liquidate. Stalin also harbored an intense personal dislike of Bukharin on account of the latter's intellectual superiority.*

These excerpts from Larina's book shed light on the treatment of the family members of prominent political prisoners, as well as the character of the show trials and Stalin's role in them; her recollections further illuminate Stalin's personality and legendary duplicity.

Larina was imprisoned solely on account of having been Bukharin's wife. It was the policy of the Soviet regime (a policy adopted later by other Communist systems) to arrest as a matter of course all close relatives of individuals accused of serious crimes against the state. As Larina testifies, this included the wives of old revolutionaries, high-ranking military officers, and collective farm chairmen, and even those of NKVD (political police) personnel.

It was a peculiarity of Communist systems to accuse many of their most dedicated supporters, including some of their founders, of implausible conspiracies. Family members were guilty by association, tainted by kinship ties. Bukharin was "supposedly guilty of spying and wrecking; the attempted dismemberment of the USSR; the organization of kulak [more prosperous peasant] uprisings; conspiratorial ties with German fascists . . . the murder of Kirov . . . and even an attempt to poison Nikolai Yezhov," among other things. Like the vast majority of such defendants, he confessed most of the imaginary crimes of which he was accused. (How such confessions were extracted from prominent political prisoners and their trials prepared is discussed in the readings by Beck and Godin, Arthur London, Eugene Loebl, Paul Ignotus, Lena Constante, and others.)

From *Anna Larina*, This I Cannot Forget: The Memoirs of Nikolai Bukharin's Widow, *trans. Gary Kern, © 1993 by Anna Larina. Russian edition © 1988, 1989 by Anna Larina. Used by permission of W. W. Norton & Company, Inc.*

It was another characteristic of Soviet repression directed at former high-ranking officials (such as Bukharin) that their arrest was preceded by gradually mounting criticism of their views or activities, demotion, and finally public denunciation (usually in the press), followed by arrest and culminating in a didactic trial. (In Hungary, such trials were called "conceptual," since they were intended to illustrate particular political propositions.)

The major stimulant of these trials was Stalin's determination to discredit and annihilate all potential competitors for power; the alleged conspirators were also accused of sabotage and blamed for prevailing economic problems and scarcities.

．　．　．　．　．

Who jealously conceals the past can hardly be on good terms with the future. . . .
Aleksandr Tvardovsky

In December 1938, I was returning to an "investigative prison" in Moscow following a year and a half of arrests and imprisonments. First came exile in Astrakhan, then arrest and imprisonment there; next, I was sent to a camp in Tomsk for family members of so-called enemies of the people; on the way, I was held in transit cells in Saratov and Sverdlovsk; after several months in Tomsk, I was arrested a second time and sent to an isolation prison in Novosibirsk; from Novosibirsk, I was transferred to a prison near Kemerovo, where after three months I was taken out and put on the train for Moscow.

At this time, the wives of many major military and political figures were being recalled from the camps and prisons and returned to Moscow. The purpose was not to lighten their sentence but, on the contrary, to lengthen it—or even to dispose of the ones who had witnessed real crimes, in contrast to the false crimes attached to them. Among the women I chanced to meet in these years were the wives of three generals—Yan Gamarnik, Mikhail Tukhachevsky, and Iyeronim Uborevich—as well as Lyudmila Shaposhnikova, wife of Mikhail Chidov, second secretary of the Leningrad District Party Committee, who had worked under Sergei Kirov.

．　．　．　．　．

The Tomsk Camp, December 1937–March 1938

I spent only a few months in the Tomsk camp, but it was there I had to endure from afar my husband's ordeal—the infamous "Bukharin trial"—and his execution. There, too, I began to feel sharply the tragedy of that time and came to perceive it, quite apart from the horrors I personally experienced, as the tragedy of the entire Soviet nation. In our camp alone, there were some four thousand wives of the men now known as traitors to the motherland. Far from being unique, the Tomsk camp of confinement was one of many.

The only males there were the prison guards in their black overcoats, counting and recounting us every morning, and a latrine cleaner, Uncle Kaka—so dubbed by Yura, a two-year-old boy confined to the camp with his mother.

We wives were quite diverse in terms of moral and intellectual qualities, as well as the levels of our husbands' former positions and political careers, but a common denominator had marked us out for this camp. Among us were the wives of such old revolutionaries as Aleksandr Shlyapnikov and Béla Kun, the wives of such military men as Iona Yakir and his younger brother (both shot), the wives of the directors of the Party and the soviets in the union republics, the wives of collective farm chairmen and of ordinary collective farm workers, the wives of the chairmen of village soviets and of NKVD personnel from Genrikh Yagoda's tenure as chief, as well as the sisters of Tukhachevsky. In common, we were all confined for our associations with "enemies of the people," though not one of our husbands or brothers had ever been any such thing. Each of us was officially labeled a *chesir*, or "family member of a traitor to the motherland."

In the mind of the camp command, I suppose, most of us *chesirs* had a kind of abstract "enemy" quality, because they themselves had no idea what was actually going on in the country. They merely saw a continuing flow of transports of prisoners, one after the other. The people had become their own enemy.

And when the command—for the most part, a drab, poorly educated lot—encountered the wives of their famous former leaders, they felt they were dealing with special enemies. One incident proving this is burned into my memory. On my second day in camp, our jailers made the "ordinary" *chesirs* form a circle in front of the barracks and put me and Yakir's wife, Sarra Lazarevna, in the center. A red-cheeked commandant who had come from the Gulag administration shouted at the top of his voice:

"See these women? They're the wives of the most vicious enemies of the people. They helped our enemies in their traitorous acts, yet here, just look at them, they still turn up their noses. Nothing pleases them, nothing seems right to *them*."

It would have been odd to be "pleased" at being confined in a camp, but in fact, we had not had time to turn up our noses and were even relatively happy. After a long, tormenting forced journey that included stops at transit prisons, we had finally (or so we thought) reached our destinations, and no physical labor was required of us at the Tomsk camp.

Having shouted out these terrible words with great passion, the hardy, self-satisfied officer headed for the prison gates. Horrified, the convicts began to disperse. Although some began to shy away from Sarra Lazarevna and me, most were disgusted with this performance. We ourselves were in shock. It felt as if we had run the gauntlet. Unable to move, we stood stock still in the bitter frost until someone led us back into the barracks, to our cold corner by a window encrusted with snow. Around the walls, the two levels of bed boards were completely packed with women. The previous night had been real torture. No one could find a comfortable position. Almost every woman lay on her side, and when someone wanted to shift her position, she had to wake her neighbor so that they could turn over together, thus initiating a chain reaction of awakenings down the line.

Now the barracks was like a cracked beehive. Everyone was buzzing about what had happened. Some got nasty: "The Bukharins and Yakirs have messed everything up, and now we and our husbands must suffer because of them." But the rest cursed the Gulag commandant, and many advised us to write a complaint to Moscow. Of course, Sarra Lazarevna and I understood that this would be pointless. That night, we sat on the edge of the plank bed, wide awake. Our places filled instantly with sleeping bodies, but neither of us felt like sleeping, or even living, at that moment. We conversed softly amid the sweet snoring of slumbering women.

General Yakir had been shot on June 11, 1937. On September 20, his wife and fourteen-year-old son were arrested in Astrakhan, where they had been living in exile. (I had been arrested in Astrakhan on the same day.) Even before this latest disaster befell her, Sarra Lazarevna Yakir had been barely hanging on to life.

Now it was December. I had yet to endure the execution of my husband and awaited it with foreboding and in ignorance. No correspondence was allowed. (Later, we would be permitted to write a single, solitary letter to ask for warm things and inform the recipient that we could receive packages of food once a month. We would not even be permitted to write a letter confirming the receipt of such packages.) Toward morning, Sarra Lazarevna and I woke up our neighbors so that they would make room for us, but no sooner did we finally drop off to sleep than it was time for the morning count.

We lined up in a row, and the duty officer, a young lad, began the roll call: "Las' name, firs', middle, year of birth, article, term. . . . Las' name, firs', middle, year of birth, article, term. . . ."

Obediently, the women gave their name and date of birth. For the article under which they had been sentenced and the term of imprisonment, they recited like this:

"*Chesir*. . . eight years."

"*Chesir*. . . eight years." (Now and then, only "five years.")

Chesir sounded less derogatory than "family member of a traitor to the motherland." And for the few among us who had little schooling, it meant nothing at all. They had trouble memorizing the full phrase for their official stigma.

When he came up to me, the duty officer shouted out with special emphasis, "Aha! Las' name?"

"Larina," I answered. Only that name was written on my documents, but, though I did not know it yet, both Larina and Bukharina were set down as surnames in my dossier. For some reason, no one had ever asked my surname during transport. Here, my married name had apparently been entered on the roll.

"Larina!" he screamed. "What, keeping your spy name silent?"

It was not hard to guess his meaning, so I answered, "Bukharina. Only if it's a spy name, then your name is Chinese."

Everyone froze in fear. Sarra Lazarevna, standing beside me, poked me in the side.

"Want to go to the cooler, do you? To the cooler? You haven't been yet, but you'll go."

I was not sent to the cooler, but you can see how I spent my first days in the Tomsk camp.

That morning, Sarra Lazarevna and I left the stuffy barracks and walked through the compound for fresh air and distraction from our thoughts. In the frosty haze, we could see the Siberian sun shining blood-red. ("A sun fit for war," said the women.) It lightly tinted the snow, which was still free from footprints, virginally pure right up to the fence, since it was forbidden to walk there. At the corners of the fence, hastily thrown together with wooden beams, stood the watchtowers from which the guards (still called marksmen) followed our every movement. Should anyone edge just slightly toward the fence, there would be the cry "Halt! Who goes there?" For this reason, the path leading from the dismal barracks to the kitchen became our only thoroughfare. It was always packed with women, many of whose faces were stamped with suffering, confusion, and fright. In jest, we named this walkway after Leningrad's grand boulevard, Nevsky Prospekt (there were a lot of Leningraders among us), or "Main Street in a fit of panic." To keep from freezing, the crowds of unfortunates hurried along the Nevsky at a fast clip. Most of us were dressed in torn, quilted jackets and cold boots. Those arrested during the summer wrapped themselves in the cloth blankets of the camp, replacing their lightweight skirts and scarves.

Catching sight of me in the crowd, Lyudmila Kuzminichna Shaposhnikova called out from afar. A friend of my parents, she had known me since I was a child. Blond with greenish eyes and a winning, big-hearted smile, she had not lost her charm in the camp. Belying a pampered look, which concealed her already advanced years, Lyudmila Kuzminichna was strong-willed and faced her new misfortunes with equanimity. An old Party member, "risen from the ranks of the workers" (as we used to say back then), she had managed a perfume business in Leningrad. Once, together with Vyacheslav Molotov's wife, Polina Zhemchuzhina, she had gone to America and been received by President Franklin Roosevelt. Because few Russians traveled abroad in those years, this event stuck in my mind. Lyudmila Kuzminichna was a camp favorite. She naturally commanded authority among the *chesirs* and had been chosen for the most responsible post, that of running the kitchen.

She had a warning for me, "Be very careful . . . don't talk openly about what goes on in the camp . . . keep quiet about Nikolai Ivanovich. The situation here is rotten, as you saw for yourself with that Gulag officer yesterday. The spy network is well developed. A lot of low-life women will try to win their freedom by getting you to talk about dangerous subjects, and you can be dragged off to Section Three for interrogation. You have to be extra careful; this is a hard time. And you must survive! As for myself, my days are numbered. They won't let me live. . . ."

"What do you mean 'numbered'?" I naively objected. "You got eight years, just like the rest of us."

"There will be more. The eight years will be extended."

Shaposhnikova explained that she was being taken to interrogations in the camp and would most likely be sent back to Moscow. I could make no sense of this.

"But why?" I asked. "Why?"

"I know a lot, that's why."

As she spoke, she glanced around to see if anyone was nearby, but we were alone.

"A Leningrader," I thought, "close to people who worked with Sergei Kirov. She herself says she knows a lot. How do the closest comrades of Kirov explain his assassination?"

I couldn't miss a chance like this.

"Lyudmila Kuzminichna! What actually happened to Sergei Mironovich? What do you know about it? They must have talked with you about it there in Leningrad. How much do they really know?"

"Ah, so that's what you'd like to know!"

She looked at me for a long time, her face reddened, nervous, and distraught. Finally, she exclaimed, "What questions you put to me! Can one really talk about this?"

"I think we can, Lyudmila Kuzminichna. *We* can!"

"Yes, yes, I'm going to die anyway, but you must go on living. I'm not afraid for myself, but for you. However . . . can you keep as silent as the grave?"

Naturally, I insisted I could. She was persuaded.

"Zinoviev didn't need to get Kirov. This came down from the very top, on orders from the Boss. [That's exactly how she put it.] After Kirov was shot, many Leningraders understood this. Chudov did, too."

By this time, I already understood that Zinoviev had not needed Kirov's death, but a variety of scenarios still seemed possible to me. When Kirov was murdered, in December 1934, I was not able to think my way through to a conclusion. But after my arrest, while in the Astrakhan prison, I found myself entertaining the most terrible thoughts. Even so, now that my rising suspicions were confirmed, I could only gasp, "How horrible!"

"Horrible? And why is the murder of Kirov any more horrible than all the other murders? His was an easy death, murder from around the corner. Sergei Mironovich didn't die as an 'enemy of the people,' as a 'spy.' He suffered no tortures. Will the murder of Bukharin be any less horrible? Better not think about it.... You have a lot of horrible experiences ahead of you."

"But whom did the Boss rely on?"

"I won't tell you. Time will tell."

Having said this, Lyudmila Kuzminichna changed the subject, reminiscing about a summer we had spent together in Mukhalatka, in the Crimea—she with her husband, Mikhail Semyonovich Chudov, I with my father. To my surprise, she recalled some juvenile lines of verse I had written then for Chudov [whose name derived from the word for "wonder" or "miracle"]. He was a tall, powerful man with broad shoulders. At age fifteen, I facetiously called him Ilya Muromets, the great bogatyr (or hero) of the old Russian epics.

> What a miracle, what a miracle,
> To us has come Uncle Miraculous.
> Uncle is a worker of wonders,
> A Leningrader bogatyr.

"A bogatyr like that," Lyudmila Kuzminichna mused, "a bogatyr, and he was blown away like a piece of straw." Mikhail Semyonovich had been executed a few months before. She rubbed away a tear, and we parted quickly, before drawing too much attention from the other strollers on Nevsky Prospekt.

Shaposhnikova would indeed be sentenced a second time and shot....

·　·　·　·　·

How Stalin Toyed with Bukharin—The Bukharin Trial

If it is possible to rate life's experiences in order of difficulty, then without doubt the months of interrogation preceding my husband's arrest, more than the trial itself, were the most unbearable for me. At the time, early in 1937, my mind had not yet become accustomed to the horrendous accusations against him: plotting a "palace revolution," planning terror against Stalin (and against Lenin, too, back in 1918). Nor had I, or Bukharin either, adjusted to the inexplicable and terrible cross-examining of several defendants at once. I will never forget that February night when a snowstorm raged as I accompanied Bukharin, enfeebled by a hunger strike, to the Kremlin for the famous meeting of the Party's Central Committee, the February-March plenum of 1937. His trial there was the logical culmination of what had obviously begun for Nikolai Ivanovich back in August 1936, when his name was mentioned along with those of Tomsky, Rykov, Radek, and others at the trial of Zinoviev.

Today, we understand that, immediately after the death of Lenin, Stalin had begun preparing his traps very carefully, but in those days it would have been considered the wildest fantasy to imagine that differing ideological views within the Party would one day be represented as the acts of criminals and bandits. I say this even though the so-called Bukharinist Right Opposition had been routed after 1929 and Nikolai Ivanovich ceased to occupy a leading position in the Party, and even though he felt oppressed at always being in Stalin's sights and under his fire. For example, Stalin baited Bukharin by suggesting to him that his former young political protégés, who had been denigrated with the term *shkolka* and driven away, many to work outside Moscow, had turned into counterrevolutionaries. He also set the Press Department of the Central Committee against Bukharin, as well as the editor of *Pravda*, Lev Mekhlis, with whom Nikolai Ivanovich had frequent run-ins. After my husband was appointed chief editor of *Izvestiya*, in 1934, Stalin telephoned from time to time to hand down various directives. For example, Bukharin and Radek were ordered to write "destructing" articles ("destructing" is exactly how he put it) about the late Bolshevik historian and revolutionary Mikhail Pokrovsky.

Once, Stalin called Bukharin and chewed him out because the author of some article, gushing with praise, had written that Stalin's mother called him Soso [the Georgian equivalent of Joe or Joey].

"What's this 'Soso' business?" demanded the enraged Stalin. It was impossible to understand what had set him off. Was it the mention of his mother, to whom (as I had heard) he never paid the slightest attention, or did he believe that his mother, like everyone else, should call her son the "Father of All the Peoples" and the "Corypheus of Science"?

Yet, simultaneously, Stalin "petted" my husband. In the spring of 1935, at a banquet for graduates of the military academies, he gave this toast: "Let us drink, comrades, to Nikolai Ivanovich, and let bygones be bygones!" At a banquet for young officers, this was a toast not to a military leader but to the disgraced, but still beloved, Bukharin! The audience drank and burst into stormy applause, which swelled, as we are accustomed to say, into an ovation. Nikolai Ivanovich was completely taken by surprise. This was Stalin's way of testing the people's attitude. With him, everything was calculated, every step—no, every inch of every step. Of course, this is obvious *now*, but then no one, including my husband himself, suspected a thing. The toast was considered a sincere expression of Stalin's attitude toward Bukharin.

To take another example, Stalin phoned in the summer of 1934 to congratulate Nikolai Ivanovich on a speech about poetry he had given at the First Congress of Soviet Writers. Stalin was especially pleased by Bukharin's analysis that the poet Demyan Bedny was in danger of falling behind the times. Another time, Stalin phoned in the dead of night, waking us up. When I went to the telephone, I heard three words: "Stalin. Call Nikolai!" Nikolai Ivanovich said to me, "More trouble again," and uneasily took the receiver. But there was no trouble. Stalin, not sober, had called to wish us well on our marriage. "Nikolai, I congratulate you! You outspit me this time, too!" Nikolai Ivanovich did not ask about the phrase "this time, too," but did want to know how he had "outspit" Stalin, who replied, "A good wife, a beautiful wife, a young one . . . younger than my Nadya!" This is the way he talked, even though by then she was no longer among the living. After pranks of this kind, we had learned to expect trouble the next day. Nikolai Ivanovich became accustomed to this nerve-racking business, to a certain degree, and up until August 1936 was able to master it with his natural joie de vivre. But beginning at that point—that is, with the Zinoviev trial—the accusations against him became so terrible that his life-sustaining forces dried up before my very eyes.

I had been waiting for Bukharin's trial for a whole year, but I was sent to the camp before it began. I knew the sentence would be death; I prayed for the quickest possible end so that my husband's sufferings would be over. And I nourished the feeble hope that Nikolai Ivanovich would leave life proudly, declaring loudly (as he had at the February-March 1937 plenum), "No, no, no! I will not lie about myself!" This hope was born entirely of my great love for him.

But it was unfounded. I already understood very well that any of the accused brought to trial would confess to crimes they could not have committed.

Usually, we got no newspapers in camp, but in the first days of March 1938 a guard brought in papers reporting the trial of Bukharin and those charged with him. Giving me a mean, contemptuous look, he shouted, "Read, read who you are!" handed the papers to the barracks *starosta* [head woman], and left, slamming the door. The *starosta*, Zemskaya by name, always reminded me in both appearance and name of a snake [*zmeya*]. She was also, of course, someone's wife. In Leningrad, she had been a public prosecutor; in camp, she was an informer. She once caused me trouble by reporting that I had in my possession a book stamped "Library of N. I. Bukharin" with the very suspicious title *Dangerous Liaisons*. This was, of course, the lively and witty novel about high-society libertines written by Choderlos de Laclos, the eighteenth-century French author and political activist. An excellent edition of the Russian translation had been released in the early 1930s by Academia, the Soviet publishing house. I cannot recall now why I had that particular book with me. After Zemskaya snitched, my things were searched and this world-famous classic was confiscated and declared "counterrevolutionary."

Now, instead of passing out the newspapers to us prisoners, the *starosta* sat on the upper bed boards, right across from me, and read them aloud. When she read the prosecution's charges against Bukharin specifically, she sometimes broke off and glanced in my direction so that she could later report my reactions. She had complete coverage of the trial of the accused men, except for the newspaper reporting Nikolai Ivanovich's concluding statement. I was very interested to know whether this was mere coincidence or whether something was being withheld.

Before my husband's trial, I thought I had more or less prepared myself psychologically for it by reading the initial evidence against him. The documents had been sent to him before his arrest, when he was still under investigation. But the accusations leveled at the trial surpassed all expectations in vulgarity and monstrosity. In them, the criminal fantasies of Stalin (those reading the charges were his pawns) reached their apogee. The sheer mass of crimes alleged against Bukharin could not possibly have been committed by only one criminal in his entire lifetime—not just because one lifetime would have been insufficient, but because he would certainly have failed after the first few.

Nikolai Ivanovich was supposedly guilty of spying and wrecking; the attempted dismemberment of the USSR; the organization of kulak uprisings; conspiratorial ties with German fascists, as well as German and Japanese intelligence; terrorist hopes of murdering Stalin; the murder of Kirov; a terrorist act against Lenin in 1918, previously attributed solely to the Right Social Revolutionary Fanny Kaplan, but her hand now shown to be Bukharin's hand; the executions of the long ailing, nonfunctioning Vyacheslav Menzhinsky [nominal chief of the political police from 1926 to 1934], Valerian Kuibyshev [chief of the Party's Central Control Commission], and the writer Maxim Gorky; and even an attempt to poison Nikolai Yezhov [then chief of the NKVD]. As if to say, "Well, how could you fail to take care of an old pal?"

After the recitation of charges against all of the accused, Vasily Ulrikh, the chairman of the Military Collegium of the Supreme Court, asked whether or not they admitted their guilt. Only one, Nikolai Krestinsky, was able to declare, "I do not."

Tears shot from my eyes at these words. This was a moment of transcendence and pride in him. It seemed to me that I could actually see Krestinsky's kindly face with his myopic eyes peering through thick glasses. His denial of guilt would not endure. He was soon forced to "confess"—that is, to lie—but this moment put a considerable dent in the progress of the trial.

I had been sitting as the *starosta* began her reading, but finally, in order to avoid the stares of curious women, I lay down on the bed boards and pulled the cover over my head. Blood was flowing from my nose; I had a terrible headache. Sarra Yakir, inseparable from me, moistened a towel with cold water, put it under my nose, and said softly, "Deaden yourself, deaden yourself. You have to try not to notice anything. Follow my example. . . . I am already dead to everything!"

Suddenly, Zemskaya broke off her reading and shouted in a commanding voice, "Bukharina! Come here and wash the corridor! It's your turn today!"

In fact, it was not my turn; moreover, the *starosta* could see my condition. She knew I could not wash the corridor. She simply wanted to report my refusal, which would be added to my characterization as a counterrevolutionary.

113

Sarra spoke up. "Don't you worry, Zemskaya. I'll wash it for her."

And, though exhausted herself, she went off to wash the dirty and interminable corridor.

In my condition at that moment, in a barracks where no fewer than a hundred women fixed their stares upon me, and when I could not take a newspaper into my own hands and reflect upon what had just been read, could not make even the most elementary analysis of that squalid travesty of justice, all of the accused seemed to have the same face. Except for Krestinsky. In fact, in my imagination, Nikolai Ivanovich looked much more abject than when, many years later, I was able to read the account of the trial and his final words for myself. As the *starosta* read on, I even began to have doubts that the man in the dock was really Bukharin and not some stand-in made up to look like him. His admissions were so monstrous that if he had made them to me in private I would have thought him insane. Indeed, many people at the time did think that there were stand-ins at the trial, that this Bukharin was not Bukharin. But as the reading continued, my initial doubts rapidly dissolved. I knew Nikolai Ivanovich too well not to recognize his style and character. Besides, using imposters would have been too crude and risky a subterfuge in general, and with Bukharin in particular. Indeed, the very events of the trial, which included an altercation with the chief prosecutor, Andrei Vyshinsky, made the supposition of a stand-in untenable.

Many years afterward, when I had returned to Moscow, the writer Ilya Ehrenburg confirmed that it was definitely Nikolai Ivanovich in the dock. He told me that he had attended one of the court sessions and sat near the accused men. At certain intervals, he recalled, a bailiff would come over to Bukharin and lead him out, then bring him back a few minutes later. No one else was taken out like this. Ehrenburg suspected that Nikolai Ivanovich was being given injections to weaken his will-power.

"Maybe," he said, "it was because they feared him more than the rest."

Ehrenburg had been given his ticket to the trial by the satirist Mikhail Koltsov, editor of the satiric paper *Krokodil.* "Go, Ilya Grigoriyevich, and take a look at your buddy!" he had said in a hostile tone. But Koltsov, too, would suffer Bukharin's fate. . . .

· · · · ·

The Last Good-bye and the First Search

The fateful day of February 27 arrived. Stalin's secretary Poskryobyshev telephoned that evening and informed Nikolai Ivanovich he was required to appear before the plenum.

We began to say farewell.

Ivan Gavrilovich was in terrible condition. Debilitated by suffering for his son, the old man lay in bed most of the time. At the moment of parting, he began to have spasms, his legs involuntarily jerking up, then falling back to the bed, his hands shaking, his face turning blue. He looked as if he were about to give up the ghost. But the trembling subsided, and he once again asked his son in a weak voice:

"What's going on, Nikolai, what's going on? Explain it!"

Before Nikolai Ivanovich could respond, the telephone rang again.

"You're holding up the plenum," Poskryobyshev snapped, executing his master's command. "They're waiting for you."

I cannot say that this caused Nikolai Ivanovich to hurry up very much. He found time to say good-bye to his first wife, Nadezhda Mikhailovna. Then it was my turn.

The tragic moment of our terrible separation, the pain that lives still in my heart to this very day: I cannot do them justice. Nikolai Ivanovich fell to his knees before me. With tears in his eyes, he begged forgiveness for my ruined life. He urged me to raise our son as a Bolshevik—"A Bolshevik without fail!" he said twice. He asked me to fight for his vindication and to remember every single word of his testimonial letter, then to deliver it to the Central Committee when the situation should change. "And it definitely will change," he said. "You're young, and you'll live to see it. Swear that you will do this!" I swore.

He got up from the floor, embraced me, kissed me, and said finally, with great emotion, "See that you don't get angry, Anyutka. There are irritating misprints in history, but the truth will triumph!"

A nervous chill went through my body, and I felt my lips trembling. We understood that we were parting forever.

Nikolai Ivanovich put on his leather jacket, his hat with ear flaps, and turned to the door.

"See that you don't lie about yourself, Nikolai!"

That was all I could say in farewell.

Having seen my husband off to "purgatory," I hardly had time to lie down before they came for the search. Now there was no doubt. Nikolai Ivanovich had been arrested.

A whole squad came, a dozen or so persons, including a doctor wearing a white smock over his NKVD uniform. A search with a physician in attendance! An unprecedented event! Just see how humane they are!

The leader of the search party was Boris Berman, chief of the NKVD Investigative Department. He would be shot later. He came to my search as if to a banquet, wearing a stylish black suit, white shirt, and a fine ring on his finger, and sporting an elongated little fingernail. His smug expression revolted me. The instant he entered my room, he asked, "Any weapons?"

"Yes," I replied and gestured toward the drawer of the nightstand. I wanted him to retrieve the revolver with the inscription "To the Leader of the Proletarian Revolution from Klim Voroshilov."

Berman suddenly seized me by the hand in an overbearing manner, exactly as if stopping me from grabbing the gun to shoot him. Then he took the revolver from the drawer, read the inscription, and smirked, evidently because he had found an unexpected trophy for the Boss.

"Any more?"

"Yes."

There was a German hunting rifle that Rykov had brought back from Berlin as a gift for Nikolai Ivanovich.

Then Berman wanted to know where Bukharin's archive was kept. I asked for clarification: What exactly did he mean by "archive"? Absolutely everything, it turned out. To reach the study, we had to pass through Ivan Gavrilovich's room; there, the physician was sitting beside the old man. In the study, I found a crowd of men and two women, all hard at work. From the safe, they pulled out the minutes of Politburo sessions and the stenographic records of Central Committee plenums; they were emptying out all of the drawers of the desk, as well as the cabinets that held documents related to Bukharin's many years of work at *Pravda*, *Izvestiya*, the Comintern, and the Scientific Research Center. They were also clearing out all of his publications: books, pamphlets, speeches. Meanwhile, from the room where we had spent the last, tortured months together, they took the folder with Lenin's letters and the rough draft of the Party program (the proposal passed at the Eighth Party Congress, in 1919). In one desk drawer, they discovered several letters Nikolai Ivanovich had written me in my childhood, mostly descriptions of nature, and the handwritten manuscript and typed copy of his poem in memoriam of Sergo Ordzhonikidze. These letters and manuscripts were seized, too, despite my protests to Berman that they were "documents unrelated to the investigation." (But, then, what could actually be related to such a scandalous "investigation"?) In fact, everything was cleared out, down to the last scrap. It was all heaped into a huge pile in the study, a mountain of paper that was then labeled "the archive." Like barbarians, the search party destroyed Nikolai Ivanovich's honest and energetic life's work, in order to wipe the true portrait of Bukharin from the face of the earth and replace it with the defiled one to be presented at his trial (if not quite as besmirched as Stalin and his sycophants would like). Then a truck pulled up to the back door. As I watched from the kitchen window, they filled it to overflowing and drove away, evidently to the NKVD.

But Berman remained behind with the two women and a few of the men. Then began the demeaning procedure of the personal search.

They lifted Ivan Gavrilovich up from his bed. Stunned and depressed, he stood shaking in agitation while they rummaged through his pockets and turned them all out on the bed. I did not see the search of Nadezhda Mikhailovna. They entered the baby's room, but Nanny Pasha was in a fighting mood and would not let them frisk her. She shoved one of the NKVD women aside and shrieked, "Get back! Get back! You won't find anything here, you shameless louts!" Yura slept on, undisturbed. When they tried to go to his bed, I determinedly blocked their path, but they did search his cradle.

I was spared a personal search since I was in my nightgown; in fact, I stayed in it to the end. But both my bed and Nikolai Ivanovich's were subjected to meticulous probing.

Going on midnight, I heard a sound in the kitchen and went to take a look. I was overwhelmed by the scene that greeted my eyes. It seems the "officials" had worked up a hunger and had fixed themselves a feast. Since there were too few places at the kitchen table, they were sitting on the floor. Newspaper was laid down as their tablecloth, and thereupon sat an enormous ham, and some sausage and eggs were being fried on our stove. In horror, I rushed back to my room. Immediately, I recalled a sentence I had recently memorized in Bukharin's testament: "At the present time, the so-called organs of the NKVD are in the main a degenerate organization of unprincipled, dissolute, well-kept functionaries." True, these are the people who execute these outrages, but who corrupted them? I could hear them laughing merrily in the kitchen.

Then Berman popped into my room to invite me to share their supper. "You're not eating anything, Anna Mikhailovna. Could it be that you've decided to follow Bukharin's example and announce a hunger strike?" he asked.

I boldly replied, "I'm not about to announce a hunger strike, but I won't eat at the same table with you or sit on the same floor."

Berman smiled ironically and informed me that he was leaving and that only the "worker lads" would remain.

I asked where I could find out about Nikolai Ivanovich. "From me," he answered readily and gave me his name (which I had not known until then) and telephone number.

Soon the "worker lads," having eaten their fill, began to sing. Ivan Gavrilovich's room was closest to the kitchen, and I wonder what he thought, hearing all this. Afraid that this merry group would awaken the baby, I went to the kitchen to quiet them down. These NKVD "officials" had no intention of apologizing but, to my delight, said that they were leaving, anyway. A hush fell over the apartment. Not everyone left, however; the women remained behind. They were under orders to turn the pages of all of the books in Bukharin's huge library in hopes of finding something compromising. This page turning lasted for days. Several times, I went into the immense somber room with arched ceilings and shelf after shelf of books that was the study, and there the women kept turning, turning, turning the pages of books. I cannot believe they were able to turn them all. When they left, they sealed the glass doors of the bookcases.

For several days afterward, I lay in bed like a dead person. This was the reaction that set in after such prolonged nervous tension. And for a long time, the imaginary rustle of turning pages tormented me.

Nadezhda Mikhailovna, wearing the medical corset without which she could not move from place to place, crawled into my room. Neither of us could realistically console the other as we shared our impressions of the search, made gloomy prognoses of the fate of Nikolai Ivanovich and Rykov, and, with pain in our hearts, watched over Yura. He crawled around the room looking for his father, calling out for him.

Eventually, though drained of energy and spirit by many months of torture, I tried to gather up my strength. I had to look after the baby, who had been deprived of a proper mother's care for half a year. And I had to work fast to learn what was happening to my husband before the *vertushka* telephone was disconnected. Berman's number could be dialed directly only from this device. A week after the arrest, I decided to phone.

A man's voice, which I recognized as his, answered, but when I identified myself, he said, "Berman is not at work." I began phoning daily. Coming to recognize my voice, the chief of the NKVD Investigative Department would not even bother to ask who was calling but immediately answer that he was not in. Eventually, I had enough of this and shouted, "Why are you lying? I recognize your voice!" Berman hung up immediately. But he phoned back the same day, undoubtedly after getting authorization from Yezhov. He read off a list of books Nikolai Ivanovich had requested from home, the German books of fascist ideology he had bought in Berlin in 1936. I was given permission to break the seal on the bookcase.

"Bring the books to Investigator Kogan," Berman said. "A pass will be ordered up for you."

Just as I was about to leave, Kolya Sozykin phoned and offered to go along with me. On the way, he bought some oranges for Nikolai Ivanovich, perhaps with funds appropriated for this purpose by the NKVD. He left me at the entrance to the famous building on Lubyanka Square.

Investigator Kogan was sitting in a small but long and narrow room, more like a coffin than an office. He greeted me with conspicuous civility.

"Well now, Anna Mikhailovna, just last evening I had a chat with Nikolai Ivanovich in this room. He has a sweet tooth, your husband. When we had tea, he took six lumps of sugar in his glass."

"That's funny. He never did that at home. Evidently, he has developed a longing for sweets because of his bitter life."

I handed over the oranges and the books.

"What do you mean, a bitter life? We treat Nikolai Ivanovich well, so there's no need for you to bring oranges. Better to give them to the child."

But I did not take them back.

Kogan handed me a little note written in Nikolai Ivanovich's hand:

"Don't worry about me. They are looking after me, and watching after me, in every way. Write how you are there. How is the boy? Take some photographs of yourself with Yura and send them to me. Your Nikolai."

"Exactly as if Nikolai Ivanovich were in a sanatorium here," I ventured timidly, so struck was I by the phrase "looking after me, and watching after me."

"He even has the opportunity to work," said Kogan, holding out to me a manuscript page from a chapter of Bukharin's book *The Degradation of Culture under Fascism*.

Noting the title, I remarked, "Doesn't it seem paradoxical to you that the fascist hireling Bukharin is writing an antifascist book?"

Kogan turned red. "That's not for you to decide! If you insist on discussing matters related to the investigation, today will be the last time we meet. If not, then I will permit you to call me from time to time, and to come here to find out how Nikolai Ivanovich is doing."

The investigator reminded me to answer my husband's note. I wrote briefly that we were all feeling "not bad," and said a thing or two about Yura. I promised to bring photographs. Kogan insisted that I add that we were still living in our apartment. I refused, since I could not divine the hidden significance of this, and told him that I was only waiting for the day when I could get out of the Kremlin.

I was still sitting down as we said good-bye; the investigator firmly pressed my hand. I glanced at his face and was surprised to see unspeakable remorse in his eyes.

I got up to leave.

"My telephone number, the telephone, Anna Mikhailovna, write it down!"

But he wrote it down himself on a little piece of paper. He asked me not to abuse the privilege, to call no sooner than two weeks from that day and be ready to bring along the photographs.

On that date exactly, with the photos in hand, I tried to contact Kogan. I was unsuccessful, and after many more telephone calls, his successor informed me, "Investigator Kogan has been sent on a long trip. There is no point in telephoning for him any more."

Anyone who survives from that time will recall what was meant by "a long trip." I was no longer permitted to telephone for information about Nikolai Ivanovich or to give him the photographs.

My Testimony

Anatoly Marchenko

ANATOLY MARCHENKO (1938–1986) was a Soviet worker from a poor working-class family who received eight years of schooling. He became radicalized by the mistreatment he received by the authorities for his involvement in a nonpolitical brawl (described in the beginning of the excerpt that follows). Subsequently, his failed attempt in 1960 to escape from the country led to a lengthy imprisonment, and his rebellious nature earned him special punishments. He was twenty-three when he was sentenced to six years for "high treason"—a charge attached to attempted illegal border crossings. There was no provision for appealing the sentence.

His account provides many details of prison camp conditions in the post-Stalin period, allowing us to note differences as well as similarities between the earlier and the later era. Under the successors of Stalin there was a semblance of legality; Marchenko was assigned a lawyer who actually tried to defend him, unlike earlier years, when the defense lawyer echoed the views of the prosecutor. Marchenko was defiant in court, unlike the compliant defendants of the Stalin era, who were softened up during long pretrial detention. But bureaucratic arbitrariness continued to determine the fate and daily living conditions of prisoners. The quality and quantity of food remained deplorable, and food rations were reduced when production norms were not met, just as in the old days. Chronic starvation was routine.

The conditions described here appear worse than those recorded in One Day in the Life of Ivan Denisovich *partly because Marchenko often faced special punitive treatment (see "The Cooler" and "Special Regime") because of his defiant behavior. Particularly chilling are the descriptions of self-mutilation and suicide attempts among the many prisoners seeking to escape the intolerable conditions. Self-mutilation, widely reported in the Gulag, appears to have been a peculiarity of Soviet camps. Prisoners displaying tattooed slogans denouncing the authorities or political leaders were also characteristic of the post-Stalin Soviet prison culture. Of further interest are Marchenko's unusual*

From Anatoly Marchenko, My Testimony *(New York: Dutton, 1969).*

observations about the attitudes and conduct of the guards and their firmly internalized obedience to authority.

Marchenko's main conclusion—one reached in other similar accounts—is that "it isn't too difficult . . . to reduce a man to the condition of a beast, to force him to forget his own human dignity. . . ." He died in prison.

. . . . .

The Beginning

My name is Anatoly Marchenko and I was born in the small Siberian town of Barabinsk. My father, Tikhon Akimovich Marchenko, worked his whole life as a fireman on the railway. My mother was a station cleaner. Both of them were totally illiterate and my mother's letters always had to be written by somebody else.

After eight years of schooling I quit school and went as a *Komsomol* volunteer to Novosibirsk to work on the hydroelectric power station there. This was the beginning of my independence. I was made a shift foreman with the drilling gang, traveled around to all the new power station sites in Siberia and worked in mines and on geological surveys. My last job was on the Karaganda power station.

It was there that I first fell foul of the law. We young workers lived in a hostel and went dancing at the club. In the same settlement lived some Chechens who had been exiled from the Caucasus. They were terribly embittered: after all, they'd been transported from their homes to this strange Siberia, among a strange and alien people. Between their young people and us constant brawls and punch-ups kept breaking out and sometimes there was a knife fight as well. One day there was a huge brawl in our hostel. When it had all died away of its own accord the police arrived, picked up everyone left in the hostel—the majority of those involved had already run away or gone into hiding—arrested them and put them on trial. I was one of the ones arrested, and they took us away from the settlement, where everyone knew what had happened. They sentenced us all in a single day, with no attempt at finding out who was guilty and who innocent. Thus it was that I found my way to the terrible camps of Karaganda.

After that the circumstances of my life turned out in such a way that I decided to escape abroad. I simply could see no other way out for me. I made my run together with a young fellow called Anatoly Budrovsky. We tried to cross the border into Iran, but were discovered and captured about fifty yards from the border.

That was on October 29, 1960. For five months I was kept under investigation at the special investigation prison of the Ashkhabad KGB. All that time I was kept in solitary confinement, with no parcels or packages and without a single line from my family. Every day I was interrogated by KGB investigator Sarafyan (and later Shchukin): *why did I want to run away?* The KGB had entered a charge of high treason against me and therefore the investigator was not very pleased with my answers. What he was after was to get the necessary evidence from me, wearing me down by interrogations, threatening that the investigation would go on until I had told them what was required of me, promising me that in return for "worthwhile" evidence and an admission of guilt, I would have my twice daily prison rations supplemented. Although he didn't get what he was after and got no material whatsoever to support the charges, either from me or from any of the forty witnesses, nevertheless I was tried for treason.

On March 2–3, 1961, our case came before The Supreme Court of the Soviet Socialist Republic of Turkmenia. It was a closed court: not a single person was present in that huge chamber, except for the court officials, two guards armed with tommy guns at our backs, and the guard commander at the main entrance. For two days they asked me the same questions as they had been putting during the investigation and I gave them the same answers, rejecting the charge. My fellow escapee, Anatoly Budrovsky, had evidently not been able to stand up to the interrogations and solitary confinement and had yielded under pressure from the investigator. He gave evidence against me, thus shielding and saving himself. The evidence of forty other people was in my favor. I asked why the court paid no attention to this and was told: "The court itself decides what evidence to believe."

Although I refused any defense, my lawyer attended the court and pleaded my case. He said that the court had no grounds for convicting me of high treason: no trust could be placed in the evidence of Budrovsky in that he was an interested party and was being tried in the same case. The court ought to take account of the evidence of the other witnesses. Marchenko could be convicted for illegally attempting to cross the border, but not for treason.

I refused to take up my right of having the last word: I did not consider myself guilty of treason and had nothing to add to my evidence.

On March 8 the court pronounced its sentence: Budrovsky got two years in the camps (this was even less than the maximum in such cases, which was three years) for illegally attempting to cross the border, while I was given six for high treason—this too being considerably less than the permitted maximum penalty—the firing squad.

I was then twenty-three.

Once more I was taken back to prison, to my cell. To tell the truth, the length of my sentence made no impression on me. It was only later that each year of imprisonment stretched out into days and hours and it seemed that six years would never come to an end. Much later I also found out that the label of "traitor to the Homeland" had crippled me not for six years but for life. At the time, however, I had only one sensation, and that was that an injustice had been committed, a legalized illegality, and that I was powerless; all I could do was to gather and store my outrage and despair inside me, storing it up until it exploded like an overheated boiler.

I recalled the empty rows of seats in the chamber, the indifferent voices of the judge and prosecutor, the court secretary chewing on a roll the whole time, the silent statues of the guards. Why hadn't they let anyone into the court, not even my mother? Why had no witnesses been called? Why wasn't I given a copy of the sentence? What did they mean: "You can't have a copy of the sentence, it's secret"? A few minutes later a blue paper was pushed through the little trapdoor for food: "Sign this to say that you've been informed of your sentence." I signed it and that was that. *The sentence was final, with no right of appeal.*

I went on hunger strike. I wrote a statement protesting against the trial and sentence, pushed it through the food trap and refused to accept any food. For several days I took nothing into my mouth but cold water. Nobody paid any attention. The warders, after listening to my refusal, would calmly remove my portion of food and soup bowl and bring them back again in the evening. Again I would refuse. Three days later the warders entered my cell with a doctor and commenced the operation known as "forced artificial feeding." My hands were twisted behind my back and handcuffed, then they stuffed a spreader into my mouth, stuck a hose down my gullet and began pouring the feeding mixture— something greasy and sweet—in through a funnel at the top. The warders said: "Call off your hunger strike. You won't gain anything by it and in any case we won't let you lose weight." The same procedure was repeated on the following day.

I called off my hunger strike. And I never did get a reply to my protest.

Several days later a warder came to fetch me. He led me via a staircase and various corridors to the first floor and directed me through a door lined with black oilcloth. A little nameplate said: "Prison Governor." In the office inside sat the prison governor at his desk, beneath a large portrait of Dzerzhinsky;[1] on the couch were two men familiar to me from the investigation of my case, the legal inspector of prisons and the head of the investigation department. The fourth man was a stranger. One glance at him and I shuddered, so unnatural and repulsive was his appearance: a tiny little egg-shaped body, miniscule legs that barely reached to the floor, and the thinnest scraggy little neck crowned by an enormous flattened globe—his head. The slits of his eyes, the barely discernible little nose, and the thin smiling mouth were sunk in a sea of taut, yellow, gleaming dough. How could that neck hold such a load?

They told me that this was the Deputy Public Prosecutor of the Turkmen Republic, and invited me to sit down. The conversation was conducted in an informal and familiar tone. They asked me how I felt and whether I had ended my hunger strike. Thanking them for their touching delicacy and interest I informed them that it was ended and asked in turn: "Can you tell me, please, when and where I will be sent?"

"You are going to a Komsomol[2] site. You'll be a Komsomol worker," answered the monster, absolutely wreathed in smiles as he enjoyed his little joke.

I felt unbearably revolted. On me, who had been sentenced by them for treason to my country, it somehow grated to hear them utter these words here, in this office, and to see their cynical sneers. They all knew perfectly well what it meant. And I knew too.

Back in my cell I thought of the various sites I had worked on. Outside every one there had been a camp, barbed wire, control towers, guards and "Komsomol workers in reefer-jackets."[3] I recalled how as a nineteen-year-old youth I had been sent on a two-month assignment to Bukhtarma power station. The quarters where we free workers lived were at Serebryanka, some way away from the site, and the camp was there too. Both we and the camp convicts were taken to each shift and back again by train. The "free" train consisted of five or six ancient four-wheeled wagons. It used to stop about fifty yards from the guardhouse and then we would show our passes to the soldier on guard duty and walk through the entrance passage. After this they would open up the gates and the endless train with the cons on board would roll straight inside the site perimeter. This one was not like ours with its hopeless little four-wheelers, but consisted of big, strong, eight-wheeled cars into which the cons were packed like sardines. On every brake platform sat a pair of tommy gunners and the rear of the train was brought up by an open platform full of soldiers. The soldiers would open the doors, drive out the cons, herd them away from the cars, and line them up five deep. Then began the count by fives: the first five, the second, the third, the fifteenth, the fifty-second, the hundred and fifth . . . counting and recounting. Suddenly there would be a mistake and they'd start counting all over again. Shouts, curses, and yet another recount. After a thorough check the cons would go to their work places. Then, when the shift was over, the same thing would take place in reverse order. I had worked side by side with them, these "Komsomol workers in reefer-jackets." I used to get my pay, go to dances on my days off, and never think a thing of it. Only one incident had embedded itself in my memory.

One day at the beginning of August one of the watch towers had suddenly started firing in the direction of the river Irtysh. Everybody downed tools and ran to the riverbank, crowding up against the fence, with the free workers and cons all mixed up together. They tried to drive us away, of course, but we stayed put and gaped. A swimmer was already more than halfway across the river, closer to the opposite bank. We could see clearly that he was having difficulty in swimming and that he was trying to go as fast as possible. It was a con. It seemed he had bided his time till the dredger stopped working and then had crawled through the pipe and plunged into the Irtysh some way out from the shore. They hadn't noticed him at first and by the time they had opened fire, he was already a long way off. The guard launch had already set off in pursuit and now was about to catch up with the fugitive; it was only about a dozen yards behind, but the officer with the pistol in his hand was for some reason holding his fire. "Well, if he shoots and kills him and the con goes to the bottom, how's he going to prove afterwards that he hasn't escaped?" explained the cons in the crowd. "He's got to have either a living man or a body to show them."

Meanwhile the fugitive reached the far shore, stood up and staggered a few steps. But the launch's bow had already struck the stones and the officer leapt out and found himself within two paces of the con. I saw him raise his pistol and shoot him in the legs. The con collapsed. Some tommy gunners ran up and as they stood there and in full view of the crowd on the opposite bank the officer fired several times into the prostrate prisoner. The crowd gasped and somebody swore obscenely.

The body was dragged over the stones like a sack and tossed into the launch. The launch set off downriver in the direction of the camp.

Now I couldn't help but think of Bukhtarma and this incident, and also other sites. No matter where they sent me now I would always be a "Komsomol worker," I would be soaked and frozen during the checks, I would live behind barbed wire, I would be guarded by armed guards with sheepdogs; and if I couldn't bear it and tried to escape, I would be shot down just like that fellow in the Irtysh....

. . . . .

The Cooler

I had caught a chill in the Karaganda camps already and had received no treatment. Since then I had suffered from a chronic inflammation of both ears, which from time to time would become acute. This time it was also my ears that caused the trouble. My head was splitting in two, I had shooting pains in my ears, it was difficult to fall asleep at night, and painful to open my mouth at meals. On top of that I had fits of nausea and dizziness.

I went to the camp medical post, although the old hands warned me that it was useless, that the ear specialist came once a year and summoned everyone who had complained of ear trouble during the past year to come to him at the same time. There were quite a few. "What's wrong?" "My ears." Without further ado the specialist would note it down in his notebook and write out a prescription for hydrogen peroxide. No further inquiries and no proper examination, and there was no chance of being excused from work—it was out of the question. Only if you turned out to have a high temperature would they consider excusing you from work for a few days.

I appealed to the doctor several times and each time heard only insulting assertions that since I didn't have a temperature I must be well and therefore was simply trying to dodge work. And at the end of June, for failing to fulfill my norm, I was given seven days in the PC or punishment cell, in other words the cooler. I found nothing surprising in this: given that I was failing to fulfill my daily norm, the cooler was inevitable. At first they call you up in front of your company officer to listen to a sermon about every con having to redeem his sin in the eyes of the people by honest labor.

"Why didn't you fulfill your norm?" asks the officer when his homily is finished. This when he can see that the man in front of him can barely stand up. "Sick? How can you be when you've got no temperature! It's very bad to pretend, to dissimulate, to try and dodge your work." And just to make the point clear he gives you several days in the cooler.

Now what did the punishment cell look like in 1961? First there was an ordinary camp barrack block, divided into cells. The cells were various: some were for solitary, others for two people, five, or even twenty, and if necessary they would pack up to thirty or even forty in them. It was situated in a special regime camp about a quarter of a mile from camp ten. A tiny exercise yard had been specially fenced off; it was pitted and trampled hard and in it, even in summer, there was not a single blade of grass—the least shoot of green would be swallowed at once by the starving cons in the cooler.

The cells themselves were equipped with bare bunks consisting of thick planks—no mattresses or bedding were allowed. The bunks were short, you had to sleep bent double; when I tried to straighten out, my legs hung over the end. In the center of the bunk, running crosswise and holding the planks together, was a thick iron bar. Now what if this bar had been placed underneath the planks? Or set in a groove, if it had to be on top, so that it didn't stick out? But no, this iron bar, two inches wide and almost an inch thick, was left sticking up in the very middle of the bunk, so that no matter how you lay it was bound to cut into your body, which had no protection from it.

The window was covered with stout iron bars and the door had a peephole. In one corner stood the prisoner's inseparable companion, the sloptank—a rusty vessel holding about twelve gallons, with a lid linked to it by a stout chain. Attached to one side of the tank was a long iron rod threaded at the other end. This was passed through a special aperture in the wall and on the other side, in the corridor, the warder would screw a big nut on to it. In this way the sloptank was fixed immovably to the wall. During toilet break the nut would be unscrewed so that the cons could carry the tank out and empty it. This procedure took place daily in the morning. The rest of the time the sloptank stood in its appointed place, filling the cell with an unspeakable stench....

At 6:00 a.m. came a knocking at all doors: "Wake up! Wake up for toilet break!" They started taking us to get washed. At last it was our cell's turn. However, it was washing only in name. You had hardly had time to wet your hands when you were already being prodded from behind: "Hurry, hurry, you can get all the washing you want after you've been released!" Less than a minute is the regulation time for a con to wash in, and whoever fails to get washed has to rinse his face over the sloptank in the cell.

And so, back in our cell once more, we waited for breakfast—alas nothing but a name: a mug of hot water and a ration of bread—fourteen ounces for the whole day. For dinner they gave us a bowl of thin cabbage soup consisting of almost pure water, in which some leaves of stinking pickled cabbage had been boiled—though little enough even of that found its way into the bowl. I don't think even cattle would have touched this soup of ours, but in the cooler the con not only drinks it straight from the side of the bowl, but even wipes the bowl with his bread and eagerly looks forward to supper. For supper we got a morsel of boiled cod the size of a matchbox, stale and slimy. Not a grain of sugar or fat is allowed to prisoners in the cooler.

I hate to think what we prisoners were driven to by starvation in the cooler. Return to camp was awaited with even greater eagerness than the end of your sentence. Even the normal camp hunger rations seemed an unimaginable feast in the cooler. I hate to think how I starved in there. And it is even more horrible to realize that now, even as I write this, my comrades are still being starved in punishment cells. . . .

The time drags agonizingly between breakfast and dinner and between dinner and supper. No books, no newspapers, no letters, no chess. Inspection twice a day and after dinner a half-hour walk in the bare exercise yard behind barbed wire—that's the extent of your entertainment. During inspections the warders take their time: the prisoners in each cell are counted and recounted and then checked with the number on the board. Then a meticulous examination of the cell is carried out. With big wooden mallets the warders sound out the walls, bunks, floor, and window bars to see whether any tunnels are being dug or any bars have been sawn through and whether the prisoners are planning to escape. They also check for any inscriptions on the walls. During the whole of this time the prisoners all have to stand with their caps off (I will explain later why this is done).

During the thirty-minute exercise period you can also go to the latrines. If there are twenty of you in a cell, however, it is difficult to manage in time. There are two latrines, a line forms and again you are chivvied: "Hurry, hurry, our time's nearly up, what are you sitting around for!" If you don't manage it, there's always the sloptank back in the cell, and they never let you out to go to the latrines again, not even if you're an old man or ill. Inside, during the day, the cell is stifling and stinks to high heaven. At night, even in summer, it is cold—the cell block is built of stone and the floor is cement: they are specially built that way so as to be as cold and damp as possible. There is no bedding and nothing to cover yourself with, except for your reefer-jacket. This, like all your other warm clothes, is taken away when you are searched before being stuck in the cooler, but they give it back to you at night.

There is not the slightest chance of taking a morsel of food with you to the cooler, or even half a puff's worth of cigarette butt or paper or the lead of a pencil—everything is taken away when you are searched. You yourself and the underwear, trousers, and jacket that you are forced to take off are all poked and prodded through and through.

From ten o'clock at night till six in the morning you lie huddled on your bare boards, with the iron bar digging into your side and a cold damp draught from the floor blowing through the cracks between them. And you long to fall asleep, so that sleeping, at least, you can forget the day's torments and the fact that tomorrow will be just the same. But no, it won't work. And you can't get up and run about the cell, the warder will see you through the peephole. So you languish there, tossing and turning from side to side until it is almost light again; and no sooner do you doze off than: "Get up! Get up! Toilet break!"

Incarceration in the punishment cell is supposed to be limited to not more than fifteen days, but the officers can easily get round this rule. They let you out to go back to camp one evening and the next morning condemn you to another fifteen days. What for? A reason can always be found. You stood in your cell so as to block the peephole; picked up a cigarette butt during your exercise period (that one of your camp friends had tossed over the fence to you); answered a warder rudely. . . . Yes, you can get a further fifteen days for absolutely nothing at all. Because if you really rebel and allow yourself to be provoked into making a protest, you get not simply fifteen days in the cooler but a new trial by decree.

In Kargal I was once kept in the cooler for forty-eight days, being let out each time only so that a new directive could be read to me ordering my "confinement to a punishment cell." The writer Yuli Daniel was once given two successive spells in the cooler at Dubrovlag camp eleven for "swearing at a sentry"—this happened in 1966.

Some men can't bear the inhuman conditions and the hunger and end up by mutilating themselves: they hope they will be taken to hospital and will escape, if only for a week, the bare boards and stinking cell, and will be given more human nourishment. While I was in the cooler, two of the cons acted as follows: they broke the handles off their spoons and swallowed them; then, after stamping on the bowls of the spoons to flatten them, they swallowed these too. But even this wasn't enough—they broke the pane of glass in the windows and by the time the warders had managed to unlock the door each had succeeded in swallowing several pieces of glass. They were taken away and I never saw them again; I merely heard that they were operated on in the hospital at camp number three.

When a con slits his veins or swallows barbed wire, or sprinkles ground glass in his eyes, his cellmates don't usually intervene. Every man is free to dispose of himself and his life as best he can and in whatever way he wishes, every man has the right to put an end to his sufferings if he is unable to bear them any longer.

There is also usually one cell in the punishment block that is filled with people on hunger strike. One day, as a mark of protest, a con decides to go on hunger strike, so he writes out an official complaint (to the camp governor, the Central Committee, Khrushchev—it is all the same who to, it has absolutely no significance; it's simply that a hunger strike "doesn't count" without an official complaint, even if you starve to death anyway) and refuses to take any more food. For the first few days no one takes a blind bit of notice. Then, after several days—sometimes as many as ten or twelve—they transfer you to a special cell set aside for such people, and start to feed you artificially, through a pipe. It is useless to resist, for whatever you do they twist your arms behind your back and handcuff you. This procedure is carried out in the camps even more brutally than in the remand prison—by the time you've been "force-fed" once or twice you are often minus your teeth. And what you are given is not the feeding mixture that I got at Ashkhabad, but the same old camp skilly, only even thinner, so that the pipe doesn't get blocked. Furthermore the skilly you get in the cells is lukewarm, but in artificial feeding they try to make it as hot as possible, for they know that this is a sure way of ruining your stomach.

Very few men are able to sustain a hunger strike for long and get their own way, although I have heard of cases where prisoners kept it up for two to three months. The main thing is, though, that it's completely useless. In every instance the answer to the protest is exactly the same as to all other complaints, the only difference being that the governor himself comes to see the hunger striker, insofar as the enfeebled con is unable to walk:

"Your protest is unjustified, call off your hunger strike. Whatever you do, we won't let you die. Death would save you from your punishment and your term isn't up yet. When you go free from here you are welcome to die. You have made a complaint, you are complaining about us to the higher authorities. Well, you can write away—it's your right. But all the same it is we who will be examining your complaint...."

And this was the sanatorium I had been sent to on account of my illness. I served my seven days and came out, as they say, holding on to the walls—they had worn me to a shadow. Nevertheless, despite my weakness, I still had to go out to work the next day in order not to earn myself another spell in the cooler....

. . . . .

Special Regime

During my first spell in the cooler I hadn't really got to know either the camp or the men in it, except for my cellmates. But now, during my second stay in the cooler and subsequently on remand, awaiting trial, I and my companions not only got a closer look at the special regime but also got to know a few of the cons doing special. In some of the camps I stayed in later, and also at the prisoners' hospital, I met many cons who had at some time done special, so that I know very well what it amounts to.

The living zone of a special regime camp is equipped with cell blocks about eighty yards long and twenty-five to thirty yards wide. A long corridor runs down the middle of the block from end to end, while a transverse corridor divides it in half. Both corridors terminate at each end in doors that are equipped with a variety of locks and bolts. The long corridor has rows of doors on either side that lead into the cells, these being the same as you find in the punishment block: plank bunks, bars on the windows, a sloptank in one corner, and doors equipped with shuttered peepholes (the shutters are on the outside, of course, so that only the warders can move them—otherwise the cons might look out into the corridor). The cells are divided from the corridor by double doors: on the corridor side there is a massive iron-lined door double-locked with a conventional lock and a padlock; the door on the inside, which is also kept permanently locked, consists of a grille formed by heavy iron bars set into a heavy frame, as in a cage for wild beasts. Set into the barred door is a food trap, which is also kept locked and is opened only when food is being served. The barred door is opened only to let cons in and out, for they are driven out to work, in the words of Captain Vasyayev, so as to pay for the bread they eat.

The appearance of the living zone in a special regime camp is completely different from that of an ordinary or strict regime camp: the zone is completely deserted. After work everyone is kept under lock and key until morning, until the parade for work again. The whole of your free time is spent in the cells, with the warders padding noiselessly up and down the corridors in their felt knee-boots, eavesdropping, and peering through the peepholes. . . . But who are the people held on special regime, behind thick bars and behind locked and bolted doors, behind rows and rows of barbed wire, and behind a high wall? What fearsome, bestial bandits are these?

Officially, special regime, like prison, is reserved for particularly dangerous and hardened offenders, and also for cons who have committed an offence in camp. That is the rule for ordinary, everyday criminals: first normal regime, then intensified, then strict regime, and finally special regime or prison. Politicals begin their camp career at once on strict regime—we are all "particularly dangerous" from the very beginning, so that for us the path to special regime or prison is significantly shorter.

You can also get special regime as part of your court sentence—for a second political offense. The most common course, however, is for cons to come here from strict regime camps—either for escaping (if, of course, they're not shot on being caught), or attempting an escape, or else for refusing to work, failing to fulfill the norm, "resisting a guard or a warder." . . . To become a bandit or a vicious hooligan in camp is easier than falling off a chair: all you have to do is preserve an elementary sense of your own dignity and one way or another you are certain to end up as "a vicious wrecker of discipline," while developments after that depend entirely on the whim of admin—will they limit themselves to administrative measures of correction or have you tried in court again?

Here is an example. I have already pointed out that in the cooler they don't give you a chance to have a decent wash; and there isn't the remotest chance of being allowed to clean your teeth—do it back in the cell, if you please, over that stinking sloptank. The very desire of a con even to do such a thing provokes righteous indignation and anger on the part of the warder: what, a common criminal, and he's talking of cleaning his teeth! But they don't even let you have an ordinary wash. No sooner have you wet your hands in the basin than: "Enough! Back to your cell!" And if you don't step back on the instant they grab hold of you and pull you away. At this point, God forbid that you should resist even instinctively or ward off the hand that is dragging you away from the basin. The warders will then drag you into the guardroom and start insulting you, mocking you, prodding you. They only want one thing—that the con should bear all this in silence, submit, so that it is clear for all to see: the con knows his place. And if you dare to answer an insult or a blow—there's your "vicious hooliganism" for you, "resistance to the representatives of law and order," followed by a report to the prison authorities, a new trial, and sentence by decree, which can be anything up to and including the death penalty. At the very least your term will be extended and you'll be put on special regime.

Somewhat later, in the Potma transit prison, I met several cons from camp ten who had been sent to special regime camps or to prison for "organizing a political party" in the camp. Chinghiz Dzhafarov said something, a stool pigeon squealed to the fuzz (a KGB detective in this case): and they started to round people up—not only those who took part in the conversation, but also anybody who happened to be around and might have heard it.

In practice any con that the authorities take a dislike to is liable to end up on special regime or in prison—if he's too difficult, say, or independently minded, or popular with the other cons. Everybody has more than enough of such crimes in his book as failure to fulfill the norm or breaking the camp rules. And sometimes it's simply a matter of chance, the result of sheer bad luck. After I had been taken out of camp ten, for instance, it was decided for various internal reasons to transform it from a political into an ordinary criminal camp. But what to do with the political prisoners? Some of them were distributed to other political camps, but the majority were sent to a special regime camp—it was the closest to hand. And on my way back to the camps in 1963, as I passed through the familiar territory, I saw that several new cell blocks with barred windows had been added to the special regime camp. Inside were my comrades from camp ten.

Iron bars, bolts, extra guards, confinement to cells outside of working hours—all this, of course, is only part of the corrective measures applied to these particularly dangerous offenders. Here the work is also heavier than in the other camps.

First you build a brick factory, for instance, and then you have to work in it. A brick factory even in normal conditions is no bed of roses, and in the camps it is even worse. The main machine is the celebrated OSO—two handles and one wheel plus handbarrows, and that's the extent of the mechanization. Working in the damp and the cold, the cons get soaked and freezing; then comes the long, long roll call. One cell at a time they are taken from the work zone to the living zone. Before passing through they are thoroughly searched, one by one, while the rest are forced to wait all this time in the rain, the snow, or the frost, stamping their feet to keep warm. Finally they are back in their cells with not the slightest chance to warm themselves or change their boots or clothing: all they have is what they stand up in, both for work and for indoors in the cell after work—filthy, damp, and sweaty. Somehow or other the con tries to dry out his clothes overnight with the warmth of his own body; before he's finished, however, it is already morning, time to get up, parade for work, and again it's hurry-hurry, don't stand around, if you don't fulfill your norm you go on punishment rations. And the norms are such, of course, that it is impossible to fulfill them, so that any con can at any time be punished for falling short of them.

The main punishment and the strongest corrective measure in the camps, easy to carry out and well tried in practice, is starvation. On special regime this measure is particularly sensitive: parcels and packages are in general forbidden. All you can get from the camp shop is toothpaste, toothbrushes, and soap; in order to buy tobacco you have to write a special application to admin and then it's up to them to decide. No food from outside is ever allowed in, all you get is rations. And everyone knows what camp rations are like: you won't quite kick the bucket, but you won't be in a hurry to shit either—you've got nothing to shit with. And even then, if you don't fulfill your norm, admin can put you on punishment rations—the same as in the cooler.

And so men sentenced to special regime camps live for years in these terrible, inhuman, indescribable conditions. It isn't too difficult, it seems, to reduce a man to the condition of a beast, to force him to forget his own human dignity, to forget honor and morality. On top of this the cells are apportioned in such a way that there are never less than two stool pigeons to each cell—to report on their comrades and each other. But what can a stool pigeon gain on special regime? First, he doesn't get put on punishment rations; secondly, he may not have his visits cut out. Here a con is permitted one visit a year lasting up to three hours—this is usually reduced to half an hour, and more often than not is not allowed at all. The main thing, though, is that admin can make representations to the judiciary for a prisoner to be transferred from special regime back to strict regime before his time is up, for "starting on the road to rehabilitation." Not before half his term is served, true, but still it's a hope! Somehow to break out of this hell six months or a year ahead of schedule, this is the lure that leads men to become informers and provocateurs and to sell their comrades.

I have already mentioned self-mutilation in the cooler and such cases are even more frequent on special regime. Men gouge their eyes out, throw ground glass in them, or hang themselves. At night sometimes they slit their veins under the blankets; and if their neighbor doesn't wake up soaked in blood, yet one more martyr is freed of his burden.

One day three cons agreed to put an end to themselves in the usual way, that is with the help of the sentries. At about three in the afternoon they took three planks from the brick factory and placed them against the wall. The sentry in the watch-tower shouted:

"Stand back or I'll fire!"

"By all means, and deliver us from this happy life," replied one of the cons and started climbing. Having reached the top, he got entangled in the barbed wire there. At this moment there was a burst of tommy gun fire from the tower and he slumped across the wire and hung there. Then the second man climbed up and calmly awaited his turn. A short burst of fire and he fell to the ground at the foot of the fence. The third man followed and he too fell beside the first.

I was told later that one of them had remained alive, he had been seen in the hospital at camp three. So at least he had escaped from special regime for a time. The other two, of course, had escaped forever, shot dead on the spot. In general this suicide was just like many others, differing only in that it was a group affair. Individual instances are common, and not only in special regime camps.

A sentry who picks off such an "escaper" in this way gets rewarded with extra leave to show admin's gratitude. But the attitude of the other soldiers to the marksman doesn't always coincide with admin's. Once, in camp seven in the autumn of 1963, a sentry shot a routine suicide case, a fellow who was ill, when he was on the wall. He got his leave all right, but he was black and blue when he set off for home: that night the other soldiers had organized a little farewell party for him, though under a different pretext, of course.

On the whole, many soldiers are ashamed of this type of service and don't even tell their families that they are guarding prisoners. Sometimes it happens that when you get talking to one, and he's sure you won't give him away, he'll say quite openly what he thinks of the camps and his duties:

"In a year I'll be free again and this fucking military service can go to hell."

The way he talks it is clear that his three years are as much a prison sentence to him as the con's years inside. So you say to him:

"But if they order you to, you'll shoot me too, and if you're up in the watch tower you'll fire on a con just the same, even when you know he's not escaping but simply doing it in desperation...."

"Of course," he agreed. "If they order me I'll fire and I'll shoot to kill. What else can I do when it's an order?"

"Yes, what can we do?" says another.

"I don't like the idea of being put inside myself," replies a third.

Many soldiers perform their duties out of fear, and not because they're conscientious. And when Burov, Ozerov, and I were beaten up, the soldiers did it more for show than in earnest. The warders, though, are a different kettle of fish. It's true they're not conscientious and work only for the money, but they try to suck up to admin, try to last out till they're pensioned off, and try not to get thrown out beforehand; then they also like to be praised and they hope, perhaps, for promotion to senior warder. Moreover their absolute power over the cons corrupts them (and the higher administration too for that matter)....

. . . . .

Self-Mutilation

Here is one out of a number of similar stories, from which it differs only in its originality. It took place before my very own eyes in the spring of 1963. One of my cellmates, Sergei K., who had been reduced to utter despair by the hopelessness of various protests and hunger strikes and by the sheer tyranny and injustice of it all, resolved, come what may, to maim himself. Somewhere or other he got hold of a piece of wire, fashioned a hook out of it and tied it to some home-made twine (to make which he had unraveled his socks and plaited the threads). Earlier still he had obtained two nails and hidden them in his pocket during the searches. Now he took one of the nails, the smaller of the two, and with his soup bowl started to hammer it into the food flap—very, very gently, trying not to clink and let the warders hear—after which he tied the twine with the hook to the nail. We, the rest of the cons in the cell, watched him in silence. I don't know who was feeling what while this was going on, but to interfere, as I have already pointed out, is out of the question: every man has the right to dispose of himself and his life in any way he thinks fit.

Sergei went to the table in the middle of the room, undressed stark naked, sat down on one of the benches at the table and swallowed his hook. Now, if the warders started to open the door or the food flap, they would drag Sergei like a pike out of a pond. But this still wasn't enough for him: if they pulled he would willy-nilly be dragged towards the door and it would be possible to cut the twine through the aperture for the food flap. To be absolutely sure, therefore, Sergei took the second nail and began to nail his testicles to the bench on which he was sitting. Now he hammered the nail loudly, making no attempt to keep quiet. It was clear that he had thought out the whole plan in advance and calculated and reckoned that he would have time to drive in this nail before the warder arrived. And he actually did succeed in driving it right in to the

134

very head. At the sound of the hammering and banging the warder came, slid the shutter aside from the peephole, and peered into the cell. All he realized at first, probably, was that one of the prisoners had a nail, one of the prisoners was hammering a nail! And his first impulse, evidently, was to take it away. He began to open the cell door; and then Sergei explained the situation to him. The warder was nonplussed.

Soon a whole group of warders had gathered in the corridor by our door. They took turns at peering through the peephole and shouting at Sergei to snap the twine. Then, realizing that he had no intention of doing so, the warders demanded that one of us break the twine. We remained sitting on our bunks without moving; somebody only poured out a stream of curses from time to time in answer to their threats and demands. But now it came up to dinner time, we could hear the servers bustling up and down the corridor, from neighboring cells came the sound of food flaps opening and the clink of bowls. One fellow in the cell could endure it no longer—before you knew it we'd be going without our dinner—he snapped the cord by the food flap. The warders burst into the cell. They clustered around Sergei, but there was nothing they could do: the nail was driven deep into the bench and Sergei just went on sitting there in his birthday suit, nailed down by the balls. One of the warders ran to admin to find out what they should do with him. When he came back he ordered us all to gather up our things and move to another cell.

I don't know what happened to Sergei after that. Probably he went to the prison hospital—there were plenty of mutilated prisoners there: some with ripped open stomachs, some who had sprinkled powdered glass in their eyes, and some who had swallowed assorted objects—spoons, toothbrushes, wire. Some people used to grind sugar down to dust and inhale it—until they got an abscess of the lung. . . . . Wounds sewn up with thread, two lines of buttons stitched to the bare skin, these were such trifles that hardly anybody ever paid attention to them.

The surgeon in the prison hospital was a man of rich experience. His most frequent job was opening up stomachs, and if there had been a museum of objects taken out of stomachs, it would surely have been the most astonishing collection in the world.

Operations for removing tattoos were also very common. I don't know how it is now, but from 1963 to 1965 these operations were fairly primitive: all they did was cut out the offending patch of skin, then draw the edges together and stitch them up. I remember one con who had been operated on three times in that way. The first time they had cut out a strip of skin from his forehead with the usual sort of inscription in such cases: "Khrushchev's Slave." The skin was then cobbled together with rough stitches. He was released and again tattooed his forehead: "Slave of the USSR." Again he was taken to hospital and operated on. And again, for a third time, he covered his whole forehead with "Slave of the CPSU." This tattoo was also cut out at the hospital and now, after three operations, the skin was so tightly stretched across his forehead that he could no longer close his eyes. We called him "The Stare."

In the same place, in Vladimir, I once happened to spend several days in a cell with Subbotin. This was a fellow the same age as myself and a homosexual. There were few homosexuals in Vladimir and everyone knew who they were. There was nothing they could earn there. He had been classed as a "political" after being in an ordinary criminal camp and making an official complaint—thus "letting the tone down." One day, after having sent about forty or fifty complaints to Brezhnev and the Presidium of the Supreme Council and to Khrushchev and the Central Committee of the Communist Party of the Soviet Union, he swallowed a whole set of dominoes—twenty-eight pieces. When the whole of our cell was being led down the corridor to the exercise yard—he had swallowed the dominoes just before our exercise period—he clapped himself on the stomach and said to one con from camp maintenance who was coming the other way: "Listen, Valery!" I don't know whether Valery really heard the sound of dominoes knocking together in Subbotin's stomach, but he asked him: "What have you got there?" and Subbotin drawled "Dominoes."

The doctors wouldn't operate on Subbotin. They simply ordered him to count the pieces during defecation, saying that they would have to come out on their own. Subbotin conscientiously counted them each time and on his return to the cell ticked off in pencil on a special chart the number that had come out. No matter how diligently he counted, however, four pieces still remained unaccounted for. After several days of agonizing suspense he washed his hands of them: if they stayed in his stomach it was all right as long as they didn't interfere, and if they were out already, then to the devil with them.

One Day in the Life of Ivan Denisovich
Aleksandr Solzhenitsyn

ALEKSANDR SOLZHENITSYN *(1918–) is doubtless the best known not only among the authors included in this volume but among all those who have written about repression in the Soviet Union or in any Communist state. It was he who introduced the term "Gulag"—a Russian abbreviation of "main administration of camps." Until the publication of his writings in the West in the early 1970s few people in Western countries were aware of the existence and nature of Soviet concentration camps, although—as several selections in this volume indicate—he was by no means the first to chronicle their existence and characteristics.*

His exceptional impact is probably the result of several factors. One is the encyclopedic coverage and sweep of his narrative describing the Soviet penal system in his best-known work, The Gulag Archipelago. *Its three volumes cover every aspect of the Soviet political-penal system: chronological, geographical, economic, political, and experiential. Not only was he himself an inmate for eight years (arrested in 1945 for a disrespectful reference to Stalin in a letter written during World War II), he also obtained the testimonies of other inmates about conditions in the prison camps. The Nobel Prize he was awarded in 1970 greatly enhanced his reputation, and his exile from the USSR in 1974 made him even more visible, as did his occasional public statements while abroad. He lived in the United States from 1974 until 1994, when he returned to post-Communist Russia.*

His style of writing—a powerful blend of eloquence and understatement—has been another ingredient of his success. However, the key to his wide impact is most likely to be found in the increased receptivity of his audiences: by the late 1960s and early '70s Western illusions about the progressive and benign character of the Soviet system had largely disappeared. While it was possible after World War II (in 1946) to publicly ridicule and accuse Viktor Kravchenko (a Soviet official who defected in 1944 and wrote I Chose Freedom*) of*

From Aleksandr Solzhenitsyn, One Day in the Life of Ivan Denisovich, *trans. Max Hayward and Harold Hingley,* © *1963 by Henry Holt and Company. Reprinted by permission of Henry Holt and Company, LLC.*

perpetuating falsehoods about Soviet repression—with many distinguished Western intellectuals joining the official Soviet campaign of denigration—by the early 1970s the climate of opinion was different. Khrushchev contributed greatly to this new climate by revealing and denouncing (some) of the crimes of Stalin in his famous speech in 1956. While his concern and compassion was limited to the Communist victims of Stalin's campaigns of terror, including especially the falsely accused defendants in the 1930s show trials, this was the first official Soviet admission of the system's failings and the first authoritative confirmation of the hardly noticed voices that had earlier described the specifics of Soviet terror and repression.

Khrushchev further contributed to lifting the veil of secrecy from Soviet repression by allowing the publication (in a journal) of One Day in the Life of Ivan Denisovich *in 1962, the first writing published in the Soviet Union to disclose conditions in the Gulag (and excerpts from which follow).*

Subsequently, Khrushchev and his successors judged Solzhenitsyn a threat to the Soviet system, and no other writings of his were published in the Soviet Union. He became the subject of public denigration in the official media and was at last exiled. During his stay in the United States Solzhenitsyn became a somewhat controversial figure because of his strong religious beliefs, critiques of American mass culture, and views of Western decadence.

The excerpts that follow convey with exceptional force, clarity, and specificity the routine deprivations suffered by the camp population and show how human beings can be reduced to a handful of basic and simple human needs (food, warmth, sleep, rest), their life revolving around the daily efforts to meet them. In a sparse, matter-of-fact style, the story presents a typical day of an inmate while providing insight into the lives and outlooks of the captives and the many spurious reasons for their detention.

· · · · ·

Reveille was sounded, as always, at 5 a.m.—a hammer pounding on a rail outside camp HQ. The ringing noise came faintly on and off through the windowpanes covered with ice more than an inch thick, and died away fast. It was cold and the warder didn't feel like going on banging.

The sound stopped and it was pitch black on the other side of the window, just like in the middle of the night when Shukhov had to get up to go to the latrine, only now three yellow beams fell on the window—from two lights on the perimeter and one inside the camp.

He didn't know why but nobody'd come to open up the barracks. And you couldn't hear the orderlies hoisting the latrine tank on the poles to carry it out.

. . . .

Shukhov never slept through reveille but always got up at once. That gave him about an hour and a half to himself before the morning roll call, a time when anyone who knew what was what in the camps could always scrounge a little something on the side. He could sew someone a cover for his mittens out of a piece of old lining. He could bring one of the big gang bosses his dry felt boots while he was still in his bunk, to save him the trouble of hanging around the pile of boots in his bare feet and trying to find his own. Or he could run around to one of the supply rooms where there might be a little job, sweeping or carrying something. Or he could go to the mess hall to pick up bowls from the tables and take piles of them to the dishwashers. That was another way of getting food, but there were always too many other people with the same idea. And the worst thing was that if there was something left in a bowl you started to lick it. You couldn't help it. And Shukhov could still hear the words of his first gang boss, Kuzyomin—an old camp hand who'd already been inside for twelve years in 1943. Once, by a fire in a forest clearing, he'd said to a new batch of men just brought in from the front:

"It's the law of the jungle here, fellows. But even here you can live. The first to go is the guy who licks out bowls, puts his faith in the infirmary, or squeals to the screws."

He was dead right about this—though it didn't always work out that way with the fellows who squealed to the screws. They knew how to look after themselves. They got away with it and it was the other guys who suffered.

Shukhov always got up at reveille, but today he didn't. He'd been feeling lousy since the night before—with aches and pains and the shivers, and he just couldn't manage to keep warm that night. In his sleep he'd felt very sick and then again a little better. All the time he dreaded the morning.

But the morning came, as it always did.

Anyway, how could anyone get warm here, what with the ice piled up on the window and a white cobweb of frost running along the whole barracks where the walls joined the ceiling? And a hell of a barracks it was.

Shukhov stayed in bed. He was lying on the top bunk, with his blanket and overcoat over his head and both his feet tucked in the sleeve of his jacket. He couldn't see anything, but he could tell by the sounds what was going on in the barracks and in his own part of it. He could hear the orderlies tramping down the corridor with one of the twenty-gallon latrine tanks. This was supposed to be light work for people on the sick list—but it was no joke carrying the thing out without spilling it! Then someone from Gang 75 dumped a pile of felt boots from the drying room on the floor. And now someone from his gang did the same (it was also their turn to use the drying room today). The gang boss and his assistant quickly put on their boots, and their bunk creaked. The assistant gang boss would now go and get the bread rations. And then the boss would take off for the Production Planning Section (PPS) at HQ.

But, Shukhov remembered, this wasn't just the same old daily visit to the PPS clerks. Today was the big day for them. They'd heard a lot of talk of switching their gang—104—from putting up workshops to a new job, building a new "Socialist Community Development." But so far it was nothing more than bare fields covered with snowdrifts, and before anything could be done there, holes had to be dug, posts put in, and barbed wire put up—by the prisoners for the prisoners, so they couldn't get out. And then they could start building.

You could bet your life that for a month there'd be no place where you could get warm—not even a hole in the ground. And you couldn't make a fire—what could you use for fuel? So your only hope was to work like hell.

The gang boss was worried and was going to try to fix things, try to palm the job off on some other gang, one that was a little slower on the uptake. Of course you couldn't go empty-handed. It would take a pound of fatback for the chief clerk. Or even two.

Maybe Shukhov would try to get himself on the sick list so he could have a day off. There was no harm in trying. His whole body was one big ache.

Then he wondered—which warder was on duty today?

He remembered that it was Big Ivan, a tall, scrawny sergeant with black eyes. The first time you saw him he scared the pants off you, but when you got to know him he was the easiest of all the duty warders—wouldn't put you in the can or drag you off to the disciplinary officer. So Shukhov could stay put till it was time for Barracks 9 to go to the mess hall.

The bunk rocked and shook as two men got up together—on the top Shukhov's neighbor, the Baptist Alyoshka, and down below Buynovsky, who'd been a captain in the navy.

When they'd carried out the two latrine tanks, the orderlies started quarreling about who'd go to get the hot water. They went on and on like two old women. The electric welder from Gang 20 barked at them:

"Hey, you old bastards!" And he threw a boot at them. "I'll make you shut up."

The boot thudded against a post. The orderlies shut up.

The assistant boss of the gang next to them grumbled in a low voice:

"Vasili Fyodorovich! The bastards pulled a fast one on me in the supply room. We always get four two-pound loaves, but today we only got three. Someone'll have to get the short end."

He spoke quietly, but of course the whole gang heard him and they all held their breath. Who was going to be shortchanged on rations this evening?

Shukhov stayed where he was, on the hard-packed sawdust of his mattress. If only it was one thing or another—either a high fever or an end to the pain. But this way he didn't know where he was.

While the Baptist was whispering his prayers, the Captain came back from the latrine and said to no one in particular, but sort of gloating:

"Brace yourselves, men! It's at least twenty below."

Shukhov made up his mind to go to the infirmary.

And then some strong hand stripped his jacket and blanket off him. Shukhov jerked his quilted overcoat off his face and raised himself up a bit. Below him, his head level with the top of the bunk, stood the Thin Tartar.

So this bastard had come on duty and sneaked up on them.

"S-854!" the Tartar read from the white patch on the back of the black coat. "Three days in the can with work as usual."

The minute they heard his funny muffled voice everyone in the entire barracks—which was pretty dark (not all the lights were on) and where two hundred men slept in fifty bug-ridden bunks—came to life all of a sudden. Those who hadn't yet gotten up began to dress in a hurry.

"But what for, Comrade Warder?" Shukhov asked, and he made his voice sound more pitiful than he really felt.

The can was only half as bad if you were given normal work. You got hot food and there was no time to brood. Not being let out to work—that was real punishment.

"Why weren't you up yet? Let's go to the Commandant's office," the Tartar drawled—he and Shukhov and everyone else knew what he was getting the can for.

There was a blank look on the Tartar's hairless, crumpled face. He turned around and looked for somebody else to pick on, but everyone—whether in the dark or under a light, whether on a bottom bunk or a top one—was shoving his legs into the black, padded trousers with numbers on the left knee. Or they were already dressed and were wrapping themselves up and hurrying for the door to wait outside till the Tartar left.

If Shukhov had been sent to the can for something he deserved he wouldn't have been so upset. What made him mad was that he was always one of the first to get up. But there wasn't a chance of getting out of it with the Tartar. So he went on asking to be let off just for the hell of it, but meantime pulled on his padded trousers (they too had a worn, dirty piece of cloth sewed above the left knee, with the number S-854 painted on it in black and already faded), put on his jacket (this had two numbers, one on the chest and one on the back), took his boots from the pile on the floor, put on his cap (with the same number in front), and went out after the Tartar.

The whole Gang 104 saw Shukhov being taken off, but no one said a word. It wouldn't help, and what could you say? The gang boss might have stood up for him, but he'd left already. And Shukhov himself said nothing to anyone. He didn't want to aggravate the Tartar. They'd keep his breakfast for him and didn't have to be told.

The two of them went out.

It was freezing cold, with a fog that caught your breath. Two large searchlights were crisscrossing over the compound from the watchtowers at the far corners. The lights on the perimeter and the lights inside the camp were on full force. There were so many of them that they blotted out the stars.

With their felt boots crunching on the snow, prisoners were rushing past on their business—to the latrines, to the supply rooms, to the package room, or to the kitchen to get their groats cooked. Their shoulders were hunched and their coats buttoned up, and they all felt cold, not so much because of the freezing weather as because they knew they'd have to be out in it all day. But the Tartar in his old overcoat with shabby blue tabs walked steadily on and the cold didn't seem to bother him at all.

They went past the high wooden fence around the punishment block (the stone prison inside the camp), past the barbed-wire fence that guarded the bakery from the prisoners, past the corner of the HQ where a length of frost-covered rail was fastened to a post with heavy wire, and past another post where—in a sheltered spot to keep the readings from being too low—the thermometer hung, caked over with ice. Shukhov gave a hopeful sidelong glance at the milk-white tube. If it went down to forty-two below zero they weren't supposed to be marched out to work. But today the thermometer wasn't pushing forty or anything like it.

They went into HQ—straight into the warders' room. There it turned out—as Shukhov had already had a hunch on the way—that they never meant to put him in the can but simply that the floor in the warders' room needed scrubbing. Sure enough, the Tartar now told Shukhov that he was letting him off and ordered him to mop the floor.

Mopping the floor in the warders' room was the job of a special prisoner—the HQ orderly, who never worked outside the camp. But a long time ago he'd set himself up in HQ and now had a free run of the rooms where the Major, the disciplinary officer, and the security chief worked. He waited on them all the time and sometimes got to hear things even the warders didn't know. And for some time he'd figured that to scrub floors for ordinary warders was a little beneath him. They called for him once or twice, then got wise and began pulling in ordinary prisoners to do the job. . . .

．　．　．　．　．

The air outside hit Shukhov. The cold and the biting mist took hold of him and made him cough. It was sixteen degrees below, while his own temperature was ninety-nine above. He had to fight it out.

Shukhov trotted off to his barracks. The yard was absolutely empty. There wasn't a soul to be seen. It was that short, blissful moment when there was no way out any more, but people kidded themselves that there was and that there wouldn't be a roll call. The escort guards were sitting in their warm barracks, leaning their heads against their rifles—it was no picnic for them either to kick their heels on top of watchtowers in this freezing cold. The guards in the main guardhouse threw some more coal in the stove. The warders in the warders' room were finishing their last cigarette before going out to search the prisoners.

The prisoners—they were now dressed in all their rags, tied around with all their bits of string and their faces wrapped in rags from chin to eyes to protect them from the cold—were lying on their bunks on top of their blankets with their boots on, quite still and with their eyes closed. Just a few seconds more until the gang boss would yell: "Fall out!"

Nearly all the men in Barracks 9, including Gang 104, were dozing. Only the assistant gang boss, Pavlo, was busy, moving his lips as he counted something with the help of a small pencil. And on a top bunk the Baptist Alyoshka, Shukhov's neighbor, neat and cleanly washed, was reading his notebook in which he had half the Gospels copied down.

Shukhov raced in but didn't make a sound, and went to Pavlo's bunk.

Pavlo raised his head. "Didn't they put you in the cooler, Ivan Denisovich? And are you still alive?" (They simply couldn't teach Western Ukrainians to change their ways. Even in camp they were polite to people and addressed them by their full name.)

Pavlo handed him his bread ration from the table. There was a little white heap of sugar on top of it.

He was in a great hurry, but he answered just as politely (even an assistant gang boss is a big shot of sorts, and more depends on him than on the Commandant). He scooped up the sugar with his lips, licked the bread clean with his tongue, and put one leg on the ledge to climb up and make his bed. He looked at the ration, turning it, weighing it in his hand as he moved, to see if it was the full pound due him. Shukhov had had thousands of these rations in prisons and camps, and though he'd never had a chance to weigh a single one of them on a scale and he was always too shy to stick up for his rights, he and every other prisoner had known a long time that the people who cut up and issued your bread wouldn't last long if they gave you honest rations. Every ration was short. The only question was—by how much? So you checked every day to set your mind at rest, hoping you hadn't been too badly treated. ("Perhaps *my* ration is almost full weight today.")

"It's about half an ounce short," Shukhov figured, and he broke the bread in two. He stuck half inside his clothes—into his jacket, where he'd sewed in a little white pocket (the factory makes prison jackets without pockets). He thought of eating the other half, the one he hadn't eaten at breakfast, right away, but food eaten quickly isn't food. It does no good, doesn't fill you. He made a move to shove his half-ration in his locker, but changed his mind again. He remembered the orderlies had already been beaten up twice for thieving. The barracks was as public as the courtyard of an apartment building.

So, not letting go of the bread, Ivan Denisovich pulled his feet out of his felt boots, neatly leaving his foot-cloths and spoon inside them, climbed up bare-footed, widened the little hole in his mattress, and hid the other half of his rations in the sawdust. He snatched his cap off his head, pulled a needle and thread out of it (this too was hidden carefully because they also checked prisoners' caps at inspection; once a warder had pricked himself on the needle and had been so angry he'd almost smashed Shukhov's head in). Three quick stitches and he'd sewed up the hole where the ration was hidden. Meanwhile the sugar in his mouth had melted. Shukhov's whole body was tense: at any moment the work-controller would start yelling in the doorway. Shukhov's fingers moved like lightning while his mind was running ahead thinking what he had to do next.

The Baptist was reading the Gospels not just to himself but almost aloud. Maybe this was for Shukhov's benefit (these Baptists love to spread a little propaganda):

"But let none of you suffer as a murderer, or as a thief, or as an evildoer, or as a busybody in other men's matters. Yet if any man suffer as a Christian, let him not be ashamed; but let him glorify God on this behalf."

One great thing about Alyoshka was he was so clever at hiding this book in a hole in the wall that it hadn't been found on any of the searches.

With the same swift movements, Shukhov hung his overcoat on a crossbeam, and from under the mattress he pulled out his mittens, a pair of thin foot-cloths, a bit of rope, and a piece of rag with two tapes. He evened the sawdust in his mattress a little (the stuff was heavy and hard-packed), tucked in his blanket all around, threw his pillow into place, then climbed down barefooted and started putting on his foot wrappings—first his good new foot-cloths and then on top the ones that weren't so good.

Then the gang boss cleared his throat loudly, got up and shouted:

"Snap out of it, 104! Out-si-ide!"

Right away everyone in the gang, whether snoozing or not, yawned and made for the door. The gang boss had been in camps for nineteen years, and he wouldn't chase you out to the roll call one second too early. When he said "Outside!" the time had really come. . . .

· · · · ·

They said even the Commandant was scared of Volkovoy—let alone the prisoners and warders. Not for nothing was he called Volkovoy.[1] And he always looked at you like a wolf. He was dark and tall and scowling, and always dashing around. He'd come at you from behind the corner of the barracks, shouting: "What's going on here?" You couldn't keep out of his way. In the early days he carried a whip of braided leather as long as his arm. They said he beat people with it. And he'd sneak up behind someone during the evening roll call and let him have it in the neck with his whip. "Get back into line, you scum."

Everybody would back away from him. The fellow he'd whipped would take hold of his neck and wipe off the blood and keep his trap shut so as not to get shoved in the cooler on top of it.

Now, for some reason or other, he'd stopped going around with the whip.

When it was freezing, the frisking routine was not so tough in the morning—though it still was in the evening.

The prisoners undid their coats and held them open. They marched up by fives, and five warders were waiting for them. They put their hands inside the prisoners' coats and felt their jackets. They patted the pocket (the only one allowed) on the right knee. They had gloves on, and if they felt something odd they didn't yank it out right away but asked, taking their time: "What do you have there?"

What did they hope to find on a prisoner in the morning? Knives? But knives don't get taken out of camp, they get brought in. What they had to watch out for in the mornings was people carrying a lot of food to escape with. There was a time when they were so worried about bread—a six-ounce ration for the noon meal—that an order was issued for each gang to make itself a wooden box and put everybody's bread together in it. It was anybody's guess why they thought this would help. Most likely the idea was to make things even tougher for people and add to their troubles—you took a bite out of it to put your mark on it, and threw it in the box. But all these hunks looked alike anyway. It was all the same bread. Then all the way you worried yourself sick about not getting your own piece back. And sometimes you got into a fight with people over it. Then one day three fellows escaped from the building site in a truck and took one of these boxes with them. So the bosses had all the boxes chopped up in the guardroom and then they went back to the old system.

In the mornings they also had to look out for anyone with civilian clothes under his camp uniform. They'd long ago taken away these clothes and they said you'd get them back when your sentence was up. But nobody'd ever been let out of this camp yet.

And another thing they checked for—letters you might try and slip to someone on the outside to mail. If they searched everybody for letters, they'd still be at it by noon.

But Volkovoy shouted to the warders to give them a real going over, and the warders quickly removed their gloves, told the men to open their jackets (where each man had taken a little of the warmth from his barracks) and undo their shirts. Then they began to feel around to see whether extra clothes had been put on against regulations. Each prisoner was allowed a shirt and vest, and anything extra had to come off—that was Volkovoy's order passed down through the ranks of the prisoners. The gangs that had gone ahead were lucky—some of them had already been checked out through the gates. But the rest had to open up. Anyone with extra clothing on had to strip it off right there in the freezing cold!

The warders got busy, but then they had trouble. The gates were clear now and the guards were yelling: "Come on, come on!" So 104 got a break from Volkovoy. He told them to report if they had anything extra and hand it to the stores that evening with a note explaining how and why they'd hidden it.

Everything on Shukhov was regular issue. Let them look, he had nothing to hide. But they caught Caesar with a woolen shirt, and the captain with some kind of jersey. The captain kicked up a fuss, just like he used to on his ship—he'd only been here three months.

"You've no right to strip people in the cold! You don't know Article Nine of the Criminal Code!"

They had the right and they knew the article. You've still got a lot to learn, brother.

"You're not Soviet people," the captain kept on at them. "You're not Communists!"

Volkovoy could take the stuff about the Criminal Code, but this made him mad. He looked black as a thundercloud and snapped at him:

"Ten days' solitary!"

And a bit quieter, he said to the chief warder: "You can see to that in the evening."

They didn't like putting people in solitary in the morning because it meant losing a day's work. So let him break his back all day and shove him in the cells at night.

The punishment block was nearby, on the left of the perimeter, a stone building with two wings. They'd finished building the second wing this autumn—one wasn't enough. The prison had eighteen blocks divided into small solitary cells. The rest of the camp was made of wood—only the prison was stone.

The cold had gotten under their shirts—there was no getting rid of it now. They'd just wasted their time wrapping themselves up. And Shukhov's back ached enough as it was. If only he could lie down in a hospital bed right now and sleep. That was all he wanted. With a nice heavy blanket. . . .

. . . . .

Shukhov took off his cap and put it on his knee. He dipped his spoon in both his bowls to see what they were like. It wasn't bad. He found a little bit of fish even. The gruel was always thinner than in the morning—they had to feed you in the morning so you'd work, but in the evening they knew you just flopped down and went to sleep.

He began to eat. He started with the watery stuff on the top and drank it right down. The warmth went through his body and his insides were sort of quivering waiting for that gruel to come down. It was great! This was what a prisoner lived for, this one little moment.

Shukhov didn't have a grudge in the world now—about how long his sentence was, about how long their day was, about that Sunday they wouldn't get. All he thought now was: "We'll get through! We'll get through it all! And God grant it'll all come to an end."

He drank the watery stuff on the top of the other bowl, poured what was left into the first bowl and scraped it clean with his spoon. It made things easier. He didn't have to worry about the second bowl or keep an eye on it and guard it with his hands.

So he could let his eyes wander a little and look at other bowls around him. The fellow on the left had nothing but water. The way these bastards in the kitchen treated a man! You'd never think they were just prisoners too!

Shukhov started to pick out the cabbage in his bowl. There was only one piece of potato and that turned up in the bowl he got from Caesar. It wasn't much of a potato. It was frostbitten of course, a little hard and on the sweet side. And there was hardly any fish, just a piece of bone here and there without any flesh on it. But every little fishbone and every piece of fin had to be sucked to get all the juice out of it—it was good for you. All this took time but Shukhov was in no hurry now. He'd had a real good day—he'd managed to get an extra helping at noon and for supper too. So he could skip everything else he wanted to do that evening. Nothing else mattered now.

The only thing was he ought to go see the Latvian to get some tobacco. There might not be any left by morning.

Shukhov ate his supper without bread—a double portion and bread on top of it would be too rich. So he'd save the bread. You get no thanks from your belly—it always forgets what you've just done for it and comes begging again the next day.

Shukhov was finishing his gruel and hadn't really bothered to take in who was sitting around him. He didn't have to because he'd eaten his own good share of gruel and wasn't on the lookout for anybody else's.

But all the same he couldn't help seeing a tall old man, Y-81, sit down on the other side of the table when somebody got up. Shukhov knew he was from Gang 64, and in the line at the package room he'd heard it was 64 that had gone to the Socialist Community Development today in place of 104. They'd been there all day out in the cold putting up barbed wire to make a compound for themselves. . . .

·　·　·　·　·

Shukhov went to sleep, and he was very happy. He'd had a lot of luck today. They hadn't put him in the cooler. The gang hadn't been chased out to work in the Socialist Community Development. He'd finagled an extra bowl of mush at noon. The boss had gotten them good rates for their work. He'd felt good making that wall. They hadn't found that piece of steel in the frisk. Caesar had paid him off in the evening. He'd bought some tobacco. And he'd gotten over that sickness.

Nothing had spoiled the day and it had been almost happy.

There were three thousand six hundred and fifty-three days like this in his sentence, from reveille to lights out.

The three extra ones were because of the leap years....

EASTERN EUROPE

Albania
✿ ✿ ✿

The Last Days of Freedom
Nika Stajka

Communist Albania under Enver Hoxha was in all probability the most brutally repressive of the European Communist states, in part because of its isolation from other Communist countries its rulers considered insufficiently orthodox. Thus, Albania rejected post-Stalin Soviet Union and neighboring Yugoslavia and China, too, after a brief alliance. Isolation presumably contributed to its rulers' besieged mentality, but quite possibly there was also a cultural element, in that a violent political culture preceded the Communist takeover and contributed to high levels of repression.

This excerpt from Nika Stajka *(1925–) details with shocking specificity the types of torture used against political prisoners and the exceptionally brutal working and living conditions in the Albanian Gulag.*

. . . . .

1. *Shooting by firing squad*—this is the easiest method and way that the Communists utilize, after having tortured their enemies, although these, in many instances, are not guilty from a Marxist point of view; they are eliminated by a volunteer firing squad. Volunteers in the squad are not Communists; they aspire, through their hypocrisy and barbarism, to be "good Communists." We have the example with the "son of the Serreqi yogurt peddler," who was always punctual to shoot those sentenced to death with his automatic rifle, especially the Catholic clergy.

Those sentenced to die were hauled on trucks to the place of execution; thus, they were spared, up to a certain point, from assaults from the fanatic subservients of the Communist Party.

The contrary happens in the army, where anyone sentenced to death, although tortured in the cells of the security section in his own barracks, is attacked by a crowd of crazy soldiers.

From Nika Stajka, The Last Days of Freedom *(New York: Vantage Press, 1980).*

Once their enemies have been executed, the Communists try to make them disappear completely, erasing all traces of where they were thrown or buried. The place behind the Catholic cemetery in Shkodra where the Communists executed by shooting almost all their enemies is recognized as an "execution place," but nobody can say where anyone was buried. Their bodies are perhaps buried together in some common grave, and the ground is ploughed immediately after to even up the surface.

2. *Hanging*—the difference between shooting and hanging depends on the idea that each person may have about these two manners of forcibly ending a human being's life. It is very important for the Communists, though, because they satiate either way their bloody instincts of vengeance against their enemies. To kill the enemy by shooting him is a "duty," but it respects him to the last minute, until death; to hang the enemy is offending him until the last moment of his life. Shootings took place on the outskirts of the city, behind the Catholic cemetery; but hangings were performed in the city square, known as *"Dugajet e Reja"* (the new stores). Everything was prepared ahead of time, so people realized the day, the time, and who was going to be executed.

The sentenced walked between the prison and the execution place, through the streets that led to the place prepared for him. I believe that what he had suffered in the cells of security was nothing for him; hanging, which awaits him, shall be nothing, either, compared to what he must endure after he leaves prison, on his way to the execution place. It can be said that he is more dead than alive when he reaches the place where death is awaiting him, not so much because of fear about what he expects but because of what the populace does to him. Guards do not try, at all, to defend him from the affronts that the mob inflicts on him since they also want to look "active" in helping the people against this "enemy of the people," against this "trash."

Spitting, rotten eggs, tomatoes, stones, etc., are the weapons of the crowd against the prisoner; while some pull him to one side, others push him, knock him down, tear his clothes up, beat him, and the poor person must go on walking, tied up, falling and raising with the help of the guards who accompany him.

The "young female guerrillas" distinguished themselves in these kinds of crimes.

3. *Mysterious disappearances*—many of those who were arrested in the first days, when the Communists took over, disappeared in a mysterious way. The "silent executions," that is, those who were shot without trial, were always known by the people, but there were others who disappeared into absolute mystery.

Who could imagine what has been of the first ones arrested by the Communists, who were seen in the isolation cells of the Tirana jail in 1949 and 1950? Who were they? Nobody could tell since those arrestees disappeared "alive." There were many, also, who, as the security people say, died ahead of time, without having been taken in front of the "popular courts," because one of them hung himself in his cell; another one threw himself from the second or third floor of the security building, dying on the street; and many more disappeared for no apparent reason. However, we are sure, as the Albanian people are, that they no doubt died because of the tortures.

I have had many opportunities of hearing about the tortures in the cells of security during the isolation, and in many instances I have also seen, after many years, the consequences of those tortures. . . .

. . . . .

The prisoner in Communist hands finds himself also in a big dilemma, besides his tortures. What to do? Speak up or keep his mouth shut and endure everything? Whatever the decision, the security agents feel pleasure in practicing tortures on the "enemies of the people." If the prisoner starts to speak up, he must go on speaking up about all his actions, thoughts, and dreams, which in his process he must portray as realities; so his conviction is assured. However, that is not easily ended, for when he has nothing else to say, they continue torturing him and telling him: "We already knew all of that, and we know much more, so it is better for you to speak up" . . . and the tortures go on.

In other instances, if the prisoner has decided not to speak up and is able to endure the tortures, he must endure it to the end, until his torturers get tired, but only he knows what he has had to endure. . . .

There is no limit for the processing period; I have known of short lapses, but also of months and years, since everything must come out as planned by security. I personally spent 338 days in the isolation cells at the new prison in Lapraka, Tirana.

In general terms, the persons with political importance who have been arrested by the Communists have had their processes finished in a few days, in a shorter period than those who were not so important, and there are hundreds of instances; political prisoners who have had a taste of inhuman tortures have put an end to it by signing anything quickly, and thus they have ended, executed by shooting or by hanging. . . .

The kind of torture depends on the malign ability in the soul of the officer in charge of the process. However, there are persons who, having been imprisoned, affirm that there have been officers in the same Security Corps who never tortured anyone.

There have also been high-ranking officers in the Security Corps who have done everything imaginable against the prisoners; while the latter rot under the ground or in the prisons or forced labor camps, the former ones wander about the free world, living in peace, since as they say: "They did not like Communism." Such is the case with Capt. (First Class) Qemal Galip Soili, security officer with the First Division in Tirana, and Lieutenant Mithat, who were the terror of agents in the Security Corps arrested for conspiracy.

I cannot leave unmentioned the vulgar spy, idiot, and criminal, for what he did against those who, for so many years, fed him and tried to make a man out of him, and who, today, without any remorse for the past, lives peacefully in the world metropolis, where the symbol of freedom is seen, in New York; everybody knows him as Ndoc Kapaj, but he committed his crimes under his true name: Ndoc Kol Vasili, from Bardica. For the sake of those who lie under ground, I feel that I have the duty of speaking about that one, my companion for many years in the seminary, in a separate chapter of this book.

Captain Qemal Galip Soili was in charge of forcing arrested soldiers to put an end to their "proceedings"; he felt more qualified than the rest of his comrades, so he locked them up for years on end in the prisons and labor camps.

Lieutenant Mithat looked like a true and dedicated Communist, especially in charge of security matters; but, when I was still imprisoned, I noticed that Lieutenant Mithat was arrested because he had attempted to flee from Albania to Yugoslavia.

I would not like to mention the tortures for several reasons, starting with the fact that the Communists have practiced them in the most diabolical manner, as well as criminally and inhumanly. That is why we cannot portray the strength that each means of torture has in itself. I will mention the most ordinary and well known, as prisoners have related them, of course, reserving their names.

1. *The rod*—No doubt this torture has always been the most ordinary method, and the most practical one, during the centuries. This comprises the rifle butt, the whip, the wet cord, the boots, the rod proper, and even a knife.

The importance of the rod relies on the qualifications of the user. In general, as soon as the prisoner is hit, he starts to yell. That is why, while the rod or club is used inside, outside in the yard, soldiers and Security Corps members sing and dance with ear-piercing music so the people will not notice the clamor of the tortured prisoners.

Many of those tortured with clubs have been crippled for life; some have had their feet broken; others have seen their arms broken; still others have gotten their ribs fractured, and others contracted tuberculosis in a short span of time.

2. *Electric power*—generated by a hand-driven dynamo; I believe that, for the Communists, this is a first-rate torture. It is an amusement for them since they try to test the effects of this kind of torture when the two terminals are placed on different points on the prisoner's body, whose hands and feet are tied to the chair, while the prisoner is almost always naked. To each question that is asked, the prisoner must answer "yes"; otherwise, the power is started, and the prisoner begins to yell, but, being tied up, although he tries to get up crazily, in many instances only hits his head against the wall in front of him, and falls out of balance to the floor, again hitting his head and getting soaked in his own blood.

This kind of torture is said to have been applied by "comrade" Pjerin Kecira to several priests, such as Father Ciprian Nika and others whose names are reserved out of caution since they were not taken to the firing squads at that time.

The electric power is one of the most difficult tortures, since the tortured prisoner cannot control himself, as he could if he were whipped. As many of those who have tasted the whippings have said, the difficulty with the latter is with the first five or six lashings . . . since after these the prisoner passes out and keeps on enduring it as an animal! So much so, that many have remained lying down for months and have even urinated blood.

3. *The louse*—I could not say whether or not this kind of torture exists in other parts of the world, but I believe that it is a fancy torture invented by the Yugoslavian or Albanian Communists. The louse, small as it is, may cause terrible tortures. The prisoner, tied to a chair, gets his head shaved with the "zero" shaver, and if he has started to resist the questioning, denying what he is asked, an officer places on his head a louse contained in a small cup upside down. The louse, after two or three minutes turning around the edge of the cup, tries to get out and pierces its small claws into the prisoner's head skin, causing at first an annoying noise and then strong pains. This forces the prisoner to sign his "processing."

4. *The whirlpool* (Jeleku)—this torture is a variant in the use of the club. The prisoner, tied hands and feet, and curled up in such a manner that his knees are against his chin and his wrists very tight, gets a rod through his arms and under his knees; two Security agents raise the prisoner and, supporting both ends of the rod between two tables, the body thus placed is rotated with his head down and his buttocks up. Making sure that he does not slide, one of the officers tries to move him until he gets impulse and starts turning on himself, while the other one hits his buttocks with the club, anywhere it may hit. Generally, the prisoners thus tortured becomes lame for life. If the prisoner starts to yell, he does not yell very long and signs the "processing" pretty soon.

5. *The cat*—this torture was performed with women accused especially for allegedly having cooperated with the anti-Communist guerrillas. The prisoner, naked, is placed in a large bag, her hands tied behind her body; a cat is also placed within the bag. The bag is closed, and the cat is beaten with a club, so anyone can imagine what the cat will do to the person within the bag.

6. *Hanging by the hands*—this torture is generally practiced in the cell where the prisoner is locked up, his hands tied behind his body with a long rope, and the rope tied to the bars of the small window open at a height of about three meters. The torture is performed when the rope is pulled and the prisoner is forced to rise to the tips of his feet until, little by little, out of exhaustion, with no food and no sleep, he gets to be completely extenuated and falls, remaining dangling from his hands.

Only when the prisoner has reached this stage can the guard, through an order from the "torturing officer" in charge of his "processing," free him from this terrible torture, which gets repeated each time the prisoner resists accepting what is told him or what is asked of him.

This is one of the most practiced tortures on the part of the Security Corps, in the isolation cells of the "New Lapraka Prison," in Tirana.

7. *Sleep*—the prisoner is placed inside a room and within a circle drawn on the floor with chalk. Standing there, he must stay until he signs his "processing." In front of him, sitting in a chair, a Security Corps officer keeps his eyes on the prisoner, awaiting his decision. These officers are relieved in shifts until the torture ends. The prisoner, standing motionless, gets tired soon; although he tries to rest first on one foot and then on the other, but the moment comes when he cannot endure it any longer and falls. The officer kicks him twice or three times . . . the prisoner wakes up and rises, falls again, tries to get up once more, and then falls asleep when he is exhausted.

Through this terrible torture, the prisoner is ready to sign and acknowledge anything . . . including his death sentence, in exchange for his sleep. He wants to rest, to sleep. This torture lasts longer than some hours; it takes days and nights on end. One of the companions in my group was thus tortured: Soldier Jovan Jani, for a whole week, day and night. Unable to get up when he finally fell, he was taken to his cell, where a male nurse, in order to remove his woolen stockings, was forced to cut them with a razor blade, and then he was taken to the hospital to make him come to. He related all those tortures in front of everybody, when taken to court, when the "judge" asked him: "If you do not accept the 'processing,' why have you signed it?"

This kind of torture is performed when a long time has elapsed and the prisoner still resists and does not want to sign, since he does not accept what the Communists want.

8. *The lights*—maybe this torture does not have any sense or value for many, but to whoever has experienced it or is able to imagine it, this can be one of the most difficult tortures. The prisoner is sitting and usually has his hands tied behind him. Upon starting to give negative answers, the officers in charge of practicing the torture start to increase the intensity of the light little by little, which at the beginning was normal. If the negative development continues, other large and bright lights start to be turned on around the prisoner, which hurt his eyesight, since all are directed towards him. An intense heat is followed by headache and nervousness in all his body, very close to hysteria. The prisoner usually signs his "processing" as a result of that.

9. *Water*—everyone can imagine what it is to be thirsty, but being forced to endure thirst because no water is provided is something different. Forced thirst is one of the tortures that leads people to a horrible death, a very hard one. Hunger is nothing when compared to thirst. If we can endure ten days without food, we shall never be able to endure one day without water after thirst has started.

This torture is an ordinary one every day, since generally all prisoners must endure it when it goes accompanied by hunger: "No bread and no water!"

Without mentioning what is done to the prisoner in the "processing room," if he does not want to concede, he is taken to his cell, bound hands and feet, and left with no bread or water. Many hours elapse . . . also days. The tortured person does not ask for bread; he asks for water, and his petition, little by little, changes into screams of desperation, until his voice, because of thirst, tones down to swift moans, asking for "water, water, water!" The prison guards, who are usually criminal and sanguine, following the instructions of the Security Corps officer, belatedly approaches a cup with water to his mouth, telling him: "Open your mouth, you trash, enemy of the people!" and many other insults according to the custom of the prison. The prisoner does not mind what the guard tells him; he only wants a little water. As soon as the guard puts the cup to his mouth, he withdraws it and continues his speech of low and vulgar expressions: "That's enough! Shut up! It is better to put you to the firing squad . . . we are going to shoot you!" etc., but the prisoner continues asking for "water, water, water!" until the guard or the security officer make him shut up by kicking him or clubbing him; by now, the prisoner has gone out of his mind and shuts up because he cannot endure it any longer . . . he has lost all his strength. When he has reached this condition, then he is given some water.

It is hard for me to go on mentioning the tortures that are performed in the Albanian prisons, by the Communists and the so-called "Security Section," which is so infamous that everything that has happened and is still going on is blamed on this "criminal corps" for having done it against its enemies, whom they call "the enemies of the people."

Several tortures, which for us would be today ridiculous things, for those who were labeled "enemies of the people" and tasted them, were terrible.

10. *The barrel*—the prisoner was placed into a barrel that was filled with water up to the prisoner's neck; this torture was practiced during winter and the prisoner was left inside the barrel for a long time.

11. *The wire*—one of the criminal tortures invented by the malign spirits of the Security Corps. The prisoner was tied, hands behind his body, with a wire instead of handcuffs. His hands, in many instances too tightly bound, bleed in a very short time because of being swollen.

If this torture lasted for days, the wire, going into the flesh, formed an ulcer because the flesh disintegrated. This was the case with Zef Bardhoku, about whom we shall write later.

12. *The scissors*—cutting the prisoner's flesh with a pair of scissors looks like the imagination of a criminal maniac, which is adequate for the inhuman feelings of the Communists. Many persons affirm that the ex-minister of the interior in the Communist government of Tirana, the great Communist who wanted to change Albania into one of the republics in the Federation of Yugoslavian Republics, "Comrade Koçi Xoxe," tasted this torture, performed on him by his very Communist "comrades."

13. *The knife*—this is also one of the ordinary tortures, but with different consequences, according to the manner in which it is practiced.

The prisoner's flesh is opened with a knife, to pour salt and vinegar into his wounds. Anyone can imagine the results of such a torture. At the prison for the "enemies of the people," in Tirana, I met Vladimir Beristovski, to whom the Communists, among other tortures, cut the flesh in his gluteal region with a knife, for a length of ten or fifteen centimeters. This wound was still visible in his flesh after many years. In that wound, the Communists poured salt and vinegar!

14. Shooting between the fingers; hot eggs under the armpits; splinters of wood under the nails; a cigarette stuck into the eyes; drops of water dripping on the head; many also got their teeth pulled as a torture.

As we have mentioned, all these tortures, and many more that the Communists perform on their enemies, depend on the criminal imagination of each Security officer, and according to the value and importance that the Security Corps attaches to the prisoner. . . .

. . . . .

More than three hundred of us were roaming, aimless, in the prison courtyard. All communications with those "who stayed behind" were cut. All doors were locked up around us. We were given a ration of "dry bread," and the guards started to tie us up in groups of three and groups to each other. Before midnight, we were ordered to climb on the trucks, departing in an unknown direction until we went through the city of Elbasani; the "veterans" knew the way very well, and they sent word around that "we were heading towards Maliq again . . . !"

Hunger and thirst started. The bread that we were given before departing, wrapped in the few clothes that we had, was loaded in other trucks behind us. We could not ask for any authorization for personal necessities, either, since the guards had told us before departing, "Do everything now . . . we won't stop for anything en route. . . ."

This time, too, the "Maliqi swamp" was awaiting us.

Vloqisht, Pojan, Rembec, were forced labor camps known to the prisoners, but the road we were traveling this time was unknown to them. A new camp awaited us. It was located on the highway that goes by the Mali i Thate (the Mali Thate mountain) in the direction of Bilishti, close to the small town of Nizhavez.

We arrived after sundown. The guards stationed themselves around the camp, called us according to their rolls, as the trucks approached the road to the gate of the camp, in the same order that we had been tied up in groups of three, released us and counted us again as animals, then pushed us into the camp.

The "veterans" were scared when they saw the swamp . . . terror overcame them because they were the only ones who knew what was in store for us, while we were "glad" because we were not at the prison any longer. We believed that we were "free" and gave no importance to what the other ones were telling us about the situation at the camp and the work at the swamp.

"Mali i Thate" was on one side; in the front there were two small hills that obstructed our visibility, upon which some "galleys" for the guards and for the storage of materials for work had been built; on the third side, the office of the director of the camp; and on the back side, approximately at a distance of thirty or forty meters, the immense swamp of Maliqi started. The camp was square, about 100 × 100 meters, surrounded completely by barbed wire up to the height of two meters, enmeshed in the shape of a pyramid, or rather as a "continuous triangle" in a straight line. Lights were positioned twenty or thirty centimeters above the top of the barbed wire, one meter apart from each other, all around the camp. On the four corners, on the outside, the four "guard towers" were located, with four German "Scharz" ready in the direction of the camp and the guards with their rifles at hand.

Inside the camp, twelve "galleys" had been built for the prisoners, six on one side and six on the opposite one, their doors aimed at the center of the camp, at a distance of three meters, approximately, between the back of the galleys and the barbed-wire fence. There were spotlights in the center of the camp.

On one side of the camp, near the fence and opposite the two groups of "galleys," there was the kitchen, and a short distance beyond, in the same direction, near the corner of the fence, there was a big pit, covered with boards, with approximately twenty-five holes, that served as toilets for the prisoners. The holes were not covered or apart from one another. The "hospital" was located near the entrance gate.

Because we arrived late, the camp commander did not allow our clothing to be delivered to us, at least to those of us who had any . . . so we had to spend two nights and one day without eating the 200 grams of bread that we had been given before departing from the prison at Tirana; we spent that time hungry, inside the "galleys," around the bonfires that we set with the remainders of the boards used to build the "galleys."

The beautiful spring weather of Tirana changed for us to cold and ice, in the heights of Korça. I believe that nobody could sleep because of the cold, until the sun came out and started to revive us with its heat, although it could not help us against hunger. Two hundred grams of bread had to last us from the fourteenth of April, for several days, until the seventeenth, in the afternoon, when the "camp force" arrived for the first time. Naturally, this time we only got "dry bread" until the following day.

The first days were spent in conferences and "organizational meetings." In all, there were about 1,700 or 1,800 prisoners, since later on there were arrivals from all parts of Albania, from Korça, Durrësi, Vlora, Gjirokastra, and Elbasani. Those prisoners from Shkodra said that work was under way in the Peqin-Kavaja channel, with an extension of seventy-two kilometers.

We were divided into twelve "brigades" and each one had chosen his "work companions," forming groups of ten or twelve under the direction of a "brigade commander," who was a prisoner, too, but usually an ex-member of the Party or a veteran guerrilla. . . .

The camp commander, Capt. (First Class) Beqir Liçua, in the presence of the representative of the Interior Ministry (the director general of the forced labor camps for prisoners) notified us about the new "work code."

He started his speech with these words:

"It is a great honor . . . it is an extraordinary privilege . . . it is an undeserved favor . . . that the people and its government have given you, by choosing you from among so many prisoners, to afford you the possibility of coming here to work. Many of your companions, who are in the prisons, when they realize your situation and the circumstances of work, will try to come here themselves, too, but perhaps it will be too late for them. I want for you not to be scared about forced labor, but instead I invite you to overcome, with good will and courage, all difficulties . . . because our government of the people has taken care of providing you with all the necessary conditions, so you will attain success in this great 'popular action.' Don't think that the situation of the previous camps will repeat itself. Enemies and traitors, who had infiltrated up to the highest echelons of our popular government, do not exist anymore. The people, the Party, and the popular government itself have given them 'the shot that they deserved'; the just sentence . . . !" And thus the commander, talking about everything, jumping from an issue to the next, whether good or bad, not thinking about what he was saying, finally started speaking about the new "work code":

"Through a decision of the ministerial council, the Presidium of the Popular Covenant has enacted the new work code."

This "code" was published a few days after our arrival at the Maliqi Swamp. In its chapters, verses, and paragraphs there was ample reference to the "help and privileges" that prisoners would be afforded for the work that they had to do . . . but I will mention only the most relevant points that stuck in my memory after so many years.

1. Each worker-prisoner is entitled to be furnished working clothes.
2. Each worker-prisoner is entitled to be furnished personal underwear every six months.
3. Each worker-prisoner is entitled, for the winter period, to be furnished a "fur coat" every four years.
4. Each worker-prisoner is entitled to be furnished, during the year and the winter period, enough sleeping clothes, a mattress, and blankets.
5. Each worker-prisoner, according to his need and the circumstances of his work, is entitled to be furnished "working boots."

6. Each worker-prisoner is entitled to be fed on the same level with a free "worker of the Republic."
7. Each worker-prisoner who attains his daily quota is entitled to:
   a. a compensation in cash.
   b. reduction of his sentence.

Now let us see how the points of that "work code" worked in practice.

At the beginning, we were given trousers and half coats from the Italian army but in sizes other than ours. During the four years that I spent in the camps, that was the first and last time that any clothing was distributed. The "personal underwear" was distributed several times but not for all prisoners; when this clothing arrived at the camp, the "brigade commanders" came first, and they chose the best and all they wanted; then came the cooks with their helpers; then the "spies" and those whom the guards had given any privileges, as those in the "personal secret service" for every guard, "good workers," those workers with "temporary flags," etc., so many of us never took a turn to get anything. More than one half of the prisoners did not get any clothing at all.

The "fur coats" never arrived; as I mentioned above, they were replaced by the military "half coats." Mattresses and blankets arrived several times, but they were distributed in the same manner as "personal underwear," besides the fact that there were only 200 blankets and fifty or sixty large bags, called "mattresses," so the majority got nothing for the winter. Boots arrived several times but only for two or three "brigades," and either they did not fit or it was worse to wear them because in the new work sectors we worked with the water up to our knees and sometimes higher than our waistlines.

Food was always insufficient. When the number of workers reached 1,800, we were entitled to twelve kilograms of beans for the two meals of the day (breakfast and lunch); dinner consisted of "tea" only. From the two rations of beans, we only got the peelings and the coloring powder, mixed with the foul smell from the grease of the "half barrels" where they were cooked. Beans were eaten first by the cooks and their helpers, then the camp guards and their "faithful" and "spies" . . . so the rest of us were left with the stinking water. . . . A similar thing happened with macaroni. And what about the meat? We had twenty grams of meat per person (crude meat), but when it was cooked together with beans or macaroni, we had to be satisfied by thinking that there was some meat in there. . . .

As to paragraphs 1 and 2 in Article 7 of the "code" (compensation in cash and reduction of sentences), it was something ridiculous for many and a suicidal law for those sentenced by the government to twenty or twenty-five years in prison if they understood it as a "favorable law.". . . In order to attain the daily quota (a 10 percent of a twenty-four-hour day) one had to work twenty-seven days in order to get two and a half days in reduction of his sentence, or approximately thirty days a year. For anyone sentenced to twenty-five years, he had to work twenty-three years in order to obtain two years' reduction.

The "compensation in cash" when the quota was attained was 100 Lek. The prisoner was entitled to 10 percent of the 100 Lek, so when he attained his quota, he got 10 Lek, and the rest went to the "popular government." Many were satisfied with this point because the majority received monthly an approximate sum of between 100 and 300 Lek, so we could buy cigarettes with the 10 percent of our own money.

The "technical office" was organized under the direction of the "prisoner-engineers" in the camp, Namik Gjelili and Pandeli Zografi.

"Standard setters" were appointed too, in charge of monitoring the attainment of the daily quotas on the part of all "brigades."

Prisoners received the news about the new "work code" with applause and shouts, many because they believed in the "popular government" and others out of fear, still others out of hypocrisy. . . .

· · · · ·

Work started on April 20. The prisoners were headed by the camp commander, who, covered up to his waist by fisherman's boots, accompanied by the camp engineers, the technicians and "standard-setters," and surrounded everywhere by well-armed guards, went into the water of the swamp. Although the water edge was only a few meters away from the camp, the first "work sector" was almost two kilometers inside the swamp. Boots were given to four "brigades," but they were useless because the water, in many places, was up to our waists. The "work sectors" were distributed according to the brigades, companies, and squadrons . . . and we immediately started digging the ditches, small channels for the drainage. All brigades were into the water because the whole "work place" was "under water." Work got started! The main ditch was dug under water for the drainage! What I am trying to explain is something unbelievable, as it was also unbelievable for us what we were doing; it was something terrible that got to our nerves and changed our laughter into nervous hysteria since we thought that we were trying to do an impossible task . . . however, the truth is that the following day when we returned to work, water had disappeared from the surface and was running normally within the ditches that we had dug under water. The canal started at the mouth of the swamp, near the Maliqi Lake, with a width of twenty-five meters, which in several points reached two meters in depth, and a length of seven kilometers.

Along with the articles of the new "work code" and the technical regulations for the work, the camp directorate established its regulations, too, in the first place its savage and inhuman disciplinary regulations against the "enemies of the people."

1. Each worker-prisoner who accomplishes his daily quota is entitled to rest.
2. Each worker-prisoner who accomplishes his daily quota may continue to work in order to increase his cash percentage and reduction of his sentence.

During the first days, only a few attained their daily quotas, but the camp command did not take any measures against the prisoners. "It is your duty and in your interest to work…!" we were told; the "internal guards" of the brigades told us nothing, either, and the brigade commanders gave no importance to our wish and good will toward work.… The "club," which in previous camps had been the daily ordinary torture, not only was discontinued but was not mentioned, either. All "veteran" worker-prisoners were astonished!

At first, the daily work quota was ninety cubic centimeters per person, in removing and transporting mud from the canal, twenty-five meters wide, to the place of the landfill, that is, the dike twenty-five meters away.

That, although it seems a short task, was something completely unattainable.

The swamp water quickly filled the holes that were dug to get the work started and continued. The soft dirt, full of roots and algae, became thick mud and clay. In order to use a shovel, two workers had to intervene: One, on the surface, held the shovel, and the second, inside the water and the hole, had to feel with his hands the position where the shovel had to be placed … the one on the surface removed the mud … if anything was left in the shovel, both tried to remove it … all this mud was removed with other utensils or with cans or any other thing that permitted to remove it before the sector was full of the mud of those working nearby. For this reason, around every group's work sector, a dirt bank of approximately fifteen or twenty centimeters was built, and the work proceeded until we reached the bottom…; then the "standard-setter" of the brigade, the brigade commander, and the "internal guard" were called; they measured the sector, and if the measurement was approved by the "standard-setter," the bank was broken up, cleaned up, and that was the end of the daily task for the whole group. Generally, all groups had three shovels each, to fill a wheelbarrow with mud from the canal and to transport mud twenty-five meters away in order to build the dike that later on had to protect the camp against flooding.

One worker had to spread the dirt from a wheelbarrow in the space of a square meter and pack it down "well" with a piece of wood, two hundred times. This is the kind of work that had to be done with all the muddy dirt of all wheelbarrows during the eight-hour shift.

All that the camp commander had promised us, especially the "good will to work," did not last long since, with the shift from the first sector, the situation changed as well.

Each worker-prisoner is in the obligation of completing his daily work quota.

Each worker-prisoner, although he has completed his daily work quota, must go on working until his eight hours have elapsed.

The "internal brigade guards" started to get moving, the "brigade commanders" started to shout . . . and we were all scared, expecting something unusual. The "old prisoners," the veterans, warned us to be careful because the situation of earlier years was apparently going to be repeated.

In this instance, I am very sorry, but I cannot refrain from stating that the conduct of the prisoners from Korça toward the other prisoners was very unpleasant. Most of them had "full bellies"; they did not know what kind of hunger the others were enduring . . . they were close to their relatives . . . they had food! . . . while the others longed for a mouthful of food, some more of the camp ration, because we were starving.

It was not envy on the part of the "other prisoners" because those from Korça had food, so much so that no one dared to approach those who had food to see what they were eating; each one shut himself up, enduring not only hunger but also pain; because those who had food, in those days of difficulties for the "other prisoners," did not mind if the prisoners from Elbasani, Durresi, Vlora, Berati, Gjirokastra, and other places went to work every morning with empty stomachs. Later on, the morning tea was served in exchange with the evening dinner, and we had to work all day on our empty stomachs until sunset, when the bread was distributed, but this quickly disappeared . . . and those from Korça thrust themselves in "attack" against the other brigades. The Korçarian brigade was always an "attack brigade" (*brigada sulmuse*); all of them "assailed work"! In those days, all of them were "distinguished workers," but only in Maliqi, since when they found themselves in the other camps at Kavaja, Fusha-Vojgurore (Kuçove), Vlashuk, Shtyllas-Fier, etc., prisoners from Korça had it very hard, because most of them were left "foodless" since they did not get anything from their homes as earlier, in Maliqi, and many of them became spies for security, for the camp commander, and "ears" for the camp internal guards in exchange for only a half-serving spoonful of bean water or macaroni, if there was anything left. . . .

· · · · ·

By this time, friendly reader, you already have an idea about life in the forced labor camps, although I have not written almost anything, really; but this time we want to get up early, before the sun breaks. The sky was still shining with stars, or perhaps it was raining. The camp internal guard, at four o'clock in the morning, went from one end of the camp to the other blowing his whistle as a signal to "get up!" At the same time, the brigade "internal guards," with their clubs in their hands, came in striking everyone who, for one reason or another, took too long to rise from their rags. . . . All tried quickly to get through with their personal necessities . . . the "toilet holes" were all full, while three or four endless lines of prisoners were waiting their turns. . . .

164

Around the big hole for the solid waste, except on the side of the watch tower, lines of fifty or more prisoners, side by side, were getting through with their needs; the second and third groups came along, one after another. Those who came the latest, according to this routine, had to walk on the tips of their toes because urine had flooded the place. Nobody seemed impressed, though, and nobody wanted to waste any time. Everyone wanted to get through quickly! Afterward, if anyone had been able to save some water, he did his personal "cleaning" by dampening his fingertips and rubbing his eyes. All of that in fifteen minutes! Tea was distributed right away, about five spoonfuls of water that tried to smell like tea but stank like the half barrels where it was boiled. (Later on, tea was distributed for "dinner," while in the morning we had the food previously distributed in the evening.) Twenty minutes later, the whistle gave the signal for the brigades to get together near the exit gate, to get ready for work. Prisoners answered the roll call from the brigade guard. The latter, upon ending their roll calls, "presented their forces" to the day officer, while two other guards counted the prisoners who went through the camp gate, and they went in lines according to their brigades. When everyone was out, the two guards who had counted the prisoners gave their tally to the day officer; if it coincided with the count of the internal guards, the officer ordered "go to work!" Otherwise, the counting had to be started again until both figures were in accordance.

Outside the camp, formed in twelve brigades, we again awaited the order to "go to work!" with the brigade commanders and the internal guards at the heads of the lines. Three heavily armed guards led the way, one of them with a German Scharz machine gun and the other two with rifles of the same make. On the sides and around us, at a distance of fifty meters, went the other guards, with automatic German rifles, machine guns, etc., until the circle was closed.

Generally, the walk toward the work sites started around five o'clock in the morning, once the number of prisoners going to work had been verified. When the walk started, after two or three minutes, all brigades had taken the shape of a jumbled mess because each prisoner was trying to get to the center of the lines, but who could get in sooner? Clubs started to fall upon the prisoners' backs, while guards and brigade commanders yelled, "Move on! Why are you not walking?" Those in front were forced to run since those behind were pushing them, trying to run away from the club blows, so the front runners also started to get blows from the commanders and guards who opened the way. Everyone was scurrying around to get away from the blows, and between the "move ons" and the "why aren't you walkings?" from here and there, at seven o'clock everyone was ready to start working.

Back at the camp, the day officer started to take the roll call of all those who stayed behind, beginning with the camp physician, the cooks, the sick, and those on "medical leave." That ended all day activities at the camp until the brigades came back.

We worked at the Nizhaveci camp until the last day in September. The walk between the camp and the work sites took two hours each way; thus, every day, among the 1,800 prisoners, those who received the club blows changed.

No one spoke, neither to himself nor to his companion, because of the weariness, hunger, and fear of the club, the annoyance of sufferings in the camp . . . each one had his thoughts and his problems. Only the hope that "someday we would get out of there" kept us alive, although that "someday" might never come . . . or it was very far away! . . . awaiting the realization of his dreams, which influence heavily the hope for freedom, although many knew that their dreams were difficult to come true and that prisoners would probably stay where they were.

Upon arrival to the work sector, at seven o'clock, each one knew what part he had to do, and work started. No one could or wanted to waste any time; everyone struggled to complete his daily task with shovels, picks, wheelbarrows, and the big wooden piece to stir the dirt to build the dike, and those who felt stronger got into the water.

We were all "transformed"; we looked like "automats," in many instances acting without knowing what we were doing; only "working!" for fear of not being able to complete the daily quota. No one rested. No one could stand "straight." Those who worked with shovels had to hold them through the middle of the handles, and, stooped like that, they awaited. . . ! Those who pushed the wheelbarrows had to wait until they were full, holding them on both ends and await while stooped. . . ! Those who leveled off the dirt for the dike could not use that way to rest, either, because he did not have any reason to wait . . . he had to keep moving his shovel at all times or else use the *tokmak,* the wooden piece to level off the dirt. Everyone had to be moving all the time. We all had to have a special care not to use that way to rest because the brigade commanders and the internal guards were quick to start shouting and screaming "because of the consequences" . . . using the worst words and expression against the "enemies of the people," accusing us of being "irresponsible," of "having no conscience," or of "committing a direct sabotage" (*sabotim dyrek*) thus starting the yelling and the club blows.

All of these forms of treatment were used, too, at the former camps in Vloqishti, Beden, Pojan, etc.; although I did not go through those camps, I had companions who were there and told many things that I have had to set aside.

In many instances, the brigade internal guard went to help the brigade commander, although the former did not use the club because the commander had used it; in order to appear "prudent" and not "criminal," the guard ordered the prisoner to go into the water, perhaps down to his waist, leaving him there until he fell completely into the water or the mud, worn out by the cold and the leeches that sucked his blood. There were cases when a prisoner fell into the water and the internal guard sank him in the mud, drowning him in the most criminal manner.

Through the diabolical and criminal imagination of the brigade commanders and guards, prisoners were tied upside down to a post, on the canal shore, with two *tokmaks* tied to their hands; because of the weight, the prisoner stayed not only with his head upside down but also stretched by the additional weight of the two large wooden pieces. Thus he remained for hours on end until the guard ordered his feet released and the weight of the *tokmaks* made him plunge directly into the mud of the canal ... and the guard sank him quickly.

The dead, drowned, or murdered by the external guards were unimportant to them. After the brigade commanders and guards pronounced the prisoner "dead," they forced his companions, those closest to him, to throw the body behind the dike, while the other prisoners lined up with their wheelbarrows, piling up dirt and mud from the canal on his dead body ... that was the prisoner's burial.

Many prisoners were killed behind the canal dike, gunned down by the external guards while they were doing their personal necessities, and they remained squatting as they were ... their bodies were quickly covered with dirt and mud, buried forever in Maliqi.

The monotony of the daily work was changed by the "breaking of the swamp reed." A large area of the sector that the canal traversed was covered by this plant, which reached a height of two meters or better. These sectors were also the deepest for us. Before starting to work, we had to crush the reed and level off the sector, not so much to facilitate our work as to give "visibility" to the guards who stood watch around us.

All prisoner-workers, according to their brigades, formed lines and joined their arms until the last one of each brigade linked with the first one in the next brigade, thus making a line of approximately 200 meters in length. Once well linked, the "march against the reed" started. The two or three brigades in the front lines had the hardest task: to crush the reed from the root, while the other brigades went by crushing it. This way we had to get enough ground ready for all the brigades. In these sectors, the water was usually higher than our waists, so everyone would be able to imagine the kind of inhuman work that the Communists forced their "enemies" to perform at the Maliqi Swamp.

At twelve noon, there was a half-hour rest for lunch. Whoever had anything could eat, while the rest of the prisoners lay down, with their arms under their heads, looking at the sky, lost in their thoughts, until they sank into sleep for a few minutes. At 4:30 or 5:00 p.m., according to the time we had started to work in the morning, the day's work ended. ... All brigades, in their respective sectors, were counted by their commanders, and the numbers were verified when the brigade internal guard did the counting. Immediately, the brigades gathered in a wide area so the day officer could do the recounting and then went into a third place where they were again counted by two sergeants who took their stations according to their brigades. During this period, the external guards moved and took their positions in the direction of the road that we had to walk. If the count was correct, we started right away, almost running, because the guards were also tired and bored, and they wished to go back to the camp more than we did, but that made the situation harder because the clubs fell upon us with or without any reason.

There were problems when someone was missing since they immediately said: "He has fled!" and they started to take a count of us up to five times, and when we got started, there were club blows all over the place.

Upon arriving at the camp, the guard on duty blew his whistle for "lunch." All of us were ready, lined up. The "volunteers" brought the bread for the whole of the brigade. The "half barrels" of food were ready in front of the door of each brigade, but . . . we had to wait. The food could not be distributed because the day officer had to deliver his lecture . . . criticizing, suggesting, threatening, and in several instances brutally punishing someone through the brigade commanders. Time went on, and we were enduring hunger, awaiting . . . until finally the order was given to distribute food. During this waiting time, the majority had eaten the bread ration, so the "food," water colored by beans or macaroni, was sipped quickly.

One hour later, "dinner," consisting of two or three spoonfuls of hot water with the color of tea and the stench of grease was distributed.

At 9:30 p.m. the "preparation" signal was given . . . and at 10 p.m., "retreat."

During the night, nobody could go outside for any necessity; that went on up until the last months of our time at the Nizhaveci camp; it was really a complete silence because everyone was trying to get some rest.

We were all labeled as "enemies of the people," reactionaries, traitors, saboteurs, criminals, villains . . . that is why the "popular government" had no mercy for any one of us, although we had been told at first that work was a great privilege for us, with the "socialist emulation" on our empty stomachs and enduring club blows on our backs, worse off than animals, since we were all between the ages of sixteen and forty-five years, while the aged and the handicapped, unable to work, "ate the government bread as parasites." They said that "it was better to eliminate" the latter.

The work at the Maliqi Swamp cost the enemies of communism very dearly, those labeled as "enemies of the people." The swamp was drained, but it was flooded with the blood and sweat of the prisoner-workers.

Maliqi covered with its mud the bodies of hundreds of prisoners, whose names were unforgettable only in the minds of their companions in the same sufferings, while the history of modern times in our country, Albania, will show the future generations that "the big Maliqi Swamp was drained by prisoners who paid for the hate that the Communists felt against them. . . ."

When the Maliqi Swamp was drained, in 1951, certain forms of inhuman tortures that the Communists used against the prisoners were finished; they were used against political prisoners, the so-called "enemies of the people." All prisoners who went through the various camps at Maliqi, who today might be in other camps, or perhaps free, wherever they may be, they shall remember with hate their sufferings, only feeling resignation for the love of their companions who remained buried there.

The camps of Maliqi, Vloçisht, Pojan, Rembec, Nizhavec, except for the water, which worked in favor of the Communists to increase their hate, tortures, and suffering for their enemies, are no different than those in Beden, Çengelaj, Gosevogel, Uravojgurore (Kuçove), Shtyllas (Fier), Vlashuk, etc., because hunger and clubs were never separated from the prisoners.

BULGARIA

The Truth That Killed

Georgi Markov

The case of GEORGI MARKOV (1929–78) provides an unusual example of political violence perpetrated by a Communist state (Bulgaria, in this case) even beyond its borders. Markov was a prominent Bulgarian writer who until his defection in 1969 was a privileged member of the elite, well known and highly rewarded. It was precisely this insider, elite position that enabled him to observe the prevailing abuses of power and the corruption of the rulers.

After his defection he worked for the BBC in London and expressed his critiques of the regime both in his broadcasts and his writings. He received numerous death threats and in 1978 became the victim of a novel method of assassination. While waiting for a bus on the street in London he was pricked by the tip of an umbrella carried by an agent of the Bulgarian political police. The tip carried an unusual lethal poison developed for inconspicuous assassinations. He died in the hospital a few days later. Apparently his murder was ordered at the highest level—

From Georgi Markov, The Truth That Killed *(New York: Ticknor and Fields, 1984). Reprinted by permission of A. M. Heath & Co., Ltd.*

by the Bulgarian Politburo—as retaliation for his ongoing critiques of the regime and particularly its leader Todor Zhivkov, whom he knew personally.

The excerpts that follow provide on the one hand a summary of his life and death (written by his widow), and on the other descriptions of life in the Bulgarian Communist police state culled from his memoir. One section illustrates the high-handed public behavior of a military officer; a second examines "the cult of personality" as practiced in Bulgaria. These cults—modeled after that of Stalin—provided (or were intended to provide) the major source of legitimacy of Communist systems, including their policies of repression.

In these excerpts Markov also reflects on the official cultivation of hatred and the associated preoccupation with "the enemy" on the part of the authorities. It was a preoccupation that most directly served to justify political violence and coercion. Unlike many Western intellectuals, who believe that Marxism was a noble theory poorly implemented, Markov observes, "I know of no other political religion which has had a stronger impact on the baser human instincts and passions, which has given such encouragement to human vice generally, as the Communist ideology."

It should be noted that the assassination or kidnapping of prominent defectors from Communist countries was not peculiar to Communist Bulgaria but was a policy pioneered by the Soviet system under Stalin. The most famous of such assassinations was that of Leon Trotsky in Mexico City, carried out by an agent of the Soviet political police. (For examples of such Soviet assassinations and kidnappings, see Paul Hollander, The Many Faces of Socialism, *85–88.)*

· · · · ·

Introduction, by Annabel Markov

My husband Georgi Markov is buried in an ancient and beautiful country churchyard in the west of England. So old are some of the tombstones in that little churchyard that their inscriptions have almost disappeared. Those which can be read indicate that nearly all of those whose bodies lie there were local, and that most lived long and perhaps relatively uneventful lives. But my husband's plain white headstone proclaims that, in every way, his life was different. He was born in another country, Bulgaria; he met his end unnaturally, before his time; and he died, as his stone says, "in the cause of freedom."

It was on September 7, 1978, that Georgi was attacked by an assassin on London's Waterloo Bridge, some time between the early afternoon and evening. As he passed a bus stop he experienced a sudden stinging pain in the back of his right thigh and, turning sharply, saw a man behind who bent to retrieve an umbrella and murmured "I'm sorry." Georgi noted that the man sounded un-English and that when he almost immediately hailed a taxi its driver seemed to have difficulty in understanding him. But so relatively unimportant did the incident obviously seem to Georgi that when he came home that night he did not mention it. He had, it is true, mentioned it to a fellow émigré and friend shortly after it occurred. But he had not been sufficiently alarmed to call a doctor, nor had he gone to the police. It was not until the early hours of the next morning, when his temperature had risen suddenly and alarmingly, that he at last said to me: "I have a horrible feeling that this may be connected with something which happened yesterday. . . ."

But even as Georgi told the story, and displayed a small puncture mark on his thigh, I did not feel he really believed that what he had feared had at last happened. Yet this was a man who, for nine years, had felt himself to be in danger; and who, for the past nine months, had lived with the certain knowledge that his enemies planned to kill him.

Until 1969, Georgi Markov was one of Bulgaria's top novelists and playwrights, his work known throughout the Eastern bloc. He was a member of the privileged élite and an acquaintance of the President, Todor Zhivkov, even traveling to the West, on one occasion, as cultural representative of Bulgaria. Then in 1969, after just one performance of a new play, *The Man Who Was Me*, he defected. Writing in English in a diary long afterwards, Georgi said: "Whenever I look back to my past, it seems to me that the most essential part of it is locked between two events, which I still cannot connect." The first of those events took place in 1962 after the publication of Georgi's first novel *Men* when, as he wrote in that same diary, "I awoke to find myself a literary star." The second was on the day seven years later when, in great haste, he left forever the country he loved.

To begin a new life at the age of forty, having to adjust to the foreign ways of another country, is difficult enough. To do it as a writer, transplanted from everything that went into forming an experience and a talent, unable any longer to communicate in the natural medium, is almost impossible. Yet it is a measure of Georgi's essential optimism and courage that he was determined to succeed as a writer in the West also; and, despite the enforced haste in leaving Bulgaria, he was careful to take with him proof of his talent. There was *Men*, which had been translated throughout Eastern Europe and made into a film that opened the first week of Bulgarian films at the National Film Theatre in London. There were other novels like *The Women of Warsaw, Portrait of My Double*, and the manuscript of a novel which had been banned, *The Great Roof*. There were plays like *The Cheese Merchant's Good Lady*, with which Georgi had made his debut as a playwright in 1963, and *Let's Go Under the Rainbow*; and there was also *The Assassins*, a play which had been singled out for censure in an article signed by Todor Zhivkov. In that hastily gathered collection, indeed, could be seen Georgi's development as a writer over the past seven years: from *Men*, which had made him a favorite of the Party, to the novels and plays which had become so outspoken against the system that they were no longer permitted to be published or staged.

When Georgi drove out of Sofia for the last time, he felt, he later described, as if he were attending a funeral. But at that point he did not know if it was he who was, in a sense, dead, or if it was everything that he was leaving behind him. It was soon apparent what the Bulgarian regime felt. Within ten days there was an article in the Party newspaper *Rabotnichesko Delo* criticizing Georgi's works and describing them as "alien to socialist society"; within two months all his plays had been taken off the stage; and within a year he was being described in the Bulgarian press as a traitor. Three and a half years after his defection, a special court in Sofia sentenced Georgi *in absentia* to six and half years imprisonment and his property was confiscated. "We hope," a Party hack wrote, "that in the West they know how to bury dogs."

But those books and plays and short stories and film scenarios—fruits of a prodigious creative output—were not all Georgi had brought to the West. He had also brought his memories and, because he had led an extraordinarily eventful life, they constituted both an unusual and a very complete picture of life in contemporary Bulgaria. For Georgi had observed the present system from its inception, at every level. Not only had he suffered greatly from it (the prisoner in the chapter "The Justification" was himself), but he had also reaped all the benefits it could offer. Born in 1929, the son of an army officer, Georgi grew up in pre-revolutionary Bulgaria and saw the Communists take over in 1944 when he was still a schoolboy. Subsequently, as a student, he was imprisoned for his political beliefs and this episode left a profound impression on him. Georgi later said that it was at this point when, half-broken by the system, he decided to be as successful as he possibly could within it. After surviving both meningitis and tuberculosis, he qualified as a chemical engineer, running the metallurgy factory referred to in the early part of his memoirs, before finding himself, at thirty-three, one of the country's top writers. As such, Georgi got to know everyone of influence in Bulgaria and, along the way, observed at first hand the corruption of absolute power. In 1975, in a series of weekly talks broadcast by the Munich-based station Radio Free Europe, he began to share his memories with those he had left behind.

By this time, Georgi had established himself in England and managed to achieve a measure of success as a writer. He had joined the Bulgarian section of the BBC's External Services; he had also started to write for the German radio station, *Deutsche Welle;* and he had adapted old plays and begun to write new ones. *The Archangel Michael,* the first play Georgi wrote after coming to the West, won a prize at the Edinburgh Festival in 1974; and Georgi was about to begin a literary collaboration with an English friend, David Phillips, that resulted in what was intended to be the first of several novels. That could have set the pattern of a new phase of life spent concentrating on capturing a new audience in a new environment. But Georgi missed his old audience and, above all, he was a committed writer. He was elated when he learnt that his broadcasts for Radio Free Europe were being listened to by an estimated audience of five million (more than half of Bulgaria's total population), and he laughed when he heard a joke currently circulating in Sofia to the effect that the subjects of some of his broadcasts, the Party leaders, were regularly tuning in to hear all about themselves. His amusement did not give way to apprehension, either, when news came that no less a figure than Zhivkov was enraged by the memoirs (and most particularly by a series of talks in which Georgi described their meetings).

During the period when the memoirs were broadcast, Georgi would sometimes receive telephone calls from Bulgarians visiting the West who wished to express their appreciation. Then, in January 1978, there came a very much more sinister call, the purpose of which was to warn Georgi that, if he continued to write for Radio Free Europe, he would be killed. Similar warnings recurred throughout five months and then, in late May, the Bulgarian who had delivered the warnings, who professed to be a friend, came to visit Georgi personally. The decision to kill had been taken by the Bulgarian Politburo, he said; and the means with which the murder would be effected had already been transported to the West. Georgi would be poisoned with a rare substance which would be undetectable (and had, by the way, been tested in Moscow), and he would develop a high fever before his death, which would be put down to natural causes. Everything the Bulgarian said, incidentally, led Georgi to believe that his enemies would attempt to administer the poison orally, and this may have been intentional.

To know that powerful enemies have planned your death in detail would spiritually destroy most people. Not so Georgi. In nine years of living in the West, most of them in England, he had never been able to sleep in an unlocked room, had always taken care with whom he ate and drank, had kept secret any plans to travel abroad. In what were to be the last months of his life he took even greater precautions, but still managed to live as generously and as fully as he always had; and our last holiday together was not really spoilt when he received a telephone warning saying that an attempt on his life was to be made there and then, as we tried to relax with our baby on an Italian island.

I now believe that Georgi's enemies always knew exactly when they would try to kill him, and that specific threats were issued and then not carried out as part of a deliberate policy both to terrify him and eventually to make him drop his guard. ("They're playing with me," Georgi said, when he returned unscathed from that Italian holiday.) In Georgi's memoirs he stresses the importance of September 9 in the calendar of Communist Bulgaria. It was on September 9, the anniversary of the imposition of Communist rule, that Georgi, by now in hospital, suffered a terrible collapse from which he was only saved through the efforts of doctors and his own great will to live. He survived for two more days, believing that he would be able to talk with Special Branch officers, who had by then been alerted. But the poison in his system was impossible to resist.

For just a few hours after Georgi's death on the morning of September 11, it was purely a tragedy for his family and friends. By the end of the day it had become a public sensation also; and, within three weeks, the world-wide rumors that he had been murdered were confirmed. Scotland Yard announced the finding of a minute precision-made metal pellet in his thigh: exactly the same weapon as had been used in an unsuccessful attempt on the life of another Bulgarian defector, Vladimir Kostov, in Paris. At the inquest into Georgi's death the coroner ruled that he had been killed unlawfully, and the poison used to fill that pellet was identified as ricin, rare and exceptionally deadly, which is known to have been extensively researched in Eastern Europe.

It is very clear whose interests were served by Georgi's death; and a wealth of circumstantial evidence exists which heavily implicates them. But because of the nature of the weapon used, which allowed the assassin to get clear away before murder was even suspected, it is unlikely that murder charges can ever be brought (though the British police continue their investigations). What does exist for all to see, however, is the motive for the crime: and these memoirs must be almost unique in the whole field of literature from Eastern Europe in that their author paid with his life for writing them.

I remember very well the general disbelief immediately after Georgi's death. It seemed impossible to many of those born and brought up in the West that a man could be murdered for a series of broadcasts. They were lucky indeed in not appreciating what a closed society involves. Georgi was murdered because he told the truth. Not only did he question the underlying values of Bulgarian communism, and therefore Soviet communism also, but he took a cool fair look at Zhivkov, who has now been in office longer than any other East European leader. To look at a man who has encouraged a personality cult around himself as an ordinary mortal was apparently unforgivable. Indeed, the chapters in this book on Georgi's meetings with Zhivkov have been described by at least one Bulgarian émigré as "dynamite."

These memoirs have already been published in Bulgarian by means of a special fund and have received considerable acclaim. They have moved some of Georgi's countrymen to describe him as "Bulgaria's Solzhenitsyn" and, over and over again, I have been told how true they are. "We have an author in his own right and talent among the greatest in our language," wrote one Bulgarian who dared not sign his name. Georgi's theme is "the unimaginable tragedy of our people," as that same Bulgarian put it, and yet, in parts, this is a very funny book. That does not surprise me, having lived with Georgi and known him, and neither does the book's highly subtle and flexible approach. All these qualities single it out among dissident literature, as does the fact that it is the only such work to come out of Bulgaria, the Soviet Union's closest satellite state.

Spanning as they do the years from 1947 to 1969, Georgi's memoirs are, *in toto*, roughly twice the length of this English translation. Hence there were considerable problems involved in selecting the right material for a Western readership. The names of those who would mean nothing to non-Bulgarians have been cut in places, and the chapters on Zhivkov himself have also been reduced in length (we have indicated where cuts have been made). I think Georgi's authentic voice comes through loud and clear in this English translation: and, in so far as it can, so does his rich and striking use of language which so many Bulgarians have commented on. It is very clear from this book how much Georgi loved Bulgaria: not the country it had become, which he said he never missed after 1969, but the true Bulgaria where he was born and shaped and which he never forgot.

Georgi's only child Sasha does not remember her father very well because she was only two when he died. But she helps me when I put flowers on his grave and she asks about him a great deal. "Why did Daddy write those things if he loved us?" she said not long ago. I told her that Georgi believed that the Bulgarian authorities would never dare risk the scandal that might ensue if they killed him; and I told her that, above all, Georgi was a man who could not compromise or be dictated to. Through this English translation, Sasha will know the father who adored her. It is therefore dedicated to her as well as to those many, many Bulgarians for whom Georgi is a national hero.

Georgi was a man who passionately loved life and understood how it should be lived. That he was prepared to put himself in a position of great risk indicates just how greatly he believed in individual freedom. He died defending it.

. . . . .

The Truth That Killed

I know of no other political religion which has had a stronger impact on the baser human instincts and passions, which has given such encouragement to human vice generally, as the Communist ideology. A time had come in Bulgaria when men were expected to express themselves solely through the commission of evil deeds, which were justified as a dialectical necessity of the Party. And it was precisely through the practice of that evil, by causing pain and suffering to others, that some people in Bulgaria now saw that they could cut a figure in life and society, better themselves, perhaps even gain a place in history. I know of a high-ranking officer in the State Security who had once lived as a humble employee in a forestry enterprise, and who in normal times would never have left it. But his entry into the militia, followed by a long series of arrests, interrogations, torture, and testimonies extracted by force, had pushed him up the ladder of promotion to a most powerful position. In a dramatic confession, he told me once that his career began from the moment when he was sent to arrest his closest friend of whose innocence he was totally convinced.

175

I know of many people who made brilliant Party and state careers and rose to positions which they would never have reached in a free society—solely by manufacturing evil for all those who happened to stand in their way. The capacity to do harm proved to be the most useful talent of the Communist epoch, since the *evil* done to individuals always turned out to be *good* for the policies of the Party. Figuratively speaking, people were not allowed to hold out a hand to help each other, but were given every opportunity to exchange cruel blows. When we talk of the "enemy-mania" which raged in all the spheres of our society and became a fundamental element in the Communist mentality, we must not forget that not only the Party but also many citizens felt a need for it. Through it they found themselves and discovered a purpose to their lives, they lived in order to seek out, hate, and fight enemies, as if the existence of the enemy justified their own existence. Actions against the enemy were at the same time actions of self-approval. The reward was two-fold: on the one hand, the gaining of Party recognition, and, on the other, the achievement of personal self-confidence and gratification. That is why this "enemy-mania" acted like a powerful bellows fanning into a blaze fiendish feelings and ambitions that otherwise would have remained locked in the cold silence of an untapped human coal seam. If, throughout the centuries, men have felt a need for the existence of God, king, or leader, in our time many people felt the need for an enemy. Nothing is more important to the life of a Communist society than the existence of an *enemy*. Voltaire's claim that if there were no God, men would find it necessary to invent Him, had its perfect application in our society, with its need for an enemy. Without this enemy, ideology, Party, and regime became a ridiculous nonsense. Through the enemy, everything found some sort of justification. The enemy justified the terror regime and all its violence; the enemy was the excuse for the immense failures and mistakes of incompetent leaders; the enemy explained economic reverses . . . and in the most cynical way the enemy was used to defend the need for the privileges of the elite. This gigantic, terrible, dastardly, indefatigable, constant, and ubiquitous *enemy* was the magic key to the Communist regime's existence. Most public activity in Bulgaria at that time was directed against various enemies. All secret or open meetings and sessions of Party organizations or individual groups of Party members were directed against some enemy; ministerial and managerial councils were transformed into headquarters for the struggle against the enemy; the whole atmosphere in the country was fraught because of the unceasing war against the enemy.

I shall always remember an incident of a slightly later period, which nevertheless sums up the blackness of that time and the two faces of "enemy-mania"—the public and the private.

It was, I think, during 1958. My friend K and I were queuing for bread outside a bakery near the tram stop in Knyazhevo. Everything was calm and normal. The baker took the bread out and about ten of us began to shuffle forward. At this moment, a major appeared from somewhere—I learnt later that he was from the barracks at Gorna Banya. He was about thirty-seven or thirty-eight, with a reddish face and dark eyes, and he moved with marked self-confidence, hitting his boots with a small crop. Instead of joining the queue, the comrade major tried to jump it without even an excuse. The people at the front, obviously frightened, meekly made way for him. But my friend K, who could not stomach this triumph of impudence, ran forward and placed himself between the major and the bread.

"Take your place in the queue, if you please!" he said.

For a moment, the major seemed amazed that somebody had dared to challenge him; then his face grew dark red and he yelled: "Who are you to tell me what to do?"

"Instead of showing people an example, you behave intolerably!" K replied firmly.

At this, the people in the queue took courage and started to heckle the major, who, seeing that he would not be allowed to have his own way, flew into a rage.

"I'll teach you who I am!" he shouted at K, turning away and quickly walking off into the main street. The people heaved a sigh of relief and a pleasant animation set in as if every one of them had won a victory. But those of us still queuing shuddered when we saw the major returning after a minute with two militiamen in uniform.

"This one here!" he said, pointing to K.

Nearly all of us in the queue tried to explain to these representatives of law and order what had happened, and that if anyone deserved censure, it was the comrade major. But without listening to us, the militiamen seized K and, accompanied by the major who looked at us with triumphant fury, they marched him off to the militia station.

I immediately rang K's parents, and his father ran around trying to do what he could, but was not able to achieve anything that day. K spent the night in the Knyazhevo militia station and was let out only the following evening. When he came to us, his face was unrecognizable—it was covered with ugly bruises and two of his front teeth had been knocked out.

He told me that when they brought him to the station the major and one of the militia officers who was clearly a friend of his had pushed him onto the floor and brutally beaten him up.

"So you're not going to let *me* have bread, are you? *Me! Me!*" yelled the major, kicking my unfortunate friend.

But this was the end of only the first act. In the evening, they took K to the chief of the militia station himself. He listened silently to the story of my friend and even pretended that he sympathized with him.

"If you really are one of us, the major was clearly in the wrong," the station chief said, whereupon he suddenly asked: "But are you one of us?"

My friend did not know what to reply, and the chief added: "Remember that whatever you say will have to be proved!" Then he looked at him meaningfully and said: "Now, tell me the names of your friends!" K cautiously mentioned a few names of friends who had a certain political weight.

"And now, tell me who your enemies are?" the militia chief demanded.

K thought a while and replied: "I don't really know, I don't think I have any enemies."

"No enemies!" The chief raised his voice. "Do you mean to say that you hate nobody and nobody hates you?"

"As far as I know, nobody."

"You're lying!" shouted the lieutenant colonel suddenly, rising from his chair. "What kind of a man are you, not to have any enemies? You clearly do not belong to *our* youth, you cannot be one of *our* citizens, if you have no enemies! We are surrounded by enemies, and this man here claims that he has none! Where do you live? On what planet?"

Afterwards the police chief reeled off approximately the following speech: "The man who doesn't hate isn't one of us! Because one cannot live without hating! It is not possible for a citizen of ours not to have a proper attitude towards the enemy. Even in his time Christo Botev[1] used to say: "To love and to hate strongly!" And if you really do not know how to hate, we shall teach you! We shall teach you very quickly!"

And, indeed, they wasted no time teaching him. K was offered his immediate release on condition that he would become a secret informer and regularly report whatever he heard to the militia. Merely in order to get off, he signed several declarations on oath promising to serve them. After this incident, he suffered from a prolonged nervous fever and kept repeating to me that he no longer wanted to live in Bulgaria. Finally, he fled abroad.

However, what impressed me so greatly, and what I never forgot, was the diabolical declaration by the militia colonel that "You are not a proper man if you do not hate!" Probably without being aware of it, this servant of the "people's democracy" had formulated precisely the basic moral tenet of Marxist-Leninist-Stalinist ideology. Hate was the main engine, the motor of all relations between man and Party, man and state, and man and man. Only a few years were needed by these professors of the art of hate to turn fear and hatred into the main emotions of the period.

Look at any newspaper of that time, read any speech, examine the workings of any department, enterprise, co-operative farm, school, or university—and you will inevitably discover the corrosion of hatred. We students of that era were expected every day to hate Nikola Petkov,[2] Traicho Kostov,[3] Tito, Franco, Chiang Kai-shek, American imperialism, German revanchism, Yugoslav revisionism, the black Fascist past, the Church and the clergy, bourgeois remnants, the émigrés—and so on. In reality, this abstract hatred took on concrete forms: you hated your colleague because he was more gifted than you, you hated your friend because he had more success with women, you hated your chief because he was above you and you hated your subordinate because you suspected him of wanting to take your place, you hated the greengrocer and the baker because they had not kept you anything under the counter, you hated your powerful relative X because he did not let you have a passport to travel abroad, you hated your wife because she wanted a life of her own, you hated your children because they did not obey you. In the end, you hated yourself, because you could not become what you wanted to be.

Nor did this hatred remain merely an open or undeclared feeling; very often it was translated into powerful actions to which the cultured Western world referred euphemistically as "violations of the law." The better name is "terror." It seems to me that there is no closer link on earth than that between hatred and terror. And since both needed enemies, when no more enemies existed they had to be invented. In principle, everybody could be an enemy; absolutely every Bulgarian citizen had done something, however innocent, for which he could be declared an enemy at a given moment. If somebody had done nothing, then this was an even stronger reason for treating him as an enemy. I am convinced that if one day, somehow, enemies cease to exist and there is no way of inventing them, people like our lieutenant colonel will die out, for they will have nothing to live for. . . .

. . . . .

The cult of personality arrived in Bulgaria with the airplane which brought Georgi Dimitrov.[4] Never before had our country witnessed such a vulgar pageant of human abasement. The introduction and establishment of the cult should be seen entirely as part of the general movement, both spiritual and physical, which was aimed at undermining and destroying the independence, human dignity and self-respect of every individual Bulgarian. For the overwhelming majority of our people (with the exception of a handful of Party fanatics), the cult was an expression not of bigoted worship, passionate faith, or boundless devotion, but of fear. For many, the mouthing of phrases like "our beloved teacher and leader, father of all progressive humanity, Comrade Stalin" was a kind of vaccine against terror.

I remember how stunned I was by the first signs of the invasion of this Soviet-made cult. It began with the propaganda groups' incessant chanting of "Stalin-Tito-Dimitrov." Later Tito was dropped from circulation. I can testify to the ceaseless bellow: "Stalin-Stalin-Stalin!" Such parades of human voices were always organized, never spontaneous. Usually, the signal was given by a group of Party agitators and security agents. Years later, the feeling of mockery would anticipate the signal. One of my colleagues in the Polytechnic was always the first to jump up and start chanting the relevant name, forcing the Party masses to yell every two minutes. I remember a particular end-of-season performance at the National Theater. The play was called *The Exploit.* Shortly before the curtain rose, Vulko Chervenkov,[5] who at that time was King and God, entered the Royal box. The whole audience immediately jumped to its feet, incessantly shouting: "Cher-ven-kov, Cher-ven-kov. . . ." I looked at the people around me. Most were regular theater goers; they looked intelligent, with none of the grey uniformity of typical Party faces. And that is when I suddenly sensed that they triumphed in their effort to worship the man whom they deeply hated in reality, that their voices were really shouting the most degrading and hostile insults, that the incantation of the dictator's name had a quite contrary meaning. Life had forced them to participate in this circus and they did so with the exaggeration of clowns. All the while, the man above them accepted all this with imperial condescension. Afterwards, a friend said to me: "I gave him such a 'Cher-ven-kov' that his hat flew off!"

The other ritual of the cult of personality was the quotation mania. We quoted until we were blue in the face. I cannot remember a meeting or a conference where, every minute, someone would not volunteer the priceless cliché: "As Comrade Stalin says. . . . As Dimitrov says. . . . As Chervenkov says. . . ." Later the name of Lenin began to crop up; and now, when I read the Bulgarian newspapers, I see that things haven't changed much, for they say "as Comrade Zhivkov teaches us."

The mania for quoting also serves as a proof of loyalty. I know so many people who, in order to remain at the university or get a job, would be ready to repeat for the rest of their lives "as comrade ___ teaches us." But during that time there was also a flood of mockery. It was particularly in evidence in the examination papers of aspiring students, each of whom either cited non-existent quotations, or quoted in such an ambiguous way that everything plainly became ridiculous. Often what the "comrade" had said was—judged by normal thought processes—pure rubbish. Sometimes I am tempted to draw up a catalogue of the utter nonsenses, the megalomaniac phrases, and the stupid pronouncements of all these former and present deities. On the other hand, I consider that the regime deliberately forced us to repeat these inanities in order to kill off the last resistance of our personal dignity.

One of the most banal manifestations of the personality cult was the so-called "red corners." In every institution, office, or business establishment, and even in the homes of the more zealous Party members, there was the inevitable corner covered in red material in front of which stood a small bust of Stalin, Dimitrov, or Lenin, as the case may be. Sometimes all the saints were grouped together. When there were no busts, plaques were used or just photographs. Over the "red corner" there always hung a slogan. These special Communist altars to the cult of personality were subsequently left to gather dust. But I know a lot of pseudo-artists who made considerable fortunes by producing busts or plaques for this purpose. There were also the usual funny stories about offices which laid on a reserve of different busts. Today the "red corner" continues to exist in many places, with Lenin occupying pride of place.

180

Perhaps the most humiliating and inhuman expressions of the cult of personality were the political rallies, which continue to this day—albeit in a less ostentatious way. They, too, are exclusive products of the regime. Every older Bulgarian citizen remembers that parades on such a scale were quite unknown in our country before 1944. The traditional military parade on St. George's Day or the religious procession and service for the Epiphany were a thousand times more modest events than the Communist celebrations of May 1. I have often questioned the point of these pompous party carnivals. Are they not well-organized rituals, aimed at suppressing, defacing and destroying the natural instinct of every person to be himself? Perhaps there is some similarity with religious rituals. But whereas in a religion man is expected to pay homage to the spiritual image of good, to the love of his neighbor, to the aspiration towards a just and lofty life, things are quite different in the case of the Communist religion. You have to stand in line, to take up your place in the herd, then with hundreds of thousands of others you must pass in front of an elevated and distant rostrum, turn towards it, take off your hat and wave your hand in greeting while your face produces the most pleasing possible smile. Like a well-trained monkey, you are expected to bow to other human beings, who are not superior to you in any way except in the power they hold, which they have assumed without asking your consent. The leader of your group will make you shout the name of the creature standing in the center of the rostrum, while this creature, tired and bored by the four- or five-hour procession of the human herd, does not even notice you. On all sides you are hemmed in by portraits of people, who may be like you biologically but whom you do not know personally; though you are in no way convinced of their worth, you must bow to them as reverently as to your mother and father. And this very bow is the death blow to your dignity, to the consciousness that you are a being of equal worth and with equal rights, and not an animal or a slave. To recognize and value the qualities of this or that man is normal in human relations, but to fall on your knees before somebody whimpering his name negates everything you are. I stress this moment of humiliation which is a kind of death. It is the main blow which the cult of personality has dealt and continues to deal to the spirit of our people. The basic principle of the personality cult has always been "I am everything, you are nothing."

One of the most tragi-comical expressions of the personality cult was the renaming of streets, towns, villages, factories, hospitals, schools, and even mountain peaks. The ridiculous thing was that they were awarded the names of living Party figures. There was no Bulgarian town without its "Stalin" street or "Georgi Dimitrov" street. Foreign Communist parties provided material for immortalization with the names of Molotov, Tito, Gheorghiu-Dej, Tolbukhin, Clement Gottwald, and Kalinin, while the members of our own Politburo competed amongst themselves in proffering their names everywhere. I recall that I trained in a railway plant at Kostenets called Anton Yugov,[6] that I visited a factory named Tsola Dragoycheva, that I walked along a street called Vulko Chervenkov. Numerous sites and projects bore the names of many other still living Party bosses, such as Georgi Damyanov, Dimiter Ganev, Vassil Kolarov, and so on. Subsequently it transpired that some of the comrades were not so distinguished, while others (like Tito) passed out of the Communist camp, which led to all sorts of comical re-christenings until it was finally decided that only the names of dead Party leaders could be used for this purpose.

Of course, the personality cult had its hierarchy which was decreed by the Party and strictly observed. Nevertheless, while Marx was inevitably accepted as the first and the greatest, there were disagreements as to whether Stalin's image should precede that of Lenin. But even more amusing was the struggle about the distribution of the secondary positions of these self-appointed Party Olympians. Veritable wars were waged over the order of precedence in the Politburo's portrait gallery until, finally, the alphabetical order prevailed.

The Communist cult mania has always been the expression of a two-way lack of intelligence. If a handful of crippled human beings with Party tickets fanatically look up to a leader whom they identify with the Party and who fills their limited empty lives with faith and devotion, satisfying their instinct for servility, what is to be said of those whom they look up to? Often, observing these self-appointed saints at close quarters, I have asked myself if they take all this comedy seriously. Do they really believe that they are exceptional representatives of the human species to whom others should pay obeisance, as if they were gods? Unfortunately the answer is *yes*.

In character, these Party counts, marquesses, and barons were and are mediocre people, often possessing a below average intelligence. An ironic play of chance and circumstance had enabled them to occupy such elevated positions; but they lacked the necessary intelligence to perceive this and so ascribed their good fortune to their own exceptional qualities. They believed that they were worth more than the common people and insisted on being treated accordingly. This explained their inaccessibility, their unbearable pretensions, the fact that they surrounded themselves with fawning servants, their encouragement of every kind of worship of themselves and the constant demonstration that all depended on their power. Add to this the fact that they published an official Bulgarian calendar, which they had stuffed with the dates of their births and all the more important events in their lives, thus convincing themselves that they had displaced St. Iliya, St. Nicholas and St. Dimiter.

That they forced on people the cult of their own personalities was in itself a proof of their repulsive mediocrity. Not one of them was a real personality. And when they fell from power and mingled with the people, everyone was amazed by their ordinariness.

Voices from the Gulag

Tzvetan Todorov

TZVETAN TODOROV (1939–) is a philosopher, born in Sofia, Bulgaria, who has lived in Paris since 1963. He is the author of approximately twenty books encompassing philosophy, literary history, and contemporary history, including Facing the Extreme: Moral Life in the Concentration Camp *(1996), one of the few books to offer a comparative examination of the Nazi and Soviet concentration camps. Considered a major European thinker, his work and ideas were the subject of an international conference held at the University of Sheffield, England, in June 2004.*

Bulgaria was among the most repressive Communist states in Eastern Europe. An unusual feature of this repression was that it continued unabated after Stalin's death, well into the 1980s. Between 1944 and 1989 there were nearly one hundred concentration camps in Bulgaria. The camp discussed in the excerpt that follows was Lovech, which operated between 1959 and 1962. The case studies presented here are based on Bulgarian sources, including the transcript of a four-and-a-half-hour documentary film titled The Survivors.

. . . . .

Bozhidar Petrov

My father was one of the founders of Radio-Sofia. He was a director, scriptwriter, and actor. In 1962 Colonel Chakûrov told him: "You managed to escape our Popular Tribunal, so now your sons will answer for your acts!"[1]

One day there was a ringing and pounding at the front door. The blows along with the curses grew louder. I leapt from my bed and ran straight into a group of police and plainclothesmen. Their pistols were drawn, and they shouted: "You've been listening to imperialist music! Who gave it to you? Where's your tape player? You're going to confess everything!"

From Tzvetan Todorov, Voices from the Gulag *(University Park, PA: Pennsylvania State University Press, 1999). Reprinted by permission.*

183

My mother was crying, while my father tried to explain that I was a musician who played the violin, accordion, guitar. He told them that I liked authorized music. "Keep your explanations to yourself! We know which music is and isn't authorized!" They then grabbed the tape player and the only tape we had, and ordered my brother to throw his clothes on because he had some explaining to do at the police station. The tape player was never returned to us. Nor, at first, was my brother. He returned home about two years later. We heard that he had been taken to Belene. A letter arrived six months later. We petitioned and lodged legal complaints, but the courts told us that they had no file on my brother and that we should address the matter to the Ministry of the Interior. We wrote to the ministry, but never received an answer. My brother was nineteen years old at the time, and I was fourteen. It was 1957. After he finally returned home, he was drafted into the army. He was traumatized by his experiences, telling me about the beatings, the hunger, the hard labor.

Between the years 1959 and 1960 I was hauled into the Ministry of the Interior at 5 Moskovska Street seven times. They suspected me because I wore tight pants, listened to Western music, and danced to American songs. The first time followed a dance one Saturday night at a club on Gocho Gopin Street. It was around eight o'clock when a large number of cops and plainclothesmen appeared and forced most of the boys to take off our pants while keeping on our shoes. Along with a few others, I refused to obey. We were pushed into a police van parked in front of the club and taken down to 5 Moskovska Street. We entered a waiting room, where our names were called out one by one. My turn came, and I was brought to a furnished room where two police officers were waiting. "Take off those pants, you little bastard," one of them shouted. He then walked up to me and struck me in the face.

"Wait! Why are you hitting me? I've done nothing!" I cried. "These pants are new, they're mine."

"Take him downstairs," the other officer ordered.

I was taken out of the room, and a guard led me down a flight of stairs that opens onto Dondukov Boulevard. To the left and across the street was a bar, while to the right was the door through which we were brought in. We continued down a series of spiral staircases that led to a big room that contained ten or so cell doors. One was opened, and I was pushed inside. The cell was small and completely empty. There was a lamp of sorts, but it barely cast any light. It was around ten o'clock. The silence was oppressive, broken only by the opening and closing of doors.

A good deal of time passed, and it must have been past midnight when I heard the pounding of boots on the concrete floor. Someone then shouted: "Off with your coats and jackets! Roll up your sleeves, remove your shoes and socks! Roll up your pants to your knees! Are you ready?"

I then heard the key turn in the lock. "Out!" a voice commanded. The others were also being ordered out of their cells. "Lie down, with your legs in the air." Screams filled the room. "Stop your crying, you son of a bitch! Count up to fifty." Something slammed.

"Tie the son of a bitch up!"

"Stick him on the chair."

More than an hour must have passed like that; then my turn came. They forced me to lie down near the door. Stretched out on the floor, I lifted my legs as I was ordered to do. A plainclothesman stood over me, wearing a blue shirt with the sleeves rolled up and a tie.

"You're going to count up to fifty out loud, and if you don't scream too much you'll save your ass and be let go."

It started. Near me was another victim. A long rubber whip whistled and came down on the soles of my feet. How could I ever make you understand the pain? Trying not to cry too loud, I counted up to fifty.

"Stand up!" My torturer was coated with sweat. "Hold out your hands."

Sitting up, I started to get to my feet when a sharp pain knocked me to my knees. I couldn't walk, and still on my knees, I held out my hands.

"Count up to twenty," he ordered. He began to hit me while I counted. The pain was bad, but it was nothing in comparison to being whipped on the bottom of the feet.

"Now, go to the shower room. In one hour there will be an inspection. Those of you who still have bruises will be beaten again."

I crawled on my stomach toward the showers.

Inside, there were about ten others stretched out on the cement floor. My mouth was dry, and I needed water, but a mustached thug wouldn't allow me to drink. My feet were so swollen that they seemed to have been pumped with air. They had ballooned grotesquely, and I could neither walk not stand up. The cure, as it turned out, was to wet the hands and rub the feet, then stamp up and down till the swelling went down. Water ran out onto the cement from a pipe. I wet my feet and pressed them against the ground. The pain was overwhelming. Some of the others were unable to stand long enough on their feet to go through the necessary acrobatics. We finished by running in place on the cement, then in a circle around the large room, in the middle of which stood our torturers. Pushing myself to the limit, I succeeded in getting my feet "in order." I then underwent the "inspection." This meant showing my hands, slapping them together several times, then lifting my feet one after the other without lying down. If you passed the test, you got dressed and put on your shoes. One of the torturers took me outside by the stairs. At the door he said: "Go home at once. If you tell anyone what happened here, we'll bring you back."

I went home and went to bed. It was four o'clock in the morning. I didn't say a word to my parents about what had happened, as I didn't want to worry them.

A few days later, I confided to a few friends what I had gone through. They advised me to lodge a legal complaint, but I didn't dare. And it was a good thing I didn't. About two months later, I saw those who did complain: they were back at 5 Moskovska Street, strapped to chairs in the basement. I say "later" because, despite my precaution, I myself was brought back to this place six more times. At the end of the second visit, all the torturers knew me and asked me to explain to the other unfortunate victims how to "cure" their swollen feet. Some of them were so shocked and scared that they didn't keep their legs in the air. Instead, they hit their heads against the ground, screaming and begging for mercy. This broke the torturers' rhythm. When this happened, the victim's legs were put on a chair and tied between the back and the seat. Or the victim was tied, sitting down in the chair, and was then pushed over onto the ground. He couldn't move in that position, and the blows against the feet were even more painful.

There were two kinds of whips: a thick one and a thin one. But I think one was as painful as the other. There were also sandbags the size of boxing mitts. Others were punched with them, mostly in the small of the back. I cannot say how much it hurt, though, since I was never hit with them. There were seven torturers. They were always dressed in civilian clothing—ties and rolled-up shirt sleeves—and they always stank of alcohol. They picked their victims and, when they grew tired of hitting us, would have a colleague take over. Three or four of them would hit us at the same time, but it was always different, though I do not know why. I knew victims who had complained; I knew others who stayed in the basement for months because their feet could not recover; I saw corpses. When a victim couldn't reduce the swelling of his feet, the torturers stopped beating him, because he could no longer feel the pain.

One day they were beating two brothers. One of them no longer able to stand it, shouted, "Stop! He's small. Hit me instead!" His request was met and they started to concentrate on him. He suddenly cried, "Wait! I've a father who's like you."

There was a moment of silence, followed by a barrage of questions concerning the identity and profession of the victim's father. "He's a doctor who works at the local slaughterhouse."

With that, they jumped him, shouting, "And so, you're saying we're butchers, you little bastard?" The whips cracked, and the older brother was badly beaten, but the younger one was left alone. Christo and Ivan were the names of the two boys.

In 1960, the torturers grew bolder. They began to hit us all over the body. On the chest, on the back. They were like mad dogs. They no longer bothered maintaining a cover of secrecy and no longer cared about "curing" the victims. The majority of these people are now retired. I meet them in the street and they smile at me as if we were once good friends. They were "recycled" over the last thirty years and were placed in important positions controlled by the Ministry of the Interior. Georgi Pavlov was a colonel who commanded the police in Sofia. Rangelov was a colonel too, as was Bakurdzhiev, who was an advisor in the Interior Ministry. Georgiev was a colonel at Interior. I cannot remember the names of the three other torturers. But they were all Party members, were former partisans, and held important posts. They tortured me because I listened to Western music, wore tight pants, enjoyed American dancing, and because my father was a well-known figure in the world of culture before the Communist takeover.

· · · · ·

Boris Gikov

About 5:30 one morning in June 1959, there was a pounding at our door. Two plainclothesmen and a policeman then rushed into the house and carried out a search. They said they were looking for hidden arms. They found nothing and even signed a report to this effect. But they took me back to the station for a "small matter" of an identity check. I was taken to the police station at 1 Polyanov Street and locked in a basement prison cell. Nasko turned up a short time later, also brought in for a "small identity check." After a sleepless night, the two of us were loaded into a green truck and brought to the guardhouse at the central train station, where we were thrown into a cell with others who had been arrested.

The oldest among us asked why we'd been arrested and where we were being sent. But no one knew. The next day we were handcuffed and loaded into a cattle car. At one of the train stops, someone looked through a small crack in the siding and recognized the station at Pleven. But it was only after the train passengers got off and left the station that our wagon doors were opened. We were hustled into rows of three and, with guards waving machine guns all about, were led to the station's guardhouse. The building was dilapidated and grim. Once inside, our handcuffs were removed, and we were locked in cells furnished with rotting wood beds. An old man in a striped uniform who had also been arrested told us that we were bound for the Belene concentration camp. According to him, thousands of men were locked away at Belene, where they were worked to death. They were worked until they met daily production quotas that could never be met; they worked regardless of how much time it took.

We passed yet another sleepless night.

At dawn, we were told to prepare our bags. Nasko and I each had a piece of stale bread and jam brought from Sofia. The same guards put on our handcuffs, and we got into the same cattle car, which took us to the station at Levski. We changed trains, getting into one marked "Levski-Belene." It was now clear that the old prisoner was telling us the truth.

We reached Belene at ten o'clock in the morning and walked from the station to a bridge. We halted near some buildings, where officers were waiting. The guards gave them our official papers. After waiting there for two hours, we were taken across the bridge and to an island. We then picked up the pace until we reached the entrance to the camp, which was ten kilometers away. We could see barracks from the gates, but not a living soul.

We were put through a very careful body search upon our arrival. We were stripped naked, our heads were shaved, and in place of our own clothing we were given old army and prison fatigues. All of our personal effects were confiscated; I never saw them again. They then divided us into work brigades. Nasko and I were in the same brigade and in the same barracks. This was our only consolation in our grim situation.

When I say "barracks," something like sheds might come to mind. But, in reality, they were underground shelters. Upon entering, you had to climb down a couple of steps in order to reach the room itself. It was divided by a corridor, and along each side were bunk beds with shredded, rotting mats covered by fraying military blankets. About a hundred people, piled on top of one another, lived in this room. The shelter itself was built with a mixture of cob and woven branches—the same material used for animal pens. Hygiene was out of the question, since the walls were alive with thousands of bedbugs, which never left us in peace and never allowed us to sleep. The mosquitoes were nearly as bad.

To occupy our time until the return of the work brigades, we carried wood until dusk. Since we weren't yet enrolled in the camp, we ate what we had brought along with us.

The camp directors were all officers: Colonel Trichkov, Major Gogov, Captain Atanasov, Major Neshev (his wife Totka Nesheva was in command of the female prisoners), Major Goranov, and yet others whose names I forget.

I learned from veteran prisoners about the trip to Work Site No. 2 the year before. The inmates, I was told, were herded by horse-mounted guards and wolfhounds trained for this very task. Cudgel blows rained down on the defenseless victims under the pretext that they were tramping across a plantation of young poplar trees. The fact of the matter is that there was neither a plantation nor poplars. The prisoners were so panicked, and tried so hard to avoid the club blows, that they didn't stop to pick up the possessions or clothing they had dropped.

The camp was surrounded by barbed-wire fences, more than two meters high, held fast by fence posts in the shape of an upside down L, like those in the fascist camps we saw at the movie theater. Along the fence every forty or fifty meters were wooden towers. They were manned by armed watchmen with orders to fire immediately on anyone who passed beyond the warning signs on the perimeter.

Everything at the camp was done to bugle blasts. Going to bed, getting up, breakfast, lunch, roll call. The roll call took place after dinner; one could never predict how long it would last. We stood along three sides of a rectangle while a guard called out, brigade by brigade, the prisoners' first and last names. It was as if we were in prison. The length of the roll calls seemed that much longer during the cold winter nights.

In the middle of the summer the barracks were oppressive, all the more so because we were packed in like sardines. I spent that first night waiting for the bugle call at five o'clock without ever closing my eyes. Once it sounded, absolute pandemonium broke out. A hundred prisoners were trying to dress and walk at the same time. They pushed one another while rushing toward the sinks and toilets in order to be the first ones there.

At our work site alone, there must have been two or three thousand prisoners. There were, among us, political prisoners, common-law criminals, convicts, and still others. It was impossible to make sense of this jumble of people, and Nasko and I did our best to stick together. We were sent to the Eleventh Work Brigade, which turned out to be a punitive measure. Nearly all newcomers had to pass through this gauntlet.

We went to our site, accompanied by machine-gun-carrying guards and a brigade chief, who, like us, was an inmate. We were then divided into groups of two and given our daily production quota. We had to dig, load, and transport ten cubic meters of sand and dirt in wheelbarrows. The women prisoners, it seems, had a norm of eight cubic meters.

Unless you've tried, you cannot know how hard it is to push wheelbarrows full of sand. Part of the load inevitably falls out with each step. Those who couldn't fill the quota—which happened to Nasko and me several times— were recalled after dinner and had either to cut wood or to load the food silos for the camp livestock till late into the night. The veteran prisoners called this work detail "dance night," since we worked under the blaze of search lights.

Although the work schedule was intense, we managed to find enough food to stave off death. We were allowed to receive one hundred leva every three months along with a package of five kilos.[2] However, the delivery of the packages depended on the whim of the officers, who rewarded model prisoners. In five months, I received just one package. We were also allowed to send letters every three months. The letters were censored, and we weren't allowed to describe our lives in detail. About all we could write was "All is well."

So much for our rewards. As for the punishments, they were horrible. Those of us sentenced to solitary confinement were sent to a sort of dungeon with several cells. Each one was about a square meter in size. Those locked inside were forced to remain standing in water up to their ankles.

We worked for about a month on a dike, and then Nasko and I were assigned to a fishing brigade made up of sixteen men and two flat-bottomed boats. We caught the fish in a huge net with which we would block out part of the marsh. We tossed into the boat whatever we caught. We spent nearly a month on the boats, and were able to supplement our diets with fish.

A group of us, including Nasko and I, were then transferred to Work Site No. 1, which was a kilometer away from No. 2. We were divided into groups to work outdoors. About forty of us were sent to the village of Alexandrovo in order to join a project on the Osum River. We were housed in a barracks located on a small island in the middle of the river. Though we were still guarded, the atmosphere was more relaxed. After twenty or so days a torrential downpour struck, lasting three entire days and nights. When we awoke on the fourth day, water was up to our knees in the barracks. The bridge that connected us to the mainland had been swept away by the waters; not a trace of it was to be seen. We were ordered to find and reassemble the construction material. Naked down to our belts, we gathered and dragged ashore wood planks that had been caught in the branches of willow trees. The water had turned terribly cold in the down-pour, and we had to change our clothing every thirty minutes. By nightfall we had succeeded in rebuilding the bridge. This happened in early September 1959.

It was then that our group was ordered to return to Belene. It seems that instructions had been given to close the camp, which existed under the heading of "Section 0789." All the prisoners were assembled at Work Site No. 1 and told that the camp would be closed. Immediately afterward, large numbers of prisoners were released. All of us thought that we'd soon be seeing our loved ones again.

While the camp was breaking up, names were called from a list. Since iden-tification papers weren't required, Nasko answered to someone else's name and was freed. On the other hand, I ignored Nasko's prodding and waited for my own name to be called. I've long since regretted my honesty.

Following the departure of the liberated prisoners on 3 September 1959, there only remained about 140 people in the camp. We were told that we would stay to help with the harvest and that our own liberation was imminent. We waited through all of September. Finally, we would wait no longer and went on a hunger strike.

Very early one morning in the middle of October, we were loaded onto trucks covered with canvas and left for an unknown destination. I don't re-member how long the journey lasted, but we eventually noticed that we had passed through Lovech. Three kilometers or so from Troyan, we turned off the road, to the right, and entered a tunnel that led under a train track. We came to a halt at the foot of a tree-covered hill.

As we were getting out of the truck, I noticed that the guards and officers waiting for us were the same ones from our earlier camp—but even more bloody-minded and furious. "We're going to die here," I said to myself. . . .

. . . . .

Lilyana Princheva

I am a pharmacist by training and was thirty years old when I found myself in one of the camps.[3] I was released nearly six years later, having been at both

Belene and Bosna. When I think about all that can be said regarding the awful conditions, the truly awful conditions at these camps.... At Bosna, we actually lived in a stable. We worked like beasts of burden in the fields. We were constantly humiliated, and the clothes we were given were no less humiliating: they were old, tattered army fatigues. We worked from morning to night, under the blazing sun of summer and in the paralyzing cold of winter.

By far the worst thing, though, was what happened to our souls. In the camps where I was imprisoned, the prisoners didn't die and weren't killed. Those who became seriously ill were in fact sent away so that they wouldn't die in the camp. The horror of these camps was that they turned thousands of people into human wrecks. It was as if our hearts had been extinguished or ruined. Ruined by the humiliations, the hard and often absurd labor. Our work was like Sisyphus's pushing of the rock: it sapped our moral and psychological strength, our dignity, and our integrity. The Sisyphean nature of work also existed at Bosna. In the autumn, for example . . . we were taken to the fields. Arranged in long rows, we spent the entire day breaking lumps of dried soil with the backs of our hoes.

We survived, however, because we kept our humanity—and did so despite their best effort to persuade us, day in, day out, and around the clock, that we were useless, that we were vermin and a danger to society. They humiliated us and tried to sap our ability to think for ourselves. In our ranks were anarchists, Trotskyites, Agrarians, and those who refused all labels and Party affiliations. In this intolerable atmosphere of daily hardship and hard and pointless labor, we were saved by that aspiration shared by all human beings—namely, the desire for dignity, humanity, and goodness.

Let me tell you a story. One day we were working at the dike. The work was extremely hard. A bird of prey suddenly passed not too far above us, carrying an animal of some sort in its beak. We shouted, and the bird took fright and dropped its prey. Into our midst fell what turned out to be a young rooster. We picked it up and could have eaten it on the spot, we were all so hungry. But instead, we kept the rooster. He symbolized man's ability to escape from the jaws of death. We spoiled the rooster, and he became a real character, standing in front of us during morning and evening line-ups. We all loved that rooster. He became our good luck charm, our talisman. And then, one day, he disappeared. We were all worried and looked for him high and low. Finally, we understood what had happened. A new group of women had arrived the night before. There was a Gypsy among them, who had already been sent to the camp one or two times. Her name was Gina, and we were sure she was the thief. We surrounded her and asked what she had done with the rooster. Gina began to cry and said that she had broken the bird's neck in order to eat him. We forced her to give him back to us. We dug a small grave and buried him in it. We were all heartbroken, but though we were also starving, we didn't dare eat him.

This isn't the only example of the power of the human spirit. . . . For example, we all agreed that whenever a package arrived, we would give it to whomever was ill. Though starving, we wouldn't allow ourselves to eat a single thing from the package. It was for our sick comrade.

I can draw certain conclusions from all of this. The camps were not only a place of physical destruction and mutilation (for all of us, without exception, left the camps mutilated to one degree or another). They were also places where the individual's moral character and dignity were undermined. We were incessantly told that we were the scum of society and that we had to be eliminated. Many of us could not withstand both the awful physical conditions, which pushed our bodies and nerves to the breaking point, and the moral torture. There was the combination of miserable material conditions, hard and pointless labor that resembled Sisyphus's boulder, unrelenting brainwashing, the stream of total disinformation, separation from one's home, and the constant reminders that the fate of our families was in our hands. All of this turned the camp inmates into an amorphous mass, into people who had given up completely, or others who became undercover agents, or informants. In other words, into anything that the authorities wanted to turn us into.

CZECHOSLOVAKIA

❀ ❀ ❀

The Confession
Arthur London

ARTHUR LONDON (1915–86) became a Communist at age fourteen and enlisted in the International Brigade to fight against Franco in the Spanish civil war in 1936. He subsequently participated in the French anti-Nazi underground until his arrest and deportation to Mauthausen (a Nazi concentration camp) in 1942. London returned to Czechoslovakia in 1948 and became undersecretary of foreign affairs in 1949, a position he held until his arrest in 1951. He was accused, among other things, of collaboration with the Gestapo (while at Mauthausen), and later of spying for the United States and conspiring on behalf of Tito. He was tried with Slansky in the major Czech show trial of the post–World War II period, modeled on the Soviet trials of the 1930s. Of the fourteen defendants, eleven were Jewish. They were characterized by the prosecutor as "Trotskyists-Titoists-Zionists."

These didactic trials (in Eastern Europe and earlier in the USSR) served two major purposes. One was to discredit particular individuals or groups within the party leadership; the other was to support and illustrate particular propaganda themes. The charges were wholly imaginary and the defendants had to learn and rehearse elaborate scripts for the trial.

London spent six years in jail and was released in 1956, when all fourteen defendants were rehabilitated, eleven of them posthumously. He left Czechoslovakia in 1968 to live in France, where he died.

A bestseller in France, The Confession *was made into a movie by Costa-Gavras.*

· · · · ·

After three hundred yards, as I was entering the lane behind the Tuscan Palace, one of the cars overtook me and stopped dead in front of me. Six armed

From Arthur London, The Confession, © *1968 (under the title* L'Aveu) *by Editions Gallimard. English translation* © *1970 by Macdonald and Company Publishers. Reprinted by permission of HarperCollins Publishers Inc.*

men rushed up, pulled me off my seat, handcuffed me and threw me into the first car, which drove off at full speed. I struggled, and demanded to know who they were, but they blindfolded me and shouted: "Shut up! No point in asking questions! You'll know who we are soon enough!"

They were not arresting me, they were kidnapping me. It was like detective stories which I had always thought exaggerated, but now I was involved in one myself, in broad daylight, in a residential area of Prague. I even thought some subversive organization was behind it, for there had been recent rumors that the Western powers had sent armed gangs into the country and that shots had been exchanged with men from security.

I protested again, and told them to show me their papers. "Shut up! You've nothing to ask!"

The car drove through the town. I heard trams and cars passing us, and we stopped several times. The men were whispering. One of them got out and then came back. More whispering, and off we drove. I had the impression that we were driving round in a circle and the whole thing became more agonizing.

Finally one of the men started up the car and said: "We can go in in twenty minutes."

On we drove. The noises diminished and then the tires creaked on gravel. Hands seized me, pulled me out of the car and pushed me down a passage. We went up and down flights of stairs, and along corridors. After we had turned in every direction, my eyes were unbandaged, my handcuffs removed, and I found myself in a small bare room, with no window, lit by a tiny bulb burning in a corner above a table. The rest of the room was in darkness.

I was made to undress and put on some dungarees with no buttons and a pair of shapeless slippers. I asked to see a Party official immediately, but my demand was greeted with insults and threats. The few objects of value which I had on me were removed and I had to sign for them. As for my Darex coupons[1] which I put on the table—about 1,200 crowns—one of my kidnappers took them and hurried to the door. Another ran after him. "Where are you going with all that? Leave them on the table." I later discovered that all these things were stolen from me.

I was again blindfolded with a cloth tied so tight that I was stifled. I went down more corridors, up and down stairs, bumping into walls. Finally the bandage was torn from my head. I was in a cell, with a mattress and two folded blankets in the corner. Before the door was closed I received an order: "You are not allowed to sit down. Walk!"

This arrest was the worst ordeal of my life. The moment I had been handcuffed the images of twenty-two years in the Party filed through my mind, comrades—dead and alive—with whom I had fought in Czechoslovakia, in Spain, in France, in prisons and Nazi concentration camps, their confidence and their affection which I had never betrayed, my family which had performed so many sacrifices for the Party, my parents-in-law, my wife and children who were even now vainly awaiting my return.

Alone in my cell I was in despair, but at the same time, paradoxically, I felt a certain relief. After more than a year of being suspected, after the anxiety that had turned me into a hunted animal, I was at last to know what I was accused of and I would be able to defend myself. Everything would be cleared up. It was in the Party's interest. I clung to this hope in spite of the barbarous way I had been arrested. I stopped walking for a second—I felt so tired—but the door opened noisily. Two guards seized hold of me, shook me and knocked my head against the wall, "to set my ideas in order" they said, and told me they would repeat the treatment if I had another lapse of memory. The two guards were in uniform with a five-pointed red star on their caps. There was no longer any doubt: I was definitely in the hands of State Security.

Night had fallen and no light shone through the opaque glass window. I wondered where I was. Was this the notorious Ruzyn prison near the Prague airfield, of which there had recently been talk? The sound of aeroplanes close by seemed to confirm this supposition. And yet I had no doubt that I would soon be able to see one of the Party officials. Maybe Siroky, who knew my past and present work, or Kopriva, Minister of State Security, who could clarify the Field business in which he knew I had only been accidentally involved. I was sure my arrest had created a scandal. After all, I was Under-Secretary of Foreign Affairs and my colleagues would undoubtedly intervene on my behalf.

I thought about my family. I tried to imagine what they were doing in that moment. They must first have thought I had stopped for a chat with my friends, but then started to worry. Lise might have tried to telephone everywhere to be sure that I had not met with an accident, but by this time she must have been informed of what had happened to me. What did they tell her?

How sorry I was not to have been able to go home. Havel's visit meant that I hadn't been able to talk to Lise since the night before.

I heard the dull noise of an object being placed on the floor. It was soup time. I had so many prisons behind me, from Ostrava in the early thirties to La Santé, Poissy, Blois, in France during the occupation, and in each one soup time was always accompanied by the sound of bowls, the grinding of a trolley, the noise of clogs, and the shouts of the warders. Here all was silent. Outside my cell I only heard muffled steps and whispers.

I imagined a long corridor, lined with doors, and assumed that this silence was part of security methods. I had always believed that these methods must be strict to be efficient, but that they should be more humane than in the prisons of the bourgeois. I still had no idea of what was in store for me. But the steps did not stop outside my door. There was to be no bowl for me, but it didn't matter much since I would have been incapable of swallowing anything. I couldn't imagine that I would also be tortured by hunger! For the time being my main torment was the thought of the ghastly night my family must be spending. . . .

. . . . .

I was shoved against a wall, my tie and belt pulled off, and the handcuffs tightened behind my back, the steel cutting into my flesh. I was then forced into a room where my mask was removed and I was again ordered to walk up and down. The room was feebly illuminated by a naked bulb in the middle of the ceiling, and thick planks of wood were nailed to the window. This was not a normal prison, and the room was entirely empty. A coarse spy-hole had been cut in an ordinary door. I went up to the window to try to see through the splits between the planks, but I could see nothing; the planks were nailed together too closely. A kick against the door made me jump and the same voice as before ordered me to keep walking.

It was four yards from the wall to the door. The spy-hole was constantly being opened, and from time to time I could hear a short whisper behind the door. It was very cold, and I walked faster to keep warm. The handcuffs had cut into my wrists and my swollen hands were numb and frozen.

This second night lasted an eternity. The sound of footsteps echoed in other cells. Others were going through the same hell as myself. But who were they? I walked, from wall to wall, deep in my thoughts, and if I stopped an anonymous voice immediately repeated the order. So I knew that, behind the spy-hole, eyes were always watching me.

The guards came for me, put my mask on, and, after another walk through the maze, I found myself in a heated room. When my mask was removed I was blinded by the crude light of a small projector concentrated on my face, leaving the rest of the room in darkness. A voice with a strong Ukrainian or Russian accent said: "You are here for a very serious reason. The Party ordered your arrest and told us to interrogate you. I repeat that the matter is very serious indeed, a matter of international espionage and treason against the Soviet Union and the people's democracies. Your duty is to help us get to the truth. You are not the only person to have been arrested. Other important people have been implicated in the same business. You cannot count on anybody's assistance. You have been in the Party a long time and I appeal to you to help the Soviet Union and our Party. Have you anything to say?'

I listened in amazement. Who could this be? A Russian? I later discovered that it was Janousek who had lived in the USSR and had been working in the Ministry of the Interior for several years until he was fired by Ossik Zavodsky on account of the brutality of his methods—he was known to have tortured certain culprits during interrogations. He was said to be a drug addict and he nursed a fierce grudge against his former employer and all of us who were now in his hands. After losing his job he had been chosen by the Soviet advisers to work in the special branch of the security which they had created.

As I gradually grew accustomed to the dazzling light I distinguished two figures next to the man who was speaking to me. "Have you anything to say about Field," he asked, "and about the hostile activities of the volunteers in the International Brigades?" I replied that despite the shock of my arrest and the conditions of my imprisonment I was relieved to find myself face to face with someone who, in the name of the Party, was going to clear up my position. I had constantly demanded to be heard by the Party and was ready to answer any questions.

The same voice interrupted me: "Very well, then we'll draw up a report." He turned to one of the figures and ordered: "Go ahead!" and then to the second one: "Write!"

I heard the sound of a sheet of paper being placed in a typewriter and another voice which asked me: "When did you enter the American intelligence services directed by Allen Dulles? Who recruited you, and where? And with whom have you collaborated?"

I was stunned. They hadn't summoned me to explain anything. Not only was I accused, but I was also declared guilty! "Never. Nowhere. By nobody!" I shouted, and protested against the inanity of these accusations. I later discovered that I was being interrogated by Major Smola, who had been put in charge of investigating the activity of the former volunteers in the International Brigades. The first voice, Janousek's, screamed: "Shut up! I'm warning you that this business is going to have serious consequences. We have all the proof we need. We shall use methods that may surprise you but which will make you confess anything we like. Your life depends on us. Either you decide to redeem yourself by a full confession, or you insist on remaining an enemy of the Soviet Union and the Party until the gallows. So start by answering the questions you have just been asked."

I continued to protest, so Janousek called a warder and dismissed me: "Think about it in your cell. And if you don't reach the right conclusions you'll regret it."

The mask was again put over my face, and then I was placed in the cell and ordered to keep walking. I was terrified. Once more I thought of my past. . . .

. . . . .

Nobody ever told me the name of the prison I was in. From the constant roar of airplane engines I gathered that I was again in Ruzyn, the prison near the Prague airport. That was my only landmark. I was to spend twenty-seven months in complete isolation, seeing only warders and interrogators. When led from my cell to the room where I was interrogated I was always blindfolded with a knotted towel.

My cell was small and narrow. A double window with thick panes was opened a few minutes every day to air it, while I was made to stand at the other end. When I was not ordered to face the wall I could see two poplars against the sky. Later, after I had been transferred to another cell in the new building, I was not even able to see these trees, for the ventilation was such that the windows did not have to be opened.

I almost feel nostalgic when I remember the first cell. It was a refuge for me between interrogations; I could hear noises from outside: distant voices, dogs barking, birds singing. Sometimes I heard a funeral march because my cell must have looked onto the Ruzyn cemetery. There was a narrow wooden table and two stools chained to the wall, a mattress, and latrines in the corner. I learned how to tell the time from the angle of the sun's rays and the shadows, and I gradually managed to identify all the prison noises. Once again I was in solitary confinement but never before had it been like this. When I was allowed to sleep, the mattress had to be facing the spy-hole. The light was on all night and shone in my eyes. It was very cold. The dungarees I was wearing offered me no protection and in the evenings, before going to sleep, I had to fold them carefully and put them on the stool; if the warder decided they were badly folded he would wake me up any number of times to make me fold them again.

To the left of my cell was another cell whose inmates rapidly succeeded each other. I realized this because they tried to contact me by tapping Morse code or the alphabet used by the revolutionaries in the Tsarist prisons. I only knew the latter, and could therefore only answer certain calls, which were always anonymous. I never gave away my name since I never knew to whom I was talking. Twice the warder discovered me doing this: as a punishment I had to strip, and he sprayed me with cold water, made me do physical exercises, and fold and unfold my mattress several times.

Sometimes I heard violent blows against the neighboring door, screams, the hurried steps of the warders, sounds of a struggle, then a body being dragged along the corridor and stifled groans. A few seconds later the door was opened again and my neighbor was brought back. From the words whispered by the warders I understood that they had put him in a straitjacket and gagged him to give him a cold shower. Some prisoners were to keep the straitjacket on for twenty-four or even forty-eight hours, and I was soon to become acquainted myself with this sinister dungeon.

I received no mail and knew nothing of what was going on outside. I was constantly alone with my thoughts. Every morning the warder appeared for a report with his eternal: "Requests and complaints." I automatically repeated the same request: "I want to write to the Central Committee. I want an interview with a Party representative."

Although food was more regular here than at Koldeje I was always tortured by hunger, for the rations were minute. One night, seeing the ravenous looks I aimed at his sandwich, an interrogator said to me: "So you're hungry are you? Well then, confess! After that you'll get your full rations." In spite of a violent argument he offered me a piece of bread—he was a compatriot of mine from Ostrava.

The worst part was not being allowed to sleep, having to stand during the questioning, and the exhausting marches round the cell.

The prison woke up early, between five and six o'clock. We then had to get up, fold our blankets, roll up our mattresses, clean our cells, and wash. And then start walking again.

At the beginning of my stay in Ruzyn the interrogations went on day and night. They started in the morning and only ended the next day, between four and five o'clock. While the interrogator rested I was taken back to my cell where I had to walk until they came for me again. Sometimes, after making me walk all day, they came for me in the evening and the interrogation went on until morning. Then, when day broke, without being able to sleep for a second, I had to continue my hallucinatory march.

When I was allowed to sleep for the four hours to which I was theoretically "entitled" those hours were a fresh torment. I had to lie on my back, my hands alongside my body outside the blankets. If I turned round or put an arm under the covers the warder woke me up at once, made me get up, fold my bed, and do squatting exercises with my arms outstretched. He made me undress and sprayed me with cold water, and ordered me to walk. Only then could I go back to bed.

This would happen up to three or four times in a row: if not to me to a fellow prisoner, and the warders' shouts and kicks against his door would wake me up. In practice these four theoretical hours were reduced to a mere hour or two.

As I was often interrogated for eighteen or twenty hours on end I was sometimes allowed to sleep in the mornings. The interrogation which started the day before towards nine o'clock in the evening ended at four in the morning. By the time I had returned to my cell, made my bed and undressed it was half past four. I fell asleep. At half past five the alarm for the whole prison rang. So I too had to get up, wash, clean my cell, wait for the warder to bring the soap which I then had to return to him together with the bowl, the towel, and the toothbrush. At a quarter to seven I went to sleep again. But I was constantly interrupted: at a quarter past seven a warder came to open the window to air the cell; at half past seven another one came for the daily report; at a quarter to eight the first one came back to shut the window. At eight I had to get up and at nine the interrogation resumed.

Other times I came back from the interrogation at eight in the morning, and had to see to the daily drudges. I went to bed at nine, I was woken up several times, and at half past eleven I had to get up. I received my food, and again had to start walking, then the interrogation, and so on. . . .

For a long period I walked round my cell all day. At night I made my bed and went to sleep, more dead than alive, but no sooner had I closed my eyes than the warder shook me awake and took me off to the interrogation. One or two hours later I was taken back to my cell, fell asleep again to be woken up shortly afterwards, and led back to the interrogation. And so on all night.

This lack of sleep for weeks and months on end accounts for the moments of insanity and the hallucinations which I experienced. I was no longer in control of my senses; I thought I was going mad and would fall into a state of total sottishness and apathy, moving like an automaton.

I had been arrested several times during the First Republic, and then in France under the occupation. I had been interrogated by the Special Anti-terrorist Brigades in Paris notorious for their brutality. I had known the worst Nazi concentration camps, Neue Bremme, and Mauthausen, but the insults, the threats, the blows, hunger, and thirst were child's play when compared to systematic lack of sleep, this infernal torture which voids man of every thought and turns him into an animal dominated by his instinct for self-preservation.

Every physical and moral torture was carried to an extreme. I had been forced to walk continuously in the Gestapo punishment camp of Neue Bremme near Sarrebruck, before being deported to the extermination camp of Mauthausen. But there it had only lasted twenty-six days, while here it went on for months, and was made all the worse by my having to keep my arms to my sides, level with my trouser seams.

After a few hours' march, thanks to the slippers which I was given on my arrival and which were changed as soon as the soles got too soft, my feet were covered with blisters; a few days later my feet and legs were as swollen as if I had elephantiasis. The skin round my toenails burst, and the blisters became suppurating wounds. I could no longer get the slippers on. I walked barefoot, and was brutally taken to task for it. In the end this became as ghastly as the handcuffs.

One day, as I was walking barefoot, the warder was startled by the sight of my deformed feet exuding water and pus. He called a doctor who, after examining me for a few seconds, gave me some diuretics, saying that I didn't urinate enough. After six months my feet were in such a state that the interrogator who was questioning me, as a great favor, let me sit down for a few minutes.

Initially I was not allowed to see a doctor despite my requests. I spat blood for two days running, and when, towards the end of March, I was taken to the Bulovka hospital to have my pneumothorax insufflated Major Smola told me: "Don't think we're doing this for your health. No, no. We're only doing it to be able to take you to the gallows alive."

The doctor established that my pneumothorax had collapsed. He tried to fill it out but only partially succeeded. The lower part of my lung had caved in, and he diagnosed pleurisy with discharge.

The interrogations increased. At the end of my stay in Koldeje, the Security Services concentrated on making me the leader of a "Trotskyist group of volunteers in the International Brigades" and the head of the Trotskyist conspiracy in Czechoslovakia. Each new interrogation brought me fresh charges.

I was presented with more "confessions" extorted from fellow prisoners—from Zavodsky, Dora Kleinova, Svoboda, Holdos, Hromadko, Pavlik, Feigl, Spirk, Nekvasil, and others. Each confession contained charges more terrible than the last, as well as half-truths which confused the issue, and downright lies. I later discovered that the report containing Vales's "confessions" had been entirely made up by the interrogators. He didn't even know about it.

Dozens of statements were also collected against us from outside by the Security and the Party organizations. The Party's call—that everyone who had known us should help reveal the traitors—released the wave of hysteria and collective psychosis necessary for the preparation of our trial.

Every day I saw the pile of letters denouncing me on the interrogator's desk grow larger. He showed them to me happily, to increase my bewilderment and prove that I would get away with nothing. Numerous letter writers, influenced by the articles and speeches made by the Party leaders ostracizing us, interpreted normal facts as crimes. Some of them wanted to raise their credit in the Party's eyes, others acted out of fear. Many of them wrote things which they were later to regret or for which they tried to find excuses. Without suspecting it they were serving the Security Services. Whether or not these denunciations were made in good faith their consequences were the same for us. Other individuals made up whatever our accusers liked, and assured their careers and their future.

Important figures in embassies or in Party organizations, even if they hardly knew me, invented the most extraordinary stories. Some did it to disassociate themselves from me and guarantee their own safety, while others were themselves arrested, under the pretext of acknowledging receipt of their reports; the Security Services had decided that their personality fitted into their idea of the "plot" and that they too could make some useful "confessions."

Most of the letters were addressed to the Central Committee of the Party. Some of them were read to me, and others I saw myself. In one of them a member of the Cadre Department had noted in the margin: "for the attention of the Minister Kopriva," and another hand had added "for Comrade Doubek."

All this time I could still not get the Party to hear me. I felt totally helpless. The interrogators refused to draw up a report with my replies; instead they wrote daily reports for the Party in which they interpreted my refusal to sign the "confessions" as the attitude of a hardened criminal.

When, after the trial, I met Vavro Hajdu—who had been arrested some time after myself—he told me of the conversation he had had with Siroky about my arrest. To his question: "How is Gérard taking things?" Siroky simply replied: "Very badly. He has the wrong attitude." This wrong attitude was to proclaim my innocence.

I was beginning to become aware of the interrogators' impatience. At Koldeje one of them had already told me they were working night and day on my case. This had originally been to enable the Central Committee to make a statement about our arrest, but now it was so that our group should be tried as soon as possible, because a public trial had become "politically necessary." I was told that this trial should take place in May or June, and they repeated that "the political situation requires the denunciation of your criminal activity." Smola added details: "It will be a large trial before the Supreme Court. Your gang will be shown up before our working classes. You know what that means for you? The Supreme Court won't have much mercy."

As I still refused to sign my "confessions" I was now threatened with a trial *in camera.* "You'll pay for it with your head, for even if you don't confess, the pile of material we possess, and the number of witnesses against you, are enough to have you condemned. Our reports alone are enough," said Smola, and another interrogator told me: "We'll inform the prosecutor and the court. We'll be there when you're tried and we'll be the ones who address the Judge and the jury. Your sentence will be whatever we ask. *Our* attitude towards you at your trial will be determined by *your* attitude towards us now."

So they could have me tried *in camera*—and nobody would know I was innocent! This threat was more terrible than all the others. But it didn't have its full effect on me because even if my hopes diminished day by day I still refused to believe that I would never be able to explain myself. It was inconceivable that the Party could have an interest in covering up such crimes and because it was inconceivable I held my ground. I had now been caught up in this infernal machine for four months. . . .

. . . . .

My body and brain were crushed. It was like being in a mill. Round and round we went. The pyramid of my crimes rose. One man was not enough to support it, it needed a good half-dozen.

>—Trotskyist activity in Spain and collaboration with the International Commission of the League of Nations, with Field and the American Intelligence Services.
>—Collaboration in France with the French police, the Gestapo, and the American Intelligence Services.
>—Repatriation of Trotskyists into Czechoslovakia and the other people's democracies during the war so as to betray the secret organizations of the Party and their leaders to the Gestapo and prepare for the future.
>—Sending Mirek Klecan to Czechoslovakia during the occupation so as to betray Fucik and the underground Central Committee to the Gestapo.
>—The formation of a Trotskyist network based on an espionage network in all the people's democracies.
>—Being the delegate of the Fourth International in the Eastern countries.
>—Having had contacts and collaborated with the Rajk and Kostov groups.

—Having been in contact with an important group of spies in Hungary (whose name I have forgotten).

—Being the leader of a Trotskyist network in Czechoslovakia centered round the former volunteers from the International Brigades.

—Being the chief resident leader of an American espionage network in Czechoslovakia directed by Field, a direct collaborator of Allen Dulles.

—Having been in contact with Tito's men and having prepared a *coup d'état* in Czechoslovakia.

—Being responsible for the death of hundreds of Jews in France during the war.

—Collaboration with the Gestapo in Mauthausen. . . .

. . . . .

In July Major Kohoutek again threatened to arrest my wife. He told me that the Security Services had long intended to do so, and that she wouldn't be the first wife of a defendant to be in this prison. "You mustn't think that her French citizenship can protect her. On the contrary. We can easily say she's an agent of the Second Bureau, that they'd put her onto you. Believe me, I can find enough witnesses to say that."

They also attacked my parents-in-law, simple, honest people who had devoted their lives to their family, the Party. They were accused of being anti-Party cosmopolitans. If this term was usually attributed in Ruzyn to Jews, intellectuals, and comrades who had lived abroad during the war, it was particularly absurd to attribute it to my wife's parents. They had come from Spain to France at the beginning of the century. They had fled from the hard regions of Aragon whose earth was so poor that it could not nourish a peasant's family. My wife's father became a miner. He had joined the French Communist Party when it was founded in 1921. He had learned to read by painfully stumbling through the articles in *L'Humanité*. Lise's mother was a Catholic, but she managed to conciliate communism with her religion. Frédéric Ricol, my father-in-law, had brought up his children with a candid, unconditional faith in the communist ideal. For the whole family the USSR and Stalin were the incarnation of goodness, the guarantee of a happy future which would free man from servitude.

My wife's brother was also accused of being a Second Bureau spy although he had been a much respected militant communist since his youth. These continual threats against my wife affected me deeply. I was well enough acquainted with the methods practiced in Ruzyn, and I knew the Security would have no difficulty in getting false evidence and carrying out their threat. I knew there were women in the prison and I had often wondered whether Lise was one of them.

I was all the more affected by this threat because that day I had managed to read a report against my wife on Kohoutek's desk, which began with the words: "Comrade London told me yesterday. . . ." And I deduced that she was surrounded by police spies who provided the Security with continuous reports about her. I was later proved right.

This was a new psychological preparation, a new conditioning. I was only to realize later the nature of the turn my interrogations were taking. For the time being it seemed as though a more serious charge was to be brought against me than "being responsible for the Fourth International in the Eastern countries," a Fourth International "led by the Trotskyist group of former volunteers from the International Brigades in Czechoslovakia."

This trial was no longer mentioned. But now Kohoutek claimed that I had not confessed all. I had omitted some very important facts. Furthermore, my "confessions" only served to cover the real culprits and to shield them from justice.

This, he said, was because I counted on some of the culprits, who occupied important functions in the Party and the state, to help me. "Your interrogations," he concluded, "will not be over until you have confessed everything."

And the roundabout continued, the interrogations succeeding each other at an infernal rate.

Towards the end of July Kohoutek came to the room where I was being questioned by one of his interrogators, and took me to his office. There he told me that his superiors had just given him some orders concerning my case. After talking to the Party officials, they had authorized him to speak not only in their name but in the Party's name.

The Party, he said, had discovered the existence of a vast plot against the state directed by some of its leaders. He then started enumerating the names of all the members of the Political Bureau: "It's not him . . . nor him. . . ." He mentioned them all except for the Secretary General of the Party. "Do you see who I mean?" asked Kohoutek.

"You mean Slansky?"

"Yes, that's right, Slansky. You are to be interrogated about all the contacts you and the other volunteers of your group had with him; you must say all you know, and give the smallest details."

He added: "You're not the first one the Party told us to interrogate about Slansky. We already have numerous statements against him, some of which were made a long time ago." To convince me, he read a long statement against Slansky without telling me who made it.

"There are plenty of others," he went on. "Besides, you yourself have already implicated Slansky."

"I have?"

"Yes, of course. Haven't you told us that you had nothing to do with the promotion of your accomplices after their return from France? Haven't you said that Slansky himself ordered them to hurry back to Prague, that he met them personally on their arrival and subsequently gave them important posts in the Party and the State?"

My astonishment increased: "Then why have you so far always prevented me from using those explanations in my defense, and even from mentioning Slansky's name?"

He replied: "Because you persisted in denying that you were responsible for the Trotskyist group and that you had spied with Field. Now that you have signed your first confessions, the Party thinks we can go further."

Finally Kohoutek said sententiously: "Think about it, Mr London. Who do you think gave the order to arrest you and the other volunteers? We couldn't have done it without Slansky's orders. He sacrificed you because he thought he'd save his own skin by throwing you overboard."

I was stunned by the turn the situation had taken. I had in fact always thought that Slansky, as Secretary General of the Party, was, together with the other Party leaders, primarily responsible for my arrest and that of the other veterans from Spain. That was why he had systematically refused to see me when I had asked him to help me discuss my dealings with Field with the Party, why I had found myself up against that wall of suspicion for nearly two years, and why he had deliberately handed me over to Security, branding me as an enemy. Because of this he had passed over our pleas, had let us be charged for decisions taken by himself or the secretariat, and had never denied the monstrous distortions made by the Security officials of our true activities in Spain and France, all of which were known to him. . . .

．　．　．　．　．

It was still dark when we reached Pankrac, the old prison situated in a workers' quarter of Prague, not unlike the Santé in Paris. But Pankrac is self-contained, and in it both investigation and trial take place.

Accompanied by warders and interrogators, my hands chained, I was led along endless corridors into a basement with cells on either side. I was locked into one of them and the spy hole remained open, as in the French death cells. A guard stood permanently outside my door. In one corner of the cell was a mattress, in the other a chair—a warder was to sit in this chair every night I spent there. They were obviously determined to keep us alive until the verdict.

Kohoutek told me that today, 20 November 1952, the public prosecutor was going to read the bill of indictment in the presence of the fourteen defendants. After this the hearings would begin and the first to be heard would be Slansky. At that point I would be taken back to Ruzyn where I would await my turn to be interrogated. After my testimony I would take my place in the dock and remain there until the verdict.

Before the beginning of the trial Dr. Sommer, accompanied by a nurse, listened to my chest. He took my blood pressure and gave me some pills. He did the same thing in every cell and this ritual was to take place throughout the trial, sometimes even between sessions.

Shortly before nine o'clock I was taken out of my cell. The doors of the neighboring cells were opened and my fellow defendants came out into the corridor. We lined up one behind the other, between each of us the same warder we had had in Ruzyn. This was the first time that we were all together. The only man I did not know personally was Frejka.

Our line moved forward. The first was Slansky, then came Geminder, then myself, Hajdu, André Simone, Frejka, Frank, Löbl, Margolius, Fischl, Svab, Reicin, and Sling.

Their faces were closed and drawn, and they had an absent expression in their eyes. None of us looked at each other.

Again the maze of corridors and stairs. Then suddenly we came out into a huge hall, brightly lit, and filled with people. I took care not to look at the spectators because I was afraid of recognizing my wife in the crowd. I hoped my lawyer had seen her, as he had promised, and persuaded her not to be present at the trial.

By chance, as I passed the newspaper reporters, my eyes met those of a man I had known long ago in Ostrava.

We were made to stand in the dock, a warder between each of us, and a few minutes later the court entered.

I felt that I was on a stage, with my thirteen comrades and the members of the tribunal. Every one of us was ready to perform his part of the spectacle, which had been meticulously produced by the experts in Ruzyn. Not a detail had been omitted. One felt the sureness of touch that these masters of imposture had acquired through experience of numerous trials before ours. There were microphones everywhere, and the lights and electric wires running across the floor heightened the effect of the première.

The judge, Dr. Novak, opened the proceedings. Turning to us he asked, perfectly seriously, whether the delay stipulated by law to precede our appearance in court had been respected. We each replied in the affirmative. He then told us to follow the bill of indictment and the proceedings attentively and to benefit from our right to express our opinion about the various pieces of evidence. He even went so far as to tell us that we had the right to defend ourselves as we thought fit. Then he called upon the public prosecutor Urvalek to read the bill of indictment. The accusation ran: *that, as traitors, Trotskyists-Titoists-Zionists, bourgeois nationalists, and enemies of the Czech people, of the people's democratic regime, and of socialism, they created, in the service of the American imperialists and under the leadership of Western intelligence services, a center of conspiracy against the state; tried to undermine the basis of the people's democratic regime, to impair the construction of socialism, to harm the national economy; indulged in espionage activities, tried to weaken the unity of the Czech people and the republic's defensive capacity in order to break its firm alliance with the Soviet Union and ruin its friendship with the USSR, in order to liquidate the people's democratic regime in Czechoslovakia, restore capitalism, drag our republic into the imperialist camp and destroy its sovereignty and national independence.*

Not one of the defendants winced as he heard the bill which reproduced numerous "confessions and admissions" (particularly those of Slansky, Frejka, and Frank), as well as the statements of witnesses and extracts from experts' reports on economic and industrial problems. Our crimes ranged from high treason to military treason, passing through espionage and sabotage.

These charges, brought against us by Urvalek in the name of the Czech people, stated that *the conspirators did all they could to prevent the supply of our goods to the Soviet Union and the other people's democratic states, neglecting contracts and asking far higher prices for these goods than the current prices on the world market. In the capitalist states, on the other hand, they sold the same goods at considerably reduced rates in comparison with the prices for the USSR, and far below the level of the prices on the world market.*

Urvalek read some statements by Slanksy:

We impeded the development of foreign trade with the Soviet Union by ordering and importing machinery from the capitalist states, although the same machines were made in the USSR where they could be purchased cheaper. A large number of Soviet orders were refused on the pretext that Czech industry was not producing the goods required, while in fact it was producing them.

In other cases trade with the Soviet Union was restricted by deliberately high prices or by orders which were only partially accepted under the pretext that the capacity of the factory was insufficient, while the delivery of the goods was delayed. . . . The same measures were taken against orders from the other people's democracies and trade relations with these countries were thereby reduced accordingly. . . .

Urvalek at last reached the end of the list of crimes against the state and the people:

The treachery and perfidious nature of this attack against the liberty, sovereignty and independence of our country, plotted by these criminals, are all the worse since they took advantage of their membership of the Communist Party of Czechoslovakia and the confidence of the Party dear to our workers. They misused the responsibility of their high posts, in order to ally themselves with our most determined enemies, the American imperialists and their minions, in order to sell our country into capitalist slavery. The conspirators only managed to carry out their criminal activities by feigning agreement with the program and policy of the Communist Party and hiding their real faces behind a cunning mask. Even when the first members of the center of conspiracy against the state had been unmasked and put in prison that sly, double-faced Janus, Rudolf Slansky, tried to distract attention from himself as leader of the plot and pretended to be himself a victim of the subversive activities of Sling, Svermova, and others.

But although the conspirators led by Slansky succeeded in occupying important posts in the Party and the state they did not manage, as did Tito in Yugoslavia, to subjugate the supreme organs of Party and State, to usurp power and reach their criminal goals.

Thanks to the vigilance, the clear-sightedness, and intelligence of Comrade Klement Gottwald, the guide of the Czech people; thanks to the unity of the Central Committee of the Communist Party, firmly united round Comrade Klement Gottwald; thanks to the indefectible loyalty and devotion of the Czech people to the Party, the government, and Comrade Klement Gottwald; thanks to the unshakable loyalty of our people to the Soviet Union, the conspiracy has been broken and the criminals' efforts thwarted.... Loyal to the people, the government, the Party and Comrade Klement Gottwald, the organs of State Security stayed the criminal hands of the conspirators in time....

On the basis of the above-mentioned facts:

RUDOLF SLANSKY, *born 7-31-1901, of Jewish origin, of a family of tradesmen ... former Secretary General of the Communist Party of Czechoslovakia, Vice-Premier of the Republic of Czechoslovakia before his arrest*

BEDRICH GEMINDER, *born 11-19-1901, of Jewish origin, son of a tradesman and restaurant owner ... former head of the department of international relations of the Central Committee of the Communist Party of Czechoslovakia*

LUDVIK FREJKA, *born 1-15-1904, of Jewish origin, son of a doctor ... former head of the economic department of the Chancellery of the President of the Republic of Czechoslovakia*

JOSEF FRANK, *born 2-15-1909, Czech, from a worker's family ... former Assistant Secretary General of the Communist Party of Czechoslovakia*

VLADIMIR CLEMENTIS, *born 9-20-1902, Slovak, from a bourgeois family ... former Minister of Foreign Affairs*

BEDRICH REICIN, *born 9-29-1911, of Jewish origin, from a bourgeois family ... former Under-Secretary of National Defense*

KAREL SVAB, *born 5-13-1904, Czech, from a workers' family ... former Under-Secretary of National Security*

ARTUR LONDON, *born 2-1-1915, of Jewish origin, son of a tradesman ... former Under-Secretary of Foreign Affairs*

VAVRO HAJDU, *born 8-8-1913, of Jewish origin, son of the owner of a bathing establishment in Smrdaky ... former Under-Secretary of Foreign Affairs*

EUGEN LÖBL, *born 5-14-1907, of Jewish origin, son of wholesale dealers ... former Under-Secretary of Foreign Trade*

RUDOLF MARGOLIUS, *born 8-31-1913, of Jewish origin, son of wholesale dealers ... former Under-Secretary of Foreign Trade*

OTTO FISCHL, *born 8-17-1902, of Jewish origin, son of a tradesman ... former Under-Secretary of Finance*

OTTO SLING, *born 8-24-1912, of Jewish origin, son of manufacturers ... former secretary of the regional Committee of the Communist Party of Czechoslovakia in Brno*

ANDRÉ SIMONE, *born 5-27-1895, of Jewish origin, son of manufacturers ... former editor of the paper* Rude Pravo, *are charged with....*

· · · · ·

During the three hours which it took to read the bill of indictment there was total silence in the hall. From time to time we were dazzled by the light of the reflectors. We were being filmed, and would soon be shown in dark cinemas before the main feature.

The session was suspended and we were taken back to our cells. In the afternoon I was driven to Ruzyn. I was in a state of complete apathy. I was caught up in a process and I had no more human reactions than a piece of metal on a conveyor belt about to be crushed in a machine.

Two days later, on November 12, it was my turn to stand witness. In the meantime I had had to repeat my lines again. I also knew the precise moment at which I would be interrupted by the prosecutor and by the judge and what their questions would be.

As I was waiting for my turn in a box in the wings, Kohoutek came to see me. He told me that the Party leaders were following the course of the trial attentively and that they hoped all the defendants would live up to their expectations. He also told me not to forget what Bacilek had said—that my future depended on my behavior. Then Kohoutek speculated on the sentences. According to him they would be heavy, but there would be no death sentence. Even if, by some chance, there were one or two, they could always appeal. "I repeat," he insisted, "that what the Party needs at the moment is not heads but a large political trial."

As an example he gave details of the trial of the Industrial Party in Moscow. All the heavy sentences that had been passed, including the death sentences, had subsequently been commuted to far lighter ones. He spoke of Ramzin, the main defendant, and compared him to Slansky. After being sentenced to death, the Party commuted his sentence to ten years in prison, of which he only served five. He was then released for good conduct. He even added that Ramzin had received one of the highest decorations in the Soviet Union for the work he performed in prison.

His words cheered me considerably, particularly since he spoke with great conviction and seemed to believe what he was saying. I wanted to believe it too, and to convince myself I thought that during the last two years Kohoutek and all the other interrogators had shown a total ignorance of past history. When they tried to talk about it they did so like schoolboys reciting badly learned lines, repeating snatches of conversation heard between the Soviet advisers. If, as he told me, he hadn't made it up, he must have been repeating what the Soviet advisers had said. . . .

. . . . .

The carefully selected audience consisted mainly of officials from the Ministry of Security in civilian dress, and delegates picked from the factories and ministries. The latter only received tickets for one day of the trial, and they were relayed by other men every day. There were also some Czech journalists and the representatives of the central organs of foreign Communist Parties. Some of them, like Pierre Hentgès, knew me. That was why he was all the harder on me when he reported the proceedings. Had I not entered their camp to murder their wives and daughters?

The families of the defendants were not notified as to the date of the trials. It was by reading the papers or listening to the radio that they heard that their husband, father, brother, or son was being tried that day. This was unprecedented.

Between sessions the warders led us into a corridor where there were eight plywood boxes. Opposite there were two open cells, occupied by Slansky and Clementis, and then four more boxes. Our warders from Ruzyn stood before every box to prevent us from talking to each other. I was between Geminder and Hajdu, opposite Clementis's cell. We could see each other perfectly well, and ever since the first day we had exchanged friendly signs of greeting. By looks and gestures, we established a silent dialogue.

We did not all react in the same way. Geminder, for example, stared into space. He seemed deep in thought, walked like an automaton, and sat motionless in his box. He never replied to any smile or sign of friendship. Although he was an old friend of Slansky, who was in the cell opposite him, he never tried to signal to him, but looked away every time he saw him. His eyes were blank. I myself tried in vain to attract his attention. And yet we had known each other since our childhood.

I saw Slansky every time he returned to his cell. He appeared calm, despite his haggard features. He passed before all his fellow defendants, staring at something in front of him, not looking at any of us. From time to time we saw one of his interrogators join him in his cell with a plate concealed between two files. Maybe he required special food for his health.

Between sessions André Simone, who suffered from diarrhea, used to pass in front of my box to go to the lavatory. He looked very ill. His face had changed completely. He was like an old man. His jaws sagged and his chin receded. I was unable to conceal my astonishment and my interrogator explained that his false teeth had broken in prison, deforming his face, and that he had constant diarrhea, since he was unable to chew his food. What had they done to him? He had once had such an easy gait and quick wit. When Vilem Novy, with whom he had worked for many years on the editorial board of *Rude Pravo*, came to stand witness against him and the judge asked him to point out André Simone among the defendants, Novy turned to us and looked at us all, without recognizing the man he was looking for. The second time around he looked aghast as he at last recognized André Simone, a caricature of the brilliant journalist he had once known.

As for my friend Hajdu, he sat frowning in the box next to mine, nervously smoking one cigarette after the other. When his interrogator brought him a cup of coffee he replied surlily "Pass it to London," as he used to do when we lunched together. He didn't care for coffee much, but he knew that I loved it. During the sessions only a warder stood between me and him. I watched Hajdu. He was tense and scratched the palms of his hands. He, the legal expert, just muttered insults when he heard what was being said in court. When his lawyer was pleading he could hardly contain himself: "Moron, idiot, bastard!" Several times the warder between us in the dock nudged him to make him keep quiet.

Margolius was very dignified. He managed to dominate his feelings, like Frejka and Frank, whose faces were immobile. Fischl looked shattered. Löbl was calm, in control of himself. He talked at length to his interrogator between sessions.

Reicin and Svab paid attention to everything around them. Of us all, Sling was the most relaxed, the most energetic. When he saw me he greeted me, and every time he passed me he nodded and smiled. Had he not lost so much weight in these two years of prison he would have been the one who had changed least.

As Sling was giving evidence and gesticulating, his trousers which had become far too big for him fell to his feet. Seeing him in his underpants we all laughed hysterically, and he laughed so much himself that he had difficulty in continuing his statement.

Clementis was one of the ones to laugh most. He tried to calm himself by squeezing his pipe between his teeth to breaking point. Slansky laughed till tears ran down his face, and his whole body shook.

The audience and the members of the court roared with laughter. The prosecutor hid his face behind a newspaper. The members of the court plunged their heads into their files. The warders yelped as they tried to stifle their laughter. The only one not to change expression was Geminder.

But the misfortune which befell our comrade was a mere pretext. The actors of the appalling tragedy were at last allowed some form of relief.

The judge had to suspend the proceedings.

Kohoutek and the interrogators were indignant. During the interval they told us that Sling had made a clown of himself on purpose. By bending down to pick up his trousers he had managed to show his behind to the court. This proved, they said, that Sling was a frightful blackguard who couldn't give a damn about anyone or anything.

During the week of the trial the entire headquarters of Ruzyn, led by Doubek, were mobilized at Pankrac.

We got better food than usual, coffee, and cigarettes. When the session was prolonged we were given sandwiches.

There was a constant coming and going in the wings of the court between sessions and in the subterranean corridor where we had our cells. The heads of Ruzyn visited the defendants for whom they were responsible several times a day in order to keep up the morale of "their clients."

As usual Kohoutek was talkative, too talkative. He said that the Party was satisfied, that our "friends" had spoken to the Party leaders who followed every detail of the trial attentively. His own outlook was still more optimistic than before the proceedings. I tried to catch what Doubek and the other head interrogators were saying to my fellow defendants. From what I could gather they were all discussing the same thing.

When the chiefs left the interrogators again returned to the subject. They told us that their opinion was based on the conversations they had had with their superiors. According to them Sling would have one of the heaviest sentences, twenty years; Hajdu, twelve years; Löbl, twelve years; Clementis and Geminder, from fifteen to eighteen years; Slansky, twenty or at most twenty-five years; Margolius, ten years; and me, twelve.

But as the trial proceeded we became increasingly pessimistic. We feared that the last act of the tragedy would end in a far more sinister manner than we had been led to imagine.

Dr. Sommer diligently visited us and gave us tranquillizers. At night, in my cell, I could not sleep. I got up, paced round and from time to time the warder would offer me a cigarette and try to calm me. The same thing must have happened in the thirteen other cells, because I heard the sound of steps and muffled voices.

In the court the hostility was more and more marked. It must have increased with the proceedings. And then there was the evidence, the worst of which was Gusta Fucikova's. She accused Reicin of having handed over her husband to the Gestapo. Her peroration, which repeated the last words of Fucik in his book *Written Under the Gallows*, was greeted by frantic applause:

"Whoever has lived for the future and has fallen for its beauty is a figure hewn in stone. But he who, with the dust of the past, tries to build a dam against the current of the revolution, is no more than a puppet of rotten wood, even if his shoulders be decorated with gold braid. To the men whom I loved, I say: be vigilant!"

The day before the prosecutor read his charge, Kohoutek asked me what sentence I thought would be demanded. I replied that we would all be hanged. He then looked at me dully, shaking his head slowly: "That's not possible. They can't hang you all. They must leave some of you alive. And the chances are that you'll be one of them, since the charges against you are lighter than the others. Even if the sentences are heavy, what counts in all political trials is to remain alive. Don't lose hope." Even a man like Kohoutek, who was a zealous architect of this trial, seemed overcome by the tragic turn the proceedings were taking in court.

In the evenings, until late into the night, and in the morning, before the sessions, we could hear the tapping of typewriters. From my interrogator I discovered that even here individuals who were still at liberty were being questioned and having reports drawn up on them.

Sometimes, between sessions, a defendant was brought a sheet of paper so that he could make a note of the names he was to add in his evidence. I heard the names of General Svoboda, the Minister Gregor and others. Subsequently, after my release, I managed to look over the papers of this period as well as the typed report of the trial: the more outrageous anti-Semitic expressions, numerous names, and whole passages from our statements were omitted. This reserve material was kept for further trials.

On the morning of November 22, when he informed me that my statement had been postponed, Kohoutek said: "After examining Clementis's evidence yesterday, the Party decided to make him appear a second time this morning to make an additional statement about Slovak bourgeois nationalism."

So it was during the night that the last report had been drawn up with Clementis. He then had to learn his text by heart in order to be ready for the session which opened with his evidence.

The day before the prosecutor's indictment Kohoutek brought me a pencil and paper and asked me to write out my last statement before the verdict. "You must stick to the line taken in your 'confessions' and prove to the Party that you are continuing to do what is expected of you." A little later I gave him my draft. He left to see his "chiefs." Very early the next morning he returned and gave me the corrected text. Three sentences had been crossed out and others had been added. He accused me of not having thought about it enough. "And now learn it by heart. And don't change anything. Otherwise you'll regret it."

Fortunately the text was short because I could no longer concentrate. The last days I could hardly follow the proceedings.

I only snatched pieces here and there, from the otherwise dull din. I still felt that my personality was split; I was both actor and spectator in this trial. One thought obsessed me: "So that was what happened at the trials of Moscow, Budapest, and Sofia. How could I and so many other communists, so many honest people, believe in them?"

My Mind on Trial
Eugene Loebl

EUGENE LOEBL (1907–87) was first deputy minister of foreign trade in Communist Czechoslovakia until his arrest in 1949. Like Arthur London, he was also a defendant in the Slansky trial in November 1952 and among the three sentenced to imprisonment for life; the other eleven were sentenced to death and executed. He served eight years.

Loebl's case, like many others represented in this volume, typifies a peculiar feature of repression in Communist systems, namely that it often was directed against its committed supporters, including high-ranking party and government officials. This pattern originated in the Soviet Union and served particular political purposes: eliminating potential competition within the party leadership (as in the Soviet Union under Stalin) and providing examples and support for specific propaganda themes. In Eastern Europe in the post–World War II period, one such theme was the menace of Titoism (or national communism). Every effort was made to discredit Titoism by linking it to Western powers and their intelligence services.

People such as Loebl, London, and the Hungarian Paul Ignotus who served abroad or spent time abroad in exile were particularly suspect and were therefore routinely charged with spying for some Western power.

As in similar Soviet and East European trials, confessions served to prove the defendant's guilt, along with denunciations by fellow defendants, both extracted under great physical pressure.

· · · · ·

After my return, nobody was told about what had happened to me, but somehow it was in the air. People in the ministry continued to address me as First Deputy Minister, and I was still directing foreign trade, giving instructions to the commercial attachés at embassies all over the world; but now I was not allowed to leave Prague for a weekend without first getting permission.

I attended cabinet meetings, gave interviews, spoke on the radio, and negotiated with ambassadors, just as if nothing had happened. But somehow every-

From Eugene Loebl, My Mind on Trial, *© 1976 by Eugene Loebl, reprinted by permission of Harcourt, Inc.*

thing was changed. People seemed to know that I had been at Party headquarters for questioning. They had no way of knowing what had happened there, and yet I felt that they were wondering what would become of me, whether I would remain a person of influence or simply disappear.

It so happened that I had planned a dinner party for a number of friends two nights after the interrogation. Now, one by one, they or their wives called to tell me how terribly sorry they were that they would not be able to come. Each one said how unhappy he was that something had come up and that he would be looking forward to seeing me, his dear friend, sometime soon.

Everyone I met was exceedingly polite, but it was a very strange politeness. People did not know what was going to happen to me, so they were not sure they should risk being friendly to me. They all acted ambiguously, in such a way that they would be prepared whether I was given an advancement, the sack, or something worse. Many of the people I considered my best friends adopted this restricted kind of friendship, though others, whom I hardly knew, were ostentatiously friendly.

I was not offended, just somewhat saddened. I understood this behavior. In the growing polarization of our society, people were choosing their official contacts and even their friendships very carefully. Association with someone who was suspect might have serious repercussions for a man in a leading position. We were all exercising such caution; I probably chose my friends and reacted to invitations the same way.

No one knew what I was being charged with, including me. Something was happening that would either help me or hurt me, but no one seemed to know where or why, or who was going to decide. It occurred to me that maybe even the ones who were going to make the decision were waiting for some word, some explanation, some directive from above. In the meantime, nothing was what it seemed to be, no one said what they really thought—again, including me.

The day after my interrogation, I left my apartment early in the morning so I could clear up the work I had missed at the ministry. The streets were still empty, but as I passed a side street, I saw two men in a car at the corner. Looking in my rearview mirror, I saw that they were following me to the ministry.

From that day onward, I was followed wherever I went, whether to the theater, to a movie house, or even to the office of the Prime Minister or the President. I felt that everyone around me would notice that I was being followed, and this made me very nervous. But no one did, not even my wife. I remember we went to the cinema together; I noticed a man following us, but she did not.

I thought of challenging my followers, but I changed my mind. I guessed that they would reply that they were just doing their job. And, after all, it *was* their job. If I made too much of a fuss, those who were in charge would take it as a sign of bad conscience.

True, their boss, the Minister of the Interior, Vaclav Nosek, was a very good friend of mine. We had known each other since the war, when, as members of the Party cell, we were both exiled in London. But being a Deputy Minister myself, I realized that possibly Nosek would not even have been notified of such a surveillance if it was only routine. If he had been notified, and the investigation was being conducted with his knowledge, the confrontation would be very awkward, for both of us. After all, in a revolutionary situation like the one we were in, anybody's political reliability could be questioned, and it would be wrong to act offended. And if I complained, there would be a very simple answer: "No one is following you, it is just your imagination; and if someone does follow you, it is only routine."

I decided that the best I could do would be to go on working, trusting in my innocence and in the justice of the Party.

Then one evening, Thursday, November 24, the doorbell rang. I was at home listening to the radio with my son, Ivan.

I remember walking to the foyer and opening the door. The man waiting there was dressed in a leather coat with a belt, which was a standard uniform of the Czechoslovakian secret service. He showed me his identification papers. He was an employee of the Ministry of the Interior, and he told me that the Minister, Vaclav Nosek, wanted to see me.

Since there were some important things I had to do that night, I told the man that I would call the Minister and postpone the meeting until a mutually more convenient time. But the policeman insisted, saying that the Minister was still on his way home and that I would have to come with him at once.

Suddenly I knew that this was it.

I turned to my son and said good-by to him. I made the usual excuse: that I was being called to a meeting and would return soon. He went on listening to the radio. My wife would be coming home to give him dinner.

And who could tell, maybe I would be returning soon.

Outside, a black limousine was waiting. One policeman was in the driver's seat, and another was standing at the nose of the car. He opened the door and motioned me into the back seat. Then he and the man who had come to my door took their places on either side of me.

The car did not go toward Minister Nosek's house. After a few miles, we came to a roadblock manned by two armed guards. One of the men with me showed the guards a letter, and we proceeded on through a gate and across a yard to another gate. Here the man again showed the letter, and the gate opened and closed like an iron curtain behind me.

I got out of the car, and one of the men said: "Mr. Deputy Minister, in the name of the Republic, you are under arrest. . . ."

· · · · ·

Monday morning, after I had finished washing, cleaning up my cell, and making my bed, the door opened and two guards entered. They handcuffed me behind my back and led me down the corridor past rows of cells like mine. At the end of the corridor was a locked steel barricade. There the guards turned me over to an interrogating officer, who took me through the barricade and up the stairs to one of the interrogation rooms on the floor above.

It was a small office, with three men sitting behind a desk, all civilians. One of them I knew: it was Doubek, who had interrogated me at the Party headquarters. In the center sat a gray-haired man with a very narrow tie and a slight lisp. His name was Vladimir Kohoutek, and I was to see a lot of him over the next three years. The third man was a young Slovak, a former carpenter, who was Kohoutek's assistant; I have forgotten his name.

Kohoutek ordered the guards to take off my handcuffs and offered me a seat. There was a package of cheap cigarettes in front of him, and, seeing my eager look, he asked me to take one and motioned the Slovak to give me a light. The carpenter struck a match, and I eagerly inhaled the smoke.

After clearing his throat, Kohoutek reached for a file, opened it, and started asking routine questions: my name, my date of birth, my parents, my occupation, and my address. As I answered, he entered the information on a form on the desk in front of him. Then, without changing his tone of voice, Kohoutek began the interrogation.

He said that he knew that a few days ago I had been a Deputy Minister, one of the leading personalities in the country. Now, he said, I should look at myself and think about where I was.

Kohoutek had a very even voice, and this first time, as always, he called me by name: "Loebl. Loebl, sit down. Loebl, you are a traitor. Loebl, stop lying. Loebl, your cover-up won't work."

He continued by saying that I should understand that, since I had been in such a high position and was so well known abroad, this was not merely a police action. I would never have been put in jail if the very leadership of the Party had not decided that I should be interrogated. And I should realize that I had already been sentenced by the Party. Finally he said that everything depended on whether or not I would confess and tell them with whom I worked against the Party and against socialism—who gave me my orders and who were my associates. He said that my complete confession was the only thing that they were interested in.

I could not believe my ears. There were no specific charges whatsoever against me, only a request that I confess. There were no facts, no witnesses. Because I was a prisoner, I must be guilty of something, and Kohoutek wanted to find out what.

I told them that if they were so sure that I was guilty, they should indict me. Why bother with an interrogation if they already knew all the facts? Kohoutek replied that they knew I was a criminal, but that they wanted the details of my criminal activities, especially the identities of my co-conspirators. If I cooperated, the Party would be merciful; if not, I could expect the worst.

I lost my temper and shouted at him, "I have a right to know the specific charges against me!"

Kohoutek got up from behind the desk, walked over to where I was sitting, and shouted in my face: "Don't think that we are going to swallow your Jewish tricks. You want to know what *we* already know so that you can better hide what we don't know yet. Our instructions are to give you no information whatsoever; you will have to tell us about your crimes yourself."

I remember shouting back at him to take me to court and to prove his case there, if he could. I said that I knew I was innocent and that he had not a shred of real evidence against me. As far as I was concerned, there was nothing else to talk about.

To my astonishment, this worked. Seeing that I had nothing more to say, Kohoutek piped down and returned to his chair. His voice was like that of a teacher talking to a pupil.

"Everyone here is guilty, Loebl. We don't arrest innocent people. Loebl, we know you are a traitor, a spy, and a saboteur. If we didn't have proof of that, you'd still be Deputy Minister."

I did not know what to say. Again he got up and stood in front of me, and I could smell the tobacco on his breath. "Let me give you some advice, Loebl, the way I'd advise a friend. Confess everything. Now. Give us all the details. Believe me, Loebl, the Party will be merciful, and if you make a sincere and complete confession, you will not be executed."

I told him that I did not see any reason for me to be executed.

He shook his head. "You leave me no choice."

He sat down at his typewriter, pulled out a sheet of paper, and started slowly pecking at the keys.

"You want to know what our charges are? Your whole life is a charge against you, Loebl. You have been an enemy of the working class and an enemy of Socialism from the very beginning."

He opened up a file on the desk in front of him.

"Loebl, I want you to tell me your whole life story, and as you talk, I will write it down."

I told him that I had already written a biography at Party headquarters.

"I have a copy of it here in front of me," Kohoutek replied, "but now we want a *real* biography. The truth. With all the details. Loebl, we'll spend weeks on it if we have to."

Then Doubek said that he had also read what I wrote at Party headquarters, but that they had discovered that all I had said was just an attempt to hide the truth and that a new "deposition" was absolutely necessary. This time, however, it would not be I who typed it, but the interrogator Kohoutek and his assistants, and I should be prepared to give them the information in as short a time as possible.

They would interrogate me in two shifts, eight hours each. After an hour of discussion, we began to go through my biography. Kohoutek told me to begin with my childhood, and I started to dictate.

"I was born in Holic, a village in western Slovakia with a population of about five thousand. My father was a merchant, and his father was a merchant. I was one of three children."

Kohoutek interrupted me.

"The most important thing in writing this deposition is objectivity, Loebl. That's what you have to learn. You have to learn to look at your life from the outside. You are telling me one thing, but whatever you say is always being distorted by the mind of a traitor. To get to the truth, Loebl, I must clarify what you say and write it objectively and concisely. I would phrase what you have just told me this way: 'I was born into a family of capitalists in a rural part of Slovakia, and from my youth, I was taught to exploit the working class and to hate their party.'"

I told him that was nonsense.

"On the contrary, Loebl, what you said implied all this. You deny your class adherence because it exposes you for what you are: an enemy of the working class. As you see, by objectively rephrasing what you say, I can show that your whole life has molded you to be a traitor to your party and your country."

I said I had left the village to go to technical school, that I had wanted to be a designer of machines, a draftsman.

"What you mean, Loebl, is that you were a careerist who went to a technical school because you wanted to boss workers instead of making an honest living as a working man."

I said I did not have the skill to be a good draftsman and decided to enroll in the University of World Trade in Vienna.

"In other words, your real aim in life was to be an unproductive capitalist who dealt in high finance and lived off the hard work of others."

Kohoutek asked about my family, and when he heard that my brother was a lawyer who emigrated to Israel, he immediately commented, "The truth is, Loebl, that you come from a Zionist family and that you are a Zionist imperialist yourself."

It went on like this all day. Kohoutek asked me about my life, but wrote down the "objective truths": that everything I had ever done was an integral part of my sabotage and planned treason. Again and again I told him what had really happened, but he never even bothered to write it down. . . .

. . . . .

After several days of being awakened forty or fifty times during the night, my hands started trembling and I had dizzy spells. My skin hurt whenever I touched it or washed myself, and I was deeply depressed.

They also began to blindfold me whenever I left my cell. At first they just used an ordinary towel, but then they began using motorcycle goggles covered with black tape. After he had covered my eyes, the guard took me out of my cell, turned me around, and, every few steps, made me turn around again, so that I would lose all sense of direction. Each time I was taken out of my cell I was blindfolded, and this blindfolding was the most degrading experience in my whole life.

Just before Christmas, Kohoutek told me furiously that if I did not confess immediately, he would have to spend the holidays with me instead of with his family. He said that I would be spoiling his Christmas, and that if I spoiled Christmas for him and his family, he would spoil it for me. All he had to do was to give an order, and they would imprison my wife. If that didn't matter to me, I could not expect that it would matter to him.

"If you stop this ridiculous resistance and confess, we will restore your privileges. You'll get cigarettes and books, and you'll be able to sit down."

The thought that I would be able to sit down again, or sleep, or read, was almost too much for me. I would not have minded spending my whole life in prison, if only they would let me sit down and sleep and read.

I had to decide quickly what to do. I could not bear the idea that my wife might be arrested, that our Ivan would be left alone in Prague. It came to my mind that I could say that I would confess, and then, after Christmas, they would find out that I had not meant it. That way, everybody's wish would be fulfilled: Kohoutek would get to be with his family, my wife would be able to stay with our son, and I would get a cigarette and sit down.

What I did not know at that time was that my wife had been arrested the same night that I was. As I learned later, she had been transported to the women's wing of the same prison that I was in—Ruzyne—almost at the same time as I: her number was 1475. After I was set free, she told me that she had been in prison for six months but never knew that I was in prison as well. They told her that I was still Deputy Minister, and that I had decided to abandon her because of her treasonable activities. They wanted her to reveal my crimes.

On the first day of May, they had broadcast the May day parade over the prison loudspeakers. My wife's interrogator called her in and told her that, at that very minute, while she was rotting away in prison, I was sitting on the reviewing stand with the rest of the government officials. He said that I did not care for her any more. Why would she then persist in protecting me? He challenged her to confess my crimes.

But at that time, before Christmas, I knew nothing about Fritzi's imprisonment, and so, when Kohoutek threatened to jail her, I really believed that her fate was in my hands. I no longer remember everything that went through my mind, but I told Kohoutek that I would confess.

Kohoutek was ecstatic. Now that I had admitted that I was a spy and an agent of the imperialists, he gave me a cigarette, wished me a merry Christmas, and, for the first time, honored me by shaking my hand.

When I got back to my cell, I found a small table and a chair along with two packs of cigarettes, matches, paper, and a pencil.

I sat down. Nobody opened the door; nobody shouted at me to walk. I smoked a cigarette. All at once I felt like the richest and smartest man in the world. I had saved my wife and son, I could sit down and smoke—and what must I give "them" in return?

In a day or two, I would tell them that I had changed my mind. What could they do to me? . . .

. . . . . .

When he found out that I had written nothing at all, he had a fit. He shouted at the guard to take away the table, chair, and cigarettes. He even pulled a lighted cigarette out of my mouth, threw it on the floor, and stamped on it. He swore, threatened me, took all the papers, and left. He certainly spoiled my Christmas, but I guess I spoiled his as well.

After that, the interrogations became more and more painful, in every sense of the word. More than anything, it was the pain in my legs that seemed unbearable.

Some days, the interrogation consisted of only one question: "Will you confess your crimes?"

When I said I would not, I had to turn my face toward the wall and stand in that position for the rest of the day. During all those hours, my interrogator would read a book, doodle, or type something on the typewriter. Now and then, one of his colleagues would come by, and the interrogator would stand in the open door, keeping an eye on me and talking, though not loudly enough for me to overhear anything.

Standing in the corner with my face against the wall was humiliating, and it made me very depressed. Even more depressing were the documents they let me read.

A few of my colleagues at the ministry, a couple of my lifelong friends, people I had helped and promoted to good jobs, had signed depositions and denunciations in which they professed that they had always suspected me of being a traitor. Some of them accused me of having made trade agreements detrimental to Czechoslovakia and contrary to her interests. Every trade agreement naturally has aspects that are favorable to each side; no agreement has ever achieved everything that either country wanted. The writers of the depositions would pick a single item from a trade agreement and point out that it was unfavorable to socialism and proof of my sabotage.

Some of those letters might have been written with an eye toward benefiting the writer's career. But most of them had obviously been written under pressure. I knew that it was very dangerous to refuse to write a letter when asked to do so—and extremely difficult for anyone who wanted to keep his job to wriggle out of that duty. It was also totally out of the question to write favorably about someone who had spent so many months in jail.

At that time, I did not think the writers despicable. I imagined that they had been summoned by the secretary of their Party cell and told that the Party already had sufficient proof that I was a traitor. And even if they had known me as a man of impeccable behavior, they might think that I had been misleading them, as I was misleading the Party. I myself had been told that others, probably as innocent as I was, were traitors—and I had believed it. I had simply not been able to imagine that a Party member could be imprisoned without having committed any crime.

This same logic must naturally have seemed valid to my friends. As Party members, they would of course believe what the Party said. And in those days of mutual suspicion, when it was difficult to believe that there was smoke without fire, everyone would figure that a man in my position, negotiating all those contracts worth hundreds of thousands of dollars, would by the nature of his job be a constant target for temptation.

Nevertheless, these accusations depressed me deeply. Although I understood intellectually how the letters had come to be written and tried to convince myself that it did not matter, I felt the effects of this systematic snapping of the links that had bound me inwardly to my friends and collaborators. . . .

· · · · ·

One day, Kohoutek had me brought from the cell for interrogation, and, as usual, he made me stand facing the wall. Suddenly he asked me to turn around, and he said, with feeling, "You know, Loebl, I realize that it is difficult to admit here that you are a spy, a traitor, and a saboteur, but I've got to get you accustomed to it."

He leaned across the table with a friendly glint in his eyes. "Repeat after me: I am a spy. I am a saboteur. I am a traitor."

I said that I was not a spy, a saboteur, or a traitor, but he told me to repeat it, and that that was an order. I knew that if I did not obey an order, I would be punished with the cold, dark dungeon and one meal a day until I gave in. And so I repeated, "I am a spy. I am a saboteur. I am a traitor. . . ."

· · · · ·

On Kohoutek's instructions, Dr. Sommer again took my blood pressure, X-rayed me, weighed me, and gave me a thorough checkup. Although I knew I was little more than skin and bones, I was still surprised to see that the reading on the scale was barely a hundred and ten pounds; when I was arrested, I had weighed a hundred and seventy.

Sommer jotted my weight onto a chart in my file and then turned to the guard. "Put him on Diet #2. I'll clear it with Comrade Kohoutek."

The next morning at ten o'clock, the guard took me into the prison yard, and I was told that I would have an hour to walk around. While I was walking, another guard came over to me with a piece of buttered bread and some salami, which I ate.

When the hour of walking was over, they took me to Drozd's office for an hour of interrogation. Then I had lunch: some very good soup, a large helping of meat, two vegetables, and a dessert. After lunch, the guard came in and told me to take a nap.

At two o'clock, I went back for two more hours of interrogation, but this was interrupted by another guard who brought me more bread and salami. At about six o'clock, when my afternoon interrogation was over, I got a supper of meat, two vegetables, and a dessert of cheese.

This went on day after day. First they had planned my confession, and now they were planning my weight. I could even visualize the doctor setting his own target figures and doing whatever had to be done to make sure that the plan would be fulfilled.

I learned that the food I got was the same as that which the interrogators ate and on a par with the food served in the best restaurants in Prague. Some of my fellow defendants—the ones who had lost even more weight than I had—got even richer food. They were forced to drink cream three times a day and eat ham instead of salami, and they had beer with lunch and dinner. Diets were determined not according to rank, but according to weight loss.

Sometimes I was interrogated at night, but usually the interrogations amounted to only three or four hours during the day. It was still called interrogation, but it was very different from the sessions that I was used to.

Kohoutek called me into his office to brief me on my testimony. "The teachers are anxious to make sure that the defendants confess to certain particular charges and include all the necessary details in their confessions."

Here he stopped and took out of my file what must have been a list of my crimes.

"Your worst crime, Loebl, was that you tried to tie the Czechoslovak economy to the imperialist West in preparation for what you hoped would be a break from the Soviet Union. By making us dependent on trade with the West, you thought you could eliminate trade with other socialist countries and restore capitalism to Czechoslovakia."

He paused and looked down the list.

"On top of that, you were a spy who gave valuable information to agents of the West, and a saboteur who tried his best to create economic problems in Czechoslovakia so as to discredit Socialism in the eyes of the working class, both of our country and of the world at large. You were also a Titoist agent who negotiated a treaty that was highly favorable to Yugoslavia and totally unfavorable to our country. Finally, you are a Jew who always did what was in the best interests of world Jewry and a supporter of Zionism, the bulwark of Anglo-American imperialism in the Near East."

He finished reading from the list, put it back in the file, closed it, and looked at me intently.

"Your job now, Loebl, will be to work out the exact wording of your testimony with your interrogator, Comrade Drozd. You will use your previous confessions as a basis for what you will say at the trial. Lieutenant Drozd will ask you the questions, and you will have to formulate good answers."

He ordered the guard to take me to Drozd's office. When I got there, I found Drozd pacing the room and looking very uneasy. He seemed to be uncomfortable in his role as assistant director of a play the whole world press was going to see.

"You know, Loebl, this business about writing the answers for a trial has to be done just right. The teachers are perfectionists, and if things aren't done exactly as they should be, they will get very angry. They've spent weeks briefing us on exactly how to do it. You know that Kohoutek and the others were present in Budapest, and they watched the preparations for the trial to learn how to proceed.". . .

. . . . .

I kept busy writing my testimony, but poor Drozd was not able to formulate the questions, let alone the answers.

By that time, I was ready to confess whatever I had to confess without offering the slightest resistance. Even in the midst of this tragedy, I could not help seeing that the situation had all the elements of a farce: where illiterate men like Drozd who could hardly spell were producing a show that would be seen by the whole world, and, at the same time, a helpless prisoner, sentenced even before his trial began, wrote all the questions that the prosecutors, attorneys, and judges would ask, as well as all the answers that he would give them.

Throughout the preparation for the trial, the teachers were careful to see that there were no contradictions among the statements of the various defendants. The confessions were to be like pieces in a giant jigsaw puzzle: they had to form a common picture which would demonstrate that the entire country, and all the important ministries and party organs, were in the hands of traitors, and that these traitors were disciplined members of a single well-organized conspiracy. Each of the defendants had his own special part in the larger scenario, assigned to him by its authors—the teachers. . . .

. . . . .

It took two months for my testimony to be finished and approved. The next step was to learn it by heart. Every day, I had to memorize a few pages of questions and answers. In a week or so, I knew it all by heart.

We rehearsed in Drozd's office. I had to stand in front of the desk, and Drozd, sitting behind it, asked me the questions. He read what the prosecutor, defender, and judge would say at the trial, and I had to answer from memory. I was not permitted to leave out or change a single word, not even the syntax. At the smallest mistake, Drozd repeated the question, and I had to repeat the answer until it was exactly the same as in the script.

After this rehearsal, I had to read the whole thing aloud, both questions and answers, so that I would remember it better. When Drozd saw that I knew everything by heart, he informed Kohoutek, who attended a rehearsal.

Both interrogators sat behind the desk, each with a copy of the script in his hands. Drozd asked the questions, and I answered them. After a short time, Kohoutek interrupted me.

"You seem to know all the answers, Loebl, but I am concerned about how you say them. You speak as if you didn't believe what you say. It is expected that you will answer with a firm voice. Your answers should sound convincing and decisive. As you did confess of your own free will, we want everyone to see that this is so, and therefore, you should not hesitate when you answer. Your answers should sound the way you feel—that you wanted to confess, that you wanted to make up for the crimes you have committed."

I tried my best to play the role the way they wanted me to play it. Like an actor on stage, I was not concerned about whether it was the part of an honest man or a liar, a lover or a murderer, or how ridiculous the play itself was: I only wanted to do my best, play my part well, and be in harmony with the rest of the actors. I put out of my mind any thought that this trial showed the true morality of the regime and its real concept of justice.

In retrospect, what bothers me most is what I did not feel at that time—namely, that I no longer felt that I was a human being. Had I played the part out of fear or under pressure, had I hated it or been desperate at being forced into such a humiliating role, I would not feel the pain I feel now whenever I think of what happened. But at that time, I felt no shame or humiliation or hatred; I did not even make an internal protest about what was happening. It is this that still gives me a feeling of indescribable horror.

Yet I would like to stress again that I was not brainwashed. I knew exactly what I was doing. I thought, read, and learned more in those months than I had at the university. On the one hand, I read books on economics, physics, philosophy, and ethics; but on the other hand, every human value had been driven out of me, and I played my role without inhibitions.

It is frightening to think of how low I sank. It was as if I completely lost the human characteristics that are every man's legacy from the hundreds of generations that have gone before us.

Perhaps it would be better if I did not write about this, if I did not disclose how I feel today about what happened to me then. Perhaps it is just a kind of self-flagellation. But how could I write honestly if I lied about the worst part of the most horrifying experience of my life? . . .

. . . . .

The night before the trial a guard brought me my civilian clothing and shoes. The belt and the shoelaces were missing, so that I could not use them to commit suicide. I went to bed apathetic, not at all excited. If anything, I was worried about whether I would remember all my lines. I was so caught up in the show that I wanted to play my part in exactly the right way.

It was still dark when the guard came and told me to get dressed. Then another guard came, cut my hair, and gave me a shave. An hour later, I was taken to the prison yard. The night was illuminated by huge lights. In the middle of the yard, there were buses surrounded by hundreds of guards in battle dress and carrying submachine guns.

My guards led me across the yard and up the steps of the first bus. Inside, there were four cells on each side of a narrow corridor. Every cell had a small door, and inside was a chair. There was just enough room to permit a prisoner to sit without moving.

One of the guards handcuffed me and locked the door from the outside; only then did I hear three more prisoners being loaded onto the bus. Those in the cells across the corridor must have got there before I came.

After an endless hour of waiting, the bus began to move. Then it stopped again. I heard a huge door being opened, and then the engine began to roar at normal speed. Outside, I could hear the sounds of metal treads on cobblestones; I guessed that our bus was being guarded by tanks.

I knew that the trial was to take place in Pankrac, an old prison built centuries before. The courtroom was in its courthouse annex, next to the Supreme Court.

Half an hour after the bus left Ruzyne, it stopped. Another heavy gate clanged, and we were inside Pankrac.

The bus door clicked open and then the doors of the cubicles, one by one. I counted; mine was the fifth.

The large, bleak courtyard of the medieval prison was dazzlingly lit by army searchlights which were reflected on the dewy cobblestones. There must have been a good hundred soldiers with submachine guns at the ready, and a dozen armored cars loomed in the rear near the gate; the place looked like a beleaguered fortress.

My first thought was, "What are they afraid of? Is the populace going to rise in revolt to liberate us—or do they believe the Americans are going to do it?" But when that first shock wore off and I stood in the glare of those lights, I suddenly realized that after three years in prison, I was now facing reality.

There, in Ruzyne prison, isolated from the outside world, I had been led to believe that I was the center of the world and that my prison life was the only true reality. In my isolation, I forgot completely about the difference between objective reality and the artifact, the artificial universe constructed in my immurement, by my jailers and myself. From that point of view, the coming trial would be just a welcome change in my status, and whatever testimony I gave would be pointless.

But in the glare of the searchlights that were cutting the misty predawn November morning, I suddenly realized that this would be a real trial, with a real public, and that I was a defendant in this trial.

Suddenly I realized anew the existence of all those values I had abrogated under the torment before my confession.

Up to that moment, I had been afraid that Slansky or one of the other co-defendants would deny my charges and expose me; I had only hoped that everyone would confess the way I did and that nobody would perform better than I. Being beyond morality myself, I wanted to evade a confrontation with people who had retained their morality.

But now, faced with the imminence of what was going to happen to me, I desperately wanted to be moral once more. I was aware that the Other One was not my real self. I condemned my past conduct and promised myself that, once in the dock, in the presence of the public and the press, I would expose everything; I would withdraw my confession and then maybe all the other defendants would withdraw theirs. In view of the publicity of the trial, not much could happen to me; the worst they could do was hang me.

At the same time, I felt in the depths of my being that I had neither the guts nor the strength to do anything. I had the moral strength to condemn myself, but not to do something about it. It was like being someone who was half awake, who felt that he should get up but did not have the strength to do so; instead he dreamed about what he would do if he did get up. This sense of weakness, of being paralyzed and knowing perfectly well how despicable my conduct was, was one of the worst experiences of my life.

Two guards took me to a cell two or three floors below ground. It was obviously a little-used cellar that was cut off from the other cells. There was no water pipe or toilet. There was one iron bed, two chairs, a small table, and a large garbage can that I was supposed to use as a toilet. I was not left alone for a second. The guard stayed with me in the cell, but I was told not to speak to him unless I needed something.

Later that morning, they brought a washbasin and, in contrast to the meager furnishings, an excellent breakfast: real coffee with milk, ham, and buttered bread. It was the kind of breakfast that none of the members of the ruling working class could afford.

Dr. Sommer came to see me with his nurse, who was carrying a plate covered with different kinds of pills. Dr. Sommer gave me a thorough checkup and some tranquilizers, and we exchanged a few words. He was like a family doctor talking to a long-term patient. . . .

. . . . .

We walked up three flights of stairs and then down a long corridor, which was partitioned off into cubicles. Each of the cubicles had one chair for the prisoner and another for his guard. The partitions were in a row down one side of the hall so that the prisoners would have no chance to communicate with one another across the corridor.

Dr. Sommer and his nurse walked up and down the hall, distributing pills. High-ranking officers of the army and the secret police walked among the prisoners, accompanied by Kohoutek and the other interrogators; they stopped at each cubicle and exchanged a few friendly words with the accused. Several generals and colonels came to see me. They asked me how I felt and encouraged me not to be afraid of the sentence. They reminded me that the judgment of my party would be fair, and that I would be given every opportunity to make up for what I had done. They also said that, in any case, the Party would take care of my family, and they offered me coffee, cigarettes, and soft drinks. It was as if I were surrounded by my best friends.

Suddenly there was a great commotion, and, one by one, we were ushered into the courtroom.

The courtroom was a large hall with about three hundred seats. In front, there was a long bench for the judges; at the left, the bench for the prosecution; and at the right, the bench for the defense counsel. In front of the judges' bench, there were small tables for the court stenographers and many cameras and broadcasting equipment.

We defendants sat in the first three rows, framed on both sides by armed guards.

When I took my place in the dock, I saw my accomplices in the "conspiracy" for the first time; until that moment, I had not known who else would be on trial. I had known only that Slansky would be charged as the head of the conspiracy, and I had guessed that my old friend Clementis would be one of my codefendants.

Sitting next to Slansky was Josef Frank, the Deputy General Secretary of the Party. He was Slansky's assistant and a fellow member of the Politburo. In spite of his German name, he was a Czech, originally a worker but a Party functionary for many years. . . .

. . . . .

Next to Frank sat Bedrich Geminder, a very close and loyal friend of Gottwald's, and next to him Clementis. Farther down, I saw Karel Svab, the Deputy Minister of the Interior. On my bench, there was Ota Sling, the Party Secretary for Moravia, a long-time Party member who had fought in the Spanish Civil War, spent World War II in England, and would never have dreamed of opposing the Party line.

André Simone, whom some called the "Czech Walter Lippmann," sat next to him. His articles were the mainstay of the foreign-news page of the official Party journal, *Rudé Pravo*. During the war, Simone had lived in Mexico and spent several years in Paris. I hardly recognized him. He must have been about fifty, but he looked as if he were a hundred. His body was skin and bones, his face deathly pale.

Then came the Deputy Minister of Defense, Bedrich Reicin, a giant who was over six feet tall and looked even larger in contrast to the minuscule Simone. Reicin, who had fought in the Czechoslovak detachment in the Soviet Union and been decorated by the highest Soviet orders, was widely known as an agent for the Soviet army's secret service, and everybody in Prague was afraid of him.

On the other bench, I saw Dr. Otto Fischl, the Deputy Minister of Finance. Among other crimes, he was accused of permitting Jewish emigrants to Israel to take nearly all their possessions with them. Actually, Fischl had been disliked and feared because he was particularly severe with emigrants to Israel, in order to keep anyone from leaving who would not be loyal to the Party. He was so zealous that he often went on inspection journeys to the borders to make sure that customs officials obeyed the rules.

Besides the economist Dr. Vavro Hajdu and the Deputy Minister of Foreign Affairs, Arthur London, there was also my friend and the Third Deputy Minister of Foreign Trade, Rudolf Margolius. After spending the war in a German concentration camp, he had emerged with great faith in the Soviet Union and the Communist Party, and it was I myself who had advised the Minister of Foreign Trade to appoint him first his personal secretary, and not long afterward, deputy minister.

Altogether, there were fourteen of us, eleven of whom were Jews. Most of my fellow defendants had been Party members much longer than I; many had spent their lifetimes in the service of the Party, suffered imprisonment in capitalist prisons and concentration camps because of their devotion, and fought in the Spanish Civil War or alongside the Soviet Union in World War II.

The chief prosecutor and four assistant prosecutors took their places, followed by the four counselors for the defense. Then the president of the court, Dr. Novak, began the proceedings. Very formal, calm, and always dignified, he was the personification of objectivity, and he ran the show with a solemn voice.

"Will the citizen chief prosecutor read the indictment."

The chief prosecutor rose and solemnly began: "The accused Trotskyite, Titoist, Zionist, and bourgeois nationalist traitors created, in the service of the United States imperialists and under the direction of Western espionage agencies, an anti-state, conspiratorial center designed to undermine the people's democratic regime, to frustrate the building of socialism, to damage the national economy of the republic, to carry out espionage activities, and generally to weaken the unity of the Czechoslovak people and the defensive capacity of the republic.

"They did this to destroy the close alliance and undermine the friendship of the Czechoslovak people with the Soviet people, to liquidate the people's regime . . . undermine their close alliance, and liquidate the socialist form of government in the Czechoslovak Republic. Their aim was to restore capitalism and to drag the republic once again into the imperialist camp, while destroying its national sovereignty and independence."

The indictment made it clear that all of Czechoslovakia's economic and political difficulties were caused by a conspiracy of criminal individuals, coordinated by Slansky, who disguised themselves as Party zealots and placed themselves in key positions from which, in close contact with one another, they would not only be able to turn Czechoslovakia toward the West, but also put the economy into such a chaotic state that the people would cease to believe in the leadership of the Communist Party and the alliance with the Soviet Union.

After the indictment, Dr. Novak asked each of us whether we understood it, and whether we pleaded guilty or not.

Every one of the defendants was answering in the affirmative, and my turn was approaching. I wished terribly hard that I would be able to get up and say, "No."

But when my turn came and I was asked whether I confessed and admitted the crimes which were charged to me, I got up and said, "I do."

I cannot explain why I was unable to say no. I can only say that it was totally impossible. I just could not do it. The treatment had worked; it was foolproof. We played our parts in the scenario to the letter. We knew what we were doing, but we could not change it.

There were two sessions a day, morning and afternoon, during which they proceeded to question all the defendants in succession. Each night, we were transported back to Ruzyne prison in long black limousines, handcuffed and blindfolded.

My turn came on a Sunday. That particular morning, they took off my blindfold about a mile out of Ruzyne. It was a beautiful sunny day, and, as we drove through a park, I saw children being led by their parents on a Sunday outing.

In the courtroom, the prosecutor cross-examined me, and I confessed everything exactly as it had been written out in our scripts. The prosecutors, the counselors for the defense, and the judges had it all there in front of them— the questions I myself had conceived when I wrote my deposition with Drozd.

Everything went smoothly until one of the prosecutors asked a question before he was supposed to ask it; inadvertently, he had skipped a whole paragraph. I remember that I corrected his question and gave the correct answer. Practically no one noticed, but after the trial, Kohoutek told me that he was grateful that I had stuck to the deposition; he was furious with the prosecutor.

"How dare he make such a mistake! I assure you he will be severely reprimanded."

Kohoutek was very pleased with my performance. He said that I sounded absolutely convincing. But it must have been clear to everyone that the scenario of the trial was concocted; it ran so smoothly and interlocked so well. There was nothing unexpected or dramatic, such as would happen at a real trial. All of us defendants stated our crimes and our confessions in such exaggerated terms that it ought to have been obvious that this could not be our own wording.

The very smoothness of the judicial machinery ought to have alerted every thinking person to its phoniness, but I learned later that it did not. The many people who were listening to our voices on the radio, and the fifteen hundred or two thousand dignitaries, writers, newspapermen, and shock workers who were witnessing the trial were conditioned to accept our depositions and the entire trial as genuine.

True, there were only Party members present and even they had been carefully screened, but among them were French, Italian, and British Communist newspapermen who could not have been subjected to the various psychological pressures that Czechs and Slovaks were subjected to.

So the ghostly theater of the trial continued, with not only the spectators but also the nation and the whole Communist world as a terrible choir.

One day, the smoothly running clockwork of the trial had a ludicrous interruption, an event not foreseen in the script. The Moravian Party Secretary, Ota Sling, had always been slightly obese, but during his time in prison, he had lost much more weight than he could gain back for public appearance. During his cross-examination, he had to hold his trousers up with one hand, as the defendants were not permitted to keep their shoelaces or belts.

The screenwriters of the trial had forgotten to reckon with the force of gravity. In the midst of the sordid, solemn ceremony, Sling, in the heat of his confession, suddenly gestured with both hands at the same time. His black trousers slipped to the floor and left him standing in his white underwear.

The judges, prosecutors, guards, defense counselors, and defendants—everyone—burst out laughing. With this laughter, something human crept into that court, something that had not been planned. And the mirth was so spontaneous that it was impossible even for Dr. Novak to stop it. The public and judiciary personnel were still laughing when we were taken back into the long corridor for the break between sessions. . . .

. . . . .

. . . when my turn came to confess, just like the others I could not escape that deep groove that had been dug into my psyche in the years of solitary confinement, and I, too, helplessly repeated the phrases engraved in my mind.

Drozd told me that he expected there would only be two or three death sentences, and that I, who had been imprisoned far earlier than anyone else, might expect a sentence of not more than ten or fifteen years. Nevertheless, this was not my reason for confessing at the trial. I knew that if I denied the charges, I would be sentenced to death, but what made me confess was not a fear of death, but a lack of strength and willpower to act on my own.

I naturally cannot say what the motivations of the other defendants might have been, but all of us confessed exactly as we were told and taught to confess.

A hushed silence fell over the courtroom when the chief prosecutor began his final speech: "Our people's democratic court has never before dealt with a case involving criminals as base as those whom you see in the dock before you."

It was a very long speech, and he enumerated once again all the crimes and shameless confessions in which we boastfully had admitted our guilt. Finally he said:

"In the name of all of the Czech and Slovak people against whose freedom and happiness these criminals acted, in the name of peace, against which they shamelessly plotted, I demand the death sentence for all of the defendants."

He turned to the judges and raised his voice.

"Let your verdict become an iron fist that will crush these vermin without the slightest pity. Let your verdict be a fire that will burn out the roots of this shameful abscess of treason. Let your verdict be a bell ringing throughout our beautiful country for new victories on the march to the sunshine of Socialism. I demand the death sentence for all of the defendants!"

The audience answered with a standing ovation.

After a short plea from the defense counselors, we were taken back to our cells. I remember again my dual minds, one reacting to the events while the other, simultaneously, was merely speculative. During the trial, after three years of solitary confinement, I had been overwhelmed by the sudden contact with so many people. I had also been inquisitive; after my own experience, I wanted to see whether any of my fellow defendants had lost their souls the way I had. As the time passed and our sentencing drew closer, I felt my exhilaration and excitement petering out and exhaustion setting in, but this could also have been caused by Dr. Sommer's medication.

On the last day of the trial, each of us had to make a final statement to the court. I cannot remember what the others said, but I do know that I spent the whole night thinking about how to phrase my own last statement; I was acting as if it might have some significance. I did not even think of denying what I had previously confessed; there was simply no escape from the steel ring to which I felt shackled.

In their last statements, all of my codefendants once again proclaimed their guilt and confessed their crimes. Several of them actually called for the supreme punishment and assured the court and the public that whatever punishment was meted out would be just, deserved, and exemplary. The Party journalist, André Simone, even exclaimed in a ringing voice that there was not a gallows in the entire country high enough for a traitor of his caliber.

On November 27, 1952, the court pronounced sentence:

Eleven defendants were sentenced to death, three to life imprisonment.

London and Hajdu were sentenced to life, the court explained, because "the period of criminal activity was shorter than that of the others."

Loebl was sentenced to life because he was the first to be arrested, because he confessed spontaneously, and because his confession helped to unmask the conspiracy.

Besides sentencing me to life imprisonment, the court detailed the nature of my relationship with Slansky, trying to explain the inexplicable: how the General Secretary could approve my arrest even though he himself had been my boss and, at the same time, my accomplice in the conspiracy.

When, after the recess, the defense counselors flocked to our cells in the long corridor outside the courtroom, they advised us to waive the right to appeal and accept the sentence. Not one of the defendants appealed.

I must say again that in telling this story, I can only speak for myself. When I confessed, I knew exactly what part I was playing. What I said and what I did, I did and said because I did not have the strength for anything else; I was literally knocked out.

However, I have no intention of hiding behind the pressure I was exposed to. Deep inside me, I still have a feeling of guilt. I wish I could have been stronger and not given in. My denial could have influenced many of those who were listening and who were made to believe that the trial was a just one.

EAST GERMANY

❄ ❄ ❄

The Stasi

Mike Dennis

MIKE DENNIS (1940–), educated at Liverpool University, is a professor of modern German history at the University of Wolverhampton in England and chairman of the University's Russian and East European Research Center as well as editor in chief of the journal East Central Europe. *He is the author or coauthor of numerous books on the German Democratic Republic (East Germany).*

This study was chosen for information about East Germany since no relevant English-language memoirs could be found. The original footnotes have not been included.

· · · · ·

An Orwellian Nightmare

The Ministry of State Security, popularly known as the Stasi, was an integral element of communist rule in the German Democratic Republic between the ministry's establishment in 1950 to its dissolution in 1989. The GDR itself was founded in 1949, as Stalin's "unwanted child" of the Cold War. Despite the popular uprising in 1953 against the Stalinist system which had been imposed on the GDR and despite the mass exodus of East Germans to the West, the new state managed to survive until its next major test in 1961. The Berlin Wall, erected by the East German Communists with Soviet endorsement, arrested in a brutal manner the hemorrhaging of the population, thereby stabilizing the system behind the ugly barrier which soon came to symbolize the totalitarian nature of communism. A combination of social incentives, economic growth, and more subtle forms of coercion subsequently enabled the GDR's rulers to consolidate their position and, in the era of superpower détente, to gain international recognition for their country. However, the Soviet Union's retreat from empire under Gorbachev and the GDR's chronic economic mal-

From Mike Dennis: The Stasi: Myth and Reality, © *2003 Pearson Education Limited.*

aise exposed the frail legitimacy of the communist social and political order. When the Berlin Wall eventually fell, on the evening of November 9–10, 1989, it was an act of desperation by East Germany's bewildered rulers to save an obsolescent system which neither they nor their security and military forces could prevent from disintegrating under the twin pressures of popular demonstrations and mass flight.

Following in the footsteps of its Soviet counterpart, the KGB, the Ministry of State Security functioned for almost four decades as the sharp sword and trusty shield of the GDR's key institution, the ruling Socialist Unity Party (SED). Such was the ministry's power and ubiquity that one author, Alexandra Richie, refers to it as exercising, in the 1980s, "almost complete control over the captive population of East Germany." And, indeed, the comprehensive surveillance of the population by a vast army of informers and a plethora of scientific and technical devices lends substance to the claim by the historian Christoph Klessmann that George Orwell's *Nineteen Eighty-Four* was realized to a greater extent in the GDR than was ever the case in the Third Reich. When, in addition, the Stasi's success in planting agents in all areas of West German political and cultural life is borne in mind, then it is tempting to concur with Anne Applebaum's verdict that it was "the most pervasive and efficient secret service in history."

Former high-ranking officers of the Stasi seize eagerly on this notion of efficiency as part of a well-packaged defense of what they regard as the ministry's honorable and legitimate role in protecting the East German state against a legion of external and internal enemies. This kind of argument is also used to combat the denigration of the MfS as part of what the officers perceive to be a continuation into the new Germany of the traditional anti-communist doctrine of the old Federal Republic (FRG). The elements of the defamation campaign which they allege is being conducted by the mass media and the "political class" encompass forced adoptions, the murder of babies, the use of torture in MfS pre-trial detention centers and assisting terrorists in West Germany's notorious Red Army Faction. Not only does this litany of infamy—most of which can be substantiated—serve to discredit the Stasi by association with the murderers of the Gestapo but by depicting the ministry as the center of evil it adds grist to the mill of those who seek to condemn the GDR as a totalitarian state, thereby justifying the wholesale dismantling of the former GDR's institutions and the socio-economic upheaval since the country's incorporation into the Federal Republic in October 1990.

Although the self-portrayal of a dedicated, professional service class helps to sustain the officers' feelings of worth and identity in a world transformed, it too often masks the darker, repressive side of the GDR which is so closely associated with the totalitarian paradigm. One of the central sub-themes in the highly controversial debate on the applicability, and the value, of the totalitarian label to the GDR concerns the centrality of the role of the Stasi within the system. Rather than being—as its long-serving minister, the autocratic Erich Mielke, insisted—the loyal and trustworthy agent of the SED's will, the ministry is sometimes depicted as a "state within a state" whose clandestine operations were not rigorously controlled and monitored by Party organs. Egon Krenz, the former head of the SED's Central Committee Department for Security Questions and the SED's last leader, subscribes to the latter argument, partly because it helps to relieve him of some of the burden of responsibility for the Stasi's excesses and abuse of human rights. The myth of an ultra-efficient and omnipotent intelligence and security service has also come under challenge on the grounds that the Stasi was submerged in a flood of data, much of it mindless trivia. Tina Rosenberg has depicted the minutiae, or what she calls the thousands of tons of "shit" under the nuggets of gold, in graphic detail:

> The Stasi knew where Comrade Gisela kept the ironing board in her apartment... and how many times a week Comrade Armin took out his garbage and what color socks he wore with his sandals while doing it.... The Stasi kept watch on trash dumps and lending libraries—the names of those who checked out books on hot air balloons or rock-climbing equipment were of particular interest—and tapped the booths of Catholic confessionals and the seats at the Dresden Opera. Stasi cameras monitored public toilets.... Some of its dossiers on East Germans had a hundred categories of information—even the number, location, and design of tattoos. The Stasi kept a library of smells: a few hundred glass jars containing bits of dissidents' dirty underwear, so trained dogs could sniff and match the smell to an antigovernment pamphlet found on the sidewalk.

Complementary to the "drowning-men of the Stasi" thesis is the view that the ministry was incapable of controlling the disparate social, economic, and political currents in a state bedeviled by a pronounced legitimacy deficit and highly vulnerable to Western influences. One leading German historian, Lutz Niethammer, takes up this theme, arguing that the Stasi, "an uncontrolled and paranoid military bureaucracy," far from being the core of the regime should be placed at the edge on the grounds that the mass of society had either been integrated or immobilized and, furthermore, that the ministry fostered rather than reduced opposition. By the late 1980s, it had come to personify an outmoded anti-fascism and Chekist steel fist. While the interpretation of a floundering Stasi is certainly not without substance, the Stasi cannot, of course, be relegated to a peripheral role in the light of its multiplicity of functions as guardian of the verities of Marxist-Leninist ideology, its ruthless implementation of the socialist revolution of the 1950s, its upholding of the Communist power monopoly against perceived enemies at home and abroad, its crucial part in the acquisition of hard currency and scientific and technical know-how from the West, and its snooping into the intimate details of people's lives. Far from being a blunt sword and rusty shield, the Stasi was an indispensable instrument of the Communist power elites in the global struggle against their capitalist rivals in the West, even though it should be stressed that in some spheres, especially the vital one of the economy, the Stasi's autocratic minister, Erich Mielke, often resembles a Don Quixote tilting at socialist windmills.

. . . . .

The Stasi in Comparative Perspective

To what extent was the Stasi *sui generis,* at least in German history? A comparison with its nearest pre-war equivalent, the Gestapo, reveals that the Stasi soon evolved into a much larger organization than the former and was far more reliant on a structured network of agents than on the kind of voluntary "spite informers" who supplied denunciatory information to the Gestapo. For example, in 1977, the Gestapo employed probably no more than 7,000 officials out of a population of 66 million. In contrast, the MfS, a mere 2,700 in 1950, had reached 48,786 in 1971 and over 91,000 full-time staff out of a population of about 16.4 million in 1989. Furthermore, the MfS, like its KGB counterpart, housed both foreign intelligence and counterintelligence under one roof, whereas the Gestapo was but one element in the Third Reich's system of policing, state security and counterintelligence. One of the other key agencies was the Security Service (SD) of Himmler's *Schutzstaffel* or SS, and whereas SD informers reported on popular opinion, the Gestapo agents concentrated on "political crimes." The number of SD agents is difficult to assess; some historians speculate that the total may have been between 100,000 and 120,000 in 1939. And, as will be stressed in this book, during the course of the 1960s, MfS staff became increasingly professional and more proficient at subtle forms of repression; on the other hand, the professionalism of the Gestapo's early officers—a legacy of the Weimar Republic—was eroded by less qualified new recruits and the organization was caught up in the growing barbarism of the Third Reich. The contrast is captured in Heiner Geißler's differentiation between the mountain of corpses and files left behind by the Third Reich and the GDR respectively.

Other countries, too, have been unable to dispense with intelligence and security services. In the adversarial atmosphere of the Cold War, the intelligence services of both West and East experienced an exponential growth and were extremely costly to run. They generated a paper mountain of data, suffered information overload, were adept at justifying their existence and evading public accountability, and were pervaded by a conspiratorial view of the world and what Philip Knightley has called "an obligatory paranoia." They vied with each other in the use of advanced technology to spy on friend as well as foe and to turn each other's agents. Moreover, the hidden hand of the CIA extended beyond low-level covert operations such as the funding of anti-Communist trade unions, political parties and newspapers to the covert "hot zone" of seeking to overthrow governments in Iran, Guatemala, Nicaragua, and Cuba. The overthrow of the Iranian prime minister and the restoration of the Shah in 1953 and the "Bay of Pigs" fiasco in 1961 illustrate the extremes to which the CIA was prepared to go. But covert activities were also practiced at home, notably by J. Edgar Hoover, the long-time head of the FBI, who in the 1960s, according to the National Commission on the Causes and Prevention of Violence, "helped spread the view among the police that any kind of mass protest is due to a conspiracy promulgated by agitators, often Communists, 'who misdirect otherwise contented people.'" As a purveyor of the Red Scare in American politics, Hoover was not too dissimilar from Mielke as the propagator of the Imperialist Scare in the GDR.

It is little wonder that East Germany's legendary spymaster Markus Wolf stresses the basic similarity in methods and goals between the secret services of the Cold War rivals. They were, he claims, vital to the preservation of peace as they gave statesmen security from being taken by surprise. Not only was he therefore performing a task analogous to that of his West German counterparts in the BND but also, in his words, "Our sins and mistakes were those of every other intelligence agency." What Wolf conveniently downplays is that a deep-rooted insecurity pervaded the entire East German leadership class and, secondly, that a symbiotic relationship existed between beauty and the beast, that is, between his elitist foreign intelligence service and the Stasi's enormous apparatus of domestic repression. In the West, there was a clearer, though by no means sharp, differentiation between these two services—in America the CIA and FBI and in Britain MI5 and MI6. In this respect, the Stasi is closer to the KGB whose ruthless and uncompromising campaigns against real or imagined enemies at home and its centrality to the preservation of the Soviet system distinguished it from the intelligence communities of the West. The outcome of the Stasi's dual task of external intelligence and the ubiquitous system of surveillance and intimidation at home was an agency many times larger than any Western intelligence or security service, including the Stasi's West German counterparts, the BND and BfV.

One of the most striking features of the Stasi was its sheer size—91,105 full-time staff and about 176,000 informers shortly before the fall of the Berlin Wall—which, together with an elaborate system of postal and telephone monitoring, enabled the ministry to conduct an almost blanket surveillance of society. The ratio of Stasi employees to the East German population as well as the intensity of surveillance may well have been unprecedented in modern history. While the degree of monitoring and intrusion may have been exceptional, the practices were not peculiar to East Germany as the Cold War spurred the antagonists, in both the East and the West, to penetrate each other's countries as well as their own society. Yet, even the MfS has been outstripped by the electronic monitoring capability now available to modern states. At the time of writing this book, in the summer of 2002, EU governments are considering acquiring access to and storing for one year the records of personal communications, including all emails and telephone calls, a concept of universal surveillance which would have delighted the Stasi's monitors. . . .

· · · · ·

Prison Conditions

Despite improvements, conditions remained harsh in the Stasi's prisons and the specially trained interrogators utilized a variety of psychological techniques. This can be illustrated in numerous ways. When an arrest was made, usually without warning, an individual was immediately disoriented. In the early decades, prisoners were neither allowed to see the route along which they were taken by car to prison, nor were they informed of their destination. Arrest was a traumatic experience, whether it occurred at home or at work and whether it was expected or not. In the 1970s, it was common practice for the children of parents under arrest to be placed initially in one of the state's children's homes rather than in the care of relatives. Wolfgang Hinkeldey, an electrician, was arrested by the Stasi on December 11, 1976, at his home in Jena, imprisoned in Berlin-Hohenschönhausen, and proceedings initiated against him for incitement hostile to the state and for forming associations hostile to the state. Hinkeldey was deported to West Berlin on September 2, 1977, without a trial having been held. He describes what happened after he opened the door at 7:30 on the morning of his arrest:

> Three characters are standing outside.
> "You are Herr Hinkeldey?"
> "Yes."
> "Get dressed. You are coming with us to clear something up."
> That is how it is. How often have I gone through this moment in my mind. It still frightens me now. I get dressed. . . .
> A Stasi official stays in the flat. The other two take me out to a car. In front is the driver, with me in the middle behind him. My last journey through Jena ends at the Stasi building Am Anger. I have to wait. A young man watches me over his ND [*Neues Deutschland*]. Then they put handcuffs on me. I am driven away again in a car and taken to the State Security regional headquarters in Gera.

Although it was impossible to keep all prisoners in solitary confinement, every effort was made to reduce contact between prisoners other than with a cell inmate. The prison guards of Department XIV had to ensure that prisoners did not listen accidentally into conversations or radio and television programmes. The surveillance of prisoners was remorseless. Guards kept regular watch over prisoners inside the cells, usually by means of the peephole in the door, and lights might be flashed on and off during the night. Prison rooms were monitored by cameras and conversations with lawyers recorded. Defense lawyers had limited access to the relevant documentation. From the 1970s onwards, greater use was made of bugging devices. In 1987, a joint Main Department IX and Department XIV report revealed that 30,959 hours of prisoners' conversations had been recorded in that year, the first time that the 30,000 mark had been exceeded! Bugging devices were complemented by the widespread use of cell informers. In 1985, there were two prisoners for every one informer in the Stasi's two pre-trial detention centers in East Berlin; in the regions, the ratio was between 3:1 and 10:1. Among the main incentives for spying on fellow-prisoners were better conditions in cells, the prospect of an early release and "atonement" for a misdemeanor.

The treatment of prisoners gives the lie to the depiction of interrogations by a former Main Department IX officer with many years of service: "Every prisoner under investigation had his defense lawyer, everyone was able to receive visits by relatives, so if anything untoward had happened, they would not have kept it to themselves." And while he acknowledged that imprisonment was a serious encroachment on a prisoner's life, he insisted that interrogations were stressful for both parties. Contrasting personal experience of conditions and treatment in Stasi custody are recalled by a political prisoner, Gerhard J., who was eventually sentenced to imprisonment in Cottbus in the late 1970s for would-be emigration. He recalled his first impressions of the MfS detention center in the Otto-Nuschke-Straße in Potsdam, where he spent seven months. It was known as the Lindenhotel because of the lime trees which stood in the street outside; it had been used by the Nazis as a jail for political prisoners.

> I was led through a labyrinth of dark corridors and stairs. An eerie lack of space, hemmed in by ropes, red lights in every section, windows you could not see through. Then bars and more bars. Frightened and cowed I put my hands behind my back without being asked. . . . Somehow I then arrived in the cell wing, was led to the room where prisoners' property was stored, taken to the partitioned-off space at the back, and had to take off all my clothes again. I now had to come out of this partition completely naked and undergo a body search once more, but this time more thorough and extensive than on the previous occasions.

Since I was already familiar with this "striptease," I was not unduly shocked or embarrassed. But I was still rather irritated by the people standing around me and gawping. And so I had to get into all the positions they wanted, bend down, and move my limbs on command. That was not the end of it; I even had to push my penis to one side. My things were packed in a cardboard box and I was given the usual institution clothing.

Gerhard J. was then led to his solitary cell and acquainted with prison rules by an officer:

He said: "The day has fifteen hours, very long hours, as you will see! When the siren sounds, your day is finished. Then it is time to sleep. Not until this moment are you allowed to get your bed ready and lie down. You are strictly forbidden to lie down during the day."... I was pleased to hear that I did not have to clasp my hands behind my back, a practice demanded in Hungary. But to make up for that, it was explained to me that I had to get up and stand to attention when the door opened. Then it was made clear to me that I was no longer Herr J. but number 53!... Being given a number was justified as follows: "A personal number is solely for your security and to preserve your anonymity. In this way we are ensuring that other inmates cannot later hold your stay against you and turn it to your disadvantage!"

Although the crude physical maltreatment of prisoners which characterized the Stalin era became the exception rather than the rule, the MfS refined its psychological techniques. Prisoners were confronted with a range of penalties such as the withdrawal of leisure time and of the right to receive visitors, reading materials, and cigarettes. Sleep deprivation, various types of threat and disinformation were used, and a feeling of isolation and disorientation was cultivated. Deaths and suicide were not uncommon, although unexplained deaths were rare as the MfS was sensitive to possible adverse international reaction. One of the most notorious cases concerned Matthias Domaschk, who had belonged to the church's *Junge Gemeinde* in Jena since the early 1970s. It remains unclear whether his death in the MfS pre-trial detention center in Gera in April 1981 was the result of suicide or of his harsh treatment by MfS interrogators. Elsewhere acts of defiance were punished severely, thereby reinforcing the conformity of most prisoners to prison rules and regulations. Siegmar Faust, for example, received twenty-four months in solitary confinement in the MfS detention center in Cottbus for complaining to the prison authorities on behalf of his fellow-prisoners.

An interrogation was a fundamental part of any detention. It was designed

241

to clarify the nature of the alleged offense, obtain a confession and prepare the ground, where appropriate, for a prosecution in the courts. As Fricke points out, the interrogator's objective was usually to prove guilt, whatever the cost in time. The *Erlebnisbericht*, a form of record of the hearing, reflected the conception of the interrogator, even though it was signed by the prisoner. The ways in which the better-trained interrogators of the Honecker era preyed on prisoners' vulnerability and their sense of disorientation are recalled by Gerhard J. with regard to his main interrogator, a major, in the Stasi pre-trial detention center in Potsdam:

> To me he seemed like a combatant of the old guard. An old-style Communist, then. He was not in the least hurried and to my surprise not in a bad mood but polite and obliging. . . . His manner was conciliatory and unexpectedly displayed the characteristics of a normal human being.
>
> The image created by this man did not belong in this building according to my expectations and ideas at that time and did not correspond to the frightening image of the Stasi. In my state of anxiety I had expected a certain roughness and brutality and now I was being greeted in a friendly and polite way. Not only did it surprise me but also it threw me. . . . In the following interrogations, approaches or tactics this major was, at least in my case, positively avuncular.
>
> . . . The major spoke calmly to me and came across almost like a father.

Gerhard J. discovered, however, that the kind uncle rapidly transformed himself into a strict disciplinarian when he refused to comply with the interrogator's wishes. Interrogators were skilled at playing on the fears of their charges. In the case of families who had tried to flee the GDR together, the partners and children were frequently imprisoned and separated immediately afterwards. Confessions were often extracted from parents afraid that their children would be sent to a home, and interrogators sometimes sowed so much distrust between partners that a divorce ensued. A prisoner in Berlin-Hohenschönhausen in the early 1970s recalled that forged letters were presented to him during the interrogations, from which he formed the impression that his fiancée had left him. In general, interrogators were adept at threatening prisoners—especially women with children—with repercussions for family members. A female prisoner, Christina Müller, writes of her time in custody in the MfS prison in Leipzig in the early 1980s:

> The investigating officer showed no sign of human emotions—
> on the contrary. When he had found the vulnerable spot he ex-

ploited it in order to put me under pressure. They used any means they could to destroy people's morale and to make them compliant, even with lies. They went so far as destroying the trust between married people. I myself suffered especially from being separated from my son and I worried about how he was coping with suddenly being alone.

The damage to their health suffered by so many prisoners at the hands of the Stasi is described by Rudolf Piseur, who was kept in custody for over six months in the late 1970s:

The never-ending, nerve-shattering interrogations last more than six months. My psychological and physical decline is being accelerated by the well thought-out and cunning interrogation methods that are pre-programmed again every day and deliberately use lies, slander, false statements, and blackmail in abundance. So I can expect fifteen years to life in prison. At every conceivable opportunity the Stasi threaten me with this punishment. Gradually I come to believe it. Any contact with the outside world, even with my family is strictly prohibited. I do not receive any news from outside. . . . Impotent rage, apathy take possession of me. I suffer a chronic nervous breakdown. Fortunately, I survived a heart attack, and the interrogations continue.

· · · · ·

Who Were the Officers?

The full-time MfS officers in the Honecker era were overwhelmingly male and tended to have a lower level of formal educational qualification than their peers in the Party and the other state organs. They were committed both ideologically and politically to "real existing socialism," did not eschew the material benefits of their position, and were recruited primarily from families with roots in the SED, the MfS and the other security forces. While significant variations existed in individual social profiles, the general pattern was that of a relatively self-contained, self-recruiting, and exclusive elite.

The average age of MfS full-time staff increased gradually over the decades from 28.0 years in 1950 to 35.7 years in 1983, although, as a result of the expansion of the ministry, there was a steady replenishment by younger cadres. The generation which entered the MfS in the 1950s gradually took over the key posts in the ministry. By 1982, two-thirds of staff came from this group, as opposed to 22 per cent in 1969. After the death in 1982 of his First Deputy Minister, Bruno Beater, Mielke was the sole survivor of the older generation of KPD cadres at the summit of the MfS.

Although the proportion of female staff in the MfS was a relatively high 25 per cent in 1954, this declined gradually to 15.8 per cent in 1971. Changing little throughout the Honecker era, women's participation in the MfS was 15.7 per cent in 1989 or, in numerical terms, 14,259. Women were relatively well represented in services and administration, for example, the Medical Service, the Finance Department, and the Main Department Cadres and Training, as well as in operational units such as the Central Coordinating Group and ZAIG. They were, however, less prominent in those units which were directly engaged in work with IMs, where their share was only between one-sixth and one-fifth. There was a perceptible gender differentiation, with women concentrated in secretarial and typing posts. In general terms, the nearer the top of the ministerial hierarchy, the less visible were women. They achieved a peak in 1978 of 4.5 per cent of all MfS leadership cadres, only for this to fall to 3.8 per cent ten years later. No woman ever became head of a Main Department and in 1988 only 1.8 per cent were in charge of a department. In an interview given in 1993, a former MfS officer and mother of three recalled that: "The functions which were associated with a lot of work but little honor were always filled by women. Because they had children, women were not put in functions which were really important."

The low participation of women in leadership positions as well as the distribution of jobs by gender can be explained in part by the numerous burdens typically borne by GDR women in the home and at work. A former secretary and an assistant in an intelligence evaluation group stated, in an interview in July 1990, that women with children were regarded as an element of "instability" in the MfS and that they felt guilty when they had to take time off work to look after sick children. As many were married to MfS staff, this added to rather than provided relief from their countless burdens. Moreover, in the militaristic Stasi, a veritable bastion of male chauvinism, women were deemed to be too "gossipy" for the conspiratorial work of a Chekist.

Data compiled by the Stasi on the occupational, educational, and family profile of the full-time personnel have to be treated with caution as they were often manipulated to demonstrate the preponderance of "workers" in an organization which prided itself on being the sword and shield of the SED, the self-appointed representative of what was defined in ideological terms as the most progressive force, that is, the working class. According to Stasi materials, the working-class origins of personnel fell from 92.3 per cent in 1962 to 78.9 per cent in 1988, while that of white-collar employees and the intelligentsia rose from 3.9 per cent to 10.6 per cent and from 0.6 per cent to 6.6 per cent respectively. However, an analysis of 400 doctoral candidates of the Law School probably provides a more realistic picture of distribution by social group. The proportion from working-class families declined markedly from 91.2 per cent in the early 1950s to 51.8 per cent in the later 1970s and, even more telling, immediately prior to joining the MfS, only 13.1 per cent were classified as workers. The majority were recruited from the SED and the state apparatus, from the armed forces and the mass organizations and from among pupils and students.

The declassified files of the Main Department Cadres and Training underscore the significance of the armed forces and the Guard Regiment as sources of recruitment. 20.7 per cent of MfS full-time personnel in 1988 came from the National People's Army, 2.7 per cent from the People's Police and as many as 39.6 per cent from the ministry's own regiment. In the 1970s, as the children of Stasi personnel reached maturity, the ministry drew increasingly on these offspring to restock the ranks. Two former HV A officers confirm this process of self-reproduction:

> So in the HV A as well the practice became common of reducing the work to bring on the next generation to a kind of "internal reproduction." The department was particularly keen to recruit colleagues who were the children or at least the relatives of other members of the Ministry of State Security. Irrespective of the particular individual, that ensured "quality" and it guaranteed that these candidates did not have any contact with the West.

Predestination by family can be traced in the comments of Andreas K., a lieutenant in the Main Department Protection of Individuals, who joined the MfS in 1978:

> ... and I got to know the MfS through my father. He was the leader of a District Service Unit and I have to say he had a work collective in which each person was there for everyone else. That impressed me and also motivated me even as a boy. The families were integrated, we children played together, you felt a sense of security even as a young man.

Not only did the ministry recruit heavily from the security and armed forces, but the concentration of Stasi families in apartments in the Lichtenberg and Hohenschönhausen districts of East Berlin narrowed social and cultural horizons. Sample survey data from 1989 on the political affiliation of MfS staff and their parents underline this point and indicate why the ministry constituted a bedrock of loyalty to "real existing socialism": 79.1 per cent of the fathers and 56.2 per cent of the mothers of MfS employees were members of the SED and only 9.3 per cent came from homes in which neither parent belonged to a political party. The ministry was one of the favored destinations for the children of Politbüro and Central Committee members. In 1986, eight of the twenty-one full members and the five candidate members of the Politbüro had at least one child in the MfS. This indicates that the political elites were able to use their influence to place their progeny in key positions at a time when social mobility was slowing down. With regard to MfS full-time staff, the survey also revealed that in 1988 over four-fifths were members of the SED and only 6.1 per cent were not affiliated to any party. While this might have buttressed loyalty to the SED system, it undermined critical reflection and ideas on reform.

A marked improvement in qualifications occurred over the decades. Those with a higher education qualification rose rapidly in the 1960s before a slowdown in the growth rate from the mid to late 1970s onwards. Whereas only 1.6 per cent had such a qualification in 1950, by 1975 the figure had risen to 9.1 per cent and to 11.9 per cent in 1988. The general improvement in the formal educational qualifications of the officer corps, facilitated by a plethora of further educational and training programs, reflected the Stasi's drive for a more professional and competent administrative staff, a development which was also observable elsewhere in GDR society. The contrast between the level and intensity of training at the beginning of the 1950s and the Honecker era is instructive. In the earlier period, short basic courses in German and Marxism-Leninism were introduced in an improvised manner to raise the low standards. By the time that Honecker came to power, not only were staff receiving a grounding in the arts of political policing as well as a thorough training in Marxism-Leninism, organized by the SED Party organ in the ministry, but they were also able to take advantage of an array of opportunities provided by residential, distance-learning, and correspondence courses. In the first quinquennium of the 1970s, the latter was the mode of study of over three-quarters of all trainees.

Several Main Departments had their own training institutions. HV A provided instruction in foreign intelligence work at its school in Belzig until 1986, and subsequently at Gosen. At the apex of the system stood the Law School (*Juristische Hochschule*) in Potsdam-Eiche. In 1955, it changed in status from a college to a university (*Hochschule*); the term "Law" or "Juridical" was added ten years later. By the mid-1960s, it was running numerous initial and further training courses for leading cadres and in 1968 it was granted the right to award its own academic degrees. While the professional and educational level of MfS staff undoubtedly improved, it remained lower than in other major organs and the programs were intended to boost efficiency, not to create a critical reform potential. The dissertations written by Stasi officers as part of their university training illustrate this: they were task oriented and primarily concerned with the smoother functioning of security operations.

· · · · ·

246

The Life-Style and the Mindset of the Stasi Service Class

Alexandra Richie has sought to capture the life-style of the Stasi officer class:

> If they were successful, they could rise high in the system, and by GDR standards the rewards were high. Employees earned OM2,000 per month (a very high wage); they had access to special shops; they could travel abroad; they could bring friends and relatives in from the west through a hidden door in Friedrichstrasse; they had access to western literature, magazines, newspapers and pornography; and they lived in the most luxurious apartments or villas. The Stasi could enjoy a vast entertainment and leisure network, which included twenty-three separate vacation spas, exclusive hospitals and sports complexes with swimming pools, modern gyms, tennis courts and saunas. Officials were given a Lada and a driver, while generals got sleek new Citroens for official and private use. . . . Some had yachts and motorcycles and shopped at the *Leiterläden* (special shops) for western jewelery, champagne and *haute couture*.

Although personnel undoubtedly enjoyed many perks, the officers' lifestyle was less uniform and often less privileged than that depicted by Richie. There were elites within elites, as can be seen from salary and bonus differentials. Salary depended on length of service, function, and rank. The ministry's top earner was Mielke, with 76,062 GDR Marks per annum. Members of the Guard Regiment and the East Berlin Regional Administration received a "capital city" supplement. In 1983, the average monthly salary in GDR Marks of the officers in East Berlin was 1,541 and in the Regional Administrations 1,371. By 1988, this had risen to 1,818 and 1,700 respectively. In the latter year, the average for all GDR employees was 1,280. Given these differences, it is not surprising that many staff desired to move from the District Service Units where pay and status were inferior. Differentials in supplementary payments according to rank were not inconsiderable; in 1987, a soldier received 220 GDR Marks, a sergeant 450, a captain 550, a colonel 600, a major general 1,000 and a senior general 1,400. Additional benefits included very low levels of taxation on income and generous pensions as well as the possibility of a new apartment and access to a range of consumer goods beyond the reach of most ordinary East Germans.

Financial and other material considerations, while by no means insignificant in earlier decades, seem to have played an increasingly important role for service in the MfS during the 1980s. After the collapse of communism, one officer lamented that his original idealism was not shared by some colleagues, who were motivated only by their monthly salary. However, material inducements were not the only motives but were usually linked, in varying degrees, to political conviction, the attractions of membership of a powerful and elitist organization, and the excitement of espionage. The MfS, especially its Law School, devoted considerable effort to identifying these motives as well as to ways of strengthening the officers' belief in the ultimate victory of socialism and of fostering their hatred of the enemies of socialism. Once in the employ of the ministry, officers were required, according to the cadre guidelines of 1964, to adhere to the rules of conspiracy, lead an exemplary private life, raise their children in the spirit of peace and socialism, and conduct themselves in a disciplined manner. Discipline was strictly enforced throughout the ministry and, as all staff from waitress to minister held a military rank, it was based on strict military principles. Officers were required to swear a solemn oath "to be an honorable, brave, disciplined, and alert soldier, to obey military superiors without question, to carry out orders with determination, and never to reveal military and state secrets."

The memoirs of, and interviews with, former MfS officers provide an insight into motivation, albeit with the qualification that they are not free of the methodological problems inherent in any such personal reconstruction of the past. Motives and values covered a broad spectrum: the desire to preserve peace, to serve the honorable and worthy cause of socialism, to continue the anti-fascist struggle of the KPD and to pursue a chosen career in a dedicated manner. Markus Wolf speaks for most of his former comrades in his stubborn defense of HV A as a "normal" foreign intelligence service dedicated to peace and the protection of socialism from surprise attack and an atomic war launched by the West. He asserts that his own communist past and his intensive political and ideological training in Moscow, together with his Jewish origins and the prominence of ex-Nazis in the Federal Republic, bound him to the GDR and shaped his perception of his work in the MfS as a link in the country's anti-fascist chain both before and after 1945.

One of Wolf's colleagues in the top echelons of the domestic arm of the Stasi's service class, Rudi Mittig, arrived in the MfS via a different route. He had served in the Wehrmacht during the Second World War and was, at that time, a believer in fascist ideology. Subsequently, he came to admire anti-fascist fighters such as Mielke and was determined to protect the GDR's socialist order against its Cold War enemies. When he joined the MfS in 1952, he was perhaps performing an act of contrition for his fascist past. A later generation's values are reflected by a lower-ranking officer, a lieutenant who enlisted in 1975. His motivation, he claims, was not driven primarily by material considerations, but by American imperialism's aggression in Cuba and Vietnam and by his wish to prevent war and to protect the GDR.

One fundamental criticism of these views is that they are too uncritical of the Stalinist past and the less than honorable East German present. Although Markus Wolf has admitted to having qualms about the excesses of Stalin, the methods pursued by the Stasi and the shortcomings of the GDR, he has sought to rationalize his position by reference to the grand ideals of communism. Wolf justifies the East German communists' resort to repressive practices as a defensive reaction to the imperialists' efforts to destroy the GDR's socialist experiment. And as for Stalin's crimes, he pleads that "We German Communists had perhaps the most complete blind spots of all the foreigners in Moscow . . . since we had been rescued from death or imprisonment by the Soviet Union. Any other doubts about what was going on were overshadowed by events under Hitler's regime, and I was incapable of seeing our socialist system as a tyranny." Determined to ensure that "Nazism would never infect the Germans again," he appealed to the greater cause by quoting the lines from Bertolt Brecht's play *The Measure Taken:*

> *What baseness would you not commit,*
> *To stamp out baseness?*
> *If you could change the world,*
> *What would you be too good for?*

. . . . .

Mielke's Unofficial Collaborators: An Army of Informers

Although the MfS kept monthly statistics on its army of informers, many of the materials have not survived and a full record is only available from 1985 onwards. However, the data for the Frankfurt/Oder region are probably a reliable indicator of the general trend: whereas in 1952 only 533 informers were in the service of the MfS in the region, thirteen years later the number had increased to 2,986, reaching a peak of 4,977 in 1985. The main expert on the topic, Helmut Müller-Enbergs, estimates that about 250,000 full-time staff and about 600,000 *Inoffizielle Mitarbeiter,* that is, unofficial collaborators or coworkers (IMs), worked for the ministry between 1950 and 1989. Müller-Enbergs's figures do not, however, include the informers used by the Criminal Police.

Despite the many statistical uncertainties, the explosion in the numbers of IMs is beyond dispute. A peak of about 180,000 was probably reached in the mid-1970s before falling slightly to about 176,000 ten years later. The figures include a large shadowy group—32,282 in 1988—of IMKs (*Inoffizielle Mitarbeiter zur Sicherung der Konspiration und des Verbindungswesens*), who, usually in return for money or gifts, put their telephone, address, or apartment at the disposal of the Stasi for clandestine meetings between controllers and IMs. Most IMs spied for the units in Main Departments II, VI, XVIII, XIX and XX, with high concentrations too in the Main Department/Administration in the National

People's Army and Main Department VII. Turnover was rapid in the 1980s. There may well have been a complete turnover of IMs over the short period of three to six years in the District Service Units but probably between seven and ten years among those controlled by the Regional Administrations and by the central organs in East Berlin.

The rapid expansion of the IM network, like that of the full-time staff, is explained by the Honecker regime's determination to combat the negative effects of détente and closer relations with the West and, from the later 1970s onwards, to control the alternative political culture and the growing desire for emigration among the East German population. A deteriorating economic performance, too, gave cause for concern and prompted action against alleged spies and saboteurs. As the Stasi's "eyes and ears," the agents were regarded as the "main weapon" in the struggle against the enemy, without whom the full-time officials could not achieve their goals. According to the ministry's 1979 guidelines on IMs, they "play a key role in ensuring overall internal security in the area of operations. Their work is to a great extent preventive in nature and contributes to the early detection and implementation of new security requirements. Their work must serve the comprehensive and secure evaluation and control of the politically operative situation in their area of responsibility and provide further clarification of the question of 'Who is who?'" As the bread and butter of counterintelligence, not only were IMs deployed to combat and prevent subversion by an external enemy but also to protect socialist society against the disruption and harm caused by the "hostile" and "negative" actions and attitudes of East German citizens. Mielke referred to this latter task in his usual uncompromising fashion at a service conference in 1973:

> By means of political-operative work, in particular the work of
> IMs, greater efforts have to be made in the ministries, institu-
> tions, economic organizations and especially in the foreign trade
> enterprises to keep them free of bribery, corruption, petty bour-
> geois behavior but above all from the impact of hostile corrupt-
> ing influences.

As the enemies of the socialist state were supposedly omnipresent, then the MfS, too, had to be omnipresent—as well as omniscient. This aim led, in the opinion of the former head of the Erfurt Regional Administration, Josef Schwarz, to the principle that the unexpected had to be eliminated at all times and everywhere. The resulting scale and depth of the penetration of people's private lives as well as of the institutions of state and society, not the organization's methods, is, according to Klaus-Dietmar Henke, the historically unique feature of the MfS. The techniques of surveillance such as phone-tapping, the opening of mail and house searches, and the deployment of agents and spies to gather information and to subvert groups who were seen as a threat to the existing political and social order have been practiced by dictatorships, monarchies, and parliamentary democracies alike.

· · · · ·

Monitor and Firefighter: A Ubiquitous Enemy

Chapters eight to eleven are designed to assess the Stasi's role on the home front as an organ of surveillance, repression, and ideological policing as well as its function as an economic firefighter and moral guardian. Whereas chapters eight and nine concentrate on the Stasi's surveillance and protection of spheres which come broadly under the umbrella of the public sector such as culture, sport and the economy, chapters ten and eleven focus on those areas and groups which lay outside the immediate domain of the Party and state administration, notably the evangelical churches, the Jehovah's Witnesses, the peace movement, and fringe youth sub-cultures. The linkage between the four chapters is the Stasi's tunneling into all sectors of society and its ruthless determination to expose and, where necessary, thwart all enemies, whether potential or actual, of the socialist order. The Stasi dictionary of political-operational terms compiled for officers described this vital task as follows:

> As a whole, fulfilling the main task of the MfS must produce results to put strategic and tactical information at the disposal of the Party, to expose the enemy in his bases in the Operation Area, to disrupt and combat him, to prevent hostile activities directed against the GDR, to unmask internal enemies and to ensure the security of the GDR in all situations and to prevent damage and actions hostile to the GDR by means of preventive measures, greater vigilance, discipline and order.

The same source also provided staff with the authoritative definition of the enemy as:

> Persons who in groups or as individuals intentionally develop political-ideological attitudes and views that are alien to socialism and who strive to implement these attitudes and views in practice by deliberately creating occurrences and conditions that endanger or damage the socialist state and society generally or specifically.

The lexicon's militant language was a legacy of the fierce struggle between the German Communists and National Socialists and of the imprint of Stalinist totalitarianism on the mentality of members of the East German service class.

It was also a product of the titanic clash between communism and capitalism during the Cold War, at least until the onset of détente moderated the language of political conflict of the SED, if not of the Stasi. On the border between the two antagonistic systems, the GDR was ultra-sensitive to shifts in East-West relations and, uncomfortably aware of the many attractions of the West German model for East Germans, its leaders were constantly looking for signs of infiltration by the West. Even in the later 1980s, the MfS was still adhering to a simplistic and outmoded explanation of the causes of opposition and widespread popular dissatisfaction, attributing it to deliberate targeting by the imperialists. While the Stasi lexicon and official guidelines were written in bureaucratic and soulless jargon, the language could be crude and emotional when the mask slipped. An off-the-record statement by Mielke at a service meeting in February 1988 illustrates this point. Putting his manuscript to one side, he denounced would-be emigrants as "bandits"; eighteen months later, he was even coarser, referring to them as "filthy swine."

The image of the "enemy" encompassed a wide range of non-conformist behavior which was regarded by the ministry as having "hostile-negative" potential but which in a less authoritarian society would be far less likely to attract the attention of the secret police state. The MfS understood by "negative" persons all those who were "deviants from the Party line, held different views and were unreliable and uncommitted." Although a distinction was drawn between loosely structured "negative groups" and the more tightly organized "hostile groups," in practice it was difficult to keep them separate and the Stasi often used the hyphenated term "hostile-negative." "Negative" groups were described in the dictionary as: "loose associations of mostly young people with relatively similar interpretations of life and morals that deviate from the socialist way of life and also with views lacking clarity and conviction that are in part politically-ideologically negative." These groups were unstable and the youngsters belonging to them typically gathered together on street corners and in pubs, parks, and clubs. In the eyes of the Stasi, their "spontaneous" behavior represented a danger for public order and safety which could rapidly develop into acts of terror and "attacks on the state border." A "hostile" group, which was regarded by the Stasi as posing the greater threat, was defined as a "number of people who aim to carry out acts hostile to the Constitution or together plan, prepare, attempt or perpetrate one or more crimes against the state. Hostile groups are in direct communication with each other and, over time, develop a group structure."

Notions of the "enemy," as internalized by MfS officers, reinforced stereotyping and served as an instrument of repression. A physicist at the University of Leipzig, Günter Fritzsch, was told by MfS prison staff: "You are wrong, in here there is no democracy, dictatorship rules in our state, the dictatorship of the proletariat. This is irreconcilable class war. You are our class enemy." This kind of antagonism was upheld as one of the main characteristics of a Chekist.

Hatred was described in the MfS dictionary as "an essential determining component of Chekist feelings, one of the decisive bases for the passionate and irreconcilable struggle against the enemy," a struggle which was not just simply a matter of loathing but was bound up with the need to "destroy" or to "harm" him.

The Stasi image of the enemy was grounded in the theory that psychological characteristics are determined by external conditions and influences rather than by internal or cognitive factors. While in accordance with the regime's Marxist-Leninist ideology in that socialist society allegedly provided the preconditions for the development of all-round and productive personalities, the MfS, like other state and Party bodies, had to account for behavior and attitudes which deviated from the norm and made people susceptible to the influence of the enemy. Among the factors identified by the Stasi as conducive to such actions and attitudes were petty bourgeois egoism and careerism, antisocial or criminal behavior and grumbling. Those conditions in the GDR which enabled the imperialists to conduct political-ideological subversion against socialist society were regarded primarily as the "relics" of the exploitative capitalism of an earlier age. Although the MfS stubbornly persisted in this interpretation, it was, however, difficult to explain away the country's problems simply by reference to the capitalist legacy and to external steering by the imperialist enemy. A recognition of this dilemma can be seen in several dissertations written by officers during their studies at the Stasi Law School which tentatively acknowledged that GDR society produced a number of internal "contradictions" which caused distortions in the development of personality. Among these contradictions were poor quality accommodation, restrictions on travel, and inadequate services. Such contradictions were not deemed to be "antagonistic" in Marxist-Leninist terms but as capable of being rectified within the parameters of the existing social and political order.

· · · · ·

Tackling the Enemy—Quiet Repression and Preventive Decomposition

In the age of détente, the Stasi's main method of combating subversive activity was "operational decomposition" (*operative Zersetzung*), which was the central element in what Hubertus Knabe has called a system of "quiet repression" (*lautlose Unterdrückung*). This was not a new departure as "dirty tricks" had been widely used in the 1950s and 1960s. The distinctive feature was the primacy of operational decomposition over other methods of repression in a system to which historians have attached labels such as post-totalitarianism and modern dictatorship. This form of rule emerged out of the Stalinist era and, although the methods of control were less brutal and repressive than in the late 1940s and the 1950s, the GDR of the Honecker years was nevertheless a dictatorship of the Party elites in which coercion and injustice were endemic. The concentration on so-called "softer forms" of control in the 1970s and 1980s can be attributed to a series of interrelated factors: the stabilization of the GDR since the mid-1960s; the greater sensitivity of SED leaders to the population's needs, not least the desire for a higher standard of living; the counterproductive nature of terroristic methods; the frail legitimacy of the less prosperous "other Germany" in the East; and the GDR's search for international recognition. Although the GDR succeeded in ending its diplomatic isolation in the first half of the 1970s, closer relations with the West were a mixed blessing as it produced a massive increase in Western visitors. Furthermore, the signing of the Helsinki Accords of 1975 committed the GDR leaders to tolerating even greater movement across borders as well as guarantees for human rights. In this context, arbitrary acts and open repression appeared to threaten the gains derived from détente. Even Mielke had to adapt to the need for a more flexible system of control. He put this in his usual blunt fashion in a speech delivered in 1985: "You know that, for political as well as operational reasons, we cannot immediately arrest all enemies, although the purely legal prerequisites exist. We know these enemies, have them under control and know what they are planning." Operational decomposition was particularly appropriate for tackling those opposition groups who were associated with the churches or who had links with the West and therefore had a limited protection from more blatant forms of state repression.

The MfS dictionary summarized the goal of operational decomposition as "splitting up, paralyzing, disorganizing and isolating hostile-negative forces in order, through preventive action, to foil, considerably reduce or stop completely hostile-negative actions and their consequences or, in a varying degree, to win them back both politically and ideologically." The kind of measures which the ministry employed can be found in documents such as the 1976 guidelines on operational cases, and included: the systematic compromising and isolation of a target by means of rumor, disinformation, and deception concerning alleged immorality, excessive drinking, an "unclean past," and spying for the West; undermining their professional and personal reputation; creating fear and uncertainty through frequent telephone calls at night, inserting fictitious adverts in newspapers, sending anonymous letters, and burglary. Some victims have claimed that the MfS deliberately poisoned food and drove its "targets" to contemplate suicide. Other nefarious methods involved telephone tapping and the interception of mail, dangling the bait of travel to the West and promotion at work, provoking disagreements among opposition groups, and the criminalization of offenses such as alleged tax evasion and the disturbance of public order. Targets were also subjected to restrictions on their movement, the withdrawal of a driving license and illegal house searches.

HUNGARY

❊❊❊

Political Prisoner

Paul Ignotus

PAUL IGNOTUS *(1901–78) was a Hungarian writer-journalist who took refuge in England in 1939 "from the Nazi terror which was beginning to grip Hungary," as he put it. He described himself as "an old fashioned Social Democrat, a liberal and Bourgeois Radical." Prior to his departure he edited a left-of-center journal that made him unpopular in right-wing circles and with the government.*

After World War II he returned (in 1946) to his native country, which between 1945 and 1948 was governed by a coalition composed of the Communist Party and several noncommunist parties. In Budapest, Ignotus worked for the Social Democratic Party's daily newspaper Nepszava. *In 1947 he was appointed press attaché at the Hungarian embassy in London, a position he held for a year and a half. In 1948 the Communist Party took over the government with Soviet assistance, which included the arrest of the head of the largest noncommunist party.*

In September 1949 Ignotus was arrested by the Hungarian political police (ÁVH). He was accused of working for the British Secret Service on account of his employment by the BBC (considered by the ÁVH to be a cover organization for the British Intellience Service); he was also charged with being a contact between the British Labour and Hungarian Social Democratic Party. The ÁVH wanted him to discredit in his confessions the head of the Hungarian Social Democratic Party.

Ignotus was made to confess that he had spent his life "in a sinister campaign against the working class" and that he had conspired with British and Hungarian intelligence agents as early as 1939 to prevent the spread of communism to Hungary after the defeat of Nazi Germany. He was tried in camera in October 1950 and sentenced to fifteen years of hard labor. He spent seven years in prison. The excerpt reprinted

From Paul Ignotus, Political Prisoner *(New York: Collier Books, 1959). Reprinted by permission.*

below explains why he confessed and sheds light on the methods and policies of the Hungarian political police, which were modelled on those used by the Soviet one. Hungary at the time was tightly controlled by the Communist Party; its head, Matthias Rakosi, was officially described as "the best Hungarian pupil of Stalin."

Ignotus was released from prison during the Hungarian "thaw" in 1955 and escaped from Hungary after the 1956 revolution to settle in England for good.

．．．．．

Why Did We All Confess?

Why did we all "confess," almost without exception, at the Stalinist political police and afterwards in their courts? For myself, I wanted to live in spite of despair and exhaustion from beatings, compulsory sleeplessness and other tortures, and despite my anxiety about the fate of my relatives. Moreover, it seemed that the more absurd the confession I had to make, the more obviously false it would appear to everyone. And apart from this, my trial was held *in camera*. I felt it would be pointless to perform heroically when nobody was about except those who would beat me to death afterwards. Whether I would have "confessed" in an open trial I simply cannot tell, I do not know myself enough to judge.

Some months after my trial I was taken back to the Budapest ÁVH headquarters from my prison cell in the country town of Vác. ÁVH Lieutenant Colonel Márton Károlyi[1] received me very cordially. "How are you getting on in Vác?" I told him frankly that life was hell there; I had not expected that it would be such a "sanatorium" as had been promised by my interrogator before trial "but I should not have expected it to be so abominable as it is, sir. If an American reporter could ever take pictures of us there, they would make more powerful imperialist propaganda than anything your enemies could invent." The lieutenant colonel did not seem to be hurt. He was one of the few ÁVH officers who enjoyed my stories. "What I like about you," he said, "is that we need not trouble to ask anyone to report on your opinions. You save us the bother. I know you dislike us. But you would like to live in tolerable conditions, wouldn't you?"

"That's right, sir," I answered and did not contradict his allegations about my political hostility. Was this sincerity on my part? It may have been. But I had come to the conclusion that ÁVH officers were most irritated by the prisoners who were, or pretended to be, their comrades. For spying on other prisoners or the like, they would accept their services and reward them. But if someone hesitated about going to any lengths, he only angered them by insisting on his faithfulness to the Idea. Faithful Communists in Communist prisons—that was a thing which should be ignored, even if it happened. I felt I should play the opposite role, of the honest opponent. I stood before the lieutenant colonel simply as a man seeking his own interests. It should be a clear give and take.

"Now listen," the lieutenant colonel went on. "We want to make a series of open trials, to inculpate Social Democracy. Some of you who I think are sensible enough to know what it is about—Zoltán Horváth, Sándor Szalai, George Pálóczi-Horváth, and yourself—you would be the defendants in the first Social Democratic trial, and from your confessions the rest would follow. The verdicts of your secret trials would of course have to be quashed on some formal grounds, you needn't bother about that.... If you help us to do this, we shall consider it a great service. However disappointed you are with the conditions you found in Vác, I hope you see that I wish you well. I promise you will have better treatment, and plenty of food and cigarettes, and congenial work—translations for instance, if you like—and that you get wages to support your mother, and even permission to write to her, though you know political prisoners are not really allowed to do so. Would you like to write her a letter at once? ... Well go back to your cell and think it over, and give your answer tomorrow."

In my cell, I got decent food and cigarettes and books—none of which I had known in Vác—and the following day at an interview with Lieutenant Colonel Károlyi I said I consented. I felt that to refuse his offer would be suicide or worse. But I made up my mind to break my promise to him and to reveal everything I knew of the ÁVH tortures and the fake trials when I got a chance to talk in public.

Every day either Lieutenant Colonel Károlyi or his assistant, Lieutenant Szántó, spoke to me about the deposition which I was to make for the open trial. I pretended incessantly. I talked over with them carefully whether this or that statement about Anna Kéthly or Szakasits might be believed or not. I soon found that although they had decided now to concentrate on "credibility," they were as keen as before to include obvious absurdities. "So much the better," I thought and made cheerful use of the good books and decent food.

By then any pretense on their part that our statements must be true had gone. They would never have said that we should tell lies. But the ways of compiling the truth became quite farcical. I remember Lieutenant Szántó acting as messenger between Pálóczi-Horváth and myself, only concerned with fitting together the tales we were both concocting but never inquiring about their foundation in fact. "Pálóczi tells me we can't say he gave his spy reports to Macdonald at the BBC, since everyone knows they were hardly on speaking terms." "Well let us say that he handed them to Macdonald through Tarján," I suggested. That settled it. By the way, Pálóczi-Horváth had never been a Social Democrat but a Communist who had worked for a while on the staff of the BBC The reason for including him in a so-called Social Democrat trial was that before the war, in the service of a British agency in Budapest, he had been in touch with Arpád Szakasits, as he had with a great number of people of most different political denominations, united in resistance against the Nazis.

Simultaneously, I was working out my own plan. If the president of the court asked about my proceedings in Britain, I would start to quote one or another of my spy contacts in English, and say: "Everything we say here is a foolish lie. This is a framed trial as were all those staged by this régime. We were beaten to shreds and threatened that our relatives would be arrested and tortured if we were not to consent...." And so on and so forth. I hoped that by the time someone had checked and silenced me it would already be too late: the scandal could no longer be hushed up. I knew hell would be heaven compared with what would happen to me, and perhaps also to my mother and sister and brother in Budapest. But there must be one man, I felt, to tell the truth to the world.

Would I have done this had the trial been held? I cannot vouch for it. But I knew that when Lieutenant Szántó came to tell me that "we have decided for the time being no open trial will be held," a great stone rolled off my chest. My impression was that our depositions had been shown to Rákosi who had not found them "credible" enough to be aired. But whatever the reason, I was very glad to be released from this role of hero and martyr which I had meted out to myself.

What was the reason for the confession of others? No answer can be given which applies to us all. The accusations made by the ÁVH were fairly uniform—spying in the service of imperialists, conspiracy to oppress the working class, and so forth—and very few if any had committed what they were sentenced for. But their cases were very different both politically and psychologically.

The position of those who had committed approximately what they were accused of was easiest. In the Vác prison hospital I spent some weeks in the company of a former member of parliament, the Very Reverend Father Bozsik. After the imprisonment of Cardinal Mindszenty, he had really acted as the President of a Shadow Cabinet "in case the régime changes," and had negotiated with American diplomatic representatives. In a democratic country, of course, there is nothing wrong in heading a shadow cabinet and talking to the diplomats of any foreign power with which one's own country is not at war. But to confess as much as that was enough for the ÁVH to draw up the rest. Bozsik told me he had known about a "military line leading to Americans" but he himself had not been concerned with it. The ÁVH simply accepted his admission, linking it with the "military line" and with the murder of two or three Soviet soldiers which had happened years before and had nothing to do with Bozsik's activities. Bozsik was harshly treated, like everybody else, under police arrest and afterwards in prison; in addition, he could expect kicks from young armed ruffians whenever his occupation was asked and he answered "priest." But he did not suffer any special torture. Having agreed to confess to the truth and not to contradict the "completion" of his admissions, he was sentenced to ten years' imprisonment—substantially less than myself.

This does not mean that all right-wing people got away so easily. The most notable case is that of Cardinal Mindszenty of which I learned some details in prison and afterwards—from my first interrogator, and some Communist officials who were later imprisoned, and from other sources.

How much of the charges against the Cardinal was true? He was doubtless a frantic opponent of communism and of the republican régime established after the war, and of many a social reform it had introduced. To be against the régime was by no means illegal. Did he then conspire with the representatives of foreign powers? This depends on how one defines conspiracy. He certainly advised the Americans not to return the Crown of St. Stephen to Budapest but to deposit it at the Vatican. He was also accused of illicit dealings in foreign currency through his co-defendant, Prince Esterházy. Whether this was true is of no interest; currency regulations, as I pointed out above, were not meant to be kept in Hungary, and everybody broke them with the blessing of the government except when a scapegoat was required.

Surely it was not single acts like these which turned the fury of the government machinery against him. It was his general attitude from 1945 onwards. It is an open secret that many of his senior priests objected to his rigidity; so did some leading Jesuits. These same Jesuits were imprisoned a year or two later. The Rákosi régime persecuted religion. According to some, the Cardinal's attitude was thus vindicated. Others take an opposite view and think that it was much cleverer to be flexible and so demonstrate the impossibility of coming to terms with the Rákosi government, than to allow them to persecute religion on the pretext of "fighting Reaction."

It is also true that the Cardinal buried in his grounds a tube which contained his secret notes. It was a great triumph for the ÁVH to discover it. But the secrecy of those notes was their single interesting characteristic. When they were made public one merely wondered why they had ever to be secret.

The Cardinal had an unflinching faith in his own status, dignity, and vocation. On the question of education, but also in other matters, he was unwilling to yield to government pressure; though he was often approached by Catholics of high standing who wanted him to be more conciliatory. At the end of 1948 he made small gestures in the direction of compromise—presumably when he realized that the help he had hoped from the West was not forthcoming. But the campaign against him was already at its height, and Rákosi made up his mind to have him arrested. The Cardinal made a statement that if ever he were arrested and made any "confession" in prison, people should know it had been made under duress. He felt what was approaching. Nevertheless the fact that a Cardinal could be jailed must have come as a terrible shock to him.

To be isolated from every soul with whom one might exchange a human word, and to feel oneself at the mercy of cruel enemies, is bound to disturb anyone's mind; but chiefly the mind of a man who had filled the position and had the outlook of Cardinal Mindszenty. There is no saint who cannot be in some way broken by humiliation—especially in solitude. The Cardinal, as far as I know, was not beaten up. But his treatment was hardly less cruel than the shower of truncheons. He was deprived of sleep, and ordered to do physical jerks like other prisoners; in addition, the thugs made him a special butt for their coarse amusements. The fact that a Cardinal had the same biological needs as everybody was a special pleasure for them. They made fun of him in the most revolting way. The leader of the torture squad, Princz, pressed his buttocks to the Cardinal's mouth.

At that time—(1949) a Yellow Book was published in several languages by the Hungarian Government on the Mindszenty case. It contained the well-known charges leveled against him at his trial. It showed the secret manuscript documents found in the primate's park. It also showed photographs of documents signed by the Cardinal in ÁVH custody. Since then, as we know, the handwriting expert employed by the ÁVH has escaped from Hungary and made clear that some of these documents were forged. I was in London at the time of the trial and did not know that; but two of the documents gave away their origin beyond doubt. One was a letter addressed to the Minister of Justice, István Ries, the typical manifestation of a disturbed and tormented mind, alternately blaming and defending himself in almost incoherent sentences. This was obviously genuine—if I am wrong about it I should have to alter all my opinions of the ÁVH and congratulate them for having once, exceptionally, produced such a masterpiece of a fake. In this, truly, nothing was "confessed," except that the Cardinal was feeling miserable and wondered whether his ideas had all been right. He had every reason to feel and express himself thus. The other was a deposition starting with the phrase "I am a nobleman," then confessing he had hated the common people and been a spy. Anybody could tell at once, whether this document was forged or not, that its text must have been dictated by the ÁVH. Talking about the case with friends in London—for instance, with a left-wing Catholic priest, the Basque Dean Onaindia—I gave my honest opinion about these papers. When interrogated by ÁVH officers I confessed this crime, but it was not important enough to prove that I had acted as an "I.S. agent" so they did not bother about it.

The Cardinal's trial, it will be remembered, was a shock to those who expected him to appear in the posture of heroic martyrdom. He did admit the truth of some of the allegations against him. His manner was embarrassed and apologetic, though not servile. The first reaction in the Vatican press was that "he admitted what was true and denied what was untrue." I think this was the case indeed. Later on, those who felt disappointed that he was not more pugnacious in the dock spread the belief that he must have been doped with a mysterious drug. I think this is nonsense. I spoke to a great number of prisoners who confessed under torture, and never heard of anything like that, except for morphia injections after tortures.

But I learned much later that the reports and broadcast commentaries of the trial were edited to the extent of falsification. The Cardinal may not know this, even today, but his hosts at the American legation in Budapest might tell him. By the time he was tried, the Iron Curtain had become almost impregnable. Only very few non-Communist Western correspondents were admitted to political trials in Hungary, and these were surrounded by interpreters who had been carefully trained in the Party office. They had been told what to translate and what to forget about in unpredictable events. The version of the Cardinal's confession which reached Western readers was thus to some extent distorted; the tape made of his confessions, and transmitted by the Budapest radio, had been carefully cut. His voice, however, was genuine. In his trial the most substantial cuts and deletions had to be made from the confessions of his co-defendant, the former editor of a Catholic daily paper, László Tóth. When imprisoned he was almost deaf, and his evidence in the dock was a most pathetic sight. But he had the courage to describe the tortures which he had undergone at No. 60, naming and describing exactly the rooms where they had taken place. Later, he died in prison.

Catholic priests and non-socialist politicians were as a rule ordered to confess that they had acted as American spies. Spying for Britain was the role meted out to the socialists. In the Socialist Party, bitter factional fights had been going on before their merger with the Communists; not only between those who were for and against the merger, but also among smaller groups. Now, however, they were all united in the I.S. ring. Most fortunate among them was the man to whom the ÁVH interrogator showed a great map or diagram, representing the British Socialist World Conspiracy which had to be "revealed." The interrogator was a comparatively good-natured man who wanted his victim to save trouble. "Look here, we shall have to prove this and you are a fool if you do not help us." There was a criss-cross of lines on the map, with such captions as political line leading to the foreign office; military line leading to the British military attaché; and so forth. There were the names of well-known socialist leaders such as Kéthly, Bán, Peyer, Szakasits. . . .

The socialist questioned in this way got a hiding now and then but was far more fortunate than most of his comrades who could not get access to such helpful maps of their crimes. Usually the ÁVH started the sessions with maltreatment, partly as a way to break the morale of their victims and partly because they really hoped that the victims might thus spill something worth knowing. In any case they had nothing to lose by it. Miss Kéthly herself has told me she was not beaten up, but all other methods of maltreatment were applied to her. Since, owing to her international reputation and her sex, the crime-inventors apparently hesitated about what her role in the World Conspiracy should be, she was kept in prison for years without sentence. In a way the most fantastic case was that of Madam Ries, the wife of the former Minister of Justice. She was arrested at the same time as her husband; she was put in solitary confinement without a word of explanation and kept there for years and when the thaw came she was suddenly released. She had never been asked to confess—but I wonder whether her position was better for that.

I remember also the case of Z, a socialist intellectual of the fellow-traveling wing, who started by confessing to as many imaginary crimes as anyone could invent. He was panic-stricken, worried about his wife and children, and knew enough of ÁVH methods to judge that nothing short of ludicrous self-denigration would satisfy them. He put down such things as "The C.I.C. agent posing as an American editor, X, gave me so many dollars for disclosing the production figures of the Y armaments factory. The I.S. agent, posing as a British editor, P gave me so many pounds. . . ." This should really have satisfied the most sanguine expectations. But his interrogators were insatiable and reproached him for "not coming down to the heart of the matter." He was, as so many of us were, taken to Major Princz, and received the treatment known as "wolf's bandage." This meant tying his wrists to his knees and hanging him on a pole, head downwards. In this position they spat at him and beat him, mainly on his testicles. After such treatment, he was ordered to drink salt water so that his swollen tongue nearly strangled him. This went on for days or, more exactly, for nights. After dusk he had to crawl—for he could no longer walk—up the stairs and was "interrogated" overnight while he lay on his back on a couch. He implored his torturers to tell him what else they would like to hear from him; but the answer again and again was torture and the same shouts: "You know very well yourself, you won't get away with it until you have confessed the real thing."

He was hardly alive when Major Princz, after one of his performances, bellowed: "Now we have had enough of the nonsense you talk; you must describe how the Yugoslavs organized you in." This was indeed something which could not have occurred to Z. As a political writer, he had been in touch with a number of Western intellectuals and diplomats but hardly ever with Yugoslavs. His response, of course, was prompt. "O yes, forgive me, I quite forgot about them. . . . I shall write about that by all means. . . . But so many things have happened since, and so many names have escaped me. Could I perhaps get the list of the diplomatic corps of the Yugoslav embassy in Budapest? There is a copy at the Ministry of Foreign Affairs. If I saw that I should be able to describe the thing." "All right, now at last you are talking sense. But beware if you try to deceive us again." After a day or two Z got the list and sat down to work at once: Counselor of Legation X___itch had offered him so many dinars for this information, and Secretary of Embassy Y___itch so many for the other. Dates were given in the deposition, with diplomatic receptions where these talks had taken place. "Well you old bastard this seems all right; you could have begun like that," the interrogator patted him on the back. After a few days there was a question: "Look here, Z, you say you met Y___itch on the___. But he had not yet come to Budapest, had he?" "O yes, I forgot to point out that had really taken place by correspondence through some other agent I had seen. . . ."

This was reassuring. Z was given medical assistance: an operation on his testicles was carried out while he lay on the wooden bunk. He was allowed some months to recuperate before being tried. On the eve of his trial, the officer in charge summed up his depositions. He redictated Z's confessions about C.I.C. and I.S., dollars and pound notes, spying and socialism. He was already at the end when Z told him, "Now, sir, I think I should add that the Titoist agents. . . ." The officer interrupted him with a gesture which gave him to understand that all that was of no importance. The ÁVH had changed their minds; they had first thought of including Z in a "Titoist" trial but had later decided that he could be better used in the context of Anglo-American spying.

The Tito agents were *ex officio* arrested Communists. In addition to Yugoslav spy-links they had to confess British, German, French, American, South American, Swiss and other spy-contacts if they had spent any time before or during the war in such countries. Theirs was the most complex situation: they could not sensibly say they had opposed communism, as to some extent everybody else could. Their confessions, known now to be nonsense, were particularly puzzling to some people. Did they simply yield to threats and torture? Did they believe the promises that even if they were sentenced to death the sentence would not be carried out, and that they would be allowed to live in comfort away from the public eye? Or were they persuaded, like the hero of *Darkness at Noon,* that they owed this moral sacrifice to the Party?

It was a mixture of all this. But in general, torture was surely more decisive than one would think from the otherwise often startlingly accurate descriptions in *Darkness at Noon.* I knew some Communists in prison who had not specifically been tortured under arrest before trial but the threat had been permanent and minor samples had been given of its fulfillment. At the other extreme, for example, one was "electrified" while he sat in cold water for hours, day after day, and wrapped in a rag and beaten until his ribs were broken—all for not confessing to crimes which he could not have guessed, as they had been invented by another imprisoned Communist under duress. The average was a cross between the two.

As to Rajk, my information is that he was so shocked by the call of the three ÁVH agents who came to fetch him that at first he resisted them. They had to struggle to take him to No. 60. Then, the various methods of breaking a man were applied simultaneously. He was beaten up and tortured. He was informed that his wife was also under arrest and might also be tortured. They threatened that his baby son would as though by accident be run over by a car. He was promised "sanatorium" treatment after his "purely formal" death sentence. Meanwhile, appeals were made to his belief in communism. It was explained to him that the Party needed this great sacrifice on his part: Tito's Yugoslavia had to be revealed as the agency of a capitalist world conspiracy "which it really is," and he, Rajk, alone could convincingly perform the role of its leading figure in Hungary. Among others the Minister of the Interior at that time, János Kádár, is said to have personally called on him in his cell, bringing Rákosi's most comradely messages and assuring him of the Party's profound appreciation and gratitude in case he consented. The coaching of "accomplices" and "witnesses" was managed on similar lines. Rehearsals for an open trial were staged in the presence of the ÁVH chief, Péter. Rajk then was a nervous wreck. Now and then he forgot his lesson and was reprimanded by Péter.

At his trial, he acted perfectly as prescribed. When asked by the president of the court "And who finally foiled your attempts?" he answered like a model schoolboy, "Great Stalin and wise Rákosi." Among all the promises they had made, there must have been one he found it hard to believe—the "purely formal" nature of his death sentence. Under the gallows he did not seem to be surprised. His last words allegedly were "Long live the Soviet Union." Was it for the sake of his wife and son? Was it meant to demonstrate that he was a better Communist than those who were murdering him? Or was he ultimately convinced, whatever his own tragedy, that his "compass" must be right? We shall never know.

Others who shared his fate did turn out to be surprised. Major-General Pálffy-Osterreicher shouted "we were deceived," and a young Communist, András Szalai, cried with the rope round his neck "I perish innocently, how can Rákosi tolerate this?" He could, quite lightheartedly. But surprises can always crop up in a "planned" society, including the surprise of a promise honored. In prison we met in comparatively good health a Communist whose hanging had been reported in the Budapest press, and there may have been other similar cases.

Many of those who had endured grave tortures to bargain off at least some of their alleged crimes felt it had been worthwhile if they had thus escaped hanging. This may have been so in certain cases—but in others, unwillingness to confess yielded a different crop. A memorable example was that of the two Szücs brothers. Both started their Communist careers in the underground movement before the war. One of them, Miklós, was my friend. He was a leading member of the London Hungarian Club during the war,[2] and afterwards correspondent of the Hungarian Communist Party paper and chief of the Hungarian government-sponsored information bureau in Britain. At first he struck me as tiresome and parrot-Communist, but I became fond of him. He was sincere and honest to the limit of Party loyalty and occasionally beyond. In the course of years he acquired a real sympathy for the British labor movement and, so long as that was possible, really hoped for a mutual arrangement "between the two workers' parties." He could hardly hide his disgust at the outrageous attacks on old Hungarian socialist leaders at the time of the merger and showed an open concern for their fate. But, needless to say, he fulfilled Party orders obediently and served the Communist government loyally. His authority among Hungarians in London was much increased after Rákosi, arriving on a Government mission at London Airport on one occasion, looked about for him and cordially shook his hands: "I am so glad to see you; you know your brother and I are old friends."

They were. Ernö Szücs was Rákosi's cellmate in Horthy's prison. After the war he became a senior official of the Ministry of the Interior and later, as a colonel, one of Gábor Péter's deputies at the head of the ÁVH. When Miklós from time to time visited Budapest, he used to stay with his brother. "Do you always see eye to eye with him?" I once asked him. "Let's not discuss family matters," he answered with a faint smile. I did not of course press the question. Among prisoners of the ÁVH it was common knowledge that Ernö Szücs was one of the great confession-forgers, together with Lieutenant-General Péter, Colonel Décsy, and Colonel Janikovsky (who was to the best of my belief responsible for my own suffering, the man who had taken me in to see Gábor Péter).

Miklós Szücs, visiting Hungary on an official trip in the spring of 1949, was suddenly ordered to appoint someone else to his post in London and to stay in Budapest as "an important post" had been found for him there. He was made director of the Technological Institute. When I last saw him, in the summer of that year, he spoke with some nostalgia of England but felt quite happy—especially, I think, as he had parted from his London girlfriend, an ardent but unattractive comrade. He was arrested two or three days before me. The order was given by his brother Ernö.

Six months after my trial I was taken once again to the Budapest police headquarters where Lieutenant Colonel Károlyi and Lieutenant Szántó started by overfeeding me, as they always did on such occasions, and went on to torment me with threats and questions—this time about the "spy-links between the Szücs brothers." As an agent of the I.S., I must know that the British authorities, once having learned of the family ties between Miklós and Ernö, made use of them. In spite of my worries and jitters, I was unwilling to give conclusive evidence and was ultimately left in peace about them without getting the promised "hiding." I learned the background and sequel later.

Lieutenant-General Péter fell out with his Colonel Ernö Szücs, according to some informers, because even Ernö Szücs thought that his chief overdid the fabrication of evidence. Péter announced to Rákosi his suspicions of a "spy-contact" between the two brothers. Rákosi authorized him to arrest Ernö Szücs. From then onwards the Szücs brothers were alternately tortured and brought together to confess. Their belief was that if they yielded they would be executed. They were taken to a spot in ÁVH headquarters known as the *lefolyó*—the drains. At that spot the bodies of victims were made liquid with an acid and then let down the drains into the sewage of the city. A former assistant of Colonel

Ernö Szücs, having witnessed a bit of the scene, was horror-stricken and ran to Rákosi: "Comrade Rákosi, I don't know what to say, Comrade Ernö Szücs is being beaten up over the *lefolyó*. . . ." "What?" Rákosi exclaimed, "those people are simply mad, what did you say? Awful. I'll ring them at once to stop that. You go back now to assist the Comrade Colonel." The man hurried back and at the entrance to the ÁVH was caught by the guards who were waiting for him: "You swine, you dared to squeal against us to Comrade Rákosi?" He was terribly beaten up and later interned. The bodies of the Szücs brothers meanwhile vanished down the *lefolyó*.

I cannot vouch for the truth of all details in this story.[3] But the essence of it—that the Szücs brothers were beaten to death by the ÁVH for their unwillingness to "confess" to imaginary crimes—was admitted to me personally, at the time of the thaw in 1956, by György Nonn, then attorney general of the People's Republic, formerly private secretary to Rákosi.

There may have been some who refused to confess anything at all. Certainly some were unwilling to confess everything demanded from them. It was comparatively easy to confess lies and conceal the truth. This was to some extent what I did. During my years in the prison of the ÁVH I was in constant terror of what might next be asked from me. The interrogations were a nightmare. I leave it to the imagination of the reader to realize what it was like to be pestered on one occasion—in 1951 I think—by questioners who wanted me to confess that my brother and sister had acted as my informers when I had been a spy in London.

Confessions were not uniform. The behavior of prisoners was not uniform. Differences of moral strength and of mental awareness, even at the moment of prostration and fainting, manifested themselves in the various depositions. But in one thing there could be no difference between us: none of us could be dignified. In prison I often recalled the various romantic descriptions of saints and heroes who would not falter under whips and hot iron: there was, for instance, the excellent and in many ways realistic Italian film, *The Open City*, in which the Resistance hero spat in the face of his cruel interrogator, the Gestapo officer. This is just the scene which in such circumstances cannot happen. The Resistance hero, or his opposite number in ÁVH custody, by the time he faces the demands of his interrogator, is physically unable to show pride. The Gestapo or ÁVH see to that. To be proud and dignified while cigarette ends are stamped out on one's skin is surely more difficult than cinemagoers would think. But it can be tried. To be proud and dignified after being forbidden to go to the lavatory for twenty-four hours cannot even be tried. It is this sort of torture which all ÁVH prisoners had to undergo from the beginning. They were dirty, miserable, and exhausted by the time their conclusive interrogations started. Sense of honor may not have gone but their self-respect must have been crushed. Coming from damp cellars, they were shivering—in itself a bad start to dignified composure. Many of the Frenchmen guillotined under the Terror behaved magnificently. But even they trembled. "Tu trembles Bailly," a guard sneered at the great scientist, and former Mayor of Paris, seeing him on the way to the guillotine. "Oui, parcequ'il fait froid," Bailly answered, so that the crowd should hear. But no crowd attended the interrogations at No. 60. Proud gestures in the circumstances would have been grotesque and silly as well as suicidal.

Few people are able to bear witness to that. Most rewrite in their memories the stages of their ordeals. Self-deception started even in prison. I remember the hospital room in Vác where I spent some weeks with, among others, Father Bozsik and my old friend, the former Secretary General of the Social Democrat Party, Ferenc Szeder. About fifteen of us were in that room for suspected heart trouble. We were a motley little crowd which ranged from the former Arrow-Cross Fascist Lord Mayor of Budapest to a "Trotskyite-Titoist" who insisted even there that "history will vindicate our People's Republic": the representatives of all political shades and of practically all social strata. We were treated abominably, buffeted about, threatened all the time, spied on, and fed on fodder. I asked a very soldierly former Fascist whether he had been beaten up and he answered "O no, if that had happened, I shouldn't be here; because whatever the result, if anyone dared to strike me I couldn't stop myself from hitting back."

One night our room was raided. Seventeen-year-old thugs with rifles chased us out of our beds, kicked us, abused us, and searched our beds and drawers; and one of them slapped the face of my soldierly cellmate. We all took it humbly. The day after, we started whispering about what had happened. What a shame, how disgraceful!—we all sighed. After a pause, one of us began: "But at least I had my own back," and told us a witty answer he believed he had made. We all nodded, confirming that he had been very brave. In the course of the following days some three or four of us remembered equally brave remarks we had made. If our whispers had been tape-recorded, that night of humiliations would have gone down as a heroic act of resistance. If the night itself had been tape-recorded, we should all have emerged as cowards. We were but human in a sub-human world.

The Undefeated

Gyorgy Paloczi-Horvath

GYORGY PALOCZI-HORVATH (1908–73) was a leftist Hungarian journalist who lived in Britain during World War II and worked for the BBC. He was a critic of the Hungarian right-of-center government and was strongly opposed to Hungary's alliance with Nazi Germany. He returned to Hungary in 1947 anxious to work for the creation of a democratic Hungary and joined the Communist Party. Between 1948 and 1949 he was head of the foreign language department of the Hungarian Radio Service. He was arrested in 1949, charged with espionage on behalf of Western intelligence services, and sentenced to fifteen years' imprisonment. As other readings also indicate, this was the fate of many idealistic supporters of East European Communist systems who returned from Western exile. He was released in 1954 as a result of the amnesty that followed the death of Stalin. Rehabilitated, he worked at the Hungarian Historical Study Institute until his escape in 1956. In England he was a senior editor of Irodalmi Ujsag *(Literary Gazette), the major Hungarian political-literary journal abroad after 1956.*

The case of Paloczi-Horvath is among those which illustrate how closely the policies and procedures of the East European political police were modeled on those of the Soviets. In these countries, too, the authorities persecuted groups and individuals not for their behavior or actions but on the basis of abstract theoretical considerations (see the discussion of "objective crime" in the introduction) in order to score didactic points; alleged enemies of the state had to fit into particular scenarios. Those who had lived for a period of time in the West could more plausibly be accused of spying than those without such experience.

In Hungary, the show trials resulting from such considerations were called "conceptual trials" because their objective was to illustrate particular political-ideological themes or propositions. In these cases, as in the Soviet ones, coerced confessions constituted the key, and often only, evidence against the accused. Those arrested often had no idea whatsoever why they were detained and believed that it was because of

From Gyorgy Paloczi-Horvath, The Undefeated, © *1959 by Gyorgy Paloczi-Horvath. Reprinted by permission.*

some misunderstanding soon to be cleared up. Another method imported from the Soviet Union was the use of detailed, and repeatedly written, autobiographies by the accused, which were intended to reveal his past life and all his alleged transgressions. Sleep deprivation, endless nocturnal interrogations, minimal food, unsanitary conditions, and actual torture sooner or later had the desired outcome, as the defendants confessed to the criminal roles and activities the authorities devised for them. A public, or quasi-public, trial usually followed, but not in every instance; sometimes the signed confessions were used against other defendants with or without courtroom confrontation.

· · · · ·

It was nearly midnight when the black car stopped in front of 60 Andrassy Avenue, the headquarters of Security Police. The three SP men in mufti took me to a guard's room in the basement. A young lieutenant sat at a desk. He looked at me in disgust, got up and tore the Party badge from my lapel.

"Empty your pockets!"

I had to undo and hand over my shoelaces and my necktie. Then an SP guard with rifle took me to a circular staircase which led to the cellars. The cellar corridors were brightly lit. At twelve-foot intervals stood guards with their rifles glaring at me with what I learned to know as the compulsory SP expression of loathing and hate. The cellar was cold and damp. The air was musty, everything smelt of disinfectant, sweat, and a combination of various stenches as yet unknown to me.

At the end of one of the corridors I was thrown into an icy cold cubicle three yards by four. There was a wooden plank for a bed and a bright naked electric bulb which threw a harsh light on the unclean whitewashed walls. In the iron door there was a small rectangular spy-hole which was opened and banged shut every five minutes. I stood in the middle of the cell and shivered, my heart nearly jumping out of my breast; I gulped down air as if I were suffocating.

I did not understand the reason for the brutal swiftness of my arrest. Whatever suspicions they might have against me, I was evidently under detention for questioning.

Why does everybody behave as if they took my guilt for granted, I thought. And why these cellar cubicles? Our system should not keep people in such inhuman conditions. Why brag that our Security Police uses no sort of physical coercion if they put people into such awful holes? It's good, though, that they do not torture people. It would be terrible for innocent people like myself to be tortured to give away secrets which they don't know.

How long will it last till I clear myself? I wondered. I ought to be in Rome now. The UNA World Congress had already started, there was that delay with my passport. If I can't clear up everything tonight, I shall miss the Congress.

I walked up and down, five short steps to the door, five steps to the wall. Above the three wooden planks there was a tiny window with heavy iron bars. It opened into an air shaft which probably led up to the courtyard. It must be awful in the winter, the cold streaming down on one's head. From time to time I looked absentmindedly at my nonexistent wristwatch, or reached into my pocket for a cigarette. Every five minutes the spy-hole was ripped open, a face appeared with the usual expression of loathing and hate, then it was banged shut again. All through my corridor and in the maze of corridors in this cellar empire spy-holes were banging. Heavy boots clattered on the stone floor. Five steps to the wall, five steps to the door. Above the door the naked electric light glared mercilessly into my eyes. What can they suspect me of? What nonsense is this? And why did they bring me in post-haste at midnight if they do not start questioning me right away? I hope to God I shall get an intelligent SP investigator. It would be awful if I got a cliché-mongering ignoramus. Bang, steps, steps, steps, bang, door, wall, bang, steps, clatter of boots, bang, glaring light. Growing impatience in my body, impatience and alarm.

No, this can't go on! I must lie down and try to sleep. I am going to need all my strength! I banged on the door. The spy-hole was ripped open at once. A grim face asked, "What do you want?"

"Can I have some blankets?"

"No!" Bang.

I was dressed for summer in a light linen jacket and flannel trousers. In the cellar it was cold. I stretched out on the hard planks. I closed my eyes but the lamp glared down on my face. With closed eyes one looked through blood-red light. I turned towards the wall, away from the light. Bang! A face in the spy-hole, a harsh voice: "Lie on your back. We must see your face."

I turned into the required position, putting my hands under my head. Bang! A face in the spy-hole and the same harsh voice: "Put your hands palm upwards on the plank. We must see your wrists."

They took good care that the prisoners should not commit suicide. One of the SP officers told me later, "In this building only we do the killing, nobody else." There was wire netting on the windows to prevent prisoners from hurling themselves to death. After each hearing, when they took us back to the cellar, there was a most thorough search. We had to undress completely and everything was examined for fear we might have stolen some sharp instrument with which to commit suicide. The frequent searches during the winter were further sources of torment.

I remember that night well. It was the longest night I ever spent. I soon got up and paced up and down the cubicle until they changed the guards, until the prisoners were driven out one by one to a troughlike contraption where we were supposed to wash ourselves. There was only one towel, soaking wet already and smelling of emaciated bodies. I did not use the towel. I put my shirt on my wet body. Steps, bang, steps. The prisoners were driven out one by one to the w.c., with a guard standing in the door. Then after another eternity there was a very loud clatter, the metallic clinking of pots. Out one by one again—prisoners were not supposed to see each other—to get "breakfast": half a pint of lukewarm flour soup and a piece of damp bread. I forced myself to eat up everything. Then we had to put out our dixies, and the "day" started; crouching on the edge of the wooden planks, walking up and down, counting to seven hundred between bangs on the spy-hole, never ceasing to wonder about my "case," hopeful, desperate, impatient, apathetic by turns.

In the afternoon the cubicle door was opened unexpectedly. I was hopeful that my hearing was to begin. But it was only finger printing and photographing. A wooden number plate was put under my face. Unshaven, with bloated eyes, I must have looked the typical criminal. But aren't they only supposed to do this *after* they have established one's guilt?

Back in the cubicle, I stretched myself out on my bunk and slept a while. I woke up hungry and shivering. I badly wanted a cigarette. I was thirsty. But at least it must be morning. I waited and waited, but nobody was called out for the morning wash. I banged on the door and asked for water. "Can't you wait till dinner?" Bang!

My God, it's not dinnertime yet. After many eternities dinner came—some soup and a piece of bread. I wolfed it down. Then I stretched myself out in the prescribed position and with the red glow burning in my eyeballs, burning the back of my head, I tried to sleep.

Bang! The cubicle door was open. A guard shouted, "Out!"

I came out.

"Put your hands behind your back! Move on!"

Staircase, corridors, more civilized surroundings. I was taken into an office room. Behind a desk sat a small dark-haired young man. In front of the desk four or five yards away stood a chair.

"Good evening, Paloczi-Horvath, sit down on that chair."

While I sat down, he lit a second lamp on his desk, turned it full into my face. The piercing white light made me blink.

"Tell me the story of your life, with all possible details. Let's start with your family."

I talked. He made notes. While he wrote I could glance at his wrist watch. It was just past eight p.m. when he started questioning me. At half past twelve he leaned back in his armchair:

"Now I ask you, Paloczi, why are you here?"

"I asked you that already. I am anxious to know. There must be some mistake. Or someone denounced me. If you tell me what it is, I am sure we can clear it up in no time."

"No, there is nothing to clear up. We know what we know. But it's up to you to tell us what you did. This is our method. You must realize the game is up. If you tell us now, at once, on the first hearing what we know anyhow, then we shall see that you are not a hardened criminal, just someone who slipped.... In your case a big enough slip. But if you come clean, if you co-operate with the authorities, we shall help you."

"I have nothing to tell. I did not commit anything, I made no slip, small or big."

"Well, if that's your attitude, we have means to get you to talk."

It was just midnight. He rang the bell on his desk. A guard appeared. "This man will type his autobiography till four in the morning. Then take him to the cellar, but he is not to sleep."

Turning to me, he said: "You will be given a typewriter. Write down everything you told me. And think it over. Till tomorrow you will have time to think, because you are not going to sleep."

He left. I typed. The guard had orders to prod me on with his rifle butt if I stopped typing. So I typed, half asleep, with reeling head, typed and typed, till the time came to go down to the cellar cubicle. A piece of paper had been stuck on my door. Evidently the order that I should not be permitted to lie down.

Bang. Five steps to the wall, five steps to the door, glaring light, bang, hard eyes looking in. I staggered up and down and looked longingly at the wooden plank. I would not mind the red glow in my eyeballs. Only to stretch out, only to get a second of oblivion.

Morning wash, breakfast, and staggering again. At nine o'clock in the morning I was taken up to another officer. A young man behind the desk. In front there was a chair at five yards' distance. The curtains were drawn. As I sat down, the desk reflector was turned full into my face.

"Well?" the officer said with a questioning look. "Do you like this? An intelligent man like you should realize that there is no point in resisting. You are at our mercy. We know everything about you. We have a great organization to fight against your resistance. You might be fit and strong, but nobody is fit here for long.... Don't you realize that we can do anything to you, I say, *anything*."

"Communist police cannot use methods of torture."

"That's what you believe, Paloczi. Why do you think I have this in my desk?"

He took out a long rubber truncheon and brandished it into my face.

"However, I don't like to use it, if it can be avoided.... We know all about you."

Then it started all over again—I wanting to know the accusation, he wanting me to confess. After a long debate he told me to go on with my life story. The hearing lasted four hours. Then a guard was called in and I had to type till nine P.M. till the original interrogator arrived. He questioned me till midnight, gave an order that I should type till four in the morning, then down to the cellar to stagger up and down in the cubicle.

Just before washing, they changed the guards. It must have been five-thirty a.m. Bang! I did not look at the spy-hole. Bang again. A young peasant face.

"Hey, you!" he whispered. "Come here. I'll let you sleep till they take you to the interrogator. I will put a piece of bread on your bunk. . . . Don't sign anything!" Bang!

I did not even think. I just staggered to the bunk and slept like a log.

At nine in the morning the routine started again. The two SP officers went on questioning me in turn, twice a day I had to type my life story. From four in the morning till the first hearing I had to spend the rest of the twenty-four hours walking up and down in the cubicle. This went on for three weeks. As far as the SP officers were concerned, I never slept. But every second day the young peasant guard was on duty, and some other guards were slack. And I learned to sleep while staggering up and down. Sometimes a guard let me sleep during typing hours.

During those three weeks I had to write the story of my life over and over. They made me write some eight thousand words a day. Their orders varied. They would tell me to write down my life story from 1937 to 1941. Then from 1932 to 1934. Then they picked a simple incident which I had to describe in great detail. After that 1939 to 1942, and so on, endlessly. They hoped to catch me out. But I always wrote the truth, and at the end of the second week they started to curse my blasted memory.

The young SP man who questioned me for the first time used a mixed language of Marxist textbook jargon and Budapest underworld slang. He frequently interrupted me by shouting: "boloney, bunk, bullshit," or "tommyrot." At the end I called him Tommyrot. From his style, accent, and general behavior I concluded that he must have been a shop assistant in one of the disreputable districts of Budapest or a barker in a fun fair. The only way of life and the only type of government he knew was the Communist one. He imagined the "capitalist state" as a monolithic organization run by a sort of Politbureau of monopoly-capitalists.

The capitalist political police in his mind was a Security Police with capitalist policy. Most capitalist organizations were according to him front organizations of the Secret Service or Deuxième Bureau, and so forth. Britain, for instance, was run by the Intelligence Service. Any ministry, organization, or institution which had a research department or intelligence section was naturally a secret branch of the I.S. The most sinister branches of the I.S. were, according to Comrade Tommyrot, the British Conservative Party, the Liberal Party and the Labor Party. These parties, under the central direction of the I.S., had each their own way of working toward the same end—that of betraying the working class of Britain. And through their contacts abroad they did a great deal of spying. The other important I.S. front organizations were the International Red Cross, the BBC, and the World Federation of United Nations Associations.

It was very fortunate for me that I had actually worked for a period for the BBC, that I was Secretary-General of the Hungarian UNA, and most of all, that I "worked for the British during the war." The only reason they did not start torturing me right at the beginning was that these facts alone gave them a good case against me. It helped too that in describing my escape from Hungary in 1941, I wrote at length about the day on the Yugoslav coast when the British sent us foreigners off by flying boat. Being half drunk with sleeplessness, I typed mechanically what I thought and felt. Next day Tommyrot was quite pleased with it.

"I see at least that you confess your loyalty to the British. Don't you see that after this there is no point in denying that you are and always were a capitalist at heart?"

"I don't remember exactly what I wrote last night," I replied. "It is true that those British diplomats behaved in a most humane way. The fact that I recognize their human qualities does not necessarily mean that I share their political views."

Tommyrot laughed. "Says you. . . . Why pretend that you are a Communist? Nobody believes you. We never believed you. We know that you are an agent. We exploited you while you were useful for us, but had you watched all the time."

"If you had me watched all the time since I came home, you must know that I did nothing against the regime. You must know that I behaved, wrote, and lived as a sincerely convinced Communist. And whatever you do to me, I shall stay a Communist."

"Tommyrot, tommyrot! . . . Stop making speeches! You think because you are a writer, you can get away with anything. You think because the I.S. trained you to be a Marxist, you took us in? Not even for a second! When you came back to Hungary on your agent's mission, your fate was sealed. Of course, you've taken in some people. They saved you in July. You were supposed to be in the July 6 batch of arrests, but some ideological bigwigs saved you. But on the fifteenth of August we received permission to pull you in with the next batch. You know of course that Comrade Rakosi signs all such lists?"

He talked on, but I did not hear anything he said. My head reeled. So on that day of the reception Rakosi had already signed the order of my arrest. No, I can't believe it! But I remembered the strange curiosity in Rakosi's eyes. That look. . . . God, that look made me think that Tommyrot is perhaps telling the truth. No, it can't be true. . . .

· · · · ·

The weeks passed. I was still impatient, but now I waited for the end of the police investigation. After all, sooner or later they would have to hand me over to an investigating judge, then I should learn the accusation, I could enlist legal aid, clear myself within a few days. It would never come to a trial.

During those first sleepless weeks everything was vague and blurred. Even suffering. It was a hideous feeling to be jailed by my own state, to realize that I,

274

a good Communist, was confined in a Communist jail. It was worrying that the Security Police was not the intelligent organization I imagined. The investigators were brutal and ignorant. And the reactionary talk about torture, which I had never believed for a moment, was true! Everywhere in the building one could hear screams, groaning, whimpering, sudden shrill shouts. At all hours of the day these sounds broke into your cubicle and disturbed your attempt to escape in imagination from all the horrors. There was a girl nearby who started to sob loudly whenever they took her out from her cell to be interrogated. Sometimes I heard her sobbing when they brought her back. I heard her faltering steps, the inarticulate sounds she made as each step hurt her bruised body.

Another torment was the revolting sensation of one's unclean body. I had the same shirt, light summer jacket, and flannel trousers on all the time, for weeks. Up in the interrogator's room after half an hour I still could smell the prison-cellar stench emanating from my clothes, from my body. They did not shave me and still gave no permission for the weekly hot showers other prisoners had. I felt sticky with dirt all the time.

Then "coercion" began. The first occasion would have been comical if it had not been the beginning of torture. One morning Tommyrot asked me where I met Professor Szentgyörgyi, the Nobel Prize winning Hungarian scientist during the war. I told him truthfully that I met him in Istanbul.

"You lie, you fascist swine!"

I kept silent. He asked me again, "Where did you meet Professor Szentgyörgyi?"

"In Istanbul."

"All right. I'll teach you Istanbul."

He rang the bell, whispered something to a guard, and I was taken to a whitewashed room. I was ordered to turn to the wall.

"Stand closer. Still closer. . . . All right now, stand at attention. Don't move, if you don't want to get kicked."

There I stood, my nose an inch from the whitewashed wall. They changed the guards every four hours. The guards had only one duty, to kick me or hit my back with their rifle-butt in case I moved. I stood in that position till the evening. About nine p.m. Tommyrot came in.

"Where did you meet Professor Szentgyörgyi during the war?"

"In Istanbul."

"All right, that's O.K. with me. Then you go on standing."

After the first twenty-four hours I had to take off my shoes because my feet were enormously swollen. Standing there I learned about the famous "cinema" of prisoners. By the first evening the unevenly white-washed wall had started to vibrate. The little particles, the slight cracks, the dust on the wall took on various shapes. There were mirages on the wall. My dazzled eyes played tricks on me. Soon I saw snarling, squinting, and grinning faces, eyes burning with hatred and loathing. There were hallucinations too. I heard quite clearly the banging of the spy-holes. The wall became full of spy-holes and through each a miniature SP thug glared at me. Next dawn I became quite faint. I hoped I should pass out soon. Curiously enough this thought gave me some strength; I was almost relieved. The wall cinema, which till then had been black and white, took on delicate colors. I saw all sorts of pinks, purples, and reds. Lovely girls walked away from me with a voluptuous undulating walk. They always disappeared into the infinite and then started to walk away again.

On the second evening Comrade Tommyrot asked his question again. I again answered with Istanbul.

On the third day I fainted twice in the morning. In the afternoon, when the four o'clock guard came in, there was a great commotion outside in the corridors. They had their weekly Party meeting in the big auditorium. When the building became quiet again, the guard—a young sandy-haired boy—told me, "Sit down now and try to sleep. I'll wake you up if someone comes."

I staggered to the chair and slept. It was already dark when he woke me up. There were steps on the stairway.

"Stand at attention now. And stick to the truth, whatever they do to you!"

It was again nine p.m. They took me to Tommyrot's room. As I staggered in he turned the reflector into my face but did not tell me to sit down. I stood there. Every inch of my body was hurting me, my skin, my bones, my insides. Everything in my body seemed to be terribly heavy. I stood there reeling. Comrade Tommyrot said pompously with a victorious smile:

"This will teach you, you fascist swine, that it is no use to lie to us. We knew all the time—we have it here in writing—that you met Professor Szentgyörgyi not in Istanbul but in Constantinople."

There was an explosion of anger in my head. I jumped forward, trying to grab him and shouted:

"You stupid idiot, if you don't know that Istanbul and Constantinople are one and the same. . . ."

I went on shouting. In the next second there were two guards in the room. I was manacled hand and feet to a chair. Tommyrot sat in front and spat repeatedly into my face. The spittle was flowing down my face.

This was the beginning. Later, when my solitary confinement period was over, I never talked to my cellmates about torture. I won't now either. There were many people who had a far worse time than I. There is no point in describing pain. There are so many ways to cause piercing pain to the human body. All of us prison graduates had days when we were tossed about on a stormy ocean of pain. We were alone with our agony, alone like a small abandoned star in the vortex of a hostile universe.

Torture alone did not make us "confess." Sleeplessness, hunger, utter degradation, filthy insults to human dignity, the knowledge that we were utterly at the mercy of the SP—all this was not enough. Then they told us that they would arrest our relatives and torture them in front of us. We heard women and children screaming in adjacent rooms. Was this a put-up job for our benefit? I still don't know.

After the period of torture we were sent back to our solitary cubicles to "rot away for a while." Now we were tormented by the intense cold, by the glaring bulb, and the four walls which threatened to collapse on us.

We had to be awake eighteen hours a day. There were no books, no cigarettes, only thousands of empty minutes. Now our fear was insanity. Our heads were whirling, we imagined sounds and colors. Some of us had a nightmarish feeling of being drowned. Our emaciated bodies and feverish brains produced eerie visions and hallucinations. Is it any wonder that many of us had no sound judgment, no will power to resist our tormentors?

POLAND

A Prisoner of Martial Law

Jan Mur

Jan Mur (the pseudonym of Gdansk-based author Andrzej Drzycimski, 1942–) was imprisoned in Poland when the authorities crushed the Solidarity Movement in 1981. Excerpts from his book suggest that, notwithstanding the suppression of Solidarity, the early 1980s in Poland were the beginning of the end of Polish communism. Details of prison life, especially as regards the treatment of political prisoners, make clear that the political will of the authorities was seriously weakened. There was a complementary decline in the level of intimidation among the population, including prisoners.

Compared to all other accounts in this volume, imprisonment in Poland in the early 1980s stands out as a relatively humane and non-

From Jan Mur, A Prisoner of Martial Law, *© 1984 by Jan Mur, reprinted by permission of Harcourt, Inc..*

traumatic experience. The prisoners enjoyed remarkable freedom to interact, organize, and defy the hesitant, sometimes apologetic prison authorities. Shortly after his imprisonment, Mur and others handed a list of demands to the prison authorities outlining their refusal "to submit to the routine of a penal institution." The warden pleaded with the prisoners "not to make things difficult for us." The prisoners decorated their cell with a picture of the pope and a cross they improvised from slats torn from a table. Many of them were allowed furlough for several days. Prisoners even wore inside the prison Solidarity pins that were not allowed outside.

The book suggests that the repression of Solidarity was half-hearted in comparison, at any rate, to the measures that had been taken in the past against any real or even imaginary challenge to a Communist regime.

. . . . .

Sunday, December 13, 1981

And so I am in prison—why? For what reason? What crime did I commit? I lie on my bed and constantly ask myself these questions. My companions in misfortune ask the same ones. No, I cannot forget this. All of this must be described. Not from a distance in the future, but now, every day. Something in the form of a diary, a conversation with myself. This has to make up for being separated from my loved ones. For how long? But first I should reconstruct a chronology of events.

It is after midnight and I am on my way home from the National Commission meeting. I wonder along the way if I shouldn't just disappear somewhere and not go home. But then I ask myself why I am afraid. The most they can do is detain me (for the first time) for forty-eight hours. Surely they want only to frighten the people connected with the Union, because, in the end, no one can govern this society without listening to its voice. Seeing no unusual police activity on the way home, I finally relax.

At home we have guests who are already sleeping. I eat my evening meal in peace. After two days of listening to the National Commission's deliberations, I am exhausted. I fall asleep immediately. The doorbell wakes me up. In answer to my question, "Who's there?" I hear "Police." And, indeed, I see three uniformed policemen and one plainclothesman through the peephole. I tell them to come back in the morning. They immediately try to break down the door. I open it. They burst into the entryway and surround me. At first they are aggressive, then they calm down a bit. I demand an arrest warrant. In answer, the plainclothesman, who seems to be in charge of this raid, tells me that I am being detained on the basis of some unknown Article 42. He adds that I am not being arrested but being interned. He shows me the bill of internment. I read in it that I am to be interned at Strzebielinek or Czarne. I get dressed, gulp down a little milk, and my wife gives me a bit of bread, a toothbrush and tooth-paste. I am told that everything else must be left behind. I slip my watch into my pocket anyway. My horrified children and wife look on, as they lead me out.

They take me away in a cold *Nyska*.[1] First we drive through the city, passing regional headquarters, where there are a lot of police. Then we turn onto Slowacki Street. I look at my watch: it is almost four A.M. During our trip, a young police officer tries in vain to start a conversation. I think that we are heading for the airport. I relax when we turn off at the Tri-City exit. I think then that we are going to Wejherowo. We drive through it, however, and into a forested region where a road sign with the word "Piasnica"[2] flashes by. After a two-hour ride during which we lose our way and get stuck in the snow, we drive up to a high wall. At the entrance, the sign reads: "Penal Institution/ External Division of the Wejherowo Prison in Strzebielinek." There is a high, gray wall with watchtowers in the corners, searchlights, and machine guns. My "guardian" leads me into a large room. They take my picture from three sides. They take prints of all my fingers and both palms. They tell me to sign this. I'm dazed. While waiting for whatever was coming next and later when surrender-ing my things (I have to give them everything I have including my watch), I see familiar faces. I do not remember their names. Finally, I am led into a court-yard surrounded by a high chain-link fence that ends in rows of barbed wire. Beyond the fence are five one-level pavilions joined by a corridor. There are bars in the windows. In the guard booth I am assigned a cell. I happen to see a doctor on my way there. He asks, "Don't we know each other? I can't recall." The guard leads me down a long corridor, on both sides of which are cells. There are twelve. The corridor begins and ends with a grating that reaches the ceiling. The key rattles and in a minute they have me locked behind a door that is covered with a heavy sheet of metal, or perhaps the entire door is steel. There is a row of bunks along the wall, in which are two barred windows. At first I think that I am alone, but then I spot a friend whom I had been talking to a few hours ago. Things perk up. Our cell is filling up fast. By evening we have a complete set of sixteen people, a real tower of Babel: workers, an engineer, a teacher, lawyer, journalist, secondary school student, and various Union activ-ists. Through the window, we can see women being led in. We recognize Grazyna Przybylska-Wendt and Alicja Matuszewska, both of whom are from the Presidium of the National Commission. There is Wisniewska from the Department of Intervention, Krystyna Pienkowska from Teachers' Solidarity; Halina Winiarska, an actress from the Wybrzeze Theater; Joanna Gwiazda, Joanna Wojciechowicz, and the diminutive Alina Pienkowska.

The first meal, tea, is at noon. Later, pea soup. Our table setting, if one can call it that, is two aluminum bowls, a mug, and spoon. We wash the dishes in a sink which is right next to the toilet in one corner of the cell and divided from the rest of our "apartment" by a partition. . . .

. . . . .

December 14, 15, 16: Monday, Tuesday, Wednesday

Slowly we are getting used to our new environment. Prison authorities, as we are slowly finding out, exist on a few levels of initiation. The warden of the penal institution, who holds a major's rank, can make decisions regarding everything: toilet paper, cigarettes, toothbrushes, and the amount of stools for each cell. The remaining matters, such as the required routine, our status, appeals of the internment orders, and so on are the domain of the police spokesman relegated to the affairs of the interned by the district commander of the police. We hear that the police spokesman is timid, and demands that everything be in writing to the district police commander. He avoids making any independent decisions. He introduces himself to someone as "Captain Maciuk, M.A." It seems that he is an *ubek* known in the Young Poland circles, because he personally directed searches in their apartments. His new job is certainly a promotion. The guards that watch us are also organized according to a definite hierarchy. This is obvious during our walks outdoors. The guards let us out of our cells, but in the courtyard they have nothing to say. The ZOMOs decide how we are to move around (there are marked routes for walks) and how long the walk is to last. This matter becomes a source of conflict immediately because sometimes the walks last fifteen minutes and at other times a half hour. According to rumors about the regulations, it would appear that the walks are supposed to last an hour. It seems that the ZOMOs shorten them at will.

The first walk was on Monday. We all went out. The guards and ZOMOs showed us the circle in which we were to move. We could run, throw snowballs at each other, walk—whatever anybody wanted to do. The only restriction was that we weren't allowed to get near the people running on the opposite side of the square. So we shouted to one another and exchanged a little information, but we shouted mainly to raise our spirits. The ZOMOs pretended not to hear. It was clear that they did not know what their attitude toward us should be.

The first assignment that we gave ourselves was to make a list of all those interned in Strzebielinek. Thanks to contacts made during our walks, through the Judas window[3] and through written messages left on the walkways or thrown through windows, in a little while we knew that a large group of members of the National Commission were locked up with us, as well as other Union activists from various strata of the Union membership in the Gdansk and Stupsk voivodeships. Together there were around 200 people.

We quickly came up with a few plans to avoid the rigors of prison life and to make contact with other cells, that is, to organize a life that was as free as possible. There were all kinds of ideas about how to survive and not to soften and sell out. On Tuesday we had a list of demands ready and delivered to the warden's office. No one wanted to submit to the routine of a penal institution. The first serious clash came in the evening of the second day when our guard told us to carry a stack of our neatly folded coats out of the cell. We protested. "We have not been given due process, and so we are not obligated to abide by prison rules. We demand to be informed of our status, and we demand to know the rules for the interned. Until these demands are met, we follow no rules."

The guard tried persuasion, but he got tangled up in his own arguments. On the one hand, he was our guard, on the other, he was powerless. "Gentlemen, this is how we are accustomed to doing things, it has always been this way. . . ."

The next day, the guard on duty simply posed a rhetorical question, "You are not returning your coats?" "No." He shut the door.

On the third day the Black Major, chief of the guards and warden of the institution, appeared. He stood in the doorway of the cell and a few of his men stood behind him. "Gentlemen," he said with a sweet smile, "please do not make things difficult for us. You are a very difficult cell, why all the resistance?" and he pulled a bench up to the door. We repeated our arguments, adding that surrendering our coats was an unnecessarily repressive measure. We used them to cover ourselves. It was cold and damp in our cells. The major listened with a smile on his face at first and then gradually his demeanor became more somber. He was risking his authority by carrying on this exchange in the presence of the guards. Then suddenly he refused to talk any more and interrupted our explanations, saying dryly: "Well, then. You won't put them out?" "No." "Well, then, thank you. I will remember this." And turning around, he slammed the door of the cell.

The confrontation with the major upset the cell. A heated discussion erupted on the wisdom of being stubborn in so petty a matter.

"I don't know," said J. "I personally could have given mine up. The line of my resistance is elsewhere. Coats are probably not worth the battle."

I disagreed. The battle for coats, our first victory in the camp, was psychologically significant. The incident with the major, however, had brought out the rather characteristic range of positions. Cell mates who swore "not to surrender a single button" began to waver after the warden left, slamming the door behind him, a neat move straight out of a book of guard pedagogy. Some believed that aggravating relations in this way was senseless, that, after all, it was no big deal, putting the coats out and now, you'll see, they'll show us. . . . In the end the majority decided that if the guards insisted on the coats again tomorrow, we would give them up without resistance. And in fact, the next day when the guards asked for the coats, we folded them on the bench and put them in the corridor. In the morning, our coats were returned, but they kept the bench, which was replaced with stools. We were fighting for our coats and surrendered them, and they were fighting for the bench, which made an excellent battering ram when left in the cell (as was proven in a neighboring pavilion). The affair with the coats ended.

That was just one of the fronts on which we did battle. We fought for ourselves with many much smaller actions. Many useful talents surfaced in these circumstances. It began with painting posters which we then pasted to the cell door. Most of them arose on the occasion of the anniversary of December 1970. We were also getting ready to organize a demonstration during our walk on December 16. We were supposed to stand in the middle of the courtyard and sing a hymn, "God, Protector of Poland,"[4] and the Ballad of Janek Wisniewski.[5] During the singing we were going to hold signs that read "Let no one shoot at us again," and "December 1970—we remember." Our illustrations bore religious and patriotic symbols. The Gdansk monument to dockworkers who were killed was painted on one sign. Later it turned out that similar activities had been planned by other cells without our mutual knowledge. Not knowing this, we began to call the various cells on our camp "telephone," that is, on the radiator pipe, and to tell them through the window about the arrangements. The guards probably heard our conversations and told the warden, who spoke to us that evening over the loudspeaker (called a *kolkhoznik*) and announced that all demonstrations with signs were forbidden and by force of martial law were subject to strict prison punishment. This announcement sounded rather funny in a prison cell. In the end, after talking it over with a few cells, the warden agreed to allow commemoration of the anniversary with the singing of religious songs. We did not want to stand on the square with empty hands on that day, however, so we decided to make red and white flags. This was no mean feat. At one point Janusz simply took off his sweater and then his white undershirt. We tore a fairly even rectangle out of the undershirt and colored the lower half red with the stub of a crayon that was left behind in a cabinet. We tied string to both sides of the flag so that each of our sixteen cell mates could hold it. When it was our turn to take a walk, we gathered in a circle, and opening our circle we unfurled the flag and stood in a row facing the pavilions, from which our friends watched. After a minute of silence, we sang the national anthem and the hymn "God, Protector of Poland" together with our fellow prisoners from both pavilions. The ZOMOs and guards reacted in a variety of ways. Some of them moved discreetly aside, others smoked cigarettes and did not react to the words of the anthem but simply stared at us menacingly. We felt strong, stronger with each line of those songs, and they knew it.

We spent our evenings in the cell, arranging our abode. We made a cross from slats torn from the tables. The Christ figure was made of ordinary hemp twine normally used for packages. Below we affixed a picture of the Pope. Under the cross on the wall hung our flag with a piece of black mourning ribbon attached. At eleven P.M., all the cells in both pavilions sang "All of our daily cares" through the open windows. We said an "Our Father," "Hail Mary," and "May They Rest in Peace" for those who died in December of 1970. . . .

. . . . .

Friday, March 19

There has been a lot of nervous activity in the camp for the last few days. The prisoners are removing the rest of the dried grass, a volleyball court is being prepared, and the day before yesterday, there was a search in camp for stools which were in need of repair. Finally it all became clear: a two-man delegation from the International Red Cross in Switzerland appeared. First the authorities "worked over" the members of the delegation for a few hours, and later, they unexpectedly opened our cells and encouraged us to leave them. We decided that since we had been sitting locked up in our cells up to that time, we would not take advantage of the authorities' "benevolence" now either. We all knew that the Red Cross delegation was in the camp, and that the prison authorities were trying to implement one of our first demands: open cells. The warden even tried to convince us to go out into the corridors of the pavilion, where we were supposed to meet with the Red Cross delegation and the representatives of the Ministry of Justice and the Polish Red Cross. The tension was broken by the arrival of the Swiss.

One of them, a doctor who spoke fair Polish, said that he understood what was going on but that they would like to invite us to meet with them, nevertheless. Then they came into our cells together with their Polish companions and began noting the various problems and inadequacies. There were a lot. They noticed our threadbare, dirty blankets; the tattered floor coverings; the primitive furnishings; the mold on the walls and ceiling; and the water standing in the bathroom. They were interested in the number of people in each cell, and even in the layout of the beds. They also wrote detailed reports about the health of internees and about the sanitary conditions in a few of the cells. These were also the subjects discussed at meetings with cell delegates and during individual conversations with internees. One of the doctors became interested in the matter of drinking water, about which we complained and which was located next to the camp pigsties. In the front part of a small building was a one-car garage and in the back of it was a pigsty from which manure was tossed right next door. Major Kaczmarek wanted to cover up the whole matter, but after we mentioned possible contamination of the water supply, the doctor in the company of our colleague-translator went to take a look at the building. Straight out of the pigsty ran a nice-sized rat. In the pigsty and in the cracks of the cement gutters that passed right through the center of camp, the rats had found conditions in which they could thrive.

During our talks with the Swiss, we found out that the Red Cross considers us to be political prisoners, similar to those in seventy other countries in the world. Our status is rather strange, however, in that the Hague Convention, dating from the beginning of the twentieth century, stipulates the rights of the interned only for people interned on foreign soil and not as citizens of a given country. That is why the Red Cross must count on the goodwill of the Polish authorities in its contacts with internees. This limits what they can do. Their main goal is to visit the internees and to propose the release of the most gravely ill. They are also supposed to help establish decent conditions for us in prison and to help our families, who find themselves in extremely difficult circumstances. The Red Cross delegation that came to Poland also tried to gain access to those arrested and sentenced "for continuing Union activity." The Red Cross also considers those people to be political prisoners. Unfortunately, the Red Cross has been unsuccessful in its attempts to meet with this group. The authorities will simply not allow it. The Red Cross is also getting no help from the authorities in determining the number of internees. They have received no list of names, locations of internment camps, nor, of course, any list of those dismissed from work for Union activity. The Red Cross must get all of its information from private sources, or by individual questioning of families, internees, or Church representatives. As of now they have visited one-third of the twenty-four camps still functioning. The problems are similar in all of them, even though the living conditions may vary. They assured us that they will remain interested in our fate and promised to return to camp in a few weeks if we were not released. Each transfer would be noted in a special file, so that we would not disappear somewhere. They did not, however, want to say too much about the conditions in the other camps, nor did they want to talk about Lech—about whom we inquired on several occasions—because they received permission to visit the camps only on the condition that they would not pass on any of this kind of information, and that all of their notes, outside of their personal and medical notations, could be checked. In spite of this, they were asked by internees in a few of the cells to mail letters and literary work to the West.

A few colleagues took advantage of the presence of representatives of the Ministry of Justice to get some legal advice regarding their detention and the ways of invalidating the internment decision. The only useful information we got out of these conversations was the representative's "private" statement that the way to invalidate the internment decision was to have the matter brought up by a lawyer, who must demand access to the charges. In that case the institution which interns someone must justify its decision. This reverses the method of action used up to now. It is not we who must then explain our innocence, but the police commander who is obligated to prove our "guilt." This is, however, the logic of a dreamer who believes in the fiction that the law is still functioning. So far, all the lawyers who have tried to apply this reasoning have had no luck, as they never gain access to charges. Only the phrase that the "reasons for internment have not been nullified" is being upheld.

During the Red Cross visit twenty-four persons expressed the desire to leave Poland permanently. Other information revealed that four people lost their jobs during internment, and that, in camp, there are two secondary-school students, five students from the Politechnic in Gdansk, one student from the University of Gdansk, as well as people from all professions excepting the medical.

A soon as the delegation left camp, yesterday and today, we were immediately locked up in our cells. The prison authorities would not allow the Swiss to spend the night in our cells. . . .

. . . . .

Thursday, April 15

Today they gave "passes" to freedom! Usually for a few days, but in some cases up to the maximum, one week, after "consideration" of a particular case. These passes were immediately taken by some of our colleagues, who had either serious family problems or matters that needed attention, i.e., health problems. Others took advantage of the passes to get away from here for a few days. The news that such possibilities exist was told to us by Major Kaczmarek two days ago. Not too many people know about it, however, because some of us disagree as to what the request for a pass means. One has to write a request for a pass in order to get one.

The passes were issued by the acting commander of the voivodeship. People say that this man, Colonel Paszkiewicz, will become the next commander in the near future. Paszkiewicz received people in a room where a psychologist had been installed not too long ago. The psychologist was accompanied by a dark, intelligent *ubek,* who during his talks (done individually) with internees, would shuffle through dossiers and hand his boss the more important material. Both of them were very nice and emphasized that they were not treating the internee simply as a camp number. They took into account the internee's background, his education, and professional status before internment and they did not avoid the courteous forms of address such as "Mr. Engineer" and the like. Real courtesy . . . they were interested in camp conditions and fretted over the mistakes made during the mass arrests on December 12/13, assuring us that if they had to repeat this operation on such a massive scale, which they hoped, for our sake and theirs, would not happen, then they would try to carry it out even more efficiently and without those little mistakes. They emphasized that there was not a single life lost that night on the coast in spite of the scale of the operation, and that they personally were very happy about that. They warned the internees who had gotten passes that, contrary to the practice in camp, no one was allowed to wear Solidarity or any other union pins outside the camp gates, and that commemorative ceremonies marking anniversaries of the workers' strikes were also banned, or one "could have trouble," including a sentence and prison term.

We said good-bye to our colleagues who left with passes. Some of us feel that this type of contact with representatives of the organs of repression is a manifestation of weakness and an indirect acceptance of martial law. Others feel that freedom is freedom and that there is always more to do outside of the walls than there is sitting here. What the *ubeks* think about the matter is unimportant.

I personally feel that perhaps it would be best if we demurred on the passes, but each man carries within himself the consciousness of his own limits which he cannot overstep, so that personal motives may justify applying for a pass.

ROMANIA

The Silent Escape: Three Thousand Days in Romanian Prisons
Lena Constante

LENA CONSTANTE (1909–), an artist, was "the only woman political prisoner to have endured eight years of solitary confinement in Romanian prisons." Her total sentence was "twelve years of hard labor for the crime of high treason, [and] ten for counterrevolutionary activity." She was accused of spying in connection with her work at the Institute of Folklore, which had many foreign visitors with whom she often met. The charges against her were also based on her association as an artist (painter) with the wife (a set designer) of a Romanian Communist Party leader (secretary of the Politburo) and minister of justice, Lucretiu

From Lena Constante, The Silent Escape: Three Thousand Days in Romanian Prisons *(Berkeley, CA: University of California Press, 1995)*, © 1995 by The Regents of the University of California. *Reprinted by permission.*

Patrascanu, who became the major defendant in the Romanian show trials after World War II. Constante and Mrs. Patrascanu jointly created a marionette theater in Bucharest and worked together for four years; under the circumstances, this friendship sealed Constante's fate. She served a total of twelve years and was released in 1961. She was rehabilitated in 1968 when the authorities admitted that the charges against her were totally unfounded.

Constante and the other defendants were detained and prepared for the 1954 trial for a period of five years. Patrascanu was sentenced to death and executed; other defendants were given long prison sentences. The trial was one in a series of East European show trials that took place between 1948 and 1954 at Soviet instigation, and they closely resembled the Soviet show trials of the 1930s. In these trials the main defendants were often Communist leaders popular in their own countries (as Patrascanu was), unlike the so-called "Moscovites" who returned to Eastern Europe from Soviet exile with the occupying Soviet troops and whose loyalty to and dependence on the Soviet authorities was total. These trials, generally speaking, served three purposes: (1) to eliminate local Communist leaders whose loyalty to Moscow might not have been unconditional; (2) to provide illustrations of the evils of "Titoism" (that is to say, a national communism not subordinated to Soviet interests and dictates); and (3) to consolidate Communist power in the countries concerned.

The Soviet campaign against "Titoism" or national communism erupted in 1948 following Yugoslavia's declaration of independence from Moscow. Until Stalin's death the Soviet Union did everything short of armed intervention to subvert and discredit Tito's Yugoslavia and its independent course. (In turn, Yugoslavia dealt harshly with supporters of the Soviet Union, as indicated in the Venko Markowski excerpt included in this volume.)

The following selection illustrates the varieties of mistreatment victims of these trials in Romania faced, the major and minor deprivations of prison life, and the totally contrived, staged quality of judicial proceedings.

· · · · ·

I have been sentenced to twelve years in prison. The trial lasted six days. The preliminary investigation, five years. So I've already served five years. Alone. In a cell not quite fifty-four square feet. For 1,827 days. Alone. For 43,848 hours. In a cell where each hour inexorably had sixty minutes, each minute sixty seconds. One, two, three, four, five seconds. Six, seven, eight, nine, ten seconds, a thousand seconds, a hundred thousand seconds. I have lived, alone, in a cell, 157,852,800 seconds of solitude and fear. Cause for screaming! They sentence me to live yet another 220,838,400 seconds! To live them or to die from them.

During the final days of the investigation, they had raised my hopes of being released once the trial was over. Little by little I'd come to believe them.

The shock at these seven additional years of detention shatters my brain.... I feel nothing. For two or three days, perhaps even four, I lie on my straw-filled mattress. Unconscious.

Each day, midday and evening, they bring me a bowl of blackish liquid and a thin slice of bread. I cannot swallow them. I don't even see them. My eyes are closed. Behind my eyelids, all is black. I don't feel my arms. I don't feel my legs. I am coming apart.

About four o'clock in the morning they make me leave my cell. It is April 15, 1954, of that I am certain. They order me to sign a document. I sign it. I don't know what it is I am signing. A sheet of white paper covers the words.

They push me outside. I am still wearing my prison glasses. The lenses are an opaque black. I feel the air. It is cold. They are still pushing me ... making me go up two steps.... They make me get into a police car.

I leave behind five years of detention. In those five years, they have made me change prisons four times. In each of these prisons, several changes of cell....

. . . . .

Interrogation. A militiaman has me sit in front of a small table. Across from me, a large desk. A man is there. Bull-necked. He asks me several questions. I don't know the answers. He speaks with a foreign accent. I don't know the people he's talking about. I tell him so. He accuses me of lying. Suggests in an authoritative tone that I confess everything. Confess ... what?

I thought I was in luck. Knowing nothing, I could give nothing away. I'd never heard some of the names he was talking about. He also mentioned a few names I did know, but they were those of my best friends. All estimable and respected. This was no problem for me, and I could in all sincerity answer "no." I was extremely surprised to see he didn't believe me. He persisted. Urged me to tell the truth. This went on for quite some time. Then he got angry. Shouted. Claimed he had proof that my denials were false. I become frightened. He seems sure of himself. He says it is for my own good that he is wasting his time persuading me to confess. He gives me time to think. All the time I need. I am overcome with fear.

One interrogation follows another. Several days go by in this unequal contest. His tone grows more and more menacing. I have only a jumbled memory of all this. I have all but forgotten the cell, the stairs, the office. I wouldn't recognize this man now. My memory has clung only to the sensation of my fear.

I was no longer a person. I was nothing. My truth was no longer the truth. My truth was not their truth. But what *was* their truth? It took me a long time to grasp it.

Every interrogator has the right, within limits, to use certain gambits. I knew this. The tactics may include gaining the accused person's trust, misleading him, even threatening him. Hope and fear are the interrogator's weapons. He can thus put them to use. Within limits. To go beyond these limits is inhuman. To go from threats to torture is inhuman. To strike a person's flesh is criminal.

In those first days of interrogation, I didn't doubt the investigator's good faith. I took his questions to be sincere. Honest questions, from his point of view. A correct attitude, from his profession's point of view. Back in my cell, I racked my brains. What arguments could I come up with to persuade him? To show him his mistake. I really had nothing to tell him. Not about myself nor about the others.

My denials are fruitless. All they do is infuriate him. He studies me with eyes filled with hate. The eyes of a madman. I am beginning to doubt myself. Have I lost my mind? My fear is compounded by a new torture.

The guards hustle me into the office several times a day. At any hour. Even in the middle of the night. The stairs, the interrogator, the questions, the threats, the fear.

He embellishes his sadism with words designed to trap me. He speaks of duty, mission, the public good. It is easy to trip over these words. To be skinned alive by them. Shed blood, or even die from them. For him, anything goes. For him, everything is permissible. To impose "his" truth becomes his singular goal. For this madman, the law doesn't exist, because he is the law. And he is justice, too. And vengeance. He is God.

After a few days, he punishes me.

As usual, after the wake-up call, the guard opens the door and takes me to the toilet. In the corridor, a small sink, a sliver of soap, a dirty hand towel, a grimy comb with broken-off teeth, full of hair. This is where I wash my hands and face. I feel soiled.

The guard always has me follow him. This time, he doesn't take me back to my cell. He stops where the corridor makes a right angle, and he opens a door, motioning me inside. He shuts the door. The key turns. It's just a cubicle, three by six feet. The steeply pitched ceiling comes down to about three feet above the floor. There is only a square yard of floor space where it's possible to stand up straight. A cement floor. In the far wall is an opening to the outside. About a foot high and two feet wide. This dormer window is boarded over. I can't see it, but I feel it with my hands. The guard slides open the tiny judas window. Warns me that I am forbidden to sit on the floor. I must remain standing.

It is January. Our winters are severe. The cubicle is unheated. Through the chinks come gusts of wind, icy blasts. I am wearing only a thin pleated skirt, a blouse, and woolen jacket. I'm cold. I cross my arms over my chest. Press my legs together. I'm cold. I don't have room to walk. I can take only one step. When I attempt another, I bang my head on the sloping roof. I do some exercises. This is even worse. My whole body is freezing. I manage to loop my skirt between my legs, draw it up in front, and tuck it into my waistband.

I grow colder and colder. My teeth start chattering. Every so often the judas opens. The guard looks at me. Around noon, I guess, he cracks the door and hands me a thin slice of bread.

For those first few hours I suffer only from the cold. Suddenly I feel tired. I have been standing for hours. Almost without moving, for want of space. Leaning now against one wall, now against the other. My feet ache. My ankles swell. I am dreadfully cold. I am chilled to the bone. Tired. I am tired. I am tired unto death. I begin to mumble: I'm tired to death . . . tired . . . tired . . . so tired. To forget the feeling, I concentrate on the idea of tiredness. This litany lulls me to sleep. I manage to sleep a few seconds. Standing up. Without swaying. A fist raps on the door. Jolts me awake.

I don't know how many hours I've been here. I don't know whether it's night or day. That first evening, in the corridor, I'd seen a telephone on the head guard's table. It rings at all hours of the day and night. It's the summons to the interrogation room. Then one of the seventeen cells opens. Muffled footsteps pass in the corridor. Go up the stairs . . . I abhor this telephone. Out of a dread of the interrogation room. As soon as I hear its shrillness, I cease feeling cold or fatigue or sleepiness. Nothing. I wait anxiously for the guard's footsteps. I feel only my fear.

Words take time. They can't tell it all at once. How can this anxiety be expressed? I would need a single word. A word that creates a synthesis. A crushing blow of a word. A thunderclap word. A blood-soaked word. Shrieked from a throat choking with anxiety. The waiting in the hollow of my stomach. My heart squeezed by horror. The dread that tugs in my chest, high up, a place, a point on the left, where usually there is nothing. My heart. A flesh word. A blood word. This word does not exist.

So many words that so far say nothing. How can I express the despair? The revolt? The physical pain in my heart? The pain obliterates everything. Nothing further goes on in my mind. Nothing in that strange place that I find hard to locate. High up. No. In back of my eyes. Higher yet. So much higher it is almost outside this other disgusting self, my body. No. Nothing in the head. Everything happens only in that lump of insentient flesh, mute and as a rule nonexistent. Suddenly in the hurt, the pain, the fear, I feel assailed by my heart. I knew it was there. Theoretically. Now it is all that exists. It hurts. To the point of wanting to scream. And my belly and my bowels clench, clench harder, and harder yet, without stopping. . . .

. . . toward me? No. A door opens. Not mine. Again I am cold. So, so cold. I shiver. My teeth chatter. With a little noise. Pathetic. I am pathetic. Dirty, bristly, trembling from head to toe, hungry. Locked up in a cage, outside the law, outside time, I was truly pathetic. With such need for someone's, anyone's, pity. But I was alone, alone, all alone.

Nonetheless, I was the center of the world. This world existed all around me, *for* me, only because I was becoming aware of it. Accepting it, wasn't it I who made it real? To accept its reality was to accept my suffering. I had to disown it in order to live. To destroy it in order to survive it. In this dungeon of a cell for unending hours I became aware of my duality. I was two. For I was here and I saw myself here. I was two. For I couldn't go through this bolted door and yet I could be elsewhere.

The interrogator had ordered me to reflect and remember what I feigned— he said—not to know. On the contrary, I had to forget, forget everything, starting with him. No longer would I hear the click of the judas. Nor see the guard's eye. Nor "realize" the cold. Nor feel the hunger. I had to escape. Flee. Unable to get to the other side of the wall, escape from myself. To leave this body, now only a torment, behind. This miserable, hungry flesh. Repudiate my body's "me." No longer endure its pain. Nor tremble with its fear. My body could only be here. Me, I could be elsewhere. My body didn't have space to move its aching feet. But, *I* would grow wings. The wings of a bird. The wings of the wind. The wings of a star. And I would get away.

This was the beginning of a long apprenticeship. Escape is no easy thing. Only gradually did I succeed in learning. By going through distinct stages.

I couldn't bear the fatigue any longer. I allowed myself to slide along the wall. I flexed my knees. I hunkered down, crouched into a ball. I faintly hear the sound of the judas. It opened. It closed. The guard said nothing. He went away. Crouched on the floor, curled over with my forehead against my knees, my arms hugging my legs, I fall asleep. Like a dog. Worse than a dog. A dog can drag itself off in search of shelter. Be lucky enough to find a garbage can. Get a crust of bread, a bone. Dogs are to be envied. Humans pitied.

I am awakened by the cold. The cement floor is ice. I laboriously stand up. I rub on the cement with my right sole. Fatigue. I shift from one foot to the other. I warm my place. Again I crouch down. From time to time, I repeat the routine.

A knock at the door. "Get up!" I get up. It's the next morning. A guard takes me to the toilet. There it is warm. The wooden seat is warm. I would like to stay there. Sitting. Not leave. He raps on the door. Back to the cell. Through the half-opened door, someone hands me a thin slice of bread. A bowl of water.

The telephone. . . . This time it is for me. The office again. The hangman. And he asks me if I have done some reflecting. I can't answer. My teeth are chattering. I can't stop them from chattering. I can't stop trembling. A guard brings me a cup of tea. He orders me to drink it. I raise the cup. My hands are shaking. Drops fall on the table at which he has me sitting. I finally manage to get the tea down. It has warmed me up a little. Not much, but I have stopped trembling.

He speaks. Of his rights. Of his power. Of the force he represents. Of his own patience. Of the infinite patience of this force. He says that everything depends on me. On my good will. On my sincerity. He knows about my "criminal" doings. All my offenses are known to him. They've got hold of all the proof. They can convict me and sentence me. If I persist in my denials, I will be judged and sentenced along with the other defendants. Sentenced to death. If, however, I agreed to help them by telling the whole "truth" about the others accused, he would release me from prison. He cannot free me right away but he promises me excellent living conditions. They would satisfy all my desires. They would provide me with a house, clothing, food, books. Until the trial. Witness for the prosecution. I would be a witness for the prosecution. Then, freedom. The choice was mine. Either the overlooking of my crimes, or my death. He gives me more time to think. And space. The cell. . . .

· · · · ·

Shivering from the cold, I weighed another possibility. Perhaps he had received a false denunciation about me. Even so, what should his attitude have been? To make inquiries. To discover the truth by asking precise questions. No. This investigation had been faked. Leaving the limits of any law out of consideration.

The truth, he had only to create it. His aim was to create a wholly different truth. How? Through the force of words. For words can say something or they can say its opposite. Join or separate. Express or conceal. Create or destroy. Words can deceive. Betray. Kill. Words can do anything.

At noon, the guard gives me a little hot liquid and a slice of bread. The heat from this make-believe soup, from this doubtful-tasting water, is pleasant. Friendly.

The minutes continue to creep by. Heavy, ice-cold. Now and then the phone rings. I hear steps. Muffled voices reach me through the door. The judas opens. The judas shuts. Prison life.

I am sleepy. I even manage to fall back asleep. Standing. Struck down by fatigue. Mainly, however, I make an effort to think logically. To dispel the fog that takes possession of my mind. To reflect. To understand.

Witness for the prosecution . . . witness for the prosecution. . . .

These were frightening words, and I was mortally frightened by them. In plain language this meant accusing one or all of the other defendants. Accuse them how? Accuse them of what? Why accuse them?

But who were these accused? All I was sure of was three arrests. Had they arrested still others? How could I manage to convince this man that I knew nothing incriminating about anyone? For I was still giving him the benefit of the doubt.

What must I do? Or say? It is possible to provide evidence of a perpetrated act. But what evidence is left by an act never done, never even contemplated?

Only four-and-a-half years later, at the first session of the trial in court and hence after about 1,650 days, did I see that there were eleven of us defendants. Only then did I also learn what we were accused of. Of the eleven defendants, I knew only four. The six others were completely unknown to me. Five men and a woman.

One of the four was my best friend, Harry Brauner. We were married after leaving prison. I knew his life, all the way back to childhood. Almost twenty years. I knew he was as innocent as I was.

The second, H. Torosian, had become close to the Party toward the end of the war. Out of friendship for Lucretiu Patrascanu. To combat fascism. He had made many sacrifices. Risking his life.

The third, Herbert Zilber, a longtime member of the Party, had never prompted any great fondness in me, but I admired his intelligence. In my youth I had a mania for intelligence. The snobbery of intellectuals. I prized them above all. I have recovered from that since then.

Patrascanu, the number-one defendant at the trial, was one of the most important members in the Party. Secretary of the Political Bureau. I had worked with his wife for four years. Both of them had been Party members since they were young. For a long time illegally. Both she and I had worked hard to launch a marionette theater. The first in our country. She was a set designer; I, a painter; my companion, a musician. He had helped us. The three of us were together most of the time. During the weekends and vacations, it was all four of us. I had admiration, respect, and great affection for this man. I saw the Party only through his eyes. I knew about the underground work he had done to get the country out of the war against the Soviet Union before it was too late. The important role he had played in the first months of the change of alliance and regime. I knew that since then he had had more and more ideological problems with other Party members. That he had been gradually shouldered aside. I knew that his intellectual lineage was doing him harm. Even more harmful was the trust he had inspired in a whole people. Or nearly. He was the sole person to be received anywhere in the country with unequivocal good will.

I knew something of his views. I guessed that he disagreed with certain of the Party's decisions. Overhasty. That he wanted a pluralist government for these early postwar years, which were made harder yet by the country's partial destruction and Hitler's pillaging, and appreciably worsened by the huge war reparations demanded by the Soviet Union. He did not approve of the excessive purges or the unbridled acts of revenge. It was a long way from this to believing him a traitor to his Party and his country, and I could not believe it. At the interrogator's request, however, I was supposed to accuse him. Me. Why? Simply because this man was asking me to?

But who was this man? What did he represent? Despite my lack of political experience, I could answer this question. We were no longer a free country. I knew on whose behalf he was acting.

This is now clear to everyone. We had been only marionettes in the classic government trials. Didn't every country in Eastern Europe have one of its own?

· · · · ·

By the end of the investigation, I had reached some understanding of this technique. Moreover, before my arrest I had read a book, Arthur Koestler's *Darkness at Noon*. This was in fact one of the interrogator's complaints. I had committed the capital offense of reading a book. That book. This view has had its precedents in the course of history.

Once I was freed, I read Arthur London's *The Confession*. A book about a trial. About a technique. Only then did I finally grasp what was puzzling me. Everything had been the same. Down to the tiniest details. No new stroke of imagination. No attempt at modification. A lesson well learned and recited by heart. . . .

· · · · ·

Bit by bit, the silence weighing down on the prison became palpably oppressive. Yet it was time for the wake-up. This total silence hung over me like a threat. I would no longer risk pausing too often. The danger was there. My whole body sensed it. What was the explanation for this silence? Now and then I looked up at a small window set high in one of the walls of this cellar. It was as black as the silence. As black as my heart. As black as my fear. My anxiety was becoming more pronounced. What was the explanation for this silence? Had everyone left? Were they all dead? But the guard at the judas was very much alive. I waited for the first glimmer of early light in the window. Intently. So I reckoned the approximate time from my to-and-fros. Giving each step a second, I took twenty seconds to make a round trip. Sixty seconds, that is to say a minute, for three full trips. In the end, 180 trips an hour.

I made these 180 treks with a few pauses for rest, and the silence still reigned. The window was black as ever. Daylight was still far off and I finally understood that I had been allowed only two hours' sleep. No more than two hours.

Thus they coerced me into doing three periods of walking a day. Twenty-four hours divided by three. Each of these eight-hour segments involved six hours of walking and two for rest. I had begun at eight in the morning. First rest from two to four in the afternoon. Second period from four in the afternoon to ten at night. Rest for two hours. Midnight. He had woken me up at midnight. At night. In the silence, in this concentration-camp space, nothing but me. Me and the guard.

I was sleepy. A need for sleep. A vital need for sleep. Passing by the faucet, which I had left turned on slightly, I refreshed my eyes with a few drops of water that I'd catch as I walked.

I walked, asking myself: why? Why not stop? Why not dare to stretch out on the bed? Why not fall asleep?

Drunk with sleep, stumbling with each step, I finally sat on the edge of the bed. Perhaps I forgot to count to eight, perhaps I passed out. . . .

The guard bursts into the room, club in hand. He rushes over to me—I'm already on my feet—and he begins hammering with his club on my ankles and calves, shouting: "Walk, you piece of shit, or I'll break your legs! Walk, unless you want to go home as an official notification!"

Under these brutish blows, my muscles tense up, my whole body rebels. As though jerked by an electrical discharge, my feet hurriedly resume the pace.

It was nighttime. He has nothing to do. Perhaps he too is sleepy. He has found a way to take his mind off sleep. Seated on a chair, his stick in his hand, he intently watches me make the transit, laughing at the jumps I make to evade him. He pounds hard. On my anklebones, on my calves, but no higher than my knees. I cannot hold back my tears. They run down my face. Mingle with the mucus streaming from my nostrils.

This guard was young. He couldn't be over twenty. But he was short. He was ugly. They had made him a jailer. Given him a club. And the right to use it. Good wages. A privileged situation. All this didn't fit him very well.

He finally began yawning. He stretched out on the bed, still watching me. But at last he closed his eyes. The club slipped to the floor. He began snoring. I went to the faucet. I drank a little water. I washed my face. The pain was bearable. Close enough to him to be able to make sure that his eyes were closed, I remained motionless for some time. Struggling against the fascination of the club and his head. . . .

Several days go by. All alike. Each day the doctor gives me an injection. To strengthen me? To weaken me? I shall never know. He gives me a piece of sugar before injecting me.

I'm afraid of their threats. I'm afraid to stop. I'm afraid. What new punishment will they invent to punish some possible resistance? Soon. . . .

It is after eight in the morning. I have just begun the walking period. A guard comes in. He looks furious. He swears at me. He is going to be punished because of me, because of his lack of vigilance. I too will be punished. Just wait.

Ten minutes later, three guards come in followed by the boss. Tell me to take off my shoes. Get on my knees on the bed. Not along the bed. Crosswise. My feet hanging over the side. My face to the wall. I take off my shoes. I kneel. I can't see them. My heart is pounding. From fear. Behind me they are hatching a plan. Against me. They're going to do something to me. What are they going to do?

I hear some cloth crumple. A metallic sound. The boss's voice. Don't I cry out. He has told me not to cry out. Are they going to beat me again? I don't understand. I hear some noises. Cutting the air. One snap, two, three. Pain. Pain.

One of the guards is whipping me. The soles of my feet. With all his might. With his leather belt. His heavy leather belt. With its heavy metal buckle. With his belt he whips the soles of my feet. Shocks of pain. Waves of pain. My body writhes. The other two guards grip my shoulders. One on the right. The other, the left. They hold me with all their strength. It's over.

They have me sit on the bed. I can now see them. All four of them. See one of them rebuckling his belt. With the metal buckle. See his sweaty face. Red. His drunken face. Hear his rapid breathing. The guards leave. The boss speaks:

I must obey. He had ordered me to walk without stopping. I had stopped. He had warned me that any pause would be punished. I was punished. They are stronger than I. They know everything. They can do anything. I must resume walking. How long this walk will last will depend on me. They do not know the word pity. I should decide once and for all to confess everything. So as to end the agony. To remain peacefully in a cell. Lying on a bed. Like the others. At last, I resume walking. "Like the others?" The little cell was now occupied by Harry.

I got up. I resumed walking. Without even trying to put on my shoes. I was in too much pain. The soles of my feet were too swollen. The blows had caused me searing pains. Now the pain stretched out in time. I was in pain all the time. I was in pain every second. How can I describe the pain? The soles of my feet developed large blisters filled with water. Like those left by a burn. But I still had to walk on them. I tried walking on my heels. To walk on the sides of my feet. Nothing worked. I was in pain . . . .

I couldn't see the prison. They always made me go through the corridors wearing opaque black-lensed glasses. A guard gripped my arm, nudging me right or left. Toward the offices, toward the cell.

The cell was about forty square feet. Filthy walls covered with graffiti. Some half erased, others still legible. Sometimes moving words. Attempts at a calendar. An iron cot, a straw mattress, a clean sheet, a coarse homespun blanket. A table, a chair. No window, a dim bulb diffusing a yellowish light through the room day and night. This light, combined with the pale reflection of the daylight coming through a square aperture above the door, gave me a vague nausea.

The surveillance was permanent and complete. For the whole year I spent there, for all those four hundred days and four hundred nights, the iron flap of the peephole in the door silently slid to the right. Every two minutes, an eye filled the round hole. The eye looked at me. Every two minutes. Then the shutter abruptly slid back with a metallic click. Every two minutes. Continually. For four hundred days and four hundred nights. For 576,000 minutes I was subjected to this assault and this clicking about 288,000 times.

The regulations affixed to the wall were peremptory.

It was forbidden, under threat of punishment, to remain in bed after five o'clock in the morning.

It was forbidden, under threat of punishment, not to be in bed after ten o'clock at night.

It was forbidden to sit on the bed between five in the morning and ten at night.

In bed, it was forbidden to have one's hands underneath the blanket.

If, while sleeping, I was bothered by the cold and covered my arms and hands, a rap on the door woke me up with a start.

It was forbidden to sleep during the day.

It was forbidden to cry.

It was forbidden to shout.

It was forbidden to laugh.

It was forbidden to sing. On threat of punishment.

It was not forbidden to sit on the chair.

It was not forbidden to stand. It was not forbidden to walk in the cell.

I had lost a great deal of weight. I was tired. My feet hurt. Because I was unable to remain stretched out in bed, the chair produced sores in a few days. Painful sores. When they hurt too much, I was obliged to stand up and walk around in the cell. I took four steps up to the wall, made a U-turn, four steps to the door, U-turn, the peephole would open, four steps to the wall, the peephole would close, U-turn, door-wall, door-wall, four steps, four steps, peephole, door-wall, wall, wall.

The interrogation resumed with another interrogator. Young, handsome, self-important, cruel. His was a hard job. Without explicitly asking me to lie, he had to get me to state that I had been a spy. To do this, he skillfully supplied me with information. It concerned actions supposedly committed by me and denounced by the other defendants. All this was false. I grasped his tactics. His strategy. Pushed over the edge by threats, by punishment, by fear and suffering, I was to accuse myself. By taking in his information, I was to build the scaffold of a credible guilt. A fierce, unevenly matched struggle between the two of us.

At the time, the interrogator was the absolute master of the person accused. To achieve his collaboration, to force him to "recall" or forget, make up, to lie, to frighten him or give him hope, finally to punish him, the interrogator could order whatever changes he pleased in the regimen. First of all in diet, of course. For the better, for the worse, or to the limit of survival. My first punishment was hunger. This punishment went on for four hundred days. I was hungry for four hundred days. A nagging hunger. Degrading. Bestial. A hunger that twisted my stomach. Piercing my belly with cramps. Flooding my face with tears.

I was given three cups of water a day. In the morning, the first cup was the only thing for breakfast. At midday, the second cup came with the single dish for lunch. On an enameled iron plate, two or three mouthfuls of meat surrounded by a little questionable liquid. Sometimes, the meat was replaced by some quarters of potatoes, seven or eight prunes, or three spoonfuls of noodles or polenta. I was also given a small slice of dark bread, wet and indigestible. At six o'clock, the same meal and a third cup of water. Between the evening meal and the next midday meal, nothing. Eighteen hours of starvation. It was forbidden to keep even a crust of bread to stave off one's hunger during these hours. Aromas of a roast of meat, cheese, and coffee wafted through the door. Exacerbating the hunger. For there were "rich" diets for those who had managed to satisfy their interrogators.

I was tormented by hunger day and night. Only in dreams did I get some feeling of satiety. After the dream of going home, the dream of food is the second kind of dream of the prison cell. Mainly I dreamed of eating cakes. The sugar of which I was totally deprived and my mouth kept the memory of it on awakening.

In the morning I barely moistened my lips in the first cup of water. I sacrificed my thirst to an even more pressing, more imperative need. To create the illusion of cleanliness. By pouring out this water drop by drop, I moistened a bit of rag. Each week I received a little piece of laundry soap. With the wet rag moistened with the black, evil-smelling soap, I rubbed the whole of my body as best as I could. Hiding myself in the blind spot of the cell, to the left of the door.

The wait for the interrogation session evoked a permanent fear. The guards walk with furtive steps. The steps of a spy. But the steps of those who fetch you for the interrogation make noise. I hear them resonating from a distance. The sound approaches. Holding my breath, I listen for the sound of each step. I count them. The steps come closer and closer. Fear grips my throat. My heart stops. Ever closer. I am bathed in sweat.

Sometimes, the steps halt in front of one of the cells ahead of mine. Other times they continue to approach. My cell is the next to last along the corridor. One more step, yet another, closer, ever closer. I am just a mass of tense flesh. Of flesh oozing fear. They arrive. They are in front of my door. They go past my door. They go off. The corridor makes two turns, for there is a second row of cells after this one. My corridor leads to the courtyard, the other to the street. My body releases. Comes apart at the joints. My neck droops. My shoulders slump. I feel my arms fall to the floor. My sweat turns cold. My heart goes back to beating normally. Slowly everything goes back into place. Slowly I re-create myself. Not for long. The prison is packed. No leisure. Quite the contrary. Industriousness, much industriousness. And everything begins all over again.

It was the sour odor of these accumulated layers of sweat that I wanted to clean off with this now-gray rag. The sour odor of my sweat. The disgusting odor of my fear.

Sometimes, however, the footsteps don't go past my cell. The intervals between two interrogations are irregular. A few hours, a few days, weeks, months. The time of day? Never the same. Morning, evening, night. The key goes into the lock. The key turns. Turns in my bowels. The latch in the door goes down. The door opens. A hand presents me with the glasses. I put them on. I stretch the elastic around my head. I can't see anything. The hand grabs my arm. Hauls me out of the cell. Away from my shelter. Away from my safety. To the offices. To the interrogator. To terror.

An interrogation session could last five minutes or it could last an hour, or much more. I managed to conceal my fear. I could make my face a mask. Control my voice. I could even make my eyes vacant. But I couldn't keep the sweat from oozing from my armpits. I couldn't keep it from making rivulets that ran down my arms. In the crook of my elbow. Nor the palms of my hands from collecting the sweat from my armpits. And with its nauseating odor.

Only once a week could I take a shower. Quickly. Just enough time to get wet. To soap up. Fast. To have time to rinse, for suddenly the water was shut off. During this time the door was left ajar. A guard stood there. Always. I pretended not to see him. Still, certain gestures were hard to make in front of this voyeur. When I didn't have time to rinse away the remaining soap from my body, I wiped it off with one of the wet sheets lying on the floor. I was not the first to use it.

Every morning, after wake-up call, I was taken to the toilet. I suffered from constipation. Because of the lack of food. The food ingested was utterly insufficient. My digestive system held on to it as long as possible. Squeezing it. Evacuating only the completely indigestible bits. The evacuation of these nuggets, small hard black rocks, was slow and difficult. It sometimes happened that I was unable to do so for ten days in a row. Moreover, I didn't even have time for it. After a few seconds, the guard urged me, shouting, to leave.

The anteroom of the toilet had a small sink for washing up. Still in a rush, I washed my hands and face, but didn't always manage to rinse out my rag. A sackcloth towel hung from a nail. A single towel for the whole prison. Over fifty cells.

Soon I had pimples filled with pus on my forehead. Then all over my face. I couldn't see them. There wasn't a single mirror in the prison. But I could scratch them. My fingers always came back to them. I couldn't keep from touching them. They spread to my shoulders. Then my arms became covered with them. The interrogator used them as an occasion for obscene sarcasm.

The pimples made me even more depressed. I couldn't stop squeezing them with my fingernails to lance them of their pus. This became a habit. A kind of morbid source of relish. And each time I was demoralized by it.

I was forbidden to retire before ten at night. When an old rusty gong sounded down the corridor. For a long while I was kept awake by the anxiety, hunger, and physical pain. The straw in the mattress was brittle and full of twigs. I was scrawny. Lying on my back, the sores on my buttocks hurt. Lying on my side, my hips began to hurt.

The endless murky glow of the light bulb continued to nauseate me. The mournful stillness weighing on the prison at night oppressed me from all sides. From time to time a train went by on the edge of town. Its whistle, piercing the night, made sleep impossible. Made nostalgia more poignant.

There were also the crickets. Usually, they were small and black. They could be heard chirping in the corridor, in the cell. Under the bed. The monotonous chirping tickled my brain. Lent a dull voice to the silence of the prison night.

I still remember the monster cricket with the same dread. It was loathsome. A huge green and yellow bug clinging to the wall. As repulsive as vomit. The time was around 4:30 in the afternoon. Suddenly I see it near me, on the wall. It is an outgrowth of the prison. Horror makes me lose my head. What if it leaps on me? I am being ridiculous and know it. But I can't stand to have this thing near me. I scurry over to the door. The peephole immediately opens. In a jerky voice I beg the guard to open up and take the awful thing away. I can see it on the wall. He doesn't even answer. He closes the peephole. Goes off. I knock again. He comes back and says merely: "Wait!"

I often heard this word. It was their only response. "Wait!" I had to address the guards formally. They always answered as though I were a dog: "Wait!" when I asked for water. "Wait!" if I asked to go out to the toilet between "programs." "Wait!" It was always, "Wait!"

I wait. He doesn't open the door. The animal begins to move. I feel I am on the verge of a nervous breakdown. I feel I am on the verge of madness. The animal moved. On the wall it slowly moved the three angular segments of its oily, greenish legs.

In the cell I had an enameled metal chamber pot. Without a lid. The inside was coated with a thick chalky crust. Giving off a strong smell of urine. I was allowed to use it when I couldn't wait for the "program." I held off doing so because of the stench I would have to put up with until the "program." That was the only time I could go empty it and give it a quick rinse. I always brought it back with some water inside to hold down the odor.

I had the idea of drowning the bug. I picked up the chamber pot. I put the edge of it against the wall just beneath the monster. Suddenly raising the pot, I made the thing fall inside. Horror! It began wriggling about in the water. Hitting the sides of the pot. Jumping. Its carapace was hard. Loud thumping on the metal. Its movements faster and faster. The noise grew louder and I had nothing to cover the top. If it managed to jump out, I could never catch it. It would hide under the bed. During the night, it would leave its hiding place. Would leap up on the bed. Would leap on me. The only thing I had to cover the pot was my jacket. But the bug would jump up and touch it. I could never wear the jacket again. This animal caused me too much disgust.

I hurriedly rapped on the door. I would prefer any punishment to this presence. A guard rushes up. My face must look terrified and terrifying. He must let me out at any cost. At any cost he must let me empty the pot into the toilet. If he doesn't open the door immediately, I'll start shrieking. I'll call for help. I'll rouse the whole prison.

We were all there in great secrecy. Shouts were particularly forbidden. We always had to speak very softly. So as not to be recognized by our neighbors. . . .

. . . . .

On the tenth day, alas, they sent me to the lower dungeon. Early in the morning a guard handed me the glasses. For the first time pushed me to the right all along a corridor. I stumbled down some twenty steps. Below, another corridor, with a musty smell. A right angle. The key. A second key and, taking off the glasses, I look despairingly at the wall of my new cell. The black cell.

A permanent twilight filled the cell. The air was saturated with the damp cold of the rainy days of autumn. The feeble rays from the light bulb only vaguely pierced the darkness. There too, the bed, the table, the two stools were just blocks of cement. Above the bed, barely three feet above, a cement slab served as a second bed. The cell really had two doors. A first full door and a second, lower door that was just a grillwork with thick iron bars. This was in fact just a deep cellar. For me, a subterranean living space to inhabit for eight months.

Those eight months, as well, I drag them out from their stagnant gray mists. No point of reference. Nothing happened to break up the hideous monotony of days, all alike from one to the next. Here and there some pale halos pierce the fog. In this primordial twilight, it seems to me that I was merely the ghost of some creature who lived long ago, very far off, somewhere in I didn't know what shattered and forever-annihilated world.

. . . the tenth day. . . . A metal plate with a little of something unidentifiable on it. A slice of black bread. After a few days I was hungry. By the end of the month I was starving. Once again, seventeen hours of hunger to keep in check. To endure. At midday and in the evening I forced myself to chew slowly the two tiny portions, for in facing the empty plate, my hunger became even more acute. I got into the habit of keeping a crust of bread for the torment of the next morning. I broke it into fourteen very small pieces, more like large crumbs. During the night, the crumbs dried. Became hard. I had seven hours to deceive my hunger while waiting for lunch. Around every half-hour I took one of these nuggets of bread in my mouth. I couldn't bite, suck, or swallow it. Just let it become soaked in saliva, as slowly as possible. Melt in my mouth. . . .

. . . . .

I stumbled from fatigue, hunger. I rested on the stool. I couldn't stay there for long. The cold of the stone soon pervaded me. Toward the end of the day I could only mechanically repeat the beginning of the play. Finally, everything got mixed up. I felt the night squeezing against the walls. No more escape possible. It was the hour of the trap. I was caught. I could no longer struggle against myself. The hour of solitude and sadness. The hour of despair.

At ten o'clock I was finally allowed to collapse on the block of cement. I was barely separated from it by the few inches of straw. Because of the upper bunk I had a sense of lying in a niche of a mausoleum. There, the darkness became denser, almost black. Sleep eluded me. Words, scraps of verse swirled in my head. Sometimes the solution vainly sought all day came to me in a flash. I would even wake up in the middle of the night, trying to remember a fugitive verse, heard in a dream, and whose loss I regretted. Also, weird images often appeared behind my closed eyelids. Faces formed and were transmuted into other faces. Surreal cavalcades cantered by, unfolding like images in films, fantastic images in black and white. . . .

・　・　・　・　・

I suffered terribly from bad teeth. The cause was undoubtedly the anemia brought on by the lack of nourishment, the complete absence of fruit, green vegetables, and dairy products. I vainly asked the interrogator for medical care. At night the pain was excruciating. I had to give up stretching out in bed. For a whole month I could only sleep sitting up. My gums were purulent. One after another my teeth decayed. All it took was a crust of bread to break the walls of a bad tooth. The sharp points cut into my tongue and drew blood. My front teeth began to crumble. Sometimes a crumb penetrating deeply in the cavity made me sweat with pain. I had had a toothbrush. I didn't have it anymore. One day in the previous cell I was brushing my teeth with soap, spitting the water into the chamber pot. I could not be seen from the judas. A guard, unable to observe me, rapped violently on the door. Being unable to answer him, my mouth filled with the foul-tasting laundry soap, I had shown him the toothbrush through the judas. Seeing the handle of the brush an inch from his eyes, he took mortal fright and accused me of trying to put out his eye. I was hugely pleased at having terrorized him, but the toothbrush was confiscated. I cleaned my teeth with broom straws. I had to do this very carefully. But I still sometimes managed to touch a live nerve. The pain was agonizing. To calm it down, I had only cold water or the heat of my palms. Twice, the interrogator gave me two sedative tablets, claiming that in doing this he was breaking "regulations."

I spent the whole summer focused on the pain. I watched out for it. I felt it come on insidiously. It was a tide that gradually covered everything, a paroxysm that made a hole in my brain. Then just as slowly it receded. Allowing me a few hours' respite. Of sleep, when the lull occurred at night.

I could sometimes conquer the pain through work. In a poem, of which I recall only a few lines, I tried putting my sufferings into stories. I imagined a cockroach boring into my skull. Relentlessly gnawing away at my brain's gray matter, it gorged on my thoughts, my memories, transforming present and past into "white brain dust," and all my thoughts, even forgotten and lost, were just a torment.

I wasn't always alone in the cell. I sometimes had a visitor. Worrisome. The guard handed out slices of bread well before meal-times. To put off starting in on it, I set it down far away from me on the floor on a blank sheet of paper. One day I was in the middle of drawing when I heard a sharp noise, very close by. I pricked up my ears. The noise was repeated. It was coming not from the corridor but from my Turkish toilet. The section of wall half-hid it from me. I leaned over a little and saw a filament, a sort of long, very thin worm hurriedly wiggling back and forth. Hardly daring to breathe, I leaned over a little farther. It was awful to see. My slice of bread had been stolen by a big fat rat. It was now trying to get it through the round hole of the toilet. The hard crust of bread hit against the sides. The rat's tail wiggled. I saw its claws clutching at the bread. It finally managed to get the bread through and together they vanished. Too bad about the bread, but having a cellmate of this kind filled me with fear and loathing. I called the guard. I complained. He began laughing and slammed the judas closed. I had several visits from the rat, but I had taken precautions. Finding nothing more to make off with, not even bread crumbs on the floor, he scurried away for good.

YUGOSLAVIA

Goli Otok: Island of Death

Venko Markowski

In this memoir, VENKO MARKOWSKI (1915–88) sheds light on the little-known repression in Tito's Yugoslavia that was directed at Communists loyal to the Soviet Union following the break between Tito and Stalin in 1948. At that time, Yugoslavia chose a path of "national communism" and independence from the dictates and influence of Moscow. Consequently, "Titoist" and "Titoism" became the most common terms of political abuse in every Soviet bloc country and figured prominently among the accusations put forward in the East European show trials.

From Venko Markowski, Goli Otok: Island of Death *(New York: Columbia University Press, 1984). Reprinted by permission.*

Markowski, a poet and avowed supporter of the Soviet Union, was charged with inciting antigovernment feeling in one of his poems. He was sentenced in 1956 and released in 1961. Between 1965 and 1988 he lived in Bulgaria, where he was a member of the parliament between 1971 and 1988.

Tito's government chose the inhospitable, barren island of Goli Otok in the Adriatic to imprison its political prisoners. Markowski's account reveals that the mistreatment meted out by UDBA (the Yugoslav political police) rivaled similar practices in the Soviet Union and other Communist states.

According to the author, even after the normalization of relations between the two countries (under Khrushchev) pro-Soviet prisoners remained imprisoned on Goli Otok.

• • • • • •

Letter Eight

You ask where I am. I am on Goli Otok. Until 1948 no one even knew that such a place existed. It is an island in the Adriatic, an island that is subjected to strange and changeable weather. If there is a storm brewing, even in the heat of summer, it is as cold as winter here. But if it is sunny, even in the midst of a severe winter, it is like the hottest of summers. The island is nothing but rocks, rocks that are enveloped in a spectral silence during our blood-red sunsets. The sinister squawking of the seagulls tears the silence like a knife. The mute sea suddenly falls calm, and for a moment one feels lost in the most terrifying corner of the world's most awful dungeon. One feels as if one has entered the anteroom of a terrestial hell. . . .

It is possible for such an inhuman jail to be hidden from human eyes in the middle of the twentieth century? Can this have occurred in a country whose leaders fought for a brighter future, for the happiness of their people, for equality among all those people?

What in fact is Goli Otok? What is its history? Did Satan himself come to earth to create it? Is man such a hellish creature that he can create this diabolical inferno?

Shadows—not real human beings—dwell on Goli Otok; shadows of our former freedom fighters. On Goli Otok human beings are reduced to things, to numbers; they are treated as mere quantities; they live in rags and tatters. From dawn to dusk a sorrowful train of people moves back and forth across the desert that is Goli Otok. Their eyes are sunken; their hands have been broken in inhuman toiling. Their legs drag as if bound by heavy chains. Their heads are bent low. They don't talk, they don't even look around. Each of these shadows is a loose page torn from a shattered life.

Who are these people? Where have they come from? What crime did they commit? Are they really criminals? It appears that they have committed the most heinous of crimes. When the Nazi villains invaded their country they fought the invader with their bare hands. They robbed the invader of his weapons and took to the paths of the partisan movement. They have come to Goli Otok from every part of the country. Their crime is that in front of their relatives, before the investigating authorities, and at their trials, they stated openly and clearly that they stand firmly by the Soviet Union, and that the Soviet Union and its peoples have brought light to mankind and saved humanity from the cruel Nazi pestilence. Those sent to Goli Otok are the bravest of the brave, the most resolute; they are the bricklayers of the revolution. And in the dark of night, while they were asleep, the UDBA agents came to seize them, dragged them from their homes, and hurled them pitilessly to the butchers who humiliate them, degrade their most sacred feelings, deprive them of their very humanity. Many of them have already been swallowed up by the sea. Many others lie half-buried under the stones on Grgur Island. Many were clubbed with planks and spades out in the open during the night and then thrown into pits to die. When the sea is calm and the waves drop off to sleep, the cries of those who still cling to life can be heard. . . .

Not even Hitler treated his enemies in this way. Nero did not slaughter the Christians as cruelly. Where did such malice come from? The people who perpetrated these dark deeds fought side by side with their victims against the common enemy. Which hand will bring them together in an anonymous mass grave? Which hand will place the gravestone? Which will engrave their names on a cold marble slab?

As time passes, they begin to fade in my consciousness. . . . They seem apparitions in a frightening dream. . . . Inhabitants of some awful desert. . . . Men who have come to this most terrible corner of the earth to pour out all the anguish and suffering they have experienced.

Goli Otok is populated with ghosts. Here the air is as heavy as cold steel. Everything is ugly and frightening. As if speaking in some mute, fateful language, everything says: we were once alive, but now we are dead; we were happy once, but now we are filled with grief; we were once a rushing river, but now we are a stagnant swamp, a mournful desert.

The criminal has stolen everything from these brave men, smothering their brave souls. But he has not been able to rob them of their belief, the belief that they shall yet see the end of the one who has committed this terrible crime against them. He has not managed to crush their hope that they will live to see their Pilate disgraced. This contemporary Pilate wears snow-white gloves to hide his bloodstained hands. He lines the country's roads with virginal flowers, while slowly, cruelly, he kills his weak, shackled victims.

Time is an unforgiving judge. The farther away an event is, the more strongly and strikingly it shakes our memory, pervading the secret corners of our souls. It embraces our life and as if it had happened yesterday. Everything comes alive, everything calls for revenge, everything looks to the day of judgment.

There is no mound big enough to hide the truth. Truth cannot be substituted for a lie. Lies are the ornaments of Pharisees. The lie is the sister of calumny. Many witnesses can be coerced into silence, but not time. What has occurred lives on in the book of memory. The book of the past lives in the blood, and the language of the blood is frightening. Silence echoes loudly; it echoes and grows powerful, becoming a kind of conscience. And this conscience saw the murderer in that evil hour when he stabbed his victim in the back.

Here, at Goli Otok, there are professors and students; young men and broken old men; workers and peasants; generals and soldiers; public figures and former statesmen; ex-ministers and Party leaders. . . .

Also at Goli Otok is that peasant who, after selling his wheat at the market, went to a tavern for a drink. A stranger asked him: "Uncle, if you have two glasses, one of which is Russia and full, the other of which is Yugoslavia and empty, from which one would you drink?" "From the full one, of course," he answered.

That man had never been involved in politics.

Also at Goli Otok is the colonel who said that Jovanka's legs were sexy. And also the general who was betrayed by his own small children for shooting at the portrait of the supreme commander.

A terrible, cruel, and inhuman system reigns at Goli Otok. Only after the individual has been sentenced does the inquest begin. On Goli Otok it was largely the prisoners themselves—those apostates who had submitted utterly to the will of the authorities—who were used to break the others, to destroy the honor and decency they were trying to preserve. At first many of the "trustees" had been honorable people who struggled against the insidious pressure brought to bear on them by the Goli Otok system. At first they would have preferred to have their necks broken on the rocks rather than show even a moment's weakness before the authorities. But gradually, little by little, they were worn down; they submitted and accepted as the truth those things they knew to be false.

After the normalization of relations between Yugoslavia and the Soviet Union, it became increasingly difficult for even the most committed of Communists to continue their resistance. Many of them became disheartened and started to "repent." But a minority held fast to their convictions. To help them resist the enormous psychological pressure to which they were subjected, they began to turn toward China. For them this was a time of epic struggle; struggle between truth and fraud. They knew that a deceitful sham was being perpetrated, but could not fully grasp how something of this magnitude had come about. Perhaps they had been deluded from the very beginning. Had the extraordinary victory of the national liberation struggle led them to believe in impossible ideals? They realized that something out of the ordinary was taking place but were unable to grasp its exact nature. But, as time passed and the "normalization" of Yugoslav-Soviet relations did not bring about their release from the "Wire" (this is how the inmates referred to the inside of the Goli Otok jail), they realized that it had all been a fraud.

Later, when the French Communist Party demanded the liberation of political prisoners in Yugoslavia, the prisoners at Goli Otok understood that they had been wrong to waver in their faith in the USSR. Khrushchev had misled not only the Soviet Union, but all the parties that believed in the Bolshevik Party, the Party of Lenin. When Mao Tse-tung turned against the Soviet Union and looked for support from the LYC, the number of apostates at Goli Otok decreased. Their belief in the Soviet Union grew stronger and they became more united, more tenacious, more committed to their ideals. The number of "bandits" again increased ("bandit" is the name given to a prisoner who from the beginning to the end of his sentence remains intransigently opposed to the authorities).

Darkness cannot hide the deeds of men. Water doesn't wash away the stains. . . .

. . . . .

Letter Nine

Guarded by policemen and agents we disembarked at Goli Otok. As we get off the ship we are greeted by a large group of convicts. They kick us and beat us. UDBA agents move about, seemingly prepared to cope with any emergency. Our reception party fills the air with roars and threats, and above it all one hears a howl more terrible than that of a hungry wolf.

Not even the Roman emperors treated their victims in this manner. Even the madman Caligula cannot be accused of having brutalized his subordinates and prisoners of war like this. To encourage the Romans to rise up and destroy the gladiators, Praetor Licinius Cras first plunged his dagger into Roman blood. In order to destroy communism in Yugoslavia, Tito, the secretary of the League of Communists of Yugoslavia, destroys and humiliates Yugoslavia's most worthy sons. Among the prisoners on Goli Otok I recognize the leaders of the First Proletarian Brigade, from which the Yugoslav army later emerged. Here are the brave men of Sumadija's battalion. Here are the worthiest members of the Partisan movement.

Even the most shameful and degrading exile in the time of the Roman Empire was lighter and more humane than exile to Goli Otok. The great Roman poet Ovid, author of the *Metamorphosis,* was treated far better during his imprisonment. He was able to write his wonderful *Pontiki* during his exile in Dobrudja, on the Black Sea coast. On Goli Otok every lyre is muted. All inspiration is suffocated. Among the thousands who perished here was Yugoslavia's talented lyricist Veles Peric. Another poet, Marko Vranesevic, who had already served time on Goli Otok, killed himself to avoid arrest by UDBA and a return trip to Goli Otok. Many of the prisoners on Goli Otok were utterly emaciated specters, too weak to lift a stone big enough to crush their skulls.

We new convicts were forced to run between two rows of men. As we ran, these crazed and enraged men poured buckets of filth on us, threw stones, spit, even whipped us. And all the time they cursed and threatened us: "Bow your heads, you bandits! This is your final home; none of you will leave here alive."

As the blows rain down upon us, our steps become slower and heavier. One of us falls and the rest of us quickly run over him; we are being chased like a herd of wild animals. The tide of running men carries me along. One moment I too am almost trampled underfoot, the next I almost break free of the surging crowd. My thoughts are scattered and I cannot collect them. I am terribly agitated and cannot calm myself. I try to breathe in deeply, but lose my wind. One of the men in the gauntlet prods me in the ribs while another kicks me.

We are being chased along a steep rocky path. The sharp pointed stones pierce our leather soles. Our feet begin to bleed. Now none of us utters a word. Everyone has joined in beating us—convicts, commanders, policemen, UDBA agents. One of those standing in the gauntlet aims a blow at one of us new arrivals but then doesn't hit with all his might. Immediately they start to beat him too, because he showed a momentary weakness, because his blow was less than wholehearted. Why did this one man show mercy? Did he recognize an old Partisan comrade at whose side he had fought? Or did he recognize a friend with whom he had worked, shared his last penny, made plans for a better, happier, more human life?

Suddenly I spotted my old friend Moma Djurié among the convicts. I could not believe my eyes. Sharp questions tore at my brain. Can he really be here as well? But wasn't he the commander of the Marshal's bodyguard? What is happening here? One can hardly know whom one will encounter next.

I felt that time itself had run off the rails. It was as if the earth had suddenly opened up, sky and earth fusing together to avoid seeing this frightful human tragedy.

The silence grows more and more oppressive. Ugly clouds press close against us and furious waves slam against the island's shore. The island is dead and mute. I hear only the sound of feet pounding across the sharp rocks.

Everything is forbidden us at Goli Otok. It is forbidden to look around, to listen, and, of course, to speak. Even sighing is forbidden us. A single word can be punished by a whip, a fist, or by brass knuckles. The gauntlet seemed endless. As we ran it seemed to get longer, steeper, harder to traverse. Our hearts beat out an irregular pulse; it was as if icy hands were about to rip them out.

Our brains boiled as if they had landed in hell's fiery furnace. My eyes saw nothing, as if a thick fog had suddenly enveloped us.

Suddenly, like a sharp bayonet, a siren pierced the awful loneliness. Everyone was startled; everyone wondered where the noise was coming from. Soon the mystery was solved. Another steamer full of people was coming from Rijeka. The wail of the ship's sirens drowned out the screams of its frenzied cargo. Some of the passengers refused to disembark, their sharp cries piercing the air. "Where are you taking us? We won't go any further!"

Pistol shots rang out, the sea was stained with human blood. I heard desperate shouts: "Have mercy. I can't breathe. My hand is shattered. I am not a criminal. Stop, you murderers!" But nobody replied.

The guards forced the passengers onto the beach; those who refused to move were simply tossed off the ship like sacks of flour. The new prisoners are shaking with terror; brand new wrinkles lace their foreheads; one man's hair has turned white during the trip here. Tormented, driven mad by the tortures they have suffered, they laugh sinisterly and rend their clothing, spitting and cursing.

What have we come to? Torturing our own children as if they were cattle, harnessing them to a heavy yoke and dispersing them to these monstrous islands. Blue sea, open your unplumbed deep and swallow us. Why should the rocks, the sea, the birds mock our fate? Return our conscience! You villains, you stole it at night in the cells, but the cells are more human than you; their dark corners protect us. You robbed our hearts, but our faith will live on even in these ravaged hearts. That faith glows and broadens; its flames will burn all this dirt to ashes. The agents and the policemen are shaking; indeed, the stones themselves are shuddering too. For nobody can come near the newcomers. They are as dreadful as erupting lava, as strong as lightning; as violent as the merciless elements. Their anger is the anger of those who have been deceived. Their revenge is the revenge of villages that have been burned down and pillaged. Everything is struck dumb in their presence. Their eyes blaze like fierce bayonets; behind their silent mouths hide broken human traces. . . . The moaning of their souls echoes cries from time immemorial.

Who will demand just revenge for all their suffering? Who will take them by the hand and lead them back to their burnt and deserted homes, as a mother leads her child? Sinister birds call above their deserted hearths. Even the most evil of curs were struck dumb in front of the scoundrels from UDBA.

Lawlessness reigns from Rijeka to the Dojran Lake and anyone who raises his voice in protest is immediately crushed. The villages remember, remember the burned houses, remember the devastated huts and hovels, the torn shirts of the people, remember the mothers dressed in mourning cursing their fate. Even the plague took pity on children. Even our invaders spared the children when they burned and pillaged our villages. Even the Ottoman yatagan, which fell on the heads of rebellious men and women, made an exception for the

309

children. But these twentieth-century cannibals have long since forgotten family and kin. They are as ready to kill their own families as they are to betray their motherland.

The evening falls, keeping one eye open. Blood-stained, the Adriatic is calm. The moon passes by astounded; fearing the ugly sight, it doesn't look down. Our heroes have fallen without benefit of arms to defend themselves. Sad words echo through the darkness. A sorrowing Yugoslavia mourns and searches for its kidnapped children. The sobs are laced with Montenegrin, Croatian, Serbian, Bulgarian, and Slovenian curses, curses that recall the conjurations of earlier centuries, when the people rose up against the wild invaders. This long and wordless song in the eerie silence re-invigorates the weak. It restores some light to their smashed faces, and revives the faith that had been prostrated.

Wrapped in a blood-stained cloak, Goli Otok sinks into an uneasy silence. People sleep wide awake. Songs and sad psalms seem to emerge from the depths, as if in Old Testament vigils. Our worn-out souls lose themselves in dreaming, secretly singing and pouring out their sadness. The stars weep with grief, and their tears turn into dew and shine on the cool stones. The night has hardly come and it is already over. The stars have hardly come up when they dim and disappear. The siren has hardly signaled sleep and now it is hooting, roaring, thundering, resounding over rocks and sea and waking the dead-tired eyelids. The new day begins with the tortures that are particular to Goli Otok....

．．．．．

Letter Thirteen

The red-hot ball of the sun hangs low over Goli Otok, bathing the island in infernal heat. There is neither the slightest breeze nor a hint of cooling shade. The old white-headed professor from Ljubljana University kneels over the burning-hot gravel in silence, sweat pouring from his body, his cheeks, and eyes. I hear him sigh and whisper, "Once there was a Yugoslavia, but it is no more." Under the scorching sun, his eyes dim; dizziness overcomes him and he falls down in a faint. Two guards run over and pick him up; holding him by the arms they force him to kneel on the sharp stones in the terrible heat.

"Where am I?" asks Professor Cene Logar, staring blankly at the guards. "Who has brought me to this place?"

The guards sneer at him, " *You* are the one who is responsible for your being here. And it is entirely up to you whether you will ever return to the university. You frittered away the people's trust."

The old man falls silent. But his eyes are brimming with a terrible anger. He grinds his teeth and then, all of a sudden, spits at the guards, "Bloody bastards! Even here you can't let an honest man alone!"

Not far away another prisoner stands, stripped to the waist and with a box full of stones hanging from a rusty wire that has been looped around his neck. He is a Hungarian from Vojvodina who had been accused of serving the Hungarian king when he was a young man and who has now been accused of being a spy for Rakosi. Consumed with a terrible fever, he gasps for air and then utters an inhuman cry: "Stop torturing me! I am burning up with fever. My skull is splitting in half!"

The guards call a doctor, an UDBA doctor, who feels the prisoner's forehead and says, "he has a slight fever."

The doctor then puts a thermometer under the prisoner's arm, waits a minute, and looks at it in shocked surprise. "You must have done something with the thermometer," he says. "It is impossible for it to indicate a temperature of 40.5° C. after only a minute." But the next time the thermometer reads 41° C. Clearly the prisoner has sunstroke. The doctor takes an aspirin out of his pocket, gives it to the convict, and makes him swallow it without any water, merely wetting it with saliva.

We are not permitted to have drinking water here. We can take a drink of water only when showering. And for this reason no one pays any attention to how dirty he is; everyone puts his mouth under the shower nozzle to drink himself full, storing up water for the coming week.

By this time Professor Logar was already sprawled unconscious on the blood-stained rocks. The heat is terrific, as if flames dart out of the stones, lick his feet, caress his blood-stained knees. His eyes open from time to time, but otherwise he does not move. He is staring off into the distance, across the hills toward Ljubljana, toward the monument to France Presern. He regains consciousness and asks: "Where are you, Kardelj? Can't you see what kind of Yugoslavia you have forged? Didn't both of us fight for this Yugoslavia? Didn't we tell people that they would be able to speak openly? What has happened? Oh, Kardelj, Kardelj! You would bring even Presern himself to rot on this evilly named island if he were alive."

At that moment a terrible cry slices through the tense atmosphere. A tall, stout, 65-year-old Montenegrin is being force-chased[1] by five people. The convict is carrying a deep box of stones which weighs eighty to ninety kilograms. He holds the heavy box by its handles, but it is also attached around his neck by a wire; he cannot rid himself of this terrible burden even by letting go with his hands. Behind him are five strong men, chasing and beating him in an attempt to make him run faster. "You will cough up your mother's milk and confess everything," they yell at him. "We too were stubborn at first; we are Montenegrins, too."

Turning back toward them, the convict answers: "I know nothing. I told all I know in court. I now have only my honor left, and that is what I live for. I'm not like you."

Enraged by these words, the five men now chase him even harder: "We will tear the flesh from your bones and then you will speak. Nobody will come to your aid here. We are your gravediggers. It's up to you and you alone how you pass your days at Goli Otok."

Raising his eyes to the sky, the Montenegrin utters a painful cry: "Do you see this, God? Is there no power that can put an end to my humiliation?"

Sometimes I think that everything that happens here happens according to some prearranged plan. At that very moment the warden of Goli Otok prison emerged from the administration building, dressed in plain clothes and carrying a whip. Feigning anger, he addresses the five men who are force-chasing the Montenegrin: "Stop! Why are you torturing this man? What has he done to you? What old scores are you trying to settle?"

One of the five answers the warden: "He is the most stubborn enemy of socialist Yugoslavia. His conduct undermines the Montenegrins' faith in Tito. He has done greater damage than the fascists. And if he is not broken he will continue his subversive activities here as well. Warden, with his tricks he could fool the devil himself!"

"Leave him alone!" the warden responded. "Enough for today. Give him a chance to think it over." And turning to the Montenegrin, who stood there harnessed to his box like an ox, the warden said: "Come with me. We are, after all, fellow men; we will reach an agreement. Furthermore, we were comrades during the war. No reason to pay the bill for someone else's exploits!"

The Montenegrin immediately calmed down, put down the box, and followed the warden into the administration building.

Here on Goli Otok we run, harnessed to our boxes, just like horses harnessed to a wagon. I too am harnessed; I too am chased. Forced-chasing is the most terrible of all punishments. The fingers quickly develop deep cuts; their flesh begins to hang down in strips. The wire around my neck cuts into the flesh until the blood begins to gush forth. We fall down, one after the other, but we are still in our accursed harnesses. Nevertheless, our pride does not allow us to beg for mercy. We hide our exhaustion, camouflage the pains that wrack us. We do not want the enemy, who until yesterday was our friend, to comprehend our weakness. And so we run on. The handles of the boxes cut through the bleeding flesh until they strike at bare bone.

The apostates urge us to come clean, to confess everything. They remind us that they too were once put through these same tortures, and insist that whether we want to or not, whether we live or die, we will confess everything to the authorities who rule the sinister island of Goli Otok.

Our fresh wounds hurt, and yet, somehow, they do not hurt. Later on, at night when our flesh has cooled down and when the salt from our sweat has penetrated our wounds—then we will know what terrible teeth these wounds have. A wound will hurt awfully once salt has penetrated it; indeed, salt is the most dreadful torture in the world. It is even worse than the "Jesus" straitjacket, a torture in which the victim is stretched out just as Jesus was on his cross, with only the tips of his toes touching the ground. And torture with salt is even worse than the torture in which the convict is put in a cell filled with water and forced to squat all night on one leg over a bed of spikes. But the human soul is harder than stone. Pain is what hardens it. The soul is the master of the body; it will decide when and how the flesh will be stripped off.

Before the evening inspection the room supervisors come to us with their mock concern. These supervisors are convicts who have proved their absolute loyalty to the warden and the examining magistrates. They know that the shortening of their own sentences depends on a continued display of such abject loyalty. They come to us smoking cigarettes and try to strike up a conversation. Sometimes they are hesitant, as if they don't know how to begin, as if they have never had to perform such a task. They are anxious to have us understand them correctly; they want us to know that everything they do is for our own good, for the good of the force-chased. "Comrades," they begin, "you cannot smash a wall by banging your head against it. We all went through this before you; look, we still have the scars on our foreheads. Anything that you confide in the warden or the examining magistrates will be kept in strictest confidence; these men are as tight-lipped as the grave. Trust them; they are our fathers!"

Some of our group, who had been the most brutally tortured, spit right in their faces. "We didn't come here to lose our self-respect," they began. "We entered the struggle out of self-respect, and we are willing to die here in order to preserve it. Better to die an honest death than to live in dishonor. To crawl like a snake between people's boots, to be avoided by young and old, to be crushed like a loathsome being—that is not life."

In the dark of night some of our number are put in a sack that is weighted with a heavy stone; noiselessly they sink into the unplumbed depths of the Adriatic.

Others are sent to Isolation, a building as frightening as the gaping jaws of the vilest dragon. The walls are thick, the floor is wet; dirty water drips from the ceiling day and night. Muffled moans and screams pierce the sinister silence. Many of those who are brought here are broken and emaciated when they leave. Many disappear in the basement cells. Many cough up even their mother's milk.

Sometimes the prisoners held in Isolation must spend the entire night mopping the floors of the long corridors while the guards kick and curse them: "Make it shine like the sun. When we turn the lights off it must shine brightly. You who defamed and shamed our country must now scrub the earth you have soiled. You thought our leader would be afraid of your threats, of the saber-rattling you instigated along our borders. But we have proved that we are valorous; there are cowards among us to be sure—*you* are the cowards!"

In the morning the first sunbeams sneak furtively through the small, barred windows high up on the walls of our cells. The siren wakes the prisoners in

Isolation. Exhausted, reduced to mere shadows, the men prepare for the most dreadful of Goli Otok's tortures—the quarries.

Outside, forced-chasing is already under way. The chasers take turns, some of them stopping to catch their breath and then returning with redoubled fury, pouring out their impotent hatred on the prisoners. They say that more than one convict was found trampled to death along the path of the forced-chasing—they were simply tossed into the ditch, left to rot unburied. Diabolical ravens circle over the exposed bodies in a gloomy burial dance. Their terrible caws shatter the silence; that cawing is as frightening as Goli Otok itself. . . .

Letter Forty-three

My dear,

Every prisoner who has been on Goli Otok and been subjected to its severe regime has something special to remember: one will remember that his hand was cut off; another, that his leg was broken; a third, that his eye was gouged; and a fourth remembers that his golden teeth were knocked out with a fist. Some left their bones behind; others, their health; still others—the graveless—have left shadows that wander about at night, breaking the silence, and kindling mournful grave lamps in the dark void.

The story of Goli Otok is dark and terrible. It is a story written in blood, watered with sighs, strung with curses—a story so terrible that its telling can wake even the dead.

Little by little, time sweeps all things into oblivion. The murderers depend on time to cover their tracks, to help them escape the pillory.

Goli Otok lacked a lot of things: from food to rest, from the mere right to meet with others to the possibility of engaging in sincere conversation. Although it was an open prison, it was secured by three hundred padlocks and surrounded by three hundred chains. A sinister pair of UDBA eyes was stationed at each corner; a carefully concealed officer stood at alert on each road and crossroad. No one had any illusion of escaping. Anyone could kill you without being held responsible; anyone could stab you in the back; anyone could rob you and you had no one to complain to. The authorities and the informers ("the ears") carried out the orders of Belgrade: "If anyone refuses to accept our way, we shall make him do so. Our law rules here and any violation will be punished; every incidence of stubbornness is disastrous and any hesitation is fatal."

The silence is deeper than the silence of the dead.

In the years since the prison was constructed, no one is known to have escaped, in part because the sea around Goli Otok is infested with sharks, which are far more dangerous than mines. The only known escape was that engineered by Branko Mileusnic, a man from Prilep who had worked as an assistant to the examining magistrates for a long time. They became so accustomed to him that they took it for granted that his "reeducation" was complete. One year on May 1, while everyone was celebrating, Branko Mileusnic boarded the steamer to Rijeka, allegedly on a business trip. He was helped by the fact that those who work for the Administration wear clothes much like those worn by civilians. From Rijeka he managed to take the train to Gevgeli. The Administration did not realize he had run away until the next day, at which point they dispatched telegrams saying that he was a dangerous criminal. Mileusnic was able to reach Salonika Bay and was about to board a steamer for Africa when the Greek authorities apprehended him and sent him back to Yugoslavia, delivering him to the Yugoslav frontier authorities.

This case of Branko Mileusnic was cited as proof that even the most perfidious criminal could not escape from Goli Otok. The authorities needed to have Mileusnic back not because they would miss one prisoner more or less, but because they needed to prove that anyone who ran away would be caught immediately and returned to Goli Otok.

Despite the presence of so many prominent political, military, and social personalities, Goli Otok was poorly organized. But this was what the authorities wanted. Nobody trusts anybody else, everyone keeps everything to himself. Those who had been organized in Party organizations on the outside are crushed by chaos here at Goli Otok. Beset by doubts, insinuations, false reports, internal spying, and disntegrating marriages, they have been reduced from complete personalities to mere shadows.

But even in this chaos there were forces that planned for the organization of an underground Central Committee.

In Yugoslavia Party congresses were being held. The old threats against Cominform members were heard again. Political prisoners who had been released, Cominform supporters, lived in constant fear. They could not rid themselves of the thought that they were about to be arrested, sentenced, and returned to Goli Otok. The more strong-willed left the country: Vlado Dapcevic, Moma Djuric, Milan Kalafatic, Mileta Perovic, and many others were among them. In their new countries, they raised their voices in protest on behalf of those still imprisoned at Goli Otok.

But this made the authorities take even more severe measures against us. Now we were not allowed to read any newspapers. No news was broadcast over our radio loudspeaker. We were being kept in total ignorance. What news we got had to be squeezed through the eye of a needle; letters were generally our only source of political information. Sometimes, however, the common criminals, reeducated by us and working in the Administration, were able to supply us with newspapers, where we could read about attacks against Yugoslavia.

There is one extraordinary story about a common criminal who, determined to get some newspapers, slapped the doctor in the face and thus distracted the attention of the Administration officer. The criminal said: "Chief, is that the way to reform us? I am sick and burning with fever (he had artificially inflated his temperature with a raw potato) and he doesn't want to examine me." And while the chief and the doctor argued, the convict managed to take the newspapers from the table and hide them under his shirt.

Thus the carpentry workshop, where people from Isolation worked, was informed about the recent events in the world. No one suspected that the common criminal might supply the political prisoners with newspapers.

The experience one gets behind a prison's walls is a constant testing process; in time certain stable values emerge from the constant trial and error. Life, sorrow, and joy, having and not having—they all go hand in hand, they are all a vital part of our experience. I lack words to describe how our eyes shine when we receive news.

My dear, only a few more weeks and, if our luck holds, we shall see each other. It is up to the authorities, you know. You cannot trust them, cannot know what they think about your being released. Perhaps the public prosecutor will pass a new sentence, sending me to some other island, imprisoning me in a room for three. But I don't believe it will happen. They are afraid of me. But another corpus delicti will be needed, and they may well consider me. If my silence means I'm disseminating propaganda against the foundations of the SFRY, then it is possible I will be sentenced again. But if keeping silent only means keeping your mouth shut and holding your tongue behind your teeth, then it is not in vain. Let's hope that time will soon end our hesitations, our endless speculating and our exhausting guesswork.

Send a telegram before you come. Thus I shall know that you are on your way to Goli Otok. If I am not given the telegram, you should not worry; that would mean only that they don't want to let you come to Goli Otok, that they prefer to torture me with doubts to the last moment.

Bring clothes and an overcoat for me. It is winter, you know, and if the forecasts are correct it will be a severe one. They say various omens portend a bad winter: a great ground swell has made the sea bulge, and birds are breaking their wings.

I will see you soon.

CHINA

Mandarin Red

James Cameron

JAMES CAMERON (1911–85) *was a prominent British journalist who was also active in the Campaign for Nuclear Disarmament. He was chief foreign correspondent of the* London News Chronicle *and the author of several books. One of the first Western journalists to be allowed to travel to Communist China, he visited on behalf of the* News Chronicle *in 1954.*

This short excerpt from his Chinese travelogue offers an outsider's unusual glimpse of a Chinese prison. Although it was a conducted tour in what was probably a model prison—or at any rate, one presentable enough to show to a Western journalist on short notice—this selection is still valuable as a rare eyewitness report of a Chinese prison housing political offenders. Cameron responded with appropriate skepticism to the official narrative with which he was provided.

• • • • •

It is possible that if anyone had told me, a week or two earlier, that I should shortly find myself behind the walls of a Chinese political prison I might have found the thought improbable, not to say pessimistic. However, so it came to pass; and the fact that I did not emerge from bondage already under contract to write my horrifying reminiscences is due to the fact that I spent most of the time taking tea and small cakes with the Governor.

It was possibly an odd way of dallying with hellfire, but I found it instructive, strange, and sad.

It so happened that in making my official requests for sight-seeing facilities I included, as a forlorn and rather ironic postscript, such unlikely expeditions as Lhasa, the border province of Sinkiang, and the nearest political prison. I shall doubtless go to my grave without seeing either Lhasa or Sinkiang, but it is fair to say that I was in the jail in next to no time. This was in its way characteristic of the obscure workings of the Chinese official machine, which could be unbearably slow over matters that seemed of little importance, and almost preposterously prompt when least expected. I recall once casually asking one

From James Cameron, Mandarin Red: A Journey Behind "The Bamboo Curtain" *(Penguin Books).* © 1955 by James Cameron. Reproduced by permission.

of the Information staff what the postage-rate was between Peking and Paris. After profound self-examination he said that he would refer the matter to the Ministry of Communications. (I cleared the point up myself in five minutes by merely going to the post office.) Yet the high authority produced the prison overnight. It was a simple question of approach. After some time in China I learned the secret of keeping abreast of affairs, which was: never in any circumstances to make an enquiry at that office, called 'Information,' of which I have already had too much to say. Casual questions in the street were occasionally useful: direct demands to the Foreign Office were almost invariably met; at a pinch one could retire to one's bedroom and dream up the answers for oneself. All these methods were more rewarding than asking information from Information. Approached at the proper level the government never, to my knowledge, let me down. At the Information level all was mystification and obscurity.

So one day we drove to the prison.

It lay outside the walls of Peking, in the complicated maze of suburbs that sprang up and multiplied almost while you watched; a huddle of buildings set up forty years ago by a local war-lord for the convenient disposal of his opposition. It had been inherited by the Kuomintang, who maintained it in business, while allowing such infinitesimal amenities as the warlord had installed to decay, so that when the People's Republic took it over in the ordinary course of events as part of the fittings of feudal China, it was not a place even to put a landlord in. The Communists retained its purpose, which was not substantially different from that of the warlord, but they spruced up its accommodation and drastically modified its methods.

At the best, however, I am no fanatical amateur of jails.

In this dispiriting establishment—where, as everywhere else in the New China, man and woman met on equal, if depressing, terms—the regime claimed to 'treat' its dissidents and 'reform' the unreliable. To hear the Governor, a sprightly angular man called Liu Hsiang-Chun, speak in chiding terms of his counter-revolutionaries and criminals, while the armed guards manned the observation towers outside, it seemed a system somehow born of Heinrich Himmler out of Hans Andersen.

We arrived through a gate like all prison gates, for even under communism they had not yet got around to growing roses round the door. There was a moment's colloquy between my escorts and the turnkeys, while a few searching glances were cast around the interior of the car. In a little while we were walking through alleys of Production Graphs and Model Workers' attestations and demands for the liberation of Taiwan, exactly as in every factory throughout the nation, though perhaps a trace more touching in this context.

For anyone who, like myself, had always thought of revolutionary jails as uniquely situated among the ice-bound salt mines of Siberia, this was in some sense a shock: the prison was, quite simply, a great textile factory. It is true to say that there was a massive wall, and on top of that an electrically-charged wire barrier, and armed men stood at the door.

"But please note," said the Governor, "that they're all outside. Security, you know. Inside, we run affairs our own way."

I wandered around the place quite openly, though with the rather shamed embarrassment one must feel, as a free man, in zoos and prisons. No one gave me more than the one brief guarded glance that is the prisoner's acknowledgment of a stranger.

At first glance the jail seemed to be dedicated much more to production than to reform—to begin with I could see little but weaving sheds, an uproar of looms through a thin cloud of dust; dyeing sheds; long rooms filled with knitting machines. Everyone appeared to be desperately hard at work.

"And that is the manner of their redemption," said the officer who was with me, "the policy is reform through production". . . in the clattering weaving sheds, the knitting benches; men and women making striped socks eight hours a day; they had tried to oppose the irresistible, now they were working their passage back to orthodoxy among the thudding looms.

There were two thousand convicts in the Prison of the People's Court of Peking. A hundred and thirty of them were women. Two-thirds of the total were classified as "counterrevolutionaries," which technically included four categories. There were straightforward Kuomintang agents. There were committeemen of counterrevolutionary leagues and associations. There were "bandits," or saboteurs of State property. There were "counterrevolutionary Landlords and Despots." They were serving sentences up to life, though I was assured that the average was something under ten years. Almost every one of them had been sentenced for crimes committed "before the Liberation."

Outside in the courtyard the off-duty shift was occupied in the desperate sort of leisure of captive people—playing basketball with a wild zeal, leaping and clapping and making over-emphatic gestures; reading in corners; doing physical jerks in solitary corners. At one side a thirteen-piece orchestra under a young conductor who, they told me, was serving life, for sabotage—was rehearsing for the weekend concert. They played moderately well, stealing glances over their shoulders. It all seemed so fortunate—the band was there, the basketball team was there, the P. T. zealots were there, and I was there. I felt it was inhuman to stay: while I was standing by with the Governor how *could* they relax?

The Governor said: "There are four stages of re-education. First there is the explanation of their crime. That is not always easy for people whose standards of behavior are improperly adjusted. Then there is labor education. After all, few of them ever had jobs of any kind. Then there is production technique—merely how to use the machines. Then there is the Current Events class, the classes for correct ideological thinking and the simpler Marxist-Leninist principles. For the illiterates, there is culture. We aim to teach them at least two thousand characters."

"Do they all respond?" I asked.

"Most of them. Some take longer than others. They get remission of sentence for productivity, and improvement in ideology. They can see their relatives once a fortnight for half an hour. They can be fairly comfortable on the whole, if they seriously try to reform their backward political ideas."

"And if they are obstinate about that?"

"There are, of course, penalties," said the Governor. "The most serious punishment here is Social Rebuke. That is to say, the critical attitude taken up towards the offender by the more progressive comrades, which manifests itself in an atmosphere of disapproval." He sounded, for one curious moment, like the solemn principal of some Progressive school.

"And if they are stubborn enough to be unmoved by that?"

"Very few are," said the Governor. "However, there are privileges which can be removed—supplementary gifts from their families, and so on. Or their sentence may be reviewed—that is to say, increased. There is no form of physical punishment here; it is considered to be useless ideologically."

"But people are executed, from time to time?"

"That is as may be," said the Governor. "It is certainly not in *my* province. We have no capital punishment here. I do not know where it is done, if it is done."

The separate men's and women's living blocks radiated out in spoke fashion from a central hub, or lobby; the warlord had employed modern ideas in prison architecture. Most of the cells slept twelve people, ranged tightly together on trestle beds. The usual slogans and portraits of Mao Tse-Tung were on the lime-washed corridor walls, and a huge communal mosquito net hung overhead, sagging here and there under little accumulations of bird droppings. Apart from that everything was starkly and almost aseptically clean, though palpably in need of repair. At one end of the corridor was a notice advising the prisoners that winter was approaching, and to be sure to put on enough blankets at night.

As I left an empty cell I saw the edge of a piece of paper protruding from under a pile of mattresses—I picked it up to see what this twilight counter-revolutionary wrote in the long nights, but it was only a little obscene drawing.

The officer said: "We don't ever lock the cells." Sure enough, the hasp of the door was broken off. "They can't get out, anyway. They might as well circulate and talk."

The food, he said, was enough. "By no means too much, but enough. Every day a pound of vegetable, a third of an ounce of oil, half an ounce of salt, a variable ration of rice and flour, with four ounces of meat once a week."

Back in the factory the machines clattered and thumped; some men plunged hanks of yarn into vats filled with scarlet dye, like blood. The expressionless men and women fed the knitting machines, churning out socks of violent candy stripe—you saw those socks all over China; the factory's norm was reckoned, alarmingly, at four thousand dozen pairs a week. Men and women worked together; the gaudy socks piled up all around them with a strangely frivolous effect. Nobody spoke.

"We've had no escapes, ever." said the Governor, "no physical punishment, and no escapes. Death? Maybe four or five a year. Then, when the prisoner is—re-educated, and freed, the Labor Bureau tries to get him a job outside. As a matter of fact," said the Governor, suddenly, and fantastically, "some don't want to leave. They ask to stay on when their time's up. In that case, we just keep them at work, and pay them the standard union rate. Yes, we have about a hundred and fifty men here who could go any time they liked. They have separate quarters. I suppose they *like* it."

I was about to suggest that the gunmen on the towers, the electric fence around the walls must be as much to keep out of this idyllic scene as to keep them in, but I didn't. The Chinese officials were kindness itself, and psychologically as elastic as a rubber band, but they do not joke with the book.

So we had more cups of tea, and all the blue-suited cadres came to see me off, just as the factory stopped and the unknown political prisoners moved across the yard. They wore shirts and vests and colored kerchiefs and patches. It was odd, I thought, driving back through the grey tiled streets, that the people in jail are the only ones in China not in uniform.

Prisoner of Mao

Bao Ruo-Wang

BAO RUO-WANG *(Jean Pasqualini, 1926–77) was born in Beijing. The son of a French (Corsican) father and Chinese mother; he retained French citizenship. He studied at a technical college in Shanghai, specializing in machine tool operation. In 1945 he was employed by the U.S. Marines as a driver, interpreter, and "civilian specialist for local affairs" for the military police. Later he worked as a "civilian liason" with the Criminal Investigative Division of the U.S. Army. He married a Chinese woman. In 1953 he served as a "personal assistant to an officer of a Western embassy." Such jobs and connections made him suspect in the eyes of the authorities and an obvious candidate for subsequent charges of spying.*

In 1954 he was summoned to the Bureau of Public Security (the Political Police) and warned to "act in a law-abiding way." He was arrested in 1957 for unspecified "counterrevolutionary activities." His interrogation lasted for fifteen months. He wrote a 700-page autobiography and confessed to all the fabricated charges. He was sentenced to twelve years' imprisonment, to be spent with "units of Reform Through Labor," but was released in 1964 when France and Communist China established diplomatic relations; he served seven years. After his release he lived in Paris and taught Chinese at university level.

His account is particularly informative of both the specifics of the Chinese treatment of political prisoners and the principles underlying their treatment. As the text indicates, utilitarian and ideological motives converged as the regime attempted not merely to punish its supposed enemies and make use of their labor but also to crush them psychologically.

In the period discussed in Ruo-Wang's book (the late 1950s and early '60s), the Chinese political system came closer to approximating the purest forms of totalitarianism than any other similar system, excepting North Korea and Cambodia under Pol Pot.

· · · · ·

From Bao Ruo-Wang and Rudolph Chelminski, Prisoner of Mao, © *1973 by Jean Pasqualini and Rudolph Chelminski. Used by permission of Coward-McCann, Inc., a division of Penguin Group (USA) Inc.*

On the afternoon of Friday, November 13, 1964, a political prisoner was released at the Chinese border checkpoint of Shumchun, the principal land entrance to Hong Kong. He was hardly important enough for any consideration:
There were no delegations to meet him, no press, no relatives. Only the usual
English colonial policeman was there at his post on the other end of the Lo Wu
Bridge. Across the way he could see the uniformed Chinese busying themselves around the grey brick buildings of the frontier station and beyond that
the Shumchun freight yards, where steam locomotives ferried back and forth,
drawing boxcars covered with slogans in huge Chinese characters. "Long Live
the General Line," the slogans read, "Long Live the People's Communes" and
"Long Live the Great Leap Forward."

At precisely 1:30 p.m. the policeman saw at the far end of the bridge the
man he had been notified to meet. He had a typically Chinese face set off by
black-rimmed glasses, walked with a busy, hunching gait, and appeared to be
in his mid-thirties. The grey woolen suit he wore was obviously government
issue, and the collar of his white shirt was absurdly too large for him. He crossed
the bridge with a face void of expression, never looking back. All the policeman knew of him was that he was a French citizen and that his name was
Pasqualini. All that must have appeared rather odd, considering his thoroughly
Asiatic appearance.

That prisoner was myself. I was about to start my new life in the West with
six Hong Kong dollars in my pocket—U.S. $1. I was on my way to France, my
homeland even though I had never set foot there. Nineteen sixty-four was the
year that France and the People's Republic of China officially recognized each
other, and it was as a special "gesture of extraordinary magnanimity" that I, a
passport-holding French citizen, benefited from remittance of the remainder
of my twelve-year sentence and deportation. By then I had spent seven years
in Chinese prisons and forced-labor camps. As I crossed that bridge I was leaving behind an entire culture into which I was born, every friend in the world, a
wife who had had to divorce me for her own sake, and two sons whom I shall
probably never see again.

But I had learned about *Lao Gai*.

Lao Gai—short for *Lao Dong Gai Zao*[1]—is a twentieth-century invention, an
institution presented to humanity by the Chinese Communist theoreticians. It
means Reform Through Labor.

In our fair and pleasant world there is no shortage of countries that have
built their modern civilizations on a foundation of deportation areas, concentration camps, and prison farms. The Soviets have been especially notable
achievers in this line. Their complex of forced-labor camps was impressively
vast in its prime, but it was brutally cruel, unsophisticated—and inefficient—
compared to what the Chinese developed after the victory of the revolution in
1949. What the Russians never understood, and what the Chinese Communists knew all along, is that convict labor can never be productive or profitable

325

if it is extracted only by coercion or torture. The Chinese were the first to grasp the art of motivating prisoners. That's what *Lao Gai* is all about.

Those seven prison years I lived—often in abject, despairing misery, sometimes literally starving, and always haunted by hunger, in perpetual submission to the authority not only of guards and warders but even more so to the "mutual surveillance" of my fellow prisoners and even to my own zealous self-denunciations and confessions—constitute my own story, of course, but far more important, they are the story of the millions upon millions[2] of Chinese who endured the camps with me and are still in them today. I am their only spokesman. The story of *Lao Gai* has never been told before.

Let us avoid polemic here; the purpose of this book is neither to slander the People's Republic of China nor to invent fantasies for the CIA. What follows on these pages is only what I personally lived and saw and heard about from others. I don't pretend to be a scholar, but I was born and raised and spent thirty-seven years of my life on Chinese soil. And what I learned about the prison system came firsthand.

There is a simple, basic truth about the labor camps that seems to be unknown in the West: For all but a handful of exceptional cases (such as myself) the prison experience is total and permanent. The men and women sentenced to Reform Through Labor spend the remainder of their lives in the camps, as prisoners first and then as "free workers" after their terms have expired.

Labor camps in China are a lifetime contract. They are far too important to the national economy to be run with transient personnel. It was convicts who reclaimed and made flourish the vast Manchurian wastelands which had defeated all past efforts and which today still offer the only convincing proof that a Sovkhoze-style state farm can operate profitably; convicts who began China's plastics industry and run some of her biggest factories and agricultural stations; convicts who grow the very rice Mao eats.[3] To achieve these successes one thing was indispensable: a stable supply of manpower, willing to work hard. With this assured, the Chinese reached a goal that had eluded even Stalin—making forced labor a paying proposition. China surely must be the only country in the world whose prisons turn a profit. It is an exploit of which they can be rightfully proud.

"A living hell" is the popular image inevitably conjured up by the idea of Communist labor camps. There is truth in the image, of course, but it is distorted because it is incomplete. The reality, the most exquisite irony that I discovered as the years slipped by, was the same that had already been testified to by the survivors of Stalinist camps: Not only is the society within the camps in many ways purer than the larger one outside, but it is also freer. It is in the prisons and camps that the notions of friendship and personal freedom are the most highly developed in China.

There is an impressive fund of partial knowledge and downright misinformation in the West concerning China, in spite of the many doors that have recently been opened; when it is a question of her prison system, that fund absolutely overflows. There has been no shortage of Westerners—journalists, priests, businessmen, soldiers—who have spent some time in confinement on the mainland and written books about the experience. Almost all of them were hampered from the start by the basic fact of speaking little or no Chinese. But even more important, being round-eyed foreigners, they invariably received special treatment—their own private cells or rooms, different rations, and isolation from Chinese prisoners. No Westerner has ever been allowed to visit the camps, not even Mao's friend Edgar Snow. And certainly none has ever won the doubtful honor of being selected for Reform Through Labor.

I did because the police authorities for all intents and purposes considered me as just another Chinese. I was a very rare animal—a foreigner born in China, speaking the language like a native, with the face of a Chinese. A snake in the grass, the interrogators called me, and they had a point.

I'm a strange mixture. I have confused people for years. My name, Pasqualini, comes straight from my Corsican father, an adventurous character who left his native island at the turn of the century (in something of a hurry, as I understand it; I have often wondered if he had been involved in some sort of vendetta), joined the French army and eventually found himself on garrison duty in Peking—those were the days when just about every Western power had a piece of poor, humiliated China. With the end of the war and demobilization my father elected to stay on in China. He went into business for himself and took a Chinese wife. As their only child, I grew up first as a Chinese boy with my playmates and then as a Westerner when I attended Peking's French Public School and three different mission schools, run by the Marist brothers and the Salesian fathers. It was, as my jailers often pointed out to me later, a most thoroughly rotten and reactionary, bourgeois education. . . .

．　．　．　．　．

It finally happened on a freezing Friday night two days after Christmas. Six weeks earlier the police had told me I must remain in or around the house until further notice; ever since, I had been waiting for the other shoe to drop. When it came down, the only sound it made was a soft, very polite knocking at the door. I was reading in bed and my wife was already in a deep sleep. I jammed on my old slippers and shuffled over to the door.

"Yes, who is it?"

"Lao⁴ Chia, from the police precinct."

Well, that was certainly friendly enough. For a brief, hopeful instant, I felt a surge of optimism: Maybe it meant things were going to be okay. I was, as the Chinese say, having illusions. As I swung the door open, a harsh rush of cold air hit me and I was literally propelled backward into the room by five grim and very determined visitors—three large cops in padded blue winter uniforms, each one bearing a pistol, Chia, and a dour, expressionless woman from the Street Security Committee. No one was being polite now. Their theatrical entrance and the stamp of their booted feet woke my wife, who looked up, squinted and asked what was the matter. Stupid and panicked, all I could mumble was the usual ritualistic "nothing." It was the understatement of my life. The tallest of the policemen planted himself ceremoniously in front of me and another stood by my side. The third sat gingerly on the edge of the bed. Chia and the security woman, obviously enjoying her work, barred the door.

"What is your name?"

"Pasqualini."

He didn't like that. "What is your Chinese name?"

"Bao Ruo-wang."

"Your nationality?"

"French."

That was all he needed for the moment. Slowly and carefully he opened his briefcase, extracted a printed card and unfolded it to show a photograph of myself stapled to one corner. Enunciating with studied clarity, he spoke the magic formula:

"Bao Ruo-wang, known also under the original name of Pasqualini, you have been discovered to have been engaged for a lengthy period of time in various counterrevolutionary activities and to have violated the laws of the People's Republic of China. I hereby announce your arrest in the name of the law. This is the warrant for your arrest."

The word "arrest" was a cue. The cop at my side seized my wrists with surprising force and the third bounded forward from the bed and snapped a pair of steel cuffs over them. The tall one, very much the leader, thrust the warrant at me to sign, which I did, awkwardly.

"And put down the time, too." He consulted his watch. "Forty-seven minutes past nine."

They frisked me and made a cursory check of my papers until they came upon my passport. It went into the briefcase.

"Take him away," the tall one ordered.

As they hustled me out, I caught one last glimpse of my wife. She was terrified. "Go, and learn your lessons well!" she cried.

God, she had certainly learned *her* first lesson in a hurry. But what else could she say under the circumstances? In China one is expected to react in a certain correct manner to every given situation. Prison is not prison, but a school for learning about one's mistakes. What counts is not what a thing is, but what you call it. By being refractory, or failing to show the proper spirit, my wife could have been imprisoned herself, for having knowingly lived with and harbored a counterrevolutionary. The two kids were still sleeping as the door closed.

It was in a black Russian Pobeda that I rode to my first rendezvous with prison, jammed in the back seat between two Sepos—Security Police. There was no traffic whatever, and we sped easily past the Drum Tower, the back of the Winter Palace and finally into a small, twisting back road. It was the entrance to the famous Tsao Lan Tse Hutung—Grass Mist Lane Prison. The Chinese have the most poetically named jails in the world. Through a side door we swept into a wooden-floored reception office, where I was left with a surly young guard for my first taste of arbitrary authority and my first lesson in humility.

"Squat!" he ordered. "Head down!"

To help me along he shoved my head roughly down until my chin touched my chest. Five minutes of tomblike silence, and then he whistled and made a gesture for me to stand. Meticulously he searched me again, taking papers, my ball pen, and identity card. He put it all in a little heap, drew up the list, which I signed—with his pen. Once again, he invited me to squat. I contemplated the floor until another guard appeared to trot me across the compound to an empty office where there was a chair for him and a ridiculously tiny stool in the corner, as if meant for an evil child. For twenty minutes we sat in silence, the guard reading a book—not Mao, I noticed. The phone rang, he grunted a few unintelligible answers, and we were off again, with me leading the way (the prisoner, I was learning, always goes first, for obvious reasons). What we came to was finally the real thing—a true prison block. A fat little warder with bulging black eyes was already waiting for us. In trio we padded down a corridor lined with thick, look-alike wooden doors. Halfway down the row he stopped at one of them, pulled back the latch and looked over at me. We went in together.

The place was lit by a single twenty-five-watt bulb high in the ceiling, and I could make out a long row of men sleeping on a communal shelf-bed that ran along the entire back wall. The warder shook a prisoner awake and told him to make room for me; somehow, heaving and pushing around him, he managed to make a little clearing not more than a foot and a half wide. The warder turned and went out. I took a brief look at my surroundings. The cell was no more than eight feet deep and about twenty feet wide, and the shelf-bed took up all the space except for a narrow walkway in the front. Set in the whitewashed brick walls were two small, barred windows with panes thickly frosted over; on the ledges underneath were two neat stacks of books, pamphlets, and newspapers. A pair of tar-lined iron buckets sat in the far corner, one on top of the other. The men sleeping in front of me appeared disheveled but clean. Each one lay on a pallet-like mattress with a thin cotton quilt over him; a few had even placed coquettish little pieces of cloth under their heads to keep the pillow clean.

The prisoner who had been awakened for me put a finger to his lips and motioned me to lie down. In my state of mind, I would have obeyed anyone. I took off my shoes and clambered up onto the shelf. As I was arranging myself, the warder suddenly appeared again with a quilt. He tossed it over me and went back out. I lay staring at the ceiling, too confused and depressed to sleep.

My wife, I knew, would be in for a rough time, but maybe she would be able to find a job. What worried me most was the kids, who from now on would have to face their schoolmates with the stigma of a counterrevolutionary father. My wife wouldn't be able to shield them from it indefinitely. It wouldn't be easy. . . .

I huddled miserably under the quilt as the north wind swept past outside the window and the cell grew chillier. The only heat was from a warm stovepipe, which poked into the cell over the door, crossed the room above our heads, and then ran out the back wall through a hole by the window. Sleepless as I was, I sat up and crept across to the tar buckets to take a leak. Just as I started thundering nicely a chorus of angry shushings arose behind me. So apparently pissing at night was against the rules. I shuffled guiltily back and drew the quilt around me. What a hell of a way to start my new life.

I must have finally dozed off, because it seemed only a minute before a whistle was blowing furiously out in the corridor and everyone, before I could even collect my senses, was on his feet. Utterly astonished, I watched for the first time the incredible precision of reveille in a Chinese prison. Two men stood at either end of the bed and began folding pallets and quilts into neat, triangular stacks not unlike the napkins in a Chinese restaurant. Another one crouched down, dragged a glazed terra-cotta basin from under the bed and began ladling cold water into six enamel wash basins. While six prisoners were occupied washing their faces at the basins, four more brushed their teeth over the slops bucket in the far corner. At precisely the right moment four of them changed places with four of the face washers and received a fresh scoop of water. The silence was total, except for the spittings and splashings. No one said a word. Not knowing what part I was to take in this mechanism, I simply held my place by the bed and watched.

After everyone had finished, the basins were emptied into the slops bucket and the piss bucket, which two others in turn toted over to the door. My cellmates fell into a precise line behind the buckets. Automatically, I joined them, not sure what the line was for. We were eighteen in all. I should have guessed: We were making our morning trip to the latrine. We marched silently out, down the corridor and out a side door, across a courtyard, into another building facing ours, out again and onto a little pathway that ran along the side of the prison's high outside wall. At the end of the path were two long cement trenches, very clean. Above the other end of the ditch rose a watchtower from which a Sepo stared blankly down at us, Kalashnikov hitched up his shoulder. Poor bastard, if a bunch of prisoners shitting was the most interesting thing he had to look at, his life couldn't be a very rich one. Even out here the organization continued, and the two men with the slops buckets set briskly to cleaning them with little pieces of broken brick. We marched back to the cell, climbed up on the bed, sat cross-legged and began the meditation period in which we were to ponder our sins. We were exactly like a flock of Buddhist monks. . . .

. . . . .

It doesn't take a prisoner long to lose his self-confidence. Over the years Mao's police have perfected their interrogation methods to such a fine point that I would defy any man, Chinese or not, to hold out against them. Their aim is not so much to make you invent nonexistent crimes, but to make you accept your ordinary life, as you led it, as rotten and sinful and worthy of punishment, since it did not concord with their own, the police's, conception of how a life should be led. The basis of their success is despair, the prisoner's perception that he is utterly and hopelessly and forever at the mercy of his jailers. He has no defense, since his arrest is absolute and unquestionable proof of his guilt. (During my years in prison I knew of a man who was in fact arrested by mistake—right name but wrong man. After a few months he had confessed all the crimes of the other. When the mistake was discovered, the prison authorities had a terrible time persuading him to go back home. He felt too guilty for that.) The prisoner has no trial, only a well-rehearsed ceremony that lasts perhaps half an hour; no consultation with lawyers; no appeal in the Western sense. I say in the Western sense because there actually is a possible appeal, but it is such a splendidly twisted, ironic caricature that it is worthy of the best talents of Kafka, Orwell, or Joseph Heller. We shall see that later.

Very soon I realized that I could expect no help from any quarter. My wife was petrified with fear, poor, and in danger of being locked up herself. At the time France had no diplomatic relations with People's China and the Quai d'Orsay certainly wasn't prepared to make any trouble over me. I was nothing more than a half-breed who happened to be holding a French passport by luck of birth. I was no Jenkins, and no one was going to war over my ear. . . .

My brain was flailing away trying to get all this business straightened out when, unexpectedly, I was called for a second interrogation. Again, I was taken aback and unnerved. Why another session at 8 p.m.? Everyone had indicated that they always took a few extra days to digest the material from the first session. The only explanation I could find was that my output that morning had been completely unsatisfactory, and that they were planning to try again, from another angle. And how right I was. It was pitch dark when a cop—a new one this time, but with the same fat pistol—led me away through the maze of passageways and corridors. My apprehension mounted as we crossed the big courtyard in silence, and it was an almost friendly sight when we came upon the green door marked "41st." I barked out my name and trotted in, head down, aiming crab-like for the stool in the corner.

"Don't sit down." It was the interrogator who spoke. "We're going somewhere else this time."

I stood studying the floor for another five minutes before another Sepo came in. We trooped out en masse. This time I had the privilege of four guards and four big pistols. We pushed bravely off into the night, me blindly leading the way as always, left-right, left-right. We came up before a huge, three-story structure that I took to be some kind of administration building, then inside and across a big, sparsely furnished meeting hall. I found myself at the head of a flight of red brick steps, lit dimly and twisting steeply downward. Down I went, boots creaking behind me. An iron gate stopped us, but one of the guards came forward with a key. I could make out another set of steps, even darker, plunging into the penumbra. The walls were closer, too, barely the width of my shoulders. With each step the air seemed to grow damper, warmer, and more sickly. I felt as if I were walking into a plague. My mouth was dry. I was scared as hell. At the end of it all was a wooden door sheathed in iron.

"*Baogao!*" someone ordered behind me. "Report!"

I shouted out my name and the door flew open. Two men in blue padded uniforms were there to jerk me inside and at the same time lock my arms behind me. There were ten more little steps down, then an opening, and then—I found myself in a torture chamber.

I don't think a person screams when he is terrified. The first instinct is to freeze up. It's not possible, I thought, it's not possible, but there was a tiger bench before me, just as bright as life. I contemplated it numbly and felt cold. A tiger bench is a simple device, really, just a sort of articulated board. The client is tied firmly in several places, and then the bench can be raised in many different and interesting ways. Eventually it is the hip bones that crack first, I have been told. Next to the bench were water and towels, indispensable accessories for that great classic, the water torture. The towel goes over the prisoner's face and the water is poured gently on it. The man suffocates or drowns. It is a handy little torture, because it is light and portable. It is a technique that was much in vogue during the war in Vietnam. I looked around and saw bamboo splinters and hammers, and even a set of chains heating over a coal fire. I think I would have sunk to the floor if the two cops weren't supporting me by my arms. His face a stone mask, the interrogator stepped up before me. The faithful scribe followed, notebook in hand. And finally, after a long theatrical pause, I discovered the truth of this routine.

"This is a museum," he said. "Don't be afraid. We wanted you to have a look at this place so you could see how the Nationalist reactionaries used to question their prisoners. Now we are living in a different era. We are in a socialist society, under the humane regime of Chairman Mao and the Chinese Communist Party. We do not use such crude and inhumane methods. People who resort to torture do so only because they are weaker than their victims. We, on the other hand, are stronger than you. We are certain of our superiority. And the methods we use are a hundred times more efficient than this."

He looked over the room with disdain, looked back at me for a long moment, then ordered the guard: "Take him away."

Long Live Chairman Mao, I thought as I shuffled out. From that moment on, my interrogations started going smoothly.

The next time I saw the interrogator he had a bit of psycho-political explaining for me.

"You see, Bao, the reason you became frightened when you saw our museum the other night was that your mind has been poisoned by imperialist propaganda. What we showed you was just our way of letting you know that it is only the criminal Chiang Kai-shek regime that ever used torture. Now that you have learned the lesson you will see that the only way for you is to confess. It saves so much time for you and me. And there are so many advantages."

"What do you want me to confess?"

He looked pained. "We don't tell people what to confess. If we did, it would be an accusation and not a confession. Don't you see that we are giving you a chance? We already know everything about you, Bao. We want you to confess only to give you the opportunity to obtain some leniency. If what you tell us tallies with what we already know, then I can give you my word that you will be leniently treated. But if you tell us only five or ten per cent, then you'll never go home."

"Where do I begin?"

"There are many ways. Some people prefer to start with the most important things and then work their way down to the details. But most are the opposite—they start with the trifles and little by little work their way up to what is really important. You might say they try to save the best part for the last. That's all right with us. We know we will get it eventually. And then there are some people who suffer from loss of memory and can only talk about the most recent things; they don't seem to like to talk about their past. It's all up to you, Bao. We have lots of time. Only one thing: Don't try to make fools of us. I can promise you it won't work."

I began the story of my life, from age eight onward. The interrogator hardly interrupted again and listened with complete attention. The scribe took it down in Chinese characters with admirable speed and precision. That session lasted six hours in all. As the sessions continued the gaps between them gradually grew larger and larger. I had plenty of time to think, to observe my new home and to slip into its routine.

Our little world of Grass Mist Lane was so poetically named, I learned, because there had once been a Buddhist monastery on the spot, razed by the Nationalists to make way for the prison. The great, square compound was itself divided into four smaller squares or sub-compounds, each with its own courtyard. They were called, naturally enough, the South, East, West and New compounds. The whole thing was surrounded by a brick-and-plaster wall about twenty feet high, topped by the inevitable electrified barbed wire. Each compound was divided into blocks and each block into cells and offices, storerooms, and so on. The cells varied in size. In Block A of the West Compound, where I spent my entire interrogation, the cells were designed for twenty men. The floors were concrete, the bars on the windows, stout wood, and the windowpanes were covered on the outside, to block the view and make the feeling of isolation complete.

From the first time I saw it I was amazed by the organization of life in Grass Mist Lane. Every one of us had a certain housekeeping job to carry out, and a time for it. Our existence was governed by a routine as fixed and unvarying as the seasons. Confessions and interrogations occupied five days of the week, with Sunday free for political study and meditation and Tuesday for cleanup. Two cellmates would scrub the floor then, while the rest of us remained on the communal bed and cleaned windows, curtains and walls, or else mended clothing. Another detail would take the cotton quilts to the courtyard to be sunned. If some of us had ripped or worn through quilt, pallet, or jacket, the cell leader could request needle and thread.

Tuesday was also the day for shaving and nail trimming, both jobs performed with the same little pair of nail clippers. It took me an hour to take off my beard with the clipper, whisker by whisker, but when I was done it was as close a shave as if I had done it with anything as potentially dangerous and forbidden as a razor. Each cell kept a little box for toenail parings, passed around from man to man as he snipped himself. At the end of every month the warder collected the boxes and turned them over to the central prison authority for sale to the outside. Mixed with other equally exotic ingredients, the toenails were used in traditional Chinese medicine. I never did know what they were supposed to cure, but it was enough that they paid us a movie every four months—a dreary propaganda movie, to be sure (there are no others in China), but it was still a break from the routine. . . .

· · · · ·

The natural complement to the study meeting is the struggle. It is a peculiarly Chinese invention, combining intimidation, humiliation, and sheer exhaustion. Briefly described, it is an intellectual gang-beating of one man by many, sometimes even thousands, in which the victim has no defense, even the truth. The first struggle I ever met with indirectly took place in the cell adjoining ours a few months after I arrived at Grass Mist Lane. The entire cell was working over a newly arrived prisoner, and the din of their shouts was so passionate that our peaceable study session was hopelessly derailed. The technique, as I heard it, was a thing of utter simplicity: a fierce and pitiless crescendo of screams demanding that the victim confess, followed by raucous hoots of dissatisfaction with any answer he gave them. The horrible, ear-splitting din continued for a couple of hours, and it ended only when the man was led away in chains to solitary.

A guard slammed open the slot in our door, and Loo beckoned us over one by one to get a glimpse of the spectacle. There was plenty of time; he could barely move. His feet were in fetters, an iron bar a foot long, ringed at both ends to pass around the ankles. Bolts held the rings fast; two chains rose from the middle of the bar to the wrists, which themselves were joined by another chain. In all, the outfit weighed thirty-two pounds. The prisoner was obliged to carry the vertical chain from his feet looped several times, since it was long enough to drag on the floor and that was forbidden.

The struggle was born in the thirties, when the Communists first began making headway in the great rural stretches of China. Developed over the years by trial and error, it became the standard technique for interrogating the landlords and other enemies who fell into the hands of the rebellious peasants. There is a system and a very real rationale behind it all. The Communists were and remain extremely formalistic: A man must be made to confess before he is punished, even if his punishment has been decided beforehand. The captured landlord was pushed, shoved, or carried to a handy open area and forced to kneel and bow his head as dozens or hundreds or thousands of peasants began surrounding him. Screamed at, insulted, slapped, spat upon, sometimes beaten, hopelessly confused, and terrorized, no victim could hold out for long.

The Speak Bitterness meetings were in the same psychological vein. As they were liberated from serfdom, the peasants were invited to testify to the horrors they and their families had undergone at the hands of their class enemies. Like mad mirror images of revivals, Speak Bitterness campaigns drove the participants to vociferous frenzies of hatred, which was precisely the intention. Orwell had perhaps heard of them when he wrote of the daily "Five Minutes' Hate" in *1984*. The reasoning is simple: To kill an enemy you must hate him. Without hatred it is only murder.

Of course struggles continue to be used in prisons today, both as punishment for improper attitudes and as a tool for extracting confessions. But they are also prevalent in ordinary civilian life. In a half-dozen or so campaigns of political zeal that had swept over China since 1949, Struggling became a fact of life for everyone. As in prison, a man might be struggled for something he had said weeks or even months earlier; for in civilian life, too, scribes are present to note down what is said. Or he might be trapped by one of the omnipresent denunciation boxes which proliferate in every city. A foreigner might mistake them for mailboxes, since they are painted bright, optimistic red, slotted at the top, and padlocked closed. Underneath is a shelf space for standard forms and above it a little notice in Chinese characters: "Denunciation Box." The forms are neatly categorized:

> Name and address of denunciator
> Address of employment
> Name and address of person being denounced
> Age
> Sex
> Date of birth
> Native of what province and town?

Physical traits: hair, eyes, height
What are his hobbies and pastimes?
What special knowledge does he possess?
How did you come to know him?
What are your relations with him?

Separate pages are provided for the actual denunciation. One denunciation per page, please. The police collect from the boxes daily. Denunciation boxes also exist in prisons and camps, and there are also the so-called Constructive Criticism Boxes.

If a denunciation leads to a struggle, the victim is well advised to submit immediately, because there is never any time limit to a struggle: It can go on indefinitely if the leaders of the game feel that not enough contrition has developed. Like all the other non-physical interrogation techniques, the purpose is to bring the victim to accept anything that may be judged for him. Thus a struggle is rarely resolved quickly; that would be too easy. At the beginning, even if the victim tells the truth or grovelingly admits to any accusation hurled at him, his every word will be greeted with insults and shrieks of contradiction. He is ringed by jeering, hating faces, screaming in his ear, spitting; fists swipe menacingly close to him and everything he says is branded a lie. At the end of the day he is led to a room, locked up, given some food, and left with the promise that the next day will be even worse.

Often there will be a day off, on Sundays for instance, but this, too, is an exercise in sadism. Locked in his room, he will be perpetually surveyed by at least one of the struggle team. If he happens to look out the window, the guard will rebuke him for allowing his mind to wander from his problems, which must totally occupy his thoughts. If he nods off to sleep, the guard will grab him by the hair and jerk him awake. After three or four days the victim begins inventing sins he has never committed, hoping that an admission monstrous enough might win him a reprieve. After a week of Struggling he is prepared to go to any lengths. . . .

. . . . .

I took another important step along the road to the camps late in December, when I was urgently summoned back to the interrogation center for my version of what is known in China as a trial. Being the period of the Great Leap, the order of the day was still to do everything "quickly, well and with economy." Consequently, the court came to me, in a free room back where I had started everything in Grass Mist Lane. I was only one of many to be tried, and the atmosphere around the huge, dossier-covered table was one of bustling efficiency.

"This is not an interrogation," the prosecutor announced. "You are here for your trial. You are not obliged to say anything. You will answer only when you are told to. We have chosen someone for your defense."

The usual clerical preliminaries of name, former address, etc., took only a moment, following which the prosecutor read aloud my Statement By My Own Hand and his own official inculpation:

You have been charged with the following crimes—
1. Collecting information for imperialist powers.
2. Engaging in illegal activities and transactions prejudicial to the economy of the state.
3. Spreading rumors with the intention of creating confusion among the masses.
4. Slandering, calumnizing, and insulting the Chinese Communist Party, the Chinese People's Republic and the leadership thereof.
5. Distributing imperialist propaganda with the intention of discrediting the Chinese People's Republic and the people's democracies of the socialist camp; and in a vain attempt to corrupt Chinese youth.
6. Undermining the good relations which exist between China and various friendly nations.

I admitted that I had nothing to retract from my statement and that the accusations were true and just. The prosecutor called on my defense lawyer, a young fellow of about thirty in a Mao suit. His plea was concise and to the point:

"The accused has admitted these crimes of his own free will. Therefore, no defense is necessary."

The prosecutor sent me back to my cell and urged me to devote my time to furthering my studies before sentencing.

About a month passed before anything more happened. During that dreary time the only thing I remember with any clarity was a struggle session in which I was a direct participant. The cells were emptied and about a thousand of us were herded out into a big courtyard next to the main building. The cadres instructed us to go to the latrines quickly, since the meeting was to start at 1:30 sharp and there would be no departures allowed. Off we trooped, heads bowed, in silent pairs. The guards had prepared things for us by laying straw mats on the frozen earth as an elementary protection against the dampness. Everyone was bundled up as warmly as he could, but we had no proper winter clothing; right from the start we were shivering as we huddled together. A ring of soldiers surrounded us. Up on the roofs the guards were silhouetted against the pearl-grey February sky.

Our victim was a middle-aged prisoner charged with having made a false confession. He was an obstinate counterrevolutionary, a cadre shouted out to us through a cardboard megaphone. For his actions he was to serve as an example for all the rest of us. Perhaps, he said, our enthusiastic participation could help him along to a full and frank admission of his sins. I never did learn the man's name. He sat in the little open space without a mat, head bowed. We surged around him and began.

"Down with the obstinate prisoner," we screamed. "Confess or face the consequences." These sorts of imprecations may sound slightly comical in English, but in Chinese they are terrifyingly real and fraught with menace—especially in the framework of a prison where a man has no counsel or friend. And when a thousand men are shouting at once.

Every time he raised his head to say anything—truth or falsehood, that wasn't our concern—we drowned him with roaring cries of "Liar!" "Scum!" Or even "Son of a bitch!" This time there was no one to reproach us for this breach of the rules, as Loo had done in the study sessions.

"Is he telling the truth?" howled out the cadre, hopping energetically from foot to foot.

"No!" We all hooted in derisive unison. The struggle continued for three more hours like this, and with every minute that passed we grew colder, hungrier, and meaner. A strange, animal frenzy built within us. I almost think we would have been capable of tearing him to pieces to get what we wanted. Later, when I had the time to reflect, I realized that of course we had been Struggling ourselves at the same time, mentally preparing to accept the government's position with passionate assent, whatever the merits of the man we were facing. Our victim finally reached a point where he couldn't bear it any longer. He raised his head and cried out directly at the guards:

"Don't waste their time any longer. Punish me according to the regulations."

It was a request that was defiant at the same time. The guards came forward with the chains he had earned by his obdurate attitude. In front of us they hammered home the rivets to his fetters and irons.

A week afterward the warder called me to his office to show me a document, written in Chinese, in which I formally requested the honor of going to a labor unit and waived my right to stay on in the Interrogation Center. I signed instantly. Within a few days I was transferred to the Transit Center. Anthony Liu came with me. We had joy in our hearts. . . .

· · · · ·

On April 13, my big day finally arrived—the sentence. I was folding 4,500 leaves by then and already dreaming of making it to 6,000 so I would be eligible for heavy rations. In the afternoon a guard called out my name and told me to go to the warder's office. I dropped my bamboo stick and jumped up without even bothering to consider my appearance. I was a pretty unappetizing sight. Since it was hot and close in the cell, I was wearing only a pair of grey shorts, a dirty white undershirt and slippers. By now the best I could do for my boil was to cover it with my old handkerchief. It wasn't a very sanitary solution, but at least it might keep the lice out of the wound. I hopped over the piles of book leaves and hurried down the corridor. In the warder's office I met a handsome young man in an olive drab jacket and blue pants.

"This is a representative of the People's Court," the warder said. "He wants to see you."

After the usual formalities—name, former occupation, address—he opened his briefcase and brought out a sheet of paper covered with Chinese characters.

"You have been called here to hear your sentence," he said. He began reading from the paper. "The accused is charged with having participated in the repression of the Chinese people by having been a faithful running dog of the imperialist powers, with engaging in illegal activities and black marketing, with spreading rumors with the intent of creating confusion among the masses, with slandering the Chinese Communist Party and calumnizing its leadership, and with distributing imperialist propaganda with the intent of corrupting the Chinese people.

"The accused, having admitted all these crimes by himself under his own free will and under no pressure whatsoever, the People's Government hereby sentences you, Bao Ruo-wang, to twelve years' imprisonment, counting from the date of your arrest on December 27, 1957. You will carry out this sentence in units of Reform Through Labor."

Long Live Mao, I thought. It could have been life or twenty years, and I was getting only twelve. What a relief! I think that at that moment I truly loved Mao, his police, and the People's Courts.

My particular sentencing process was unusually straightforward and free of ruse, probably because I was a foreigner. The Party decided I had earned twelve years and that exactly is what they gave me. This was quite different from the usual sentencing procedure, as a fellow prisoner, a former judge, explained to me in the camps several years later.

First, he said, there is nothing in China to limit the sentencing power of the government. The common analogy is the rubber band—a sentence can be stretched or abbreviated, depending on dozens of nonobjective factors. A man sentenced to life might well become a free worker before his cellmate who was sentenced to ten years. A committee of three or four persons who know the prisoner makes the judgment of sentence. One of them might be a policeman who had been watching him on the outside, another the interrogator and another his scribe. Together they decide on a fitting sentence and then, depending on their attitude toward the accused, begin embroidering on it. If, as in my case, the actual sentence was twelve years, they might announce twenty to him, or even life. As always, the prisoner is told that he can lighten his sentence by making the necessary efforts and showing himself to be a model for the others. So perhaps after one year of furious effort he will be rewarded by a gift from the state: a sentence reduction from life to twenty years. Radiant and grateful, he becomes even more so the perfect prisoner, and after three more years he is reduced to only fifteen years. Two years later the sentence is reduced to ten years—ten more years only! Since he has already served five and continues to behave with zeal and gratitude, they wait until he has served seven more (to make his original twelve years). It is at this moment that the government, in its generosity, decides on an amnesty. Twelve years instead of life! The man becomes a free worker with a song in his heart, thinking only of helping to build socialism.

Another interesting invention of the Chinese Communists is the suspended death sentence—the execution to be carried out only if the prisoner misbehaves himself in some manner determined by his warders. It tends to make model prisoners. Lo Rui-Qing, formerly China's number one policeman (he was stripped of his powers during the Cultural Revolution, and I wonder where he is now), took it upon himself one day in 1959 to explain and justify the system:

> Among the punishments to be meted out to the criminal elements of our country there is one sanction called "capital punishment with two years' suspension of execution and forced labor with observation of the effect." Imperialists have denounced this as a most cruel punishment. We say that it is the greatest possible clemency. The criminals themselves understand this. Capital punishment with suspension of execution gives a last chance for reform to these persons living under the sword of the government. In fact, most of the criminals who receive this punishment are saved. Where was there ever, in ancient or modern times, in China or abroad, so great an innovation? Where in the capitalist world can such a humanitarian law be found? (*People's Daily*, September 28, 1959.)

"Do you have any objections to this?' the court representative wanted to know. Of course I did not.

"Do you wish to appeal?"

God, no. Bartek and all the other horror stories I had heard had cured me of that. "No,' I said with emphasis. "I realize I have the right to appeal, but I am satisfied with my sentence. I do not wish to appeal. I only wish to sign my name."

"Raise your right hand," he ordered me. "Do you hereby accept that you were given a fair and just trial and a just sentence?"

"I do."

"Sign."

When I got back to the cell I was bursting with joy. I told Howe that I was the happiest man in the world. He agreed that the sentence seemed an unexpectedly good one. The soup tasted good that night. Only after the lights went out did I begin thinking of what lay before me. Ten more years. It began to seem longer and longer. . . .

. . . . .

At intervals throughout the year—it depended on how production was going—the cells were directed to organize their individual ration-voting sessions. Ration voting was one of the worst aspects of the penal system, for it tended to isolate one prisoner from another and create a tension that dovetailed perfectly with the officially sanctioned Mutual Surveillance. It got us in the belly, the one place where we were all vulnerable. Each cellmate was bidden to assess the other, and when he voted, he was told that he should consider attitude toward work as well as output. The form for the meetings was universal. One by one, going by our lineup and sleeping positions rather than alphabetical order, we made little individual speeches describing our past work, plans for the future, and finished with a request for food. The others then commented and voted. One of the early sessions I experienced will give a good idea of how the system works.

"My name is Bao Ruo-wang," I began in the proper form. "I am here for counterrevolutionary activities. The government has assigned me to folding book leaves and at present I am on the light-duty ration. Since I am now up to 4,500 or 5,000 leaves a day and since I don't think I'll be able to reach the target set by the government in the near future, I guess I should stay on my light ration."

Two cellmates briefly commended me for my positive attitude in continuing work while I was in pain from my boils, but it was too much to expect that I would get off without negative comment. Citizens are supposed to criticize each other; prisoners even more.

"Bao Ruo-wang has been commendable in his attitude," someone piped up, "but we must remember that rations are not awarded on the basis of attitude alone. His production figures are low. Two weeks from now, if he doesn't make it to the target, the warder will probably punish him. So wouldn't we look bad if we voted him such high rations now?"

Even worse was to come. It was a guy named Liu, a real sour bastard. Liu loved to talk for the record; and he had a high voice to boot—the classical shithead.

"I think Bao should be demoted," he squeaked. "He's always making funny remarks. Does he think he's in a hotel? He's here to be punished, not to enjoy himself. He came here in the middle of February, and we're now almost into May. Should he still be eating light rations? That's a waste of government food. It's shameful. He probably thinks he can just coast along and still get well fed. There are other prisoners who just arrived a month ago and are already up to six or seven thousand leaves a day."

Silence. Howe looked around but no one had anything more to say.

"I have nothing more to add to this myself," he finally said, "except to ask that any time one of you feels compelled to throw out accusations, let him keep in mind what his own production figures are. We don't want any polemics or personal arguments. All we are trying to judge here is what rations Bao should eat until the next meeting. One of you suggested heavy rations and another suggested that he be put back on punishment level. Let's take a vote. Who votes for heavy?"

One hand went up. I appreciated the gesture, but I never had figured to stand a chance for that.

"Light?"

Everyone but Liu and myself (the prisoner whose case is being considered never votes) raised his hand. So I was all set: light rations until the next session. . . .

* * * * *

At the end of that week Old Yeh interrupted our section's smoke break with an announcement.

"I've just come from the brigade leader's office," he said. "The eight of us have been assigned the job of burying the dead. I guess they figure that since we're already doing the dirtiest work, we wouldn't mind taking on the burial detail, too. In return we will all draw maximum rations, get an extra meal when we work at night and be able to keep small things we find on the bodies, like cigarettes and soap bars."

The very next night we had our first assignment, some poor unknown from among that pathetic batch of arrivals. We heaved him fully clothed into our little handcart with the bicycle wheels and hustled him up to the graveyard on the hill. It was a beautiful evening, with a red sunset and the cicadas singing in the trees. The hole was ready. We dumped him in as he was—there were no more coffins in those days—covered him with his sleeping mat and quickly filled the hole. Small Pan looked on in horror. He didn't touch his shovel. When we came back, we got two extra pieces of bread.

The next morning we were called in from the pigs for another one. This time we had to dig the hole ourselves. While four of them went off to start digging, I and the others fetched the body. This one had been a cripple, but by the looks of him he was an intellectual from a good family. His coat was clean and his coverlet was silk. We gathered his fountain pen and books to send to his family and heaved him into the cart. My toe ached with each step up to the graveyard. I had hurt it several days earlier and now it was infected. That was going to cause me more trouble later, but for now my only concern was to bury our unfortunate classmate.

As I approached the graveyard I saw a strange scene. Everyone was standing around the freshly dug hole and suddenly one of them—it turned out to be

Small Pan—detached himself from the others and threw himself at the feet of the guard witnessing the burial. Two of the men in the section, Shau and Chang, pulled him away.

On the way back Yeh told me Small Pan had gone a little bit crazy when he saw the body coming. He begged the guard to send him back to Peking, even to the Transit Center if they wanted. He was sure he would die if he stayed on in Northern Precious Village. The poor little bastard was right. Of course we had to struggle him back in the hooch. No one wanted particularly to do it, but the guard had given us orders. We compromised by giving him a group criticism session, avoiding the rancor and insult of a struggle. We advised him to go to the warder and make a clean breast of his doubts and explain his attitude.

Small Pan agreed and left the room at about 8 p.m. to give it a try. When he came back, he was in tears. Pan cried more and more toward the end of his life. Yeh yelled at him to cut it out—weeping in prison was a sign of resentment, as if the government were oppressing him in some way. Small Pan stood there in that little peaked cap he had made out of extra pieces cut from his jacket, his shoulders heaving in grief.

"How would you feel if the warder threatened to put your ration down to eighteen catties a month?" he sobbed.

Eighteen catties. That made about twenty pounds. Yeh didn't press the point. "Sit down and do your lesson," he said.

The infection in my toe soon spread up my leg through the lymph glands and formed a gruesome boil on my groin. When it started bubbling, I had to go see the doctor. At least he was honest with me. The combination of my TB and the bad rations made the boil extremely dangerous, but it still wasn't the time to operate. We could do nothing but wait. Panicked at the thought of a generalized infection finishing me off, I went to see "One-arm" and made an exceptional request to be transferred back to Peking. If I was going to die, I told him, I wanted to be near my family. He gave me a scolding for my improper attitude and ordered me to write out an admission of ideological fault. I should have known better.

In the burial detail we had a brief experience with the magic black box, an invention of some zealous cadre. Coffins had long since disappeared, since the wood was urgently needed for other purposes, but the authorities of Northern Precious Village evidently felt that form should be served nonetheless. The result of their concern was the black box—a special, reusable coffin with a sliding bottom. We would place the box directly over the hole and then, so to speak, pull the rug out from under the corpse, which would pile headlong into its final resting place. Warder Wang finally did away with this grisly pretence, and I admired him for it.

One night late in August we got a call that there was a fresh corpse for us. Half our section was away doing something else, it turned out, so there were only four of us left. Two of them went to dig the grave, but the one who was supposed to help me had cramps and couldn't leave the hooch. I went to the Black Shed alone, pulling the rickshaw cart behind me. The Black Shed was a special place reserved only for prisoners who were dying. When a prisoner was in his last hours, he was carried there to expire alone, out of sight of the others. It was better for morale. Often there were two or even three of them in there at a time.

The guard who had called me out helped me load the corpse, still in its bedclothes, into the cart, but then he took off. I was left to carry out the burial alone. More than a mile, I had to walk with it behind me. The moon was nearly full but I didn't look back. His head thumped against the side boards as we climbed the path; it was as if he were still alive and protesting. When I buried him, his eyes were still open. The next morning I asked "One-arm" to make sure I would never have to do a night burial alone anymore. In September we averaged two deaths a day and by October most of those three hundred who had come from Peking on July 25 were dead.

Summer was finished in the middle of September. The sun was still warm when it showed itself, but the skies were almost constantly cloudy and the rains came more regularly. When the cold became acute, Yeh gave me a tip— snuggle up to the pigs for warmth. Far from running away, the animals actually seemed to enjoy our company in such close quarters. I huddled next to their opulent black flanks, watched the rain, and pondered the vagaries of fate that had brought me there.

Throughout the whole time with the pigs, my pal Koo kept hustling and helping me out as he had done in the days of the wheat harvest in Branch Farm Three. A master scavenger, he set something of a record one week by catching a chicken and then a hedgehog, which he shared with me and a few other friends. That was, of course, counterrevolutionary behavior, but little matter. Longman cooked the animals in the classic peasant style, first gutting them and then applying big gobs of sticky mud around them to make a ball of clay. The ball hung for a few hours over a fire and when Longman broke it open, it fell away from the cooked chicken, pulling the feathers with it. A little wild garlic and some salt from the horse trough made it a memorable feast.

I finally had my operation in the first week of October. Naturally there was no anesthetic, and since the doctor was not a practitioner of acupuncture, I had only a rag to bite on as he opened up and lanced my boil. The operation was a success, though, and I could feel myself getting stronger with each of the five days of rest that "One-arm" gave me. I passed the time loafing around the cell and reading periodicals in the library. Now I could watch the progress of the burials on Hsiung's cemetery chart with a professional eye.

On October 13, I was out in the fields with the pigs when Yeh told me the warder wanted to see me. When I got back to the compound, I saw a wooden horse cart in front of his office. And Longman was standing there! Something was up. Because of our good efforts and our positive attitude, "One-arm" told us, we were being transferred back to Number Three Farm. We were a rare oddity, Koo and I. The traffic to Northern Precious Village was almost entirely one way; we were some of the few to go back to the living.

"Zheng chü," said Old Yeh, who had come to see us off—Keep striving.

"Sure, Yeh," I said. "And good luck to you."

I never saw Yeh again. I suppose the burial detail eventually got him. . . .

Bitter Winds: A Memoir of My Years in China's Gulag

Harry Wu

HARRY WU (1937–), *imprisoned between 1960 and 1979, is among the best-known former Chinese political prisoners. He came from a prosperous, Westernized family. His father, educated in the American Missionary College, was assistant manager of a bank and later owned a knitting-yarn factory; his mother came from a landowning family. Harry Wu attended a missionary school and later the Beijing Geology Institute. Both his background and his reluctance to participate in required political activities at the university led to his arrest during the so-called anti-rightist campaign. Also held against him was his reluctance to hand over his personal diary to party officials. During the "Hundred Flowers Campaign," when criticism of the regime was officially encouraged, he spoke his mind, as did others; such candor too was held against him. Anticipating arrest, he planned to escape with a small group of others, but the police learned about the plan. Ultimately he was charged with "counterrevolutionary crimes" and sentenced to "reeducation through labor." He was released nineteen years later.*

In 1985 he left China. He has been an associate of the Hoover Institution at Stanford University since 1988. In 1992 he started the

From Harry Wu (with Carolyn Wakeman), Bitter Winds: A Memoir of My Years in China's Gulag, © *1994 by Harry Wu. This material is used by permission of John Wiley & Sons, Inc.*

Laogai Foundation, which is devoted to documenting forced labor and human rights violations in China. As a U.S. citizen he returned to China twice in 1991 and once in 1994. On one of these trips, accompanied by a CBS television film crew, he managed to produce a documentary about Chinese labor camps. On his fourth visit in 1995 he was arrested at the border and held for two months on espionage charges; after being sentenced to fifteen years he was expelled, probably in large measure because of U.S. pressure (including pressure from Congress). His release was also linked to the possibility that Mrs. Clinton might have otherwise refused to attend the forthcoming UN Conference on Women in China.

Both before and after his detention in China, Wu has lectured widely on the Chinese Gulag both in the U.S. and in other countries. He has also testified before various U.S. congressional committees.

· · · · ·

As soon as I took a seat in my classroom on June 6, Comrade Ma began to speak. I had never heard her tone so cold. "Today we discuss Wu Hongda," she declared. "First we ask him to explain his absence. It appears that he stayed away from Beijing for nine days without permission in order to avoid the rectification movement. Now that he has returned, he must be criticized. Second, we ask him to explain the poisonous ideas he spoke on May 3." With a shudder I realized that this criticism meeting was devoted entirely to me.

Comrade Kong, the Youth League member in charge of propaganda for the Party branch in our class, followed Comrade Ma's lead. "Why has Wu Hongda tried to escape from the rectification movement when everyone understands how important this campaign is to our country's political life?" he asked sternly. "I think the answer must be that he is afraid of making mistakes and wants to avoid criticism. I also think he is a liar. We all can see that he has deceived the Party and that he has not told the truth about his actions or his thoughts."

My explanation about Meihua's apparent distress, like my protest that I had received the dean's approval before leaving, had no impact. I had gone to Shanghai without permission from the Party branch, the six or seven activists in the room chorused. I had not responded to the certified letter and had returned to campus only under pressure, only after receiving two telegrams. I was to confess my true intentions in escaping just at the height of the political movement. "The rest of us welcomed Chairman Mao's teaching, and we have tried hard to help the Party correct itself, but we all remember what Wu Hongda said in May," accused one Youth League member. "Those were poisonous ideas. They show that Wu Hongda opposes the goals of socialism!"

The atmosphere in the classroom grew tense. I realized that opinion had turned overwhelmingly against me. No one dared counter the denunciations of the six or seven students trusted by the leaders. The meeting ended promptly at five o'clock with Ma's "conclusion."

"Wu Hongda," she instructed, her voice tense, "you come from the bourgeois class, and you have many bourgeois ideas and actions to account for. You must be honest and make a serious self-criticism to the Party. In one week you must complete your thought summary in two parts, the first analyzing your escape and the second analyzing your poisonous ideas."

"Don't use the word 'escape'!" I interrupted.

Ma stood up from the table at the front of the room, her jaw rigid. "Now is not the time for you to talk," she shouted. I had never seen her face so hard. "Write your self-criticism and turn it in to the Party branch."

Not wanting to join my classmates heading toward the cafeteria, I walked around the campus for a few moments alone, trying to figure out what was happening. Why had my girlfriend left me? Why had I been singled out for criticism? Why had the attitude of my classmates turned hostile? Angry and upset, I decided that in my self-criticism I would accept responsibility for staying away longer than five days and that I would admit I should study Chairman Mao's teachings harder, but nothing more. I was stubborn, and I believed that I had done nothing wrong. I returned to my dormitory, wrote three pages, and handed them to Ma that evening. . . .

. . . . .

The anti-rightist campaign reached its climax at the Geology Institute in mid-September after the students and faculty members returned from the summer's field research. One by one the Party leaders picked out those they intended to accuse. At the end of September, Zhang Baofa, one of my classmates who was the son of a landlord and a frequent critic of the Party during the rectification movement, received a rightist "cap," or label. One lunchtime I saw posters denouncing his "counterrevolutionary rightist crimes" spread across the signboard outside the cafeteria. That afternoon we all had to attend a serious criticism meeting. Early in the proceedings Comrade Ma asked me to speak out and offer my comments. I deferred, claiming I could no longer recall Zhang's opinions, but later she returned to me. By then all twenty-eight of my classmates had spoken, and I too had to "show my attitude." I could not remember any of Zhang's statements, I hedged, but according to what my classmates had alleged, I believed that his opinions were incorrect and that he had opposed the Communist Party. Having achieved a unanimous opinion, Comrade Ma dismissed the meeting.

A week later I learned that Liu, another student in my grade, had been capped because some of his classmates had reported to the Party branch that his personal diary contained "reactionary" and antisocialist thoughts. After an investigation he too was labeled a counterrevolutionary rightist. The next day Ma and Kong asked me to turn over to them my own diary. Angry and worried,

I replied that my diary was personal, that I had written nothing except thoughts about my personal relationships. They continued to pressure me. "If what you say is true," Ma countered, "then show it to us. We won't blame you for your personal feelings. We want to help you, and this is a chance for you to prove yourself." In fact, I had never written about anything remotely political in my diary, but I had often given voice to my deepest feelings about Meihua. I vowed inwardly to resist and prevent the Party from intruding on the one remaining private sphere of my life.

Finally Kong pounded the table. "Since you persist in refusing the Party's help, we no longer request but order you to turn over your diary." I had no choice. I could not defy the Party's command. Three days later they returned the diary to me without comment. Had they found any counterrevolutionary statements, I knew they would have retained my notebook as evidence. At that I grew very angry.

"You found nothing, as I told you, but you wouldn't believe me," I shouted. "You have violated the constitution and violated my human rights by forcing me to surrender what is only a personal diary."

Ma stood up. "Remember what you have said," she commanded me ominously. "Are you accusing the Communist Party of violating the constitution?"

"Not the Party, but you," I repeated. "You have violated my rights."

The moment passed, but the pressure on me increased when Ma ordered me to turn in the rewritten thought summary that I had never completed the previous June. Now I was to include every detail about the influences on my thought from childhood, including my family life, my middle school experience, and my class background, in order to explain my counterrevolutionary rightist actions and opinions. Hearing such a serious accusation so soon after the incident with the diary, I became truly frightened. I knew that if I were actually accused of counterrevolutionary actions, I could be sent to hard labor in the countryside or even to prison.

Ma's words early in October indicated another escalation of the charges against me, and her use of the word "rightist" outraged me. The Party might disagree with my views, I thought, but I had never done anything wrong or committed any crime. I certainly did not see myself as an enemy of the socialist system, and I didn't understand how they could brand me with the severest political label. I still sincerely wanted to work hard for my country, and it seemed preposterous to consider me an "enemy of the people." I did not realize then that within each university and each department, a quota of rightists had been set, and that it was the task of each Party Committee to select the designated number of people to label.

At lunchtime on October 20, a week after I had turned in my thought summary, a crowd around the large bulletin board outside the cafeteria pulled back as I approached. The students stared at me awkwardly. No one spoke. Then I saw the banner, written in large characters, proclaiming "Wu Hongda's

Counterrevolutionary Crimes." Below this headline, six newspaper-sized sheets of pale green paper itemized my offenses. My eyes kept returning to the large red *X* crossing out my name, a designation usually reserved for criminals who had been executed. Here the *X* signaled that I had been removed from the "ranks of the people" and relegated to the political status of outcast and enemy. . . .

. . . . .

My history of counterrevolutionary mistakes would deny me the privilege of working in a college or a government office. But I expected that the school authorities would find some practical use for my training, especially after a faculty committee gave my senior thesis on the water supply for the plant the highest mark and a special commendation. I thought I might be sent to a remote industrial facility to do mineral testing or perhaps to a field station in the far northwest to collect soil samples. My living conditions would hardly be easy, but at least I could have a fresh start, apply my technical knowledge, and contribute to the development of my country. Little did I realize the folly of such plans.

On April 27, Kong sought me out in the cafeteria. With graduation nearing he rarely accompanied me anymore, so I grew wary when he asked politely whether I had finished eating and could follow him outside for a talk. The sky was gray with clouds as Kong clasped his hands behind his back and led me slowly around the expanse of hardened mud that served as a playing field. He spoke predictably, almost casually, about the necessity of reforming my thoughts. All the while I watched the overcast sky and wondered about the reason for this idle talk. I feared that the authorities had somehow learned about the escape plans made the previous fall. After an hour Kong looked at his watch. It was almost nine o'clock when he announced that we had to attend a meeting.

Over the past two years I had been summoned often to group criticism sessions. Out of habit I took a seat in the back row of the classroom, hoping that this morning would bring merely a repetition of previous proceedings. Then I looked up. On the blackboard, beneath the colored portrait of Chairman Mao, the chalked characters "Meeting to Criticize Rightist Wu Hongda" stared back at me. My stomach tightened. Then Wang Jian strode to the front of the room. Normally Kong and his fellows from the Youth League branch office chaired these criticism meetings themselves. Some people sat stiffly, while others turned awkwardly to look at me. Wang's opening words broke the silence: "Today we meet to criticize the rightist Wu Hongda." A chorus of allegations sprang from the audience.

"Wu Hongda still refuses to reform himself!"

"He opposes the Party, he must be expelled!"

"Down with Wu Hongda, he must now show us his true face!"

For perhaps twenty minutes the accusations continued. I stared straight ahead until Wang Jian signaled for me to stand. "According to the request of the masses and with the full authority of the school," he intoned, "I now denounce, separate, and expel the rightist Wu Hongda, who has consistently refused to mold himself into a good socialist student and has chosen to remain an enemy of the revolution."

Precisely at that moment a uniformed Public Security officer appeared at the doorway. "Representing the people's government of Beijing," he declared as he stepped to the front desk, "I sentence the counterrevolutionary rightist Wu Hongda to reeducation through labor." He motioned me forward and pulled a piece of paper from his jacket pocket. My eyes fixed on the blood-red badge beside his lapel. How could this be happening, I wondered.

"Sign here," the officer commanded, pointing to the bottom of the form. His hand seemed purposely to cover the body of the document, preventing me from seeing the charges for my arrest.

"I wish to see the accusation against me," I replied, guessing that my year-old plan to escape had been discovered.

"Just sign your name," he repeated.

"It is my right," I asserted, suddenly feeling bold, "to be informed of my crimes."

"The people's government has placed you under arrest," he countered impatiently. "Whether you sign or not doesn't matter."

I knew that signing the warrant meant agreeing with the decision for my arrest, and I tried to stall, hoping that someone in the room would support my request to know the charges against me. Anger and fear rose in my throat. No one spoke. With no other choice, I bent to scrawl my name. I knew that anyone arrested for trying, even just planning, to escape was usually shot.

The officer grabbed my arm to lead me across the playing field toward my dormitory room to collect some clothes and bedding. My cheeks burned in shame when I saw my former teammates practicing for a baseball game. "Please let go of me," I asked. "I won't run away. There's no place for me to run." The officer released his grip. He even seemed to reassure me.

"Don't worry too much. We all have to change our thoughts. Maybe after three months or six, you'll come back and be given a job. Work hard at reforming yourself, and you'll return a new socialist person." . . .

. . . . .

I finished tying a few belongings inside my quilt, and the angry officer guided me to a waiting school jeep. At the district police station, a duty officer took my fingerprints and removed my keys and watch, my shoelaces and belt, even my library card.

"This can't be happening," I thought to myself again. "There must be some way out."

Outside they motioned me back to the jeep, where I sat alone for perhaps two hours. I thought about trying to escape, but many police walked around inside the Public Security compound. Finally the driver appeared, then a guard leading a second prisoner, who climbed in beside me on the hard rear seat. He looked dirty and disheveled. I felt insulted to be thrust alongside a common criminal, no doubt a vagrant from the countryside picked up for stealing food from a Beijing market during this time of famine. We rode in silence for more than an hour. I could see nothing outside the olive green canvas roof. The screech of brakes signaled our arrival at the Beiyuan Detention Center, which I soon learned was a holding facility for prisoners awaiting relocation to the labor camps. . . .

. . . . .

Three days later I huddled for warmth in a group of thirty prisoners on an open truck bed bumping across the mountains north of Beijing, beyond the Great Wall. Snow started falling as we left the detention center in mid-afternoon. It was October 25, 1960. Cold and very hungry, I pulled up the collar of my heavy, padded overcoat. At each corner of the truck bed, a security guard stood watch to prevent escape attempts. We were not permitted to stand or stretch. The occasional thud of a rifle butt striking a prisoner who had raised his head or ventured a word with his neighbor broke the silence of the journey.

I hugged my knees, kept my head down, and began to think intently. My optimism about being transferred had turned to dread. For weeks I had longed for a labor camp assignment because of the promise of work and extra food, but the harshness of the guards on the truck told me my expectations of better treatment were probably mistaken. I still could not believe that my words or actions at the Geology Institute warranted this kind of punishment. I also could not imagine what would finally happen to me. I had received no sentence, nor would I ever face trial. Reeducation through labor was an administrative, not a judicial, penalty. It could be applied and extended without reference to a legal code.

For half a year I had survived on little food. Each day at the detention center had brought study classes and struggle meetings, with only brief periods to walk in the fresh air. How long would I remain a prisoner? Was I really a criminal? I began to wonder whether I truly was in the wrong. Perhaps my ideas had brought harm to the majority of the Chinese people. Perhaps I really had opposed my motherland when I criticized the Communist Party. I stared out across the dark sky and the falling snow and wondered where I was headed and what would become of me. Though I had largely forgotten my Catholic faith, at this moment of adversity I instinctively prayed to God to forgive and protect me.

"Climb down! Get out of here!" shouted one of the police guards. By the time the truck reached the Yanqing Steel Factory, many of the prisoners felt stiff from the cold. When they didn't move immediately, the guards kicked them off the truck bed. They rolled like stones. Half jumping, half rolling, I hit the frozen dirt on my feet. My knees wouldn't bend, and I collapsed as a shock of pain traveled up my legs.

We limped in a ragged group toward a far corner of the factory yard. A prisoner approached us, astonished at the sight of newcomers. "Why have you come here?" he asked. "All production has stopped. We are waiting to move somewhere else. And now more come?" He walked away, shaking his head in disbelief.

As I tried to absorb the meaning of his words, the cold and my hunger confused my thoughts. "I want to labor, I believe I can labor. Besides, a human being has to do something. I need food. If I work, maybe they will give me more food. But that prisoner says all work has stopped here. Does that mean no food?"

The Yanqing Steel Company, I would soon learn, was administered by the Beijing Public Security Bureau. Incorporating not only a steel factory but a brickworks and two small iron mines about five miles apart, it operated as a state-owned production facility using prison labor. Its prison name and number were unknown to local residents. By the time I arrived, the production facility had been abandoned. The economic failures of the Great Leap Forward meant that in North China electricity could be supplied only to Beijing and to certain important industries and universities. Without electricity, the steel factory had no need for iron, and thus the mines also lay idle. The entire compound was part of the industrial sector that the government had declared temporarily "dismounted from the horse."

Why had we come? The Beijing Public Security Bureau had apparently ordered all of the labor camps under its jurisdiction to accept some of the overflow of newly arrested prisoners from the city. No preparations had been made for our arrival, no additional shelter or provisions had been made available. In camps whose production had been "dismounted" from the economy, there was no work to be done. There was also a severe shortage of food.

We arrived at the steel factory at around six o'clock, and we simply squatted on the snow-dusted ground. We had eaten nothing since leaving the detention center that afternoon. Finally some trucks appeared again at the gate to the yard, and the security guards climbed down to call out a list of names. One of them was mine. I wondered where on earth I would be taken next.

Night had fallen and, still without food, I felt the cold ever more sharply as I huddled in the truck with the other prisoners. In the darkness we wound up a narrow, rutted mountain road and then descended steeply into a rocky gorge. When we reached a wooden gate, two policemen stepped out into the cold from a small guardhouse. The snow flurries had stopped, and a few stars hung high above the rugged rock walls. The only other light came from dim flood lamps above the doors of buildings stepped into the mountainside. We stood in the bitter wind while the guards counted us, called our names, and transferred our files. Still no food.

"You sleep up there," shouted a guard against the wind, pointing up the hill to the farthest cluster of buildings. "It's ten o'clock, too late to do anything more tonight. We'll see to everything tomorrow." The trucks backed around and rumbled away. The only remaining guard pulled up his collar against the wind and hurried away to his own quarters as we headed for the barracks.

At the end of October north of the Great Wall, the wind slices through the mountains. I felt bitterly cold, but I stood for a few moments looking up at the sky, amazed at our freedom. There were no guards and no walls. We had been given no regulations. I realized that escape must be all but impossible from this desolate canyon.

We climbed up the path to examine our lodgings, hoping to get warm. Each building measured about fifteen feet by fifty feet. A crude wall divided the structure into two rooms. The windows, crosshatched with vertical and horizontal slats, had once been covered with paper. The doors blew freely in the wind. It was obvious that no one had lived here for a long time.

My squad chose the rear section of one building because it seemed the most sheltered. Kangs faced each other on opposite walls beneath the windows. The night was too black for us even to consider searching for wood to start the small stoves beneath the kangs that could warm the brick platform. Gusts of wind rustled the remaining shreds of window paper.

I moved quickly to be the first to occupy the far corner and stay as much out of the wind as possible. Xing's words came back to me. You have to take care of yourself, don't be concerned about others. My energy drained away. I sat with my back to the corner, my arms clasping my quilt tightly around my shoulders. All night I hovered near sleep and waited for morning, whatever it would bring.

Just after sunrise a guard's voice yelled, "Come out, come out!" I had never seen such a barren landscape. Steep rock cliffs rose on all sides. The row of barracks had been cut into the rock near the top of a small cleft at the base of an almost vertical mountain. On the opposite side of the cleft at about the same height, I could see the mouth of the Yingmen Iron Mine. A railroad track, rusty with disuse, led from the mine entrance to an ore-loading station.

A footpath led from the guardhouse below past the barracks and around the cleft of the mountain to the mine entrance about 400 yards away. Along the path stood several sheds. The guard pointed out the prison kitchen, the repair and maintenance shops, the security office, the confinement cells, and a separate police kitchen and police living quarters. Treeless and vast, the rocky mountain slopes made prison walls unnecessary. The rough dirt road we had traveled the previous night provided the only access to the outside world.

A guard appeared on the path with an older duty prisoner carrying a bucket and ladle. Each new arrival got two ladles of thin corn gruel. "How's it going?" the guard asked as we rapidly swallowed the porridge.

"We're too cold," someone complained.

"How can we sleep in the wind?" another asked.

"It's always cold in North China in the winter," replied the guard indifferently. "You'll get used to it." And he started down the hill.

Again I heard Xing's words. "We need paper for the windows," I called out.

"Wait. I'll see what I can find," the guard called over his shoulder. He returned at around ten o'clock, carrying some newspapers but without any wheat paste. If he had brought any, we would have eaten it.

"What about tacks?" someone asked.

"There aren't any tacks," the guard answered.

"Then what should we do?" we asked together.

The guard shrugged his shoulders and smiled helplessly. "I don't know."

"We're cold. We need something to burn under the kang," I persisted.

"Go out and look for weeds and grasses."

We set out to search the desolate hillsides for fuel, but we were too hungry and cold to look energetically. I could see the effort was futile, so I returned to the barracks and wrapped up in my quilt. Keep yourself warm, I thought. Don't get too cold. Save energy. Don't move around. Sleep, just like a bear in winter.

That afternoon a security director from the factory appeared in our barracks. "What's the problem?" he asked with no trace of sympathy. The guard who had brought the newspapers conveyed our request. "I approve two pounds of wheat flour from the storehouse," he answered, writing the order quickly in a small notebook.

A guard accompanied the duty prisoner who carried up a small bucket of wheat paste that had been cooked in the prison kitchen. He watched carefully as we set to work, but I managed to swallow a few handfuls when he was watching someone else. Even before we had finished gluing the paper to the window slats, I could see that the newsprint was too thin to be very effective. It blocked only a little of the wind.

In these primitive surroundings two hundred of us began to eke out an existence. The guards bothered to count us only in the evening. They didn't seem to worry about our escaping. We didn't have enough energy, and there was no place to go. . . .

. . . . .

That evening we had our first meal of solid food since leaving the detention center. The duty prisoner handed us two wotou made of corn chaff mixed with very rough sorghum. The buns were cold and rock hard. We got no vegetables, and no one even hoped for oil or meat.

After a week of this diet, my bowels stopped moving. Most of the other prisoners had the same problem. The sorghum had hardened in our intestines, causing sharp pain. The weakness caused by our hunger compounded our distress. The only way to move the bowels was to reach inside the rectum and pull out the hardened sorghum lumps.

One morning I noticed the police cook carrying a basket of cabbage down the path from the mine. Pulling out the sorghum balls had begun to cause bleeding from my rectum, and the pain was sharp. I knew I needed vegetables in my diet to relieve the distress. That night while the other prisoners slept I sneaked from the barracks and in the darkness followed the path around the end of the cleft to the mine entrance. I could smell the musty scent of cabbage as I drew closer, but then I saw a rusty iron lock across the gate. I returned empty-handed and greatly disappointed but nonetheless pleased with my new boldness. I was beginning to understand how to stay alive.

A month had passed when one morning a guard called the prisoners to stand in lines outside the barracks. Without explanation, he paced back and forth, choosing several men from each squad. He motioned with his hand for me to step out. "Follow me," he said to the ten of us as he headed toward the mine.

With production halted, the mine served as a root cellar to store the huge heads of cabbage that provided a mainstay of the prison guards' diet. Every week to prevent spoilage, the cabbages had to be turned, the outside leaves removed, and the rotting heads separated from the others in the pile. The guards had decided to assign this job to a select group of prisoners.

We followed the young police captain into the mine where stacks of cabbages lay against one wall. He positioned himself between us and the entrance, and we began rotating the heads and pulling off spoiled leaves. Not half an hour had passed when I saw one of my workmates tear out the tender inner leaves from a large cabbage head and quickly stuff them into his mouth. Another prisoner did the same, then a third. In spite of my hunger, I hesitated. Like most Chinese, I had never considered raw cabbage edible. Then I realized I had to seize any chance for extra food. I tore out a cabbage center, and a wonderful flavor, fresh and sharp, filled my mouth. I could feel the cabbage settle satisfyingly in my stomach. . . .

·　·　·　·　·

In early August of 1961, the Beijing Public Security Bureau instituted a new policy to counter a growing demoralization within the labor camps. The rising number of deaths over the summer at the height of the nationwide famine had bred a sense of desperation and panic among labor-reform subjects. Insubordination, fights over food, and escape attempts at Qinghe Farm and at other camps had made prison management difficult. In order to lift morale and maintain stability, the Qinghe headquarters decided that those who had reached an advanced stage of starvation would be sent to a different compound within the sprawling prison complex, out of sight of healthier inmates. What had previously been known as section 585 was renamed the Prison Patient Recovery Center.

I listened carefully when the Qinghe commander explained the new policy. "According to the decision of the Central Committee of the Communist Party," he announced, "and also according to Minister of Public Security Luo Ruiqing, all labor camps will use strong management to prevent vicious and malignant incidents involving prisoner uprisings in the camps. To the best of our ability in this situation, we will try to do the best for you and improve your lives. You must take care of your health and follow good sanitation in order to reduce the risk of disease.

"To this end, the Qinghe Farm headquarters has decided to establish a patient recovery camp for sick prisoners in both the western and eastern sections. At these camps we will offer special treatment in order that prisoners will recover more quickly and return to labor. Only through labor can you reform and become new socialist people. If you cannot labor, you cannot reform yourselves. So we want to give special attention to all sick prisoners. In the western region, section 585 will be the patient recovery camp. We hope that there you will become more comfortable and regain your health, return to labor, and never forget to reform yourselves and become new socialist people."

The first group left for the new recovery center in late August. Over several weeks the clinic doctors examined every prisoner in section 583. They checked our weight, our blood pressure, and our other vital functions, then divided us into three ranks. I never learned the medical criteria for the different categories, but I could see that those assigned to the first rank looked the closest to death. A second group of prisoners left for 585 in mid-September and a third in early October. . . .

．　．　．　．　．

It was nearly noon, and I saw prisoners scattered around the yard, standing or sitting against the barracks walls, trying to soak up some warmth from the autumn sun. Many looked scarcely human. The brow bones above their eyes protruded under tightly stretched skin. Their mouths hung slightly open below hollowed cheeks. Their gaunt necks seemed unnaturally long. Their blank faces gave no sign that they had noticed our arrival. With a start I wondered whether I looked the same.

In the year and a half since my arrest, I had never seen myself in a mirror. I stared down at my washboard ribcage and realized that I must have looked equally wasted and unkempt, with my face unshaved, my hair long and uncombed. Those people must once have been doctors or teachers, factory workers or peasants, I thought, each with his own heaven and hell, his own hopes and problems. Now they are virtually indistinguishable. If Chairman Mao were to spend a year in the camps, he would look no different. My anger flared briefly. Were these the new socialist people that Chairman Mao wanted to create? Was this the glorious result of reforming yourself through labor?

Inside the barracks that first evening I surveyed my fellow prisoners more closely. Several of my new squad mates had begun to swell, some in only one leg, some in both, one already above the waist. I was one of the few not yet affected by edema, but I feared their fate awaited me. Perhaps my own emaciation was more extreme than I knew. I recoiled from the thought that these ravaged people were my mirror.

Why had I been sent to this place where all the prisoners seemed so seriously ill, so close to starvation, I wondered anxiously. I thought back to the prison doctor's examination in August, when my weight had been just over eighty pounds and my blood pressure very low, sixty-five over eighty-five. The fluid in my lung no longer troubled me, but I felt very weak and always cold. Perhaps I had lost my resistance to disease. Perhaps my condition was dangerous. I fell into a troubled sleep.

At ten o'clock on my first morning in 585, a tall, balding cook named Wang, stern and almost toothless, arrived with two buckets of gruel hanging from a shoulder pole. I guessed from the bitter taste that we were eating a mixture of half cornmeal and half food substitute, probably ground corncobs. While it clearly lacked nourishment, the warm liquid felt soothing and filling as I drained my bowl. Then a duty prisoner handed me a small packet made out of folded newspaper that contained two ounces of what he called "health, richness, and relaxation powder." I had never heard of this tonic, but it tasted slightly sweet. Others said that it was mostly ground yellow beans with a bit of sugar. I watched some of the prisoners mix the powder into their gruel, while others ate it right from the envelope. I felt grateful for even this meager source of protein. . . .

. . . . .

The gruel and the bean powder had given me a small spurt of energy. I squinted as I stepped into the sunlight.

Walking slowly, we made our way around the compound yard. At 583 the identical barracks had held two thousand inmates, but these seemed about half occupied. I estimated that about twelve hundred men had been transferred to 585 over the past six weeks. It looked to me as if at least half had already lost the ability to move about.

Inside the latrine I could see two prisoners tending small fires. What could they be cooking, I wondered, when no one is permitted to leave the compound to search for food? We all had matches left from our cigarette rations in 583, and they could have gathered dried leaves and scraps of paper as fuel, but I couldn't guess what they would find to boil. I drew closer, and they watched me carefully, like wolves ready to defend their food. One prisoner said that he was braising his wotou in water to make it expand. "That way you feel fuller," he declared. I thought of our food-imagining evenings. The other more fortunate prisoner was boiling a small handful of wheat flour that he must have received in a package from a family member. He had added just enough flour to his pot of water to make his stomach feel fuller. How many ways we found to satisfy our need for fullness, I thought.

I turned back toward the yard to see three prisoners rush toward a duty prisoner carrying a wooden bucket of food. The three men fell to their knees to lick up some spilled gruel from the hard-packed mud. I remembered vividly the moment nearly a year before when Xing had lapped up the Spring Festival soup, unable to control his urge for food. I also thought of the opening scene of *A Tale of Two Cities*, which I had read in middle school, when starving Parisians lapped up spilled wine from between the cobblestones on the streets. . . .

· · · · ·

In 585 the days passed differently than at any camp I had known before. There was no labor, no political study, and almost no fighting. I saw only one actual fight during those first weeks, like a slow-motion film with the prisoners' fists hardly clenched, falling powerlessly through the air, as if paper men were trying to strike each other when they could have just blown each other down.

Without the energy or the will to move about, we lay hour after hour with our heads to the wall beneath our quilts and with our chipped enamel bowls on either side of our pillows, one for urine and the other for food. I felt more comfortable without clothes, and most of the other prisoners also lay naked unless they had to get up. Hardly anyone spoke. We rarely even walked the short distance across the yard to the latrine since our bowels moved only every three to five days. Usually we knelt on the kang to urinate and then emptied the bowls outside twice a day. I seemed to grow steadily weaker. . . .

· · · · ·

During the study session that evening, the duty prisoner shouted from the doorway, "Wu Hongda, report to the security office!" My squad members seemed to assume I was being called to discuss the following day's labor assignment, but I knew I might never come back.

Sitting around the table, their cigarette smoke filling the air, Captain Gao, Captain Wu, and Administrator Ning looked up as I stood in the doorway. The tiny office was already too crowded for me to enter. "Report what happened last week on your day off when you went to pick peaches," Gao commanded.

"I want to confess right away," I began immediately, not permitting myself time for second thoughts. "I was the one who mailed the three letters. It had nothing to do with Guo Jie and Chen Quan."

They exchanged glances. Captain Gao looked at me intently. "We have already investigated the incident. We believe it unlikely that you did this, so we have placed Chen and Guo in confinement to force them to tell the truth. What more do you want to tell us?"

I knew that Fan Guang would already have reported working alongside me for the entire morning while Guo and Chen had picked in trees farther away.

Thinking rapidly, I explained that Fan Guang had picked peaches from the trees adjacent to mine part of the time but that he had not been able to keep me in sight continuously. "While Fan Guang was busy, I swam over to the other side of the canal," I reported. "It took me only fifteen minutes to mail the letters."

Administrator Ning yelled to the duty prisoner, "Call Fan Guang!" A moment later Fan appeared and confirmed that during some periods of time, he had not actually been able to observe me working.

"Release Guo Jie and Chen Quan!" shouted Gao. "Return them to their squads, and have the kitchen provide them with food. Tomorrow they return to labor. Place Wu Hongda in confinement."

Many times I had seen from a distance the row of ten confinement cells along the southern edge of the prison compound. As the duty prisoner marched me closer, I could see that a brick wall screened the barred cell openings from outside view. A rough path led alongside the doorways, where the duty prisoner who supervised this section grabbed my arm, opened one of the barred gates, forced my shoulders down, and pushed me inside. Expecting to be able to stand up after I stooped through the entrance, I nearly fainted when my head banged hard against the cement ceiling in the darkness. The iron bars grated against the floor as the guard shoved my feet inside. Then the key turned noisily in the lock.

Feeling the shape of the cell with my hands, I tried to move my head toward the entrance. The structure was about six feet long, three feet wide, and three feet high, slightly larger than a coffin. It smelled dank and moldy. The night was silent, and I didn't know if prisoners occupied any of the other cells. I wondered if anyone could hear me if I shouted. Squatting on my haunches, I tried to minimize contact with the cold cement floor. Without even straw beneath me, I quickly grew chilled, but I concentrated on planning my confession, determined to leave this concrete cage at the captain's first visit. The fact that I had not been handcuffed gave me hope that my treatment would not be too harsh. I fell asleep curled up with my back against the wall.

At daybreak I crawled over to sit beside the iron gate. I could see nothing but the loose stones and weeds that covered the pathway between the line of cells and the brick wall. I wished I could see the sky. Then I thought about the animals I had visited as a child at the Shanghai zoo.

Outside the gate beyond my reach stood a metal bucket. I shouted for someone to come so that I could relieve myself. I shouted louder, then raised myself up on all fours, but it was hard to urinate with my back pushed against the ceiling. Finally I slid off my pants and sat on the ground. The urine spurted against the iron bars. That was my most important activity during the first day of captivity.

On the second day I waited, but again no one came to bring food or water. A sharp pain grew in my stomach, and my throat felt sticky and bitter. When night fell, I moved toward the inside corner of the cell, trying to escape the mosquitoes that swarmed near the gate. Confused images flashed across my mind mixed with fragments of memories from my childhood as I tried to sleep.

On the third day, the special duty prisoner arrived sometime around noon. He looked about fifty years old, with a strong body and an expressionless peasant's face. "Wu Hongda!" he called.

"Yes," I answered, my voice already sounding weak.

He squatted and moved close to the gate to look inside. "Are you okay?"

I crawled to the bars like a dog. "When will they give me food?"

"Usually after the third day. That's the rule." His voice conveyed no feeling, and I wondered vaguely how many suffering prisoners he had attended.

"Can I have water?" He didn't answer, just stood up and walked away.

Early on the morning of the fourth day, he returned. Without speaking, he opened the gate to let me out, and I crawled to his feet to accept a bowl of water. I gulped two mouthfuls, then sipped the rest. He asked if I wanted to use the metal toilet bucket. Strangely I felt the urge to have a bowel movement and I struggled to stand up, but I could squeeze out only a few drops of urine. "I want to confess to the captain," I pleaded.

"I'll report to the authorities," he answered and locked me inside.

He returned in half an hour carrying a bowl of corn gruel and a piece of pickled turnip the size of my thumb. With trembling hands, I drank the thin porridge, then scraped the sides of the bowl with the turnip. Before long Captain Gao appeared.

"What did you want to say to me?" he asked, his voice almost casual. I tried to remember my prepared speech and explained in a humble voice that I had only wanted to inform Chairman Mao of our situation and to ask him to end my years of labor reform so that I could return to work and help with the goal of building socialism.

"You call that a confession?" Captain Gao yelled. "You believe that you have not committed a crime? You believe that you can decide the Party's policy and choose where you want to be sent?" He strode away. That evening a second bowl of gruel appeared.

On the fifth day my body began to tremble. I feared that I could not survive the continued contact with the cold concrete floor. Until then I had tried to stay curled in a corner, touching the ground as little as possible, but I no longer had the strength to maintain that posture. I could only sprawl on the ground, allowing the cement to absorb my body heat. In the morning when the duty prisoner brought another bowl of gruel and unlocked the door, I had to drag myself to the opening to drink the soup. I had no strength to move outside, nor did I have the urge to use the toilet bucket. Urine would occasionally trickle down my leg, but I no longer noticed the wetness or even the smell.

On the sixth day when the bowl of morning gruel appeared, I called out weakly, "I want to confess to the captain." I knew that confinement terms usually lasted seven days, and I intended to apologize to the Party and express my repentance to secure my release. But Captain Gao never came. I began to hallucinate. Childhood memories mixed with illusions. I got into a fight with the neighborhood children. I sneaked into the Summer Palace in Beijing to catch carp in the lake. I kissed Meihua during summer vacation. I saw my stepmother's long, white hands.

On the morning of the seventh day, Captain Gao appeared. The duty prisoner carried along a low stool so that Gao could sit beside my gate. I managed to drag half of my head and shoulders out of the cell.

"Are you making progress with your self-criticism?"

"I am guilty," I cried. "I committed a crime against the Party, a crime against the people. I failed to follow the government's instructions to reform myself, and so I committed a new crime. I beg the government's forgiveness, I beg for a second chance...."

"Describe from the beginning how you wrote those letters," Captain Gao shouted.

I explained how I had taken the letters with me when I went to pick peaches, how I had sent Fan Guang away, how I had sneaked across the prison boundary to reach the postbox across the canal. I struggled to make my thoughts coherent and my voice strong.

"If you want to leave this confinement cell today," Captain Gao threatened, "you will confess not only that you resisted reform but also that you conspired with a counterrevolutionary clique. You will confess the plot hatched by your enemy group. Otherwise you will not leave here!"

He told the duty prisoner to place a second bowl of corn gruel beside my head. "Drink the soup and then confess. I warn you that the government's patience is not limitless!"

Prostrate at Captain Gao's feet, I swallowed the soup. A surge of strength returned. "I know I have not lived up to the Party's trust," I confessed. "I promise I will never do it again. I understand the wisdom of Chairman Mao's teachings. I am a 'die-hard element,' and I must undergo reform for a long time to become a new socialist person. I beg the Party for a second chance...."

A kick from Captain Gao interrupted me. "Stop talking nonsense! I already know about your counterrevolutionary clique. I warn you to report what you have done with your die-hard group. Otherwise you will stay in confinement." He left immediately. The duty prisoner pushed my shoulders inside, locked the gate, and carried away the stool.

Clutching the bars, I called out, "Help me! Tell Captain Gao I want to confess further. Tell him I beg the Party for another chance...."

"It's against the rules. You missed your chance. I can only report emergencies." I heard him walk away.

Darkness enveloped me, and for the first time I knew despair. I had endured the hunger, the thirst, the cold, trying to hold on until the seventh day.

Now I felt utterly abandoned, as insignificant as an ant on the pavement. No one would care if I were crushed beneath a shoe....

. . . . .

On the eighth morning the duty prisoner found me collapsed at the back of the cell. When he shouted, I didn't respond. After a few minutes he crawled inside to drag me to the gate. "Drink your soup!" he ordered, but I kept my eyes shut. I would no longer accept their food. I pushed the bowl away, and the gruel spilled onto the cement.

"Oh," exclaimed the duty prisoner, "now he wants to die!" He left to report, then some hours later brought a second bowl, but I didn't move. That afternoon Captain Gao returned. "It's up to you whether you eat or starve," he declared. "The Party and the government do not fear your threat of suicide." I heard him leave, but I didn't open my eyes.

On the ninth morning I heard Captain Gao's voice outside my gate. Through squinted eyes I could see that he had brought along four prisoners and a clinic worker. "Wu Hongda!" he shouted. "I see that you want to resist the Party and the government to the end. I see that you want to cut yourself off forever from the people. Drag him out!" The duty prisoner reached in and pulled me through the gate.

"The Party's policy is to transform you into a new socialist person. The government holds itself responsible for you. We will use revolutionary humanitarianism to save you from the path of death and to keep you from cutting yourself off from the people!"

Then the four prisoners pinned me to the ground, and the duty prisoner, with his strong peasant hands, held my head. The clinic worker fed a rubber tube into my nostril, forcing it in inch by inch. I felt a stabbing, burning pain, and my throat tasted salty. "Far enough," he muttered as he began to pour a thin gruel through a funnel into the tube.

That afternoon I lay on the concrete floor and swallowed the blood that dripped from my nasal cavity down my throat. The Communist Party's revolutionary humanitarianism had kept me from death.

On the tenth morning Captain Gao appeared again. I never opened my eyes, but I could tell from the voices that he had brought along a different group of prisoners. Maybe he wanted others to benefit from this lesson in re-education, I thought vaguely.

"Wu Hongda!" he called. "Have you straightened out your thinking? Do you want to continue to alienate yourself from the people or are you ready to walk on the bright path of confessing and receiving leniency?"

I did not respond. Again the duty prisoner held my head. "Today change to the right nostril," he said as he fed in the tube. I seemed to feel less pain the second time.

When the prisoners released their grip on my arms and legs, I felt a slight pressure in my right hand. I realized dimly that someone had passed me a small wad of paper. I didn't move. I heard the team leave, and the duty prisoner pushed me inside.

Smoothing the paper, I narrowed my eyes and recognized Zhao's cramped handwriting. "Go ahead and confess. Only Guo and Chen. No need for sacrifice." I rolled up the note and swallowed it immediately. True to his word, Zhao had made a plan to help me.

On the eleventh morning I heard again the approach of footsteps and recognized Captain Gao's voice. "I'm ready to confess," I called out weakly. "I'm ready to eat."

"What is it you want to confess?"

I tried to speak, but the pain in my nose and throat turned my words to a low grunt. Captain Gao told the duty prisoner to support my head so I could speak. The shift in position brought a gush of blood from my nose and mouth.

"Remove him!" ordered Gao. "Send him back to his company and give him three days to write a full confession. Tell the kitchen to prepare sick-list rations. If he doesn't confess completely, he will return."

The ordeal had ended. For two days I could not move from the kang. No one could express sympathy to me, but I could see concern in my squad mates' eyes. They would offer me a drink of hot water or a small piece of wotou. Guo caught a frog in the fields and the second night managed to hand me a bowl of tender, steamed meat. Gradually my strength returned, and I felt amazed at my body's resilience. I felt no hatred for my captors, no desire for revenge. I was alive. Nothing else mattered.

Before my release Guo and Chen had already undergone separate struggle meetings and criticized themselves before their squad members. The police believed the case had been handled successfully and treated my written confession as a formality. They had intercepted the letters quickly, discovered and severely punished the ringleader, prevented a suicide, and extracted a full confession. They considered the matter closed. On my sixth day out of confinement, still weak but largely recovered, I returned to labor. It was September 17, 1965.

Red in Tooth and Claw: Twenty-Six Years in Communist Chinese Prisons

Pu Ning

PU NING (1917–) is a prolific and famous Chinese writer who has often been compared to Solzhenitsyn because of their shared "passion for documenting the evil deeds perpetrated by the Communists; they are also both serious literary artists" (C. T. Hsia). In 1958 he was forced to make self-criticism; in 1960 he was sent to the countryside to undergo "labor reform" for a year and two months. In 1969 he was imprisoned for over one year; subsequently, he was forced to do hard labor under community supervision. In 1978 he was "rehabilitated," and in 1983 he was allowed to move to Taiwan.

In Taiwan, Ning met Han Wei-tien, a former high-ranking officer of the Chinese Nationalist Army who participated in anticommunist underground activities on the mainland and after his arrest in 1951 spent twenty-six years in Chinese Communist prisons and labor camps. Wei-tien was actually sentenced to life imprisonment, and his wife was forced to divorce him (as was a frequent practice in such cases). The verdict also noted that he "refus[ed] to be frank, bore grudges without repentance, and chose to be stubborn to the last." He was released in 1976. After his release he wrote a detailed journal recording his life and imprisonment. Pu Ning suggested that he rewrite the story and subsequently turned Wei-tien's experiences into Red in Tooth and Claw, *excerpts from which follow.*

Pu Ning's narrative suggests that there were many similarities between the goals and practices of the Soviet Gulag and its Chinese counterpart. In China too, forced labor was used extensively for economic and strategic military purposes and human lives were considered expendable, lavishly and wastefully used to accomplish economic goals, especially given the scarcity of appropriate machinery. The narrator in this reading worked in remote areas near Tibet building the road from Hsining, capital of Tsinghai Province, to Lhasa, and later in the Telingha Labor Corrections farm located in the basin of the Gobi desert.

. . . .

From Pu Ning, Red in Tooth and Claw: Twenty-Six Years in Communist Chinese Prisons, © *1994 by Pu Ning.*

Starvation was endemic. Inmates were classified according to their "crimes" and usefulness and fed accordingly. Injured workers received only two-thirds of their ration. It was forbidden to utter the word "hunger"; doing so could lead to being accused of "spreading rumor in order to bring about anarchy." Overall, conditions were probably worse—in the period described below, at any rate—than in the Soviet camps, and the guards appear to have been more brutal. Conditions improved after Mao's death and the political changes that followed (the same process took place in the Soviet Union after Stalin's death).

. . . . .

The cell was twenty-odd meters deep. It was cylindrical, about one meter in diameter and walled with bricks made from yellow clay. On its top was a one-inch-thick round wooden cover divided into two even sections. Each section was joined to an iron chain, the other end of which was fastened to the brick balustrade surrounding the cell.

Early in the winter of 1967, four ganbu[1] and three guards took me to the well from an interrogation room of the prison house at Telingha, in the Tsaidamu Basin, where I had been cross-examined for a long time. I remember thinking it was already as cold as deep winter.

The well was in a large fenced yard. At each corner of the yard a fully armed cadre stood guard over the well and the prison house nearby. As soon as I was brought to the well, one of the cadres who had been irritated by my answers during the cross-examination angrily commanded the guards, "Drop him down!" Then he turned to me and said in a tone of warning: "Reflect well on what you've said while you're down below! We'll come back later to ask you more questions."

A basket was brought, made of willow branches strung with four thick cords and tied to a thick rope more than twenty meters long. Willow baskets are a traditional craft of the peasants of the North. It was to be my personal elevator. I dared not hesitate, but stepped into the basket slowly and sat in it without stirring. At one point I risked giving the commander a cold smile. However, I knew I could dare no more than this if I meant to live. A guard then came with a key, opened the lock on the iron chain of the wooden cover, and lifted the cover. Another guard came and unfettered my hands. With a third guard, they grasped the long thick rope tied to the basket and began to let me down slowly into the well. But when I was yet some meters above the bottom, they let me drop—purposely, I guessed. With the shock of the fall, I passed out.

When I regained consciousness, my whole body was aching, but I thought I was lucky to be still alive. I knew I was to be imprisoned at the bottom of the well until I was willing to tell the Communists what they wanted to hear. Now, as I looked around, I found that darkness had enveloped everything: they had again covered the well.

I had neither matches nor a lighter. I was trapped in the dark. After considering my plight for a while, I began to crawl, groping. Then I sat up to think again. Suddenly, I noticed a foul smell. I studied the smell uncomfortably for a time before I realized that it was only the smell of urine and feces. This well had been a cell for other prisoners before me. They had eaten, slept, and excreted all in the same place. I reached out my hands and touched the ground to "see" if I had crawled into anything unmentionable. I had, and I had already rubbed my clothing in some of it.

The bottom of the well was like a cave. Near the surrounding wall, I could not stand up without hitting a protrusion, but I could stand upright and jump as high as I was able in the central part, where the shaft of the well rose up to the top. Estimating with my groping hands, I guessed my living space was about two meters in diameter. This made me a bit thankful to the designer: If the space had been any smaller, I might not have been able to stretch out comfortably when I lay down.

Fortunately, the well was dry. I cleaned my hands by rubbing them against the wall and then lay down for a long rest.

About two hours later I heard noise coming from the top of the well. Then half of the well-cover was lifted. Some light shone down, enabling me to see that the bottom was covered with pebbles and broken pieces of stone in sand. As the light was dim, I supposed it was getting dark outside.

Then I saw a basket being let down from above. When it reached me, I found there was a mug inside. It was my evening meal. I took the mug out of the basket and looked at its contents: some rice gruel with boiled Chinese cabbage. But I found no chopsticks. This was probably to prevent me from killing myself by swallowing them. Before I could finish the thought, the basket was lifted up and the well was covered again. The dim light had been with me for no more than five minutes. Suddenly very hungry, I finished the food at once. While eating, I held the mug all the time. I never put it on the ground for fear of what it might touch.

I didn't feel too bad that afternoon and evening. I believed that they probably wouldn't keep me imprisoned there for a long time. Besides, I was too tired for any quick or appropriate response to my situation. As I lay on the ground, I felt the pebbles and broken pieces of stone hard and uncomfortable underneath my body, but the thick cotton clothes I wore prevented them from hurting me. The most unpleasant thing was still the smell. I wondered why the former occupants hadn't tried to keep the cell cleaner. Was it because they came for such a short time? Were they so disheartened by their plight that they had no will to do anything? Or were they so weak that they had no strength to stir at all? Before I finished puzzling this out, I realized that I had lost any sense of the smell, though the disgusting atmosphere had entered deep in me.

On the whole, my first night in the well-cell was full of ease compared with my nights above, which were full of pains, both physical and mental. For fourteen years I had either been sick or forced to labor like an animal. I had had very few days at the prison when I did not feel the pressure ready to crush me as surely as a huge rock. Now I was alone in the cell. I thought I might be able to get a good long rest if they did not bother me. In this dark world, I thought, I would be free from the weary life outside and even the struggle to maintain my dignity. No one, I believed, could understand how I cherished this chance of having someplace entirely to myself.

That night I slept soundly. I even had the sweetest dream of my life. I dreamed I had been released and led by a divinity to a new world, a new Arcadia. When I awoke the next morning, I still fancied I was enjoying my life in that blissful land, until a dull pain intruded. But still, even though I was not in the world of my dreams, just to be away from the Communist leaders' whistles and whips, from having to labor in chilly weather was enough compensation for the lightless imprisonment.

Sometime the next morning, another succession of noises came from the top of the well. I was given a mug of gruel for breakfast. Again, I had about five minutes of daylight while a basket was let down and then lifted up through the half-open cover of the well.

After finishing breakfast, the first thing I did was try to clean the ground of my "home." I rid my garment of the dirt which was stuck to it, then used my hands as brooms and gingerly swept the floor. I collected all the filth in one corner. When the work was done, I scooped up a handful of sand and scrubbed my hands with it. I finished by rubbing my hands on the wall, to make sure that they were as clean as possible. It was a pity that I had nothing to dispel the unpleasant smell emitted from the corner of filth, which I decided to use as my temporary "toilet." After cleaning the ground, I found I could further improve it by removing the jagged stones to make it smooth. As I had time to spare, I took great care in carrying out my improvements. Finally, I had a little space which I could call both my seat and my bed and which I believed was tolerably comfortable for one used to the meager comforts of prison life.

In my school days I had read the adventures of Robinson Crusoe, and the Englishman's plight on the deserted island naturally came to mind. I was, like him, isolated from the outside world, but I was even more alone than he. He had at least had a dog for a companion, while I had nothing but dirt and stone. What made me, the "well-bottom Crusoe," even more miserable was that the space in which I dwelled was too limited to allow me any real activity at all. I saw no daylight except during the few minutes when they brought me my meals, but I could not spend all the long hours of endless night in sleep. I spent most of my time thinking. Very often this mental exercise carried me very far into the past. . . .

· · · · ·

Shanghai's Tilan Bridge Jail was the biggest jail in Asia. After 1949, when the Communists had taken China, the jail became a monster's den full of skeletons, and a magician's cage for turning human beings into wild animals. Its concrete buildings, as formidable as citadels, were built in the twenties by a construction bureau of the British Concession. Until 1949, its eight prison houses were named Chung, Hsiao, Jen, Ai, Hsin, Yi, Ho, and Ping. (After that year, the eight houses were numbered from 1 to 8 instead.) Each house had five stories, and each story had eighty-eight cells. An entire house could accommodate 2,200 prisoners. So the eight houses together could take in 17,600 prisoners. Later, an all-female prison house capable of holding 7,200 women was added. Still later, another prison house with a capacity of 6,000 was incorporated into the complex. Ultimately, Tilan Bridge Jail became a leviathan able to devour a total of 30,800 criminal minnows, so to speak. Besides the ten main prison houses, the jail complex boasted a hospital, a factory, and a large cooking works.

As you walked down any floor of the prison houses, you saw on both sides of the corridor a long succession of cells, the design of which was much like that of an American chicken farm. Each side of the corridor had forty-four cells, each of which was three meters long and one and a half meters wide. Such a small cell was often crowded with three to six prisoners. To get to the cell, you stepped into an aisle that led to all the other cells that were on the same side. The aisle looked very long, but it was so narrow that it barely allowed two people to pass each other. On the other side of the aisle, there was a horizontal iron pipe more than one meter above the floor. The pipe extended to all the other cells on the same side. Below the pipe were many horizontal iron plates constructed a few inches apart. Behind the iron plates was barbed wire, through which you could see another iron pipe and many more iron plates. After you crossed all the iron barriers, you came to another aisle. Only after you crossed the second aisle did you at last reach the "cage" for the "birds."

In the center of each prison house, from the top floor to the ground, there was a large circular opening ten meters in diameter. Looking down from the top floor from the edge of the opening, the guards could see clearly what was happening on each level below. Should there be any need, they could speak to everyone from this point. Beyond this was a thick concrete wall over three meters high. Beyond the wall there were eight towers where guards watched the surroundings day and night. Not even a bee, they said, could escape without being seen.

The immensity of the jail can be inferred from the fact that meals were sent to prisoners by a small train. It took eighty criminals to wash the tin boxes used to serve meals at the jail every day. These criminals washed the boxes at a long sink only one meter high, which forced the washers to bend down to work. After two hours in such a position, almost all the washers were doubled over, not unlike dead lobsters.

A jail often brews the thick and unpleasant atmosphere of a grave or a funeral parlor. The Tilan Bridge Jail was like that but it had also something special, something uniquely its own. Unlike most other jails, the Shanghai jail was very quiet. It was so quiet that you would be terrified by the silence as soon as you entered. Sometimes you might even be led to doubt that your ears were still working. For how could a gargantuan jail jammed with more than thirty thousand prisoners maintain such an unearthly hush? Its perfect silence made one think of the dead stillness at the bottom of the sea. The horror produced by the ruling Communists, I think, was best suggested by the jail's lack of noise. Once you were behind the bars of Tilan Bridge, you would never forget its atmosphere. It made you feel as if you were pickled in a mysterious element, mundane yet unbearable. The taste and the smell of imprisonment kept surging in your senses. There were times when you felt that all the walls had feet and were walking steadily and dismally toward you and that once they reached you they would hug you, pressing on your chest, your back, and your head, hugging you and pressing on you again and again until you thought your bones would break and your flesh would burst.

The overactive imagination was never entirely without material. For one thing, you no sooner entered your cell than you found twelve regulations written on the wall. Instantly, the twelve regulations were like twelve eyes watching over you, and your senses were immediately strained. These twelve rules were:

1. Sit still and behave well.
2. Resistance to repentance will bring ruthless reprisal. Criminal leaders will never be excused, though forced followers may be condoned.
3. Merits will always be rewarded. Great merits may result in release.
4. Stick to the regulations. No discussing them and no acting against them.
5. Obediently observe one another and quickly report anything suspicious to the managers.
6. Discuss no cases and exchange no addresses. Never call one another brothers. Do not attempt to build up affection.
7. Make no noise. Do not shout "Report!"[2]
8. Never shelter anyone, nor conceal anything.
9. Do not try to cultivate any feelings of unity. Do not send gifts or share food among yourselves.
10. No tête-à-têtes and no gestures of any sort.
11. Live regularly. Never stay up too late and never rise too early.
12. When meeting visitors, no private conversations and no shaking of hands are allowed.

Such rules are like so many cords or ropes constricting you. But what constricted us even more tightly was the space. A prison cell in Tilan Bridge measured 2.5 meters in length and 1.3 meters in width. When the British ruled here, such a cell held at most three prisoners. But when the new management took over, the same space was often crowded with six men, sometimes seven. It was also occupied by a stool, a stand, and a shelf. The space left for the poor jailbirds, if you can believe it, was so limited that six occupants were invariably forced to sleep all on one side, keeping their legs and bodies straight. They were so tightly packed together that to turn over was always a collective action; no individual could hope to roll over in his sleep without the others' cooperation. Even at midnight, supposedly the quietest hour of all, the terrifying silence of the jail would be broken by sounds of swearing and cursing—because some troubled sleepers were struggling for sleeping space. But the biggest problem was if you woke up and had to relieve yourself: You didn't dare to just get up and go. Once you left your place, it would immediately be occupied by the ones sleeping beside you. And once your sleeping space was occupied by the others, the only way to regain it was to wake everybody up and ask for a total rearrangement of the shared space. In fact, those who could not refrain from getting up during the night often roused their fellow sleepers, causing arguments. The wardens never seriously punished such arguments, although they broke the jail's silence and were obviously against the rules. Actually, the "managers" of the jail were only too happy to have some quarrels among the jailbirds. They thought quarrels prevented the prisoners from uniting and made them eager to spy on each other.

Crammed into such small cells, the inmates naturally had no room to exercise. During the day, we just sat and ate and excreted. We were asked to sit all day long. Worse still, we were told to sit cross-legged with our hands on our knees and our heads bent down in a manner of meditation. This position was held from early morning till nine o'clock in the evening, when whistles were blown to signal bedtime.

One summer, it was said, the weather was very hot. There were bedbugs in the cells. One hungry bug crawled onto a sitter's foot and bit him. The sitter could not bear to be so ill used by such a tiny creature and slapped at it. Just as the prisoner struck at the insect, a prison guard was going by. He singled out the offender at once.

"What do you mean by doing things like that, you bastard?" the guard shouted.

"The bug was biting me, you know. I had to—"

"You had to revolt?"

"It really hurt."

"You bastard, what an aristocratic thinker you pretend to be! Not yet corrected? We proletariats have been bitten by all sorts of bugs the year round, and we think nothing of it. How can you make such a fuss when these little things are kissing you? Are you still an elitist? Are you still particular about your hygiene? It seems you're as anti-revolutionary as ever. Don't you know your crimes? Write, write down your self-criticism quickly! Otherwise, I'll make you eat those manacles!"

This anecdote illustrates the true nature of the first regulation, "Sit still and behave well." But the poor guy in the story was lucky; the guard was obviously in a good humor. It if had been otherwise, even as a minor offender of Regulation One the prisoner would have had his hands fettered at once. He would have been forced to "keep digging out the roots of his anti-revolutionary ideas" and condemned for "revolting against prison regulations, agitating malcontents for an uprising, and attempting to annihilate communism."

Those who were asked to write down their self-criticism were already in a sort of danger. Later on, their self-criticism might become evidence of their crimes. And in most cases such "evidence" could bring about severer penalties, even capital punishment.

Even if the inmates had not violated any regulations, they were often called individually to the police office and were pressured into disclosing their fellow inmates' "unlawful" words or actions. For the Communists such disclosures were grounds for a "suspect" being shackled, confined in a "rubber cell," or even put to death.

Every day the prisoners had only half an hour to "fang fang," that is, to take a breath outside the cells. Prisoners were given just two meals a day, one in the morning and the other in the afternoon. The morning meal was a small amount of a very thin porridge made from a little rice in a lot of water. Two hours after you ate, or rather drank, that gruel, the gnawing feeling in your stomach would return. The afternoon meal was always boiled rice with a little vegetable, never with any meat. Cooked with neither oil nor salt nor any other seasonings, the meal really had no flavor at all.

Every prisoner was allotted a ration of rice each month. There were three different allotments based on the prisoners' ages and statures. The big allotment was twenty-two jin of rice per month; the medium, twenty jin; and the small, eighteen jin. The rations were barely enough to keep the prisoners from starving. But if a prisoner could survive his first five years in the jail, he would be considered fit to live on. He would then be entitled to such meager amounts of food three times a day, and he would be given more rations and even be allowed to eat enjoyable food (one jin of dry meat and ten apples per month), legally sent to him by his family or friends.

No inmate at Tilan Bridge Jail ever stopped feeling hungry. . . .

. . . . .

Prison House No. 7 of Tilan Bridge Jail was a special prison for those convicts considered particularly dangerous. Before I was sentenced I had been in House No. 1. I had once pretended to commit suicide there, though, so I was considered dangerous and moved to No. 7. There I thought I would suffer more severely. But some ten days after I came to No. 7 (toward the end of August that year), we heard, quite unexpectedly, a loud and clear broadcast from the building's loudspeakers.

"Listen, men. You are soon to go to a new environment. There, everything is better. There, you can have meat for meals, and you can eat your fill. There, you will all get fat because you will be well fed. There, you will have fresher air and can have enough exercise. In a word, you had better go there rather than stay here for good."

The words were obviously from a "leader," who purposely softened his usually rough tones. The broadcast was repeated twice, and the next day a female voice repeated the same message. The third day it was a man's voice again. For three days the broadcast penetrated our ears like bullets, although it had been so toned down as to make it sound like music or even like a nightingale's song.

We knew we were about to be sent somewhere for "labor correction," but we did not know where. Finally, the day came when each of us was given a suit of thick black cotton clothes along with a cotton cap. They also promised to give us each a leather suit later. These signs showed that we were to be sent to the Northwest or the Northeast. . . .

．　．　．　．　．

The first day on the train, we were each given a loaf of black bread, which we found too dry to chew. We had little water to drink and were often very thirsty. At midnight we stopped at a station where we found well-armed guards standing on the platform. We were told to carry our common commodes out of the train, clean them, and carry them back with two big barrels of water for each compartment. After a long day's thirst, we all drank the water and filled our canteens with it as happily as one who sees rain after a long drought. But by the next day we suffered from thirst again, as each of us had to make do with only one mouthful of water for the day.

There were four small windows on the ceiling of each compartment. The windows were blocked with fine iron bars to prevent escape, so the circulation of air was hindered. Day and night, watching from our crowded compartment through the four small squares of barred windows, we saw only three kinds of skies: bright sky, cloudy sky, and dark sky. As to the passing landscape, we could see nothing except when the train stopped and the iron doors were opened for a moment. We were often allowed to stay on the platform for a while if the train stopped at night, though there was nothing to see but a few lights glowing in the dark. Soon we were sent to the train again and buried in the iron coffins, which offered no egress.

Each cattle car was about ten pings and held about seventy or eighty of us packed as tightly as sardines. Day and night, whether we were sitting, standing, or lying, we could never straighten our legs and were always in close contact with one another. Flesh stuck to flesh. In such an overcrowded space, the air was always dirty, and we never had enough oxygen. What came into our mouths and noses was mostly carbon dioxide. Ammonia emanated from the commodes and our sweating bodies twenty-four hours a day. There were times, indeed, when we felt we could no longer breathe.

Some of us began to get sick. Fever, headache, dizziness, diarrhea, and stomachache were the most common symptoms. Those who started vomiting were left vomiting until they dirtied themselves, their nearby fellow sufferers, and the already filthy compartment. Those who suffered from diarrhea had to crawl or run over the others' bodies and rush to the commodes. If they were too slow, they just ended up emptying their bowels into their shorts or pants and polluting our small living area. As for those with fever, we could not help them in any way; there wasn't space enough for them to lie down for a good rest.

The train ran ten days and ten nights from Jen-zu to Hekou in Kansu Province. We took turns reclining, sitting, and standing. In any position, we jostled, squeezed, and stuck to each other. When we stood or sat, we were like so many candles on a candelabra. Only we did not burn with light. We just consumed our energy and got sore legs, which gradually grew worse until we lay down and had them massaged for a while.

I believe horses, cattle, hogs, and sheep were better treated on the train than we were. For they were treasures alive. And they were more used to being penned up and conveyed by such vehicles. When we arrived at Hekou, more than half of us packed in the iron cans had fallen ill. Fortunately, however, the sick were all sent off to a hospital there. The ten days' journey was for us only a prelude to our new nightmarish life. I had a presentiment that even though I had been lucky enough to escape the diseases, I would not be so lucky with the nightmares to come....

. . . . .

The plateau in the west of Chinghai Province (about two hundred li from Huang-yuen) has an average height of two thousand meters above sea level. It is a composite of high mountain ranges. When you looked up at the mountain tops or down into the valleys, you could really feel the sublimity of nature and see its beauty. But we were not sightseers. We were road-builders. For us, those sublime and beautiful hills and vales were obstacles we had to overcome. According to the lunar calendar, the three months from the middle of the Tenth Month to the middle of the next year's First Month are the coldest months of Chinghai. After the Eleventh Month, the skies never clear. Blizzards are frequent. Snow covers the lowlands as well as the uplands, the grass as well as the trees. Before the snow comes, you can see a little winding path leading to Hsining, the capital of Chinghai. It was an important route for the Mongolian and Tibetan hordes of the old days, and is still an important passage for the wandering nomads there. On a good day, you can see camels, yaks, or sheep driven along the path and appearing between the peaks. When we arrived there, part of the path was only one or two feet in width, and the whole path was thickly covered with snow. We were asked to widen the path so that two trucks could pass each other on the road. You can imagine how tremendous a task it was.

And you can imagine how the task was made more gargantuan by the fact that we had no modern machines of any sort. To build the road, we had only pickaxes, shovels, hammers, baskets, and carts. We dug through layers of ice, shovel by shovel. We cracked the ice plates with pickaxes and cleared the ground with spades. We ate away huge rocks bit by bit with hammers and chisels. We tied baskets with ropes to poles and loaded the baskets with earth or ice, rocks, or gravel. We shouldered the poles with loaded baskets. We removed all the bumps in the road and used these to fill in the holes, all with our hands. We occasionally used carts to carry sand, soil, and gravel for the same purpose. We also carried buckets of water to sprinkle on the pavement before we smoothed it with whatever heavy object (not necessarily rollers!) we had on hand. All this was manual labor indeed.

But this was not all you would see while we were at work. There were also some unexpected scenes.

"Thud!"

A poor fellow fell to the bottom of a deep valley. Some said he plunged in on purpose.

"Whoosh! Crack! Crash!"

By a precipice, a man in black clothes and a black cap was said to have fallen, carelessly. It was getting dark. In the dark places "careless" laborers kept falling from crags or cliffs. And nobody seemed to care. Then there was a miracle. With a series of rumbling sounds, rocks big and small, earth high and low, trees, moss, and men, all moved and rolled and glided and slid. Some minutes later, on a hillside, corpses loomed pitiably. We could not tell exactly when the earthquake occurred. We had lost our sense of time. In our world we had only two colors other than red—black and white. We also had only two sorts of time, daytime and nighttime. We thought the "miracle" happened during the dark time, for we did not see it very clearly.

But we knew why men continually fell. There were those who fell to kill themselves. Such were people in despair. They often fell at a good site, on the brink of a steep face of rock, perhaps. From there they needed only one jump to fall straight to the bottom without having to be bothered by ivy leaves or branches. From there they could imagine themselves as eagles descending down and down and down on their prey.

There were also those who fell because the "leaders" forced them. These were often "stubborn" prisoners, whom the "leaders" were not satisfied merely to blame, curse, and threaten. Hence, when the time came, they were forced to fall (probably with guns). Such men never fell at good sites. When they fell, the nearby trees and rocks rushed in to mangle them.

The third class of people who fell were those who had a poor sense of balance. They did not know they would fall. They just worked and walked until suddenly, one slip, and they had lost their chance to complain that it was too dark to see anything.

The fourth group fell, of course, because of a natural disaster, a disaster that probably happened because Heaven and Earth were not happy about being constantly annoyed by us: "How could you dig, strike, and crack all the time?" they might ask. If you want to be exact about the total number of casualties, I can tell you only this: Each group had at least several dozen and at most several hundred. Not too heavy a number, was it?

If you construct a road on a plain, you can at least stand securely, but on the plateau, the ground rises and falls abruptly. The slopes are often difficult to climb, not to mention to walk or stand on. When the snowy season comes, the slopes become so slippery that even to climb them is dangerous. We were asked to build a road on such slopes.

It is superfluous to emphasize how difficult it was for us to crack ice, shoulder baskets, carry stones, etc., on such uneven ground. It is not superfluous, I believe, for me to repeat that we were asked to build a road there by hand, without any modern machines. I believe twenty thousand bees can build a big hive very easily in a tree. But I do not believe the same bees can build the same hive easily in the water. We were like so many bees there. We were also asked to build, in an alien environment, what was beyond our ability to build. So we were not sensibly exploited at all. If you want to squeeze any meaning out of that fanatic enterprise, you ought to view it from a different angle. You must know that we were not only being exploited, we were also being punished and tortured.

Later, they sent rollers to us. These were not machine-operated rollers, but rollers to be pulled by horses or donkeys, each weighing over a thousand kilograms. But instead of letting beasts do the work, the Communists ordered us to pull the rollers back and forth over the uneven ground. In doing this work, we were not just tortured, we were humiliated too. For we were treated no better than beasts. . . .

. . . . .

The north wind blew constantly over the plateau. Our clothes were useless against it. It chilled our hands, our legs, our souls. We wielded the pickaxes, the shovels, all the tools in our hands, up and down, back and forth, high and low; we exercised ourselves in every possible way, every possible direction, hoping that we could thus keep warm and hold back the chill of the north wind. But we failed. We had no more strength. As we stopped plying our tools vigorously, the wind began again to bite into our flesh and bones. We were exhausted. We were numbed. The weak ones, aged or sick, suddenly fainted away. Some of us dropped, never to rise again, and falling snow began to cover the bodies with white shrouds.

By the time we reached the site for work early each morning, we had already begun to shudder from the cold. We stretched out our hands to pick up the tools we had left on the ground the previous night. (The Communists dared not let us take the tools back to the tents at night for fear that we might use them for rebellion.) But our hands were so stiff that they didn't even take our own orders. Besides, the tools were already buried deep beneath the previous night's snowfall. We strove to remove the ice. Then we held our tools tightly. Much too tightly, in fact. For we suddenly realized that our palms and the tools had been glued together. I did not know what to do next. I simply shook and pulled my hand off the tool with brute force. A layer of skin from my palm was pulled off too. My palm began to bleed. I wiped the blood with my coat sleeve. I also wiped the tool. Then I started to work.

My case was not the worst. Many others' hands were chapped from the cold, many had slits on their hands as long as babies' mouths, and the raw flesh there, they said, was deadly quick to pain. After eighty or ninety percent of us had got frostbite or chilblains on our hands, the Communists reported the situation to the higher officials, and we were each given a pair of cotton gloves.

The time we suffered most during the day was toward noon. By then we were already too hungry to do anything. But we dared not stop toiling, especially when a leader passed by. There were times when we were able to see our lunch boxes which had been sent to our working place, but the leaders refused to allow us to rest and eat immediately. On the contrary, they bade us work harder and try to finish the job at hand. Actually, they wanted us to wait until the meal was freezing cold so that we might suffer even in eating. We knew their maliciousness. But what could we do? We could only go on toiling until they blew the whistles.

Eating lunch was indeed a painful thing for us. The loaves of "woh-woh toes" had by then frozen as hard as stone. And we were so hungry. How we wanted to get them down into our stomachs immediately. But we couldn't. Besides some vegetable leaves, we had only some pickle and a little cold water for soup. We had nothing tasty or warm enough to help us chew the tough bread. Therefore, by the time each of us had finished getting down the "two hard stones," it was already time for the leaders to blow the whistles again, signaling us to resume our drudgery.

"Cold comes before frost, and chill comes after snow." This saying applies to our experience on the plateau. During the cold seasons on the plateau, we occasionally had one or two sunny days. But to see the sun did not necessarily mean that we felt warmer. A sunny sky after a heavy snowfall was often accompanied by a strong northwest wind. That wind was the coldest of all, sharper than a razor. Once our faces were exposed to it, they would soon start to shed layers of skin. So, during the cold periods, we were really afraid to see the sun and hear the wind.

It was often difficult for us to say how or why our fellows died. Many starved to death. But many froze to death, I believe. In fact, all sorts of deaths could be reduced to two primary reasons: hunger and cold. Some died exhausted. Others died spitting blood. Some killed themselves by jumping into the valley. If such people had been sufficiently fed and adequately sheltered, they would not have come to such ends. To die from hunger or cold is of course not to die a "natural" death. But after we had seen so many deaths in the cold time and in the cold place, we gradually became accustomed to seeing people dying or dead. We developed "cold eyes." We even developed a philosophy toward death. We thought all deaths were natural deaths. We were like flowers. Flowers can wither, be blown away, be stamped on, be nipped, or be scorched. All ways that lead them to death are natural in the world of nature. The same with us human beings. To be tortured to death has been natural in human history, too.

Even with this knowledge, we shuddered in the shadow of death. After all, we were no real philosophers. We still hated the Communists for their whipping, cudgeling, and shooting. We regarded them as cruel death dealers. In the eyes of the Reds, our lives were insignificant substitutes for things insubstantial. For them our lives were no longer lives, but opportunities for torture, means of creating climaxes for tragedies.

I looked up ahead and saw the Sun Moon Mountain Range with its crags, cliffs, peaks, and precipices all steep and all covered with snow. As I looked farther, I saw the Mo-tien Ling, even loftier and more precipitous than the Sun Moon Mountains, with a summit capped with a thicker layer of ice. Then I looked at the rugged ground I was standing on and thought: "How can we ever build a road over this?" With this thought I looked at the mountains again; I suddenly felt that the mountain peaks were all devils' or monsters' heads gazing at me. I looked at myself and my fellow laborers. Our flesh was too thin and our bones too weak, and every pore of my skin felt the chill. . . .

. . . . .

The second half year of 1960 saw the greatest number of deaths from starvation. Every day, from every Big Team, more than thirty corpses were conveyed to a yard by cart. That yard became a horrible place. When passing it, we experienced a spine-chilling gloom. We did not even dare to cough in the presence of that "graveyard of cadavers." At night, if a queer sound was heard from that direction, we would imagine that ghouls were feeding on the corpses, or that the starved were still groaning for food even after death. Every week, every day, every hour, one corpse after another, each stiff as a tree trunk, fell before our eyes. We could not believe that death could come so easily. The dead bodies were like raindrops, and we stood in stormy purgatory for three years on end.

In those years, starvation became a sort of mental manacle, depriving us of our freedom to think. We could not for a moment forget its threat. It seemed to be continuously putrefying the air and making it difficult to breathe. How we longed to swallow that sinister word along with the morsel of food allotted to us! During the slow torture of starvation, we became sick enough to imagine a fire burning our bodies, or a pump forcing out every bit of liquid.

If you saw us, you would find each face starved into a pale mask, without flesh or life. Such faces were little different from those of the departed. No matter its shape, the face of a starvation victim is covered by only a fragile layer of skin. The eyes are hardly eyes but rather the pits of nuts fitted into sockets of bone. Such eyes shed no light. Yet, they bespeak the urgency of their owner's case. Although ghastly, they are more serviceable than the mouth, for they plead better than any words.

Some fellows were still alive when they lay down at night, and at dawn they were dead. They had become icy bodies with stiffened limbs. Nobody knew the exact time they had yielded up their last breaths. If you went close enough to examine the corpses, you might find the eyes of some of them wide open, while others still clenched their teeth. These phenomena occurred so frequently to the dead at the farm, one wondered if they were significant gestures. We speculated that a man who died with his eyes wide open had died somehow unsatisfied or unavenged, and a man with clenched teeth had not yet ended his hatred. Or, perhaps, the starved were still straining their eyes to find food, and, finding none, could only bite their teeth together tightly.

The search for food was everybody's priority in those times. The kitchen became a magnet. On our farm, many stronger fellows gathered there to rob the food senders. It is hard to believe that men on the brink of death could still be so energetic, but they struggled out of their beds, staggered up to the kitchen door, and lay in ambush there, waiting for the moment when the bamboo hampers of loaves were carried out of the kitchen. They were all prepared to steal. One day these starving plunderers snatched the loaves away, and afterward many suspects were imprisoned in special cells, and kept constantly in close custody until they died. Strife was inevitable among these men. Three to five people died every day fighting one another for food at the kitchen door, or in the yard. They did not fight with clubs or fists, but merely pushed each other with their remaining strength. That push was often enough to knock down one's opponent and deprive him of his life.

Death took a great variety of forms among the starved. In addition to those who were pushed in fights there were those who simply stumbled and fell, shattering their fragile bones while happily biting off their first pieces of "woh-wah-toe." There were those who, having finished their own meals, took quick, shy glances at others who were still eating, and found their mouths watering profusely and their hearts straining a little too much. They didn't recover from these strokes.

The starving criminals still had to labor, but the weaker and more miserable tried to save their energy by evading hard work. They actually did not toil as much as they rested, and their tasks were often not completed. At the end of each day, when they were walking back for the night's rest, they had no strength to walk steadily, and each wanted to rest his hand on someone else's shoulder while they walked in line. But no one could allow such a fatal burden on his weak shoulder, and all staggered along alone.

Back at the tents, no one felt he was still himself. It is strange that hunger can cause so much pain in your body. It seems like a vise pinching all your bones, which feel dislocated for lack of flesh and sinews. Your head, hands, feet, even your belly and bowels, are no longer where they normally are. You are tempted to cry out loud but haven't the strength. When experiencing extreme hunger, one can barely utter an audible sound.

Before dinner time, some of the prisoners gathered outside the kitchen. They were not allowed in but could stay outside for a short while watching the preparation of dinner. They watched with their dull eyes sunken in their big sockets. They watched attentively the way the kitchen workers mixed together flours of different colors (usually white and black), made it into dough, shaped it into loaves of bread, and steamed the loaves in a tight basket and sieve of bamboo. Occasionally, a breeze might blow some of the escaping steam out of the kitchen. The steam, with its accompanying smell of food, became a treat for the "hungry ghosts" waiting outside. They inhaled it with avarice. And they deluded themselves into believing that some form of food had already entered their bodies.

At last, one kitchen worker would strike an iron plate with a stick, giving the signal that dinner was ready to be served. At this everybody was cheered, though each would be given only two loaves as small as one's fists. The two small loaves were swallowed down quickly by each "gluttonous criminal." If someone were slower than his peers in devouring the bread, he would be watched and envied. His neighbors would stare at him greedily, hoping that some crumbs might fall unexpectedly onto the ground so that they could snatch up the godsend for themselves. But such a thing never happened. When anybody swept the ground with his eyes, the best he could grab was perhaps a discarded rotten leaf of Chinese cabbage, and that leaf was regarded as a treasure. When the lucky finder thrust it into his mouth, he probably believed it was his savior, too.

The threat of starvation, like any other prolonged frightful threat, is liable to cause insanity. But how can you believe the insanity I saw in our famine-stricken area? Hunger drove many men so mad, they took their enamel basins to the fertilizer pits, and fetched back basinfuls of night soil. They then washed the dirty stuff with water again and again in order to pick out the undigested grain that remained in the excrement. Strange to say, they did find a lot of such grain and ate it for supper.

How did they come to know that such "treasure" was there to be found? The criminals were divided into different classes, allotted different tasks, and treated quite differently. The first-class prisoners were those Party leaders, officials, or officers who had committed "errors"—Communists were seldom said to have committed crimes, and they were seldom openly called "criminal" although they could become prisoners. Such prisoners, when undergoing "labor corrections," were often assigned to work as kitchen managers, prison doctors, carpenters, masons, ironsmiths, tailors, cleaners, keepers of grain yards or barns, and members of watering teams. Since they were engaged in such "lighter and nobler" work, they were said to be undergoing "great labor corrections." And those "great laborers" often enjoyed privileges unshared by other classes. They were not guarded by armed men, they had bigger allotments of rations; they were often free to take a walk inside or outside the prison house; when they worked outdoors, they had more freedom; they were not followed everywhere and watched over by guards. Thus, they often crept to the grain yards or barns and stole grain. The keepers of the yards or barns normally overlooked their pilfering, for they were pilferers, too. The pilferers often had no opportunity to cook the grain before they ate it, however. Whenever they failed to digest the grain because of diarrhea or other diseases, therefore, the grain would be passed out whole and sound. Knowledge of this situation made the grain prey to the insanity of the "hungry worms" who came out clutching their enamel basins.

The "high-class laborers" usually did not dare to steal too much grain at one time, but the more daring ones often had grain to sell or to exchange for clothing or tobacco. The kitchen managers or workers had, of course, food for sale or exchange. They stole flour, bread, and edible oil. They were therefore the patrons of the "rich" starving criminal laborers who could obtain regularly from their families some amount of daily necessities. During the three years of great famine, while the poor and law-abiding prisoners starved, the wealthy ones and the cunning Communists managed to dodge the brunt of the "natural disaster."

As for the miserable ones, their plight was almost too horrible to describe. For me, the most terrifying thing was done by the watering team. They took advantage of the hours they were out working to dig out the newly buried men who had died of starvation. The dead bodies were usually buried in the salty ground within the confines of the farm. In winter the graves were dug to only one meter's depth, while in summer they were dug to two meters. But in all seasons, the bodies were dumped into the graves and covered with only a thin layer of sandy soil. Therefore, it was fairly easy to dig out a newly buried corpse.

Nobody wanted to believe what the watering team did with the dead bodies they excavated, but it was true; they sold them as meat. Although the starved men had little flesh left, it was considered safer to eat than the flesh of those who had died from disease. The watering team cut the remaining flesh from the arms, thighs and breasts of the newly-buried corpses. The meat was then exchanged for clothing, tobacco, and other daily necessities. The transaction was of course, very secret. The "seller" usually pretended to be selling horse meat, camel meat, or the meat of an unknown rare animal. The "buyer" would not inquire into the nature of the meat offered. When you are on the brink of starvation, you don't mind eating mouse meat or lizard meat. In fact, any meat is a delicacy to someone willing to eat even soap or cotton.

So, many ate dead men's flesh cooked or raw, and counted themselves lucky. But such meat was not healthful, although tasty to the eaters, and some time after eating a large quantity of it the eater might swell up and die, only half suspecting he had fed on his former fellow laborers.

The hungry "birds" ("Birds will die for food," goes a proverb of ours) who had no money or barter had no chance to taste the meat offered by the watering team. After they got tired of supplementing their diet with weeds or herbs, they often resorted to theft. If they couldn't steal meat directly, they would steal others' money or possessions to barter for this precious commodity. As a result, loss of money or other valuable things became a daily threat to all the prison laborers. Some people thought that staying in the tent might be a way to protect their belongings, but they were unable to because suspending their labor (even for sickness) would, according to the regulations, cost them half of their daily allowance of food (two loaves of bread would be reduced to one). Under such circumstances, many people decided the only way to protect themselves was to steal. If your jacket were stolen, for instance, you would try to steal one from someone else. This practice naturally added many more cases of theft to the already growing list, and no day passed without quarrels, curses, and despair among the laborers.

The conditions were grim. There was a man named Chang He-lin who was from Hunan Province, where he had been a security officer. He was about fifty, and at Telingha he belonged to the Second Middle Team of the First Big Team of criminal laborers. I was then in the same unit, and I noticed he was absent one day when they called the roll. When they noticed him missing, the leaders sent two malicious men to find him. He was sick in bed, and they dragged him naked (he didn't wear any clothes in bed) to the gate of our camp.

"Why didn't you get out and work?" the leaders asked him. He couldn't reply. He only showed them his pale face and two closed eyes.

"We'll shoot you if you refuse to work."

But he still made no answer.

"All right, take him to the work site!" the Communists shouted.

He remained silent. Some of his fellow laborers laughed at his nakedness while others shed tears for him. Then the two malicious men brought a big basket and pole. They put him into the basket, hung it on the pole and carried him to the place where we were to labor that day. It was very cold then (it must have been several degrees below freezing), and on the way to the worksite, Chang froze to death. That fulfilled the leaders' threat: "Sick or dead, all malingerers must be taken to their place of work."

Jiuzhen Prison—A Tibetan Account

Tenzin Choedrak

Tenzin Choedrak (1922–) was a Tibetan physician practicing traditional Tibetan medicine when he became one of the personal physicians of the Dalai Lama in 1954. He was arrested during the Tibetan uprising against the Chinese occupation in 1959, held without charge, and finally sent to a succession of prisons and prison camps. He was sentenced to seventeen years of hard labor. Released in 1976, after completing his sentence he returned to medical practice. In 1980 he was allowed to leave for India, where he has been living ever since.

His account illuminates the brutal treatment of political prisoners, especially those suspected of supporting or sympathizing with Tibetan demands for autonomy and religious freedom. His arrest was also part of the Chinese campaign to purge Tibet of individuals who held high positions in Tibetan society or government prior to the Chinese occupation.

. . . . .

On October 15, 1959, the prison's [the maximum-security PLA prison in Lhasa] seven hundred inmates were drawn up in long files surrounded by Chinese troops, in the southern quad. Seated at a small table before them, the camp commander spoke. "Among you there is a very stubborn group who persist in telling lies and refuse to recognize the truth," he said. "We have decided to send them for further study in China. Conditions are far better there than here. Food is more plentiful, and their needs will be amply provided for." The results of seven months of interrogation were then read out: four prisoners were to be released and twenty-one would be sent to work at the hydroelectric plant at Nachen Thang. The seventy-six men bound for China were to leave within two weeks. The prisoners, however, were not told who had been selected for the last contingent until three days before their departure. At that time, on the morning of October 29, Dr. Choedrak was informed that he had been picked. Because neither charge nor sentence had been given him, he didn't actually believe he was going to China. Instead, he assumed that the selected

From Tenzin Choedrak, "Jiuzhen Prison—A Tibetan Account," in Geremie Barmé and John Minford, eds., Seeds of Fire: Chinese Voices of Conscience, *© 1986 by Geremie Barmé and John Minford. Reprinted by permission of Hill & Wang, a division of Farrar, Straus and Giroux, LLC.*

prisoners were to be taken somewhere nearby and, under one pretense or another, executed, their separation having been for this purpose only.

The next day Tenzin Choedrak's handcuffs and leg irons were removed and, along with the seventy-five other men, he was driven to the Norbulingka [the Jewel Park, the old summer palace of the Dalai Lama]. Quartered there for two nights and a day, Dr. Choedrak gradually made the acquaintance of his new prison mates—all of whom had held high positions in Tibetan society and government. The men were of one mind: even if China was, in fact, their destination, singled out as they were, there could be little doubt that their remaining time was limited. Their fear increased when, on the morning of their departure, they were permitted to bid farewell to their relatives. As dawn broke the prisoners were brought near a wall, from where two or three at a time were called to a window for a strictly allotted few minutes with their families. Despite Chinese threats to cancel the meeting if a single Tibetan showed emotion, everyone wept. The guards then ordered those who had yet to go forward to console their relatives. They were fortunate. They were going to the motherland itself—to receive education. On the far side of the wall the families—all of whom had brought food, clothing, and blankets—were assured that their relatives would be living under the best possible conditions in China. Nonetheless, the prisoners were permitted to accept the gifts. . . .

. . . . .

Their farewells completed, the prisoners were directed into two roofless troop trucks, a soldier mounted on the corners of each. A truck bearing a machine gun aimed at the Tibetans led; another, carrying ten soldiers and a second machine gun, took up the rear. With no room to sit, the thirty-eight prisoners in each truck stood shoulder to shoulder and stared in silence as the engines started and they were driven off, their wives throwing dust and crying after them the traditional phrase for dispelling sorrow, "Let all of Tibet's suffering be gone with you! And now be done!"

Dr. Choedrak and his companions were indeed en route to China. November 1 had been earmarked for a massive transfer of prisoners from the capital; numerous convoys had already set out ahead of them and as they passed Drepung, the road behind filled with six more trucks, transporting three hundred young monks from the monastery, all thirteen and fourteen years old. Grown to ten trucks and over four hundred people, the convoy headed north for Damshung, and its first major stop, Nagchuka. For the entire journey, the prisoners, forced to stand, were whipped by the late autumn wind as they repeatedly crossed 15,000-foot passes. Nighttime provided little respite. Jammed into the largest quarters available in whichever village they stopped in—often, for convenience sake, a single room—half the men had to sit on one another's laps for lack of space. Every night was punctuated by loud yells as arms or legs were trampled. Those who had to relieve themselves could do so only in their bowls, which they then had to hold so that nothing would spill. Irritability was heightened by the drastically reduced rations, now down only to a cup of boiled water and six steamed flour dumplings a day.

On the eleventh day, the column halted on the north shore of Lake Kokonor. Herded into boxcars on a railroad, the prisoners rode east, toward Lanzhou, the capital of Gansu province. Though few had seen a train before, they were too exhausted to care. Together, they sat in silence bunched against the cold, watching the light dance between the slats of the cars' walls. After one day they arrived at Lanzhou, and the two groups were separated. While the young monks remained on board to continue farther into China, Dr. Choedrak's group was placed in trucks and driven north once more. Though Lanzhou had been the jumping-off point for the Great Silk Road for centuries, the surrounding countryside was empty, perennially ignored by the Chinese and populated only by the Hui, Moslem people, now a minority themselves. On the city's northern edge, the silt-filled Yellow River ran west to east. Beyond lay Mongolia, its alien nature attested to by the ruins of the Great Wall and the edge of the Gobi Desert.

It was toward an outcrop of the Gobi, the Tengger Desert, that the prisoners were driven. A giant tract of flat rocky debris, the Tengger served as a springboard for windstorms and fierce winter gales which rifled the featureless land between it and the Wall. This forlorn expanse was traditionally spoken of as having "three too-many's"—too much wind, sand, and rock—and "three too-few's"—too little rain, grass, and soil. It had always been an area of transit—Mongols passing through, north to south and back on pilgrimage to Tibet, traders moving east or west on the Silk Road. The Communists, however, had found a new, seemingly ideal use for the region—as a vast zone for prisons.

The number of prison camps dotting the barren landscape of northern Gansu and Amdo (renamed Qinghai by the Chinese) was known only to those in Peking. Nevertheless, the general estimate was that these two provinces contained a vast sea of prison camps housing up to 10 million inmates, a "black hole," as a 1979 *Time* magazine article dubbed it, "from which little information ever reached the outside world or even the rest of China."

Owing to its 300,000 square miles of inaccessible terrain, Qinghai had been designated, soon after 1949, as the future site of most of China's prisons. In the early fifties, small camps, holding a few hundred prisoners, had begun as tent compounds surrounded by barbed wire—sometimes electrified. As their first task, the inmates had constructed their own prison walls out of brick or mud. By the middle of the decade, these had given way to colonies of prisons—fortress-like compounds lining dirt roads for miles at a stretch. Containing from 1,000 to 10,000 inmates each, the archipelagos provided the backbone of the system. The strip north of Lanzhou, for which Dr. Choedrak's group was destined, was considered the worst. It was followed in severity by four zones, two north and one south of Qinghai's capital, Xining, the fourth, four hundred miles due west, on the way to Xinjiang. Prisons and labor camps, though interspersed with nomad flocks, distinguished the entire countryside.

At sunset, the Tibetans passed through a ragged village of packed-mud houses, by a few stunted trees. Five miles beyond, they caught their first sight of Jiuzhen Prison. Four fortress-like stockades, set a sizable distance from one another, constituted the camp. Approaching one, the trucks passed staff quarters and a group of outbuildings behind which the prison's twenty-foot-high five-foot-thick brick walls stretched a half-mile long by 1,000 feet wide. Two guard towers rose on either side of the red flag raised over the gate in the eastern wall; one was positioned at the center of the western wall. Within stood seven cellblocks, housing 1,700 prisoners, in either fourteen- or twenty-seven-man rooms, built in files down the central yard. The kitchen ran along the western wall; the toilets were in a block in the southwest corner. A single notice board hung to the left of the gate. In the main, the prisoners were Chinese and Hui of high social standing: ex-officers of the Moslem warlord Ma Bufang's army, as well as doctors, professors, judges, civil servants, and other members of the intelligentsia now marked as reactionary. It was clear there was no hope for escape: the area was far too barren and remote to live alone in for more than a few days. . . .

· · · · ·

The day following their arrival the men were acquainted with Jiuzhen's rules. Communication, save for practical necessities, was forbidden. "This is a maximum-security camp for those who have committed the worst crimes," the guards informed them. "No spreading of reactionary rumors will be tolerated." On the basis of recommendations by the officials who had accompanied them, a "progressive" leader was appointed from each group of ten to fifteen prisoners. Although the leader lived side by side with his cellmates he was exempt from *thamzing* (Tibetan for "struggle"). In return, he was required to report the most minute occurrence down to potentially significant looks exchanged between their prisoners. Accordingly, from the first days of their new life in Jiuzhen, a second invisible prison held the men, a virtual moratorium on all human contact. The only statements made were for the informer's benefit and were stock phrases such as: "The new Communist leadership is so much better than the exploiters of the past." Or: "The conditions here are truly excellent, we are really enjoying it."

Each day, before dawn, the prisoners were mustered. Once in line before their cells, they were led in a rousing propaganda song, the first verse of which began: "Moscow has announced revolution so the imperialists are shivering with fear." They were then marched to work in the fields, returned briefly for lunch and, after the day's labor, required to sing again before dinner, which was served, as were all meals, in the cells by the kitchen staff. Following dinner, political "study session" lasted until ten o'clock, after which they slept. Every ten days each prisoner was subjected to a private interrogation session. In addition, prisoners were randomly taken to a small room in the staff quarters outside of Jiuzhen's walls where, for an entire day, four interrogators would question the man in turn, trying to wear him down by probing for "crimes" in the smallest details of his past life. Otherwise not a moment was spent away from the group, which was marched to and from the toilet as well as the worksite by armed guards.

It was the middle of the "three lean years," and Jiuzhen's produce was not for the prisoners' own consumption but that of the staff and the army units in the region. Guarded by the PLA, who shot on sight any man crossing his field's perimeter, each prisoner, equipped only with a shovel, had to break enough barren ground daily, including irrigation ditches, to be suitable for cultivating thirty pounds of wheat. The soil was turned a foot deep, covering an area of roughly 4,000 square feet. The task was so daunting that, even with clear soil, a strong man could barely manage to complete it. More often, the earth was hard and stony. In this case, after they had removed the larger rocks, the prisoners were ordered to fetch sand and clay from a nearby area in pairs: they used a long bamboo pole from which two baskets were hung suspended between them. The new earth was then mixed in with the old. Speed was of the essence. A point system rewarded those who completed their quota. Those who did not were punished. On returning from collecting sand, the inmate received a blue or a white slip of paper. Tabulated at day's end, the slips determined the number of baskets he had carried. The next day a red flag would be placed beside the field of the best team, whereas all those groups who had failed to approach its level were given increased labor time and a longer nightly meeting. Stretchers were always on hand for the frequent cases of collapse. If a field was close to the pickup point for sand, sixty trips could be made in a day, running both ways; if far, no more than twenty-five. . . .

· · · · ·

With the arrival of summer, arid desert heat replaced the dry cold. Prisoners were issued baggy, gauze-like cotton uniforms. On the morning of May 1, 1960, six months after the Tibetans' arrival, the kitchen staff came to their cells bearing the usual basket of dumplings and a bucket of greens. The dumplings, though, were the size of an egg. When the prisoners asked why they were so small, they were told that rations had been cut from sixteen and a half to eight and a half pounds a month. Henceforth, three dumplings a day were given and they were no longer even made from wheat. To save yet more grain Jiuzhen's authorities had instituted the mixing of indigestible roots and barks with the food. Three types were most easily identified. The first was rotten bark taken from trees in an area of low-lying hills far from the camps. After it was powdered and mixed with the dough, the dumplings were tinged red; they left a heavy, painful feeling in the stomach. If ingested over too long a time the bark produced bleeding sores inside the stomach and intestines. After eating them for even a few days many of the men found blood in their stools. Chaff was also mixed in and, in the autumn, a further additive which destroyed the semblance of a bun altogether. This consisted of waste material from soybeans. With the kernel of the bean removed to make tofu for the staff, its remaining skin was steamed to form a sort of porridge mixed with flour. The gruel was so loose, though, that the steamer itself had to be brought to each cell, where two spoonfuls per man were dispensed. Over the winter, meals had included the exterior layers of cabbage and other leafy greens, their interiors already taken by the guards. Now a native plant with flat green leaves topped by a yellow flower was used. Collected by periodic details, the plant was boiled in water and one ladle's worth for each man given out. Altogether, a single meal comprised little more than a mouthful of food.

Hunger governed the prisoners' every thought. Order broke down. The strong bullied the weak over who had received a large ladle of greens. Even when the Chinese took to skimming off each spoonful with a chopstick to make sure all the portions were of uniform size, the men's anguish about potentially unequal allotments focused itself as an obsession over the size of their bowls. There had never been a standard issue of containers. Thus, each man used what he had been permitted to retain from his relatives' gifts or, failing that, from containers he had somehow managed to pick up from guards. The assortment was varied. Dr. Choedrak had brought a mug as well as a washbasin. As the mug proved too small to eat from, he secretly procured a pair of scissors from a brigade of ex-prisoners, kept on as laborers, who lived outside Jiuzhen's walls. With these, he cut down the high sides of the basin so that it fit fully over his face and could easily be licked clean. Most were not so fortunate. Some had cups, others tin cans, the rest metal ashtrays—given out by the Chinese. Those worst off possessed only pieces of wood in which crude indentations were carved. Eventually, the men devised a system for randomly exchanging containers after the meals were portioned out and just before they ate. In this way, some measure of peace was restored, though as the next month unfolded it mattered little.

With the beginning of summer, the first symptom of starvation appeared: extreme enervation. While walking, their knees frequently buckled, and a number of the men found themselves unable to stand once they had fallen. Even if they managed to sit, their legs would not carry them until after a few hours of rest. By July one and all resembled living skeletons. Ribs, hips, and shin bones protruded, their chests were concave, their eyes bulged, their teeth were loose. Gradually their eyebrows and hair, once shiny and black, turned russet, then beige and then it fell out, the hair coming loose from the skin with just a slight pull. Each morning, those who could rise placed both hands against the wall and inched up, carefully balancing their heads in an effort not to fall. Once erect, they would edge dizzily through the straw down the back of the *kang* toward the cell door. From there they would go to the toilets by supporting themselves against the window ledges and walls of the buildings en route. From now on no one could walk securely, much less run for baskets of sand. Leg joints felt locked in place; feet were dragged along, too heavy to lift. When the men returned to the prison at night, they lowered their bodies gingerly onto the platform, this time only one hand against the wall, the other used to steady the head; tilted to the side, its weight was sufficient to bring one crashing down, unable to check the fall. . . .

. . . . .

For the prisoners, a death occasionally provided an increase in rations—for a single day at least. If they were lucky, the loss could be hidden from the guards and the deceased's ration obtained. Dr. Choedrak himself benefited from this. Waking one morning, he noticed that the man lying next to him was unusually still. He nudged him, listened closely, and realized that he was dead. By then, the prisoner on the fellow's far side had realized the same thing. By mutual consent, they managed to partially cover the dead man's head with his blanket, telling those around—and the Chinese, when they arrived—that he was too sick to move. By this, they obtained an extra portion of food, which they discreetly shared between themselves after the kitchen staff departed.

As the death rate increased the Tibetans began to consume their own clothes. Leather ropes, used to tie the bundles brought from Tibet, were cut into daily portions with stones and shovels. Each piece was slowly chewed during work, in the hope that some strength could thereby be gained. Small leather bags were put to the same use. Dr. Choedrak owned a fur-lined jacket, which had proved invaluable through the first winter, but in the course of the following summer he was compelled to eat it. He began with the fur. As winter came again, he managed to secure a small quantity of brush with which to make a fire under the *kang*. Piece by piece, he roasted the rest of his coat. Walking to and from the fields, prisoners picked as many plants—dandelions were a favorite—as they could eat, scavenged leaves from the few trees in the area, hunted for frogs and insects and dug for worms. One worm was particularly sought after as a source of grease, there being no fat of any kind in the diet. White, with a yellow head, the inmates nicknamed it "Mapa," after the best, most tasty form of *tsamba* mixed with butter.

A more constant source of food was the refuse discarded by Chinese guards. Crowds of prisoners would gather around bones or fruit rinds thrown by the roadside. Those lucky enough to have arrived first masticated their finds for .hours to make them last. The results of this scavenging, though, could be perilous. One day Dr. Choedrak was assigned—in company with a low-level government official named Lobsang Thonden—to work on a garbage pile outside the prison walls. It was in a large area where the camp's waste was mixed in with human excrement before being taken to the fields as fertilizer. Together, the two men shoveled the feces into trunk-sized baskets, which were then carried off by their cellmates. As he shoveled, Lobsang Thonden came upon a small baby pig—pigs were kept by the staff—dead and almost completely decomposed. When the guards were not looking Lobsang retrieved it and whispered to Dr. Choedrak, "We should eat this. It might help us." Wiping the excrement from it, he pulled the pig apart to see if there was any edible flesh to be had. A portion about the length of an index finger remained, still red, between the shoulder blades. He then decided to take it back to the prison to eat more palatably with the evening's greens. Dr. Choedrak admonished his companion to consume the meat immediately. On one count, Tenzin Choedrak pointed out, he was so weak that it would be of instant benefit; on the other, if it was discovered during the check at the prison gate, there might be trouble. Lobsang Thonden ignored the advice. Instead, he placed the meat in his back pocket, where, as Dr. Choedrak had warned, it was found a few hours later at the evening check. The Tibetan's small piece of meat infuriated the prison guards. That night he was threatened and abused; the next day work was delayed and a public *thamzing* involving the entire camp was convened in the prison yard. Lobsang Thonden was brought forward and tied by the special method used to twist the shoulders in their sockets. The camp commander shouted indignantly: "Taking such unclean food is a grave insult to the Chinese Communist Party and to the nation itself. Eating anything that can be found is a direct attempt to abuse the government. The conditions and rations here are very good. Such an insult cannot be ignored. It must be corrected by *thamzing*." "Activist" prisoners jumped up to beat and "struggle" Lobsang Thonden in the usual manner, repeating the charges against him. Soon, however, he collapsed. Afterwards, he could no longer walk or care for himself and was taken to the hospital. There, for the one and a half inch of flesh, he died four days later.

Despite such harsh reprisals, the prisoners had nothing to lose and were little dissuaded. On one occasion a group of Chinese inmates attacked the kitchen staff—all of whom were fed to the point of being portly—as they were leaving the kitchen carrying baskets of dumplings. Grabbing all they could, the men ate as they ran away; yet by that night each had been identified and punished. Unprovoked cruelty was common as well. While Dr. Choedrak was in the toilet one day, a Chinese prisoner came in to relieve himself. The man was so weak that when he squatted down, he fell on the floor, foaming from his mouth, unable to move. A guard entered. He began kicking the prisoner, berating him for lying in the toilet until, in a minute's time, he died on the spot. Taunting was a favored means of abuse. Dr. Choedrak witnessed a Chinese inmate being dragged helplessly to the fields, the guards reproaching him for being "too lazy to work." After moving about listlessly for a few minutes, he simply collapsed and died. On another occasion Chinese inmates were discovered eating a donkey's head which they had retrieved from the same pile of feces and garbage that Lobsang Thonden's pig had been in. Handcuffed and severely beaten, they were brought in front of 900 prisoners for *thamzing*. The prison staff railed at them, "You Kuomintang officials have badly abused the poor people under you, and now you're even abusing the Communist Party by eating a donkey's head. This is why you're dying, because you don't know how to look after yourselves." Twice Dr. Choedrak himself received *thamzing* for "insulting behavior" concerning food. In one instance he was caught eating cabbage leaves from the manure pile. The other involved his training as a physician. With the traditional Tibetan doctor's vast knowledge of plants, he quietly advised prisoners what to eat and what not to eat in the fields, despite the risk of such unapproved communication. Discovered, he was brought to trial once more on the grounds that his actions were premeditated provocation of the authorities, who maintained throughout that the entire camp was receiving "ample sustenance".

Dr. Choedrak's advice, though, was badly needed. Prisoners ate anything they came across. Some items were not so dangerous. One cellmate managed to find the knee joint of a small sheep. There was no meat on the bone, but for an entire month he kept it hidden under his bedding, taking it out each night for a few precious gnawings. On New Year's Day, to demonstrate magnanimity, a single mule was boiled for the entire prison. A friend of Dr. Choedrak, a steward for a noble family in Tibet, noticed that the water the animal was cooked in had been thrown by a staff member onto a refuse pile not far from the kitchen. Though not the toilet proper, this was a place where prisoners also went to relieve themselves, and the whole area was covered with pools of urine. Regardless, Dr. Choedrak's friend ran to the mound with his mug and collected all the surface dirt he could, in the hope that some of the boiled water could be strained out of it. He showed Dr Choedrak the soaked mud and asked if he thought this would benefit him. Like every prisoner, the steward had been suffering from an inability to sleep, difficulty with his vision and a constant loud rushing noise in the ear—all caused, according to Tibetan medicine, by the rising of "lung" or wind, which was produced by starvation. Dr. Choedrak agreed that if he could succeed in getting some of the soup water separated from the mud and urine, it would help to repress the "lung." The man did so and actually felt better for a short while. But other cases were not so salutary. People were dying in the most horrible manner from abrupt dysfunctions in their digestive tracts. A prisoner named Gyaltsen Dagpa, whom Tenzin Choedrak was unable to assist, perished when his intestines burst. For weeks he had been indiscriminately picking and eating whatever wild grass he could find. Soon he had a bad case of diarrhea and after a few days a viscous jelly-like substance emerged with his stools. Then, only water was ejected. At this point, whenever the man ate or drank he would scream from the excruciating pain. Soon the pain became constant, and he could no longer consume either liquids or solids. For two days he lay on the *kang* clutching his stomach, screaming, and then he died. Dr. Choedrak deduced that the interior lining of the man's intestine had been scraped away by the roughage, accounting for the viscous substance. Once worn through, the intestine then burst—at which stage, when the man drank water, it passed into his abdomen, causing intense pain. At the very end, when nothing at all emerged, the internal wound had disrupted the digestive tract entirely and become fatal. Another man, named Teykhang Chopel, succumbed when his sphincter cracked apart due to the hard indigestible objects lodged in his intestine.

Though he knew what not to eat, Dr. Choedrak could not endure such conditions long. As the anniversary of the Tibetans' first year at Jiuzhen arrived, he too collapsed and was taken to the hospital—a place visited at one time or another by all the prisoners. It was here, during an intermittent stay lasting three months, that he gained a view of camp life outside the isolation of his own group's daily existence. The hospital itself—no more than a barren room—existed as such in name only. There was virtually no medical equipment or supplies except for a few ointments for applying to wounds and some Chinese herbs said to help digestion. On occasion, when a patient was in the most dire condition, a shot of glucose would be administered or a mug of carrot juice given. The main function of the hospital staff was to dispose of the dead, many of whom had perished on its premises. Staff members were mostly prisoners who had received the jobs as a reward for being "progressive." It was, in fact, a substantial dividend. Not only did the assignment replace grueling field labor; it also provided a veritable cornucopia of extra food, the staff routinely disguising deaths and thus continuing to receive the dead men's rations. . . .

· · · · ·

At the beginning of 1961, Tenzin Choedrak was released from the hospital and resumed work. His recovery was due not only to rest but also to his own form of cure. He had noticed one symptom shared by all those who died: severe diarrhea. In most, a thin watery stool was constantly emitted; to absorb this flow, a rag had to be kept in the pants. In Tibetan medical theory, Dr. Choedrak knew, the digestive power or heat of the stomach is the key to health, the level of digestive heat determining not only metabolism but, through it, the harmonic function of the three humors. In Jiuzhen, however, this heat had been subjected to a twofold attack: from the severe cold and the consumption of coarse, indigestible material with no grease or fat. To increase his digestive heat, Dr. Choedrak quietly practiced, for half an hour each night, an advanced form of meditation—called Tum-mo Bar Zar, literally meaning "Rising and Falling Heat." After his cellmates had gone to sleep, Dr. Choedrak visualized purifying energy—in the form of white light—suffusing him, drawn in with each inhalation to a point just below his navel. Picturing a triangular flame the size of a rose thorn, he imagined it extending up the central channel of his body, through the tantric energy centers at the navel, stomach, heart, throat, and crown of his head where, burning away the layers of mental impurity, it released a fountain of clear, nectar-filled light which returned, blissfully, down his body. He would then conceive all of the sufferings experienced in prison to be washed away, replaced by the ineffable joy embodied in the light. "In the beginning, one just imagines all this," he recalled. "But after five or six months there was an unmistakable improvement, a slight rise in body heat. I was very weak, but I never had any more diarrhea or other digestive problems. Also, despite all the suffering we experienced, the meditation gave me more courage. I had no more fear, I just accepted my fate."

· · · · ·

. . . Despite the breakdown of conditions within their domain and the chaos without, the Chinese prison officials never deviated from their policies. With hundreds of prisoners already dead, executions—a constant feature of the camp—continued to be carried out. Charges were never specified. The names of those to be shot would simply appear on small posters periodically glued to the prison walls, beside such observations as "stubborn" or "suffers from old brains." When the executions had been carried out—they were not, as in other prisons, held publicly—a red check would appear next to the names of the executed, and the poster would be left up for some time as a warning. Then in the nightly meeting the officers would repeat a well-worn observation: "If one reactionary is destroyed, that is one satisfaction. If two are destroyed, that is two satisfactions. If all the reactionaries are destroyed, then you are fully satisfied."

Q1—A Twentieth-Century Bastille

Wei Jingsheng

WEI JINGSHENG (1950–) is one of the most courageous and best-known Chinese dissidents, at any rate in the Western world; inside China he is far less known given the official control of the media of mass communications. He exemplifies an uncommon willingness to defy an oppressive police state as well as the capacity for a remarkable political-ideological transformation.

Coming from a family of loyal party members (his father had a high position in the Foreign Ministry) and educated at elite party schools he joined the Red Guards at age 16 during the Cultural Revolution, traveled widely in China and was a dedicated supporter of Mao. In 1969 he enlisted in the Peoples Liberation Army. He was trained as an electrician and in 1973 he worked in the Beijing Zoo. By 1978 he was a dissident, active in the post-Mao Democracy Movement. He attracted attention for his poster on Democracy Wall calling for "The Fifth Modernization" by which he meant democratization.

In 1979 he was arrested, charged with "counterrevolutionary propaganda and incitement," and giving information to a foreign journalist about the Sino-Vietnamese war. He was sentenced to fifteen years and spent much of it in solitary confinement. In 1993 he was released on probation, rearrested in 1994, and charged with attempting to overthrow the government. In 1997 he was released and deported to the U.S. Ever since his exile he has been active in pro-democracy movements abroad championing civil rights and political freedoms in China. His best-known book Courage to Stand Alone *(a collection of prison writings) was published abroad in 1997.*

The following excerpt (written in 1979) provides detailed information about "China's top political prison", Q1, where he spent many years and about the treatment of political prisoners.

• • • • •

. . . .

From Wei Jingsheng, "Q1— A Twentieth-Century Bastille," in Geremie Barmé and John Minford, eds., Seeds of Fire: Chinese Voices of Conscience, © *1986 by Geremie Barmé and John Minford. Reprinted by permission of Hill & Wang, a division of Farrar, Straus and Giroux, LLC.*

If you go a short way down the main road in Changping County, in the countryside due north of Peking, you will come to a hot springs resort area set in the most picturesque scenery. This is the famous spa, where, according to tradition, the Manchu Empress Dowager used to come to take the waters.

Continue further north a few minutes, and by the roadside you will see a large sign in several languages: Foreigners Prohibited. The innocent traveler will take this to be a military zone and go on without giving it another moment's thought. But anyone who knows the truth will instantly experience a sense of terror, for just beyond the sign lies China's top political prison: the infamous Qin Cheng No. 1—Q1.

You won't find Q1 on any map, and you will only ever hear it referred to as No 1. The local farmers know nothing of this huge maximum-security complex. There is only a vague sinister rumor circulating that the Japanese once constructed a prison in the area.

To the north a lonely but well-maintained asphalt road leads straight to the prison. The main entrance and the gatehouse beside it seem perfectly ordinary. A stranger wandering by would suspect nothing unusual. A huge screen wall inside the open gate makes it totally impossible for the casual passer-by to catch even the slightest glimpse of the "view" beyond. . . . On this huge screen is inscribed a single quotation from Mao Zedong, on the subject of Proledic— the Dictatorship of the Proletariat.

Behind the screen wall is a building of several stories with an archway in the middle of it, beyond which lies the main part of the prison proper, enclosed within a three-meter wall, topped by electrified barbed wire. The rusty iron gate inside the archway is a chilling sight. Just reflect for a moment on all the people opposed to Mao and his dictatorial policies, who passed in through this gate never to return; or on all Mao's former followers, who were sent here under a cloud of suspicion; many of them entered here, but few were fortunate enough to re-emerge. Even the shock of release could be fatal. After 1975 it became the practice to put newly released political prisoners in hospital for a short stay before their actual release, in the hope that this would make the transition less violent. Those who enter through this double iron gate are usually atheists, but the ones lucky enough to leave have had a taste of what it's like to be cast into a "modern hell." People even jokingly call it the Atheists' Gate to Hell.

There are sentinel boxes on either side of the gate. If you have permission to visit the Underworld, you will be allowed to continue from this point on down Hell Alley, a T-shaped asphalt road that lies within the enclosure. It slopes gradually towards the north. The land to the east and west is laid out with symmetrical compounds, all painted the same color. A lot of the compounds to the west have fruit trees growing in them, and to the east, further down the road, is an area of newly constructed housing. These new buildings were put up after the Cultural Revolution to accommodate the rapidly increasing number of high-ranking political prisoners. They are one of the prison's showpieces of "modernization."

Each building has a small door that opens directly onto the road. The road leads to a hillock covered with chestnut trees, and in the spring and summer it is a scene of lush greenness. The buildings are neatly laid out. In fact the environment has a natural beauty and tranquility that make it ideal for rest and recuperation. And yet it is in this place that indescribable suffering is inflicted on countless Chinese families. Their loved ones have come to this beautiful and secluded spot to be subjected to the cruelest torture imaginable; former inmates and their relatives are left with harrowing memories of what happens within the walls of the compound, and their agony leaves its imprint on their features for the rest of their lives.

Q1 is completely isolated from the outside world. Only former prisoners, their families, and close friends ever know or talk about it. The prison is run by Section 5 of the Ministry of Public Security, and it is even kept a secret from the regular police force. The guards are very carefully selected, and have to be below a certain age. Prisoners report never having seen guards over twenty. They are replaced in batches at frequent intervals.

Prisoners are divided into four categories, according to the level of their monthly keep—theoretically 8, 15, 25 or 40 *yuan*. In actual practice widespread corruption means that no prisoner receives his entitlement. For example, a prisoner's official monthly ration of grain may be 17.5 kilos, but because he never takes any exercise, he cannot possibly eat even half of it. The entire amount is still purchased, however, and according to one version the guards use the surplus to feed their pigs, which are in turn sold to supplement the guards' own diet. Such stories of corruption and embezzlement abound. The whole situation could be summed up by saying that the "legal" expropriation of the prisoners' allowances has come to be considered a routine and reasonable practice at Q1—and at other prisons. Some of these "routine practices" double as punishment: starvation, for example—the lightest and most common form of punishment meted out at Q1. First the prisoner is starved, then he (or she) is given a bowl of cold noodles with great blobs of fat floating in it, to "make up" for all the missed meals. Ninety-percent of prisoners fed in this manner suffer from diarrhea and nausea as a result and have to miss the next few meals until they recover.

This superficially "civilized" form of torture has been institutionalized at Q1: it serves as a punishment and at the same time as a means of enriching the warders' diet. Small wonder that it is carried out with such zeal.

Each inmate has a separate cell, one meter by three, containing a sink, a chamber pot, and a plank bed with a thin cover. Their black prison uniforms are replaced every six months. When the winter uniform is issued, the summer one is called in. With the delays in the clothing department, this often means that prisoners are still sweltering in their padded winter clothes in May. There is a small window in the door of each cell, which serves as an observation hole, and as an opening through which food, a needle and thread, or the newspaper can be passed. Some prisoners are allowed to read the Marxist-Leninist classics, or the *People's Daily,* but this is considered a great privilege. Ordinary prisoners who "co-operate" are allowed to engage in a number of unpaid activities such as making rope or straw-hats, to keep themselves from becoming stiff. But the ones who make a bad impression on the prison staff are subjected to all sorts of punitive or restrictive measures. They may, for example, be denied the right to exercise, whether outside or within their cell, for as long as six months at a stretch. A former deputy director of the PLA Academy, who had been deputy chief of staff during the Korean War, was kept immobile for six months, after which he was no longer able to walk at all.

The exercise area is approximately one hundred meters square, and is quite separate from the cells. It is laid out in rows of connected squares, like rice paddies in Southern China. The endless walking and running has worn the grass into a circular dirt track. The exercise area used to be divided by bamboo partitions, but these were replaced in the late 1960s by a high brick wall which separates two rows of connected compounds, and is patrolled by guards with rifles.

The inmates' lives are governed by all sorts of irrational regulations. They have to sleep facing the door. It is forbidden to turn the other way, and if a prisoner happens to do this while sleeping, he is woken up, repeatedly if necessary, until he learns to face the observation hole. There was a Tibetan who had to sleep on one side of his face for more than ten years. One of his ears became swollen and numb, and finally infected. He tried sleeping on the other side, but was repeatedly woken up and abused by the guards until, driven beyond endurance, he finally went berserk and tried to strangle one of them. In the end he was granted special dispensation to sleep facing the other way.

Sanitary conditions are very poor. Soap is not provided at all, and bathing is permitted only once a month, regardless of the season. A few privileged prisoners are given semi-annual physical examinations.

Living conditions at Q1 are enough in themselves to destroy an ordinary man's will. If one did not know that most of the inmates were among the finest people that modern China has produced, one could easily mistake the place for a lunatic asylum, or a penitentiary for prisoners sentenced to death. What an irony! These prisoners are gifted individuals who joined the Communist Party to fight for the freedom, prosperity, and peace of China and of all of mankind; they devoted the better part of their lives to achieving and maintaining power for the Party. Many of them were imprisoned in the past by the Party's enemies: now they are being detained by the very party they helped to create. They are at the receiving end of modern techniques of torture. Every day they face psychological and physical destruction.

The torments of daily life are not enough to break the will of these stalwart people. Q1 is therefore equipped with modern instruments which cause terrible pain in the head during interrogation. When the pain becomes unbearable, and the prisoner is writhing around on the ground, the pain suddenly ceases only to resume again just as suddenly; and so on, until either a confession is extracted or the interrogators conclude that their techniques are proving ineffective. There are other more antiquated but still highly effective methods of torture. For example, the exposing of a prisoner night and day to a strong light; after a while this can cause severe mental disturbance, even complete insanity.

One of the people tortured at Q1 was Wang Guangmei [widow of former head of state Liu Shaoqi]. She had been given the bright light treatment over a long period, and suddenly one day, while eating her bread and cabbage soup, she is said to have gone out of her mind. She was visited by an old friend, the wife of a high official, who said she looked so terrible that she could hardly recognize her. She was haunted by the sight and, at considerable risk to herself and her family, she protested to Chairman Mao. Her letter to Mao, together with the general indignation among high-ranking cadres, eventually led to a change in command at the prison. The public security people were replaced by PLA Unit 8341 (the Palace Guard of Mao and the Central Committee) and Q1 became a "relatively civilized" institution.

Someone may object that I have only cited extreme cases, and that none of these are the really common forms of torture. That is perhaps true. The most common torture of all is simply to beat the prisoner up. Normally he is called out and surrounded by a group of men who then proceed to kick him and beat him up until his head bleeds, and he can hardly breathe. One high-ranking cadre who was released from Q1 had scars all over his head. Another even more common form of torture is to forcibly administer heavy doses of drugs—under the pretext of some mental disorder. The drugs themselves in fact produce a state of grave mental imbalance. Sometimes the inmate has to be sent to hospital for "further treatment." One person who had this treatment recalls that after being given the drugs he began talking to himself all the time, for days on end, even while he was eating. Naturally, these monologues were recorded for use during future interrogations. Among the hospitals that cooperate in such practices are the Fuxing Hospital [this is the hospital where Wei Jingsheng himself is reported to have been subsequently "treated"], Hospital 301, and Anding Hospital in Peking. The relevant sections of the hospitals are officially called "clinics for senior personnel." The Anding "clinic" is in the suburban area outside Desheng Gate and it is simply called Clinic 5. A visitor there once saw a stocky middle-aged man with a zombie-like expression on his face, his whole head pitted with scars, walking somnambulistically forward in a straight line. If he had not been pulled to a standstill by a guard he would have walked straight into the wall. These prisoners, who fought against dictatorship from youth, who dedicated themselves to the cause of freedom and human rights, have now been subjected to these "advanced" methods of investigation, and have been brutally tortured, to the point where they have lost all sense of reality.

The KMT special agent in the film "Red Crag" was a bungling amateur when compared with the adepts who work in Q1. The techniques of torture used by the KMT in the '40s were advanced for their times; the techniques employed by the Communist Party since the '70s are positively futuristic.

Someone may in all innocence suggest that this is not unlike what happens in the Japanese film *The Chase*. Actually, it is quite different: one is a film, the other is real life. In *The Chase* the villain commits his villainy by stealth but gets caught and punished in the end; in Q1 the villainy is being perpetrated in broad daylight by the government, and high-ranking officials periodically receive "invitations" to "inspect" the premises. Nearby, foreign tourists are sampling the delights of the Great Wall; but the Chinese officials who have the fortune to visit Q1 are enjoying recreational activities of a radically different kind.

These inhuman methods naturally provoke violent reactions among the prisoners. Some inmates, unable to endure the hardship inflicted on them, attempt suicide. Others go on hunger strike. The Panchen Lama once refused to eat. He declared that he had no wish to live any longer, and he requested that his corpse be "delivered to the Central Committee." The guards will not countenance such defiance. They show no sympathy for cases like this. Usually after a prisoner has been on hunger strike for about a week, he is given a severe beating, may have a few teeth knocked out, and then he is forced into a "pacifying suit"—a tight rubber straight-jacket, which is extremely narrow at the shoulders and chest, and joined together at the sleeves and legs. The suit is then inflated, making breathing virtually impossible. These suits are particularly effective in immobilizing refractory elements. If these methods are still not effective, prisoners are force-fed large quantities of liquid.

Prison terms at Q1 generally run for more than ten years, and many die there while serving their sentences. Hardly anyone was released before the 1970s, which is why one never heard the place mentioned. It was extremely rare for anyone to be allowed to visit.

Before the Cultural Revolution generally one was not notified when a person was thrown into Q1. Relatives did not know where their loved ones were or whether they were alive or dead, or what condition they were in at all. Even warders are ignorant of the names of their prisoners, who are identified by number rather than name. When they fail to obtain information from the Ministry of Public Security, relatives normally consider that the person has permanently disappeared. Likewise, prisoners are given no information about their families, though they generally assume that since they are in prison the Party authorities on the outside will certainly be giving their families hard time. They will have every obstacle put in their way, every trick the bureaucracy can manage will be played on them, and they will have no one to help or protect them. The anxiety a political prisoner experiences can only be comprehended by those who have been through the same thing themselves.

A human being is more than just flesh and bones. Even atheist materialists must recognize the existence of the human spirit. But what kind of spiritual existence is there for the inmates of Q1? Some former inmates recall not being allowed to converse with anyone at all. Sometimes, even at the risk of being punished for "troublemaking," an inmate may abuse a warden just to provoke him into conversation. Interrogation provides inmates with their only opportunity to talk. One man, after ten years of confinement, was so overwhelmed when he heard his name spoken during an interrogation, that he was literally unable to speak. Many strong-willed men still show deep-seated symptoms of psychological damage after their release, even though they have not actually been subjected to prolonged physical or mental torture. After a decade of solitary confinement, some still cannot speak properly, even a few years after their release.

But even in this oppressive spiritual environment, the human mind continues to function. Whoever invented the various forms of "mental therapy" employed in Q1 understood that a prisoner in circumstances like these is bound to be concerned for his family and friends, to worry about his wife and children. The most effective way to break a prisoner's will, to destroy his spirit, is to keep him in an unbalanced state of mind: to make sure that he is unable to obtain information about his family and friends, so that he torments himself with the thought of how they are being discriminated against on his account. The aim is to keep the prisoner mindful of his own impotence to help them, and to cause him to torture himself with the knowledge that their suffering is a result of *his* offences against the authorities.

The proverbial saying, "force is the tactic of the petty man; psychology the way of the adept," is borne out by reports from many released prisoners. During their confinement they were told things like: "Your wife has remarried and is getting on very nicely in her new home. . . . Your son has committed an offence against socialist order, but he was not jailed. Instead he has simply been sent to a labor camp for re-education. . . . That most attractive daughter of yours has been receiving a lot of attention from young men. . . . Your other children have been ill, but the government is 'doing everything possible' to treat them . . . etc., etc." Afterwards prisoners often discover that the stories were completely untrue. So why were they told such lies in the first place? Just so as to inflict further pain and anguish.

In some important cases, they find a woman who is physically similar to an inmate's wife, and get her to flirt with the man. It is one of the oldest stratagems in the book although perhaps it is employed as nothing more than another form of torment. . . . Anyway, the people at Q1 resort to every conceivable means to squeeze the "last drop of surplus value" from these hapless souls.

In 1975 many long-time Party members suddenly had what they thought was a stroke of good luck. As part of Deng Xiaoping's "rehabilitation" movement, they were released from Q1. But such sudden and overwhelming joy can be dangerous, even fatal. . . . To "ensure the safety and well-being" of these people, the Central Committee adopted a policy of temporary exile. Those who left Q1 that year had first to spend a period of time in hospital to absorb the shock of re-entering society. Then in 1977 hospitalization was no longer considered necessary. Instead, the prisoners were sent to remote towns in the countryside, where the quiet surroundings would likewise "soften the shock" of liberation. The places of exile were selected according to the Three Nots for the relocation of political unrealiables: 1) *not* in Peking or at large city; 2) *not* near any major transportation junction; 3) *not* in a place where the prisoner concerned had once lived or worked. Most political prisoners have probably been exiled in accordance with the regulations, with the exception of such rare cases as the Panchen Lama and a small number of people close to Party leaders.

Release is no easy or pleasant affair either. Before leaving Q1, the prisoners are confronted with a number of groundless accusations. A final "case summary" is then drawn up showing why your decade incarceration was well deserved. Upon release, you were expected express gratitude for Chairman Mao's leniency: after all, your case, which in fact represented a "contradiction between the People and the Enemy," was now being treated as an "internal contradiction with the People" [Maoist gobbledegook for the conversion of a serious political crime into a pardonable offence]. Therefore you are not expected to complain if your activities are restricted and you are sent off to a faraway village. Former Peking Mayor Peng Zhen, former State Planning Chairman Bo Yibo [both key Party leaders once more], and many other prisoners were dealt with in this manner. Bo Yibo was more courageous than most. "In the past I erred by following the directive of the Central Committee," he declared and promptly added: "If I obey the Central Committee this time, shall I be committing another error? To avoid the possibility of any further errors, it would be best if I declined to carry out the Central Committee's decision altogether?" Bo simply refused to leave Q1. Since then, so it is said, the preliminaries have been dispensed with, and political prisoners are sent directly in exile.

Once he sets foot in Q1, a prisoner loses all sense of normality; when he leaves he assumes that exile will be comfortable by comparison. But is there really much difference between being in Q1 and being in exile? The food ration still operates on a four-tier system of 200, 120, 80 and 60 *yuan*. In Q1 prisoners are constantly guarded by armed wardens; in exile they are constantly watched over ["taken care of" to use the official expression] by local workers. Take for example the Russian widow of Li Lisan. She was accused of being a Soviet spy and sent to Q1 for seven or eight years. Upon her release she was exiled to Yuncheng in Shanxi Province, where the local commune provided two young people to "take care of" her. As she was an old woman, she requested a transfer to Peking, to live with her daughter and grandchild. Permission was finally granted in December 1978.

Or take the case of one of the organizers of Tibet's earliest Communist organization—the East Tibet Democratic Youth League. Because of his contacts with the Soviet and Indian Communist Parties in the 1940s, he was falsely accused of having illicit relations with foreign countries and was imprisoned at Q1 for eighteen years. In 1978 he was released and sent to a small town in Sichuan province. Even to go to the doctor's he needed to be accompanied. He had to be constantly "looked after" by someone assigned to him by the United Front Ministry—although he had a son and daughter living with him who were quite capable of seeing to his needs.

These two instances are relatively mild. Some exiles, it is said, are still not allowed to receive visits from their friends and relatives. For them exile is nothing more than an extension of Q1, a further extension of the Party's consistent and all-embracing policy toward prisoners.

I have revealed the brutal terror of Q1 not merely as a plea for the innocent prisoners incarcerated there. These young men and women who dedicated their lives to the Chinese revolution and dared oppose Mao's barbaric dictatorship, do indeed deserve our respect and emulation. But the most profound lesson to be learnt from Q1 is that the dictatorship of the proletariat does not exist in our country. Instead what goes by the name of the proletarian dictatorship, this Proledic, is manipulated by a small group of tyrants as a tool to oppress the proletariat. The tool has been used so effectively that all of the dictator's opponents have been eliminated, even his "close comrades-in-arms" from the era of the Long March.

It is inevitable that dictators resort to barbaric measures. Dictatorship cannot justify its oppressive methods; it can therefore only maintain itself by the use of force. The instruments of repression are not only directed against the masses, they must be used to quell any and all internal opposition. Dictators show no mercy even towards comrades who once fought at their side. One can almost say that those who lost their lives during the revolution were the lucky ones. They are honored as heroes who fought for freedom and peace; and they have attained true peace of mind. They have been spared the fate of being tortured by their comrades, and did not live to see their relatives being maltreated. They need not constantly tremble in fear at the thought of the next day's torment.

Dictators can create any number of political excuses for eliminating their opponents. They talk glibly of "class enemies," "counterrevolutionaries," "rebels," and "traitors." Dictatorship needs these labels, and it needs prisons like Q1. Or to put it the other way round, if political imprisonment was somehow made impossible, then one of the indispensable tools of dictatorship would have been removed. So we are dealing here not just with the humanitarian implications of imprisonment for the individual, but with the significance that such imprisonment has for the basic rights of the people as a whole. In order to avoid the disastrous consequences of dictatorship, one must first eliminate the conditions that create it and sustain it, including the dehumanizing system of political imprisonment and persecution.

Born Red

Gao Yuan

GAO YUAN (1952–) was a Red Guard during the Cultural Revolution in China, a political movement initiated by Mao that acquired a dynamic of its own and produced many rival factions. The political violence generated by this movement was quite distinct and different from the centralized, government-controlled varieties found in other Communist states, as well as in China before and after the Cultural Revolution. There are some similarities with the ethos of the Soviet purge period, insofar as during the Cultural Revolution, too, the authorities encouraged citizens to give priority to political loyalties over personal and familial ties; in China, as in the Soviet Union, individuals sought personal safety in the fantastic accusations and denunciations they leveled against their fellow citizens, and in both settings many high-ranking functionaries abruptly and dramatically lost their power, status, and privileges—and sometimes their lives as well. But a good deal of the violence in China came from decentralized mobs, which entailed a degree of spontaneity and unpredictability.

Instigated and sanctioned by Mao, the movement was directed against elements in the party bureaucracy, which he intended to shake up and reinvigorate by the mass participation of young people, mostly high school and college students. In fact, the Cultural Revolution degenerated into quasi-anarchy, mass hysteria, political witch hunts,

From Gao Yuan, Born Red: A Chronicle of the Cultural Revolution, © *1987 by the Board of Trustees of the Leland Stanford Junior University. All rights reserved. Used with permission of Stanford University Press, www.sup.org.*

and orgies of public violence and humiliation. Much of it was directed at authority figures, such as teachers.

Gao Yuan's father was a veteran Communist functionary (head of his county government) who, like others in a similar position, came under attack by the Red Guards for his alleged lack of attention to the class struggle and for being insufficiently revolutionary.

The book from which these selections were taken is based on the author's diary.

Gao Yuan studied engineering in China but later worked as a journalist. He came to the U.S. in 1982 and obtained a master's degree in journalism from the University of California at Berkeley and an M.B.A. from Stanford University. He lives in Palo Alto, California.

· · · · ·

At our next assembly, three strangers sat on the auditorium stage beside Secretary Ding. They were introduced as a work team that would be investigating the progress of the Cultural Revolution at Yizhong. The young woman in charge of the team was exemplarily red and expert. She had graduated from Beida in history and already was a vice-head of Yizhen county. Accompanying her was another college graduate in his early thirties and a dour-looking older man.

The team made rounds of the school over the next couple of days and then issued a report pronouncing Ding Yi's supervision impeccable. Fangpu was required to write a public apology. I went looking for Fangpu after the poster appeared and found him in the library. "I went along as a tactical maneuver," he confided to me. "It doesn't mean that I have changed my mind."

Although the work team had defused Fangpu's assault on Ding Yi, it lifted the ban on criticizing teachers. The team also suspended classes altogether so we could make Cultural Revolution full time. Once again, posters about teachers proliferated. Their tone grew harsher. "Down with Big Traitor Lu!" said one headline. Lu, who taught senior-level history, had done underground party work in Shanghai before liberation. He had once been arrested by the Kuomintang, and the poster charged that he had taken the occasion to betray some of his comrades to the enemy. Another poster was headlined "Ultrarightist Zhu is Rubbish!" Zhu taught senior Chinese. The poster said he had not shown repentance since being labeled a rightist in 1957. It referred to him as "Eclectic Zhu" because he wrote essays that blended Confucian, Mohist, Logician, and Legalist thought.

Another read "Leng, Reactionary Student of American Imperialist Leighton Stuart, Must Confess to the People!" The target was an old philosophy teacher, an eccentric bachelor who wore a Western-style suit to class. Leng had graduated from Yenching University, founded by Americans and later absorbed by Beida. The poster alleged he had made underhanded deals with the last U.S. ambassador to China.

More posters appeared about our physics teacher, Feng, accusing his father of representing American aggression in old China. Feng's two little children played happily around the posters. Each time they recognized their father's name, they would point and yell proudly, "There's another one for Papa!" Feng wrote a reply, saying his own mother had been a victim of U.S. imperialism. The American navy officer had raped her, insisted she marry him, and then abandoned the whole family. Next to this account, Feng hung a large framed photograph showing a Caucasian man in uniform, with his pretty Chinese wife and several children. One of the children was Feng himself. This family history and the picture attracted a big crowd. No more posters about Feng appeared after that.

The attack on Teacher Shen resumed with renewed vigor. "Ferret Out Old Fritter Shen!" one poster said. It said Shen had been born into a big landlord family and had gone to Hong Kong after liberation to escape political retribution and to make lots of money by working for a foreign company. Yuanchao wrote a poster claiming that Shen had insulted his father, the veteran of the Long March. Yuanchao had once written on an English test "My father is a cock," instead of "My father is a cook." Shen had cited the mistake in class as an example of carelessness. Yuanchao charged that Shen had read the sentence aloud in a deliberate attempt to tarnish his father's reputation.

More criticism of Teacher Li went up as well. One poster, which began "Rip off Li's revolutionary insurgent mask!" claimed that our Chinese teacher had not really intended to lead his troops in an uprising against the Kuomintang. Instead, it gave the following version: Li's troops were guarding Chiang Kai-shek's residence in Nanjing, the Kuomintang capital. Just before the People's Liberation Army crossed the Yangtze River to take the city in the spring of 1949, Li went on vacation somewhere north of the river. While he was enjoying himself visiting brothels, his men revolted of their own accord and went over to the Communist side. Li was stranded and had no choice but to surrender. When I remembered how the tale of a Communist heroine had moved Teacher Li almost to tears, I was not sure what to believe.

One morning, the news spread swiftly across campus that Leng, the lackey of the American imperialist Leighton Stuart, had cut his throat. He had bungled the suicide attempt, slicing his windpipe instead of an artery. Other teachers found him on the ground outside his single room and an ambulance rushed him to the Army Hospital. He survived but did not return to school.

Leng's drastic action silenced the criticism aimed at him, but not that against others. Old Fritter Shen now was said to have raped a serving girl at his landlord family's estate while he was a youth, and to have written counterrevolutionary poetry in English as well as Chinese. Teacher Li was accused of corrupting students' minds with his tricks of balancing a rifle and riding a bike without moving. He also was said to have told other teachers dirty stories about visiting brothels in Shanghai. I was feeling more and more disappointed with Teacher Li.

Some teachers began to expose other teachers, producing furious poster battles. Liu and Yang waged one such battle on the wall inside the bell tower courtyard. Yang said the rightist Liu did not really know much about geography but just threw out bits and pieces of bourgeois trivia to dazzle his students. Liu charged Yang with having an affair with the wife of an army officer while her husband was fighting in Korea. The exchange attracted a lot of attention. Neither won the battle, since their posters provided students with more ammunition to use against both of them.

Other teachers followed Feng's example and wrote explanations, confessions, or self-criticisms in hopes of arousing sympathy. Sometimes students took these as evidence of bad faith, accusing the teachers of making false admissions in order to get by—"crossing the sea under camouflage," as the first of the Thirty-Six Stratagems put it.

The concern with the Three Family Village became buried under layers of posters about teachers. Students first concentrated on those with bad family origins, such as landlord or capitalist, or bad personal histories, such as counterrevolutionary or rightist. Later, these factors did not seem to matter. Anyone who had ever said anything suspect in class was fair game.

I liked almost all my teachers and did not want to attack them, but neither did I want my classmates to think me an unrevolutionary misfit. Finally, I decided to criticize Teacher Wen. Although she always spoke to me in a kind and gentle way, I had grown weary of her lectures about being red and expert, and still felt she was singling me out. I entitled my poster "Denouncing Wen Xiu's Persecution of Me" and posted it in the bell tower courtyard. It ran for thirteen pages on sheets of paper more than a meter high. . . .

. . . . .

Shuanggen wrote a poster too, accusing Wen Xiu of maltreating him. His poster got more attention than mine, because he called Wen Xiu "the daughter of a filthy capitalist's whore." Our homeroom teacher's old mother, who lived with her on campus, had a frightening, ravaged face. According to Shuanggen, the old woman's deformity was the result of syphilis she had contracted as a prostitute in Shanghai. "Wen Xiu masquerades as a learned intellectual," Shuanggen wrote, "but her family status is really lumpen. . . ."

The *People's Daily* had called upon us to "sweep away all ox ghosts and snake spirits." Caolan, the monitor of class 85, and Congfang, the class's Youth League secretary, decided to organize a unified action against Teachers Shen and Li. Little Bawang was the most enthusiastic. He suggested we take inspiration from Chairman Mao's report on the peasant movement in Hunan province, written in the 1920s, which described how the peasants had put dunce caps on the heads of local tyrants and evil gentry and paraded them through the streets.

The class split into active and passive contingents. The activists took up ink bottles, brush pens, paper, and paste buckets and trooped off to the Teachers' Building. Little Mihu carried two dunce caps made of white paper, topped with white tassels of the type used for funeral decorations. Little Bawang had two wooden boards. The rest of us followed and watched as Li and Shen were dragged out of their offices and onto the porch. "What's the matter? What's the matter?" Li was saying. "What's the matter?" Little Bawang yelled. "We're here to sweep away you ox ghosts and snake spirits!" The two were capped, and the boards were hung around their necks. Li's board identified him as "Reactionary Kuomintang Colonel and Chiang Ching-kuo's Running Dog." Shen's said, "Vile Progeny of the Landlord Class and Imperialist Spy."

I tried to push my liking for Li out of my mind and concentrate on his crimes. The latest posters had accused him of yearning to "change the heavens," to return to the old days, to restore Kuomintang rule. One poster even said that one night in 1962, when Chiang Kai-shek was raising a hue and cry about counterattacking the mainland, Li had donned his old colonel's uniform. . . .

. . . . .

As I thought of these things, I began to hate Teacher Li. Yet part of me still liked him. I stayed some distance from the porch and tried to hide from his view among the growing crowd of students. "Students, let's talk things over," Li was saying now. Little Bawang motioned to him to stop talking. A struggle meeting was about to begin. Li and Shen stood on the porch with their heads lowered. Caolan led the crowd in shouting slogans: "Leniency to those who confess, severity to those who refuse!" "Li, make a clean breast of your crimes!" "Shen, confess or be damned!" "Long live the Great Socialist Cultural Revolution!"

"Speak!" Little Bawang yelled at Li. "How many people did you kill before Liberation? What crimes did you carry out for Chiang Ching-kuo? Speak!" Other students echoed his commands.

"I killed no one," Li said. "I was guarding Chiang Kai-shek's residence. Chiang Ching-kuo was my chief. I was a battalion leader under his command."

"Did you kill any Communists?" Little Mihu shouted excitedly.

"No, never. I didn't like Chiang Kai-shek's killing. That's why I ran away with my soldiers and surrendered when the People's Liberation Army came to Nanjing. My brother, who crossed over earlier, had a lot of influence on me. He can testify to that. He works in the provincial government. . . ."

"Li is not honest," Little Bawang cut in. "Li is playing tricks with us. Don't be taken in by this cunning fox."

"Down with Li!" Caolan shouted, holding both fists high. "Down with Li!" voices chorused up and down the porch and through the crowd.

Suddenly, with a plopping sound, the paste bucket was upside down on Li's head. The sticky brown mixture of sweet-potato flour and water, still warm, oozed down Li's shoulders and over his back and chest. Little Bawang picked up a broom and began knocking on the bucket. Shen was trembling and bow-ing his head very low, almost to his knees. I wished he would confess his crimes as soon as possible and get the ordeal over with. But he appeared too frightened to talk at all. The students on the porch then ordered both teachers to start marching. They paraded Li and Shen around the campus, shoving and pushing the two teachers with almost every step. Li, unable to see with the bucket on his head, stumbled and fell several times.

Following class 85's revolutionary action, other classes began to organize struggle meetings and parades. The wooden slogan boards grew larger and heavier, the dunce caps taller and more elaborate. Some students hung bricks on the boards to make it harder for the teachers to stand up. One group of first-graders made a cap of sorghum stalks as high as a two-story building for their homeroom teacher; they had to support it with long poles as they marched him around.

The list of accusations grew longer by the day: hooligans and bad eggs, filthy rich peasants and son-of-a-bitch landlords, bloodsucking capitalists and neobourgeoisie, historical counterrevolutionaries and active counterrevolutionaries, rightists and ultrarightists, alien class elements and degenerate elements, reactionaries and opportunists, counterrevolutionary revisionists, imperialist running dogs, and spies. Students stood in the roles of prosecutor, judge, and police. No defense was allowed. Any teacher who protested was certainly a liar.

The indignities escalated as well. Some students shaved or cut teachers' hair into curious patterns. The most popular style was the yin-yang cut, which featured a full head of hair on one side and a clean-shaven scalp on the other. Some said this style represented Chairman Mao's theory of the "unity of opposites." It made me think of the punishments of ancient China, which included shaving the head, tattooing the face, cutting off the nose or feet, castration, and dismemberment by five horse-drawn carts.

At struggle meetings, students often forced teachers into the "jet-plane" position. Two people would stand on each side of the accused, push him to his knees, pull his head back by the hair, and hold his arms out in back like airplane wings. We tried it on each other and found it caused great strain on the back and neck. Still, some students insisted that it was far more humane than the methods the Kuomintang reactionaries and American imperialists had used to torture the Communists at the infamous Sino-American Cooperation Organization Prison in Happy Valley, near the city of Chongqing. The novel *Red Crag* detailed some of those tortures: bamboo splints under the fingernails, electric shock, the rack. A few students even argued that we should use a bit more force. After all, weren't many of these bad eggs Kuomintang and American agents?

At one meeting, Little Bawang and other activists in my class gave History Teacher Yang a jet-plane ride and a yin-yang haircut. We all knew how proud Yang was of his swept-back Chairman Mao hairstyle. I had heard that he washed his hair with cold water every morning and ate walnuts to make it shine. Teacher Yang displayed a stony expression as the students shaved half his scalp. The next day, he was nowhere to be found. The rumor was that he had run away to stay with relatives. His disappearance alarmed the work team, which issued a new order: from now on, we were to keep watch on the teachers at night.

Virtually none of Yizhong's 200 teachers escaped attention in our big-character posters, and almost anyone who was criticized had to stand before a chanting crowd at least once. After attacking the most obvious bad elements first, students went on to milder cases, even a few from excellent family backgrounds. A young teacher from a worker's family was charged with emphasizing academics over politics, and a young woman of poor-peasant origin was criticized for wearing high heels, proof that she had betrayed her class. Each apologized in a public meeting. . . .

· · · · ·

Not until evening did Grandpa tell us that Mama had been hiding just next door. An old lady who was on very good terms with Grandpa lived there. Papa had told Mama that he could not evade the rally, but perhaps she could. On new year's eve, she had left their room just before the rebels put sentries at the door, brought Yiyuan to us, and gone next door. For a night and a day, she had lain on the neighbor's kang with a quilt over her head.

The old lady's son, who had joined the crowd of ten thousand at the middle-school drill ground, described the rally to us. Thought guards had dragged Papa onto a makeshift stage and ordered him to kneel down. Papa refused, saying that he had never knelt down in front of anybody, not even his parents, and that he did not know how. The Thought Guards kicked him behind the knees and pulled his hair to force him down. He was held in a jet-plane position for two hours. The rebels took turns holding his arms up like wings and planting their feet on his back. Qin Mao and other rebel leaders made speeches denouncing him as Lingzhi county's biggest capitalist-roader. Finally, they put a feudal-style official's black cap from a Beijing opera costume on Papa's head and then took it off to symbolize his removal from office. When the rally was over, Papa could not walk. He had to be carried offstage.

Grandpa, my two sisters and three brothers, and I sat around the table in silence, listening to the account. After our informant had left, Grandpa swallowed more opium-licorice pills and tried to cheer everyone up. "Don't be upset, children," he said. "When you take off the official cap, your whole body feels light. Papa can breathe easier now. They want to ruin our Spring Festival, but let's not give them the satisfaction. Come on, let's make *jiaozi!*"

Making jiaozi, steamed dumplings, had always been our central Spring Festival ritual. "Nothing is more comfortable than lying in bed; nothing is more delicious than jiaozi," the saying went. We would wrap them late on new year's eve, put them out in the courtyard to freeze, and boil them on new year's morning. Zhihua, who was becoming an accomplished cook, prepared the dough and set it aside. He chopped the pork into fine shreds, while I minced the scallions and cabbage. Grandpa combined the ingredients with just the right amounts of soy sauce and sesame oil. Zhihua rolled the dough into long ropes, which he cut into slices to be flattened into circles. The rest of us folded in the filling as fast as he could supply us with wrappers.

Mama arrived when we were almost finished, her eyes swollen, her hair uncombed. "Papa has bruises and a backache," she said in a flat voice before we had even asked. "I've sent for a doctor. Otherwise, everything is all right. Yiyuan can come back with me." As she led my little sister out the door, she added, "Don't offend the other kids when you go out to play. On second thought, you'd better just stay at home."

At midnight, we lit our firecrackers outside the house. We fell asleep to the staccato of firecrackers popping all over town and awoke to the same sounds. Weihua and I ate our jiaozi in haste and headed for the government courtyard. Two red paper lanterns and a sign saying "Happily celebrate Spring Festival in revolutionary style!" hung over the front gate.

Papa lay in bed, covered with two quilts. Mama and Yiyuan sat at his side. The top of the desk looked like a pharmacy shelf. "Papa, we brought you jiaozi," Weihua said, holding out a tin lunchbox.

Papa raised himself with difficulty. "Have you eaten yet? How are they this year? Mutton or pork?"

"Pork," I said, looking over the bruises on his face. "We got a whole quarter of a pig."

"Good, good. Put them there on the stove. When I get hungry, I'll eat."

"Papa, are you in much pain?" Weihua asked.

"Not much. When we were fighting the Japanese, our medics sometimes operated on wounded soldiers without anesthesia. The men would pass out from the pain. That you could call pain."

Papa's haggard face took on a glowing expression. "How I miss those days!" he said. "We all had one goal: to drive the Japanese out of China. Nobody cared about rank or personal gain. Everybody was ready to lay down his life. When we had one corn pancake, we all shared it. Where is that spirit today? Why are we conducting these endless struggles?" He lay back on the pillow again. . . .

. . . . .

I could not convince my classmates of my innocence. At last, they let me get up from my knees and ordered me to submit a written confession. I wrote that when my father had led a guerrilla unit against the Japanese he had known Yang, then a district military commander; that I had heard many stories about Yang's service as commander of the advance force on the Long March; and that I felt sorry for Yang and hoped for his reinstatement. I knew this feigned sympathy totally contradicted Chairman Mao's revolutionary line, for Chairman Mao himself had ordered Yang arrested. Nonetheless, it satisfied my class-mates.

The reversal that we Red Rebels yearned for did not occur. By the time the shrubbery atop the city wall was turning green again, the pro-93rd Army side had taken over Yizhen county's new administration. The deputy political com-missar of the County Military Department, who had fled to Shimen to seek refuge when the other department officials sided with the 901, had returned to become chairman of the County Revolutionary Committee. Fangpu was vice chairman. Weihua's classmate Hezui could strut about even more proudly be-cause his Red Army veteran father was a committee member. By contrast, my classmate Yuanchao's father, also a Red Army veteran, had been forced to re-sign as head of the Army Hospital because he had leaned toward the 901. He was planning to retire to his hometown in Jiangxi province. Yuanchao and his sister Kangmei had gone ahead to look for a house.

Fangpu also became a member of the standing committee of Shimen prefecture's Revolutionary Committee. My former editor Qiude assured me, "The higher the helicopter rises, the harder it will plunge to the ground." But Fangpu's political career seemed to be on an ever-rising trajectory.

By the time the lilac bushes burst into purple blossom, we were involved in a new campaign. Chairman Mao had made a speech saying that factionalism was not completely bad. Proletarian factions should fight bourgeois factions, and proletarian factions could unite with one another, but not with bourgeois factions. This inspired the Twelve-Force Typhoon campaign, intended to de-fend the newborn proletarian revolutionary committees against class enemies. The time was still not ripe for a grand revolutionary alliance.

The Twelve-Force Typhoon made a broad sweep across Yizhen, targeting landlords, reactionaries, counterrevolutionaries, capitalist-roaders, "diehard madmen," and "anti-army elements." All the villains accumulated since lib-eration, plus the leaders, activists, and unrepentant members of the losing fac-tion, had to put on white armbands with black characters identifying their crimes.

Ding Yi, still "number-one capitalist-roader and counterrevolutionary re-visionist," Mengzhe, "black chieftain of the madman's hodgepodge," and Jinfeng, "tramp and concubine of the black chieftain," took countless more jet-plane rides on the stage of the school auditorium. The disgraced teachers were also dragged out again. I saw Zhubajie knock Teacher Li down in a rice paddy and submerge his head under the muddy water. On another occasion, I saw him drumming on Teacher Liu's bald head with a stick. Not long afterward, Teacher Liu went to the army hospital with bleeding ulcers and had three-fourths of his stomach removed.

East-Is-Red Corps students made Red Rebel students put on white armbands and kneel down before Chairman Mao morning, noon, and night. The noontime sessions were often held outside for other students to see on their way to lunch. Although the weather had turned warm, some of the Red Rebels still wore their thick padded winter clothes for protection. Once-proud warriors like Xiangsheng, now labeled the "black cripple general," and Chunfei, "black madman ambassador," crouched and kowtowed submissively while their classmates kicked their buttocks.

Their submissiveness may have saved their lives. One who did not submit was Yongrui, former director of our arsenal. Her classmates harassed her in countless ways, making it impossible for her to eat or sleep. One day, I saw her washing her bowl over and over again at the sink in the dining hall. The bowl was covered with ink. A few days later, I watched her struggle to stand upright while her classmates pulled her hair to force her head down. When she had weakened, the students threw her onto the classroom floor and kicked her unconscious. She revived and asked to go to the toilet. She could not stand up. Many onlookers had gathered, but neither I nor anybody else dared to help her. She dragged herself outside toward the lavatory. Later in the day, Red Rebel students found her body on the path. She was buried outside the north city wall with the others who had died ingloriously.

Perhaps my classmates had decided that I posed no threat, or perhaps they respected Papa's status, for even Zhubajie left me alone. Erchou escaped the dragnet too. Nonetheless, we took precautions. One night, we dug up the blindfold and ropes that had bound Zongwei and threw them down the well in the bell tower courtyard.

Weihua was not so lucky. At first, his classmates merely made him apologize to Chairman Mao, without even making him kneel down. Late one night, however, a group of students beat him up again. One of Weihua's friends woke me early the next morning to tell me. He said that Weihua had disappeared. I finally found him lying on a bench at the bus station waiting for the next bus home. His jacket was torn and his face was covered with cuts. Hezui and Huahuagongzi had laid another trap, enlisting the aid of younger students to throw Weihua off guard. When the bus came, I helped Weihua to a seat and told him to see a doctor as soon as he got to Lingzhi. He nodded absently. I later learned that he had fainted the moment he stepped into the house. He stayed in the local hospital for a week recovering from internal injuries. . . .

· · · · ·

On market days, all the victorious organizations in the county paraded their Twelve-Force Typhoon victims through the streets of Yizhen. The County Revolutionary Committee enlarged the marketplace and built a permanent stage for struggle meetings. The movement reached its height in mid-June, with a rally attended by ten thousand people. Mengzhe and other top leaders of pro-901 factions stood on the stage, held by armed police. Several hundred "special guests" with white armbands knelt on the ground between the stage and the audience. The authorities were "killing the chicken to scare the monkey," as the old saying goes. They sentenced some of their captives to jail terms and others, including Mengzhe, to labor reform. A policeman kicked Mengzhe behind the knees to make him fall, pulled his arms behind his back, and snapped a pair of shining handcuffs on his wrists.

After the rally, the typhoon subsided. Some former Red Rebels were dispatched with the ox ghosts and snake spirits to grow vegetables by Rear Lake. Others were allowed to take off their white armbands and rejoin their classmates. The East-Is-Red Corps even absorbed some of its old adversaries into its organization by creating a new class of members. The original members were now called Red Guards and had the right to wear red armbands. The new ones were fighters and could not wear red armbands. Although Erchou and I never applied, we were named fighters anyway. Now we could mix with our classmates and attend most of their meetings. We remained in our own room but could enter the room next door at will.

I resumed reading radio manuals and experimenting with new circuits. Erchou made woodcuts of Chairman Mao on the tops of broken desks. Meanwhile, for the boys next door life had become aimless and boring. From time to time, they brought in a couple of teachers and made them slap each other or crawl on the floor. At night, they would light campfires outside the dormitory to attract cicadas and eat those that plunged into the flames. One day at noon, I stepped into their room to find them engaged in collective masturbation. Lying in bed stark naked, their penises displayed like a row of antiaircraft guns, they were competing to see who could shoot the highest.

The school Revolutionary Committee declared that we would have a two-month summer vacation, the first since the summer of 1965. Weihua had returned to school. Fearful that his old enemies would beat him a third time, I persuaded him to go home early. On the last day before vacation, I faced his enemies instead.

Hezui and Huahuagongzi had one of their flunkies summon me to a room in the Teachers' Building. When I told them that Weihua had left, Huahuagongzi grabbed the front of my shirt and said, "You brothers are playing tricks!" Letting go of my shirt, he opened a folding fan with the flick of a wrist, closed it again, and used the folded fan to poke me in the chest. I backed up a few steps. He kept poking me until I had backed up all the way across the room. He struck me on the head with the fan and yelled, "Halt!"

I had stopped beneath a portrait of Chairman Mao. Pointing to the picture, Huahuagongzi ordered, "Confess your crimes!" Just as I had seen my comrades do during the Twelve-Force Typhoon, I bowed three times to Chairman Mao and said, "Great leader Chairman Mao, I apologize to you, for I did not study your works well, and I took the wrong side in the great winds and waves of class struggle. . . ."

I went on and on until Huahuagonzi ordered me to stop. He ordered me to sweep the cement floor. I did so. He ordered me to sprinkle the floor with water to keep the dust down. I went to the dining hall and brought back a bucket of cold water. I sprinkled the floor. As long as they did not beat me, I did not mind humoring them.

When I had finished my tasks, Hezui pointed to a washbasin and said, "Drink a basin of cold water to refresh yourself, and then you can go." He laughed as he filled the basin from the bucket and placed it on a desk in front of me. I drank a third of the water and put the basin back on the desk. Huahuagongzi rapped me on the head with his fan. I picked up the basin again and drank some more, very slowly. My stomach was starting to ache. I put it down again and said, "I can't take anymore."

"Stop pretending," Hezui said. "I know you can finish." I forced down some more, letting as much as possible flow down my chin and inside my shirt. When the basin was two-thirds empty, Huahuagongzi got impatient and dumped the rest on my head.

"Now," he said, "go get the worst person at school and bring him back here."

"How do I know who the worst person is?" I said. "You have to tell me. If I don't satisfy you, you'll be angry."

"It doesn't matter; just get the one you think is the worst."

I walked slowly out of the building as I contemplated this demand. It would be a difficult decision, for whoever I sent them would be their next amusement. I went to the recreation building and found Eclectic Zhu. No sooner had he trotted off to the teachers' building like a goat than I regretted my choice. Eclectic Zhu might be an ox ghost and snake spirit, but he had never harmed me. I chased after him. My bloated stomach slowed me down. Eclectic Zhu got to the room before me. I put my ear to the door and heard Huahuagongzi say, "Why are you here?"

"A student said you wanted me."

"You motherfucker, who wants an ox ghost and snake spirit like you? You've been struggled against so much that you stink! We want those madmen! Go away, you motherfucker!" My guilt assuaged, I retreated to my room, collected my things, and set out for the bus station.

As I passed Rear Lake on my way to the small north gate, I saw Mengzhe's secretary, Jinfeng, working in a tomato patch. She was barefoot, with her pant legs rolled up to the knee. The back of her blue jacket was wet with sweat, and her hair clung to her sunburned face. She still wore her white armband. Nobody was guarding her. She was working all alone and could easily have run away. "Sister Jinfeng, why don't you flee?" I said.

She turned to me. "Thank you, but I don't want to leave. I want to be near Mengzhe," she said. "Anyway, where could I go? I don't have food coupons or money. People would know what kind of person I am. They would pick me up right away and send me back." She was right. She looked shabby and beaten-down. With one look, anybody in the county could guess that she was from the defeated faction.

"Sister Jinfeng, take care of yourself," I said. "The clouds will pass and the sky will clear." I shook her hand, and left without looking back.

Autobiography of a Tibetan Monk
Palden Gyatso

PALDEN GYATSO (1933?–) became a monk at age ten and was arrested in 1959 during the Chinese campaign against religious institutions and monks in Tibet. He spent a total of thirty-one years in a variety of prisons and labor camps (years punctuated by escape and rearrest) for his religious beliefs and for his advocacy of Tibetan independence.

Gyatso lived among prisoners who were "forced to steal food meant for pigs. . . driven to chewing and eating used leather items, . . . bones of different dead animals, mice, worms, and grasses" (A. M. Rosenthal, "You Are Palden Gyatso," New York Times, April 11, 1995.) He was tortured by electric shock and boiling water; an electric prod was shoved into his mouth, and he was made to wear leg shackles for more than two years.

He witnessed the execution of prisoners and reports that "their families would be informed of the execution by means of an invoice on which such expenses as the number of bullets fired and the length of jute rope used to bind the prisoners were itemized." A similar practice was also reported during the Cultural Revolution, when relatives of the executed were billed for the cost of the bullets used in the execution. Gyatso's father was beaten to death.

Gyatso was released in 1992 and in 1993 escaped to India, taking with him instruments of torture he acquired and which he produced during a U.S. congressional hearing. Since his escape he has traveled widely, devoting his life to exposing the Chinese atrocities in Tibet. He has also testified at the UN Commission on Human Rights in Geneva.

From Palden Gyatso and Tsering Shakya, Autobiography of a Tibetan Monk, © *1997 by Palden Gyatso and Tsering Shakya. Used by permission of Grove/Atlantic, Inc.*

In his preface to this book, the Dalai Lama wrote that "Palden Gyatso's testimony is one of the most extraordinary stories of suffering and endurance. He was arrested when he was a twenty-eight year old monk . . . and was released . . . when he was nearly sixty."

. . . . .

In June 1959 three Chinese officials came to the village, accompanied by an interpreter. They announced that everyone had to exchange their Tibetan currency for Chinese paper money. The Chinese officials set up a temporary office dominated by two large metal trunks full of new Chinese banknotes, and the villagers queued up to hand over their Tibetan money in exchange for these crisp new denominations.

We heard that the Chinese had taken over Gyantse monastery and arrested all the monks. But still I felt secure in Gadong. Our monastery had not participated in the revolt and my own involvement in the Lhasa uprising was insignificant. Of what could the Chinese possibly accuse us? In July I went back to Ingon to fetch Gyen Rigzin Tenpa and he was welcomed back to Gadong with great ceremony. Strange to think that only a few months before we had walked into the monastery like beggars.

One morning I was reciting a text in my room when I heard a slow drumbeat coming from the Temple of the Wrathful Deities. I stopped chanting. Then someone knocked on my door. A novice came in and told me that all the monks had to gather in the courtyard. He was very agitated. Outside, in the courtyard, the monks were looking up at the Chinese soldiers standing along the outer walls of the monastery, their guns fitted with bayonets. Some monks were bringing a table out into the courtyard. An old monk told us to place flowers on the table and a novice was sent to fetch pots of flowers. The Chinese officials said nothing; they just observed the preparations we were busy making for them. We offered them tea, as is customary. They declined. . . .

. . . . .

The senior Chinese official stood up. He announced that "reactionary bandits" had betrayed the unity of the motherland and kidnapped the Dalai Lama. He spoke fast, brandishing a fist. He said that Gadong monastery had to declare where its loyalties lay. Then a local Tibetan called Samling stood up beside the official and said that Gadong had been associated with reactionaries. He said that the monastery too had "betrayed the unity of the motherland." Samling, speaking in the Lhasa dialect, said that monks must cleanse their minds and learn to identify the real enemies of the people. He scolded us as a teacher would a child who had been making mischief. He paced up and down as he made these bizarre accusations. . . .

. . . . .

415

Everything happened so fast. In Tibet there is an expression "the heart jumping out of the mouth" and that's how I felt. We were gripped by fear. I looked at Gyen Rigzin Tenpa. His eyes brimmed with tears. But the shackled monks before us gave no indication that they were afraid. There was a question in their expressions: "Why are you doing this to us?" These were the faces of innocent men.

The Chinese official stepped forward and Samling translated what he said. He pointed his finger at the monks and accused them of being in league with bandits. The monks stood silently, their heads bowed, while the official walked past them, screaming abuse. Then he warned, "There are some among you who have still to confess their crimes and submit to the will of the masses." He told us we were wolves dressed in sheep's clothing but that soon he would root us out. It was only a matter of time. The monks were led away at gunpoint. They were locked in a room in the monastery.

We had to attend a "study session." More Chinese officials had arrived, guarded by young soldiers. The officials wore blue Mao suits with a pen stuck in the right-hand breast pocket like a badge. Some had several pens in their breast pockets and it seemed to us that the pens were an insignia of rank: whoever had the most pens must surely be the most senior. The Communists said that everyone should wear the same uniform as a sign of equality. But they displayed seniority by other means. The suit of a high-ranking officer simply had more pockets. The Chinese were far more conscious of rank and status than the Tibetan officials they were in the process of ousting.

The "study session" was conducted by a Chinese official called Zhu xi. He was the local Committee Chairman and his dark complexion and chapped skin suggested that he had been in Tibet for a long time, for that dry, broken skin is the signature of Himalayan winds. Zhu xi's lesson concerned the recognition of "the three exploitative classes."

"The Tibetan people," he said, "have lived beneath the weight of three mountains. Today we have cast aside those three mountains. We have arrived at a new chapter in Tibetan history. The exploited masses have overthrown their master, a master who has lived for centuries on the fat of the masses. Now the sky and the earth have changed places!"

Again we were bewildered. We were simple village monks and the official's jargon meant nothing to us. Exploited masses? Three mountains? What *was* he talking about? He began to explain.

"Listen carefully," he continued. "The three burdens which weigh on the backs of the masses like mountains are the old feudal government of Tibet, the aristocracy, and the monasteries. These three classes have oppressed and exploited the Tibetan masses for centuries."

We still didn't have any idea what he meant by "exploited."

"Do you recognize your exploiters?" the official asked. We shook our heads. The official paused, searching for an analogy. Then he said, "The exploitation of the masses is like a carpenter using a plane to shape a block of wood. The masses are the wood. The exploiter is the carpenter."

Our faces remained blank. The official lost his composure. He interpreted our incomprehension as obstinacy. The session ended with another warning that we should cast away "old thoughts." We were told we had "green brains." This was another phrase coined by the Chinese. It would later become a term of abuse. . . .

. . . . .

. . . [They] themselves [had] been subjected to study sessions. The new lot were more authoritative and more crisply dressed. Gyen and I waited in the courtyard while the *shag* was searched. Gyen's belongings caused the Chinese to get very excited. We saw a young Chinese soldier thrusting a photograph into the hands of a senior officer. They disappeared into a room. Twenty minutes later they emerged and came towards us. The officer in his smart blue suit and supercilious manner told us that, incredibly, there were still those who refused to admit to their crimes and continued to conceal their treacherous activities from the Party and the people. It was clear that he was referring to me and Gyen. . . .

. . . . .

A soldier took me to a small room which had belonged to a monk but was now being used solely for the purpose of interrogation. It was bare but for three wooden stools and a high wooden box which served as a table. Folded papers had been placed under one side of the box so that it sat level on the uneven stone floor. Two guards stood at the door.

The officer introduced himself as Liao. His face and lips were dry and chapped—that signature, again, of the Himalayan wind. There were wide gaps between his teeth. He smoked cigarette after cigarette, lighting one from the embers of another. Gyaltsen, the officer's Tibetan interpreter, sat on one of the rickety stools, waiting for instructions.

Liao's manner was severe and indignant; he spoke in a kind of bark. "You have concealed your identity for a long time," he said. "You had ample opportunity to confess your crimes. Our Party workers have been extremely lenient. Still you have chosen to hide your crimes from them. This is very serious. And now I learn that you opposed the motherland and took part in the Lhasa demonstrations."

He paused to suck on his cigarette. "The Communist Party will be lenient so long as you admit to your errors. The Party will ignore your—misjudgments. . . ."

. . . . .

"You have to acknowledge that your teacher was a spy," Liao insisted.

But I was resolute. I refused to make the false allegation the Chinese were attempting to draw from me. Several hours passed. Liao became irritated by my persistence. Then he said something that I would later recognize as a standard caution. I would hear it many times during my imprisonment. Liao's voice was suddenly gentle and I could hear the translator take on that tone like some secret passed from one man to the other.

"Do you know the Party policy?" he asked.

"No," I replied.

Liao stressed that the Party's policy was leniency: they would be willing to forget my crimes if only I confessed to them. But if I resisted, he said, then the Party would "fight back." I said once more that Gyen Rigzin Tenpa was not a spy. Liao's voice sharpened. He insisted that Gyen Rigzin Tenpa *was* a spy.

"You can say what you like," I said.

Before I could breathe in, Liao's open palm had caught me on the side of the face, knocking me backwards. The two guards who had been standing by the door came forward and grabbed my arms. I saw the interpreter, Gyaltsen, step back. He looked frightened. The guards began to kick me.

"Do you confess?" asked Liao. "Do you?"

"Do whatever you want with me!" I shouted. I was enraged. I'd lost my senses.

The guards held my arms behind my back, tied them with a rope, then threw the end of the rope over a wooden beam. They pulled down on the rope, hoisting my arms up, wrenching them from their sockets. I screamed. I began to urinate uncontrollably. And I could no longer hear anything beyond my own screaming and the thuds of the guards' fists landing on my body.

After a while a guard untied the rope and before I could think straight Liao began to question me again. He wanted to know if I was ready to confess. I said that I had nothing to add to what I'd said earlier. Liao signaled to the guards. They put me in handcuffs and shackled my feet together with a chain. "Think carefully," said Liao, looking me straight in the eyes. "Confess."

They took me to another room and left me there alone. Later that afternoon a Tibetan man brought me some food. "Why don't you confess?" he whispered. "They'll kill you if you don't confess."

The interrogation went on for several days. I went over my story again and again, explaining my connection to Gyen Rigzin Tenpa. The Chinese were not interested in my involvement with the uprising. All they wanted was for me to implicate Gyen as a spy. But how could I do that? In Tibetan Buddhism the bond between teacher and student is based on devotion and trust. I looked to Gyen as my mentor. How could I betray him and live with a clear conscience? And what if the Chinese had not sent Gyen back to India at all? If the Chinese were keeping Gyen prisoner somewhere and I denounced him as a spy, what then? I had nothing to confess.

One morning I was woken early. Guards dragged me into another room. A tall Chinese official came in, wearing a long padded woolen jacket that indicated a senior rank. This man would later become chairman of the notorious Drapchi prison. He was known as Chairman Yin and I would always recognize him by his large nose. Yin was followed into the room by a young girl who, to judge from her two gold teeth and soft Lhasa accent, seemed like the daughter of a wealthy Lhasa merchant. But she had forsaken traditional dress for the uniform of the Chinese cadres. Later I would discover that this young girl was in charge of a prison in Lhasa. Her name was Dolkar.

The Chinese officer had a pistol in a holster on his belt. Dolkar began to ask me questions, beginning with my name. She took out a notebook and recounted some details about me. I nodded, confirming that the details were correct.

"We know all about you," she said. Dolkar looked at me and, seeing the bruises that darkened my face, asked me what had happened. I didn't reply. Dolkar spoke quietly to Yin in Chinese and ordered the guard to take off my handcuffs and the chain that shackled my legs. . . .

. . . . .

At about ten o'clock on that first morning, I was summoned to another interrogation. The Chinese officer wore the earth-colored jacket of the soldier's uniform, but his trousers were the blue of a senior official. I can see him now, his cropped hair and large, round face. . . .

The interrogation started gently. They began with the usual question: *Do you know the Party's policy?* What came next was as inevitable as a refrain. If I confessed, the Party would be lenient. If I refused to confess, the Party would be violent. The interpreter gave these phrases the gentle, rhythmic quality of poetry.

"Do you understand the meaning of leniency?" the Chinese officer demanded.

I did not reply.

"Leniency," he went on, "does not mean that the Party can turn a blind eye to every crime committed by a reactionary. If someone deserved to be executed and the Party chose to sentence them to life imprisonment, that too should be regarded as leniency."

I nodded my head, though not because I agreed.

The next day I was taken into another, darker room. A shaft of light shone through a single, narrow window and by this light I could make out the tools that lay on the table by the wall, the large stick and the lengths of rope. In the corner of the room there was a heap of handcuffs, chains, and leg irons.

The Chinese officer launched into a volley of questions about my life since the age of eight. Once more my answers were noted down and compared with statements I had made previously. The interrogator listened quietly, occasionally asking me to clarify some minor point. The tools remained on the table, the shackles in their pile in the corner of the room.

By the fourth day we had got to the events of 1959. The officer was more alert now and analyzed every statement I made. He was especially interested in discovering if the Lhasa uprising had been organized and, if so, by whom. He repeated certain questions over and over again: *Who instructed you? Who were your friends?* I did not realize then that every person I named immediately became a suspect.

I insisted that no one had told me to go to the demonstration outside Norbulingka, the Dalai Lama's summer palace, on March 10. Without warning, the officer banged his fist violently on the table. He picked up a handcuff and dangled it in front of my face. I blinked at every slight motion of his hand.

The officer began to question me about Gyen Rigzin Tenpa, accusing him repeatedly of being an Indian spy. But strangely the mention of Gyen's name was a source of strength to me. When the officer said he had evidence against Gyen I knew that he was bluffing. I told him he should question Gyen directly. I refused to say anything more. The officer tapped on a notebook, saying, "All the evidence is in here." Still I refused to corroborate their accusations.

The officer picked up a pen, placed it on the edge of the table and pointed to it. He told me that I too was on the brink and that confessing was the only way to save myself. This was my last warning. Two guards began landing blows on my back with the butts of their rifles. I slid from the chair on to my knees. My whole body was shaking.

The Chinese officer shouted, "Confess! Confess!" Dhundup, who had joined the Chinese in beating me, translated the officer's commands into our native tongue.

The Chinese were demanding that I denounce my own spiritual teacher. But how could I do anything that would bring harm to Gyen Rigzin Tenpa? I had no idea what had happened to him, whether he had been detained or deported to India. As far as I was concerned, I had done nothing that could be considered politically significant. I had nothing to confess. And no amount of beating could induce me to implicate Gyen Rigzin Tenpa in these preposterous accusations.

It was only later that I realized what great emphasis the Communists placed on confession. All meetings began by extolling the virtues of confession and the futility of resisting the People's Liberation Army. I remember a Chinese officer comparing Tibetans resisting the PLA to eggs smashing against the face of a cliff. But every prisoner had to confess his guilt. The Chinese did not believe their work was done until the prisoner confessed.

Whenever a Tibetan was arrested some charge would be found to keep him in prison. Then the Chinese would use every trick in the book to extract a confession from him. They would talk to his family, his friends, anyone who had had the slightest contact with him. And if this didn't work they would find someone prepared to denounce him as a reactionary. Sometimes they black-mailed those closest to him in the whole world. . . .

. . . . .

At first I was baffled by the authorities' insistence on obtaining admissions of guilt. Soon I realized that it was an important element of Communist Party policy. An admission of guilt was like saying, "The Party is right and I am wrong." It did not matter to the Party whether the confession was genuine or not. All that mattered was that it proved to the Party that one more enemy of the people had been eliminated.

I admitted that I had been present at the Lhasa uprising. This did not seem very important to me. After all, if the Chinese intended to arrest everyone who had taken part in the Lhasa uprising then they would surely have had to round up the entire population of Lhasa. But no amount of beating could in-duce me to denounce Gyen Rigzin Tenpa. So I was charged with taking part in the March uprising in Lhasa.

One morning we were all made to line up in the courtyard. A number of new Chinese officials had arrived. One of the senior officers stood on a step and announced that the investigations had been completed. We had been found guilty by the military court. Since the Lhasa revolt, the whole of Tibet had been under military control and the jurisdiction of military courts.

My name was called and I stepped forward to receive a single sheet of paper. The headings were written in red ink; the rest was in bold black Chinese characters. "Gyantse Military Division" was the only thing written in Tibetan. I had no idea what the document was. When the meeting came to an end we all rushed towards the young Tibetan interpreter with our pieces of paper. The young man glanced at the papers one by one and read out the number of years specified on each document. When he looked at my piece of paper he shouted, "Seven years."

I wasn't frightened by the announcement of my sentence, because all this time I had a strange, abiding feeling that this predicament would soon be over and I would be released. I was not alone in this: the prisoners shared the belief that we would all be freed as soon as the Dalai Lama returned to Lhasa from India. I had no inkling then that I would be imprisoned for more than thirty years.

We received our formal sentencing from a Chinese military court. There had been no hearing and the flimsy document was the only sign of any kind of procedure. All decisions had been made behind closed doors. There was no right of appeal. I had been sentenced to seven years' imprisonment and classed as a reactionary, a label which would apply for three years after the end of my sentence, as would the deprivation of all political rights.

Now that the Party had won, the official interrogation came to an end and there were, for the moment, no more beatings. But the questions went on and on. We were interrogated daily, asked what we were thinking and whether we still opposed socialism. Under communism, we were told, imprisonment was not just a punishment but also an opportunity to reform ourselves through labor. This was our first task: to reform the way we thought. I was to let go of all that I remembered of the old Tibet and learn to cherish the new socialist society. Our labor was to contribute to the building of that new society.

So we were put to work. Every morning we lined up in groups for a roll call, then marched out to an open field which was normally used for grazing horses. The villagers had identified the field years ago as barren and difficult and had reserved it, wisely, as a grazing area. But the Chinese decided that the land should be ploughed and cultivated. In the cold spring of 1961 six of us were forced to carry a huge metal plough to the field. We had to devise a means of pulling the plough. We tied ropes to its axles, three of us pulling on each side. A young PLA soldier stood on the back of the plough, adding his weight so that the blades would sink into the ground.

The soldier was enjoying himself. He rode the plough like a chariot and when he felt we were not pulling hard enough he cracked a whip of flex-wire across our backs. Our only break was for lunch, but even this included socialist education. One of the officials would read from the *People's Daily* and then talk about other socialist countries and their leaders. We had to learn the names of our "fraternal" nations: Albania, Bulgaria, Czechoslovakia, Poland, Romania, Yugoslavia. The Soviet Union was on the list too; it was still a friend of China at that time. We also had to memorize those countries which were considered the enemies of socialism. These were headed, of course, by imperialist America and Britain.

We had to learn the names of the great socialist leaders: Marx, Engels, Lenin, Stalin, and Mao. Huge portraits of these men hung in prominent positions in the prison. Stalin was particularly revered. Later, during the Cultural Revolution, Mao's portrait occupied the most prominent wall....

· · · · ·

Chinese officials thought carefully about which sort of shackle they should use on which prisoner. Everything they did had some link to socialist ideals. Our imprisonment and the punishments and occasional rewards that were handed out to us all showed the power of the Communist Party. Every speech and question began with a eulogy to the Communist Party. For the Communists, physical confinement was a means of gaining control of our thoughts. Every meeting began with a lecture on the need for prisoners to reform their ideas and beliefs. They told us that we had to learn to cherish the Party in our hearts and minds. But the cuffs could not control the way I thought. My religious training brought me peace of mind. Physical restraints were only the outward sign of imprisonment; I still had the power to give my thoughts free rein.

One day I was approached by Yeshi Wangyal, our cell leader. Everyone called him Gyantse Pa-la, or father, because although he was only in his late forties Yeshi already behaved like an old man. He took his responsibilities seriously, always warning us not to get into trouble with the authorities and making sure that no one was listening to our conversations. Yeshi told me that he had just attended a meeting of all the cell leaders at which it had been announced that everyone involved in the escape would be subjected to a *thamzing*.

I had witnessed quite a few "struggle sessions" since the Chinese first invaded. My own family had been subjected to a *thamzing* on account of their class background. The Party claimed that these sessions allowed the people to vent their anger at landlords and other representatives of the exploiting class. The *thamzing* always started with a verbal condemnation and usually developed into beatings. Chinese officials watched the proceedings from a distance, as though they were street brawls. They hardly ever intervened in such violence because to them it demonstrated "the wrath of the serfs." This absolved the Party and its officials of all responsibility. If anyone was hurt, it was a consequence of the people's anger, not the Party's.

The villagers, the prisoners, the work units—we were all watched over by the Chinese cadres and anyone who did not participate in the *thamzing* with the required enthusiasm was sure to get a visit from Party officials, either that same evening or the next day. The official, with an expression of deep concern, would say that he had noticed you had not shown *nam-gyur yag-po*, a pleasing face. This meant that you were a marked man. At the next meeting you would be forced to pull some innocent person by the hair and shout abuse at them, and by that you would demonstrate your love for the Party and your support for the people. Almost all Tibetan high lamas and officials were subjected to this form of violence. The *thamzing* was, more than anything else, a display of the Party's power.

At Gyantse there was also a monthly meeting called "rewards and punishments," during which prisoners who had "reformed" were rewarded and those who had failed to reform were punished. The punishments mostly took the form of a *thamzing*. Gyantse Pa-la's warning helped prepare me for such punishment, though I was still apprehensive; no one ever knew quite what would happen in these meetings.

My turn came on a Monday morning. The Chinese officials were seated at a large table in the open yard. The compound was surrounded by soldiers, their guns fitted with bayonets, as well as by lines of warders. We were brought out into the yard and made to stand in rows while we waited for an announcement. My heart pounded. The gathering looked too ceremonial for a struggle session. Six months had passed since our escape and we had still not been sentenced. I thought I might be sentenced to death, since prisoners bound for execution were often shackled to stop them committing suicide.

A tall, unfamiliar official stood up and announced that this was to be a "reward and punishment" meeting. A Tibetan warden shouted; "The prisoners who escaped from Norbukhungtse, come forward!" I and my companions shuffled forward from the crowd, dust rising from our heels. We stood in front of the tall official. The other prisoners were instructed to sit down and we were made to turn and face them.

A young Tibetan interpreter stood up and denounced us. He said that we were reactionaries who had betrayed the motherland and opposed the people. The young man must have been from Gyantse, for he spoke the local dialect with a smattering of the new socialist jargon. He urged the other prisoners to expose our crimes and set themselves to punishing us for turning our backs on the people's government. The prisoners, like a chorus, began to shout, "Eradicate reactionaries! Eradicate reactionaries!" The voices of 2,000 Tibetan prisoners rang in our ears. When the shouting finally died down, a burly prisoner approached us, rolled up his sleeves and started to make a vigorous denunciation. I thought he was going to hit me.

"Why should you want to escape?" he asked. He said that under socialism prison was a place in which we could reform and educate ourselves. We had betrayed the Party and the country. Again he asked each of us, in turn, "Why should you want to escape?"...

"The reason is obvious," I said, and began to list all my grievances, including the mass starvation of prisoners. The officials present were clearly uncomfortable, while the prisoners were secretly delighted by my defiance. They all knew why I had escaped. The burly prisoner looked startled by the response his question had provoked. The wardens instructed him to return to his seat.

Then the warders summoned another prisoner, called Thangtse Worpa. At the time of the Lhasa revolt, Thangtse had been a minor civil servant in the Gyantse district. He had been imprisoned because of his class background. He was determined to prove himself as useful as he could to the Chinese. In prison he had a reputation for beating other inmates, so I was frightened when he walked up to me. He praised the Party and socialism, then asked me, "Why should you have wanted to escape?"

"I escaped because I feared I would die of starvation," I replied.

Thangtse hit me hard on the left cheek and I fell to the ground. He put his hand on my neck and pushed me into the dirt. He said, "The earth is the Party and the blue sky is the people, and between the earth and the sky there is no escape for you."

Thangtse went up to each of the prisoners in turn, pulling their hair, spitting in their faces and ranting like a madman. A guard told him not to hit the prisoners, but this was just a show of benevolence intended to suggest the Party's magnanimity, for nothing that happened at those meetings was not part of the Party's strategy. If someone was beaten, they were beaten with the full authority of the Communist Party.

The *thamzing* came to an abrupt end and a senior officer stood up to read out our sentences. We were now described as the "big guilty" prisoners. The officer read out my sentence first: "Palden Gyatso from Panam County eight years, to be served consecutively, with a further three years of deprivation of all political rights." I did not know what to feel. I was glad that I was not going to be executed. But now I would have to serve a total of fifteen years in prison.

Others received similar sentences. The old man Gyalpo was already serving a twenty-year sentence and so his term was not increased. But his ankles were shackled in the heavy iron bands linked by a chain just two rings long. The officials announced that he was to remain in these shackles for four years. . . .

. . . . .

By the end of 1963, life in the prison had settled into a routine. The Chinese had become more organized. After the war with India, our jailors had a renewed confidence and meetings became displays of arrogance and pride boosted by China's achievements. We were told again and again that the Tibetan refugees in India were all living as beggars and that sooner or later the Dalai Lama would be returned to China.

My life had fallen into a pattern of work and meetings and sleep. We were woken by a reveille when the sun rose and we rushed to get out of the cell, no matter how cold it was outside. That movement into the open air gave all of us a fleeting sense of freedom. And the fresh air would blow into the cell, which would by then be rank with the stench of the sanitary buckets.

Pairs of prisoners took it in turns to empty the buckets by pushing a pole through the handles and resting it on their shoulders. Perhaps the only bonus of being shackled was that I did not have to perform this task. All the night soil was tipped into a huge pool in the far corner of the prison and in the spring this manure was used as fertilizer on the fields. After the reveille, during the two hours before we were marched to work, labor reform prisoners would deliver two kettles of weak black tea.

Each prisoner received twenty-four *gya ma* of *tsampa* per month—about twenty-five pounds. The daily ration was distributed every evening and had to last the entire day. Prisoners who worked in the stone quarry received extra rations as their work was physically more demanding. After the Sino-Indian war there was a slight improvement in the food situation. Prisoners who had relatives nearby were allowed to receive food parcels once a month, although sometimes the guards kept these parcels for their own use.

At midday a bell rang for lunch and we returned to our cells. More black tea was brought in by the labor reform prisoners. The only good thing about the tea was that it was hot. A handful of tea-leaves had been added to the water to give it some color, but it was completely tasteless. We had two precious hours to ourselves.

The prison officials took a break and slept during those two hours. We learned to concentrate all our thinking and relaxation into that brief span. I would sit at the end of the platform bed and recite prayers and texts from memory. Some prisoners went to sleep and others chatted about their past and exchanged stories about their families.

It was difficult to establish friendships in the cell because the authorities ensured that no one got the chance to know anyone else very well. All the prisoners changed cells every three months. This way there was no opportunity for conspiracy. New friendships were quickly broken up and different faces greeted you each morning. You never knew when you would see old friends again. Several criminal convicts were placed in the cells to serve as informers. They were vigilant and alert to any idle chat about socialism. Their surveillance was constant. If a prisoner made so much as a casual remark about prison food, this would be reported as a defamation of socialism.

We were supposed to work six days a week and have Sunday as a rest day, but this was never observed. Although there was no work on a Sunday, the day was taken up with meetings and study sessions. These meetings were traps. Supervising officials took a note of every comment we made and these notes were added to our personal files. The study sessions were no more or less than periods of indoctrination. We all preferred manual labor to these meetings. . . .

· · · · ·

I knew, of course, that I had committed no crimes. But each prisoner had to master the skill of making confessions which were pleasing to the Party. I used to rely on the technique of admitting to some minor transgression, wrapping this confession in a grand ideological explanation. So I might say that I had gone to the latrine frequently to avoid work, thus subverting socialism and hampering production. Then I would declare my desire to contribute to increased production. It was the moment we were asked to accuse and criticize others that caused us the most anxiety.

At this particular meeting the cook was ordered to criticize someone and he happened to criticize me. He transformed my casual remark in the kitchen into a defamation of socialism and a celebration of the old feudal society. My choice of verse was fashioned as an attempt to bring back the old feudal order.

I was made to stand up and a guard gazed at me with exaggerated astonishment. "You insolent reactionary," he said. "How dare you compare the conditions of the feudal age with those of the new society?" He then asked the assembled prisoners if they thought that conditions were better before the arrival of the Chinese. He announced that in the old society prisoners were never fed but were left to starve in dungeons, whereas in the new society even criminals who had pointed a gun at the Party were given the chance to reform.

I kept quiet. There was no point in trying to explain myself. Once accused there was no defense. I was instructed to examine my thoughts and conduct. "We will be watching you," the guard told me. "You must make a clean break with feudal sentiment and embrace the new society." And then for eighteen days I was interrogated about whether the old society was really better than the new socialist era.

I had been in prison for five years but I had still not got used to the prison regime. The loss of freedom is so tangible. My work in Drapchi was not physically demanding, but the fear of being criticized was a constant source of mental torment. To make things worse, I had no contact with my family. We were not allowed to write to each other, because any form of communication with the outside world immediately aroused suspicion.

At the same time, our families were being forced to denounce us. Any communication with a political prisoner was considered a criminal act. A Party official would visit the family and subject them to what was called "re-education". He would ask them if they stood with socialism and the working people or with "reactionaries who oppose the Party and split the unity of the motherland". Of course, there was only one answer to that question.

It was far safer for everyone to forget their loved ones. We all learned to live as though we were orphans, with no parents or brothers or sisters or even friends in the outside world. This was perhaps easier for me as a monk than it was for some other prisoners. I was used to being solitary. I had no strong ties, no memories of a wife or children tugging at my heart. There were many cases of wives remarrying in order to prove that they had completely severed ties with their reactionary husbands. The Party liked this sort of public declaration.

In February 1966 I was transferred once again to another prison. When we heard the order to pack our bags we all feared that we were about to be dispatched to Kongpo, in the southeast, near the Burmese border. Prisoners there lived in the middle of dense rain forest, so distant from Lhasa or any other center of authority that guards administered beatings and other punishments at will.

A prisoner was never told why he had been transferred. This moving of prisoners was carried out not only for administrative reasons but with the specific aim of preventing them becoming a cohesive group. The Party saw conspiracies everywhere.

Every few months all prisoners had to move dormitories so that no one was in the same cell for long. If the authorities suspected that two prisoners were becoming friendly, they were immediately separated. Any good act of human kindness was frowned upon. A friendship was officially described as a "sugar-coated bullet," especially if it were between people from working-class and land-owning backgrounds. I remember that a former Tibetan aristocrat was immediately subjected to a *thamzing* when he gave a cigarette to a convict. This was described as an attempt to buy favor with the working class....

. . . . .

I was moved many times, from cell to cell and sometimes to a different brigade. One cold February morning I was moved to Sangyip, a new prison named after a small village situated at the bottom of a narrow valley about fifteen miles northwest of Lhasa.

The valley's steep slopes protected Sangyip from the worst of the winds and it was to grow into a vast prison complex, with three separate jails as well as the training school of the People's Armed Police and the center of administration for all the prisons in Tibet. But in 1966, when I was taken there, the Chinese had opened only two prisons: Outritu and Yitritu, meaning prisons number Five and One. I was sent to Prison Five, which was divided into five brigades. My brigade camped in the open and went to work wherever our labor was needed.

All the prisoners were housed in tents surrounded by thick scrolls of barbed wire. Guards patrolled the perimeter day and night. Each tent, which might contain up to fifteen prisoners, made a unit. My unit carried out odd jobs like painting, breaking stones and making bricks at the construction sites.

At night the temperature plunged below freezing and we huddled together for warmth. Often I could not sleep, so fierce were the blasts of wind against the tent. We woke each morning to find a thick frost stiffening the tarpaulin.

The Chinese were busy constructing the prison buildings which would soon dominate Sangyip. It was clear that they were preparing for the arrival of many more prisoners. I was initially given the job of reducing large boulders to rubble with a heavy hammer, though later I had the easier task of painting window frames.

The weekly meetings, held in the tent, were a constant source of worry. After six years in prison it was a struggle to come up with new things to confess and the day before the meeting I'd have to think hard for some fault I could admit to. Usually I would fall back on a confession of laziness, and say that I'd been avoiding work, thus hampering socialist production. If I was lucky, the cell leaders would accept my confession and dismiss it with a reprimand. Sometimes they would keep harping on some minute transgression, accusing me of opposing the Party. There was no more serious crime.

In the spring of 1966 I sensed some change in the Party's policy. Every day, during our lunch break, there was a group reading of the *Tibet Daily*'s editorial and a discussion. Usually the discussion was a matter of denouncing the target of that particular editorial: imperialist America one day, Russian revisionists or Indian expansionists the next. We just followed whatever view was officially approved and expressed in the paper.

But that spring the editorials became much less clear-cut. They were full of vague denunciations of class enemies and revisionists. The Chinese officials were confused by the editorials as there were no clear guidelines as to whom the articles were attacking. Later, when I began to understand how the Communist Party operated, I realized that the lack of clarity in the *Tibet Daily*'s editorials was an indication of uncertainty or power struggles among the Party leaders. This confusion was the beginning of the Cultural Revolution.

One day in May we were ordered to stop work and dismantle our tents. We were bundled into trucks and taken back to Sangyip prison. Only three of the five brigades were housed permanently inside the prison, but that afternoon it was brimming with people. A Tibetan officer ordered us to pitch our tents right there in the open yard. Each unit raced to find a spot and soon the dirt of the yard was invisible beneath this new township of canvas.

May was an unusual time to hold such a gathering. Usually prisoners were gathered together only in winter, when the Chinese would hold a "reward and punishment" meeting that lasted for a whole month. My experience had shown that dramatic changes were normally the precursors of bad periods.

So it was hard to sleep soundly, with all the tents pitched close together and the fear of what lay in store. The next morning, at reveille, there was none of the usual rush. There were no guards chasing us out of the tents. Instead we just lolled about the yard. Even cell doors had been left ajar.

Then a group of officers marched into the yard and the leader of each brigade ran through a roll call. A senior Chinese officer took charge of the meeting. He said that Chairman Mao had personally instructed that every man, woman, and child in China should take part in the Cultural Revolution and purge the Party of revisionists.

We were issued with a small booklet containing the "Sixteen Point Directive" by Chairman Mao. The Chinese officer warned us sternly that we were expected to memorize the points, make it clear where we stood and wage war against all enemies of the Party. I was amazed by the speed with which the authorities had produced the booklet and its Tibetan translation. The speed was an indication that the new campaign had to be taken seriously.

It was also announced that we were expected to give voice to our doubts and criticisms. Mao himself, apparently, had decreed that no one would be punished for expressing their views. The officer who told us this did so in a gentle melodic voice and appeared to be sincere. But I was not convinced. I kept thinking of the preamble that had become familiar from all my interrogations: *If you confess, you will be treated leniently.*

We were so desperate to speak out that this promise of leniency was enough to entice many prisoners to make complaints and give voice to feelings they had kept secret for many years. We had kept quiet about our lack of freedom, about intimidation in the weekly meetings, about the cruelty of cell leaders. Most of all we longed to be able to talk freely to each other without the fear that our words would be twisted into defamations of socialism or the Party. The promise of leniency was, of course, no more than a trap, a tactic the Chinese would later call "luring the snake out of its hole." That promise was the beginning of the Cultural Revolution, the revolution that for the next ten years would plunge Tibet into the deepest hell. . . .

. . . . .

As a reactionary who belonged to the exploiting class, I was an easy target. In prison, as outside, the only beneficiaries of the Cultural Revolution were those classified as "poor peasants." Criminal convicts from a poor background were treated far more leniently and became cocky in their new-found status. We Tibetans called them "thick necks." Those "poor peasants" were said to have a clean political background: they were untarnished by the desire to restore feudal privileges. Criminals strode around the prison like the elect, and although they were not exempt from criticism themselves, you had to be very careful, because they could easily deflect any accusation by saying that it was an attempt to victimize the working class.

On both sides of the prison walls your worth was now dictated by your class background. If a criminal convict worked hard, criticized regularly, and declared his enthusiasm for the class war, he might soon earn remission and be released.

By the end of 1967 the meetings had become litanies of petty accusations and admissions of trivial faults. The punishments were as cruel and violent as before. Even the way we sat was criticized. When we adopted the traditional cross-legged posture, which was supposed to emulate the Buddha in meditation, we were immediately accused of showing feudal respect to the Buddha. Instead we were forced to emulate PLA soldiers by squatting on the ground. I found squatting very uncomfortable and I'm sure that all Tibetan prisoners thought it was a stupid idea. The unfamiliar posture made our weak legs shake. After a few minutes I would have to get up, pretending I was fetching something.

In the spring of 1968 I was sent to work in a brick factory near the prison. Several months passed with neither criticisms nor beatings. Evenings were spent studying. This invariably meant reading Mao's "Little Red Book." One evening, as I was reading, two soldiers and a Tibetan official called Chung la, our brigade leader, came into our dormitory. Chung la had a dark complexion and quick temper.

One of the soldiers, a senior officer, began to speak. "The Party has been kind and patient," he said, with a note of exaggerated indignation. "The Party has given all reactionary criminals a chance to reform themselves, but still they oppose the people and the Party. These criminals are like butchers who have sheep's heads on display but only sell stringy goat meat."

He had a gift for melodrama, this soldier. But we knew that such a sudden outburst could mean only one thing: that one of us was to face the severest punishment. Even the cell leader was afraid. His failure to report the smallest violation could easily be regarded as an act of complicity. The senior officer glanced at the other soldier, who immediately called out, "Palden Gyatso." I froze.

All the faces around me relaxed as soon as my name was called. My cellmates sighed with relief. I had no idea what I was supposed to have done. I stood up and walked to the middle of the room. The officer demanded my confession. He accused me of "firing missiles wrapped in wool."

"Confess! Confess!" he shouted. Some prisoners would have been so shaken that they blurted out their innermost secrets. I knew that I had to stay calm and keep quiet, waiting for the officer to reveal the nature of the charge. The soldiers were angered by my silence. The officer ordered the cell leader and another prisoner to take hold of my hands.

They pushed me down by the neck and began to twist my arms behind my back. "Bow your head!" the officer shouted. "You insolent reactionary!" A chorus of "Confess! Confess!" rose up from the prisoners around me. But still I kept silent. Two more people came into the cell, a prisoner and a guard. The cell leader pulled me up by the hair. He pointed to the prisoner who had just come in and asked me, "Do you recognize him?"

I recognized him. His name was Rigzin and he came from Lhasa. We were in the same brigade and I'd seen him quite a lot around the compound. He'd also been sent to work in the brick factory, but I couldn't understand what the connection between me and Rigzin could be. "Yes, I do know him," I said to my interrogator.

The cell leader pushed my head down and Rigzin was told to begin his condemnation. "Evil reactionaries like Palden," he said, "have never been reconciled to the defeat of feudalism. They dream in secret of resurrecting the corpse of feudalism." Then Rigzin revealed the crime I had apparently committed. He said that earlier that afternoon I had made the "ritual of water offering." This was a ritual performed by all Tibetans: you simply dip your finger into water and then sprinkle it into the air as an offering to the deities. I had not performed this ritual since the Cultural Revolution began, knowing full well the consequences in store for anyone caught doing such a thing.

"Do you admit to this?" the officer asked.

"I never made such an offering," I replied angrily.

The officer turned to Rigzin and told him to reveal the exact details of my crime. I couldn't believe my ears. Rigzin described how I'd dipped my hands into a stream and then tossed them in the air. I recalled the incident rather differently. After work, we walked back to the prison along a narrow, clear stream. I dropped my glove into the stream and bent down to retrieve it. I had cupped my hands to take a drink of the cool water. It was so refreshing that I splashed some water on my face. Then I shook the water off my hands to dry them.

Rigzin contorted this simple act into a religious ritual. The officer immediately ordered the other prisoners to subject me to a *thamzing*. My fellow prisoners rushed forwards and started to punch me on the back and sides. Some of them kicked me too. The cell leader wound an old, thick rope around my body, pinning my arms to my sides. I couldn't move. Blow after blow landed on my chest and arms and shoulders and on my ribs. The prisoners knew that if they didn't hit me hard they would themselves be guilty of hesitancy in support of socialism. I could not even raise my hands to protect my head.

I had watched prisoners die during a *thamzing*. An old, gentle man called Sholkhang Yonten, the thirteenth Dalai Lama's scribe, had refused to condemn His Holiness and was subjected to a beating. He fell unconscious and died on the way to hospital.

I would have welcomed a quick death. I told the guards to kill me. They were shocked by my audacity and replied with a blow to the side of the head and a kick in the ribs.

When the beating eventually came to an end the guards were panting like dogs. There was a stench of sweat. I fell to the floor. The cell leader untied the rope and with the rope gone I was able to breathe normally. As the guards were leaving the room, the officer looked back at me and said, "Don't think your case is finished. We'll go on investigating until you confess to your crime."

I crawled into bed. Gradually the pain subsided and I drifted into sleep. The next morning it was my turn to fetch the tea from the communal kitchen. My face was swollen and my ribs and arms were covered in bruises. All my cellmates could see that I was in serious pain. Each one of them would have been willing to take my place were it not for the fact that such a gesture would be characterized as "fraternizing with a reactionary" or "showing sympathy for an anti-socialist criminal." So my fellow prisoners just watched as I struggled to lift the bucket and walk out into the courtyard. . . .

. . . . .

I remember that, at some time during my ordeal, yet another prisoner committed suicide. He was known as Mei Metok, a reference to the large moles on his face, and he'd been a monk at Namgyal monastery in Potala. Mei had been arrested in 1959 for taking part in the Lhasa uprising and at the time of his suicide he too had been the subject of a *thamzing*.

Mei worked with me in the brick factory. A dirt track led from the factory to the prison gate. Each day, marching to and from the factory, we walked alongside the track, through the dust thrown up by passing trucks. Mei marched three rows in front of me. One evening, returning to our cells, Mei broke out of the orderly line and threw himself beneath a truck that had just come in through the main gate. The truck stopped, but too late. I remember Mei's foot jerking violently, then resting motionless on the dirt track. I looked away. We were ordered to march on to the prison in quick step. . . .

. . . . .

Our daily existence was so harrowing that we had learned to appear indifferent to beatings and torture. But I was beginning to feel the strain. The mental burden, the load of anxiety that went with every new day was starting to crush me. I too considered following the example of Mei Metok. Back in the cell the *thamzing* began again, but the beating was less rigorous this time. Even Chung la seemed subdued.

For a fortnight I refused to make any confession. I stuck to my story. The officer at last gave up and said that my case would be dealt with during the annual assessment meeting. I think that my stubbornness won me the admiration of my cellmates.

The annual assessment meeting took place each winter. All the prisoners assembled and reports compiled by the brigade leaders were read out. Those "diligent" prisoners who had informed on others would usually be rewarded with a picture of Mao or a copy of his "Little Red Book." Prisoners who had apparently failed to "reform" themselves were rewarded with increased sentences. Each year a number of prisoners were sentenced to death for failing to reform.

We were woken one morning in November 1970 by the sound of the large metal gate grating on the ground. The gate was rarely opened. This was followed by the brigade leader's voice shouting at the guards, telling them to wake up the prisoners. The cell door was flung open and the guards rushed in, prodding us awake and out of our beds. We assembled in the yard. It was still dark outside, the sky a scattering of thousands upon thousands of stars. The icy wind cut into our faces. We heard the sound of trucks coming into the prison and our cell leader told us we were being taken back to Drapchi to attend the annual "reward and punishment" meeting. We knew this meant an execution.

It was still dark when we got to Drapchi. We jumped down from the trucks and guards instructed us to sit on the muddy ground. More trucks arrived and hundreds of prisoners disembarked. The residents of every prison around Lhasa had been summoned to this meeting. At dawn we were marched through into the prison courtyard. On the surface of the yard the numbers of each prison and brigade had been written in chalk.

An officer told us the three rules of the meeting: no talking, no sleeping, no visits to the latrine. We welcomed the warmth of the dawn sun. Officials from the judicial bureau emerged from their rooms and sat down on a long bench before us. One of them gave a signal and guards brought out those prisoners who were about to be executed. I was relieved that I had not been chosen and at the same time repelled by what was about to happen.

Armed guards dragged in the prisoners one by one, tightly bound and gagged with jute ropes. A large piece of wood hung from their necks filled with Chinese characters I could not understand. I guessed that they gave the names of the prisoners along with details of their supposed crimes. More and more prisoners were dragged out into the yard with these same wooden panels hanging from their necks. Soon there were more than fifty standing before us.

A guard signaled to the cell leaders and activists began to chant, "Death to counterrevolutionaries!" Then a thousand voices joined in this shout of condemnation. . . .

* * * * *

I heard my name being read out by an officer on the podium. I was ordered to come to the front and face the prisoners kneeling motionless, awaiting execution. One of them was grabbed by the hair, face pulled up to mine. She was an old woman, deep-wrinkled and toothless. Her face was swollen and bruised. She could hardly breathe. Even today the memory of her makes me shiver.

Two guards took hold of me and pushed my head down. The woman's name was read out, followed by a list of her "crimes": how she had opposed the motherland, engaged in counterrevolutionary activities and sought to overthrow the dictatorship of the proletariat. But I was not concentrating on her crimes, because her name alone had caused my heart to jump.

She was Kundaling Kusang la. I had heard that name many times before. Kundaling came from one of the great aristocratic families in Tibet and was widely admired for her bravery in standing up to the Chinese. She had organized and led the massive women's demonstration in Lhasa on March 12,1959, and I had heard that during *thamzing* she had insisted on declaring that Tibet was an independent country. She was the heroine of the Tibetan uprising of 1959. . . .

* * * * *

I was startled by the presence of a soldier beside me. He placed his hands on my shoulders. My brigade leader appeared in front of me.

"Palden Gyatso," he said.

My throat was dry, but he did not expect a response. "Do you know," he went on, "that you are teetering on the brink of a cliff? You are *this* far—" the distance between his thumb and forefinger—"from these prisoners." He gestured to those awaiting execution. But I was so overwhelmed by fear and disgust that his threats hardly registered in my hearing.

The meeting dragged on and on. Readings of prisoners' case histories continued well into the afternoon. It was announced that the Party had decided to deprive these criminals of the right to live. In thunderous voice the audience demanded death for counterrevolutionaries and death for all enemies of the people. The prisoners were herded into the back of a truck. The truck drove slowly past each of the assembled brigades before coming to a halt at a trench five feet deep that had been dug by prisoners just outside the prison gate. The officers climbed on to the walkway on the prison wall to get a better view. Some of them watched through binoculars.

The prisoners were forced to kneel at the edge of the trench. Then they were shot by a firing squad. The force of the shots toppled their bodies into the trench. Soldiers took aim again and fired at close range into prisoners who had been only wounded in the first volley. Silence is more absolute than usual after a minute of such gunfire. Fifteen people were shot dead that day.

Their families would be informed of the execution by means of an invoice on which such expenses as the number of bullets fired and the length of jute rope used to bind the prisoner were itemized. . . .

. . . . .

In the spring of 1991 we received news that a foreign delegation was to be brought in to inspect Drapchi prison. The sudden improvement in prison conditions was a clear sign that the arrival of the delegation was imminent. In April the kitchen suddenly filled with a wide variety of fruits and vegetables. Chunks of meat and fat appeared in our diet. For a week the criminal convicts were assigned to the task of making the prison look beautiful. All the buildings were given a fresh coat of paint. All the prisoners were given new uniforms.

CAMBODIA

A Cambodian Odyssey

Haing Ngor

HAING NGOR *(1940–96), the son of a businessman from a prosperous Cambodian family, attended medical school and practiced medicine in Phon Penh before the Khmer Rouge expelled the population of the city. It was a peculiarity of the Cambodian regime to suspect and consider Westernized (and thus corrupted) those who were highly trained professionals. Such qualifications were a serious liability, and Ngor did his best to deny that he was a doctor. (By the same token, wearing glasses was also a dangerous act in Communist Cambodia because it suggested higher education and expertise.)*

Ngor lost most members of his family during the years of terror. He himself was repeatedly arrested and tortured. In 1979 he escaped to Thailand, and in 1980 he came to the United States. He had a part in the movie Killing Fields *and won both an Academy and Golden Globe award for his performance. In 1996 he was shot and killed in an apparent robbery in Los Angeles.*

The excerpts reprinted here are among the most illuminating we have about conditions in Pol Pot's Cambodia and the regime's treatment of its civilian population. Especially noteworthy is the portrait of Chev, a killer who "killed to feel good about himself," that is, to satisfy his conscience by committing politically motivated murder.

• • • • •

The Wheel of History

Thousands and thousands and thousands of people filled the street, plodding south, where the Khmer Rouge told them to go. Thousands more stood in windows and doorways, unwilling to leave, or else came out from their houses offering flowers or bowls of rice, which some of the guerrillas accepted with shy country smiles and others coldly ignored. Car horns blared. From distant parts of the city came the chattering of assault rifles and the occasional boom of artillery. The fighting wasn't over, but white bed sheets hung from the buildings as signs of truce and surrender.

From Haing Ngor, A Cambodian Odyssey *(New York: Macmillan, 1987). Reprinted by permission.*

The Khmer Rouge strode through the boulevard, tired and bad-tempered, armed with AK-47 rifles and clusters of round, Chinese-made grenades on their belts. Their black uniforms were dusty and muddy. They had been fighting all night; some had waded through ditches. A few specialists carried the big tubular rocket-propelled grenade launchers on their shoulders, accompanied by soldiers carrying the elongated grenades in backpacks. Here and there were *mit neary*, the female comrades, firing pistols in the air and shouting harshly at the civilians to hurry up and leave. They were young, the Khmer Rouge, most of them in their teens. Their skins were very dark. Racially they were pure Khmers, children of the countryside. To them Phnom Penh was a strange, foreign place.

Directly in front of me a guerrilla, with the wide-eyed smile of a boy with a new plaything, tried to take a motorcycle for a joyride. He revved the throttle to maximum rpm. As he released the clutch, the front wheel skitted left and right and then the machine lurched forward from under him and into the crowd. He picked himself up from the pavement and walked off scowling, leaving the bike on its side and pedestrians holding their legs in pain.

I put my Vespa in neutral and walked it into the street. No sense starting the engine and wasting gasoline. The crowd was shoulder to shoulder. There was no chance of getting through.

A Khmer Rouge shouted, "You have to leave the city for at least three hours. You must leave for three hours. You must leave for your own safety, because we cannot trust the Americans. The Americans will drop bombs on us very soon. Go now, and do not bother to bring anything with you!" . . .

. . . . .

Something beyond understanding was happening. Between our hopes of liberation and the scowls on the guerrillas' faces, between their order to leave the city "for three hours" and knowing that it took three hours to move three blocks was a chasm that our minds could not cross. We could only sense that some enormous event was unfolding and that we were part of it, and our fates were no longer ours to choose. . . .

. . . . .

Every morning the local Khmer Rouge soldiers assembled to recite their code of behavior, which went like this:

1. Thou shalt love, honor and serve the workers and peasants.
2. Thou shalt serve the people wherever thou goest, with all thy heart and with all thy mind.
3. Thou shalt respect the people without injury to their interests, without touching their goods or plantations, forbidding

thyself to steal so much as one pepper, and taking care never to utter a single offensive word against them.

4. Thou shalt beg the people's pardon if thou hast committed some error respecting them. If thou hast injured the interests of the people, to the people shalt thou make reparation.

5. Thou shalt observe the rules of the people when speaking, sleeping, walking, standing, or seated, in amusement or in laughter.

6. Thou shalt do nothing improper respecting women.

7. In food and drink thou shalt take nothing but revolutionary products.

8. Thou shalt never gamble in any way.

9. Thou shalt not touch the people's money. Thou shalt never put out thy hand to touch so much as one tin of rice or pill of medicine belonging to the collective goods of the state or the ministry.

10. Thou shalt behave with great meekness toward the workers and peasants, and the entire population. Toward the enemy, however, the American imperialists and their lackeys, thou shalt feed thy hatred with force and vigilance.

11. Thou shalt continually join the people's production and love thy work.

12. Against any foe and against every obstacle thou shalt struggle with determination and courage, ready to make every sacrifice, including thy life, for the people, the workers and peasants, for the revolution and for Angkar, without hesitation and without rest.

Every morning, when the recitation was over, the same young Khmer Rouge soldier shuffled out of the line and walked to our vicinity of the village, to keep watch over us. He slept each night in a hammock slung from the poles of an open-sided shed behind our house. He wore an old green Chinese-made uniform with a Mao-style hat. His trousers had a hole in the seat. There were rips along the cuffs and more rips at his elbows and collar. There was no pen in his pocket, meaning he was the lowest grade of soldier, like a private.

In spite of his shabby appearance he was full of revolutionary fervor. Several times a day when the mood struck him he fired his AK-47 into the air and began yelling slogans: "Long live our victory! Down with U.S. imperialism! Long live the independent, peaceful, neutral, nonaligned, sovereign, uh, peace, uh, peaceful, neutral Cambodia!" He usually stumbled over the longer slogans because he wasn't very bright and he didn't know what some of the words meant. His rifle fire made us nervous, but gradually we realized that he didn't mean us any harm. He had a wide, round, smiling Cambodian face. Beneath the tattered uniform and the political indoctrination was an uneducated country boy. . . .

. . . . .

In Tonle Batí the Khmer Rouge made us go to *bonns*, or brainwashing sessions, the same as in the village Huoy and I had just come from. They were always at night and usually in some mosquito-infested clearing in the forest. One evening, however, the Khmer Rouge leaders held a special *bonn* in the *sala* or hall next to the temple itself. We in the audience sat on the cool, smooth wooden floor. Soldiers had rigged a loudspeaker system powered by truck batteries. Standing near the microphone were cadres with the usual black cotton trousers and shirts, plus red headbands and red kramas tied like sashes around their waists. Outside, a light rain fell. One of the costumed men stepped to the microphone and spoke.

"In Democratic Kampuchea, under the glorious rule of Angkar," he said, "we need to think about the future. We don't need to think about the past. You 'new' people must forget about the pre-revolutionary times. Forget about cognac, forget about fashionable clothes and hairstyles. Forget about Mercedes. Those things are useless now. What can you do with a Mercedes now? You cannot barter for anything with it! You cannot keep rice in a Mercedes, but you can keep rice in a box you make yourself out of palm tree leaf!"

"We don't need the technology of the capitalists," he went on. "We don't need any of it at all. Under our new system, we don't need to send our young people to school. Our school is the farm. The land is our paper. The plow is our pen. We will 'write' by plowing. We don't need to give exams or award certificates. Knowing how to farm and knowing how to dig canals—those are our certificates," he said.

"We don't need doctors anymore. They are not necessary. If someone needs to have their intestines removed, I will do it." He made a cutting motion with an imaginary knife across his stomach. "It is easy. There is no need to learn how to do it by going to school."

"We don't need *any* of the capitalist professions! We don't need doctors or engineers. We don't need professors telling us what to do. They were all corrupted. We just need people who want to work hard on the farm!"

"And yet, comrades," he said, looking around at our faces, "there are some naysayers and troublemakers who do not show the proper willingness to work hard and sacrifice! Such people do not have the proper revolutionary mentality! Such people are our enemies! And comrades, some of them are right here in our midst!" There was an uneasy shifting in the audience. Each of us hoped the speaker was talking about somebody else.

"These people cling to the old capitalist ways of thinking," he said. "They cling to the old capitalist fashions! We have some people among us who still wear eyeglasses. And *why* do they *use* eyeglasses? Can't they see me? If I move to slap your face"—he swung his open hand—"and you flinch, then you can see well enough. So you don't need glasses. People wear them to be handsome in the capitalistic style. They wear them because they are vain. We don't need people like that anymore! People who think they are handsome are lazy! They are leeches sucking energy from others!"

I took off my glasses and put them in my pocket. Around me, others with glasses did the same. My eyesight wasn't too bad, just a little nearsighted and astigmatic. I could still recognize people at a distance, but missed some of the details.

The speaker retreated from the microphone and stepped back into the line of cadres dressed like him, with the red kramas around their waists and the red headbands. A hiss in the loudspeaker system gave way to tape-recorded music, a strange march with chimes and gongs finishing out the phrases, the same kind of music I had heard in the exodus from Phnom Penh. Definitely music from Peking, I decided. The cadre began a stylized dance to it, raising their hands and dropping them in unison, as if using hoes. When the second stanza of the music began they changed position and mimed pulling on the handles of giant wrenches, as if tightening bolts on industrial machinery.

I watched in surprise. I had never seen a dance that glorified farm work and factory labor.

Another speech began, about the development of the economy and how we were all going to have to work hard for Angkar and how laziness was our enemy. "Angkar says, if you work you eat. If you cannot work you cannot eat. No one can help you." The country was going to be self-sufficient in filling all its needs. It was not going to rely on the outside world for anything.

Then the second dance began, with the same sort of alien music. This time the female comrades danced in unison, moving with masculine vigor instead of feminine grace, mimicking rice harvesters slashing rice stalks with their knives. Then came another propaganda speech, and after that came another dance, one after the next.

At the end of the last dance all the costumed cadres, male and female, formed a single line and shouted "BLOOD AVENGES BLOOD!" at the top of their lungs. Both times when they said the word "blood" they pounded their chests with their clenched fists, and when they shouted "avenges" they brought their arms out straight like a Nazi salute, except with a closed fist instead of an open hand.

"BLOOD AVENGES BLOOD! BLOOD AVENGES BLOOD! BLOOD AVENGES BLOOD!" the cadre repeated with fierce, determined faces, thumping their fists on their hearts and raising their fists. They shouted other revolutionary slogans and gave the salutes and finally ended with "Long live the Cambodian revolution!"

It was a dramatic performance, and it left us scared. In our language, "blood" has its ordinary meaning, the red liquid in the body, and another meaning of kinship or family. Blood avenges blood. You kill us, we kill you. We "new" people had been on the other side of the Khmer Rouge in the civil war. Soldiers of the Lon Nol regime, with the help of American weapons and planes, had killed many tens of thousands of Khmer Rouge in battle. Symbolically, the Khmer Rouge had just announced that they were going to take revenge. . . .

* * * * *

Later a new interrogator, one I had not seen before, walked down the row of trees holding a long, sharp knife. I could not make out their words, but he spoke to the pregnant woman and she answered. What happened next makes me nauseous to think about. I can only describe it in the briefest of terms: He cut the clothes off her body, slit her stomach, and took the baby out. I turned away but there was no escaping the sound of her agony, the screams that slowly subsided into whimpers and after far too long lapsed into the merciful silence of death. The killer walked calmly past me holding the fetus by its neck. When he got to the prison, just within my range of vision, he tied a string around the fetus and hung it from the eaves with the others, which were dried and black and shrunken.

Each tree in the orchard had its prisoner, and each prisoner had a different means of punishment or death. The sturdy man who chopped off my finger and the other who disemboweled the pregnant woman were only two of the specialists on the prison staff.

Never had I seen deliberate killings before, carried out by professionals, in front of terrified spectators who knew that their own turns to die would come soon. Never, never, never. There had been cruelty in the Cambodia of Sihanouk and Lon Nol. There had been torture in their prisons. Lon Nol troops had done barbarous things to civilians of Vietnamese descent, and also to captured Khmer Rouge. But I knew of nothing like this, no cold-blooded pleasure in such a broad range of torture and murder techniques. . . .

* * * * *

. . . Chev *was* a killer himself. More than once, as I recovered from my wounds, I watched Chev accompany the soldiers to the afternoon arrests. He stood around pretending to inspect the canals until the soldiers and prisoners were out of sight. Then he nonchalantly followed them with a hoe over his shoulder, stopping now and again with the pleased expression of a man who is enjoying his afternoon stroll. There were never any gunshots later. Chev used his hoe to kill. The next day he was invariably in a cheerful mood, walking around energetically without his hoe. He killed to feel good about himself. If he purged enough enemies, he satisfied his conscience. He had done his duty to Angkar.

Why? Why did they kill so many? For the Khmer Rouge in general, from the lowest-ranking soldier to the burly interrogator who had chopped off my finger to the ever-smiling Chev, the act of killing other human beings was routine. Just part of the job. Not even worth a second thought. However, there were differences in their backgrounds, and in their motivations. The low-ranking soldiers, for example, were young and uneducated. Few of them had any independent sense of right and wrong. In the civil war they had been trained to kill Lon Nol forces. When they were ordered to kill "new" people on the front lines they obeyed automatically, without thinking much about the difference. For some of them, of course, and for the prison interrogators, there was an element of *kum-monuss* in what they did. But the prison interrogators were older and higher-ranking than the soldiers, like the two-pen rank of the burly man who chopped off my finger. Officers like that didn't kill just to obey, or to get revenge. They enjoyed it. They were sadists: Torturing others was the ultimate proof of their own power.

But for Chev and other front-lines leaders there was a more sophisticated reason for killing, and that was political necessity. When they talked about sacrificing everything for Angkar, they meant it. Whatever got in the way of Angkar's projects had to be eliminated, including people. To them, though, we weren't quite people. We were lower forms of life, because we were enemies. Killing us was like swatting flies, a way to get rid of undesirables. We were a disappointment to them because we never finished the projects on time, because we didn't work hard for twenty hours a day, because we were constantly wearing out and getting sick.

The worst thing was that the killings seemed so normal. Maybe not normal, but inevitable. The way things were. To us war slaves, the old way of life was gone and everything about it half forgotten, as if it had never really existed in the first place. Buddhist monks, making their tranquil morning rounds, didn't exist anymore. Three-generation families, where the grandparents looked after the little children, didn't exist anymore. Shopping for food in the markets and staying to gossip. Inviting friends over to eat and drink and talk in the evening. It was all gone, and without that pattern we had nothing to hold on to. Demoralized, split apart, like atoms removed from their chemical compounds, we let the Khmer Rouge do what they wanted with us. We didn't fight back. In the fields we were two thousand men and women with hoes, and Angkar was only two or three brainwashed teenagers with rifles. Yet we let the soldiers take us away. Why? Because it was in our nature to obey leaders. Because we were weak and sick and starved. Because it was *kama*. We did not even know why, but we submitted to them. . . .

. . . . .

After four days and four nights with no food or water they let me down and untied the ropes. The circulation returning to my arms and legs brought a pain that was worse than the numbness and hotter than the fire. I fell over on my back and didn't move.

They tied my hands and feet. They tried to make me kneel, but I fell over and they grabbed my hair and shook my head until I saw the plate in front of me. On the plate was fresh rice with two small salted fish on top.

"Are you a doctor?" a faraway voice asked. "A captain?"

I tried to form words, but my mouth wouldn't work. In front of me was the plate heaped with rice.

"No," I whispered. "Give me water. Then shoot me."

"If you tell the truth. Just tell Angkar the truth, and you will have water and rice."

Blood had trickled into my mouth from my cracked lips. "Just *shoot*," I croaked. "Please, I can't bear it. Please, Angkar, if you don't trust me, just shoot. I will be happy to die. Just shoot."

"Big mouth!" the guard exclaimed. He shouted to other guards, telling them to come over. They pulled me to a sitting position. Just before they put the plastic bag over my head, I glimpsed the pregnant lady next to me. She already had a bag over her head and she was kicking convulsively with both feet. They tied the bag around my neck, I couldn't see anything, and they pushed me and I fell over again. I tried to breathe, but the plastic got in the way of my mouth and there was no air and I went wild, struggling to get the bag off, but I couldn't and my feet were kicking and I couldn't see. Then they pulled the bag off and I took great gasping lungfuls of air.

They took the bag off the pregnant lady next to me, but it was too late. She had died of suffocation. A guard ripped her blouse apart and pulled down her sarong. Then he picked up his rifle, which had a bayonet attached. He pushed her legs apart and jammed the bayonet into her vagina and tried to rip upward but the pubic bone stopped the blade so he pulled the bayonet out and slashed her belly from her sternum down below her navel. He took the fetus out, tied a string around its neck and threw it in a pile with the fetuses from the other pregnant women. Then he reached into her intestines, cut out her liver, and finally sliced her breasts off with a sawing motion of his blade.

"Good food," he remarked to the other guards. Then he bent down between her legs where the wound was still quivering and he said, "Ha! Look at this! Her cunt's laughing." The other young guards came and looked and stood around, grinning. The flies whooshed around the body of the poor woman, whose crime had been marrying a Lon Nol soldier.

I lay on my side without moving. They would disembowel me next, just for fun. It was nothing for them to cut someone open. Just a whim. They would come for me soon. But the seconds turned into minutes and then they walked away with the woman's liver and breasts. "Enough food for tonight?" said the nearest one, and another said in a voice that was fainter and farther away, "Yes, I think so. Probably enough."

Time passed. Five minutes or five hours, I did not know the difference. A rubber-tire sandal shoved my shoulder and then I was on my back looking up at a guard. He said, "This one isn't dead yet. Give me some water to pour up his nose."

Another guard came over and I found myself staring at a thin, brown-colored waterfall descending from a pail.

The muddy water splashed down near my nostrils and some of it went into my mouth, which was partly open. I started to choke and cough but at the same time my mouth began to work and I swallowed. I had never tasted anything so good. A change come over my body, a stirring of strength. He kept pouring and pouring in a thin, steady stream to get into my nose, and some of it did, but I tilted my head back and it filled my mouth and I swallowed again and again. The water also got in my eyes, but I blinked and concentrated on the brown water pouring down.

When the guard emptied the pail and walked away, I felt much better.

At twilight, the guards untied us and helped us walk back to the jail. Of our group of eighteen, only five of us were still alive, and none of the women. My feet and legs were covered with blisters, which popped underneath as I walked.

They gave us watery rice, and after four days with no food it was like a banquet. Then they dragged us by the arms into jail and locked us into the pens again. The next day I expected to be killed but they gave me a bowl of watery rice again, and the same the day after that.

They made me work around the prison. I gardened and raked and saw the "new" people coming in and only a few of them leaving alive. In the daytime vultures wheeled overhead. At night, the wolf-like *chhke char-chark* snarled and growled as they ripped the flesh of corpses outside.

Then they loaded me into an oxcart and drove me to another jail with thatch walls. Here the prisoners plowed rice fields and tended oxen and ate the rations of watery rice. It was like the front lines, except harder, and we were all terribly emaciated, with arms and legs like sticks. I spent two long months at this place, living from one day to the next.

Then I was released. . . .

To Destroy You Is No Loss

JoAn D. Criddle and Teeda Butt Mam

JoAn D. Criddle (1936–) is a freelance writer and editor residing in Davis, California. She and her husband sponsored Teeda Butt Mam, a Cambodian refugee, and her family of thirteen, providing them with temporary accommodation in their own home. The experience led her to help Mam and her family to put into writing their experiences during the Pol Pot regime. They are also authors of Bamboo and Butterflies: From Refugee to Citizen *(1992).*

Teeda Butt Mam (dates not available) came from a well-off Cambodian family; her father was an official in the Cambodian government before the Communist takeover. She and her family were among the residents of Phnom Penh expelled from the city and sent to the countryside to become forced agricultural laborers. Her father was killed because of his position in the former government, while she and the rest of the family survived four years of inhumane treatment before escaping to Thailand and eventually making their way to the U.S. She and her husband live in California and became U.S. citizens in 1986.

. . . . .

Author's Note: *Although this book is written as a first-person narrative it is in fact a biography, not an autobiography of my dear friend, Teeda Butt Mam. With Teeda's permission, I've taken the liberty to speak in her voice because it allows the story to be told with greater force and in fewer words.*

—JoAn Dewey Criddle

From the privacy of our balcony, we noticed a trickle of residents from other districts trudging down the streets. By early afternoon, the trickle had become a flood. Rumor had it that everyone must prepare to leave the city. At once! The Angkar "requested" it. Soldiers claimed whatever pleased them by pointing weapons at the owner and suggesting he loan the object to Angkar Loeu. In our neighborhood, no soldiers came to enforce an order to leave, so my father

From JoAn D. Criddle and Teeda Butt Mam, To Destroy You Is No Loss: The Odyssey of a Cambodian Family *(Dixon, CA: East/West Bridge, 1996 [1987]). Reprinted by permission.*

and brothers-in-law chose to disregard the mass evacuation as a false rumor. Without real conviction, we invented explanations for the movement of so many people burdened with large bundles. Perhaps they were merely villagers anxious to return home, perhaps they had done something to incur the wrath of the Khmer Rouge and had been kicked out. They were evicted squatters, slum dwellers, perhaps. As more and more frightened people crowded the streets, it became apparent that the order to leave was no rumor, but did it mean everyone?

Herded along by the Khmer Rouge, frightened residents streamed toward the four main thoroughfares leading to the city outskirts. The din on Monereth Boulevard and Mao Tse-tung Road could be heard even in our tightly shuttered home. Those moving too slowly, turning aside to rest, or even stopping to adjust their loads were threatened by gun-wielding soldiers. With occasional shots fired overhead, the masses were kept moving.

Shaken by what had happened during the past few hours, our family sat down to dinner shortly after two. While we were eating, a neighbor rushed in to report that the entire city was to be emptied of residents for three or four days while the Khmer Rouge "cleaned up Phnom Penh." We analyzed possible meanings of "clean up." It could mean clearing the city of snipers and reputed CIA-led resistance. Perhaps it meant removal of all the filth and rubble three million residents and tons of rockets had inflicted on the city. A passerby, running to warn friends and relatives, yelled that everyone must leave quickly because the Americans were preparing a massive bombing of Phnom Penh. No one was sure if this or any other explanation was correct, but all those fleeing the city seemed anxious to comply at once.

Papa, as chief provider and undisputed head of our extended family, felt differently. He did not believe that anyone—not even this mysterious Organization on High—could possibly empty an *entire* city of three million people. The idea was absurd. Where would they all go? How could they all be fed, sanitation provided? What reason could the Khmer Rouge have for wholesale evacuation? They might well be planning to remove all the recent refugee-squatters from the parks, alleys, and temporary camps around the city, he argued, even those from slums and heavily damaged areas. But not *everyone*. It made no sense. The Butt family, he decided, would remain quietly behind our shutters until the confusion passed.

Family members were accustomed to agreeing with my father. He made final decisions in our home not only by reason of his patriarchal position, but also because he was a wise man who held our interests and needs above his own. He was a kind, gentle husband and father, much loved and respected.

Several times during the long afternoon, soldiers with portable loudspeakers drove through our neighborhood, issuing conflicting orders. One said people must leave immediately. The next that everyone should prepare to leave tomorrow. Papa chose to wait and see, and hope. At 4:00 p.m. the first official announcement of victory was broadcast, followed immediately by a formal order to evacuate.

The order was distressing. Even more alarming to my father and brothers-in-law was the victory statement itself: "This is the United National Front of Kampuchea. We are in the Ministry of Information. We have conquered by arms and not by negotiation. Long live the extraordinary revolution of Kampuchea."

By arms and not by negotiation. That arrogant statement left little hope for compromise with the former government or moderation in stated Communist goals. Our bubble of optimism burst. Darkness falls swiftly near the equator: there is little twilight at Cambodian latitudes. Political darkness fell just as fast.

Solemnly, we ate an evening meal of leftovers prepared in the gathering darkness. No lights were turned on or candles lit this first night under the new regime. Soorsdey, the children, and I went to bed early. It had been a long, draining day. Still, I could not sleep. I lay listening fearfully to the continuing bedlam in the streets while my mind sifted the day's happenings.

Mum's youngest brother, a forest ranger, lived near Thailand, just one kilometer from the border. He had urged us a few weeks before to leave Phnom Penh and stay with his family in the quiet frontier village. However, Leng needed to be at the airport daily; Keang had his work with the Ministry of Information. Papa felt he should keep his office open and stay abreast of final decisions even as the government collapsed. Wives and children refused to go without husbands and fathers. Besides, all we owned, all that was familiar, was in Phnom Penh. So the kind offer had been turned down and, though we did not know it yet, the borders were being sealed.

Under cover of darkness, many of our neighbors buried treasured items in their gardens, secured valuables inside walls, pried up floorboards to create secret vaults. Jewelry was sewn in skirt hems and jacket linings; radios, cameras, silver bowls, candlesticks, and silverware were concealed in bags of rice and beans. Not my family; my practical mother had packed our things weeks before.

From my bedroom, I heard Mum make her usual nightly round of the house. Even in the dark, she moved with assurance, pausing at each door. My frail grandmother slept deeply, as did the serving girl who shared her room.

In contrast to the unusual quiet in which I woke, I drifted to sleep amid noises my shuttered windows could not keep out: the insistent cries of hungry children, the distant moans of weary families trying to settle on the hard pavement, the angry shouts of black-uniformed youths. . . .

· · · · ·

Khmer Rouge soldiers were on the streets when I awakened before dawn. Four-to six-man patrols moved through the avenues and alleys of Phnom Penh evicting everyone from homes, shops, and shelters. No delays were permitted. No requests allowed. Troublemakers were killed on the spot. Often, animals were slaughtered to intimidate owners.

Already, on this second day of evacuation, orphanages and monasteries, hotels and hospitals, stood empty. Within hours of the takeover, people staying in these places had been driven from the city at gunpoint. Doctors and staff were killed if they resisted expulsion. Hospital patients too weak to walk were shot in their beds. Others, carrying still-attached plasma bottles, hobbled from the wards. Hospital beds, filled with the sick and dying, were pushed through the streets by relatives and friends.

For nearly four hundred miles, the border between Cambodia and Thailand curves through mountains, jungles, and across rivers. The Khmer Rouge methodically evacuated all villages within five miles of the border, creating a no-man's-land that extended from the southern fishing villages on the Gulf of Thailand to the ancient Khmer temple of Preah Vihear in the north and beyond.

Borders with Laos and Vietnam were likewise secured, and all roads into the country closed, jungle paths booby-trapped and mined. The Cardamon Mountains and the Elephant Range to the southwest completed the cordon. A lethal web was being cast over Cambodia. Angkar Loeu, the spider at the center, was even then issuing the orders that would entrap each citizen in servitude and fear. For millions of my fellow countrymen, this web would become a shroud.

North, south, east, and west, the four official exits from Phnom Penh filled with people. Friendship Highway, built with U.S. aid during the Vietnamese War, had once transported military supplies eastward from the port city of Kompong Som through Cambodia to Vietnam. Now it carried the human flotsam of civil war.

With first light, a thorough emptying began street by street, block by block, house by house, from the center of the city outward. The rich, the poor, the sick and lame, filed past our door. Mum packed additional supplies. Papa urged us to remain quietly inside as long as possible. Mearadey and Rasmei pressed him to leave. If the neighborhood was emptied, we could more readily be singled out. Better to move now and be part of the faceless mass, they reasoned.

Papa was reluctant to leave the shelter of our yard. "If we leave our home, we will never return." There, he had said it. . . .

· · · · ·

During those first days of the evacuation, people unable to keep up were clubbed. However, once the Khmer Rouge had the entire population moving like a herd of dumb oxen, it took only shouts and occasional prodding to keep us in line.

In peacetime, Phnom Penh, with its stylish shops, sidewalk cafés, cream-colored mansions, walled villas, tropical foliage, and tree-lined boulevards, had always seemed elegant, but the alleys hid cardboard and corrugated-tin hovels where the poor eked out a miserable existence. Until our march from the city, however, I'd had little knowledge of this other world. Now I rubbed shoulders with not only those who'd recently fled the advancing Khmer Rouge, but also with peasants who had abandoned their villages earlier for the promise of wealth in the city. These poor people had been reduced to selling vegetables on the street, pedaling the three-wheeled pedicabs, or driven to begging, prostitution, theft. Many had been unwell and underfed even before being forced to make this grueling march back into the countryside. By the third day, many impoverished peasants began to die.

Stifling heat, lack of food, and bad water also took their toll of the old, the infirm, and the young. Dysentery and dehydration were felling many. Water supplies had been shut off to encourage residents to leave the city, so those not carrying their own water were soon reduced to drinking from ponds and ditches. Though my family used bottled water, little Tevi soon became deathly ill. Mearadey tried to ease her pain, but we were not allowed to stop long enough to care for her properly.

Inching along Monivong Boulevard, we finally reached Keang's old law school. It had taken us four horrendous days to travel less than two miles. We took shelter in classrooms where Keang had sat for exams. Charred remains of desks littered the tiled floors where refugees cooked rice. The corners of rooms were used as toilets.

My English school, next door, was a stinking shambles. Windows were smashed, the lovely grounds trampled, trees destroyed. Textbooks had provided fuel and light for squatters. That I could understand, but I could not understand the Khmer Rouge's wanton burning of books. Stacks of books had been simply tossed out library windows and set afire. Even the law library was destroyed.

Most books in Phnom Penh's many libraries were in French. Ever since our independence from colonial rule twenty-two years before, Cambodians had felt resentful of continued French influence. But French was undeniably our second language, the language of the educated. It was the language that made contact with the outside world possible. But it wasn't just hatred for the French that prompted the Khmer Rouge to burn books; it seemed to be hatred for any learning. Books written in Cambodian were also tossed to the ravenous flames, and bookstores, newsstands, and stationery shops torched. Rare, priceless volumes in special collections had been eliminated without a second's thought. Even illiterate peasants, filing past the burning books, were devastated by the senseless destruction.

Money was also burning. At first people grabbed fistfuls of bills from the burning piles in front of banks. The soldiers laughed. Money wouldn't be needed in the new Cambodia, they said. This was a new era, a starting over, year zero— *Tchap Pdum Pee Saun*. Angkar Loeu would take care of us from now on. They told refugees to throw their useless riels into the flames. A few gullible people believed the soldiers and unburdened themselves of bulky money bags, but most, ourselves included, refused to believe that our hard-earned riels were totally worthless, even though it had recently required a shopping bag of bills to purchase a bag of rice.[1]

As food shortages increased, rice became the measure of value. A car or costly watch was the price demanded for a fifty-pound bag. More often, no proffered wealth could pry rice from a lucky owner.

Famished refugees chewed leaves and even tree bark to dull hunger pangs. Stripping the once majestic teak, jacaranda, and Nandi flame trees, they boiled leaves and bark in polluted water to make tea. Years before, Prince Sihanouk had spent large sums on spacious parks and grandiose public buildings, with the goal of making Phnom Penh rival Saigon as "the Paris of the Orient," but it was the gracious tree-lined boulevards that provided so much of the city's charm. As we shuffled toward the bridge that spanned the Bassac River, rows of denuded trees stood as battered sentinels of our broken nation. . . .

· · · · ·

Two and a half weeks after eviction, a call was issued for men in certain categories to return to Phnom Penh to begin the reconstruction. Those encouraged to volunteer included former government leaders, military officers, doctors, lawyers, business leaders, educators and professional men, and skilled workmen such as engineers, plumbers, electricians, and mechanics. Families of these men were to remain in the temporary camps a little longer.

A wave of hope rippled through the crowd as the truck-mounted loudspeaker blared this announcement. Former government officials, especially, felt the need to show support for the new regime and many stepped forward. Mothers and children urged their men to register so Phnom Penh would be ready before the monsoon rains came, for already the winds were shifting from the northeast to the southwest, bringing occasional showers. Within the month, much of the delta would be a quagmire.

Papa and my brothers-in-law wanted to sign up, yet felt constrained to wait. They had no desire to volunteer for what might be prison, exile, or execution. During the past few weeks, we had witnessed a level of dishonesty, brutality, and capriciousness that defied understanding. Such behavior, coupled with our aversion to Communist philosophies, made us suspicious. The men were in a quandary. Was the call to rebuild genuine, or was it merely a means of identifying certain men for reprisals?

Though Keang, Papa, and Leng decided to wait, they continually took stock of their alternatives. Every day they watched the army of recruits file toward Phnom Penh. Once Papa noticed an important colleague's familiar blue Peugeot station wagon inching its way along the congested road toward the city. Hoping at last to get reliable information, he hurried through the crowd, trying to attract his friend's attention. The man sat in the front seat next to a Khmer Rouge driver.

A brief look of recognition crossed his somber face, then his terror-filled eyes looked straight ahead. Papa glanced from the man's stricken face to his lap and saw that he was handcuffed. In the rear seat, a soldier held a pistol to his head. Papa melted into the crowd, his questions answered.

Two days later, a Voice of America broadcast reported that eighty-five government officials had just been executed. We learned much later that bodies of thousands who had answered the call to rebuild were stacked in public buildings such as Toul Sleng High School. They had been tricked to their own executions.

After the men had left, allegedly to restore Phnom Penh, portable loudspeakers blared the awful truth—there would be no return to the city for us.

"Leave!" they ordered. "Go find a place in the villages. . . . Cities are evil; technology is evil; money and trade are evil. . . . The strength of a nation is in its working men and women, not in the parasites of cities who live off the labor of the peasant. . . .Everyone must work in the fields. . . . Plant rice so the nation can prosper. . . . Only those who work will eat. . . . All are dependent upon the Organization on High."

With hope of returning to the city gone, we recognized the cruelty of the lies we'd been told. A few weeks under Khmer Rouge rule had impressed on all of us that we were dealing with vengeful, irrational masters. Those foolish enough to challenge the decisions of Angkar in public seldom did so twice.

One woman, beside herself with worry, timidly asked an officer how she could send funds to her son studying abroad if the Cambodian riel was no longer recognized. I listened closely, for Uncle Ban also had a son studying in France. Sneering, the officer said it was not a concern of the Angkar and would no longer be a concern of hers; communication with the outside world had been severed.

In the new Cambodia, the officer loudly boasted, there would be no modern means of communication. No mail service or telephones. No newspapers. No border crossings. No trains, cars, buses, or planes. The evil ways of the Western world were outlawed, all ties to the past abolished. This was a new era—Year Zero.

Not many occupations would be needed. No merchants, no bankers, no teachers, lawyers, or civil servants, no doctors, dentists, or dressmakers trained in the corrupt ways of the West. No railroad engineers, pedicab drivers, cooks, waiters, maids—not even truck drivers or housewives. These people had been leeches on society, consuming the harvest of the true laborer. "True labor" was in agriculture, fishing, and a few other basic occupations directly related to food production.

Reeling at this latest revelation, we tried to find some logic in the demand that everyone work the land. We certainly did not possess the necessary skills, having been trained in other areas formerly considered important. We could not grasp the full intent of these pronouncements.

Papa reasoned that these rash decisions would be reversed once leaders considered the ramifications. He continued to offer words of encouragement: "If we hold on a little longer, surely we can awaken from this world of unreality where good is bad, right is wrong, and our training is deemed not only worthless, but evil."

Noting the humility and quiet dignity of a passing Buddhist monk stripped of his saffron robes, Papa admonished us to practice our Buddhist teachings. Be peaceable. Drive out hatred, desire, and dissension. Strive for inner peace. Others might be able to control the environment, even the physical body, but not the mind.

A new edict came. Everyone was told to select a village quickly, or else be assigned one. Return to ancestral villages was encouraged, but those forced to the east, as our family had been, were to continue in that direction. My parents were determined, nevertheless, to seek refuge in the Khum Speu area to the north, where Samol's parents lived and where Uncle Ban's and Uncle Suoheang's families hoped to return to their abandoned homes. Keang also had ties to Khum Speu because he'd been a high school teacher there shortly after he married Mearadey.

Uncle Ban, his son Si Ton, and my other cousins were not yet willing to abandon their vigil. They hoped that the renewed movement of the population might give them an opportunity to learn the whereabouts of their missing loved ones. We left supplies, wished them success in their search, and hoped they could catch us en route to Kompong Cham Province. Grandmother Butt bid them a tearful good-bye. It was especially hard for her to leave Si Ton, her twenty-seven-year-old grandson who had always been so solicitous of her. We took turns pushing the car, starting the motor only to ascend the occasional hill. We decided to try skirting Phnom Penh by using back roads along the Mekong River.

We were no longer merely homeless refugees. We'd been given a new designation by Angkar— "People of the Emigration"—as if that title altered our homeless, miserable state.

The winds shifted. Cambodia knows only two seasons, the wet monsoon, and the dry monsoon. Hot, moist air blew in from the Indian Ocean, temperatures and rain would increase through June, July, and August, then taper off through September and October. Six feet of rain would fall in the delta during the six months of the wet monsoon. The rains began.

Slogging through the wet countryside, the beaten populace finally accepted how futile it was to continue carrying heavy items that could not be used in grass huts. One by one, prized possessions were abandoned. Rice paddies filled with TV sets, air conditioners, refrigerators, sewing machines, furniture, bags of money, even cars.

Some citizens could not bend with the loss of wealth and the specter of hardship. A Chinese merchant told us he had saved nothing but two bags of riels. His fortune was good for little more than fuel to cook a pot of rice. He tied the bags around his neck and drowned himself in the Mekong.

Fearing enslavement or death at the hands of the Khmer Rouge, a professor and his wife and children consumed lethal doses of poison, climbed into the family car, and drove it headlong into the river.

The rest of us plodded on toward the years of servitude ahead. Slowly, we learned that the Khmer Rouge had left little to chance in their movement of people. From the very first day, what had appeared to us as mass confusion and chaos had been a single-minded effort to empty the city as rapidly as possible, regardless of cost in suffering or loss of life. The leaders were determined to redefine society overnight. Their bold and truly diabolical scheme was beyond our wildest imaginings during those first chaotic months. Mass evacuation had been deliberately conceived to throw us off balance and to prevent organized resistance.

The Communists needed this psychological advantage. They were surprisingly few in number for an army that had just toppled our American-backed republic through prolonged military battle. By their own probably exaggerated count, they had only four thousand regular soldiers and fifty thousand guerrillas to control a population of approximately eight million.

Without deception and swift action, the Khmer Rouge could never have subdued so many of us with so few. If we had guessed that eviction from our homes was something other than a temporary necessity, or that slavery and starvation were to be our fate, we would have resisted more desperately. But our awareness came too late; we could no longer muster effective resistance.

Feeding us a series of lies, keeping us on the move, overwhelming us with the effort of mere survival—all these Khmer Rouge tactics were similar to those of the Nazis in dealing with the Jews. But never before had such strategies been turned against an entire nation; never had a country enslaved its own people so thoroughly; never had a society without cities been attempted on so grand a scale.

Within weeks, Angkar Loeu was able to break down societal structure and all but the closest family ties. Weaker members of the population, those who would have burdened the regime, died quickly. And military leaders, government officials, and the educated—the greatest potential threat—were either killed or incarcerated. Spies reported minor infractions and kept people from trusting each other. Some men taken to be "searched" never returned.

Soldiers seized identification papers of those they caught in the random searches. In the name of Angkar, items on the proscribed list such as radios, pens, medicine, jewelry, watches, money, expensive Western clothing, and even eyeglasses were claimed. Most of these "luxury" items were destroyed on the spot. Like everything else, the purpose of their destruction seemed to be to intimidate, to bewilder, to create debilitating anxiety.

Women were searched less rigorously than men. We took advantage of this in hiding valuables. I hid my gold necklace in my jacket lining. Mearadey insisted on keeping our birth certificates, graduation papers, and other documents, though she knew she was taking an enormous risk. Keang begged her to destroy them, but she felt sure education would someday be highly prized again, and she wanted documentation. . . .

. . . . .

I was tired of constantly being admonished to emulate the docile water buffalo. Water buffalo made no demands. They worked hard all day, yet never complained and seldom got sick. They subsisted on grass. Unthinking, they did the bidding of their masters. These dim-witted animals were more highly esteemed by Angkar than any villager.

I was also weary of being compared unfavorably with bamboo; so versatile, pliable, and useful. And I resented being likened to a single grain of rice—insignificant.

According to Angkar Loeu, each person should aspire to be like one grain of rice in a huge bowl—no different from any other grain and insignificant by itself. No one was to esteem himself above another. No one was irreplaceable. Only in being part of the whole did one have value. Remove one grain of rice and the bowl would be just as full.

Unsubtle allusions to the "eyes of the pineapple" insured that everyone would endeavor to remain indistinguishable from all others. No one wanted one of Angkar's many eyes focused on him.

Though talkative and friendly by nature, I had become wary and silent since coming to Khum Speu. I mentally reviewed everything before I spoke. It was best to play dumb. I tried never to stand out except by working extra hard. I never volunteered for anything or complained where it could be heard by those outside my family, or my closest friends. I took no initiative. Whenever I was asked a question, I answered, "I don't know," even when I knew the answer or had an opinion. I acted impressed by everything the leaders told me, as though their thoughts were profound. I dutifully sang the Communist songs, did my work in silence, watched old village girls, and tried to act as they did. . . .

. . . . .

It was hard to keep track of time; life was the same from day to day, month to month: work and fear. In dry weather, I labored on dam projects with my youth crew and often lived away from home. In the rainy season, I worked closer to Speu. There were few days or experiences that stand out.

During evenings when we camped at the dam site, I wove hats from palm fronds for my family or as barter items. Usually, however, I was too spent to do anything not required. At least away from the village we were not subjected to nightly indoctrination sessions. They were far more oppressive than work. To come back to the village muddy and exhausted after a long day in the fields, I dreaded the nightly meetings where the entire village of several hundred people met for three or four hours of numbing speeches and confessions. I dared not be absent, nor let my head nod or my eyelids droop as I sat on the hard, backless benches in the communal dining pavilion.

Meetings began with a few rousing Communist songs, that no one dared refuse to sing with gusto. In Phnom Penh, I'd loved to sing along with records or the radio. I'd known all the popular American and English songs by heart. Now I limited my singing to the requirements of evening meetings or to humming a satiric refrain while I worked.

After the songs, evening meetings settled into the first order of business— *kosang,* a formal warning that a person had displeased Angkar. Anyone could charge another with real or supposed failings. Old villagers had some opportunity to discuss their alleged crimes before being punished. New villagers were expected to "confess" without knowing the charges. It was a dictum of Angkar that in our society of comrades, the faults of another were only pointed out to help that person improve; therefore, the "guilty" were expected to submit to the humiliation of a *kosang,* then "reconstruct themselves" into good people by confessing and repenting. Most often it was new villagers who needed reconstructing.

For a minor infraction, a *kosang* usually brought denial of food for the next day, reduced rations, or extra work. A person was "called to see Angkar" or sent for "reeducation" if they committed a "serious crime" or after they'd received several *kosangs.* Prisons and work camps for intractable citizens were almost nonexistent. Either a person was an asset, or he was an expendable liability. Old villagers were usually deemed capable of mending their ways; new villagers were often ruled incorrigible.

Children were encouraged to report failings in their parents and other adults; their word was taken as fact. An envious neighbor, or one harboring a grudge, could cause trouble or even death by accusing his enemy of failure to live by some Khmer Rouge rule. Seldom did anyone receive more than a couple of *kosangs* of a serious nature. The most common serious crimes were stealing food, keeping a private hoard of rice, or dwelling on the past. Even asking to stay home when ill could bring the serious accusation of laziness.

In addition to facing accusations by others, we were expected to confess areas in which we had failed to do our best for Angkar. If a person did not stand up often and admit his own failings, he could be certain others would point them out. My family actively sought for trivial things we had failed to do well, so we would have something to confess that would not bring serious repercussions, yet would show that we were trying to improve.

During the final part of the meetings, we were bombarded with local lectures or broadcasts from Phnom Penh. Often our illiterate leaders, not expected to think for themselves or offer original ideas, simply spewed forth strings of Communist sayings about the need to increase production.

Another favorite lecture theme was renunciation of personal desires for group goals. Renunciation of material goods, wealth, education, family ties, and religion were all recurring subjects. Angkar wanted all villagers to cease to be concerned with themselves, to strip away pride and envy. Individualism was to succumb to collectivism.

Sometimes there were theatrical performances by children at evening meetings. We were expected to give these productions our solemn attention. These embarrassingly amateur plays depicted gory scenes in which loyal, valiant Khmer Rouge were beaten and tortured by diabolical Lon Nol soldiers, with the Khmer Rouge always triumphing in the end. Villains wore black moustaches and made awful grimaces to indicate their wicked nature. Other revolutionary themes were similarly treated. I had no firsthand knowledge regarding the inhumane treatment of Khmer Rouge soldiers or villagers by Lon Nol's army, but the barbaric acts they committed in these plays were identical to those the Khmer Rouge perpetrated against us.

I joined a group of villagers one evening in a jungle clearing to watch a propaganda film extolling the close ties between Cambodia and China. It featured Pol Pot and other leaders who had traveled to Peking, and I was curious to see just what the men behind the awesome Angkar Loeu looked like. To my surprise, they were ordinary-looking men, about the age of my father. I felt an emotional letdown when I saw how unexceptional they looked. The incessant propaganda had led me to believe that The High Organization was composed of super-humans. Looking at these grinning men, it was hard to imagine any of them willfully ordering the backbreaking labor, suffering, and death I saw each day....

．　．　．　．　．

"Playing around with women" was one of the more serious crimes. Under Angkar, all sex offenses were serious but almost nonexistent. Unmarried couples were forbidden to speak words of endearment. Homosexuality was virtually unknown and condemned if discovered. Rape was beyond comprehension.

Premarital or extramarital sex brought the death penalty. Not many were killed for adultery; most people were too tired to find or be a willing partner.

Repeated quarreling with a spouse brought enforced separation or possible death. But there wasn't much quarreling either. All a person wanted was to eat and sleep after an exhausting day of work. It takes energy to fight or make love, and few had the stamina for either.

Along with the awesome words "Angkar Loeu," which had come to imply some godlike creature who capriciously meted out death and seemed to know my every thought and action, there was another phrase that filled me with fear and a sense of helplessness.

The dreaded phrase was *lut-dom*. *Lut* is the part of metal processing in which a rod of metal is placed in a fire until it is red-hot and pliable. *Dom* means the hammering—when the hot metal is put on the anvil and pounded into shape, any shape desired. *Lut-dom* described the way people were expected to be molded by Angkar into the pure Communists of the future. If, after heating and hammering into shape, they still refused to conform, they were either "re-heated" in the fire of evening political meetings and everyday struggle, or disposed of.

Whenever leaders referred to the Wheel of History—implying that the inevitable era of communism had arrived—I could not help but conjure up the awful image of a huge wheel grinding me under as it rolled slowly but relentlessly forward. "The new Cambodia is like a train gathering speed," we were told. "Nothing you do will stop it. If you try to step down or stop the rushing train, you will be crushed under its powerful wheels." I had become unwilling baggage aboard the train of this alien ideology, yet I could find no way to get off. After almost two years under Angkar, the future seemed a gaping, black tunnel rushing to swallow me. . . .

* * * * *

The Khmer Rouge continued to rank society's members according to those most worthy of emulation and those who were the greatest enemies of the people. According to that system, our family was on the enemy list.

"Federalists," the first category of enemies, included members of the royal family, all government workers, even policemen on the streets—anyone with "authority." These were considered unredeemable and all were to be killed. Papa had been in this category, as were Keang and Leng, if it were but known.

Traitors in the second group were "Capitalists and Speculators": businessmen, intellectuals, students, teachers, professionals such as doctors and lawyers, plus technicians and skilled laborers. In this category, most were to be eliminated, but some were deemed capable of reeducation and could be spared. According to his biography, Keang belonged to this group.

Of the three categories of farmers, big plantation owners generally were killed if found. They had farmed many acres, owned equipment, and employed others. Especially damning was their employment of others. It was self-evident "exploitation."

Middle-level farmers had owned land and equipment, but had not used the labor of others. Mum's oldest brother fit this description. She especially worried about him because he was an outspoken critic of the new regime. Many in this group, however, were not killed, just stripped of possessions and humbled. Poor farmers were classified with factory workers and manual laborers as the proletariat. Leng's biography listed him as an unskilled laborer; everyone sought that classification.

Mum worried that Mearadey and Rasmei would be widowed if the backgrounds of her sons-in-law were discovered. Above all, she agonized about her "precious Ne and Da"—the nicknames by which Soorsdey and I were known within the family. We came home each night so exhausted we seldom spoke. Our existence consisted of working, eating, and sleeping. But Mum's worst fear was that Ne or I would be forced to marry a soldier as some friends' sons and daughters had been made to do.

It was considered unpatriotic to refuse a soldier's marriage proposal. It was possible to turn away the first few offers, but if refusals continued, a girl was accused of feeling superior and might even be put to death. Since Angkar didn't allow divorces, a person could be trapped for life with an unwanted partner. Already Mum had turned away hinted proposals, especially for Soorsdey. But it was only a courtesy that she was even asked. Parents no longer had to be consulted. Ne was almost nineteen and I had turned sixteen in August, four months after the takeover. We were considered good-looking, desirable girls, despite our efforts not to draw attention to ourselves.

Mum's poor health brought her into close contact with old people in the village; she worked with them. In addition to weaving, spinning, and baby-sitting, the ill and elderly made bamboo baskets, braided rope, and performed other tasks around the village. Though life was physically less rigorous for them, it was equally bleak. They had grown up in a society that revered its old. Now the Khmer Rouge made them feel useless. Traditional family attention and pleasures of their twilight years were denied them. They'd expected to spend old age as wise, senior members of loving family groups, free to visit Buddhist temples regularly, and contemplate the next world. Instead, their days were filled with long hours of toil, and their wisdom was scoffed at by their captors. They were treated like flotsam, serving no practical function in a society that cared only for "useful" objects.

One pleasure remained to them. Pol Pot had not denounced the chewing of betel nuts and leaves. This pleasant-tasting, mildly narcotic plant dulled the pain and loneliness of many, especially old peasant women. My mother, like most women from the cities, shunned the teeth-blackening, lip-staining habit, and was repulsed by the bright red spit. But now my mother understood the need old people had to drug their senses, so she never condemned those who found solace in the betel nut.

One way we could get Mum's mind off our current troubles was to start her talking about the past. The deep lines around her mouth and eyes would soften as she reminisced about her youth, her marriage, and life as a young woman in Phnom Penh. She treasured the memories of her traditional upbringing....

. . . . .

There is a human tendency to believe that nothing really bad can happen to you—to the other person, perhaps, but not to you and your family, particularly when you've done nothing wrong. When the relocation orders came, former city residents had even felt that their superiority over old villagers was at last being acknowledged. Everyone had cited instances of actual relocations, reassuring themselves that it was a common Communist practice. So, like sheep, we had willingly, happily, assembled in town squares throughout the nation, and impatiently waited for trucks or ox carts to haul us away.

As the magnitude of the slaughter became known, a deep depression overtook me and I questioned my own survival. I, too, would be moldering in the pond if I had joined Si Ton. My clothes, too, would have been part of the mound dumped in West Speu had Mum and I joined my friends. It seemed such an ugly twist of fate that Si Ton, coming from a less prominent family, should be a corpse in a reeking reservoir, yet I lived. No wonder the chief had not dared move Keang from the district against orders.

I had no explanation for being alive except for the leader's lingering doubts about Mum and me being part of Keang's family. Mum was grateful—not for her life, but for mine. She immediately set up her little shrine again in the back of the hut to offer thanks.

I could not bring myself to pray, could not bring myself to believe that it would be possible to continue to remain alive; not when, one by one, my close friends with less prominent fathers were killed with their families. Loved ones on every side had been murdered. Those death trucks had been meant for Mum and me! Angkar was stalking us. What was our crime?

A black shroud of speechless horror enveloped me as piece after gruesome piece of evidence accrued. Suspicion. Distrust. Gut-twisting terror. Each person clutched his thoughts more tightly to himself. Everyone worked harder. We dared not complain. We had never before felt so totally beaten, so much like slaves at the mercy of diabolical masters. Each time we had told ourselves it could not get worse, but it had. Like walking dead men, we waited our turns in mute silence. Any person or event out of the ordinary filled us with panic.

Like repeated blows of a hammer, I learned almost daily of the death of yet another relative or close friend, and of the nonexistent new villages where they had supposedly gone. Silently, I berated myself, tortured myself, for being so gullible. *Why* had I allowed myself to believe the lies? Would I *never* learn?

My mind returned again and again to the deaths of loved ones. My fiancé and his whole family were dead; only one brother, studying in Paris, had been spared. Papa was surely dead. Leng's brother and sister-in-law and their two children were dead. Leng's mother was dead. His other brother was probably dead. Grandmother was dead. Mum's brother, his wife, and six children were dead. Uncle Suoheang's daughter and her three children were dead. Many other relatives were dead. My two best friends were dead. No doubt even Blacky and Brownie had long ago starved or been shot. Everywhere I turned there was death.

I mourned for the murder of my fiancé and the marriage that would never be. How flimsy had been the cloak of protection in which I'd smugly wrapped myself as his bride-to-be. How suddenly it had been torn away.

All of Uncle Ban's children had been outstanding students. Now, except for my cousin in Paris, all eight children and their parents were dead or missing.[2]

. . . . .

Up to the time of the first harvests, men had been punished for acts of rebellion, real or suspected, or eliminated because they had held positions in the former government. We had thought oppressive measures would diminish once former officials had been identified, rooted out, and removed, as Papa had been. Despite the frightening slogans and the continued harsh treatment, we had not fully grasped that the lives of this generation did not matter; what mattered was Angkar Loeu's "plan" and the future utopian society of which its leaders dreamed. To Angkar, we *were* just grains of rice. Insignificant.

Cambodia, we were instructed, could still renew itself, even if all but two Cambodians were destroyed, as long as those two were not contaminated. In bitterness, some whispered that the killings would stop only when Pol Pot and his wife, Khieu Ponnary, were left as the "two uncontaminated Cambodians."

I could not shake the dread I felt every time a soldier or a *srok* leader entered the village. It could only mean trouble for someone. Keang's mentor was dead, himself a victim of the purge. Would Keang again be summoned by Angkar? Would explanations be demanded from Mum and me about our failure to relocate? Surely someone would question Leng's continued presence in Prey Tayo. From one quarter or another, we were sure death would strike.

Before 1977, Keang had held out some hope for the future. Surely the day would come when the leaders would feel secure enough to return some trappings of civilization to the masses. None of us even remotely believed that any longer. None, it was clear, would live to see that day.

Slogans took on new meaning when the incredible plans of Angkar to wipe out not only the past, but most of the people from that past, became apparent. If someone complained about conditions, he was curtly told, "To destroy you is no loss."

The message was now chillingly clear. Complaints ceased; we had a claim on nothing, not even life.

Hungry people wanting more food were told to "ask Angkar."

"Who is Angkar Loeu?"

"Why, the people, of course! It is everyone; it is you. Go ask yourself."

At the nightly meetings there were many analogies to common trees. We were told, "If you are wise, you will plant a hedge of *kor* trees around your hut."

Everyone knew this play on words meant that if we wanted to live, it would be well to insulate ourselves with a wall of silence.

Another tree invoked was the banyan. This large tree is subject to disease. If decay is noticed in time, it can be scraped away, leaving the good wood to develop into a full-sized trunk again. But if the diseased part is not cut away, the tree weakens and dies.

Leaders justified destruction of "diseased elements" of the old society, even the killing of people touched by those diseased elements—their families. We were told repeatedly that in order to save the country, it was essential to destroy all the contaminated parts. Society would again become viable only when all corrupting influences were cut out. It was essential to cut deep, even to destroy a few good people, rather than chance one "diseased" person escaping eradication.

Rather than slowing down, each year the purges and paranoia had spread to encompass more and more people in ever-widening circles. There seemed to be no end to those who could be considered an enemy of Angkar Loeu; no end to those who might add their spilt blood to Angkar's expanding, crimson pool.

The national anthem of Democratic Kampuchea, sung at each nightly meeting, was meant to stir us to increased efforts, dedication, pride, loyalty. Instead, it took on a macabre new meaning and filled me with revulsion.

> *Bright red Blood which covers towns and plains*
> *Of Kampuchea, our motherland,*
> *Sublime Blood of workers and peasants,*
> *Sublime Blood of revolutionary men and women fighters!*
>
> *The Blood changing into unrelenting hatred*
> *And resolute struggle. . . .*

Stay Alive, My Son

Pin Yathay

PIN YATHAY (1944–) *was director of public works in the Ministry of Public Works in Cambodia before the Khmer Rouge seized power. He was educated in civil engineering at the Polytechnical Institute in Montreal, Canada. He and his family were among the inhabitants of Phnom Penh forcibly evacuated by the Communist authorities. He escaped from Cambodia in June 1977, after living for two years and three months under the Pol Pot regime. During the Pol Pot terror he lost seventeen members of his family, including three sons, his wife, both parents, and a brother and sister and their families.*

Following his escape he worked as a consultant in France for five years and later as a project engineer with the Asian Development Bank based in Manila; since 1990 he has been principal project engineer with the French Development Agency based in Paris.

· · · · ·

[T]he rains had begun. We slept in the open on mats, near the work site, so urgent had it become that we complete our task. We had no tents. We just lay out on our mats beneath the trees, soaked. The place swarmed with mosquitoes. We shivered the nights away, huddling around fires built both for warmth and to keep away the insects.

I could see, moreover, that all our labor was going to waste. No one had surveyed the site, there were no plans, and no one kept records. The Khmer Rouge seemed to think that revolutionary fervor could replace the laws of physics. In each section thousands of men and women dug, obeying the orders of their local leaders, but without anybody even checking that the canal we were building ran downhill away from the lake. The banks were made up of loose earth, without any attempt to compact them. If water ever actually flowed along the canal, it would wash the banks away in no time.

Occasionally, at meetings, some particularly brave (or foolhardy) technician would try to tell the Khmer Rouge how the work should be done. The reply was always the same: "You don't know anything about the revolution. We

From Pin Yathay (with John Man), Stay Alive, My Son, © *1987 by Pin Yathay. Used by permission of the publisher, Cornell University Press.*

do. Why do you try to tell us what to do?" Qualifications were declared to be useless. Diplomas were *saignabat*, "the invisible signal." What counted was physical work. That was *saignakhoeunh*, "the visible signal." That was tangible. Therein lay honor.

As time went on, I thought more and more about something old Ta Bun said to me one evening during one of our meetings at the pool. I had come to trust him now, and we made regular exchanges, my clothing for his sugar. "The predictions of Puth are coming to pass," he said, with a knowing nod and penetrating look from his wrinkled eyes.

Puth was a nineteenth-century sage who prophesied that the country would undergo a total reversal of traditional values, that the houses and the streets would be emptied, that the illiterate would condemn the educated, that infidels —*thmils*—would hold absolute power and persecute the priests. But people would be saved if they planted the kapok tree —*kor*, in Cambodian. *Kor* also means "mute." The usual interpretation of this enigmatic message was that only the deaf-mutes would be saved during this period of calamity. Remain deaf and mute. Therein, I now realized, lay the means of survival. Pretend to be deaf and dumb! Say nothing, hear nothing, understand nothing!

This canal will never carry water, I thought, and kept quiet.

· · · · ·

There were, nevertheless, hints of better times to come.

Some time in August 1975, during a political meeting, the Khmer Rouge chief announced that money was to be reintroduced towards the end of the year. He even posted the prices of some commodities—a kilo of beef, a dozen eggs, a kilo of rice.

This welcome news confirmed the rumors of political change. One of my neighbors was a teacher, Leang, who had arrived in the pagoda two months before us. Leang, a tall thin man with a wife and two children, had been a member of the central committee of the Democratic Party, the main opposition party under Lon Nol. His former eminence gave him certain privileges, and he was allowed to go fishing, not simply for himself but also for other residents in the pagoda. He used to borrow my nets, the ones I had acquired after leaving Cheu Khmau, and we often fell into conversation. From Leang I learned a little more about the Khmer Rouge.

He confirmed that there were two main factions, both of which had their own sanctuaries. The Khmer Rouge east of the Mekong were favorable to Sihanouk. These were the moderates, and they wore khaki. The other faction, the Maoists, the implacable puritans of the Khmer Rouge movement, who were hostile to Sihanouk, came from the south-west, where we were. They dressed in black. According to Leang, Sihanouk would act as arbitrator in this internal conflict. When he did so, we would all return home.

His confidence, born of years of lecturing, puzzled me. How could he be so certain? Where was Sihanouk? What did his power depend on? How could he exercise influence?

As it happened, Leang's information was correct. Sihanouk returned from Peking that September. We never knew it and his return changed nothing, but the rumors—true or not—conferred on Sihanouk the status of national savior. We came to believe that he alone could overcome the ideological quarrels and restore some of our liberties.

Soon, I was sure, the schools and universities (at least) would reopen. They could do without engineers to build bridges, but how could a country live without schools and universities? What had happened to my educated friends who had joined the other side? I couldn't imagine all those who'd joined the Khmer Rouge being resigned to the denial of education. Logically, we would proceed to a more moderate and forward-looking society.

My confidence was boosted from another source, a Khmer Rouge officer I met through Chan, who worked on the canal in my group. Chan, a former trader of about forty, had been in Phnom Penh when the city fell and had been unable to return to his wife and children in Battambang. He had headed south to join his parents in the village a mile from the pagoda, but as a New Person had to live in the pagoda itself—the Khmer Rouge discouraged family senti-ment since it undermined their ability to control New People. But while we were building the canal Chan often used to sneak away to visit his parents during lunch hour. Sometimes he invited me along, for the two of us got on well. He was a tough, stocky man, who had a habit of glancing about him as he talked, as if on the look-out for trouble; it was a habit that made me glad he trusted me. The two of us would slip away to his family's house, where we would gorge ourselves on pumpkin and palm-sugar, supplied by his elderly peasant parents.

There, Chan introduced me to the Khmer Rouge officer, Mith (Comrade) Pech, who was married to one of his cousins. Pech was a highly placed man in the provincial communist hierarchy. He had a motorcycle and the cut of his clothes showed his importance, as did the two pens which he proudly exhib-ited in his breast pocket. He was thirty-eight years old, and had completed his Baccalaureate before joining the underground. I was never sure whether he had joined the Khmer Rouge freely or had been forced into it against his will. Indeed, there was much about him that was mysterious. I never saw him smile. But Chan assured me that I could ask him anything I wanted.

One thing, of course, obsessed me. Were we going to return to Phnom Penh?

"Yes, I think that you'll be returning soon," he said "But I have no formal information on this subject. We must always, no matter what happens, respect the orders of Angkar."

He appeared to be straightforward, but I dared not tell him the whole truth about myself. I was still a "technician of a Public Works Department." I told him that I hoped that one day they would make use of my skill.

He replied evasively, "It's possible . . . but first you must be re-educated. This stage of your education is still not over. We think that we can make use of the technicians in a year's time. Don't worry. We are Cambodians like you. We will not abandon you."

That was something. It was the first time that a fixed period for our penitence had been mentioned. Had the possible reintroduction of money any significance? No, that didn't mean that the New People had completed their ordeal. I said I thought that the engineers, doctors, and teachers would be more useful in their real occupations than in the fields. "No, no, you must all finish your re-education. You may be fully re-educated at the end of one year if you do not commit any errors, if there are no blots, no faults found by your leaders. Execute the missions which Angkar requests that you accomplish, correctly, without cheating." We were clearly not on the same wavelength, but at least there was an end in sight.

Why the confusion over the return to our birthplace, I insisted, why did we have to stop at Sramar Leav?

My questions seemed to tax his patience. He scolded me for asking. "Angkar is master of your destiny. It is important that you know it. Angkar has many detours. Angkar is not to be predicted. It might bypass different stages without prior notification. Do not believe that what Angkar says will be for ever. It may change at the next turn. It may proceed in leaps and bounds. But Angkar always has its reasons." He spoke allusively, in parables, like a monk. I began to see that we could not be sure of anything. From one day to the next everything could change and expectations could be contradicted. The paradoxical nature of the organization troubled me.

There was one other question I wanted answered. While we were in Cheu Khmau, we had heard explosions from the frontier area. Were we at war with Vietnam? My question elicited the first good explanation of Khmer Rouge policy.

"You know, undoubtedly, that Vietnam is not totally revolutionary. It did not order the evacuation of the cities, as we did. We know that it is dangerous to leave the cities intact, inhabited. They are the centers of opposition, and contain little groups. In a city, it is difficult to track down the seeds of counter-revolution. If we do not change city life, an enemy organization can be established and conspire against us. It is truly impossible to control a city. We evacuated the city to destroy any resistance, to destroy the cradles of reactionary and mercantile capitalism. To expel the city people meant eliminating the germs of anti-Khmer Rouge resistance. This is but one of the aspects of our dissension with the Vietnamese."

So now I knew for certain—there was no point in thinking of going to Vietnam.

But we had to get out. It was not so much the work on the canal that convinced me as what happened after work stopped. There came a time, after several weeks, when the canal was declared finished. There was to be a big political meeting and celebration, which sounded promising. We were all marched up along the levee to a huge field outside a village. There were thousands of people all walking in a huge column. At one point, there was water lying in the canal, and with a certain satisfaction I saw that here at least the canal must be sloping uphill. There would be no chance of water running anywhere from the lake unless there was a huge amount of it. And if there was that much water, if the rains were that heavy, then the canal would not be needed.

The meeting was presided over by the chief of the whole district. He was a powerfully built, grim-looking man with cold eyes, who had a reputation as a slave driver. Word had also spread about his origins. He had been a drunk, a thug, a small-time crook who had found respectability as a Khmer Rouge fighter and had proved his courage in the battle for Phnom Penh. The revolution had turned him into a leader.

Strangely, his oratorical qualities were undeniable. But instead of congratulating us, his speech was the same as all the others. "You must work hard," he said, "Then Angkar will look after you." All the old phrases. We sat and listened in stunned silence. A glance at my brother Theng and people near by was enough to show that we all felt the same. We had made a superhuman effort, but apparently Angkar couldn't care less about that. All Angkar wanted was yet more work. . . .

. . . . .

As I walked back to fetch the rest of the family and our baggage, the awfulness of our position struck me. Beneath a scattering of big trees, the jungle was a mass of saplings, thick undergrowth, tall grass, and thorns. There was no heavy canopy to protect us against the rain.

Without any clear idea of what I was doing. I began to clear the undergrowth with my tall young cousin, Sim, whom I had taken under my wing. Any spread leaves and mats on the damp earth as a base to take care of the children. Sim and I went off to cut poles, make holes to stick them into, and dig drains. Sim as usual worked as if he didn't have a care in the world, and even began cheerfully whistling a song that had been popular just before the revolution— "I'm rowing a boat! Rowing a boat! Rowing a boat!"

"Be quiet, Sim!" I said, glancing round, "You'll draw attention to yourself, silly boy." He should have learned by now not to show any sign of happiness.

In the afternoon, we managed to tie a few poles together with vines and get the beginnings of a thatch on. There were no walls. Then I packed the floor of the hut with stones to make the ground as firm as possible, and covered this bumpy base with a carpet of leaves.

Towards the end of the afternoon, a loudspeaker called us for food. With the other men of the family, I went back down the trail. We gathered round a table, thousands of us, waiting for our names to be shouted out.

As dusk fell, I set about making a fire. The wood was as wet as the ground but I still had my two lighters left over from Phnom Penh, and, after scraping away the damp surface of the branches with my knife to reveal the dry wood within, we succeeded in burning a few branches to boil our rice.

We had never been in such a terrible situation as this. Before, we had always stayed in houses raised on piles, traditional houses protected from the damp. Our hut, set in the shade, would always be wet. It certainly was then. Even before dark, it began to rain again. Soon, the carpet of leaves and the mats over them were impregnated with water. We wallowed in a bog, freezing and worn out. Staud was now permanently sick. The other two children just stood or squatted sadly, watching us. As we huddled round the fire, Any and I looked at each other without speaking, and wept. No one spoke. Tears were the only words we needed, tears not so much for ourselves as for the children.

Those first three days were a nightmare. As soon as I stopped work on the hut, I fell silent, transfixed by our misfortune, numb with cold and fear, overwhelmed with gloomy thoughts. Only young Sim remained lively, indifferent to the discomfort. He was strong, with no responsibilities, and nothing seemed to bother him. It was Sim who was the driving force behind the building of the hut. He seemed to run everywhere, collecting wood and tic-vines.

While he worked, I checked up on my parents, who were with the other twelve members of our group three hundred yards up the trail. For the time being they all seemed well. Theng and Sarun, assisted by Vuoch and Keng, had started to build a house that was much more solid than ours. Their site was better as well—a clearing, shaded by two big trees, on a slope down to a stream. Srey Rath was outside playing with Theng's two boys, Visoth and Amap. My father was his usual stoical self, claiming in an off-hand way that he was fine. After all, he said, he had never expected anything better of the Khmer Rouge. But my mother, lying on a mat beneath a part of finished thatch, had been worn out by the journey. She forced a smile for me, and said she would be all right in a day or so. Only Lao, who had always been the most active of the women, seemed too downcast to do anything. She just sat beside her exhausted mother, hardly glancing up at me. Somewhat reassured, I walked back down the trail to see how Sim was getting on with the house.

Near our rudimentary home, another house was going up. Three sturdy men were working on it, tying roof poles together, and laying on thatch. To my amazement and delight, one of them was my old friend Chan. I had been wondering what had happened to him. I had last seen him walking off in the rain towards the Watt Ang Recar pagoda. Somehow, in that two-week wait in the pagoda, we had missed each other. Now, there he was again, slapping my shoulders in welcome, as delighted to see us as I was to see him. He introduced me to the two men he was sharing with—Keo, a former customs officer, who had managed to send his wife and mother abroad before the fall of Phnom Penh, and Sun, a science graduate and a teacher about my age. They were clearly a resourceful trio, and were building a large hut, with a fine ridged roof.

Work started on the fourth day, by which time our houses were ready. The first task was to clear the forest, chopping trees and dragging them aside. Veal Vong, as our camp was called, was right in the middle of uncut jungle. There were no existing rice fields anywhere near by. We had to create our own. The pattern was much the same as before—wake up at six a.m., a break for food between noon and one p.m., work until six p.m. However, for the first time we were supervised by armed guards during our working hours. As we chopped trees, pulled up bushes, uprooted the stumps, and piled them into heaps beside the cleared land, the Khmer Rouge would suddenly appear to watch us, causing us to redouble our efforts.

As I discovered, wandering the trails and standing in line for food during those first few waterlogged weeks, there must have been five hundred or six hundred families in our camp, scattered over two or three miles of forest paths—nearly five thousand people in all.

Nor was the great exodus over yet. For several weeks after our arrival, thousands and thousands more, all city people in their tattered city clothes, all as distressed as we had been, filed past our hut, plunging deeper into the forest, to make new fields as we were doing. We watched them in silence, as we had been watched on our arrival. Always the same poignancy, the same drawn and mortified faces, the same tears, the same little dramas as friends and families met and parted, never to see each other again. So many people, so many wracked bodies, so many unsmiling faces. I began to wonder if we were part of some gigantic extermination program, for the decrease in rations and the increase in forced labor could only lead to hundreds, perhaps thousands, of deaths. If this was purification, it was purification by the survival of the fittest.

As the days went by, I became ever more worried about the children. They had completely lost their carefree ways. They no longer played, not even with their cousins, Theng's two boys. They became silent and wary. Staud's condition worsened day by day. His feet were swollen, and he became weak. He no longer seemed to have the energy to cry. His state of health began to obsess us, and we fed him any little extra rations we could lay our hands on. At my heart-felt request, Any was exempted from work to look after him.

. . . . .

It was not long before the dying started. Even in the first week, I saw several people carrying corpses down the trail. It was hardly surprising, given the amount of people in the forest near us, and their state of health. The dead were buried in the forest, at the edge of our newly cut fields. I was told it was because the Khmer Rouge thought that the corpses should act as fertilizer for the future crops. Cremation, they said, was mere waste. You had to gather the wood, make a pyre, and attend the funeral—a waste of wood, labor and time. In Veal Vong, a corpse had its uses.

At first, these sights made little impact on me, obsessed as I was with my own problems. I hardly knew the families involved.

One evening, though, Staud's fever became worse. During that night it rained violently, so heavily that our roof of branches and leaves opened. Water cascaded on to us and ran over our mats, flooding the floor. The only way to avoid it was to squat, holding our clothes off the ground, or dangling them over branches and twigs leant against the uprights. But after a while, I gave up, and asked my three neighbors to give Any and the two younger children room for the night. They agreed readily enough.

When I returned home next day, Any was cooking the rice. Staud was all curled up, dozing on the mat.

"How is he?" I asked. "Has he eaten?"

"He doesn't want anything. He just lies there," replied Any sadly.

Indeed, the poor little boy looked terrible, like one of those children on famine relief posters we used to see in Phnom Penh. He was nothing more than skin and bone, his stomach bloated, his feet and legs swollen. The other two children were squatting near by, weeping softly, and shivering, waiting for their rice soup.

Suddenly, Staud called "*Mak! Mak!*" (Mummy! Mummy!)

"What is it, Staud?" said Any, going across to him. "What's the matter, darling?"

Silently, he moved his hand, beckoning her closer. She sat right beside him, and patted him. He closed his eyes again. After a few minutes, she took him up and cradled him. He said nothing, sleeping in her arms.

Half an hour later, he twitched, as if he was having a dream.

"Staud!" she said. "Staud, wake up!"

He didn't respond. I shook him to wake him. Again, no response.

Any already knew the truth and was weeping bitterly, in silence.

"Yes," I whispered, "He's dead."

For several minutes, I was too stunned to do anything, too battered by exhaustion and grief. Then I tried to take Staud from Any, and after a while she let me have him. I laid the poor emaciated little body down on a mat. Any sat beside him and cried.

Now I became aware of the two other children, shivering, not yet realizing the enormity of what had happened. I put my arms around them. It was as if I was in a coma, unable to move, unable to re-establish contact with life, fixed there between my two children, holding them to me, with my baby boy dead and my wife incapacitated with grief. At last, I thought, he is free. He no longer has to endure this infernal existence. At least he died quietly, in his sleep, without pain. I hoped we would be as lucky.

The thought brought me back to reality. I laid the two boys down on their mats and covered them with a blanket, then lay down beside Any and held her in my arms, feeling her body wracked by sobs. My mind began to wander. What would I do with the body? How would I be able to help Any and the children cope with their loss? Eventually, I drifted into an exhausted sleep.

Next morning, I told Any I would have to go to the village chief, to excuse myself from work, to get permission to bury Staud.

"No," she said, and I knew her mind had been working over the same ground as mine the night before. "No, he must be cremated. To bury him would be to abandon him in the forest. He would be lost for ever. I will collect the ashes and carry them with me wherever I go." She looked up, haggard with grief and lack of sleep, her eyes red with tears.

"No one has been cremated here," I said. Then, to console her: "Don't cry. He is free. We will have other children. It is a relief for him."

"Do something, my dearest Thay," she begged, her voice breaking with sobs. "I don't want him to be buried in the forest. We can't abandon him here. I want him to be warm. . . . Staud was always too cold. . .let him be warm now. . .I don't want to leave him. . .I want to take him with me."

"All right," I said. "All right."

I was nervous of asking the village chief for permission to perform the cremation, but Chan, who got on well with the chief, volunteered to speak for me. Permission was granted, as an exceptional favor. The chief even came across to our hut to offer his condolences to Any, who was still weeping beside the body.

Leaving her to her grief, I walked up the trail to tell my parents what had happened. They both hurried back with me to offer Any consolation but, clearly, Staud's death came as no shock to either of them. "Death will come to all of us if things go on like this," said my father, his face set.

In the afternoon, Sim and I built a funeral pyre three feet high, forty yards back from our hut into the forest. I helped Any put Staud in the best clothes we had—shorts, T-shirt, even shoes. We laid him on the sticks and set fire to it.

The fire burned all afternoon, Any watched for a while, her face lined with grief, and then retired into the house. Sim just sat there, staring into the fire in silence. Later, in the evening, when the fire was burning low, the others came to watch the dying flames and sit for a while with Any. When they had gone, I collected the ashes in a small bag, which I laid gently by Any.

She had been right to insist on cremation. It helped to cope with grief.

. . . . .

A few days later, during lunch, my father came across to talk to us as he often did, bringing bad news—Theng's mother-in-law had died that day. It had been very quick. She had developed a fever the night before and died that morning. I had hardly addressed more than a few words to her through all the last months, but the suddenness of the death brought home to me how vulnerable we all were. One day, a child, the next an adult; when would it be my parents' turn, or Any's, or the other children, or my own?

Now, death came with increasing frequency in the forest around us. The bodies were buried all around the edge of the clearings by grave-diggers appointed by the village chief. Grave-diggers became necessary because the families had become too weak to dig the graves themselves. It was not a bad job, for it meant being exempted from work for a day.

There was no relief from the unrelenting labor, except for the tedious political meetings and a day off every ten days. Time was measured now by the numbers of deaths per day in the people round about us—four deaths, five deaths, sometimes as many as ten deaths a day.

Hope died, and was buried along with the corpses. Mourning became part of our slavery.

·　·　·　·　·

As conditions worsened—the rice ration after several weeks was dropped to one can for six people each day—a new economic system, barter, ensured survival of a sort.

It appeared that three or four miles away, there were villages occupied by Ancients, as well as many other camps established by newcomers like us. We had frequent contact with both Ancients and New People, for New People, supervised by Ancients, were often sent into the forest to cut bamboo. Columns of people would stream past our hut in the morning carrying cooking pots, with small bags of food at their waists, returning in the evening laden with bamboo. Often, a casual greeting would lead on to conversation, and thus contacts and friendships developed. The Ancients received rather more rice than we did, and in addition were allowed to grow their own food. And we, the city people, had possessions—mainly clothes, but also jewelry, watches, the occasional radio—that were of interest to the peasants, who were willing to exchange their rice for our goods. Regular contacts with passers-by ensured that everyone knew the relative value of their goods.

Strangely, it became clear that the Khmer Rouge were also feeding rice into this black market system, and profiting from it to acquire goods for themselves and their families. Where did all this rice come from?

Eventually, the explanation got around. The amount of rice to be distributed was calculated on the basis of the census carried out on our arrival. But the only people who knew the actual number of survivors were the Khmer Rouge themselves. They simply never reported many of the dead. Rice for those who had died kept on arriving. Thus, the worse we were treated, the more deaths there were, and the more rice the Khmer Rouge had for themselves.

These embezzlements institutionalized the black market in which the Khmer Rouge themselves played a vital role. A sort of exchange rate was established—the equivalent of ten cans of rice (rice was always measured in terms of condensed-milk cans) for a pair of trousers, four cans for a shirt, six cans for a cotton sarong, fifteen cans for a silk sarong. A *tael* of gold—just over one and a quarter ounces—bought thirty to forty cans' worth. Automatic watches were much in demand, both by the Khmer Rouge and by the Ancients. A good wrist-watch could fetch sixty to eighty cans' worth of rice. My radio was now out of batteries, and I didn't think it worthwhile to buy more on the black market, so I offered to exchange it. I received twenty-five cans' worth of rice for it.

A few city deportees acted as brokers, among them a contact of mine who had been one of my subordinates in the Public Works Department. He took the risk of meeting the relatives of the Khmer Rouge (for the Khmer Rouge themselves could not be seen to be playing a part in the system). He would negotiate the deal and, as his profit, take a share of the rice. If, for instance, I parted with jewelry to the value of one *tael* of gold, in exchange for which he received from the Khmer Rouge forty cans' worth of rice, he would pass on thirty-five cans. The system actually worked fairly well. The local Khmer Rouge, or, rather, their wives and their parents, respected their promises on the whole. They recognized that this illegal exchange could only work on the basis of confidence and discretion.

All of us resorted to bartering: my father, Theng, and Keng (acting on behalf of poor Sarun) as well as myself. Thus both households held together, and I was able to feed not only my wife and children, but also my cousin Sim.

Sim was drafted into a youth brigade a couple of weeks after our arrival at Veal Vong, and was based in a camp elsewhere, two or three miles away. But every evening, he sneaked back to have dinner with us. He wasn't meant to do it, and would have been severely punished if he had been found out, but that didn't bother him. He was quite happy to take the risk. "Anything for a little extra food!" he used to say, with a carefree smile. Though his rice ration was larger than ours, because he worked correspondingly harder, he could always do with more. We were happy to oblige. He had always been a willing worker, never showing a sign of unhappiness. His arrivals in the evening brought a little joy into our bleak lives. It was about the only thing that made Sudath and Nawath smile.

Having brought considerable quantities of clothing and jewelry with us, we were amongst the lucky ones. Some people at Veal Vong had nothing at all—no medicine, no clothing, no jewelry, no dollars. You would think, therefore, that they were outside the system. But even they found a niche to supplement their rations. The best way was to specialize in the search for food. On our day off—once every ten days—we were allowed to gather what we could from the forest. Those who wished, therefore, could turn themselves into expert gatherers. Some tracked down land crabs, some caught fish with lines or traps, some collected mushrooms. They then exchanged their delicacies for rice.

Yet still the people died. First malnutrition and exhaustion undermined them. Strangely, the men succumbed more easily than the women. Perhaps it was to do with the amount of work; or perhaps they were not so able to withstand the shock of having their world destroyed, of no longer being in control of life; or perhaps, in these grueling circumstances, the women possessed some deep-seated strength that was normally hidden.

And among the men it was the harder workers, the apparently stronger ones, who tended to succumb more quickly. Often, they were the once well-off, over-eager to prove they had set their old ways behind them. Weakened by their efforts, they fell an easy prey to any one of a number of illnesses—diarrhea, dysentery, beriberi, malaria.

Secondly, food-poisoning was a common cause of death. Rice soup was mixed with polluted stream water, or unknown wild plants, or mushrooms. Especially mushrooms. There were a number of different species, and we didn't know much about them, learning from hearsay how to differentiate the edible ones from the poisonous ones. For those who chose wrongly, death arrived quickly—vomiting and stomach pains were quickly followed by diarrhea and death. Before eating any mushrooms, I made sure that other families had already eaten some of them before us. I wasn't about to risk the children's lives for the sake of mushrooms.

· · · · ·

Then I began to notice the disappearances.

The first one I noticed was Ming, a Vietnamese neighbor. There were several Vietnamese families in the village, all of whom had been told they would be able to go home soon. Somehow, the time never came.

Ming was a tall, strong character with a wife and four-year-old child. I liked him. His wide smile and broad shoulders always seemed to carry some comfort. One day he confided to me that he had found a crafty way to make his ration grow. In the evening, during the rice distribution, he went up to the bags, and, as people pressed around awaiting their turn, he stuck a special craftsman's knife—a long hollow tube with a sharpened end—into one of the bags. Out flowed the rice into his waiting scarf. By the time he told me of his trick he had got an extra six cans' worth of rice. But the next time he tried it, one of the Khmer Rouge spotted him. He was seized and led away for "re-education," and his wife was left anxiously awaiting his return.

Day after day she waited. Days turned into weeks, and still he didn't reappear.

Then I noticed that a number of former Republican officers who had tried to conceal their identity had vanished. A couple of times, a worried wife asked me, "Have you seen my husband? He went off to cut bamboo and I haven't seen him for two days." I thought perhaps they had escaped.

When Sim failed to appear one evening, my uneasiness increased. We were expecting him as usual, and he just didn't come. We shrugged, and told the children he would be along as usual the following evening. "Yes, he's probably got some extra work, silly fellow," I said. But he didn't come the next day either, or the next. No one had seen him. I wondered if perhaps he had fallen ill. A week passed, then two weeks, then a month.

I suppose I suspected what had happened, but didn't like to admit it to myself. There came a day, however, when I saw the truth, and could no longer deny what had happened to Sim and the rest.

I was with my neighbors cutting bamboo shoots, perhaps two miles from my house, deep in the jungle. Ahead of me I saw an ideal bamboo tree—a dozen separate stems, with a number of tender little shoots growing up between them. As I approached it, I noticed a strange smell. Then, almost at my feet, I saw a shape and a patch of dark blue. I looked closer.

It was the body of a man in a dark blue shirt, face down, and badly decomposed.

I stood back, feeling shocked, but not surprised. It was like the confirmation of something I had known for a long time. I thought: it's too close to the village. It's been put there on purpose to frighten us. That thought was even more frightening than finding the corpse.

Later, an acquaintance told me about Sim. He had been spotted by Khmer Rouge on his way to our house, and taken away into the forest for "re-education."

"What harm am I doing?" he had protested. "I'm just going to my cousin's to eat, the way I always do. What harm is there in that? No one has ever stopped me before, I didn't know I was doing anything wrong. Please comrades, now I know it's wrong, I'll never. . . ."

"No, no comrade, you are an anarchist, you do not obey orders. You must come with us."

He had simply vanished. I was told he must have been cudgeled to death like so many others, to save bullets and prevent anyone hearing anything.

Poor naïve Sim. An anarchist, the brigade leader told the rest of his group, an anarchist who loved his freedom too much. We never told the children. He simply disappeared from their lives.

Children of Cambodia's Killing Fields

compiled by Dith Pran

DITH PRAN (1942–) is a Cambodian refugee who spent four years in forced labor camps and escaped to Thailand in 1979. He lost fifty relatives in the terror, including his father and four siblings. His life is portrayed in the movie Killing Fields. *He has been a photo-journalist for the* New York Times *since 1980 and is the founder and president of the Dith Pran Holocaust Awareness Project.*

The recollections of these children confirm that the Cambodian regime was probably the most brutal and inhumane of all the Communist systems represented in this volume. It attempted to carry out the most ambitious scheme of totalitarian social engineering by depopulating urban areas (through the forced relocation of their residents) and by "mount[ing] history's fiercest ever attack on family life," as is observed by Ben Kiernan in his introduction to this volume. Children were routinely taken away from their parents and their upbringing was entrusted to the party-state, or Angkar (the Politburo, which included the regime's leading elites). Angkar had to approve of all marriages. Loyalty to one's family was discouraged and punished—loyalty to the political authorities was demanded and rewarded. Children were encouraged to spy on their families when in a position to do so.

Children and adolescents shared the hardships of the adult population—manual labor in agriculture and insufficient food, clothing, and shelter. They were also exposed to the spectacle of violence meted out against the putative enemies of the system.

. . . . .

The Unfortunate Cambodia
Sarom Prak

Under a light of a candle in my unit in Sungai Besi Camp in Malaysia, at two a.m., I am sitting alone thinking about my life in the past and in the future. I

. . . .

From Children of Cambodia's Killing Fields, *compiled by Dith Pran,* © 1997 Yale University Press.

have been living in this detention camp for seven years without any resolution. I ask myself, "Why am I alone? Who or what made me be alone like this?" This is a very complicated question that I try to explain to everyone I know, particularly Cambodian people, so that they don't forget why.

From 1975 to 1979, I was a slave in the Pol Pot regime. The whole country was annihilated by the Khmer Rouge during their years in power. When I recall the brutal massacre of millions of innocent people, I am dreadfully terrified.

After the Khmer Rouge takeover in April 1975 in Cambodia, at least 2 million people were driven into the countryside. Men, women, and children were banished from the cities by Khmer Rouge soldiers. Angkar divided us into city people, whom they called "new," and country people, who were called "old." This was the first time I had heard of the Khmer Rouge. During the leadership of the Khmer Rouge all of Cambodia was put into vast forced labor camps. Most temples were destroyed, and many monks and nuns were killed. They broke the sentiment between wives, husbands, and children. They segregated them into separate work groups, and everyone had to eat in communal dining halls near where they worked. We were not allowed to see each other. If we wanted to meet our parents or relatives we had to escape from the camp secretly. We were chastised seriously if the Khmer Rouge got word of this.

I was in a camp in Takeo province. All of us were awakened at 6 a.m., and we labored until our first meal, at 11:30 a.m. The Khmer Rouge permitted us to eat one can of rice mixed with the skins of potatoes. This fed 200 persons. After that we continued working again from 1:30 to 6 p.m. Then we were again fed a meal. At night we labored from 7:30 to midnight. If one of us pretended to be ill he was allowed to eat only a bit of gruel. If he was always sick, he would disappear. When his relatives would ask where he was, the Khmer Rouge would reply rudely that he'd been sent to Angkar. No one came back when the Khmer Rouge sent someone to Angkar. Lamentably, all of us were coerced to labor without stopping in the rain and under the hot sun. During this time there were many kinds of work, including digging a trench and canal, making a dam, and so on. We were the Cambodian slave labor.

In this Communist regime nobody could marry without approval from Angkar. Men were not able to propose to any girls. Angkar compelled some people to marry even though they had never seen each other before. Angkar prepared a wedding party for seventy to 100 couples every now and then in Takeo. The forced marriages were a good way for some of the people who had power—like the soldiers, the chiefs of villages and districts—to molest young girls until they got pregnant. Many of these girls were forced to marry these men, and sometimes they were killed because of being afraid to marry them. Flirtations, adultery, and love affairs were reasons for execution. No one could complain or argue with them. If someone dared to do this, he or she would disappear.

The Communists practiced killing several million innocent people. The young Khmer Rouge soldiers not only butchered strangers but also their own parents. The principles of Angkar implanted this idea into the minds of the soldiers: "We were born by virtue of the sexual passion of the parents, so we don't respect them. If the parents do something wrong, we must kill them."

The Khmer Rouge killed many of the new people after telling them to load up the salt from some province or another. They gathered the people together, took them to an isolated spot, and killed them. The people had thought they were going somewhere to work, but none came back.

"When I went into the jungle near the hamlet to look for wood for the communal dining halls, I saw many bones and dead bodies," said a villager. At another location in the district were more bodies. This is where my father was killed. My father was a captain in the army from the time Cambodia was a French colony. The Khmer Rouge accused him of being a CIA agent for America. Then they executed him.

At that time I lived in a pagoda in Takeo. About 100 meters to the east of the pagoda I saw dead bodies appearing from the pits because wolves ate them at night.

Before they were butchered, some innocent people were coerced to dig small pits for themselves. None of us had the energy to fight back because we didn't have enough food to eat. After the new pit was ready, the young soldiers tied the arms of their victims and ordered them to kneel near the edge of the pits. Then the young soldiers began to hit them with heavy hoes, thick bamboo sticks, or axes.

During the killings there were shouts of pain and moaning. Blood ran from their nostrils, ears, and mouths as the objects crushed the backs of their heads. Some victims were not yet dead when the soldiers pushed earth over them. Throughout the country, large pits had been dug by the laborers. Then trucks carried the blindfolded prisoners to be dragged to the edge of the pits. One by one the prisoners fell into the pits after being hit.

The Khmer Rouge killed teenagers. They held their arms up, disemboweled them, and cut out their livers and gall bladder and put them into sacks. Some of the Khmer Rouge soldiers ate the livers of their victims. The young boys moaned and shouted out in pain. They disfigured the bodies and slashed the throats of young children and babies. The Khmer Rouge tore the babies into pieces.

Some people who accidentally broke the knives, hoes, axes, and plows they were working with were slaughtered by the Khmer Rouge. Generators were used to electrocute some men. Others were beheaded with machetes. The Khmer Rouge used pincers to cut off the nipples of women, and they took their fingernails out. In some places they forced people to take off their clothing. The Khmer Rouge collected the clothing to distribute to people and said that the clothing was a present from Angkar. Some people recognized their relatives' clothes, but none dared to say so or to ask any questions about them.

In 1977, I moved from the 105th district to the 109th district in Tram Kak district, Takeo Province, with the other people. In this area there was a killing center to the east of the hamlet at the rice field. When the executors slaughtered people, they generally switched on a blaring loudspeaker because they didn't want the villagers to hear the shouts of pain and moaning. After a while, when the villagers heard the loudspeaker they knew that the Khmer Rouge were slaying people. So the villagers who lived around a killing center wept bitter tears quietly.

Every nook and cranny was demolished by the Communist Khmer Rouge. During this time, there were no planes, no train service, no mail. There was nothing.

I am a survivor of the Communist regime. I have undergone bitter suffering for many years in Cambodia. So I take every opportunity to notify others and insist that people in all four corners of the earth fully realize what happens when people slay other human beings. I am not you and you are not me, but we are all human beings. Life is not something to sell.

Living in the Darkness
Rouen Sam

I can never forget the Khmer Rouge Communist regime. When I was fourteen years old the country collapsed and the Khmer Rouge forced people to leave town. We had to go to the jungle at gunpoint. The Khmer Rouge were telling us that we had to leave only for three days because the United States was going to drop a bomb. They said they would clear out the town until the enemy was gone. They told us not to bring any belongings except for a few, for we would be back in three days.

Our family didn't take much. We didn't prepare. My father was very old and said not to bring very many things. The Khmer Rouge went straight to our family. "Leave now. If you don't leave, we are going to shoot you!" I ran to pick up my books so that when I came back I would be prepared for school. I went and said good-bye to my coconut tree and mango tree and then to my house, the place that brought me fun and joy. Then I cried. My father was standing there looking at me, and he said sadly, "Don't worry. We are coming back. You will not lose your tree."

We walked about twenty kilometers on the dusty, dry road, and the Khmer Rouge, dressed in black, walked behind us with guns pointed. Their shoes were made of tire rubber, and they wore red and white striped scarves. They harassed and humiliated us. They said that I was stupid because I was riding my bike and carrying my chemistry and history books, along with a book that had been a gift from my teacher. "Who is going to come back and study?" They laughed in a sinister way. Then one of them told me to give them my books so they could tear a page in which to roll a cigarette. I had sisters and I was afraid they would hurt them, so I didn't say anything and gave them the books. They tore up my books and then began to smoke.

The Khmer Rouge leader, Me Kong, put our family into a place they used to store rice seed. At this time we had eight in our family, and we never saw the sun unless we were sent outside. It was a place with no windows and a very small door. It was made of wood and bamboo. Cow dung was used to paint the dwelling. Inside were many scorpions and spiders. They fell from the ceiling, biting my family. The place smelled, especially when it rained. After a while we were all told to go to work in different places. Our family was broken up.

They put me with others my age and had me work in the field to watch the cows. Every day I watched the cows, and after I fed them at night I went to the place where the children lay on the ground to sleep. We didn't have a roof, wall, or bed. We slept on the ground. I worked so hard and got so little to eat. We only ate one meal a day, at lunch. Angkar measured each serving, only about a cup and a half, which was mostly broth and maybe two tablespoons of rice. They also gave us a small piece of salt to suck on as we ate. Sometimes we didn't even get salt. We fought each other for it.

One day as I was watching the cows eat grass, I noticed that a few of my cows were missing. I smelled something like a dead animal. My cows were running toward the smell, and I followed them. By the time I got there the cows were licking the dead body's clothes. Some were standing there sniffing. It was a human body that had just been killed. You could see her long black hair and the string around her hands. I looked around and saw people who had been shot and their heads were smashed in. There were at least one hundred people dead. This was the place they took people to kill. I was very scared because if I couldn't get the cows back, I would be killed or punished. I whistled for the cows to come and we hurried back.

I saw so many of the prisoners they took to kill. The prisoners were blindfolded, and their hands were tied behind their backs. I thought they had done something wrong. I didn't realize until I had been moved to a different place what really was happening.

One place I remember clearly is Thunder Hill. One day at this camp they called all the kids to come to a meeting. We had to walk in a line across ponds and creeks. Our clothes got wet, but it didn't matter because we were used to it. We had to go single file because Angkar was afraid we would escape.

On the way I saw my two younger sisters. They were in different camps than I and were also being forced to go to the meeting. I saw my youngest sister from very far away and we tried to look at each other. I couldn't ask her how she was doing; we only stood and stared at each other. We weren't supposed to get out of line and had to look straight ahead. I tried to recognize their walk. Both of them were so skinny and didn't have good pants to wear. My younger sister wanted to cry when she saw me, but crying was forbidden by Angkar. I turned away from my sisters so the Khmer Rouge wouldn't see her cry and discover that we were sisters.

The meeting took place at the temple. They had all of us sit in line. The children sat in front. We looked like grandmothers and grandfathers, we were so thin. We were too tired to smile, laugh, or cry. We were so dry that we had no tears left.

The meeting started. They called the two prisoners. "If someone betrays Angkar, they will be executed. We want everyone to know that these people are bad examples, and we don't want other people to be like this." Two of them walked the prisoners to the middle, which was in front of us. Angkar talked with a microphone. He told us to come to the front so we could see those who had betrayed Angkar. They deserved this. All the kids like me were forced by the leader to sit in front to see one of the prisoners. Angkar said, "If anyone cries or shows empathy or compassion for this person, they will be punished by receiving the same treatment."

Angkar told someone to get the prisoner on his knees. The prisoner had to confess what he had done wrong. Then the prisoner began to talk but he didn't confess anything. Instead, he screamed, "God, I did not do anything wrong. Why are they doing this to me? I work day and night, never complain, and even though I get sick and I have a hard time getting around, I satisfy you so you won't kill people. I never thought to betray Angkar. This is injustice. I have done nothing wrong! Arthmel Atsasna." In Cambodian this means that Communists destroy their own people, culture, religion, and ancestors. "You kill people without reason. This is injustice!"

Suddenly one of them hit him from the back, pushed him, and he fell face to the ground. It was raining. We sat in the rain, and then the rain became blood. He was hit with a shovel and then he went unconscious and began to have a seizure. Then Angkar took out a sharp knife and cut the man from his breastbone all the way down to his stomach. They took out his organs.

When I saw this I felt so shocked, like I was blind. It felt like they were hitting me just as they hit the prisoner. The person that cut him open took a sharp piece of wire and stuck it in what I think was the liver and bowels. They tied the organs with wire on the handlebars of a bicycle and biked away, leaving a bloody trail.

Angkar calmly told us over the microphone, "All girls and boys, you have seen with your own eyes. If someone feels compassion or sympathy for the enemy that has just died, then you will be punished just like him." My spirit and mind were gone somewhere already. I know I saw them carry the bloody organs away. Now I wondered if this was true, did it happen? I was now a prisoner in my mind and my body.

My mind says, "Don't remember, because this could be me." The air smelled like blood. Clear rain drops coming from the sky became blood. I was enraged and shaky this first time I saw a killing. I said to myself, "Oh, my God." My mind shut down. My eyes didn't even blink. Then Angkar told us to get in line, and we all headed back to the place we lived.

When we returned Angkar called all of us for another meeting before we were allowed to eat. I felt very sorrowful, angry, and hurt that I couldn't help this person who died unjustly. They told us to be strong. They brainwashed us into not following the dead prisoner's path, to continue to work like thunder.

That night I couldn't sleep. I remembered the face of the prisoner, his words, and what they had done to him. It was cruel and inhumane. I was so angry inside. I couldn't forgive them for what they did to their own people. At 3:30 a.m. I hadn't fallen asleep yet, and then the whistle blew. I had to get up and get in line.

I was at so many camps, and again they moved me. Here my job was to fix the small dams that supplied water to the rice fields. If there was too much water the rice would spoil and die. If this happened we would be punished and not get any rice. Sometimes I had to dig in the small creek in order to get clay for the dam. I was very small, and I had to swim to get the clay out of the creek bed. I then had to swim with the clay to where the dam was.

The water was full of leeches. I was afraid of the leeches and had trouble doing my job. Angkar told me to be fast and work hard. If I didn't, they were going to send me to some place from which I'd never come back. "We will send you to eat dirt or eat the shovel we use to hit people with. You'll die." So sometimes I just let the leeches stay on me. When they are filled with blood they fall off.

My Mother's Courage
Arn Yan

During the 1970s, a great tragedy happened to the Cambodian people. I can remember this now, and I will not forget it for the rest of my life. In 1975 there was intense fighting between the government soldiers and the Khmer Rouge guerrillas. The Khmer Rouge took power. Everybody was extremely happy to get the new government. They hoped that they would have more freedom, liberty, and peace. But all they had been hoping for was gone.

My father had hoped that our family would stay together and that there would be no more killing. But only fifteen days after the Khmer Rouge took control of Cambodia, my father was accused by a cadre of being a former soldier or colonel of Lon Nol. He was really a cattle dealer between provinces. Before they killed him, they played a game with him. The killers let him eat all he wanted and then called him up to a small room and interrogated him about military matters. He knew nothing about these matters. He had never joined the army. When he didn't answer them, they hit and punished him by covering his head with a plastic bag and putting his head upside down in a jar full of water so that he lost consciousness several times.

After three days of interrogation, the man who called himself the King of Death made the decision to have my father killed. At that time, the faces of fifteen of the victims were covered with a dark cloth. One of the killers started telling those people to get on the truck. Everybody knew that they were going to be killed soon, but all they could do was plead with the murderers. Even though they all tried their best to beg not to be killed, their efforts were worthless.

When they arrived at the killing field, their faces looked pale. The killers told these innocent people to get off the truck and stand near the curb of Highway 5. Then they started counting "1 ... 2 ... 3 ...," and told them to run down to the field as they counted. The killers pointed their rifles at each of them and pulled the triggers. That was the end of my father's life. He was killed when he was forty-five years old. My mother has been a widow since.

Ten days after he died my mother went to ask one of the cadres about my father, "You told me that my husband would be coming back this week but it has been three weeks already." The man answered, "You don't have to worry about those betrayers. They will be coming back next week. They are so busy with their work. Don't ask me anymore about your husband." When my mother heard this she knew that my father had been killed. At that time I was about seven years old and I wondered why she didn't eat but just cried. I asked her, "What is the matter with you?" She answered by smiling with tears dripping from her face.

Three weeks passed by. My father didn't come back. I started asking my mother, "Where is Dad, Mom?" She didn't say anything to me. She just covered her face with a handkerchief and cried. When I saw that she was crying, I began to cry too. The next day she woke up early in the morning and went to the killer's office. When she arrived one of the killers came up and started asking her, "What did you come here for?" She answered, "I just want to know about my husband. You told me he would be coming, but now it has been five weeks already."

The man answered, "What! That's not your problem. That's your husband's problem. You don't have to know about those kinds of things." She knew that he was dead so she replied, "Why don't you send me to where my husband is staying?" The man turned to the group of people standing around and said, "If anybody is related to the men that aren't here, please come over to me." The rest of the people were told to go back home. There were about fifty people left, including my family.

Meanwhile, one killer stood up and spoke directly, "Please don't ask anymore about all those people who went to help Angkar two months ago. You know they were betrayers and they were former Lon Nol soldiers. They all were sent to death." In the meantime, all the victims' relatives cried, shouted, and yelled at that stupid man. "How come you killed my husband! He wasn't a soldier. He was a rice farmer." The Khmer Rouge cadre announced, "if anyone wants to know some more about their husbands, come to my office tomorrow night." A lot of people went back, but my family didn't. We were afraid of being killed. We later learned that the people who did go back to the cadre were killed.

In June 1975, I was called to work as a grass carrier. I worked seven days a week from six o'clock in the morning till noon. They gave us about a twenty-minute break during lunchtime. We worked again from twelve-twenty until six in the evening. All the children from six to ten years old had to go to work. They divided us into groups according to age. I sometimes worked fourteen hours per day. That was hard for me.

During 1975, the first year of the Khmer Rouge control, we had enough food to eat. But from 1976 to 1978 we didn't have enough food to eat and we weren't allowed to cook for ourselves. They had to cook for us and we had to eat together in groups of ten to fifteen people. Sometimes I didn't get my ration because I didn't finish my work on time and my food was thrown away. We ate gruel, rice mixed up with a banana stump, and one can of rice was put into the big pot. That one can of rice fed one hundred children, and we could hardly find a grain on the plate. All that we could find was the stump of banana. This didn't make us healthy. After we ate, we got sick a lot from diarrhea, cholera, and stomachaches. Day by day, hundreds of children and adults died from starvation, and this was just in the small village where I lived.

One day I was very sick and starving to death. I didn't go to work. I just stayed in the children's cottage. One of my group leaders came up to me and spoke in a loud voice, "Why don't you go to work?" I responded, "I am sorry. I can't go to work." He asked me again, "What's the matter with you?" I answered, "I'm sick. I'm hungry. I don't have any strength in my body at all. Please forgive me, sir!" I said this kneeling down on the ground with my two hands held up to him. I hadn't finished what I was saying when he picked me up. He smacked and kicked me until I dropped to the ground. I lost consciousness for a couple of hours.

When I woke up, my face and body were covered with blood. I could hardly walk, and I was very scrawny because I hadn't eaten food for two days. I was sent to the hospital to be treated. In the hospital they didn't have any real medicine. All they had were fake medicines and traditional medicines made from tree leaves, stumps, and roots. Some traditional medicine could help us, but others didn't have any effect. None of the medications helped me.

One week later my mother heard that I was in the hospital. She was shocked. She came to visit me but she didn't recognize me because I was very, very skinny. The moment she saw me she cried and said to me, "What can I do for you? I don't have anything left besides my body." She came to visit me every day and packed some kind of food for me whenever she came. She got some medicine for me by exchanging valuable things like diamonds, gold, necklaces, earrings, and bracelets that she had hidden in the ground around our hut. She came to visit me by stealing time from her work. If the soldiers had known, she would have been in big trouble. After I got some medicine from her, I started to feel a little bit better. When I felt back to normal I was called to work in the children's team again.

One year later, in 1976, I was sent to another province to work on transplanting rice, pulling out rice seedlings, and carrying bunches of rice. That was the hardest year in my village. People went to work every day and worked really hard in the fields but they didn't get enough food to survive. All the crops that they grew were sent to China.

Sometimes I was out of rations, so I had to go out and steal all kinds of vegetables and fruit, such as potatoes, papayas, pumpkins, and watermelons. They were planted at the place where many people were buried in shallow graves. I went out almost every night to steal with my friends. I remember one rainy night when all the people around me were sleeping, and I asked one of my friends, "Do you want to go to steal with me?" He said, "No! Are you crazy?"

Nobody wanted to go because it was very dangerous and quiet there. Wild animals like wolves, snakes, monkeys, and tigers lived there. When I went, there was only the sound of these animals. Even though I was very scared and knew I would be killed if I was caught, I was determined to eat. Nothing is worse than starving. I didn't care about being arrested and being killed. That night I was so filled up that I couldn't walk or go back to the work camp. When the sun rose I woke up and walked straight to work. One of my group leaders came up to me and asked, "Where were you last night?" I told him that I had gone to my mother's house. He didn't hit me this time, but I was punished by being put to work for twenty-four hours in the field. Everybody went home except me, but luckily I finished all the work he required me to do.

The year 1977 was the worst year for people in Battambang province. They grew a lot of rice, but there was a big flood that destroyed all the crops that had already been planted. There was nothing left in the fields but water, seedlings, and straw. Day after day, we had almost nothing to eat. There was no rice or vegetables. We had some cassava, stump of papaya, lilies, and fish to sustain us. In 1975 they had required at least seven to ten people to live in one hut. A few years later there was nobody in those small houses anymore. In one house, at least five people died, and in some houses there was nobody left. They were killed, and others died from starvation, disease, and lack of medication. At the hospital no one was educated, so most of the time sick people weren't helped. The Khmer Rouge killed the doctors, professors, teachers, lawyers, and high-ranking people.

One thousand Cambodians were left in my village. About six thousand had died. The village was so quiet. In some huts everybody had died and nobody buried them. The bad smell spread all over the village. Sometimes I drank water with a bad smell and with blood floating in it. Nobody could do anything for anyone else even if they were friends or close family members. All they could do was to survive by getting food to eat.

Early in 1978 one of my cousins was killed because he made a small mistake. In the morning he went to work plowing and raking the field. He saw a fish swimming in the water. He stepped down from the plow to catch the fish and put it in his pocket. One of the Khmer Rouge leaders was watching from behind him. He dragged my cousin down from the plow, telling him, "You're supposed to come to work. You're not supposed to come to catch fish." The man hit my cousin on his head and neck with a bamboo stick until he died.

When they put you to work, you worked. They had somebody follow you all the time, keeping an eye on you every second. Before that man hit my cousin, my cousin said, "Please forgive me, sir. Please don't hit me. I won't do it again." At the time, I was carrying rice seedlings to transplant in the field. I didn't know my cousin was being beaten and killed. I thought it was somebody else. After he was killed with the bamboo stick, one of my friends came up and whispered, "Arn, do you know what happened to your cousin?" I said I didn't know. "Arn, if I tell you, don't get surprised, okay?" He told me that the man they put on the dike who was hit and died was my cousin. I said, "What? The man with the bloody body on the dike, he was my cousin?" He answered, "Yes."

When I saw that he was lying in the field, I was so depressed, and I asked myself what he did wrong. I could do nothing besides feel very sorry for him, bless him to go to heaven, and hope that God takes care of him. From then on, every second we were working the killers always came behind us. They wouldn't let people go to work from one place to another. If we wanted to work somewhere else, we had to ask them. If we didn't ask, we would be in big trouble. They punished us by sending us to jail or by killing us. Their doctrine gave us no human rights, no sympathy, and no freedom to do anything. Sometimes we made only a small mistake but they pointed us out to the killers and we would be killed.

The Khmer Rouge tortured and killed people in many different ways. They sometimes pushed people's heads into a barrel full of water. Sometimes they pulled out the fingernails. Other times they dug three holes in a triangle shape and buried all of the people's bodies except for the heads. Then they put a pot on the heads and burned a fire until the people died. Sometimes they put people in a pot covered with a lid and built a fire.

Many times they killed people by cutting out their livers with a knife. They buried the bodies but used the livers and gallbladders to make traditional medicine for fevers. Often they ate the livers. Sometimes they hanged people, and sometimes they covered their heads with plastic bags. Babies were thrown up in the air and came down on bayonets. Other times they grabbed babies' feet and hit them on tree stumps.

I survived the Khmer Rouge largely because my mother really cared about me. She stole rice and vegetables. When she knew I had stolen something, she told me not to do it again. She said, "I am old and I will be dead someday. I don't want you to die." Even though she stole every day, there still wasn't enough for us to eat. Luckily, we are alive today, and we lost only my father and my brother. But for the rest of my life I will not forget these unimaginable, tragic events that have happened to me.

The End of Childhood
Seath K. Teng

"Come with me. I'll take you to the village to play with all the other children, and before dark, someone will take you back to your mom." This alluring statement changed my life as a child for almost three years. The time that I started to realize and become interested in the world was when I faced the most hateful things in life. At the age of four I was robbed of my normal childhood. I was separated from my family to face the cruelty and hatred of the Khmer Rouge.

My family was separated from each other to work in different places. Until the end of 1975 we were able to live with our mother. One morning, while my mother, sister, and I were pulling weeds at the watermelon farm, we saw two Khmer Rouge soldiers approach us. They came to take my sister to the village. I wanted to be with her. I had never been away from her, so the two soldiers took both of us. They said that we could come home any time we wanted. But this wasn't the case at all.

When we got to the village there were many children already there not much older than me. I saw my grandmother and my aunt. I ran to them but one soldier pulled me back, telling me to be still. I cried, throwing both my arms at my grandmother and aunt to take me, but they didn't come. The feeling of rejection was burning inside me. I thought that both my grandmother and aunt didn't love me. All I could think about was my mom, and being away from her made me cry more and more. I was fortunate at that time because I had my sister. She was my only comfort until they took her away from me.

After the Khmer Rouge got all of the children, they took us to long shacks made of bamboo with a roof made of palm leaves. In the middle was an open area where all the meetings were held. Before they assigned us a place to sleep, they held a long meeting. We all sat in the open square listening to the loud intercom. The Khmer Rouge soldiers told us not to love our parents or to depend on them because they are not the ones who supported us. They told us to love the new leaders and to work hard so that our country could be prosperous. If we didn't do as they said, we would get a severe beating for punishment. After the meeting they made us cheer and keep repeating that we love, work hard for, and respect our new government.

They then took us to sleep in the long shelter. They made us sleep in a row. In one shelter there were two rows of children sleeping with their feet facing each other. We slept on a bamboo floor with no sheets, no cover or pillow. The Khmer Rouge soldiers slept in their hammocks high above us.

Early in the morning, before sunlight, they shouted and whistled for us to get up and get in line to go to work. We were very tired, and some of us didn't get up on time. If we didn't get up they would pull us up on our feet and threaten to beat us if we were slow again. Every morning before sunlight we all went to work without anything to eat. We did a variety of work depending on the jobs that needed to be done.

I remember that we did most of the jobs in the rice field. We grew so much rice, but they fed us so little. What we did depended on the season. The adults did all the planting. What little piece of the rice plants the adults dropped, we had to gather and give them back to plant. To do this we had to stay in muddy water all day. The only time we came out of the muddy water was around noontime, when it was time to eat our first meal. We only had one set of clothing. We slept in it wet or dry.

In the harvesting season we picked up the rice strands that the adults dropped when the plant was cut. This time of the year was hard for us because the rice field was very dry and the rice stubs cut our bare feet. This physical pain to our feet we could endure. The most terrible pain we had to endure was hunger pain. Our meals were always rice porridge with salt. The Khmer Rouge soldiers fed us only two meals a day. They gave us one bowl for every four children. As Charles Darwin put it, it was survival of the fittest. Whoever could eat the fastest got more to eat. They didn't give us a spoon, either. We just used our hands.

Besides working in the rice field, the children pulled weeds from the vegetable garden. Sometimes the Khmer Rouge took us to the mountain to collect rocks for building bridges. If we didn't do our job we would get a beating and not be allowed to eat our meals. To eat, we had to work hard. If we were really sick and couldn't work that day, we were allowed to eat only one meal with extra liquid in our rice porridge. They said we didn't provide any labor and that we were lucky to eat for free.

We worked seven days a week without a break. The only time we got off work was to see someone get killed, which served as an example for us. Eighteen years have passed, and I can still remember one of these killings vividly. Sometimes I have nightmares about it. I remember a day we were working in the vegetable garden pulling weeds. In the middle of working, the whistle blew and the soldiers told us to stop. They said we had to go to a meeting to see the punishment of a traitor. When we got there they made us sit in front near the victim so we could get a close look at what was going to happen.

In the center of the meeting place was one woman who had both of her hands tied behind her. She was pregnant and her stomach bulged out. Before her stood a little boy who was about six years old and holding an ax. In his shrill voice, he yelled for us to look at what he was going to do. He said that if we didn't look, we would be the next to be killed. I guess we all looked, because the woman was the only one killed that day. The little boy was like a demon from hell. His eyes were red and he didn't look human at all. He used the back of his ax and slammed it hard on the poor woman's body until she dropped to the ground. He kept beating her until he was too tired to continue.

We were taught not to love or respect anybody besides the Khmer Rouge government. If we were caught hugging or talking intimately to our parents, we would get a beating. I didn't get a beating for this because I never saw any of my family members. During the time I was at the children's workplace I never thought about my family. I was brainwashed from all the meetings we had to attend.

There were incidents of children running away from this place. They never succeeded. They were caught and brought back. Whenever that happened there would be a meeting, and one of the soldiers would tie up the runaway. After that the Khmer Rouge would point at the children. Whoever was pointed at had to do the beating. If we didn't participate or if we didn't beat severely enough, we would be the next victim and also be beaten. To save ourselves from being hit, we hit hard. After the beating they left the bloody kid there and starved him until they put him to work again. While these beatings took place they made us shout, saying they deserved it because they were traitors and were a bad example for everybody.

At the reeducation meetings, I believed the Khmer Rouge soldiers when they told us that our families did not love us. I kept in my mind the first time I was at the village, when I cried, wanting to go to my grandmother and aunt, and they didn't come to me. At the time, I didn't know that the Khmer Rouge government made us behave this way.

I was told later, toward the end of 1978, that we were free to leave the children's workplace. I had no idea where my family was and felt very lucky that my sister found me and took me to our parents. I was almost seven when I saw my parents for the first time since I was separated from them three years earlier.

Imprinting Compassion
Sophea Mouth

If an individual has been exposed to a violent environment, is that individual prone to violence? Can the effect of violence be so strong that it destroys human compassion? A violent environment need only have a short-term effect on human compassion, as it did with me, because compassion cannot be destroyed, it can only be paralyzed temporarily.

A man was holding a sharp ax rotated backward in his right hand, and with his left, he had a firm grip on another man's shoulder. At that instant, the edge of the ax cut open the man's chest. Blood spurted and I heard a roaring groan, loud enough to startle the animals. I stood there smiling deceitfully in shock because it was the first killing I had seen.

491

After the cadre had opened up the man's chest, he took out the liver. One man exclaimed, "One man's liver is another man's food." Then a second man quickly placed the liver on an old stump where he sliced it horizontally and fried it in a pan with pig grease above the fire that one of the cadres had built.

When the liver was cooked, the cadre leader took out two bottles of rice-distilled whiskey, which they drank cheerfully. I was too young and the cadres didn't allow me to participate in their celebration, although I had no desire to taste human liver.

I considered myself an observer only. One of the cadres had taken me in and had accepted me as a trusted member who could and would be willing to obey commands and share whatever information I could get out of the workers.

As I sat and observed those men using small bamboo stakes to poke the slices of the liver frying in the pan, I thought that they were savages. Their eyes were bloodshot—perhaps they were intoxicated from what they had eaten—and they scowled at me. As soon as they caught me looking at them, they asked me to examine the corpse closely. The odor from the blood was so strong that I threw up.

The cadres exposed me to the killing because they wanted to test my loyalty toward them and Angkar. If I showed any reluctance toward seeing their ruthless behavior, they wouldn't have been convinced that I had assimilated into their culture.

This was one of the incidents that touched my heart profoundly. I was paralyzed, unable to move freely knowing that this could happen to me or my relatives. My heart was pounding like a drum.

Though the incident affected me, I had to cope with my life. I did not become a violent person. How much of an effect did the incident have on me? Did it alter my behavior and my compassion entirely? The answer is no, and something that happened to me before the Khmer Rouge came to power, when I was about ten, helped me to remember why.

During the civil war I was sitting below my grandmother's house, which was on stilts. A girl walked straight toward me. She was wearing rags. On her back was a cloth sack sewn together with a white thread. Her complexion appeared to be pale, perhaps from undernourishment, and her cheeks no longer had a glowing look. She was a walking cadaver. After I observed her thoroughly, I was speechless, not because I was disgusted by her appearance, but because she aroused my pity. My initial reaction was to adopt her as a part of my family. I thought that she wouldn't have to go around begging anymore if she was my sister. Even though she was around my age, she addressed me as a superior. "Sir, would you spare me a couple cans of rice?"

I looked her in the eyes. Her eyes suggested that she had been through a great ordeal. They had a look of desperation. I asked her where she was from. She said, "I used to live in Kompong Cham Province and I have been begging for food about nine months. My house was destroyed by the bombing, and the bombs killed my father and two of my brothers. My mother is recovering from injuries to her legs."

Without hesitation I took her cloth sack and went into my house and filled it with about ten pounds' worth of rice. I was very careful not to let anyone in my family know that I had taken some rice and other canned goods and given them to a beggar. I feared that my parents would punish me. Still, I was willing to accept the consequences. I offered to help carry the rice to the place where she was staying because I wanted to find out if what she had said about her family was true.

When she stopped at the edge of the city, I asked where she was staying. She said, "Right here." When I looked in the direction she was pointing, I saw two poles supporting a piece of plastic. Under the plastic was a woman with two amputated legs and a torn blanket covering her body. The mother was curious as to who I was, and the girl explained that I had been very generous to her.

The mother looked at me and said, "Thank you, nephew, for helping me and my daughter. I wish to bless you with all the luck and glory that your fate will not be like mine." I couldn't speak, but tears had reached my cheeks and I wiped them off repeatedly.

Angkar's indoctrination was an attempt to destroy all my compassion for another human being. Angkar believed that an individual must destroy this "negative" feeling if she or he is to serve the party. At one point I began to accept what Angkar had to offer. I accepted their ideas not because my compassion had been destroyed by the indoctrination but because I wanted to live. I was not mad and I was not confused. My mind was clear and I knew what I was doing. I used my wit to deal with the cadres. I was subtle in almost everything I did. I fooled the cadres many times. I had to pretend that Angkar was right and that it was justified in whatever it did. Deep inside, though, I knew I could never kill anyone. Angkar's indoctrination still causes me to have nightmares.

My feelings for my family help explain my actions. I remembered when the cadre forced my mother to leave her home. She refused, and the cadres shot her right in the neck. She fell to the floor and blood rushed out and there was a puddle of blood on the floor. I was determined not to cry—not that I didn't feel horror, but my heart was frozen.

Later I learned that the cadres had arrested my father. He was a former military leader, and they were going to execute him. He managed to escape during the execution lineup. He came to my aunt's farm to join us, and we lived as farmers for several months. Then Angkar decided to purge people with wealthy backgrounds. My father tried hard to conceal his identity. He lied to the cadres that he was a peasant, but the cadres were still suspicious of him.

A peasant woman who didn't like my father claimed to know his identity, and she reported it to Angkar. Angkar then concocted a scheme to kill my father without alarming the villagers. They reassigned him to a distant zone, but everyone knew that those who were reassigned never returned. It was Angkar's usual killing tactic. Fortunately, my father was sick and couldn't go. His life was spared, but he lived in constant fear.

In the midst of the confusion Angkar took away my older brother, my oldest sister, my two younger sisters, and my youngest brother. Angkar forced them to dig canals, to transplant rice, and to carry baskets of dirt to build dams. My older brother said that Angkar starved him. Angkar gave him a daily ration of one bowl of rice gruel and he had to supplement his diet by eating raw field crabs or whatever he could find when the cadres weren't looking. My youngest brother had to stay in the indoctrination camp. My sisters were in a similar situation. They became emaciated from starvation and intensive labor.

Since I lived among peasant farmers, I didn't experience the kind of pain the others experienced. I mostly observed pain. I wanted to help those who were not as "fortunate" as I was by whatever means possible and went out of my way to help others.

The Pol Pot regime turned some people into fierce human beings. I know several refugees who used to be killers that are now leading religious lives. When I asked them why they did what they did during the Pol Pot regime, they said they didn't have any choice, and that is why they didn't think about morality when it came to obeying orders.

For me, I value other people's lives as much as I love my own. I could not kill anyone because Angkar told me to. Whatever decision I made, it was not to hurt or kill anyone, but to serve and to protect them whenever I could. Neither the cadres nor Angkar could convert me against my will. Now, compassion is mine.

The Tonle Sap Lake Massacre
Ronnie Yimsut

A pointy object poked at me very hard and woke me up from the muddy bottom of the canal. I slowly opened my eyes to look at a soldier, who continued to poke me with his oversized AK-47 rifle. He was no older than twelve, just a few years younger than I was, but much, much fatter. He was yelling angrily for me to get up from the mud. "Go ahead and shoot me," I said to myself. I was ready to die. It was hopeless. I finally pushed my weak, skinny body up from the mud and wearily walked toward where my group was congregated. It was our time to go, at last. I began to have mixed feelings about the sudden relocation plan. Normally we would stay in one place for weeks or even months at a time before they shipped us out again.

They ordered us to file in rows of four. A small group of soldiers who were to escort us was made up of all ages. Some were as young as ten. There were only five of them to escort what was left of my original group of people. By then there were only seventy-nine of us together. During five awful days at this place, eight of us had died, including six children and two elderly men. I wondered why there were so few of them if they were going to kill all seventy-nine of us.

The oldest soldier came over in front of us and spoke loudly so that everyone could hear him. He told us that we were being moved to Tonle Sap, which meant "Great Lake," to catch fish for the government. He also said that there would be food to eat there. Suddenly people were talking among themselves about the news. We were all very skeptical about this miraculous news, but it made sense, since most of us were once commercial fisherman at Tonle Sap. They told us just what we wanted to hear. The food, the chance to catch and eat fresh fish from the lake, and to get away from the misery. It all sounded too good to be true. I was completely fooled by the news. And so were the rest of the people.

They took us south over a familiar muddy road toward Tonle Sap, which was about six or seven miles away. The longer we were on that road the more relaxed we became. Perhaps they were telling us the truth? We seemed to be headed in the right direction. There were only five of them and they can't possibly kill all seventy-nine of us . . . could they?

After about three miles of walking they asked us to stop and wait for the rest of the group. People were very weak, and the three-mile hike took its toll. Another child died on the way. The soldiers allowed the mother to bury her child. It was another twenty or thirty minutes before the rest caught up.

They wanted us to move on quickly with the setting of the sun. They first asked all the able men, both young and old, to come and gather in front of the group. The men were then told to bring all kinds of tools, especially knives and axes, with them. They said the men needed to go ahead of the group to build a camp for the rest of us. The men soon lined up in single file with their tools in hand. I watched my brother, Sarey, as he walked reluctantly to join the line after saying good-bye to his pregnant wife. I told him that I would take good care of Oum, my sister-in-law. The group disappeared shortly as the sky darkened. That was the last time I saw Sarey and the rest of the men again.

The sky was getting darker and it grew chillier. The notorious Tonle Sap mosquitoes began to rule the night sky. After about thirty minutes or so, the two soldiers that had led the men away returned. They quickly conferred with their fellow comrades about something not far away. One or two of the people from my group overheard something quite unbelievable, and the shocking news quickly spread among the people within the group. I learned that they said something like, "a few got away." It only meant one thing: the men were all dead except for a few who managed to escape.

It was about seven or eight o'clock at night when we were ordered to move on again. By this time the children who still had enough energy to cry were crying and screaming as loud as they could. It was mainly from hunger and exhaustion, but also from the attack by the swarming mosquitoes. Above the cry of the children I could hear the sobbing and weeping of the people who had lost their loved ones. The odds were stacked against us. If we didn't die of starvation, exhaustion, or mosquito bites, there was a good chance that we would be killed by the soldiers.

The thought of coming face to face with death terrified me for the first time. I thought about escaping right then but after long consideration couldn't do it. I didn't have the heart to leave my family, especially my pregnant sister-in-law, who was already a week overdue. Besides, where would I go from here? I would eventually be recaptured and killed. If I was to die, I preferred to die among my loved ones. There were plenty of opportunities for me to escape, but I just couldn't do it.

I reluctantly trekked with the rest of the group, with my sister-in-law Oum holding onto my right shoulder and a small bag of belongings on my left. It was ironic that night. We knowingly walked toward our death, just like cattle that were being herded to the slaughterhouse. Even the children seemed to know it. But I still had a little hope despite everything I had seen and heard.

A few miles before we were to reach Tonle Sap they ordered us to turn off to the west instead of continuing down south as planned. It was a very muddy, sticky road. My feet seemed to get stuck in the mud every single time I put them down. Progress was slow and cumbersome. A few people got stuck in the mud, which was just like quicksand, and the soldiers came over to kick and beat them. I never knew if they made it. I was busy helping Oum and myself move forward and didn't really care anymore.

All that time I was trying to calm myself down and keep a clear mind. Oum was beyond help. Her quiet weeping had now became a full-blown scream. She was in bad shape physically and emotionally. She said that she had a stomach cramp or was in labor, she wasn't sure. It was to be her first child. She didn't know much about childbirth or contractions, and neither did I. All I could do was to drag her across the muddy flat so that the soldiers wouldn't come and beat us to death. It was pathetic.

We were no more than 300 yards off the main road when they asked us to sit down on the edge of a small shallow canal that ran east to west. Both of our legs were stretched forward, and we had to shut up or they would beat us up. In a matter of minutes a large group of soldiers numbering more than fifty suddenly emerged from a hidden place in the nearby forest. It was really dark by then, but from their silhouettes I could tell that they were soldiers with AK-47 rifles, carbines, and large clubs in their hands. One began to shout loudly to us as the rest surrounded the group, their rifles aimed directly at us. People began to plead for their lives.

The soldiers screamed for all of us to shut up. They said they wished only to ask a few questions. They said they suspected that there were enemies among our group. They claimed there were Vietnamese agents in our group, which was a bogus claim since we had known each other for many years. It was a tactic, their dirty trick to keep us calm, weak, and under control. It was very effective because all the strong men who could have risen against them were the first to go. What was left of the people in my group were women, children, the sick, and the weak. They had us right where they wanted us. It was a pre-meditated plan.

A soldier walked toward me and yanked a cotton towel from me and shredded it into small strips. I was the first one to be tied up tightly by the soldiers with one of the cotton strips. I was stunned and terrified. I began to resist a little. After a few blows to the head with rifle butts, I let them do as they pleased with me. My head began to bleed from the cuts. I was still semiconscious. I could feel the pain and the blood flowing down my face. They were using me as an example of what one would get if they got any kind of resistance.

They quickly tied the rest of the people without any problems. By this time it was totally chaotic, and people continued to plead for their lives. I was getting more and more dizzy as blood continued to drip across my face and into my right eye. It was the first time that I had tears in my eyes, not from the blood or the pain, but from the reality that was setting in. I became numb with fear.

I was beyond horrified when I heard the clobbering begin. Oum's elderly father was next to me, and his upper torso contracted several times before it fell on me. At that moment I noticed a small boy whom I knew well get up and start to call for his mother. And then there was a warm splash on my face and body. I knew that it was definitely not mud. It was the little boy's blood and perhaps brain tissue that got splattered from the impact.

The rest let out only a short but terrifying sound, and I could hear their breathing stop. Everything seemed to happen in slow motion, and it was so unreal. I closed my eyes but the terrifying sounds continued to penetrate my ear canals and pierce my eardrums. The first blow to hit me came when I was lying face down on the ground. It hit me just below my right shoulder blade. The next one hit me just above the neck on the right side of my head. I heard fifteen more blows, and the victims landed everywhere on my skinny body.

Fortunately, I didn't feel them until much later. I didn't remember anything after that, and I slept very well that night. I woke up to the sound of mosquitoes, which were still buzzing like bees over my body. Only this time there were tons of them feasting on my and the other people's blood. I was unable to move a muscle. My eyes were open, but my sight was blurry. I thought I was blind. I was disoriented. I couldn't remember where I was. I thought I was sleeping at home in my bed. I was wondering why there were so many mosquitoes. Where was I? Why couldn't I move? I was still tied up with the cloth rope.

After a few minutes I was able to see a little, but everything else was still blurry. I saw a bare foot in the line of my sight, but I didn't know whose it was.

Suddenly reality set in at full blast and I broke into a heavy sweat. The memories of the event came rushing back and smacked me right in the head. I realized what the sharp dull pain was all over my body and head. I was very cold. I have never been so cold in my entire life. Fear ran rampant in my mind. I suddenly realized where I was and what had happened. Am I already dead? If I am, why do I still suffer like this? I kept asking myself those questions over and over, but could only come to the same conclusion. I am still alive. I am alive! Why? I couldn't understand why I was still alive and suffering. I should have been dead.

The faint light of dawn broke through, revealing my shivering, blood-soaked body in the mud. It must have been about four or five o'clock in the morning on January 1, 1978. "Not a happy New Year today," I thought. It was still dark and cold. My motor skills came back little by little and I was able to move with great difficulty. I pushed myself to sit up by hanging onto the pile of dead bodies. I began to work to untie myself from the cloth rope.

I broke the rope after a few painful tries. My eyesight came back, but after seeing the scattered bodies lying in every direction, I wished that I was blind. Some were beyond recognition. Some were stripped completely naked. Bloodstains that had already turned a dark color gave the area a new dimension. It definitely was not a sight for sore eyes.

I wanted to look for my relatives but was unable to turn around. My neck was stiff with pain. My head hurt, oh, it hurt so bad. I could only feel around me with my hands. Everywhere I touched was cold flesh. My hands were both trembling and I couldn't keep them from shaking. I cried my heart out when I recognized a few dead bodies next to me. One of them was Oum and her unborn child. I suddenly remembered the bare foot I saw when I woke up. It was hers. Her elderly father and two sisters were all part way on top of each other and side by side as though they were embracing just before they lost their lives.

I couldn't go on. My cry turned to a sob, and it was the only sound around besides the mosquitoes, which continued to torment my almost bloodless body. I began to fade and feel as though my life was slipping away. I passed out again on top of the dead bodies.

I woke up to the sound of people coming toward the killing field. I sat up and listened closely. I began to panic. "They are back to finish me off," I told myself. "They are going to bury me alive!" They might as well, I thought. I've nothing to live for. Technically I was already dead. I was ready to give up as the voices were getting closer and louder when my survival instinct finally took control. I pushed myself, inching my way toward nearby bushes. I was no more than twenty feet away from where I was earlier and commanded a good view of the area. The people soon arrived at the site. I was right. They were back with a new batch of victims. Most of the people were men, but a few were women. Their hands were all tightly bound together with rope.

One of the soldiers gave a command. In broad morning light, I was again witnessing the slaughter of humans. In just seconds they were all clobbered to death just like the rest of my family and friends, whose bodies were still scattered on the muddy ground. My heart just stopped. My entire body shook convulsively and I wanted to throw up. My left hand squeezed tightly over my mouth so that I wouldn't accidentally cry out and give myself away. I felt as though I had gone through the same ordeal all over again. My mind just couldn't take it anymore. I went blank and passed out again.

It was not until the next night that I was really awake. More people were coming toward me again. I assumed that they were more victims to be killed. I didn't wait to find out. I decided then that I wanted to be alive. I began to slip away from the area by crawling on my elbows and knees. I was no longer bleeding, but I knew that I was in bad shape. I was hungry and very thirsty. My lips cracked like mud in the hot sun. I had to find water soon or I would die of thirst. I worked my way west along the shallow dried-up canal and then turned north. By this time it was really dark and chilly again. I found myself in the middle of impenetrable brush and forest. I went back and forth trying to find a way through the thick forest and ended up back where I started, near the killing area.

For the next seventeen days, I hid out in the forest. I slept only at day time, spending my night raiding one village after another for whatever I could find to eat. My injuries healed quickly and I began to put on some weight thanks to the food that I stole from the surrounding villages. I never stayed in one place long. I was on the move and always watching out for any sign of danger. I knew that they were searching for me, and I was able to keep a step or two ahead of them. They always counted bodies, and if one was missing, they searched and usually recaptured the escapees. For seventeen days I was the king of the jungle.

I stumbled accidentally onto a group of escapees who were also hiding in the forest. I almost got killed because they thought I was a Khmer Rouge spy. The only thing that saved me from certain death was my recent injuries.

We headed for Thailand. After fifteen days of hiking the 150 miles we found ourselves in a Thai jail and then in prison. The Thai authorities considered us political prisoners because we arrived after they closed the border.

Over 600 others like us were kept in a 75-by-75-meter cell. The living conditions were bad and the treatment we got from the Thais was even worse, but I'd rather be in a Thai prison than in the forced labor camps with the Khmer Rouge anytime. At least we were fed and clothed like human beings. Because I was the youngest of the prisoners, I got better treatment. I got to know some of the guards really well, and within four weeks at the Thai border I gained over twenty pounds. I was under eighty pounds when I arrived there.

We all spent five months in the Thai prison before we were moved to a refugee camp near the Thai-Cambodian border. I waited for a recruitment drive for freedom fighters to fight the Khmer Rouge while I was in the refugee camp, but they didn't accept me because I was "too young and too skinny." I even told them that I was almost eighteen, but it was no use. I couldn't go back to fight, and staying in the camp would only lead me to suicide. I had nothing to live for. I thought that I should end my life just like my fellow refugees who had already killed themselves. But that was too easy! I was a survivor.

My life began to turn around when a CBS news producer named Brian T. Ellis showed up at the camp one day. I was interviewed for a documentary film called *What Happened to Cambodia*, which was later broadcast in the United States. Mr. Ellis took me outside of the camp for the very first time in months. I tasted freedom and I liked it a lot. That day with Mr. Ellis was special and I have never forgotten it. My life began to change for the better after Mr. Ellis left. I now had a reason to go on living. It was a chance for a new life.

VIETNAM

South Wind Changing

Jade Ngoc Quang Hu'ynh

JADE NGOC QUANG HU'YNH (1957–) grew up in South Vietnam during the war. In 1974 he enrolled at the University of Saigon, where he studied until 1975, when he was arrested and sent to a reeducation camp. He escaped from the camp and Vietnam in 1977 (to Thailand) and subsequently came to the U.S. For six years he worked in various unskilled jobs (including fast-food service and housecleaning). In 1987 he obtained a B.A. from Bennington College, and in 1992 he received an M.A. from Brown University. He currently lives in Bennington working on various books assisted by an NEA grant. In addition to the volume excerpted below he is coeditor of Voices of Vietnamese Boat People: Nineteen Narratives of Escape and Survival *(2001).*

. . . . .

On April 21, 1975, President Thieu resigned and left for Hong Kong. A month before Tran Van Huong took over, he had transferred his huge assets to his brother, the ambassador to Hong Kong. General Ky delivered a speech at the Catholic church saying that he would stay to fight with the people, but after the speech, he disappeared fast. Duong Van Minh became president; his first important act was to order all foreigners to leave the country within twenty-four hours, while he prepared negotiations. Nobody seemed to care about our country anymore, nobody cared for our people anymore, and I tried to run away from the coming execution. What could I expect from these opportunists? Everyone lost hope. Soldiers left their units to go back to their families, hoping they could help them with something.

We were standing on Phan Thanh Gian Avenue watching people scurry back and forth, when an M-48 tank appeared at the intersection, lurching around like a mad dog, shooting into the air with all the ammunition it had left. The tank stopped and two soldiers popped out of the hatch. They jumped to the ground, tore their uniforms off and threw them down in the street, and ran. An army jeep raced around with a speaker announcing the news. Duong Van Minh had unconditionally surrendered and was asking all the southern soldiers to put down their weapons.

From Jade Ngoc Quang Hu'ynh, South Wind Changing, © *1994 by Jade Ngoc Quang Hu'ynh. Reprinted with the permission of Graywolf Press, Saint Paul, Minnesota.*

The northern army thundered into the presidential palace with a T-54 tank, knocking down the gate. They tore down the southern flag with three red stripes on a yellow background. Over the palace they raised their red flag with one yellow star in the middle. It was April 30, 1975, the last day of the Republic of Vietnam. The whole city turned chaotic. A Russian Molotova truck carrying northern soldiers barreled into the city and shooting broke out here and there. Many people ran out into the street to welcome the new comrades, the new government for a new future, but no one knew what it would lead to. It was to be the darkest day for the southerners. The war was over for Americans, but a new revolution, a new regime, and a new Vietnamese class conflict had just begun.

My friend Hanh and I went to Vung Tau to search for a way to escape, but to no avail. The new government ordered all the southern soldiers, officers, security, police—anyone who was at all related to the southern government—to report to a certain place. I told my aunt that I was leaving for home because I thought it would be safer there, with my family in a small town. I went home to Vinh Binh, but I couldn't see any of my brothers because they were all stranded in different places. A public speaker on a telephone pole along the road announced the order for everyone to register with the new authorities, no matter if you were a teacher, student, or civilian. They ordered people to give up their books, magazines, tapes, newspapers. Any literature in the South was to be destroyed. If any was found in people's homes, the literature would be confiscated and the people would be executed.

In Vinh Binh, we had to go to a meeting every day to receive a new education from the Communist Party. The secret police were everywhere, checking on people. If they suspected anyone of anything they would arrest him or her.

Every week we had to go to the meeting at Ward eight and march on the hot street with thousands of sweating people chanting "Long live Ho Chi Minh, long live the Communist Party!" The black tar melted under our bare feet. We had to welcome the new government by singing their victory song as we held up the red banner with the Communist Party sign. We had to carry Ho Chi Minh's picture in front and yell out loud to condemn the betrayers who followed the U.S. and the southern government.

I remember one day very clearly. We had marched to the soccer field. We stood in front of a platform in rows, blending in with the secret police. One of the VCs stepped up to the microphone to direct the program. The new national anthem played. The master of ceremonies introduced an executioner in a cowskin-colored uniform. The executioner pulled some papers from his briefcase and read from them. With a stern and cold expression he announced the name, the age of the person, the city where he lived, and told us that this young man was working for the CIA.

"He is our traitor, he is against our party, our government, and our people! Is he guilty?" he shouted into the speaker.

"Yes, yes!" everyone shouted.

"Take him out for the people to see who he is," he ordered the guard.

The guard stepped off the platform, then pulled up a young man about my age, clean and handsome, with his hands cuffed at his back. I guessed he was one of the southern colonels' or generals' sons. I wasn't sure, but by looking at him I could guess what kind of class he was from.

"Are we going to execute him?" he yelled into the microphone again.

"Yes, yes!" the crowd shouted.

Then, the executioner moved on to another paper with another name appearing on his list and the process began again. When he reached ten people, he stopped in order for the comrades to tie the prisoners up at poles in front of us. He ordered the guards to take off their blindfolds and asked them, "Do you have anything to say for your last request?"

"We don't have any guilt. We love this country! Long live the Republic of Vietnam!" the prisoners all shouted as loud as they could. It was like an electric wave being sent through us.

The guards blindfolded them. Several yelled that they didn't want their eyes covered. The guards held their guns up, aimed at the young men, and shot them. I saw their blood sprinkle all over as their bodies shook while their heads fell to one side and they died. I felt as if I was being pushed closer to the pole.

"Long live Ho Chi Minh! Long live the Communist Party!" the executioner shouted into the microphone, applauding.

The execution had sparked the crowd. They repeated what the executioner said and clapped their hands to worship the leader without any hesitation.

Later, we marched to the cemetery to watch as they used a bulldozer to raze all the southern soldiers' graves.

"These people are against us. They are traitors and we have no place for them!" the VC leader yelled to us. He turned to a children's group assembled there. "If any of you know someone who is in hiding or betraying us, you have to report to the secret police at once. You are our future. You are the children of Uncle Ho, you are following in his footsteps."

The bulldozers revved, and the smell of decay thickened the air. Coffins broke as the bulldozers ripped through them, and worms crawled out. We could not move until they ordered us to leave.

On Sunday, May 15, 1975, the secret police invaded our house and threw us out. They searched under our beds, in every closet and every corner of the house where they thought they might find valuables, even in the toilet. They let each of us take one shirt and one pair of pants. My mother held her shirt and pants while pleading with them for permission to burn some incense at the altars for our ancestors for the last time. The VC consented. She lit the long sticks, and moved about the altars, placing them in the incense burners. She kneeled and bowed to pray.

As she bowed to four directions, I saw her glance to see if any of the Viet

Cong were watching her. Then, quickly, she rose, stepped behind the statue, and from a small hole in the wall snatched a fabric belt filled with jewelry, which she bundled into the roll of clothes she was carrying as she sat down again. Later it would buy our food. My parents, older and younger sisters, and two youngest brothers went back to the village. They put my father on the people's court to execute him. But people defended him, saying that he was rich because he had worked hard and not because he had received land from my grandfather. He narrowly escaped death. All of my brothers were placed in labor camps. I didn't know whether my brother, the pilot, had escaped or was killed. There was no news. I pleaded with the police to let me return to my school. They agreed.

I came back to Saigon, hoping to blend in with the big crowd, staying with my aunt's family.

One day, my aunt asked me to go to the black market to buy some food. I walked down the street where they sold goods, and I didn't know that the police had raided the area. A policeman ran by chasing someone, but his quarry escaped, and he stopped, his chest heaving. He turned to me.

"Where are your papers?"

I showed him my identification. He took it and looked at it, his eyes hot, the skin of his face mottled with frustration.

"What is your occupation?" the policeman asked.

"I am a student."

He grabbed my hands and handcuffed them at my back, pointing his AK-47 at my ribs and commanding me to move. People stared at me as we began to walk. I didn't know what my crime was. The VC policeman jailed me at the ward shelter for a week and ordered me to write a confession every day, listing all of my background from my great-grandfather's generation to the present. They moved me into a big group with many southern soldiers who had been sent to them for "reeducation." In early June 1975, a few months after my eighteenth birthday, I was sent to a labor camp. No one knew what had happened to me. I could see my aunt's face, waiting for me to bring back the food to cook a meal that would never be....

. . . . .

My first taste of a labor camp was at Hiep Tam town, the site of a U.S. helicopter field abandoned after the war. It was about twenty-five acres with three barracks, three watch towers, several bunkers, and over thirty chopper garages made from sandbags, where the Americans had hid the helicopters. Several barbed wire fences circled our camp to keep us from escaping. The VC packed more than 500 prisoners into each of the barracks, which had no toilet and no place to wash. A guard told us that we would only be here from three to ten days, and then we could go home to our families. Yet I also heard them whispering to each other, and laughing: three to ten days for them, but three to ten years for us.

At first, they treated us nicely and encouraged us to tell the truth in our confession papers, so that we could go home. Nobody knew that at the end of the month our papers would become "evidence" that would allow them to sentence us to serve time in a "reeducation camp." A lot of the prisoners were trapped with this gimmick, but I told them a lie and stuck with it through my time in jail.

They divided us into groups of twenty prisoners each, gave us three axes, and ordered us to convert the whole air field into a garden. We took turns using the ax to break the tar-and-cement runways piece by piece, piling the broken rock into one spot under the boiling sun. Our hands blistered but we weren't allowed to stop. We formed a line to transfer the dirt and soil from the rice field to the newly uncovered ground to make a garden. We dug two wells about twenty-four meters deep to get water, dumped the sand out of the sandbags and tied pieces of bags together to make a rope for the well. We sewed the rest of the sandbags together to make walls for our barracks. After six months, our hands had turned numb and the big heavy axes had been ground into tiny hammers.

Every night the guards held a meeting at which we were expected to criticize ourselves about how poorly we had worked that day. Each group had to pick the laziest one and a guard would punish that person by putting him in a small metal box of connex which the Americans had used to store their ammunition. We had to take turns appointing someone to receive this kind of punishment, because if we didn't pick someone out, the guard would tell us that we weren't honestly criticizing each other and more trouble would come. The metal box was over-hot during the day and freezing at night; everyone had to taste this torture at least once during our time at the camp. You were lucky to be let out in two days, and fortunate to be alive if they put you in the box for a week.

We began to grow vegetables: lettuce, tomatoes, cucumbers, corn, beans, and peppers, but the crop wasn't good because the soil was dull and too full of clay. The guard ordered us to "increase our production," but how could we? They announced a slogan: "With our human labor we can turn rocks and pebbles into rice." The guard said that if we could reach a set level, they would release us and let us go home. Everybody was happy again when they heard the word "home," after a long, depressed period at the camp. At the meeting the guard told us: "Use your human waste as fertilizer. We do this in the North every day."

We dug a rectangle in the soil about one foot deep for our toilet and every day twelve people would squat around the rim to do our business. On the other side, a few meters away, other prisoners watched and waited to catch our excrement in a big ladle, competing against each other for a piece of shit to fertilize our vegetables, afraid that if we didn't make our vegetables grow bigger we would get in trouble. One prisoner ran over to the hole where we were squatting and put his ladle beneath one of the prisoners.

"What are you doing?" the squatting man shouted at him.

"It's okay. Just do your business. I just want to make sure it all gets into my ladle."

"Go away!" he yelled angrily. "I cannot shit if you are around. I'll kill you if you talk anymore."

The whole group, which had been squatting there stood up, pulling up their pants, ready to threaten him. He ran back to the other side to wait.

When they got the fertilizer, they mixed it with water and showered the vegetables. It seemed to be working very well since the vegetables were growing bigger. Sometimes we just covered the toilet hole with soil and dirt and built a garden over it and dug another toilet at other sites in the camp.

We didn't have any newspapers, magazines, or books to read, but there were plenty of stories in our barracks, things that actually happened to us or to people we knew. There was a former Green Beret captain who slept two beds away from me. He had a beautiful young wife who came to visit him, but she didn't have any money to bribe the guard to let her see her husband. The guard chief told her that if she wanted to see her husband she would have to sleep with him first. And if she refused, he would single him out for "special treatment." Afraid, she did not see how she could refuse. One day, she told her husband that she couldn't come to visit him for six months—she was having a hard time taking care of the children at home. But in fact, her stomach was growing rounder: she gave birth to a baby girl. She resumed her duty, visiting her husband and this time she brought their four-year-old boy to see his father. She wanted to hide the truth because she knew it wouldn't help her or her husband at all in this situation. She didn't know whether her husband would forgive her or not if he knew what she had done. The boy had a conversation with his father the former captain, who was presently a prisoner.

"What do you do at home?" the captain asked. "Are you a good boy?"

"Yes, I'm a good boy, father," he said proudly. "I play and watch my little sister for mother."

The captain knew that he hadn't slept with his wife at all and how could his wife have another baby? Was she a prostitute, he thought. How could she do something like this to me? The captain looked at his wife helplessly, without a word, and tears fell. His face reddened, he stood up and ran back to his barracks while his wife ran after him to beg his forgiveness.

"It isn't my fault. I didn't do anything wrong. I love you and I have to support the children. Nobody helped me. I was always faithful to you, but after Saigon fell, and with you locked up in here, what could I do? The guards can kill you anytime they want but I wanted my son to have a father."

The husband looked at her, then shut the barracks door on his wife and child. The guard came to take her into the booth for his usual payment.

That night, the captain killed himself by biting off his tongue. I didn't know if he died because he felt he had nothing to live for anymore or if the shame of losing face in front of everyone was too much for him. No one except the captain will know exactly what he went through. . . .

. . . . .

The area around the labor camp began to change: we were turning the jungle into gardens. We grew sugarcane, bananas, corn, lettuce, tomatoes, hot peppers, and yucca root. We had the right to grow them but not the right to eat them. Like when the guards said we could defecate, but not urinate, on pain of castration. We tended the garden and watched the produce grow, our mouths watering. I felt like I was half dead and half alive.

We harvested the corn, salads, and cabbages, sorted the good and bad, and brought them to the highway for the VC to take away to sell. We didn't know where or to whom. We had to steal anything we could eat; we even picked edible leaves we found on the road or wherever we worked. We caught crickets or lizards and ate them raw because we could not let the guards see this. If the guards saw you, you would find yourself at the "guillotine center," the place where the VC held our meeting each evening. The guard tied the thumb of your left hand to your right toe and the right thumb to your left toe and let you stay at the guillotine center for a few hours, donating blood to mosquitoes. If the guard wanted to kill you he would leave you there all night. You died in horror, your face sunken, pale as a banana leaf from loss of blood, your mouth wide open. I could tell you about beatings, but they seemed almost routine: we were beaten whenever the guard felt like it.

I didn't know what to think anymore. I became numb and indifferent. I lived day by day and consoled myself with the thought that perhaps I was being punished for being cruel to others in past lives. I missed my family terribly and I wondered what had happened to them. What was my mother doing right now? I bet she was crying and I hoped she hadn't become blind because she was getting old. She had eleven children and eight of them were in jail. What did she think? How could she bear that kind of life? How about father? I bet he was worrying as always and getting skinnier. I knew he wouldn't cry. What could I say to my sisters and brothers? I prayed to my Buddha to help them and myself. I heard the temple gong bang with its harmonious and warm sound, soothing me.

"Hey, I'm starving. Do you want to cook some yucca root?" Hung whispered. We were squatting in our hut.

"We don't have any," I answered.

"We have plenty in our garden." He smiled sarcastically.

"You mean we're going to steal again?"

"No, it's ours. We grew them. The guard didn't grow them."

"But they have a right to beat us up if we eat our crop," I said.

"Don't be a scaredy-cat. Let's go."

We woke a few other prisoners we trusted, and told them to build a fire for boiling water. Hung and I sidled out into the night, then crawled under the barbed wire fencing and into the garden. It was midnight. I recognized some of the stars in the sky. The weather was cool and it wasn't too dark.

We crept along the dike to the yucca root garden where we would dig some. I felt a cold chill when I stepped on the dewy grass. Hung found a spot and began digging a hole beneath the yucca tree, cutting the roots with his pocket knife. He put them in a bag and covered the hole up to make it look as if nothing had happened. He gave me the bag and moved to another spot to get some more. We could not get all the root in one spot because the tree would die and the VC would know. We took a little here and there from the furrow. And then I heard footsteps. I snatched a piece of soil and skipped it towards Hung, then jumped behind a bush nearby. I didn't know if Hung had received my signal. Several flashlights appeared, moving closer to our spot. I heard the sharp sound of metal cocking. I held my breath and tried to stop my beating heart, which seemed so loud the guard would notice.

"Come out with your hands up," one of the guards shouted and pointed his flashlight.

I stayed put, since I didn't feel any gun pointing at my back. They always bluffed—that was their trick. Everything became quiet and the guard moved along the furrow. He called out to his comrade walking along the garden, then disappeared into the dark. I lay in the bush not too far from the furrow, waiting a while before I made my move. I felt something thud on my back and thought it was Hung's signal for me to go back. I held the yucca bag and crept along the dike until I arrived at the hut. I gave the bag to my neighbors to cook the roots. They peeled off the skin and put them in the boiling water.

"What took you so long? Where is Hung?" one of them whispered.

"Hung couldn't get out because of the guard." I answered with broken breaths.

Four prisoners stood at each side of the hut to watch for the guards. We sat down in a circle around the fire. We were afraid someone would see the sparks from the fire even though it had been placed in a hole in the ground. We opened our mouths, sucked in the cooking smell, and exhaled with our noses, like we were some sort of filter machine.

"Smells good. Is it done?" one of the inmates asked in a low voice.

"Almost. Keep watching," I said.

I wondered what was happening to Hung.

"What can you do with the yucca skin?" someone asked.

"I'll bury them," I said.

I dug a hole in the ground and buried the skin to keep the guard from finding the evidence. It was almost morning now. I heard some shooting in the distance. We shared the yucca root and buried the fire. Hung still wasn't back.

When day broke, the camp was strangely quiet with no activity at all, though it was broad daylight. Strangely, there were few VC to be seen as if they were all meeting somewhere. Worried about Hung, I decided to go to the bathroom, our "communication center." I waited in line for a toilet, in the overpowering smell. I tried to identify a familiar face, to communicate with someone. I sat in the toilet finally and my connection sat next to me. I asked him about Hung. He said he didn't know. I asked him why we hadn't gone to work that day and why the guards weren't saying anything. He said there was some fighting near the border but he didn't know for sure who was fighting. I asked him if anyone in the camp was missing. He answered no. I asked him to check on Hung and let me know. We left the toilet.

Our group didn't report that Hung was missing because that would be dangerous for him if he had escaped. He would need all the time he could get. Besides, we could take advantage of the situation. The guards ordered us to dig trenches and holes around our camp and inside our huts. They told us that the Cambodians had attacked the border and that if any fighting reached our camp we would need to take cover in the trenches and holes. They said that they were protecting us from the Cambodians. I thought, if the Cambodians attack again, I will escape in the chaos. The morning went by; the situation was still tense. We had a meeting at the guillotine center and Chu Tu, one of the guards, pulled me to the side.

"Don't hide in the trenches," he paused, his face weary. "The trenches and holes are targets for grenades."

It figures, I thought, and the VC said they were protecting us. I thanked Chu Tu but still suspected him. Chu Tu was a southerner who had joined the North to fight the French in 1945, and had stayed there until the fall of Saigon when he returned to the South. He was the assistant chief for our camp, but it seemed that all the power was in comrade Son's hands. Chu Tu seemed to carry a big resentment against the North; I had used this to get to know him, hoping to turn him against comrade Son, hoping the more numerous VC guards might rebel against the Northerners. I went to the "communication center" to pass Chu Tu's warning on to my fellow prisoners, and ask them if there was a way we could take advantage of the situation.

I learned from them what had happened to Hung. He had escaped, but was captured by guards from another camp nearby. They held him and tortured him before sending him back to our camp.

That evening, the guards came to our hut and escorted twenty-four of us to the "guillotine center." They ordered us to stand in a circle, beat each other, and yell, "You have to report to a comrade if someone escapes." We kept hitting each other until we couldn't move our hands. Our skin bruised and swelled. They pulled our arms back and tied our toes to our thumbs and left us in the sun to burn. They didn't give us any food or water for a whole day. I felt terribly hungry and cold, but there was nothing to eat; I swallowed my saliva, in pain.

The more pain I felt the more I hated the VC. I couldn't stand the color of their uniforms; it looked like the color of a cow and I named them "yellow cow" meaning uneducated and stupid . . . every negative thing I could think of. I became determined to escape. I could not stand this pain any longer.

My body grew colder, even though it was hot and humid in the afternoon. My stomach growled. The hungrier I felt the colder I got. I wished they would just shoot us.

Hung was sent back to our camp, half dead with torture marks. His whole body was skin, bones, and bruises. It seemed like they would never heal. His eyes were sunken beneath messed-up hair which he didn't care to comb. Hair was growing everywhere on his face. He looked like an old man when he walked, his back hunched. I could imagine all his bones broken to pieces. He seemed like a dead ghost wandering about the camp. His clothes had holes everywhere. He appeared to have no energy, no feelings, no life any longer. We gave him medicine and asked him to take it, but he didn't say much. We looked at him, knowing he wouldn't survive.

He told us how they tormented him in the other camp. They filled up a barrel with water, put him in it, and closed the lid. They hit it with a stick for a minute and then took him out. He said he didn't know anything but blood, which came from his eyes, nose, ears, and mouth. Besides that, he had to cut trees down and carry them back to the camp. Hearing his story, I felt like I couldn't breathe because something clogged my throat as if someone had put a bag over my head and tied it to suffocate me. We tried to help each other as we could. I didn't know when it would end.

The guard mixed us with different inmates in a different hut. I was in a new hut with different prisoners, not sure of the make-up in this new group. Luckily Hung was here too. I watched them slowly, and reacted. They gave me some water and roast sweet potato as a sign of welcome.

The next day we went to work on the rice paddy. I had an easy job irrigating water into fields while two prisoners put ropes around their necks and pulled the plow behind with one inmate holding it to make furrows. Some picked weeds and grass and dug a little trench for the water to run. This was a new area that the VC had assigned to us. I observed it very carefully, searching for ways of escape. . . .

Hearts of Sorrow

James M. Freeman (ed.)

JAMES M. FREEMAN *(1936–) received his Ph.D. from Harvard University in 1968. He teaches anthropology at California State University in San Jose. Freeman is coauthor of* Voices from the Camps: Vietnamese Children Seek Asylum *(2003) and author of two anthropological studies of India. He was awarded the American Book Award for* Hearts of Sorrow *in 1990.*

· · · · ·

Prisoner Without Trial: 1975–1976
Narrator 12: Ex-ARVN Colonel

In this chapter, the colonel describes his first year as a reeducation camp prisoner. He recalls his initial shock as he and others are treated, not with the respect they are accustomed to, but as prisoners, and their belated realization that they have been betrayed. He describes the rotten and inadequate rations, misunderstandings between the guards and the prisoners, punishments, indoctrination sessions, and limited attempts at resistance by the prisoners. Of particular interest is how quickly, easily, and effectively the Communists were able to round up and control their prisoners. The remarkable fact is not that there was resistance, but that it was so muted: the prisoners-to-be docilely reported as ordered and were then transported to reeducation camps; they were controlled by a handful of guards and cadres; in most camps they cultivated the very crops that supported the camps: in effect, the prisoners and their families paid for their own imprisonment.

In mid-June 1975 I heard the announcement that former military officers were required to go for ten days of political study. We were told to bring just enough money and clothes to cover that period.

Close to midnight some 2,000 to 3,000 of us were called to a schoolyard

From James M. Freeman, ed., Hearts of Sorrow: Vietnamese-American Lives, © *1987 by the Board of Trustees of the Leland Stanford Junior University. All rights reserved. Used with permission of Stanford University Press, www.sup.org.*

and separated into groups of forty to fifty men. Most of them were doctors, engineers, and teachers who had been in the Army of the Republic of Vietnam. Also among us was a chef from a famous restaurant in Cholon, the Chinese section of Saigon. Because of this, I thought we were going to get VIP treatment. Now I realize that this was to lull us into unsuspecting complacency.

Around 2:00 a.m., Chinese military trucks arrived. We were loaded into them and canvas coverings were placed completely over us so that we could not see outside. We sat for hours unable to move or even turn in that crowded, suffocating space, while the loading continued. Some men needed to urinate; the guards would not let them off the truck, so the men urinated into empty bottles or nylon bags and kept it. All of us were unhappy. Some of us realized that our darkest days were coming. I felt insecure about what was to become of us.

Around 5:00 a.m. the convoy moved. People who sat near the corners of the canvas opened it a little to look out and report to the rest of us where we were going. The smokers among us were very obstinate. Despite the strong objections of others, they tried by any means to smoke, even though we were in a confined space. With this began a split between officers in the same truck: they became strangers to each other.

For seven hours we traveled nonstop. We were hungry, thirsty, and very unhappy. Finally we came to an abandoned military camp which we recognized to be Long Thanh, the rear base of the 18th Division of the ARVN. The two guards in our truck, youngsters about eighteen years old, called to us to step down, stand in rows, and wait until our names were called and checked. The words they used were a shocking insult to us. They called us "Elder Brothers," but we who were in our forties and fifties were not used to such informality and familiarity from kids. As former officers and officials, we expected to be able to relax and be comfortable, not to be treated as army privates, told to line up and follow the orders of a youngster. It was a deep shock for us.

Some of us needed to urinate. Our guards refused permission categorically until all the prisoners had been checked to see that none were missing. All of us were thirsty, for we had not expected that we would need to bring water. We had figured we'd be having a feast cooked by that Chinese chef! Since they were illiterate, the PAVN (People's Army of Vietnam) did not know how to write our names correctly or form a list. They were unaccustomed to command. With their northern accent, they mispronounced our names. As they messed things up, they got angry and shouted at us....

· · · · ·

For lunch we were handed some rotten rice, originally from a U.S. food aid program. It had been sitting in bags in the jungle and had turned green. There were no pans or firewood; we were told to collect what we could and cook our own food. In addition, we were given a small bag of instant noodles and told to cook it in a big pan of boiling water; this would be soup. Ordinarily one person would consume that bag of noodles; now it had to be distributed to fifty or sixty people. Every one of us was discouraged. While in the field, all combat officers of the ARVN from captain on up had an orderly who had taken care of cooking, washing clothes, and other tasks. Now we ourselves had to cook rotten rice. Thus began our lives as reeducation prisoners.

We were short of everything: water, food, tobacco, drink, and other things. Because we thought we would be gone only ten days, and that we would remain in Saigon during that time, many prisoners did not bring mosquito nets, and this was the worst of all. We sat through a long night of darkness without light. Some men told funny stories to dispel the gloom; others lost their morale.

The Communist cadres did not need to prompt us; we all began to insult President Thieu, Vice-President Ky, and other officials of the former Republic of Vietnam who had flown off and left us behind. We began cursing them that first day; we still curse them.

After a few days of settling in, some prisoners were able to persuade the guards to buy them cigarettes, food, sweets, and even to send some letters to family and friends in Saigon. Some of them bribed the guards so generously that they received supplies from their families quite regularly and lived royally. This really split us apart. They never shared with us, never, and we suspected that they were antennae working for the Communists. Just a few succeeded in having their families come to visit them; the rest of us suspected them because of that. Those who were poor had no supplies at all. We'd gather and speak indirectly and sarcastically at those rich people. We'd invent stories that seemed to be about someone else, but actually were about the man right next to us. And we told stories that insinuated without directly accusing them.

Some prisoners were so *vile* that they became the servant orderlies of the rich officers, attending to their every want, washing their clothes, cooking, bringing water for the bath. For this they received food, tobacco, and other things.

Because at Long Thanh we were at a rear base, there was room for 10,000 prisoners, and that's about what we had. The guards were outside the fence; we were on the inside. Each day we had to provide a squad or platoon to do labor work at the headquarters of the Communist cadres outside our enclosure. We rotated the men who did this. To get there, we had to pass by the guards, and whenever we were outside, we had to keep in line under a leader chosen by us.

Most of us were older officers who had to wear spectacles. These were quite new and strange for the guards. North Vietnam is poor; never had these guards seen spectacles until they saw us with them. When our leader came to the gate, he had to stop and shout, "Everyone stand at attention!" Then we gave a military salute to the guard. He was very proud of this moment and not in a hurry for us to move on.

One day, the guard said angrily, "All of you take off your hats, but you *never* take off your spectacles! You are not polite to me. All of you must take off your spectacles!" He was a man from the countryside, the sort that wants to show off but makes the wrong criticism in trying to appear sophisticated.

We stood at attention and took off our spectacles while he shouted. When he finished, our group leader shouted out his report: "Honor to report, Mr. Cadre. Cell Number Three has ten persons going to labor work." Our leader then had to continue by calling out the names of the workers; to do this, he had a piece of paper with their names written on it. Instinctively he put on his spectacles to read.

The Communist private soldier stopped him and ordered, "Take off your spectacles!" Our leader did so, but he could not read the paper, so we simply stood there. Such incidents happened many times.

Each morning, around 6:00 to 6:30 a.m. we heard the beating on a piece of metal that indicated the lifting of our nightly curfew. Thousands of us were inside the fence, but our latrines were outside. We were not allowed to use them until the curfew was lifted. Also, each section of one thousand men had only two or three rows of latrines, and they were very old and quite dirty. Each morning, men would arise at 4:00 or 5:00 a.m. and wait in line for the signal to use the latrines. Some of the men had stomach aches, not so much from dysentery, which is common in the North, but from colic.

From 6:00 to 7:30 a.m. we went to the latrine, boiled water, and if we had food saved from our dinner, we ate it. Those whose families had given them supplies ate some food and coffee or tea. No breakfast was given. Some prisoners stole food from others. Because we had no room on the floor, those with extra food had to hide it somewhere else. They'd look for an empty sandbag or rice bag, hide food in it, and hang it from the corrugated iron roof. Because of the subtropical climate, the food spoiled quickly; if the owners didn't eat it, others would steal it.

Everyone was selfish for many reasons. When our families sent supplies to us, usually they included money and a message. My wife sent me dried bananas. Inside each one she rolled a banknote that was so thin it looked like a stick. In the bottom of a bottle of meat cooked in fish sauce, she put a message wrapped in nylon. Sometimes we shared or exchanged food; if someone found money, he usually kept it, but if he found a letter, he gave it to its rightful owner. The letters were dangerous, for we never knew when a prisoner might inform the cadres. We had a few informers. We found out when the rest of us were sent North; they remained in the South.

Around 7:30 a.m. we had to study and discuss political lessons at our quarters under the supervision of the cadre; he was in charge of about sixty of us. Some of the cadres were lazy, but they also had an inferiority complex and were afraid of showing up because we would embarrass them. In discussion we might raise questions not sincerely, but with the intent to insinuate jokes and insult them. Still, the Communists were able to destroy any resistance by us or even planning for resistance because they rotated and mixed our units every three to six months.

Our lessons continued until noon, when we cooked and ate our noon meal of soup and rice so rotten it smelled when cooked. When possible, we relied on the supplies from our families.

In the afternoon, we had no discussion. Instead, we were supposed to participate in meditation, in which we thought over the lessons of the morning. In fact, we used this time to gamble, wander around, and make homemade knives, musical instruments, and domino sets. From time to time, the guards would confiscate these.

Dinner was cooked in a common kitchen for the whole subdivision, but this kind of meal most of us could not eat: rotten rice, some vegetable soup with no meat or fat but just salted water cooked with spoiled vegetables. Only the poor could eat that. Although it was forbidden, most of us cooked in our quarters using special stoves we fashioned out of milk-powder cans. With its top, we used it as a pot for cooking, but when needed, it became our stove. For fuel, we collected nylon bags in which families had sent food supplies. These bags were an efficient fuel. We cooked in the corner, with a blanket or mat covering the outside and a guard to watch for cadres.

If we were caught, we were sent into the connex, a type of big metal storage box left by the U.S. units in Vietnam. They were high enough to stand in and they had a door. Minor infractions of camp rules, such as gambling, fighting, cooking, or stealing, brought four days to a week in the connex.

For serious misbehavior such as resistance to political discussion or to cadres, our heads were shaved, we were given only one-half ration of food, and a small, half-size milk can of water a day. The shaved head was the mark of a person who had resisted a cadre's order. This was a corporal punishment: for Asian people, this is a very grave insult. Some of our officers were very proud of themselves. They saw themselves as high-ranking versus the low cadres. When they passed one another, our officers didn't salute the cadre; they'd turn aside, or they'd dare to spit in the cadre's presence. This was a big insult, a very serious one for North or South, Communist or Nationalist. When called to headquarters for criticism, these officers argued back, giving insinuating insults to the cadres or even to communism. This earned them shaved heads.

In the connex, a prisoner could move, but he was not comfortable. In the daytime there was no air: the sun, the heat of the other men, sometimes a whole gambling party of ten prisoners crowded into the connex, made the atmosphere suffocating. At night it was cold; also, we had no bathing, and we were not allowed to leave to use the latrine. We had to urinate and defecate in improvised containers left inside the connex. Once a day the guards rotated and checked us. If the guard was friendly, he might leave the door open for a while, or even throw in a half-smoked cigarette.

For very serious punishment, a prisoner might be left in the connex for an indefinite period of time. Because he had made a political insult during our political discussion classes, one man was left inside the connex for two months. He became so seriously ill that they put him in a hospital for prisoners. For a long time we heard no news about him, for the Communists try to keep information from us. Later while working outside the compound, we met other prisoners and exchanged information on various people. From that we heard that he had been transferred to another unit.

In my group no one attempted to escape, but in others they did. After we had been in the camp for some time, some of the young men were recruited to cut firewood. Three young officers tried to escape and were immediately caught. They were beaten a few times with rifle butts. The following day the guards selected one prisoner from each subdivision to dig three graves. The Communists did this intentionally so that when the gravediggers returned to their groups, they would spread rumors that someone was dead or dying. At this point we did not know what was happening, since the events were half secret, half public. This made us worry, put us in a state of uncertainty, which is what the Communists wanted.

The next morning we were told to stay at home; there would be no political meetings, no labor. Loudspeakers were set up in every subdivision of the camp. At 7:30 a.m. the loudspeakers blared, informing us to listen to the tribunal for judging the three officers who tried to escape.

The tribunal lasted for five hours. Then came the announcement, very solemn, intended to intimidate everyone: the three evaders were convicted; all three were sentenced to death by firing squad. We had to listen to the loudspeaker until the shots rang out.

This had a big impact on us. For about three days we felt very sad. Many prisoners made comments and speculated about this event. The cadres held a special political session to discuss the incident; then we were supposed to comment on our own feelings and impressions of the event. And certainly everyone lied. But this event had a very powerful effect on us; no one else in our camp attempted to escape. Elsewhere they did. My nephew-in-law Lieutenant Chien was shot and killed while attempting to escape from Hoc Mon Camp....

. . . . .

We were supposed to live by the phrase, "Labor is glorious." The Communists intended to have all of our units working in the fields or cutting firewood. But the fields were small and the prisoners many, so numerous that the Communists had to select us. Work became a *symbol*, a *ritual* act. In six months my unit was sent out only three or four times....

. . . . .

During the six months that we stayed in the southern camps, the Communists used political study sessions, with confessions for each lesson, and informers mingled among us to sort us into different categories of acceptance or resistance to reeducation. Those whom they considered dangerous were sent to the North.

The confessions went along with about ten political lessons. I don't remember much about them except some of the titles. One lesson commented about the extent of our crimes, our so-called crimes against the nation and people of Vietnam. All of these crimes were imaginary and exaggerated. During study and discussion sessions, the cadre in charge of our unit would try by all means to force every one of us to speak, to give an account of past activities in the army. He did not hesitate to press those who could present a good account of their lives. As many crimes as we could relate, the cadre pressed further, and suggested that the others had to imitate those examples and not hide anything from their past activities.

Quite a few of the prisoners were innocent enough to report officially during this kind of discussion every kind of crime they were supposed to have committed in the past. While the cadre directed the discussion as chairman, two secretaries recorded every word of the confessions. One former province chief announced that he had two roles, one civilian, and one as chief military officer of his sector, through which he had conducted many operations. He listed the number of Communists killed, houses burned, and villages destroyed. Everyone had to confess his own past activities in one way or another.

Some of us who were older and more experienced tried to avoid confessing. We did this by choosing our words so that in the end it was not a confession at all. We said that what we did was done for particular reasons. If we had been more inhuman we would have been more destructive to human populations. When we got orders to destroy a hamlet, we called our artillery to fire into the forest, burning it instead.

I told the cadre that I was an artillery man. Like air and navy men, those in the artillery were considered the most wicked because their power of destruction through technology was tremendous. I confessed the truth, but tried to minimize my crime. "I commanded artillery, but during this time there was no war, so I just trained my soldiers. There was no fighting, so I did not commit any crime at all. When war flared, I was sent for training in the U.S.A.; then I was transferred to staff, so I didn't harm anyone. I just surveyed. I also participated in the overthrow of the Diem regime. Then I was sent into exile as a military attaché, where I just performed ceremonial functions that did not harm anyone. When I returned to Vietnam, I served as a liaison officer in charge of protocol, so I think that with such activities I did not commit any crime at all."

The cadre was not at all pleased with my confession. He said, "Even a surgeon, a doctor in a military unit, commits a crime. It is not necessary to hold a weapon to commit a crime. The contribution of any kind of effort is also a crime. Your crimes are so many that they could be compared to the leaves of the trees in the jungle, or the stars in the sky!"

What the cadre wanted was for us to say certain conventional things. Then he would say, "I am very pleased that every one of you used the same expression to condemn yourselves."

The Communists were very smart. They'd use these confessions to categorize us. Also, they made us confess, not privately, but publicly. This created a kind of emulation encouraging each of us to confess the best of himself, which meant the worst for himself. And the informers among us tried to be friendly. If by mistake we gave them too much in confidences, they gave this information to the Communists.

At that time in the South, all of us expected to be returned home in a short time. The cadre insisted always that the length of time of our reeducation depended solely on ourselves, not on anyone else. We ourselves were to blame if we were not released. If we behaved correctly during our time of reeducation, if we made serious confessions, if we cooperated with the cadres efficiently, which meant if we denounced the next fellow, then we would have great hope to go home sooner than anyone else. All the time, this was the only story the cadre preached. And we believed him. . . .

. . . . .

Harshest Incarceration: 1979–1981
Camp Number Six, Nghe An Province, Central Highlands

When the Vietnamese Communists foresaw their clash with the Chinese, they quickly evacuated all of the reeducation camps along the northern border. Because I had been denounced as a CIA agent, I was classified as among those who were most dangerous, and I was in the first group of prisoners to be moved to Nghe An Province in the Central Highlands. Ironically, the very informer who had falsely denounced me was also sent South with my group. Of the men in my northern camp, only a dozen or so made the trip with me; the other 300 men sent with us were from other camps. We were sent to many places before making the long journey to Nghe An by truck.

We were taken to Camp Number Six, located in an arid mountain area near the Laotian border. This camp had been a French prison for the detention of Vietnamese revolutionaries. During the time of Communist rule, the prison had been used to house civilian criminals. Now they converted the prison into a detention center for South Vietnamese officers of the old regime. The criminals were moved next to us to a site where a new jail was built of light materials such as wood and bamboo. The civilian criminals were much better off than we were because we were put in the old buildings of brick, stone, and iron, which in summer kept the heat in, and in winter retained the chill. It was both terribly hot and cold. We were further depressed and terrified when we found that our guards were from the Public Security Agency, for they are brutal, like the KGB of the Soviet Union.

We were locked in small rooms in which we were so crowded that there was not enough sleeping space for everyone at once. We had to build platforms to stack people for sleeping. About eighty or ninety people would be locked into a room six meters wide and about twice that long. In rooms that measured eight by twenty-four meters, the Communists put 150 to 200 men. Our own clothes and blankets were not enough to keep us warm, and we had nothing else. We made our own extra clothing with U.S.A. sandbags. That helped us quite a bit.

To add to our misery, we found that fish were swimming in the well we used for drinking water. This revealed that the well was polluted, since the fish had found an underground channel leading from the nearby lake into which we drained the waste from our latrines. That was our only source of drinking water during our entire internment. . . .

. . . . .

In Nghe An, prisoners were punished by being put in a small cell with no light, where they remained for ten days or more with one leg chained, with half the food ration, and with all correspondence and family packages denied. Two Catholic priests were put in these isolation cells in 1979. When I left in 1981, they still were in there.

For beating our own company leader and informer, the two men were put in the cells for fifteen days. One of the men was a writer and former director of military television in South Vietnam. Shortly after his release from the cell, he cut a vein in his wrist, poured his blood into a cup, and suddenly threw it into the face of the great informer, our company leader. This was a great insult. All of us were taken by surprise and quite afraid. At first, we thought that the company leader was wounded and bleeding. He himself was so terrified that he rushed to the small window with iron bars to call the guards for help. Again the writer was sent to the isolation cell. The next day, every one of us was furious at the company leader, who now was isolated all by himself: we ignored him, turned our backs on him, and would not speak to him. We avoided look-ing at him, even though he had the full support of the head instructor [of a group in a reeducation camp], a man of the Public Security Agency. . . .

. . . . .

One time, we were ordered to select peanuts for future planting. Seven Moun-tains watched us closely so that we would not steal and eat the peanuts. One of the prisoners stole some and was caught by Seven Mountains, who started to criticize him. The prisoner responded by shouting back loudly and pulling out his shirt in an insolent manner to show that he had hidden nothing. Seven Mountains lost face in our presence. He thought for a while, then ordered the prisoner to go to his office, located some fifty meters away. We listened to the sounds of beating and shouting. When the prisoner returned, his face was bruised. We were upset by the incident.

The prisoners who were treated most brutally were the criminals: thieves, brigands, murderers, and government officials who had been caught misman-aging funds. Although they were isolated from us in the jail area, we worked side by side with them in the fields. They knew how to plow the land, so we took orders from them and got advice, since we were unskilled labor. Mostly they duped and cheated us. They'd promise to help sell our clothing, watches, and rings, but then they just swindled us. Some of them were always unfriendly, but others faked friendliness to make a profit off of us.

One time, a number of the criminal prisoners stole some of our clothes in the field and were caught wearing them. For this, the cadre and guard beat them with rifle butts until they got tired. One of the criminals fainted after being kneed and kicked in the stomach and smashed with rifle butts on his shoulders and head. This was the first time we had seen that sort of beating, since we political prisoners were not supposed to be beaten.

The cultivation of rice did not benefit us, for we could not eat it uncooked. The vital thing to do when we stole food was to eat it immediately, to fight hunger. We preferred to cultivate corn, manioc, sweet potatoes, peanuts, and beans, for then we had a chance to steal food.

The cadres and guards had had long experience in dealing with prisoners. Because they knew that the loss in these kinds of crops was heavy, they devel-oped many preventive measures. Peanuts were considered high quality crops. To prevent insects, particularly crickets, from destroying the seeds, the Com-munists put the peanuts in a concentrated DDT solution. This impeded both insects and prisoners. The peanuts mixed in this concentrated solution smelled very strong. The peanuts were brought out and distributed to prisoners only very late in order to avoid the loss. Can you imagine—we, the educated offic-ers who can realize how much danger the DDT solution is, nevertheless ate those peanuts raw, covered with DDT. But we did not become ill. There was an unexpected effect: the DDT killed all of our intestinal worms! So it helped! To fight the hunger and to kill the worms. . . .

. . . . .

No one thought of escape. There was no way. To the west was Laos, also under Vietnamese Communism. To the east, an escaping prisoner would have to ford rivers before reaching the grand road. Along the way, he would meet a hostile local population. Nghe An had been the cradle of revolution for centuries and centuries. We do speak Vietnamese, but our accent was of the South, which betrayed us very easily to those people who speak the central accent. . . .

. . . . .

During the first year, each prisoner in our reeducation camp was given a monthly ration of sixteen kilograms of uncooked rice, along with vegetables, fish, and a small amount of meat. In the second year, our ration of rice was cut to twelve kilos. For rice they substituted flour, corn, and a coarse grain that is fed to horses and pigs. We had to cultivate our own vegetables. By that second year, we were better organized and planted kitchen gardens. But the funny thing is, if we grew more vegetables, they cut our rations; if we grew fewer vegetables, they gave us larger rations.

I remember one day when a prisoner went to the jungle, killed a huge snake six meters long, and dragged it back to camp. All of the men in Platoon B had a good meal that night. I was not part of that group, but I lived very close to them. At the end of the month, the Communist financial officer called the leader of Platoon B to his office and said, "For the next two months, Platoon B will get less dry fish and vegetables. You've had too much meat this month."

"What meat?" asked the platoon leader.

"Snake meat."

The platoon leader replied, "We caught it in the jungle."

"The meat belonged to the government," said the official.

From then on, if any prisoner caught something, he ate it in the jungle, or he cut it up, sneaked back to camp with it, and ate it without letting the Communists know.

Each morning when we passed through the bamboo gate on our way to jungle work, we had to report to the sentry, telling him how many of us were going out to work, to what unit we belonged, and what our work assignments were for that day. We were not allowed to use the word "comrade" to the guard, but had to call him "Elder Brother." He used the same term for us. When returning through the gate, we had again to tell the sentry how many prisoners were with us, even if we had just gone out and come back. Prisoners who were carrying things might go back and forth ten times, and each time the first man in line would report to the sentry. The rest of us had to stand there, no matter how heavy a load we carried. We could neither put it down nor proceed until the guard gave us permission. To punish us, some guards forced us to stand for long periods. Any prisoner who walked through and reported without slowing down was punished.

Every day a few of us out of the group of 800 were made to stand for over an hour. This happened to me twenty times. During these punishments, prisoners fainted from exhaustion, for it was easier to carry wood while walking than to stand with it. Some of the men had made many trips, and often had carried a single load for over an hour. They were tired and would forget to stop for the sentry perched high atop a tower. Then they were made to stand still and hold that load for one or two hours. At that point, they collapsed. This never happened to me, but about thirty men in my unit of 200 fainted, particularly in the second year, when they were starving and weak. When that happened, the sentry would give us permission to carry the men into camp, then return and bring in their wood, in addition to our own loads. The sentries were low in rank; this was their only opportunity to punish us. The sentries from the North were harder on us than those from the South.

As the days went on, our standard of living became worse and worse; many prisoners died. In my group of thirty, two men died; some groups had more and some had less who died. The causes were first that we were forced to do very heavy work while receiving very little food. We quickly became exhausted; we deteriorated fast. Second, many people had dysentery. Third, because of diet deficiencies, particularly lack of meat and milk, many people developed rheumatism and other crippling and paralyzing diseases that looked like polio. Finally, although we had doctors, we had no medicines and no surgery room. The amputation of limbs was done with a handsaw, without anesthesia. I know of six prisoners in our battalion who had their limbs taken off in this way. Several of them died from infections. (For a Viet Cong surgeon's report of performing amputations without anesthesia during the war to save Viet Cong soldiers, of whom 50 percent survived, see Mangold and Penycate 1985: 189.)

The reason they lost their limbs in the first place was infection. While working in the jungle, they would get a slight injury. Because we had no medicines, infections developed: pustules grew, the infection spread until the arm or leg was full of gangrenous pus. Then the limb had to go. The prisoner was put in sick bay. Inside a mosquito net they cut off his limb, applying the only medicine they had, hot water. The patients cried loudly because there was nothing to stop their enormous pain. Everyone in the camp heard their terrible screams. Then their stumps became infected, and they died. Because we were often switched from one group to another, I did not see all six of these men die, but others told me what happened to them. We knew when someone had died because we had to wrap a mat around the corpse and bury it. In the second year, we made wooden coffins for those who died.

In that first year, Ngo Nghia, a former first lieutenant of a parachute troop, was sentenced to die for killing a Communist soldier while trying to escape from the camp. I was forced to witness his execution. He was twenty-six years old. Since that time, a lot of people in the U.S.A. have collected money for his widow.

Because we were moved around so much, we often didn't know what happened to those who resisted. Often they would disappear at night, never to be seen again.

But I do remember one incident that happened during my third year as a prisoner. A French radio-television representative came to visit the camp, along with seven or eight other people. To prepare for this, two days earlier the Communists told a twenty-one-year-old second lieutenant, a former student at the University of Saigon, to deliver a speech for the TV crew. The Communists wrote the speech for him: "We prisoners have been treated very well; we have been given good food and shelter and have received good lessons to study. All of us former ARVN soldiers recognize that we are guilty, and that we made too many mistakes against the People. We thank the Communists for coming to our country to liberate South Vietnam."

Instead of reciting these prepared words, he gave his own speech, written with the help of his friends, which contradicted everything that the Communists wanted him to say: "We are treated badly; we have no medicine and not enough food. We are forced to do heavy, exhausting labor."

When the Communists heard this, they called out. "Who is still CIA among you?" As soon as the reporters left the camp, the Communists beat that lieutenant for a long time. Then they handed him a prepared confession. He tore it into pieces.

That was the last we ever saw of him. The following day, one of the reporters came back to the camp and asked to see the lieutenant. The guards said, "He is not here anymore; he's gone."

Each day, each man assigned to wood cutting was supposed to cut down one tree and bring back one log four and a half meters in length and twenty-three centimeters in diameter. No man could carry that heavy weight, so the Communists explained, "We don't ask you to carry it by yourself. We ask six of you to cut down one tree, carry it to camp, return to the jungle, and get the rest: one tree for each man."

Sometimes we worked until midnight, for if we didn't finish, we were put in the connex. Depending on the seriousness of the offense, we'd be kept there for one day, three days, sometimes over a week. Each day we received a small amount of water and one-half of a meal. Before they'd let us out, the Communists would force us to sign a confession and promise to do better in the future.

I was put in there three times for three days each. I just sat there with the others who were being punished and thought about the corruption and cowardice of our former generals and president, who had left us behind. There wasn't enough food; I was starving, and my head began to ache. I became dirty, itchy, and like the others in the connex I developed rashes, since there was no water with which to bathe. There was a small hole in the connex, through which friends handed us a can to use for urinating. Also, they would bring us little bits of food, which they would hand through the hole. Each time they came, they were accompanied by a Communist guard, who would not let them talk with us. In the connex we had no blankets, and we got very cold. We also were covered with mosquito bites; we were itching all the time, and we frequently became ill. What made the connex terrible for us was that it was so bitterly cold in the cold season, and so unbearably hot in the summer. We dreaded the cruel torture of the connex. . . .

· · · · ·

Buddhism Under Communism: 1975–1978
The Closing of the Orphanage

Fifteen days after the fall of Saigon, the Communists sent four people to visit the orphanage that I ran. First they asked me questions about my activities, the financial situation of the orphanage, and about all of the property belonging to the orphanage. They addressed me not with terms of respect, but as "Elder Sister," which was less respectful.

One month later, they sent five men to mix with the children and ask them questions: "Are you satisfied?" They tried to find if the children were unhappy with me, if I had anything to hide, if I had exploited them. They needed evidence to accuse me and evict me. Then the men made an inventory of all the items in the warehouse, and from that time took over control of the orphanage. They let me stay, but would not let me do anything. They kept the key; I became just an employee without any authority. I was not even allowed to speak with the children. . . .

· · · · ·

Monks Denounced

One day I was told to attend a ward meeting. When I arrived, a Communist official handed me a piece of paper and said, "We brought you here to denounce the six senior monks we have arrested. Write your opinions!" He did not address me by my title as a Buddhist nun, but in a more familiar, less respectful way.

I hesitated, but a monk near me wrote, "Buddhist monks contribute to the well-being of society."

After reading it, the Communist official said, "No! Write it to accuse the *traitors* who have been arrested!"

The monk wrote another general statement. "Be calm. The government will only punish those who commit crimes and reward those who meet government goals." This monk wouldn't betray his teacher, who was one of the six arrested monks.

Then the Communists brought in their agents who claimed to represent various groups: a woman's association, Catholics, and a Buddhist association. One after another they stood up and said, "Those monks are traitors. They have plotted revolution against the government. Punish them!"

For their third and final step, the Communists handed around a people's petition, prepared in advance, which enumerated all types of wrongdoing the accused traitors were said to have made. Then the officials asked, "Do all the people agree?" Everybody at the meeting automatically raised their hands. "Then sign the petition!"

My heart was beating wildly. I feared that the Communists would insist that the first and most important signature be that of the monk whom they had ordered to write the denunciation. If he signed first, he would betray not only Buddhism, but his own teacher, who was like his father. If he refused to sign, he would break up the meeting and himself be condemned. But the Communists asked an old man to sign first. He was said to represent senior citizens. Next, they asked a representative of veterans. The monk was placed tenth. This is how the petition received its signatures.

In this atmosphere, the Vietnamese Communists declare that they allow freedom of religion, while in fact they discourage it. They encourage sons to denounce fathers, students to accuse teachers, and novices to betray their monks. This is very difficult. If you press the trigger of a gun, at least you kill someone fast. But this other way is a slow death, much more terrible. After three years of living under Communist rule, I realized that they intended to destroy religion. It was then that I decided to escape.

The majority of those who escape do so not to improve their economic or material life but because life in their homeland has become unbearable. They spend a fortune to escape, even though life for most of them is not easier in America. They come here for freedom. They wanted to stay in Vietnam, to help rebuild the country after years of war, but they were not accepted.

Whenever people visited me, they complained about the Communist invasion of their privacy. They were especially upset that nobody could trust anybody, for Communist agents were everywhere in disguise. The agents would say something critical about the government, and if you agreed, they would report you. If they went to your home and saw you talking with another person, they would immediately separate you and ask you both to write on a piece of paper what topic you had discussed, and turn you in if your reports were in disagreement. So whenever we began a conversation, we first agreed on a fictitious subject that we would describe if we were forced to report it. If Communists suddenly appeared, we would switch to that topic. Parents dared not talk to their own children, for the next day the children might involuntarily reveal something to their friends at school. Even husbands and wives became wary of one another.

I had lost all freedom. I could not talk. I could not circulate freely. This was no life at all. . . .

. . . . .

Bien Hoa Jail: 1981

When I returned home from six years in reeducation camps, I was told that each Saturday morning I must report to the ward office with a written account of my activities during the past week.

For four weeks I observed these regulations obediently, but I found that I could not stand it. Besides reporting every weekend, I had to put up with many visits of the Public Security Agent of my street. He looked for me too many times during the week, and bothered me too much. He was very modest, a Southerner, and very polite with me, but younger than my youngest son. I had to spend too much time playing host to him, offering him tea, our best cigarettes; it was too much.

In early May, I decided to flee the country with my two sons. In 1980 they had been caught and imprisoned for attempting to escape from Vietnam, but had been released after five months. They had no desire to remain another day in Vietnam. We went to Ca Mau, the southernmost part of Vietnam. We put down half of our fare to escape, some nine taels of gold, more than nine ounces.

For this trip, we carried three or four shirts and a pair of trousers, but no food or water, since the organizers of the escape had promised to provide them. They warned us not to carry provisions, since this would attract the attention of the Communists.

Around 5:00 a.m. about 100 of us got into a big riverboat, and we started towards the sea. Just as we were about to leave the mouth of the river, we heard the firing of small arms. A small boat came aside and someone ordered us to come over to the riverside. We waited for almost twenty-four hours. The next morning, around 2:00 a.m., the guards searched each of us. About two hours later, I noticed that my younger son had secretly fled. He had pretended to go to the latrine, but kept going. An hour later, I heard a lot of shots fired very close, and people screaming. I was terrified that my son had been shot. A few moments later, the guards dragged back three young men, but with relief I saw that none were my son.

An hour after that, the women and children of our boat pointed to a strange sight; they laughed, but also expressed fear. A tall man covered entirely with mud walked towards them with his hands up. A Communist soldier marched behind him, shoving the muzzle of his rifle into the prisoner's back. Barking dogs followed. The prisoner was my twenty-four-year-old son. While others laughed, I looked on terrified. The soldier ordered my son to go to the river and wash off the mud, which covered him up to his eyes. When the women and children had seen him like this, they had thought he was a ghost.

After he washed, the soldiers tied my son's hands behind his back around a tree. I could not keep away my tears. Around 10:00 a.m. the sun was very high already. He was exhausted, and the sun beat down on him. Water ran out of his nose and mouth. The women saw this and were so moved that they implored the cadre in charge to permit me to give him a hat. The cadre instead ordered others to carry my son to the shade. By that time he had collapsed. He had a very deep cut on his toes. I and my older son helped the younger one to lie down in a house nearby. Everyone rushed in to help. A nurse said, "The shop next door sells some alcohol; it is necessary to get some to clean his wound."

Late that afternoon, all the passengers of the boat were moved to the district prison without exception: women and children went along too. The prison actually consisted of two buffalo stables, one for the men, and the other for the women and children, very uncomfortable because of the rain and the mosquitoes. . . .

For two months we remained in that prison. My wife visited us not only to provide us with rice, but to figure out how to get us released. The prison was much more crowded than the reeducation camps, and we had to lie in mud. Around fifty men were put in a room that measured five by eighteen meters. Since there was not enough room to lie down, we built a small platform. The room for women and children was slightly larger, but also small.

We did not have enough mosquito nets. No work was required of us, and those with money could manage to get food from the outside. Otherwise the inmates did not have enough food. They received only some rice and salt, along with dirty canal water, which people used for cooking, bathing, and going to the latrine.

Although the Chinese organizer of our escape had fled, the Public Security Agent whom he had bribed to allow us to escape had been caught. He was a very rich man, but he was also in jail. My wife and other women went to this man's house and threatened to denounce his wife. Fearing this, that woman bribed officials to get me released. It took two months. My wounded son, who looked like he was eighteen years old, told officials he was a student, and they released him. I told officials that I was a photographer and so they released me. There was no trial. My oldest son remained in jail for another three months. Early one morning, he escaped. He had been in Con Dao prison for five months, now in Ca Mau prison for three months. With this ended my first attempt to escape. In all, I made six attempts before I finally succeeded.

On my third attempt, I was caught but released soon afterwards. When I was caught on my fourth try, I was put in jail in Bien Hoa for nine months. That was truly horrible, a living *nightmare*. The Bien Hoa facility is one of no less than thirty reeducation camps and prisons that are found in Dong Nai Province.

Bien Hoa prison, also known as Reeducation Camp Number Five, formerly was for female prisoners under the Republic of Vietnam. It was built with money from the United States Agency for International Development (USAID) and is located on the outskirts of Bien Hoa city. The concrete flat roof of the wards is low, roughly seven feet high inside. Each ward is about seven by twenty-one meters in size; originally it was furnished with twenty-five to thirty wooden beds for inmates. Windows and doors were covered with iron bars, and the doors were left unlocked except at night. The female inmates were allowed to walk around the inside yard of the quadrangle jail.

Because of the great increase of prisoners in the new Communist regime, the jail housed both males and females along with their children. Some wards contained eighty to 100 political detainees and criminals. I was put in such a room. No longer were there beds; everyone had to sleep on the concrete floor in three rows, like sardines in a can.

Never in all of my prison experiences have I experienced such a terrible detention as in the Bien Hoa jail. The crowding into small rooms and the oppressive heat from the low ceilings and from the animal heat of the inmates made this a suffocating horror, especially at night. Between 6:00 p.m. and 7:00 a.m. the iron doors were shut, and we were locked in that narrow space. The iron door had no opening, no bars. For thirteen hours we would lie low on the floor; we breathed not oxygen, but carbon dioxide exhaled from the inmates lying next to us, much too close to us, and we became intoxicated! And we also got the worst scabies! Everybody busied himself with thinking about the barred door, thinking about how to save a place to get some fresh air when we heard the clanking of the jailer's bundle of keys as he fumbled to find the appropriate key to this double-locked ward.

In my early days in the prison, I mistook the jailer's behavior for contempt or even fear of the prisoners. Every morning, the jailer would swiftly put himself behind the door when he opened it. Later I realized that he hid himself there to avoid the blow of hot, suffocating human stench which was thrown out with the opening of the door. The low concrete roof absorbed the heat of the sun during the day and discharged it at night, along with the heat emanating from 100 human bodies. During the summer days in this tropical country, the inmates were confined in a virtual gas chamber.

Because of the shortage of food, the feeding of inmates was the worst possible: rice of lower quality and, when that ran out, dried corn. These were served with a little salted vegetable soup. With this sort of food and in these living conditions, inmates were kept alive at the lowest rate, well below cattle and pets. To spare the administration the feeding of the inmates, the officials authorized the families of the prisoners to visit them and bring them food once or twice a month depending on their detention status. Those who were pending release and were eligible to do daily labor could receive two visits.

For the first few months, I remained in this jail cell permanently without getting out, except for interrogation. Officials would call to ask me my identification and then to discuss the fact of my being caught on another of my boat escape attempts. In fact, my elder son, now in Canada, had taken a different route to get to the same boat. He had succeeded while I had failed and been sent to jail, again with no trial. For those who try to flee the country, there is no trial, just jail.

I feared that I was not safe in the jail. Whenever I heard the iron door of the jail cell creak open I felt sick; I shuddered with fear. A newcomer, a captured boat person sent to jail, might be pushed into the cell, recognize my true identity, and denounce me to the Communists. The officials had no idea who I was.

I had given them a false identity. They did not know that I was an ex-reeducation camp prisoner who had evaded reporting weekly to the PSA office. So on top of all the horrors of the cell, I was constantly threatened by the fear of being discovered and also the nagging mental doubt that this time my wife could do nothing to liberate me.

In this prison, we were jailed along with many kinds of detainees. Most of them were criminals: murderers, robbers, rapists, and delinquents. This added to our misery, for the criminals would threaten us for food, money, tobacco, and clothes. We feared they would use force; also, they knew the Communist cadres better than we did, and they had a good relationship with them. We feared that the criminals would denounce us falsely any time that they liked. Our best policy was to be modest and to comply to their will; we gave them what they demanded. The next largest group was boat people. Finally, there was a small group of political prisoners. At its highest point, the Bien Hoa prison held some 1,500 detainees. These included twenty Catholic priests and ten Buddhist monks, most of them captured boat persons.

The prisoner who had been detained longest in a cell was Le Ba Dung, a Jesuit priest. After 1975, Brother Dung found no more reason to stay under the Communist regime, so late in that year, he attempted to escape by boat from Vung Tau. He was caught carrying a briefcase full of documents that, he told me, were politically unfavorable for the new regime. Because of that, he had been accused of being a CIA agent and was sent to the Bien Hoa jail.

Most of the boat people were released after a short time, no more than one year. The exceptions were the Buddhist monks and the Catholic priests. In particular, priests do not have a chance to be released once they are detained because they are considered by the Marxist-Leninist regime to be like a narcotic poison.

Brother Dung had been in jail since 1975. For five years he was kept in solitary confinement with one of his legs shackled. For five years he was unable to stand up; he could only sit or lie down on a wooden board. He defecated and urinated in a container which another inmate would clean out every day under the supervision of a guard. Twice a day a half-ration of food was shoved through a small hole. Family supplies and visits were completely forbidden. Under these conditions, Brother Dung lost any notion of time. Imprisonment like this was reserved for those indefinite-term prisoners condemned for high treason, but without a trial or verdict. Most of these prisoners were Catholic priests.

In 1980, Brother Dung became seriously ill, so he was taken to the prison dispensary, and later transferred to Ward Number Seven, where I met him. At that time, he was unable to walk, partly because of his illness and partly because of his long confinement in chains. The years of isolation without speaking to anyone also changed his mentality. He was like a savage restive to society, and he was considered the principal troublemaker of the ward. He was against the other old Catholic priest who was in Ward Number Seven. I was the only one with whom he had sympathy. Even so, I tried to avoid talking with the priests too long or frequently lest informers in the ward take me for a camouflaged priest. Later I found that Brother Dung was released in 1982 as part of an amnesty.

In the fourth month, I was transferred to Ward Number One. This is a ward for inmates pending release. There I was ordered to sweep the rectangular yards of this section of the jail twice a day and to cook extra private food for all the inmates of that ward. Because of this job, I was able to go around and see many places and people in the prison. This was interesting indeed, but it also was a great threat for me; now there were more inmates in other cells who might recognize me from my former social life and denounce me unintentionally.

In fact, one person did recognize me. He tried to remind me where we had met. I said falsely, "Oh yes, I remember you. We met in prison once before!" Anyway it was mandatory that I do this work, so the only way to minimize the danger was to keep my eyes hidden most of the time under a traditional conical palm-leaf hat used by countryside farmers. On the hat I painted a half-serious, half-joking note in large characters, "Silent Mouth," and I kept dumb to most of the questions of the inmates. In South Vietnam, there is a sect of Buddhist monks who beg for food but never respond to comments or questions. So people recognized my behavior.

My wife again tried to get in touch with the right people to bribe them. After nine months she succeeded, and I was released on the eve of Christmas. However there was no way I could go home. For over a year, I had been delinquent in reporting weekly to the PSA office, so I had to remain in hiding. I would remain for a few days or weeks at the house of a friend, then move on to the house of another, all the time looking for an opportunity to escape once more.

The Vietnamese Gulag
Doan Van Toai and David Chanoff

DOAN VAN TOAI *(1945–) was a student leader and journalist in South Vietnam and critic of the anticommunist government before the Communist takeover; he was arrested as a procommunist. Nevertheless, he was once more arrested shortly after the Communist victory in 1975. At first it appeared to be a case of mistaken identity, but the matter was never clarified. Like many other prisoners in Communist states—including those supportive of the system—he never understood the reasons for his arrest. He was repeatedly assured that the reasons would be clarified and was advised to wait "for the judgment of the Revolution." Like those in Chinese prisons, he too was told that everything "depends on your sincerity." And like other political prisoners in Communist states, he too had to write and rewrite his autobiography.*

He spent close to three years in prison and prison camps, and in his discharge papers the reasons for both his arrest and release were left blank. He was allowed to leave for France in 1978, and in 1979 he moved to the U.S., where he continued to be an advocate for civil rights in Vietnam. He is the author or coauthor of several other books dealing with the Vietnam War.

In recent years he has served as director of a program of international development in Asia.

DAVID CHANOFF *(1943–) holds a Ph.D. in English and American literature from Brandeis University. He is the coauthor of thirteen books, five of them concerned with topics related to Vietnam. He has also published numerous articles in the* New York Times Magazine, Washington Post, Washington Quarterly, New Republic, *and the* American Journal of Education. *He has taught at various*

From Doan Van Toai and David Chanoff, The Vietnamese Gulag *(New York: Simon and Schuster, 1986). Reprinted by permission of the authors.*

universities in the Boston area, most recently in the anthropology department at Tufts University.

. . . . .

On the evening of June 22, 1975, less than two months after the fall of South Vietnam, there is a concert in Ho Chi Minh City, formerly known as Saigon.

Vietnam's National Orchestra has come here from Hanoi. At 8:00 p.m. it will perform at the Grand Theater—formerly the home of South Vietnam's parliament. For the past week it's been impossible to get tickets. Ages have passed since the southern capital has heard a classical concert played by a real symphony orchestra. I'm thirty years old, and I've never heard anything but third-rate bands featuring electric guitars and syrupy songs with the most astonishingly affected lyrics. American ersatz. As for traditional Vietnamese music, it's been killed off by the war.

But that evening I'm at the Grand Theater, thanks to some Communist party friends who are repaying a favor. The Vietnamese National Orchestra isn't the Berlin Philharmonic. But for the first time I am enjoying a true professional orchestra, over a hundred musicians, live. I'm amazed. So this is one of the luxuries peace has to offer, this peace I have never known.

The orchestra has just finished a Beethoven concerto. I am in heaven. The master of ceremonies now announces that a ballet performance will follow. That's when I notice the four *Bo Dois* (soldiers) in their green uniforms at the end of my row.

One by one they are taking away the people sitting between me and the aisle, and talking to them. The *Bo Dois* are obviously looking for someone. When my turn comes, one of the soldiers leads me to the lobby. I'm curious about what they want, but calm. In the lobby there are maybe ten more soldiers, all from the North, to judge by their accents. One of them, very young, eighteen at the most, shouts at me, clipping his words, "Is your name Toai?"

"Yes," I say. I'm about to add "why?" but before I can, he takes a step forward and slaps me. Then one of the others holds him back, and I'm quickly surrounded and hustled up the stairs toward the manager's office on the second floor. As I'm being rushed along, struggling to keep my balance, I remember when I raced up these same stairs five years ago at the head of several hundred university students—members of the Saigon Student Union. We were about to take over the National Assembly building, to demand that a number of our imprisoned comrades be freed. That episode had earned me a stay in President Thieu's jails.

The Communist party and the NLF[1] certainly know all about my antiwar activities as a student leader. They know that even though I had never formally joined either one of them, I was always their ally. What could they possibly want with me now?

In the manager's office I'm forced to stand in front of a North Vietnamese

Army lieutenant. While *Bo Dois* on both sides pin my arms, the lieutenant stares at me and asks, "Are you Ngo Vuong Toai?"

I suddenly understand. Now I know what's wrong. About ten years ago, Ngo Vuong Toai was president of a small anti-Communist student organization that was a front for the Thieu government, and probably the Americans as well. It was commonly known that the NLF had condemned him to death, and in 1966 they tried to assassinate him. Toai had been wounded in the stomach and had barely survived. Afterward he left his little group and went to work directly for the government, in the well-guarded offices of the Ministry of Information.

Obviously there's been a misunderstanding; I'm being mistaken for this other Toai.[2] "No," I tell the lieutenant. "I'm not Ngo Vuong Toai. I don't have anything to do with him. I'm Doan Van Toai. I was vice-president of the student union. I fought against the puppets. I worked for the Front. I've been in jail for it. Now I'm working with the PRG Finance Committee.[3] You can verify everything with Colonel Nguyen Ngoc Hien and with the Association of Patriotic Intellectuals."

I take a certain pride in listing my titles and credentials. I watch for the effect, waiting for the apology I so richly deserve. The lieutenant is obviously embarrassed. He's been told to arrest a certain Toai, who was supposed to be at the concert. Apparently he has the wrong man.

But while I watch him trying to decide what to do, something else occurs to me. How did I happen to be in the very row he was told to search? Is this really just a simple misunderstanding? Somebody who knew I was at the concert has to be involved. What are the chances that the *Bo Dois* would know exactly where to find me, yet mistake me for Ngo Vuong Toai? Not so good, I think.

Meanwhile, as far as the lieutenant is concerned, my person matches all too well the individual described in his orders. Or at least I'm not so bad a fit as to be dismissed out of hand. So he reacts as any policeman would. "Not the right Toai? Maybe so, maybe not. Take him in and we'll check it out."

Outside the theater, I'm ordered to climb on the back of a Honda motorcycle, and accompanied by two other Hondas, we speed off to the police headquarters on Tran Hung Dao Boulevard. I haven't given them a bit of trouble. Although I'm beginning to have some doubts about what's really happening, I'm still convinced it's a misunderstanding that I'll be able to clear up quickly. Several years earlier I had read the first volume of Alexander Solzhenitsyn's *Gulag Archipelago.* I vividly remember chapter two, entitled "Arrest." Even in the Vietnamese translation, the writing was dazzling, memorable—though I had dismissed the substance of the book as propaganda. But now the words come back to me, the thoughts of someone who's just been arrested. "Who, me? What for?" "It's a mistake, they'll clear it up." But that was in Russia. Who knows whether things like that really go on there? Anyway, this is Vietnam, the new Vietnam.

At police headquarters I wait in the hallway, guarded by three *Bo Dois*. I listen as the lieutenant discusses my case with the duty officer. The lieutenant is trying to unload this potential embarrassment on the officer. This may not be the Toai he was told to arrest, but he's not sure. "We'd better keep him." But the duty officer doesn't want any trouble, doesn't want to be saddled with the responsibility of arresting the wrong person—someone who might be able to cause problems. But the lieutenant says, "Look, you'll have even more problems if you don't lock him up and he turns out to be the right guy."

The discussion goes on forever, until both men suddenly realize it's already eleven o'clock. That puts an end to it. At this hour there's no way anybody can disturb a higher-ranking officer to resolve the matter. Better to lock up the prisoner until tomorrow, when they can ask someone what to do.

So I'm pushed up to the desk.

"You are Doan Van Toai?"

"Yes, Doan Van Toai! Not Ngo Vuong Toai, the one you were supposed to arrest. I protest this treatment. I demand. . . ."

The duty officer cuts me off with a wave of his hand and says loudly, "We'll clear it all up in the morning. Right now, you're under arrest."

"Under arrest!" Now I'm beginning to get excited, raising my voice. "That doesn't make any sense. I'm not Ngo Vuong Toai. I never collaborated with the puppets. I was a student opposition leader. I spent time in jail. Can't you understand that? This treatment is unacceptable!" By now I'm shouting. "How can you arrest me? What am I supposed to have done?"

The officer has been drumming his fingers on the desk, not looking at me. Now he raises his eyes and says in a formal tone, "You are accused of suspicious acts."

"Me? Suspicious acts? What suspicious acts? Who has denounced me? I demand to see the liar who denounced me!"

Already I know I don't have a chance. Any more discussion with this low-level nonentity is useless. It doesn't make any difference to him that he might be jailing an innocent man. I'll have to explain myself to somebody else, somebody in charge. Meanwhile, this individual is reciting a catechism to me.

"If the revolution decides to arrest someone, it has its reasons. If a mistake is made, that will be acknowledged. Be patient and wait for the revolution's judgment. While you wait, you'd better keep your voice down."

I start to protest again, but my heart's not in it. This representative of the revolution has decided I should be locked up. So I'll be locked up. If I keep shouting, they'll beat me. That's pretty clear.

A *Bo Doi* removes my belt and searches my pockets, taking my wallet. It's ten minutes before midnight, according to my watch, which I glance at as the *Bo Doi* pulls it over my wrist. Then two of them push me down a hallway with doors on each side, cell doors. The air is heavy, stale with the smell of unwashed bodies. Snoring comes from behind the doors. I have the feeling that the place is full. . . .

. . . . .

Solitary confinement. No letters, no books, no pen or paper. Three paces up, three paces back. Each day becomes a slow-motion nightmare that has to be lived to its end. But the end brings no relief. Day and night merge.

Like prisoners the world over I count the days, scratching a line each morning on the back wall near the corner. I force myself to keep up the memory exercise, but it becomes an act of will. My yoga is going downhill too. I tire quickly. It's the food, I think: two bowls of rice a day, no vegetables, no meat. I have less and less energy, and find myself growing apathetic.

But my mind is wonderfully focused anyway, preoccupied with the same questions: "Why have they put me here? When are they going to question me?" I develop a monomaniacal urge to explain myself, going over and over the phrases I will use, honing them until I think I've found the exact wording that will be most effective, then changing it as yet a more felicitous expression or tone occurs to me. I imagine a scene with a high-ranking prison official and try to divine if he will be sympathetic or cold as I sit opposite him, cogently describing my meritorious life—making it easy for him to acknowledge the mistake that's been made. "If a mistake has been made, the revolution will acknowledge it." Isn't that how the duty officer put it before they locked me up?

Every time I hear a *Bo Doi* in the hall I ask to speak to someone in charge. But they always have the same answer: "Be patient. You're not the only one. The officials are very busy."

"How busy can they be?" I think to myself. "How many souls do they have dying by inches in their cells, waiting for a turn?" I've just scratched the forty-fifth nick on my wall calendar. Have they had forty-five days' worth of prisoners to talk to before me?

Yoga still helps me fall asleep, but it's becoming increasingly difficult. I begin to feel a despair I have never experienced before, a choking sensation in my upper chest and throat.

Then, on the morning of the forty-sixth day, there's a knock on the door and the peephole opens.

"Number five! What is your name?"

"Doan Van Toai."

"Doan Van Toai, prepare yourself to go to work!"

Work is the Tran Hung Dao term for interrogation. I can't believe it. Suddenly the *Bo Doi* looking in through the peephole shouts: "*My nguy* [American puppet]! You're naked! What do you mean by that? Are you a dog?"

The fact is that I have only the shirt and pants I was arrested in. To keep them clean I sleep naked. And sometimes I don't bother to put them on at all.

It's not exactly as if I'm on display to the world in here. But the idea of a naked prisoner has upset the *Bo Doi*'s sense of propriety. He's furious at this breach of good taste.

"Get dressed! Now!" he hisses.

I do, as fast as I can. Then the door opens, and the *Bo Doi* pushes me roughly down the hall. I begin to sway, dizzy from walking straight ahead for more than three paces.

An iron door swings open. We go left, then left again, stopping in front of an office door, which the *Bo Doi* opens gently, announcing, "Prisoner Toai."

"Bring him in," says a voice.

"Attention!" shouts the *Bo Doi*, turning toward me. Then, looking important, he signals me to go in.

As I step into the office I feel a wave of relief. The scene I've been imagining for a month and a half is about to take place. Finally I'm with someone I can talk to, someone who will tell me I don't have to stay here anymore.

This someone is sitting behind a desk at the back of the room, thumbing through a sheaf of papers. I greet him respectfully: *"Kinh thua Bac."* Literally, this means, "I salute you, Uncle." There's no family relationship implied, only polite deference. But my greeting elicits no response, just a continued leafing through the papers—my file, I suppose. I can see it's quite substantial already. Then, without raising his eyes from the file, the *can bo* tells me to sit down, indicating the chair seven or eight feet in front of his desk.

I sit. Several minutes go by, the silence broken only by the shuffling of papers. At last the *can bo* raises his head and smiles at me. He's about fifty years old, with a pleasant, friendly face.

"How are you?" he asks solicitously. "Are you sleeping well? Is your appetite all right?"

I feel almost as if I'm in a doctor's office. I hear myself say, "My appetite's all right, *bac* [uncle]. But there's not enough food." Then I catch myself. My appetite's hardly the issue I want to discuss. Still respectful, I say, *"Bac,* I'd like to know why I'm here! I haven't..."

With a quick gesture, the *can bo* cuts off the complaint that is starting to boil up inside me.

"You must understand, prisoners eat the same food we do. Our country is poor... you know that. Good. Now, are you ready to answer my questions?"

"Ready? *Bac,* I've been ready for forty-six days! Every time I could, I've asked to speak with someone, to prove that..."

Again I'm cut off.

"Perfect! You must answer honestly all the questions I'm going to ask. One of these days you will be released. I'm absolutely sure of that. But it all depends on you, on your sincerity. The revolution is lenient with those who recognize their mistakes. But we are harsh with those who are obstinate and lie to us."

I restrain myself from jumping up and attacking him. Instead, in the most measured terms I'm capable of I express my indignation.

"What mistakes? My father was a teacher in the underground. I organized demonstrations against Diem when I was in high school. I was one of the student leaders against Thieu. I even went to jail for it. I didn't break any laws after liberation. What mistakes are you talking about?"

Again the hand rises, signaling me to be silent. I'm at this smiling *can bo*'s mercy. I shut up. All patience, all gentleness, he explains that he is acquainted with some of my activities against the old regime. But "certain points" have to be clarified.

"Which points?" I ask.

He smiles. "What's important here is that you tell me everything, truthfully. I understand you were born in Cai Von. . . ."

· · · · ·

The door is set into a blind wall. Above it is a red signboard. In bright yellow letters on this signboard are the words *Khong Gi Quy Hon Duc Lap Tu Do* (Nothing Is More Precious Than Independence and Liberty). Of all the slogans Ho Chi Minh used to exhort his people, this is the most famous. So embedded are these words in the nation's subconscious that signs like this are invisible. Perhaps that is why they have been chosen to mark the entrances of all liberated Vietnam's prisons and reeducation camps. Or perhaps some high official with a taste for irony ordered it. Having read that the Nazis marked their death camps "*Arbeit Macht Frei*," he started looking around for some Vietnamese equivalent—and there it was: "*Khong Gi Quy Hon Duc Lap Tu Do.*"

Until 1975, few Saigonese had ever heard of Le Van Duyet Prison, even though it had been sitting right there in the pleasant Giadinh suburb for thirty years. The reason was that Le Van Duyet was small potatoes. Even at the height of the Thieu repression, it had sheltered only some two hundred souls. Chi Hoa, Saigon's central prison, sometimes bulged with as many as eight thousand. If some relative or colleague disappeared, you went to Chi Hoa to search, not to some place like Le Van Duyet.

When I entered Le Van Duyet on September 6, 1975, two thousand prisoners—ten times the former number—inhabited its cells. (You could not say they "lived" in them.) After I had been there for a while, my job enabled me to count them. At the same date, Chi Hoa housed forty thousand—only five times the previous high.

Underneath the red-and-yellow sign two sentries lolled. Otherwise there was nothing to set Le Van Duyet off from the neighborhood bustle. On one side the prison shared a wall with the Ho Ngoc Can High School. On the other it abutted Giadinh's City Hall. Each day, directly in front of the prison door the Chi Lang Boulevard market came alive with the haggling of vendors and housewives. Across the boulevard stood the Le Van Duyet memorial, erected to honor the nineteenth-century Vietnamese hero whom the prison commemorated. Legend insisted that Le Van Duyet's bravery was such that upon seeing him tigers would flee for their lives. By the old regime's last years, the Giadinh temple built in the hero's honor had become the center of a cult. Officers' wives would go there to prostrate themselves and pray for their husbands' protection or promotion. Newly engaged couples would swear fidelity under the hero's aegis. ("If you betray me, may Duyet kill you.")

Collective cell number two, which I share with my friend Nguyen Van Hien and sixty others, is located in what is now called Zone A. In former times Zone A was Le Van Duyet's only cellblock. It contains nine collective cells and ten individual cells. The collective cells hold approximately sixty prisoners each. In what had originally been Le Van Duyet's large courtyard, the new regime has erected two new cellblocks, Zones B and C. Zone B contains five collective and twenty individual cells; Zone C, sixteen collective and fifty individual. With only the remnants of a courtyard, there's no place for prisoners to walk or exercise. Life in Le Van Duyet is a permanent lockup. In the twenty-two months I will spend here, various jobs and tasks get me out of my cell from time to time. Other prisoners are not so fortunate.

A large number of Le Van Duyet's inmates are former Communists or Front members who went over to the Thieu side under the *Chieu Hoi* (Open Arms) program. The old regime had announced that over 250,000 guerrillas turned themselves in during the years following the Tet defeat. Captured, disillusioned, or just sick to death of fighting, they had responded to Saigon's standing offer of amnesty and resettlement. After April 30, those who hadn't left the country faced an especially grim future. In the rush of events since liberation I hadn't thought much about the fate of these *hoi chanh* (ralliers). Now I was sharing it.

Nguyen Dich Nha, cell two's leader, was a *hoi chanh*. Ten years before he had been captured during a commando raid against an American facility in Saigon. First he was condemned to death, then pardoned and sent to Con Son Island—which was scarcely better than death. Unable to deal with the horrors of that place, he saved himself by recanting his allegiance and going over to the government. After his release, he had married and opened a little shop in the capital. Now he is here, among the first to be arrested after Saigon's fall.

Nha has been made head of cell two because he lives in a state of perpetual terror and so is useful to the *Bo Dois*. Not only does he have a guilty conscience about having betrayed the revolution to save his skin, he is also keenly aware of the "blood debt" he owes his former comrades, who might collect it at any time. To the other prisoners he is irritable and nasty. In front of the *Bo Dois* (to whom he tells everything) he trembles obsequiously. Both groups despise him.

As in all the cells, number two's prisoners are divided into groups of between ten and fifteen individuals. Each of these is called a *to*, and each *to* chooses its own representative. The representative is responsible for everything that happens among the *to*'s members. He watches over their behavior, apportions their food, and represents them to the cell leader, who in turn is the only one authorized to talk to the guards.

The object of this system—and often the result—is to divide the prisoners by creating jealousies, rivalries, and quarrels among the various *tos*. With sixty-two of us jammed together, nothing could be easier. Irritable, tense, and excruciatingly idle, the inmates are ready to fight about nothing, and often do. Inducing arguments over food, water, or sleeping privileges is child's play. In this way solidarity among the cell's prisoners is undercut, and the authority of the head prisoner/informer and the guards is reinforced. The Romans knew the approach as "divide and conquer." In Le Van Duyet it is called "training a dog to bite other dogs."

Among ourselves we often talked about the contrast between prisoners' behavior now and what it had been in earlier times. There were hundreds of examples of how militant prisoners in Thieu's jails had made life hard for their keepers, who often wouldn't even dare enter their cells. One of my *to* comrades, formerly an inmate at Phu Quoc (a prison island near the Cambodian coastline), told me about how his collective cell had literally torn an informer to pieces and hung his remains from the ceiling. The guards had been forced to use vomiting gas to storm the cell and get the body out. In the six months it took before the administration gave up the investigation, not a single prisoner had talked.

Of course I had never received anything like the full treatment in Thieu's prisons, but regardless, I was inclined to think that the new regime's methods were simply smarter than those of the old prison masters. I had gotten a foretaste of one of the favorite ploys back in isolation at Tran Hung Dao, when they threw old Professor Thong into my cell. The full-blown procedure was more elaborate. As a way of gathering information and sowing distrust among the prisoners it was brilliant; you could never even tell whether they were using it or not.

It would start with a piece of information gleaned from a stoolie, something about one of two close friends in the cell. Perhaps the stoolie has overheard some compromising fact that one friend had told the other during one of those endless, intimate talks with which friends filled their days. (With everyone squatting or sitting cheek by jowl, a determined eavesdropper could pick up anything.) Now the *can bo* checks the information against the prisoner's interrogation report, including his one or more autobiographies. If it is truly new and incriminating, say an act against the state that the prisoner had not confessed to, the *can bo* then sits on the information for ten days or two weeks. At the end of that time, he calls the prisoner's friend in for interrogation, discussing with him some entirely different subject. Two days later, the prisoner himself is called, and the *can bo* accuses him of his former crime. ("We know that during May 1975 you spread slanders about the state!") The prisoner wonders how they found out. The only person he's told has been his friend—and now he recalls vividly that two days earlier the friend was here with this very *can bo.*

If the prisoner is not really close to his friend, chances are good he will denounce him on the spot in a desperate attempt to ward off the consequences of his crime. Even if the two have been faithful intimates, a seed of suspicion has been planted. Two days later, a *Bo Doi* will come into the cell and announce loudly that Prisoner X (the friend) should prepare for a visit from his wife. Now the whole cell suspects X has said something he shouldn't have during his recent interrogation, and that this is the payoff. The subject of the ploy is not only sure of that, he is convinced he knows exactly what information his former friend, the Judas, has sold.

But it isn't just the dog-eat-dog techniques that undermine prisoner solidarity and morale. In my own experience, I tell the others, formerly everyone was proud to be a prisoner. We had such contempt for the puppets, and we idealized the revolution. Being arrested then was a badge of honor. Now, no one has any ideals left; how could they? But we can't completely erase the "idea" of the revolution from what is, or what might even yet be. So in spite of ourselves, we wonder if in some way we aren't guilty. Because to acknowledge once and for all the inhumanity of the revolution is to admit that our ideals are as dead as dust and that our past struggles, whatever their purity and courage, were (even as we fought) being compounded with shit by those we honored. No, it's easier to hope in some corner of our minds that maybe we really are guilty.

To the hard-bitten Phu Quoc prisoner there is a more prosaic explanation: isolation. Under Thieu, the prisoners had hope—hope in their comrades, their families, their lawyers perhaps, the opposition, the newspapers, international agencies; hope for negotiations, hope for victory. Maybe most of these hopes were illusory, but they still gave the prisoners something to hold on to, something to nourish the spirit of resistance. "At Phu Quoc I even saw International Red Cross representatives once." He says it softly, with a touch of awe—like a man who has once witnessed a miracle and knows it won't come again. "Of course, they weren't shown everything; but it boosted the hell out of our morale just to know they were around."

Of course he's right. Even the Con Son tiger cages had been discovered by a visiting delegation—of Americans, no less. They created such an international furor that Thieu and his cronies had been forced to exercise some restraint and caution. Now there's no International Red Cross and no world opinion. Our families don't even know where we are, or if we're dead or alive. We are lost men. We have already disappeared from the face of the earth.

"Dai Dollars," one of the cell's bona fide criminals, confirms the Phu Quoc veteran's analysis. "Dai Dollars" is a hardcore thug, a hired killer from Cholon who told us he had been arrested fifteen times during the Thieu years. Each time he had managed to get out, thanks to the protection and bribes of his friends. In those days "Dai Dollars" had had nothing but scorn for the guards, people who were meaningless, or who at worst could always be paid off. The legal system had worked for him. Lawyers and judges could be bought or intimidated by the crime lords who employed him; investigations could get sidetracked, evidence lost, witnesses might refuse to come forward. So when he was inside, he ruled the roost. It was said that he had even strangled one of his cellmates in Chi Hoa.

Whatever he might have done in Thieu's Chi Hoa, "Dai Dollars" with his elaborate tattoos is as meek as a lamb in the new Le Van Duyet. One of his gangster friends, "Nam Heo" (Number Five Swine), had met an untimely end shortly before Hien and I arrived. He had beaten up a "political" who had insulted him, and subsequently had been hauled off to an isolation cell. For two days he screamed out his defiance. On the third day there was silence, and that was the last anybody had seen of him. "Nam Heo's" passing was no great loss to anyone, but it had made "Dai Dollars" thoughtful. With no legal system to exploit, he knew he was as defenseless in this place as the simplest delta peasant boy.

Under cell leader Nha's gimlet stare, the atmosphere in number two is tense and heavy. Nha stays in a corner by himself, observing everyone's activities—not that there's much to observe. We wake up at six in the morning and go to sleep at ten at night. We are not allowed to read, write, or lie down. Napping is prohibited, as is talking in groups. What Nha sees mostly is quiet conversations between individuals and a lot of glazed-over expressions, whose owners have retreated into the worlds of daydream and memory.

The only periods of "relaxation" are mealtimes, when it is permitted to talk freely. So in spite of the constant, gnawing hunger, we make the miserable bowlful of red rice last as long as possible, relishing whatever discussion or entertainment we can provide each other. In this regard, cell two is fortunate to number among its residents Thanh Viet, one of the South's best-known comic actors. Any audience will do for him, even one as motley as this, and his joking and good humor are infectious.

It was his joking that landed him in here in the first place. When the female lead in one of his stage farces was being seduced by a sweet-talking gigolo, Viet had yelled at her, "Don't listen to what he says. Look at what he's doing!" The audience had laughed uproariously. "Don't listen to what they say. Look at what they do" was the single slogan that Nguyen Van Thieu bequeathed to posterity. By "they," of course, the dictator had meant the Communists. At least one theatergoer, however, found Viet's use of the phrase distasteful. Now he was in jail for "spreading counterrevolutionary slogans inspired by American puppets."

My regard for golden-toothed Hien has only deepened. We are together all the time, and with nothing to do but talk, our friendship has flowered into the richest I've ever shared. We have long, soul-to-soul discussions. Hien's natural authority commands the respect of all the prisoners. Even the guards show their deference in little ways. The situation has aggravated the misanthropic Nha into a silent rage. But he doesn't dare attack Hien directly. God only knows what protectors the former official might still have on the outside. So by default I become the object of Nha's ill temper. Any occasion at all will do. If I talk too loudly, I'm admonished; if I stand in the wrong place, I get a reprimand. Despite my irritation, I keep quiet, doing my best to avoid or ignore the cell leader's yelping voice.

One morning toward the end of October, two *Bo Dois* shuffle into the cell bearing stacks of new, green pajamas. For the first time in four months I can change clothes. Since my arrest I have been wearing the same shirt, pants, and underwear, which I wash as often as possible and which are now miserably frayed. Putting on the brand-new prisoner's uniform gives me a distinct physical pleasure. What luxury there is in the feel of new, clean cotton!

For a few minutes number two becomes a giant, packed dressing room as the prisoners strip down and lovingly get into their new outfits, amazed at their luck. In the hallway we can hear *Bo Dois* bustling around and calling out to each other. Several times the door opens and one of them sticks his head in to see how the dressing is getting on and to yell orders about making sure the cell is clean. Also to remind us curtly of the rules: "Everybody in his place! No talking!"

No mistake about it, inspection's in the air. A fever of excitement comes over the cell. Hopes leap.

"What if it's the Red Cross?"

"If it's the Red Cross we'll tell them we're starving!"

"We can't write to our families!"

"Where are our lawyers?"

"Are we going to have trials?"

"If it's the Red Cross, I'm going to tell them everything. The hell with it! What's to lose?"

"Shut up!" screeches Nha, watching anxiously out the partially opened door. "Everybody up!"

The door swings in, the inspectors appear. Shit . . . they're all Vietnamese. For a moment a barely audible groan ripples the air.

"Attention!" Nha shouts. "Cell number two, sixty-two men present!" We straighten our shoulders in a military parody, sticking out our shrunken chests. Worse than monkeys in a zoo, I think. At least monkeys could show them their asses!

The head inspector is Tu Tuan, the prison warden. He's wearing a uniform with four stars underlined with double gold bars, showing he's a colonel in the North Vietnamese Army. Behind him there's another officer and four civilians.

They all squeeze into the cell. Suddenly one of the civilians looks at Hien. "What?" he says, "you here?"

"For five months," Hien replies calmly.

The civilian inspector is visibly shaken, but he recovers quickly. He doesn't ask Hien why he's behind bars—better not get into that. Instead he says, "Do you know your father died?"

The familiarity of the tone says that these two aren't just passing acquaintances.

"I know," answers Hien, his face expressionless.

"Do you want me to write your mother?"

In a low voice, trying to make this exquisitely public conversation as private as possible, Hien says, "She probably knows already. If not, it's better you don't tell her anything."

"All right." The inspector's voice takes on a tone of forced breeziness. "Okay, if you need anything, you'll let me know, huh?"

That's it. A few more moments of looking around, and the door pulls shut behind them. Everyone sits down, silent and depressed. Also a bit awed at the interchange between Hien and the inspector. Hien just folds his hands in his lap and stares down at them. When after a few minutes talk in the cell starts up again, I say, "Hien?"

He looks at me, his wrinkled face showing a kind of bitter satisfaction. "There," he says. "There you have a true *can bo*. No untoward curiosity, no compromising intervention, friend or no friend. But you know, he's one of the most courageous. Some of them wouldn't recognize their own fathers if they met them in prison—especially their own fathers!"

With this, Hien falls silent, losing himself in thought. A bit later he says, "I should know. When I went on inspection tours at Hoa Lo [Hanoi's central prison] I didn't have the slightest doubt that everybody there was guilty. A true revolutionary has to have absolute trust in the party, right?" The gleam is back in his eye. "And the party's infallible, right?" A flash of gold. Hien the ironic, once more in complete control. . . .

· · · · ·

Food, I am coming to see, is a drug. Cut it down sufficiently, and people often react like addicts in withdrawal. Even those with the best backgrounds and training can do irrational things for a handful of rice. In our cell a former minister of the Diem government and dean at Saigon University dishonored himself by trying to steal a spoonful of *nuoc mam* fish sauce from another prisoner. He was thoroughly beaten up for his trouble. Not too long afterward, the engineer Lam Truong Thi was caught taking someone else's share of rice. He too was beaten up, then thrown into isolation by the *Bo Dois* who came to investigate the commotion. There, during the night of July 14, 1976, he committed suicide out of shame, somehow managing to slash his wrists.

Both of these attempts were irrational. Nothing is watched more jealously than the rice, from pail to bowl to mouth. The "apportioner" might use a subtle trick or two to help a friend get a trifle more, but outright stealing is impossible. Only those who are being driven insane by their hunger would even try.

Starvation also leads to the death of Tran Tien Tai, a twenty-five-year-old student. Apparently, the last time we had soup, Tai's good friend, a mathematics professor named Linh, gave Tai his share, and now it is time for Linh to have two portions. But Tai turns a deaf ear to Linh's remonstrations and brings the bowl up toward his mouth. Seeing this, Linh tries to grab it, and in the scuffle Tai's lip is cut. Furious, he throws the bowl at Linh, and the two are at each other's throats.

In the few seconds before their neighbors can intervene, the damage is done. A guard passing the cell hears the brief uproar, and in a minute the door swings open and four *Bo Dois* are standing there pointing their guns at us. Linh and Tai are still enraged, and when one of the *Bo Dois* barks out, "Who started the fight?" they fall to accusing each other. Without trying to determine who is lying, the *Bo Dois* handcuff them both and lead them away.

The next morning a *Bo Doi* comes into the cell and orders us to get dressed; that means putting our green pajamas on over the underpants that are the only clothing most of us ordinarily wear. We are only told to do this prior to one of the rare visits from an official. A little later Lieutenant Ban makes his entrance, accompanied by two armed *Bo Dois*. In his high-pitched, officious voice he proclaims the verdict: "Prisoner Nguyen Van Linh, a reactionary criminal, and Tran Tien Tai, who attempted to leave the country illegally, have violated prison discipline. According to the regulations, the penalty imposed is two months' solitary confinement on one-half food rations. In addition, Tai will receive thirty blows with the cane."

Isolation I know can kill you. But the prospect of thirty blows with the cane makes us all cringe. For this punishment—a rare one—is administered by a specialist in torture by the name of Tu Cao.

This Tu Cao is a tall, lean, horse-faced individual of about fifty who the prisoners think has "the face of a killer." He is said to have been a torturer in the French jails twenty-five years ago. And some of the Le Van Duyet inmates have personally experienced his ministrations as prisoners under Diem and Thieu. Arrested shortly after the Communists entered Saigon, Tu Cao had soon resumed his profession . . . talents such as his do not lie fallow long. Anyone who survives his caning is at best half-alive. Tu Cao boasts of having caned more than two thousand prisoners in the course of his career, and of having killed one hundred of them.

Under the *Bo Dois*' close watch, cell seven's forty-five-plus prisoners line up in the oppressive stillness of the courtyard. Tran Tien Tai is brought out, stripped to his underpants. He is ordered to lie on the ground, face down.

With a vile smirk on his face, Tu Cao checks the flexibility of his instrument, a rattan cane about four feet long and a half inch in diameter. He bends over and feels Tai's shrunken hips and thighs, no doubt to gauge their resistance so he can administer his blows most effectively. Tai is not to be beaten to death.

As Tai feels the touch of Cao's fingers, his eyes widen in fear. He is lying with his right cheek on the ground, staring at us as if in mute appeal. I feel my heart turn to water, but it is forbidden to look away. This lesson is meant for us as much as it is for him.

After an eternity, the *can bo* snaps his wrist in a quick downward movement and says: "Begin!"

Tu Cao raises his arm and strikes, once . . . twice . . . three times. Between each blow he pauses for what must be a half a minute. The anguish in those thirty seconds is palpable. The whole world seems to hold its breath waiting for the next blow.

At the fifth, Tai can't hold it in anymore. As the rattan cracks down onto his upper thigh he screams, "*Troi oi! Chua oi!*"

The *can bo* stretches out his arm toward Tu Cao: "Stop!"

I feel my tensed-up muscles suddenly relax. Around me I am aware that my cellmates are breathing convulsive little sighs of gratitude. The *can bo* is going to be satisfied with five!

Then, in a dead cold voice, he says, "The regulations specify that the prisoner shall not cry out during physical punishment. The first five blows do not count. We'll start over."

I have the feeling my blood is congealing. Thirty-five of those blows, the whistling cane slashing down through the heat, the smack as it cuts into Tai's skin and bones. Tu Cao looks at him and says, "You heard that? No shouting!" Then he begins. "One!" Thirty seconds. "Two!" Thirty seconds. "Three!" Thirty seconds.

Tai has closed his eyes and clenched his jaw tight. Not a sound comes out of him. Every thirty seconds the blows slash down on his buttocks and thighs. I want to scream, "Faster! Faster! Get it over with!" But the animal knows his job. The *can bo* watches, his face impassive, his eyes flicking from one of us to another. Tai seems unconscious. He's probably fainted—so much the better for him.

"Twenty-nine!" "Thirty!"

"Get up!" orders the *can bo.* But Tai remains motionless. A little stream of blood is trickling down his lips into the sand.

The *can bo* raises his voice a pitch: "You refuse to obey?"

Suddenly Tu Cao is down on his knees holding Tai's wrist. Now it's the horse face that shows panic. "It's unbelievable," he stammers. "Unbelievable."

Still holding the limp wrist, he puts his ear next to Tai's nose and mouth. "I think . . . I think he's dead, sir." He seems frozen with fright. He was not supposed to kill this prisoner.

I feel the relief of exhaustion. At least Tai's ordeal is over. After that beating I feel sure he wouldn't have survived more than a day or two in the isolation cell.

Tu Cao has now turned the body over in the dust. He pries Tai's mouth open and stares into it. "Sir," he exclaims to the *can bo*. "He committed suicide! He bit his tongue and swallowed it. That's why his mouth is bloody!"

The *can bo* walks over and squats down while Tu Cao keeps the mouth open. Then he stands up facing us. "Prisoner Tai died voluntarily," he says. "It was not the revolution that killed him. The revolution does not wish to kill, but to reeducate. We do not torture prisoners as the puppets did. If we must punish them, it is like a father punishing a son, to educate him. We do this publicly, as you can see. If Tran Tien Tai is dead, it's because he decided to kill himself, as you all witnessed."

But the *can bo* feels very uncomfortable about this. Shortly after we return to number seven, a *Bo Doi* brings in a prepared statement for the cell leader to sign. "I, Nguyen Hau Nghi, representative of cell seven, am witness to the fact that prisoner Tran Tien Tai committed suicide by swallowing his tongue."

Lost Years: My 1,632 Days in Vietnamese Reeducation Camps

Tran Tri Vu

> *TRAN TI VU (a pseudonym; dates not available) was a lieutenant in the South Vietnamese army and as such was subject to "reeducation" after the North Vietnamese victory in 1975. He estimated the total number of such prisoners at approximately one million; they included, in addition to former military officers, civil servants, "capitalists," and members of the old political parties and religious groups. According to an official statement at the time of his detention, the period of "reeducation" for junior officers and civil servants was supposed to last for seven days; he packed accordingly, but his sentence became four and a half years.*
>
> *As in China, "reeducation" in Vietnam largely consisted of political indoctrination, combined with manual labor, but it was pursued without the same degree of tenaciousness and without the Chinese technique of "struggling."*

. . . . .

Into a rucksack I put those things needed for a seven-day stay[1] at the camp: two pairs of trousers, shirts, a mosquito net, a blanket, a piece of canvas to be used for a sleeping mat, toothpaste, soap, medicines (for colds or dysentery), and money. The money I tucked away very carefully.

When taking leave of my wife and little daughter, I tried to put on a calm appearance. But both my wife and I had the premonition that this departure would be an ill-fated one. Seeing my child babbling away happily, my heart ached at the thought of their uncertain future.

Earlier, before I was due to present myself to the authorities for "reeducation," a *Bo Doi*[2] had come twice to my house and urged me in a soft voice to report in good time.

Before I decided to take the risk, I made careful inquiries into this business of "reporting for reeducation." The information I had gathered was full of contradictions. Some said all servicemen attending previous seven-day reeducation sessions had returned safely home, but that smacked too much of commu-

From Tran Ti Vu, Lost Years: My 1,632 Days in Vietnamese Reeducation Camps, *Indochina Research Monograph 3 (Berkeley, CA: Institute of East Asian Studies, University of California).* © *1988 by The Regents of the University of California. Reprinted by permission.*

nist propaganda. Still, that was what I told my wife to reassure her. One person whose accounts I felt I could trust was Duong Cong Hien—a tricky chap though—who had connections with communist officials in Hanoi. After the fall of South Vietnam, he announced that his family had been awarded a first-class medal posthumously for his father, who had fought and died in the war of resistance against the French. Hien's uncles were all high-ranking cadres in the North. However, he was sincere enough to reveal that reeducation would take quite a few years. "No less than that, I'm afraid," he said.

On the eve of the deadline to report, a communist cadre, followed by a bunch of kids, came to stand in front of my house. With his loudspeaker pointed in our direction, he read the official order. Then he and the kids shouted slogans praising the "clement" policy of the "Revolution" and condemning the stubbornness of those who refused to report for reeducation. For people like me, it was very clear that if we did not report, we would not be left alone.

I was to report to Nguyen Lam school near Cholon.[3] When I arrived, I stopped to read the notices that covered the gatepost, then someone shouted shrilly in a voice that sounded like a child's: "Why don't you go in to report? What are you waiting for?"

Then came a more affable voice; "Come in! We are about to call it a day." This was the voice of a cadre sitting at a table in the center of the schoolyard. Behind him was a group of people sitting on their heels. I approached the cadre. "Name?"

"Tran Tri Vu."

"Rank?"

"Reserve lieutenant."

"'Lieutenant' is enough. Why complicate things with 'reserve'?"

Giggles came from the group of squatting persons followed by a shout from the *Bo Doi* with a child's voice, "What are you fellows laughing at?"

The old cadre, more calmly: "Order, please!" Then, to me, "Branch?"

"Officer seconded to the Education Department."

"Another of those fellows! Don't you know which branch you belong to when you have not been taught to pilot a plane or drive a tank? You are infantry, understand? You're like the others who declared they have been 'seconded' in an attempt to conceal their actual branch. Isn't that so?"

"Oh no! I—"

"Enough! Go and sit there, behind the others."

I joined the squatting group of men who looked at me with mocking smiles. Later on, this "seconded" business caused me to be reprimanded time and again.

We remained squatting until our legs grew numb and until the group grew large enough that the *Bo Doi* decided to move us. The new place was a classroom.

"This is where you stay for the time being," the *Bo Doi* said. "If anybody wants to go out, he has to ask the guard in the corridor; you cannot go out unless you've got his permission. Two persons at the most will be allowed to leave the room at one time. Got it?" Somebody answered yes in a low voice, but the *Bo Doi,* as if vexed, repeated angrily. "Have you understood?" Seeing that he meant business, everybody replied yes in a loud voice. The *Bo Doi* then ordered the group leader, who had been appointed before I arrived, to sit at the door facing the group, as if to watch over us. The *Bo Doi* returned to the schoolyard.

The leader of our group was Pham Van Tuong, a dentist and medical corps lieutenant. We introduced ourselves all around. The man who arrived minutes before me was Nguyen Van Long, a lieutenant in the Rangers. He introduced himself by saying, "I've a lot of 'blood debts' to pay, I'm afraid."

It was then 6:00 p.m., June 26, 1975. The people in the room responded to the situation as their ages and natures dictated. Middle-aged persons remained silent, their hearts heavy with worry; the younger ones seemed not too worried and tried to make fun of the discipline that had just been imposed on them. But the jokes did not make many of us laugh. Long said, "Those child-soldiers have been particularly harsh today."

"You're right," I concurred. "They are very short-tempered."

We were talking in low voices when a *Bo Doi* appeared and spoke through the door before proceeding to another room to repeat his order: "Be ready for dinner. Put your belongings in order. When going out, remain in line and obey the order of the guard."

A van with the words Ai Hue Restaurant painted on its sides was parked in the yard. Someone clapped his hands, and a shout came in reproof: "Don't you fellows know how to keep discipline?"

Someone complained, "How can they joke under the circumstances?"

Long said teasingly, "Oh, come on! Let them have a little fun!"

Later, I was told that the person who had complained was Mr. Cuc, the oldest member of our group. "We have to avoid being insulted," he explained; "that would be a great humiliation for us."

"We have already suffered humiliation," Long countered. "Is there any greater humiliation than losing the war?"

Everybody in the room intervened noisily. "Now, come off it." "Leave him alone."

Long looked at me with a smile, but I shook my head, uneasy at what had happened. As fate would have it, Long, old Mr. Cuc, Tuong, and I were destined to be together for a long time.

Dinner that evening was characteristic of the irony of our situation. The restaurateur was one of the most famous in Cholon. Food was served on expensive china. The waitresses wore the usual shiny black trousers and white Chinese coats embroidered with the name of the restaurant. But the rice was brown rice, and the food consisted of fried pickled cabbage, fat meat cooked with brine, and thin cabbage soup. The only things reminiscent of the restaurant's normal cuisine were the tiny saucers of soy sauce and pickled red pepper. The waitresses told us that the *Bo Doi* had come to their restaurant and asked that meals be prepared for people reporting for reeducation. The *Bo Doi* provided the rice and some money, but the restaurateur still suffered a great loss. Said one of the waitresses with a laugh, "Our boss had to comply for fear of the consequences. After all, we have to support the Revolution, don't we!"

We ate our meal standing around the school tables. As we picked out the husks left in the rice, some tried to joke about the restaurant buying brown rice by mistake.

After the meal, we were brought back to the classroom, and two by two we were allowed to go outside to relieve ourselves. At eight o'clock we were ordered to keep silent and go to sleep, but we continued with our muffled conversation. Those who had come the day before told me to lie down on the floor wherever I liked. Most of us had brought along a large piece of cloth to serve as a blanket. Half of it was now used as a mat, the other half as a blanket and a protection against mosquitoes. A few had managed to hang their mosquito nets. By midnight, the whole room was quiet except for some snoring. I could not sleep; hundreds of questions kept turning around in my head. I felt an unusual need to urinate. I asked to go out and was led outside by a *Bo Doi*. The scene there was extraordinary. The place was crawling with *Bo Dois*; every five meters two of them were standing guard. When I got back to the room, I still could not sleep. It appeared that old Mr. Cuc and I were the only persons still awake in the room. Mr. Cuc was counting beads on his rosary and silently saying his prayers.

Suddenly, hurried footsteps were heard in the corridor. I looked at my watch: 1:00 a.m. A *Bo Doi* came into each room in turn; his voice was not too loud, but it was enough to cause everybody to awaken in alarm, "Everybody get up and prepare for maneuvers."

Long, still not quite awake, shot back, "The war is over. What do we need maneuvers for?"

Nobody paid any attention to him. All were busy putting things into their bags. The corridor outside was full of *Bo Dois*. One of them, paper in hand, entered the room. "Are you people team no. 6? Where's Pham Van Tuong? Get your people out and have them stay in line in the yard. Stand at the position assigned to your team. Hurry up with your preparations!"...

．　．　．　．　．

Then one afternoon we were ordered to get ready to assemble in the yard, giving rise to conjecture and speculation. Some said that a great number of vehicles had arrived at noon; were they to take us back to Saigon? Others told us a *Bo Doi* had revealed that we would be scattered to various places because there were too many here at Trang Lon. A few worried about money that, in violation of the rules, they had managed to give the *Bo Doi* for the purchase of food; if we had to go now, the money would be irretrievably lost. We had to wait until late in the evening before the *Bo Doi* arrived and ordered us to assemble for roll call. To the naïve question of whether we should bring our luggage with us, a childish-looking *Bo Doi* shouted, "What for? Are you mad?"

After we assembled, we had to wait for the other units to arrive. This was the first time the whole D4 was gathered together. At last a *Bo Doi* gave the order. "Everybody prepare to greet the camp leader!"

Only then did we realize that the camp leader was the short fellow who often came to our shed to chat with us. He said his name was Ha. As he was the only fat *Bo Doi*, we nicknamed him Fatty Ha. We sat down on the ground at his instruction; after looking us over, he declared, "I have been too busy organizing things concerning your life here and have not had the opportunity to participate in your activities. Now, my superiors judge that it is time I told you a number of things you ought to know. First, I shall inform you of the regulations governing reeducation; second, I'll be giving you explanations on some of the issues that may be raised; finally, we shall all participate in a constructive working session." He then called out to another *Bo Doi* to ask him to read the regulations; they began "Democratic Republic of Vietnam—Independence, Freedom, Happiness."

As the *Bo Doi* read on, the sound of whispered comments increased. Some observed that the appellation Provisional Government of South Vietnam was not used in the official document. Others drew attention to the presence of more and more *Bo Doi* around us. Suddenly, there was a shout. "Stop! No more reading, please! There's too much disorder!"

Fatty Ha stepped forward and said, "I want to draw your attention to the fact that the regiment's commander will be coming to observe our meeting. Therefore, you must listen attentively, in complete silence. This is very important. Now, comrade, go on with your reading!"

The more we heard, the more silent we became; everything we heard was appalling. Following rules on "clean eating, neat living" came regulations permitting us to write home once a month to "boost the morale of our families," to watch movies (North Vietnamese propaganda films, of course) once every quarter, to have visits by relatives. And if we showed good will and progress in reeducation, we would be allowed to go home soon. We were transfixed with fear. When the *Bo Doi* had finished reading, tumultuous protests and queries rose from our ranks.

"Why did you say that reeducation would last only seven days?"

"You don't wait long to cheat us, do you?"

"Remember! The communiqué [on reeducation] is still there! The ink hasn't dried yet!"

There were shouts from the *Bo Doi*'s side, too. At the same time, they moved to surround us, their rifles pointed in our direction. Two orders followed. "Everybody stand up! Now, sit down, everybody!"

Having given us the order to sit in lines, Fatty Ha again stepped forward to say, "You should learn to keep order at every meeting. From now on, any disorderly conduct shall be severely dealt with!" Then he spoke about the clement policy of the "Revolution" and kept repeating. "Your crimes deserve the death penalty. But the Revolution, out of clemency, has permitted you to be reeducated; after completion of your reeducation you will be sent back to your families."

What we had feared had become reality. The communiqué had been worded in ambiguous terms to lure as many of us as possible into reporting for reeducation. The speech ended with explanatory replies to our queries, for example, no one had said that our reeducation would take only seven days, the communiqué had urged us to bring a seven-day supply of food for the travel, just in case, and so on.

At this point, Fatty Ha burst into laughter. The *Bo Doi* standing behind him guffawed. Within our ranks, somebody swore loudly, and a voice rose. "How clever the Revolution is!"

A *Bo Doi* shouted, "You don't know how to keep quiet, do you?"

As an introduction to the meeting proper, Fatty Ha said, "As you are not yet familiar with the 'revolutionary' way of life, some of you, even after some time in this place, are still careless in your speech and actions, which denotes a real resistance to progress. You are here to be reeducated in order to become progressive socialists, and as such you will be returned to your families, we hope soon."

With these words, which seemed to come right out of a manual, he began a detailed enumeration of the offenses committed by us since our arrival at the camp. Each unit was mentioned in turn in the indictment. When our turn came, we were quite amazed because all the details were true. They included words we had used to make fun of the Revolution and such acts as asking the *Bo Doi* to buy things in town for us and using more water than necessary when cooking rice in order to obtain a thin soup in addition to the cooked rice. Although no names were mentioned, we all knew perfectly well which offense applied to which person among us. In particular, the charge related to some words considered "offensive" applied to the very words I had said to Long only and no one else, "Although the *Bo Doi* are 'revolutionaries,' money has the same effect on them as it has on us." I had told him this when he hesitated to ask the *Bo Doi* to make a purchase for him; I knew they vied with each other to oblige us in order to make some profits out of the dealings.

As he went on, Fatty Ha became more and more violent to the point of uttering threats. "Remember this: The Revolution is clement, but it does not mean the Revolution does not know how to punish as they deserve those of you who are obstinate enough to resort to psychological warfare here. Don't be surprised if later on severe and pitiless measures are taken against the culprits."

Then, in more conciliatory tones, he promised to overlook past offenses if the culprits showed sincere repentance. Concluding this "constructive" session, he told team leaders to look among their members for musical people who would be taught revolutionary songs, which they in turn would teach their companions to sing. "From now on," he said, "when beginning and ending a working session, we shall sing those songs to create an enthusiastic atmosphere that will no doubt bring good results."

The session ended late at night. Although the weather was fine, our hair and shirts were wet from dew. On the way back to our shed, nobody felt like talking; we were all upset, frustrated, and worried to the point of fear. It was now quite certain that our reeducation would take a long time, not seven days, not one month.... We were all the more worried because we had proof that the "eyes and ears" of the Revolution were among us. Most of us were exposed for offenses we had committed. As for me, I was convinced that Long was the "mole"; no doubt about it!

It had been our habit to gather every night for some talk, but that night, without a word being exchanged, everybody spread his mat and got into his mosquito net. The silence was heavy. I could not sleep. Hundreds of questions, hundreds of thoughts went through my head. Around me, nobody seemed able to sleep. From time to time, someone turned over and sighed deeply. Someone swore angrily; another moaned as if in high fever. I did not expect such reactions after the first session. As far as I was concerned, I had learned an important lesson. From now on, I would constantly be on my guard vis-à-vis my companions; I would not confide my thoughts or joke with anybody. I had not expected Long to be so evil-minded. I thought he was a straightforward young fellow, as youth must be. Who would have suspected he was such a scoundrel! He had introduced himself as someone owing a debt of blood to the Revolution. He insulted the communists and was abusive about communism and very often made fun of the *Bo Doi*. All this had been meant to trap us into revealing ourselves.

The next day I got up early as usual, washed, then had a cigarette while waiting for daylight. But many of my companions arose late. Tuong, our team leader, had to urge them many times to roll down their mosquito nets, put things in order, and clean the place. Some had fever and could not get up. As usual, the *Bo Doi* came to call the roll. Those who were in good health had to stand in line in the courtyard and wait for the *Bo Doi* to finish counting the sick who remained in the shed. It was a day unlike the other days. Everyone looked sullen and worn out; everyone kept a stubborn silence and avoided talking to one another. The atmosphere was heavy. When time came to cook our meal, the kitchen team members called out to each other to go and fetch the daily ration of rice. My companions on the carpentry team and I went to the *Bo Doi's* shack to repair some tables and chairs. Coming across Long, I behaved as if I had not seen him. Mealtime was at 10:00 a.m. Each of us was given his share, which we ate in silence, each absorbed in his own thoughts. Only the young ones, who seemed not to care much, were chatting away in their corner.

Each day, food was supposed to be distributed twice, at 10:00 p.m. and 4:00 p.m., but usually there would be some delay. The camp medical orderly used to make his rounds of the sheds daily to take down the names of the sick and distribute medicine. On this day, he found more people reporting sick than usual, and he revealed that the number of sick people in the other units also had increased considerably. As usual, he gave his patients tablets bearing Chinese characters. A pharmacist among us tasted them and declared the drug was some sort of quinine.

The day dragged on at a snail's pace. Food was distributed later than usual because the work parties came back late. In the evening a *Bo Doi* came for roll call, after which he declared, "You have to have faith in the Revolution. After a period of reeducation you will be sent home. Reeducation cannot begin yet because we still have no suitable place for it. We have to wait until a meeting room is available."

After roll call, each went silently about preparing for bed. As I was not in the habit of going to bed early, I sat fanning myself with a piece of thick paper, hoping for a fresh breeze. Long came to sit beside me. Neither of us spoke. At long last, he said, "Why is everybody so silent tonight? You, who usually are so calm, also seem worried."

"I am not worried. Since coming to this place, we have been taken good care of by the Revolution. So why should I have to worry? By the way, when making your report to the Revolution to acquire merit, don't forget to report truthfully what I am now telling you."

"God! So, you suspect me of having reported on you, don't you? I swear—"

"Don't swear! I sincerely hope the Revolution will release you sooner than the rest of us. But, please, do not be so wicked as to harm other people. The words 'The revolutionaries are as greedy as we are' were those I said to you and only to you. Yet you had the heart to report fully my words."

"Good Lord! You suspect me to be the informer, and I suspect somebody else. I used that phrase when talking to Chiem Van Trung, Ong Tran Thinh, and Vo Tai. When Fatty Ha mentioned it, I knew I had been reported on."

I looked at Long, trying to read his thoughts. I didn't expect him to be that clever. Indeed, he was quick to come to his own defense. It seemed best that I not make an enemy of him. I said, "Fine, if you didn't report on me. Let's drop the subject. However, from now on, don't ever disclose anything to anyone because the 'eyes and ears' of the *Bo Doi* are everywhere. The proof is they know everything."

"Yes, I am really worried. Everybody in the kitchen team suspects everybody else of being a mole. The rice soup affair was first suggested by others; I had nothing to do with it."

Feeling that a long talk with him wouldn't do me any good, I pretended to be sleepy and retreated to my bed. Beside me, old Mr. Cuc was saying his prayers, his voice lower than usual....

. . . . .

Each day while we worked at clearing the camp, a few of us would be detailed to look for metal sheets to be used in erecting a hall where reeducation sessions would take place. Preparations for reeducation made everybody glad because they renewed our hope of being allowed to return home at the completion of the "course."

As we waited impatiently for reeducation to begin, life became harsher, especially where our daily fare was concerned. We had only salt to eat with rice; fish was distributed on rare occasions and in negligible quantities. After a short time at the Long Khanh camp, everybody had become all skin and bones. One day I came across Chiem Van Tuong as he was sawing the end off an ampule of "calcium corbiere" solution. Only after much urging on my part did he disclose that he had asked the male nurse at the infirmary to buy tonic for him. The next day, I got permission to go to the infirmary with Tuong; the result was very satisfactory. I gave the nurse some money for which I could obtain any tonic I wanted. In addition, I asked him to buy some sugar for me, if that was possible. I stressed that it did not matter if the price was high, provided he could get the sugar.

The following day, I put on a loose shirt to go to the infirmary. The nurse said, as he handed me a small parcel, "I have used up the money you gave me. Take care when taking this back; we'll be in big trouble if you don't!" I went back to our shed, bending my body as if I was suffering from stomach pains and clutching the package hidden inside my shirt. I thrust the parcel deep inside my rucksack and only opened it when nobody was around. It contained a box of calcium solution and twenty-seven tablets of brown sugar, weighing approximately one kilogram.

The sugar looked dirty but when I put it in my mouth, it tasted oh, so delicious! I had never suspected that sugar could be so succulent, so refreshing! From that day on, at each meal. I surreptitiously took out a half-tablet of sugar, which I ate with rice. My body became much stronger. From time to time, my diet was enriched with a chunk of roasted snake. So, I had sugar and I had meat! Consequently, I was able to keep my spirits up better than most of my companions. In particular, I was one of only six detainees not infected with scabies out of a total of sixty-two. In the whole camp, over 90 percent of the inmates were estimated to be infected.

The scabies situation became worse and worse. There were moments when I thought that some of my companions had contracted leprosy because they had sores all over their bodies, oozing smelly pus that caused their clothes to stick to their skin. Whenever they took their clothes off, blood and bits of skin came off in various places, and it was very painful. We had to ask some men to take care of the most serious cases and do such chores as draw water from the well and boil salted water for them to wash their bodies. They could not do these things themselves, for their hands were covered with suppurating sores. Besides, we did not want them to use the well or wash themselves near it for fear of contaminating the water, which, among other things, was used for cooking.

Things got even worse when the nurse's purchasing of medicine and other goods in the local market was discovered. At first, the number of people involved was small, and the transaction was limited to the purchase of medicine. Perhaps the experience some of the *Bo Doi* had gained at Trang Lon caused discipline at this camp to be much more stringent. Each time we tried to enter into conversation with a *Bo Doi*, we got answers that smacked of propaganda, one identical to another. The case of the nurse was an exception, and it constituted our only way to communicate with the outside world. But gradually, both we and the nurse became careless and the transactions too conspicuous. Finally, he was transferred to another unit and was said to have been subjected to disciplinary measures.

Actually, the action taken against the nurse originated from a rivalry between factions of the *Bo Doi* themselves. Our battalion—coded D4—had three individuals addressed as commanders. At first, we were amazed at the command structure of the *Bo Doi*'s armed forces and were unable to understand why there should be that many commanders in one unit. Later, it was explained that this was because of the fixed division of duties among the three. The political commander, with the rank of commissar, represented the Party; the military and administrative head was called the executive commander; and the supply and distribution of food and other necessities fell under the responsibility of the logistics commander. The military commander of D4 was a Southerner named Hung; the political commissar, Sau, was also from the South; the logistics commander, who was also in charge of our reeducation, was a Northerner.

While at work clearing the camp or doing various chores, we usually witnessed instances of rivalry between the Northerners and Southerners. For instance, the Northern commander would change orders that the other two had given us. When Commander Sau instructed us to clear an area to widen a pathway, the Northerner told us to hoe up the place to plant sweet potatoes instead; sometimes, while we were working under Commander Hung's order, we would suddenly be told by the Northern commander to stop work and follow him to do something else. If we ventured to remind him of Hung's order, the reply would be, "Forget it! Just follow me!" Hung, on hearing our explanation for not doing our assigned work, would shake his head but show no other reaction.

One day, when the nurse—a Northerner—was in the midst of selling medicines and other goods to us, one of the Southern commanders, as if just passing by, entered the infirmary and caught him in the act. The next day, the nurse did not show up and an instruction was issued for those of us who had given money to him to inform the camp administration and get a refund. Quite a few men who had given money to the nurse, and even letters for him to stamp and post in town, became so fearful of being discovered that they lost sleep and appetite.

From then on, we were deprived of almost everything. From time to time, some vegetables or sea fish were distributed, but the distribution was irregular and the quantities minimal. Besides, those with scabies were afraid of eating sea fish. As for me, I still had a few packets of instant noodles left; these I ground into powder, using an empty bottle, and ate as a substitute for salted ground sesame. My provision of sugar, though used sparingly, was finally exhausted, and I chided myself for not having saved some in anticipation of sickness. Some of the men craved sugar so much that they plucked the stems of dried maize and chewed them because their sweet taste was vaguely similar to sugar cane.

Each day, I was detailed to search for usable metal sheets to cover the roof of a big building, probably a former meeting hall. But metal sheets were hard to find, and the work dragged on endlessly. The 1975 rainy season had arrived, and only a quarter of the roof was covered. The majority of the inmates worked at hoeing a plot of land to plant peanuts, but their progress was slow. Most of them had never used a hoe before, and with their bodies weakened by scabies and malnutrition and their morale low, they very easily succumbed to fatigue. Some developed fevers after only a few days of this work. I had played tennis in my early youth and I seemed to have more bodily strength than most of my companions. Besides, roofing the meeting hall required less physical effort than hoeing the ground.

A fellow in my team named Binh was a mechanical wizard; he first tried his hand at turning metal sheets into water pails. Later the *Bo Doi* asked him to make suitcases for them. The suitcases he turned out were very solid and pretty, but quite heavy; an empty one would weight as much as seven or eight kilos. Binh suggested using aluminum sheets instead, and, as a result, I was instructed by the study monitors to search for aluminum sheets, which were even harder to find than metal ones.

Despite the strict discipline at the camp, which forbade transactions between the *Bo Doi* and the detainees, we suspected that some of the *Bo Doi* were not averse to making some profit by buying things for us. A number of them also managed to make extra money by other means. One day, I saw a *Bo Doi* steal into the area where we lived, pull down some still usable metal sheets, carry them over to the fence, and put them down on the ground. He then attached to each sheet a long cord and slid the end of the cord under the fence. I did not grasp the purpose of this maneuver until the next day, when I got up on the roof of the building to do my usual work and saw two *Bo Doi* drive a three-wheel Lambretta scooter up to the fence. They simply tugged at the rope and the metal sheets slid slowly and smoothly over the grass onto the road. In an instant the scooter, loaded with the sheets, was gone. Only then did I understand why whole metal sheets were so hard to find and why so many roofs and walls were devoid of them. Because aluminum sheets were light, of a good size, easy to move, and, especially, could be sold at a very high price, almost none could be found. Still, we had to hunt for them now to make suitcases for the study monitors! From time to time, we came across one; if it was part of the roof of a shed detainees lived in, we had to wait until they were out at work to remove it and replace it with a much heavier corrugated iron sheet, all under the supervision of a monitor. . . .

. . . . .

On the eve of the day the "course" was due to begin, the team leaders were summoned to a meeting to discuss preparations. The communist cadres called the business of going to the classroom to study *"len lop."*[*] When the great day arrived, we were told to put on clean clothes. In the lecture hall we had to stand in perfectly straight lines. The platform was full of *Bo Doi*, most dressed about the same but a few of them wearing red military badges. We stood facing the stage, waiting. When a man who appeared to be a high-ranking cadre entered the hall, an order was shouted, "Everybody! Get ready to greet the commandant!"

We watched as he took his seat in the middle of the platform. He must have commanded a unit higher than a battalion as we knew by sight every cadre in the battalion responsible for our camp. Nobody gave military salutes, which was surprising among soldiers; they simply stood at attention. (Only much later did we see them drill in marching and saluting.) A monitor shouted an order, "Let the team leaders present their teams!"

One after the other, the team leaders stepped forward and reported the number of persons in their teams, the number present, the number of absentees, and the reason for the absences.

This first session already promised to be thorny. The commandant, seeing that more than one hundred were listed as absent angrily demanded, "Who gave them permission to remain in their barracks? Reeducation, for them, is a matter of life and death. How can they be absent from the class?" He turned to the *Bo Doi* sitting beside him and ordered him to go to the barracks, check on those who had reported sick, and see that all except those who were seriously ill came to the meeting hall. Half an hour later the presentation of teams resumed. The number of absentees was now reduced to a little more than forty, the latecomers being those seriously infected with scabies. They were unable to sit down, so they had to stand at the far end of the hall when the teams were given permission to sit.

The commandant waited until then to make his introductory speech. He spoke through a loudspeaker that would have been much more effective in a smaller room. He stressed that in reeducating us, the Revolution aimed at equipping us with a stock of knowledge and the proper logic to serve as a basis for us to determine our position vis-à-vis the People. He concluded, "I would like to emphasize advice that will be repeated over and over again, and that advice is from now on, you will speak and act exactly the way the Revolution teaches you to do. You must absolutely not think, speak, or act in any other way. Decidedly, you have to speak and act according to the teachings of the Revolution only."

He then introduced the cadre who would give us the first lesson, saying, "Let me introduce to you the comrade instructor who will give you the first lesson: 'U.S. imperialism has ultimately and permanently failed in its war of aggression against Vietnam.'"...

．　．　．　．　．

A discussion session followed the three-day lecture. Groups of fifteen sat in circles on the ground; and to prevent us from drifting into small talk, the *Bo Doi* and study monitors sat down near us. But as there were many more of us than them, they had to move from one group to another about every half hour. Therefore, the "discussions" actually took place only when the *Bo Doi* were near, and the informers, fortunately, did not report on this cheating. When we did "discuss," we took turns to speak in support of the instructor's assertion that the Americans had lost the war. But we had no conviction in what we said, and several times we were forced by the monitors or instructor to speak out with more enthusiasm....

．　．　．　．　．

The lesson involving self-assessment of guilt and self-indictment brought about much bitter reflection. The atmosphere in the camp was heavy and fraught with menace. In forcing us to acknowledge our many offenses, was it not their intention to cast us into a future they had already decided on? No one among us felt there was any prospect of comfort and security in the days to come.

Usually at the start of a study session, the monitors would ask us to sing in unison, while clapping to a beat, such revolutionary songs as "Solidarity" or "As if Uncle Ho Was Present in the Great Victory Celebration." But now, we clapped and hummed through the songs as a matter of form, and threats by the *Bo Doi* did not produce more enthusiasm. The cadres seemed to realize what was behind our reluctance, which was probably why the third lesson took place in a much more relaxed atmosphere. This time the instructor, younger than the other two, from time to time enlivened his lecture with a joke. The lesson began with a statement that became unbearably tedious as it was repeated over and over. "Vietnam is a country endowed with a fertile land and 'forests of gold and seas of silver.'" The lesson listed Vietnam's potential in terms of land, sea, and, especially, mineral resources. The instructor gave a few examples that made us clap our hands and laugh out loud because they were so idiotic and ludicrous. For instance, he said, "Residue from Hongay coal, which we spread over the surface of roads, is in great demand by the Japanese, who plan to convert this material into as many as 117 articles of merchandise! You see, only one item that we discard as waste material is sufficient to arouse the lust of the Japanese imperialists. But in order to safeguard our sovereignty, instead of selling it, we prefer to wait until we have the capability of manufacturing the goods ourselves!" Speaking about the Vietnamese language, he told a story of a Cuban specialist, a member of a construction support team, who was filled with admiration when he went through the Quang Tri area and heard a woman scold her child with "You naughty boy, you're such a vandal!" because he thought that even when showering abuse, the Vietnamese language still sounded like music. Hearing this, we all clapped our hands in derision. Somebody swore in exasperation, wondering why he did not choose a quotation from our treasure of famous poems if he wished to discuss the language. . . .

· · · · ·

The subject of the next lesson was "The Vietnamese Labor Party is the Party that has led the Vietnamese people from one victory to another and to final victory." Roughly speaking, it recalled that in the course of our history there had been a great number of struggles aimed at either winning back or defending national independence, including resistance movements against the French; but these were all short-lived. The Vietnamese people had to wait until the formation of the Party in 1930 to be able to secure continuous and permanent victory. In discussing this propaganda, all we had to do was praise the party, and everything went smoothly for us.

The final lesson dealt with the topic "To love one's country is to love socialism." It served to coerce people into admitting that socialism—and only socialism—could truly protect the fatherland. When discussing the lesson, many of us raised the question of why many non-socialist countries were independent and their nationals living in comfort and happiness. This was rejected at once by the instructor, who said there was no country that was truly independent and no people living in happiness unless socialism had been adopted. He noted that in non-socialist countries there were still strikes and fights for pay raises, which proved that their nationals were not yet living in happiness. Only in socialist countries were there no strikes. He pointed to the USSR as an example of a socialist country where people lived in complete happiness and said that as a consequence, it had been noted that the USSR had achieved the most success of any country in the world. The discussion ended with everybody expressing the hope that Vietnam could catch up fairly quickly with the Soviet Union. Having enumerated outstanding Soviet achievements and affirming that the Soviet Union was first in everything, the instructor said, "I've noticed that many of you, though outwardly accepting what I've told you, inwardly still have doubts. It's because you are so fearful of the Americans and admire them so much that you can't see anybody more capable than the Americans."

We applauded. The instructor, thinking we were showing appreciation for his remark, also clapped his hands and said, "That's true! When you admire the Americans so much that you worship them, you tend to be blinded by your feelings—"

A ripple of applause and laughter went through the audience. The irony was that from the very beginning of the reeducation period, the *Bo Doi* had spoken with awe about the Soviet Union out of all proportion to reason so that listeners were either amazed or irritated. Some *Bo Doi* even stated that "when the Americans brought their B-52s into the war, they had no inkling that the Soviet Union had already deployed sophisticated weapons 'in the clouds,' and when the bombers arrived, they were immediately shot down."

The Soviet Union was set up as a perfect model of socialist achievement. Still, the instructor did not bring much enthusiasm into his argument in support of the idea that "to love one's country is to love socialism," nor did he seem to mind much our lukewarm attitude during the discussion.

After more than a month of this kind of political education, we felt completely drained. Sitting all day in the lecture hall or staying around our shed to participate in the discussions or write the "results obtained" papers, we had little time for physical exercise. Although our diet had been improved by a relatively regular supply of food, every one of us had become obviously thinner. Then we were informed that we would have to rewrite our personal histories, taking into account recent developments and the fact that we have been "equipped with new concepts and logic."

We all felt we were in for an unpleasant surprise and we were right. The instructor explained that this time, besides the necessary account of past history, we also had to assess, politically, each member of our families as well as the things we had done in the past. Finally, the account was to be brought before the group for "constructive criticism," which meant that members of the group would "help" by making accusations so that "each could see more clearly his own offenses."

In making declarations about relatives, we had to mention their guilt as well. For example, when I stated that my grandfather had been a district civil servant, I had to add that he belonged to the feudalistic social category; my father, who had been a teacher in the days of French colonization, had to be considered a member of the intelligentsia, therefore, a lackey of the French imperialists. If a man's father had been a farmer, he had to specify whether he belonged to the "landlord" category (if he owned his own rice fields) or was a "poor farmhand" (if he worked the land for the owner). Similar social categories were applied to all occupations. The cadres who supervised the writing kept impressing us with the implications of each of us having to make three copies of the account, one to be sent to our place of birth, one to our present address or former employer, and the last copy to the central government. The officials at these places would evaluate the account for accuracy and note untrue or incomplete statements. This caused many of us to write and rewrite, over and over, for fear of being accused of insincerity. The whole business was a headache, and then came the reading of the account before one's group, followed by a critique and assessment of the writer's sincerity and willingness to acknowledge his guilt. Whole mornings had to be devoted to reading and criticizing the accounts; at the most, three papers could be got through at each session. At the end of the session, every remark about or criticism of an account had to be written down on a piece of paper and attached to it.

In the hope of acquiring merit in the eyes of the Revolution, some people became very cooperative. They went so far as to accuse others in their group of downgrading their previous ranks to minimize their guilt. One could never have imagined that reeducation could lead to such degradation!

On the evening of the day that we finished criticizing the accounts, Long sat down to talk with me. He confided his fear that when his account was sent to his native place, it would be discovered that his father was not a poor farmhand, as he had declared, but was in fact a landlord. I relieved his worries somewhat by expressing my doubts about the feasibility of sending such an enormous number of documents to various destinations for checking.

"According to my estimates," I told him, "the number of civil servants on reeducation amounts to tens of thousands; the number of officers must be in excess of 100,000; 'capitalists,' members of political parties, and religious groups also would total more than 100,000. The sum total of all the accounts would amount to more than a million. They wouldn't have enough personnel and cadres to deal with this business of checking up on each and every one of us."

Long told me later that many men believed the Revolution eventually would do the checks because they would not have to tackle the whole task at once but could take their time about it; they also might examine only the accounts of people they were ordered to pay special attention to.

During private talks with one another, we discovered that the majority of inmates, in their desire to be left alone for the time being, had accused themselves of the most serious offenses they could think of. A number of men who had not occupied any important position or who came from poor families and consequently had no grounds for self indictment had, as a last resort, invented such offenses as "opposition to communism" or "hatred of communism" as a result of watching pictures of the great massacre of the civilian population by the communists during the Tet Mau Than (1968) offensive in the ancient capital of Hue. Much against our will, we accused ourselves in very strong terms to avoid having such harmful remarks as "attempt to hide past offenses" or "unwillingness to show repentance" entered into our records.

Like all things, the study period too came at last to an end. To me, it had been like a nightmare, assessing my own parents and grandparents, representing them as members of certain social categories, and accusing myself of offenses I had had no idea of. And yet, after doing this, we were still not free of anxiety or the fear of being accused of something. I wanted to forget about the whole affair, if only to give relief to my mind, but many were so obsessed by this business of writing their past histories and judging their offenses that they behaved like dotards. Some would complain to anyone willing to listen: "My guilt was such that it will be difficult for me to be pardoned by the Revolution!" Depending on his nature, each person had a different attitude in the face of a given situation. There were those who seemed not to care what happened; at night, they would lie down and sleep soundly as usual. Others, when faced with a problem, would worry incessantly, their faces haggard from sleeplessness and despair.

A week after we had completed our political studies, we were ordered to assemble in the yard. A *Bo Doi* called out the name of Tanker Quang, told him to return to his shed, pack, and get ready for "transfer to another camp." The rest of us were told to stay where we were, lined up in the sun, thus preventing us from getting news to our families through him. Nobody was fooled by this "transfer" business; everybody knew that Quang was being released because of his father-in-law's intervention.

The fact that only one person was released at the end of the political studies worried all of us. Up to now, if few had been allowed to return home, it was because we had not yet been reeducated; things should be different now that we had been through political indoctrination, yet nothing had changed. Some of the men tried to elicit a clue from the monitors but only got noncommittal answers to questions. "Don't worry!" they told us. "Rest assured; you'll be released in due course. Surely, some will be released earlier, some later than the others. You cannot go home all at the same time because the offenses committed by one person are different from those of another." Worries grew as the days passed without further releases; many risked putting direct questions to high-ranking cadres they chanced to meet. Meanwhile, it was rumored that a great number of inmates at other camps had been released, but I believed the rumor had been spread by the cadres themselves to try to alleviate our worries and impatience, maybe to prevent a possible mutiny.

One day the *bodoi* summoned us to the meeting hall where a cadre from regimental headquarters attempted to explain that our reeducation was not yet completed; we had just finished the first stage; his superiors were making preparations for the second stage. When we raised questions, we got only vague answers. We made it clear that we were not satisfied. Finally, the cadre said, "I have been instructed by my superiors to come here to give you the necessary explanations. I have told you everything my superiors wanted me to convey to you, but you are not satisfied. Well, I'll personally tell you this, as a friend. You cannot return home at this moment. Outside, a campaign for the building of our new society is being launched; the People will not leave you alone if you return among them now! It's better to bide your time. Stay here, continue with your reeducation, wait until you get good results, and return home at the opportune moment. You want me to specify how long it will take. I don't really know, so I cannot tell you. However, I can tell you this much, on my honor as a communist: although your reeducation cannot be completed in a short time, it will not take a very long time either. So, be patient and apply yourselves to your studies."

Hearing these tortuous tautological explanations, most of us realized that we had no hope of being released after reeducation. Our confinement no doubt was indefinite! Our spirits had never been lower than at this moment. . . .

CUBA

Before Night Falls

Reinaldo Arenas

REINALDO ARENAS *(1943–90), a well-known Cuban writer, was allowed to leave in 1980 in the Mariel boat exodus, which Castro used to remove "socially undesirable elements," such as criminals, homosexuals, and the mentally ill. Arenas succeeded in getting out as one of these "undesirables."*

At age fifteen he joined Castro's guerillas to fight the Batista regime, but he subsequently became critical of Castro's policies. He attended the University of Havana and worked at the National Library. Arrested in 1973 as a "counterrevolutionary" and vocal critic of the regime, his homosexuality was also held against him. The Cuban government, like some other Communist systems, made the repression of homosexuals a high priority. They were dismissed from "cultural organizations" or responsible positions on the ground that their behavior "did not fall within the political and moral parameters" the job required. Many were sent into forced-labor camps. In El Moro prison (which Arenas describes below), "homosexuals were confined to the two worst wards . . . below ground at the lowest level. . . . Gays were . . . treated like beasts." Arenas was charged not only with being a CIA agent and dissident but also with "the corruption of minors." In Cuba, as in other Communist states, political dissidents were often also charged with non-political crimes in order to discredit them morally and better legitimate their mistreatment.

Arenas further antagonized the authorities by smuggling his critical writings abroad and maintaining contact with Western intellectuals sympathetic to Cuban dissidents. After prolonged mistreatment by the political police (also described below), he agreed to make the humiliating confession demanded of him, admitting to being a "counter-revolutionary" and promising to avoid contact with Westerners and never to write again anything critical of the Cuban Revolution, as well as to reform his sexual orientation.

The antihomosexual policies of Communist states await further research and examination (for one early study, see Allen Young, Gays

From *Reinaldo Arenas,* Before Night Falls: A Memoir, *trans. Dolores M. Koch,* © *1993 by the Estate of Reinaldo Arenas and Dolores M. Koch, English translation. Used by permission of Viking Penguin, a division of Penguin Group (USA) Inc.*

Under the Cuban Revolution, *San Francisco, 1981). These policies seem to have been part of the puritanical sexual morality promoted by these systems in their earlier stages. (Such an orientation has greatly diminished in Cuba since the 1990s, as the government now permits prostitution partly because of the hard currency it brings in from foreign tourists.) The official hostility toward homosexuality presumably also stemmed from traditional Latin American cultural attitudes unrelated to the official values of Marxism-Leninism. These policies (like all others) were probably further stimulated by Castro's personal preferences and machismo.*

The excerpts to follow are especially informative of the high degree of repression the Cuban government inflicted on intellectuals and its intolerance of free expression.

The policies of the Castro regime have induced an exceptionally high proportion of the population to leave the country, even in comparison with similar exoduses from other Communist states. Cubans have left legally when possible, and when prevented from doing so they have made desperate and often life-threatening attempts to reach the shores of the United States using the most rudimentary flotation devices, including rafts fashioned from old tires. Such escapes have been common from the earliest days of the system and continue to occur at the time of this writing. According to Arenas, "merely to own a floating object was proof enough that one wanted to leave Cuba and this could mean eight years in jail." Over 10 percent of the population has left Cuba, legally or otherwise, since 1959.

This excerpt, in addition to describing the experiences of Arenas, also summarizes the notorious case of Padilla, another well-known Cuban writer who was subjected to a show trial and coerced into a confession along the lines of the Soviet and East European show trials.

In addition to his autobiography, Arenas has written eight books of fiction.

· · · · ·

The Padilla "Case"

State Security chose Heberto Padilla as the sacrificial lamb. Padilla was the irreverent poet who had dared to submit a book critical of the Revolution, *Fuera del juego,* to an official competition.

Outside Cuba, Padilla had already become an international figure who therefore had to be destroyed, and with him, all other intellectuals in the country who had similar attitudes.

Padilla was arrested in 1971, as was his wife, Belkis Cuza Malé. He was locked up in a cell, intimidated, and beaten. Thirty days later he emerged from that cell a human wreck. Most of us Cuban intellectuals were invited by State Security, through UNEAC, to hear what Padilla had to say. We knew that he had been arrested, and were surprised to learn that he would speak. I remember that UNEAC was under close surveillance by undercover cops; the only persons allowed to enter and hear Padilla were those whose names appeared on a carefully checked list. The night Padilla made his confession was sinister and unforgettable. That vital man, who had written beautiful poetry, apologized for everything he had done, for his entire previous work, throwing the blame upon himself, branding himself a despicable coward and traitor. He said that during his detention at State Security he had come to understand the beauty of the Revolution and he had written some poems to spring. Padilla not only retracted all he had said in his previous work but publicly denounced his friends, and even his wife, all of whom, he claimed, also held counterrevolutionary attitudes. Padilla named them all, one by one: José Yanes, Norberto Fuentes, Lezama Lima. Lezama had refused to participate in Padilla's apology. While Padilla was giving out names of counterrevolutionary writers, Virgilio Piñera started sliding down from his chair and sat on the floor, as if trying to become invisible. All those whom Padilla named, between sobs and chest beatings, had to come up to the microphone next to Padilla, accept the blame for their errors, and state that they were unworthy people and traitors to the regime. All of this, of course, was put on film by State Security, circulated in intellectual centers throughout the world, and shown especially to those writers who had signed a letter complaining of Padilla's wrongful arrest, such as Mario Vargas Llosa, Octavio Paz, Juan Rulfo, and even Gabriel García Márquez, now one of Fidel Castro's most important standard-bearers.

All the writers mentioned by Padilla filed past the microphones making their confessions. Pablo Armando Fernández's confession was long and sickening; he accused himself even more violently than Heberto Padilla had done. César López was also there, and he confessed all of his ideological errors. Norberto Fuentes did also, except that at the end, when the proceedings seemed to have concluded as planned by State Security, Fuentes asked for the floor and returned to the microphone. He said that he did not agree with what was going on, that Padilla was in a very difficult position and had no choice but to make his confession, and that he, Norberto, felt very differently because he worked hard and, for being a writer, had to starve. Moreover, he did not consider himself a counterrevolutionary for simply having written several books of short stories, imaginative or critical; and he ended by pounding the table with his fist. The State Security officers stood up and I saw some of them reach for their weapons. Norberto Fuentes was silenced by shouts and threats of violence.

While the shameful spectacle of Padilla's confession was taking place, Castro's government was organizing what was called the First Congress of

Education and Culture, which significantly concerned everything that opposed what its title implied; it was evident that what he wanted was to put an end to all Cuban culture. Even positions concerning fashion were dictated there. Fashion was being identified as ideological diversionism and a subtle penetration by Yankee imperialism.

The cruelest attacks of that congress were unleashed against homosexuals. Paragraphs were read labeling homosexuals as pathological cases, and more important, it was decided that all homosexuals who held positions in cultural organizations should be immediately severed from their jobs. The system of *parametraje* (parameterization) was imposed; that is, every gay writer, every gay artist, every gay dramatist, received a telegram telling him that his behavior did not fall within the political and moral parameters necessary for his job, and that he was therefore either terminated or offered another job in the forced-labor camps.

Agricultural labor or gravedigger jobs were the kinds of work offered to the "parameterized" intellectuals. It was evident that a dark cloud had descended upon Cuban intellectuals. By then it had become impossible even to think of leaving the country. Since 1970 Fidel had been proclaiming that all those who wanted to leave had done so. Thus the island became a maximum-security jail, where everybody, according to Castro, was happy to stay.

Every artist who had a homosexual past or who had slipped politically ran the risk of losing his job. I remember the case of the Camejos, who had created one of the most important Cuban artistic institutions, the Guiñol [Puppet] Theater. Along with most of the actors and puppeteers in that group, they were suddenly parameterized and their theater destroyed.

Agents of State Security, such as Héctor Quesada or Lieutenant Pavón, were now in charge of the witch-hunt. The raids had resumed and the splendid big boys of State Security again dressed up as obsequious faggots and went out to arrest anyone who dared look at them.

One of the hottest scandals of the moment was Roberto Blanco's arrest and public trial. He had been a very important theater director in Cuba during the sixties, but had recently made the mistake of admiring the erect phallus of one of those splendid big boys of State Security; handcuffed, his hair close-shorn, Blanco was escorted to a public trial held in the very theater of which he had been the director.

Public humiliation has always been one of Castro's favorite weapons: the degrading of people in front of a public always eager to make fun of any weakness in another, or of any person who had lost favor. It was not enough to be accused; you had to say you were sorry and beat your chest before an audience that would applaud and laugh. After that, shorn and handcuffed, you had to purify yourself of your weaknesses in a sugarcane field or by doing some other agricultural work.

One arrest followed another. Even a writer who had won national poetry awards, such as René Ariza, was suddenly sentenced to eight years in jail, accused of ideological diversionism. Another writer who had won awards, José Lorenzo Fuentes, was also sentenced, but to thirty years in jail. El Beny had also been detained, for corruption of minors or something like that, and was by then at a forced-labor camp. Others, of course, tried to get out of the country by any means available. Esteban Luis Cárdenas jumped from a building into the Argentine embassy; he did fall into the patio of the embassy, but Cuban authorities, not inclined to respect any diplomatic treaty, went in and dragged him off to jail.

How many young people have died, and are still dying, trying to cross the Florida Strait or simply gunned down by the coast guard of State Security? Others opted for a more foolproof way to escape, that is, suicide. The poet Martha Vignier chose this option; she jumped from the roof of her home and smashed herself to bits on the pavement....

· · · · ·

Prison

Morro Castle is a colonial fortress built by the Spaniards to defend the Port of Havana against corsair and pirate attacks. It is a dank place, sitting atop a promontory. It had been converted into a prison. The building is of medieval construction, with a drawbridge that we had to cross to enter. We walked through a long, dark tunnel, then the portcullis, and finally entered the prison itself.

I was taken to the booking station, a cell where prisoners are classified according to crime, age, and sexual preference, before being taken inside to serve their time. Strangely enough, neither the officer of State Security who had apprehended me and who was expecting a promotion nor even the high official named Víctor was allowed through the portcullis. They may have been as shaken as I was and for that reason were not able to pull rank to get in; besides, they were in civilian clothes. So in all that confusion, I entered with my ID in the name of Adrián Faustino Sotolongo, the compass, my watch, and all my hallucinogenic pills.

In that cell there were about fifty prisoners; some were in for common crimes, others had been in traffic accidents, and still others were political prisoners. What struck me most in the prison was the noise: hundreds and hundreds of inmates were marching on their way to mess hall; they looked like strange monsters, yelling and greeting each other. It sounded like a unanimous roar. Ever since my childhood, noise has always been inflicted upon me, all my writing has been done against the background of other people's noise. I think that Cubans are defined by noise; it seems to be inherent in their nature, and also part of their exhibitionism. They need to bother others; they can neither enjoy nor suffer in silence.

That prison was perhaps the worst in all Havana. The toughest criminals were sent there; the prison held mostly common criminals, with only a small section reserved for political prisoners who were awaiting trial or sentencing.

I wanted very much to keep the watch and give it to my mother, so I hid it in my underwear. An older prisoner, whom I later befriended, and who had already been through various jails, advised me to hide the watch quickly. When I showed him the compass, he remarked how amazing it was for me to have entered the prison with that instrument. Eduardo—that was his name—told me that some prisoners had been sentenced to eight years simply for possessing a compass, and that I should flush it down the toilet immediately to remove all proof of ever having had it.

The hallucinogenic drugs that I still had could be lethal if taken in excessive doses. I was afraid of torture, and afraid of compromising my friends, some of whom had taken great risks on my account. I therefore took a number of those pills with a little water. After taking them, I lay down near a rough but good-looking trucker who had committed God knows what kind of transit violation. I did not expect to wake up again, but three days later I regained consciousness in the prison hospital: in a wing full of people with infectious diseases. The doctor told me it was a miracle that I was alive; they had expected me to remain in a coma and die of a heart attack.

From now on, all my old energy, with which I had enjoyed hundreds of youths, would remain locked up next to two hundred and fifty criminals. . . .

I arrived at El Morro with an infamous reputation not as a political prisoner or a writer but as a rapist, a murderer, and a CIA agent; all this gave me an aura of respectability, even among the real murderers.

As a result, I slept on the floor only the first night after my arrival at ward number 7, to which I had been assigned and which was not, in fact, for gays but for prisoners convicted of various crimes. Homosexuals were confined to the two worst wards of El Morro: these wards were below ground at the lowest level, and water seeped into the cells at high tide. It was a sweltering place without a bathroom. Gays were not treated like human beings, they were treated like beasts. They were the last ones to come out for meals, so we saw them walk by, and the most insignificant incident was an excuse to beat them mercilessly. The soldiers guarding us, who called themselves *combatientes,* were army recruits sent here as a sort of punishment; they found some release for their rage by taking it out on the homosexuals. Of course, nobody called them homosexuals; they were called fairies, faggots, queers, or at best, gays. The wards for fairies were really the last circle of hell. Admittedly, many of those homosexuals were wretched creatures whom discrimination and misery had turned into common criminals. Nevertheless, they had not lost their sense of humor. With their own sheets they made skirts, and with shoe wax obtained from relatives they shadowed their eyes; they even used lime from the wall whitewash as makeup. Sometimes when they were allowed on the roof of El Morro to get a bit of sun, they made it into a real show. The sun was a rationed privilege for prisoners; we would be taken out for about an hour once or twice a month. The fairies attended as if it were one of the most extraordinary events of their lives, which it almost was. From the roof we could see not only the sun but the sea as well, and we could also look at the city of Havana, the city of our suffering, but which from up there seemed like paradise. The fairies would dress up for this occasion in the most unusual ways and wear wigs made out of rope, which they obtained God knows how. They wore makeup and high heels fashioned from pieces of wood, which they called clogs. To be sure, they no longer had anything to lose; maybe they never had anything to lose and therefore could afford the luxury of being true to their nature, to act queer, to make jokes, and even to express admiration to a soldier. For this, of course, they could be punished by not being allowed out into the sun for three months, which is the worst that could happen to an inmate. In the sun one could kill the ticks, get rid of some of the fleas and lice, which lodge in the skin and burrow beneath it, making life miserable and sleep impossible.

My bunk was the last in a row, next to a skylight. It was pretty cold there and when it rained, water came in. The beam of the Morro Castle lighthouse would come in through the skylight; it was difficult to sleep with that intense light shining on my face every two or three minutes. Added to this were the noises the prisoners made, and the lights of the prison itself, which were never turned off.

I slept embracing the *Iliad,* smelling its pages. To keep busy, I organized French lessons. There were, of course, no books for the lessons, but little by little we managed to get some paper, pencils, and other items. I would give the lessons from my bunk. It was very difficult to pronounce clearly and make yourself understood in French in the midst of the clamor, but they did at least learn a few sentences, and at times we could even have a dialogue in French. The classes had a more or less set schedule, after meals, and on occasion lasted up to two hours. In a prison there are always people, young and old, interested in learning something, and even murderers could enjoy the French language.

On the other hand, not all the prisoners were murderers. There was, for example, an unfortunate father with all his sons, who had been sentenced to five years because they had killed one of their cows to feed the family, something Castro's laws did not allow. Still others were in jail for killing cows they did not own, to sell the meat on the black market. There is so much hunger in Cuba that people would quarrel desperately over those few pieces of meat on the black market, sold at sky-high prices. . . .

Summer came and the unbearable heat exploded. Heat in Cuba is always unbearable: humid and sticky. But if one happens to be in a prison by the sea, with walls more than a yard thick, no ventilation, and two hundred and fifty people in one room, the heat becomes really intolerable. The bed ticks and lice of course reproduced at alarming rates, there were clouds of flies in the air, and the stench of shit became even more pungent.

Outside in the city, and along the Malecón Shore Drive, the 1974 carnival festivities were taking place; this was the festival Fidel had made into a party in his own honor around the 26th of July. The prisoners all wanted to get out and be able to drink beer and dance to the beat of the drums; it was the greatest happiness those men could dream of, and yet many of them would never again be able to experience such joys.

The fairies organized their own little carnival in their ward, with drums made from pieces of wood or iron. They would dance the rumba in that hot ward; the highlight was when someone sang *Cecilia Valdés*. He sang very well and his soprano voice echoed through the prison to the words: *"Si . . . Yo soy . . . Cecilia Valdés"* [Yes . . . I am . . . Cecilia Valdés]. He could have been the star of any zarzuela or musical comedy.

The inmates were impressed listening to that queer, who said his name was Yma Sumac. Gonzalo Roig would have been proud to have such an accomplished interpreter. The carnival would last until daybreak, when the soldiers entered the gay ward and beat them into silence, thus ending the celebration. On one occasion, Yma Sumac was dragged out all covered with blood; it was said that another queen, who also wanted to do *Cecilia* but did not have the voice for it, had stabbed him. We never saw "her" again.

After six months at El Morro I still had not been brought to trial; others had been waiting for more than a year. One day a guard called me to the gate. I walked out with no idea why they would be calling me. I was then escorted to a small room where I saw my mother; she had managed to get in to visit me. When my mother came close to me and hugged me, she was weeping. Feeling my prisoner's uniform with her hands, she said, "Such heavy material . . . how you must be suffering from the heat." Those words moved me more than any other remark; mothers always have that enchanting way of treating us as if we were children. We hugged each other and cried; I took advantage of the opportunity to ask her to see my friends and warn them to be careful with those manuscripts of mine they were keeping for me; she promised to visit them. I could not explain to her what that place was like, but told her that I felt good, that I would probably be out soon, and that she should not come to see me again but wait for my release. When she stood up, I realized how old she had become in those six months; her body was bent and her skin had lost its smoothness. . . .

. . . . .

Villa Marista

We arrived at Villa Marista, headquarters of State Security. Once inside, they brought me to an office, removed all my clothes, and gave me yellow overalls. They took off my slippers and gave me another pair, and then sat me down on what looked like an electric chair, full of straps for the arms and legs. Yes, it was a sort of tropical electric chair. There I was photographed and fingerprinted. Then I was taken to the second floor; in passing I saw the small cells with a single bulb that stayed lit day and night above the prisoner's head; I realized, without a doubt, that this was worse than being in the hands of the Inquisition.

I was assigned to cell number twenty-one, and shoved inside. The small hatch through which one could look out on the hallway remained shut. In that place you could not tell day from night; the bulb remained on at all times. The toilet was a hole in the floor. For four days I stayed there without seeing anybody. On the fourth day I was taken out and led to the interrogation room.

A lieutenant who said his name was Gamboa started the interrogation by asking me if I knew where I was. I answered that I knew I was at State Security. Then he asked, "Do you know what that means? It means that here we can make you disappear, we can wipe you out, and nobody will know; everybody thinks you are at El Morro, and there are many ways you could die there, you could easily get stabbed." Of course I understood what he said: I understood why I had not been taken directly to State Security but to El Morro; to all my friends I was at El Morro, even to my mother, whom they had intentionally given a pass so that she would see me there. Now, if they murdered me, people would think I had died at the hands of some killer at El Morro and that I had never been at State Security.

It was difficult for me not to be confused by the thousands of questions that were thrown at me. Sometimes the interrogators started at dawn and would continue all day; then I would not be questioned for a week and it seemed as if I had been forgotten, only to be taken again to the same officer. That man did not believe a word I said. Sometimes he would leave in a rage, and I would remain alone in that interrogation chamber; sometimes another officer would continue the questioning.

There were many Russians at State Security, which was under the absolute control of the KGB, like a branch office. The Soviet officers were more respected and feared than the Cubans, everyone saluting them as if they were generals; perhaps they were.

Lieutenant Gamboa stressed again and again how isolated I was, saying that all my friends had abandoned me and no one would do anything for me. He also dwelt on my sexual relations with Rafael Arnés. He started out by asking me how my lover was doing, and I had no idea whom he meant because there had really been so many. He then told me that he was referring to Arnés and asked me various questions about him, some very intimate. Security always wanted to know as much as possible about any individual, even though he might have close ties to the agency, in the event he should lose favor or they might want to get rid of him. At that point, I had nothing to say about Arnés.

"And what about the Brontë sisters?" the officer asked me one afternoon. I realized then that one of the people who had been informing on me for many years was Hiram Prado; the Brontë sisters were the Abreu brothers, and only Hiram Prado knew that I called them affectionately by that name. The lieutenant knew of our meetings at Lenin Park and about our friendship. I was not too surprised to learn that Hiram Prado was an informer; after living so many years under that regime, I had come to understand how humanity disappears bit by bit in everyone, and how human beings break down in order to survive. Informing on others is something most Cubans do every day.

After my release from jail I learned that Hiram Prado, under pressure from State Security, had visited most of my friends to find out where I was hiding while I was a fugitive. He even went to see my mother.

The night I knew for certain that Hiram Prado was an informer, I returned to my cell rather depressed.

One day a strange noise came from the cell next to mine; it sounded as if a piston were releasing steam. An hour later I heard bloodcurdling screams; the man had a Uruguayan accent and he was yelling that he could not bear it anymore, that he was going to die, that they should stop the steam. I then understood the purpose of the pipe sticking out near the toilet hole in my own cell; its function had been a mystery to me. It was a tube through which steam could be released into the prison cell, which, being tightly shut, would become a steam room. To release steam was a method of torture similar to fire; the closed cell full of steam could almost suffocate a person. Every now and then a doctor would come in, take the prisoner's blood pressure, check his heart, and say: "You can give him a little more." The steam would continue to build up, and when he was about to die from a heart attack, he would be removed from his cell and taken to the interrogation chamber.

My neighbor was subjected to this torture for over a month. I would knock on his wall and he would knock right back. In all truth, he was being murdered. Nobody could resist those incessant steam baths in that state of semi-starvation. After a while the baths stopped. I thought maybe he had confessed or perhaps died.

I was switched to a cell that was even worse than the one before. I felt that this was in punishment for my lack of sincerity with the lieutenant who was questioning me. However, the accusations made against the government by my foreign friends were having an effect; although my keepers continued to threaten me, they also feared foreign public opinion. Of course, they did not let me out of the cell. They wanted me to make a confession stating that I was a counterrevolutionary, that I regretted the ideological weakness I had shown in my published writings, and that the Revolution had been extraordinarily fair with me. In other words, a confession that sounded like a conversion, and of course, a commitment that I would work for them and write optimistic books. They gave me a week to think it over. I did not want to recant anything, I did not think I had to recant anything; but after three months at State Security, I signed the confession.

Needless to say, this only proves my cowardice, my weakness, the certainty that I am not the stuff of which heroes are made, and that fear, in my case, had won over moral principles. But I was comforted by the fact that in the communiqué I had written in Lenin Park to the International Red Cross, the UN, UNESCO, and many other organizations that never published it, I stated that my accusations against the regime of Fidel Castro were absolutely true to fact, even if at some point I denied them. I did know the moment might come when I would have to recant.

When I told the officer that I agreed to write a confession, he himself gave me pencil and paper. My confession was a long one; I talked about my life and my homosexuality, which I detested, about having become a counterrevolutionary, about my ideological weaknesses and my accursed books, the likes of which I would never write again. I actually recanted all I had done in my life, my only hope for redemption being the possibility that in the future I could join and become part of the Revolution and work day and night on its behalf. Needless to say, I was requesting rehabilitation, that is, to be sent to a labor camp; and I committed myself to work for the government and write optimistic novels. I also praised the henchmen who had informed on me, stating that they were wonderful people whose advice I should have always heeded: Portuondo, Guillén, Pavón; they were heroes. I took advantage of the occasion to state all the worst I knew about Hiram Prado, but they paid little attention to me because his work as an informer among the intellectuals and in Havana's underworld was so important to them.

After I had finished writing my confession, the lieutenant took his time reading it. Three days later he came to my cell to congratulate me. He seemed euphoric, and it was evident that he had been pressured by his superiors to have me sign the confession and get me out of there. I later learned that the foreign press had reported my disappearance and that I was not registered as an inmate in any of Havana's prisons; it was time for State Security to move me back to El Morro. Four months of isolation had gone by.

My confession, of course, did not mention anyone still in Cuba who could have been harmed, or the names of any of my friends in other countries. It all amounted to my admitting that I had been a counterrevolutionary who smuggled his manuscripts out of Cuba and had them published, and to my promising, now repentant, that I would never again have any contact with the rest of the Western world or write a single line against the Cuban Revolution. I also promised to reform my sexual behavior.

Once my confession was signed, I was returned to my cell. I have seldom felt more miserable. About fifteen days later I was transferred back to El Morro and had another interview with Lieutenant Gamboa. Lieutenant Víctor was also present and he seemed to waver between being infuriated and being friendly. Neither man could really have thought that my confession was sincere, but then, they could never have expected any truthful declaration to come out of a torture chamber.

While I was writing my confession they insisted I include that I had corrupted two minors, the two hoodlums who had stolen our clothes—mine and Pepe Malas's—at the beach. By the way, Pepe Malas never went to jail, because he was an informer for State Security. He was released as soon as he identified himself at the police station, while I was sent to jail.

I would be tried for a serious common crime, corruption of minors. There was even talk of rape. By convicting me of a common crime, they would avoid an international scandal. Keeping me in jail for at least eight years, the system would manage to obliterate me and separate me from the literary world.

During the days following my confession, one of the soldiers on guard in the hallway would sometimes stop to talk with me; I imagine he had been so instructed by Lieutenant Gamboa. That good-looking mulatto would open the hatch and at times talk with me for over an hour; he would scratch his testicles and I would get sexually excited; I would often masturbate while he was walking by my door.

One night while I was asleep, he came in and asked me for a match. Of course I was not allowed to have matches in jail. We talked for about five minutes and he left. Perhaps he wanted to make me feel uneasy and test my signed resolution. From that night on, I dreamed that he would enter my cell and we would make love. Perhaps he knew that I masturbated watching him, and maybe it amused him. Anyway, our conversations kept getting longer until I was transferred out.

Before my confession I had a great companion, my pride. After the confession I had nothing; I had lost my dignity and my rebellious spirit. On the other hand, I had made a commitment to the lieutenant to collaborate in any possible way, and they could ask me to make a public appearance to read my whole confession. Moreover, after my confession they could also obliterate me physically.

Now I was alone in my misery; no one could witness my misfortune in that cell. The worst misfortune was to continue living after all that, after having betrayed myself and after having been betrayed by almost everybody else. . . .

. . . . .

Mariel

Around the beginning of April 1980, a driver on the number thirty-two bus route drove a bus full of passengers through the doors of the Peruvian embassy asking for political asylum. Strangely enough, all the passengers on the bus also decided to ask for political asylum. Not one of them wanted to leave the embassy.

Fidel Castro demanded that all the people be returned, but the ambassador from Perú stated that they were on Peruvian territory, and according to international law, they had the right to political asylum. Days later, during one of his fits of anger, Fidel Castro decided to withdraw the Cuban guards from the embassy, perhaps trying in this way to pressure the ambassador to give in and force the people out of the embassy.

This time he miscalculated. When it became known that the Peruvian embassy was no longer guarded, thousands upon thousands of people, young and old, entered the grounds asking for political asylum. One of the first to do so was my friend Lázaro. I did not believe in the possibility of asylum because the news was even published in *Granma*; I thought it was a trap, and that once all the people were inside the embassy, Castro would arrest them. As soon as he knew who his enemies were—that is, all those who wanted to leave—he could then easily put them in jail.

Lázaro said good-bye to me before going to the embassy. The following day the embassy doors were closed again, but there were 10,800 people inside and 100,000 more outside, trying to get in. From all over the country, trucks were arriving full of young people who wanted to get in, but at that point Fidel Castro knew he had made a big mistake by withdrawing the guard from the Peruvian embassy. Not only was the embassy closed but only people living in Miramar were allowed near the site.

Electricity and water to the embassy were cut off, and for 10,800 people, 800 food rations were delivered. In addition, State Security smuggled in numerous undercover agents who went as far as to murder former high government officials requesting asylum. The area surrounding the embassy was scattered with Communist Youth Organization and Communist Party IDs, discarded by the people inside.

All the world press agencies were wiring the news, but the Cuban government tried to play down the incident. Even Julio Cortázar and Pablo Armando Fernández, stalwart champions of Castro who were in New York at the time, declared that there were only six or seven hundred people inside the embassy.

One taxi driver drove his car at full speed trying to break into the embassy, and was machine-gunned down by State Security; wounded, he still tried to get out of his car and into the embassy, but he was carried away in a patrol car.

The events at the Peruvian embassy were the first mass rebellion by the Cuban people against the Castro dictatorship. After that, people tried to enter the U.S. Interest Section office in Havana. Everybody was seeking an embassy to get into, and police persecution reached alarming proportions. In the end, the Soviet Union sent a high official of the KGB to Cuba, to hold a number of meetings with Fidel Castro.

Fidel and Raúl Castro had personally taken a look at the Peruvian embassy. There, for the first time, Castro heard the people insulting him, calling him a coward, a criminal, and demanding freedom.

It was then that Fidel ordered that they be gunned down, and those people—who had gone for fifteen days with almost no food, sleeping on their feet because there was no space to lie down, trying to survive amid the filth of their own excrement—faced up to the bullets by singing the old national anthem. Many were wounded.

To avoid the danger of a popular uprising, Fidel and the Soviet Union decided that a breach must be opened to allow a number of those nonconformists to leave; it was like curing sickness by bleeding.

During a desperate and angry speech, accompanied and applauded by Gabriel García Márquez and Juan Bosch, Castro accused those poor people in the embassy of being antisocial and sexually depraved. I'll never forget that speech—Castro looked like a cornered, furious rat—nor will I forget the hypocritical applause of García Márquez and Juan Bosch, giving their support to such a crime against the unfortunate captives.

The port of Mariel was then opened, and Castro, after stressing that all those people were antisocial, said that precisely what he wanted was to have that riffraff out of Cuba. Posters immediately started to appear with the slogans LET THEM GO, LET THE RIFFRAFF GO. The Party and State Security organized a "voluntary" march against the refugees at the embassy. People had no choice but to take part in the march; many went with the hope of perhaps being able to jump the fence and get inside. But the marchers could not get close, not with three rows of cops between them and the fence.

Thousands of boats full of people started to leave for the United States from the port of Mariel. Of course, not all those at the embassy who wanted to leave were able to do so, but only those whom Fidel Castro wanted to get rid of: common prisoners and criminals from Cuban jails; undercover agents whom he wanted to infiltrate in Miami; the mentally ill. And all this was paid for by the Cuban exiles who sent boats to get their relatives out. The majority of those families in Miami spent all their resources renting boats to rescue their loved ones, and when they arrived at Mariel, Castro would often fill their boats with criminals and insane people, and they could not get their relatives out. But thousands of honest people also managed to escape.

Of course, to be able to depart from the Port of Mariel, people had to leave the Peruvian embassy with a safe-conduct issued by State Security, and had to return to their homes and wait until the Castro government gave them the order to leave. From that moment on, State Security, not the Peruvian embassy, was making the decisions as to who could leave the country and who could not. Many resisted, not wanting to abandon the embassy, especially those most involved with the Castro regime.

The mobs organized by State Security waited outside the embassy for those leaving with safe-conducts and in many instances tore up their permits. Besides losing their right to exile, they were beaten up by the rabble.

Lots of people were physically attacked, not only for being at the Peruvian embassy but merely for sending telegrams asking their relatives in Miami to come for them at the Port of Mariel. I saw a young man beaten unconscious and left on the street just as he was coming out of the post office after sending one of those telegrams. This happened daily, everywhere, during the months of April and May 1980.

Twenty days later, Lázaro returned from the embassy and was hardly recognizable; he weighed less than ninety pounds. He had gone to a lot of trouble to avoid being beaten, but he was starving. Now all he could do was wait for his exit permit. The day it came, I accompanied him in a taxi to where the documents were being issued, and he said to me: "Don't worry, Reinaldo, I am going to get you out of here." When he left the taxi, I saw the mob attack him and hit him on the back with steel bars as he ran under a shower of rocks and rotten fruit; in the midst of all that, I saw him disappear toward freedom, while I remained behind, alone. But in my building almost everyone wanted to leave the country, so it felt like a sort of refuge.

During that civil strife, terrible things were happening. To escape being beaten by the mob, one man got in his car and drove it into some of the people who were attacking him. An agent of State Security immediately shot him in the head, killing him. The incidents were even published in *Granma*; to have killed such an antisocial person was considered a heroic act.

The homes of those waiting for exit permits were surrounded by mobs and stoned; in the Vedado, several people were stoned to death. All the terrors suffered for twenty years were now reaching their peak. Anyone who was not Castro's agent was in danger.

Opposite my room someone had put up various posters reading: HOMO-SEXUALS, GET OUT; SCUM OF THE EARTH, GET OUT. To get out was exactly what I wanted, but how? Ironically, the Cuban government hurled insults at us and demanded that we leave, but at the same time prevented us from leaving. At no point did Fidel Castro open the Port of Mariel to all who wanted to leave; his trick was simply to let go the ones who posed no danger to the image of his government. Professionals with university degrees could not leave, nor could writers who had published abroad, such as myself.

However, since the order of the day was to allow all undesirables to go, and in that category homosexuals were in first place, a large number of gays were able to leave the island in 1980. People who were not even homosexual pretended to be gay in order to obtain permission to leave from the Port of Mariel. . . .

The Politics of Psychiatry in Revolutionary Cuba

Charles J. Brown and Armando M. Lago (eds.)

CHARLES J. BROWN (dates not available) is a human rights activist who has worked for Freedom House, Amnesty International, and the U.S. State Department. ARMANDO M. LAGO (dates not available) has a Ph.D. in economics from Harvard and was a founding member and president (1990–94) of the Association for the Study of the Cuban Economy. He taught at Catholic University in Washington, D.C., from 1968 to 1976, where he worked on a study of "the human costs of social revolution."

While the use of psychiatric prisons in the Soviet Union was widely known and criticized, there has been little information about or awareness of similar practices in Castro's Cuba. The volume here excerpted is a unique and authentic source of information, based as it is on the testimony of refugees who had personally experienced these practices.

It remains to be learned what if any part the Soviet example played in the Cuban use of psychiatric methods in the treatment of political prisoners. As in the Soviet Union, in Cuba critiques of the system were defined either as pathological (hence the use of psychiatric methods) or as a reflection of hostility conditioned by class interest, which called for a purely punitive response.

The cases presented in this volume include individuals of widely varying ages, social backgrounds, and occupations. Many had been arrested repeatedly and detained in a variety of institutions, penal and psychiatric. It is characteristic of these detentions that, as Amnesty International reported, "people not suffering of any psychological disorder are held together with violent psychopaths and seriously disturbed people, making their stay a very traumatic experience. . . ."

Those subjected to psychiatric treatments had in common that they had criticized or rejected the regime; some were outspoken dissidents, others merely made some incautious political remark. There were among them those who tried to escape from the country.

From Charles J. Brown and Armando M. Lago, eds., The Politics of Psychiatry in Revolutionary Cuba, © *1991 by Transaction Publishers. Reprinted by permission of the publisher.*

Periods of detention ranged from weeks to months and years. The most common forms of "treatment" were electroshocks and the extensive use of psychotropic drugs (antipsychotic medications normally used in the treatment of serious mental illnesses, such as schizophrenia, and to control hallucinations). As used in Cuba, these medications often caused disorientation and had a variety of other debilitating side effects.

There was little pretense that those arrested were given treatment for genuine psychiatric problems; rather, these practices were either purely punitive or designed to break the wills of more defiant prisoners.

The excerpts printed below provide insight not merely into the case histories of the particular individuals who had these painful experiences but also illuminate characteristics of the Cuban political system, as for example the widespread use of informers linked to the Committees for the Defense of the Revolution. There is unmistakable evidence in these pages of the inhumane arbitrariness and brutality with which the political police have sought to control the Cuban population, especially those unwilling to conform.

. . . . .

The Teenager

José Alvarado Delgado
OCCUPATION: student
DIAGNOSIS: sane
CONFINEMENT: 1 month
ELECTROSHOCKS: 3
PSYCHOTROPIC DRUGS: yes

Born in Havana on June 10, 1964, José Luis Alvarado Delgado attended Enrique Masa and Manolito Aguiar Workers' Pre-University High Schools in Havana. On November 22, 1980, the sixteen year-old Alvarado sought political asylum at the Colombian Embassy in Havana. A Cuban guard at the Embassy arrested Alvarado and turned him over to State Security agents, who took him to their headquarters at *Villa Marista* in Havana. He was held in a small, cold cell, and interrogated continually for one week. His interrogators threatened to send him to the Havana Psychiatric Hospital (Mazorra), warning that violently insane patients would rape and beat him.

When Alvarado refused to cooperate, he was transferred to the Carbó-Serviá ward of the Havana Psychiatric Hospital (Mazorra). At their first meeting, his psychiatrist spent more time asking him about his detention than his mental health. Their second meeting consisted of a battery of exams, including an encephalograph and an intelligence test. During their third meeting, the psychiatrist told him:

> that I did not have any psychiatric problems and that State Security had taken me [to Carbó-Serviá] because I had not wanted to sign a self-incriminating confession. "But you knew these things already," she said. "If you do not cooperate, it will be worse for you."

Later that same day, an orderly and one of his inmate trusties seized Alvarado, placed a rubber bit in his mouth, and forced him to undergo electroconvulsive therapy until he became unconscious. When he regained consciousness, he discovered that the shocks had caused him to lose control of his bowels. When he protested, members of the hospital staff held him down and force fed him psychotropic drugs. From that day on:

> I was forced to take psychotropic drugs three times daily. . . . The reaction was immediate. You felt like everything around you slowly was losing its animation. You felt far away. You could walk, eat, and talk, but they were involuntary reflexes. The moment would come when you could not remember anything—neither your name nor that of the friend beside you. It was like being awake and dreaming at the same time. The real was confused with the unreal.

Alvarado later told Don Schanche of *The Los Angeles Times*: "They used the psychiatric hospital to destroy the will of the person."

When he continued to refuse to sign a self-incriminating confession, a State Security agent warned him that "whether you want to or not, sooner or later you will give in." Enraged, Alvarado struck the agent. Several inmate trusties seized him and, following the orders of one of the doctors, took him to the punishment cells of the Castellanos ward. At odd hours of the day and night, one of the orderlies or one of the inmate trusties would spray the prisoners with water. Alvarado was forced to undergo a second session of electroshock therapy, and force fed additional large doses of psychotropic drugs. After three days in Castellanos (and a total of three weeks in Mazorra), Alvarado concluded that if he did not sign a confession, he "would be totally destroyed." Upon signing, he was sentenced to one year in jail, which he served at the Combinado del Este Prison in Havana. He was released on November 22, 1981, one year to the day after he had sought asylum.

On March 22, 1982, Alvarado was arrested while trying to send photos that he claimed would document Cuba's training of Latin American subversive groups to the United States Interest Section in Havana. Once again he refused to cooperate with State Security or sign a confession. After a brief detention in *Villa Marista*, he was returned to Carbó-Serviá, where during a one week stay he was subjected to a third series of electroshocks and large doses of psychotropic drugs. By the time he was returned to *Villa Marista*, he had lost part of his memory, and could not control his automatic reflexes. Alvarado later said that he was so disoriented that when the authorities handed him a confession, he signed it. He was sentenced to six years in prison. For one week he was held in solitary confinement in the maximum security wing of La Cabaña Prison. He later was transferred to the Combinado del Este Prison in Havana. On May 30, 1986, he was released on parole.

On June 25, 1986, Alvarado gave an interview to a Reuters correspondent in Havana. He spoke about his own experiences and denounced the incarceration of other political prisoners. In late August, he was arrested and accused of breaking the conditions of his parole. Authorities alleged that he had tried to obtain a visa from the United States and had tried to obtain asylum in the Venezuelan Embassy. He was sentenced to an additional year in prison, and was ordered to serve the last two years of his earlier sentence. Alvarado spent the next eighteen months in solitary confinement in the infamous "Rectangle of Death" maximum security ward of Combinado del Este Prison. He was released on March 19, 1988.

In October 1988, he was arrested and detained for two days for complaining that the Cuban government would not give him an exit visa. On March 20, 1989, he was arrested and detained briefly while trying to make arrangements at the Swiss Embassy for his departure from Cuba. He finally managed to leave Cuba for Europe on April 9, 1989.

· · · · ·

The Refusenik

ESTEBAN CÁRDENAS JUNQUERA
OCCUPATION: educator
DIAGNOSIS: psychotic
CONFINEMENT: 24 days
ELECTROSHOCKS: none
PSYCHOTROPIC DRUGS: yes

Born July 16, 1946 in Ciego de Avila, Camagüey province, Esteban Cárdenas Junquera graduated from Manuel Azcunce High School in Tarará, Havana province, in 1963. In 1966, after three years in the School of Education at the University of Havana, he was expelled for "anti-Soviet attitudes." In March 1970, he was arrested for refusing to serve in the Cuban Armed Forces and detained in Morro Castle Prison in Havana. In May, he was transferred to the

Castellanos ward of the Havana Psychiatric Hospital (Mazorra), where doctors diagnosed him as a "psychotic personality with the ability to differentiate between right and wrong." During his three-week stay, he was given five hundred milligrams of chlorpromazine on a daily basis and was forced to watch while electroshocks were administered to other dissidents. Cárdenas later said that he believes the purpose of his internment was not to cure but to frighten and demoralize him. He since has described the inhuman living conditions in Castellanos. Human excrement covered the floor. He shared two towels and one bar of soap with nineteen criminally insane inmates. Under the supervision of the orderly Heriberto Medero two inmate trusties named "Mayarí" and "Caballo" conducted a reign of terror.[1] After twenty-four days in Castellanos, Cárdenas was returned to Morro Castle, tried, and sentenced to six months forced labor on a crew assigned to Havana's Metropolitan Park Program. After his release, Cárdenas began to work as a temporary at the Center for Information and Study of Culture. In May 1971, he was arrested and charged with vagrancy. Because his name was not on the Center's official payroll, he was found guilty and sentenced to one year in prison. After serving his term at El Príncipe Prison and performing forced labor on a dairy farm in San José de las Lajas, he won his appeal and was released. In 1972, he worked for *Bohemia* magazine for nine months until he was fired for "ideological deviationism." In 1974, he worked as an advisor on literature to rural schools in Jagüey Grande, Matanzas province, until he again was fired for "deviationism." From 1975 until his arrest in 1978, he worked in the Publications Department of the National Library in Havana. In March 1977, he was detained for seventy-two hours at State Security Headquarters at *Villa Marista* for his allegedly "revisionist" writings. On September 2, 1977, he was arrested and detained for three hours at *Villa Marista* in Havana. Although he was accused of plotting to leave Cuba illegally and kidnapping a government official, he was released. On March 21, 1978, Cárdenas sought asylum in the Argentinean Embassy by jumping into its garden from an adjoining roof. He broke his ankle during the attempt. The Embassy called the police. State Security agents arrested him and carried him from the Embassy grounds. He was sentenced to fifteen years in prison, of which he served twenty months. Released on October 13, 1979, he came to the United States in January 1980. He currently resides in Miami, Florida.

. . . . .

The Businessman

EUGENIO DE SOSA CHABAU
OCCUPATION: business executive
DIAGNOSIS: none
CONFINEMENT: 5 months
ELECTROSHOCKS: 14
PSYCHOTROPIC DRUGS: yes

Born in Havana on August 8, 1916, Eugenio de Sosa Chabau attended schools in Cuba, the United States, Great Britain, and Switzerland, and studied diplomatic and consular law at the University of Havana. He was a member of the Board of Directors of the daily newspaper *Diario de la Marina,* and presided over the Santa Regina Sugar Mill as well as cattle ranch operations. In December 1959, he was arrested for conspiring to depose the Castro regime and was sentenced to twenty years in jail and an additional twenty years under house arrest. Over the following years, he was confined to several prisons, including the Isle of Pines and La Cabaña. He was one of the *plantados,* prisoners who refused to participate in reeducation programs or wear the uniform of common prisoners.

In 1977, after seventeen years in prison, de Sosa was taken from Combinado del Este Prison to State Security Headquarters at *Villa Marista* to be interrogated on information he allegedly passed to "counterrevolutionary exiles" in 1963. He was stripped and placed in solitary confinement in a small, unlit cell. Psychotropic drugs were mixed in with his food; when he discovered a half-dissolved tablet in his food, he stopped eating.

One day, he was interrogated by a State Security officer, who told him that one of his daughters (whom he had not seen in over fifteen years) and his granddaughters were flying in from Texas to visit him. The officer told him that the visit was "a gesture of mercy of the Castro government" before his execution. A few days later, de Sosa was taken to the barber and given clean clothes. When he entered the room, however, he found not his family but the same State Security officer, who told him that there had been a terrible accident involving the plane, and that his daughter and granddaughters were dead. (De Sosa later discovered that both the visit and the death of his family were a hoax.) Enraged, he struck the State Security officer. As de Sosa later put it, "when I was told of the 'tragedy,' I believed it. . . . I wanted to die." The guards beat him savagely, telling him he would be shot the next day at La Cabaña Prison.

That night, however, he instead was taken from *Villa Marista* and driven through Havana. At one point, he was forced to lie down on the floor of the car. When he was removed from the car, he discovered that he had been trans-

589

ferred to the Carbó-Serviá ward of the Havana Psychiatric Hospital (Mazorra). De Sosa later described Carbó-Serviá as "a snakepit writhing with the violent and insane."

> There were about eighty men in this ward, all violently disturbed. The smell of urine and excrement was sickening. There would be brawls among the patients every so often and shattered, bloody bodies had to be carted out. During my stay there, five patients were killed in brawls....

One day, several young boys, the oldest of whom probably was no more than sixteen, were brought into the ward:

> [The boys] had been caught writing anti-government graffiti on some building walls, and a "judge of the people" declared that to do such a thing they must be insane and in need of psychiatric treatment. Before the day was over all the boys were systematically gang-raped by more than thirty patients in the ward. To this day I can hear their cries for help and see their bloody bodies as I stood by in impotent rage. Not a single staff member intervened.

During his time in Carbó-Serviá, de Sosa was subjected to fourteen sessions of electroconvulsive therapy. As he later described, most electroshocks were applied with little or no regard for the health or safety of the patient:

> My first encounter with group electroshock treatments occurred one night when I saw a team of four men, directed by a man called Mederos who was dressed as an orderly, enter the ward. Six patients were grabbed and rubber pieces stuffed into their mouths. They were thrown to the floor in a row side by side. Right there, on the floor, the electrodes were applied to both sides of their heads and the shocks [were] applied. Six bodies started to contort one by one.... The shocks were applied to the temples of the patients, but to me they applied most of the shocks to the testicles instead.

He later told Lourdes Meluza of WLTV-TV in Miami that electroshocks "felt like thunder, an explosion."

After five months, he was returned to Combinado del Este, where he remained until his release on November 15, 1979. He arrived in the United States on January 18, 1980. He now is an independent associate with the Calmaquip Engineering Corporation in Miami, Florida.

. . . . .

The Filmmaker

Nicolás Guillén Landrián
Occupation: filmmaker/artist
Diagnosis: unknown
Confinement: 5 years
Electroshocks: 20
Psychotropic drugs: yes

A filmmaker, artist, and poet, Nicolás Guillén Landrián was born in 1938 in Camagüey. He is the nephew of Cuba's late poet laureate, Nicolás Guillén. He graduated from Escuelas Pías High School and enrolled in the University of Havana, where he participated in the Revolution. In 1962, Cuban authorities accused him of trying to leave Cuba without authorization and sentenced him to two years at a "rehabilitation farm" on the Isle of Pines. After a year, he developed a nervous disorder and was allowed to complete his sentence under house arrest, but not before being confined for a brief time in the Galigarcía Hospital (later known as Centro de Salud Mental) in Havana, where he underwent twelve sessions of electroconvulsive therapy (ECT) under anesthesia.

In 1970, Guillén was arrested and detained briefly in Combinado del Este Prison in Havana. In 1973, the National Film Institute (ICAIC) expelled him for films "inconsistent with the goals of the revolution." ICAIC authorities had discovered that his documentary, *Coffea Arábiga* (*Arabian Coffee*), contained a scene showing Fidel Castro climbing a mountain while the Beatles' song, *Fool on the Hill*, played in the background. Another factor in his expulsion was his refusal to participate in a film intended to discredit the poet Heberto Padilla. Unable to make a living as a filmmaker, he did odd jobs in the construction industry. In 1976, Guillén was accused of "ideological deviationism" and of conspiring to assassinate Fidel Castro. The latter charge apparently was based on an offhand remark made at a party. Taken to State Security Headquarters at *Villa Marista* in Havana, he was held without trial and interrogated for six months. In 1977, he was sentenced to two years in Combinado del Este Prison. Confined to the psychiatric unit of the Combinado del Este Prison hospital, he was given large doses of psychotropic drugs. His health broken, he was sent on the recommendation of State Security to the Carbó-Serviá ward of the Havana Psychiatric Hospital (Mazorra), where the orderly Heriberto Mederos supervised the administration of eight sessions of ECT without anesthesia. He was returned to Combinado del Este, from which he was released in 1979. In 1980 (about six months after his release), Guillén was accused of attempting to send abroad a document condemning human rights abuses by the Castro regime. Charged with "being dangerous to the Cuban Revolution," he was sentenced to four years in Combinado del Este Prison.

In November 1981, the political prisoner Rafael Saumell was transferred to the psychiatric ward of the Combinado del Este Prison hospital. There he met Guillén. Saumell later recalled that Guillén's doctor was Jesús Edreira, M.D.,[2] and that the nurse Natalia Figueroa forced Guillén to swallow several medications four times each day: twenty-five milligrams of chlorpromazine; trifluoperazine;[3] and trihexyphenidyl hydrochloride.[4] Each day, Figueroa would search Guillén's bunk to make sure he had not hidden the pills. Saumell remained in the ward with Guillén until May 1982, when he was transferred to La Cabaña Prison. Guillén was released in 1984.

From the time of his release from jail in 1984 until the end of 1989, Guillén's family kept him confined (on the recommendations of State Security) in the Havana Psychiatric Hospital (Mazorra) for six out of every seven days. He nonetheless remained active in the Cuban Committee for Human Rights (*Comité Cubano Pro Derechos Humanos*). At the end of 1989, he was allowed to emigrate to Miami, Florida. Since that time, he has become well-known in the emigré community for his paintings.

· · · · ·

The Civil Servant

GUALDO HIDALGO PORTILLA
OCCUPATION: civil servant
DIAGNOSIS: paranoid schizophrenic
CONFINEMENT: 69 days
ELECTROSHOCKS: 8–12
PSYCHOTROPIC DRUGS: yes

Born in Bayamo on August 21, 1951, Gualdo Hidalgo Portilla graduated from Luis A. Turcios Lima High School in Bayamo. He first enrolled at Holguín University; he later transferred to the School of Humanities at the University of Santiago, from which he graduated in 1978 with a degree in philosophy.

In 1976, Hidalgo was named a Professor of Philosophy at the Camilo Cienfuegos Vocational Military School in Holguín—despite the fact that he had not yet received his degree. By 1977, he had been promoted to Director of the Department of Philosophy. Later that same year, however, he was fired as a result of his failure to join the Communist youth. For the next year he taught training programs in the construction industry.

In October 1978, Hidalgo joined the Political Studies Department of the Provincial Power Assembly in Holguín, eventually being promoted to Department Chief. In this position, he was privy to policy briefings held in Havana on a wide variety of topics. It was his responsibility to explain new policies to provincial administrators, and to develop educational and training plans for the province. He also taught political economy and history of philosophy for state industry executives at the National School of Economic Administration (*Escuela Nacional de Dirección de la Economía*) in Holguín.

Hidalgo still held these positions on May 15, 1981, when he sought asylum at the British Embassy in Havana. He was arrested by Cuban authorities, who accused him of attempting to kidnap the British Ambassador in order to obtain asylum. He was taken to State Security Headquarters at *Villa Marista* in Havana, where he was interrogated for twenty-seven days.

On June 11, 1981, Hidalgo was transferred to the Carbó-Serviá ward of the Havana Psychiatric Hospital (Mazorra). He was diagnosed as paranoid schizophrenic by Oscar de la Rosa, M.D. He remembers his experiences in Carbó-Serviá as the worst of his confinement: "Prison is nothing compared to Carbó-Serviá."

Hidalgo has stated that he received between eight and twelve electroshocks during his stay. He does not remember the exact figure because, as he later noted, "one of the characteristics of electroshock is that it erases short-term memory. When you receive several electroshocks, it is almost impossible to remember how many there were." The shocks were administered by a common prisoner with no professional training; often they were given to patients on a whim, sometimes as entertainment, sometimes as punishment.

Hidalgo was forced to ingest large doses of psychotropic drugs. He was unable to identify what the drugs were. Those who refused to take the drugs were threatened with beatings by gangs of criminally insane inmates. The combination of electroshocks and psychotropic drugs resulted in a number of side effects: memory loss; convulsions; muscular rigidity and a loss of muscular coordination; vertigo; and confusion. Hidalgo later commented that the large doses of psychotropic drugs "were more adequate to kill horses than to treat humans."

After sixty-nine days in Carbó-Serviá, Hidalgo was returned to *Villa Marista* on August 20, 1981, where he remained until October 15, 1981.

It continues to be unclear whether Hidalgo ever was tried or convicted of any crime. On July 31, 1981, the Cuban government announced that Hidalgo had been tried for his alleged actions at the British Embassy but had been found not guilty by reason of mental illness. Hidalgo since has stated, however, that he never appeared before a tribunal or court of any kind. Despite his supposed exoneration, Hidalgo spent the next two years (October 1981 to sometime in 1983) at Combinado del Este Prison in Havana, and the following three years in the Provincial Prison in Holguín, from which he was released on the order of the Minister of Interior on May 15, 1986. Despite the claims of the Cuban government to the contrary, Hidalgo alleges that he was tried *in absentia* and convicted of "actions against the Chief of a Diplomatic Representation." To this day, he still does not know the terms of his conviction or sentence.

After his release from prison, Hidalgo survived by doing odd jobs in Holguín. He left for the United States on June 13, 1990. He lives in New Jersey with his wife and son, and has begun work as an operator in a print shop.

· · · · ·

The Union Activist

Jesús Leyva Guerra
Occupation: seaman
Diagnosis: paranoid schizophrenia
Confinement: 39 months
Electroshocks: 24
Psychotropic Drugs: yes

Born in Santiago de Cuba in 1947, Jesús Leyva Guerra worked for many years as a seaman in the merchant marine. He became active in his union, and helped forward complaints about working conditions to the appropriate authorities. When they failed to respond, Leyva began to participate clandestinely in dissident activities. In 1978, Leyva was denounced by his brothers (who are State Security officials) for allegedly engaging in illegal foreign currency exchanges. He was sentenced to ten months in prison, the first seven of which he spent in the Havana Psychiatric Hospital (Mazorra). He completed his sentence at the Combinado del Este Prison in Havana.

In 1981, Leyva was arrested and charged with *salida ilegal*, attempting to leave Cuba illegally, under Article 247 of the Cuban Criminal Code. Sent to the Gustavo Machín Psychiatric Hospital (Jagua) in Santiago de Cuba, he was diagnosed as paranoid schizophrenic by Carmen Betancourt, M.D. and confined for two months. In 1983, Leyva was arrested for distributing dissident literature. Shipped once again to Machín, he was examined by Enrique Font, M.D., who re-diagnosed him as paranoid schizophrenic. He was subjected to six sessions of electroconvulsive therapy in ten days. He was released after a three month confinement.

In 1985, Leyva was arrested and charged with attempting to seek asylum at the Ecuadorian Embassy in Havana. He was sentenced to three months in the Carbó-Serviá ward of the Havana Psychiatric Hospital. Transferred to Machín, he again was re-diagnosed as paranoid schizophrenic by José Perez Milán, M.D., and given large doses of psychotropic drugs. He spent one month at Machín before being released. In 1986, while on a hunger strike to protest labor conditions at his place of work, Leyva was arrested and sent to Machín. Reexamined by Orlando Lamar-Vicens, M.D., the hospital's director of security, he was given six electroshocks and heavy doses of psychotropic drugs. He was released after five months.

In November 1987, Leyva was arrested moments after leaving the home of the human rights activist Elizardo Sánchez Santa Cruz. Confined for nine months in Machín, he was given a new psychiatric evaluation and additional doses of psychotropic drugs. On 14 July 1988, Leyva was arrested in Santiago de Cuba while collecting information for the Cuban Committee for Human Rights (*Comité Cubano Pro Derechos Humanos*) and the Cuban Commission for Human Rights and National Reconciliation (*Comisión Cubana de Derechos Humanos y Reconciliación Nacional*), two unofficial human rights groups operating within Cuba. Taken to Machín, he immediately began a hunger strike that would last eight days. Diagnosed once again by Lamar-Vicens, he was forced to undergo twelve sessions of electroconvulsive therapy and ingest large doses of psychotropic drugs. Leyva later stated that during this stay, he also suffered additional interrogations and beatings at the hands of Captain Carlos del Toro of the Ministry of Interior. He was confined to Machín for a total of nine months.

In *Human Rights in Cuba: The Need To Sustain the Pressure*, Americas Watch's Mary Jane Carnejo states succinctly the hypocrisy not only of Leyva's confinement, but of confining any sane dissident to a psychiatric hospital:

> If Leyva has been confined to treat any mental illness he may suffer, why has he been held in the judicial ward of the hospital? If he has been held in the judicial ward because he has criminal charges pending against him, what are they? If it is because he is considered by judicial authorities to be dangerous to himself or to society, has he actually caused harm to himself or another person, or is this a form of preventive detention?

In an October 1989 interview with *Miami Herald* correspondent Liz Balmaseda, Leyva stated that the electroshocks and large doses of drugs were so frequent that he remembers very little of his stay. "Later they told me I ate on the eighth day of my hunger strike, but I don't remember." In a 1990 interview with Lourdes Meluza of WLTV-TV, Miami, he said that "the effects [of electroshock] included swelling of the lower and upper extremities and burned temples. . . . I was not able to recognize my family or my wife, and I secreted blood through my penis."

His wife, Elba, was horrified by what she found when she came to visit him at Mazorra. He was so disoriented that he failed to recognize her and sat down at a table with strangers. His arms and legs were swollen and his temples had electrode burns. "He was out of it, like a drunk, dead gone," she said later. "He would drool all over himself."

Elba and others complained to hospital officials, who told them that Leyva was "crazy" and that the hospital was trying to cure him. When *Los Angeles Times* correspondent Don Schanche asked a government official to comment on the complaints, the official "responded by shrugging his shoulders and rolling his eyes, then warned that it was dangerous for foreign journalists to interview human rights dissidents without first advising the government."

On April 20, 1989, after a little over nine months in detention, Leyva was released. In October 1989, he, along with his wife Elba and their two children, emigrated to the United States. They currently live in Miami, Florida.

· · · · ·

The Truck Driver

José Morales Rodríguez
Occupation: truck driver
Diagnosis: none
Confinement: 18 days
Electroshocks: 14
Psychotropic Drugs: yes

Born in Victoria de las Tunas in 1939, José Morales Rodríguez was an independent truck owner-operator. In 1960, he was accused of conspiring against the government and sentenced to six years, which he served in the Boniato, Holguín and La Cabaña Prisons. Near the end of his term, a year was added because he would not cooperate with authorities. In 1970, he was arrested in Victoria de las Tunas and accused of conspiracy, serving one year in Holguín without a trial. In 1973, he again was arrested, serving nine months in Holguín and Santiago de Cuba Prisons without a trial. On June 21, 1981, he was arrested and accused of participating in a conspiracy to assassinate Fidel Castro. During his interrogation in Victoria de las Tunas, he was placed in a water tank and given electroshocks. In July, he was taken to the Gustavo Machín Psychiatric Hospital (Jagua) in Santiago de Cuba, where he was given fourteen electroshocks and large doses of psychotropic drugs. As a result, he experienced severe memory loss. After eighteen days in Machín, Morales was returned to Victoria de las Tunas and placed under house arrest, where he spent the next seven years. In March 1989, he was allowed to leave Cuba. Today he lives in New Jersey, where he works in construction.

· · · · ·

The Musician

Julio Vento Roberes
Occupation: musician
Diagnosis: acute paranoia

CONFINEMENT: 5 years
ELECTROSHOCKS: 16
PSYCHOTROPIC DRUGS: yes

Born on December 28, 1932, Julio Vento Roberes began studying music at age seven, graduating in 1948 from the *Academia Municipal de Música* in Matanzas. Vento was a flutist, composer, and soloist with the Matanzas Symphony Orchestra and National Orchestra of Cuba. His hobby was cartooning. On August 27, 1964, while attempting to leave Cuba, he was arrested in Havana and jailed for two years, first at La Cabaña and then at San Severino Castle. On February 4, 1977, Vento was arrested in Matanzas after leaflets advocating political and civil rights and featuring his cartoons were posted throughout Matanzas. He was found guilty of distributing enemy propaganda under Article 108 of the Cuban Criminal Code and sentenced to five years in prison. Vento instead was committed to the Carbó-Serviá ward of the Havana Psychiatric Hospital (Mazorra) for the entire five year term. He was diagnosed as suffering from acute paranoia as well as "delusions that he was a defender of human rights." He was subjected to sixteen sessions of electroconvulsive therapy (ECT) and large doses of psychotropic drugs at the hands of the orderly Heriberto Mederos. Vento has said that when he showed the electrode burns on his forehead to Oscar de la Rosa, M.D., the attending psychiatrist, de la Rosa objected that the ECT had not been medically prescribed.

During the Mariel boatlift in 1980 (while Vento was in Mazorra), his wife was expelled from Cuba. This left Vento's children, Jesús (seven years old at the time) and Walkiria (two years old) without parental supervision. At first, they lived with relatives. Cuban authorities eventually ordered them placed in the home of Juan Enrique Quin-tana Alvarez, a Ministry of the Interior official based in Matanzas, who formally adopted them. At the end of his term, Vento was not released. He again began to draw political cartoons. On October 10, 1982, while still in confinement, he was accused of distributing leaflets with anti-Castro caricatures and of writing letters abroad complaining that he had not been released from the Havana Psychiatric Hospital at the end of his term. He was found guilty of distributing enemy propaganda under Article 108 of the Cuban Criminal Code and sentenced to eight years in Combinado del Este Prison in Havana. Until early 1986, he was held with a group of *nuevos plantados,* but then was moved to another part of the prison. During his time in prison, he became a member of the Cuban Committee for Human Rights. In 1987, Vento was included on a list of prisoners to be released to a delegation from the U.S. Catholic Conference. Told he would have to leave without his children, he chose to remain in jail. On August 22, 1988, Vento was forcibly taken from prison and flown directly to the United States. He now lives in Tampa, Florida.

· · · · ·

The Cadet

EDUARDO YANES SANTANA
OCCUPATION: military cadet
DIAGNOSIS: unknown
CONFINEMENT: 1 month
ELECTROSHOCKS: none
PSYCHOTROPIC DRUGS: yes

Born in Havana on September 30, 1945, Eduardo Yanes Santana attended high school at José Ramón Rodríguez Technological Institute and as a cadet at Ceiba del Agua Military Academy. Upon graduation he enrolled in the School of Humanities of the University of Havana, but did not graduate. Yanes was arrested on April 13, 1964 because of his opposition to compulsory military service. Sent to La Cabaña Prison, he served two and one-half months for insubordination and twelve months for failing to register for military service. He next was arrested in 1966 and held in isolation for forty-seven days in State Security Headquarters at *Villa Marista* in Havana. Transferred to a forced labor battalion under the control of the Military Units to Aid Production (UMAP), he was sent to a UMAP camp at KILO 9 near Morón, Camagüey province. Captured while trying to escape, the authorities beat him savagely. In early 1967, as a result of his continued defiance of UMAP authority, Yanes was sent to the Camagüey Psychiatric Hospital. He was held for four days and kept under constant sedation; no physician ever diagnosed or treated him. After a failed escape attempt, he was transferred first to La Cabaña and then to Morro Castle where he served fifteen months.

Early in 1969 he was taken to the Habana del Este Naval Hospital in Santa María del Mar, Havana province. He was examined by a group of psychiatrists and released. In the latter half of 1969, he was accused of "failing to integrate into Marxist society" and held for one month in the Castellanos ward of the Havana Psychiatric Hospital (Mazorra). The orderly Heriberto Mederos threatened him with electroshock treatments. Although Mederos did not carry out this threat, he did force Yanes to watch while he and one of his aides, a criminally insane inmate nicknamed "Caballo," gave electroshocks to others. Inmates were doused with water and forced to lie down on a wet floor. The shocks would continue until the inmate went into convulsions and became unconscious. Although it was winter, Yanes and the other detainees had to bathe outside with ice-cold water at five o'clock in the morning. Yanes also was forced to ingest psychotropic drugs. During his stay at the hospital, Yanes was not examined by a physician. Upon his release from Castellanos, he was confined for six months to El Príncipe Prison. One month into his stay, he was sentenced *in absentia* to an additional eighteen months for being "highly dangerous." He spent the last four months of this sentence in the Quivicán Penal Prison.

Late in 1978, Yanes was held for ten days at State Security Headquarters in *Villa Marista*. While there, agents attempted to recruit him to spy on other dissidents. In 1980, Yanes was one of many who sought asylum at the Peruvian Embassy.[5] He left for Costa Rica on April 16, 1980 and came to the United States on July 12, 1980. Before his departure, all of his manuscripts were confiscated. He now resides in Miami, Florida, where he owns and manages a ceramic tile installation firm. He is completing work on a collection of his poems and a memoir of events at the Peruvian Embassy.

· · · · ·

The Physician

F. MARIO ZALDIVAR BATISTA
OCCUPATION: physician
DIAGNOSIS: anxiety
CONFINEMENT: 15 days
ELECTROSHOCKS: none
PSYCHOTROPIC DRUGS: yes

Born on May 4, 1946 in Holguín, Oriente province, Fulgencio Mario Zaldívar Batista attended the Instituto de Holguín and the Marist Brothers High School in Holguín. He studied medicine at the University of Oriente, later transferring to the University of Havana, from which he graduated as a Doctor of Medicine in 1972. Zaldívar practiced sports medicine, later working in the Aleida Fernández Cherdie polyclinic in Marianao, a municipality in Havana Province.

On December 20, 1979, Zaldívar was arrested at the Barlovento Marina and accused of attempting to leave the country illegally under Article 247 of the Cuban Criminal Code. During his initial detention and interrogation at State Security Headquarters at *Villa Marista* in Havana, he was tortured and confined to an ice-cold cell.

On March 14, 1980, he was transferred to the Havana Psychiatric Hospital (Mazorra). He was diagnosed as suffering from anxiety and confined to the Carbó-Serviá and Castellanos wards. Each day, Zaldívar and the other inmates were forced to swallow a one hundred milligram tablet of chlorpromazine:

> Everyone was forced to take the pill. They would look into our mouths to make sure that we swallowed it. If we didn't, criminally insane inmates would beat us up in return for privileges granted by the staff.

Zaldívar experienced mental confusion, disorientation, drowsiness, weakness, incoherence, and diarrhea as a result of the chlorpromazine.

Since his release, Zaldívar has discussed some of the things he witnessed while at Mazorra: gross and indiscriminate use of psychotropic drugs, usually administered forcibly by other inmates; inhuman living conditions; the use of psychiatric techniques against sane individuals; and the mixing of political dissidents with the criminally insane. Zaldívar also has emphasized that he found it particularly disturbing that all of this was being done under the supervision of professional medical personnel. After fifteen days in Mazorra, Zaldívar was returned to *Villa Marista* for twelve days of interrogation. Blindfolded with a black hood over his head and bound by a rope tied tightly around his neck, he was beaten and kicked until he lost consciousness. He eventually was transferred to the Combinado del Este Prison in Havana where, eighteen months after his arrest, he was told that he had been sentenced *in absentia* to four years in prison. From May 1980 to early 1982, he was confined to Combinado del Este. During his stay there he experienced cardiac valve problems as a result of bacterial endocarditis. He then served six months in La Cabaña Prison. The final two years of his sentence were spent in Holguín and Playa Manteca Prisons. Zaldívar was released at the end of 1983. On 18 December 1985, he left Cuba for Panama. He now resides in Miami, Florida, where he is studying for the Medical Board exams. He has published a book of poems composed in prison.

· · · · ·

My Personal Testimony on Psychiatric Abuse in Cuba
Ariel Hidalgo Guillén

My name is Ariel Hidalgo. I graduated with a B.A. in history and was a high school teacher of Marxist philosophy and political economy. I am also the author of *Origins of the Workers' Movement and Socialist Thinking in Cuba* which has been included in the bibliography of humanities at the university level in Cuba. On the 19th of August 1981, because of my disapproval of the Cuban government's organized repudiation of those who left via the port of Mariel in 1980 (a position which cost me my teaching post), State Security agents searched my house. After their search, I was taken to Havana's Center of Security Investigations, better known among Cubans as *Villa Marista,* where they accused me of "enemy propaganda." The basis for this charge was, among other things, my collaboration on a manuscript which was a leftist critical analysis of the social system ruling Cuba entitled *Cuba: The Marxist State and the New Class.*

On the 9th of September, after twenty days of interrogation, I was handcuffed, placed in a car and driven to what at the time was an unknown destination: the Havana Psychiatric Hospital.

I was placed in an area closed off with iron bars which I later found out was called Sala Carbó-Serviá. Upon seeing the inhuman expressions of the inmates, my first impression was that I was entering a cage of gorillas. Once inside, I realized that I was at the complete mercy of a hundred men—convicts from different prisons, the overwhelming majority of whom were violently insane. Among them were murderers and rapists. The doctors never crossed the shadows of the bars, and the orderlies only entered when they had to remove someone forcibly to be subjected to electroshock treatment.

From sunrise to sunset, a group of leaders, self-appointed by use of force, made the majority of the inmates stay outside on a small patio six meters long enclosed only by iron bars and offering no shade from the sun. The worst part of this, however, was not the lack of protection from the elements. It was having to share such a small space with eighty or ninety psychotic people. During that time, I had to stand, not only because of the lack of space, but also because the floor was covered with excrement, saliva, sperm, et cetera. The most repulsive acts imaginable took place there, including rapes and beatings of defenseless elderly persons.

They only let us enter for a few minutes to eat. Shortly before meal time, dozens of people would push for the door and upon its opening a deafeningly loud horde would descend upon the two large tables in a space within Sala Carbó-Serviá designated as the dining room. When you entered, the food already was on the tables. Plates were so close together to one another, that people had to climb on top of each other in order to eat. The surge of people entering immediately made everything even worse. Some inmates got two or three plates; the strong took the food away from the weak. Some, in their desperation to get one or two rations to eat, ran on top of the tables, stepping on plates or knocking them on the ground. If I succeeded in getting a plate of food I had to eat surrounded by insane people. Because of the savagery of my neighbors, it was an effort to keep the food down.

At night, I could barely close my eyes for fear that some maniac would try and take advantage of my sleep to commit some outrageous act. Lighting on fire the socks of sleeping prisoners was one of the principal ways to pass the time. Some of the more deranged prisoners masturbated and urinated on those who slept.

I was kept there for ten days during which I was taken out of the ward on only one occasion. It was for half an hour, during which I was given a psychiatric evaluation. Looking back on it, if someone killed me in one of those violent disagreements which were so common, I think my murder would have gone unpunished.

As an additional anecdote, I would like to add that after five days in the Sala, a sane young man was added to our number. I say sane because of the expression of terror on his face upon entering, which, I imagine, was similar to that on mine when I arrived. He sat down by the bars next to the entrance and, like an ostrich burying its head in the sand, hid his head in his folded arms. I asked him about himself. He told me that he was a pediatrician named José Arturo García (I think he is already in the United States) and that because of a few words said to a girl friend in jest, was charged with planning the murder of President Fidel Castro.

Since there were no beds available, I gave him my mattress to sleep on, and slept on the frame. After talking to him for a long while (he calmed down when realized that he was not alone in his sanity) he confessed, "If you had not spoken to me, I would have killed myself."

(signed)
Ariel Hidalgo (Guillén)

Against All Hope

Armando Valladares

ARMANDO VALLADARES *(1937–) is probably the best-known former Cuban political prisoner in the West. Valladres spent twenty-two years in prison. Arrested in late 1960, he was released in 1982 because of international pressure that included a personal request from President Mitterand of France to Castro.*

Valladares was arrested because of his freely expressed critiques of the regime at his place of work (a postal savings bank attached to the Ministry of Communications). He became classified as a "counter-revolutionary" and "potential enemy of the revolution." Having attended a Catholic school was also held against him. During his trial he was accused of unspecified acts of sabotage. From the notorious La Cabaña prison (in Havana) he was transferred to the prison complex on the Isle of Pines. This was followed by the Boniato Prison, the harshest of all, where the "diet was designed to bring on deficiency diseases and metabolic disorders."

His experiences in the Cuban penal system testify to the unusual brutality and vindictiveness with which political prisoners have been treated there (including the frequent infliction of bayonet wounds by the guards—an activity not reported in other Communist systems).

Cuba, unlike the Soviet Union and its East European satellites, introduced an ambitious "political rehabilitation program" for its political prisoners. Its goal was to extinguish any overt defiance of or hostility toward the system; self-criticism was encouraged and rewarded. As Valladares put it, the goal of the program was "the moral annihilation of the prisoner, the destruction of all his principles. . . ." By the same token, those like Valladares who refused to participate in this program were treated with special harshness and denied medical care.

A failed escape from the Isle of Pines further aggravated his treatment and added ten years to his sentence. As a result of his prolonged and varied mistreatment, Valladares suffered from many ailments, was confined to a wheelchair, and had to be put through a lengthy and intensive program of rehabilitation before his release. He lives in Spain.

From Armando Valladares, Against All Hope, © *1986 by Armando Valladares. Reprinted with permission.*

Because of the constant firing squads the prison at La Cabaña had become the most terrible of all the jails. But added to that terror of death came another—the terror inspired in us by the early-morning "inspections."

Captain Herman F. Marks, an American whom Fidel Castro had appointed head of the garrison of La Cabaña and official executioner, was the man who fired those *coups de grâce* and carried out the inspections. When he was drunk, which he was very frequently, Marks would order the garrison to form up in full military gear and attack the prisoners. He called the prison his "private hunting reserve." Another of his amusements was to stroll through the *galeras* and call out to those who were to be tried for offenses which carried the death penalty; he would ask them behind which ear they wanted the *coup de grâce*. He had a dog he took with him to the executions so the dog could lap up the dead men's blood. Years later he returned to the United States.

For the inspections the platoon of soldiers, armed with wooden truncheons, chains, bayonets, and anything else they could use to beat us with, would erupt into the *galeras* shouting and striking out blindly. The order was that we prisoners were to come out of the cells the instant the cell doors were opened. But when the cell doors would be opened, the angry mob of soldiers would rush in like a whirlwind, meting out blows at random. Prisoners, also like a whirlwind, would be trying to get out into the prison yard, and so a knot of prisoners and guards beating them would form at the door, since we couldn't all fit through the door at the same time. We were always in mortal terror of those inspections. We would be gripped by panic, desperation, and, worst of all, confusion—we would try to escape unharmed, but that was virtually impossible, since outside in the patio a double file of guards armed with rifles and fixed bayonets made sure that no one failed to receive his quota of blows and kicks.

Hundreds of prisoners ran or staggered out in all states of dress and undress, some even naked. When we were all out, they rushed us and began beating us with even more ferocity. The more the guards flailed and yelled at us, the more furious they became, their faces growing more and more horrible and deformed with hatred and sadism. Up on the roof a line of soldiers, including women, their rifles cradled in their arms, contemplated the spectacle. Among the soldiers up there was always a group of officers and civilians from the Political Police, and, of course, conspicuous, Captain Marks.

About three o'clock one morning in the days after my trial, which I will talk about in a moment, the cry of "Inspection!" woke us all up. Men were shouting the terrifying word from the *galeras* nearest the main gate. Almost instantly the prison yard filled with guards, but they didn't open the cell doors. That was strange—soldiers were just standing there before the bars. But when they opened the doors and gave the order to come out, on the double, the blows began. They did not go inside the *galeras*. They beat us outside. One of us, a seventy-eight-year-old man named Goicochea who could hardly walk, was pushed, fell to the ground, and fractured his thigh. But no one picked Goicochea up; no one even stopped to help him.

We ran around him, trying at the same time to dodge the soldiers' blows and not to trample him. We ran toward the front wall, where we always formed up under the yells of the guards armed with rifles and fixed bayonets waiting for us there. At that inspection, as at some others, platoons were present from the National Revolutionary Police, which collaborated with the garrison at La Cabaña. This time the inspection had a special purpose. Months before, the Revolutionary Government had begun a campaign to collect money to buy arms. Castro's own slogan at the beginning of 1959—"Arms? For what?"—had been utterly forgotten, and now the rage to arm Cuba was spreading over the land. The government had asked the people to contribute money and jewelry—rings, pendants, gold chains—to the defense coffers.

Because of the terror, anguish, and blind panic the inspections always gave me, I had forgotten to grab my watch when I ran out. I always hid it inside a shoe when I went to bed, but like everyone who possessed a watch I always took it out with me during these inspections. It was a matter of prudence—if you left it the soldiers would find it and "confiscate" it for sure. And if you dared to report the "loss," the soldiers invariably took it as an accusation of thievery against themselves; the consequences to the prisoner are easily imagined. As I had run out of my cell I had realized that I had left the watch. No doubt about it, I had thought, I might as well give it up for lost. It had been a gift from my father.

But now all the prisoners were being stripped of their watches, pendants, chains, and wedding rings anyway. One by one, as we entered the *galeras*, completely naked, they took our jewelry. The officers shouted, egging on the pillaging by the soldiers, "Let's go! You people have to contribute to buying weapons and airplanes just like everybody else!" If one of us dared not to turn over a piece of jewelry he was beaten even worse.

All the jewelry was dumped into a canvas bag. When we returned to the *galeras* there was a huge mess of clothing and personal articles strewn down the passageway. Now that we were safe, out of reach of the guards, the prisoners began to rage against them, accusing them of being thieves and robbers. When I picked up my shoes under the cot, I was amazed to find my watch, which had escaped the search. What should I do now? Suddenly I was frightened, frightened to have in my possession my own watch. What if the garrison troops saw it and jumped to the conclusion I'd hidden it from them? They might feel I had intentionally mocked or tricked them, even defied them. Good Lord, what to do? I stood there dazed and bewildered, holding the watch, while some of the prisoners around me looked at it incredulously and asked, "How did you manage to sneak that one by?"

I was now paralyzed with worry. I would have to hide the watch as though I had stolen it. I toyed with the idea of going to the door, calling the guard over, and very politely turning it over to him. I would explain what had happened. That way I would avoid reprisals, but that seemed a weak and even cowardly thing to do. I decided not to do that, and I think that somehow that decision was what determined all my future conduct. I would always act according to my own set of values, because reprisals would be more bearable than the reproaches and censures of my own conscience.

Every morning at sunrise La Cabaña awoke to the same question—"Who will they shoot today?"

After the morning headcount they opened the cells and we congregated in the prison yard and waited in the interminable line for breakfast. The youngest member of our particular group was Carlos Alberto, who was underage, although he was taller than any of us. Carlos Alberto had married very young, and his wife, Linda, had brought their daughter, Gina, to the last visit, when she was only a few months old. Carlos and I had made our attempt to escape from the jail at Political Police Headquarters, so the possibility, or rather virtual certainty, of our being executed always hung over our heads. Because of that and because of his age, Carlos Alberto's family had requested that he be transferred to a jail for minors.

A few days after his trial he was called to the main gate with his belongings. He was being sent to a prison outside Havana. Within a few weeks, somehow supplied with a hacksaw, he cut through the bars of his cell and escaped. He managed to enter the Venezuelan embassy, and after months of pressure the Cuban government allowed him to leave the country.

Carrión, Piñango, Boitel, and I were jubilant at Carlos Alberto's escape—one man fewer in that hell! When days before I had thought of Linda and the months-old baby girl, I couldn't help being overwhelmed by grief for them. I remembered Juan José and Pedrito, and I thought about their little children, whom I had played with during the visit, and who a week afterward had been left fatherless. Gina, at least, would not be an orphan.

The authorities did not bother to notify the families of the men they had executed, so that quite often the mothers, wives, and children of executed men appeared at visiting time asking to see them. A wrenching silence would fall. The prisoners would look at one another, as though saying, "You tell them." Sometimes the family interpreted that silence perfectly, and they would open their eyes wide in pain and shock and break into tears.

When Julio Antonio Yebra's mother found out about her son's execution, she exclaimed with extraordinary self-possession and integrity, "If the death of my son were the last blood shed by these firing squads, I would accept his death without another word."

But he would not be the last. Thousands and thousands more would follow Julio Antonio. . . .

· · · · ·

Men who had been sentenced to death did not return to the *galeras* after their trial. They were led to tiny cells located down at the end of *galera* 22, alongside the cells for Revolutionary Army soldiers sentenced to prison terms for robbery, drug abuse, and so forth—"common crimes" as opposed to "political crimes." The prisoners sentenced to death would have to walk down the entire length of the *galera* of those common prisoners. The common prisoners were kept separate from us political prisoners by the little yard surrounded with high fences just at the main gate. We could see them from our yard, but there was no chance of physical contact with them.

It might have been that they thought they could score some points with the prison guards, or it might have been that they were actually channeling their hatred of those who stood up against the Revolution that many of them had supported, and still supported. For whatever reason, all through that walk, those common prisoners, "delinquents," really criminals, would harass the men sentenced to death, who would have their hands tied behind their backs and be led by guards; they would insult them, spit at them, throw things at them, push them. And it was not solely those few moments of walking down the *galera* which were exploited by the common criminals to harass the political prisoners. There were even some who would follow them to their cells on that improvised Death Row, to which the common prisoners had access, and keep on insulting them, screaming at them there, denying them in their last hours the peace and seclusion that would have allowed them to pray, meditate over their lives, be still.

The guards did nothing about the harassment. The authorities did not even deign to disguise their approval of those proceedings. On the contrary whenever there were political prisoners on Death Row, the authorities would pass out liquor to the common criminals to get them drunk so they would sing the "Internationale" and crow about the triumphs of the Revolution and the beating the counterrevolutionaries had taken and were taking.

Some of the prisoners spoke to the authorities and requested them to put a stop to the delinquents' standing in front of their cells insulting them and yelling at them. But the authorities had not an iota of compassion for them. From the moment the condemned men came out of the tribunal trials with their hands tied behind their backs and began walking to the cells of that Death Row, their escorts pushed and shoved them, mocked and laughed at them. The guards even stripped them of their shoes and threw them to the common prisoners, who fought over them like vultures.

And when the platoon of guards led them to the firing squad, the farewell the political prisoners received from the common prisoners in *galera* 22 was cries of *"Viva Fidel Castro! Viva la Revolución!"*

When the van with the members of the firing squad passed through the entrance which opened into the moats, the unmistakable sound of its motor would be heard throughout the *galeras* and of course in Death Row, where the men knew the decisive moment was at hand. Throughout the *galeras* the murmur of voices in prayer would begin. Otherwise we prisoners, lying on our cots, kept an oppressive, painful silence, a silence made even more painful by our absolute impotence to prevent the death of one who until a few hours before had shared with us his hopes, his dreams, his troubles. A throng of images and thoughts whirled through our heads during those moments: his fatherless children, his widow, his mother prostrate with grief. And the thought too, which made us shiver, that the man the firing squad awaited could well be any one of us. Often I would suddenly see myself with my hands tied, gagged, led into the moat . . . descending those steps to the wooden stake before the wall of sandbags, the spotlights trained on it . . . officers shoving me against it and pulling a piece of rope tight around my waist . . . the soldiers raising their rifles and deafening thunder echoing all along the moats. . . . That could happen to me; I expected it. Every night I rehearsed that journey. I could see every inch of it in my mind. I knew the route by memory—every step, the wooden stake. . . .

There were nights when there would be ten or twelve executions. You would hear the bars of the man's cell door and someone coming to the bars to see his friend and cry out to him the last goodbye. There was no way to sleep in the *galeras*. That was when God began to become a constant companion of mine, and when death became a door into the true life, a step from the shadows into eternal light.

The blows of the hammers nailing together the wooden coffin would echo from the stone walls of the moats. The corpse was not given over to the relatives so they could hold a wake and funeral or accompany it to the holy ground of a cemetery. Instead, a van with INRA (National Institute of Agrarian Reform) painted on its side took the body to Colón Cemetery, where it was buried in a common grave, in a plot reserved for that purpose by the Ministry of the Interior. In the van would be an officer from the Political Police and several soldiers. The body was buried without a marker or headstone or anything else to identify it. The family did not even have the sad privilege of knowing where their loved one was buried.

But it was not only corpses that disappeared; some detainees were secretly subjected to interrogations and, when the authorities had finished, taken directly from Political Police Headquarters to the firing squad. We could see that happen sometimes from our *galeras*. Once when I was in the prison yard with a group of my friends, I saw them take down a gagged man with his hands tied behind his back. He was dressed in olive green. They shot him hurriedly. He had not come out of that prison; no one knew who he was. And that happened many times—men were executed and buried secretly. . . .

· · · · ·

Knowing that we were, so to speak, sleeping on a mattress full of explosives destroyed many prisoners' nerves; some went completely mad. They felt they were trapped, and they gave way to sheer animal panic. On two nights we were awakened by the blood-curdling shrieks of prisoners who threw themselves over the sixth-floor railing onto the prison yard below. One of them had been in the jail for two years. The other had arrived with the last consignments of prisoners from Oriente province. I remember that this latter prisoner's name was Arturo; I had spoken with him several times.

Every time the group of technicians under Lightning's command went down into the basement, several prisoners would be seized with hysteria.

"They're down there! They're sure as hell gonna blow us to smithereens! I hope they don't connect us up by mistake!"

Dozens of men lived in that state of anxiety. They kept watch on their own (they would hardly sleep), and they practically leaped out of their skin if it grew too quiet outside. They had evolved a grisly interpretation of a too-silent night—the guards on post had received orders to evacuate because they were going to set off the TNT.

And in the aftermath of the Bay of Pigs failure, not only our psychological state, but living conditions generally in the prison became much more severe. Even food was much scarcer. At that time, they would bring in vats full of greasy water with some vegetables floating in it—potatoes, pumpkins, yams—frequently dirty and rotten, at that. We found out from men working in the kitchen, who belonged to Circular 4, that one hundred pounds of foodstuffs per day were allocated for the six thousand prisoners on Isla de Piños—that worked out to less than a pound for every fifty prisoners. And that was the extent of our food. The bread had not a drop of fat or lard in it, just salt, and not always that. Its texture was so rubbery that you could stretch it out to more than a third longer without breaking it.

Filth, cockroaches, and rats continually appeared in the food.

The hot sugar water they served as breakfast was prepared with sugar dyed green. The sacks the sugar came in had a notice printed on them: NOT FOR HUMAN CONSUMPTION. It was waste sugar, swept up off the factory floors or picked up with shovels, and it was full of trash and impurities. It was meant to be used as cattle feed.

It was during those months that guanina came to Isla de Piños. The guanina bush, related to the tree called fustic which produces a strong yellow dye and is sometimes slightly toxic, yields a small bean somewhat like a lentil, and about the same color, but it tastes terrible. It has a strong, bitter taste of bile—another of its relatives is called, for good reason, the kidney tree. Campesinos sometimes used it as a substitute for coffee. It, like the green sugar, was ordinarily used for cattle feed, but only when mixed with other grains, since it has hardly any nutritional value of its own. It is not used for human consumption. But that didn't matter much to the prison authorities.

There was a man named Vivas Bartelemí in our Circular. He had been a medical student who had gone as a member of a diplomatic mission to Communist China, and he had appeared in the newspapers in a photograph shaking hands with Mao Zedong. Somebody started a rumor that he had bought the guanina during his trip to China. Vivas thought that was funny. Knowing his sense of humor, I suspect he himself had something to do with the spread of the rumor. Irony seemed to crop up all around Vivas. He had been fighting against Batista and was taken prisoner during the Revolution. When Castro came to power, Vivas was arrested again and confined to the same Circular he had been in before.

One of the dishes they served us was guanina with cornmeal ground very fine, but still full of worms, and very bitter-tasting. The rice also had worms, and a very unpleasant taste—they didn't wash it before cooking it. It seemed that any foodstuff that had spoiled was sent to Isla de Piños, for us to eat. It was about that time that macaroni and spaghetti began appearing constantly; this food became the staple of the Cuban people, as it also did, of course, for the prisoners, for the next twenty years. But you should not imagine a tasty dish of macaroni Italian-style. What they served in the jail was boiled with a little bit of salt until it all stuck together in a gummy paste; that was all. You had to cut it into pieces to serve it, and even to be able to swallow it, you had to add sugar. The sale of cooking oil, spices, and salt that we had taken advantage of before was now suspended. There was no protein whatsoever in our diet. So not only was our food unbearably monotonous and unspeakably foul-tasting, it lacked all vitamins and other elements necessary to the organism as well, and that would have further consequences later on, when the effects of vitamin and protein deficiency were felt by all of us.

One day they called us out in groups of twenty-five to take us to the records office, which had been set up in the back part of Building 5. We went up some steps leading to a large room. They shaved my head, took clippings of hair around my temples, and fingerprinted me several times. They went all over my naked body, looking for tattoos, marks, or scars which might be used to identify me. Then they photographed me and gave me my prisoner number—26830. From then on, my name would not mean anything to the garrison, and I would be just a number.

We were made to sign a card authorizing the prison to open and read our correspondence. One man refused to sign, so the guards were sent for. They beat him until he signed. There was another prisoner, named Mitre, who couldn't be forced to sign. He was a calm, quiet man, but he had an indestructible will.

Given all these conditions, who could have been surprised when one rainy, stormy night in July, Cheo Guerra, Pedro Carlo Osorio, "El Mexicano," Edmundo Amado, and two other men decided to escape. They cut through a window on the hospital side of the Circular. The rain was coming down in sheets; the sound of it was deafening and the spotlights were useless, since the curtains of water cut off their light. The men managed to climb down without any trouble, but they got no more than a few yards away. Someone had seen them. An intense burst of fire, muted somewhat by the sound of the rain, sounded the alarm. They were captured, and on the spot, dripping wet in the driving rain, they were given a brutal beating. The soldiers, blind with rage, couldn't even wait to get them to the punishment cages, where they were to spend many months. That was Cheo's second visit to the dungeon-like cells, and it would not be his last.

The next morning, Lieutenant Julio Tarrau, the prison director, came in at the head of the garrison. Wielding his Russian Makarov pistol, which no one had ever seen him shoot but which he thought gave him more authority, and which certainly gave him more courage, he screamed at us, "I'll kill any son of a bitch that moves. Stand in front of your cells, at attention!"

The garrison, which amounted to some two hundred soldiers for that search, filled the prison yard. The first wave entered without firearms, carrying only bayonets and truncheons. Behind them came the guards armed with rifles and fixed bayonets.

"Okay!" Tarrau began speaking again. "Everybody strip! Everybody take off your clothes and stand there in front of your cells!"

Carrión and I stripped. In the next cell, ex-Captain Tápanes-Tápanes, from the city of Cárdenas, and his cellmate Chávez followed suit.

There was someone on the fourth floor who did not take off his underwear. Lieutenant Tarrau screamed at him to come downstairs. The atmosphere grew even more tense, more frightened and expectant. Thousands of eyes were fixed on that man slowly walking down the stairs. In everyone's mind was the same question—and it was almost like a plea there was no longer enough time for: Why didn't you take off your underwear like everybody else?

When the man came to the prison yard, Tarrau himself shoved him, and a group of guards fell on him. The prisoner struggled, but only for a few seconds. The hail of blows flattened him, and staggering, almost unable to walk, he was dragged and shoved out toward the punishment cells, while they ripped his underwear from him in shreds. He had not even reached the main gate before he was naked.

A murmur of protest and indignation arose throughout the Circular. Tarrau shot his pistol into the air, and the guards cocked their rifles. You could hear the bolts of the machine guns click too, as the guards in the tower cocked them and took aim at the prisoners before the cells. The rifles' power of persuasion silenced us. We learned later that the prisoner hadn't wanted to take off his underwear because when he was fighting in the mountains with Castro's troops an enemy mine had torn off his member and destroyed one testicle.

The spectacle in the Circular beggared description. All you could do at the moment was stare—there were hundreds of completely naked men formed into a surrealistic legion, standing at attention in perfect formation.

"First floor, down here!" Tarrau was the only one giving orders. He was livid with rage. *He* was the director, and these prisoners had tried to escape on him.

We began to descend, and he ordered us to stand in front of the wall next to the washbasins. Some of us were randomly clubbed and pushed. When we were all downstairs, the garrison went up into the cells. Five or six hours later we were still standing there; several older men's ankles and legs were swollen and inflamed. No one was allowed to raise his head, under threat of being beaten and dragged off to the punishment cages. Some of those who couldn't resist the temptation to look up to watch the destruction of our possessions were caught at it and brutally beaten and then spent months naked in the punishment pavilion.

When the soldiers were finally finished with their work and the bars of the main gate closed behind the last guard, we were released from our formation. In the prison yard, in front of the showers and washbasins, there were piles of clothing from all the cells on all the floors. Several inmates later took charge of sorting the clothing and calling out the owners' numbers. We headed back to our cells. More than a thousand naked prisoners filled the stairways. We were all eager to be the first to arrive, less to see what the guards had done than to cover ourselves....

There is nothing more humiliating or more degrading than forced nakedness before your oppressors—you feel especially vulnerable. The authorities knew that, and they used our nakedness against us, another in their arsenal of psychological weapons. The interrogators from the Political Police never failed to keep prisoners, both men and women, naked. They took the women in naked for interrogations by groups of officers. If for a man it's embarrassing to be forced to stand there completely stripped before a phalanx of interrogators, for a woman it is much more terrible, and many of the suicides and attempted suicides among the women were triggered precisely by that humiliation. Even today the government still employs this practice with women political prisoners. When they are confined to solitary, they are completely undressed and then officers from the jail, Prison Headquarters, and the Political Police stop by to see them.

We arrived at our cells. On the floor, all jumbled together and scattered, were the few things we owned—underwear, socks, uniforms, and our pillows. Over the heap they had poured the little *gofio de trigo* and sugar we had left, our only reserve of real nutrition, which we very carefully doled out so as to keep down our hunger a little. Then, on top of all that, they had poured out the water from the pails.

Dozens of cots had been slashed by bayonets, and in some cells they had mixed salt and washing detergent into the food.

This had been the reprisal operation which never failed to follow an escape or escape attempt....

. . . . .

In one corner of each cell, in the center of a slight depression, was a hole that served as a latrine. A piece of bent tubing above it was our shower. The control knob itself was outside the cell, and the guards on duty controlled it. The cells were completely empty, so the granite floor was our bed. Each cell measured about seven feet long by six feet wide. Years later, I would be in many other punishment cells, and these on Isla de Piños were the largest of all.

I was sent into cell 1, Boitel into 3, Ulises into 5, and Brito into 7, so there was an empty cell separating each occupied one. Lieutenant Paneque and two guards took charge of me.

"You have to take off all your clothes. It's an order from upstairs." He said this without his usual arrogance and despotism. He couldn't stop worrying about the possibility that we would accuse him. I think he must have decided not to bring up the subject directly because he was always accompanied by other soldiers. His superiors weren't allowing him to be alone with any of us even for a moment. After I found out what had happened, I grew certain he was being watched, and that it was only because he was a member of the Party that he hadn't been jailed at once. They were just waiting to interrogate us.

I began to take off my clothes, sitting on the floor. The men who had captured us hadn't even bothered to search me, so I still had the knife strapped to my leg with rubber-band "garters"; I was also wearing under my shirt the T-shirt with the bottles of vitamins, the water-purifying tablets, the matches, and all the rest.

They didn't even let me keep my underwear. I sat there, completely naked, in the darkness of the cell. It was cold, and I was suffering from the throbbing pain in my leg. The swelling was black. When the soldiers had left our cells and closed the main barred gate that opened into the outside hallway, Boitel called us and asked us what cells we were in. There was no confusion for me because I was in the first one. Ulises was the only one who didn't know exactly which cell he was in. He hadn't thought to look at the number painted in black above his door.

I don't know exactly how much time had passed—an hour, maybe—when they brought us food. I will never forget it. There was white rice and tinned Russian beef with sweet potatoes. It wasn't the food the Circulars were given, of course, but rather the food the soldiers themselves ate. After the meal, several officers in uniform came to each of us. They threw clothes in and ordered us to get dressed, they were going to take us out. Leaning on Brito and the wall, hopping along on one leg, I crossed the interior patio, and we went into the main room of the building.

They had set up long tables with typewriters. Dozens of soldiers made way for us. The whole off-duty population of the garrison and their officers were packed into the room. A middle-aged woman was sitting before one typewriter.

She was the judge of Nueva Gerona, and she was going to read the charges against us. To an untutored spectator, this could easily have appeared to be a perfectly correct legal proceeding. (And indeed the reading of charges was performed, but we were never taken to trial. One day the sentence came to us from the tribunal. It had sentenced us to ten years more in prison for the crimes of breaking our original sentences and damage to state property. This last charge against us reflected the crime of cutting the bars of the windows.) Commander Gálvez, the local chief of the Political Police, and other officers in civilian clothing who had come from Havana questioned us at length.

The men from the Political Police tried to get us to tell them how we had obtained our uniforms, the hacksaw blades, and the other equipment. Our answer was always the same: the fat common prisoner, the one called Chito, had been the link who had provided us with the necessary materials. They knew as well as we did that no such person existed, but there was no way to shake us from that response. The interrogation began to get complicated when they asked us how we had gotten out of the presidio. None of them believed our detailed explanation of how we had gone out through the guardhouse. It really seemed so impossible to accept.

"We know there are soldiers who helped you men in this escape attempt of yours," one of the civilians, a Political Police agent, said. "And we know more about that than you think we do. You were taken out and left outside the security cordon, out of danger," he added.

Boitel and I, who were sitting next to each other, simply looked at each other. We didn't want this to get so involved that we would wind up in a situation we had never intended and that really didn't interest us in the least. Implicating a nonexistent Chito hurt no one; now it was obvious that our interrogators believed guards had aided us, and that meant *innocent* men were being implicated.

There was a great expectancy among the soldiers that surrounded us; they were hanging on every word, almost hypnotized by the course things were taking.

The discussion grew heated. Our explanation was always the same—we had gone out through the guardhouse.

"You know all these details—the guardhouse, the ditch behind it, all that—because you can look out the window of the Circular and see it. Dozens of prisoners could give us the same description."

That seemed a perfectly logical assertion, so they kept going over and over those moments, until at last I remembered the large iron gear wheels hidden among the weeds in the yard, over which I'd almost fallen when I was pretending to urinate to give Boitel time to find the ditch. There was no way to make out those wheels from the Circular. I described them to the officer. He looked at me skeptically, called over another of the civilians, and they left the room. Soon he was back. He had been in the guardhouse yard and could see for himself that the wheels were there. Only then did they believe the story we were telling them.

We learned later that the lieutenant in charge of the searches, a man called Tareco, or "Odds and Ends," another of those bullying types the prison was full of, was sent off to a work farm, sentenced to ten years in prison for laxity in pursuit of his duties in the searches. They held him responsible for our smuggling in what we needed for the escape. They never did learn how we managed to do it. Only now, after more than twenty years, are the facts being brought to light in this book.

Guards returned us to the cells and stripped us again. They didn't close the cell door, and that detail caught my attention. I was sitting on the floor; outside I heard the voices of several approaching soldiers. Three or four of them, or maybe five—I'm not sure how many—appeared before my open cell. Now that the interrogations and all the paperwork were finished, they were going to settle accounts with us, collect what we owed them for having tried to escape. Since the light bulb in the hallway was at their back, I didn't realize they were armed with thick twisted electric cables and truncheons.

"Stand up! We're going to make sure you never even *want* to try to escape again!"

My stomach tightened more than ever before. I felt such pressure in my chest that I could hardly breathe. In my months of prison I had learned only too well what these reactions were—they were fear, terror, and in only a few seconds the vision of what was about to happen passed through my mind.

They were already beating my friends. I heard the dry thud of the blow on their naked bodies and the cries and curses of the guards.

"Stand up, faggot!" the guard shouted again as he raised his arm. Suddenly, everything was a whirl—my head spun around in terrible vertigo. They beat me as I lay on the floor. One of them pulled at my arm to turn me over and expose my back so he could beat me more easily. And the cable fell more directly on me. The beating felt as if they were branding me with a red-hot branding iron, but then suddenly I experienced the most intense, unbearable, and brutal pain of my life. One of the guards had jumped with all his weight on my broken, throbbing leg.

I could not sleep that night. My back burned and stung as though it were on fire, and the pain in my leg was almost enough to make me faint. Thus, Lieutenant Tarrau's threat had been carried out, the threat he had made only a few hours before in his headquarters office, that we would pay. . . .

. . . . .

The next morning, they welded the doors shut. Lieutenant Cruz, head of the Political Police, told us Castro had personally ordered it done. We were told we'd stay in those cells not for months, but for years.

The military doctor was a Communist who tried to look like Lenin, wearing the same kind of goatee. He was more than six feet tall, had very white skin, and was heavy. His name was Lamar. He wore the uniform of a doctor, but he was a sadist. When I asked him for medical care, he looked through the peephole, stared at my leg, and told me he hoped it turned into a good case of gangrene, "so I can come in myself and cut it off."

That frightened and worried me. I was afraid I would get an incurable infection. My leg was still very swollen and inflamed, and all around the ankle and the calf, the swelling had taken on a blackish color and was shiny from being so stretched and swollen.

Absolutely no one could enter that hallway. The Security Corps was carrying out an investigation aimed at discovering and detaining all our contacts and collaborators. They brought in Oruña and Sierra from Circular 3, the two prisoners who had been in charge of the radio. They had been betrayed by another prisoner. The arrival of Oruña and Sierra allowed us to find out all the things that had happened after our escape.

I couldn't stand up, so I moved about sitting down, dragging myself along on my buttocks. The situation grew more difficult when they named as our personal guards the soldiers who had been on duty at the guardhouse the night of the escape. The guards overseeing the punishment cells, then, were guards who were being punished themselves. The fury and sadism of those men defies description, especially the tall blond young man who had been on duty at the machine gun, singing campesino songs—he considered us responsible for his disgrace.

This guard found himself a five-gallon pail, like those used to wash the floors, and took it in to the common prisoners to urinate and defecate in. When he had it about half full of filth and urine and dirty water, he added a little water to it and climbed up to the chain-link ceiling of the cells. Since I hadn't been able to sleep the night before because of the cold, I had taken advantage of the relative warmth of noon to lie down in one corner to try to sleep a little. I was exhausted not only by sleeplessness but pain as well.

The shock of the cold was what woke me. I was bathed from top to bottom and sitting in a caramel-colored, foul-smelling puddle. Down my face and neck were sliding pieces of excrement. I was the first of us prisoners to receive the impact of that bath, and it took me so off guard that I opened my mouth in surprise. Chunks of excrement fell into my mouth. The guard was above my head, on the other side of the chain-link. I saw the enormous soles of his boots. He was looking at me with loathing. He did not say a single word. Neither did I.

With my index finger I flicked some remains of the excrement off my shoulders and thighs, and I dragged myself over to the latrine to turn on the shower. It was turned off from outside. I called the guard. He didn't answer. Then I shouted to Boitel and the others and told them what had happened. They began to scream, "Water! Water!" The blond guard, the same one who had thrown the excrement on me, came into the hallway and ordered us to shut up. He said there was an order from higher echelons to give us water only to drink, and that only at mealtimes.

A little while later another soldier arrived with a wrench and closed off the taps located in the hallway, out of our reach, putting as much force into the wrench as he could. For more than three months the taps were closed. In all that time, we were not permitted to bathe, even once. There were only those baths of urine and shit that the guards bestowed on us from the ceiling.

The filth dried in my hair and on my body. The terrible smell of it filled the cell.

There are certain things one never thinks about when one reads or hears about a prisoner confined in a cell under the conditions we were kept in; there are things that are simply inconceivable outside a jail. And among those things are a man's bodily functions. We had to relieve ourselves there, in that hole in the ground in a corner of the cell. But when we were done, there was absolutely nothing to clean ourselves with, no water or soap or paper or even a piece of cloth. We had to use our fingers for toilet paper—there was no other way.

Boitel was shouting and arguing with a guard. I didn't know what it was all about.

"Come down here and do that, you coward. You people are despicable! You just do it because you've got that uniform on. Otherwise, you wouldn't dare!"

"What's happening, Boitel?" Ulises asked.

Boitel told us he had been jabbed with a pole. Actually, I didn't understand what he was talking about until the guard walking along the roof of the cells came to mine. He had a long wooden pole, rounded at the end, and I immediately understood what had happened.

Boitel had been sleeping, and the guard had slyly stuck the pole through the holes in the chain-link ceiling and poked him with it to wake him up. From that day on, the "Ho Chi Minh poles" would be used to torture us and send us to the verge of madness. There was no way to escape them, since the guard, up on top there, dominated the whole cell, and he could prod us whenever he wanted. The end of the pole was blunt and didn't wound us, but it hurt, and it didn't let us sleep. That was what they wanted.

There was only one guard who didn't prod us, and when every three days he came on duty in the area, we could sleep six straight hours. But as soon as his relief came, the new man went up onto the chain-link ceiling, pole in hand, and started prodding us. Then he went down; in an hour he came back up again, and once more, the sudden awakening.

I was utterly exhausted. The lack of sleep and the tension were seriously affecting me. I sought God then. My conversations with Him brought me a spiritual strength that gave me new energy. I never asked Him to get me out of there; I didn't think that God should be used for that kind of request. I only asked that He allow me to resist, that He give me the faith and spiritual strength to bear up under these conditions without sickening with hatred. I only prayed for Him to accompany me. And His presence, which I felt, made my faith an indestructible shield.

They continued slopping the pails of urine and excrement over us. In the cold winter mornings, they would also throw freezing water at us. That was unpleasant, but at least it cleaned some of the excrement off the cell floor. Little by little, the latrine, without water to flush out the fecal matter, grew full. As soon as night fell, cockroaches took over the walls and floors and crawled all over my body, and their ticklish creeping often made me jump awake. . . .

· · · · ·

The authorities had so far not considered taking us out to work barefoot. . . .

Or so I thought, until that morning when all of us who habitually stayed behind were called out to the prison yard. A small group of sick prisoners, wrapped in blankets and shivering with cold, or their breathing labored by asthma, were forced to go form up outside the building. Then, when the military leader of the Circular had taken all the platoons out, he ordered the sick men back inside, to stand with those of us who did not have clothing or shoes. I waited there with the rest of the men. I amused myself during those minutes observing Saturn, which came out every morning about that time. Gang 20, to which I belonged, went out last to the quarries.

There were about eighty of us formed up in that contingent. Some of us had on only underwear; some were wearing sandals, but most of us were barefoot: men who were staying behind knew that neither shoes nor clothing had arrived in the warehouse yet, so some of the sicker men had given their shoes to healthier men, workers. Only two percent of the prison population could stay behind, not go out to the work fields, on account of sickness. If there were thirty sick men, we had to select the twenty to remain in the building and the ten who, sick or not, would go out to work. They would be dragged out if necessary, but they had to leave the building and go to work.

It struck me as strange that they had not yet ordered us to go back to our cells. That was when a platoon of guards arrived led by Juan Rivero. He had been one of our guards in the punishment cells. Rivero was one of those soldiers whose rank goes to their heads—he was made head of the punishment-cell block and then head of Internal Order and then director of his own concentration camp. He stood there a few moments looking at us, sneering. When the inspection was over, he called the head of the Circular over and asked him for the list of the sick men who had formed up in the front rank, just at the little roadway which led off to the main entrance of the prison. He examined the list and made a gesture with his head. The leader of the Circular ordered the sick men back inside.

Another platoon arrived then, brandishing bayonets, and we were ordered to line up two by two. From that moment on, you could feel the hostility. We marched off toward the main exit of the prison. The guards escorting us on each side were wielding their bayonets and shouting and threatening us. We walked by the soldiers' houses and the headquarters buildings. We went on through the barbed-wire gates at the main entrance, and turned to the right, toward the east. Moment by moment the violence grew.

They had already beaten several men, and those heading up the files were shoved along and told to march faster. The walk was trying, because most of us were barefoot. The thorns and burrs simply wouldn't allow us to walk as fast, let alone as comfortably, as the guards with their boots on.

That area was totally new to us; we had never worked there. I was slightly familiar with it, though, from the time we were making our preparations for our escape attempt. I had taken notes on it as I studied it through the telescope. Over that way was where the "Turd Bowl" was located, a ditch where all the sewage from the prison emptied, not only sewage from the prisoners but also from the headquarters installations, the military housing, the shops, the hospital, the barracks, and all the rest—the excrement of some eight or nine thousand people. When we were studying the possibilities for our escape, at one point we considered using the sewers, and I investigated the ditch. At the opening of the sewer a man from inside the Circular could crawl through the pipe, but farther on it narrowed and a man's body wouldn't fit. The people who built the prison had even thought about the possibility of a prisoner's trying to escape that way one day.

In spite of the fact that we were headed directly toward the ditch, it never occurred to me that that might be our destination. When we came to a stand of undergrowth, a little reddish-earth path appeared. Another platoon was waiting for us there, armed like the others with rifles and fixed bayonets. They joined the cordon. The look of this began to worry me. The shoves and the blows on our backs and heads continued. Lieutenant Juan Rivero was marching out in front with two sergeants and a soldier who was not wearing a cap. By the quality of his uniform, we all knew that he was an officer from the Political Police. I felt an almost uncontrollable dread.

We were already accustomed, like Pavlov's dogs, to react to known stimuli. A search was terrible, but we knew what was going to happen. We knew we might be beaten on the stairways as we were leaving, as we were coming back in, but we were prepared for whatever came. Not now. Now we were completely in the dark about what was happening and what might happen.

We crossed the little creek. Murmuring pines surrounded us. The ground here was very rocky. At intervals little islands of sharp spiky rock seemed to float along the surface of the ground. The rocks, called "dog's teeth" in Cuba, were made of millions of microscopic crusts of plankton. We would try to avoid them, but they grew denser and denser. It was becoming almost impossible now to find footing free of those rocks. We finally came to a barbed-wire fence. The first men who tried to get through it by holding apart the strands and crawling between were beaten to keep them from doing that. The guards wanted us to vault the fence. That meant we landed with our bare feet on the other side of the fence, on top of the sharp rocks. The whole purpose of that was to injure the soles of our feet, to make us cut our feet to ribbons on the rocks.

For some men the pain of a rock piercing their foot was so great that they staggered and fell to their knees, and when they stood up again, their knees would be bloody too. The second a prisoner fell, the guards started brandishing their bayonets and yelling at him to run. I caught hold of one of the fence posts and jumped over holding on to the wood to soften my fall. I didn't calculate how near the fence that would make me land. As I landed on the other side, my right ankle, whose bones had been out of place since I was injured in the escape, gave out on me. My left knee buckled. I swiveled involuntarily and crashed into the barbed wire. The barbs ripped into my knee, tearing my pants leg and the skin, and left scars I still bear. Then the guards made us run.

If the rest of the men felt as I did at those moments, they were terrified. A thousand ideas added fire to my terror. I thought we were going to be machine-gunned, since we were outside the prison grounds—far from the prison, in fact. It would be easy enough for the guards to say that it was a mass escape attempt.

Blood from my knee stained my pants, and the stain was growing. When we came to the sewage ditch, our feet were bruised and mangled, many of us had, as I did, scratches and scrapes, and we were exhausted and terrified. What we saw then, though, practically made us retch. The ditch was six or eight yards wide at its widest point. On its surface floated islands of excrement. Above the shit were clouds of green flies. The smell of sewage, of those disgusting miasmas, filled the air.

The squad leaders, at an order from the officer from Political Police, attacked us. They shoved us with their hands and rifle butts and forced us to wade into that horrible ditch. I fell into the sewage headlong—someone had pushed me from behind—and I could not keep the filthy water from filling my mouth and eyes. The pretext for that torture was that we had to clean the bottom to keep the canal from becoming obstructed. In some places the water reached as high as a man's chest or even his chin, depending on his height. The bottom was irregular; there were sharp drop-offs, so that you'd suddenly sink over your head if you took a wrong step. You had to pick something up off the bottom—a rock, a little trash, anything even if it was just a little handful of mud, and take it over to the side of the ditch where the guards were waiting to beat you. The uncomfortable position they had to stay in, squatting down, and the fact that we prisoners had only our heads sticking out of the water meant that the guards would hit us in the face, necks, and on our shoulders. Many men were bleeding from the cuts and wounds.

The scene was indescribable. If you didn't plunge in deep enough, you'd be pulled out onto the bank and beaten. As long as we were out in the middle of the ditch, it wasn't so easy to hit us with their bayonets, so some of the soldiers found long sticks to hit us with at a greater distance. Other guards, wanting to join in the fun of the punishment, threw rocks at us. Then the order to advance toward the narrowest part of the ditch came. It was precisely there that a layer of excrement covered almost the entire surface, damming up the water. The water was flowing sluggishly through a small opening. We waded forward through that sea of shit. Every time we submerged, we had to push aside the excrement so we could get our heads above water. Our hair was full of it. Our ears and the wounds on our feet and those caused by the garrison's bayonets were open doors to infection and contamination. It delighted the guards to see us plunge our heads into those filthy waters. They never let a chance go by to poke us with a bayonet or push our heads down into the water with their boots. Nothing after this can be worse, I thought as I begged God to give me strength to resist, to endure. They had already struck me several times, and the cuts on my knee were burning, irritated by the fetid water.

We were so black that from a distance of only one or two yards, you couldn't recognize even your best friend. We looked as if we'd been dyed in a tank full of ink.

Toward noon, they took us out of the ditch. I felt I'd passed a new test—that had been a bestial punishment. We prisoners looked at each other in silence. We were battered, unrecognizable men covered with filth and detritus. The sun burned down, and our hair and clothes, matted with excrement, started drying out. The guards were taking a little rest. We had to stand in the sun.

Juan Rivero and the officer from the Political Police were strolling nearby contemplating our state with undisguised satisfaction. They gave the order to march, and we marched off, some of us limping, others leaning on friends' shoulders. It was a parade out of some surrealistic vision. Thirst had made my throat scratch, but when I recalled the gulps of filthy water I had swallowed, I felt nauseated. I wanted desperately to get back to the Circular and take a bath and quench my thirst. We were exhausted, almost at the end of our physical strength.

But they weren't leading us back to the prison. We were heading away from it, toward the coast. They gave the order to halt in front of a well where we could get some water to drink. But not a single one of us moved, and we were very thirsty. It was a spontaneous reaction of repudiation, of rejection. The soldiers insisted, and even brought over a can filled with several gallons of water. No one drank. Thinking that perhaps fatigue and the gnawing hunger of months and months might be used to humiliate us still further, Juan Rivero said that he was going to bring us lunch. But we weren't having any of that, we weren't going to eat in that state of filth. One of the prisoners answered him, "Juan Rivero, down with communism!"

The defiant prisoner hadn't finished his sentence when the entire garrison fell on us, beating us with rage and fury. And they ordered us to double-time back to the lake the ditch emptied into. That stretch had an indescribable brutality about it. Our legs, swollen by hours in the putrid water and then standing in the sun, would not obey. Anyone who fell was savagely beaten. Almost dragging ourselves, putting forth what was for us a titanic effort, we arrived. The little lake was a bowl full of excrement. The ground it was dug out of had excellent drainage, so it absorbed almost all the water, and what was left was a gigantic deposit of shit. But it was not just human excrement. There was also the filth of five hundred or so pigs from a hog farm nearby, which gave off an unbearable stench. There were also bloody cotton wads in it, the sanitary napkins of the women guards, and bandages that had almost certainly come from the hospital, and all sorts of other filth. There the swarm of flies made a constant almost musical background buzz.

Mario Morfi had been beaten more than almost anybody. They had flown into a rage with him, and Juan Rivero had given orders to beat him again and again. So when Morfi entered the lake after those long hours in the ditch, he came down with a cramp. His exhausted legs wouldn't respond, and he began to sink into the shit. He tried to grab on to some support, which did not exist, to stay afloat, but it was no use. He called to his nearest comrades to help him. The closest men tried to help, but the guards were still incensed with Morfi and they flew at the other prisoners to keep them from reaching him. They yelled at the prisoners to leave him alone, he was all right, he was just faking the cramp so that he could get out of work. I cannot remember witnessing a more horrifying scene in my life than that one. I was some fifteen yards away from the sinking man. All we could do was watch him slowly going under. The guards had loaded and cocked their rifles. They threatened to shoot anyone who tried to get close enough to help Morfi. He kept sinking—down to his shoulders, his chin, his nose. Almost involuntarily, almost without realizing what they were doing, his friends standing closest by, even under threat of being shot by the squads, started running to help their comrade drowning in the filth. Morfi had lost consciousness; nothing but the top of his head was above water. Calimano and Kelo got there first. Others followed. The guards didn't fire, but they did beat the men who ran to his aid. Morfi was pulled out of that sickening quicksand-like lake, and they carried him away, along with another prisoner wounded in the leg by a guard we called Mosquito—for his skinniness and long legs.

Morfi was dazed and semiconscious. He had still not recovered when he was thrown into a truck which had come to bring food to the garrison. We persuaded them to let another prisoner, Franco Mira, one of the Bay of Pigs invaders who died a little later in jail, accompany the wounded men to the Circular, in case they needed any help on the way. Franco tried to give Morfi a little water, to see if he would regain consciousness, but one of the guards kicked away the jar and cried, "Let the son of a bitch die! That'll be one less of you bastards to take care of!"

We stayed about two hours more up to our necks in that shit. And then they marched us back. I cannot recall a longer or more painful march or a return more fervently desired. All I was thinking about was taking a bath and disinfecting my cuts and wounds. I knew the danger they posed, since they had been infected by sewage and shit.

It was the last hours of afternoon. Our wounds, covered with excrement, dried. The excrement in our ears and hair dried too. That poisonous water produced infections in our eyes; there were several cases of hepatitis, and a whole series of digestive disorders. Morfi got an ear infection from all the filth in his ears. His eardrum perforated, and he had problems with balance for the rest of his life. . . .

. . . . .

Of all the prisons and concentration camps in Cuba, the most repressive was Boniato Prison, on the extreme eastern end of the island. Perhaps in the past it had not been so bad for other prisoners, but it has been and will always be for political prisoners. Even today, when prison authorities want to put a group of prisoners through the worst imaginable experiences, when they want to perform biological or psychological experiments on them, when they want to hold prisoners completely incommunicado, to beat and torture them, the jail at Boniato is the installation of choice.

Built at the lowest point in a valley, surrounded by military encampments, far away from towns and highways, it is the ideal location for their plans. The cries of tortured men and the bursts of machine-gun fire are heard by no one; they fade away into the solitude of the place, are lost in the hills and valleys. Relatives are often as far as seven hundred miles away, so they're very seldom standing at the prison entrance asking for news. And if after a long exhausting pilgrimage they manage to arrive at the outskirts of the prison installation, the guards send them back home. The isolation of a jail may be one of its main advantages, and the jail at Boniato is the most isolated of all the prisons in Cuba.

Our trip to Boniato was the worst we had ever made. The police van held twenty-two prisoners uncomfortably, but the authorities crammed twenty-six of us inside.

I was in a cage with three other men. Since we couldn't all sit down at once, I crawled under the wooden seat and curled up. I knocked continually against the other men's legs. I fell asleep with the rocking and rolling of the vehicle and slept until Piloto, nauseated by the smell of gasoline and the rocking of the truck, began to vomit. The only thing to hold the vomit was my aluminum drinking cup, so I gave it to him. About two hundred miles farther on, in the city of Santa Clara, they gave each cage a can to urinate into. I got under the seat again. Urine kept splashing out of the can and wetting my legs from the rough braking and the potholes in the road. Piloto was still very motion-sick, but we didn't have anything to give him to control his nausea. One of the prison vans broke down as we were coming into Camagüey. The trip took more than twenty-five hours.

At last the caravan stopped at the entrance of Boniato Prison. When the door opened, I saw a great billboard saying "CUBA—FIRST FREE TERRITORY IN AMERICA."

They took us out of the trucks and led us to Building 5, Section C. Taking advantage of the tumult of prisoners and guards, I managed to hand a package I was carrying to Enrique Díaz Correa, who had arrived previously and was already inside. Had I not given him the package with the pen point, a tiny photo of Martha, some small sheets of onionskin, and a jar of ink made in the prison, I would have lost it all in the search, since they stripped us and even looked under our testicles.

A circle of hostile faces and fixed bayonets surrounded us, but there were no beatings. The food that afternoon was served in tins that had contained Russian beef. It was three spoonfuls of boiled macaroni and a piece of bread. That was February 11, 1970.

That day saw the beginning of a plan for biological and psychological experimentation more inhuman, brutal, and merciless than anything the western world had known with the exception of the Nazis' activities. Boniato and its blackout cells will always be an accusation. If all the other human-rights violations had not occurred, what happened at Boniato would be enough in itself to condemn the Cuban regime as the most cruel and degrading ever known in the Americas.

We were locked up in forty separate cells. To go to the latrine you had to call the soldiers. I thought it was strange that we had not been counted at dusk as was usual in the jails. My cell had a burlap cot, but it sagged like a hammock.

At sunrise the garrison flooded the hallway. They came in shouting and cursing. It was the same as always; they had to get all heated up to come in. They beat on the walls and the bars with the weapons they were carrying— rubber-hose-covered iron bars (so they wouldn't break the skin), thick clubs and woven electrical cables, chains wrapped around their hands, and bayonets. There was no justification, no pretext. They just opened the cells, one by one, and beat the prisoners inside. The first cell they opened was Martín Pérez'. I remember his big husky voice cursing the Communists, but without saying a single dirty word. I got close to the bars to try to look out, and a chain blow made me jump back. I was lucky it hadn't hit me in the face.

They opened cell number 3, number 4, number 5. As they approached my cell, I trembled inside. My muscles contracted spasmodically. My breathing came with difficulty and I felt the fear and rage that always possessed me.

Some men, their psychological resistance wasted away already, couldn't contain themselves, and before the soldiers even entered their cells they began to shriek and wail hysterically. Those shrieks multiplied the horror. The soldier that opened the bars to our cell was armed with a bayonet. Behind him were three more, blocking the entrance. I saw only that one of the guards was carrying a chain. They pushed us to the back of the cell so they'd have room to swing their weapons. We tried not to get separated, because we knew that was the most dangerous thing you could do. That was when they would kick you and knee you in the groin. They knocked me to the floor, and one of them kicked me in the face and split my lower lip. When I recovered consciousness my head was lying in a pool of blood. My cellmate was bleeding through the nose and his hand was fractured near his wrist.

Several men were seriously injured. One of the Graiño brothers had his cheekbone fractured by Sergeant "Good Guy"; he spit out broken teeth. He'd been beaten so brutally his face looked like one huge black eye. Pechuguita, a peaceable little campesino from Pinar del Rio, had his head split open; the wound was so large it took twenty stitches to close it. Every man, without exception, was beaten. The guards went about it systematically, cell by cell.

After the beating the officers and a military doctor passed through to examine us. They took wounded men out of the cells, but right there on the spot a medic with a little first-aid cart sewed up and bandaged the wounds. When they finished bandaging us they said, "Don't say we didn't give you medical treatment!" and put us back into the cells, where we waited for our next beating.

I was bruised all over. My face was swollen and bloody. I could hardly stand up for the pain all over my body. They had given me the worst beating of my life. But what had affected me most was waiting for them to come to my cell and beat me. That did more damage to me than the blows themselves. A thousand times I wished I had been in the first cell. That way they would come in, beat me, and go back out again. I wanted it over with once and for all so I wouldn't have to go through that torture of waiting and dreading. My nerves were destroyed by it.

The guards came back in the afternoon, almost at nightfall, and the nightmare of the morning was repeated—beatings, cell by cell, with more wounded men the result. We could communicate with the other sections of the building by shouting back and forth, so we traded the names of the most gravely wounded men.

Odilo Alonso woke up the next morning with his head monstrously swollen; I would never have imagined that anyone could have looked so grotesquely deformed. His ears were so swollen he looked as though he were wearing a helmet. After three days of those two-a-day beatings, many men could no longer stand. Martín Pérez was urinating blood, as was de Vera, and other men's eyes were so blackened and swollen shut by the blows that they could hardly see. But that didn't matter to the soldiers—they beat men again and again.

Sergeant Good Guy, whose real name was Ismael, belonged to the Communist Party. He had a big Pancho Villa moustache. Whenever the garrison came in to beat us, he cried *"Viva Communism!"* madly, over and over. It was his war cry. He would tell the other soldiers to beat the wounded on top of their bandages, so that nobody could say that the soldiers had beaten them more than once. Another sergeant did exactly the opposite—he would beat the wounded men on their bare skin and say with a sneer, "I wanna see 'em sew you up again."

Odilo was getting worse and worse. The blows to his head had affected him horribly. His ears were leaking pus and bloody liquid, and his face was monstrously inflamed. Finally he could no longer stand erect. It was only then that they took him to the prison hospital.

They gave not so much as an aspirin to even the most seriously wounded men. They didn't take any prisoner out of the section unless he was in danger of death. They didn't try to kill us quickly; that would have been too generous a gesture to have hoped for from those sadists. Their object was to force us, by means of terror and torture, into the Political Rehabilitation Program. To do that, they were slowly and inexorably destroying us. They would take us to the very brink of death and keep us there, without letting us cross it. We had even been vaccinated against tetanus, so they could bayonet us, wound us with machetes and iron bars, and break our skulls, sure that at least we wouldn't contract tetanus.

The attitude maintained by our group was discussed in the magazine *Moncada,* the official organ of the Ministry of the Interior, in an article written by the head of Jails and Prisons, Medardo Lemus. He wrote that our resistance was a major block to the plans the government had for enlisting all prisoners in the Political Rehabilitation Program, and that our rebelliousness and especially our refusal to conform with prison discipline was a bad example for the other prisoners. The authorities therefore saw themselves obliged to separate us from the rest of the penal population.

But men could not stand up forever to the daily beatings, the terror, the psychological tortures, and some took on the uniform. Those desertions caused us great pain. It was as though the authorities were pulling off pieces of our own bodies. I felt diminished every time one of our men left; years of terror, misery, and the dream of freedom had united us.

The capacity to stand up to something like that is very difficult to gauge. Men who had stood up to the Castro dictatorship in all-out combat in the mountains or in the cities, who had gone in and out of Cuba clandestinely in missions of war, who were full of bravery and heroism, could not, unarmed, confront the terror, the lack of communication, the solitary confinement for very long, and they finally gave in. But that might have been better in one sense, because that way our position solidified. Our bodies grew thinner day by day, our strength slipped away, our legs were beginning to look like toothpicks, but inside, the foundations of our spirits, our faith and determination, grew stronger and stronger with every blow of a bayonet, with every ignominy, with every harassment, with every beating.

Every afternoon at dusk the thundering voice of the Brother of the Faith, as we called Gerardo, the Protestant preacher, echoed through those passages, calling out to the prayer meeting. They tried to keep us from our religious practices, to interrupt, silence the prayers, and that cost us extra quotas of blows. The first time this happened the guards unleashed a beating in the midst of the prayer meeting, cell by cell, but as soon as they left the beaten men continued singing, and the other prisoners followed their lead. The guards moved back and forth and handed out blows in what seemed to be a different dimension from the one in which we were praying and singing hymns to God. In the cell in front of mine, I watched guards kicking two prisoners lying on the floor. Those prisoners also began to sing and pray as soon as the guards had left. Now those men over there, who had been singing before, were being beaten. And so the surreal scene went on. Above the shouting and tumult, the voice of the Brother of the Faith was singing "Glory, glory Hallejujah!"...

Twenty Years and Forty Days: Life in a Cuban Prison

Jorge Valls

JORGE VALLS *(1933–), teacher and poet, "ran afoul of the Castro regime soon after it took power, both for refusing to register for the draft and for his insistent defense of a friend who was being prosecuted on political charges."*

Like many other political prisoners under Castro, Valls participated in the resistance against Batista and was arrested several times under his rule. In 1955 he became a founding member of the Revolutionary Council, one of the groups organizing armed resistance against Batista. He went into exile in Mexico in 1958 (for the second time) and returned early next year after the victory of the revolution. From early on he was disturbed by the repressive policies of Castro, which included the mistreatment of many former supporters and leaders of the anti-Batista struggle.

Convicted of "activities against . . . the state and leading anti-government organizations" in 1964, Valls was imprisoned and released twenty years later in 1984. Castro personally participated in his trial (just as he did in those of other important political prisoners, such as Huber Matos). As noted in the foreword to Valls's book, "The presence of so many of Castro's former allies among the long-term political prisoners signals another characteristics . . .[of] the Cubans' political prison system: the active, personalized and often vindictive involvement of Fidel Castro himself in using the prisons to punish old friends and settle old scores."

Valls was among the political prisoners who refused to participate in the "reeducation" programs and were therefore given especially harsh treatment.

Valls left Cuba in 1988 and now lives in Miami, Florida.

. . . . .

From Jorge Valls, Twenty Years and Forty Days: Life in a Cuban Prison, *© 1986 Human Rights Watch.*

Arrest and Interrogation

It must have been a little before midnight when State Security, the Cuban political police, arrived at the house where I was visiting, banging at the door and shouting loudly. "But what is this?" the mistress of the house kept saying. I was used to night arrests, but it still gave me a hollow feeling in my stomach. They had come to arrest someone else, another visitor who was a fugitive, but they asked everyone for identification, which at the time took the form of a draft card. I told them I didn't have one, so they took me in to State Security as well.

It is hard to convey the all-powerful nature of Cuban State Security, also known as the DIER (the Revolutionary Army Department of Investigations), the G-2, or simply "the department." State Security is officially a branch of the Ministry of the Interior, which oversees the country's prisons and, for many years, any legal procedures stemming from political charges.

In Cuba, it is not the political police who serve the government, it is the government that serves the political police. They are the ones who decide whether a person will be investigated, arrested, kidnapped or executed. A Cuban citizen can be arrested anywhere, at any time, without anyone knowing, and kept locked away at State Security for a few hours or a few years. The courts are subordinate to State Security, which retains the evidence and decides which prisoners will be tried and which will be released.

State Security headquarters were in "Villa Marista," which used to be a religious school and monastery. From the outside it still looked like a school, with gardens and playgrounds. But inside, it had been turned into a labyrinth of corridors, offices, sweatshops, and cells.

The agents noted my name, address, and other personal details, then took my picture with a number at the bottom. When they asked me why I didn't have a draft card, I answered, "Because I didn't register." When they repeated the question, I explained, "Because I am not ready to take up arms to serve a totalitarian government." The agent in charge typed up his investigation, and ordered the others to take me back to the cell.

I walked through a long corridor with cells on each side, hermetically closed with large steel doors and enormous locks. They reminded me of the iceboxes in a morgue where the corpses are kept.

I went into my cell, stripped of everything except my glasses. They had taken away my clothes and my belongings, even the gold chain I used to wear around my neck. I began to dress myself in the overalls they handed out to all the prisoners.

My cellmate was a tall, strong fellow with a kind gaze. Later I learned he was a garbage man who did not know how to read and write. At night he would stand by the concrete shutters that did not let any light pass in, talking to God.

We talked about anything and everything, he and I, except about whatever it was that had gotten us into jail—there were eyes and ears everywhere, provided by modern technology. But we did exchange the most ancient identifications: who we were, where we came from, what we did. And finally we would talk about God and our loved ones. Sometimes it is only when they expect the worst that human beings discover their best qualities.

The next day I was taken to be cross-examined. They had given me a small card with a number along with the overalls. For the guards, one has no name, just a number, and the guards were just as anonymous to us. They guided me along the labyrinth, through the corridors and up the stairs, until we reached a room furnished only with a desk and two chairs, air-conditioned and soundproofed.

The interrogating officer came in. He was young, in his thirties, and said his name was Rosell. He didn't show any interest in getting my confession about clandestine organizations or activities. They already knew about my life down to the smallest detail. Not that I was so unusual; my father was a suit salesman and my mother was a piano teacher. I had been a student until the university was closed in 1957, leaving me one year short of my degree. I had worked as a schoolteacher since I was a teenager. But what really mattered to my interrogators was their belief that I was against Castro even before he took power, and I told them they were right.

The officer said, "Since you have decided to oppose us, we will oppose you." The cross examination lasted for over two hours. Elementary questions were repeated over and over again, and my life and my opinions were reexamined.

Several times the interrogator insinuated that they knew something shameful about my private life, my "sex life," to be specific. At first I just let it pass to see how far he would go, but finally I had to stop him. "What do you know about Jorge Valls!" I shouted. "Have you ever heard the name of Jorge Valls mixed up in a scandal? You don't know what you're talking about."

He seemed ashamed and tried to apologize. "It's just that you have a lot of enemies," he said. "It must be that," I answered, and it ended there. State Security often tries to blackmail prisoners with their private lives. Sometimes they do it with intelligence they've gathered, but sometimes they know nothing and keep guessing in hopes of tripping you up.

There were more sessions. Once I was taken to see a woman who had supposedly been arrested some months before and was now accusing me of "counterrevolutionary activities." She was part of a couple who had made contact with me outside. The two had never inspired any confidence in me. They had asked me for money and offered me the leadership of an anti-government organization, but I didn't have any money to give, and had refused all of their proposals. Now they were trying to implicate me. It must have been one of the many conspiracies organized by State Security to fish for disaffected people.

All of this was a waste of time; they knew why I was there, and I did too. Finally they led me to an office and told me to sign a paper listing the charges against me. I looked at it quickly. I wasn't going to sign anything accepting any charges other than not registering for the draft—I knew that the usual sentence for draft evasion was three years. But after my first interrogation this offense wasn't mentioned any more, and it wasn't listed in the charges either.

The agents suggested that my situation was difficult, and that it could go as far as execution. They told me I should "retract" my behavior (I didn't know what that meant) and collaborate with the police department. I refused, smiling, thinking that if you cannot prevail in a just cause, at least you can suffer for it.

A little while later a special vehicle took me to the infamous prison for political offenders, La Cabaña. Inside the car I found an old friend from past struggles, and it made me very happy. But we did not talk much along the way.

State Security was nothing new for me. I had been there in 1960, '62, and '63. My arrests were never justified. In Cuba the political police may arrest a person and hold him indefinitely, whether he has committed a crime or not. I know of someone who was captured with an arsenal of thirty machine guns and released a few days later, and others who were not involved in anything who spent long years in prison or were even executed.

One night in 1960, State Security came to my home. A family, friends of my parents, was visiting. The agents searched my room and my papers thoroughly. When I arrived, a little after midnight, they took my father, his friend, and me to State Security. The women were placed under house arrest. We spent more than three days in jail. No explanation was offered as to why we had been arrested or why we were released; we were expected to be grateful because they let us go.

In 1962 I tried to leave the country in a ship full of lumber that was sailing from the Isle of Pines. We were stopped near a place called Carapachibey and placed under arrest by a group of soldiers who appeared to be under the command of a Czech officer. First they took us to a military base. Then they transferred us to Havana, where we were held for thirty days and then released.

In 1963 I wanted to study certain areas in the Oriente province of archeological interest. I was captured near Imías by the G2 branch of the political police. They took me to their headquarters in Santiago de Cuba, where I was kept in jail for two weeks incommunicado and interrogated for many hours. They questioned me about events in my life that took place when I was fourteen. Later they transferred me to Havana, telling me that if nothing could be found against me, they would release me. They did, but I had been "disappeared" for more than a month. No one knew what had happened to me.

State Security had its own techniques. They would put prisoners on benches, separated from each other by walls, like a stone box. There they waited endlessly until they were called. The walls were painted with spots, and after staring at it for a while, you would start seeing things. They would often keep a prisoner in extremely low air-conditioned temperatures, so that by the time the cross examination took place he would be shivering with cold.

But the worst thing was the loss of time perception, and hope. The cells were artificially lit and the prisoner was called or fed at very irregular intervals. After a while you wouldn't know whether it was day or night, still yesterday or already tomorrow.

This unhinged some people. One such case took place at the State Security headquarters in Santiago de Cuba in 1963. We were being kept in cells in a large room, but the walls did not reach the ceiling; instead, they were covered with a grill, like a cage. From my cell I could hear the voice of a man. He sounded like a very old peasant from deep in the hills. He asked the guard for the time. The guard answered it was 1:00 p.m., though I calculated it to be very late at night. The farmer, astonished and afraid he was going mad, said, "Then what you brought me is lunch and not dinner?" The guard affirmed this. Later I could hear the old man babbling under his breath, "But why does this have to happen to me?" Near dawn I was awakened by the curses of the guards: the poor peasant had committed suicide.

Once, during a brief moment when the guard was away, I was able to speak with another prisoner whose face I never saw. He told me that he had been there for more than eight months and that no one on the outside had any idea where he was.

Losing hope was the worst thing. If you ended up with State Security, no one knew what happened to you, and no one could make any efforts on your behalf. You could be disappeared for a week or for years.

Prisoners were subjected to various interrogation techniques. Beyond a certain point, a prisoner either succeeded in keeping silence about absolutely everything, with the risk of schizophrenia, or he was capable of confessing that he had eaten his own mother uncooked—though a confession wouldn't help his situation.

Beatings and physical torture were common, but the most serious abuse was the "depersonalization" treatment. It was carried out in endless interrogations, in which the prisoner was asked the same question (such as name and address) hundreds of times. They deprived the prisoner of sleep until he started to talk and act like a zombie; they disoriented him by serving breakfast at 8:00, lunch at 6:30, and dinner the next day, and so on.

They would go to great lengths to confuse a prisoner. A guard might ask him, "What would you like for lunch?" The prisoner would answer, "Anything."

"No, no," the guard responds, "you must say what you want."

Finally the prisoner says, "Chicken." After a while the guard comes back with a piece of chicken—that would fit into a thimble. The prisoner supposes that it was a joke and waits a few minutes. The guard comes back.

"Are you bringing me lunch or not?" the prisoner asks.

"But that was your lunch," the guard answers. "Just what you asked for. Anything else?"

If the prisoner keeps playing the game, the guard will keep bringing thimblefuls of different dishes until the officer in charge gets bored.

There were many stories like this. That's why it wasn't surprising if a prisoner with no previous experience in State Security tried to kill himself after forty-five days. He's talked and he doesn't know what or how much he's said. But he knows he will never be the same. . . .

· · · · ·

In La Cabaña, 1964

I refused to register for the draft because I believed that the military was being used against the people, instead of on their behalf. Since 1952, Cubans had lived in a continuous state of violence. A citizen had no faith in his protection under the law; he merely survived at the whim of the powers that be. The years 1959 to 1965 were the most violent in Cuba's history, even bloodier than the nineteenth-century wars of independence, for many people who fought against Batista were also opposed to the establishment of a totalitarian state.

In 1963 the government established the draft. Many of us knew that it was not created to defend the nation against a foreign invasion. We believed that the new armed forces were to serve as an instrument of repression.

To accept military service would mean lending ourselves as instruments to kill our brothers. There were already tens of thousands of prisoners, and their number was increasing rapidly. They made up a whole new social class, the wretched of the earth, made up of representatives of many different strata of society—peasants, workers, students. Many of us were willing to go to jail as the last place a man could hold out for his principles. . . .

We awoke at dawn. Now I could see the place in better light. It was a large rectangular galley with a grill; on the other side, there was a large pit. Great moisture stains crept across the ceiling. Men were sleeping on the floor, although some of them had cots brought by their families.

At the end of the room were the toilets, blocked off by partitions. The galley was composed of three levels. The first one, with the entrance grill, opened to the courtyard. The only one who was allowed to live there was the "major," a representative chosen by the convicts who had to deal with the officers. We lived in the second level, which was connected by a tunnel through a thick wall. The opening that led to the third level was blocked by a thick steel door. Behind it there were some other prisoners, even more cut off than we were. The only source of air was through the back grill facing the pit, and it was extremely warm.

There were about seventy prisoners, of great variety. Some were very old, in their sixties and seventies; others didn't look more than sixteen. The majority were in their thirties, and almost all of them had belonged to the revolutionary army or fought in the war against Batista. Many had just arrived from State Security and hadn't been sentenced yet, others had already spent several years in jail and were there for punishment or some other unstated reason. We were all supposed to be there on a temporary basis.

Among the prisoners were old friends of mine, some of them dear friends I hadn't heard from for several years. They told me of Marcos's last moments. In the street you still heard the persistent rumor that they hadn't killed him, that that was an invention and that they were keeping him hidden away. Now that I knew he was dead, his death was more incomprehensible than ever. The prisoners, who had strange ways of learning the truth, told me some of the details: his last meal was guavas and cheese; he was executed at 3:45 a.m.

Aside from my grief for Marcos, I found prison an elating experience. It was the only "free territory" in Cuba, the only place where you could say anything you wanted and not be afraid of arrest. Of course, they could still execute you, but we were used to the thought of death.

While we were talking, someone started to sing a Mexican *ranchera* in a rough but expressive voice. The song had those metaphysical lyrics, all about death, with little yelps that are like the cry of a soul wounded by another's evil. Several of the prisoners found it upsetting. "Why does he have to sing that?" someone exclaimed.

I was pained by his complaint, and looked at the singer. He was a young man with thick hair, who had been brought a short time before with two other prisoners. It was obvious that the three of them had spent a long time in State Security. I asked if anyone knew why they were there.

"Trying to escape from the country," they said. "But a bad situation. Apparently some people were killed."

A few days later they were taken from the cell and shot. The young man had had his reasons for singing that song. . . .

If I recall correctly, there were eleven galleys with numbers from 7 to 17, all facing a walled patio. Each galley had a domed ceiling of ancient Spanish military construction. A large grill marked the front entrance, and a smaller grill faced the pit in back.

The rooms were about twenty meters long and less than eight meters wide. Near the entrance were two toilets, one with a tank for sitting. There was also a small cubicle with a sort of shower and a sink. They were separated by thin walls and had a small wooden door or a piece of hemp cloth hung like a curtain. On one side there was a urinal where two men could stand at a time, and a big washing stand. Three meters behind the grill were iron beds, stacked in bunks of four, leaving a space of less than forty centimeters between bunks and a central passageway about two meters wide.

Three hundred and four people lived within this space, and they were forbidden to stand less than three meters behind the entrance grill unless they had special permission. Each prisoner had his belongings in a bag that hung from the bed or from a nail on the wall. Three hundred and four men would not all fit at the same time, so some had to stand while others tucked themselves inside the niches of the beds. At night, those who had no bed would fit themselves on the floor like pieces of a puzzle, under the beds and in the passageways. We could neither stretch nor bend too much, and once we were in a position it was difficult to change it. If someone had to walk from the back to the front grill, he would have to find the tiny spaces between bodies and tiptoe in order not to step on his neighbor's face or chest.

It was summer, and the warmth was asphyxiating. The air was foul with sweating bodies and accumulated dirt. The beds were filthy and crawling with bugs, though we found we could reduce their population by passing the iron pieces through fire. . . .

Even going to the toilet at night was a problem. I remember one old man who had been brought in a few days before, and was given a place to sleep way back in the galley. Once, long after midnight, he woke up with diarrhea. After calling the guard he had to go through the galley, stepping over the bodies of the other prisoners, until he could reach the toilet that was near the entrance. He was a very old man, and walked hesitantly, barely missing the prisoners lying in his path. But he could not control his bowels, and he dripped from one end of the galley to the other. The poor man felt like dying of shame, and his unintentional victims could do nothing more than wait patiently until the next day.

Settling for the night was not at all easy. First we had to spread a blanket or some papers on the floor because it got so cold at night, and then slide our bodies partly under the beds. We would sleep next to each other trying our best to save space. If one of us wanted to change positions, he had to sit up. Every night the rats would pass, brushing our heads. There was one I used to feel coming and going; I couldn't imagine where the little animal was headed, but after her trip she didn't bother me any more.

A young lad used to sleep a little ways behind me, a peasant boy of fifteen or so. The cold floor was bad for him and he would cough all night long. He was very thin and we would look at him with pessimism.

Night was no time for rest. On the contrary, that was when the horrors began. At nine or so the executions would start, in the pit behind the galley on the other side of the grill. Although we couldn't see the shootings from my galley, we could hear even the slightest sound. The still of the night and the echo of the pit made them even more pronounced.

We knew exactly when the light was turned on. We could hear the squad come marching, and the car that brought the convict pulling up. Then there would be the sound of a door opening and footsteps in the night. We could hear the prisoner being tied to the pole, his last cries, the command to fire, the volley, and finally the shots ringing out; then the squad retiring and the corpse being taken away. The last sound would be the screech of the night bird coming to peck at the pieces of flesh that still clung to the pole and the wall.

After the silence call it was strictly prohibited to talk, but prisoners would grunt, pant, mumble curses, and so on. Some would pray the whole time the execution was going on. This was repeated almost every night, and usually a whole group was shot, prolonging the session. Sometimes it happened at midnight, sometimes at three or four a.m.

At sunrise the prisoners would rage in despair and impotence. Some would curse the air, and we would get into fights with each other at the least provocation. We had to bite our lips hard, over and over again, we had to pray for a way to go on in this pit of human misery without our brains bursting and without hating ourselves too much.

The daytime was never quiet. There was always some pretext for the guards to come into the galley to push us out with beatings or bayonets, for inspection or some other meaningless activity. When we were deadly tired, we would finally fall asleep, our brief truce with reality, until we were rudely awakened for new rattlings of our bones. . . .

There were four circular buildings and two square buildings in the Isle of Pines prison. I was assigned to one of the first category, a round building with a conical zinc roof. The openings in the grilled windows looked like holes in a rotten cheese. Inside, a guard kept watch from a tower in the center, which looked out on five stories, with a hundred cells each. The first floor was raised more than three meters off the ground, and there was a sixth level next to the roof without cells, just open space divided by steel beams.

Since there were two men per cell, there were easily more than a thousand men in each building. The square buildings were supposed to be even larger. So the figure of 8,000 prisoners, counting those who were living in the hospital and other areas, is a very conservative estimate. Bearing in mind that there are many other prisons in Cuba, it is not unreasonable to guess that there were at least thirty to thirty-five thousand prisoners in the total prison population. No one except the government can say exactly how many prisoners there are in Cuba at any given moment; there are so many places to keep them and so many kinds of prisoners that our numbers are always mistaken.

Surrounding the prison and scattered throughout the island were farms, pastures, and quarries connected with the prison, as well as workshops of every kind and a large tract of land that was used for gardens, firing ranges, and storage sheds. . . .

Who were we, the prisoners? A number of us, a little under ten percent, were ex-military men from the Batista period. A very few people were there because they had been wealthy or had something to do with Batista, or perhaps had demonstrated a negative attitude towards the revolutionary process.

But the overwhelming majority of us—I would say around 85 percent—had participated in the fight against Batista, either directly or as sympathizers. The civil violence that took place between 1952 and 1958 had involved practically every Cuban. It had been more than a struggle against a greedy, corrupt government; it had been a movement for national reform, and everyone projected his own highest ideals on the process. Even many of the soldiers who defended Batista's power wished they were on the other side, longing for the radical transformation that would turn us into an efficient, humane society.

Of everyone who was involved in the revolution, the bravest and most committed were the peasants. The farmers, who had started to get involved in the fight against Batista, were now participating in large uprisings against the new government, which had alienated them with its plans for land expropriation and state farms. They were determined to take part in deciding the national destiny, something that had always been decided for them in the past.

The mobilization of the peasants was contributing to some new cultural developments. The Castroite organizations would sing military marches and chant slogans, but the peasants would express themselves in folksongs, called "corridos," with lyrics that celebrated the deeds of local heroes like Waldo Ramírez. Another popular form was the "decima," a short satirical poem that could be improvised as the singer went along.

The peasants came to jail in groups. Each guerrilla left dozens of executed comrades behind, and was accompanied by collaborators from all over his area. Each of these groups formed its own "guara," or brotherhood, like a family of warriors.

There were young mestizos from the mountain ranges of the east who had never come down to the lowlands before; peasant troubadors who had traveled through the hills singing at the peasant feasts (called "changüís"). There were old men who had never set foot on asphalt pavement and boys who had won their manhood amid the smell of gunpowder and the startling surprises of guerrilla warfare.

There were many city people too. A large number of union leaders who had won their battles against Batista and lost to his successor came with strings of followers. They represented every industry: sugar mills, bakeries, oil refineries, urban transportation, electricity plants, etc.

Then there were the students. Some were so young that they couldn't have done anything against Batista but chant revolutionary slogans or thrill to the intrigue of clandestine life. They entered prison in bunches. There were also professors and professionals. Some prisoners pursued a university education in prison. Every sector of society was present, from circus performer to priest, from violinist to nuclear engineer.

These men had come to live in buildings housing more than a thousand people, in open galleys where the farthest point was nearly 100 meters ahead.

They lived without wife or mother, but many times they would come with their sons, brothers, or cousins. (Their wives and mothers would be in the women's prison.) Every ideological current was represented as well. Catholics, Protestants, Jews, practitioners of santería (a kind of Cuban voodoo), atheists, Masons. Politically, they ranged from extreme conservatives to trotskyists and anarchists. Nonetheless, they did not group themselves according to party. They would sit and talk, curing the world's problems a hundred times a day, always ready to die for their opinions. Yet they would grow old without the chance to even write the chronicle of their passion. . . .

But the dominant experience of "The Island," as we called it, was defined by forced labor and irrational brutality. From the beginning, the guards had been trained to hate us. They were taught that we were murderers, traitors, capitalist exploiters, torturers from the past, CIA agents, and ten thousand things more. They were led to believe that any harm inflicted on us was an act of social justice, a sort of holy vengeance for a thousand abstract sins. Thus a guard could beat a fifteen-year-old boy bloody, holding him to blame for the horrors of slavery that took place centuries before; or for the crimes and torture committed under Batista.

The corporals who guarded us were chosen because they were debauched or perverse. There was one who would beat the prisoners terribly, and then run to masturbate behind some bushes. Another smoked marijuana.

Food was very bad and very scarce. Our daily fare was corn flour or macaroni boiled with salt, and some soup that was supposed to have peas but was closer to hot water. Saturdays and Sundays we were only given vegetable broth. They gave us coffee and a piece of bread before sunrise. Every few months our families were allowed to send us small quantities of roast flour, powdered milk, chocolate, and sugar. It was usually enough to provide us with about three spoonfuls of a mixture daily for a month. A piece of meat would fall into our plates every few months, or perhaps fish or eggs.

People fainted from hunger, their blood pressure dropping dangerously low. I remember one occasion when they brought a very thin soup to the field where we were working. The rule was that meals had to be tested by a convict before serving it to the rest, and it was my turn to test it. It was spoiled, bitter, and I reluctantly told the others, "I don't think it's safe." But another convict snatched the spoon away from me, saying, "Give me that. You don't know anything." He took a spoonful of soup, tasted it quickly, and said, "It's all right. Serve it." I bowed my head sheepishly. They were hungry.

The lights from the tower and the dispensary were our only source of light. For those who worked in the field, reading was almost impossible, since they had to leave before sunrise and return after sunset. Nonetheless, the students would get up before sunrise and study the best they could. Most of their work had to be oral.

Mail was an unusual luxury. Once in a while they would give us a letter, perhaps one for every twenty that were sent to us. We were allowed to send one letter every two months, at most.

Much has been published elsewhere about forced labor. It was simply a pretext for treating us badly. We had to work in quarries and fields; sometimes we would be taken to the swamps to pull out sunken logs or roots.

I was among a group that had to work like animals in a tomato field. As hungry as we were, if we wanted to eat tomatoes we had to steal them, and we were brutally punished if we were caught in the act. On the other hand, the tomatoes had been sprayed with an insecticide that caused dysentery. Once the tomatoes were harvested, they were abandoned to spoil.

We had to cut the grass with a machete, somehow without touching a pumpkin stem that lay among the weeds. Once, when a prisoner accidentally nicked the stem, the guard swung his bayonet at the prisoner's neck and almost severed his ear.

All of us were systematically beaten, some more, some less. Some were beaten because they were weak and unable to work, but the expert farmers also got their share.

One day we were hoeing furrows when the prisoner next to me fell a few steps behind. The guard stuck his leg with the point of his bayonet. The blood poured down into the soil, which became mud as I hoed. Another prisoner fastened his handkerchief around the man's thigh to serve as a tourniquet, but he lost the use of that leg for the rest of his life. Months later he was hobbling around with a crutch made out of a rough stick.

In the summer of 1965 I was taken to the hospital because I could not work any more. I had a bad lung from a case of pneumonia that left me with emphysema. I was so exhausted that I slept for days, unable to stay awake for more than an hour in the evening. There was another convict in the room who was a man of about forty-five. His face was crumpled, prematurely old, engraved with deep furrows of fatigue. They sent him back to the field, and a few days later he was found dead. A collapse, they said. He died of exhaustion.

Another prisoner was operated on for an ulcer. I don't know why they cut him open the way they did; he was splayed from the top of his stomach to the bottom of his abdomen. Two weeks later he was sent back to the field. We were planting sweet potatoes when the corporal came by. Without warning, the corporal pounded his fist into the man's stomach. He bent double, his eyes bulging. We went on working.

Youths, especially if they were handsome, were in the worst position. There was one, about twenty-two at the time, who was sitting on the ground bare-chested one day, picking out newborn tomato plants. I saw the corporal standing to the side, looking at him. Then he walked up to the boy and pierced his arm with his bayonet.

The blacks were also singled out for special abuse. "You nigger," the guards would say, "how could you revolt against a revolution that is finally making human beings out of you?" They always got more than their share of the beatings and bayonets.

One day I had to stay in the compound because I was sick. Around ten in the morning the grill opened and an unconscious body was thrown into the arena. It looked like a corpse, covered from head to toe with dark mud, so that you couldn't even tell if it had eyes or a mouth. The doctors came down, and we learned that the unconscious man was covered with excrement. He and some others had been taken to "work" in a sewage ditch. They had been forced to sink in the mire, over their heads, until they lost consciousness. Then they brought them to our building and threw them on the floor like a bundle. Many of the men in that group contracted different infections that lasted for the rest of their lives.

One corporal had the bright idea that prisoners should cut grass with their teeth, and made them do it.

One day, in Brigade No. 5, where I was working, one of the prisoners had been bayoneted early that morning. He was lying on the ground like a wounded animal, unable to move. Beatings and bayoneting had been frequent. Someone whistled and we tightened our grip on our machetes and hoes. We left the furrows and started towards the corporal. He shouted, and the guards circled us with their loaded rifles. We stopped just in front of the corporal, and he shouted that we had to stand in line because we were to be taken back to the compound. We stood in line and climbed onto the trucks.

There was one work brigade that was taken to the quarries every day to break stones. Most of its members had been guerrillas, and the corporal who was in charge of them enjoyed punishing them. He was a primitive man; he hardly knew how to talk. One day there was a big storm with lots of thunder and lightning while the men were working. The corporal was struck by lightning and fell unconscious to the ground. The prisoners took him in their arms, massaging his heart and giving him artificial respiration until he regained consciousness. A short time later, the corporal was transferred.

Once a truck that carried the prisoners out to the fields overturned. Some were wounded, many bruised, but there were no fatalities. . . .

During the time we were there a number of prisoners were mutilated. Some lost a leg, others an eye or an ear. Then prisoners began to court disaster. First, a convict had bees sting him until his whole body was swollen. Another one injected petroleum into his leg so it would be ruined and he wouldn't have to work. One day in the field I heard a man saying he was going to "find a way out." A while later I heard his voice whispering from behind some rocks. "Cut, cut," he was saying, "don't be afraid."

"But one is enough," another voice answered.

"No, both," insisted the first. A second later I saw the prisoner walking across the field holding his two chopped-off fingers in his other hand like a trophy. "Corporal, an accident! The machete slipped and cut off my fingers!"

The corporal sent him to the hospital, and another prisoner gave him a paper bag for his fingers.

Since there were hundreds of students, we held a student congress where the students discussed their political points of view. Since there were so many union leaders, we held a workers' congress where they debated the nation's problems from a labor perspective. When someone asked them what doctrine was the most helpful for workers in achieving their goals, they answered, "The sayings of José de la Luz y Caballero," a Cuban Christian ethical philosopher of the nineteenth century. They meant that all the workers needed to confront their problems was a clear mind and a tempered will.

Violence reigned. Inspections were as violent as those in La Cabaña, though perhaps less humiliating. The guards would rush into the compounds, and the convicts would run out, sliding down the handrails from floor to floor in their haste. Once a man had both legs broken in the tumult.

Many times we would talk loudly while we worked so the guards could hear us, reminiscing about the battles we'd waged and revolutionary comrades who had been killed. The young soldiers would finally find themselves sympathizing with us, and accepted our offers to share our snacks. They would warn us when the corporal was coming.

We, the prisoners, were not defeated in spirit, and in many ways we represented a threat to the regime. We were the most politically conscious sector of the population. There were so many of us that every family in Cuba had some kind of connection to someone in prison. We included dissident revolutionary leaders from every faction. Our numbers grew by the thousand, and soon the population of political prisoners, more than any battalion or political party, was the intellectual and political equivalent of the country's capital. That made us very dangerous. Abuse in the fields became more frequent. The authorities began to kill prisoners without any provocation or pretext, as though it were a deliberate tactic. . . .

It was 1968. Just a few days after the first visit we were allowed after leaving the Isle of Pines, we noticed some unusual developments. Officers we had never seen before began to appear on the patio. Someone said he had seen trucks unloading some strange bundles. Suddenly a group of soldiers, heavily armed, entered the patio, coming towards the galleys. But it didn't look like an inspection; first, there were too many of them, and second, they were too orderly.

It was something worse: a change of uniform. We were going to be given the same uniforms as the convicts in the reeducation plan, which were indistinguishable from those of the common criminals. Many times we had witnessed how the prisoners who had accepted the "plan," either out of physical weakness or personal circumstances, were humiliated and vilified on a daily basis. They were used against their fellow prisoners. They were cast in the most ridiculous roles, as though they were in a play where they had to say the worst about their old friends; spend their days singing and joking in the face of the starvation and beating we endured. They participated in calisthenics, where men of forty-five and fifty, veterans of wars, would jump around like teenagers, ending their exercises by kneeling before the authorities, bending their heads and waving a red handkerchief. But only two or three out of a hundred would receive a reduction of their sentences. The only real benefit for the rest was a bit more food and comfort.

On the other hand, they faced a much more subtle danger. Accepting such a role meant dividing your mind in half, unhinging it. After a while, you couldn't recognize yourself. The ghosts of insanity and suicide were too vivid.

A group of us refused to wear the uniform of the common prisoners. We were called the "*plantados*," a term that was borrowed from the Cuban peasants; it meant people who "dug in their heels." We were all prisoners who were not involved in the reeducation plan, either because the authorities considered us hopeless, or because we refused. We went without the humble luxuries that accompanied the plan. Over time we achieved a special status, symbolized by our yellow uniform. Every time the officials convinced a political prisoner to accept a common blue uniform, they regarded it as another victory for the revolution, and another blow against the stubborn *plantados*.

For those of us who were in La Cabaña, the great underwear controversy began quietly. They made us pass by a guard, who asked us if we accepted the new uniform or not. If we answered yes, he would give us a blue uniform and we would take off the yellow one. If we said no, we would just leave our yellow uniform and march into another galley in our underwear. All our belongings were lost.

We spent months without clothing. Winter rushed in through the bars of the back grill, and there was nothing we could use to warm ourselves or the floor where we had to lie. I started to practice some yoga to control my shivering, but I still couldn't sleep. They would give us one strip of toilet paper (about 50 centimeters) a day, and we always had to ask for it. They forbade us visits, mail (to send or receive), sunshine, books or any printed matter, contact with other galleys, etc. Medical attention was given only in emergency cases. No clothes, no furniture, no belongings of any kind. We were naked troglodytes in a twentieth century cave.

Months went by, but most of the convicts refused to give in. Part of the group, myself included, was taken to Guanajay, a prison that had previously been for women.

Guanajay was the most civilized prison we had been in. It was a group of buildings surrounding a small park. We lived in cells for two, not too small, each equipped with a washstand. There were showers outside the cells, though we were not permitted to use them; we were not permitted to leave our cells. But they were clean, and they didn't have bugs.

One day the guards came with the news that common convicts were going to serve our meals and clean the place. We said that was unacceptable. They persisted, so we went on a hunger and thirst strike. The guards came and yanked us out of our cells, breaking some heads, arms, and fingers in the process. Then they threw us in the dungeons, aching and completely naked, now without even our underwear.

You can survive a hunger strike for the first few weeks with less distress so long as you can drink water. You get weaker, and every few days you feel yourself sinking into a deeper level of weakness, until other signs of deterioration appear. But in a thirst strike, you are aware of greater damage within a few hours. Your mouth becomes abraded like a blister. You feel as though you are burning up inside. Your nervous system is so upset that you lose your senses of perception, and you may easily lose control of your conscious mind.

We spent seven days like that. On the eighth, the conflict was resolved: the common convicts were taken away. It was not a moment too soon; only a few hours earlier, one of the strikers who had a brain lesion started having a nervous episode, a fleeting schizophrenia. They took us back to our cells.

During these confrontations between prisoners and penal authorities, medical attention was not available. You could only receive it if you surrendered your position.

If there is one thing that is really intolerable, it is a toothache. One day I woke up with a sore molar that was hammering at my jaw. There was no possibility of a dentist, not even of the help of another prisoner. There was no aspirin to be had. So many hours later, my molar broke into pieces, and the pain increased to an unbelievable level. More than seventy-two hours passed. But then the pain began to subside on its own.

I proved something that I had heard about, and which was going to be of great importance to us in the future: no matter how great the pain, it always has a limit beyond which you will feel nothing more. Either you will die, or the pain will stop hurting. This is also the key to understanding the torturer's mentality. He will torment the victim, not to destroy the victim, but to excite him, tease him, until he destroys himself.

One day we were taken back to La Cabaña, and some weeks later, many of our comrades who had refused the blue uniform were brought in from different prisons. They told us the story of their odyssey after they left the Isle of Pines, and we heard about other prisoners scattered in different prisons in Havana and Pinar del Río.

In some places, the prisoners had been controlled by judo holds or beaten until they lost consciousness, then dressed in the blue uniform and tied up with rope. As soon as the prisoner recovered consciousness and got unfastened, he would pull off the clothes. Then everything would start all over again. Some prisoners suffered broken arms, legs, heads, and injured spinal chords in the struggle. After that, they were taken away naked and subjected to long starvation treatments. They were kept without water so they had to drink from the latrine, and live in filthy conditions that an animal would have shunned. Then they were displayed, naked, unshaven, starved, and bruised, to women soldiers to provoke even deeper humiliation.

One captain from the Ministry of the Interior ordered the guards to take an eighteen-year-old boy, absolutely naked, to the galley of the worst criminals, expecting them to rape him. The young convict shouted that he would defend his honor with his life. The common convicts told him, "No, we know who you are, you're a political. We won't do anything to you. We respect you."

Another youth spent months being beaten; then, without warning, he was taken in his naked, dirty, bearded state to a room where he found his parents and fiancée, who had been brought by the officers to blackmail him. He fell into a state of nervous collapse.

The prisoners who had been to Pinar del Rio had firsthand knowledge of the children's prison. Boys of eleven, nine, or even younger, had been jailed for their "crimes." They would try to escape, and the guards would chase them over the roofs as they would try to defend themselves with stones. Those children would cry to the political prisoners that they, the children, were going to liberate them: children prisoners, ragged, toothless, eating out of old tin cans like dogs, battling the soldiers, screaming in their soprano voices, "Politicals, don't be afraid, we'll rescue you!"

After they brought us back to La Cabaña, our conditions suddenly improved. We could smell that something was going on. The Minister of the Interior had been changed. The new one had been in La Cabaña recently, and had talked with some of the prisoners.

One afternoon, a short time later, the guards came in with some bundles. They were going to give us the yellow uniforms back again. We had proven that the apparatus of power could prevent a man from doing something that he wanted to do, but it could not force him to do something that he didn't want to do. . . .

· · · · ·

The Trap

The next seven years, from 1970 to 1977, were the most alienating of all, because we were cut off from our people. Prisoners, who are segregated from the rest of the world, form a culture unto themselves, and develop a unique point of view. When we were cut off from the other prisoners, yet not reintroduced to the rest of the world, it was like abandoning us to the power of the mirror: we became completely self-referential, uncertain of whether "I am I or I am the other."

We spent these seven years in an isolated place where we were cut off from everyone except each other and the guards. The few doors and windows were covered. If a prisoner was allowed to see a visitor, the visit took place on an individual basis, with a selected relative, always the same one, with a guard watching closely. If we had to see a doctor or a dentist, we were escorted, one by one, and the rest of the personnel, guards and prisoners, were pushed away so no one could see us or speak to us. To move us meant a major operation. To wave to someone, even at a great distance, was a risk.

The prisoners had a difficult time with each other because of the close quarters. If a group of people who were fond of each other were forced to live in a hermetically closed house, without any privacy or any view to the outside, they might be happy for a few weeks, but a few months later, it would become an annoyance, and after that, a hell. It was the exact opposite of a monastery, where one is present by choice, protected from the world. In prison we were there under duress, and lived under constant threat.

First we were taken to the 6th Section of El Príncipe. This place, which used to be the mental ward of the prison hospital, was made up of two large areas, two smaller ones, four cells and a patio. The cells and the smaller areas were locked; the rest was ours. The patio was separated from the inside by a grill and surrounded by a twelve-foot wall. It was always watched by a special guard from the tower, and the windows were covered with a fine wire net that did not allow even a mosquito in or out. The entrance grill was covered by a thick piece of canvas. At the top of the wall, some seven or eight meters up, there were some holes from which we could see the central patio of the castle, but only a good athlete could climb and peep, and that with the risk of falling and breaking his neck.

The same night we arrived, Pedro Luis Boytel was brought in. He was as shrunken as a corpse, and agitated. He was coming from one of his long hunger strikes, and had been confined to a hospital room for years.

More than a year later, my friend Silvino Rodríguez was brought from Boniato. Rather than a corpse, he was like some strange kind of monster. His skin was like ash-colored paper from a deficiency of certain vitamins; his face was lean and tight, his nerves hypersensitive. He had spent the past year in Boniato, inside a filthy cell with the door and window walled shut so no light at all could enter. They had systematically beaten him. When he finally collapsed from hunger, he was taken to a hospital and fed the minimum required to stay alive. As a result, he suffered some very bad spasmodic pains, for which he was given an analgesic and sent back to his cell.

Unaccustomed to light or a space larger than two by three meters, he found it difficult to stand or to walk. Despite his courage, or perhaps because of it, he had the manner of a hunted animal, always ready for a leap to its death. He told us of those who had nearly died of starvation in Boniato; of the constant danger of an "incident" or an "accident" that led to a convict's death.

For those of us in El Príncipe, the food was not so bad, and the space was rather large, with lots of fresh air. But little by little something else was happening to us. Our monthly visits began well enough, but every time the authorities wanted to plague us, something would happen. The guard would watch us from a few steps away, inhibiting us from enjoying the little taste of freedom we so badly needed. Sometimes he would come and sit right in front of us, like a toad, and the visit would be ruined because privacy was impossible. When one of us kissed his wife, the guard would interrupt on the slightest pretext. When they wanted to deprive us of a visit they would provoke us, either in the inspection or during the visit.

There was a notable incident of violence during this period that took place during an inspection that seemed to be directed at confiscating religious objects. In the end they insisted on searching us naked, without underwear. There were some older prisoners who had spent years without a visit as punishment for refusing to undergo such a search. Now, when they refused, the guards seized them, locked them in a neck hold, and pulled down their clothes. One of the prisoners who tried to defend himself was badly beaten, and apparently suffered some broken ribs. . . .

Prisoners were taunted in other ways as well. Those with stomach diseases were supposed to receive a special diet, according to the doctor's prescription. One day the meal would be in order, the next day it would not, and the third day it wouldn't come at all. Every day we repeated our arguments with the guards, without much result.

The oldest man among us, who was near seventy, was supposed to receive a special diet because of his age and various diseases. One day they came and told us that he would no longer receive his special diet, by orders of the Ministry, not the doctor. I, on the other hand, who was apparently all right, was going to receive a special diet. Of course, I refused. It was their way of tormenting the old man.

Over time, our minds began to fail. I tried to dedicate most of my time to meditation and to prayer, but my ability to concentrate was growing weaker by the day. I was never alone, but never really with anyone else either, and my sense of reality began to dissolve without any reference points. We were rarely allowed to read a newspaper, and then it was the government paper, *Granma*. Visits were so tense that we ended up talking nonsense. We would go through our entire stock of personal stories in our minds in a few weeks. How could we maintain a sense of reality if we couldn't even be with other prisoners?

I began to lose control of my memory. My mind would insist on returning to events from many years earlier, friendships and activities from when I was sixteen and belonged to the youth committee of the Symphony Orchestra. The memory of my friendship with two young women became obsessive— whatever happened to them? It was impossible to find out, but I could not erase them from my mind. . . .

It was early in the morning when all of the alarms in El Príncipe began to ring and the loudspeakers began to blast. All the prisoners were going to be locked up. Three convicts had escaped two days ago; two of them had been captured and were going to be tried that afternoon.

The escapees were very young. They had been initially arrested for trying to leave the country. Now it was said that they had wounded or killed a guard in their attempt to escape. They were captured a few hours later, and were taken back to El Príncipe amid insults and beatings. A vicious crowd, the worst of them women, was shouting obscenities at them. Apparently the mother of one of the prisoners had been brought for her son's trial.

Microphones and loudspeakers were installed everywhere inside the prison. The place chosen for the trial was the ancient chapel, now turned into a doll factory. The show began after midday. The prosecutor and the judges competed in insulting the prisoners, and the mob would rise and roar, demanding their death.

The usual procedure required the authorities to administer a paraffin test that would show traces of gunpowder on the prisoners' hands to prove their responsibility for the guard's death or wound, but since the test results weren't available, they were ruled unnecessary. When the defendants were allowed to answer the accusations, they denied the charges bravely but hopelessly. The sentence was going to be read.

The mob was shouting "Paredón, paredón"—"To the firing wall!" The sandbags had already been heaped in place. The sentence was read. The mob cried in triumph, and struggled to get the best place to watch. The firing squad took its place facing the sandbags, and the convicts were brought out. They had to jump over a small fence. They were quick and nimble; they laughed as they leapt. We could hear the command, and the crack of gunfire. The coup de grâce. One of the victims resisted death, twisting on the ground, and the officer kicked his head. The mob bellowed and clapped.

Afterwards, they cleaned up the patio. The sandbags remained for a little while; a few hours later they were taken away. But the pool of blood lasted for several days. . . .

But the most important experience in the Combinado was the discovery of a new generation of prisoners. Our generation of prisoners was a generation that cut its teeth on rebellion. When we went to prison in 1964, there were thousands of youngsters, many of them children, who were involved in the civil violence that was wracking the country: uprisings in the hills, urban guerrilla activity, terrorism, sabotage, etc. Hundreds of youths who were fourteen or sixteen when the government changed were psychologically involved, in one way or another, in the actions against Batista that continued on against Fidel Castro. The regime had always explained our existence by saying that we had grown up without a "revolutionary consciousness," that our point of view was formed before 1959, and was solidified before they had a chance to turn us into the "new man."

But by 1977 we learned that youngsters who were brought up to be the "new man" were appearing in the reeducation plan as well. The majority of men in the plan were now twenty to twenty-five. Even if they had been born before 1959, they were still brought up in state boarding schools from that time on. They belonged to families that were partly or totally integrated into the government, and they personally had taken part in the state's political organizations. For them, the era before 1959 was a vague legend, and we who had been the youth movement of 1959 were "old men."

They brought in ten or twelve of these new youngsters every week. They were hot-blooded, rebellious youths, who had had firearms training since childhood. They threw themselves into violent, hopeless battles with the troops, which often showed some self-restraint in dealing with them. These boys were not easy to handle. They were brave and would try anything. It was preferable to manage them with guile.

They had been imprisoned for a variety of reasons. Some were in for taking part in primitive conspiracies; some for carelessly criticizing the government; others, for complicated plans to escape the country; yet others for dissenting from the government's official line. One unfortunate eighteen-year-old was mentally retarded and anatomically pubescent (with undescended testicles), condemned to remain a child until his death. He had come from a home for the mentally retarded, and no one ever knew why he had been sent to prison.

In Cuba, everything that is not forbidden is compulsory. The only way to express criticism is through rebellion, and this could take place in the most unexpected ways. One youth had snatched a microphone during a public rally and shouted a speech. Another had tried to hijack a plane with a pistol.

One young man had been considered promising until he resigned from the Communist Youth Organization and publicly expressed his discontent. During his interrogation, they asked him, "So you considered seeking asylum in a foreign embassy?" The youth answered, "Well, I'd thought of it." And so he "confessed," without ever taking the first step towards seeking asylum.

One young man had uttered a forbidden phrase in his workplace, and another had been a "hippie" and composed songs. Young soldiers were imprisoned for joining conspiracies. The cases of attempted escape from the country deserved to be written up as an anthology of fantastic stories; they included poets, novelists, and painters.

One fifteen-year-old schoolboy was sentenced to prison because he had thrown an egg at a classmate in a quarrel; his classmate and a teacher had then denounced him as being anti-government. Another student was imprisoned for five years for having drawn a U.S. flag on his notebook with the motto, "Long live Nixon!"

This new generation, created by the state, was revolting against it. But they did not believe in us old fellows, nor did they have any reverence for the past.

They had not lived it, and they were sick of the tales. They did not believe in ideologies or authorities, and did not regard any instruction as valid. The only thing they respected was courage.

Although they called us the "old men" and accused us of contributing to the situation that was smashing them, they were eager to talk to us about a number of things: religion, politics, sex, philosophy, art, flying saucers, and so on. The prison authorities wanted to prevent all contact between them and us, but the youngsters were cunning, and nimble as fishes. They had invented a thousand tricks to evade the guards, and they would come to us to share a new song as well as exchange ideas. They despised labels, and judged a man for the way he behaved towards his fellow man.

Because of that, and because they were too many to be crushed, the government tried to corrupt them. They had them caged like animals, without anything to read or anything to do besides stare at each other and fight. There were always pills available for them to drug themselves, or machetes that came mysteriously to hand during a fight. The government infiltrated agents to instigate quarrels. Homosexuality, rape, and prostitution ran rampant.

But I also learned that a new world had developed in prison over those years, parallel to and independent of official Cuban society, but much richer and more human. "Prison literature" grew into a genre, circulating among prisoners as well as on the outside. For years, my friends and I had been smuggling our writing out of prison. We copied it in tiny handwriting on the thinnest paper we could find, folded it, and wrapped it in nylon. The little "bullets" would be passed from hand to hand, first out of the galley, then out of the prison, finally out of the country. The prisoners produced poetry, short stories, and essays in considerable quantity and quality, and clandestine literature circulated all over the country in manuscript. The writing was not restricted to political topics, nor was it reduced to anti-government propaganda. On the contrary, it attempted to probe the human soul, combining religious mysticism with irony and rationalism. It was strictly forbidden, and when the authorities came across it they destroyed the manuscripts and sent the readers as well as the authors to prison.

But that was in 1978 and 1979, and there were rumors that political changes were on the way. We heard mention of dialogue, and stories of Cubans coming and going to visit relatives who lived abroad. Some prisoners who had finished their sentences more than five years earlier were being released. We started to dream. . . .

It was about three in the afternoon on June 18th, 1984 when we noticed some unusual activity in the officers' headquarters. I was called up. My friends warned me, "it must be State Security." The officer went straight to the point: State Security had come for me, and perhaps it had something to do with my freedom. I should take only a towel and a toothbrush—the same baggage they required when you went in for a "treatment." I went back to the cell and told the prisoners within hearing distance what had happened. "Be careful, it's a treatment," one of them warned.

Another said, "And if they really let you go?" I shrugged. I couldn't afford to think about that. My sentence had been completed forty days earlier, on May 8. The next day I was called to the officer's room. "You know you have finished your sentence." Sure I knew. "And you know how things are." I knew that too. Then we had spoken of different matters.

Now they took me to the director's office. He told me I was going to go free. He gave me a pair of trousers, a shirt, and a razor. Something went loose inside me and started to flutter. I cut my face shaving, and got dressed in the new clothes. They took some photos of me, and at sunset, they took me to State Security in Santiago. The officer was trying to be gentle. I told him, "If I am going to be released, then I'm leaving. I've got some friends in Santiago I'd like to see. And I'd like to visit the shrine of the Virgin of El Cobre. So good-bye."

"No," he said. "You are free, but tonight you have to stay here with us. If you want, we can take you sightseeing in the city." Oh, I thought, not so soon; I'd better be careful.

That night, in a State Security vehicle, I was taken out to see Santiago, in polite but rigorous custody. I was allowed to speak with my friend by phone. It was near midnight, and I still didn't know what my real situation was. I gazed at Santiago from a hill with several State Security officers. They showed me an amusement park, praising it in their stilted, peculiar style: "It can handle x number of children per afternoon. It has x number of machines that rotate x number of times per minute. . . ."

The next morning I was taken to Havana by plane. An officer was waiting for us at the airport. "We are going to release you, but for the moment, you will stay at State Security," he said.

We arrived at "Villa Marista," the State Security headquarters, following a long journey by plane and by car. I had motion sickness; I was dizzy with a terrible headache and an upset stomach. The officers had left me sitting on a bench. Half an hour later, a different official came for me and started treating me as though I were a newly arrested prisoner. They took my clothes away, and left me facing the wall. Then they drove me through the building, whistling at me like an animal. It was painfully familiar. I asked for a doctor.

They locked me up in a dirty cell. Time passed, and I fell asleep. When I woke up I was feeling worse. I called, at first as politely as I could, but they paid no attention. I called again, and eventually I was shouting and banging on the door. The guard came in and told me to shut up. I said I needed to see a doctor as soon as possible. Finally they took me in for an injection. But it didn't help, and a few hours later I was shouting and banging on the door again. Then they came to take me for an interview.

They led me to a room where some high-ranking officers were waiting. I entered, angry at the way I had been treated. For several minutes we held a heated conversation. Then we gradually grew calmer—they more than I. They informed me that I was going to be released and would be sent to Caracas on Friday.

Throughout the conversation, I noted that they had accurate information about my family, both inside and outside the country. They said they were interested in taking me to certain places they considered "achievements of the revolution" before I left the country, so I "wouldn't take away a bad impression of Cuba."

An officer came in to write down my name and personal data for a passport. "Why do you want to abandon the country?" he asked. "To breathe," I answered.

I returned to the first group of officers, who asked me if there was any special place in the city I would like to visit. I didn't hesitate. "The University," I answered. One of the officers smiled. "I knew it," he said.

The next day, in civilian clothes, accompanied by two State Security agents, I went to see "Lenin Park," "Lenin High School," and a model hospital.

We were standing in the park when I saw a little bus painted with black and yellow stripes. "This is a 'zebra'," they explained. "We're building a zoo where the animals will run free, and people will be able to view them from these buses." Then he looked at me and said, "You know, so they don't live in such inhuman conditions." I was stunned.

At Lenin High School the principal offered me detailed statistics on how well everything was working. It was a luxurious school with many gardens, museums, and playgrounds. I was remembering the case of Osvaldo Figueroa's daughter, who was expelled from that school because her father was a political prisoner who would not accept reeducation. I thought of the way it had turned her against her father.

The hospital had such a luxurious lobby that it looked like a first-class Mexican hotel. The three places were indeed attractive samples.

When we got to the University, they had the good taste to leave me alone. I walked under the laurels in the plaza and past the columns outside the Rector's Office. I slowly climbed the big stairway and went to the Student Association room. The door was closed. Then I went to the Law School. It was closed too. "No trespassing," a voice said from inside. "Who are you?"

"Don't worry," I answered. "I'm just a ghost." I went to the School of Architecture, where I had often gone to see José Antonio Echevarría, a student leader who had been killed in 1957. I wasn't allowed to go in there either. We left.

At three in the afternoon, they left me in a room at the Hotel Riviera in Havana. I took a shower and dressed in the clothes they had given me. The hotel was in the Vedado, my old neighborhood. I went downstairs and took a walk. The sidewalks were the same, but the trees were much older, I marvelled at the buses, the lights, the people in brightly colored clothing. I went to the church I used to attend as a child. "Didn't you used to live at? . . ." asked a man working in the yard. I looked into his eyes; I hadn't recognized him, but he had recognized me.

Later I heard my first mass in years, in the chapel near the river where eleven old ladies had been praying for me, and were still praying. I stayed to talk with a priest who had been my friend since we were young.

That night I finally saw my relatives, or at least those who were still alive. It was odd how things had changed; where I had left eight, I found four; where I had left four, I found ten.

I spent Wednesday afternoon, Thursday, and Friday wandering around my city. I tried to visit as many friends and relatives as I could. Everything looked beautiful, but something had changed. I was standing on a corner with my godmother waiting for a bus. I was saying, ". . . because in Boniato. . . ." when someone discreetly tapped my arm. "You shouldn't mention that."

I went to look for an address. Seven people, one after the other, told me they didn't know where it was. Later I discovered I was standing in front of the house, and that all seven knew it perfectly well.

On Friday the State Security agents took me to the airport. Just before I got on the plane, a Spanish journalist interviewed me. "Are you going to Holland to accept the Rotterdam Prize?" I shrugged, perplexed. "What's that?"

Literary prizes were the farthest thing from my mind, but there were a few surprises in store for me. Cristina had been released from prison in 1970. We got married in 1979, and the following year she managed to leave the country. She devoted herself to an international campaign to win my freedom, and published a volume of my prison writings in exile. So much of it had been lost; I estimated that only one line in a hundred was smuggled out over the years. Now I learned that my poetry had won five prizes, including the Grand Prix at the 1983 International Poetry Festival in Rotterdam.

That night I touched earth in Caracas, a city that I love. Before that, I had needed to touch my roots, my land, my people. That is all.

Cristina and I celebrated our wedding night in Rotterdam, on June 27, 1984.

NICARAGUA

The Civil War in Nicaragua

Roger Miranda and William Ratliff

ROGER MIRANDA *(1953–) fought against Somoza with the Sandinistas and in 1982 became executive assistant to army chief Joaquin Cuadra. Between 1982 and 1987 he was chief of staff for the Minister of Defense Humberto Ortega, one of the leaders of the regime. He has lived in the United States since 1987 and was the chief contributor to the coauthored volume from which the following reading is taken. He is currently branch chief with the U.S. Securities and Exchange Commission.*

WILLIAM RATLIFF *(1937–) is a research fellow and curator of the Americas Collection at the Hoover Institution. He is author or coauthor of numerous books on Cuba, Nicaragua, and Latin American affairs, including* Inside the Cuban Interior Ministry, Castroism and Communism in Latin America, The Soviet-Cuban Presence in East Africa, *and most recently,* China's "Lessons" for Cuba's Transition? *He has taught both Latin American and Chinese history in numerous universities in the United States and abroad.*

The excerpt reprinted below examines the police-state aspects of the Sandinista regime with special reference to the Ministry of Interior and the political police. It also provides specific examples of the treatment of dissent from and opposition to the regime, including the use of government-controlled mobs.

. . . . .

The Sentinel of the People's Happiness

With the program of deception described above, the FSLN has worn a cloak of virtue that fooled or at least confused people around the world. In essence, the Sandinistas' public position was that their government represented all Nicaraguans except for a few reactionaries who wanted Nicaragua to continue as their personal fiefdom, even if without Somoza, in the service of American

From Roger Miranda and William Ratliff, The Civil War in Nicaragua: Inside the Sandanistas, © *1993 by Transaction Publishers. Reprinted by permission of the publisher.*

imperialism. The Sandinistas claimed that to guarantee the rights of the vast majority sometimes meant terminating the rights of the counterrevolutionary few. But as time passed, the "few" became the vast majority.

The comandantes unhesitatingly relegated to themselves alone the authority to decide what ideas, people, and groups were acceptable in the new Nicaragua. To implement their decisions they needed power, as Arce had said in his 1984 speech on elections. The main institution established to exercise this power, to maintain domestic control and conformity, was the Ministry of the Interior (MINT) under Comandante Tomás Borge, who in true Orwellian terms described the ministry as the Sentinel of the People's Happiness. One writer described Borge as "the little man with the voice of a poet [and] the eyes of a zealot" who "appreciated the nuances, even the beauty of pain."[1]

MINT grew enormously larger and more pervasive under the Sandinistas than its counterpart had been under Somoza. It was the main institution of formal and informal repression, its activities ranging from the legitimate keeping of order through publication of the party paper *Barricada* and censorship of opposition media to manipulation of justice, torture, and assassination. MINT never achieved the total power it sought, but its influence was widespread and intimidating.

The major divisions of MINT were the State Security (DGSE), the police, the Directorate V intelligence operatives, patterned on Cuba's General Directorate of Intelligence (DGI), the Tropas Pablo Ubeda (until it was moved from MINT to Defense in the mid-1980s), the monitors of the media and, more informally, the mobs. MINT also manipulated the judicial system. In this chapter we will discuss the widespread repression of rights and freedoms of those who did not agree with the comandantes.

. . . . .

Rights, a Matter of Strategy

In one of his moments of candor, Interior Minister Tomás Borge told a visiting OAS mission in October 1980 that "the most important thing is our strategic, historic decision to be in favor of human rights." That is, the FSLN was not interested in human rights because it supported human rights per se, though in another passage to the OAS, Borge claimed it did, but because the Sandinistas decided that attention to human rights would advance their long-term political objectives. That is what Borge meant by a "strategic" interest.[2]

In the spirit of Marxism-Leninism or almost any arrogant ideology, support for human rights can, with a perfectly clear conscience, be manipulated to serve broader interests. Before July 1979 the Sandinistas, along with many others, rightly condemned the violations of the Somoza government, though sometimes even then they did so deceptively, as when Jesuit Father Fernando Cardenal told a U.S. congressional committee in 1977 that he came only as a churchman "in the name of the barefoot lowly peasants of Nicaragua." He gave no indication that he was a member of the FSLN or that his testimony was based on documentation provided by the Sandinista National Secretariat, a deception he admitted in 1983.[3] And even as strategic interests clearly dictated the condemnation of human rights abuses by their enemies, so they also justified accusing enemies of abuses they did *not* commit and violations by the Sandinistas themselves.

. . . . .

The Guardians of Happiness

The most important institution in terms of control and repression around the country was State Security, strongly influenced and supported by Cuba, which by the mid-1980s had some four thousand members, making it about ten times larger than Somoza's secret police had been. The DGSE chief was Lenín Cerna, who quickly became the personification of Sandinista repression. He was cunning and malicious, vain, prone to overeating—so always on a diet or exercising—and like Humberto a dog-lover who had four Dobermans.

The DGSE was divided into several sections, including F-1 (Operations), F-4 (Ideological Orientation), and F-8 (Mass Organizations). DGSE ties went into all aspects of society with a complex web of people and institutions, including informers, interrogators, squads for kidnapping or carrying out the "dirty work" of the government, special jails for holding hostages, the Sandinista Defense Committees, and the like. It used blackmail, lies, harassment, provocation, imprisonment, psychological or physical torture, and execution to achieve its objectives.

However much State Security learned from the Soviets and Cubans, many of its techniques, like those often used by the Sandinista People's Army, were learned from Somoza, though they were more pervasive and at times more sophisticated. Cerna often claimed that "physical torture was a primitive method used by Somoza. We have much more scientific ways to make a prisoner talk," alluding to the de-personalization and psychological torture the Nicaraguans had learned from the Cubans. But EPS chief Humberto Ortega admitted privately, "We have to follow the example of the old Somoza's policy of the three Ps—plata (money), palo (stick), and plomo (bullet): that is, money for friends, a stick for waverers, and a bullet for enemies." And the DGSE itself used a lot of the "primitive" palo and plomo too, as seen in Cerna's personal beating of sixty-year-old Sofonias Cisneros—who was accused of lacking respect for the educational policies of the comandantes—and in many other instances noted in this book.[4]

The most feared jail, in many respects, was El Chipote, an underground detention and interrogation center dug into the hill directly behind the Intercontinental Hotel in what had been downtown Managua. The name was taken from the mountain called that in northern Nicaragua, which in the 1930s had been the headquarters of Sandino. This facility was used mainly for political prisoners, who were usually confined there for a couple of months that were certain to be, at the very least, highly intimidating. One Sandinista official who worked with Borge said, with no little understatement: "People are afraid just of going into El Chipote because it has a somewhat fearsome reputation. That has a psychological impact by itself."[5]

. . . . .

Death and Imprisonment

From the beginning, "exemplary punishment" was considered a "low cost" but effective way to gain and keep order and control in the country. It was used to eliminate and intimidate committed enemies of the regime, but also to warn those who supported the revolution that it would be dangerous to waver or shift sides. Ironically, many of the people whose rights were violated to the point of disappearance or death were precisely the workers and peasants the Sandinistas professed to represent. One extensive, on-the-spot study of labor relations under the Sandinistas concluded that "harassment, intimidation, arrest, and even killing, of workers and peasants who peacefully criticized or protested Nicaraguan government policies was a regular event inside Sandinista Nicaragua."[6]

Some exemplary executions were aimed at individuals in order to intimidate a larger number, while others involved killing more people, playing to a still broader audience. We will give several examples.

Former guardsmen, some of whom had committed serious crimes, and alleged Somoza collaborators, were the first to be made examples by imprisonment and execution. At least thirty prisoners at La Polvora jail in Granada were killed in the months after the revolution and two mass graves were later found outside the city. The Interior Ministry, which had made Granada an unofficial detention center, tried to block investigations by CPDH. But making an example of guardsmen continued. Many hundreds of guardsmen, mostly in their early twenties or younger, were charged with nothing more specific than illicit association and "membership in a criminal organization," but in perfunctory trials they were given ten or more years in prison.[7]

One of the most widely publicized assassinations by State Security forces was of Jorge Salazar, a businessman who had supported the overthrow of Somoza but was considered a threat as early as the *72-Hour Document* because he had very effectively organized small coffee growers. Salazar became involved in a conspiracy against the government and the easiest way to silence him was with death. While unarmed, he was ambushed and murdered in November 1980 by security agents.

It is fairly well known that sixteen prisoners died "trying to escape" from the Zona Franca prison at the end of June 1981. But the details have been hidden. A group of prisoners took several guards hostage. Borge and Walter Ferrety, then chief of the Sandinista police, arrived with some EPS units prepared to provide support as needed. After some clashes between MINT units and the prisoners, which left several of the latter wounded, Borge said he would spare their lives if they would put down their weapons. When they put their arms down, Ferrety immediately shot several men in front of Borge and the remainder were summarily executed.

The execution of prisoners who caused trouble was particularly important because there were so many prisoners in the country and the Sandinistas wanted to cow them into submission. Thousands of people involved in or suspected of antigovernment activity were killed or arrested and held in inhumane conditions in state security prisons. Some 785 people were reported "disappeared" to CPDH between the fall of Somoza and September 1980, though the rights organization said that the actual number was probably closer to three thousand. While some of these people were later accounted for—reappeared, found dead, etc.—many were not, and more disappeared as time passed. Among the disappearances reported to CPDH in the first five years of the Sandinista government, 342 remained unresolved in 1984: 170 from 1979, thirty from 1980, and 170 from 1981–83. And many of the disappeared, especially peasants, still were unreported. Also, the human rights organization concluded that some ninety-seven people died inadequately explained deaths ("trying to escape," "heart attacks," and the like) between 1981 and 1984 after having been arrested by civil or military authorities.[8]

Some seven thousand people were being held in the Zona Franca, Cárcel Modelo, and other prisons in early 1987, about half of them political prisoners, far greater numbers than were held during the Somoza period. Many prisoners were peasants, some twenty-five hundred of whom were arrested and jailed in 1986 alone, according to CPDH, for refusing to join Sandinista defense organizations, for actually or allegedly supporting the Contras, or for resisting the resettlement programs which involved some hundred fifty thousand peasants between 1982 and early 1987. Some of these prisoners simply disappeared, some "committed suicide," and many were shot "while attempting to escape."[9]

In many respects the most flagrant and systematic repression by the Sandinista government was the nearly genocidal program launched almost immediately, largely for strategic reasons, against the Miskito, Sumo, Rama, and Creole peoples on the Gulf coast. Traditional organizations and institutions on the eastern coast were forcibly replaced by Sandinista Defense Committees, the EPS, DGSE, other FSLN entities led and/or accompanied by substantial numbers of Cubans. In February 1981 the heavy-handed repression brought war that continued throughout the decade at varying levels in loose cooperation with Contra forces in Honduras and Costa Rica, interspersed with the "peace negotiations" discussed below. The EPS and Interior Ministry also carried out a program which over several years often brutally resettled some twenty thousand people, while driving fifty thousand into exile in other countries.[10]

A different kind of "example" occurred in September 1987. Roger Miranda's black phone—the one that carried only calls from Humberto Ortega—rang and the chief, unusually agitated, said only, "Miranda, come to my house immediately," and hung up. In six years with Humberto, Miranda had never received a call like this one. When he arrived, Humberto took him to one of the trees in his private garden where someone had carved "FDN," the acronym for the Honduras-based Contras, into the trunk. Ortega growled, "Miranda, I want you and counterintelligence to investigate this immediately and find out what bastard has the balls to write this in the patio of my house." Miranda met with Lt. Col. Omar Halleslevens, chief of counterintelligence, and within a couple of days the latter concluded it had been done by a gardener who had worked in the house for years. Counterintelligence tortured him to find out if he was part of a broader plot, but concluded he had acted alone and had no contacts with the Contras.

Still, when Ortega was told, he ordered, without pause, "the sonofabitch must be killed." When asked if he didn't think the punishment excessive, he shouted and waved the report in Miranda's face, "What the fuck do you expect me to do when this bastard writes these signs in my own garden!" He would not reconsider. In part he had been personally insulted in his own residence. But also, he felt he had to show the hundreds of servants and security personnel who served and protected him, and had heard of this incident, that any such insult or insubordination meant death. After considering various ways to kill him, Humberto decided that counterintelligence assassins should make him die "accidentally from a falling tree," but gunshot wounds in his back left his family unconvinced by the official story. The gardener's pregnant wife was given some money and told there would be an investigation, but there never was.

• • • • •

Other Exemplary Punishments

Individuals who criticized the government were not always killed or "disappeared." Often they were beaten up instead of, or as a prelude to, being thrown in jail.

A week after the Esquipulas II peace accord was signed in August 1987, an opposition rally was broken up with unusual force, the police using electric prods. Lino Hernández, the head of CPDH, and bar association president Alberto Saborío, were jailed for three weeks. The calculated brutality of the attack on an opposition event at Nandaime on July 10,1988 surprised even those who expected the worst from Borge's forces. "They had come to teach the opposition a lesson," wrote Stephen Kinzer. The police fired volley after volley of tear gas into the crowd. Kinzer wrote that just before he too was attacked, and knocked unconscious, he "could see Sandinista police officers kicking and beating people. Never had they broken up a protest with such sustained violence."[11] Thirty-nine protesters, members of opposition political parties who were demonstrating with official authorization, were arrested and held in prison for months after their "trial" by "popular tribunals."

Sometimes people were blackmailed, as was the case with Bernardo Martínez, known as Bernardo de Cuapa. Martínez was famous because the Virgin had supposedly appeared at his house in the town of Cuapa in Chontales province, causing it to become a pilgrimage site. But Martínez was also a subtle critic of the government. State Security, concerned with his popularity, decided to take action against him, but knew it could not do so openly. So agents gained his confidence and one day, taking advantage of his fondness for drink, lured him to a hotel room where he was drugged. Rendered almost unconscious, he was raped by the state agents. Later he was shown a doctored film of the incident in which he was made to appear a willing participant. Bernardo was told that if he did not stop criticizing the government and halt his claims regarding the apparition of the Virgin of Cuapa, the tape would be made public. He was silent thereafter.

The Sandinistas made extensive and often very effective use of spies and undercover agents. One former national guardsman, José Efrén Mondragón, had his career as a Contra commander sabotaged by a woman who lured him back to Managua; for a while he campaigned to get other Contras to defect, but in time he was brutally assassinated. One of the most effective undercover agents was Pedro Espinoza Sánchez, known as *El Pez* (the fish), who penetrated and sabotaged several opposition groups in and outside of Nicaragua, bringing many to their deaths. Other Sandinista agents were well known to be spies, among them Marieluz Serrano (Nancy), who spent many months with Edén Pastora, an old friend of her family, while Comandante Cero was on the Southern Front in the early 1980s.[12]

The relationship between the Church and the Sandinistas in this predominantly Roman Catholic country was very complicated, but it boiled down to this: the cultivation and utilization of highly politicized Christians—the "popular" church—for political purposes, on the one hand, and the manipulation and when necessary the harassment and repression of those who believed the Church should stand above partisan politics, on the other. Increasingly during the decade of the 1980s, the FSLN charged that the traditional church, headed by Cardinal Miguel Obando y Bravo represented only the middle and upper classes, at the expense of the poor. The Sandinistas undertook active measures to discredit the Church and its leaders, one of the most common being the manufactured incident intended to defame a clergyman. For example, Fr. Amado Peña, one of the most important working-class priests in Managua, was set up twice by government agents to make him appear a counterrevolutionary conspirator, preaching peace as a priest but secretly plotting armed insurrection against the people's government.

· · · · ·

The Mobs and "Collective Justice"

The common cop-out when a death or atrocity could not be covered up or blamed on the Contras was the same as when evidence was found of military aid to the Salvadoran guerrillas: the government claimed the action had been undertaken by individuals or groups acting on their own, beyond the government's control. There was a logic to this, for many Nicaraguans *did* have very strong and often justifiable resentments against the Somoza regime and the National Guard, but the government systematically used and directed repression rather than trying to reign in these and manufactured resentments, and did so for many years.

Tomás Borge professed government innocence to the OAS in October 1980. He said FSLN leaders had told the police, the security forces, and the army: "'Don't commit abuses; don't be disrespectful to anyone; don't hit prisoners.' Because often they did hit prisoners or kill prisoners." He said that a "tiny minority" of guardsmen had been killed but added, "It was like Fuenteovejuna," alluding to the Lope de Vega drama in which a whole village admits having risen up and killed an oppressive tax collector as an act of spontaneous, collective justice.[13]

The most common instrument of "spontaneous collective justice," which in fact was government planned and often coordinated, was the mob. The "turbas" were gangs that, beginning in early 1981, beat up individuals, broke up political meetings and church services, and ransacked private property. More active in some periods than others, they were unofficial instruments of Sandinista "revolutionary terror" and one of the early signs that the Sandinistas had their roots in the politics of Somoza.

One of the first major targets of the turbas was Alfonso Robelo, who had been a member of the original government Junta but resigned in early 1980 and subsequently was lambasted as a lackey of the right. Robelo got authorization to hold a rally of his National Democratic Movement (MDN) in Nandaime on March 15, 1981. But on the night of March 14, EPS trucks transported turbas to the roads leading into the city to prevent MDN demonstrators from getting into town; on the next day the mobs destroyed MDN party headquarters, burned the home of the party's local leader, and vandalized other homes. The government blamed all the trouble on MDN provocateurs. On March 15, the main headline of the FSLN paper *Barricada* proclaimed: "People's Victory: Provocateurs Turned Back." The next day the National Directorate released a long statement, which said in part: "The Sandinista Front reaffirms it will respect the will of the people, in whatever form the people may express their will." If provoked, it went on, "and its means of expression produces acts that could be classified excessive, the only ones responsible are the provocateurs who have questioned everything about the Revolution and confront a people who have decided they will not go one step backward along their historical road."[14]

One of the most controversial events in the FSLN's relations with the Church was the visit of Pope John Paul II to Nicaragua in March 1983. The pope stated in advance that his visit was to be pastoral, not political, but the FSLN looked on it as a supremely political act. The FSLN decided to disrupt the pope's visit when it became clear he would not speak out against the Contras, but rather would follow the Nicaraguan church in criticizing the "popular church" and in calling for unity among Nicaraguans. The National Directorate instructed the Regional Committee of the FSLN in Managua to control transportation and access to the July 19 Plaza so as to make it hard for believers to attend the pope's mass, while at the same time making sure there were enough hecklers in strategic positions to disrupt the meeting and create a climate of hostility toward the pope. Predictably, the pope's sermon and communion were broken by amplified heckling and chanting, some of it coming from the comandantes themselves, while the pope's microphone was turned down. In fact, the vast majority on hand loved the pope and popular tensions with the government increased as a result of this manufactured incident. After leaving Nicaragua, the pope condemned the Sandinista regime for its sacrilegious behavior. But Minister of Culture Ernesto Cardenal told *Playboy* magazine (September 1983) that the pope had gotten just what he deserved.

The Interior Ministry used the turbas many other times, among them: in mid-1983 on the Salesian school in Monimós, which had established its revolutionary bonafides in the war against Somoza, because priests there dared to criticize government repression of the Miskitos and their church; in 1984 on Arturo Cruz and other opposition candidates in the presidential elections that year; and in 1988 after the escalation of atrocities in the wake of the Directorate's above-cited defense of "revolutionary violence," in Nandaime and other parts of the country.

· · · · ·

Twisting Justice

But the Sandinistas went beyond saying they were not responsible for violations of human rights. They asserted that human rights and legal norms were scrupulously respected under their government and even claimed that those who were caught deliberately violating norms of proper behavior on their own were punished. But they said this largely to cover their own systematic violations of those very rights and norms.

Between July and October 1979 the National Directorate adopted a vengeful attitude toward former national guardsmen and other supporters of the dictator who were accused—sometimes quite accurately—of crimes against the Nicaraguan people. But many people were blacklisted simply for reasons of personal vengeance. Special Courts were set up as a cover for executions and regional military chiefs were given the names of the condemned. During those months hundreds were executed around the country, often in public, on direct orders from Humberto Ortega, who was acting on behalf of the Directorate. What the tribunals actually did had little to do with justice. A delegation from the United Nations International Commission of Jurists, which made an early inspection of the courts, was openly sympathetic to the Sandinistas. But its secret report to the Sandinista leaders included sixteen "frank" comments, beginning with:

> It is unavoidable that an impartial observer reach the conclusion that the Special Tribunals constitute exceptional tribunals dispensing political justice with only the appearance of legality, abandoning elemental principles of the democratic penal process. These tribunals . . . in reality comply with the old rule of war, according to which the victors punish the losers.[15]

This judgment gave the lie to Borge's often-quoted statement that the Sandinistas are "implacable in battle but merciful in victory." In fact, on orders of the National Directorate, executions of Guardsmen occurred throughout the country: in Masaya, in Managua, León, Estelí, and in several other cities.

Only in Granada, a city that was generally lukewarm in the fight against Somoza, did the executions under the direction of Salvador Bravo draw significant criticism. In August 1979, in response to the negative publicity, Humberto himself assumed the position of a judge imparting justice and made Bravo the scapegoat for what Ortega himself had ordered. The captain was emotionally shaken by the betrayal, and in December 1981, by which time he had been promoted to captain, he committed suicide.

In 1983 the Special Courts were replaced by Anti-Somocista People's Courts (Tribunals), which operated outside the regular court system. This court consisted of three members of the FSLN. According to Stephen Kinzer,

police and security forces, using the People's Tribunal to legal-
ize their actions, arrested and imprisoned everyone they suspected of ties to the Contras. . . . Human rights advocates were
entirely justified in complaining that the People's Tribunal routinely sent defendants to jail on the basis of flimsy evidence or
hearsay.[16]

CPDH reported in early 1987 that some two thousand people had already
been "tried" in these courts and another two thousand were then awaiting trial.[17]

In late 1983, when peasants resisted brutal land collectivization in Pantasma,
a village in the northern part of Jinotega, a virtual reign of terror, consisting of
robbery, rape, and murder, was imposed by the local representatives of the
Department of the Interior. When the deaths of dozens could no longer be
hidden, the FSLN put accused government representatives, including some
members of the EPS, on "trial" and sent them to jail. But the sentences were
simply for propaganda purposes: very soon the top perpetrator was sent to
study in the Soviet Union and the others were set free. Not surprisingly,
Pantasma and Jinotega in general provided many of the unit leaders and fighters in the Contra army.

Daniel Ortega told the *New York Times* that twenty soldiers were sentenced
to prison for abuses committed during the evacuation of Miskito Indians, and
that at least five had been executed.[18] In July 1987 Tomás Borge insisted before
a large conference of international reporters in Managua that the FSLN did
not tolerate violations of human rights. Reacting in part to several recent media articles on Sandinista rights abuses, he acknowledged that "some of our
compañeros have committed serious crimes against the people on the Atlantic
coast," and added that in Nicaraguan jails over the past eight years "there have
been mistreatments and even killings, in isolated form, especially in the theater of war." He then said that these "isolated" incidents had led to the arrest
and sentencing of 2,318 members of the EPS and Interior Ministry in the previous *six months* alone.[19]

Fleeing Their Homeland

A Report on the Testimony of Nicaraguan Refugees

THE FOLLOWING is a report about Nicaraguan refugees and the reasons for their flight based on their testimony. The information was collected and published by a fact-finding mission of the Puebla Institute (located in New York City). The Puebla Institute is a lay Roman Catholic human rights group concerned primarily with the freedom of religion as defined by the relevant United Nations Declaration.

. . . . .

Introduction

The idea for a human rights investigation focusing on Nicaraguan refugees came out of a visit to Nicaragua in November 1986 by the Puebla Institute's executive director. In talking to local Catholic priests and lay leaders in rural Nicaragua, Mr. Davis heard account after account of harassment and persecution which was leading Nicaraguans—both Catholics and other Christians—to flee the country. It became apparent that many Nicaraguans were seeking refuge abroad and that theirs was a human rights story left largely untold.

For these reasons the Puebla Institute sponsored a fact-finding mission to Central America in early 1987 to examine the Nicaraguan refugee question. The objectives were to establish the best estimate of the number of Nicaraguans who have gone into exile since 1979, when the Sandinistas assumed power, and, through first-hand testimony, to document reasons for Nicaraguan emigration.

Freedom of religion is the principal focus of the Puebla Institute. In conducting the refugee investigation, therefore, the Institute was particularly concerned with the question of religious liberty. Indeed the Puebla delegation found that some of the refugees had left Nicaragua because of difficulties related to freedom of religion and conscience. We also found, however, that Nicaraguans had fled their homeland for various additional reasons, and we discuss this testimony as well in this report.

From Fleeing Their Homeland: A Report on the Testimony of Nicaragua Refugees to Conditions in Their Country and the Reasons for Their Flight *(Puebla Institute: Washington, 1987). Reprinted by permission of the Puebla Institute.*

This report does not cover all questions of human rights in Nicaragua. It is limited to the violations reported by the refugees interviewed

The Puebla Institute's fact-finding delegates were Ronald Radosh, a professor of history at the City University of New York, and Nina Shea, lawyer and Washington Director of the Puebla Institute. Ms. Shea is the author of this report.

The Puebla Institute expresses its gratitude to the office of the United Nations High Commissioner for Refugees and the governments of Costa Rica and Honduras for granting the Institute access to the refugee camps.

Summary and Conclusions

The findings of the Puebla delegation were startling. The numbers of refugees from Nicaragua were much larger than we anticipated. The Puebla delegation found that by early 1987, over 300,000 Nicaraguans, or at least ten percent of the total Nicaraguan population, had left their country since 1979, and that the exodus was continuing at high levels. In 1986, large increases in the total Nicaraguan refugee population were documented in both Honduras and Costa Rica, border states of Nicaragua. By the end of 1986, Honduras had 24,195 registered and an estimated 30,000 to 100,000 unregistered Nicaraguan refugees. Costa Rica had 21,954 registered and an estimated 85,000 to 100,000 unregistered Nicaraguan refugees. Another 150,000 Nicaraguan refugees are estimated to be in the United States.

The refugees gave seven basic reasons for why they left Nicaragua [number five is omitted here—*ed.*]. These are:

1. RESTRICTIONS ON FREEDOM OF RELIGION AND CONSCIENCE

Refugees active in Protestant or Catholic evangelistic movements described experiences of harassment and discrimination by the Nicaraguan government. From several individual refugees, the Puebla Institute heard first-hand complaints of one or more of the following abuses:

> —prohibitions on preaching, evangelizing, or attending prayer meetings;
> —detention on the basis of religious affiliation;
> —pressure on prisoners in detention to give up religious beliefs, including belief in the existence of God;
> —discrimination by the government in dispersals of food and medicine rations or in education opportunities because of religious beliefs;

—coercion or intimidation to join Sandinista organizations or to incorporate into religious instruction Sandinista ideology that the religious activist believed conflicted with his faith;

—pressure, including threats of further detention, to spy on other members of the congregation;

—denial of conscientious objector status to religious pacifists.

Such incidents demonstrate restrictions on religious freedom. Under international law, religious freedom can never be abridged, even in a state of emergency.

2. Sandinista Military Attacks Against Civilians

The Sandinista military has indiscriminately and without warning bombed and/or strafed civilians and their homes and farms in at least thirteen separate air or ground assaults in Nicaragua's conflictive southern Zelaya region since 1984. Though insurgent troops are active in this region, the refugees denied that the insurgents were present at the time of the attacks. The refugees provided the names or descriptions of nine persons, including young children, old men, and a woman, who were killed in the attacks.

The refugees described the air attacks as consisting of some combination of grenades, rockets, automatic fire, and explosives dropped from up to six MI 24-Hind or other helicopters, Push-Pull planes, and/or a single-engine plane. In some cases, the refugees said that, after the air attack, Sandinista army "search and destroy" battalions arrived on foot to carry out what appeared to be mop-up operations. The most recent attack the Puebla delegation heard about was a surprise aerial bombardment of the village of Punta Gorda on December 9, 1986.

According to the refugees, the Sandinista forces made no attempt to limit attacks to military objects, to distinguish between military and civilian targets, to warn civilians, or to otherwise minimize civilian casualties. Injury to civilians was not merely incidental to attacks on proper military targets; rather civilians and their property were directly and deliberately hit by Sandinista fire.

A Sandinista counterinsurgency policy of "draining the sea" emerges from the thirteen assaults documented by the Puebla delegation. This strategy aims at killing or terrorizing and driving out those who could lend support to guerrilla forces. This constitutes a violation of the Geneva Conventions, as well as of basic human rights to life and security of the person.

3. ARBITRARY ARREST AND DETENTION

The Nicaraguan government has used detention without charges or even minimum due process as a method of harassment or intimidation. From the refugee testimony, a picture emerges of a long-standing and widespread Sandinista practice of preventive detention without due process, especially in parts of the countryside where contras are present. Particularly vulnerable to such abuse are *campesinos* who are not active in Sandinista organizations.

Over the past five years, since a state of emergency was first invoked, political detainees have not had the rights to be informed of charges, to consult with attorneys upon arrest, to have family visits, to be judicially processed or released within a certain period, or to avail themselves of the legal remedy of *habeas corpus.*

Arbitrary detention, that is, detention without even minimum due process, regardless of the existence of a state of emergency, violates international human rights law.

4. TORTURE AND ILL TREATMENT IN DETENTION

Some refugees reported being tortured in Nicaragua's State Security detention centers, where detainess are held before trial or release. Such facilities are off-limits to independent observers and others. Five methods of torture most commonly cited by the refugees were severe beatings during interrogation; prolonged deprivation of food and/or water; mock executions; believable death threats against the detainee or his family; and extremely harsh conditions of confinement such as those found in "hot cells," cells partially filled with filthy water, or in closet-like cells Nicaraguan prisoners call "La Chiquita." In most instances, former detainees reported being subjected to a combination of these, as well as other torments. These reports conform to those documented by other human rights groups, and together demonstrate a pattern of torture occurring over the past several years in Nicaraguan State Security detention facilities throughout the country.

Despite repeated appeals by the Inter-American Commission on Human Rights of the Organization of American States and others, the Nicaraguan government has persisted in its denial of access to State Security facilities to such independent groups as the International Committee of the Red Cross and in its suspension of *habeas corpus* for State Security detainees. Having failed to adopt these basic safeguards, the Nicaraguan government must bear full responsibility for what occurs inside its prisons. Therefore, the Nicaraguan government is responsible for torture. Under international law, torture is never justifiable. . . .

6. ECONOMIC HARDSHIPS AND REPRISALS

Other refugees told the Puebla delegation that Sandinista economic policies forced them to leave. Several refugees described being economically squeezed because they refused to join Sandinista farming cooperatives. Others complained about their financial problems working with the co-ops. Hardships from these economic programs became unbearable for some, and they left. In the words of one sixty-five-year-old farmer from Nueva Segovia: "In the co-op, whatever we produced, the Sandinistas took away. Life was hard. But if you weren't part of a co-op, they wouldn't sell anything to you."

However onerous economic policies may be, they are not, in themselves, human rights violations under international law. Some refugees, however, described oppressive economic measures that amounted to reprisals for religious or political beliefs. Explaining why he left Nicaragua in 1986, one refugee said: "I refused to go to the meetings of the Sandinista Defense Committees because I am not a Communist. If you're not organized as a Sandinista, you can't work. If you can't work, you can't live." His and other similar experiences reveal political or religious discrimination, in violation of basic human rights. Some of these cases are discussed in the chapter on Restrictions on Freedom of Religion and Conscience.

7. FORCIBLE RESETTLEMENT

The government's resettlement policies also forced some into exile. The Nicaraguan government began forcibly resettling Miskito Indians in 1981 as a counterinsurgency strategy. In 1985, after strong international protest, the government declared the policy a "mistake" and allowed some Indians to return home. In the same year, the government announced a new policy to resettle thousands of other Nicaraguans, particularly non-Indians, as part of its counterinsurgency strategy. In 1986, Amnesty International observed that "compulsory relocation of rural populations remains an element of government policy in response to the continuing armed conflict."[1] While the actual numbers involved are unknown, it is clear that many thousands have been affected. Time magazine reported that 500 families in Nueva Guinea were relocated in the first quarter of 1987 alone.[2]

Some of the refugees told the Puebla delegation that the Nicaraguan government had confiscated or were about to confiscate their family-sized farms and had ordered them to move from their villages into state-run farms and settlements under the resettlement program. These refugees had refused to comply and sought refuge in Honduras instead. One farmer, fifty-one-year-old Rafael Arauz, said that the government seized his ranch and coffee *finca* four years ago, along with twenty other farms in his area and told him and his neighbors to go live at a government settlement in Matagalpa. He said that the

Sandinistas gave no reason for the order, no fighting had occurred in the area at that time, and that he had had no previous problems with the government. Like the others we spoke to, he was outraged by having to turn over his property to the authorities. When faced with the bitter choice of farming for the government that had taken his land or becoming a refugee in Honduras, he opted for the latter.

Nicaragua's forcible resettlement policy has received little international attention. It is a harsh policy and entails such human rights concerns as (1) whether the government's motives in carrying out the policy are legitimate; (2) whether individuals have been subject to any ill-treatment during the relocation; (3) whether the conditions under which these individuals are being resettled are analogous to imprisonment without due process or for discriminatory reasons; and (4) whether the government has plans to restore the confiscated properties to the owners. Since the answers to these questions are to be found only through an investigation within Nicaragua itself, the Puebla Institute does not address them in this report. We plan to do so in the future and urge other human rights groups to do likewise. . . .

Arbitrary Arrest and Detention

Nearly one third of the approximately eighty adult men we interviewed in the refugee camps in both Honduras and Costa Rica had been imprisoned by the Sandinista government at one point or another over the past six years. Most had been accused of collaborating with the contras, though few had been formally charged with any offense. Most had been held without trial or other due process and were released as suddenly as they had been arrested. They reported being arbitrarily detained without charge for periods ranging from several days to fifteen months. Some were detained repeatedly. Jose Esteban Marin, a refugee from Nueva Segovia, reported being detained six times between 1980 and 1983 without ever seeing a judge. These cases conform to the pattern of arbitrary detention in Nicaragua observed by the Inter-American Commission on Human Rights of the Organization of American States and other human rights groups.

Most former detainees said they did not know for certain why they had been held but some thought it might have been because they had not actively participated in Sandinista organizations, such as the Sandinista Defense Committees and, therefore, were viewed with suspicion by the government. The great majority were peasant farmers or preachers who asserted that they were not active in any political organization or labor union, Sandinista or otherwise.

In detention, they were interrogated about contra activity in the area, pressured to become informers for the government, and threatened with re-arrest should they refuse to cooperate. Many of the farmers reported similar detentions of other men in the area either at the same time, in what amounted to mass round-ups, or in separate, individual arrests. Some reported they were ill-treated or tortured during interrogation while in detention at State Security facilities (see chapter on torture). All expressed deep bitterness and resentment over being detained. Some went into exile immediately after they were released. Some joined the contra forces (and later resigned).

They viewed these temporary detentions as unfair and an affront to their dignity and independence. But more fundamentally, the detentions, particularly for those held for longer periods, threatened their own and their family's survival. As the heads of family-run farms, where crops and herds need daily tending, their absence had severe economic consequences for the entire family. In some cases, where all the men in a family were rounded up at one time, the situation became so acute the family was forced to abandon their farm and seek refuge and relief assistance outside the country even before the men regained their freedom.

An example is Genaro Centano, a middle-aged coffee farmer and rancher from Matagalpa. Centano, his wife, and seven children had been in the Honduran camp for three years. Their industriousness was attested to by the small plot around their shack in the camp, which they had cultivated and in which beans and other crops were flourishing. Centano said that he had at first cooperated with the Sandinistas, belonging to the Sandinista agricultural cooperative and working with the political committees. He said after a while he became disillusioned because he was used to managing the growing and selling of his crops himself. He withdrew from the co-op, which aroused Sandinista suspicions. He said the Sandinistas falsely called him a contra and arrested him in 1983. He was detained for a year, being held for six months in a local jail and then six more months in a State Security detention center. He said he was not mistreated but was ordered to report on his neighbors to the authorities. Without ever being tried, he was released. He immediately left for Honduras where his family had fled after having to give up their farm.

Other cases of arbitrary detention, that is, detention without due process, are addressed throughout this report.

From their collective testimony, a picture emerges of a long-standing and wide-spread Sandinista practice of preventive detention without due process. Men who are not active in Sandinista organizations and who live in rural areas where there is contra activity are particularly vulnerable to this abuse. Our finding is consistent with that of the Inter-American Commission on Human Rights of the OAS, as articulated in its 1986 annual report:

> According to information provided to the Commission, the effects of the state of emergency have been felt particularly harshly in rural areas where the armed groups fighting against the government are operating. Mass detentions of peasants have increased, in an effort to prevent them from collaborating with or

being used by those groups. The peasants are pressured to join the various grass roots organizations (*organizaciones de base*) controlled by the Sandinista Front, and if they do not do so, they become suspect and may be held in prolonged detention during which time, it has been denounced torture, occurs to oblige them to inform about the movements of the armed groups. The commission has been informed that mass round-ups of peasants have occurred in Nueva Guinea, Nueva Segovia, Jinotega, Matagalpa, and Esteli.[3]

Over the past five years, since a state of emergency was first invoked, political detainees have not had the rights to be informed of charges, to consult with attorneys upon arrest, to have family members visit, or to be judicially processed or released within a certain period. Under the state of emergency the writ of *habeas corpus* is not available to them. They, therefore, have no way to remedy a wrongful detention. The suspension of *habeas corpus* violates international human rights law.

The Puebla Institute does not dispute the right of the Nicaraguan government to imprison anyone who has been found guilty in a fair proceeding of security-related offenses or other crimes, be they contras, their collaborators, or anyone else. However, the Sandinistas' use of detention without charges or without even minimum due process as a method of harassment or intimidation is not justifiable even in a state of emergency. The Nicaraguan government is in violation of articles 9 and 14 of the International Covenant on Civil and Political Rights and articles 7 and 8 of the American Convention on Human Rights, which set forth the prohibition against arbitrary arrest and detention.

Torture and Cruel, Inhuman, or Degrading Treatment

Some of those who had been imprisoned, whether with due process or not, reported torture and cruel, inhuman, or degrading treatment while in State Security detention centers. Former prisoners said such abuses were used to coerce confessions, intimidate, or to force individuals to spy for the state.

Under international law, the prohibition of torture is considered so fundamental that torture is never permissible, regardless of the existence of a state of emergency or the charges against a detainee. International law defines torture as:

> Any act by which severe pain or suffering, whether physical or mental, is intentionally inflicted on a person for such purposes as obtaining from him or a third person information or a confession, punishing him for an act he or a third person has com-

mitted, or intimidating or coercing him or a third person, or for any reasons based on discrimination of any kind, when such pain or suffering is inflicted by or at the instigation of or with the consent or acquiescence of a public official.[4]

There is no foolproof test for verifying any allegation of torture short of having independent human rights observers in the torture chamber itself. However, certain factors can serve as indicators of how reliable a particular report is.

In its investigation, the Puebla Institute found reports of torture credible when (1) the testimony concerning torture was first hand, coming directly from the alleged victim, and was not mere hearsay; (2) the Puebla delegation was able to cross-examine and question the alleged victim; (3) reports of a particular type of torture were specific and reoccurring, so as to indicate a pattern on the part of security officials and not merely an isolated abuse; and (4) opportunity for torture existed, such as when a detainee was held incommunicado. The Puebla Institute also took into consideration any scars or disfigurement on the alleged victim tending to corroborate reports of physical torture. Scars cannot be made a requirement of proof, though, since torture can be psychological as well as physical in nature, and even in cases of physical torture there may be no scars. Indeed some types of physical torture are employed precisely because they do not leave marks.

These four conditions are met in each of the cases described below. The Puebla Institute interviewed and directly questioned the alleged victims. Reports of torture were described in detail, and certain types of torture evidenced a pattern.

The methods of torture most commonly reported by the refugees were: severe beatings during interrogation; prolonged food and water deprivation; mock executions; believable death threats against the detainee or his family; and extremely harsh conditions of confinement, such as those found in so-called "hot cells," cells partially filled with filthy water, or in closet-like cells nicknamed "La Chiquita" by Nicaraguan prisoners. In most instances of torture, former detainees said they were subjected to some combination of these, as well as other torments. It is the cumulative impact of the treatment that we find "severe" and unquestionably rising to the level of torture in these cases.

Every refugee who reported abuses said they occurred in the detention centers of the Nicaraguan State Security, where detainees are held and interrogated before being charged and tried or released. Not every refugee who was in State Security detention reported abuses. Nor were abuses alleged to occur exclusively in State Security facilities; a few refugees told of abuses while imprisoned in the National Penitentiary system, where prisoners are held after charges have been brought.

Ample opportunity for torture exists in the State Security detention centers. Amnesty International reported that Nicaraguan State Security detainees are frequently held incommunicado for two to four weeks or longer after arrest while interrogation takes place.[5] Neither relatives nor their lawyers are allowed to visit the detainees during this period. Furthermore, the Nicaraguan government does not give any independent individual or group access to any State Security facility. It has even barred from State Security cells throughout the country the International Committee of the Red Cross, which routinely conducts humanitarian visits to prisoners and detainees worldwide on a strictly confidential basis with the host government. The state of the detainees' security is ever more precarious since *habeas corpus,* the legal remedy whereby the well-being of the detainee can be ascertained, is not afforded to political suspects under Nicaragua's state of emergency. All of these features of Nicaraguan State Security detention fit into Amnesty International's classification of "preconditions of torture."

In denying a request of the independent New York-based Lawyers Committee for International Human Rights to visit detainees at the State Security facility in Managua, Interior Minister Tomas Borge (whose jurisdiction covers the State Security) explained that "the presence of a stranger could interrupt the process of interrogation and persuasion."[6] While interrogation is a legitimate activity of any government, torture is not. It is incumbent on the Nicaraguan government to adopt measures to safeguard against occurrences of torture and other abuses in its State Security detention centers and other prisons. The Puebla Institute endorses Amnesty International's recommendation that "it is vital that all prisoners be brought before a judicial authority promptly after being taken into custody and that relatives, lawyers, and doctors have prompt and regular access to them."[7]

Ten reports of torture from Nicaraguan refugees of particular concern to the Puebla Institute follow:

1. Justo Pastor Alvarado, a sixty-three-year-old coffee farmer from Las Manos, Nueva Segovia, was detained by State Security in 1985 for eight days without charges or trial. During interrogation, which focused on contra activity in the area, he was beaten with rifle butts and told that if he did not cooperate he was going to be killed, along with his two sons (who were not in detention). Fearing for his own and his sons' lives, he left with his family for Honduras upon release.

2. Juan Gonzalez, a forty-eight-year-old farmer from Punta Gorda, Zelaya, said he was arrested and held without charges or trial by State Security for seven days in 1984. Throughout that time he was interrogated about contra activity in the area, while kept blindfolded and bound. He still bears scars around his wrists where he said he had been tightly shackled. He said he was beaten with rifle butts by his interrogators, was repeatedly threatened with death, and at one point State Security interrogators thrust the barrel of a gun

into his mouth and threatened to pull the trigger. He reported that for the entire week he was denied food and water.

3. Pablo Rayos Membreno, a forty-eight-year-old farmer from Punta Gorda, Zelaya, was detained for nine weeks without charges or trial in 1984. He spent a week in detention in Guadalupe and Puerta Esperanza and two months in the State Security detention center of Humedades in Chontales. In the latter facility, he reported being beaten with rifle butts, being hooded until near asphyxiation for twenty-four hours during interrogation, and being deprived of food and water for six days. He described being confined for eight days in a small cell he called "La Chiquita." The cell was so narrow he could not sit or lie down, and it was filled to mid-calf level with filthy water, causing his feet to swell. He said that once his interrogators told him if he did not "confess" to contra involvement, he would be executed. They blindfolded him, took him outside, and put a gun to his temple. They did not carry out the threat and he was subsequently released.

4. Jose Ramon Gonzalez, a forty-year-old farmer from Esteli, said he was imprisoned in 1980 for two years on a security offense conviction. He said State Security in Ocotal beat him on his legs with a metal stake causing scars that he showed the Puebla delegation. He was then transferred to La Barranca State Security detention center in Esteli, where he reported being twice injected with a yellow-colored drug which caused him to become temporarily deranged.

5. Jose Esteban Gonzalez, a thirty-two-year-old farmer from Nueva Segovia, reported being hooded, kicked, beaten, and denied water for four days while in State Security detention for three months in 1982. He said he saw three other prisoners shot in cold blood by officials at a detention facility in Murra during this period. He recognized one of the victims as a person he grew up with named Pablo Acuna.

6. Jose Gabriel Herrera, a thirty-seven-year-old farmer from Cantayaguas, Jinotega, was imprisoned for four and a half months in 1982 until he was brought before a court which acquitted him of charges of collaborating with the contras and ordered his release. He said that during interrogation State Security tortured him with electric cattle prods and threatened to kill him. He left the country upon release.

7. Rosaleo Arias Gonzalez, a thirty-four-year-old farmer from Jinotega, was arrested on March 4, 1982, and served a two-year sentence on counterrevolutionary charges. He reported that during State Security interrogation he was kept in a dark cell for three months, deprived of food and water for more than a week, savagely beaten with rifle butts, resulting in cracked front teeth and a permanent lump on his head, which the Puebla delegation observed. He was then placed in a crowded, hot, and poorly ventilated cell with thirty others, where he fainted. He also gave the following description of a mock execution he was subjected to while under investigation:

The State Security guards took me in the middle of the night to a place outside the prison and placed me next to a hole in the ground. They tied my hands and feet and began kicking me. I fell down and one of them kicked me in the ribs until I rolled over into the hole. A guard then pointed an AK [rifle] at me while the others debated among themselves out loud how to kill me. They finally decided on burying me alive and began throwing dirt on top of me. After all I was not killed but taken back to my cell.

8. Two cattlemen in their twenties from Chontales told the Puebla delegation they were close friends, were both active in the early 1980s in Alfonso Robelo's former political party, the Democratic Nicaraguan Movement, and had been arrested together in 1982. They were convicted on counterrevolutionary charges and given a three-year sentence, which they served. They were initially taken for investigation to the State Security detention center in Juigalpa where both reported being beaten, deprived of food and water for over a week, threatened with death, subjected to mock executions, and put separately in small, dark, unventilated cells. One of them described his treatment as follows:

I was captured on the 7th of November in 1982. I was sent to a cell in the State Security in the city of Juigalpa where they tortured me physically as well as psychologically. I don't know how long I was there inside La Chiquita. You don't know if it is day or night. It is a little cell, as tall as one is, that is, exactly the size of a person. There is no window of light and no air comes in. In about twelve days I was given only one glass of water and no food at all. They cover the floor of this Chiquita with pine sol, a chemical that doesn't allow you to breathe. I fainted. From there they took me twice to a doctor's office where I regained consciousness. The doctor gave me water and found the lack of it was why I passed out.

After La Chiquita I was taken to the investigation cells where I was tortured some more. They put on a very bright light bulb and headphones with tapes of people screaming and groaning and pointed guns at me. One night they took me to a desolate place with a shovel and pick. They told me to start digging my grave. Since I didn't tell them what they wanted to hear they began to torture me severely with beatings. They only hit me in soft spots where there wouldn't be any signs if I went to testify to the Red Cross or another organization. They then took me back to my cell. After two months my family came to visit me. Then they gave me permission to bathe. I hadn't bathed for the two months.

677

9. A forty-four-year-old man from Chinandega told the Puebla delegation that he was arrested on March 1, 1982, and served a three-year sentence on counterrevolutionary charges. After arrest, he was taken to Quinta Ye, the State Security facility near Leon. There, showing the Puebla delegation deep scars around both thumbs, he said he was hanged by his thumbs for two days with just his toes touching the ground and beaten by guards with brass knuckles. He then described spending the following six weeks in various cells under extreme conditions:

> I was taken to a completely dark cell where I saw no light for 28 days. At the end of the period they took me out for interrogation in front of very bright lights with 300 to 500 watt bulbs. Then they put me in a cell for nine days that was filled with cold water, dirty with human excrement, up to my ankles. I was not given any water to drink, just enough to wet my lips every 24 hours. My feet swelled and I developed a reaction in my lungs which I still have. I was then taken to a very small cell where I was forced to stand, which had a floor covered with pine sol. After two days in this cell, I was taken out and put in a dark hole in the ground, which was covered by a metal lid. It is called the "hot cell." It is just large enough for one man. It had excrement from past prisoners and there were lots of ants. For four days I was kept there without any food or water. It was very hot during the day and very cold at night. On the fourth day there, I was taken out and put in a large cell. After 90 days of captivity, they took me out to shoot me near a breadfruit tree, near a well. They asked me for my last wish. I told them I had already asked God. Another command came. They took me back into the prison to a dark cell. Fifteen days later, my family found out where I was and visited me. In 105 days I had lost 87 pounds.

10. A twenty-two-year-old man from Chinandega was released from prison on June 4, 1985, after serving a three-year sentence on counterrevolutionary charges. He reported that after arrest State Security beat him with rifle butts and submerged his head in a basin of water until he lost consciousness during interrogation. He said that at Quinta Ye detention center he was subjected to forty-five days of hoodings, beatings, and electric shocks with cattle prods. He also said:

> They told me my mother was also captured. They played tapes of a woman's voice crying and shouting. I found out later that she had not been arrested. For 11 days I was without water, I only was able to sip a few drops once in a while from a tiny pipe

in my cell. For nine of those days I was completely abandoned.
No one came near me. I wasn't given any food.

These ten refugees, along with other refugees interviewed by the Puebla delegation, describe a variety of forms of torture being used by Nicaraguan Security officials. We take seriously and are concerned by all charges of torture, including those reported by only one or two refugees—e.g. torture by electric shock, hoodings, injections, hangings, and other means. The Puebla Institute is confident, however, after reviewing all the evidence, that the Nicaraguan State Security repeatedly and deliberately employed at least these five types of torture: severe beatings, usually with implements; mock executions; believable death threats; prolonged food and water deprivation; and harsh conditions of confinement.

The Puebla delegation did not try to document systematically all reports of torture by the refugees, but rather interviewed refugees at random. These cases, therefore, represent a sample of torture reports from former detainees and prisoners. They are not isolated examples. These same five types of torture have been recounted in recent cases of Nicaraguan detainees documented by other human rights organizations.

For example, the International League for Human Rights, in its July 1986 *Report on Human Rights Defenders in Nicaragua,* describes a number of cases of torture from the past three years. Among them are the severe beating and mock execution suffered by Sofonias Cisneros, the head of the Christian Parent-Teachers Association, at the hands of the State Security Director himself, Lenin Cerna; and the simulated execution of the Reverend Jimmy Hassan, the National Director of the evangelical Campus Crusade for Christ.

In its February 1987 report, *Human Rights in Nicaragua, 1986,* the Americas Watch describes numerous State Security detainees who in 1985 and 1986 were beaten with rifle butts or other instruments, held in La Chiquita, and/or deprived of food for extended periods. The Americas Watch reported, for example, that Tomasa Hernandez, a Social Christian Party leader, who was pregnant when arrested, was held for two months in early 1986 in extreme conditions in State Security cells and was deprived of food for twelve days. After her release, she suffered a miscarriage.[8]

Amnesty International, in its March 1986 report, documents prison regimes in which water or food was withheld from the detainee, State Security officials convincingly staged threats against the detainee or his relatives, and detainees were subjected to extremely harsh detention conditions, compounded with the deprivation of basic amenities such as paper for toilet use, clothes, and soap. In light of these reports Amnesty wrote the Nicaraguan President Daniel Ortega in June 1985 to "stress its concern at the extraordinary *de facto* powers accorded the State Security Service under the state of emergency and the consequent scope of abuse of these powers."[9]

The Inter-American Commission on Human Rights of the OAS, in its 1986 annual report, expressed "profound concern" about "the constant reports received on deplorable conditions in Nicaraguan prisons," where "those jailed for political reasons are forced to suffer additional privations." The Commission also protested the "brutal beatings" of some political prisoners.[10]

The Puebla Institute believes that taken together these reports evidence a long-standing practice of torture, occurring over the past five years, by the Nicaraguan State Security in its detention facilities throughout the country. Reports of torture date from 1980 to 1986 and come from detainees in urban as well as provincial jails, including the State Security centers in Managua, Chontales, Ocotal, Esteli, Murra, Leon, and Juigalpa.

Despite repeated appeals by the Inter-American Commission on Human Rights of the OAS and human rights groups, the Nicaraguan government has persisted in denying the International Committee of the Red Cross and others access to State Security facilities, and has maintained its suspension of *habeas corpus* remedies for State Security detainees. Having failed to adopt such basic safeguards, the Nicaraguan government must bear full responsibility for what occurs inside its prisons. The Puebla Institute, therefore, concludes that the Nicaraguan government is responsible for torture in violation of Article 7 of the International Covenant on Civil and Political Rights and Article 5 of the American Convention on Human Rights.

NORTH KOREA

The Aquariums of Pyongyang

Kang Chol-Hwan

KANG CHOL-HWAN *(1968–) is the author of the only English-language account of the North Korean Gulag based on personal experience. The scarcity of such writings reflects the tight controls the North Korean regime exercises over its population. Such an account becomes available only when the author can smuggle it abroad or when he himself can escape. Until a few years ago, this possibility did not exist for North Koreans. However, since the 1990s a famine has compelled an increasing number of North Koreans to escape into China (which borders North Korea in the north), a situation made possible by the apparent decline of vigilance among the border guards and their increased corruptibility.*

It has been distinctive of the North Korean political system that the collapse of Soviet communism has had no discernible impact on it; unlike other surviving Communist states, such as China, Vietnam, and Cuba, North Korea has not become less repressive politically or more liberal economically to any significant degree. It has retained not only its police- and garrison-state aspects, but total government control over the economy and an extreme and bizarre cult of personality as well. The undiminished compulsory worship of the supreme leader persists, first Kim Il-sung, and following his death in 1994 that of his son Kim Jong-il. North Korea may be the only remaining truly totalitarian state in the world.

North Korea has also been distinguished among Communist states by its aggressive, militarized foreign policy: in 1950 it invaded South Korea, and since the end of that war it has committed many acts of aggression, ranging from border incursions to the assassination of South Korean politicians and the kidnapping of South Korean citizens. It has also maintained the third largest military force in the world, notwithstanding its severe economic problems and the pitiful living standards of the vast majority of its people.

North Korean repression has had some unique features, such as the removal of the physically disabled from the capital (Pyongyang), public

From Kang Chol-Hwan, The Aquariums of Pyongyang, © *2001. Reprinted by permission of Basic Books, a member of Perseus Books, LLC.*

*executions in the prison camps, and the compulsion of the entire
population to actively participate in the worship of the Supreme Leader,
expressed, among other things, in the wearing of badges with his image.*

*The author of the excerpts that follow was, with his family, in a
North Korean prison camp from age nine to nineteen. His family were
among the North Korean émigrés who returned from Japan to North
Korea after World War II and were initially given privileged treatment
but subsequently came under suspicions of disloyalty. As in many other
Communist states, the entire family of the suspect (the author's
grandfather) was dispatched to a camp without judicial formality. After
his release, the author succeeded in escaping to China and, much later,
from China to South Korea, where he currently resides.*

* * * * *

During his morning visit, the brigade leader had assigned my father and uncle
to an agricultural work team, to which they were to report at 6:00 a.m. the next
day, the same time my sister and I were to be in school. Our half workday
would begin at 1:00 p.m. The schedule would remain unchanged until we
reached the age of fifteen, at which point we would be considered adults and
assigned to full work duty. Before our new routine could begin, however, we
had to go to the supply office for our uniforms. We all showed up there together to try on the meager selections of hand-me-downs. The experience left
us all feeling a little ashamed. As we shed our old clothes, we could feel our
former civilian lives slipping away, those lives in which we wore ties and clean
shirts, briefs, and comfortable socks. From this point forward, our wardrobes
would consist of a purple jacket and a pair of pants, both coarsely sewn from a
rough, heavy cloth. The uniforms were fitted with a great number of buttons
and resembled the Chinese prison outfits I later saw on television and in the
movies. Wearing this uniform for the first time was strange enough, but seeing
my father and sister in them was stranger still. When it rained a few weeks
later, we were in for another unpleasant discovery: the clothes shrank as soon
as they got wet. Now they weren't just uncomfortable, they were downright
ridiculous, too. Not that any of the veteran detainees ever noticed. These uniforms were distributed to us in mid-August and were meant to serve us through
the entire year. A few prisoners told me the camp had precise rules regulating
distribution of linen and uniforms. If these rules existed, they certainly weren't
followed while I was there. In all my time in Yodok, I only received uniforms
twice, and though they quickly came apart, they were all I had to wear—day
after day, year after year, in field, mine, forest, and mountain.

During our years of detention, rags were often the only clothing we had.
Our garments eventually reached such a repulsive state that the guards had no
choice but to let us wear our old clothes from the "outside." It wasn't long
before these became so tattered and grimy as to be indistinguishable from our

uniforms. After a few months in the camp, the appearance of our rags bothered us no more than they did anybody else. The only thing that mattered was keeping warm. When the winter cold set in, we put on everything we could get our hands on, hoping against hope that the layers of rags might protect us. We were also constantly on the lookout for ways to steal more clothes. Working on a funeral crew, we never buried a corpse without first stripping it naked. Apart from the cold, the worst part was underwear. The camp authorities provided us with briefs and undershirts, but their cloth was so rough that it rasped our skin, causing us to itch and sometimes to develop open wounds, such that we soon found it preferable to go without them. I ultimately came up with the idea of recycling my old tattered briefs into linings, sewing them to the inside of my camp-issued underwear. As for socks, our annual quota of one pair never lasted long, despite my grandmother's ceaseless and often miraculous darning.

At night, after a brief dinner of corn, we all scrambled immediately off to bed, thinking of the day to come, our first day of work in the camp, a day that would surely be difficult. For me it was simply horrible. . . .

．　．　．　．　．

The spring of 1979 had arrived. It was my second spring in the camp, and it followed a winter that camp veterans counted as mild. Spring is a hard season for the detainees of Yodok, the worst, I believe. Many withstand the cold of winter only to perish in the season of rebirth. Children and the elderly are most afflicted. The prisoners often called it "the yellow season," because people felt out of shape and weak at the slightest physical exertion; they suffered from dizzy spells and in the most severe cases saw the sky as yellow instead of blue. Those who were unable to protect themselves in the preceding months died. The key was to take advantage of the fall, when fruit and vegetables could still be found, to consume like bears in hibernation, eating enough to get through winter and fight through spring. That's the most important thing I learned in school. I didn't learn it from my teachers, of course, but from fellow students, some of whom had already been in the camp for close to three years. They explained that to survive, one had to steal corn and soybeans, to do it methodically, systematically, eating as much as one could in the fall and stashing the rest against the harder times of the seasons to follow. There was no other way to survive.

Our corn rations were extremely meager: adults who worked from sunup to sundown had a daily allowance of 500 grams; others, including children, were allotted 400 grams. Vegetables were not distributed at all, and the few cabbages and turnips we managed to grow in our little plot were nowhere near enough to feed a household. Despite the risks of getting caught, we wound up stealing whatever we could get our hands on. We stole from the vegetable fields, from the agent's plots, from the cornfields. We also took advantage of logging expeditions to gather wild berries, which could only be found up in the mountain, since around the villages everything was picked clean. The detainees were like goats: they devoured everything. Whatever they didn't eat right away, they dried and ate in the winter; and when any kind of animal fell into their hands, they ate that, too.

Despite these precautions, more than a hundred people died in our village every year—out of a population of two to three thousand. Many former Japanese residents were interned in 1976 and 1977, the year of my arrival in the camp. That period and the months that immediately followed were among the most murderous I ever knew at Yodok. The newly arriving prisoners were usually the first to die. If you made it through the adjustment period, though, you could expect to live for a good ten years more. The most important thing was fighting malnutrition, which was more punishing than even mistreatment by guards. Most of the camp's diseases were not very serious, but in our weakened state a simple cold could kill. Psychological factors doubtless also played a role. Those who once lived in Japan were accustomed to a comfortable, modern existence and consequently suffered more than the others. For them, the adjustment to normal North Korean life had already been difficult enough. Many had hardly negotiated this transition when they suddenly found themselves transported to a concentration camp! The arrest itself was a brutal shock, a terrible blow to their spirit. These were people who pinned their every hope on Kim Il-sung and his brand of communism, and from one day to the next they saw themselves thrown into a camp, labeled traitors and sons of criminals, and treated as the lowest of slaves. It was more than many of them could take.

I almost died during my first months in the camp. The primary reason was the corn. Despite my grandmother's tireless efforts to make it appetizing, after a certain point I just couldn't digest it anymore. My problem was not in the least extraordinary: everyone struggled with it, though women for some reason had an easier time. I didn't know of a single man who didn't suffer at least one serious bout of diarrhea during his stay in Yodok. The ordeal, which generally lasted two or three months, would leave one thin and greatly weakened. The diarrhea was made all the worse by the ghastly conditions of the latrines. The filth was unspeakable. With the sparkling whiteness of our Pyongyang bathroom still fresh in my mind, just the sight of the small stinking huts was enough to make my stomach turn. There were only seven outhouses with four places each for an entire village of two to three thousand people. We did our business Turkish style, squatting over a tank we did our best not to dwell upon. No paper, of course. Each visitor had to come prepared with his own supply of sufficiently wide leaves. Bean and sesame leaves worked best. In July, during the rainy season, there was the danger of overflow; but it was much worse in winter, when the excrement froze and gradually built up toward the lip of the latrine. The detainees then were forced to choose between chiseling away at the growing mountain of excrement with a pickax or getting up in the middle of the night and digging a new hole of their own. If you chose the latter, it was worthwhile keeping track of the location, because you might later want to retrieve what you buried and use it to fertilize your vegetable bed. . . .

. . . . .

In the spring of 1981, I was assigned to help bury the bodies of prisoners who had perished during the previous winter, when the frost-hardened earth had made timely interment difficult. As with any detail, the work was carried out after school; but since it was considered somewhat unusual, we were rewarded with a few noodles to supplement our ration of corn. This would have sufficed to make interring bodies a desirable detail, but the work offered another very practical advantage. The burial team could strip the corpse of its last remaining clothes and either reuse them or barter them for other essentials. But the fringe benefits came at a price. Since Korean tradition requires that people be buried on a height, we had to carry the bodies up a mountain or to the top of a hill. We naturally preferred the hills at the center of the camp to the steep mountain slopes near Yodok's perimeter. Their proximity allowed us to follow tradition without traversing tens of kilometers. But the neighboring hills eventually became overcrowded with corpses, and one day the authorities announced we would no longer be allowed to bury our dead there.

We thought the order had been given for health reasons, but we soon found out how wrong we were. I was walking back to the village with my team one evening after a day of gathering herbs up in the mountains, when we were overtaken by a terrible stench. As we walked on, the odor grew stronger and stronger until we finally came upon the cause. There were the guards, bulldozing the top of the hill where we'd buried so many of our dead. They actually dared to set upon corpses! They didn't even fear disturbing the souls of the dead. An act of sacrilege held no weight for them compared to the possibility of growing a little more corn. As the machines tore up the soil, scraps of human flesh reemerged from the final resting place; arms and legs and feet, some still stockinged, rolled in waves before the bulldozer. I was terrified. One of my friends vomited. Then we ran away, our noses tucked in our sleeves, trying to avoid the ghastly scent of flesh and putrefaction. The guards then hollowed out a ditch and ordered a few detainees to toss in all the corpses and body parts that were visible on the surface. Three or four days later the freshly plowed field lay ready for a new crop of corn. I knew several people from my village who were assigned to plant and weed it. Apparently, it was horrific work. Since only the larger remains had been disposed of during the initial cleanup, the field-workers were constantly coming upon various body parts. Oddly enough, the corn grew well on the plot for several years running.

That scene frightens me more today than it did back then. At the time, I remained relatively calm before that spectacle of horrors, which is perhaps the most telling indication of just how desensitized I had become. The more I witnessed such atrocities and rubbed shoulders with death, the more I desired to stay alive, no matter the cost. Maybe I didn't have it in me to become a snitch or turn on my friends, but I had lost much of my capacity to feel pity and compassion. I developed a savage will to live and a disregard for everyone around me. I also learned to control my emotions in front of the guards, which was very much in my self-interest. Trickery had come to play an ever larger role in my life. I used it to procure food, catch rats, steal corn, fake work while doing nothing, and get along with the snitches.

I wasn't alone. A few weeks after the bulldozer incident, I came across a group of people from my village standing around a woman who was loudly weeping and venting her sorrows about something. As I joined the crowd, I gathered she was lamenting the death of a relative, whose body was apparently still in the family hut. "Ah, why did you die so quickly?" she kept saying. "Why did you depart this cursed world?" The unhappy woman must not have noticed that a well-known snitch was in the crowd, as well as the leader of one of the work brigades. Her son, who was also there, saw the danger and tried desperately to catch her eye. It took him a while, but he finally did it, at which point the mother did a complete turnabout. "Oh," she continued without the slightest transition, "why did you leave this world, which had become so happy under the wise governance of our Great Leader?" No one dared to laugh, but after that, neither could anyone cry. . . .

· · · · ·

If I were to improve my nutritional intake and realize my dream of becoming the family's provider of meat, the better option was rat. One of my coworkers—a camp veteran—was the first to introduce me to the dish, going so far as to demonstrate its proper preparation. Despite my revulsion, I couldn't resist the odor of grilled meat—which was not deceptive, because the rat was truly delicious. Though the rodents were everywhere, trapping them was difficult, especially because most were quite small. The other challenge was figuring out how to reuse the traps, since the first captured rat left behind a smell that warded off the others. After much experimentation, I discovered that the smell could be eliminated by passing the contraption over a fire. By this time, however, I was already perfecting my newest trap design, which used wires strung across the entrance of the rats' nest to snare and strangle the animals as they tried to exit. My clever little invention was completed in 1982, and thanks to its increased catch, I was able to supplement the family's small food ration.

Mi-ho made less fuss about eating her first grilled rat than I did. True, I initially lied to her about the nature of the meat, but when I later told her the truth she wasn't the least bit disgusted. The poor girl was so hungry. She was suffering from pellagra, and that dish may have been her last shot at survival. At my urging, the entire family eventually took to eating rat. My uncle was the hardest to convince, but after a few months of demurring, the day came when his hunger pains were just too sharp and he, too, relented. That was the last time I saw him turn down a piece of grilled rat meat. The Yodok rats, it should be said, were fine specimens—much finer than any rat I ever caught in Seoul—and since they reproduced quickly, they were the only food product in the camp that was never in short supply.

I was not the only prisoner in Yodok to hunt rats. There were many devotees of the sport, and each had his or her own technique for trapping and preserving the game. I discovered that a friend of mine had turned his hut into a full-blown breeding ground. The other kids and I had noticed that he was always in good shape, while we, despite our little supplements, remained hungry and thin. Was he stealing food? Was someone giving it to him? Fearing that we had begun to suspect him of collaborating with the guards, the boy called us over to his hut one day for an explanation. His family was allotted two rooms, just as we were, but instead of using all their living space, they all squeezed into one room and left the second space entirely for the rats. To attract them, my friend had stolen corn from the fields and spread it on the floor. The plan worked perfectly, and the number of nests multiplied. The only maintenance required was sprinkling a little corn on the floor every few days. Whenever he got hungry, all my friend had to do was grab a wire trap and fish out a rat. It was a veritable pantry, the secret to his robust health.

Another of the camp's rat hunters prospered by taking advantage of his job as the watchman of the corn depot. The vast corn storage area which was surrounded by barbed-wire, contained about a hundred small wire-mesh silos, into which the prisoners emptied their harvest at the end of each day. Prisoners were allowed to enter the area freely, but the guard always patted them down on their way out. Everyone envied the guard's job, especially because the man who held the position was chubby—indeed almost fat—which only helped fuel speculation about his diet. People said that he always had meat in his mess tin. While most prisoners were sure he was doubling as a snitch, they also suspected him of stealing corn. Security eventually got wind of the rumor and sent guards to search the man's hovel. What they discovered was a large receptacle packed tight with salt-cured rat meat. The guards couldn't be more pleased with the man's ingenuity and fervor in controlling the population of the corn-thieving rats. The complaints of his libelers only helped shore up his position.

All the meals and extra rations provided me by the rats gradually changed my view of these animals. I began to see them as useful, even precious, on a par with chickens and rabbits. I was truly grateful for their existence, and still am. Absurd though it may seem to those who have never known hunger, I actually felt a connection with them. I remember an encounter I had with a rat in our hut one night. Raising my head from my mattress I saw him staring at me from between two floorboards. We were locked in each other's gaze, staring into each other's eyes for what seemed a long time, until the spell broke and he scurried away. Before entering the camp, I had thought of rats as scary and disgusting. Today I think of them as touchingly kind animals. . . .

. . . . .

Criticism and self-criticism sessions were nothing new to me. Such meetings took place in every North Korean school, Yodok's included. But outside the camp, these ideological exercises tended to be peaceable and rather formal in nature. Nothing much happened if you didn't criticize well enough or happened to criticize too sharply. At Yodok, the stakes were much higher. Punishments consisted of hours of nighttime wood chopping, even for ten- and thirteen-year-old children.

The atmosphere was strained. You could feel the fear and hatred spreading through the room. The kids were not as adept at controlling their emotions as adults, who knew that the wisest thing to do was accept whatever criticism they received. The adults understood that it was just a routine that had nothing to do with what their fellow prisoners really thought of them. Soon enough, the criticized person would have to criticize his criticizer. Those were the rules; there was nothing personal about it. Yet the faultfinding of peers was hard for kids to accept, especially if it struck them as unfair. They would get angry, argue, interrupt each other. While the short Wednesday meetings, which lasted only twenty minutes, were hardly long enough to cause major damage, the Saturday afternoon sessions, which went on for nearly two hours, were considerably more lively and tension-filled. A special session also could be called if something unusual took place in school. The substance of adults' criticisms was basically the same as the children's: "I wasn't careful enough during work hours . . . I arrived late yesterday because I was being careless, etc. . . ." The major difference was that the children's sessions were conducted among one's classmates.

As for the adults, each work team had its own location for Wednesday sessions, while on Saturday the different teams met together in a single large building, on whose walls hung the portraits of Kim Il-sung and Kim Jong-il. At the far end of the room was a platform with a table where the prisoner sat to present his self-criticism. Next to the table stood two guards, along with a representative of the prisoners. There were no other chairs in the room. The other prisoners sat on the floor in groups of five, clustered with their fellow team members. The assembly hall was always overcrowded. Some prisoners dozed off, others became nauseous from the intensity of the body odor that hung in the air—there was no soap at Yodok.

Sometimes we met in smaller groups to prepare our Saturday presentation in advance. Four of us would discuss our misdeeds for the week, while the fifth team member took notes. Afterward, the report was presented to a camp administrator, who selected the week's ten most "interesting" cases for presentation before the entire village. The prelude to the ceremony varied somewhat, but the main action was always the same. The wrongdoer would step onto the platform, his head bowed, and launch into his self-criticism with a fool-proof formula such as, "Our Great Leader commanded us," or "Our Dear Leader has taught us." The offender then cited one of the head of state's great "Thoughts," relating either to culture, youth, work, or study, depending on the offense committed. A typical criticism went something like this:

"At the famous conference of March 28, 1949, our Great Leader stated that our youth must always be the most energetic in the world, in terms both of work and study. But instead of heeding the wise reflections of our respected comrade Kim Il-sung, I twice arrived late at role call. I alone was responsible for this tardiness, which demonstrated neglect for the luminous reflection of our Great Leader. From now on, I will wake up a half hour earlier and make myself equal to the task of fulfilling his orders. I will renew myself and become a faithful warrior in the revolution of Kim Il-sung and Kim Jong-il."

Then it was up to the presiding security agent to decide whether the self-criticism had been satisfactory. If it had been, the prisoner could proceed to the next step: criticizing someone else. If his criticism was found wanting, the agent would ask a member of the audience to expand on the criticism proffered. If the accused tried to defend himself, a third prisoner, and, if necessary, a fourth, was selected to take up the assault. Self-defense was never wise, because the review couldn't end until the prisoner admitted his faults. Once a prisoner relented, we moved on to the next pre-selected case. The session lasted from an hour and a half to two hours, running from 9:00 p.m. until about 11:00 p.m., which wasn't always enough time to get through all ten cases. If time ran short, the agents consolidated the wrongdoing of an entire team, or several of its members, into a single presentation. A member of the guilty team would then present the self-criticism on behalf of everyone involved.

The sessions were so conventional and formalized that it was hard to take them seriously—despite the perfect silence imposed by the hard gaze of the guards. We were like bored kids in a class they find meaningless. The smallest distraction would set us off. It happened several times that audience members let out an audible fart in the middle of a self-criticism. A little nothing like that was all it took to shatter the ceremony's contrived solemnity and send the guards into a fit of rage. Sometimes they pretended not to hear, but other times they demanded to know who the culprit was. "Who farted?" they screamed. "The person who farted stand up!" If no one confessed, the guards kept us seated there until the criminal was identified, which eventually he always was. The prisoner would then be pushed toward the self-criticism table to expiate his fart with a mea culpa, at the end of which he usually received a week's worth of supplementary work details.

We dreaded these long meetings that shortened our nights needlessly. They were too much of a sham to ever take seriously, but that's not the way camp authorities saw it. They were always reminding us that "work alone can't root out your rotten ideology. You need control." What they meant was ideological control, and maintaining it was in part our responsibility. Hence, on arriving at adulthood, we were given three notebooks in which to trace the development of our ideological healing: "The Politics of the Party Notebook," "The Revolutionary History of Kim Il-sung and Kim Jong-il Notebook," and the "Life Assessment Notebook." All three accompanied us to the criticism sessions, so we could jot down all the lessons we learned.

To help advance our edification and reeducation, we also attended two classes a week to learn revolutionary songs and deepen our understanding of the life and thoughts of Kim Il-sung. The curriculum (called "the teachings") consisted largely of listening to articles read out loud from the *Rodong Sinmun* newspaper, of which three copies arrived weekly at the supply office. We weren't allowed to read the paper ourselves, because the direct word of the Party was reserved for security agents. Reprobates that we were, it would have been dangerous to expose us to more than a few pre-selected articles, and even these needed to be interpreted for us by the agents. With our rotten ideology, we were quite capable of misunderstanding their true intent. To say "interpreted" really gives the agents too much credit. All they ever did was pound us over the head with the Great Leader's most tired platitudes. "I read you this article because the Americans and their puppets in Seoul are once again threatening war. The imperialists' appetite for conquest threatens the peace, and to withstand it we must be ideologically armed."

I don't know whether the guards believed everything they said, but when they raised the possibility of a new war, some of us got nervous. We had always been told that if "the imperialists and their lackeys" ever invaded North Korea, the camp's personnel would kill us before the enemy arrived. I still had hopes of leaving Yodok one day. I had no desire to be shot by guards without having the pleasure of seeing them run for their lives. These sorts of threats sent a chill up my spine, but they made very little impression on the older veterans. "Whatever Will Be, Will Be" was their motto, and whatever happened outside the camp was of no interest to them.

Still under the rubric of our ideological reeducation, the agents sometimes tested our allegiance to Kim Il-sung by making us sing endless verses of "The Song of General Kim Il-sung." Part of the song goes, "In North Korea a new spring is everywhere on its way." *"Pang-bang kok-kok"* means "everywhere, without exception." I remember one old prisoner in the camp who had emigrated from Japan, like my parents, and who spoke Korean with a heavy accent. Instead of singing *"pang-bang kok-kok,"* he accidentally used a slightly different semantic form— *"yogi chogi,"* four syllables that mean "scattered in disorder" that have a rather negative association with filth and trash. The people who heard his slip began to laugh so hard they cried. As a consequence, he was criticized and labeled an "ideological deviant" and was almost sent to the sweatbox.

At the beginning of every year, we had the privilege of having Kim Il-sung's extended New Year's address read to us. The speech was the focal point of a two-day event featuring an absurd recitation contest. It could have been worse, though. It was January—a time when the thermometer often dipped well below 0°F—and instead of being outside we were gathered in a well-heated room. On the first day, we transcribed the speech in one of our notebooks, while the guards walked around to make sure we were making an effort. The next day, we worked on memorizing the speech by heart. The biggest challenge was figuring out how to doze off without being caught. The guards really only expected us to study the Great Leader's message and to regurgitate a few quotes. To keep us honest, they picked a handful of prisoners to recite what they had learned. The top three contestants won prizes—considerable ones, given our condition. The winner got a coat, the runner-up, a pair of socks, and the second runner-up, a pair of gloves. The kids' recitation contests were held in class, with the winner receiving a short reprieve from the usual work schedule.

My memory of these speeches has blurred somewhat, but I remember that they always started with an account of the previous year's accomplishments in agriculture, industry, the armed forces, and so forth, and ended with a list of "goals for the future." Somewhere in the middle came a nod to the Koreans residing in Japan, who under the clairvoyant leadership of Han Duk-su were continuing to lead a courageous battle in the heart of enemy land. There was also the inevitable mention of the South Koreans, who were suffering a cruel separation from the motherland and toiling under the yoke of America's lackeys. . . .

. . . . .

Having reached majority—as defined in the camp—I was obliged to begin attending a ceremony I would have preferred to skip. Yet few things were optional at Yodok, least of all the things that were most awful. Many public executions had taken place over the preceding years of my internment, but as a child I was not allowed to see them. Two of my more curious friends had once sneaked into an execution and described it to me afterward. The story left me feeling hollow and disgusted, which is the way my father and uncle always looked when they came home from one of these events, their faces hard and unnatural. They would skip their dinner and just sit there, never saying a word about what they had seen. If I pressed, they just shook their heads, and observed that "Yodok is no place for human beings."

The first public execution I saw was of a prisoner who had attempted to escape. We were dismissed from work early that afternoon so we could attend the execution. The whole village was there. The skies were rainy and gray—as I always remember them being on execution days. The event took place at a spot called Ipsok, a beautiful little elbow on the river, which turned into an island during the heavy rains. *Ipsok* means "large elevated boulder," which is exactly what the spot was: an enormous rock, as big around as a house, standing by the shore.

Three desks were set up for the occasion: for the head of the camp, the village chief, and the military guards. As the prisoners arrived they took their seats on the ground in front of the desks. Farther off, a small truck was parked under a tree. I was told that that was where they were keeping the condemned man. I felt anxious. The older veterans sat chatting. A few wondered aloud about who the man might be. Most talked about other things. Several prisoners used the time to gather herbs. Attending a few executions was all it took to render the experience perfectly banal.

Finally, the head of the camp stood up to read the condemned man's resume. "The Party was willing to forgive this criminal. It gave him the chance here at Yodok to right himself. He chose to betray the Party's trust, and for that he merits execution." During the silence that followed, we could hear the condemned man scream his final imprecations in the truck. "You bastards! I'm innocent!" Then suddenly his cries stopped. We saw two agents pull him down from the truck, each holding an arm. It must have been ages since he had last eaten. All skin and bones, it looked as if he were being floated along by the guards. As he passed in front of the prisoners, some shut their eyes. Others lowered their heads out of respect. A few of the prisoners, especially the younger ones, stared widely at the barely human figure, hardly able to believe their eyes. The unhappy being who walked to his death seemed no longer a member of the family of man. It would have been easy to mistake him for an animal, with his wild hair, his bruises, his crusts of dried blood, his bulging eyes. Then I suddenly noticed his mouth. So that's how they shut him up. They had stuffed it full of rocks. The guards were now tying him to a post with three pieces of rope: at eye level, around the chest, and at the waist. As they withdrew, the commanding officer took his place beside the firing squad. "Aim at the traitor of the Fatherland . . . Fire!" The custom was to shoot three salvos from a distance of five yards. The first salvo cut the topmost cords, killing the condemned man and causing his head to fall forward. The second salvo cut the chords around his chest and bent him forward further. The third salvo released his last tether, allowing the man's body to drop into the pit in front of him, his tomb. This simplified the burial.

That unfortunately wasn't the worst spectacle that I beheld at Yodok. In the fall of 1986, a condemned prisoner who didn't have enough pebbles stuffed into his mouth, or had somehow managed to spit them out, began proclaiming his innocence and screaming that Kim Il-sung was a "little dog"—one of the worst things you can call someone in Korean. To shut him up, one of the guards grabbed a big rock and shoved it into the man's mouth, breaking his teeth and turning his face into a bloody mess.

In October 1985, two prisoners were executed by hanging. The victims were members of an elite military unit that had succeeded in fleeing the country. They were well trained and very familiar with the terrain. One of them got as far as Dandong, China, at the mouth of the Yalu River, before he was stopped by Chinese security forces and sent back to North Korea. The Korean authorities had searched for them everywhere, even in the camp. For two weeks, Yodok's prisoners were mobilized in the effort and forced to scour the camp grounds every afternoon. In our heart of hearts, we were grateful to the fugitives for the work-free afternoons. We thought of them as heroes. Their escape had accomplished the unimaginable. All of us were rooting for them and hoping they might tell the world about what was happening at Yodok. But it was not to be.

It wasn't until we were called to Ipsok one morning that we learned they had been caught. Adding to our surprise were the gallows that had been erected in place of the usual execution posts. Our two heroes were brought forward with their heads sheathed in white hoods. The guards led them up to the scaffold and slipped nooses around their necks. The first fugitive was nothing short of skeletal, but the second one, the one who had gotten as far as Dandong, looked like he still had some reserves of energy. Yet he was quicker to die. The other one clung to life, wriggling at the end of his rope like some crazed animal. It was a horrible sight. Urine started trickling down both their pants. I had the strange feeling of being swallowed up in a world where the earth and sky had changed places.

Once both men were finally dead, the two or three thousand prisoners in attendance were instructed to each pick up a stone and hurl it at the corpses while yelling, "Down with the traitors of the people!" We did as we were told, but our disgust was written all over our faces. Most of us closed our eyes, or lowered our heads to avoid seeing the mutilated bodies oozing with black-red blood. Some of the newer prisoners—most of them recently arrived from Japan—were so disgusted they couldn't cast their stones. Other inmates seeing an opportunity to rise in the estimation of camp officials, chose especially large rocks, which they hurled hard at the corpses' heads. The skin on the victims' faces eventually came undone and nothing remained of their clothing but a few bloody shreds. By the time my turn came, stones were heaped at the foot of the gallows. The corpses were kept dangling on the ropes all through the night, guarded by security agents, who made sure no one would try to bury them. To keep warm, the sentinels built a fire, which still smoked in the morning as crows began circling above the lifeless bodies. It was a ghastly scene. Awful.

Whose decision had it been to replace the firing squad with the gallows? The agony of hanging seemed terribly long—and the stoning ceremony was simply bestial. Yet the horror it produced was not unintended. The authorities wanted us to cringe at the very thought of escape—just as they longed to exact revenge against the fugitives who had briefly evaded their grasp. When the manhunt was still on, they had offered a reward to whomever found the fugitives first. They had sent their agents out with orders not to come back empty-handed. Once the fugitives were captured, the guards, who had suffered many threats and great physical weariness because of the escape, were ready to make the condemned men pay.

I attended some fifteen executions during my time in Yodok. With the exception of the man who was caught stealing 650 pounds of corn, they were all for attempted escape. No matter how many executions I saw, I was never able to get used to them, was never calm enough to gather herbs while waiting for the show to begin. I don't blame the prisoners who unaffectedly went about their business. People who are hungry don't have the heart to think about others. Sometimes they can't even care for their own family. Hunger quashes man's will to help his fellow man. I've seen fathers steal food from their own children's lunchboxes. As they scarf down the corn, they have only one overpowering desire: to placate, if even for just one moment, that feeling of insufferable need. . . .

. . . . .

Alone in the heights, I escaped the abuse of guards: the blows, the forced labor, the sweatbox. Beatings didn't appear on the official list of sanctioned punishments, but they were the camp's most common currency. No trifle was too small to serve as a pretext for a beating—of a child or an adult. For example, the South Korean government used balloons to drop leaflets on their northern neighbor. Upon finding such a leaflet, a prisoner was supposed to turn it over to a guard or tear it up right away without reading it. The problem was, despite the paper's weight and roughness, it was much prized for its potential hygienic use. One day, a newly arrived and still unsuspecting prisoner happened upon one such crumpled sheet and rushed to hand it over to a guard. The agent looked very smug at first, but as he began to unfold the sheet, his expression suddenly changed. The paper had already been used. The guard beat the hapless prisoner with such furor that he was unable to move for several days.

I somehow was always able to dodge such thrashings and avoid the camp's most dangerous work details. Not all children were so fortunate. In the spring of 1986, three of my schoolmates were transferred to the gold mine, where their job was setting and detonating dynamite. They had to light the fuse first and run for cover second. They must have been especially tired one day, because they didn't manage to get very far before the blast went off. Two of them were killed. The third, who was partially protected by a turn in the tunnel, had half his face blown off. Poor kids! The guards had no scruples about how they used them. They actually preferred children for the job, because they were smaller and quicker. Gold mine accidents were second only to malnutrition as Yodok's leading cause of mortality. They were responsible for more deaths than even the felling of trees, not to mention the innumerable casualties that resulted from cave-ins and mishandled tools.

Soft-skinned city boy that I was, I was lucky to get out of there alive. Yet the harsh living conditions and never-ending work were precisely what saved me, because they left me no time to dwell on my condition. My every minute was accounted for. There were lessons to follow under threats from brutalizing instructors, trees to chop down, sacks of gold-laden earth to haul, rabbits to watch, fields of corn to harvest. My life was absorbed entirely in my efforts to get by and obey orders. I was, fortunately, able to accept my condition as fated. A clear-eyed view of the hell I had landed in certainly would have thrown me deeper into despair. There is nothing like thought to deepen one's gloom.

Yet I wasn't always able to repel the feeling of misfortune. I had dreams in which I died or witnessed the death of another prisoner, crushed by falling trees, for example, or stoned, like the unlucky hanged fugitives. At night, all the scenes I tried to erase from my memory returned: the cries of pain, the disfigured faces, the crushed limbs. When my eyes closed, the doors that shut out my fears and memories opened wide. Occasionally I saw Pyongyang again, something that caused me strange and useless pain; at times I wondered whether the camp was the dream, or Pyongyang. I was a bit like Zhuangzi (Chuang Tzu), who wakes up asking himself, "Where does reality start? Where does the dream end? Was it I who dreamed of being a butterfly, or the butterfly who dreamed of being me?" My obsession with death was not confined to nightmares, but sometimes appeared in daytime, disturbing my fanatical desire to survive. Death often seemed preferable to the hell all around me; but the thought of the cold wet earth that would swallow me was enough to turn me back toward life.

As the years passed, another feeling began to disturb my daily existence: the feeling of injustice, which grew sharper when I considered the discrepancy between everything I had been taught and all that I was living. My opinions evolved much as had my grandmother's—surprise gave way to a sense of injustice, which in turn transformed into indignation and silent denunciation. We had always been taught to think and speak in accordance with our Great Leader's irrecusable axioms, but the guards' actions continually contradicted them. I had memorized almost entirely *A Letter to New Korea's Much Beloved Children,* which Kim Il-sung wrote for the occasion of the Day of Children, "who are the treasure of our country and its future. . . ."[1] And yet I was being made to pay for my grandfather's crimes. I was no longer the jewel in Kim-Il-sung's eye. I was a prisoner: filthy, tattered, hungry, spent. All those beautiful words had been flouted with perfect impunity.

Why had we been cut off from the world? Why had we been labeled "redeemable" if we weren't to be given the means of reintegrating into the life of the country—especially since every bit of news in North Korea was filtered through state propaganda anyway? All attempts to communicate with the outside were severely punished. One prisoner who had wealthy family members living in Japan managed to get in touch with them by bribing a guard; when camp authorities found out, the guard became a prisoner. Even our own release—which we had been awaiting for years—was only announced to us at the last possible moment.

ETHIOPIA

Breakfast in Hell

Myles F. Harris

MYLES F. HARRIS (1940–) is a British physician who was on a relief mission working with the Red Cross in Ethiopia in 1984 (at Camp Bati) at the height of the famine. He is also author of Tomorrow is Another Country, *a monograph on modern immigration and a contributor to various British publications. He is currently consulting editor of the* Salisbury Review.

During his stay in Ethiopia, Harris was in good position to observe the destructive and repressive policies of the Communist authorities. Emblematic of the character of the regime is the visit of its leader Mengistu to a refugee camp, described in the beginning of this excerpt.

Harris took good measure of the political system, noting that its representatives were "people whose sole aim appeared to be the preservation of the throne at the expense of the people. An aim they pursued without compassion, sentiment or guilt." In pursuing these objectives, the regime was ably assisted by the East German political police ("a secret police force with one of the finest pedigrees in suppression in the world") in learning how to "kill off all those suspected of opposition and even those who could . . . oppose the regime in the future."

Not allowing victims of "the Red Terror" proper burial (as on the occasion when corpses littered the streets of the capital, Addis Ababa) was another measure devised to shock and humiliate the Ethiopian people, for whom burial was an exceptionally important ritual.

These selections (as those which follow from D. W. Giorgis) also highlight the important personal role played by Mengistu in the brutalities his regime perpetrated.

· · · · ·

Reprinted with permission of Simon & Schuster Adult Publishing Group from Breakfast in Hell: A Doctor's Eyewitness Account of the Politics of Hunger in Ethiopia, *by Myles F. Harris, M.D. Copyright © 1987.*

Bati, Wollo Province, Ethiopia 1984

In the autumn of 1984 the Red Cross set up a camp on the edge of the Ethiopian desert at a town called Bati in Wollo province. Bati, 250 miles north of Addis Ababa by road, stands at the entrance to a pass in the foothills of the great Ethiopian plateau, a plateau that rises over ten thousand feet to mountains that hold the remains of the ancient Kingdom of Abyssinia, now the Socialist Republic of Ethiopia. Through Bati came traders, missionaries, and the handful of European explorers who survived the crossing of a fearsome desert, the Danakil, that stood between Bati and the sea, a three-hundred-mile crossing alive with nomadic tribes who prized the testicles of their enemies as a proof of manhood. Few outsiders managed it.

In 1984 Bati was dying, its market empty, its people starving. In a valley outside the town, thirty thousand peasants from the surrounding countryside had gathered to die with it. Beyond them in the desert a sporadic war continued between the nomads and the Provisional Military Government, known as the Dergue.

I had arrived in Bati from the south of Ethiopia in November to work in a makeshift hospital in the camp. My job was to supervise the rescue, from among the thirty thousand refugees crammed in that narrow valley, of those too ill to walk the last hundred yards for help. But today an outbreak of meningitis obliged me to go to the provincial capital to examine some specimens I had taken from two of the victims. Giorgis, an Ethiopian male nurse, stood in for me for the day.

I should have known something was going on as I drove away from my small country hotel near the camp; every few hundred yards along the road small groups of soldiers with light machine pistols lounged in the scrub or squatted on their haunches on the edge of the road. But I assumed it was just another rumor of a guerrilla attack. The week before the rebels had raided Bati and carried off a minor commissar. And this morning at breakfast the nurses had said that they had seen soldiers on the ridges between the hotel and the camp. These troops, I thought, must have been part of the same detachment.

When I got back that evening I heard what had happened from Tula, one of the Finnish Red Cross nurses. She said that Gabre Mariam, the camp administrator, had been jumpy all morning, constantly changing the chalked statistics in the briefing office, glancing at the tattered Ethiopian flag flying in the center of the feeding area, fiddling with a tie nobody had ever seen him wear before. The reason soon became obvious. About eleven in the morning, troops began to appear on the low hills surrounding the valley where we had set our camp with its tent hospitals, feeding stations, water wells, and blanket distribution center. Just after noon a convoy of vehicles, preceded by a half-track, began to sink down the hill toward a river known as *Mot*, or "Death," which marked

the western boundary of the camp; it presaged a visit from a high official. Bringing up its rear were four green Soviet trucks filled with soldiers.

They were crack troops. The nurses said you could see it in the speed with
which they spread over the camp. Within a few moments of arrival they were
everywhere: inside the hospital; crouched in twos or threes at the crossways
among the tent lanes; ranged along the walls of the outpatients. They even set
up a machine-gun post among the mass graves on a hill to the north of the
camp. The Red Cross flag, prohibiting the entry of armed soldiers within the
area of its jurisdiction, hung limp above the gate.

It wasn't the first time this had happened; armed troops had already been
in the camp a week before when they had taken away five thousand starving
people. The European nurses staged a walkout. The Ethiopian nurses might
have gone with them except that they would have incurred ten-year prison
sentences.

Giorgis told me the rest. In the center of the convoy that brought the troops
was a white jeep, which he assumed carried an important visitor. But when it
drew up at the entrance to the feeding center its only passenger was an army
private who sat rigidly in the back seat, a decoy in case the guerrillas attacked.
Then the steady ticking of a helicopter engine began to nag at the edge of the
horizon. Five minutes passed before Giorgis saw it coming, not, as he would
have expected, from the south over the mosque and the empty marketplace
with its steel gallows, but low over the hills from the north, sliding and bucking
in the hot currents of air that licked a dead dry earth even drier. It circled,
fuselage tipped over to squint at thirty thousand pinched faces looking up at it
from the dust, then swung in over the disused soccer field behind the feeding
center. There it hovered, nose slightly in the air, while a small squad of troops
deployed themselves below it. Only when they were in position, guns pointed
at the starving crowd, did it slowly begin to descend in a fury of thick brown
dust which parted occasionally to reveal the word AEROFLOT painted in white
letters on its camouflaged fuselage.

The machine hopped twice then settled, and the pilot switched off his engine. In the silence that followed there was a rasping sound, a door opened, and
a short aluminum ladder slid to the ground. One by one, five well-fed men in
officers' uniforms with red flashes on their lapels, eased themselves down onto
the dry gray earth, looked around, then turned to the door. There was a pause,
then another figure emerged, ran down the steps, and, surrounded by the five
staff officers, all of whom dwarfed him, began hurrying toward a small delegation of officials standing beyond the circle of soldiers.

The Emperor had arrived. Mengistu Haile Mariam, Strength of Mary
Mengistu, Chairman of the Military Council of the Provisional Military Government of Socialist Ethiopia, Secretary General of the Council of Peasants
and Workers of Ethiopia, President of the Armed Forces of the Democratic
Peoples of Ethiopia, Chief of Staff of the Air and Land Forces, General in

Command of the Bureau for Armed Struggle against Imperialist Aggression in Tigre and Eritrea, Head of the Security Advisory Committee.

It was a Napoleonic scene. The tiny Emperor surrounded by his field marshals surveying the site of a truly twentieth-century battlefield, a famine camp. A battlefield with an invisible enemy whose opening shots had been fired half a century ago. Once nature had used war to adjust the delicate balance of land to people, but today, with the population doubling every twenty years on what had already doubled twenty years before, famine had become her general.

The leader was shown inside one of the tents that served as a shelter for the seriously ill, packed so close that those who died in the night had to be left next to the living until morning. The party stood there for a moment among the smells and the flies—Mengistu's generals uneasy under the dull indifferent eyes of fifty dying children. Outside where once there had been trees, grass, grazing camels, oxen driven by small boys down red dusty lanes lined with sorghum and millet, the little Napoleon's ambitions, his insane military adventures, the tribute he was forced to pay to his Slavic colonial masters, and above all the mirage of socialist collective farming, had transformed the landscape into a desert. Food alone would cure these children, although many were even beyond that. But here in Bati, 250 miles from the capital, there was little food, a wrecked hospital, one doctor, twenty nurses, and two packing cases of rudimentary drugs. Mengistu looked at the children, turned to Giorgis, and said, "Why do you not give them all blood transfusions?"

A unit of blood cost one hundred dollars, enough to feed all the children in the tent for a month. The nearest blood bank was in the capital and, besides, produced only enough blood for one person in every thousand in the country. In a radius of two hundred miles from where Mengistu stood there were eight million people starving to death. In any case, blood was not the treatment for malnutrition, although he could at least be forgiven for not knowing that.

Giorgis said to me afterwards, "Such men do not know the peoples." I stared up at his thin face. It was smiling apologetically at having such a fool for a king. I looked away . . . embarrassed to find myself near to tears. . . .

· · · · ·

The following morning Svensen held a meeting. We sat around the long breakfast table, spooning Bulgarian jam onto slabs of dry bread and listened to him. It was not a meeting about the dead child—deaths lay outside his prerogative (besides what was one more among so many?)—but about cooperation.

It was not a brief meeting, but among all the verbiage it was possible to separate several strands, all of them incompatible. Svensen had been told to cooperate with the local administration and to make sure that we did. But for us that meant cooperating with the very people who had brought about the disaster in the first place, people whose sole aim appeared to be the preservation of the throne at the expense of the people. An aim they pursued without compassion, sentiment, or guilt. No state in Africa seemed free of this legacy of the Middle Ages. Yet Geneva still clung to the pious hope that education, investment, and example would improve the attitude of the rulers toward the ruled, even though the history of the whole continent's steady decline provided evidence quite to the contrary. It was not even a matter of a few steps backwards, a few steps forwards, providing a net gain. It was a relentless and purposeful descent into chaos. We were, although we did not know it at the time, on the edge of that chaos. But before we were plunged into it we were being treated to a ringside seat at its causation. Traveling in Ethiopia at the time was like examining a patient with the symptoms of a sinister disease that somehow came in an unfamiliar sequence. It was going to be some weeks before I realized exactly how fatal a prognosis the peasant farmers had. Yet all the clues were there.

The smallest unit in the district was the *kebeli,* loosely based on a village and its surrounding land and functioning as a farmers' association, a type of cooperative. Under it the peasants still had a modicum of land tenure, but gradually it was being eroded in favor of large farms with "mass" labor. Slowly but surely the simplest decisions would edge their way upwards, propelled by a craven fear of misinterpreting the party line. In the end everything, even the number of chickens per household, would be decided by a central planning committee of Communist bourgeoisie in Addis. And this explained the fertile fields and the lack of food. There had been a drought for one year, but a year's drought is within the capacity of the peasant to survive. The paralysis came from another cause. A whole complex peasant economy developed over the centuries had been deliberately destroyed to make way for central planning. Everything was paralyzed. There was nothing to sell, nothing to buy, and nobody dared decide when to plant or when to reap. The only currency now was the grudging permissions issued on school exercise-book paper by the local sub-commissar.

I stumbled on confirmation of this secret tragedy a week or two before I left Sodo. We visited a small village near Habicha. Unused green land lay all about it, yet starving children queued for West German flour and French biscuits. In mime I asked the villagers why they did not plant crops. Three of them looked pointedly at a party poster in crude red and purple fading upon the worm-eaten door of what once was a village church. One of them began to laugh, then somebody said something in Wollaitinia, and the laughter spread. They were still laughing when we left.

The country was in the grip of a dogma that insisted on collectivization as an article of faith. To abandon it would be to surrender, and to surrender meant a reckoning. Not only with ferocious neighbors who, although in a similar or worse plight themselves, were quite willing, even longing, to go to war—but also with the relatives and friends of all those the regime had murdered, imprisoned, and enslaved over the last horrible ten years. Numbers that run into tens of thousands.

Eight years earlier Mengistu had begun to fear for his throne. Demands were being made for popular elections, a bicameral legislature along British lines, and an elected president. Abandoned by or abandoning his American allies he turned for help to a political doctor whose prescription has never varied, the Soviet Union. For the Moscow cure, the patient must become a convert to communism, swallow a Soviet base or two, and accept obligatory military aid. The military aid is never the latest, always expensive, and quite often does not work. But in Ethiopia's case, excited perhaps by the prospect of controlling the entrance to the Red Sea and therefore putting a hand on the West's windpipe, the Suez Canal, they made one exception. They sent him a small unit of the East German Volkspolizei.

Unlike their military aid there was nothing secondhand or useless about the Volkspolizei. What the Russians were giving Mengistu was a secret-police force with one of the finest pedigrees in suppression in the world, with roots going back to the great imperialist Bismarck and reaching forward into the twentieth century to an apogee under Hitler. At the time of the Ethiopian terror in 1964, many senior Volkspolizei officers had in fact been serving members of the Gestapo. For, at the end of World War II, the capitulation of half of the Third Reich to the Russians had meant little more for them than adjusting a detail of uniform, swapping a swastika for a red star, before it was business as usual.

The inheritors of the tradition of Kristallnacht and the Final Solution advised Mengistu to hold a classic set piece terror that would kill off all those suspected of opposition and even those who could, if they wished, oppose the regime in the future.

Equally importantly, they told him to kill a leavening of completely innocent people, so that a yeast of fear would spread through the country. For as Stalin said, "If we only arrested the guilty, what would the innocent fear?"

But it was not just a matter of persecuting the innocent. The Volkspolizei explained to Mengistu that every terror must be tailored to suit its victims, otherwise the memory of it would too quickly pass. Not only individuals, but nations, always held something particularly sacred or dear, and if he wanted to be remembered he must add some special, uniquely Ethiopian, flavor to it.

So Mengistu searched his heart for the most terrible thing he could do to bring his people through fear to the truth of Marxism-Leninism, and he thought of burial. Ethiopians hold burial to be one of the most important rites in life. To lie unburied, to be forgotten in death, is so awful that even today, those who whisper to you their memories of the Terror, can hardly bring themselves to speak of this part of it. Before Mengistu only the cruelest of chances would let a man die alone, and even among strangers the dead were always accorded proper burial. Even in the north during the great hunger, every one who died was carefully laid out, washed, shrouded, and buried, even when those in the

706

burial party could hardly stand for lack of food. So the little army major added his own twist. He ordered that the bodies of the slain should lie unburied like Creon's nephew and his generals on the plain of Thebes, and that anyone who attempted to defy his edict would themselves be slaughtered. One morning the people of Addis woke to streets filled with corpses and a sky dark with vultures. The Red Terror had started.

And he was remembered, and not only by Ethiopians. Five years later, on the other side of the world, I heard an Egyptian doctor who had lived in Addis during the Terror describe a nightmare journey to a United Nations cocktail party in the city. There were hardly any street lights then, and throughout the five miles their Mercedes weaved past the dark shapes of bodies lying in the broken, rutted roads. But worse was to come. As they approached the center they saw that the lamp-posts were strung with corpses, not of men, but of young schoolboys who had tried and failed to rescue their fathers' and brothers' bodies for burial. And so it was a terror both peculiarly German and yet Ethiopian, a whole city turned into a tropical Lidice. Behind the little Negro with an expression of perpetual surprise on his face, stood the ghost of Heinrich Himmler.

When it was over, of the five thousand students at the University and Colleges of Addis Ababa, only fifteen hundred were still alive.

Mengistu did all this in the name of the collective. Now we sat in a hotel in Sodo and tried to reverse one small part of it. An elderly Swedish colonel, a nun, an English nurse, a girl from Denmark, a Finn, and a middle-aged doctor.

Not surprisingly the meeting achieved nothing, except a series of secret resolutions by each of us to go his own way. As one of the officials listened to us talking about the death of the child yesterday I saw his eyes narrow at our distress. To people from poor countries Europeans are surprisingly sentimental. . . .

· · · · ·

The absurd politics had come to mean less and less as the days passed. By the time we arrived in Bati it was far too late to do anything—even if we had had the power—about the ravages of incompetent agricultural policies, brutal Party hacks, the desert war, simple indolence, or even plain greed. Once again the peasants had been abandoned to the judgment of nature. We could only temper its merciless revenge.

Prisoners say their days pass with frightening speed, one indistinguishable from the next, while the weeks and months crawl by. So it was with us. Each day was unchanging, set against a fixed landscape devoid of color. A world of gray dust, black rocks, and dry, fissured watercourses looked down on by bare hills. Life became a relentless competition between exhaustion and depression, its pain avoided by always thinking of the future: getting home to Europe, the first meal in Geneva, a visit to a large shop, winter clothes, a clean lavatory.

Petty illness plagued us and a tired numbness hung to each leg so that the endless walking through the dust ate at the nerves. In the valley the air never moved. Only at night did a slight cooling bring relief.

The day had as always begun and ended in the graveyard with the muezzin's cry: "There is only one God but God, and Muhammad his prophet. . . ." In the morning as the voice, coughing slightly now from weakness and a chest infection, trailed away on the loudspeaker, the gravediggers set out from the camp toward the five low hills to the north. They carried long crowbars, a few shovels, and many picks, for the desert here is iron hard. As they passed across the square in front of the hospital, people fell back in front of them, as from a procession of priests or magicians, set aside, marginals of society. For everyone who watched them knew the hands carrying those picks and bars might well carry their corpses tomorrow, even this evening, easing them onto the circular shelves they dug ten feet below the ground. Only the ferengi knew they would never be touched by these men, even in death.

The diggers were building a new city on the five iron hills above the camp, five hundred circular towers of carefully stacked stone topped with sloping roofs of earth, a city of the dead. Each house in the city was made by digging a circular hole, then cutting a shelf around its wall—on the shelf they would lay the bodies. Usually by ten a.m. three such holes had been made. Then the men rested, often in the waiting graves, eating small chappatis made from wheat flour, smoking vilely smelling cigarettes or chewing chat, a stimulant that wipes out sleep.

After they had rested, their leader would go to a tent at the head of the hill where the clerk, by now half crazy with the same drug, would have prepared a list of the night's dead, carried by relatives up the hill toward a square tent of black plastic. Adults were carried here, the aged, and above all children, borne in the arms of their fathers, heads flung back, small feet swinging. In the black tent they were numbered, their names recorded, each given a shroud made from a flour sack, then laid in rows to wait.

Their people would come to bury them in the afternoon, gathering around the pits to shuffle and weep while the gravediggers laid each body head to toe on the circular shelves. When there was no more room, the pit was filled with stones. By five the small houses, each containing perhaps twenty inmates, would be shut forever. The survivors, usually four, sometimes only one, and sometimes that one a sole surviving child, would make their way back to the camp. From the town the muezzin would cry out again from the tall mosque, among lengthening shadows. Jackals, hyenas, and a strange catlike animal not unlike a sphinx, that remained clearly visible in the day just outside of accurate focus, would stir themselves for the night's work.

Each morning we ate breakfast on the hotel veranda looking across the road to a range of low scrub-covered hills patterned with empty dried-out terraces. A herd of camels about one hundred strong made its way down a defile, their young scurrying about at the rear, fed back into the pack by small boys with long poles like fishing rods. We heard the muezzin's dawn cry as an army truck in Russian camouflage backed up to the guard post of the satellite station and disgorged the morning watch. Deep in the base of the valley an old man walked, half bent, in a flourishing garden at the side of a narrow flowing river, his plants the only living things to be seen aside from camels, humans, and kites. We drank our first glass of the Kursa's fresh orange juice. The food would falter, at times run out, but the orange juice supplied from the garden below us was always available.

At eight we left for the camp, taking the road through Bati.

The town was three kilometers away, clinging to the side of a brown, tree-less hill. It had not changed since our arrival two months ago. Long, struggling terraces of corrugated-iron shapes, a mosque, a potholed, dust-filled street surging with an aimless crowd of peasants, beggars, party officials, camels, don-keys, and soldiers in green fatigues. The terraces led down to a river that cut a deep trench in a stretch of gray sand, its black greasy water slipping slowly from rock pool to rock pool before vanishing around the corner of the hill toward the desert.

When we had first arrived the camp was hardly noticeable. Something that, driving through the town, the casual traveler would have hardly noticed, al-though close up it was unforgettable. The entire floor of the valley had been covered in a mass of gray, ragged shapes which, indistinguishable at a distance from the mud-gray sand, became a sea of skeletons draped in gray sacking, hideous caricatures so bereft of flesh they seemed mere collections of triangles shrouded in cloth. Unwittingly or instinctively, they had formed themselves into groups of about two hundred, separated by narrow paths to carry out the dead, admit more in their place, or allow the stronger to wander scavenging for food, shelter, or scraps of bush to light a fire at night. The lucky ones had built small wigwams of cloth and paper, inside which the sickest member of the family lay or sat, their filthy rags flapping like Tibetan prayer flags. Around the families a steady procession of weakened, staggering women and children headed back and forth from the river, carrying certain death in the jars on their shoulders, for with schistosomiasis the water brought other more sudden plagues such as bacillary dysentery, typhoid, and hepatitis.

Now, two months later, there were lines of white and khaki tents stretching to the low ochre hills a kilometer away. We pulled up in a hollow square of corrugated buildings, its entrance guarded by two men with Red Cross armbands and thin wands of bamboo. A pump chattered to itself inside a tin shed fifty yards away. The square was almost empty save for a few latecomers pulled along by ragged mothers toward a building in the far corner. From it came the roar of five thousand children. Under the supervision of Tula and Inge the first feeding of the day was in progress.

Mikael, the Red Cross supplies officer, a middle-aged man with close cropped hair and a permanent smile, stood in the yard watching stripped eucalyptus poles being unloaded from a ten-ton truck. He had built this strange, corrugated laager against the famine. We talked about the various problems. Two trucks of flour had vanished near Dese, the blankets supplies were now adequate, thanks to a consignment from the London *Daily Mirror*. Two of the cooks were in prison for fighting. The German stoves were hopeless and the cooks were going back to wood-fired cooking.

The refugees were fortunate in Mikael and another Ethiopian called Gabre Mariam, the Red Cross's chief delegate to the district. Neither spared himself. Within weeks, working with a vast army of local carpenters, peasants, electricians, and clerks they had transformed the valley from a deathtrap into a partial haven. The nightmare of the officials faded.

The chief nurse Deresa, a man of about twenty-three in a long doctor's coat with a half belt at its back, joined us. His face was badly scarred by acne and he had a high-pitched, squeaky voice that added an urgency to everything he said. He was our second head nurse. The first one, Hailu, had been arrested by the commissar of Bati, charged with too close an association with foreigners and imprisoned in Kembolcha prison. Deresa, like Hailu, came from the rebel-held province of Tigre which both had been forced to leave because of the fighting.

We usually assembled at about eight in the clinic, a corrugated-iron shed put up by Mikael soon after we arrived. A Kawasaki motorcycle with a bright yellow gas tank leaned on its stand outside. Behind an upturned tea chest, Marcos, a long-faced, serious man in tortoiseshell spectacles, was dispensing medicines to a queue of peasants. He rose to shake hands, his narrow face overcome with shyness. Although a nurse, he had recently begun medical studies at Addis University, but family problems and lack of money had forced him to quit temporarily. He had been taken on by the Red Cross for a few months. Deresa called the nurses together.

Most of them were, like him, refugees from the north. The local health department, not knowing what to do with them, had ordered them to Bati. They were all men and except for one, all under twenty-five. They watched me anxiously, straining at my English while Deresa translated. Six of them were called Ali, one Wolde, and a thin, vacant-looking youth with a silly grin, Kirobel. There was an old man, Desta, long and thin with a set somber face. He came from Mekele and had worked for a German missionary hospital in the town until they were forced out five years ago by a government anxious to demonstrate its revolutionary fervor. Since then he had lived in retirement. Deresa began to read out a list of duties from a ledger, pulling with his free hand at the belt of the white coat he had inherited from Hailu.

Hailu's arrest was still a mystery to me. He had been there to greet me when I first came. A big, chubby-faced man with tightly cropped hair. The first day he had insisted on coming with us to the hotel for lunch but when the moment came he lost his nerve and sat apart at another table. His courage, even if it had failed slightly, set a seal on our friendship. Lunching with the ferengi was for vetted party men, and I suspected he had tried to break a secret rule.

We had worked hard that first month, although we had almost nothing, just a truckful of medicines and a small frame tent from which to dispense them. Each morning we would set out to visit thirty thousand tribesmen. Organizing them in rows, calling up the stretcher bearers to carry away the sick, arguing with the local officials, getting workmen to put up more and more tents. At night Hailu was always there, groping among the rows of dying people in the tent we used as a hospital, holding a tiny kerosene lamp to the pinched faces, searching for the dying, putting up drips, distributing blankets. He taught the untrained assistants how to feed the children, kept the tent sweepers to their jobs, made the mothers bring water and food from the kitchens for the children they had despaired for.

He began to teach me Amharic. His school English improved by leaps and bounds. He was always asking questions about England. What was it like? Did everybody have a car? He warned me about spies. Did I know that the Party had told him to report on me? Everybody, he said, had to present written accounts of conversations they had had with the foreign aid workers to the police. I must be very careful.

But things are never what they seem in Abyssinia and if you are wise such remarks put you instantly on guard. The old emperors maintained a tradition of agents provocateurs that the new regime has continued. Agents in restaurants, taverns, even in the street, approach strangers with seditious remarks—agreement produces handcuffs. I remained silent, and now he worried me slightly, much as I liked him. . . .

· · · · ·

We were standing, making idle conversation outside the kitchen among the smells of wood smoke, faffa, and wheat, when Tula suddenly pointed to the low hills around the camp. On the skyline at every hundred meters stood the silhouette of a soldier holding a machine gun or rifle. They had not been there when we arrived ten minutes before and it seemed that they had risen to a single order from behind concentration points deliberately set just below the hills. We heard the sound of powerful engines and turning toward the road from Bati saw a long convoy of army trucks heading down the narrow road toward the camp. The sanitarian and a thin party official passed us, carrying new, powerful, loudspeakers.

Hailu had appeared, his face tense. He gestured toward the noise of the loudspeakers. "They are telling everybody to assemble in the football field, even the sick."

Slowly, over the next three hours, harangued by party officials and soldiers in their midst, a confused horde of frightened people shuffled toward the assembly point. Those who refused to leave their tents were dragged out by the soldiers; a few who tried to escape were rounded up and taken away by some of the encircling cordon of armed troops.

By eleven o'clock nearly five thousand people stood, sat, or lay in the relentless sun, while the small gray shapes of officials moved between them selecting—on what basis we had no idea—those for resettlement. These were formed into long desperate lines. Requests to let us bring back the seriously ill were met with deliberate incomprehension. Soldiers stood between us and the assembly point. And it was not only the inmates they took, but all our trained cooks, guards, and orderlies. At noon the lines began to move into the back of the trucks. Old men eased up on insect-like limbs, squalling babies, dying children, mothers, fathers.

Three convoys were slowly formed. The first, with about two thousand refugees, began to leave after two, grinding up the hill past a heavy machine gun the soldiers had positioned on the far side of Mot, the "Death River." As they swung it about, the sun winked on the long mustache of bullets on either side of its breech. The trucks turned right along the road toward the highlands. The second, full of Afars, left an hour later. They still had their guns. Woubshet Tulu was not so foolish as to risk a shootout with them. The tribesmen looked unconcerned, even pleased. At the top of the hill the convoy turned left toward the Danakil. They were getting a free lift home.

About five hundred—nearly all men, but some women and a few children—made up the last convoy. Among them were most of our cooks and unskilled workers. But they were not going any farther than Bati; when the convoy reached the center it turned down the hill and vanished among some old school buildings invisible from the camp. Within the hour a rumor seeped across "Death River" that Tulu had set up a new camp in the town. On what criteria he had chosen its inmates—he had separated many families in doing so—there was silence. Hailu thought they might be going to an army labor brigade in the north and were waiting in Bati for the arrival of their officers. But nobody was sure how Tulu was going to feed them, provide them with water, or dispose of their waste. It was too depressing to think about.

We had found Tulu the following morning, red-eyed, taciturn, and uncommunicative, sitting on a large desk in the sanitarian's office. Abruptly he had announced that from now on the number of deaths in the camp was a military secret. He would inform us of the daily totals, but we were not to approach the tucul, count the dead, or go near the graveyard. Information like that was sensitive and could be used by the Ethiopian government's enemies. At the word "enemies" the red eyes paused fractionally on me.

It was not worth arguing. The Red Cross supplied food to the gravediggers and the corpse washers. We would find out. I asked him if he wanted anything for the new camp. That was also a military installation, and we were not to go near it, but he would like one tent. We gave it to him.

Where were we to get new cooks and orderlies? I asked. Tulu paused for a moment and studied his elastic-sided boots. He would send an approved list tomorrow morning. They would not be the ones from the new camp.

A week later a VW minivan pulled up in front of the hospital tents. The driver got out and put his hand on the door. I do not think I can ever listen to the sound of the sliding door of a VW van without remembering. The driver pulled it back and five skeletal figures tumbled onto the sand, three lay still, barely breathing, one of them vomited. Two began to crawl on hands and knees toward the nearest tent. One made a dry gasping sound over and over again. Marcos bent down. "Water, he asks for water." They were some of the fifteen hundred men that had been held in custody in the town by the commissar.

That afternoon Gabre Mariam, the camp's chief Ethiopian Red Cross delegate, and I had gone to see him in his small room hidden among a jumble of stone offices the Italians had left behind. Outside, crowds of tribesmen, waiting for food and grain, sat in orderly rows, watched by armed soldiers. Small clusters of camels, sheltering under what trees were left, sneered at their optimism with down-turned mouths and flared nostrils. Several farted. A soldier read numbers to the crowd in uncertain Amharic.

If Tulu was frightened by what had happened he gave no sign of it. But he never took his eyes off Gabre Mariam. Woubshet Tulu was a drinking man, not well educated, and advised by foolish locals who could have stepped from the pages of Gogol's *Dead Souls*. Everything frightened them: the guerrillas, the Party, the famine, the peasants, the ferengi. Particularly party intellectuals like Gabre Mariam, university graduates with clever words, theoreticians, lily-livered, abstemious. The camp had all the marks of a decision reached deep in the commissar's resentful cups late one night.

In Sodo I would have suspected Gabre Mariam of a power play. Here was the local commissar caught out in a spectacular mess in front of a ferengi, just the circumstances in which a lean, earnest, young party man can demand his head and be rewarded with his job. But Bati was not like that, nor was Gabre Mariam that type of official. No party official wanted Bati. In the last six months it had been attacked twice by guerrillas from the Danakil who had summarily executed a local party snitch and blown the bank to pieces. The wreckage still stood—blackened beams and twisted metal girders.

After a few tense pleasantries the commissar spread two fat hands and said, "Food, we require the Red Cross to give us food."

"Can we see the camp?" He shrugged, rose, and beckoned us out to his broken-down Fiat.

It took ten minutes to weave through the back streets of the town. At the barbed-wire gates a soldier turned a key in a rusty padlock. Tulu said defiantly, "You thought you could prevent the will of the people?"

It reminded me of a Japanese prisoner-of-war camp. Barbed wire, a single hut, and as an afterthought one tent in the center set aside for the sick. At one end was a tall brick wall with a deep ditch gouged by past rains running along its base. There were a lot of people in the ditch trying to shelter from the sun. Two were dead, one rigid in the fetal position. The tent was no better. Old men, children, young women—the indifference of total starvation written on their faces—lay dying from pneumonia, measles, or dysentery. While I stood there an old man with grizzled white hair gave a slight sigh, turned over, and died.

Gabre Mariam was gray with fear and anger as he said, "We must close this place. We will need to send some nurses up to move the patients." There could be no greater contrast between Gabre Mariam and the brutal commissar. One night over coffee he had touched my arm and said, stumbling with embarrassment over the words, "I know you laugh at these things, but Lenin said, give us the organization and we will do the job." Now he was seeing a dreadful reality.

The commissar lit a roll-up and nodded his head. The sudden agreement did not surprise me. With the foreign press visiting Bati so frequently now, he stood a daily risk of his camp being discovered. If that happened the Party would show him no mercy.

But afterwards Gabre Mariam shook his head. "You know, Tulu is not a good man, and he does not want these people now because he says they are no longer fit to work—imagine this man!"

We never were able to discover how many of the inmates died, because Tulu had their bodies brought in the evenings to the mass graves and secretly buried among our own dead. It explained his orders to keep the death rate a secret from us. That had been eight weeks ago. Since then he acted only once more, to arrest Hailu. After that he spent more and more of his days immersed in the yellowing files in his small office and the nights drinking himself to extinction. But on my last day he never turned up. It was not unusual. His drinking made it difficult for him to come ever since he had once seen me looking at the slow tremor of his hands and his yellow-tinged and terrified eyes. He had cirrhosis, and I suspected the expression on my face reminded him that it was deadly. Two days after I left he was found dead in the bare room he occupied in what was once the Italian governor's residence during the Fascist occupation. He lies now on the hill with the thousands he sent on before him. Maybe God will show him mercy. . . .

Red Tears

D. W. Giorgis

D. W. GIORGIS *(dates not available) was not a political prisoner in a Communist state but a highly placed official in the Communist government of Ethiopia. His position provided an excellent vantage point for witnessing the repressive practices of that system. He worked for the regime for twelve years and was highly familiar with its leaders, policies, and their results. His gradual disillusionment motivated him to seek exile and to write an account of the policies he came to deplore. His account is of particular interest since little is known in the West about the repressive character of Communist Ethiopia and its disastrous agricultural policies, which greatly contributed to the country's infamous famine. His book also sheds light on the contribution made by the personal qualities of Mengistu (head of the state and supreme leader) to the generous use of political violence.*

Giorgis was "an active participant" in the 1974 Ethiopian Revolution, a senior member of the ruling party, deputy foreign minister, and head of the famine relief operation between 1983 and 1985. In all these capacities he worked closely with and came to know well Mengistu Haile Mariam.

Giorgis's book pays special attention to the connections between the collectivization of agriculture, forcible population movements, and famine—policies similar in both ideological inspiration and outcome to those in the Soviet Union in the early 1930s. In addition to being a model, the Soviet Union gave generous military and economic support to Ethiopia; military assistance was also provided by Cuba.

The account provided by Giorgis strongly suggests that the highly repressive character of the regime derived from ideologically inspired certainties and radical intolerance, from the "arrogance and self-righteousness of the leadership never allow[ing] the possibility of admitting error," as well as from the power-hunger of its leader. 2.5 million Ethiopians fled Communist Ethiopia. The Communist regime was overthrown in the wake of the Soviet Union's disintegration.

. . . .

From D. W. Giorgis, Red Tears: War, Famine and Revolution in Ethiopia *(Trenton, NJ: Red Sea Press, 1989). Reprinted by permission.*

Preface

The Ethiopian famine of 1984–85 moved the conscience of the world as has nothing else in recent memory. This book is the story of the victims of that famine—the story the world never heard, or perhaps only occasionally glimpsed through uncertain or misleading reports in the Western press. It is the story of a regime that, instead of saving its people, ignored their cries for help, and through its unfeeling, lethal programs caused suffering and death to a degree no one ever imagined possible. It is also the story of the efforts of dedicated Ethiopian and international humanitarian agencies to rescue the people abandoned by the regime.

I was more than a spectator to these events. As an active participant in the 1974 Ethiopian Revolution and a senior member of the Marxist-Leninist Party, I worked closely with Mengistu Haile Mariam, the Head of State of Ethiopia. I was his Deputy Foreign Minister; I was his chief political representative to the troubled province of Eritrea; and finally, I headed the entire famine relief operation between 1983 and the end of 1985. Many people have asked: "Isn't it a tragedy that you are now in exile, and are now condemning the government and political system you were part of for twelve years?"

Neither my involvement nor my departure is a tragedy. Like others, I had a vision of a better Ethiopia, and I did my best to make that vision a reality. Never to have had a vision of a better life for my people, or to have had a vision and ignored it are, to my mind, terrible tragedies indeed; but the failure to achieve an objective is not failure in the greater sense. The question is not, therefore, why I or other officials stayed with the government so long, but why we had to leave it. I could have left Ethiopia earlier; but when there was still a possibility of influencing policies and decisions, I felt it would be wrong to abandon my people in their time of distress. My tragedy is that I can no longer help my people from within. And that is the tragedy of many Ethiopians.

I was at first an enthusiastic participant in the 1974 Revolution. I was caught up in its emotions, excited by its potential for improving life in our country. Like many others, I supported its spirit and initial objectives despite the many mistakes that were made. There must inevitably be mistakes: the mark of a good government is the ability to admit them and learn from them. You can trust a politician who honestly says, "I was wrong, now let us go on from here." That never happened in Ethiopia.

The men of the Coordinating Committee of the Armed Forces gathered for the first time in June 1974 in Addis Ababa with a sincere desire to bring genuine, desperately-needed change to Ethiopia. They were for the most part honest men who were doing what they thought was best for the country. I feel proud and honored today to have been a part of that beginning. I was one of a group of Ethiopians who had a vision of creating a peaceful, united, prosperous nation. In pursuing that vision we worked for justice, equality, freedom, and independence, and we and the majority of the people believed in what we were doing. I have made concessions and given the leadership and particularly Mengistu the flattery they demanded, but I have also challenged the regime in the only ways possible. As our actions in Eritrea and during the great famine clearly demonstrated, my colleagues and I took measures and made decisions that the regime disliked, in a style that sharply contrasted with its cruelty.

Many of us around Mengistu were willing to go to great lengths for the nation, to sacrifice our energies, personal ambitions, and our lives for the good of the people. We worked under difficult circumstances. The traditions of hundreds of years of feudalism could not be erased in one stroke. The regime's interpretation and implementation of Marxism in the context of Ethiopian realities hindered democratic evolution and belittled democracy as something bourgeois and fake. It legitimized absolutism and enabled Mengistu to emerge as a traditional autocrat without even the constraints of our traditional institutions.

The stirring beginning, the blind idealism, the power struggles, the ignorance and manipulations, the executions, and the final sinking into a tyranny far worse than that with which we began—all these events and developments need to be recorded and critically analyzed for posterity. With its errors and advances, this period is a crucial one which has had, and is having, a greater impact on the well-being and unity of the Ethiopian people and the survival of the nation than any other single period in our history.

After emotions subsided, many of us saw the impracticality of our ideals. Tempered by the realities, we were willing to correct our mistakes. But the arrogance and self-righteousness of the leadership never allowed the possibility of admitting error. Like the characters in George Orwell's *Animal Farm,* the leaders of the Revolution have evolved into the New Masters; learning to walk upright, they have enslaved those they pledged to liberate. The Revolution brought the promise of a better life both for the individual and for society as a whole; but that promise has been betrayed in the most inhuman way imaginable.

In writing this book, I first set out with the limited goal of recounting only the events connected with the great famine; but I soon realized that the story would not be complete without an understanding of the large framework of the Revolution and the continuing internal unrest. I have therefore included histories of the Revolution and the internal conflicts. Since I was often close to or at the center of events, I will relate these matters through a description of my own involvement and experience.

Ethiopia needs an honest history, and I hope my efforts here will inspire others who have witnessed the tragedy to record what they have seen for the benefit of posterity. There are only a few of us who were on the inside left alive to tell the true story. I hope that knowing the truth will make all Ethiopians question themselves and their beliefs, and that we will grow wiser by examining our past. The current rulers entrenched themselves more deeply behind their errors; we must build a better future on the ruins of our mistakes.

This, then, is the story of the Ethiopian holocaust—why it happened, the efforts made to stop it, and what it has left behind.

. . . . .

Red Tears

Mengistu, in fact, began to manipulate events from the day the Emperor was overthrown. He gradually started solidifying and broadening his power base inside and outside of the Council, especially among members from the Third Division, which he represented. He relied on the private soldiers, making empty promises to individuals in return for support against the officers. Mengistu began to undermine Amman's authority. Working behind his back, he made many crucial decisions on his own and attempted to carry them out. At the same time he subtly induced the Council to challenge Amman, especially over the Eritrean question. Amman wanted a peaceful settlement with the rebels, while Mengistu wanted to crush them militarily.

General Amman's popularity was well deserved. He was basically an intelligent, honest man, who in the absence of Mengistu's intrigue might have remained in power for a long time. Amman resented Mengistu's manipulation and refused to be a mere puppet of the Council. He was ambitious and wanted real authority as Head of State; but he found his position weakened by the constant scrutiny of the Council and Mengistu, who was acting more like the Head of State. The fact that Amman was an Eritrean was used against him; his honest views on the civil war were twisted by Mengistu into a virtual accusation of treason. In mid-November Amman resigned and went to his home, refusing to appear when summoned before the Council unless it first recognized his authority as Chairman.

Mengistu went to Amman's home on the morning of November 23, to give the impression that he was trying to talk to him out of his position. Later that day Mengistu personally decided to have Amman arrested along with the twenty-two young officers who had shown opposition to Mengistu's bid for power. At Mengistu's order, an army unit was dispatched that evening to arrest Amman at his home. In the ensuing shoot out, a number of officers supporting Amman were killed. Amman committed suicide in full uniform, covered with all his decorations, just as armored personnel carriers and hundreds of troops smashed their way in. I learned of this the next morning from Major Daniel Asfaw who had led the unit sent to Amman's home. I knew Daniel well and had shared an army barracks room with him. He and some Council members who later became my close associates filled me in on what happened later at the Council meeting.

Mengistu, nervous at his own audacity, but more determined than ever with all this blood on his hands, convened the Council that night to explain his actions. Perhaps deciding that aggressiveness was the best defense, he boldly recommended that since there were demands from intellectuals for the execution of former officials under arrest in the basement of the Palace of Menelik, the Council might as well decide on their fate and announce it all to the public the next day along with the execution of Amman.

The Legal Committee, which was in the process of establishing procedures by which these people could be brought to justice, was caught unprepared by this sudden, wild proposal. Mengistu changed the entire atmosphere of the meeting with a call for revenge, crying that the Ethiopian people wanted it and expected it, and that if the Council failed to make this decision, the Revolution would never be able to bring about reform.

Council members were too inexperienced and unsure of themselves to oppose his will. Those who honestly opposed the call for blood found it difficult to speak out. They feared they might be lumped in with the prisoners and killed along with them.

The names of the prisoners were called, one by one, and members were asked to comment. No real evidence was presented. Most members of the Council didn't know the accused; they were just names. They had no idea whether the accused had committed the crimes ascribed to them. Proof consisted of the Council members saying anything that popped into their heads, including rumors. Then those in favor of execution were asked to raise their hands. Over one hundred names were read. Fifty-nine people, including members of the royal family, former cabinet members, and senior officials, were sentenced to death this way.

The Legal Committee, chaired by Captain Mikael Gebrenegus (a police captain and lawyer), was horrified at this turn of events. The members invited Mengistu to their office after the vote and asked why they couldn't continue with legal procedures against the prisoners. Mengistu replied that it was necessary to execute a few immediately, to demonstrate that the Military Council was serious. Seeing that they were unhappy with his decision, he asked if they could at least immediately convict those responsible for covering up the recent famine. Their reply was that it couldn't be done in a week or even two, that it would take time. Mengistu grew angry at their opposition and insisted that the decision of the Council be carried out. He left the room furious at the Legal Committee's efforts to thwart what he felt was a landmark event in the Revolution.

That same evening the condemned men were dragged from the Palace basement and loaded onto military trucks. Lt. Colonel Daniel Asfaw and Major Getachew Shibesi (now a brigadier general in charge of Mengistu's personal security) were in charge, at Mengistu's order. What particularly angered many of us later was the cruel way the prisoners were executed. When the trucks reached the Central Prison, the soldiers were so nervous that all sense of order vanished. As the first resisting prisoners were pushed down from the truck, the soldiers opened fire with machine guns. Many of the victims were still alive after the first volley. More and more prisoners were pushed out, and as bodies piled up on the ground and the wounded screamed, they were sprayed with bullets again and again until all were dead. They were buried in a mass grave on the prison grounds.

Most educated people and revolutionaries believed that these prisoners had committed serious crimes and wanted them tried and punished, but were shocked at the announcement of their sudden execution. As a young lawyer, I was being considered for the post of one of the judges at their trial. I was terribly depressed by this event. I felt we had missed an opportunity to establish the rule of justice at the outset.

The death of Amman was an unfortunate chance event that had extremely important consequences in shaping the character of the Ethiopian Revolution. The Military Council did not intend to kill Amman or force him to suicide. On several previous occasions, the Council had arrested almost at will every important imperial official; they simply announced the names of the officials, who rushed to report to the military barracks. But this plan failed when Amman resisted and died fighting, and the Military Council was panic stricken. Their panic and terror allowed the massacre of 1974, which consecrated them to power at the expense of the Ethiopian concept of "officiality," which was desecrated. "Officiality" in Ethiopia has a sacred value, but concomitantly the office bearers are expected to adjudicate fairly as representatives of divine justice. This was why members of the royal family and other officials had not resisted their arrest. The death of Amman and the execution of the unpopular dignitaries, and their denunciation as enemies of the Revolution, clearly demonstrated the confused state of mind of the leaders of the Military Council; this kangaroo justice portrayed them as a vicious collection of murderers. As a result, discussion of political issues and criticism of the government became impossible. People swallowed their bitterness and the country sank into a new era of fear and terror. Some fled the country and others took up arms. This explains why we have several liberation movements. It also explains why some people stay with the government despite their abhorrence of it. In short, you are in the government or in jail, if you are lucky.

The Revolution had begun with a famous slogan and song: "Without blood, without blood. . . ." It was what nearly everyone sincerely wanted—a bloodless revolution. This massacre ended any hope for a peaceful revolution. On November 24 Mengistu had more officers suspected of counterrevolutionary activities executed.

Mengistu expected a spontaneous mass rally after the announcement of the executions, but they shocked the entire population. It was the understanding of this deep shock and resentment of the people that forced the Council members to be more cautious. Around the city many started wearing civilian clothes instead of uniforms. They changed to unmarked cars, they used body-guards and always carried their guns. They realized some segments of the population were so angered by what had been done that they might try to retaliate against the Council. It is important to note, however, that because of the secrecy in which the Military Council worked, few among the general population knew that Mengistu was responsible for the executions.

. . . . .

The Red Terror

Mengistu now moved against the civilian groups. He had studied the factions of the radical intellectuals and proceeded to play them off against each other. By this time the EPRP and MEISON were regularly gunning down each other's leaders on the streets of Addis. Shortly after his coup, Mengistu decided to deal with the terrorism of the EPRP once and for all by distributing arms to the Urban Dwellers' Associations, the *Kebeles*.[1] In a speech on February 5, immediately after the execution of General Teferi Benti and six other PMAC members, Mengistu stated:

> As a result of the determined and decisive step taken yesterday
> . . . against the internal collaborators and supporters of the ELF
> [Eritrean rebels], EPRP, and EDU, our Revolution has advanced
> from the defensive to the offensive. Henceforth we will tackle
> our enemies that come face to face with us and we will not be
> stabbed from behind by internal foes. . . . To this end, we will
> arm the allies and comrades of the broad masses without giving
> respite to reactionaries, and avenge the blood of our comrades
> double- and triple-fold.

"We shall beat back White Terror with Red Terror!" was Mengistu's cry. Three months later at a May Day rally he shouted, "Death to counterrevolutionaries! Death to the EPRP!" He suddenly produced two bottles of blood (actually colored water) and smashed them to the ground to show what the Revolution would do to its enemies.

Mengistu's call to take up arms against all reactionaries was nothing more than an invitation to anarchy. He publicly gave all "progressives" what he called the "freedom of action" against enemies of the Revolution as defined by him and his political mentors of MEISON, who were out to settle scores with the EPRP. All this was rationalized by quoting that ultimate authority, the Russian Revolution, where similar measures had been taken to consolidate the leadership of Lenin and the Bolsheviks in 1918.

Mengistu assumed that by arming the Urban Dwellers' Associations he was arming men and women loyal to him. He was mistaken. Many of these civilians supported the EPRP and now had the weapons to attack MEISON or anyone else they wanted. The Red Terror began. It was gang warfare with arbitrary executions, lynchings, and street massacres. No one was spared: men or women, young or old were gunned down in broad daylight or dragged out of their homes at night and killed. Bands of men attacked anyone they suspected of holding opinions other than their own. Many high school students were among the dead. Bullet-ridden bodies were left in the streets, or publicly exhibited to try to intimidate rival factions. It is said that Mengistu originally had a list of more than a thousand people to be eliminated in the Terror. Many others close to Mengistu seemed to have lists of their own. The Red Terror claimed thousands of victims across the country.

Through it all, Mengistu denied responsibility. He stoutly maintained that it was the factions killing each other off. Thus the Red Terror was a perfect instrument for discrediting his political rivals, eliminating their threat to his power, and at the same time portraying himself and the Council as the only alternative for the leadership of the Revolution.

By the middle of 1977, most of the leaders of the EPRP and other factions were dead. Thousands of Ethiopians were jailed, thousands more had been executed, and still more forced to flee for their lives. Most of them were highly educated political moderates—skilled, sincere citizens, the kind of people Ethiopia needed to build its new society. Mengistu was now in complete control with MEISON as his ally.

During the Terror MEISON, which had extended its cells throughout the nation, began secretly conspiring against Mengistu and the Military Council so that it might assume power in its own right. It became clear that Haile Fida had great personal ambition. In September 1977, during the Somali invasion, the leaders of MEISON concluded that whatever the outcome of the war their position would be weakened. They anticipated defeat at the hands of Somalia and did not want to be associated with it. On the other hand, if Mengistu were victorious, he would be more popular than ever, leaving them a reduced role. This led them to declare their open opposition to the Council. Mengistu denounced this as a betrayal of Ethiopia and launched a campaign against MEISON. Haile Fida went into hiding but was found and imprisoned. A few members changed hats immediately and stayed with the Council as mentors. One of the leaders, Alemu Abebe, has now even managed to become a Politburo member. All the other leading members either fled or were executed.

One final challenger to Mengistu's leadership remained: his friend, the Deputy Chairman Colonel Atnafu Abate. Atnafu's conservatism and naïveté betrayed his rural roots. He never seemed quite equal to the cunning of the city-bred hardliners. A nationalist who believed that tradition, culture, and religion should play a key role in uniting the people, Atnafu considered Marxism alien to Ethiopian values. He believed the Military Council should strive for unity, not encourage the divisions and bloodshed which the extremists insisted was necessary. He made no attempt to hide his views. His ideas and the blunt way he expressed them were clearly contradictory to the mood and the thinking of the time.

He made one final attempt to halt what he perceived as a terrible mistake. At a meeting of the Council he made a speech that began: "Dear friends, I want to say what is on my mind and relieve myself of a troubled conscience." He proceeded to calmly reject the ongoing internal conflicts and the mass killings. He suggested that Ethiopia should have a non-aligned foreign policy and balanced relations between East and West. He expressed his dismay at attempts to make Ethiopia a Communist country and the growing tendency to criticize religion as a factor retarding development. He called for reconciliation between all classes of society and stated that it was the Council's responsibility to introduce policies of reform, not policies of conflict.

This was a direct challenge to Mengistu. It was a bold move, but also very naïve. Atnafu knew full well what Mengistu was capable of. The examples of Amman, Teferi, and the others who had challenged Mengistu's authority were still fresh in his mind, but he must have thought his own power base within the Council would be enough to protect him.

Mengistu responded aggressively, condemning Atnafu's suggestions as reactionary and incompatible with the objectives of the Revolution. He was supported by others on the Council. Mengistu talked to Atnafu twice during the next few days, asking him to go before the Council to renounce his statement—knowing full well that Atnafu would never agree to this humiliation. Atnafu ought to have been prepared for what followed, but he seemed to think Mengistu wouldn't dare to move against him. The third time Mengistu asked to see Atnafu in his office in the Palace of Menelik was November 13, 1977. Before Atnafu could even take his seat, he was dragged off by one of Mengistu's executioners and shot in the basement, in the same place where Teferi Banti and his six supporters had been massacred. All of Atnafu's bodyguards, drivers, assistants, and any soldiers or officers closely associated with him, were rounded up and killed in the following days.

Mengistu's leadership in the Council has never been challenged since. A footnote to this story is that the man who executed Atnafu, and many others, was promoted from major to colonel, and lived within the Palace compound for years as a trusted associate of Mengistu. Recently he has been purged. He must realize that he knows too much. He walks the streets waiting for the inevitable moment when he will be dragged off to his death. . . .

· · · · ·

Propaganda

As in all strict Marxist states, power is maintained by controlling access to information. *Serto Ader* is the official Party paper, but the English-language *Ethiopian Herald* and the Amharic *Addis Zemen* are also under the complete control of the Ideological Department of the Party. Every piece of writing goes through rigorous censorship. Under the new state structure, the Ministry of Information will vanish and there will be one Committee of Propaganda and Information within the Party's Ideological Committee, controlling all mass media.

The few at the top try to protect their power by mystifying the public with propaganda. The result is cynicism. When information is controlled by the state, no one believes anything anymore. People suspect that everything they hear is propaganda; even if it is true, they don't believe it. Because people have no reliable information, rumors sweep across the country, fostering general disillusionment. The public tends to become detached. The constant repetition of slogans, denunciations, exhortations, condemnations, harangues, warnings, and glorifications of the ruler, dehumanizes people by robbing them of a chance for independent thought and judgment.

· · · · ·

Terror

The entire country is in the grip of terror. Mengistu's loyal followers are his executioners, led by the "Gang of Four." Chief among them is Legesse Asfaw, who will play a major role in this account. Legesse is the most dangerous man the revolution has brought to power. He is Mengistu's trusted servant, the head of the Organization Department of the Party, who has personally or through his private secret police killed and jailed hundreds of innocent men and women. He barely completed his elementary schooling before becoming a sergeant in the army, but now his ego is beyond belief. He is arrogant, crude, and cruel, and will stop at nothing to get what he wants. He and Mengistu must take most of the blame for the mass murders and misdirection of the Revolution, for the flight of millions to safety in other countries, and for virtually every wrong the country has suffered in the last thirteen years. Legesse is the reincarnation of a 15th-century warlord who has been given the 20th-century power to commit murder and wreak havoc on an unprecedented scale. The prospect of Ethiopia's future with him in a position of control is truly blood chilling.

There is also Alemu Abebe, presently a member of the Political Bureau; a veterinarian by profession, educated in the USSR; and an intellectual opportunist, prepared to receive lectures from Mengistu on any subject, including veterinary medicine. He was Mengistu's chief political mentor during the Red

Terror and still feels proud of what he did then as Mayor of Addis Ababa. He personally ordered the execution of hundreds with Mengistu's explicit or tacit approval.

Shewandagan Belete, the former head of the leftist faction LEAGUE, a shabby and repulsive character, is now a member of the Politburo. He lives in constant fear of Mengistu because his life was spared when all the other LEAGUE members were executed. He will do anything Mengistu tells him to.

Finally there is Shimelis Mazengia, a member of the Politburo and head of the Ideological Department. He is a young man with no previous experience in public affairs or extensive formal education. A former elementary school teacher, he lacks any understanding of the complexities of politics. His knowledge of Marxism is very superficial, yet his answer to every problem is to quote Marx or Lenin. Over the years Shimelis has become Mengistu's chief speech writer. He is very eloquent, using the Amharic language beautifully, but what he says has no real substance. He is especially good at coining new words and filling speeches with Marxist jargon. He is very cold and shrewd. It is difficult to get to know him; he does not talk much, and when he does he exposes his ignorance and lack of experience.

The men who actually do most of the killing are Mengistu's personal bodyguards and his death squads who live in the Palace of Menelik; they have turned the Palace grounds into a mass grave. Mengistu expects their absolute loyalty and secrecy. If they relax in their roles and start talking, he has them killed. Many of the members from the early death squads are long dead. Mengistu could not risk putting them in jail for fear that they would talk.

These men and others like them on the Politburo and in different parts of the country are Mengistu's personal power base. These people will go to any lengths to keep Mengistu in power because they have everything to lose from a change of government.

As in Hitler's Germany, Mengistu's words have the force of law. Nothing has to be in writing. Sometimes his statements and wishes are followed by laws, regulations, and elaborate justifications to give an outward appearance of legality; but that is not a necessary provision. Massacres and gross violations of fundamental human rights have often been committed on simple oral instructions from Mengistu.

The secret police and death squads create an atmosphere in which murder and abduction are likely to occur at any moment. The laws that do exist, like the 1987 constitution, make the category of political crimes a broad one. There are arbitrary measures against all deviants, and arbitrary definitions of deviancy. Opponents of the regime are isolated, jailed, and eliminated. Resistance is paralyzed. . . .

. . . . .

The Tenth Anniversary Celebration

Four days of ceremony, banquets, elections, celebrations, and parades. Four days of pageantry in the midst of horror. Everyone was forced to celebrate, but on the face of every spectator was disgust. The people detested this show, this piece of theater that mocked their suffering. There was a sense of fear. The air was charged with tension and security forces were on full alert to guard against a protest, a demonstration, an attack on one of the installations, perhaps even an attempt to topple the government.

People asked themselves, was all this pomp really necessary? It was more than evident that starvation was rampant within the city. Bread lines had been getting longer every day in September until, miraculously, the arrival of foreign dignitaries brought simultaneous plenty into the capital: the lines disappeared and the shelves were full. No one was deceived, however. Everyone knew the senseless celebration was costly.

In Congress Hall, Mengistu was elected Party Secretary in a travesty of democracy. In effect, he elected himself.

At the first meeting of Congress on September 5, we were to elect the Central Committee from among the members of Congress. There were one thousand of us in the Congress, most of us unknown to one another. How were we supposed to elect a Central Committee? Mengistu went to the podium and announced that he had a list of 120 people to propose for the Central Committee. He read the list. My name was on it. A pre-designated member of Congress then made his way to the podium and read something to this effect: "Members of the Congress, there is no person in the country that knows us better than the Head of State, Mengistu Haile Mariam. He has a brilliant capacity to know people. He knows our contributions and weaknesses, our needs and our abilities. I therefore propose that we accept his nominees."

Another member then made a similar statement to second the motion. Mengistu picked up the two written statements and said that he assumed these were the opinions of everybody else. Tumultuous applause. He banged his gavel and announced that the 120 people had been elected unanimously to form the Central Committee.

The newly elected Central Committee was then supposed to choose the smaller Politburo from among its members. We all adjourned into another hall and there went through the same charade again. Mengistu read a list of seventeen proposed names. Someone among us in a pre-assigned role again made a statement that Mengistu had chosen exactly the right people, that nobody could know us better, etc., and he was seconded by another member. Applause, gavel ... and Mengistu introduced the members as unanimously elected.

Then, while we waited in the Central Committee Hall, the Politburo members went into an adjoining room to elect the General Secretary of the Party. The suspense was minimal. They came back in fifteen minutes having unanimously elected Mengistu General Secretary of the Workers' Party of Ethiopia, Commander in Chief of the Armed Forces, Chairman of the Council of Ministers, and of the Provisional Military Administrative Council. We applauded enthusiastically when the decision was announced to us.

In other totalitarian Third World countries the leaders assume an air of modesty and announce that 99 percent are in agreement. But Mengistu's Ethiopia had achieved perfection—every decision was 100 percent. After my defection, in one of my letters to Mengistu I mentioned how ridiculous this unanimity appeared to the outside world, and he seems to have taken it to heart.

Mengistu appeared before the full Congress and was introduced to the members as the General Secretary. Then we all had to sit and listen while a member of the Politburo, Amanuel Amdemichael, the elderly Chief Justice of Ethiopia, an Eritrean and former governor of that province under General Amman in 1974, read a biography of Mengistu that made his life sound like the second coming of Christ. He was "the saviour of Ethiopia, brilliant, generous." Childhood stories were told of this prodigy, this gift to the Ethiopian people. It was disgusting. Amanuel Amdemichael lost the respect of everyone for so willingly playing a part in this travesty. Mengistu sat there listening, the picture of humility, as though he had never heard a word of it before. In fact it had been written under his direction and he had corrected the final version himself. Afterward, as he stood and addressed the assembly, an embarrassed smile hovered around his mouth as he mumbled modestly: "I don't deserve this praise. . . ." It was low comedy in the worst possible taste.

That same day Mengistu addressed the Congress and the nation in a five and a half hour televised speech. He talked about the Revolution, the achievements, the difficulties. It was a boring, repetitive, boastful pontification. But I had to admire the energy of the man—to be able to speak that long with genuine enthusiasm, with a sincere belief that what he was saying was true.

It was a battle to keep our eyes open, but it was even worse for the visiting heads of state who were seated right up front where everyone could see them. Samora Machel of Mozambique, Kenneth Kaunda of Zambia, Robert Mugabe of Zimbabwe, Ali Nasser of South Yemen, Daniel Arap Moi of Kenya, DeSantos of Angola—all representing countries that had their own serious problems at home—all had to sit there and listen to the head of one of the least developed and most troubled countries on the continent brag about what he had done for five and a half hours. More than one head of state was nodding before it was over.

The most striking aspect of the speech was that there was no mention of the famine ravaging Ethiopia. At one point, for a minute and a half Mengistu talked about the recurrence of drought in general on the continent, which he called a "constraint to the successful implementation of agricultural policies." He did not mention the famine or ask for any sort of food aid. I was shocked, because a few days before I had spoken with Shimelis Mazengia, who drafted all of Mengistu's speeches, and we had agreed that Mengistu would acknowledge the existence of the famine and use the opportunity to extend an appeal to the international community. Obviously, that section had been deleted....

. . . . .

The Failure of Collective Farms

The biggest reason for national underproduction has been the imposition of collective farming. Collectivization is the linchpin of Ethiopia's socialist agricultural policy. The theory is that the sooner individual plots are done away with, the better for the economy. In 1987 there were 5.6 million hectares (94 percent of total farmland) under cultivation by individual families; only 2 percent was collectivized. According to Mengistu's ten-year plan, by 1994 an incredible 52.1 percent of all farmland will be collectivized—with a simultaneous increase in production by collectives from 2 percent to 49.6 percent of the national total. This is a ridiculous proposition. Collectivization requires a complete change of attitudes and values. It requires massive government investment and planning at the highest level. Above all it requires that peasants be convinced that their lives will be better without the church or mosque, without traditional community life, without owning land or tools—without, in essence, being the persons they are. The government believed it could accomplish all this with the snap of a finger.

In the early 1980s there was a sudden rush to collectivize. Competition was fierce among regional administrators and Party representatives to win the honor of creating the largest number for any region. At the height of this push I was in Eritrea, where rebel activity and the antagonism of the people made a collectivization program impossible, at least in my judgment. During Central Committee meetings we heard reports from regional COPWE representatives of the peasants' remarkable desire to organize into producers' cooperatives, and to set up the corresponding service cooperatives that would provide them with tools and consumer goods. They would tell how eager the peasants were to join, how smoothly and rapidly the transition was being made, how the peasants felt they couldn't work hard enough to make Ethiopia prosper. It was what Mengistu wanted to hear. It made him swell with pride at the new Ethiopia he was creating. But during our tea breaks I heard the same people whispering appalling stories of the instructions they received from Mengistu and Legesse; of how they were ordered to use any means necessary to force the peasants to join the collective farms; of the repression used to make collectivization successful in the eyes of the regime; of the execution of peasant leaders bold enough to speak out against it; of how dissidents were rounded up and sent to border areas as peasant militias. Many people fled to the Sudan as refugees or joined armed opposition movements during these months.

Collectivization has been a terrible disaster in Ethiopia. Demoralization has been the biggest harvest. None of the "collectivized" peasants showed enthusiasm for their land or their work. They felt they had been snatched from their homes and herded into slave camps. Those who were allowed to remain on their individual farms also stopped working: the fear of being forced off their property at any moment made their work seem futile.

Despite the energies devoted to propaganda, indoctrination, and encouragement, collectivization has created almost universal resentment among the peasants. Both in the South and the North there is bitter opposition to it. Rebellions were suppressed brutally in 1981 in several places, notably Gojjam and Arsi, and hundreds were executed without trial.

Even though the number of collectivized farms is small, their effect on nationwide production has been catastrophic. These farms are given more fertilizer per hectare than peasant farms; they are given more land per household, they are given tractors and more draft animals than the rest of the peasants. But for all the attention they get, productivity is extremely low and almost no surplus is produced for market.

Collectivization is destroying the nation. National unity is an extension of family unity, and collectivization destroys family and community traditions; it rips families out of their communities and forcibly transplants individuals to alien soil. People lose the sense of who they are. They feel exiled in their own country. Collectivization does not unite, it alienates. Nothing is the same on the collectives, there are not even any churches or mosques. New structures, new obligations, and new attitudes are hurriedly substituted for older values, but as the old ways are outlawed, the new ways find no roots—the peasants are left floundering with no sense of identity at all.

· · · · ·

The Failure of the State Farms

By the time of the Revolution several large, very productive commercial farms had sprung up in many parts of Ethiopia, particularly in the Rift Valley around Humera, Awash, and Mattemma. The early draft of the land reform plan exempted these farms from nationalization. The experts realized that the government would not be able to successfully manage these farms, and that premature nationalization would destroy their productivity when it would be needed most.

The Military Council, at the urging of its radical mentors, refused to accept the recommendation of the experts and nationalized these farms. They were placed under state management in 1976 and designated the "State Farms," containing at that time approximately 70,000 hectares. Subsequently they were expanded in an attempt to counter the growing shortages of grain in urban areas, and by 1982 had grown to nearly 250,000 hectares—4 percent of all cultivated land in the country. In 1983 their production was 6 percent of the national total. The performance of the state farms had proven to be a total failure. . . .

. . . . .

Conclusion

Few countries in Africa are endowed with the natural wealth and potential of Ethiopia—but our country lies on the road to annihilation. Ethiopia used to be called the bread basket of Africa, now it cannot even support itself. Even with good weather the country produces an average of only 6 to 7 million tons of grain, leaving a 1.5 to 2 million ton deficit that must be made up from foreign imports or donations. Since that amount is never obtained, millions every year are exposed to famine and malnutrition. And when even minor irregularities in the climate occur, the entire country is plunged into famine. No action the government has taken since 1974 has done anything to improve these prospects.

Ethiopia will never come out of this tailspin unless policies change and priorities are altered. Politics must be set aside in order to deal with our most crucial emergency: saving our soil from an irreversible degradation that would leave Ethiopia a desert.

Mengistu and his circle are not worried. In meetings he always dismisses the problem, saying that the tide will turn, that Marxism will overcome nature. Frank discussions have disappeared. Research is seen as an impediment to quick development. The most qualified people in the country are not consulted; instead, it is always that inferior sort of man who makes adherence to ideology or to individuals the highest priority who is called upon. These are the "experts" used to justify Mengistu's capricious policies. Planning and analysis are disregarded in favor of spontaneous decisions involving millions of dollars. The inevitable results are total failures—failures from which no one can learn because they are immediately hushed up and treated as though they never took place.

Of all the failures of the regime, the biggest is their absolute disregard for humanity. Even the Soviet Union is acknowledging this lack in its own system. Mr. Gorbachev has recently stated:

> It is essential to change over from predominantly administrative to predominantly economic methods of management at every level, to broad democratization in administration and to activating the human factor in every way. . . .[2]

The new *glasnost* policy of Gorbachev may have a great effect on all the client states. It is easy for Gorbachev to initiate new programs. He can confidently disassociate himself from the policies of past leaders. It is not so easy for other Communist leaders to follow his lead—they can't criticize their own past policies. And it will certainly be difficult for Mengistu, who has just completed the establishment of his rigid Marxist-Leninst Party and new state structure based on the old Soviet system; and who believes he has a historical mission to prove that Stalin's system of control was right, not just in the economic sphere, but in every aspect of life. Mengistu's rigid, doctrinaire policies are only just being implemented. It is unlikely that he would dismantle the machinery by which he manipulates the people and replace his vision of a controlled Ethiopia for Gorbachev's more open society. . . .

． ． ． ． ．

Mengistu's Resettlement Campaign

In the beginning of October 1984, before the general donors' meeting described in Chapter 4, Mengistu called me into his office. He told me, out of the blue, that he was planning a massive national resettlement campaign. He planned to move 300,000 families, 1.5 million people, from Wollo and Tigray to Southwestern Ethiopia in nine months. I was amazed at these numbers. He said that this was the opportune moment to implement this project, which he claimed to have been considering for a long time, since the people couldn't refuse. They were helpless. They had no property, no tools. If we moved them now they would be entirely under our control and depend on us for everything.

His rationale for the program was: 1) to establish model producers' cooperatives (collectivized farms); 2) to place people who had accepted the Revolution along sensitive parts of the border; 3) to promote integration of various tribes and nationalities; 4) to develop vast fertile areas that would produce food surpluses; 5) to remove the unemployed and *lumpenproletariat* from the urban centers; 6) to use the settlement areas as rehabilitation centers for politically undesirable people from all walks of life; and last but not least, 7) to depopulate rebel areas in order to deprive the guerrillas of support.

It was one of those rare moments when he becomes relatively frank and one gets a glimpse of the real Mengistu. I told him that it would be a fatal mistake to attempt to settle 300,000 families in nine months. I told him the RRC did not have the resources, that land use surveys on new sites had not been made, that we would not get that many volunteers, and that it would drain our resources from the most pressing problem of the hour—emergency relief. He refused to see my points. He said that he would support my agency with the necessary manpower and financial backing. He argued that the RRC could mobilize international support. I was instructed to draw up a tentative operational plan.

Mengistu was overflowing with enthusiasm as he told me all this. It was clear that he considered this project to be the panacea for all the ills of the country. Mengistu loves campaigns, and this was something he could sink his teeth into—creating new committees and agencies, launching campaigns, emergency measures that would mobilize the entire nation with himself at the top. That is why the country's direction is haphazard. So much depends on the whim of Mengistu. He gets some bizarre idea, the next morning there is a meeting where he unveils his latest brainchild, and before we know it we are plunged into a campaign with people working eighteen to twenty hours a day, ignoring their other duties, prodded on by Chairman Mengistu's slogans on the importance of this campaign for the Revolution.

I knew that this new resettlement scheme would totally sap the energy and resources of the country. It was true that in the ten-year plan conference I had stated that 15,000 *people* a year would be too little; but now, barely one month later, he had decided to move 300,000 *families*, a hundred times as many people, in only nine months. What was worse, he was trusting his own caprice instead of thorough planning. His official reasons for launching the resettlement campaign were given in an interview in December 1986 with German TV reporter, Hannah Gadatsch:

> Resettlement and villagization, among other strategies in our ten year plan, belonged to a list of measures conceived with the general aim of countering conditions of underdevelopment and in particular of modernizing and raising productivity in the agricultural sector. The plan was intended to have been carried out later and in stages, but the drought forced us to speed things up. We had to save the lives of people in deadly danger. The resettlement plan had to be implemented very quickly and as an emergency measure.

This was a lie, as anyone knew who had seen the ten year plan discussed and approved just two months before. Mengistu's resettlement plan was the result neither of research nor of long term planning. It was a spontaneous act designed to take political advantage of the people's suffering, and a chance for Mengistu to present himself as a concerned leader. It was an exercise in utter hypocrisy.

My staff and I worked day and night to come up with a workable plan. None of us believed that this huge mass movement could be accomplished in such a short time without serious repercussions on the emergency relief program and on the other national priorities. So, with all due respect to the Chairman, we presented a plan for moving and settling 73,400 families in two years. We indicated in our plan that even if we were successful in moving this many people, ultimate success would depend on a key factor: that the holdings be private and not collectivized.

We presented our plan to Mengistu's aide just before the weekly Politburo meeting. A couple of days later, I had a call from the aide at ten a.m. telling me to appear before Mengistu at once with my two deputies. We were apprehensive. When senior officials are summoned "at once" to the Chairman's office, they usually call their wives or closest relatives and leave a last message, just in case. Several people ordered to his office in this manner were never heard of again.

The three of us were ushered into his office with its huge color picture of Lenin, its photos of Mengistu and Castro; its rich red carpet, velvet seats, and gifts and ornaments from various heads of state. Mengistu was all business. We were told to sit. For once he got right to the point.

"I have invited you here in the middle of a hot discussion in the Politburo. I ordered a break so that I could resolve this problem with you. You will remember that I instructed Comrade Dawit to submit a plan for settling 300,000 families from Wollo and Tigray. Instead, you have based your plan on 50,000 families, saying that 300,000 is an impossible target. The Politburo has found this outrageous. I would like to find out whether you all concur in this opinion?"

A terrifying question. Who knew what the consequences would be if we said the wrong thing? I took the floor and tried to explain our recommendations. My senior deputy in charge of rehabilitation, Taye Gurmu, backed me up. Taye was a professional who always knew what was possible and what was not. He was a frank person who has paid the price for his honesty with abuse from Legesse. My other deputy, Colonel Habtemariam, was a hardworking man whose work was clouded by his bureaucratic approach. He contributed a lot to the administrational aspect of the RRC, but when dealing with the Politburo he often proved too timid. Now he was unable to deal with the pressure of the situation and stammered out that there was no reason why 300,000 families could not be moved if it that was what the Chairman wanted.

This was exactly what Mengistu wanted to hear. He acted as though it were the seal of approval from an expert; he ordered full preparations to be made at once, telling us that the senior Politburo member Legesse would be in charge. No discussion was allowed. Mengistu said he had to go back to reconvene the meeting. Just before he left us, he said, almost as an afterthought: "by the way, plan for 500,000 families, not 300,000."[3]

It was terrible. There was no way to move that many people in one year. Even worse, Legesse was the head of the operation. Legesse—the most heartless, arrogant man in the government; uninformed, uneducated, and yet inflated with his own ego and self-image. He was the most unsuited of any man in the government to run the program. Confused and shocked, we went to the RRC office to call a meeting of all the department heads, planners, and economists. After prolonged discussion, we were all agreed that Mengistu's plan was beyond the capacity of the RRC and beyond our mandate. The furthest we could go was the settlement of 73,400 heads of families in two years. This was our estimated figure of displaced people and people in the shelters who would volunteer to be moved, and the maximum that our resources and available land would allow.

In an elaborately prepared document which we forwarded to the Supreme Planning Committee, we explained why we would be unable to undertake this task; why in principle it would be wrong to begin such a massive venture while the RRC had other equally urgent priorities. Immediately after, I was informed that the planning and execution of this massive new resettlement program would be taken over by the Central Planning Committee and the Politburo. Various ministries and agencies were given responsibilities. Those most involved were the Ministry of Construction, Ministry of Agriculture, Ministry of State Farms, the Water Resources Commission, and the provincial party secretaries. The RRC was given the job of feeding the settlers and providing relief items, tents, tools, medicine, and seed. . . .

· · · · ·

The Failure of Resettlement

The negative results of the resettlement campaign cannot be measured simply by the number who died; compared to famine deaths, that figure is very small. By far the greatest agony for the settlers was the forced separation from their loved ones. Of the estimated 700,000 settlers (250,000 families) still in the various camps, half are separated from one or more family members. In the beginning of 1986 the RRC initiated a program of reunification. Social workers went around to all the camps to try and locate separated family members. Some were found. But in many cases, with the husband dragged off to a settlement site, whatever was left of the family wandered into cities or villages where they thought they would be safer and were never heard from again. It is hard to imagine what these people went through. The anguish of being torn away from your community . . . the indescribable torment of escaping death from famine only to lose your husband, wife, or children forever by such a senseless act of brutality. I saw it in the faces of the settlers. After the agony, after the tears, a numbness sets in and life becomes meaningless.

This is only one of the reasons why the settlement sites will never be self-sufficient. Even those who are with their families are not motivated to work. They cannot relate to forced collectivization programs where nobody owns anything, where a family cannot own land or tools, where the entire produce of their labor goes to the cooperative and families get back only enough to live on.

There are no churches or mosques on settlement sites. The whole idea of these settlements was to create the New Society without that "opium of the masses," religion. The leadership proclaims mankind's domination over the

God of nature: but in a country where faith is so much a part of the people's lives, they feel demoralized without it. The peasants will never be productive in the settlements. They are lost souls. They miss their communities, their land and tools, their churches and mosques, their family members. They will never view the settlement sites as anything more than concentration camps...

. . . . .

The Ethiopian Diaspora

Since the Revolution, 2.5 million Ethiopians have fled to neighboring countries, the Middle East, or other parts of the world. In the last three years, the exodus has become a flood. According to the UNHCR report of June 18, 1987, there are 677,000 Ethiopian refugees registered in the Sudan; it is generally accepted there are an additional 150,000 who are not under the auspices of the UNHCR. The same UNHCR report shows 700,000 Ethiopian refugees in Somalia and 15,000 in Djibouti, bringing the total in these three countries alone to 1.5 million. Kenya, Egypt, Saudi Arabia, Italy, Sweden, the USA, Canada, and Great Britain have taken the larger portion of the other one million refugees; but there are few countries in the world that have not taken in some Ethiopian refugees. I came across one in Nicaragua as a member of the Sandinista force which liberated Managua in 1980. I have found others in Sri Lanka, Australia, and Thailand, and was told that there were even a few in Iceland and Alaska. This is the Ethiopian diasopora and it may be just beginning. It is terribly depressing for me to think that so many Ethiopians have scattered throughout the world in the past thirteen years—and that the problem is practically unnoticed by the world.

These refugees are not starving peasants looking for food. Many educated senior officials are fleeing a government they fear will turn against them. In the last thirteen years, twenty-one ministers, eighteen deputy ministers, and twenty-six ambassadors have defected. Since I left the list includes my deputy, Berhane Deressa; the Ambassador to France and former Minister of Justice, Getachew Kibret; Foreign Minister, Goshu Wolde; the Ambassador to Sweden and former Minister of Interior and Minister of Defense, Taye Tilahun; the Ambassador to Japan and former Minister of Domestic Trade, Abebe Kebedde; and hundreds of other officials. The defections continue.

Ethiopia is losing its best minds. It is said that there are more Ethiopian physicians in the United States than in Ethiopia, and more still in Europe. Students sent to study in the Soviet Union and East European countries don't return home. In the summer of 1985, of 365 Ethiopians who completed their graduate work in the Soviet Union, only fifty-one returned to Ethiopia; the others found their way to the West.

Notes

Introduction

1. There is no great mystery as to what these states had or have in common. "Communist" is used throughout not in the Marxist, theoretical sense—i.e., the highest stage of development (following socialism) in which the state withered away, etc.. Rather, I refer to Communist systems as those which have in common: (1) official self-legitimation based on some version of Marxism-Leninism interpreted by the supreme leader in power; (2) one-party rule by a party usually called "Communist"; (3) state control of the economy and mass media; and (4) a powerful and large police force concerned with "political crime" and instrumental in keeping the system in power. Many of these states were at least initially modeled on the Soviet Union and were, with a few exceptions, allied with it through much of their existence. Most of them were also totalitarian for long periods of time. The Soviet Union gradually ceased to be totalitarian following the death of Stalin; the same process took place in China following the death of Mao; some Soviet Bloc countries in Eastern Europe (Hungary, Poland) likewise ceased to be totalitarian during the 1970s and '80s. Sandinista Nicaragua has never been totalitarian. The crucial distinction between totalitarian and authoritarian systems lies in the fact that the former do not tolerate any autonomous social institution or group and seeks to politicize every institution and relationship and to abolish the distinction between private and public; such systems claim to be led by an infallible ruling party and leader (surrounded by a cult) and they repress not only those opposed to them but all those judged to be capable of such opposition; historically, they also attempted to create a new socialist or Communist man.
2. In September 2000 I asked a class of over 300 students (at the University of Massachusetts, Amherst, campus where I taught) how many of them learned anything about repression in Communist countries in high school. Not one hand was raised. I also asked how many of them had heard the word "Gulag"—four of them had. There is little doubt that these findings could be duplicated at college campuses around the country; nor would the level of information be different among other segments of the population.
3. Arthur Waldron, "Mao Lives," *Commentary,* October 2005, 31.

4. Few such museums exist in the former Communist countries. An attempt was made in Russia by private citizens to preserve a former prison camp ("Perm 36") as a museum. The article reporting this noted, "There are virtually no films or photographs of the Soviet prison system" (Alessandra Stanley, "Lest Russians Forget, a Museum of the Gulag," *New York Times*, October 29, 1997). Anne Applebaum has also observed that "Russia does not have a national museum dedicated to the history of repression" (Applebaum, *Gulag*, 568). Hungary has one such small museum at Recsk, the former labor camp. There is also in Budapest a recently opened "House of Terror," a museum devoted to both Nazi and Communist atrocities.

5. For a discussion of these discrepancies, see Paul Hollander, "Soviet Terror, American Amnesia," *National Review*, May 2, 1994, and by the same author, "Comparative Moral Reassessments of Nazism and Communism," *Partisan Review*, Fall 1995. See also Alain de Benoist, "Nazism and Communism: Evil Twins?" *Telos*, Summer 1998. For a further searching examination of this asymmetry, see Anne Applebaum, "A Dearth of Feeling," *New Criterion*, October 1996. See also Oskar Gruenwald, "The Other Holocaust: Twentieth Century Communist Genocide," *Journal of Interdisciplinary Studies*, 2000, Vol. XII, No. 1/ 2.

   Three authors made the most memorable and lasting contribution to dispelling ignorance about Soviet repression. Aside from Solzhenitsyn and his monumental *The Gulag Archipelago* (New York: 1978), Robert Conquest devoted much of his life and many books to documenting these matters. The recent (2003) publication of Anne Applebaum's *Gulag: A History* (New York)—an encyclopedic and highly original treatment of the subject—has been another milestone and sheds new light on the subject. See also Galina M. Ivanova, *Labor Camp Socialism: The Gulag in the Soviet Totalitarian System* (Armonk, NY: 2000). Of further interest is Veronique Garros et al., eds., *Intimacy and Terror: Soviet Diaries of the 1930s* (New York: 1995). See also O. V. Khlevniuk, *The History of the Gulag: From Collectivization to the Great Terror* (New Haven, CT: 2004).

6. Jonathan Rauch, "The Forgotten Millions," *Atlantic Monthly*, December 2003: 28.

7. See for example, Steven Lee Myers, "As Its Past Is Exhumed, Russia Turns Away," *New York Times*, October 20, 2002. Anne Applebaum has noted: "More notable than the missing monuments . . . is the missing public awareness" (Applebaum, *Gulag*, 568)

8. For a similar undertaking, see Lawrence L. Langer, ed., *Art from the Ashes: A Holocaust Anthology* (New York: 1995). See also Donald T. Critchlow and Agnieska Critchlow, eds., *The Enemies of the State: Personal Stories of the Gulag* (Chicago: 2002), a far more limited but informative undertaking containing ten such stories.

9. ". . . the bare facts lose their power over our senses and emotions if they are not presented in a coherent and *artistic* manner" (John Garrard, "Gulag Literature," *Problems of Communism*, November-December 1982: 77).

10. The handful of scholarly works comparing Nazi and Soviet policies of extermination include I. L. Horowitz, *Taking Lives: Genocide and State Power* (New Brunswick, NJ: 1997); T. Des Pres, *The Survivor: An Anatomy of Life in Death Camps* (New York: 1976); R. J. Rummel, *Death by Government* (New Brunswick, NJ: 1994); Tzvetan Todorov, *Facing the Extreme: Moral Life in the Concentration Camps* (New York: 1996); Ian Kershaw and Moshe Lewin, eds., *Stalinism and Nazism* (Cambridge, MA: 1998). Eric D. Weitz, *A Century of Genocide* (Princeton: 2003), compares Nazi, Soviet, Cambodian, and Serb genocides. Comparative essays on instances of genocide may also be found in Robert Gellately and Ben Kiernan,

eds., *The Specter of Genocide* (Cambridge and New York: 2003). A unique personal account of both Nazi and Soviet incarceration is provided by Margarete Buber-Neuman, *Under Two Dictators*, trans. Edward Fitzgerald (London: 1949). See also Barbara Harff amd Ted Robert Gurr, "Toward Empirical Theory of Genocides and Politicides: Identification and Measurement of Cases Since 1945," *International Studies Quarterly* (1988): 32. See also Samuel Totten and Steven L. Jacobs, eds., *Pioneers of Genocide Studies* (New Brunswick, NJ: 2002).

11. In Stephane Courtois, Nicolas Werth, Jean-Louis Panne, Andrzej Paczkowski, Karel Bartosek, Jean-Louis Margolin, *The Black Book of Communism: Crimes, Terror, Repression* (Cambridge, MA: 1999). Cited below as *Black Book*.

12. As Stephane Courtois writes: "[T]he revelations concerning Communist crimes cause barely a stir. . . . Why such a deafening silence from the academic world regarding the Communist catastrophe, which touched the lives of about one-third of humanity. . . ?" (*Black Book*, 17). See also Doris Lessing, "The Strange Case of the Western Conscience," in *The Wind Blows Away Our Words* (New York: 1987).

13. According to R. J. Rummel, an American academic specialist of genocide, Communist governments in this century killed 95 million people. Of these, the Soviets were responsible for 39 million and China under Mao for 45 million. These figures exclude all famine victims except those who died in the Ukrainian "terror famine" (R. J. Rummel, "War Isn't This Century's Biggest Killer," *Wall Street Journal*, July 7, 1996). See also Rummel, *Lethal Politics: Soviet Genocide and Mass Murder since 1917* (New Brunswick, NJ: 1996), xi.

Tony Judt ascribes 20 million victims to the Soviet Union, 65 million to China, and a combined total of 6 million to Cambodia, North Korea, Vietnam, and Eastern Europe (Tony Judt, "The Longest Road to Hell," *New York Times*, December 22, 1997). Robert Conquest estimates the victims of Soviet mass murders at between 15 and 20 million (*The Great Terror*, 525–35). An article in the *New York Times* attributes 54.7 million victims to the Soviet Union between 1917 and 1987 and 35.6 million to China between 1949 and 1987 ("Genocide Is Bad for the Economy," December 14, 1997). Roger Cohen put the figure at "upward of 8 million." See his "1945's Legacy," *New York Times* "Week in Review," May 15, 2005. In *The Road to Terror* (New Haven, CT: 1999), J. Arch Getty and Oleg V. Naumov conclude that the Soviet system was directly responsible for only 2 million "excess deaths" (591–92). The authors put Dmitri Volkogonov's estimate at 3.5 million (589), although Volkogonov wrote that "altogether 19.5–22 million Soviet citizens fell victim to Stalinist repression" (*Victory and Tragedy: The Political Portrait of Stalin*, Hungarian edition, 413). Anne Applebaum, in her *Gulag* (578–86), while leaning toward the higher estimates emphasizes the difficulty of arriving at reliable figures even with the help of archives.

14. André Gide considered these establishments "one of the noblest and most successful experiments in the Soviet Union and a great achievement." Subsequently he was dismayed to learn "that only informers—those who betrayed their fellow convicts to the authorities—were granted the privilege of living in this model settlement [Bolshevo]." (Richard Crossman, ed., *The God That Failed* [New York: 1959], 166). See also Jerzy Gliksman, *Tell the West* (New York: 1948), 163–78, and Paul Hollander, "Socialist Prisons and Imprisoned Minds," *National Interest*, Winter 1987.

15. Simon Sebag Montefiore, *Stalin: The Court of the Red Tsar* (London: 2003), 76, 84.

16. *Belomor: An Account of the Construction of the New Canal Between the White Sea and the Baltic*

Sea, M. Gorky, L. Auerbach and S. G. Firin, eds. (New York: 1935), vi. For a study of these Soviet literary endeavors, see Cynthia A. Ruder, *Making History for Stalin: The Story of the Belomor Canal* (Gainesville, FL: 1998). For a critical examination of such writings, see Dariusz Tolczyk, *See No Evil: Literary Cover-ups and Discoveries of the Soviet Concentration Camp Experience* (New Haven, CT: 1999).

17. His letter was reprinted in the appendix of Gustav Herling, *A World Apart*, 252, an excerpt of which is included in this volume.

18. Shirley Hazzard, "'Gulag' and the Men of Peace," *New York Times Book Review*, August 25, 1974.

19. Frederick L. Schuman in his review of Kravchenko's *I Chose Freedom*, ("Horrors of Bolshevism Inc.," *New Republic*, May 6, 1946) called him a "Soviet renegade" and a "politically unworthy careerist," and the book "the latest spicy dish from the Redbaiters kitchen." In turn Malcolm Cowley "impugned the character and testimony of Walter Krivitsky," another high-ranking defector. (*New York Review of Books*, 1/14/1999: 48).

20. Noam Chomsky and Edward S. Herman, "Distortions at Fourth Hand," *Nation*, June 25, 1977. In *After the Cataclysm* (Boston: 1979), the same authors affirm their skepticism, writing of these massacres that the "evidence is slight and unreliable and informed opinion ranges over quite a wide spectrum" (290).

21. Getty alleged that "[s]econd-hand personal memoirs, gossip, novels and lurid accounts by defecting spies eager to earn a living in the West are soberly reviewed in scholarly journals, cited in footnotes and recommended to graduate students" ("The Politics of Repression Revisited," in J. Arch Getty and Roberta T. Manning, eds., *Stalinist Terror: New Perspectives* [New York: 1993], 40–41). Earlier, Getty became famous (or notorious) for his striking underestimation of the victims of the Soviet purges in his *Origin of the Great Purges* (New York: 1985).

22. See note 95 concerning Kristof. The difficulty of interesting Westerners in North Korean repression has been illustrated by the lonely efforts of a German physician: see James Brooke, "One German and His North Korean Conscience," *New York Times*, March 19, 2002. A remarkable recent volume given little attention in the U.S. confirms the worst stories of refugees. See Kang Chol-hwan and Pierre Rigoulot, *The Aquariums of Pyongyang: Ten Years in a North Korean Gulag* (New York: 2001), a portion of which is excerpted here.

23. To be sure, there are a few Holocaust deniers (or minimizers), such as David Irving, but they are widely considered cranks and are well outside the mainstream of Western scholarly and public opinion.

24. Lance Morrow, *Evil: An Investigation* (New York: 2003), 12-13, 16

25. See Aleksandr M. Nekrich, *The Punished Peoples* (New York: 1978), and Robert Conquest, *The Soviet Deportation of Nationalities* (London: 1960). On these deportations, see also page 418 of Montefiore, *Stalin*. For the Chinese mistreatment of Tibetans see the selections from Choedrak and Gyatso reprinted here.

26. Michael Scammel argued to the contrary: "[T]he arbitrary categories of 'kulak' and 'bourgeois' did not allow for redefinition or re-education any more than did the category of Jew to the Nazis. . . . [O]nce the class determination was made, the only hope for the victims lay in the relative sloppiness of Russian administrators compared with the discipline and efficiency of the Germans ("Conceptual Vagueness," Letter, *New York Times*, December 28, 1997).

27. Richard Pipes, *Vixi: Memoirs of a Non-Belonger* (New Haven, CT: 2003), 58.

28. Alan Ryan, "The Evil Empire," *New York Times Book Review,* January 2, 2000; Weitz, *Century of Genocide,* 236–37; Michael Ignatieff, "Lemkin's Word," *New Republic,* February 26, 2001: 25; George Steiner, *In Bluebirds Castle,* (New Haven, CT: 1971), 43; Ian Buruma, "Divine Killer," *New York Review of Books,* February 24, 2000: 20.

29. Morrow, *Evil,* 210-11, 246, 59.

30. George Steiner, *In Bluebird's Castle* (New Haven, CT: 1971), 43; Ian Buruma, "Divine Killers," *New York Review of Books,* February 24, 2000, 20. For a new, definitive study of Mao, see Jung Chang and Jon Halliday, *Mao: The Unknown Story* (New York: 2005). The authors' estimate of his victims is 70 million.

31. Charles Simic, "The Golden Age of Hatred," *New York Review of Books,* October 23, 2003: 42.

32. David Chandler, *Voices from S-21: Terror and History in Pol Pot's Secret Prison* (Berkeley, CA: 1999), 6–7, 77–78.

33. *Black Book,* 16, 217.

34. Quoted in *Black Book,* 15.

35. Elena Bonner, "The Remains of Totalitarianism," *New York Review of Books,* March 8, 2001: 4.

36. Quoted in Theodore Draper, "A New Nadezhda," *New Republic,* July 1, 1996: 31.

37. Paul Berman, "Five Lessons from a Bad Year," *New Republic,* June 28, 2004: 29.

38. For a rare volume on this topic, see Iris Chang, *The Rape of Nanking: The Forgotten Holocaust of World War II* (New York: 1997). Resulting in large measure from the impact of this volume, there has been "a sudden burst" of interest in the topic, as noted in James Dao, "Parents' Nightmare, Children's Quest," *New York Times,* May 16, 1998.

39. Chang, *Rape of Nanking.*

40. Nicholas D. Kristof, "Japan Confronting Gruesome War Atrocity," *New York Times,* March 17, 1999; see also Sheldon H. Harris, *Factories of Death: Japanese Biological Warfare 1932–45 and the American Cover-Up* (London: 1994); Ralph Blumental, with Judith Miller, "Japanese Germ-War Atrocities: A Half-Century of Stonewalling the World," *New York Times,* March 4, 1999; Ralph Blumenthal, "Revisiting World War II Atrocities: Comparing the Unspeakable to the Unthinkable," *New York Times,* March 7, 1999; and Toshiyuki Tanaka, *Hidden Horrors: Japanese War Crimes in World War II* (Boulder, CO: 1996).

41. Barbara Crosette, "The Mystery in Borneo At the 'Massacre Place,'" *New York Times,* February 3, 1987.

42. The "collective toll" of the two atomic bombs was estimated to be between 110,000 and 200,000 in the "Opinion Journal" of the *Wall Street Journal,* August 5, 2005, in an article titled "Hiroshima."

43. D. W. Giorgis, *Red Tears: War, Famine and Revolution in Ethiopia* (Trenton, NJ: 1989), 3. See also the excerpt from Giorgis in this volume; "Up to 100,000 Said to Die in Ethiopia Resettlement," *New York Times,* November 21, 1985; and Jane Perlez, "Ethiopia Drives Its Peasants Off the Good Earth," *New York Times,* September 12, 1898. It was reported by an anthropologist witnessing these events that the Ethiopian government preferred to use trucks for resettlement rather than for distributing badly needed food for the starving (V. L. Barnes-Dean, "Ethiopia Using Trucks for Resettlement," Letter, *New York Times,* July 16, 1985).

44. "To Die in Afghanistan," *Helsinki Watch Asia Watch,* New York, December, 1985: 1.

45. "[T]he Soviets have a clear and consistent policy of taking reprisals against civilians for

military actions by the Resistance.... [B]ombing is a key part of pacification strategy: the government tells the villagers that if they join pro-government organizations and prevent the Resistance from operating in their area they will be safe from bombing..." (Rosanne Klass, ed., *Afghanistan: The Great Game Revisited* [New York: 1987], 340, 341).

46. Quoted in Lee Braddock, "Moral Unequivalence," *Policy Review,* Summer 1988: 49.

47. Klass, *Afghanistan,* 337, 348.

48. Michael Barry, "Afganistan—Another Cambodia?" *Commentary,* August 1982: 31–32.

49. Klass, *Afghanistan,* 349.

50. "Tears, Blood and Cries: Human Rights in Afganistan Since the Invasion, 1979–1984," *Helsinki Watch,* New York, 1984: 136

51. "Afghanistan: Torture of Political Prisoners," Amnesty International, New York, 1986: 11, 15–16.

52. Barry, "Afghanistan—Another Cambodia?" 33.

53. Milovan Djilas, *Conversations with Stalin* (New York: 1960), 95; see also 110–11.

54. Ibid., 111.

55. Wolfgang Leonhard, *Child of the Revolution* (Chicago: 1958), 462.

56. Along the same lines, in the same conversation with Djilas, Stalin alluded to his "quarrel" with Trotsky and Bukharin, which ended in having both of them murdered on his instructions (Djilas, *Conversations with Stalin,* 75)

57. Norman Naimark, *The Russians in Germany: A History of the Soviet Zone of Occupation, 1945–1949* (Cambridge, MA: 1995), 74, 108. For a German personal account of such atrocities, see Hans von Lehndorf, *East Prussian Diary, 1945–47* (London: 1963). See also *A Woman in Berlin: Eight Weeks in the Conquered City* (New York: 2005).

58. Naimark, *The Russians in Germany,* 86.

59. Ibid., 132–33.

60. Ibid., 72–73. In the post-Stalin period, Lev Kopelev became a well-known dissident who later emigrated to Germany.

61. Alexander N. Yakovlev, *A Century of Violence in Soviet Russia* (New Haven, CT: 2002), 174.

62. Krisztian Ungvari, "Sovjet Jogsertesek Magyarorszagon 1945–ben" [Soviet violations of Human Rights in Hungary in 1945], *Magyar Nemzet* (Budapest), November 29, 1997.

63. Both *The Black Book* and Rummel, *Death by Government,* put the figure at over one million.

64. Eric Reeves, "Don't Let Oil Revenues in Sudan Fuel Genocide," *Toronto Globe and Mail,* May 4, 1999.

65. See, for example, Norimitsu Onishi, "A Brutal War's Machetes Maim Sierra Leone," *New York Times,* January 26, 1999.

66. Quoted from Tzvetan Todorov, *Hope and Memory: Lessons from the Twentieth Century* (Princeton, NJ: 2003), 91. Applebaum, *Gulag,* xviii–xix, xx, xxi. Post-Communist studies of the former Soviet Union have been rightly characterized as possessing "a tone of bland neutrality that... blurs the otherness of Soviet society" (Martin Malia, "The Archives of Evil: Soviet Studies After the Soviet Union," *New Republic,* November 29–December 6, 2004: 39). Of course, in this context "otherness" refers to the repugnant qualities of the Soviet system these authors have been reluctant to recognize or dwell on.

67. Tony Judt, "From the House of the Dead: On Modern European Memory," *New York Review of Books,* October 6, 2005, 14.

68. Alain Besançon, "Forgotten Communism," *Commentary,* January 1998: 25. See also a volume on the debates among German historians about the uniqueness of the Holocaust,

Forever in the Shadow of Hitler? Original Documents of the Historikerstreit: The Controversy Concerning the Singularity of the Holocaust (Atlantic Highlands, NJ: 1993).

69. Benoist, "Nazism and Communism," 181.

70. Herbert C. Kelman, "Violence without Moral Restraint," *Journal of Social Issues* 29, no. 4 (1973): 25, 29. For a volume replete with similar omissions and one-sidedness, see Nevitt Sanford and Craig Comstock, eds., *Sanctions for Evil* (San Francisco: 1971).

71. "Perspectives on Obedience to Authority: The Legacy of the Milgram Experiments," *Journal of Social Issues,* Fall 1995.

72. I was moved to write a letter to Mr. Keen about the one-sidedness of his presentation, to which he did not respond.

73. See note 13. According to Alexander Yakovlev, "the number of people in the USSR who were killed for political motives or who died in prisons and camps during the entire period of Soviet power totaled 20 to 25 million. And unquestionably one must add those who died of famine—more than 5.5. million during the civil war and more than 5 million during the 1930s" (Yakovlev, *The Fate of Marxism in Russia* [New Haven, CT: 1993], 234).

74. Sydney Schanberg's belief was typical of the Western limits of imagination and the Western liberals' view of the the Khmer Rouge before its defeat by the Vietnamese: a few days prior to the entry of Pol Pot's troops into Phnom Penh, he wrote that "it is difficult to imagine how [the] lives of ordinary people could be anything but better with the Americans gone" (quoted in Leopold Labedz, "Of Myths and Horrors," *Encounter,* February 1980: 43.) Later on, Schanberg did become a critic of the Pol Pot regime, as he apparently came to realize that things could and did get worse for ordinary people after the Americans were gone.

75. Quoted in Labedz, "Of Myths and Horrors," 43.

76. Martin Malia, "The Lesser Evil?" *Times Literary Supplement,* March 27, 1998: 3. See also his "Foreword: The Uses of Atrocity," in *The Black Book.*

77. Ibid.

78. Edward Shils, "Authoritarianism: 'Right' and 'Left,'" in R. Christie and M. Jahoda, eds., *Studies in the Scope and Method of the Authoritarian Personality* (Glencoe, IL: 1954), 33–34.

79. Todorov, *Facing the Extreme,* 132; Todorov, *Hope and Memory,* 35–36, 37.

80. Benoist, "Nazism and Communism," 182.

81. Quoted in Robert Conquest, *Reflections on a Ravaged Century* (New York: 2000), 10–11.

82. Malia, "Foreword," in *Black Book.*

83. François Furet, *The Passing of an Illusion* (Chicago: 1999), 496.

84. Milovan Djilas, *The Fall of the New Class* (New York: 1998), 306.

85. David Remnick, "The Exile Returns," *New Yorker,* February 14, 1994: 73.

86. Malia, "The Lesser Evil?" 4.

87. Benoist, "Nazism and Communism," 186.

88. Ian Buruma, "Divine Killer," 22.

89. In Benoist, "Nazism and Communism," 186. The same point was also made by Vladimir Farkas, a former high-ranking officer of the Hungarian KGB, in a conversation with the editor of this volume. Farkas wrote a book about his experiences and beliefs (*No Excuse* [Budapest: 1988]) that is not available in English.

90. Hollander, "Soviet Terror, American Amnesia," and "Comparative Moral Reassessments of Nazism and Communism."

91. For a volume devoted to the question of the uniqueness of the Nazi mass murders, see

Alan S. Rosenbaum, ed., *Is the Holocaust Unique? Perspectives on Comparative Genocide* (Boulder, CO: 1996). See also chapter 8 in Isidor Walliman and Michael Dobkowski, eds., *Genocide in the Modern Age* (Westport, CT: 1987). A generally unknown technique of mechanized execution reportedly introduced by Yezhov in the Soviet Union during the Purge period was described in *Comrade X* (London: 1956) by G. A. Tokaev, a high-ranking scientist (involved in the design of military aircraft) who defected in 1947: "Walking in front of the executioners, the victim entered a corridor about six feet high and two feet wide.... [D]eath [was] provided by one of two methods: shooting by automatic weapons built into the walls, released at a certain point where the victim inevitably trod on a spring section of the floor, or by levers, released in the same way, which crushed him.... [A]fter death, the machinery tipped the body into a furnace ready to cremate without delay" (100).

92. Robert Conquest, "Unearthing the Great Terror," *Orbis*, Spring 1989: 240.
93. Kristin Gustavson and Jinmin Lee-Rudolph, "Political and Economic Human Rights Violations in North Korea," in Thomas Henriksen and Jongryn Mo, eds., *North Korea After Kim Il Sung* (Stanford, CA: 1997), 132; Christopher Hitchens, *Why Orwell Matters* (New York: 2002), 73, 75. See also Abraham Cooper, "Toxic Indifference to North Korea," *Washington Post*, March 20, 2005.
94. See, for example, Brooke, "Defectors from North Korea Tell of Prison Baby Killing"; and, by the same author, "Little Girl Puts Human Face On Plight of North Koreans," *New York Times*, August 21, 2002.
95. Nicholas D. Kristof, "Survivors Report Torture in North Korean Labor Camps," *New York Times*, July 14, 1996.
96. Judt, "The Longest Road to Hell." See also Alan Riding, "Communism and Crimes: French Bristle At Best Seller," *New York Times*, November 21, 1997. This article describes the controversy *The Black Book* created in France by morally equating (or coming close to equating) the Communist and the Nazi mass murders.
97. S. A. Malsagoff, *An Island Hell: A Soviet Prison in the Far North* (London: 1926), 169, 174. The camps referred to were on the Solovki islands.
98. Roy A. Medvedev, *Let History Judge* (New York: 1972), 279, 280.
99. Avraham Shifrin, *The First Guidebook to Prisons and Concentration Camps of the Soviet Union* (Seewis/GR, Switzerland: Verlag AG, 1980), 35. This remarkable source of information was completely overlooked by reviewers in the United States.
100. Irving Louis Horowitz, *Tributes: Personal Reflections on a Century of Social Research* (New Brunswick, NJ: 2004), 263.
101. The nonrevolutionary Communist regimes were those established as a result of the arrival and prolonged presence of Soviet troops—namely, Bulgaria, Czechoslovakia, East Germany, Hungary, Poland, and Romania.
102. Forrest. D. Colburn, *The Vogue of Revolution in Poor Countries* (Princeton, NJ: 1994), 13–14. Milovan Djilas also believed that in Communist states "everything, including the economy [was] subordinate to ideological power" (Djilas, *Fall of the New Class*, 312).
103. Igal Halfin, *Terror in My Soul* (Cambridge, MA: 2003), 14.
104. Chandler, *Voices from S-21*, 150.
105. Simon Leys, "After the Massacres," *New York Review of Books*, October 12, 1989: 17.
106. Bui Tin, *Following Ho Chi Minh* (Honolulu: 1995), 115
107. See Peter Reddaway, *Psychiatric Terror: How Soviet Psychiatry Is Used to Suppress Dissent*

(New York: 1977); Petro G. Grigorienko was subjected to this treatment, as he recalls in his *Memoirs* (New York: 1982), see also Yakovlev, *Fate of Marxism in Russia*, 147–48.

108. Erik Eckholm, "A China Dissident's Ordeal: Back to the Mental Hospital," *New York Times,* November 30, 1999. The use of psychiatric wards in China for detaining political prisoners is also described in Liu Binyan, *A Higher Kind of Loyalty* (New York: 1990), 225–27. Concerning similar policies in Cuba, see Charles J. Brown and Armando M. Lago, *The Politics of Psychiatry in Revolutionary Cuba* (New Brunswick, NJ: 1991), which is excerpted here. In Romania, dissidents were sent to psychiatric institutions for periods ranging from a few months to several years. See Dennis Deletant, *Ceausescu and the Securitate: Coercion and Dissent in Romania, 1965–1989* (New Armonk, NY: 1995), 93–101.

109. Quoted in V. I. Lenin, *State and Revolution* (Moscow: Foreign Languages Publishing House, n.d.), 25–27.

110. Giorgis, *Red Tears,* 21.

111. Lenin, *State and Revolution,* 39, 68, 144–45.

112. Quoted in Mikhail Heller, *Cogs in the Wheel: The Formation of Soviet Man* (New York: 1988), 36. Lenin's inclination to political violence is also documented in Richard Pipes, ed., *The Unknown Lenin* (New Haven, CT: 1996).

113. Quoted in Robert V. Daniels, ed., *A Documentary History of Communism* (New York: 1960), 57. Stalin made the statement in 1937 in a speech to the Central Committee of the party.

114. Ted Galen Carpenter, "Democracy and War," *Independent Review,* Winter 1998: 436. Edward Shils also noted that "The phantasy of conspiracy requires the reality of counter-conspiracy so that in the end the world becomes an arena in which two conspiracies operate, the wicked conspiracies of the enemies and the legitimate and morally necessary conspiracy of Bolshevism" (*The Torment of Secrecy* [Carbondale, IL: 1974], 30).

115. Aleksandr Solzhenitsyn, *The Gulag Archipelago,* vol. 1 (New York: 1973), 173–74.

116. Yakovlev, *A Century of Violence in Soviet Russia,* 15.

117. Yakovlev, *Fate of Marxism in Russia,* 7, 11, 17, 29, 38, 39, 56–57.

118. Nathan Leites, *A Study of Bolshevism* (Glencoe, IL: 1953), 105.

119. Ibid., 105.

120. Quoted in Teresa Toranska, *"Them": Stalin's Polish Puppets* (New York: 1987), 88.

121. Quoted in Leites, *Study of Bolshevism,* 208, 106.

122. Ibid., 348.

123. Ibid., 352.

124. Presumably such impulsive, sadistic enjoyment of violence motivated the Japanese soldiers in Nanking as well as the participants in pogroms, lynchings, and other spontaneous outbursts of ethnic violence.

125. Leon Trotsky, *Terrorism and Communism: A Reply to Karl Kautsky* (Ann Arbor, MI: 1961), 20, 23.

126. Heinrich Himmler, for one, quite candidly addressed the problem of ends and means in the solution of "the Jewish question" in a speech to SS officers, where he acknowledged that it was unpleasant to contemplate corpses and, in his view, required strong character. (See Joachim C. Fest, *The Face of the Third Reich* [New York: 1970], 115.)

127. Zbigniew Brzezinski, "Patterns of Autocracy," in Cyril Black, ed., *The Transformation of Russian Society* (Cambridge, MA: 1960).

128. On these aspects of Mao's personality, see Dr. Li Zhisui, *The Private Life of Chairman Mao* (New York: 1994).

129. "Mengistu once confided to me that he enjoyed chairing meetings in this hall . . . because he was able to sit right above the basement where all former aristocrats whom he despised were imprisoned" (Giorgis, *Red Tears,* 126). This was by no means the only reflection of Mengistu's unappealing personality. See also Ibid., 18–21, 33–34, 332, and 352 for other examples of his megalomania and ruthlessness.

130. A remarkable and largely ignored publication provides detailed information about the exact location, size, and function of some 2000 Soviet penal institutions, which accomodated political as well as nonpolitical prisoners (see Shifrin, *First Guidebook to Prisons and Concentration Camps of the Soviet Union*). Harry Wu collected data on about 1,000 Chinese labor reform camps and estimated their total number at 3,000. He wrote that "within the last forty years a minimum of 50 million people have been sent to these Laogai [reform through labor] camps and at the present time some 10 million are in them" (undated manuscript).

131. Chandler, *Voices from S-21,* 122.

132. Upon his arrest, Armando Valladares was told by his interrogator, "[W]e have no proof . . . against you. But we do have the conviction that you are a potential enemy of the Revolution. For us, that is enough" (*Against All Hope* [New York: 1986], 9).

133. Robert Conquest wrote: "Prisoners recognized . . . that there was an 'objective characteristic' basic to the case. This might be social origins, past or present posts, relationship or friendship with someone, nationality or connection with a foreign country, or activity in specific Soviet organizations" (*The Great Terror* [London: 1968], 297).

134. Chandler, *Voices from S-21,* 44, 76.

135. *Black Book,* 186–87; see also Montefiore, *Stalin,* 203–4.

136. Jerzy Gliksman, "Social Prophylaxis as a Form of Soviet Terror," in Carl Friedrich, ed., *Totalitarianism* (New York: 1964), 61, 62, 64. Similar sweeping and vague categories of political crime were also introduced in Romania, such as "counterrevolutionary sabotage," "counterrevolutionary diversion," and "counterrevolutionary agitation and propaganda" (see Dennis Deletant, *Communist Terror in Romania* [New York: 1999], 84).

137. Quoted in Heller, *Cogs in the Wheel,* 95.

138. F. Beck and W. Godin, *Russian Purge and the Extraction of Confession* (New York: 1951), 93–98. Excerpts from this work are included in the present volume.

139. *Black Book,* 201.

140. Ibid., 188.

141. Conquest, *The Great Terror,* 283; see also 284–99. See also Gliksman, *Tell the West,* 67–72.

142. Deletant, *Communist Terror in Romania,* 213.

143. Quoted in Daniels, *Documentary History of Communism,* 41.

144. Nguyen Van Canh, *Vietnam Under Communism, 1975–1982* (Stanford, CA: 1983), 193.

145. Philip Gourevitch, "Vietnam: The Bitter Truth," *New York Review of Books,* December 22, 1994: 55.

146. See for example *Black Book,* 622. In Russia during the Civil War, people with clean fingernails were politically suspect (personal communication with Peter Kenez, a specialist on the Russian civil war).

147. Xiaoxia Gong, *Repressive Movements and the Politics of Victimization: Patronage and Persecution During the Cultural Revolution* (Ph.D. Dissertation, Harvard University, 1995), 49. See also *Black Book,* 486–87, and Andrew G. Walder and Gong Xiaoxia, eds., "Violence in the Cultural Revolution," *Chinese Sociology and Anthropology,* January 1994.

148. Martin King Whyte, "Corrective Labor Camps in China," *Asian Survey* 13, no. 3 (1973): 253–57.

149. Frank Chalk and Kurt Jonasson, eds., *The History and Sociology of Genocide* (New Haven, CT: 1990), 404.

150. Marek Sliwinski, quoted in the *Black Book*, 634, 593.

151. Gustavson and Lee-Rudolph, "Political and Economic Human Rights Violations in North Korea," 135. *The Black Book* notes that, "[a]s part of the [North Korean] regime's affirmation of familial responsibility, entire families have been sent to camps because one member received a sentence" (555). The experiences of one such family are narrated in *The Aquariums of Pyongyang*, which is excerpted in the present volume. In Communist Ethiopia, the entire royal family was imprisoned (Giorgis, *Red Tears*, 341).

152. *Black Book*, 560; see also Anthony Daniels, "Peoples Democratic Review," *National Review*, September 1, 1989: 20.

153. *Black Book*, 598.

154. Leon Trotsky, *The Revolution Betrayed* (New York: 1972 [1937]).

155. Ibid., 112, 49–50, 52.

156. Two uprisings—in 1953 in East Germany and in 1956 in Hungary—were put down by Soviet troops. The more peaceful attempt in Czechoslovakia in 1968 to create "socialism with a human face" was also thwarted by Soviet forces. The predictability of such Soviet support had come to an end by the mid-1980s and greatly accelerated the collapse of these systems.

157. See Conquest, *The Harvest of Sorrow*. Another author had this to say on the subject: "[T]he deaths of millions of Ukranians and other Soviet peoples in the famine of 1932–33 are directly attributable to Stalin's attempt to totally reconstruct society through rapid industrialization. . . . In the process he instituted a totalitarian system permeated by terror. There were mass death and overwhelming suffering as a result of excessive grain procurement but . . . [u]nlike the Holocaust the Great Famine was not an intentional act of genocide. The purpose was not to exterminate Ukranians simply because they were Ukranians." (Barbara B. Green, "Stalinist Terror and the Question of Genocide: The Great Famine," in Rosenbaum, *Is the Holocaust Unique?* 139, 156).

158. Alexander Orlov, *The Secret History of Stalin's Crimes* (New York: 1953), 28–29.

159. On the Ethopian famine, see also Myles F. Harris, *Breakfast in Hell: A Doctor's Eyewitness Account of the Politics of Hunger in Ethiopia* (New York: 1987), which is excerpted in this anthology.

160. Jasper Becker, *Hungry Ghosts: Mao's Secret Famine* (New York: 1997); see also Arthur Waldron, "'Eat People'—A Chinese Reckoning," *Commentary*, July 1997.

161. Bao Ruo Wang wrote, "[O]mnipresent denunciation boxes . . . proliferate in every city. A foreigner might mistake them for mail boxes since they are painted red. . . . Undernearth is a shelf space for standard forms and above a little notice in Chinese characters: 'Denunciation Box.' . . . The police collect from the boxes daily. Denunciation boxes also exist in prisons and camps, and there are also the so-called Constructive Criticism Boxes" (*Prisoner of Mao* [Harmondsworth, UK: 1976], 61, excerpted here). *The Black Book* also notes the existence of these boxes.

162. Arch Puddington, "Revolutionary Defense Committes," in I. L. Horowitz, ed., *Cuban Communism, 1959–1996* (New Brunswick, NJ: 1995), 493.

163. Rhoda Rabkin, "Human Rights and Military Rule in Cuba," in Horowitz, *Cuban Com-*

munism, 675; see also Puddington, "Revolutionary Defense Committees," and *Black Book,* 661–62.

164. *Black Book,* 481.

165. *Black Book,* 586–87.

166. Roger Cohen, "Germany's East Is Still Haunted by Big Brother," *New York Times,* November 29: 199; see also Timothy Garton Ash, *The File: A Personal History* (New York: 1997), and Mike Dennis, *The Stasi* (London: 2003), 90–106, an excerpt from which volume is included here.

167. The editor had some personal experience of these installations, having crossed the border illegally from Hungary to Austria in November 1956.

168. See for example Alexandr Nekrich, *The Punished Peoples* (New York: 1978). See also "Ethiopia: The Communist Uses of Famine," in Puddington, "Revolutionary Defense Committees."

169. Richard Eder, "Cuban In Landing Gear Survives Flight to Spain at—40 degrees," *New York Times,* June 5, 1969.

170. Paul Hollander, "Border Controls: An Integral Part of the Soviet Social-Political System," in *The Many Faces of Socialism* (New Brunswick, NJ: 1983). See also Orlov, *Secret History of Stalin's Crimes.*

171. People sought to escape from Communist countries on foot, by water (swimming, kayaking, on rafts), in the air (in balloons or planes), by tunneling underground, and on land using every type of transportation, including trunks of cars. They also climbed over walls, barbed-wire barriers, and crossed minefields. See Hollander, *Many Faces of Socialism.*

172. Mass escapes took place before border controls were tightened (as in the case of East Germany before the wall was built), when they were temporarily disrupted (as in Hungary at the time of the 1956 revolution), when the regime failed to take adequate preventative measures (as in the case of the Vietnamese boat people), or under unusual historical circumstances (as when Soviet slave laborers and prisoners of war in Germany after World War II refused to return). See Paul Hollander, "The Nature of Discontent with Communist Systems," in *Decline and Discontent: Communism and the West Today* (New Brunswick, NJ: 1992).

173. Arch Puddington, "Preventing the Brain Drain," in *Failed Utopias* (San Francisco: 1988).

174. See "Article 64, Treason," in Harold J. Berman, ed., *Soviet Criminal Law and Procedure* (Cambridge, MA: 1966), 178.

175. Chalk and Jonasson, *History and Sociology of Genocide,* 28; Stephane Courtois uses the term "animalization" to refer to the same process and intention (see *Black Book,* 747–48).

176. Todorov, *Facing the Extreme,* 127.

177. Eduard Shevardnadze, *The Future Belongs to Freedom* (London: 1991), 21.

178. See Paul Hollander, "Models of Behavior in Stalinist Literature," in *Many Faces of Socialism.*

179. Quoted in Tolczyk, *See No Evil,* 79.

180. Ivan Boldizsar, "Kanyargos Drava—Uj Magyar Regeny" [The Winding Drava: A New Hungarian Novel], *Szabad Nep* (Budapest), February 16, 1953; Joseph Revai, "Megjegyzesek egy Regenyhez" [Comments on a Novel], *Tarsadalmi Szemle* (Budapest), August-September 1952: 753.

181. *Report of the Court Proceedings in the Case of the Anti-Soviet Trotskyite Center,* Moscow, 1937: 696, 482, 504, 631, 473 (hereafter *Court Proceedings*).

182. Hungarian edition, Budapest, 1950, 418, 419. Vyshinsky further characterized these defendants as "a foul heap of human garbage . . . beasts in human form . . . mad dogs . . . and dregs and scum of humanity" (quoted in Orlov, *Secret History of Stalin's Crimes,* 330).

183. *Court Proceedings,* 1937, 462, 480.

184. Quoted in *Black Book,* 745.

185. The article was titled (in Hungarian) "Rajk, the Informer of the Horthy Police, Agent of the U.S. Intelligence Service, the Hireling of Tito and Rankovitch, Confesses before the Peoples Court," *Szabad Nep,* September 17, 1949. (All Hungarian citations translated by the editor.)

186. Sandor Nagy, "The Face of Scoundrels" (translation of the Hungarian), *Szabad Nep,* September 21, 1949.

187. Weitz, *Century of Genocide,* 168.

188. Aldous Huxley, "Words and Behavior," in *Collected Essays* (New York: 1960), 254.

189. Stephen J. Morris, *Why Vietnam Invaded Cambodia: Political Culture and the Causes of War* (Stanford, CA: 1999), 240.

190. Ibid., 13–14.

191. Robert S. Robins and Jerold M. Post, *The Psychopolitics of Hatred* (New Haven, CT: 1997), 249, 252.

192. Quoted in Ibid., 250. Philip Short observed: "The glorification of violence was characteristic" of Pol Pot's Cambodia. "In Pol's mind bloodshed was cause of exultation" (*Pol Pot: Anatomy of a Nightmare* [New York: 2004], 248).

193. Heller, *Cogs in the Wheel,* 64.

194. A witness of the Kuropaty mass killings testified that "[a]s a rule the people were being shot in the evenings and during the night. They were brought . . . in closed vehicles" (S. Matukovskiy, "The Truth About Kuropaty," *Orbis,* Spring 1989: 241).

195. Beck and Godin, *Russian Purge and the Extraction of Confession,* 63; Alexander Dolgun, *Alexander Dolgun's Story* (New York: 1975), 24; Edward A. Gargan, "Behind the Monstrous Walls, a Legion of Prisoners," *New York Times,* March 26, 1992.

196. More Chinese than Soviet photographic evidence of such atrocities is available. See, for example, "Witness to Mao's Crimes: A Photographer's Evidence of Cultural Revolution Brutality Come to Light," *New York Times Magazine,* June 30, 1996. See also Li Zhenseng, *Red Color News Soldier* (New York: 2003), a photographic documentation of the Cultural Revolution.

197. Giorgis, *Red Tears,* 32. These atrocities took place during the Red Terror campaign of 1977–78: "In February 1977 the government publicly ordered the security forces . . . to 'apply red terror and revolutionary justice.' . . . At the peak of the terror from November 1977 until about February 1978, an estimated 5,000 political opponents were killed in Addis Ababa alone" (*Political Killings By Governments: An Amnesty International Report,* London, 1983: 24). See also James C. McKinley Jr., "Ethiopia Tries Former Rulers in 70s Deaths," *New York Times,* April 23, 1996. On political violence in Ethiopia, see also Edward Kissi, "Genocide in Cambodia and Ethiopia," in Gellately and Kiernan, *Specter of Genocide.*

198. *Black Book,* 648–49.

199. For a rare American article on the Cuban camps, including those on the Isle of Youth, see George Volsky, "In Castro's Gulag," *New York Times Magazine,* October 18, 1987.

200. See Shifrin, *The First Guidebook to Prisons and Concentration Camps of the Soviet Union,* especially the maps.

201. *Black Book*, 499. See also James D. Seymour and Richard Anderson, *New Ghosts, Old Ghosts: Prison and Labor Reform Camps in China* (Armonk, NY: 1998). See also the excerpts included in the present volume by Wu, Pu Ning, Choedrak, and Gyatso.

202. Quoted in Julius Hay, *Born 1900: Memoirs* (London: 1974), 24. It was precisely for this reason that the show trials in Hungary used to be called "conceptual trials."

203. Quoted in Conquest, *The Great Terror,* 137. On the practices and impact of torture in China during and after Mao, see Jonathan Mirsky, "China: The Uses of Fear," *New York Review of Books,* October 6, 2005.

204. W. G. Krivitsky, *In Stalin's Secret Service* (Frederick, MD: 1985), 196–97.

205. Orlov, *Secret History of Stalin's Crimes,* 122–23.

206. Farkas, *No Excuse,* 118–19.

207. For a comparison of the Chinese and Soviet approaches to forced confession, see Edgar H. Stein, *Coercive Persuasion* (New York: 1961).

208. Whyte, "Corrective Labor Camps in China," 261.

209. Chandler, *Voices from S-21,* 123–24.

210. Alberto Carosa, "Letter from Albania: 10,300 Night is the Gulag," *Chronicles,* October 2004: 46.

211. The major work in English on the Hungarian show trials is George H. Hodos, *Show Trials: Stalinist Purges in Eastern Europe, 1948–1954* (New York: 1987).

212. Medvedev, *Let History Judge,* 285–86, 285.

213. Deletant, *Communist Terror in Romania,* 198, 200, 216.

214. Carlos Alberto Montaner, *Secret Report on the Cuban Revolution* (New Brunswick, NJ: 1982), 210.

215. Valladares, *Against All Hope,* 43, 132–38, 255, 272, 226–27, 285–88. See also the excerpt from this book included here.

216. See for example Volsky, "In Castro's Gulag," and Valladares, *Against All Hope.*

217. *Black Book,* 613, 611.

218. Chandler, *Voices from S-21,* 130–31.

219. Weitz, *Century of Genocide,* 179. On Cambodian torture, see also Chandler, *Voices from S-21.*

220. Jean Pasqualini, "Glimpses Inside China's Gulag," *China Quarterly,* June 1993: 353.

221. For a rich photographic record of such public humiliations, see Li Zhensheng, *Red-Color News Soldier* (Boston: 2003).

222. "North Korean Exodus," Editorial, *Wall Street Journal,* July 30, 2004.

223. Anne Applebaum, "Inside the Gulag," *New York Review of Books,* June 15, 2000: 34.

224. For an early discussion of such projects in Eastern Europe, see Richard K. Carlton, ed., *Forced Labor in the 'People's Democracies'"* (New York: 1955). As to the nuclear reactor in Hungary, the editor of this volume had the pleasure of participating in its construction in 1953 as a member of a "construction battalion" consisting of draft-age men classified as politically untrustworthy for proper military training and service.

225. Whyte, "Corrective Labor Camps in China," 258.

226. Jonathan Spence, "The Risks of Witness," *New York Review of Books,* December 19, 1996: 50.

227. In Spence, "The Risks of Witness," 50. In an undated personal communication, Wu estimated the total number of camps at 3,000.

228. Shifrin, *The First Guidebook to Prisons and Concentration Camps of the Soviet Union,* 10.

229. Ana Rodriguez, *Diary of a Survivor: Nineteen Years in a Woman's Prison* (New York: St Martin's Press, 1995), 28–29; Doan Van Toai and David Chanoff, *The Vietnamese Gulag* (New York: 1986), 209.

230. In Ivan Klima, *The Spirit of Prague* (New York: 1994), 138; Tolczyk, *See No Evil*, 142, 117.

231. Tolczyk, *See No Evil*, 168.

232. Gliksman, *Tell the West*, 167. Gliksman had actually seen the play in Moscow in November 1935.

233. By contrast, the Nazis made no pretense of trying to reeducate their political prisoners; their objective was either straightforward extermination or the extraction of maximum labor before death.

234. Lenin wrote: "[T]he fundamental social cause of excesses, which consist in the violation of the rules of social intercourse, is the exploitation of the masses, their want and their poverty. With the removal of this chief cause, excesses will invitably begin to *wither away.*" Lenin, *State and Revolution*, 145.

235. S. P. Pavlov, head of the Komsomol made this point ("Address by S. P. Pavlov . . ." *Komsomolskaya Pravda* [translated as *Current Digest of Soviet Press*], January 26, 1966: 10.

236. It may be noted here that in the so-called "construction battalions" in Communist Hungary, the draftees, besides performing manual labor, had to endure political seminars delivered by the political commissar (an army officer in charge of ideological matters) assigned to these units.

237. Bao Ruo-wang, *Prisoner of Mao*, 5–6. In Soviet labor camps, group pressure was used when prisoners working in groups or work brigades had to fulfill particular labor norms or quotas in order to avoid being penalized by reduction of their food rations; under such conditions the group had an interest in each member's performance.

238. Whyte, "Corrective Labor Camps in China," 259.

239. Valladares, *Against All Hope*, 92, 170.

240. The discussion that follows parallels to some degree parts of chapter 6 in my *Political Will and Personal Belief: The Decline and Fall of Soviet Communism* (New Haven, CT: 1999). For an overview of the structures that perpetrated the repression discussed here, see Jonathan R. Adelman, ed., *Terror and Communist Politics: The Role of the Secret Police in Communist States* (Boulder, CO: 1984). See also Alexander Dallin and George Breslauer, *Political Terror in Communist States* (Stanford, CA: 1970).

241. Although, as reported by Andrei Gromyko, it was Beria whom Stalin designated as "our Himmler," introducing him to President Roosevelt at Yalta (*Memoirs*,[New York: 1990]). See also Montefiore, *Stalin*, 427 about this incident.

242. Morrow, *Evil*, 118-19.

243. Quoted in Daniel Bell, "First Love and Early Sorrows," *Partisan Review*, November 4, 1981: 547.

244. Montefiore, *Stalin*, 76. Interestingly, several of the Soviet leaders "came from devoutly religious backgrounds. They hated Judeo-Christianity—but the orthodoxy of their parents was replaced by something even more rigid, a systematic amorality" (ibid).

245. Quoted in David Remnick, "The First and the Last," *New Yorker*, November 18, 1996: 120–21. The ruthlessness of Lenin is also captured in Richard Pipes, ed., *The Unknown Lenin.*

246. Hodos, *Show Trials*, 55.

247. Albert Resis, ed., *Molotov Remembers . . .* (Chicago: 1993), 265.

248. Quoted in Nate Thayer, "Day of Reckoning," *Far Eastern Economic Review*, October 30, 1997: 14, 15, 16.

249. Nicholas Kristof, "The Wounds of War: A Generation of Japanese is Haunted by Its Past," *New York Times,* January 22, 1997: 8; Seth Mydans, "70s Torturer in Cambodia Now 'Doing God's Work,'" *New York Times*, May 2, 1999: 4.

250. Piatakov quoted in Martin Malia, *The Soviet Tragedy* (New York: 1994), 268; George F. Kennan, "The Buried Past," *New York Review of Books*, October 27, 1988: 5.

251. Howard Becker, ed., *Antonio Candido on Literature and Society* (Princeton, NJ: 1995), 233; Deletant, *Ceausescu and the Securitate*, 18; Joseph Skvorecky, "Two Pease in a Pod: Why Nazis and Communists Sing the Same Songs," *Idler*, November 1986: 37; Peter Hruby, *Fools and Heroes: The Changing Role of Communist Intellectuals in Czechoslovakia* (New York: 1980), 223–24; Victor Serge, *Memoirs of a Revolutionary, 1901–1941* (London: 1963), 80.; W. G. Krivitsky, *In Stalin's Secret Service* (Frederick, MD: 1985), 143. There is much revealing detail in Montefiore, *Stalin*, about the deformed personalities of the major figures ("enthusiastic killers") in the Soviet coercive apparatus, such as Abakumov, Beria, Riumin, Yagoda, and Yezhov.

252. Orlov, *Secret History of Stalin's Crimes*, 131.

253. On the privileges of camp commanders in the Soviet Union, see Applebaum, *Gulag*, 266–69.

254. Christian Caryl, "The Undead," *New Republic*, December 16, 1996, 18; Oleg Kalugin *The First Directorate* (New York: 1994); Eugene Loebl, *My Mind on Trial* (New York: 1976), 155; Bela Szàsz, *Volunteers for the Gallows: Anatomy of a Show Trial* (New York: 1971), 70.

255. This is the central argument of Hollander, *Political Will and Personal Belief.*

256. Quoted in Patrick A. Swan, ed., *Alger Hiss, Whittaker Chambers, and the Schism in the American Soul* (Wilmington, DE: 2003), 314.

257. Colburn cited, 77.

THE SOVIET UNION

Man is Wolf to Man: Surviving the Gulag

1. Transport; shipment of prisoners.
2. Prisoner of higher status who worked for the administration.
3. Professional criminal
4. Roll call. Head count.
5. Makeshift shoes consisting of leather, canvas, wood, tire tread, or any other material bound to the foot with string.
6. Bread ration
7. "Let's go! Catch up!"
8. Boiled water

9. The place where one reaches the edge. A killer camp.
10. Medical assistant.
11. A goner. A degraded prisoner on his last legs.
12. "Wake up! Wake up!"
13. *Urka* lingo for a self-inflicted infection.

To Build a Castle

1. Corrective labor camps and prisons in the USSR are divided into four types according to their regime: "normal," "reinforced," "strict," and "special" or "specially strict," in ascending order of severity. The degree of severity defines the type and quantity of rations the prisoner receives, the number of privileges (letters, food parcels, visits) he is allowed, and the scale of punishments he can be subjected to. The type of regime is usually specified in his sentence, but it can be altered during his term of imprisonment. (Translator's note.)

Journey into the Whirlwind

1. Cheka: abbreviation of Russian for "Extraordinary Commission for the struggle against counterrevolution and sabotage," as the Soviet security service was called when it was first created by Lenin. Cheka remains a colloquial term for the Secret Police.
2. Nikolay Dobrolyubov, 1836–61, radical journalist and critic.
3. Tartar Communist writer, 1901–57.
4. According to Soviet law everybody has the right to public trial.

A World Apart

1. The Russian alphabet has no hard "H" and substitutes for it the letter "G."
2. The Second Section of the NKVD was concerned with the quotas of prisoners and their distribution among the camps. Like all other camp authorities, it was under the ultimate control of the Third Section, which, by the extensive use of informers, watched over the political behavior of the prisoners and the loyalty of the free camp officials, and decided all questions with even the slightest political aspect.
3. 1 lb. = approximately 450 grams.

My Testimony

1. Founder of the Soviet secret police, called the Cheka, then GPU, in his time.
2. The Komsomol is the Soviet youth organization.
3. Reefer-jacket is the ironic term used for the flimsy cotton-quilted jackets issued to prisoners.

One Day in the Life of Ivan Denisovich

1. *Volkovoy* is a name derived from *volk*, meaning "wolf."

EASTERN EUROPE

The Truth That Killed

1. Christo Botev was a nineteenth-century Bulgarian poet and fighter for independence from Turkish rule.
2. Nicola Petkov was the leader of the Agrarian Unionist Party, deputy prime minister in the interim government, and head of the opposition after World War II. In 1947 he was arrested, sentenced to death (falsely charged with conspiring to overthrow the government), and executed.
3. Traicho Kostov, a former high-ranking Communist official, was accused of participating in a Titoist conspiracy as well as having been an agent of the pre-Communist police (an accusation also made against Rajk in Hungary in a similar trial). He was tried on these spurious charges and executed in 1949.
4. Georgi Dimitrov was head of the Bulgarian Communist Party between 1945 and 1949.
5. Vulko Chervenko was successor to Dimitrov between 1950 and 1954.
6. Anton Yugov: Minister of Interior (Police) from 1944 to 1950; organizer of forced labor camps.

Voices from the Gulag

1. Chakûruv was in charge of the Internment and Deportation Service in the Ministry of the Interior.
2. This is based on the Bulgarian currency during this period. At that time, a monthly salary was from 2,000 to 3,000 leva. A "new lev" later replaced ten old leva.
3. This section is extracted from *The Survivors*.

The Confession

1. Coupons corresponding to the equivalent sum of Western currency which enabled the bearer to purchase in special shops where Czech crowns were not accepted.

Political Prisoner

1. No relative of Michael Károlyi.

2. His was a Magyarized surname; in London, he was known by his original surname, Szüsz He had been an engineer.
3. I have heard that in despair Miklós Szücz shouted: "I am ready to sign any confession you want."

A Prisoner of Martial Law

1. Brand name of van, small truck.
2. Site of mass executions of Poles in the fall of 1939.
3. Small opening in the cell door.
4. *Boze, cos Polske.*
5. About the seacoast bread riots of December 1970.

Goli Otok: Island of Death

1. Forced-chasing is a torture peculiar to Goli Otok. A convict is forced to run at full speed while carrying a heavy box of stones. Behind him are other convicts who beat him to make him run faster.

CHINA

Prisoner of Mao

1. *Lao Dong:* manual labor; *Gai Zao:* to change, reform.
2. How many prisoners are there? The estimates of the Chinese forced-labor-camp population vary wildly, depending mostly on the political convictions of the person making the estimate. There are even some distinguished authors, intellectuals, and academics in the West who appear to believe that there never was a labor camp or political prisoner in mainland China. At the other extreme are certain Sinologists who affirm that upwards of twenty million are being held in servitude for ideological reasons. Obviously, the Chinese government furnishes no statistics, but I can assure the reader from personal experience that the camps exist and that their population is colossal. An interesting hint of the possible scale is contained in a phrase dear to Chinese rhetoricians: "Only a small minority, perhaps five per cent, is against us; these are being forced to build socialism." No one who takes a stand against the government can remain out of jail, but if we take only two per cent as a reasonable possibility, this still gives us a figure of sixteen million prime candidates for Reform Through Labor. This figure does not include those individuals undergoing the standard three-year terms of *Lao Jiao*—Education Through Labor. These are persons who have committed "mistakes" rather than "crimes." In theory, they main-

tain their civic rights while in the camps. There are at least as many undergoing *Lao Jiao* as *Lao Gai;* in fact, probably many more.

3. At Branch Farm #3 of the Ching Ho State Farm, northeast of Tientsin. I worked to grow that rice with my own hands.

4 *Lao* is Chinese for "old" and it is commonly used, coupled to a person's family name, as an amicable form of greeting between friends or people with whom one is well acquainted. It is used in much the same way as the English saying "old chap" or the American "ol' buddy."

Red in Tooth and Claw: Twenty-Six Years in Communist Chinese Prisons

1. In the Chinese Communist personnel system, a ganbu is a cadre who often acts as the leader of a unit or as the superintendent of a task.

2. In the event of prisoner quarrels, fights, injuries, deaths, or other serious events, the inmates of Tilan Bridge were required to shout "Report!" to summon someone of authority to the scene. Generally, at the jail, a prisoner would have to say "report" before addressing anyone of authority. What the prisoner had to say was required to be of some importance. Hence the rule against careless use of the word.

CAMBODIA

To Destroy You Is No Loss

1. Between 1970 and the takeover in 1975, inflation drove the value of the riel down from 35 per dollar to 3000 per dollar. What this major devaluation meant to the everyday economy is best illustrated in considering the change in prices of basic commodities. Rice increased from 4 riels per kilogram to 1800 riels per kilogram, and the cost of a traditional soup meal rose from 3 riels to 1500 riels.

2. Si Ton's mother and his four missing sisters had been sent to Battambang Province. After three years of Khmer Rouge control, his mother and one sister died of starvation and illness within hours of each other. Si Ton's three other sisters had married in Battambang and had children. Their husbands had been executed by Pol Pot's soldiers.

VIETNAM

The Vietnamese Gulag

1. The National Liberation Front (NLF) was a political umbrella organization founded in 1960 to direct the insurgency in South Vietnam.
2. In Vietnamese the family name comes first and the given name last. But there are relatively few family names, and so the given name is most often used for identification. Nguyen Van Thieu (given name, Thieu), South Vietnam's political strongman from the mid-sixties until 1975, was known as President Thieu. North Vietnam's defense minister, Vo Nguyen Giap, was General Giap.
3. The Provisional Revolutionary Government (PRG) was founded by the insurgency in 1969 to challenge the Saigon regime for recognition in international forums as South Vietnam's true representative government.

Lost Years: My 1,632 Days in Vietnamese Reeducation Camps

1. The official communiqué stipulated that the period of "reeducation" for junior officers and civil servants was seven days. For many of them, it was seven years.
2. North Vietnamese appellation for soldiers. Throughout the book, *Bo Doi* will be used for the politicized soldier of Communist Vietnam.
3. Literally, "go up to the class." The Vietnamese language does not lack words to express the simple act of attending classes. But if the Communists intentionally coined this new expression it may carry a connotation reflecting their belief that political studies or, more precisely, the study of Marxism-Leninism elevated their ideological standing.
4. Popular and derogatory pronunciation of V.M. (Vei + Em = Vem), the abbreviation for Viet Minh, itself a short form of Việt Nam Dôc Lâp Dông Minh Hôi (League for the Independence of Vietnam). The Viet Minh was dominated by the Communists, so by the 1950s for the man in the street, "Viet Minh" most of the time was equivalent to "Communist."

CUBA

The Politics of Psychiatry in Revolutionary Cuba

1. *Mayarí* is a town in central Cuba; *caballo* literally means "horse."
2. This doctor is identified by Armando Valladares in his memoir *Against All Hope* as a psychiatrist in the Combinado del Este Prison hospital (New York: 1986), 331.
3. An anti-psychotic prescribed for "psychotic disorders [and] moderate to severe depression with anxiety...." See Gilbert I. Simon, et al., *The Pill Book*, Fourth Edition (New York: 1990), 886–89.
4. An anti-Parkinsonian agent often used to prevent or control muscle spasms caused by phenothiazines. Its side effects include blurred vision, confusion, and an increased sensitivity to strong light. See *The Pill Book*, 889–91.
5. Thousands sought asylum in the Embassy. This event began a chain of events that resulted in the massive Mariel boatlift to the United States.

NICARAGUA

The Civil War in Nicaragua

1. Christopher Dickey, *With The Contras* (New York: 1985), 64, 65.
2. Tomás Borge, "On Human Rights in Nicaragua," in Borge et al., *Sandinistas Speak* (New York: 1982), 85; Payne, "Human Rights in Nicaragua," 49.
3. See Payne, "Human Rights in Nicaragua," 50.
4. For documents on this incident, including Cisneros's statement to CPDH, see *From Revolution to Repression* (Washington: U.S. Department of State, March 1986), 59–67.
5. Kinzer, *Blood of Brothers*, 180–81.
6. Diamond, "Class and Power in Revolutionary Nicaragua," 280.
7. See Christian, *Nicaragua*, 132–34; Kinzer, *Blood of Brothers*, 78–79.
8. CPDH, "Los Desaparecidos: Un abominable crimen Somocista que debemos desterrar de la patria Sandinista," informe oficial, 3 de Octubre de 1980, 2; CPDH, "Testimonio Presentado por la CPDH a la Comisión de Derechos Humanos de la OEA," Managua, 12 de Mayo de 1984, 1, 2. On some of the peasant deaths never reported during the Sandinista government but discovered later, see Nina Shea, "Uncovering the Awful Truth of Nicaragua's Killing Fields," *Wall Street Journal*, August 24, 1990, and Sam Dillon, "A Tireless Crusader Reveals Pattern of Sandinista Abuses," *Miami Herald*, May 16, 1991.

9. CPDH, "The Human Rights Situation in Nicaragua," Special Report, April 1987, 4–5, 10–11.

10. See Nietschmann, *The Unknown War,* 15–42.

11. Kinzer, *Blood of Brothers,* 352, 382–83.

12. See Glenn Garvin, *Everybody Had His Own Gringo* (New York: [US, 1992]), 182–84; and Ratliff interview with Pastora, March 24, 1992.

13. Borge, "On Human Rights in Nicaragua," in *Sandinistas Speak,* 88, 90.

14. Dirección Nacional, "FSLN siempre respetará la voluntad popular," *Barricada,* March 17, 1981.

15. Comisión Internacional de Juristas, "Tribunales especiales que juzgan a Somcistas y colaboradores del Somocismo," Ginebra, 14. Copy in Hoover Institution Archives.

16. Kinzer, *Blood of Brothers,* 315; also 204.

17. CPDH, "Situación de los Derechos Humanos en Nicaragua: Informe Especial," Managua, April 1987.

18. Kinzer, *Blood of Brothers,* 275.

19. United Press International, "Borge admite torturas y asesinatos," *La Nación,* San José, Costa Rica, 26 de julio de 1987. Among the articles published just before Borge's remarks were William Branigin, "Pattern of Abuses Laid to Sandinistas," *Washington Post,* May 18, 1987, and James LeMoyne, "Peasants Tell of Rights Abuses by Sandinistas," *New York Times,* June 28, 1987.

Fleeing Their Homeland

1. Amnesty International, Nicaragua: The Human Rights Record, March 1986 : 11.

2. Jill Smolowe, "Coping with the Contras," *Time,* March 30, 1987: 39.

3. *Annual Report of the Inter-American Commission on Human Rights 1985–198:* 174.

4. UN Convention against Torture and Other Cruel, Inhuman, and Degrading Treatment or Punishment.

5. *Nicaragua: The Human Rights Record, op. cit.:* 19.

6. Lawyers Committee for International Human Rights, Nicaragua: Revolutionary Justice, April 1985: 106.

7. Amnesty International, "12 Point Program for the Prevention of Torture." Available from Amnesty International.

8. 72–73.

9. Nicaragua: The Human Rights Record, op. cit.: 21.

10. Op. cit.: 174.

NORTH KOREA

The Aquariums of Pyongyang

1. The letter dates from May 5, 1946. See Kim Il-sung, *Complete Works,* vol. 2 (Pyongyang: 1980), 193, foreign language edition.

ETHIOPIA

Red Tears

1. The *kebeles* were the Revolution's new political, administrative and security units. They existed in the rural areas too, and have been translated there as "Peasant Associations."
2. Gorbachev, as quoted in a *New York Times* review of *Perestroika.*
3. The official number we preferred to use was 300,000, even though in the Central Committee both figures were used. The idea was that if the first phase of the movement succeeded, the target would be increased to 500,000.

About the Editor

Paul Hollander, who escaped from Hungary after the defeat of the 1956 revolution, got his B.A. from the London School of Economics and his Ph.D. in sociology from Princeton University. He is professor emeritus of sociology at the University of Massachusetts at Amherst and an associate of the Davis Center for Russian and Eurasian Studies at Harvard University. His books include *Soviet and American Society: A Comparison*, *Political Pilgrims*, *Anti-Americanism*, *Political Will and Personal Belief: The Decline and Fall of Soviet Communism*, and *Discontents: Postmodern and Postcommunist*. He is also the editor of *Understanding Anti-Americanism*.